PRINCIPLES OF AUSTRALIAN EQUITY AND TRUSTS

Second Edition

PRINCIPLES OF AUSTRALIAN EQUITY AND TRUSTS

Second Edition

PETER RADAN

BA, LLB, PhD (Syd), Dip Ed (SCAE)
Professor of Law, Macquarie Law School, Macquarie University

CAMERON STEWART

BEc LLB (Hons) (Macq), Grad Dip Juris (Syd), Grad Dip Leg Prac
(NSW College of Law), PhD (Syd), FACLM (Hon)
Professor of Health, Law and Ethics and Director of the Centre of Health
Governance, Law and Ethics, Sydney Law School, University of Sydney

LexisNexis Butterworths
Australia
2013

LexisNexis

AUSTRALIA	LexisNexis Butterworths
	475–495 Victoria Avenue, Chatswood NSW 2067
	On the internet at: www.lexisnexis.com.au
ARGENTINA	LexisNexis Argentina, Buenos Aires
AUSTRIA	LexisNexis Verlag ARD Orac GmbH & Co KG, Vienna
BRAZIL	LexisNexis Latin America, Sao Paulo
CANADA	LexisNexis Canada, Markham, Ontario
CHILE	LexisNexis Chile, Santiago
CHINA	LexisNexis China, Beijing, Shanghai
CZECH REPUBLIC	Nakladatelství Orac sro, Prague
FRANCE	LexisNexis SA, Paris
GERMANY	LexisNexis Germany, Frankfurt
HONG KONG	LexisNexis Hong Kong, Hong Kong
HUNGARY	HVG-Orac, Budapest
INDIA	LexisNexis, New Delhi
ITALY	Dott A Giuffrè Editore SpA, Milan
JAPAN	LexisNexis Japan KK, Tokyo
KOREA	LexisNexis, Seoul
MALAYSIA	LexisNexis Malaysia Sdn Bhd, Petaling Jaya, Selangor
NEW ZEALAND	LexisNexis, Wellington
POLAND	Wydawnictwo Prawnicze LexisNexis, Warsaw
SINGAPORE	LexisNexis, Singapore
SOUTH AFRICA	LexisNexis Butterworths, Durban
SWITZERLAND	Staempfli Verlag AG, Berne
TAIWAN	LexisNexis, Taiwan
UNITED KINGDOM	LexisNexis UK, London, Edinburgh
USA	LexisNexis Group, New York, New York
	LexisNexis, Miamisburg, Ohio

National Library of Australia Cataloguing-in-Publication entry

Author:	Radan, Peter.
Title:	Principles of Equity and Trusts: cases and material.
Edition:	2nd edition.
ISBN:	9780409331240 (pbk).
	9780409331257 (ebk).
Notes:	Includes index.
Subjects:	Equity — Australia.
Other Authors/Contributors:	Stewart, Cameron.
Dewey Number:	346.94004.

Typeset in Myriad Pro and Minion Pro.

Printed in China.

Visit LexisNexis Butterworths at www.lexisnexis.com.au

CONTENTS

PREFACE TO THE SECOND EDITION

In writing the second edition of this book we were, of course, required to take into account new cases and legislation that have come into being in the three years since the publication of the first edition. Of the many new cases referred to throughout this edition perhaps the most significant Australian cases are the High Court of Australia decisions in *Equuscorp Pty Ltd v Haxton* (Chapter 5), *John Alexander's Clubs Pty Limited v White City Tennis Club Limited* (Chapter 9), *Andrews v Australia and New Zealand Banking Group Ltd* (Chapter 14), *Byrnes v Kendle* (Chapter 16), *Aid/Watch Incorporated v Commissioner of Taxation of the Commonwealth of Australia* (Chapter 18); the decisions of the Full Court of the Federal Court of Australia in *Grimaldi v Chameleon Mining Pty Ltd (No 2)* (Chapters 9 and 28) and *Australian Competition and Consumer Commission v MSY Technology Pty Ltd* (Chapter 22); and the decision of the Court of Appeal in Western Australia in *Westpac Banking Corporation v The Bell Group Ltd (In Liq) (No 3)* (Chapters 9, 12 and 28). In the United Kingdom, the decisions of the Supreme Court of the United Kingdom in *Jones v Kernott* (Chapter 19) and of the Court of Appeal in *Pitt v Holt* (Chapter 20) are also important. The most significant legislative development has been the introduction of the *Australian Consumer Law* which has a particular relevance to the area of statutory unconscionability (Chapter 11). Apart from the updating of the book, we also took the opportunity to refine and improve the text and expand on the breadth of analysis.

In preparing this edition Peter took primary responsibility for the writing of Chapters 1–7, 10–14, 22–27 and 30–31 and Cameron took primary responsibility for the writing of Chapters 8–9, 15–21 and 28–29. This edition is based upon materials available to us as at the end of September 2012.

As with the previous edition of this book, we must acknowledge the support of our families, friends and colleagues. Once again, the support, love and enduring patience of our wives, Sybil Radan and Nerida Stewart, and our children, Rade, Andrija and Alexsandra Radan and Maxwell, Hannah, Beth, Angus and Eadie Stewart, were indispensible to the completion of this edition of the book.

At LexisNexis, we wish, in particular, to thank Geraldine Maclurcan, Kerry Paul, Jocelyn Holmes and Tim Vaughan-Sanders for the skill, care and efficiency with which they converted our manuscript into a book.

Peter Radan
Cameron Stewart
2 October 2012

PREFACE TO THE FIRST EDITION

In the early 1970s, observant users at the University of Sydney law library, upon entering a place to which, to quote an old Serbian proverb, 'even the king must walk', would have noticed a graffiti item which boldly declared:

> They say crime doesn't pay — that's why I'm studying equity.

The few, if any, who took this advice seriously, would have found precious few Australian books in that law library dealing with the subject that would 'pay' as promised. More than likely they would have pored over established English texts such as *Hanbury* or *Pettit*. *Jacobs*, as it has always been known, the first edition of which was published in 1958, would have been a partial exception in so far as trusts were concerned. So too with Spry's *Equitable Remedies*, first published in 1971. Sir Frederick Jordan's masterly *Chapters in Equity*, correctly described by Sir Anthony Mason as 'for many decades the most authoritative exposition of equity in New South Wales',[1] could have been consulted, but it would not have been of much assistance to students, such as one of the authors of this book (Radan), who were then trying to come to grips with the series of lectures they had survived that dissected the 10 speeches given by their Lordships in the then recent cases of *Pettitt v Pettitt*[2] and *Gissing v Gissing*.[3]

However, the winds of change were brewing. Three members of what the current Chief Justice of New South Wales has referred to as 'an international bastion of evangelical equity scholarship [in New South Wales]'[4] were busy writing the first edition of what has, since its publication in 1975, almost universally been known as *Meagher, Gummow & Lehane*.[5] This blockbuster of a book saw off its established English counterparts in much the same way that Lillee and Thompson saw off their English counterparts in that year's glorious summer of cricket.

Now in its fourth edition, *Meagher, Gummow & Lehane* is a deeply learned and scholarly treatise which, in highly opinionated terms, asserts the view that equity's doctrines and remedies are, and should remain, distinct and separate from those of the common law. It has relentlessly opposed any suggestion that the legislative fusion of the formerly separate courts of common law and equity mandated, or at least facilitated, the fusion of the principles of equity and the common law.

Meagher, Gummow & Lehane has become for equity purists what the 12 volumes of *The Fundamentals*, first published from 1910–1915, are for conservative evangelical Christians. Even for those who do not subscribe to the school of 'evangelical equity scholarship', *Meagher, Gummow & Lehane* is an important work, and no serious Australian scholar or practitioner in the field can

---

1. Sir Anthony Mason, 'Supreme Court of New South Wales: Opening of Law Term Judges' Dinner' (2008) 82 *Australian Law Journal* 839 at 839.
2. [1970] AC 777.
3. [1971] AC 886.
4. J J Spigelman, 'Lord Mansfield and the Culture of Improvement' (2008) 82 *Australian Law Journal* 764 at 766.
5. R P Meagher, W M G Gummow & J R F Lehane, *Equity, Doctrines and Remedies*, Butterworths, Sydney, 1975. The second and third editions were published in 1983 and 1992 respectively. The fourth edition by R P Meagher, J D Heydon and M J Leeming was published in 2002.

ignore it. The same can be said of *Jacobs*, which, since its second edition, published in 1967, has been written by one or more of the authors, from time to time, of *Meagher, Gummow & Lehane*.

This, however, is not to say that *Meagher, Gummow & Lehane* and the school of 'evangelical equity scholarship' from which it emerged do not have their critics. Thus, Wilson, writing in 2004, said:

> The most recent edition of *Meagher, Gummow and Lehane's* has adopted an almost religious tone, devoting itself to the 'rooting out of error' and the repulse of 'cultural vandals' with suitably Jesuitical fervour … [Its] authors are conservatives in a fi eld whose history provides few firm foundations for an assertion that 'it was ever thus'.[6]

The 'cultural vandals' to whom Wilson refers are those who reject *Meagher, Gummow & Lehane's* views on the relationship between common law and equity and suggest that a fusion of their principles is, and should be, taking place. The manner in which they are attacked in *Meagher, Gummow & Lehane* has also drawn criticism. Thus, Justice Michael Kirby (as he then was), after referring to its various 'purple passages', observed:

> Those familiar with the successive 'rooting out' of heretics in England under the later Tudors will recognise the *genre* of this denunciatory writing. Burning at the professional stake would seem too kind a fate for such doctrinal rascals.[7]

In the decades since the appearance of *Meagher, Gummow & Lehane*, Australian scholarship in equity has flourished in terms of general equity texts, specialist monographs and articles. The field now also has its own specialist journal — *The Journal of Equity*. The present volume is but a modest contribution to this array of work. Although we stand apart from the school of 'evangelical equity scholarship', we acknowledge its infl uence and importance. Nor, in our view, are we doctrinal rascals (even though, admittedly, some passages of this text were written with a wry smile). Nevertheless, we do acknowledge the significance of scholarship that is less evangelical in inspiration and less fervent in tone. We hope that we have been fair to both approaches.

The research and writing of this book has been an arduous, but rewarding, experience. However, its completion was not solely the result of our efforts. Indeed, it is hardly likely that it would ever have seen the light of day but for the support and encouragement of our families, friends and colleagues.

First, and foremost, we must acknowledge the love, support, encouragement and, most of all, the understanding of our wives, Sybil Radan and Nerida Stewart, and our children, Rade, Andrija and Aleksandra Radan and Maxwell, Hannah, Beth, Angus and Eadie Stewart. Over the last few years, this book has been as much a part of their lives as it has been a part of ours. It is to them that it is dedicated.

In a variety of ways, a number of our friends and colleagues generously provided their time and expertise in assisting us to complete the book's manuscript, thereby making it much better than it would otherwise have been. We thus express our heartfelt thanks to Fiona Burns, Ros Croucher, Bryan Horrigan, Patricia Lane, Andrew Lynch, Keith Mason, Shae McCrystal, Nicola McGarrity, Tim Paine, Patrick Parkinson, Joellen Riley, Greg Tolhurst and Ilija Vickovich. We also acknowledge the valuable research assistance provided to us by Zoe Hutchinson, Rowan Platt and Andrija Radan.

---

6. Peter Wilson, 'Unconscionability and Fairness in Australian Equitable Jurisprudence' (2004) 11 *Australian Property Law Journal* 1 at 3.

7. Hon Justice Michael Kirby, 'Equity's Australian Isolationism' (2008) 8 *Queensland University of Technology Law & Justice Journal* 444 at 449.

At LexisNexis we wish, in particular, to thank Kate Hickey, Elise Carney, Annabel Adair, Jocelyn Holmes and Geraldine MacLurcan for their support and understanding, as well as efficiency in turning a manuscript into a book.

Although this book is a collaborative effort that reflects a considerable degree of discussion and analysis of its contents, each of us did, nevertheless, take the lead in writing individual chapters. Furthermore, its writing was informed by the experiences we both have benefited from in academia and private practice. For the record, Peter took responsibility for writing Chapters 1–7, 10–14, 22–27 and 30–31,[8] and Cameron did the same for Chapters 8–9, 15–21 and 28–29.

This book is based upon materials available to us in Sydney to the end of October 2009.

Peter Radan
Cameron Stewart
17 November 2009

---

8. Some of these chapters, or parts thereof, were also written for, and published as part of, his contribution to P Radan & J Gooley, *Principles of Australian Contract Law*, 2nd ed, LexisNexis Butterworths, Sydney, 2010.

TABLE OF CASES

References are to paragraphs

D

G

Hancock Family Memorial Foundation Ltd
  v Porteous [2000] WASCA 29 .... 28.98,
  28.134
Hancock v Watson [1902] AC 14 .... 18.159
Hannah's Will, Re (1939) 34 Tas LR 45 .... 18.79
Hanson v Keating (1844) 67 ER 537 .... 2.29
Hardey v Tory (1923) 32 CLR 592 .... 18.73,
  18.74
Harding (dec'd), Re [2007] 1 All ER 747
  .... 18.92
Hardoon v Belilios [1901] AC 118 .... 20.52
Hardy v Attorney-General [1903] 1 Ch 232
  .... 18.123
Hargrave v Schumann; Application of
  Gnitekram Marketing Pty Ltd [2010]
  NSWSC 1328 .... 20.62
Hargreaves v Rothwell (1836) 48 ER 265
  .... 7.60
Harmer v Federal Commissioner of Taxation
  (1991) 173 CLR 264; 104 ALR 117 .... 21.19
Harmood v Oglander (1803) 32 ER 293 .... 15.7
Harpur v Levy (2007) 16 VR 587 .... 16.14,
  16.15
Harrigan v Brown [1967] 1 NSWR 342
  .... 24.60
Harris v Digital Pulse Pty Ltd (2003) 56
  NSWLR 298 .... 3.16, 3.18, 3.19, 3.22, 8.125,
  8.129, 26.31, 26.34, 26.35, 26.36, 26.37
Harris v Harris [2011] FAMCAFC 245
  .... 21.30
Harris v King (1936) 56 CLR 177 .... 17.112
Harris v Smith [2008] NSWSC 545 .... 7.90,
  30.6
Harrison v Harrison (No 2) [2012] VSC 74
  .... 28.52
Harrison v Schipp [2001] NSWCA 13 .... 21.77
Harry Simpson and Co Pty Ltd v The
  Companies Act, Re (1964) 81 WN (NSW)
  207 .... 7.49
Hartigan Nominees Pty Ltd v Rydge (1992)
  29 NSWLR 405 .... 20.62, 20.82, 20.84,
  20.90, 20.93, 20.103, 20.105, 20.149
Hartigan v International Society for Krishna
  Consciousness Inc [2002] NSWSC 810
  .... 10.22, 10.47, 10.77

Hasham v Zenab [1960] AC 316 .... 23.1
Haslam v Money for Living (Aust) Pty Ltd
  (2008) 172 FCR 301 .... 4.10
Hastings-Bass, Re [1975] Ch 25; [1974] 2 All
  ER 193 .... 20.150, 20.153, 20.154, 20.157,
  20.162, 20.166, 20.167, 20.171
Hatch v Harlekin Pty Ltd [2008] WASC 167
  .... 20.102
Hatfield v TCN Channel Nine Pty Ltd (2010)
  77 NSWLR 506 .... 24.13, 24.44
Havelock v Havelock (1881) 17 Ch D 807
  .... 17.4
Havyn Pty Ltd v Webster [2005] NSWCA 182
  .... 13.30
Hawker Pacific Pty Ltd v Helicopter Charter
  Pty Ltd (1991) 22 NSWLR 298 .... 12.51
Hawkes v Wilkie [2012] NSWSC 1039 .... 17.86
Hawkesley v May [1956] 1 QB 304; [1955] 3 All
  ER 353 .... 20.82
Hawks v McArthur [1951] 1 All ER 22 .... 28.26
Hawthorn Football Club Ltd v Harding [1988]
  VR 49 .... 24.64
Hay's Settlement Trust, Re [1981] 3 All ER 786
  .... 20.142, 21.7
Hayden v Teplitzky (1997) 74 FCR 7;
  154 ALR 497 .... 25.17
Hayden, A v (1984) 156 CLR 532: 56 ALR 82
  .... 8.99
Hayim v Citibank NA [1987] AC 730
  .... 21.39
Hayman v Equity Trustees Ltd [2003] VSC 353
  .... 20.43
Healey v Brown [2002] EWHC Ch 1405
  .... 28.50
Hearn v Younger [2002] WTLR 1317 .... 20.154
Heartwood Architectural Timber & Joinery Pty
  Ltd v Ors & Redchip Lawyers [2009]
  QSC 195 .... 25.19
Heath, Re [1936] Ch 259 .... 17.106
Heathcote v Hulme (1819) 37 ER 322 .... 21.81
Hegarty, Re [2011] NSWSC 1194 .... 18.169
Heid v Reliance Finance Corporation Pty Ltd
  (1983) 154 CLR 326; 49 ALR 229 .... 7.14,
  7.16, 7.27, 7.28, 7.29, 7.30, 7.31, 7.33, 7.105,
  7.106, 7.107

TABLE OF STATUTES

References are to paragraphs

WESTERN AUSTRALIA

Part I:
History and Nature of Equity

1

THE HISTORY OF EQUITY

INTRODUCTION

1.1   A basic grasp and understanding of the historical development of equity and the English Court of Chancery, which administered equitable principles, is important for two reasons. First, the meaning and content of equity cannot be understood without this historical knowledge. Second, this historical knowledge explains the place of equitable principles in our general body of law.

EQUITY AND CONSCIENCE

1.2   The origins of the word 'equity' can be traced to the Ancient Greek word *epeikeia* as used by Aristotle in his *Nichomachean Ethics*, where he said:

> [E]quity, although just, and better than a kind of justice, is not better than absolute justice — only than the error due to generalization. This is the essential nature of equity; it is a rectification of law in so far as law is defective on account of its generality ... [E]quitable man ... is one who chooses and does equitable acts and is not unduly insistent upon his rights, but accepts less than his share, although he has the law on his side. Such a disposition is equity: it is a kind of justice, and not a distinct state of character.[1]

1.3   The Latin translation of *epeikeia* is *aequitas*. In *De Legibus*, Cicero viewed *aequitas* as a spirit of justice which interpreted the law according to right reason rather than by words alone, when he wrote:

> Justice is the one; it binds all human society, and is based on one Law, which is right reason applied to command and prohibition. Whosoever knows not this Law, whether it has been recorded in writing anywhere or not, is without Justice.[2]

1.4   This notion of equity became associated with the Court of Chancery in the early fourteenth century and gave a name to the body of principles subsequently developed by that court. However, the Aristotelian concept of equity is, as MacNair notes, 'merely one of the standard approaches to the judicial interpretation of legal rules, ie to consider their larger purpose in order to identify their application (or not) to the facts at issue' and thus offers 'no explanatory power in relation to

---

1.   Aristotle, *Nichomachean Ethics*, 1137b (J A K Thomson translation, Penguin Books, Revised edition, London, 1976, p 200). Aristotle's concept of *epeikeia* is discussed in G Watt, *Equity Stirring, The Story of Justice Beyond Law*, Oxford, Hart Publishing, 2009, pp 27–9.
2.   Cicero, *Laws I*, XV, 42 (C V Keyes translation, William Heinemann Ltd, London, 1928, p 345).

the particular activity of the Chancery'.[3] It is in fact the concept of 'conscience' that underpinned the emergence of equitable principles. As early as the middle of the fifteenth century, plaintiffs in Chancery readily invoked 'the law of conscions, which ys law executory in the Courte for the default of remedy by Courtes of the Common Law'.[4] The concept of conscience and the nature of equity are more fully discussed in Chapter 2.

THE HISTORY OF EQUITY IN ENGLAND

1.5   There are two broad views on the origins of equity in England. One view is that the jurisdiction of the Court of Chancery originated in the development of the law of trusts. However, the more orthodox view chronicles equity's emergence as the result of various defects in medieval common law. The essence of this view is, as MacNair colourfully puts it, 'that a sort of sclerosis of the common law had set in, as a result of which it failed to adapt to new developments in society and economy, and the Chancery provided remedies for these problems'.[5]

The sclerosis of the common law

1.6   The initial reference point in the orthodox account of equity's historical development in English law is the Middle Ages and, in particular, the reign of the Norman King, Henry II (1154–1189), who centralised the administration of justice in England into the hands of the Curia Regis or King's Council. The council consisted of the king's tenants-in-chief and such other persons as he chose to appoint. It was responsible for all three branches of government, namely, the legislature, the executive and the judiciary.[6] By the reign of Edward I (1272–1307) the administration of justice began to be distributed between the three common law courts that developed out of, and eventually separated from, the King's Council. The three common law courts were Common Pleas, King's Bench and Exchequer.[7]

1.7   During the early period of its development, the common law was characterised by its capacity to innovate and maintain flexibility to meet changed circumstances. This situation was a natural consequence of the fact that the legal system in England was in its infancy and appropriate responses to problems took time to settle. The common law courts retained their discretionary powers to grant remedies, and relief was granted on the basis of principles of abstract justice, rather than by following earlier decisions involving similar circumstances. In effect, the common law courts gave effect to the idea that is at the heart of equity, namely, 'the idea that law should be administered fairly'.[8] Adams has described the position of the administration of justice at this time as follows:

---

3.   M MacNair, 'Equity and Conscience' (2007) 27 *Oxford Journal of Legal Studies* 659, p 661.

4.   Quoted in C Ogilvie, *The King's Government and the Common Law, 1471–1641*, Basil Blackwell, Oxford, 1958, p 35. For a detailed exploration of the early development of the notion of conscience in equity see D R Klinck, *Conscience, Equity and the Court of Chancery in Early Modern England*, Ashgate Publishing, Farnham (UK), 2010.

5.   MacNair, 'Equity and Conscience', note 3 above, p 664.

6.   A S Green, 'The Centralization of Norman Justice Under Henry II' in Association of American Law Schools (ed), *Select Essays in Anglo-American Legal History, Vol I*, Little, Brown, and Company, Boston, 1907, 111.

7.   W L Carne, 'A Sketch of the History of the High Court of Chancery from Its Origin to the Chancellorship of Wolsey' (1926–1927) 15 *Georgetown Law Journal* 426, pp 428–34.

8.   W S Holdsworth, 'The Early History of Equity' (1914–1915) 13 *Michigan Law Review* 293, p 293.

Common Law and Equity originated together as one undifferentiated system in the effort of the king to carry out his duty of furnishing security and justice to all the community by making use of his prerogative power through his prerogative machinery. The identity of the two systems at the beginning, their origin in the same prerogative action, can be clearly seen in this: the essential characteristic of Equity procedure of a later date is that it begins with a petition asking the king to interfere to secure justice where it would not be secured by the ordinary and existing processes of law. But it was the essential characteristic of all Common Law actions in the eleventh and twelfth centuries that they began with a petition asking the king to interfere to secure justice where it would not be secured by the ordinary and existing processes of law … [T]he man who wished to have the advantage of the king's prerogative procedure and the use of the king's machinery, that is, who desired a remedy not provided him by the ordinary judicial system, must ask for it and obtain permission to use it; and the permission must be granted in so demonstrable a way as to authorize or command the royal officials to act in the case. This authorization and command is the original writ in an action.[9]

1.8   However, as time progressed, the interests of precision in the legal system began to outweigh the concern for the universal redress of wrongs. By the end of the fourteenth century the common law had become static and ceased to respond to changed social conditions. The common law courts abandoned their discretionary powers and became increasingly bogged down by a near slavish adherence to precedent and a morass of procedural technicalities. The resultant formalism and insistence on technicalities removed the inherent equitable principles from the common law and necessitated a new system that could respond to the changing demands of society. This need was met by what eventually emerged and was known as the Court of Chancery (Chancery) which administered what emerged as the principles of equity. It must be kept in mind that, in developing these principles, Chancery always presupposed the existence of common law principles and rights. Indeed, the equitable principles that emerged were fundamentally concerned with the manner by which parties exercised their common law rights. In this light, it was not surprising that this equitable jurisdiction of the chancellor was generally accepted within the English legal fraternity.[10]

The early Court of Chancery

1.9   Initially, litigants who were dissatisfied with the common law courts began to petition the king directly. By the terms of the medieval coronation oath, the king swore 'to do equal and right justice and discretion in mercy and truth'.[11] The king in medieval times was thus seen as having the power and duty to right a wrong for which there was no existing remedy. These petitions sought the king's intervention on a petitioner's behalf. They had no prescribed form and were usually submitted by letter, or, at times, were even made orally. No fee attached to the petition. The procedural simplicity and lack of expense stood in stark contrast to existing common law procedures.[12]

9.   G B Adams, 'The Origin of English Equity' (1916) 16 *Columbia Law Review* 87, pp 91–92.
10. Ogilvie, *The King's Government and the Common Law*, note 4 above, pp 25–33; A Cromartie, *The Constitutionalist Revolution, An Essay on the History of England, 1450–1642*, Cambridge University Press, Cambridge, 2006, pp 17–18.
11. Quoted in D R Coquillette, *The Anglo-American Legal Heritage, Introductory Materials*, Carolina Academic Press, Durham NC, 1999, p 185.
12. Carne, 'A Sketch of the History of the High Court of Chancery from Its Origin to the Chancellorship of Wolsey', note 7 above, pp 442–4.

1.10   By the middle of the fourteenth century, the increasing number of petitions saw the king delegating his authority to deal with them to the Lord Chancellor, the king's principal legal officer and 'keeper of the king's conscience'.[13] By the end of the fourteenth century the Lord Chancellor's authority to deal with such petitions was firmly entrenched.[14] Until the end of the fifteenth century, Chancery was the principal bureaucratic institution in England, with only a minimal involvement in legal work. However, the increasing volume of legal cases to be resolved by the chancellor transformed the medieval Chancery. Its administrative and judicial functions separated with the latter becoming, by the 1430s, one of the central courts of the realm. By the late Middle Ages, the Chancery Court had become 'a responsive, quick, inexpensive, and desirable avenue of recourse for those who felt that they had been wronged in ways that no other jurisdiction could remedy'.[15] It was this court that developed and administered the principles of equity.

1.11   The Chancery Court was a one-man court in that the chancellor was responsible for its decisions. However, the reality was that he had a staff of masters and clerks who did much of the work in hearing and deciding the cases brought before the court. The number of these officials was soon fixed and remained relatively constant throughout its history as a separate court. But, with the growth of its jurisdiction over time, Chancery became severely understaffed. This contributed significantly to the eventual problems with, and criticisms of, Chancery that continued to bedevil it through to its abolition as a separate court as part of the reforms in the administration of justice in the 1870s: see 1.40–1.44.[16]

1.12   However, Chancery was not the only court that administered equitable principles, although it was undoubtedly the most important. For a time during the Tudor period the Court of Requests operated a form of 'poor man's Chancery', and the Court of Exchequer entertained a relatively small number of equity cases from the time of the English Civil War in the mid-seventeenth century until its equity jurisdiction was abolished by statute and transferred to Chancery in 1841.[17]

1.13   The emergence of Chancery as an increasingly important court coincided with the long period of war between England and France, commonly referred to as the Hundred Years War (1337–1453). Whereas French and Latin had, until then, been the languages of politics and the law,[18] the Court of Chancery, from its inception, conducted most of its proceedings in English. This accounted for much of its early popularity as many litigants could not speak French or Latin. It was the English of the Court of Chancery that subsequently served as the basis for standardised written English.[19] As Lerer notes:

---

13. Shakespeare referred to the Lord Chancellor's role as the keeper of the king's conscience in a number of places including in the dialogue between the Archbishop of Canterbury and Henry V at the start of *The Life of King Henry V*: Watt, *Equity Stirring*, note 1 above, p 52.
14. Watt, *Equity Stirring*, note 1 above, p 51.
15. T S Haskett, 'The Medieval English Court of Chancery' (1996) 14 *Law and History Review* 245, p 311.
16. Carne, 'A Sketch of the History of the High Court of Chancery from Its Origin to the Chancellorship of Wolsey', note 7 above, pp 454–8; J Baker, *The Oxford History of the Laws of England, Volume VI: 1483–1558*, Oxford University Press, Oxford, 2003, pp 182–6.
17. H Horowitz, 'Chancery's "Younger Sister": the Court of Exchequer and its Equity Jurisdiction, 1649–1841' (1999) 72 *Historical Research* 160.
18. On the languages used in the early development of the law in England see J H Baker, 'The Three Languages of the Common Law' (1998) 43 *McGill Law Journal* 5.
19. J H Fisher, 'Chancery and the Emergence of Standard Written English in the Fifteenth Century' (1977) 52 *Speculum* 870, pp 872–80.

From the 1380s until the 1450s, Chancery taught a house style of spelling, grammatical forms, lexical usage, and idiom that characterized the papers coming out of many of the royal offices ... Chancery English had an impact on the rise of printed documents in Britain. When Caxton set up his print shop in Westminster, he located his business not in the commercial part of London ... but the site of the court. Caxton adopted Chancery-style spellings and word forms when he came to print not just official or intellectual texts but literary ones as well. His early volumes of the English authors Chaucer, Gower, Lydgate, Malory, and others, calibrated themselves not to the older spelling habits of the scribe but to the newer conventions of Chancery. Caxton's achievement was to take a standard of official writing for a literary standard.[20]

1.14　During the early period of Chancery's development as a court, the medieval chancellors, in making decrees, saw themselves as administering a legal system defined by the common law. As Milsom has observed, at this time there was 'no equity as a nascent body of rules different from those of the common law'.[21] Each case was decided on the basis of its own particular facts, with decrees only binding the parties to the case. Chancellors were not greatly concerned with precedent. It was not until 1557 that the first reports of Chancery cases were published. This contrasted with the practice of common law case reportage, which dated back to the reign of Edward I. As Baker notes:

> [The chancellors] were reinforcing the law by making sure that justice was done in cases where shortcomings in the regular procedure, or human failings, were hindering its attainment by due process. They came not to destroy the law, but to fulfil it ... [The chancellor's] court was a court of conscience, in which defendants could be coerced into doing whatever conscience required in the full circumstances of the case.[22]

1.15　In this period of Chancery's development, the character and personality of the chancellors had a marked influence on the justice administered by that court. Most chancellors were ecclesiastics, usually an archbishop or a cardinal.[23] Holdsworth describes the way they resolved disputes as follows:

> The equitable jurisdiction of the Chancellor ... was based upon an application of the current ideas of the canonists of the fifteenth century regarding the moral government of the universe to the administration of the law of the state. The law of God or of nature or of reason must be obeyed; and these laws require, and, through the agency of conscience, enable abstract justice to be done in each individual case, even at the cost of dispensing (if necessary) with the law of the state.[24]

1.16　In the early stages of the development of Chancery's jurisdiction, petitions for relief dealt principally with procedural concerns relating to the administration of justice in the courts of common law. For example, a petitioner may have had concerns about abuses connected with the selection of a jury. Subsequently, petitioners sought relief on the basis that common law principles

---

20. S Lerer, 'Late Middle English (ca 1350–1485)' in H Momma & M Matto (eds), *A Companion to the History of the English Language*, Wiley-Blackwell, Chichester, 2008, 191, pp 192–3.
21. S F C Milsom, *Historical Foundations of the Common Law*, 2nd ed, Butterworths, London, 1981, p 84.
22. J H Baker, *An Introduction to English Legal History*, 3rd ed, Butterworths, London, 1990, pp 117–118.
23. It was only during the reign of Henry VIII (1509–1547) that the first common lawyer was appointed as Lord Chancellor. This signaled a continuing trend. The last ecclesiastic to be appointed to that office was Bishop Williams who was chancellor for a short period after the fall of Sir Francis Bacon in 1621.
24. Holdsworth, 'The Early History of Equity', note 8 above, p 295.

were defective or to provide a new remedy where there was none at common law.[25] This was the first time that the English legal system developed an alternative dispute resolution system to overcome the deficiencies of the established legal system. In recent times the same process is evident with the enactment of consumer protection legislation and the proliferation of alternative dispute resolution programs and tribunals as a response to widespread dissatisfaction over the quality of, and access to, traditional courts.[26]

Uses and trusts

1.17   Important to the growth of the Chancery's jurisdiction was the recognition and enforcement of the 'use', a term derived from the corruption of the Latin expression *ad opus*, which means 'on behalf of'. The system of uses related to transfers of land for the benefit of others and pre-dates the enforcement of uses by Chancery. Thus, the *Domesday Book* of 1086 contained numerous references to people holding land on behalf of others.[27] Another early example related to Franciscan monks, who were forbidden by their vows of poverty to own property, whereby a person wishing to provide a home for such monks granted the land to a group of nominees to hold for the use of the monks.[28] Uses were recognised and enforced by the ecclesiastical courts, but began to disappear from ecclesiastical records in the mid-fifteenth century.[29] Thereafter uses began to be enforced in Chancery. Although they were not enforced by the common law courts, 'uses were by no means invisible to the common law … [C]ommon lawyers talked about uses in the king's courts and in chancery as if creating uses, enforcing uses, and transacting about uses were an ordinary and essential part of their learning and craft, their common law'.[30]

1.18   Over time the use was transformed into the modern trust. In relation to the trust, Maitland wrote that '[o]f all the exploits of Equity the largest and the most important is the invention and development of the Trust'.[31] Whether the trust was, as Maitland asserted, 'a natural outcome of ancient English elements'[32] with 'nothing quite like it in foreign law',[33] is a matter of academic debate. The fact that the word 'trust' drives from Anglo-Saxon words dealing with truth, clearly suggests at least some connection between the institution of the trust and some similar Anglo-Saxon concept.[34] However, it is also likely that the development of the use/trust was influenced by some pre-existing foreign model. Blackstone claims that the use was a clerical adaptation of the Roman *fidei*

---

25.   Carne, 'A Sketch of the History of the High Court of Chancery from Its Origin to the Chancellorship of Wolsey', note 7 above, pp 437–41.

26.   P W Young, 'Equity, Contract and Conscience' in S Degeling & J Edelman (eds), *Equity in Commercial Law*, Lawbook Co, Sydney, 2005, 489, p 501.

27.   G P Verbit, *The Origins of the Trust*, Xlibris Corporation, 2002, pp 27–37.

28.   F W Maitland, *Equity and The Forms of Action at Common Law*, Cambridge University Press, Cambridge, 1929, p 25.

29.   R H Helmholtz, *The Oxford History of the Laws of England, Volume 1, The Canon Law and the Ecclesiastical Jurisdiction from 597 to the 1640s*, Oxford University Press, Oxford, 2004, pp 421–3.

30.   D J Seipp, 'Trust and Fiduciary Duty in the Early Common Law' (2011) *Boston University Law Review* 1011, p 1037.

31.   Maitland, *Equity and The Forms of Action at Common Law*, note 28 above, p 23.

32.   Maitland, *Equity and The Forms of Action at Common Law*, note 28 above, p 6.

33.   Maitland, *Equity and The Forms of Action at Common Law*, note 28 above, p 23.

34.   Watt, *Equity Stirring*, note 1 above, pp 121–2.

commissium.[35] The *fidei commissium* was a device invented to pass benefits to an heir through the medium of a trusted friend in circumstances where some legal impediment precluded the heir from taking the benefit directly. Maitland doubts there is any connection between the development of the use/trust and *fidei commissium*.[36] Lupoi asserts that the trust grew out of the *confidentia* structure employed in the civil law system in several places in Europe.[37] Holmes argues that it originated in the Germanic *salman* or *treuhand*.[38] Vernit's detailed study on the foreign influences of the origins of the trust comes to the following conclusion:

> [I]f the English trust was the end result of a foreign conception it is more likely than not that the foreign influence was the *waqf* … More importantly, when Maitland said of the trust 'there is nothing quite like it in foreign law' he appears to have been mistaken. There was something very much like it in foreign law — the Islamic *waqf* — and it had existed full blown for more than 500 years before the English trust.[39]

1.19 The *waqf* is a 'permanent dedication by a Muslim of any property for religious or charitable purposes, or for the benefit of the *waqf*'s founder and his descendants, in such a way that the owner's right is extinguished and the property is considered to belong to God'.[40] The *waqf* developed in Islamic society 'for exactly the same purposes as English trusts'. These were, as is discussed below (see 1.22–1.25), 'to avoid taxes, to avoid confiscation of property by the sovereign and to avoid the strictures of the laws of bequest and inheritance'.[41]

1.20 Whatever may have been the extent of foreign influences on the development of the use and later the trust, the Court of Chancery was fundamentally guided by the idea of good conscience in their enforcement. This was most clearly exemplified in Christopher St Germain's treatise, most commonly known as *Dialogue Between a Doctor and Student*, first published in Latin in 1528 and later in English in 1531. Central to St Germain's theory of law and equity was the notion that 'equitable interventions in the name of good conscience, which were sometimes necessary to mitigate the rigour of the common law, were designed to reinforce, not to contradict, general legal principles'.[42] For St Germain, equity was not outside the law, but resided implicitly in it.[43] According to Holdsworth, St Germain's influential text became 'the basis and starting-point of the English

---

35. W Blackstone, *Commentaries on the Laws of England*, Vol II, Clarendon Press, Oxford, 1766, pp 327–8.
36. Maitland, *Equity and The Forms of Action at Common Law*, note 28 above, pp 32–3.
37. M Lupoi, 'The Civil Law Trust' in R F Atherton (ed), *The International Academy of Estate and Trust Law, Selected Papers 1997–1999*, Kluwer Law International, London, 2001, 35, pp 39–40; M Lupoi, '"Trust and Confidence"' (2009) 125 *Law Quarterly Review* 253.
38. O W Holmes, 'Early English Equity' (1885) 1 *Law Quarterly Review* 162, pp 163–4.
39. Verbit, *The Origins of the Trust*, note 27 above, p 286. See also A Avini, 'The Origins of the Modern English Trust Revisited' (1995–1996) 70 *Tulane Law Review* 1139. Whether or not the *waqf* served as an inspiration for the trust, it did inspire the names of various towns in parts of Europe occupied by the Ottoman Turks. Thus, *vakuf*, the Slavic version of *waqf*, is seen in the names of several Bosnian towns, including Gornji Vakuf, Donji Vakuf and Skender Vakuf.
40. J Hussain, *Islam, Its Law and Society*, 3rd ed, Federation Press, Sydney, 2011, p 146.
41. Verbit, *The Origins of the Trust*, note 27 above, p 281.
42. S K Dobbins, 'Equity: The Court of Conscience or the King's Command, the Dialogues of St Germain and Hobbes Compared' (1991) 9 *Journal of Law and Religion* 113, p 124. For a detailed analysis of St Germain's conception of conscience see Klinck, *Conscience, Equity and the Court of Chancery in Early Modern England*, note 4 above, pp 44–67.
43. J A Guy, *Christopher St Germain on Chancery and Statute*, Seldon Society, London, 1985, pp 71–2.

system of equity'.[44] Part of this was due to the fact that the text enabled the new breed of increasingly common law trained chancellors to comprehend and apply the principles that their ecclesiastical predecessors had developed.[45]

1.21 At the time when uses began to be enforced by Chancery, a transfer of land was called a *feoffment*. A transferee of land for the use of some other person was called a *feoffee to use*. The *feoffee to use* was required to hold the title to land for the benefit of that other person, the *cestui que use*. A conveyance of land to a *feoffee to use* would direct the transferee to hold the land for the benefit of the *cestui que use*. The common law did not recognise the rights of the *cestui que use*, holding that the *feoffee to use* was the owner of the land: *MCC Proceeds Inc v Lehman Bros International (Europe)* [1998] 4 All ER 675 at 691. However, the chancellors, by focusing upon the conscience of the *feoffee to use*, recognised the claim of the *cestui que use* and enforced the use against the *feoffee to use*. In so doing the chancellor was not denying the common law rights of the *feoffee to use*. Rather, he was preventing the unconscientious exercise of common law rights by the *feoffee to use* and compelling him to exercise such rights for the benefit of the *cestui que use*. Furthermore, a third party who took a conveyance of the land from the *feoffee to use*, with the knowledge of the existence of the use, was bound by the use.[46]

1.22 The popularity of uses and Chancery's enforcement of them was driven by two major circumstances. First, the use provided men with more sophisticated ways of dealing with their assets than was permitted by the ancient rights of primogeniture and dower that were recognised by the common law. The right of primogeniture mandated that, upon the death of the owner of land, the land passed to his eldest son to the exclusion of all other children. If the deceased had only daughters, the land passed to the daughters in equal shares.[47] The absence of children or relatives ultimately meant that the land was forfeited to the feudal lord. The right of dower conferred upon the deceased's surviving wife an estate for the term of her life of one-third of the deceased's freehold land. Not all land-based interests in property were dowerable. For example, leasehold interests were excluded from the ambit of dower. The system of uses enabled one to avoid a wife's dower rights. If land was conveyed to a *feoffee to use* for the benefit of a male *cestui que use*, upon the latter's death no dower rights would pass to his wife. This was so because dower only applied to legal estates owned by the husband at his death, and not to his interest as a *cestui que use*.

1.23 The importance of the use in this context was somewhat diminished with the passing of the *Statute of Wills* in 1540 which permitted landowners to determine who would inherit land by means of a will. The statute was something of a political compromise between Henry VIII (1509–1547) and English landowners, who were growing increasingly frustrated with the system of primogeniture and the Crown's control of land.

---

44. W Holdsworth, *Some Makers of English Law, The Tagore Lectures 1937–38*, Cambridge University Press, Cambridge, 1938, p 96.
45. Holdsworth, 'The Early History of Equity', note 8 above, p 296.
46. The point relating to the third party led to the development of equitable doctrines linked to the 'bona fide purchaser taking for value and without notice'. Indeed, it can be said that the 'bona fide purchaser' was equity's counterpart to the common law's 'reasonable man' (later 'reasonable person').
47. Because the rules of primogeniture prevented the division of lands to be inherited, other sons tended to seek a place within the Church or a good prospect for marriage, that is, a female heir.

1.24   The second factor behind the popularity of the use was its important function of enabling the avoidance of feudal incidents in land ownership. These incidents were important sources of the king's income, which operated as taxes payable when land passed from an owner to his or her heir. To limit the burden of such taxes, land could be conveyed to a number of *feoffees to use* as joint tenants, resulting in no taxes being paid until the last of them died. This was because the legal title of a deceased joint tenant did not descend to his or her heir but merged with the title of the surviving joint tenants. It was, perhaps, not surprising that a common lawyer such as Sir Edward Coke was later to remark that 'there were two Inventors of Uses, Fear and Fraud; Fear in times of Troubles and civil Wars to save their Inheritances from being forfeited; and Fraud to defeat due Debts, lawful Actions, Wards, Escheats, Mortmains, etc'.[48]

1.25   The diminution of the king's coffers that was a consequence of the system of uses eventually triggered a royal response in the form of the *Statute of Uses* which was enacted in 1535 and came into effect in 1536. This statute was one enacted by an unwilling parliament at the behest of a strong-willed and determined king in the form of Henry VIII. The statute effectively turned the use into a legal estate to which was attached the liability for payment of feudal dues. The response to the *Statute of Uses* was the development of the 'use upon a use', which effectively sought to restore the pre-*Statute of Uses* position. Although initially not upheld, Chancery eventually did recognise the use upon a use: *Sambach v Dalston* (1634) 21 ER 164.[49] With the abolition of feudal dues by the *Tenures Abolition Act* of 1660, there was no major reason not to recognise and enforce the use upon a use. The importance of the use — or trust as it was now increasingly being called — as a means of minimising tax liabilities declined. It has been only in relatively recent times that the trust has assumed a function similar to that of its predecessor in the field of minimisation of tax liabilities.

1.26   The system of trusts began to be employed in a number of ways that were significantly different from those of its progenitor, the use. In the days before the development of the modern corporation, trusts were used as convenient ways to accumulate large sums of capital for major projects. In many ways trusts presaged the split between ownership and control that is the defining feature of the modern corporation.

1.27   An important and more private application of the trust was as a device to preserve and protect the property, and hence the political, economic and social power of England's landed aristocracy.[50] Indeed, during the initial development of the law of trusts, most trusts involved land. It was only with the change from an agrarian to an industrialised economy that trusts of other forms of property became more common. The transformation of the economy saw the creation of new forms of wealth in the form of bank accounts, bonds and shares come into the hands of an emerging middle class which was just as keen as the landed aristocracy to preserve and protect its wealth through the institution of the trust. Trusts achieved this purpose by having the property vested in trustees who were experienced and qualified in managing and preserving property.[51] A related

---

48.   Quoted in Guy, *Christopher St Germain on Chancery and Statute*, note 43 above, p 75.
49.   Watt, *Equity Stirring*, note 1 above, pp 123–4.
50.   For example, the landed aristocracy dominated both of the houses of the British parliament until the end of the nineteenth century: D Cannadine, *The Decline and Fall of the British Aristocracy*, Yale University Press, New Haven, 1990, p 14.
51.   C Stebbings, *The Private Trustee in Victorian England*, Cambridge University Press, Cambridge, 2002, pp 6–8.

application of the law of trusts was the institution of the marriage settlement. At common law, 'the very being or legal existence of [a] woman [was] suspended during the marriage'[52] to her husband, with the consequence that a married woman's property was irrevocably transferred to him upon marriage.[53] According to Lord Chancellor Thurlow, the law gave the husband rights over his wife's property in exchange for the legal obligation assumed upon marriage, to provide for and support his wife: *Countess of Strathmore v Bowes* (1789) 30 ER 14 at 16. However, by means of a marriage settlement, entered into before marriage, the woman's property would be transferred to trustees to preclude the operation of the common law rule and thereby enable the married woman to effectively retain the benefits of her own property. Thus, the marriage settlement had, from its inception, the primary purpose of preserving a wife's property rights,[54] or, as Holcombe has written, 'to protect the property of … daughters from the common-law rights of husbands, and to ensure that if there were no children of a marriage the property would not pass to [the] daughters' husbands but would return to [the daughters'] families'.[55] The widespread use of marriage settlements is confirmed by a commentator in an 1863 issue of *Cornhill Magazine* who observed that they had become 'part of the regular course of affairs to which every one submits in his turn'.[56] However, the *Married Women's Property Act 1882* (UK) substantially changed the position of married women. As Yalom points out:

> From that point on, an Englishwoman could not only hold on to whatever she owned at the time of marriage or acquired after marriage, but she could also enter into contracts and sue and be sued, and dispose of her property by sale, will, or gift.[57]

As a result of the abolition of the common law rules relating to married women, the use of marriage settlements began to decline.

1.28 It has been widely claimed that the use and later the trust were protective of women by first, enabling fathers to make provision for their daughters in spite of the rules of primogeniture, and second, enabling women to retain property rights notwithstanding the common law rule that applied when a woman married. While this is true, it is only part of the story. Recent scholarship demonstrates that the use of trusts in this context also had the effect of preventing property coming into a woman's hands that would otherwise have done so pursuant to the right of dower (see 1.22) or in circumstances when daughters would have inherited because there was no male heir.[58] Furthermore, marriage settlements were usually set up in such a way as to prevent a woman from running a business in which the assets were invested. Another common feature of such settlements was that the woman was precluded from having access to the capital held on trust for her. For example, in *Re Wood* (1885) 1 TLR 192, a husband lost his job due to illness. This meant

52. W Blackstone, *Commentaries on the Laws of England*, Vol I, Clarendon Press, Oxford, 1765, p 430.
53. M Yalom, *A History of the Wife*, Pandora Press, London, 2001, pp 185–6.
54. A L Erickson, 'Common Law versus Common Practice: The Use of Marriage Settlements in Early Modern England' (1990) 43 *Economic History Review*, 2nd ser, 21.
55. L Holcombe, *Wives and Property, Reform of the Married Women's Property Law in Nineteenth-Century England*, Martin Robertson & Co, Oxford, 1983, p 38.
56. Quoted in Stebbings, *The Private Trustee in Victorian England*, note 51 above, p 11.
57. Yalom, *A History of the Wife*, note 53 above, pp 185–6.
58. R F Croucher & P Vines, *Succession: Families, Property and Death, Texts and Cases*, 3rd ed, LexisNexis Butterworths, Sydney, 2008, p 21.

that he was unable to provide for his children. His wife's application for a release of funds from her marriage settlement to pay for the education of her children was refused.[59]

1.29 Another example of the ways in which trusts were utilised arose in the context of English rule in Ireland, where legislation enacted in the early eighteenth century restricted the ownership of land by Catholics. By conveying land to trusted Protestants to be held on trust for them, Catholics could effectively undermine the legislation's stated purpose.[60]

The common injunction

1.30 One of the major remedies administered by the chancellor in the development of equity was known as the common injunction, which began to be used in the mid-fifteenth century. The effect of such an injunction was to order a plaintiff at common law to discontinue proceedings, or, if a verdict at common law had already been obtained, to prevent it being enforced. Disobedience to a common injunction resulted in imprisonment. A defendant to common law proceedings could obtain a common injunction if it could be established that the plaintiff's enforcement of common law rights was such as to amount to having acted unconscientiously. Two important features were implicit in this procedure. First, the remedy was characterised as *in personam*, in that it attached to the person of the common law plaintiff: see 2.52–2.57. This followed logically from the fact that the chancellor, in focusing on the conscience of the common law plaintiff, acted 'according to conscience'. The chancellor never denied the existence and validity of the common law rights and interests of the common law plaintiff. All the chancellor did was to prevent an unconscientious enforcement of those common law rights and interests. Second, the common injunction (and indeed all equitable remedies) was discretionary. Unless the petitioner in equity could establish unconscientious behaviour by the common law plaintiff, the common injunction was not ordered.

1.31 The common injunction effectively challenged the authority and, in a restricted sense, the validity of the decisions of the common law courts. In the context of a rapid expansion of the number of cases coming before the Chancery Court, the practice of granting common injunctions was the principal factor in the intermittent conflict that developed between the common law courts and Chancery. The chancellor's jurisdiction to issue the common injunction was challenged by the Court of King's Bench with its claim that common law courts could forbid any party resorting to any other jurisdiction for relief once a particular matter was already within the jurisdiction of a common law court.[61] A further response, as demonstrated in *Russel's Case* in 1482, was to release any person imprisoned for failing to obey a common injunction upon an application for a writ of habeas corpus.[62]

1.32 The extent of the conflict between Chancery and the common law courts depended very much upon the personal relationship that existed at any time between the chancellor and the leaders

---

59. R Auchmuty, 'The Fiction of Equity' in S Scott-Hunt & H Lim (eds), *Feminist Perspectives on Equity and Trusts*, Cavendish Publishing, London 2001, 1, pp 13–16.

60. W N Osborough, 'Catholics, Land and the Popery Acts of Anne' in T P Power & Whelan (eds), *Endurance and Emergence: Catholics in Ireland in the Eighteenth Century*, Irish Academic Press, Dublin, 1990, 21, p 43.

61. W L Carne, 'A Sketch of the History of the High Court of Chancery from the Chancellorship of Wolsey to that of Lord Nottingham (1515–1673)' (1927–1928) 16 *Georgetown Law Journal* 73, pp 104–5.

62. Baker, *The Oxford History of the Laws of England*, note 16 above, p 174.

of the common law courts. A particularly 'warm contention'[63] over the common injunction arose during the early years of the reign of James I (1603–1625). The key protagonists in the struggle were Sir Edward Coke — the Chief Justice of first, the Court of Common Pleas (1606–1613), and later, the Court of King's Bench (1613–1616) — and Baron Ellesmere — the Lord Keeper of the Great Seal (effectively the Vice-Chancellor) (1596–1603) and later Lord Chancellor (1603–1617). Two cases of the time initially signalled the ascendancy of Coke and the common law courts. First, in *Finch v Throckmorton* (1597) 78 ER 477, Throckmorton was one day late in paying rent on a lease. The Court of King's Bench declared that the subsequent termination of the lease for late payment of rent was valid. Throckmorton sought an injunction from Chancery to stay execution of the judgment. Finch appealed to the queen, who referred the matter back to all the judges, who decided that the chancellor could not examine the case after there had been a judgment at common law. The second case was *Glanvile v Courtney* (1614) 80 ER 1139. In that case, Glanvile, who had defrauded Courtney in relation to a sale of jewels to him, proceeded to enforce the agreement for sale at common law. Courtney was ordered to pay the agreed price. Courtney then appealed to Chancery, which ordered Glanvile to repay the money to Courtney. Glanvile refused and was imprisoned by order of the chancellor. However, Coke ordered the release of Glanvile pursuant to a writ of habeas corpus.

1.33 However, the setbacks suffered by Chancery in these two cases were reversed following Lord Ellesmere's decision in *The Earl of Oxford's Case in Chancery* (1615) 21 ER 485. This case was concerned with protracted litigation relating to the entitlement to certain land in London's Covent Garden. In the case Lord Ellesmere, at 486–7, declared:

> The Office of the Chancellor is to correct Men's consciences for Frauds, Breach of Trusts, Wrongs and oppressions, of what Nature soever they be, and to soften and mollify the Extremity of the Law … [W]hen a Judgment is obtained by Oppression, Wrong and a hard Conscience, the Chancellor will frustrate and set it aside, not for any error or Defect in the Judgment, but for the hard Conscience of the Party.

1.34 Following the decision in the *Earl of Oxford's Case*, the dispute between the common law courts and Chancery was referred to James I who, in June 1616, by Royal Decree ruled in favour of Ellesmere's approach, thereby upholding the validity of the common injunction and establishing the supremacy of equity over the common law.[64] In November 1616, James I dismissed Coke from office. Although the actions of James I resolved an important legal issue, it did little to resolve the increasingly strident political attacks on Chancery. James I, who came to the English throne in 1603, was the first of the Scottish Stuart[65] monarchs to rule England during the seventeenth century. The Stuart kings sought to enhance royal power and prerogatives at the expense of parliament. In this developing conflict between the king and parliament, those courts most closely associated with

---

63. E P Hewitt & J B Richardson, *White & Tudor's Leading Cases in Equity With Notes, Vol 1*, 9th ed, Sweet & Maxwell Ltd, 1928, p 621.
64. M Forthier, 'Equity and Ideas: Coke, Ellesmere, and James I' (1998) 51 *Renaissance Quarterly* 1255; Watt, *Equity Stirring*, note 1 above, pp 67–76. For a detailed account of the *Earl of Oxford's Case* see D Ibbetson, 'The Earl of Oxford's Case (1615)' in C Mitchell & P Mitchell (eds), *Landmark Cases in Equity*, Hart Publishing, Oxford, 2012, pp 1–32.
65. The original family name of 'Stewart' was changed to the French spelling of 'Stuart' by Mary Queen of Scots to overcome the difficulty French speakers had with the letter 'w'. Later English governments preferred to use the French spelling as a form of anti-Jacobite propaganda against the then exiled (and French-based) House of Stuart.

the king, such as Chancery, became the object of political attack from the opponents of absolute monarchy and the defenders of parliament. On the other hand, the common law courts became increasingly associated with opposition to the Stuarts. This political conflict between the king and parliament eventually led to the English Civil War of the 1640s, the abolition of the monarchy in 1649 and the rule of Oliver Cromwell as England's Lord Protector during the 1650s.

1.35 With Cromwell's ascendancy to power, it was hardly surprising that an attempt was made to abolish Chancery during the early 1650s. This was unsuccessful. However, there was legislation passed that dramatically reformed Chancery. These actions were motivated by the political subservience of the court to the Crown and later the Cromwellian executive, but also by claims of corruption, delay, lack of consistency, and excessive costs associated with Chancery litigation. The reform legislation was aimed at making Chancery function much as the common law courts did by means of adopting a definite body of rules and procedures. The restoration of the monarchy in 1660 meant that this reform legislation was never implemented and Chancery was thus restored to the pre-eminence granted to it by James I. Criticism of Chancery continued. The chancellor's seemingly unlimited power was most famously criticised by John Selden in his spirited rebuke first published (posthumously) in 1689, where he said:

> Equity is a Roguish thing: for Law we have a measure, know what to trust to; Equity is according to the Conscience of him that is Chancellor, and as that is larger or narrower, so is Equity.' Tis all one as if they should make the Standard for the measure we call a Foot, a Chancellor's Foot; what an uncertain Measure would be this? One Chancellor has a long Foot, another a short Foot, a Third an indifferent Foot:' Tis the same thing in a Chancellor's Conscience.[66]

The systemisation of equity

1.36 Although the restoration of the monarchy in 1660 signalled the reassertion of Chancery's importance as a court of the realm, it was also recognised that the critiques of the court were not entirely without foundation. Thereafter, Chancery started to transform itself. This process led Chancery to function increasingly in much the same way as did the courts of common law.[67] By the time of Lord Nottingham's chancellorship (1673–82) the Court of Chancery had become fixed and determinate both in matters over which jurisdiction was exercised and the principles that were applied. In *Cook v Fountain* (1676) 36 ER 984 at 990, Lord Nottingham rejected the idea that subjective notions of conscience were the proper basis of equitable jurisprudence. To him conscience was clearly defined within settled principles. This influential case proclaimed that, in its search for justice, equity's concern with considerations of certainty in the law and the doctrine of precedent had supplanted its earlier more robust and flexible approach. Thus, in *Gee v Pritchard* (1818) 36 ER 670 at 674, Lord Eldon declared:

> The doctrines of this Court ought be as well settled and made as uniform, almost, as those of the common law … I cannot agree that the doctrines of this Court are to be changed by every succeeding judge. Nothing would inflict upon me greater pain, in quitting this place, than the recollection that I had done any thing to justify the reproach that the equity of the Court varies like the Chancellor's foot.

---

66. *Table-Talk: Being the Discourses of John Selden*, London, 1689, pp 43–4.
67. S E Prall, 'Chancery Reform and the Puritan Revolution' (1962) 6 *The American Journal of Legal History* 28.

Consistent with this approach, in *Johnson v Crook* (1879) LR 12 Ch 639 at 649, Sir George Jessel, in referring to early times, opined:

> Equity Judges did not profess to make new law, and when they state what the law is, they do not mean, as might have been said two or three centuries before, that that was law which they thought ought to be law.

1.37 Holdsworth summarised the development of equity during this time as follows:

> [The] change in the character of equity is partly the cause and partly the effect of a change in the relations of law and equity. It had become clear that law and equity must recognize the fact that they were not rival but complementary systems, and that, consequently, common lawyers and equity lawyers must work together in partnership, as, for the most part, they had done before the dispute between Coke and Ellesmere. This development was made easier by the fact that many Chancellors had served as chief justices in the common law courts, and by the fact that there was no hard and fast separation between the common law and equity bars. Therefore the ideas and modes of thought of the common lawyers were becoming more in evidence in the court of Chancery. Both common law and equity were becoming settled systems; and when, at the close of the century, equity accepted the common law view of the binding force of precedents, and reports of equity cases began to appear in increasing numbers, its systematization proceeded apace.[68]

1.38 Lord Nottingham is often referred to as 'the father of modern equity' for his systematising work.[69] He was the first of a long line of chancellors who laid down, through their decisions, the general principles of equitable jurisdiction. Although holding office for only a relatively brief period of time, Lord Nottingham made profound contributions to what have become foundation principles of equity. As Moffatt observes:

> [Lord Nottingham] developed a classification of trusts, was responsible for the doctrine that there can be no 'clog on the equity of redemption' and is believed to have drafted the Statute of Frauds 1677, which in revised form still provides significant formalities requirements for the creation of express trusts or transfers of equitable interests. His influence was also instrumental in confirming the proprietary nature of the trust rather than it being merely a chose in action … Moreover, however one may choose to analyse and interpret the reason for the emergence of the 'rule against perpetuities', it is evident that Lord Nottingham's role in formulating the rule … was decisive.[70]

1.39 In this context particular mention must also be made of the chancellorship of Lord Eldon (1801–27). The exceptional length of his tenure in office, combined with his high intellectual standing and capacity for work, resulted in 32 volumes of reports of his decided cases. These cases are really the basis of modern equity. The meticulous care taken by Lord Eldon in writing his judgments meant that they were almost always regarded as authoritative. Veeder, after noting Lord Eldon's various strengths and weaknesses, makes the following assessment of his decisions:

---

68. Holdsworth, *Some Makers of English Law*, note 44 above, pp 149–50. On the acceptance of the binding nature of precedent in the Court of Chancery in the late seventeenth century see *Earl of Macclesfield v Fitton* (1683) 23 ER 392 at 392–3.
69. D R Klinck, 'Lord Nottingham's "Certain Measures"' (2010) 28 *Law and History Review* 711, argues that Nottingham's role in systematising equity was one that nevertheless allowed for significant elements of fluidity in terms of its principles.
70. G Moffatt, *Trusts Law, Text and Materials*, 4th ed, Cambridge University Press, Cambridge, 2005, p 42.

Lord Eldon's decisions ... are, in substance, monuments of learning, acumen and practical application of equity. His judgments were seldom appealed from and hardly ever reversed; and, except where the law has been since altered by statute, time has not materially impaired their authority.[71]

Not surprisingly, most contemporary equitable principles and rules have their genesis in his decisions.[72]

The Judicature Acts reforms

1.40   While equitable principles were being systematised by Lord Nottingham and his successors, great procedural deficiencies continued to impact negatively on the Court of Chancery.[73] The complaints against Chancery were much the same as those voiced against it during the Cromwellian era of the mid-seventeenth century, and stemmed principally from the lack of judges and staff, as well as its preoccupation with procedure and formal documentation.[74] None was more damning in their condemnation of Chancery than Charles Dickens in his memorable description of that court in the first pages of *Bleak House*. These deficiencies, most conspicuously on display during the chancellorship of Lord Eldon, meant that excessive delays were not uncommon and that many litigants had to settle disputes out of court rather than proceed to litigation. It was during his term in office that the first appointment of a vice-chancellor was made, although it had virtually no impact on addressing Chancery's problems. It was thus hardly surprising that Spence, in his Preface to *Equitable Jurisdiction of the Courts of Chancery*, published in 1839, wrote that '[n]o man, as things now stand, can enter into a Chancery suit with any reasonable hope of being alive at its termination if he has a determined adversary'.[75] Such were the problems with the administration of the Court of Chancery that, as late as the mid-nineteenth century, plaintiffs were attempting to avoid Chancery by approaching the common law courts for relief. Thus, in *Edwards v Lowndes* (1852) 118 ER 367 at 370, Lord Campbell CJ had to remind a beneficiary under a trust that the beneficiary had 'no action at law for money had and received [against a trustee], though he has money in his hands which under the terms of the trust he ought to pay over to the [beneficiary]'.

1.41   Similar concerns with the common law courts led to calls for a major overhaul of the English legal system. In the 1850s procedural reforms in both the common law courts and Chancery did address some of these concerns.[76] However, from then on, there was a growing call for the elimination of the separate courts of common law and equity and their fusion into a single court. This debate was largely pushed by lawyers, rather than politicians, 'with [the] lawyers generally eschewing

---

71.   V V Veeder, 'A Century of English Judicature, 1800–1900' in Association of American Law Schools (ed), *Select Essays in Anglo-American Legal History, Vol I*, Little, Brown, and Company, Boston, 1907, 730, p 735.

72.   W J V Windeyer, *Lectures on Legal History*, 2nd ed, Law Book Co, Sydney, 1957, p 268.

73.   For a detailed analysis of litigation trends and practice before Chancery see H Horowitz & P Polden, 'Continuity or Change in the Court of Chancery in the Seventeenth and Eighteenth Centuries?' (1996) 35 *Journal of British Studies* 24; Baron Bowen, 'Progress in the Administration of Justice During the Victorian Period' in Association of American Law Schools (ed), *Select Essays in Anglo-American Legal History, Vol I*, Little, Brown, and Company, Boston, 1907, 516, pp 523–31.

74.   M Lobban, 'Preparing for Fusion: Reforming the Nineteenth-Century Court of Chancery, Part I, (2004) 22 *Law and History Review* 389, pp 391–4; Watt, *Equity Stirring*, note 1 above, pp 65–6.

75.   Quoted in W R Cornish & G de N Clark, *Law and Society in England 1750–1950*, Sweet & Maxwell, London, 1989, p 41.

76.   M Leeming, 'Equity, the Judicature Acts and Restitution' (2011) 5 *Journal of Equity* 199, pp 203–4.

questions of substance, preferring to concentrate on taking forward the procedural reforms of the first half of the [nineteenth] century'.[77] An important impetus for such reform came from across the Atlantic Ocean with the example of fusion that took place in the American state of New York in 1847. A significant step in this process of fusion was the *Common Law Procedure Act 1854* which gave the common law courts some power to grant injunctions and specific performance as well as to hear and consider some equitable pleas. This legislation was followed by the *Chancery Amendment Act 1858*, more popularly known as *Lord Cairns' Act*, which enabled Chancery to order damages in favour of a plaintiff in lieu of, or in addition to, a decree of specific performance or an injunction.[78] Prior to this, a plaintiff who had been denied equitable relief by Chancery had no option but to commence fresh proceedings before the common law courts for an award of damages.

1.42   These reforms, however, were seen as insufficient as they did not address what was increasingly seen as the fundamental flaw in English law, namely, the existence of separate courts of common law and equity. The push for reform not only had the support of the lawyers, but also of Great Britain's industrial, commercial and financial interests. The latter were concerned with 'the inconsistencies and inconveniences of commercial litigation which arose from the separations of jurisdiction: the difficulties that came, for instance, from treating company directors as agents at common law and as trustees in equity'.[79] The question of reform was eventually addressed with the enactment of the *Judicature Acts* of 1873 and 1875, which abolished the historic courts of common law and equity and replaced them with one court, the High Court of Judicature. This court was divided into a number of divisions, the main ones being the Queen's (or King's) Bench Division and the Chancery Division. However, s 24 of the *Judicature Act 1873* empowered judges to give effect to both common law and equitable principles, irrespective of the division of the court to which they were assigned. The Chancery Division became primarily responsible for dealing with cases involving the application of equitable principles. Many of the reforms to the Chancery Division echoed those originally enacted in the reform legislation adopted in the Cromwellian period, but never implemented following the restoration of the monarchy in 1660: see 1.35.[80]

1.43   As will be discussed in more detail in Chapter 3, the fusion of the formerly separate courts did not similarly fuse the principles of equity and the common law. Rather, as was stated in Ashburner's famous fluvial metaphor, 'the two streams of jurisdictions [that is, common law and equity], though they run in the same channel, run side by side and do not mingle their waters'.[81]

1.44   Although principally concerned with the administrative fusion of the formerly separate courts, the *Judicature Act 1873* did deal with some issues relating to legal principle. Section 25 resolved a number areas of law in which there was a lack of clarity or uniformity, most of which involved resolving differences between the rules of common law and equity. For example, s 25(7) dealt with the different rules as to the effect of a time stipulation in a contract by giving force to the

---

77.   Lobban, 'Preparing for Fusion', note 74 above, p 390.
78.   M Lobban, 'Preparing for Fusion: Reforming the Nineteenth-Century Court of Chancery, Part II, (2004) 22 *Law and History Review* 565, pp 589–90. See also Leeming, 'Equity, the Judicature Acts and Restitution', note 76 above, pp 206–9.
79.   Cornish & Clark, *Law and Society in England 1750–1950*, note 75 above, p 44.
80.   Prall, 'Chancery Reform and the Puritan Revolution', note 67 above, p 44; Leeming, 'Equity, the Judicature Acts and Restitution', note 76 above, pp 209–11.
81.   D Browne, *Ashburner's Principles of Equity*, 2nd ed, Butterworth & Co, London, 1933, p 18.

equitable rule: see 2.24–2.25. More significantly, s 25(11) stipulated that, if there were any substantive differences between the rules of common law and equity that were not dealt with elsewhere in s 25, the equitable rule would prevail. In effect, s 25(11) gave statutory force to, and reaffirmed, the Royal Decree of 1616 issued by James I in the wake of the *Earl of Oxford's Case*.[82] Thus, in *Lowe & Sons v Dixon & Sons* (1885) 16 QBD 455 at 458, in a case relating to the rules of contribution, Lopes J said:

> At law, if several persons have to contribute a certain sum, the share which each has to pay is, the total amount divided by the number of contributors; and no allowance is made in respect of the inability of some of them to pay their shares. But, in equity, those who *can* pay must not only contribute their own shares, but they must also make good the shares of those who are unable to furnish their own contribution. Inasmuch, therefore, as the rules of equity prevail [as provided for by the terms of s 25(11)], the defendants must make good each one-half of that which Lund, Beveridge, & Co are unable to pay.

Equity in the post-Judicature Acts era

1.45 The enactment of s 25(11) of the *Judicature Act 1873* symbolised a formal supremacy of the principles of equity over those of the common law. However, the reality was that during the century that followed, the opposite was the case. Indeed, the impact of the principles of equity was in decline even before the adoption of the reforms of the 1870s.[83] For example, in 1862, in the seminal decision of *Milroy v Lord* (1862) 45 ER 185, the equitable principles relating to declarations of trust were, as Girard described it, 'put … under house arrest'.[84] Prior to this decision, if X intended to give property to Y, but the transfer had not been carried out because of some non-compliance with the relevant formalities associated with such a transfer, equity could give effect to the intended transfer by finding that X had declared himself or herself to be a trustee of the property for Y: *Ex parte Pye* (1811) 34 ER 271. However, the effect of *Milroy v Lord* was that an intended, but ineffectual, transfer of property could not be 'saved' by being treated as a declaration of trust. For a declaration of trust to arise there had to be an intention on the part of X to declare a trust of the property for Y.

1.46 The relative dominance of common law over equity in the post-*Judicature Acts* era was partly attributable to the impact that common lawyers had in administering the principles of equity, there being more of them than equity judges in the new unified court.[85] For example, a House of Lords dominated by common lawyers significantly curtailed the scope for equitable relief in relation to misrepresentations in *Derry v Peek* (1889) 14 App Cas 337. In *Maddison v Alderson* (1883) 8 App Cas 467, the House of Lords narrowed down the circumstances in which the doctrine of part performance (see 23.77–23.89) could be invoked to override the writing requirements set out in the *Statute of Frauds 1677*.[86] Girard summarises the position of equity during the latter part of the nineteenth century and first half of the twentieth century as follows:

---

82. Leeming, 'Equity, the Judicature Acts and Restitution', note 76 above, pp 211–12.
83. Young, 'Equity, Contract and Conscience', note 26 above, pp 500–02.
84. P Girard, 'History and Development of Equity' in M R Gillen & F Woodman (eds), *The Law of Trusts, A Contextual Approach*, 2nd ed, Edmond Montgomery Publications Ltd, Toronto, 2006, 13, p 67.
85. Cornish & Clark, *Law and Society in England 1750–1950*, note 75 above, pp 220–1.
86. Cornish & Clark, *Law and Society in England 1750–1950*, note 75 above, p 221.

In the decades after the *Judicature Acts*, the English courts seemed little inclined to push the frontiers of equity to supplement or correct perceived deficiencies in the common law, with the 'two streams' metaphor invoked as justification for this inactivity. Not until it was declared in the [post-World War II] era that 'equity was not past childbearing' did a certain renaissance of equity occur … In retrospect, this dictum only showed how moribund equity had been in the hands of the English judges before 1950.[87]

1.47   Illustrations of the post-World War II renaissance of equity have been particularly noticeable in the prominent examples of confidential information (see Chapter 8), fiduciary obligations (see Chapter 9) and estoppel: see Chapter 10. Writing extra-judicially, Justice Gummow, a judge of the High Court and prominent equity scholar, although welcoming this trend, suggested that in some cases these developments were imperilled 'by a failure … to resort to fundamental equitable principles'.[88] This raises a fundamental and controversial question about the nature of equity in the post-*Judicature Acts* era, a topic more fully discussed in Chapter 3. However, one can readily agree with Gummow J when he said:

[L]aw without support in values is ineffective because it is static rather than dynamic. It is from a thriving equity jurisdiction based in a thorough understanding of its principles, their necessity, and the circumstances of the individual case, that judge-made law continues to draw much of its sustenance.[89]

EQUITY IN AUSTRALIA

1.48   With the English settlement in New South Wales in the late eighteenth century, the English rules of common law and equity became the foundation of the colonial legal system in the Australian colonies. The development of Australian equity can be broken down into four main phases.

The first phase: the First Charter of Justice and the Court of Civil Jurisdiction

1.49   The embryonic Australian legal system was conceived under letters patent in the *First Charter of Justice*. While parliament had passed the Act of 1787 (27 Geo III c 2), which created the legislative basis for the establishment of the Colony of New South Wales, this Act only empowered the Crown to create a criminal court in New South Wales. By creating the Court of Civil Jurisdiction, the *First Charter* was accused by some, including Jeremy Bentham, to have been illegal.[90] Others contested this finding, and it appears that the majority of opinion was in favour of the Crown having the prerogative power to create common law courts in the colonies without legislative approval.[91] The *First Charter* empowered the Court of Civil Jurisdiction to be constituted by a Judge Advocate and two fit and proper persons, who were effectively lay magistrates. It had power to deal in a summary fashion with 'all pleas concerning interests in lands, houses, tenements, and hereditaments, and all manner of interests therein, and all pleas of debt, account, or other contracts, trespasses, and

---

87.   P Girard, 'History and Development of Equity' note 84 above, p 66.
88.   W M C Gummow, 'Equity: Too Successful?' (2003) 77 *Australian Law Journal* 30, p 34.
89.   Gummow, 'Equity: Too Successful?', note 88 above, p 43.
90.   Windeyer, *Lectures on Legal History*, note 72 above, p 302.
91.   A Castles, *An Australian Legal History*, Law Book Co, Sydney, 1982, p 95.

all manner of other personal pleas whatsoever'. It was to operate simply, without the complicated procedures which had come to characterise the common law courts in England, much like the Court of Requests: see 1.12. But importantly, the power given under the *First Charter* was purely based in common law and did not include an express power to decide equitable claims or defences. Technically, this was because the power to create a court of equity was beyond the royal prerogative and could only be created via legislation.[92]

1.50 It is perhaps not surprising that these legal niceties were ignored and that equitable doctrines and remedies were regularly applied in the Court of Civil Jurisdiction. Kercher has shown that specific performance, injunctions, refusal of penal bonds, administration of trusts, enforcement of promissory notes and marriage settlements were all either ordered or employed by successive Judge Advocates, including even Richard Dore and Ellis Bent, the first and second legally trained Judge Advocates, who must have known very well that they had acted beyond power.[93] The explosion in economic activity that occurred in the colony's second decade suggests that this illegally fused legal system was no impediment to trade and development. Indeed, if it can be argued that an efficient legal system is a necessary element of economic growth, then the Court of Civil Jurisdiction was an outright success. Kercher has shown that the court decided well over 6000 cases in its 26-year history, an extraordinary number of cases given that the population of New South Wales in this period would have likely been less than 10,000 people.[94]

The second phase: the Second Charter of Justice and the first Supreme Court of New South Wales

1.51 Arguably, the exponential increase in the court's work led to calls for a reformed legal system and for a *Second Charter of Justice*. This charter was promulgated in 1814. It abolished the Court of Civil Jurisdiction and replaced it with a Supreme Court. The *Second Charter* (like the first) was based solely on the royal prerogative, but unlike the *First Charter*, this version included an express recognition of the new Supreme Court having full power to 'administer Justice in a summary manner according or as near as may be to the Rules of our High Court of Chancery in Great Britain'.

1.52 Unfortunately, the new court was stillborn. The first judge commissioned to the court, Jeffery Hart Bent (Ellis Bent's brother), was a pompous twit and objected to having to sit with two lay magistrates. He also objected to the admission to legal practice of former convicts. A number of these former convicts, including George Crossley, were legally trained and had acted as 'law agents' before the Court of Civil Jurisdiction. By 1814, Crossley, arguably the father of the Australian legal profession, had acted as a law agent for more than 10 years, had advised Judge Avocate Atkins, and had provided guidance to Governor Bligh. Nevertheless, Bent refused to admit him, and after realising that his lay magistrates were prepared to admit former convicts, Bent, rather than resigning, decided not to sit at all. He argued that, if there were not at least two admitted lawyers in the colony, the court could not do more than hold formal hearings.[95] This meant that the court did not effectively start work until after Bent was recalled in 1817.[96]

---

92. A Castles, *An Introduction to Australian Legal History*, Law Book Co, Sydney, 1971, p 23.
93. B Kercher, *Debt, Seduction and Other Disasters*, Federation Press, Sydney, 1996, pp 11–12.
94. Kercher, *Debt, Seduction and Other Disasters*, note 93 above, pp 93–95.
95. B Kercher, *An Unruly Child: A History of Law in Australia*, Allen & Unwin, Sydney, 1995, p 33.
96. Castles, *An Introduction to Australian Legal History*, note 92 above, pp 106–07.

1.53   Bent was replaced by Barron Field, a competent lawyer and poet, who set to the task of writing rules for the new Supreme Court, that were later approved by Governor Macquarie. These established that the Supreme Court would follow the procedures of the court at Westminster as closely as possible.[97] This included the use of parchment for the engrossment of proceedings, particularly in equity. This was an incredibly expensive and cumbersome way to conduct proceedings and far removed from the simple writ procedures of the Court of Civil Jurisdiction. One of the noticeable effects on equity matters of the adoption of these traditional procedures was that the length of proceedings was greatly extended. Both Castles and Smith cite the example of *Howe v Underwood*, a case concerning a disputed trust, which was filed in 1822, but not decided until 1832.[98] It seems that the more the Supreme Court adopted formal equity procedures, the less efficient it became.

The third phase: the Act of 1823, the Third Charter of Justice and the Australian Courts Act 1828

1.54   The Act of 1823 (4 Geo IV, c 96), sometimes called the New South Wales Act, almost completed the process of bringing the creative child of Australian law into line with its British forebear. The Act separated New South Wales and Van Diemen's Land and created a new Supreme Court and Legislative Council for each colony.[99] The Act also authorised new Charters of Justice to be issued. Originally the Act was intended to be temporary, only applying until the end of the parliamentary session after 1 July 1827. But the Act was extended in operation until 1829 by 7 & 8 Geo IV c 73.

1.55   The *Third Charter of Justice* was promulgated in New South Wales on 17 May 1824, and Sir Francis Forbes was sworn in as the first Chief Justice of the 'new' New South Wales Supreme Court.[100] Importantly, the *Third Charter* granted the new Supreme Court power 'to do, exercise and perform all such Acts Matters, and things necessary for the due execution of such Equitable jurisdiction, as the Lord High Chancellor of Great Britain can or lawfully may within England'. The question of whether the Australian Supreme Courts had equitable jurisdiction was therefore forever resolved in the affirmative.

1.56   Chief Justice Forbes continued to adopt the Westminster procedural rules, even though common law and equity were dealt with by the same judges and no separate equity court had been created. In *Lord v Dickson (No 1)* (1828) NSW Sel Cas (Dowling) 487,[101] Forbes CJ, deciding the issue of who should be responsible for striking out scandalous matters in answer to a bill in equity, stated that:

> The general rules of the Equity court of England were in force here so far as they were applicable to the state of the Colony and its juridical establishment.

In any event, the equitable jurisdiction appears to have been relatively quiet in the first few years of the court's existence. Chief Justice Forbes commented that in 'an early stage of society there is

---

97.   Castles, *An Introduction to Australian Legal History*, note 92 above, p 109.

98.   Castles, *An Australian Legal History*, note 91 above, pp 111–112; M L Smith, 'The Early Years of Equity in the Supreme Court of New South Wales' (1998) 72 *Australian Law Journal* 799, pp 800–01; P W Young, C Croft & M L Smith, *On Equity*, Law Book Co, Sydney, 2009, pp 48–54.

99.   Kercher, *An Unruly Child*, note 95 above, p 69.

100. Smith, 'The Early Years of Equity in the Supreme Court of New South Wales', note 98 above, p 800.

101. T D Castle & B Kercher (eds), *Dowling's Select Cases 1828 to 1844*, Francis Forbes Society, Sydney, 2005, p 487.

comparatively but little occasion for resorting to a Court of Equity'.[102] But as the colony grew, the pressure on the equitable jurisdiction also began to mount.

1.57 Further constitutional reform came with the passing of the *Australian Courts Act 1828* (9 Geo IV, c 83), which cemented many of the principles of the Act of 1823, but clearly stated explicitly that the laws of England at 25 July 1828, both statute and judge made, were to be applied as far as possible in New South Wales and Van Diemen's Land.

1.58 By the mid-1830s, the equitable jurisdiction was in a state of disrepair with a large backlog of about 130 cases by 1836.[103] When Forbes CJ retired in 1837, Dowling J was appointed as Chief Justice and it was resolved to replace him with a specialist equity practitioner. Justice John Walpole Willis was appointed from the Chancery bar. He developed standing rules for equitable matters which were used for the next 50 years. However, his tenure was marred by his critical attitude and open disrespect for, and public criticism of, the Chief Justice's skills in equity matters. Willis J publicly admonished both Dowling CJ and Burton J for their decisions in *Neale v Solomon*,[104] a case concerning whether equitable relief should have been specifically pleaded. The *Sydney Morning Herald* reported:

> He said he had had some practice in Equity Courts, but he never heard such a decision as their Honors had come to; it was contrary to the principles of Equity, which are to do full justice to every one that comes before the Court, and not drive a party to a Court of Law. The Court, he considered was not doing Equity between the parties, and if he acceded to the judgment he should be acting contrary to the principle of all the Equity cases he had ever heard.

1.59 Willis J's acerbic attitude eventually led the Chief Justice to agree to him sitting alone on equity matters and it was not long before he started to agitate for the creation of a completely separate court of equity in the colony with its own Chief Baron in Equity, a position he hoped to occupy. The other Supreme Court judges, including Stephen J who had been appointed to replace Burton J during a leave of absence in 1839, refused to support this idea and instead suggested that all litigation could be taken by the judges on rotation. This further infuriated Willis J and he made public a letter he had somehow received from Stephen J to Dowling CJ, in which Stephen J had requested Dowling CJ's help with equity matters because he lacked confidence in sitting on them. The relationship between Willis J and Dowling CJ deteriorated until they had a fight in the judges' robing room.[105] Perhaps this fist fight is the first recorded battle in Australia between those traditionalist lawyers who believed in the strict separation of law and equity and those who saw the two as being better administered by the one court.

1.60 Willis J's demands for formal separation were partially met by the legislature in 1840 with the passage of the *Administration of Justice Act* (4 Vic No 22). This Act gave statutory recognition to the separate operation of law and equity within the Supreme Court, but it did not create any separate tribunal. The *Administration of Justice Act* created the office of the Primary Judge in Equity who was to sit alone on equitable matters. It also provided for the courtesy of first offering the position

---

102. Castles, *An Australian Legal History*, note 91 above, p 192.

103. Smith, 'The Early Years of Equity in the Supreme Court of New South Wales', note 98 above, p 801.

104. Unreported, Dowling CJ, Burton and Willis JJ, 31 March 1838, Colonial Case Law www.law.mq.edu.au/research/colonial_case_law/nsw/cases/case_index/1838/neale_v_solomon/.

105. Castles, *An Australian Legal History*, note 91 above, p 194.

to the Chief Justice, but it was expected that he would decline and that Willis J would take the position. Dowling CJ shocked everyone by taking the appointment and ordering Willis J to take up the position of resident judge in Port Phillip.[106] Willis J was later removed from office by Governor Gipps. He successfully appealed that decision to the Privy Council, but was later formally removed without pension by Royal Warrant.

1.61   Dowling CJ's victory and Willis J's eventual downfall did little to slow down the administrative separation of equity from law. From 1840, the traditional English approach to separation had taken firm root, but this did not seem to bestow any benefits in efficiency or lower costs. The Primary Judge in Equity still had to perform all his common law duties. The average time for the resolution of equity matters stretched out to five years. The *Equity Practice Act 1853*, tried to make some improvements, for example, by removing the necessity for engrossing parchments, but these did not seem to effect the necessary improvements in administration. By 1858 a legislative attempt was made to create a separate court of equity in New South Wales but it failed in the lower house. Further Acts were passed in 1865 (29 Vic No 7), 1880 (the *Equity Act 1880*, 44 Vic No 18), and 1901 (*Equity Act 1901*), primarily with the aim of introducing procedural reforms which had already been passed in England, such as the reforms regarding the recognition of legal titles and awards of damages.

1.62   The other colonies also adopted the formal separation of law and equity. Victoria legislatively adopted the separation in 1856 and Queensland did so in 1861. In Western Australia, the Supreme Court was created in 1861 with clear equitable jurisdiction and it followed the English forms of procedure. The South Australian Supreme Court began its life with separate legal and equitable proceedings and created a Primary Judge in Equity in 1867. By this time Tasmania, as it was now known, also had a single judge to determine equitable matters.[107]

The fourth phase: the judicature system reforms

1.63   In 1876 Queensland became the first Australian colony to adopt the judicature system.[108] Most other colonies followed soon after — South Australia in 1878, Western Australia in 1880, Victoria in 1883 and Tasmania in 1932. The notable exception was New South Wales, which finally passed the relevant legislation in 1970 and which came into effect in 1972.[109] It was only then, in the words of its then Chief Justice, Sir Laurence Street, that Australia's most litigious state 'advanced back to 1873'.[110] All Australian jurisdictions have in force provisions to the effect that, in the event of conflict between the rules of equity and the rules of common law, the rules of equity shall prevail.[111]

---

106. Smith, 'The Early Years of Equity in the Supreme Court of New South Wales', note 98 above, p 802.

107. Castles, *An Australian Legal History*, note 91 above, pp 347–48.

108. *Judicature Act 1876* (Qld).

109. *Supreme Court Act 1970* (NSW); *Supreme Court Act 1878* (SA); *Supreme Court Civil Procedure Act 1932* (Tas); *Supreme Court (Judicature) Act 1883* (Vic); *Supreme Court Act 1880* (WA).

110. Quoted in G E Dal Pont, *Equity and Trusts in Australia*, 5th ed, Lawbook Co, Sydney, 2011, p 6. On the introduction of the judicature system into New South Wales see Leeming, 'Equity, the Judicature Acts and Restitution', note 76 above, pp 216–22.

111. *Supreme Court Act 1933* (ACT) s 33; *Law Reform (Law and Equity) Act 1972* (NSW) s 5; *Supreme Court Act* (NT) s 68; *Supreme Court Act 1995* (Qld) 249; *Supreme Court Act 1935* (SA) s 28; *Supreme Court Civil Procedure Act 1932* (Tas) s 11(10); *Supreme Court (Judicature) Act 1883* (Vic); *Supreme Court Act 1880* (WA).

2

THE NATURE OF EQUITY

INTRODUCTION

2.1 In *Dudley v Dudley* (1705) 24 ER 118 at 119, Lord Cowper described the nature of equity as follows:

> Now equity is no part of the law, but a moral virtue, which qualifies, moderates, and reforms the rigour, hardness, and edge of the law, and is an universal truth; it does also assist the law where it is defective and weak in the constitution (which is the life of the law) and defends the law from crafty evasions, delusions, and new subtleties, invented and contrived to evade and delude the common law, whereby such as have undoubted right are made remediless; and this is the office of equity, to support and protect the common law from shifts and crafty contrivances against the justice of the law. Equity therefore does not destroy the law, nor create it, but assist it.

2.2 In a similar vein, Maitland said the following of equity:

> We ought not to think of common law and equity as of two rival systems. Equity was not a self-sufficient system, at every point it presupposed the existence of the common law. Common law was a self-sufficient system. I mean this: that if the legislature had passed a short act saying 'Equity is hereby abolished', we might have got on fairly well; in some respects our law would have been barbarous, unjust, absurd, but still the great elementary rights, the right to immunity from violence, the right to one's good name, the rights of ownership and of possession would have been decently protected and contract would have been enforced. On the other hand had the legislature said, 'Common law is hereby abolished', this decree if obeyed would have meant anarchy. At every point equity presupposed the existence of common law.[1]

2.3 Similar observations to these were made by the former High Court justice Sir Frank Kitto when he wrote:

> Equity remains also, the saving supplement and complement of the Common Law ..., prevailing over the Common Law in cases of conflict but ensuring, by its persistence and by the very fact of its prevailing, the survival of the Common Law and the enduring influence of English jurisprudence as a whole in the history of civilisation.[2]

---

1.   F W Maitland, *Equity and The Forms of Action at Common Law*, Cambridge University Press, Cambridge, 1929, p 19.
2.   F W Kitto, 'Foreword to the First Edition' in R Meagher, J D Heydon & M Leeming, *Meagher, Gummow and Lehane's Equity: Doctrines and Remedies*, 4th ed, LexisNexis Butterworths, Sydney, 2002, p vii.

2.4 The essential validity of these quotes is apparent from an understanding of the history of equity charted in Chapter 1, where it was noted that the Court of Chancery emerged as a court whose doctrines supplemented the common law where it was defective or offered no remedy. In this respect, '[u]nconscionability was and remains the fulcrum upon which entitlement to equitable relief turns': *Lift Capital Partners Pty Ltd v Merrill Lynch International* (2009) 253 ALR 482 at 507. Thus in *Legione v Hateley* (1983) 152 CLR 406; 46 ALR 1, equitable jurisdiction to relieve against forfeiture (see Chapter 13) and penalties (see Chapter 14) was based upon finding unconscionable behaviour on the part of the defendant. Mason and Deane JJ, at CLR 444; ALR 28, observed that this ruling 'conforms to the fundamental principle according to which equity acts, namely that a party having a legal right shall not be permitted to exercise it in such a way that the exercise amounts to unconscionable conduct'. In *Moorgate Tobacco Co Ltd v Philip Morris Ltd (No 2)* (1984) 156 CLR 414 at 437–8; 56 ALR 193 at 208, Deane J said that the action for breach of confidence (see Chapter 8) lies in the notion of 'an obligation of conscience'. In *Baumgartner v Baumgartner* (1987) 164 CLR 137; 76 ALR 75, the legal title to land was subject to a constructive trust (see Chapter 28) due to the unconscionable conduct of the legal owner. In *Commonwealth v Verwayen* (1990) 170 CLR 394 at 407; 95 ALR 321 at 329, Mason CJ referred to unconscionability as 'the driving force behind equitable estoppel'. In *Lift Capital v Merrill Lynch*, at 504–9, Barrett J observed that unconscionability was the basis of the equitable rule against clogging a mortgagor's equity of redemption. However, as the High Court pointed out in *Bofinger v Kingsway Group Ltd* (2009) 239 CLR 269 at 301; 260 ALR 71 at 91, although unconscionability is an underlying basis for many equitable doctrines, 'the relevant principles of equity do not operate at large and in an idiosyncratic fashion'. It must also be remembered, in the words of Young JA in *ING Bank (Australia) Ltd v O'Shea* [2010] NSWCA 71 at [82], 'that something is not necessarily against the conscience just because a judge might subjectively consider conduct "unfair"'.

2.5 In recent times, the High Court of Australia has stated that the term 'unconscientious' is a more accurate term than 'unconscionable' to describe the basis for equitable intervention: *Tanwar Enterprises Pty Ltd v Cauchi* (2003) 217 CLR 315 at 324; 201 ALR 359 at 364–5. The reason for the change in terminology has been prompted by the need to avoid confusing the general basis for equitable intervention with the specific doctrine governing unconscionable transactions: see Chapter 11.

2.6 Because of equity's role in supplementing the general law by intervening in circumstances where the common law was either deficient or provided no remedy, equity can be seen as a gloss on the common law. The extent of equity's intervention into the common law varies from area to area. Principles relating to contract law and land law have been substantially affected by equitable principles. Other areas, such as torts and criminal law, have been less affected. In the light of this it is hardly surprising that the scope of equity is not definable by general description. Rather, equity's scope can only be comprehensively defined by compiling an inventory of its contents. As has been observed, '[e]quity can be described but not defined'.[3] Thus, it was not surprising that Maitland defined equity as 'that body of rules administered by our ... courts of justice, which, were it not for the operation of the Judicature Acts, would be administered only by those courts which would

---

3. R Meagher, J D Heydon & M Leeming, *Meagher, Gummow and Lehane's Equity: Doctrines and Remedies*, 4th ed, LexisNexis Butterworths, Sydney, 2002, p 3.

be known as Courts of Equity'.[4] This is not at all surprising given that in its formative period, all that 'suits in Chancery had in common was simply that the Chancellor had opted to accept them'.[5] However, Maitland also said:

> [E]quity has added to our legal system, together with a number of detached doctrines, one novel and fertile institution, namely the trust; and three novel and fertile remedies, namely the decree for specific performance, the injunction, and the judicial administration of estates. Round these, as it seems to me, most of the equitable rules group themselves.[6]

2.7 Parkinson has suggested that equitable principles and doctrines fall within one or more of five not entirely distinct categories of unconscientious conduct. They are:

1. the exploitation of vulnerability or weakness;
2. the abuse of positions of trust or confidence;
3. the insistence upon rights in circumstances which make such insistence harsh or oppressive;
4. the inequitable denial of obligations; and
5. the unjust retention of property.[7]

EQUITABLE JURISDICTIONS

2.8 The application of equitable principles is often said to fall within one of three separate equitable jurisdictions, namely, the exclusive, concurrent and auxiliary jurisdictions.

2.9 The exclusive jurisdiction refers to matters in which equity has 'an exclusive cognizance'[8] because no relief can be obtained at common law. The best illustration relates to obligations arising under a trust.

2.10 The concurrent jurisdiction refers to matters in which both the equity and common law courts have jurisdiction to make orders. An example here concerns the enforcement of a contract where the primary equitable remedy is the order for specific performance and the common law remedy is an order for damages. Thus, equity's concurrent jurisdiction is one that supports common law rights.

2.11 The auxiliary jurisdiction is also an instance of equitable jurisdiction in support of common law rights. It is exercised when a person goes to equity 'merely in order to obtain its assistance in proceedings which they are taking or about to take in courts of law'.[9] For example, it could be by means of a quia timet injunction (see 24.54–24.58) to prevent irreparable injury to property pending a decision at law. Or it could be an order for discovery to provide better evidence and thereby facilitate proceedings already commenced at law.

2.12 Meagher, Heydon and Leeming argue that the distinction between the concurrent and auxiliary jurisdictions is one that lacks 'doctrinal validity and practical utility' with the consequence

---

4. Maitland, *Equity*, note 1 above, p 1.
5. A Cromartie, *The Constitutionalist Revolution, An Essay on the History of England, 1450–1642*, Cambridge University Press, Cambridge, 2006, p 19.
6. Maitland, *Equity*, note 1 above, p 22.
7. P Parkinson, 'The Conscience of Equity' in P Parkinson (ed), *The Principles of Equity*, 2nd ed, Lawbook Co, Sydney, 2003, 29, p 35.
8. Maitland, *Equity*, note 1 above, p 20.
9. Maitland, *Equity*, note 1 above, p 21.

that '[t]he only distinction worth drawing — and this is a distinction which has real consequence — is the distinction between the exclusive jurisdiction, on the one hand, and jurisdiction in aid of legal rights, on the other hand'.[10] The 'real consequence' to which they refer can be illustrated by the example of the injunction. When an injunction is sought to restrain the breach of a common law obligation (jurisdiction in aid of legal rights), such as a negative contractual stipulation, equity will only provide relief if damages at common law are inadequate. If common law damages are adequate as a form of relief to the plaintiff, equity will not intervene — it has no jurisdiction to do so. However, if the injunction is sought to restrain a breach of an equitable obligation (exclusive jurisdiction), such as a breach of trust, the question of equity's jurisdiction to enforce such a right does not arise because only equity can enforce equitable obligations. The adequacy or inadequacy of damages at common law does not, and cannot, arise because the common law does not recognise such obligations nor does it claim any jurisdiction in relation to their enforcement.

MAXIMS OF EQUITY

2.13   The maxims of equity are basic principles upon which the rules of equity have been established. They are not independent of one another and often overlap. Spry has written the following in relation to the maxims:

> [T]he maxims of equity are of significance, for they reflect the ethical quality of the body of principles that has tended not so much to the formation of fixed and immutable rules, as rather to a determination of the conscionability or justice of the behaviour of the parties according to recognised moral principles. This ethical quality remains, and its presence explains to a large extent the adoption by courts of equity of broad general principles that may be applied with flexibility to new situations as they arise.[11]

2.14   In essence the maxims of equity reflect and represent fundamental moral ideas or themes that lie at the heart of equitable jurisdiction. The function of a maxim is 'to provide general principles as points of departure, and not to capsule answers to specific problems'.[12] Thus, in *Corin v Patton* (1990) 169 CLR 540 at 557; 92 ALR 1 at 12, in relation to the maxim 'equity will not assist a volunteer', Mason CJ and McHugh J said:

> Like other maxims of equity, it is not a specific rule or principle of law. It is a summary of a broad theme which underlies equitable concepts and principles. Its precise scope is necessarily ill-defined and somewhat uncertain.

The most significant maxims are discussed briefly below.

Equity will not suffer a wrong to be without a remedy

2.15   This maxim is of major historical significance in that equitable remedies evolved to meet the deficiencies in the common law. For example, specific performance was decreed in relation to contracts; injunctions granted to restrain torts; and equitable accounts ordered where accounts at common law were unavailable.

---

10.   Meagher et al, *Equity: Doctrines and Remedies*, note 3 above, p 11.

11.   I C F Spry, *The Principles of Equitable Remedies, Specific Performance, Injunctions, Rectification and Equitable Damages*, 7th ed, Law Book Co, Sydney, 2007, p 6.

12.   H L Oleck, 'Maxims of Equity Reappraised' (1951–1952) 6 *Rutgers Law Review* 528, p 528.

2.16 The maxim's significance today is dependent upon the extent to which courts, especially the High Court of Australia, are prepared to adapt and extend equitable principles to meet novel circumstances. A common approach of judges is exemplified in the statement in *In re Diplock's Estate; Diplock v Wintle* [1948] Ch 465 at 481–2; [1948] 2 All ER 318 at 326, where the English Court of Appeal said:

> [I]f the claim in equity exists, it must be shown to have an ancestry founded in history and in the practice and precedents of the courts administering equity jurisdiction. It is not sufficient that because we may think that the 'justice' of the present case requires it, we should invent such a jurisdiction for the first time.

2.17 In a similar vein, in *Cowcher v Cowcher* [1972] 1 All ER 943 at 948, Bagnall J said:

> So in the field of equity the length of the *Chancellor's foot* has been measured or is capable of measurement. This does not mean that equity is past childbearing; simply that its progeny must be legitimate — by precedent out of principle. It is well that this should be so; otherwise no lawyer could safely advise on his client's title and every quarrel would lead to a law suit.

2.18 Notwithstanding the cautious sentiments expressed in these cases, it would be a mistake to assume that equity's principles have remained static and have not been developed. In the words of Kirby J in *Australian Broadcasting Corporation v Lenah Game Meats Pty Ltd* (2001) 208 CLR 199 at 271; 185 ALR 1 at 49: 'It is a commonplace that equity is a living force and that it responds to new situations. It must do so in ways that are consistent with equitable principles. If it were to fail to respond, it would atrophy.' In *Burke v LFOT Pty Ltd* (2002) 209 CLR 282 at 326; 187 ALR 612 at 643, Kirby J opined that, in developing equitable principles, courts 'should look beyond the exposition of the principles in the old cases or texts that necessarily reflect the often rigid legal environment and judicial disposition of past times'. In a similar vein, in *Mercedes Benz AG v Leiduck* [1996] AC 284 at 308; [1995] 3 All ER 929 at 946, Lord Nicholls of Birkenhead, speaking in the context of granting injunctive relief, said:

> The court may grant an injunction against a party properly before it where this is required to avoid injustice, just as the statute provides and just as the Court of Chancery did before 1875. The court habitually grants injunctions in respect of certain types of conduct. But that does not mean that the situations in which injunctions may be granted are now set in stone for all time … As circumstances in the world change, so must the situations in which the courts may properly exercise their jurisdiction to grant injunctions. The exercise of the jurisdiction must be principled, but the criterion is injustice. Injustice is to be viewed and decided in the light of today's conditions and standards, not those of yester-year.

2.19 The comments by Kirby J and Lord Nicholls are reflective of what has happened in recent times. In 1927, in *In re Wait* [1927] 1 Ch 606 at 635, Atkin LJ opined that the application of equitable principles in commercial sale of goods dealings constituted an intrusion 'into territory where they are trespassers'. However, as Millett LJ said extra-judicially in 2003: 'It can no longer be doubted that equity has moved out of the family home and the settled estate and into the market place.'[13] Recent years have witnessed a thriving development of equitable principles into areas previously considered beyond the bounds of equity. Equity judges are less occupied with cases concerning the traditional areas of real property, deceased estates, wills and settlements, and more concerned with large

---

13. Lord Justice Millett, 'Equity — The Road Ahead' (1995–96) 6 *King's College Law Journal* 1, p 4.

corporate insolvencies, mergers and corporate acquisitions and commercial disputes of all kinds. This is most noticeable in the increased application of principles relating to fiduciary obligations in commercial transactions (see 9.88–9.97).[14] However, in such cases the court will exercise restraint in applying equitable principles in the context of commercial dealings. Thus, in *Austotel Pty Ltd v Franklins Selfserve Pty Ltd* (1989) 16 NSWLR 582 at 585, Kirby P said:

> The Court has before it two groupings of substantial commercial enterprises, well resourced and advised, dealing in a commercial transaction having a great value. … This is not, of itself, a reason for denying them the beneficial application of the principles developed by equity. But it is a reason for scrutinising carefully the circumstances which are said to give rise to the conclusion that an insistence by the appellants on their legal rights would be so unconscionable that the Court will provide relief from it.

> At least in circumstances such as the present, courts should be careful to conserve relief so that they do not, in commercial matters, substitute lawyerly conscience for the hard headed decisions of business people.

2.20   In relation to the role of the judge in developing and/or adapting equitable principles, the High Court, in *Farah Constructions Pty Ltd v Say-Dee Pty Ltd* (2007) 230 CLR 89 at 151–2, 155; 236 ALR 209 at 252–3, 255–6, made it clear that trial judges and intermediate appellate courts should not depart from decisions of intermediate appellate courts in other Australian jurisdictions, nor radically change existing law unless such decisions or existing law were plainly wrong. The High Court made it clear that such changes to the law were properly within the domain of the High Court only.[15]

Equity follows the law

2.21   Equity recognises common law rights, estates, interests and titles and does not say that such common law interests are not valid. Thus, in *Leech v Schweder* (1873) 9 LR Ch App 463 at 475, Mellish LJ said that 'where a right existed at law, and a person came only into equity because the Court of Equity had a more convenient remedy than a Court of Law … there equity followed the law, and the person entitled to the right had no greater right in equity than at law'.

2.22   However, in *AMEV-UDC Finance Ltd v Austin* (1986) 162 CLR 170 at 198; 68 ALR 185 at 204–5, Deane J observed that '[e]quity followed and built upon the common law, adding its remedies by way of enforcement of the common law in some cases and granting its relief against the harshness of the operation of the common law in others'. As Cardozo CJ pointed out in *Graf v Hope Building Corporation*, 171 NE 884 at 886–7 (1930), '[e]quity follows the law, but not slavishly nor always'. Thus, equity will not permit an owner of common law rights and interests to act unconscientiously in enforcing such rights and interests. This is amply reflected in the institution of the trust. In *DKLR Holding Co (No 2) Pty Ltd v Commissioner of Stamp Duties* [1980] 1 NSWLR 510 at 519, Hope JA said:

> Where the trustee is the owner in fee simple, the right of the beneficiary although annexed to the land, is a right to compel the legal owner to hold and use the rights which the law gives him in

---

14. P A Keane, 'The 2009 W A Lee Lecture in Equity: The Conscience of Equity' (2010) 84 *Australian Law Journal* 92, pp 98–101.

15. On this issue see J D Heydon, 'How Far Can Trial Courts and Intermediate Appellate Courts Develop the Law?' (2009) 9 *Oxford University Commonwealth Law Journal* 1.

accordance with the obligations which equity has imposed upon him. The trustee, in such a case, has at law all the rights of the absolute owner in fee simple, but he is not free to use those rights for his own benefit in the way he could if no trust existed. Equitable obligations require him to use them in some particular way for the benefit of other persons.

2.23 This has the consequence, as was pointed out by Brennan J when this case went on appeal to the High Court, that '[a]n equitable interest is not carved out of a legal estate but impressed upon it': *DKLR Holding Co (No 2) Pty Ltd v Commissioner of Stamp Duties (NSW)* (1982) 149 CLR 431 at 474; 40 ALR 1 at 35.

2.24 Another illustration of the maxim relates to time stipulations. At common law time stipulations in a contract are of the essence and a failure to perform in a timely manner entitles the innocent party to terminate the contract. However, in equity a time stipulation is generally regarded as not being essential. Equity only recognises the essentiality of time if time is expressly or impliedly of the essence of the contract (*Parkin v Thorold* (1852) 51 ER 698 at 701), or, if not of the essence, is made so by the service of a notice to complete: *Carr v J A Berryman Pty Ltd* (1953) 89 CLR 327 at 348–9. Outside of these circumstances equity regards it as unconscientious to exercise the common law right to terminate for a breach of a time stipulation: *Stickney v Keeble* [1915] AC 386 at 400. As a consequence, a party in breach of a non-essential time stipulation is not by reason of that breach precluded from seeking an order for specific performance of the contract at a later date (*Michael Realty Pty Ltd v Carr* [1977] 1 NSWLR 533 at 572), although he or she will be liable to the other party for damages at common law in relation to losses arising from the breach: *Canning v Temby* (1905) 3 CLR 419 at 426.

2.25 It can be noted that as part of the reforms of the courts in the 1870s in England, s 25(7) of the *Judicature Act 1873* (UK) resolved the conflict between the common law and equity approaches to the effect of a contractual time stipulation by giving statutory effect to the equitable rules, effectively transforming a time stipulation from an essential term of a contract to an intermediate term of a contract: *Zaccardi v Caunt* [2008] NSWCA 202 at [92]. Similar legislation was subsequently passed, and now applies, in all Australian jurisdictions.[16]

2.26 Another significant application of this maxim relates to consideration. At common law consideration need not be adequate; it need only be sufficient. This rule justifies the validity of nominal consideration and equity follows the law in relation to consideration to that extent. However, equitable remedies will not be available in enforcement of a contract unless it is a contract supported by *valuable* consideration (see 2.34). Furthermore, the adequacy of consideration can be a factor in equity's exercising its discretion as to whether or not equitable relief will be granted. Thus, the inadequacy of consideration can amount to hardship and result in a court refusing an application for specific performance of a contract: *Falcke v Gray* (1859) 62 ER 250. Such situations are rare. More often, inadequacy of consideration, coupled with other factors such as fraud, misrepresentation and the like, lead a court to refuse equitable relief: see 23.58–23.59.

2.27 A somewhat different application of this maxim relates to the manner in which equity has applied limitations legislation by analogy: see 31.25–31.31.

---

16. *Civil Law (Property) Act 2006* (ACT) s 501; *Conveyancing Act 1919* (NSW) s 13; *Law of Property Act 2000* (NT) s 65; *Property Law Act 1974* (Qld) s 62; *Law of Property Act 1936* (SA) s 16; *Supreme Court Civil Procedure Act 1932* (Tas) s 11(7); *Property Law Act 1958* (Vic) s 41; *Property Law Act 1969* (WA) s 21.

Where the equities are equal, the first in time shall prevail, and where there is equal equity, the law shall prevail

2.28 These two maxims are the basis of the principles relating to the topic of priorities: see Chapter 7. The first maxim underpins the basic rule determining priority between two holders of equitable interests in the same property. Thus, where A, and subsequently B, obtain equitable mortgages in relation to the same property, in the absence of some postponing conduct by A, A will gain priority over B. In this situation, the equities being equal, A gains priority because his or her interest was the first in point of time: see 7.13. The second maxim underpins the basic rule determining the priority between the holder of an earlier equitable interest in property and the holder of a later legal interest in the same property. The holder of the legal interest will have priority if his or her interest was acquired in good faith, for valuable consideration and without notice of the earlier equitable interest. In such a situation, the equities being equal, the legal interest prevails: see 7.48.

One who seeks equity must do equity

2.29 Plaintiffs in equity must fulfil their legal and equitable obligations before seeking a remedy. The maxim represents equity's version of the biblical 'golden rule' set out in the Book of Matthew (7:12): 'do unto others as you would be done by'. The maxim emphasises that the Court of Chancery originated as a 'court of conscience'. In *Hanson v Keating* (1844) 67 ER 537 at 538–9, Wigram V-C said the following in relation to this maxim:

> It decides in the abstract that the court giving the plaintiff the relief to which he is entitled will do so only upon the terms of his submitting to give the defendant such corresponding rights (if any) as he also may be entitled to in respect of the subject matter of the suit; what these rights are must be determined aliunde by strict rules of law, and not by any arbitrary determination of the court. The rule, in short, merely raises the question of what those terms (if any) should be.

2.30 Thus, in *Langman v Handover* (1929) 43 CLR 334, the High Court approved of the decision in *Lodge v National Union Investment Co* (1907) 1 Ch 300 at 320, where Parker J held that a borrower could not be relieved in equity against securities that were illegal and void under the *Money-lenders Act 1900* (UK) 'without being put on terms by which both parties may be restored to the positions they occupied before the transaction commenced'. This approach was followed in *Verduci v Golotta* [2010] NSWSC 506 at [74], where Slattery J held that a mortgage that was entered into as the result of undue influence could be set aside in equity, but only on the condition that the borrower repaid the sum borrowed together with reasonable interest.

One who comes to equity must come with clean hands

2.31 This maxim is closely related to and descends from the maxim just discussed: *FAI Insurances Ltd v Pioneer Concrete Services Ltd* [1987] 15 NSWLR 552 at 559. It requires a plaintiff in equity not to be guilty of some improper conduct, or else relief will be denied: see 31.8–31.12. This maxim confirms that equity is not solely concerned with preventing unconscientious conduct by a defendant, but also requires conscientious behaviour by a plaintiff.

Delay defeats equity

2.32 In seeking equitable relief a plaintiff must act promptly and diligently: *Smith v Clay* (1767) 27 ER 419 at 420. Equity will not allow defendants to remain for too long in a position of not knowing whether equitable relief will be ordered against them because it would be unconscientious to do so. This maxim finds its application in the principles of laches (see 31.13–31.22) and acquiescence (see 31.23–31.24), and in the analogies that equity draws to limitation legislation: see 31.25–31.31.

Equality is equity

2.33   This maxim expresses equity's aim to distribute profits and losses in proportion to the claims and liabilities of the parties concerned. It does not mean literal equality but, rather, proportionate equality. The application of the maxim is seen in equity's favouring a finding of a tenancy in common over a joint tenancy because the latter unduly favours the person of longevity. Thus, if partners purchase land for their firm's business, unless expressly stated otherwise, equity will regard them as tenants in common rather than as joint tenants: *Lake v Craddock* (1732) 24 ER 1011. The maxim also underpins the doctrine of presumed resulting trusts (see Chapter 19). Also, equity will generally, but not always, execute a trust power of appointment equally among the objects of the power if the donee of the power has failed to exercise the power: *McPhail v Doulton* [1971] AC 424 at 451–2; [1970] 2 All ER 228 at 241–3.

Equity will not assist a volunteer

2.34   In *Colman v Sarrel* (1789) 30 ER 225 at 227, Lord Chancellor Thurlow said that a plaintiff seeking equitable relief has to have 'a valuable or at least meritorious consideration'. This requirement is expressed in the maxim that 'equity will not assist a volunteer', a volunteer being a person who has not given valuable consideration. The maxim does not require that the consideration be paid or executed: *Reef & Rainforest Travel Pty Ltd v Commissioner of Stamp Duties* [2001] QCA 249 at [10].

2.35   The rationale for this maxim is that it would not be unconscientious for equity to decline equitable assistance to a plaintiff who is a volunteer, whereas it would be so if he or she had provided valuable consideration: *Redman v Permanent Trustee Co of New South Wales Ltd* (1916) 22 CLR 84 at 96. Thus, it is the presence of valuable consideration that 'will attract the intervention of equity': *Director of Public Prosecutions for Victoria v Le* (2007) 232 CLR 562 at 575; 240 ALR 204 at 215. However, in *Conlan v Registrar of Titles* (2001) 24 WAR 299 at 338, Owen J suggested that this rationale was 'a little strange given that the common law would (and will) accept something that is entirely inadequate or lacking in actual value as being "good" consideration'.

2.36   The maxim is primarily associated with 'the rule that a voluntary covenant is not enforceable in equity': *Corin v Patton* at CLR 557; ALR 12.[17] Accordingly, specific performance will not be ordered in relation to a promise unsupported by any consideration at all, but contained in a deed: *Roxborough v Rothmans of Pall Mall Australia Ltd* (2001) 208 CLR 516 at 556; 185 ALR 335 at 364–5. Nor will specific performance be granted in relation to a contract to purchase land or an interest in land for the nominal consideration of £1: *Nurdin & Peacock plc v DB Ramsden & Co Ltd* [1999] 1 EGLR 119. In both cases the requirement of valuable consideration has not been satisfied. However, in both cases the promisor's promise is enforceable at common law by an award of damages: *Cannon v Hartley* [1949] Ch 213 at 217; [1949] 1 All ER 50 at 53–4.

---

17. For a discussion of the development of this rule see R T Macnair, 'Equity and Volunteers' (1988) 8 *Legal Studies* 172.

2.37 Two matters are of importance in understanding the operation and significance of the maxim. The first is the meaning of 'valuable consideration'. The second relates to the circumstances where the maxim does not apply.

Valuable consideration

2.38 The meaning of 'valuable consideration' has been primarily discussed by the courts in the context of legislative provisions such as bankruptcy legislation. Thus, in *In re Abbott; Ex parte Trustee of the Property of the Bankruptcy v Abbott* [1983] 1 Ch 45 at 57, Megarry V-C stated that valuable consideration means 'a consideration … that has a real and substantial value, and not one which is merely nominal or trivial or colourable'. The Australian High Court subsequently approved this statement in *Barton v Official Receiver* (1986) 161 CLR 75 at 86; 66 ALR 355 at 361–2, and *Cook v Benson* (2003) 214 CLR 370 at 381–2; 198 ALR 218 at 225. In *The Bell Group Ltd (in liq) v Westpac Banking Corporation (No 9)* (2008) 225 FLR 1 at 741, Owen J said:

> The notion of valuable consideration usually requires finding some economic worth as compared with something that is purely nominal, trivial or colourable … Valuable consideration is more than the nominal consideration that would be sufficient to support a common law contract.

This notion of valuable consideration is reflected in s 4 of the *Civil Law (Property) Act 2006* (ACT) in the Australian Capital Territory where it is stated that valuable consideration 'does not include a nominal consideration in money'.

2.39 On the other hand, valuable consideration does not mean that the consideration needs to be adequate in the sense of it being reasonably equivalent to the value of what was promised or given by the defendant. As to what amounts to valuable consideration in any given case will depend on its facts and circumstances. If the parties are at arm's length and the transaction can be fairly described as commercial in nature, valuable consideration will generally be present: *The Bell Group Ltd (in liq) v Westpac Banking Corporation (No 9)* at 741.

Where the maxim does not apply

2.40 In *Morris v Hanley* [2000] NSWSC 957 at [35], Young J said that '[w]hen one looks behind the maxim one can see that the real truth is that equity rarely helps a volunteer'. Although equity will not assist a volunteer, neither will it frustrate one or 'strive officiously to defeat a gift': *T Choithram International SA v Pagarini* [2001] 2 All ER 492 at 501. This stems from the fact that the maxim's 'precise scope is necessarily ill-defined and somewhat uncertain' and 'subject to certain clearly established exceptions': *Corin v Patton* at CLR 557; ALR 12. Thus, in *Blackett v Darcy* (2005) 62 NSWLR 392 at 397, Young CJ in Eq said:

> It must always be remembered that the rule that equity does not assist a volunteer is not a complete statement of the law and is only relevant if the donee requires the assistance of a court of equity in order to gain the property. Where the donee has gained the property (at least where he or she has not done so illegally), then there is usually no equity in the donor to recover back the money.

2.41 The most significant exception to the maxim relates to a beneficiary of a trust who can bring an action against the trustee to enforce the trust even though the beneficiary gave no consideration for the beneficial interest, provided that the trust is 'completely constituted … by a present declaration of trust or by a transfer by the settlor of the legal title to the intended trustee': *Corin v*

Patton at CLR 557; ALR 12. Another exception entitles a volunteer to enforce a *donatio mortis causa*: *Duffield v Elwes* (1827) 4 ER 959 at 971. *Donatio mortis causa* is a doctrine by which property passes from a donor to a donee upon the death of the donor where (i) the gift is made in contemplation, though not necessarily in expectation, of death; (ii) the property must be delivered to the donee; and (iii) the gift must be made under such circumstances as show that the thing is to revert to the donor in case the donor should recover: *Cain v Moon* [1896] 2 QB 283 at 286.

2.42   The rule in *Strong v Bird* (1874) LR 18 Eq 315 is another exception to the maxim. This rule stipulates that if a donor has attempted to make an immediate *inter vivos* gift of property to a donee, or a purported immediate voluntary release of a debt owed by the donee to the donor, but the gift fails because of a failure to comply with the necessary legal formalities, then, if the donee subsequently becomes the executor of the donor's estate, the gift is considered to have been perfected by the vesting of the legal title in the donee. For the rule to apply, there must be an intention, continuing up to the donor's death, to make an immediate gift: *Rutledge v Sheridan* [2010] QSC 257 at [24]–[31]. In *Matthews v Matthews* (1913) 17 CLR 9 at 19, Barton ACJ said:

> Upon consideration of the cases it cannot be doubted that there must be an attempt to make an immediate gift, and not a mere expression of intention, and that there must be a continuous intention of giving, which, after the act of making what the testator supposes to be a gift, can only mean, I think, that he believes it to have operated, and continues to mean that it should operate, as a gift, although in effect it does not satisfy the legal or equitable requirements of a perfect gift.

The rule can apply to land, including Torrens title land: *Stone v Registrar of Titles* [2012] WASC 21 at [140]. Furthermore, the rule applies in situations where there are two donees, but only one of them is appointed as the executor of the donor's estate: *Blackett v Darcy* (2005) 62 NSWLR 392 at 398. However, it has been said that the rule is anomalous and should not be extended: *Blackett v Darcy* at 398. Thus, in *Stone v Registrar of Titles* at [142]–[144], Simmonds J declined to apply the rule in the context of an attempt to make a gift of a joint tenant's interest in land.

Equity looks to the intent rather than the form

2.43   In *Parkin v Thorold* at 701, Lord Romilly MR said:

> Courts of Equity make a distinction in all cases between that which is a matter of substance and that which is a matter of form; and if it find that by insisting on the form, the substance will be defeated, it holds it to be inequitable to allow a person to insist on such form, and thereby defeat the substance.

2.44   It is pursuant to this maxim, as well as the maxim that 'equity follows the law' (see 2.24–2.25), that a failure to complete a contract on the date stipulated, time not being of the essence by express provision or by implication, will not result in a breach justifying termination. Equity will permit completion to take place within a reasonable time after the stipulated date: *Stickney v Keeble* at 415.

2.45   The maxim also explains why an equitable mortgagee is treated in equity as if a legal mortgage had been granted, with the consequence that the equitable mortgagee is able to pursue the same remedies as are available to a legal mortgagee, including foreclosure: *Carter v Wake* (1877) 4 Ch D 605 at 606. In this context, in *Theodore v Mistford Pty Ltd* (2005) 221 CLR 612 at 622; 219 ALR 296 at 302, the High Court said that 'by looking at the intent rather than the form, equity is able to treat as done that which in good conscience ought to be done'.

2.46   The maxim also has its application in the construction of express trusts in relation to the use of precatory words: see 16.26–16.27. It is also the basis of the doctrine of rectification: see 30.1–30.24.

Equity looks on that as done which ought to be done

2.47   This maxim has its most frequent application in contract cases and is the basis of the remedy of specific performance. In *Frederick v Frederick* (1721) 24 ER 582 at 583, Lord Chancellor Macclesfield said that 'where one for valuable consideration agrees to do a thing, such executory contract is to be taken as done; and … the man who made the agreement shall not be in a better case, than if he had fairly and honestly performed what he agreed to'. However, in *De Beers Consolidated Mines Ltd v British South Africa Co* [1912] AC 52 at 65–6, Lord Atkinson pointed out the limits of the maxim in this context when he said:

> The doctrine cannot in its application to contracts … be permitted to turn the conditional into the absolute, the optional into the obligatory, or to make for the parties contracts different from those they have made for themselves. What a party to a contract ought to do, within the true meaning of the doctrine, is what he has contracted to do, and nothing more and nothing less is to be taken, in equity, to be done.

2.48   The maxim is also the basis of the doctrine in *Walsh v Lonsdale* (1882) 21 Ch D 9, where it was held that a person who enters into possession of land under a specifically enforceable contract for a lease is regarded, by a court having jurisdiction to enforce the contract, as being in the same position, as between itself and the other party to the contract, as if the lease had actually been granted: see 3.28–3.38. This doctrine was applied in *Industrial Properties (Barton Hill) Ltd v Associated Electrical Industries Ltd* [1977] QB 580; [1977] 2 All ER 293. In this case A agreed to sell property to B, but a transfer was never registered. A thus remained the legal owner. B leased the property to C and a 'lease' between B and C was entered into. C defaulted under the lease, and B sued C. C discovered that B was not the legal owner and denied liability. The Court of Appeal in England held that, even though the 'lease' was defective at law, it was nevertheless an agreement for a lease and applied *Walsh v Lonsdale*. Thus, C was found liable to B. In so deciding, the court refused to limit *Walsh v Lonsdale* to cases involving only one agreement and furthermore held that the doctrine was not limited in application to where there was a contractual relationship between the legal estate holder and lessee. In this case there was no legal relationship between A and C.

2.49   Another important illustration of the maxim arises in connection with the interest of a purchaser pursuant to an uncompleted contract for the purchase of land. In *Swiss Bank Corporation v Lloyds Bank Ltd* [1979] Ch 548 at 565; [1979] 2 All ER 853 at 866, Browne-Wilkinson J said:

> [A]lthough the basis of the equity jurisdiction was and still is founded on an order in personam, the courts of equity evolved the doctrine that, in the eyes of equity, that which ought to have been done is to be treated as having been done. Thus under a specifically enforceable contract for the sale of land, the purchaser is treated in equity as the owner of the property whether or not an order for specific performance has been made … In this way the [purchaser's] rights, although founded on the ability of the court to make an order in personam against the other contracting party …, become an interest in the property itself, an equitable interest. Once the position is reached that an order for specific performance could have been made against the [vendor] if the matter had been brought before the court, thereafter the [vendor] holds the

property shorn of those rights in the property which the court of equity would decree belongs to [the purchaser].

2.50 The nature of the purchaser's interest under an uncompleted contract is not altogether clear, but was described by Deane and Dawson JJ in *Stern v McArthur* (1988) 165 CLR 489 at 523; 81 ALR 463 at 485, as a 'lesser equitable interest than ownership'. (On the nature of equitable interests in property see Chapter 4.)

Equity imputes an intention to fulfil an obligation

2.51 This maxim is of limited application. It is one basis of the doctrines relating to deceased estates of satisfaction, ademption and performance.

Equity acts in personam

2.52 This maxim dates back at least to the *Earl of Oxford's Case* (1615) 21 ER 485 at 487 (see 1.34), where Lord Ellesmere said that equity could restrain a plaintiff at common law from enforcing a judgment of that court 'not for any error or Defect in the judgment, but for the hard Conscience of the Party'. Historically this maxim is significant in that it demonstrates the different manner in which equity executed its judgments and orders as compared to the common law. At common law a judgment of damages was enforced against the property of the defendant. The defendant's assets could be realised in order to satisfy the plaintiff's judgment. In equity, remedies attached to the person of the defendant. Spry explains the historical background to this approach as follows:

> It soon became established by successive Chancellors that courts of equity would not issue decrees that disposed of or purported to alter legal rights. Clearly to have issued decrees of that kind would have resulted in a direct conflict between the courts of equity and courts of law, for in such cases both courts would have been determining the same matters but on the application of differing, and accordingly, conflicting principles. This difficulty did not arise, for in accordance with equitable principles the decrees of the court constituted merely personal directions to the defendant either to act (such as by exercising his rights at law) or not to act in a particular way. This procedure was both natural to courts that were accustomed to regard themselves as courts of conscience and also appropriate to the extent that direct conflicts with other courts were to be avoided.[18]

2.53 If a defendant in equity proceedings fails to comply with an equitable order the property of the defendant is not at risk. Rather, the defendant will be held to be in contempt of court and subject to coercive measures or constraints. In *Deputy Commissioner of Taxation v Gashi (No 3)* [2011] VSC 448 at [7], Dixon J described the court's powers to punish for contempt as follows:

> The court may punish a natural person for contempt by committal to prison or fine or both. The court may make an order for punishment on terms, including a suspension of punishment … Where the respondent is a corporation, the court may punish for contempt by sequestration or fine or both.

His Honour, at [5], also noted that the relevant considerations to be taken into account when determining the appropriate penalty for contempt include:

---

18. Spry, *The Principles of Equitable Remedies*, note 11 above, p 29.

(a) the contemnor's personal circumstances;

(b) the nature and circumstances of the contempt;

(c) the actual consequences of the contempt;

(d) the effect of the contempt on the administration of justice;

(e) the contemnor's culpability;

(f) the need to deter the contemnor and others from repeating the contempt;

(g) the contemnor's reasons for his or her conduct;

(h) the absence or presence of a prior conviction for contempt;

(i) the contemnor's financial means; and

(j) whether the contemnor has exhibited general contrition and made a full and ample apology.

In this case the defendant was sentenced to three months imprisonment for breaching the terms of a Mareva order (see 25.5–25.33). In *Dental Board of Australia v Traianou* [2011] WASC 293, the defendant was given a suspended three-month prison sentence for breaching an injunction that restrained him from practising as a dentist unless registered.

2.54   A consequence of the *in personam* nature of equitable relief is that it can be granted provided the defendant is within the jurisdiction of the court, even if the property that is the subject matter of the case before the court is outside the jurisdiction of the court. Thus, in *Richard West and Partners (Inverness) Ltd v Dick* [1969] 2 Ch 424; [1969] 1 All ER 289, specific performance of a contract for the sale of land located in Scotland was ordered because the parties to the contract were within the jurisdiction of the English court. In *Chellaram v Chellaram* [1985] Ch 409; [1985] 1 All ER 1043, the court held that London-based trustees of shares in a Bermudan company, with assets in Africa, were capable of removal by an English court, notwithstanding the foreign location of the trust property. In this case Scott J, at Ch 428; All ER 1053–4, said:

> The jurisdiction of the court to administer trusts, to which the jurisdiction to remove trustees and appoint new ones is ancillary, is an *in personam* jurisdiction … This is so … whether or not the trust assets are situated in England, and whether or not the proper law of the trusts in question is English law. It requires only that the individual trustee should be subject to the jurisdiction of the English courts.

2.55   In more recent times the concept of *in personam* has developed a broader perspective. In *Oz-US Film Productions Pty Ltd v Heath* [2000] NSWSC 967 at [13], Young J explained this development as follows:

> A court of equity basically exercises only in personam jurisdiction. That is, it makes orders against people who are present in the jurisdiction or who have submitted to the jurisdiction. The in personam jurisdiction may, in proper cases, be exercised where the defendant has property in the jurisdiction over which the Court can enforce its order. In recent times, this jurisdiction has been further developed by the presumption that a defendant is considered to have property within the jurisdiction unless the evidence shows otherwise.

2.56   The *in personam* maxim could imply that equity does not recognise interests of a proprietary nature and that all equitable interests are no more than a personal chose in action against another person. However, this is not so. Many equitable interests and rights are proprietary in nature. For example, the interest of a beneficiary under a trust is proprietary and is not limited to a personal action against a trustee. In *Baker v Archer-Shee* [1927] AC 844, a testator, being an American citizen, left property to his daughter on trust for her life. The trustee was an American corporation and the property consisted of foreign securities, stocks and shares. The income of the trust property was paid into an American bank account. No income was remitted to England. The House of Lords held that the income was taxable on the basis that the daughter's rights under the will were 'property' from which the income was derived. If the daughter's rights had been confined merely to a personal chose in action against the trustee she would not have had any proprietary interest in either the trust property or the income thereof.

2.57 Another illustration is the statutory provision in all Australian jurisdictions requiring contracts for the sale of land or any interest in land to be evidenced in writing to be enforceable.[19] Such provisions include equitable interests in land. Thus, a contract for the sale of the interest of a beneficiary under a trust where the trust property is land must be evidenced in writing to be enforceable.

---

19. See *Civil Law (Property) Act 2006* (ACT) s 204(1); *Conveyancing Act 1919* (NSW) s 54A(1); *Law of Property Act 2000* (NT) s 62; *Property Law Act 1974* (Qld) s 59; *Law of Property Act 1936* (SA) s 26(1); *Conveyancing and Law of Property Act 1884* (Tas) s 36(1); *Instruments Act 1958* (Vic) s 126(1) and *Property Law Act 1958* (Vic) s 53(1)(a); *Law Reform (Statute of Frauds) Act 1962* (WA) s 2 which stipulates that the *Statute of Frauds* s 4 1677 (UK) applies in Western Australia.

3

THE RELATIONSHIP OF LAW AND EQUITY

INTRODUCTION

3.1 As noted in Chapter 1, prior to the adoption of the judicature system, the principles of the common law and equity were administered in separate courts. This meant, for example, that equitable obligations were 'unknown' to the common law and therefore not amenable to the common law remedy of damages. Thus, in *Coroneo v Australian Provincial Assurance Association Ltd* (1935) 35 SR (NSW) 391 at 394–5, Jordan CJ ruled that a breach of the equitable obligation of a mortgagee exercising a power of sale did not attract the remedy of common law damages. In such a case the mortgagor had to seek appropriate relief from a court of equity.

3.2 On the other hand, the common law courts generally had no jurisdiction to award equitable remedies or recognise equitable defences. Defendants at common law could not plead equitable defences to an action for common law damages. Thus, in an action at common law for damages by a plaintiff for breach by a defendant of a promise to sell property according to a price determined by a third party valuer, the defendant could not raise as a defence to liability the grounds of mistake, fraud or collusion in equity. This was so even though those grounds may have provided a defence to an application by the plaintiff for a decree of specific performance: *Legal & General Life of Australia Ltd v A Hudson Pty Ltd* (1985) 1 NSWLR 314 at 336.

3.3 Furthermore, a defendant in a common law court could not get his or her matter transferred to a court of equity. The remedy for such a defendant was to obtain a common injunction from the equity court to either prevent the plaintiff from setting up an inequitable plea at common law or to restrain such a plaintiff from pursuing and enforcing a judgment obtained at common law (see 1.30–1.31). The use of common injunctions effectively ensured the supremacy of equity courts over the common law courts.

THE JUDICATURE SYSTEM

3.4 The system of separate courts of common law and equity was abolished with the introduction of the judicature system. The separate courts were fused into one court which recognised and applied the principles of common law and equity. A consequence of this administrative fusion was that the common injunction became obsolete and was therefore abolished.

3.5 In England, pursuant to s 25 of the *Judicature Act 1873* (UK) (the Act), certain specific conflicts between the rules of equity and common law were expressly resolved. Section 25(11) of the

Act, a provision rarely relied upon subsequently,[1] stipulated that, in any other cases of such conflict, the equitable rule was to apply. Similar provisions were enacted in legislation implementing the judicature system in Australia: see 1.63.

3.6 It is clear from the parliamentary debates in England concerning the Act that it was intended to serve as an administrative reform. The intention of the legislation was not to affect the dual systems of common law and equity. This can also be clearly inferred from s 25(11) which, in giving primacy to equitable principles over common law principles in cases of conflict, presupposes the continued existence of the rules of common law and equity. There was no intention in the legislation to, in some way, fuse the principles of the common law and equity into one system of law. Thus, for example, the legislation did not authorise the new court to award common law damages for the breach of an equitable obligation.

3.7 This understanding of the effect of the Act was accepted at the time by both the inner and outer equity bars in England. A number of these men would later, as judges in the English judicial system, give judicial force to this understanding of the effects of the Act.[2] Thus, in *Salt v Cooper* (1880) 16 Ch D 545 at 549, Jessel MR said of the effect of the Act:

> [T]he main object of the Act was to assimilate the transaction of Equity business and Common Law business … It has been sometimes inaccurately called 'the fusion of Law and Equity'; but it was not any fusion, or anything of that kind; it was the vesting in one tribunal the administration of Law and Equity in every cause, action, or dispute which should come before that tribunal … To carry that out, the Legislature did not create a new jurisdiction, but simply transferred the old jurisdictions of the Courts of Law and Equity to the new tribunal, and then gave directions to the new tribunal as to the mode in which it should administer the combined jurisdictions.

3.8 In *Joseph v Lyons* (1884) 15 QBD 280 at 285–6, Cotton LJ said:

> It has been argued before us that the difference between legal and equitable interests has been swept away by those statutes. But it was not intended by the legislature, and it has not been said, that legal and equitable rights should be treated as identical, but that the Courts should administer both legal and equitable principles. I think that the clause enacting that the rules of equity shall prevail … shews that it was not intended to sweep away altogether the principles of the common law.

3.9 This original understanding of the effect of the Act was echoed more than a century later in England in *MCC Proceeds Inc v Lehman Brothers International (Europe)* [1998] 4 All ER 675 at 691, where Mummery LJ said:

> [T]he Supreme Court of Judicature Acts … were intended to achieve procedural improvements in the administration of law and equity in all courts, not to transform equitable interests into legal titles or to sweep away altogether the rules of the common law.

3.10 In Australia, a similar approach was taken by Windeyer J in *Felton v Mulligan* (1971) 124 CLR 367 at 392, where his Honour referred with approval to Ashburner's famous fluvial metaphor that

---

1. F W Maitland, *Equity and The Forms of Action at Common Law*, Cambridge University Press, Cambridge, 1929, p 16.
2. R Meagher, J D Heydon & M Leeming, *Meagher, Gummow and Lehane's Equity: Doctrines and Remedies*, 4th ed, LexisNexis Butterworths, Sydney, 2002, p 44.

asserted that 'the two streams of jurisdictions [that is, common law and equity], though they run in the same channel, run side by side and do not mingle their waters'.[3] In *O'Rourke v Hoeven* [1974] 1 NSWLR 622 at 626, Glass JA noted that the Act was 'not a fusion of two systems of principle but of the Courts which administer the two systems'.

3.11   The facts of, and decision in, *Brittain v Rossiter* (1883) 11 QBD 123, serve as a useful illustration of this understanding of the impact of the judicature system reforms. In that case it was argued that a partly performed contract for personal services, which was unenforceable because of non-compliance with the provisions of the *Statute of Frauds 1677* (UK), could be enforced by application of the equitable doctrine of part performance: see 23.77–23.89. The Court of Appeal, at 129, 131, 133–4, rejected this argument because the Court of Chancery had never applied the doctrine of part performance to such contracts and, since there was no remedy either at common law or equity in such a case before the Act, there was no reason why there should be one after the Act. Another illustration is the decision in *Penrith Whitewater Stadium Ltd v Lesvos Pty Ltd* [2007] NSWCA 176, which was a case concerned with a contract that did not comply with the writing requirements set out in the New South Wales equivalent of the English *Statute of Frauds*. Ipp JA, at [39]–[47], speaking for the Court of Appeal, held that, although there was performance of the contract sufficient to attract the doctrine of part performance, a court was not thereby entitled to award damages at common law for breach of the oral contract. Prior to the introduction of the judicature system, damages at common law were not available in such circumstances. The same result applied after the introduction of the judicature system because it was merely an administrative fusion of the courts, and not a fusion of the principles of common law and equity.

3.12   However, in more recent times in England there have been judicial pronouncements on the effect of the judicature system that appear to be at variance to the above cases. The most well known is from the House of Lords decision in *United Scientific Holdings Ltd v Burnley Borough Council* [1978] AC 904 at 924; [1977] 2 All ER 62 at 68, where Lord Diplock said:

> If by 'rules of equity' is meant that body of substantive and adjectival law that, prior to 1875, was administered by the Court of Chancery but not by courts of common law, to speak of the rules of equity as being part of the law of England in 1977 is about as meaningful as to speak similarly of the Statute of Uses or of Quia Emptores. Historically all three have in their time played an important part in the development of the corpus juris into what it is today; but to perpetuate the dichotomy between rules of equity and rules of common law which it was a major purpose of the Supreme Court of Judicature Act 1873 to do away with, is, in my view, conducive of erroneous conclusions as to the ways in which the law of England has developed in the last hundred years. Your Lordships have been referred to [Ashburner's] vivid phrase ... [on] the effect of the Supreme Court of Judicature Act ... My Lords, by 1977 this metaphor has in my view become both mischievous and deceptive ... If Professor Ashburner's fluvial metaphor is to be retained at all, the waters of the confluent streams of law and equity have surely mingled now.

3.13   Lord Diplock's view has been supported by a number of courts, especially in New Zealand and Canada. In *Aquaculture Corp v New Zealand Green Mussel Co* [1990] 3 NZLR 299 at 301, Cooke P, in the context of a confidential information case, said:

---

3.   D Browne, *Ashburner's Principles of Equity*, 2nd ed, Butterworth & Co, London, 1933, p 18.

> For all purposes now material, equity and common law are mingled or merged. The practicality of the matter is that in the circumstances of the dealings between the parties the law imposes a duty of confidence. For its breach a full range of remedies should be available as appropriate, no matter whether they originated in common law, equity or statute.

This view was cited with approval by a unanimous Supreme Court of Canada in *Cadbury Schweppes Inc v FBI Foods Ltd* [1999] 1 SCR 142 at 160–1; 167 DLR (4th) 577 at 590.

3.14   On one interpretation of Lord Diplock's view, the law of trusts would be abolished because it would abolish the distinction between a trustee and beneficiary. This clearly was neither the intention, nor the effect, of the Act: see 3.8. On the other hand, it may be that Lord Diplock merely intended to say that the Act did not prohibit the further development of the principles of equity and common law.

3.15   In Australia, and in particular in New South Wales, Lord Diplock's views have been vigorously contested and debated. To a large extent this is a product of the fact that New South Wales did not adopt the judicature system until the early 1970s. In New South Wales, leading practitioners, a number of whom were later elevated to the bench, vigorously attacked Lord Diplock's views. The most notable exposition rejecting Lord Diplock's views is to be found in the leading and influential equity text, generally known as *Meagher, Gummow and Lehane* in recognition of its original three authors, first published in 1975, just three years after the judicature system came into effect in New South Wales, and now in its fourth edition.[4] It was thus not surprising when one of its original authors, Roderick P Meagher, as a member of the Court of Appeal in New South Wales, opined that the views of Lord Diplock in *United Scientific Holdings v Burnley Borough Council* were 'so obviously erroneous as to be risible': *G R Mailman & Associates Pty Ltd v Wormald (Aust) Pty Ltd* (1991) 24 NSWLR 80 at 99.

3.16   The essence of the *Meagher, Gummow and Lehane* critique of the views espoused by Lord Diplock and others is that such views fall within the domain of what they label as 'fusion fallacies'. For *Meagher, Gummow and Lehane*, a fusion fallacy arises when the decision reached in a particular case is one which could not have been reached under the separate system of courts that existed before the judicature system reforms were enacted. In particular, these fusion fallacies have led to the following:

- the administration of a remedy not previously available at common law or equity; for example, in the words of Heydon JA in *Harris v Digital Pulse Pty Ltd* (2003) 56 NSWLR 298 at 416, 'selecting a remedy from the common law range of remedies which a court of equity administering the law relating to equitable wrongs before the introduction of the judicature system would not have administered'; and
- the modification of the principles of one branch of the law by the introduction of principles from another; for example, by holding that the existence of a duty of care in tort may be tested by asking whether the parties concerned are in a fiduciary relationship.

---

4. R P Meagher, W M Gummow & J F R Lehane, *Equity, Doctrines and Remedies*, Butterworths, Sydney 1975. The second edition appeared in 1983 and the third edition in 1992. For the fourth edition, published in 2002, J D Heydon and M J Leeming appeared as co-authors in place of W M Gummow and J F R Lehane. On the background to and the emergence of this text, and the reception it has received since publication, see D Freeman, *Roddy's Folly: R P Meagher QC – Art Lover and Lawyer*, Connor Court Publishing, Ballan (Vic), 2012, pp 348–58.

3.17   Although it is quite clear that the legislation fusing the formerly separate courts of common law and equity into one court did not of itself permit what has been described by *Meagher, Gummow and Lehane* as fusion fallacies, there is nothing in the legislation to suggest that the law could not develop in such ways in the future. Such developments of the law can be contested and debated on the merits on a case-by-case basis, but to reject them simply on the basis that they involve the mingling of principles of common law and equity as they stood prior to the introduction of the judicature system serves no useful purpose in the context of any debate over the development of legal principles. As was observed by Somers J in *Elders Pastoral Ltd v Bank of New Zealand* [1989] 2 NZLR 180 at 193:

> Neither law nor equity is now stifled by its origin and the fact that both are administered by one Court has inevitably meant that each has borrowed from the other in furthering the harmonious development of the law as a whole.

3.18   The effect of the judicature reforms was recently discussed in the important decision of the New South Wales Court of Appeal in *Harris v Digital Pulse*. In that case, the issue before the court was whether exemplary damages could be awarded for breach of equitable obligations, in this case by a fiduciary: see 26.30–26.37. Mason P, at 335–9, argued that an award of exemplary damages in cases of equitable wrongs was justified. His Honour suggested that the rationale for exemplary damages in tort law could be applied by analogy to equitable wrongs, and characterised this approach as an example of 'fusion by analogy' with the law of torts. However, the majority of the Court of Appeal disagreed. Spigelman CJ, at 307–10, stressed that if 'fusion by analogy' was to be used, then the appropriate analogy was with contract law, where exemplary damages are not available. Heydon JA, in a lengthy and detailed analysis of the relevant authorities and arguments, rejected the proposition that exemplary damages should be available for breaches of equitable obligations. His Honour, at 402, also suggested that such a view, if based upon the view that the fusion of the courts allowed the new single court to award common law remedies for breaches of equitable obligations, amounted to a 'crude fusion fallacy'. His Honour, at 415, was also of the view that only the High Court could change the law in the way suggested by Mason P: see 2.20.

3.19   Notwithstanding the fact that he was in dissent on the decision in *Harris v Digital Pulse*, Mason P, at 326, was undoubtedly correct when he observed:

> No one to my knowledge advocates incorporation or borrowing by direct force of the enactment of the *Judicature Act 1873* (UK) or its Australian counterparts. That would be a fusion fallacy of a very different sort, because there is much authority supporting the proposition that the fusion effected by the statute was of an administrative and procedural character. In Ashburner's famous metaphor:
>
> > … the two streams of jurisdiction, though they run in the same channel, run side by side and do not mingle their waters.
>
> Like all metaphors this needs to be understood in context. But I shall not tarry over it, because Meagher, Gummow & Lehane's 'fusion fallacy' bogey is quite different in nature. In terms, it condemns law and equity to the eternal separation of two parallel lines, ignoring the history of the two 'systems' both before and after the passing of the *Judicature Act 1873* (UK). And it treats the permission of the statute to fuse administration as if it were an enacted prohibition against a judge exercising the fused administration from applying doctrines and remedies found historically in one 'system' in a case whose roots may be found in the other 'system'.

Both 'Equity' and 'Common Law' had adequate powers to adopt and adapt concepts from each other's system well before the passing of the *Judicature Act* (UK), and nothing in that legislation limits such powers. They are of the very essence of judicial method which was and is part of the armoury of every judge in every 'common law' jurisdiction.

Neither system consistently and automatically ignored the other before the *Judicature Act* (UK); and there is even less justification for suggesting otherwise since the fusion of the administration of law and equity. I emphasise the words 'consistently and automatically'.

3.20 Similarly, Sir Anthony Mason has written as follows:

There is no reason why the courts in shaping principles, whether their origins lie in the common law or equity, should not have regard to both common law and equitable concepts and doctrines, borrowing from either as may be appropriate, just as the courts have regard to the way in which the law has been developed by statute and has developed in other jurisdictions and, for that matter, in other systems of law.[5]

3.21 In other jurisdictions this process of shaping principles has gone much further than in Australia. For example, a number of state jurisdictions in the United States of America have recognised that the equitable defence of unclean hands (see 31.8–31.12) may be raised in relation to common law and statutory claims.[6] In this context, the American scholar Anenson[7] has written as follows:

Continued reliance on outmoded anachronisms of law and equity in order to determine the availability of unclean hands is to chase ghosts and leave courts in a constant state of epistemic failure. It also limits the legal reasoning process of judges to formulations designed in the dark days of the common law. Adherence to the increasingly irrelevant labels of law and equity additionally diverts judicial resources from the true interests at stake and deprives the law of its ability to meet the needs of an ever-changing society. Distinctions between legal and equitable defenses are dead. They were buried with the merger. It is time for courts to begin writing their obituary.

3.22 Anenson's assertion that distinctions between common law and equity are 'dead' and 'buried' does not reflect reality in Australia.[8] However, it has the ring of a call to arms for those willing to bring forward, as soon as possible, the dawning of the day 'when lawyers will', as Maitland predicted, 'cease to inquire whether a given rule be a rule of equity or a rule of common law'.[9] Furthermore, although the decision in *Harris v Digital Pulse* rejected the availability of exemplary damages for breaches of

---

5. A Mason, 'The Place of Equity and Equitable Remedies in the Contemporary Common Law World' (1994) 110 *Law Quarterly Review* 238, p 242.
6. For a detailed analysis of this development see T L Anenson, 'Treating Equity Like Law: A Post-Merger Justification of Unclean Hands' (2008) 45 *American Business Law Journal* 455. This development was explicitly rejected by Young JA (McColl JA and Sackville AJA agreeing) in *Batterham v Makeig* [2010] NSWCA 86 at [92].
7. Anenson, 'Treating Equity Like Law', note 6 above, p 509.
8. For contrasting recent discussions on this issue in Australia see M Kirby, 'Overcoming Equity's Australian Isolation' (2009) 3 *Journal of Equity* 1 and P A Keane, 'The 2009 W A Lee Lecture in Equity: The Conscience of Equity' (2010) 84 *Australian Law Journal* 92.
9. Maitland, *Equity*, note 1 above, p 20.

fiduciary obligations, Mason, Carter and Tolhurst note that '[t]he approach of the whole court was ... refreshing in its willingness to debate whether a contractual or tortious analogy was closer, rather than regarding the issue as determined a priori by the equitable derivation of the duty concerned'.[10]

LAW AND EQUITY UNDER THE JUDICATURE SYSTEM

3.23 In the wake of the introduction of the judicature system, the development of legal principles of common law and equity can be illustrated by the following examples.

Mortgagee's power of sale

3.24 A complaint by a mortgagor in relation to the exercise of a power of sale by a mortgagee has, in the absence of statutory provisions regulating the matter, traditionally been a matter decided upon in accordance with equitable principles. This is so because the sale includes the mortgagor's equity of redemption. The equitable principle has generally been formulated as requiring the mortgagee to act in good faith. However, in *Cuckmere Brick Co Ltd v Mutual Finance Ltd* [1971] Ch 949; [1971] 2 All ER 633, the Court of Appeal in England treated the mortgagee's obligations to the mortgagor when exercising its power of sale in terms of the tort of negligence with the mortgagor's remedy being a claim for common law damages. The essence of the difference between these two tests is that the *Cuckmere* test imposes a duty upon the mortgagee to obtain the best possible price for the property when sold. However, the equitable good faith duty imposes a less demanding duty on the mortgagee and does not require him or her to sell at the best possible price, although it is widely accepted that the duty of good faith requires the mortgagee to take precautions to ensure that a 'proper' price is obtained and that the interests of the mortgagor are not completely sacrificed: *Upton v Tasmanian Perpetual Trustees Limited* (2007) 158 FCR 118 at 126, 136–7; 242 ALR 422 at 429, 439–40.

3.25 In England, later cases have made it clear that the mortgagee's duties generally are equitable and have described their nature by using the traditional 'good faith' formulation: *Downsview Nominees Ltd v First City Corpn Ltd* [1993] AC 295 at 312; [1993] 3 All ER 626 at 635; *Meretz Investments NV v ACP Ltd* [2007] Ch 197 at 266–8; [2006] 3 All ER 1029 at 1097–9. On the other hand, in *Medford v Blake* [2000] Ch 386 at 102; [1999] 3 All ER 97 at 111, the Court of Appeal took the view that it did not matter 'one jot whether the [mortgagee's] duty is expressed as a common law duty or as a duty in equity' because, in all cases 'the result is the same'. In the light of this comment it is not surprising that the Court of Appeal in *Medford* at Ch 99; All ER 108, and in *Raja v Austin Gray* [2002] EWCA Civ 1965 at [16], observed that *Cuckmere Brick* stood for the proposition that the mortgagee's duty in exercising a power of sale was 'an equitable duty to take reasonable steps to obtain a proper price'.

3.26 The correctness of *Cuckmere Brick* was left open by the High Court of Australia in *Forsyth v Blundell* (1973) 129 CLR 477; 1 ALR 68. However, in *Citicorp Australia Ltd v McLoughney* (1984) 35 SASR 375 at 381, Zelling J said that, in equating the mortgagee's duty with that of negligence at common law, the reasoning in *Cuckmere Brick* was flawed. The *Cuckmere Brick* formulation was also rejected by the Full Court of the Federal Court in *Upton v Tasmanian Perpetual Trustees Limited*, at 123–5, 134–7; ALR 427–9, 437–40. Finally, it can be noted that in various jurisdictions

---

10. K Mason, J W Carter & G J Tolhurst, *Mason & Carter's Restitution Law in Australia*, 2nd ed, LexisNexis Butterworths, 2008, p 699.

in Australia, legislation regulates the nature of the duties of the mortgagee in exercising his or her power of sale. Thus, in exercising a power of sale of property of a corporation, a controller must take reasonable care exercising the power of sale in relation to property of a corporation, the controller must ensure that the property is not sold for less than its market value or for not less than the best price reasonably available in the circumstances.[11] Similar obligations are imposed on mortgagees in New South Wales, the Northern Territory and Queensland,[12] whereas in Tasmania and Victoria,[13] a mortgagee must have regard to the interests of the mortgagor when exercising the power of sale.[14]

Damages in equity

3.27   In *Seager v Copydex (No 1)* [1967] 2 All ER 415, the English Court of Appeal awarded damages for the breach of the equitable obligation pertaining to confidential information. The case does not elaborate on the basis upon which damages were ordered. It can be viewed as one in which common law damages were awarded for a breach of an equitable obligation. In *English v Dedham Vale Properties Ltd* [1978] 1 All ER 382 at 399, Slade J read the decision as being an award of damages in lieu of an injunction pursuant to the successor provisions of Lord Cairns' Act. However, this understanding of the case is dependent upon an interpretation of this legislation that permits damages to be awarded in lieu of an injunction sought in aid of equitable rights and obligations: see 26.68–26.70.

The doctrine of Walsh v Lonsdale

3.28   Perhaps the most famous example of the development of common law and equitable principles after the introduction of the judicature system is the decision in *Walsh v Lonsdale* (1882) 2 Ch D 9. In that case, the facts involved an agreement for a lease of a mill for seven years at a rent payable quarterly in arrears, with a provision entitling the landlord to demand a year's rent in advance. No lease was ever entered into in deed form and thus the lease as such was void at common law. The tenant entered into possession and paid rent in accordance with the agreement for 18 months. The landlord then demanded a year's rent in advance. The tenant failed to pay. The landlord levied for distress at common law. (The remedy of distress permits a landlord to seize a tenant's chattels and to hold them until rent is paid. If rent is not paid the chattels may be sold.) The tenant sought an injunction against the distress and damages for illegal distress. The issue before the court was whether the landlord's common law remedy of distress was permitted despite the absence of a lease at common law. Under the pre-judicature system such a result could only have occurred if there was in existence a valid common law lease. On the facts of *Walsh v Lonsdale*, that would have required the landlord to obtain a decree of specific performance of the agreement for lease. The English Court of Appeal found for the landlord, thereby holding that he was entitled to distrain.

---

11.   *Corporations Act 2001* (Cth) s 420A(1).
12.   *Conveyancing Act 1919* (NSW) s 111A(1); *Law of Property Act 2000* (NT) s 90(1); *Property Law Act 1974* (Qld) s 85(1).
13.   *Land Titles Act 1980* (Tas) s 78(1); *Transfer of Land Act 1958* (Vic) s 77(1).
14.   For an analysis of these statutory provisions see A Lark, 'Legislative Impact on the Mortgagee's Exercise of Power of Sale: The Need for Rationalisation' (2012) 20 *Australian Property Law Journal* 145.

3.29   In his decision in *Walsh v Lonsdale* at 15, Jessel MR said that, following the Judicature Act:

> There are not two estates as there were formerly, one estate at common law … and an estate in equity under the agreement. There is only one Court, and the equity rules prevail in it. The tenant holds under an agreement for lease. He holds therefore, under the same terms in equity as if a lease had been granted, it being a case in which both parties admit that relief is capable of being given by specific performance.

3.30   The decision in *Walsh v Lonsdale* has been the subject of significant discussion and debate ever since it was decided. The controversy can be seen in the first part of the judgment of Jessel MR which, if taken literally, is clearly incorrect. The judicature system did not eliminate the distinction between common law and equitable estates in property, as was confirmed in the earlier decision of *Joseph v Lyons* (see 3.8) and the statement by Jessel MR in this respect was subsequently disapproved of in *Manchester Brewery Co v Coombs* [1901] 2 Ch 608 at 617. Furthermore, the case creates the impression that a contract for a lease is as good as a lease. However, as will be seen in the subsequent discussion on *Walsh v Lonsdale*, this is clearly not the case. What the case establishes is that, until a formal lease is executed in compliance with a decree of specific performance, there exists an equitable lease only, although the parties to the lease stand in the same position as if a lease had been granted.

3.31   In truth, the decision in *Walsh v Lonsdale* was 'neither novel nor revolutionary'.[15] On the basis of the administrative and procedural reforms brought in as a result of the judicature system, the Court of Appeal in that case was able to simplify procedures to achieve what would have been reached before the passing of the Acts. However, because of the existence of separate courts of common law and equity, these proceedings would have been onerous and expensive. O'Keefe is correct when he observes:

> [T]he parties in the case [were] … spared considerable expense, delay and procedural difficulty. The Court, by treating as done what ought to be done, allowed the [landlord] to claim his right to specific performance without having first to obtain a decree and to use this equitable defence against the [tenant's] claim.[16]

3.32   The decision in *Manchester Brewery* also states the limited applicability of *Walsh v Lonsdale*. In *Manchester Brewery*, at 617, Farwell J said:

> [The decision in *Walsh v Lonsdale*] applies only to cases where there is a contract to transfer a legal title, and an act has to be justified or an action maintained by force of the legal title to which such contract relates. It involves two questions: (1) Is there a contract of which specific performance can be obtained? (2) If Yes, will the title acquired by such specific performance justify at law the act complained of, or support at law the action in question? It is to be treated as though before the Judicature Acts there had been, first, a suit in equity for specific performance, and then an action at law between the same parties; and the doctrine is only applicable in those cases where specific performance can be obtained between the same parties in the same court, and at the same time as the subsequent legal action falls to be determined.

---

15.   D O'Keefe, 'Sir George Jessel and the Union of Judicature' (1982) 26 *American Journal of Legal History* 227, p 245.

16.   O'Keefe, 'Sir George Jessel and the Union of Judicature', note 15 above, p 244.

3.33 In *Walsh v Lonsdale* the availability of specific performance of the agreement to lease was conceded by the parties and was thus not an issue before the court. However, if the issue is contested, the right to specific performance must be resolved in the plaintiff's favour. Otherwise the doctrine in *Walsh v Lonsdale* will not apply: *Swain v Ayres* (1888) 21 QBD 289 at 293–4. In *McMahon v Ambrose* [1987] VR 817 at 836–7, McGarvie J observed:

> The foundation of the principle of *Walsh v Lonsdale* was the present right to specific performance … It is based on the rationale that equity regards as done that which the parties have agreed to do and which the court regards it as appropriate to direct by an order for specific performance to be done … To treat the principle in *Walsh v Lonsdale* applicable in the absence of a present right to specific performance would be to cut it off from the rational roots from which it grew.

3.34 As his Honour pointed out, at the time when proceedings pursuant to the doctrine of *Walsh v Lonsdale* are commenced, the court must be satisfied that specific performance of the agreement for lease would be available. However, in *McMahon v Ambrose* the Full Court split on the issue of whether specific performance was available in relation to an agreement to lease which had expired before proceedings pursuant to *Walsh v Lonsdale* were commenced. The majority, Murray and Marks JJ, was of the view that specific performance was not available in such circumstances. McGarvie J dissented and expressed the view that in such cases specific performance could be ordered in the appropriate case. In *Chan v Cresdon Pty Ltd* (1989) 168 CLR 242 at 255; 89 ALR 522 at 530, the majority of the High Court expressed the view that the power to grant specific performance in such circumstances was to be 'exercised sparingly'.

3.35 A number of English cases have held that the doctrine of *Walsh v Lonsdale* applies if specific performance of the agreement for lease would have been granted at any time during the currency of the agreement: *Industrial Properties (Barton Hill) Ltd v AEI Ltd* [1977] QB 580; [1977] 2 All ER 293; *Tottenham Hotspur Co Ltd v Princegrove Publishers Ltd* [1974] 1 All ER 17. In *McMahon v Ambrose*, McGarvie J rejected this approach because, in such circumstances, there is no present right to specific performance as at the time proceedings are commenced.

3.36 Although the court must make a considered decision on the issue of specific performance, it need not formally administer the decree, but may proceed to adjudicate on the legal rights of the parties as if the decree had been administered: *Ahern v L A Wilkinson (Northern) Ltd* [1929] St R Qd 66 at 80–5. Either party may, if they wish, apply to the court for appropriate directions that the decree be administered. To this extent the doctrine of *Walsh v Lonsdale* represents a departure from the system of separate courts that existed prior to the introduction of the judicature system because at that time the separate court of equity would have administered the decree and then the common law court would have adjudicated upon the legal rights of the parties.

3.37 The ruling in *Walsh v Lonsdale* was considered by the High Court of Australia in *Chan v Cresdon Pty Ltd*. In that case Cresdon agreed in writing to lease land to Sarcourt. The agreement contained the terms of the lease as an annexure. The lease was duly executed but never registered. Sarcourt defaulted under the lease and Cresdon took action against Chan as guarantor of the unregistered lease. Cresdon's action against Chan was stated as being one taken on the guarantee 'under this lease'. Cresdon's action was unsuccessful. The court held that as there was no registered lease there was no enforceable guarantee. Cresdon's alternative claim was based upon the rule in *Walsh v Lonsdale*. This claim also was unsuccessful. In coming to its conclusion the court ruled that, although the rule in *Walsh v Lonsdale* meant that an agreement to lease gave rise to an equitable lease, it did not create a legal interest. A consequence of this is that the equitable lessee will be defeated by a bona fide purchaser of the legal estate who acquires the legal estate for valuable consideration and without notice of the equitable lease (see 7.48–7.60 on priorities).

3.38   The court also confirmed that the operation of the rule depended upon the availability of specific performance of the agreement to lease. In the circumstances of the case, two facts raised doubts as to the availability of specific performance. First, Cresdon had in the meantime mortgaged the property. Second, the lease had come to an end before the expiration of the term due to Sarcourt's breach. However, the court ruled that, even if specific performance had been available, Cresdon's action was doomed to fail. This was so because, under the rule in *Walsh v Lonsdale*, all that the agreement to lease amounted to was an equitable lease. The guarantee that Cresdon sought to enforce was of 'obligations under the lease' and the court ruled that this meant obligations contained in a legal lease. Because no such lease existed there was no enforceable guarantee.

Part II:
Equitable Interests and Transactions

4

NATURE OF EQUITABLE ESTATES AND INTERESTS

INTRODUCTION

4.1   In Chapter 2 it was noted that although equity acts *in personam*, equity nevertheless recognises rights of a proprietary nature. In this chapter the nature of equitable estates and rights in property will be analysed. Non-proprietary, or 'personal' obligations, are discussed at 15.84–15.86.

4.2   The most significant aspect of equitable estates and rights in property is their disparate and flexible nature. This is a consequence of the fact that, in the words of Viscount Radcliffe in *Commissioner of Stamp Duties (Qld) v Livingston* [1965] AC 694 at 712; [1964] 3 All ER 692 at 699:

> Equity in fact calls into existence and protects equitable rights and interests in property only where their recognition has been found to be required in order to give effect to its doctrines.

4.3   The flexibility and discretionary nature of equitable remedies is reflected in the nature of the equitable rights that these remedies have served to create. Because equitable rights are rooted in the remedies that protect them, the strength of one equitable right as compared to another will depend on the availability of equitable remedies to those asserting a claim to the subject property. Some of the rights recognised by equity will be proprietary in nature, others will not. The highest form of equitable proprietary interest is that of a beneficiary under a trust.

4.4   In this chapter the expression 'equitable interest' is used to denote a property right in equity. It should be noted that the expressions 'beneficial interest' and 'equitable estate' are often used as an alternative to 'equitable interest'. Thus, in *Commissioner of State Revenue v Serana Pty Ltd* (2008) 36 WAR 251 at 285, Buss JA said:

> The word 'beneficial', in the context of a beneficial interest in property, ordinarily denotes a proprietary interest to which a person or persons, other than the person in whom legal title to the property is vested, is entitled. That is, a beneficial interest in property usually denotes a proprietary interest held for the benefit of another or others.

4.5   In other contexts the word 'interest' may have a different meaning. In *Gartside v Inland Revenue Commissioners* [1968] AC 553 at 617; [1968] 1 All ER 121 at 134, Lord Wilberforce noted that the word 'interest' 'has to do duty in several quite different legal contexts to express rights of very different characters and that to transfer a meaning from one context to another may breed confusion'. In *Commissioner of Stamp Duties (Qld) v Livingston*, at AC 712; All ER 699, Viscount Radcliffe said:

> [T]he terminology of our legal system has not produced a sufficient variety of words to represent the various meanings which can be conveyed by the words 'interest' and 'property'. Thus propositions are advanced or rebutted by the employment of terms that have not in themselves a common basis of definition.

4.6   Thus, use of the word 'interest' must always be carefully analysed when reading cases and other textual materials in this context. For example, it may be that the expressions 'interest' or 'equitable interest' simply mean that the bearer of such an 'interest' or 'equitable interest' has some legal remedy which will, if granted, secure a right of a proprietary nature: see 4.38–4.40.

4.7   If a person has an equitable interest in property, this implies that some other person has the legal interest in that property. If one person has both the legal and equitable interests in the relevant property, he or she has no 'equitable interest' in that property as such. The reasoning behind this proposition was explained in *DKLR Holdings Co (No 2) Pty Ltd v Commissioner of Stamp Duties (NSW)* (1982) 149 CLR 431 at 463; 40 ALR 1 at 26, where Aickin J said:

> If one person has both the legal estate and the entire beneficial interest in the land he holds an entire and unqualified legal interest and not two separate interests, one legal and the other equitable. If he first holds the legal estate upon trust for some other person and thereafter that other person transfers to him the entire equitable interest, then again the first-named person does not hold two separate interests, one the legal and the other the equitable estate; he holds a single entire interest — he is the absolute owner of an estate in fee simple in the land. The equitable interest merges into the legal estate to comprise a single absolute interest in the land. It is a fundamental principle of both the common law and of equity that the holder of an estate in fee simple cannot be a trustee of that fee simple for himself for what he holds is a single estate, being the largest estate in land known to the law.

4.8   Because of the close relationship between equitable remedies and equitable interests, 'there is some circuity involved in finding the starting point for the existence of such an equitable interest, the problem being to isolate as the initiating factor the proprietary interest or the right to enforce the interest of the beneficiary': *Burns Philp Trustee Co Ltd v Viney* [1981] 2 NSWLR 216 at 223. This problem can be illustrated by the right of a beneficiary under a trust.

4.9   In *Re Transphere Pty Ltd* (1984) 5 NSWLR 309 at 311, the right of a beneficiary under a trust was described by M H McLelland J as follows:

> [W]hat is significant for present purposes is the imprecision of the notion that absolute ownership of property can properly be divided up into a legal estate and an equitable estate. An absolute owner holds only the legal estate, with all the right and incidents that attach to that estate. Where a legal owner holds property on trust for another, he has at law all the rights of an absolute owner but the beneficiary has the right to compel him to hold and use those rights which the law gives him in accordance with the obligations which equity has imposed on him by virtue of the

existence of the trust. Although this right of the beneficiary constitutes an equitable estate in the property, it is engrafted onto, not carved out of, the legal estate.

Thus, although the beneficiary has an interest in the trust property, the content of that interest is essentially a right to compel the trustee to hold and use his legal rights in accordance with the terms of the trust.

4.10   This raises the question of whether the beneficiary's right of enforcement against the trustee is a consequence of the beneficiary having an equitable interest, or whether the right of enforcement gives rise to the beneficiary's equitable interest. In *Burns Philp Trustee Co Ltd v Viney*, at 224, Kearney J suggested that the answer to this 'jurisprudential mystery' appeared to be that 'enforceability is not so much a pre-condition to the existence of an equitable interest, but rather an incident or characteristic of such interest signifying its quality or extent'. On the other hand, in *Haslam v Money for Living (Aust) Pty Ltd* (2008) 172 FCR 301 at 318, in the context of the remedy of specific performance case, Middleton J said that '[i]t is important to appreciate that the availability and the nature of specific performance is a precondition to the recognition of an equitable interest and the extent of that equitable interest in the property'.

THE COMPLEXITY OF EQUITABLE INTERESTS

4.11   The complexity of the topic of the nature of equitable estates and interests can be gauged by an examination of the decisions in *Dickinson v Burrell* (1866) LR 1 Eq 337 and *Gross v Lewis Hillman Ltd* [1970] Ch 445; [1969] 3 All ER 1476.

4.12   *Dickinson v Burrell* stands for the proposition that if A, as the result of undue influence exerted by B, conveys Blackacre by gift to B, and then assigns or devises the right to rescind the transaction to C, C can seek equity's assistance to rescind the transaction and have Blackacre reconveyed to C. Because A's right can be enforced by C against B, it is more than merely a personal right against B. It is an equitable proprietary right that, when assigned or devised to C can be enforced by C against B. The decision in *Dickinson v Burrell* means that, in order to give effect to the doctrine of undue influence, it is necessary to hold that the interest that A has is an equitable interest.

4.13   *Gross v Lewis Hillman Ltd* stands for the proposition that if A is induced to purchase Blackacre from B as the result of a fraudulent misrepresentation, and then transfers Blackacre to C, C cannot assert against B the right to rescind that A had against B. Because C is denied the remedy of rescission in this situation, the right of A must be seen as purely personal and not proprietary. Cross LJ, at Ch 461; All ER 1482, distinguished this case from *Dickinson v Burrell* as follows:

> Here, the assignee is not claiming to recover an equitable interest in property previously conveyed away by his assignor, but is claiming to throw back the property assigned to him not on his immediate assignor but on the party who sold it to his assignor.

4.14   It can be argued that the distinction drawn by Cross LJ is illogical and that C's position in both cases should be the same. However, what these two cases illustrate is that the variety of rights recognised by equity are virtually impossible to rationalise and categorise.

INDICIA OF EQUITABLE INTERESTS

4.15   In *National Provincial Bank Ltd v Ainsworth* [1965] AC 1175 at 1247–8; [1965] 2 All ER 472 at 494, Lord Wilberforce, speaking of proprietary interests, said:

> Before a right or interest can be admitted into the category of property or of a right affecting property, it must be definable, identifiable by third parties, capable in its nature of assumption by third parties, and have some degree of permanence or stability.

4.16   Lord Wilberforce's statement describes some of the characteristics of equitable interests. However, it is by no means a comprehensive list. This is so because equitable interests do not have a set of attributes that is common to all of them. At best one can merely list what attributes any particular equitable interest has and compare and contrast that list with the attributes of other equitable interests. In *Burns Philp Trustee Co Ltd v Viney* at 223–4, Kearney J observed:

> The administration of equity has always paid regard to the infinite variety of interests and has refrained from formulating or adhering to fixed universal and exhaustive criteria with which to deal with such varying situations. The approach traditionally adopted by equity has been to retain flexibility so as to accommodate the multitudinous instances in which fundamental equitable rules fail to be applied.

4.17   One of the more significant indicia of property is assignability. In *Reg v Toohey; Ex parte Meneling Station Pty Ltd* (1982) 158 CLR 327 at 342–3; 44 ALR 63 at 75, Mason J said:

> Assignability is not in all circumstances an essential characteristic of a right of property. By statute some forms of property are expressed to be inalienable. None the less, it is generally correct to say, as Lord Wilberforce said, that a proprietary right must be 'capable in its nature of assumption by third parties'.

In *Australian Capital Television Pty Ltd v The Commonwealth* (1992) 177 CLR 106 at 166; 108 ALR 577 at 615, Brennan J said:

> Although property is generally assignable, that is not universally so for, as Isaacs J said in *Commissioner of Stamp Duties (NSW) v Yeend* [(1929) 43 CLR 235 at 245], '[a]ssignability is a consequence, not a test' of a proprietary right. Assignability may therefore be denied to what is, by other tests, properly found to be property. None the less, the want of assignability of a right is a factor tending against the characterisation of a right as property.

4.18   Meagher, Heydon and Leeming[1] suggest that the proprietary nature of any equitable interest can be measured by reference to the following four criteria:

1. The power to recover the property the subject of the interest or the income thereof as compared with the recovery of compensation from the defendant payable from no specific fund.
2. The power to transfer the benefit of the interest to another.
3. The persistence of remedies in respect of the interest against third parties assuming the burden thereof.
4. The extent to which the interest may be displaced in favour of competing dealings by the grantor or others with interests in the subject matter.

---

1.   R Meagher, J D Heydon & M Leeming, *Meagher, Gummow and Lehane's Equity: Doctrines and Remedies*, 4th ed, LexisNexis Butterworths, Sydney, 2002, p 126.

4.19 It must be noted that a right that does not satisfy all of the above criteria may still be recognised as an equitable interest. However, just because some of the criteria are satisfied does not necessarily mean that the interest is an equitable interest. The following rights will be analysed against the above criteria:

• the right of a sole beneficiary under a bare trust *inter vivos*; and
• the right of a beneficiary in an unadministered estate.

The right of a sole beneficiary under a bare trust

4.20 A bare trust was defined by Gummow J in *Herdegen v Federal Commissioner of Taxation* (1988) 84 ALR 271 at 281, as follows:

> Today the usually accepted meaning of 'bare' trust is a trust under which the trustee or trustees hold property without any interest therein, other than that existing by reason of the office and the legal title as trustee, and without any duty or further duty to perform, except to convey it upon demand to the beneficiary or beneficiaries or as directed by them, for example, on sale to a third party.

4.21 The nature of the duties of a trustee under a bare trust was further detailed in *CGU Insurance Limited v One.Tel Limited (In Liquidation)* (2010) 242 CLR 174 at 182; 268 ALR 439 at 446, where the High Court said:

> The trustee of a bare trust has no interests in the trust assets other than those which exist by reason of the office of trustee and the holding of legal title. Further, the trustee of a bare trust has no active duties to perform other than those which exist by virtue of the office of the trustee, with the result that the property awaits transfer to the beneficiaries or awaits some other disposition at their direction. One obligation of a trustee which exists by virtue of the very office is the obligation to get the trust property in, protect it, and vindicate the rights attaching to it. That obligation exists even if no provision of any statute or trust instrument creates it. It exists unless it is negated by a provision of any statute or trust instrument.

4.22 However, a trustee carrying on a business is not a bare trustee: *Old Papa's Franchise Systems Pty Ltd v Camisa Nominees Pty Ltd* [2003] WASCA 11 at [57]. Finally, the fact that a trust is amenable to being terminated pursuant to the rule in *Saunders v Vautier* (1841) 49 ER 282 (see 21.48–21.66) does not mean that the trustee is a bare trustee. He or she will become a bare trustee only when the beneficiaries have, pursuant to the rule in *Saunders v Vautier*, called upon the trustee to terminate the trust: *Chief Commissioner of Stamp Duties v ISPT Pty Ltd* (1998) 45 NSWLR 639 at 651–2.

4.23 Bare trusts arise in various circumstances. These include: (i) the assignor of future property becomes a bare trustee of the property for the assignee when the property comes into existence (see 5.64); (ii) the vendor of land, upon payment of the purchase price by the purchaser, becomes a bare trustee of the land for the purchaser (*Stern v McArthur* (1988) 165 CLR 489 at 523; 81 ALR 463 at 485); and (iii) a person who holds legal title to property where the purchase price has been provided by another person is, applying the principles of resulting trusts (see Chapter 19), a bare trustee of the property for the person providing the purchase price: *Herdegen* at 281.

4.24   In relation to the above four criteria it can be noted that a beneficiary under a bare trust *inter vivos*:

1. can demand the transfer from the trustee of the legal title to the property;
2. can dispose of his or her beneficial interest to another person, subject to any statutory requirement of writing;[2]
3. can pursue the property the subject of the trust against third parties by recourse to the remedy of tracing (see Chapter 29);
4. can assert its priority of interest against all others except a bona fide purchaser of the legal estate buying for value and without notice of the beneficiary's equitable interest: see 7.48.

The right of a beneficiary in an unadministered estate

4.25   The right considered here is that of a person who is to inherit property following the death of another person from the date of death of the deceased and through to the administration of the estate. The leading case on this issue is the Privy Council decision in *Commissioner of Stamp Duties (Queensland) v Livingston*.

4.26   In *Livingston*, the facts concerned Mrs Coulson who, at her death, was entitled to a one-third share in the residue of her deceased husband's estate. The husband's estate included personal and real property in both Queensland and New South Wales. The executors of the husband's estate were domiciled in New South Wales. At the time of Mrs Coulson's death, the husband's estate had not been administered and her share had not been ascertained precisely. The Stamp Duties Commissioner in Queensland, in applying that state's succession legislation, claimed that, at her death, Mrs Coulson died owning an equitable interest in real and personal property in Queensland in relation to the share of her husband's deceased estate that she was to have inherited. The issue before the Privy Council was whether Mrs Coulson, at the date of her death, had an equitable interest in relation to her share under her deceased husband's estate. If she did, the Stamp Duties Commissioner was entitled to levy succession duty.

4.27   For the Privy Council, Viscount Radcliffe, at AC 706; All ER 696, stated that, for the Commissioner to succeed, it was necessary to show that Mrs Coulson died 'owning a beneficial interest in real property in Queensland or had beneficial property interests locally situated in Queensland'. Viscount Radcliffe noted that, pending administration of the husband's estate, his executors held the whole of the property in the estate with no distinction between legal and equitable estates. The executors had the property to carry out the administration of the estate and not for their own benefit. It thus followed, in the words of Viscount Radcliffe, at AC 708; All ER 697, that:

> [The husband's] property in Queensland, real and personal vested in his executors in full right, and
> no beneficial property interest in any item of it belonged to Mrs Coulson at the date of her death.

4.28   Although Mrs Coulson had, at the date of her death, no equitable interest in her husband's unadministered estate, Viscount Radcliffe, at AC 712; All ER 699, went on to say that her rights as a beneficiary of her husband's estate were protected because:

---

2.   *Civil Law (Property) Act 2006* (ACT) s 201(1); *Conveyancing Act 1919* (NSW) s 23C(1); *Law of Property Act 2000* (NT) s 10(1); *Property Law Act 1974* (Qld) s 11; *Law of Property Act 1936* (SA) s 29(1); *Conveyancing and Law of Property Act 1884* (Tas) s 60(2); *Property Law Act 1958* (Vic) s 53(1); *Property Law Act 1969* (WA) s 34(1).

The court will control the executor in the use of his rights over assets that come to him in that capacity; but it will do it by the enforcement of remedies which do not involve the admission or recognition of equitable rights of property in those assets. Equity in fact calls into existence and protects equitable rights and interests in property only where their recognition has been found to be required in order to give effect to its doctrines.

4.29 Viscount Radcliffe, at AC 717; All ER 702, concluded:

Mrs Coulson was not entitled to any beneficial interest in any property in Queensland at the date of her death. What she was entitled to in respect of her rights under her deceased husband's will was a chose in action, capable of being invoked for any purpose connected with the proper administration of his estate.

4.30 In the light of *Livingston* the following comments can be made in relation to the right of a beneficiary in an unadministered estate when measured against the four criteria of property suggested by Meagher, Heydon and Leeming:

1. The beneficiary's right is not an equitable interest in the context of administration of deceased estates. All the beneficiary has is the power to compel the executor to properly administer the estate. The executor has all property rights. However, the beneficiary's right to compel the executor to properly administer the estate, carries with it the right to receive property once the estate is administered. In *Re Maguire (deceased)* [2010] 2 NZLR 845 at 851, Asher J said that '[t]he executors [of an unadministered estate owe] the residuary legatees a fiduciary duty to carry out their administration tasks honestly and diligently, and the residuary beneficiaries … have remedies against the executors should they fail to carry out those duties'. Thus, in *In re Hemming, decd; Raymond Saul & Co (a firm) v Holden* [2009] Ch 313 at 324, the right of the beneficiary of the deceased's residuary estate was described as 'a composite right to have the estate properly administered and to have the residue (if any) paid to him as and when the administration is complete'. In the High Court in *Kennon v Spry* (2008) 238 CLR 3666 at 394; (251) ALR 257 at 276, French CJ described the right to proper administration of the estate as being 'connected to a real expectancy of an interest in the property'. Heydon J, at CLR 418; ALR 297, said that the beneficiary, 'while having no beneficial interest in any particular asset of the unadministered estate, is correctly described as being entitled to the appropriate share of the … estate'. More recently, in *Brennan v McGuire* [2010] FCA 1443 at [108], Rares J opined that the interest of a residuary beneficiary in the assets of an unadministered estate 'is probably best characterised as a financial resource, not as property'.

2. However, the right is proprietary in nature in relation to being transferred to others. It is a chose in action capable of transmission by will, as in fact happened in *Livingston*. Even part of the chose in action is transmissible by will: *Re Leigh's Will Trusts* [1970] Ch 277; [1969] 3 All ER 432. It is also assignable. In *Horton v Jones* (1935) 53 CLR 475, Horton looked after Jones who was old and sick. In return Jones made an oral promise to leave 'his fortune' to Horton. The agreement was never reduced to writing. Jones died and at his death had rights as next-of-kin in the unadministered estates of his four children. The estates of the children included land. After Jones' death Horton sued his estate on the oral contract. The High Court of Australia held that Horton was not entitled to the benefit of the contract. Starke, Evatt and McTiernan JJ dismissed the claim on the ground that the contract was void for uncertainty. Rich and Dixon JJ looked at the case from the perspective of the statutory requirement that

contracts involving land or interests in land had to be evidenced in writing to be enforceable.[3] In this respect it was crucial to determine whether or not Jones' rights in the unadministered estates of his children were equitable interests in land for the purposes of the statutory writing requirement. Rich and Dixon JJ said that in relation to the unadministered estates of his children, Jones had 'no right in any specific asset' in any of the estates. Their Honours, at 486, however, went on to state:

> But it is not the consequence that no right of property subsisted in the deceased, nor that no right of property subsisted involving an interest in land. The deceased possessed equitable rights enforceable in respect of the assets considered as a whole. It is true that he had no immediate right to possession or enjoyment and that his precise rights involved, at any rate prima facie, administration, and possibly necessitated conversion and calling in of investments. But, none the less, he had more than a mere equity. He had an equitable interest and it related to assets, which included interests in lands.

Given that Jones was dealing with an equitable proprietary interest in land, Dixon and Rich JJ ruled that the contract with Horton was unenforceable because of non-compliance with the statutory requirement of writing in relation to contracts involving land or any interest in land. Starke J also held against Horton on this ground as well as on the ground that the agreement was uncertain. The views of Dixon and Rich JJ in *Horton v Jones* are supported by the decision of the Privy Council in *In re Maye* [2008] 1 WLR 315. In that case, Lord Scott of Foscote, at 321, after citing Viscount Radcliffe's observation as to the nature of Mrs Coulson's rights in *Livingston* (see 4.29), said:

> This ... passage does not ... constitute a comprehensive statement of [Mrs Coulson's] rights under the will. What she was entitled to was a one-third share in [her husband's] residuary real and personal estate. It is not, in my opinion arguable that that share was other than a *proprietary interest capable of assignment by its proprietor*, of devolution as an asset of her estate on her death and of any other incidents of proprietary choses in action. [Emphasis added.]

3. In relation to the beneficiary's right to pursue remedies against third parties, Viscount Radcliffe in *Livingston*, at AC 714; All ER 700, noted that a beneficiary could recover from third parties assets that had been wrongfully withheld from the estate. This was the assertion of a beneficiary's right to a remedy in such cases, but it did not amount to a right of property. The beneficiary in such cases acts on behalf of the estate and asserts the estate's right of property. In *Re Atkinson* [1971] VR 613 at 617, Gillard J said that the beneficiary's right in such cases was an 'equity' in the sense in which that term was used by Kitto J in *Latec Investments Ltd v Hotel Terrigal Pty Ltd* (1965) 113 CLR 265: see 4.39.
4. In relation to the position of a beneficiary of an unadministered estate in the context of a priority dispute, there can be no competition with other legal or equitable interests and the priority issue does not arise because the right is not proprietary and is only a chose in action.

4.31 It should also be noted that the right of a beneficiary in an unadministered estate will also vest in the Official Receiver in the case of the beneficiary being an undischarged bankrupt. This is so

---

3. *Civil Law (Property) Act 2006* (ACT) s 204(1); *Conveyancing Act 1919* (NSW) s 54A(1); *Law of Property Act 2000* (NT) s 62; *Property Law Act 1974* (Qld) s 59; *Law of Property Act 1936* (SA) s 26; *Conveyancing and Law of Property Act 1884* (Tas) s 36(1); *Instruments Act 1958* (Vic) s 126; *Property Law Act 1969* (WA) s 34(1).

because of the *Bankruptcy Act 1966* (Cth), which by s 5(1) includes such choses in action as property for bankruptcy purposes, and by s 116, which stipulates that all property passing to a bankrupt whilst undischarged vests in the Official Receiver.

4.32 In *Official Receiver in Bankruptcy v Schultz* (1990) 170 CLR 306; 96 ALR 327, Schultz was bequeathed what was ultimately determined to be a remainder interest in a house. At the time of the testatrix's death Schultz was an undischarged bankrupt. The High Court of Australia ruled that even though the remainder interest took effect only after Schultz was discharged from bankruptcy, it nevertheless vested in the Official Receiver, because the chose in action arose at the time Schultz was an undischarged bankrupt. Schultz did not, at the time of the testatrix's death, have any legal or equitable interest in any of the assets of the testatrix's estate, but did have the right to see that the estate was properly administered. Schultz had the expectation of gaining a property interest after administration of the estate was completed. When the remainder interest in the house took effect it vested in the Official Receiver, not Schultz, even though Schultz had by then been discharged from bankruptcy. This was so because what vested in the Official Receiver at the date of the testatrix's death was the chose in action and 'the expected fruits of that chose in action': *Official Receiver in Bankruptcy v Schultz* at CLR 314; ALR 332.

4.33 The High Court's approach in this case was followed in *In re Hemming, decd; Raymond Saul & Co (a firm) v Holden*. In that case, English bankruptcy legislation stipulated that a bankrupt's estate included any choses in action that were vested in the bankrupt as at the date of bankruptcy. This meant that the trustee in bankruptcy was entitled to receive the property bequeathed to the bankrupt, even though, like Schultz, he had been discharged from bankruptcy at the time the estate was finally administered.

4.34 A final point in relation to the interest of a beneficiary in an unadministered estate is the question of determining the point of time when an estate can be said to be administered. In *Re Maguire (deceased)* at 851, Asher J said:

> The corpus of the estate and any income from it was the property of the executors until their administration role was complete. Until the will maker's debts are paid and the specific legacies met, it is not possible to identify the assets to which beneficiaries are entitled. And until that point, there is no need to distinguish between the legal and equitable estate.

4.35 The question of when an estate could be said to have been administered was considered by the Privy Council in *Hughes v La Baia Ltd* [2011] UKPC 9. In that case, George Richardson was the administrator of the estate of Isaac Richardson who died in 1946. In January 1982 George obtained letters of administration of the estate. In September 1982, the beneficiaries of the estate signed contracts for the sale of the property to Cheri Batson. This contract did not proceed to completion and in 1986 the beneficiaries contracted to sell the property to La Baia Limited, a company whose shareholders were Batson and Rosario Spadaro. The issue was whether the beneficiaries had an interest in the property sufficient to enter into this contract. It was argued that they did not on the basis that the estate was unadministered and that, pursuant to the principles set out in *Livingston*, George had the whole of the property vested in him with the consequence that the beneficiaries had no proprietary interest in the land.

4.36 The Privy Council held otherwise and upheld an order for specific performance of the contract. Lord Walker, at [27], who delivered the judgment of the Privy Council, said:

In the present case ... Isaac died over 36 years before the first agreement and over 39 years before the second agreement. As already noted, it seems in the highest degree improbable that there remained any enforceable claims against his estate, except for current legal costs and other out-of-pocket expenses of administration. There is no evidence that Isaac's estate, so long after his death, contained any assets other than the land ... In these circumstances the likelihood is that the land ... was held by George, not for the purposes of administering the estate (which had in effect already been fully administered) but as a trustee for the beneficiaries ... If that is wrong, [the beneficiaries] ... had an expectancy ... in the land, which was very close to maturing into a transmissible interest, and could be assigned in equity for value.

Lord Walker, at [34], continued and said:

Because of the lapse of time it seems very probable that Isaac's estate had by 1986 been fully administered, save only for the actual vesting of the ... land in the beneficiaries (either as tenants in common, or by way of partition). The beneficiaries had transmissible interests which were for all practical purposes interests in the land itself.

EQUITABLE INTERESTS, PERSONAL EQUITIES AND MERE EQUITIES

4.37 As already noted in this chapter, rights in equity can amount to equitable interests. The expressions 'equitable estate' and 'beneficial interest' are synonymous with the expression 'equitable interest' as used in this chapter, and mean a right in equity that is proprietary in nature: see 4.4. Equitable interests include the rights of a beneficiary under a trust, equitable mortgages, the interest of a partner in partnership assets, a vendor's lien and restrictive covenants over land.

4.38 The expression 'equitable interest' needs to be contrasted with the meanings generally ascribed to the expressions 'personal equity' and 'mere equity'. A personal equity refers to a right of access to a court of equity. It is nothing more than a right to seek equitable remedies. Such a right is personal only and cannot be assigned. A personal equity does not attach to property: *National Provincial Bank Ltd v Ainsworth* at AC 1238; All ER at 488.

4.39 A mere equity was described by Kitto J in *Latec Investments v Hotel Terrigal* at 277–8, as a right ancillary to the recognition of an equitable interest. Young, Croft and Smith JJ, state that a mere equity is 'recognised where a person is in a position to make a claim to a court of equity which, if successful, will entitle the person to an equitable interest'.[4] The fact that a mere equity may lead to an equitable interest is what distinguishes a mere equity from a personal equity. In *Westpac Banking Corporation v Ollis* [2008] NSWSC 824 at [77], Einstein J said, '[t]he critical difference, then, is between an "equity" — an in personam right in equity — which requires the intervention of the court to flower into a full equitable estate, and an equitable interest which does not because it already consists of such an estate'. Thus, 'a mere equity is a "procedural right" to have an equitable claim vindicated by curial decree, as distinct from the proprietary equitable interest so decreed'.[5]

---

4. P W Young, C Croft & M L Smith, *On Equity*, Law Book Co, Sydney, 2009, p 577.
5. L M Dargan, '*What Equity? The Classification of Equitable Interests*', unpublished Undergraduate Research Paper, Macquarie University, 2009, p 21.

4.40 In *Latec Investments v Hotel Terrigal*, the right to set aside a fraudulent mortgagee sale was held to be a mere equity. Other examples of mere equities include: (i) the right to claim an interest in property pursuant to proprietary estoppel principles; (ii) the right to obtain enforcement of an oral mortgage pursuant to the doctrine of part performance (*Double Bay Newspapers Pty Ltd v A W Holdings Pty Ltd* (1996) 42 NSWLR 409); (iii) the right to the retransfer of land where, as a result of a unilateral mistake by a vendor, the area of land transferred exceeded the area stipulated in the contract of sale (*Tutt v Doyle* (1997) 42 NSWLR 10 at 15); and (iv) the right to a constructive trust pursuant to principles laid down by the High Court in *Muschinski v Dodds* (1985) 160 CLR 583; 62 ALR 429 and *Baumgartner v Baumgartner* (1987) 164 CLR 137; 76 ALR 75. On the other hand the interest of a partner in a partnership is more than a mere equity. In this respect, in *Fazio v Fazio* [2012] WASCA 72 at [58], Murphy JA said:

> It has also always been accepted that a partner has an interest in every asset in the partnership, and that the interest is a 'beneficial interest' of its own kind (sui generis). The partner's interest before a winding-up is more than a 'mere equity' for priority purposes, even though the partner's precise entitlement (to the surplus) can only be ascertained once the winding-up of the partnership has been completed. It is a present beneficial interest in the nature of a proprietary interest.

4.41 In relation to priorities, it is clear from the decision in *Latec Investments v Hotel Terrigal* (see 4.44–4.46) that a mere equity, even if earlier in time, will not prevail against an equitable interest in the same property: see 7.18. However, it has been argued that the difficulty in distinguishing between mere equities and equitable interests warrants treating mere equities as equitable interests for the purposes of priorities.[6]

4.42 The utility of classifying equitable rights as equitable interests, mere equities and personal equities is contested. Wright has argued that the classification is dangerous and leads to too much 'attention being placed upon the labelling of the equitable interest over the more essential question of what are the attributes of that interest'.[7] On the other hand, Hepburn defends the classification of equitable rights on the basis that it 'provides structural guidance for the assessment of distinctive forms of unconscionable conduct and the application of appropriate equitable relief'.[8]

MULTIPLE CLASSIFICATION OF EQUITABLE RIGHTS

4.43 It is clear from a number of cases that an equitable right may be classified differently depending upon the context in which the right arises. This was made clear in *Commissioner of State Taxation of the State of South Australia v Cyril Henschke Pty Ltd* (2010) 242 CLR 508 at 518; 272 ALR 440 at 447, where the High Court observed that although the interest of a partner in a partnership was more than a mere equity and was sufficiently proprietary in nature to maintain priority over a subsequent equitable charge, that was not decisive of its nature in the context of the case before the court which did not concern the principles of priority in equity. A more concrete example of multiple classification of equitable rights relates to the nature of the right to set aside a fraudulent exercise of a mortgagee's power of sale. In *Latec Investments v Hotel Terrigal* this right was found to

---

6.   Dargan, *What Equity? The Classification of Equitable Interests*, note 5 above.
7.   D Wright, 'The Continued Relevance of Divisions in Equitable Interests in Real Property' (1995) 3 *Australian Property Law Journal* 163, p 175.
8.   S Hepburn, 'Reconsidering the Benefits of Equitable Classification' (2005) 12 *Australian Property Law Journal* 157, p 168.

be a mere equity in the priority context of that case, but also held to be an equitable interest for the purposes of transmission by will.

4.44   In *Latec Investments v Hotel Terrigal*, Hotel Terrigal was the owner of a hotel which was mortgaged to Latec Investments. Hotel Terrigal defaulted on its mortgage obligations. Latec Investments exercised its power of sale under the mortgage and sold the property to Southern Hotels, which was a totally owned subsidiary of Latec Investments. The mortgagee sale was thus fraudulent. A year later Southern Hotels gave MLC, as trustees for debenture holders, a security by way of a floating charge over the hotel property. Following the default of Southern Hotels the floating charge crystallised. Hotel Terrigal subsequently sought to have the fraudulent mortgagee sale to Southern Hotels set aside. In effect, Hotel Terrigal was asserting priority over MLC to the hotel.

4.45   In the priority dispute between Hotel Terrigal and MLC, the High Court ruled unanimously in favour of MLC. In separate judgments Kitto J and Menzies J effectively ruled that Hotel Terrigal's right to set aside the fraudulent mortgagee sale was not an equitable interest, but only a mere equity that could not prevail against MLC's equitable interest. Menzies J, at 291, also looked at the nature of Hotel Terrigal's right in the context of transmission by will and referred to earlier authorities, especially *Phillips v Phillips* (1862) 45 ER 1164 and *Stump v Gaby* (1852) 42 ER 1015, and said the following:

> [I]f Terrigal were a person instead of a company and the question was whether, in the circumstances here, that person had a devisable interest in the hotel property by virtue of his equity to have the conveyance to Southern set aside, *Stump v Gaby* would require an affirmative answer on the footing that, in the circumstances, Terrigal had an equitable interest in the hotel property. Where, however, the question arises in a contest between Terrigal and MLC Nominees, the holders of an equitable interest in the property acquired without notice of Terrigal's rights, the authority of *Phillips v Phillips* is (i) that the contest is between Terrigal's equity to have the conveyance set aside and the equitable interest of MLC Nominees and (ii) that in that contest, Terrigal's equity is not entitled to priority merely because it came into existence at an earlier time than the equitable interest of MLC Nominees.

4.46   Taylor J, who looked at the right of Hotel Terrigal, stated that it was an equitable interest in the context of both priority and transmission by will. However, his Honour, at 286, observed that, in the priority context, Hotel Terrigal's equitable interest was subject to 'an impediment to … title' which the court could not remove. Arguably the difference between his Honour's classification of Hotel Terrigal's right as an equitable interest, which was subject to an impediment to title, and the classification of that right as a mere equity by Kitto J and Menzies J, is one not of substance, but of semantics only.

4.47   The approach adopted by Menzies J is, however, not without its problems. In *Swanston Mortgage Pty Ltd v Trepan Investments Pty Ltd* [1994] 1 VR 672, the facts concerned whether the right to set aside a mortgagee sale of Torrens title land in circumstances where the mortgagee breached its duties in exercising its power of sale (see 3.24–3.26), gave the mortgagor an interest in the land sufficient to lodge a caveat to prevent the sale being registered. In reaching his decision that the mortgagor had no caveatable interest, Brooking J, at 676–7, said:

> [Menzies J's] approach [in the *Latec Investments* case] did enable two lines of authority to be reconciled but it does seem to me to lead to uncertainty. By reference to what considerations

will the court determine whether to treat the equitable right as constituting an equitable interest for a given purpose? It has been suggested that policy considerations may provide the answer. On the approach of Kitto J, [Hotel Terrigal] in the *Latec Investments* case could not on any view be said to have had a caveatable interest. The approach of Menzies J is more flexible and it is certainly arguable that one could, consistently with his Honour's judgment, conclude that [Hotel Terrigal] did … have a caveatable interest. Judicial attempts to distinguish between equities and equitable interests have led to criticisms of suggested circularity and the statement of conclusions as opposed to reasons for conclusions. Mindful of these criticisms, I nevertheless venture to express the opinion that on the approach of Menzies J the right of [Hotel Terrigal] … should be regarded as a mere equity for the purposes of a right to caveat … The question whether a caveatable interest exists seems to me to resemble more closely the question of priority than the question of devisability.

4.48 The comments of Brooking J have, however, attracted criticism and his ruling that there was no caveatable interest in the circumstances of that case have been rejected and not followed in a number of cases including *Patmore v Upton* (2004) 13 Tas R 95 at 106–13, *Capital Finance Australia Ltd v Bayblu Holdings Pty Ltd* [2011] NSWSC 24 at [23]–[24] and *Stone v Leonardis* [2011] SASC 153 at [40]–[50].

5

THE LAW OF ASSIGNMENT

INTRODUCTION

5.1   The essential feature of an assignment is the transfer of rights. Tolhurst states that 'a transaction is properly termed an assignment only if its effect is to transfer to the assignee the ownership of a right vested in the assignor. Transfer is the essence of assignment'.[1] A transfer can be said to occur when one person (the assignor) parts with something in circumstances where the recipient (the assignee) of that thing receives the same thing previously held by the transferor: *Lyle & Scott Ltd v Scott's Trustees* [1959] AC 763 at 778; [1959] 2 All ER 661 at 668. The result of an assignment is that the assignor no longer has the interest in the property he or she has assigned, ownership having passed to the assignee. Common examples of transfers, and therefore assignments, include a sale of goods and a conveyance of land. An assignment of property is one of the ways in which property can be disposed of. Other forms of disposition of property are discussed in Chapter 6.

5.2   A crucial aspect of the law of assignment is that of intention. For the transaction to be an assignment the intention of the assignor must be that he or she is to have no interest in the property once the assignment has been completed. If the intention is to maintain some form of ownership of the property there can be no assignment, although some other form of disposition may have taken place. This can be illustrated in the context of the creation of an express private trust. One way such a trust can be created is for its creator (the settlor) to assign property to a trustee to be held on trust for a beneficiary. In such a case the settlor does not retain any form of ownership in the property assigned. The trustee becomes the owner of the legal interest in the property and the beneficiary acquires the equitable interest. Alternatively, the creator of the trust may create a trust by declaring himself or herself to be the trustee of the property for the beneficiary. In such a case the property has not entirely passed out of the hands of the creator of the trust. He or she retains the legal interest in the property, with the beneficiary holding the equitable interest in the property. Nevertheless, there has been the disposition of property, not by means of its assignment, but rather by means of a declaration of trust.

5.3   An assignment can be recognised at common law or in equity. In this chapter the expression 'legal assignment' refers to an assignment pursuant to principles of the common law or statute. An 'equitable assignment' refers to an assignment pursuant to principles of equity. A legal assignment can only occur in relation to rights and liabilities recognised by the common law or relevant statute. If the requirements of a legal assignment are not satisfied the right or liability may, nevertheless,

---

1.   G Tolhurst, *The Assignment of Contractual Rights*, Hart Publishing, Oxford, 2006, p 32.

have been assigned in equity. Finally, if the right or liability is one recognised only in equity, it can only be the subject of an equitable assignment, although in the Australian Capital Territory a 'right under a trust' — an equitable interest — can be assigned pursuant to s 205 of the *Civil Law (Property) Act 2006* (ACT).

5.4   In an assignment of property, the nature of the assignment is important. A legal assignment gives the assignee a legal interest in that property. If it is an equitable assignment the assignee obtains an equitable interest in property. The nature of the assignee's property right is crucial in the context of competing rights to that property, a topic covered in Chapter 7. On the other hand, it can be noted that the validity of an assignment, be it a legal or equitable assignment, is important in the context of express private trusts, a topic dealt with in Chapter 16. As already noted (see 5.2), one of the ways an express private trust can be created is for a settlor to transfer property to a trustee on trust for a specified beneficiary. For the trust to be completely constituted there must be either a legal or equitable assignment of the property from the settlor to the trustee.

5.5   This chapter will examine the law of assignment under three broad headings. First, it will examine rights and liabilities that cannot be assigned. Second, it will examine the rules for a valid legal assignment. Third, it will examine the rules for a valid equitable assignment.

RIGHTS AND LIABILITIES NOT CAPABLE OF ASSIGNMENT

5.6   Certain rights or liabilities cannot be assigned. The prohibition against assignment may be the result of statutory provisions or on the basis of public policy considerations developed by the general law. This chapter will focus on the latter, in particular in relation to public pay, bare rights to litigate and certain contractual rights.

Public pay

5.7   An assignment of pay by the holder of a public office is prohibited on the basis that such pay is made to enable the office holder to maintain his or her office with decorum and propriety. However, this does not mean that public pay cannot be assigned under any circumstances. In *Arbuthnot v Norton* (1846) 18 ER 565, Norton, a judge, assigned the equivalent of six months' pay to which he was entitled to his legal personal representative upon death. The entitlement was assigned as security for an advance. The Privy Council ruled, after Norton's death, that the assignment was valid. This was so because the pay that was assigned only fell due upon Norton's death, that is, when Norton no longer held public office. Because the pay was not payable during his life, the assignment in no way diminished Norton's ability to maintain the dignity of his office. Thus, there was no infringement of the rationale upon which the prohibition against assigning public pay was based.

5.8   In the Australian Capital Territory, s 80 of the *Court Procedures Act 2004* (ACT) renders unenforceable any assignment of any salary or pension or periodical payment related to a salary.

Bare rights to litigate

5.9   A bare right to litigate is 'a right to claim damages divorced from any transfer of property': *Brownton Ltd v Edward Moore Inbucon Limited* [1985] 3 All ER 499 at 507. Bare rights to litigate include rights to sue in tort, rights to sue for unliquidated damages in contract and bare rights to sue in equity. Such rights are not assignable.[2] Debts and rights to sue for liquidated sums in contract are assignable because they are regarded as rights of property: *Fitzroy v Cave* [1905] 2 KB 364 at 373–4. It was often said that a bare right to litigate was unassignable because such a right was regarded as being merely personal and not a right of property. However, Tolhurst suggests that '[t]he better view may be that such rights are true proprietary choses in action that may not be assigned in some cases due to overriding public policy considerations'.[3]

5.10   In *Prosser v Edwards* (1835) 160 ER 196, it was said that a bare right to litigate was unassignable because it, in effect, encouraged litigation of matters which the assignor was not disposed to prosecute. In terms of legal principle, bare rights to litigate could not be assigned on public policy grounds because such assignments savoured of maintenance or champerty: *Glegg v Bromley* [1912] 3 KB 474 at 489–90. Maintenance is the support of an action by a person who has no interest in the cause of action: *British Cash and Parcel Conveyers Limited v Lamson Store Service Co Ltd* [1908] 1 KB 1006 at 1014. Champerty is the support of such an action by a person on the basis that the person receives a part of any verdict on completion: *Giles v Thompson* [1994] 1 AC 142 at 161; [1993] 3 All ER 321 at 328.[4] Historically, maintenance and champerty were regarded as torts and criminal offences. However, it is now widely regarded that the law's distaste of 'trafficking in causes of action' is not based on solid foundations and 'has long been regarded as outmoded, if not obsolete': *Owners of Strata Plan 5290 v CGS & Co Pty Ltd* [2011] NSWCA 168 at [72]. Indeed, in some jurisdictions the criminal offences and torts associated with maintenance and champerty have been abolished.[5]

5.11   The principle in *Glegg v Bromley* does not preclude the assignment of the verdict (future property) to which the assignor may become entitled as a result of the prosecution of litigation proceedings, 'provided that the assignee's purpose is not to engage or participate in the conduct of proceedings': *Cummings v Claremont Petroleum NL* (1996) 184 CLR 124 at 145; 137 ALR 1 at 14. In *Glegg v Bromley*, the assignor assigned 'all that interest, sum of money, or premises to which she is or may become entitled under or by virtue of any verdict, compromise, or agreement which she may obtain' in relation to an action in tort. In the Court of Appeal at 484, Vaughan Williams LJ said:

> I know of no rule of law which prevents the assignment of the fruits of an action. Such an assignment does not give the assignee any right to interfere in the proceedings in the action. The assignee has no right to insist on the action being carried on … There is in my opinion nothing resembling maintenance or champerty in the deed of assignment.

---

2.   In the Australian Capital Territory, s 205(1) of the *Civil Law (Property) Act 2006* (ACT) deals with the assignment of 'things in action'. A note to the legislation states that a 'thing in action' includes 'the right to sue for breach of contract'. It is unclear whether this section permits the assignment of the right to litigate for a breach of contract in all circumstances or whether it simply describes what a 'thing in action' is and does not change the existing law which permits the assignment of the right to sue in contract in the special circumstances set out in this chapter.

3.   Tolhurst, *The Assignment of Contractual Rights*, note 1 above, p 16 (n 34).

4.   For a discussion of the historical origins and rationales relating to maintenance and champerty, see *Campbells Cash and Carry Pty Ltd v Fostif Pty Limited* (2006) 229 CLR 386 at 426–32; 229 ALR 58 at 75–80. For further discussion of concepts of abuse of process and litigation funding, see *Jeffery & Katauskas Pty Ltd v SST Consulting Pty Ltd* (2009) 239 CLR 75; (2009) 260 ALR 34; *Kermani v Westpac Banking Corporation* [2012] VSCA 42.

5.   *Civil Law (Wrongs) Act 2002* (ACT) s 151A; *Maintenance, Champerty and Barratry Abolition Act 1993* (NSW) ss 3–4; *Criminal Law Consolidation Act 1935* (SA) ss 1, 3 of Sch 11; *Crimes Act 1958* (Vic) s 322A; *Wrongs Act 1958* (Vic) s 32.

5.12 In *Giles v Thompson*, plaintiffs in two separate appeals had been involved in car accidents. The plaintiffs were not at fault in either case. They contracted with a hire company which provided them with substitute vehicles, pending repairs being completed on their respective cars. A term of the contracts was that the hire company could pursue claims against the respective defendants in the names of the plaintiffs and that the company would be reimbursed for its hiring fees from the proceeds of verdicts obtained against the defendants. The hiring company provided the plaintiffs with legal assistance. The House of Lords held that this arrangement was not champertous because the hire company possessed no rights in respect of the amounts recovered by the plaintiffs. Its profits were not to be derived from the verdict, but from the hiring of the vehicles, for which the plaintiffs remained personally liable to the hire company upon conclusion of the proceedings. The fact that legal assistance was provided by the hire company did not alter this conclusion, given that the solicitors and counsel nominated by the hire company were obliged to act on the instructions of the plaintiffs and not the hire company.

5.13 However, it must be noted that there are various qualifications to the principle in *Glegg v Bromley*. In certain cases a bare right to litigate is assignable. Such cases include those involving the following:

• a genuine commercial interest;
• property with an incidental right to litigate; and
• an assignment to an insurer.

Genuine commercial interest

5.14 If the assignee has a genuine commercial interest in taking the assignment of a bare right to litigate, then the assignment is valid. In *Trendtex Trading Corporation v Credit Suisse* [1982] AC 679 at 703; [1981] 3 All ER 520 at 531, Lord Roskill said:

> [I]t is today true to say that in English Law an assignee who can show that he has a genuine commercial interest in the enforcement of the claim of another and to that extent takes an assignment of the claim to himself is entitled to enforce that assignment unless by the terms of that assignment he falls foul of our law of champerty, which, as has often been said, is a branch of the law of maintenance … The court should look at the totality of the transaction. If the assignment is of a property right or interest and the cause of action is ancillary to that right or interest, or if the assignee has a genuine commercial interest in taking the assignment and enforcing it for his own benefit, I see no reason why the assignment should be struck as an assignment of a bare cause of action or as savouring of maintenance.

5.15 For an interest to be a genuine commercial or legitimate interest, it 'must be distinct from the benefit that the person supporting the action seeks to derive from the litigation. It must be something beyond a mere personal interest in profiting from the outcome of the proceedings': *Project 28 Pty Ltd (Formerly Narui Gold Coast Pty Ltd) v Barr* [2005] NSWCA 240 at [41]. In *National Mutual Property Services (Australia) Pty Ltd v Citibank Savings Limited* (1995) 132 ALR 514 at 540, Lindgren J said that 'the expression [genuine commercial interest] refers to a commercial interest which exists already or by reason of other matters, and which receives ancillary support from the assignment'.

5.16 In relation to cases involving the assignment of a right to sue for breach of contract or debt, Lord Roskill's statement of principle in *Trendtex Trading Corporation v Credit Suisse* has been cited and applied in a number of Australian cases. In *Re Timothy's Pty Ltd* [1981] 2 NSWLR 706, Timothy's

Pty Ltd had sued Affiliated Holdings Ltd in relation to a breach of lease. Timothy's was also indebted to Bronze Lamp Pty Ltd. Timothy's assigned its cause of action against Affiliated Holdings to Bronze Lamp in consideration of Bronze Lamp releasing Timothy's from its substantial debt to Bronze Lamp. Because Bronze Lamp was found to have had little hope of being repaid on the debt except by assignment of the cause of action against Affiliated Holdings, Needham J held that Bronze Lamp had a sufficient commercial interest in the assignment and upheld its validity. In *Re Daley; Ex parte National Australia Bank Ltd* (1992) 37 FCR 390, Daley was the sole shareholder in two companies who had guaranteed the companies' bank overdrafts. The companies had claims against the bank for wrongly honouring cheques drawn by the companies. These claims were assigned to Daley. In the Federal Court at 394–5, Heerey J upheld the validity of the assignments on the basis that Daley had 'a genuine commercial interest in the enforcement of the claims by [the companies] against the Bank'.

5.17   In relation to the assignment of rights to sue in tort, in *Poulton v Commonwealth* (1953) 89 CLR 540 at 602, it was held that such rights were incapable of assignment. However, in *Beatty v Brashs Pty Ltd* [1998] 2 VR 201 at 205–15, Smith J concluded that, in the light of the decision in *Trendtex Trading Corporation v Credit Suisse*, the right to sue in tort could be assigned if the assignee had a genuine or commercial interest in the assignment. It can also be noted that a view consistent with Smith J's analysis in *Beatty v Brashs Pty Ltd* has been adopted in Canada: *Fredrickson v Insurance Corporation of British Columbia* (1986) 28 DLR (4th) 414 at 420–4;[6] *Gentra Canada Investments Inc v Lipson* (2011) 333 DLR (4th) 666 at 678. Furthermore, the English Court of Appeal in *Simpson v Norfolk & Norwich University Hospital NHS Trust* [2011] EWCA Civ 1149 took the view that an assignment of a claim in tort, including a claim for damages for personal injury, could be assigned if the assignee had a genuine commercial interest in the assignment. Speaking for a unanimous Court of Appeal, Moore-Bick LJ, at [24], observed that, although it was 'not ... possible to state in definitive terms what does and does not constitute a sufficient interest to support the assignment of a cause of action in tort for personal injury', the assignee in the case before the court had failed to establish a legitimate interest in the assignment and that, therefore, it was void.

5.18   In *Equuscorp Pty Ltd v Haxton* (2012) 286 ALR 12 at 38, 58, three of the six members of the High Court stated in dicta that the issue of the assignment of the right to litigate had been affected by the decision in *Trendtex Trading Corporation v Credit Suisse* and that decisions such as *Poulton v Commonwealth* were now subject to the genuine commercial interest principle in *Trendtex Trading Corporation v Credit Suisse*, thereby clearly indicating that assignments of tortious claims in which the assignee has a genuine and substantial commercial interest are permissible. However, in a subsequent decision of *Kovarfi v BMT & Associates Pty Ltd* [2012] NSWSC 1101 at [51]–[56], McCallum J ruled that the said statements in *Equuscorp Pty Ltd v Haxton* were made in a case that was not concerned with the assignment of a right to sue in tort and therefore did not negate the decision in *Poulton v Commonwealth*.

5.19   In relation to a bare right to sue in equity, the traditional approach has been that such a right is incapable of assignment: *Glegg v Bromley* at 489–90. However, if the principles in *Trendtex Trading Corporation v Credit Suisse* are part of Australian law as was indicated by the High Court in *Equuscorp Pty Ltd v Haxton* (see 5.18), the right to sue in equity can be assigned if the assignee had a genuine or commercial interest in the assignment.

---

6.   The reasoning of the Court of Appeal in British Columbia in this case was affirmed on appeal to the Canadian Supreme Court: *Insurance Corporation of British Columbia v Fredrickson* [1988] 1 SCR 1089.

5.20   The issue of the assignability of restitutionary claims has not been the subject of much judicial analysis. However, in *Equuscorp Pty Ltd v Haxton*, all the members of the High Court recognised that such rights could be assigned. In particular, French CJ, Crennan and Kiefel JJ, at 32, said:

> A restitutionary claim for money had and received under an unenforceable loan agreement is inescapably linked to the performance of that agreement. If assigned along with contractual rights, albeit their existence is contestable, it is not assigned as a bare cause of action. Neither policy nor logic stands against its assignability in such a case. The assignment of the purported contractual rights for value indicates a legitimate commercial interest on the part of the assignee in acquiring the restitutionary rights should the contract be found to be unenforceable.

5.21   In relation to the assignment of the right to sue for breach of statutory duties, much will depend upon the relevant statute as to whether such a right is assignable. Thus, because proceedings for damages or ancillary relief pursuant to the *Competition and Consumer Act 2010* (Cth) and the *Australian Consumer Law* can only be pursued by the person who has suffered loss or damage as a result of an infringement of any of their provisions (such as the prohibition against misleading or deceptive conduct in s 18 of the *Australian Consumer Law*), such proceedings are not assignable: *Chapman v Luminis Pty Ltd (No 4)* (2001) 123 FCR 62 at 116–7. Nor can such proceedings be pursued by the estate of a deceased person who, prior to his or her death, had suffered such loss or damage: *Pritchard v Racecage Pty Ltd* (1997) 72 FCR 203 at 218; 142 ALR 527 at 541.

Property with an incidental right to litigate

5.22   An assignment of property with an incidental right to litigate is valid: *Ellis v Torrington* [1920] 1 KB 399 at 412; *Re Kenneth Wright Distributors Pty Ltd (in liq)*; *W J Vine Pty Ltd v Hall* [1973] VR 161 at 166–7. This is because there is no assignment of a bare right to litigate, the right being incidental to a right of property. Accordingly, no issues of maintenance or champerty can arise. Thus, the right to rescind for undue influence in *Dickinson v Burrell* (1866) LR 1 Eq 337 (see 4.12) was assignable because it was incidental to the real property assigned to the assignor.

5.23   Furthermore, in *Krishell Pty Ltd v Nilant* (2006) 204 FLR 182 at 192–3, 200, it was held that a right of appeal in relation to a judgment debt, although generally not assignable, could be assigned if it was incidental to a property right. For example, if X gets judgment against Y for $20,000, but Y has a successful counter-claim against X for $5000, the court will set off the latter amount against Y's judgment debt. Effectively, X would recover $15,000. However, if X appeals against Y's counter-claim, his or her right of appeal is assignable because it is closely connected to X's interest in the judgment debt of $20,000 (X's property right) obtained against Y.

Assignment to an insurer

5.24   An assignment by an insured to an insurer of the insured's right to sue is valid if it is made in consideration of a payment made by the insurer to the insured in satisfaction of a claim pursuant to an insurance policy between them. This stems from the insurer's right of subrogation.

5.25   Under the principle of subrogation, the insurer stands in the insured's shoes. This entitles the insurer to pursue any claims that the insured has against any person in relation to the loss or injury upon which the insured has been paid by the insurer pursuant to the relevant insurance policy. Because the insurer already has a legitimate interest in the insured's right to litigate, an assignment of it to the insurer does not savour of maintenance and champerty: *Compania Colombiana de Seguros v Pacific Steam Navigation Co* [1965] 1 QB 101 at 121–2; [1964] 1 All ER 216 at 231.

Contractual rights

5.26   Contractual rights are choses in action: see 5.41. The benefit (the right to receive performance) of a contract may be assigned, but its burden (the obligation to render performance), generally, may not be assigned.[7] Thus, in *Queensland Insurance Co Ltd v Australian Mutual Fire Insurance Society Ltd* (1941) 41 SR 195 at 201, Jordan CJ said:

> As a general rule, a person may assign to another any benefit to which he may be entitled under a contract, but cannot escape his contractual liabilities by purporting to assign them, although if the contract be not of a personal nature, he may procure someone else to perform them for him. If, therefore, a contract be assigned by one of the parties, the assignee may in general compel the other party to do for his benefit whatever he would have been liable to do for the assignor's benefit, subject, however, to the obligations of the assignor being duly performed by the assignor or by someone else.

Assignable contractual rights are assignable at law or in equity. In *Pacific Brands Sport & Leisure Pty Ltd v Underworks Pty Ltd* (2006) 149 FCR 395, Sara Lee Apparel Ltd (Sara Lee) had a licence to the trade marks over clothing brands 'King Gee' and 'Stubbies'. In 2000 it granted a sub-licence of the trade marks to Underworks Ltd (Underworks) for a period of five years. A year later, Sara Lee sold its business to Pacific Brands Ltd (Pacific Brands) and assigned its contractual rights under the sub-licence with Underworks to Pacific Brands. Pacific Brands and Sara Lee attempted to novate the sub-licence with Underworks but Underworks would not agree to the terms offered. Subsequently Pacific Brands alleged that Underworks had breached the terms of the sub-licence and that, as an assignee of Sara Lee's rights under the sub-licence, it (Pacific Brands) was entitled to terminate the sub-licence. At trial, Justice Finkelstein held that, although Pacific Brands had acquired certain rights under the assignment from Sara Lee, such as the right to receive royalties, the right to terminate had not been assigned and therefore there was no right to terminate the sub-licence. On appeal, the Full Court of the Federal Court upheld the trial judge's decision, but held that his Honour had erred when he had held that various rights under the assignment were not assignable because they were not proprietary in character. Finn and Sundberg JJ, at 404, said that unless otherwise precluded, 'assignable contractual rights are choses in action; are a species of personal proprietary right; and can be transferred to a third party at law or in equity in accordance with the formal rules governing the transfer of such rights'. In this case, however, the construction of the sub-licence indicated that the rights were personal to Sara Lee and could not be assigned to Pacific Brands without Underworks' consent. Accordingly, Pacific Brands had no right of termination against Underworks.

5.27   The assignment, whether it be effective at law or in equity, entitles the assignee to sue the other party to the contract (the obligor) for damages for breach of contract irrespective of whether the breach occurred before or after the assignment. The assessment of damages in the assignee's action against the obligor has not been the subject of significant judicial analysis and the principles that are applicable are not firmly established. If the breach occurs after the assignment, the damages

---

7.   For details of the exceptional circumstances in which the burden of a contract may be assigned see J W Carter, E Peden & G J Tolhurst, *Contract Law in Australia*, 5th ed, LexisNexis Butterworths, Sydney, 2007, pp 363–4.

recoverable should reflect the assignee's loss, subject to the limitation that the damages cannot exceed what the assignor would have recovered had there been no assignment. This qualification stems from the basic principle that the obligor's position cannot be made worse as a result of an assignment of the contract. In cases where the breach occurs before the assignment, the position is less clear. The issue that arises is whether the damages recoverable by the assignee reflect the assignor's loss or the assignee's loss. Tolhurst[8] argues that, notwithstanding recent Court of Appeal decisions to the contrary in England in *Technotrade Ltd v Larkstore Ltd* [2006] 1 WLR 2926 and Australia in *Renold Australia Pty Ltd v Fletcher Insulation (Vic) Pty Ltd* [2007] VSCA 294, the better approach is that an assignee recovers damages measured against the assignor's loss flowing from the obligor's breach of contract. This is so because the assignment assigns the assignor's cause of action, and it does not have the effect of recharacterising that right as the assignee's cause of action. This means that the assignee enforces the assignor's cause of action, which in turn leads to damages being awarded on the basis that they reflect the assignor's loss.

5.28 Not all contractual rights are assignable. Contracts for personal services are generally not assignable: *Devefi Pty Ltd v Mateffy Pearl Nagy Pty Ltd* (1993) 113 ALR 225 at 234.[9] This is so because the obligor ought not be prejudiced by the substitution of the assignor by an assignee. Thus, rights under a share farming agreement are not assignable: *Moore v Collins* [1937] SASR 195. Similarly, an employer cannot assign to another person the right of services from an employee under an employment contract. As the House of Lords indicated in *Nokes v Doncaster Amalgamated Collieries Ltd* [1940] AC 1014; [1940] 3 All ER 549, an employee is entitled to choose the employer for whom he or she wishes to work. In *Pacific Brands Sport & Leisure Pty Ltd v Underworks Pty Ltd* (see 5.26) an obligation under the sub-licence to provide marketing plans and reports was intended to create an enduring relationship between Sara Lee and Underworks, so that the identity of Sara Lee was material to the obligation. As such, the personal nature of the obligation meant that the obligation could not be assigned without Underworks' consent.

5.29 Whether a contractual right is of a personal nature is a question of construction of the contract. Thus, if it makes no difference to the obligor as to whom it performs its obligations, the assignment of the benefit of the contract will not be seen as one of personal services. In *Tolhurst v Associated Portland Cement Manufacturers (1900) Ltd* [1903] AC 414, Tolhurst agreed, for a term of up to 50 years, to supply chalk to a particular cement manufacturing company which later assigned this contractual right to another company who took over the first company's business. Tolhurst's claim that the assignment was invalid was rejected because the House of Lords took the view that it could not make any difference to Tolhurst whether it supplied chalk to the assignor or assignee. However, a distinction must be made between the assignment of the benefit of a contractual right of a personal contract as a whole and the assignment of money due under it. For example, in a contract for the writing of a book, although neither author nor publisher can without consent assign the right to the other's future performance in terms of writing or publishing, that does not prevent the author assigning the right to be paid royalties: *Linden Gardens Trust Ltd v Lenesta Sludge Disposals Ltd* [1994] 1 AC 85 at 105; [1993] 3 All ER 417 at 428–9.

---

8. G J Tolhurst, 'The Nature of an Assignee's Right to Damages for Breaches of Contract That Occur Prior to Assignment' (2008) 24 *Journal of Contract Law* 77, p 95.
9. For a discussion and defence of this principle see G J Tolhurst, 'Assignment of Contractual Rights: The Apparent Reformulation of the Personal Rights Rule' (2007) 29 *Australian Bar Review* 4.

5.30　However, in some circumstances, a personal obligation in an employment contract can be assigned. In *Mid-City Skin Cancer & Laser Centre v Zahedi-Anarak* (2006) 67 NSWLR 569, Zahedi, a medical practitioner, was contractually bound by an implied obligation of confidence in relation to records on patients kept by a medical practice where he was employed. In breach of this contractual obligation Zahedi used those records to assist in compiling a list of patients for his own practice that he established after ending his employment with the medical practice. Campbell J held that the implied obligation of confidence had been assigned in equity to the purchaser of his former employer's medical practice, and that the assignee, having joined the assignor to the proceedings, could enforce the contractual obligation against Zahedi. His Honour, at 605, said:

> If one considers the contract between Dr Zahedi and [his former employer], it has now come to an end, so far as either side having ongoing obligations to provide services is concerned. However, the contractual obligation continues whereby lists of patient names and addresses which Dr Zahedi obtained … cannot be disclosed, and cannot be used except for the purposes of the [former employer]. The obligations of Dr Zahedi under that term of the contract do not require any personal interaction with the person to whom the obligation is owed, and the content of the obligation is not influenced by any action or decision of the person to whom the obligation is owed. It is not an obligation requiring Dr Zahedi to do things — it is an obligation requiring him not to do things. Dr Zahedi can perform it perfectly by total inaction. In my view, for these reasons no analogy can be drawn with the reasons whereby the benefit of a contract of service is unassignable.

5.31　Furthermore, although certain contractual rights are not assignable under general principles of law, such rights can be assigned if a contract expressly or impliedly authorises their assignment: *Devefi Pty Ltd v Mateffy Pearl Nagy Pty Ltd* at 235.

5.32　Contractual obligations that are otherwise assignable may be, nevertheless, rendered unassignable by express contractual provisions against the assignment of contractual rights. In *Owners of Strata Plan 5290 v CGS & Co Pty Ltd* at [60]–[62], Sackville AJA set out the following reason why such a non-assignability clause may be desirable: (i) it would prevent an obligor dealing with a party with whom he or she does not wish to deal; (ii) the obligor may wish to preserve set-off claims which could, if the contract were assigned, end up being prejudiced; and (iii) an assignor may be less inclined to perform his or her contractual obligations if the benefit of the contract was assigned to a third party.

5.33　A contractual provision against assignment of contractual rights is enforceable, unless it is illegal pursuant to statute or on public policy grounds, in which case it will be severable from the contract and will not preclude assignment of contractual rights. Where such a provision is enforceable, its effect depends upon its construction: *Linden Gardens Trust Ltd v Lenesta Sludge Disposals Ltd* [1994] 1 AC 85 at 104–5; [1993] 3 All ER 417 at 428. Possible effects of a breach of such a clause include: (i) the assignment is valid, but the assignor is liable for damages for breach of contract; (ii) the assignment is ineffective with the obligor still obliged to render performance to the assignor, not the assignee, although the assignor could assign the benefit of the clause after receiving it from the obligor; (iii) the assignment is ineffective with the obligor still obliged to render performance to the assignor, not the assignee, and the assignor is not entitled to assign the benefit of the clause after receiving it from the obligor; (iv) the assignment constitutes a terminating breach of contract, either automatically or at the election of the obligor.

5.34 The effect of a contractual provision against assignment of contractual rights can be circumvented by means of a declaration of trust of the benefit of the clause: *Don King Productions Inc v Warren* [2000] Ch 291; [1998] 2 All ER 608. Such a procedure results in the contracting party becoming a trustee, rather than an assignor, and the third party becomes a beneficiary under a trust rather than an assignee. The beneficiary can effectively enforce the contract by bringing an action against the obligor and joining the trustee to the proceedings: *Mizzi v Reliance Financial Services Pty Ltd* [2007] NSWSC 37 at [79]. The use of a declaration of trust to circumvent a contractual provision against assignment of contractual rights can be prohibited by a clear term to that effect in the contract: *Secure Parking (WA) Pty Ltd v Wilson* (2008) 38 WAR 350 at 377. However, a mere prohibition against assignment of contractual rights does not extend to a prohibition against a declaration of trust: *Barbados Trust Company v Bank of Zambia* [2007] 1 Lloyd's Rep 495 at 506, 513. In *Australian Zircon NL v Austpac Resources NL (No 2)* [2011] WASC 186 at [159], Corboy J ruled that, in the context of the particular contract, the word 'dealing' included a declaration of trust and thus prohibited the declaration of trust of the relevant contractual right.

ASSIGNMENTS AT LAW

5.35 The requirements for a valid legal assignment will depend upon the nature of the property being assigned. The assignment of land, goods, and debts and other choses in action will be examined below.

Land

5.36 Different rules apply to land depending upon whether the land is old system title or Torrens title.

Old system title

5.37 Except in the Australian Capital Territory (where there is no old system title land) and Queensland, and subject to minor exceptions, a legal assignment of old system title land or an interest in old system title land must be by delivery of a deed of conveyance from the assignor to the assignee.[10] In Queensland, only a written document, not necessarily in deed form, is required.[11]

Torrens title

5.38 In *Breskvar v Wall* (1971) 126 CLR 376 at 381, Barwick CJ described Torrens title as 'a system of title by registration'. Thus, a legal assignment of Torrens title land or an interest in such land requires registration of a relevant dealing in the form prescribed by legislation. No legal interest arises until and unless registration has occurred.[12]

---

10. *Conveyancing Act 1919* (NSW) s 23B(1); *Law of Property Act 2000* (NT) s 9(1); *Law of Property Act 1936* (SA) s 28(1); *Conveyancing and Law of Property Act 1884* (Tas) s 60(1); *Property Law Act 1958* (Vic) s 52(1); *Property Law Act 1969* (WA) s 33(1).
11. *Property Law Act 1974* (Qld) s 10(1).
12. *Land Titles Act 1925* (ACT) s 57(1); *Real Property Act 1900* (NSW) s 41(1); *Land Title Act 2000* (NT) s 184; *Land Title Act 1994* (Qld) s 181; *Real Property Act 1886* (SA) s 67(1); *Land Titles Act 1980* (Tas) s 39(1); *Transfer of Land Act 1958* (Vic) s 40(1); *Transfer of Land Act 1893* (WA) s 58(1).

Goods

5.39   Uniform sale of goods legislation in all Australian jurisdictions stipulates that title to specific goods sold under a contract of sale passes when intended by the parties to the contract.[13] This legislation also sets out the rules as to passing of title in various circumstances and provides that those rules apply unless the parties to the contract indicate otherwise.[14] A detailed analysis of these rules is beyond the scope of this book.

5.40   An assignment of goods at law by way of gift is effective either by way of delivery of the goods with an intention to give, or by deed of gift: *Rowland v Stevenson* [2005] NSWSC 325 at [49]–[53].

Debts and other choses in action

5.41   In *Torkington v Magee* [1902] 2 KB 427 at 430, Channell J defined choses in action as 'personal rights of property which can only be claimed or enforced by action, and not by taking physical possession'. Choses in action are a form of intangible property. They can be legal or equitable. The most common legal chose in action is a debt. Another example of a legal chose in action is an assignable right to sue (see 5.14–5.23), including an assignable right to sue for damages for personal injuries: *Simpson v Norfolk & Norwich University Hospital NHS Trust* at [7]–[9]. An example of an equitable chose in action is an interest in a partnership: *Commissioner of State Taxation of the State of South Australia v Cyril Henschke Pty Ltd* (2010) 242 CLR 508 at 516–7; 272 ALR 440 at 446.

5.42   The assignment of a chose in action was described by Lord Hoffmann in *Investors Compensation Scheme Ltd v West Bromwich Building Society* [1998] 1 All ER 98 at 117, as follows:

> [A] chose in action is property, something capable of being turned into money … [W]hat is assigned is the *chose*, the thing, the debt or damages to which the assignor is entitled. The existence of a remedy or remedies is an essential condition for the existence of the chose in action but that does not mean that the remedies are property in themselves, capable of assignment separately from the *chose*.

5.43   Originally legal choses in action were generally not assignable at law: *Owners of Strata Plan 5290 v CGS & Co Pty Ltd* at [55]. In *Lampet's case* (1612) 77 ER 994 at 997, Lord Coke said that 'the great wisdom and policy of the sages and founders of our law, have provided, that no possibility, right, title, nor thing in action, who shall be granted or assigned to strangers, for that would be the occasion of multiplying of contentions and suits, of great oppression of the people, and chiefly of terre-tenants, and the subversion of the due and equal execution of justice'. The exception to the rule was that assignments to or by the Crown were recognised. The common law rule could be circumvented in various ways. For example, the use of a power of attorney would enable a creditor to stipulate that the attorney could sue to recover the debt and also keep the proceeds of such an action.

---

13.   *Sale of Goods Act 1954* (ACT) s 22; *Sale of Goods Act 1923* (NSW) s 22; *Sale of Goods Act 1972* (NT) s 22; *Sale of Goods Act 1896* (Qld) s 20; *Sale of Goods Act 1895* (SA) s 17; *Sale of Goods Act 1896* (Tas) s 22; *Goods Act 1958* (Vic) s 22; *Sale of Goods Act 1895* (WA) s 17.
14.   *Sale of Goods Act 1954* (ACT) s 23; *Sale of Goods Act 1923* (NSW) s 23; *Sale of Goods Act 1972* (NT) s 23; *Sale of Goods Act 1896* (Qld) s 21; *Sale of Goods Act 1895* (SA) s 18; *Sale of Goods Act 1896* (Tas) s 23; *Goods Act 1958* (Vic) s 23; *Sale of Goods Act 1895* (WA) s 18.

Furthermore, as newer forms of choses in action were recognised, the common law permitted their assignment in some cases, such as patents and shares.[15]

5.44   On the other hand, considerations of mercantile convenience and necessity led equity, very early in its development, to recognise that legal choses in action could be assigned: *Sprint Communications Company v APPC Services Inc* 554 US 269, 276 (2008). No particular form of words was necessary for such equitable assignments: *Row v Dawson* (1749) 27 ER 1064 at 1064. The effect of such an assignment was to make the assignor the bare trustee of the legal chose in action for the assignee.[16] Equity intervened on behalf of the assignee by insisting that the assignor do whatever was necessary to enable the assignee to obtain the benefit of the assignment. In practical terms this means that equity generally requires an assignor to lend his or her name to any suit to recover the debt or enforce the chose in action: *APT Finance Pty Ltd v Bajada* [2008] WASCA 73 at [26]. By being joined to such litigation the assignor is bound by its result and is precluded from subsequently suing on the debt or chose in action at common law: *Performing Right Society Ltd v London Theatre of Varieties Ltd* [1924] AC 1 at 14. Being a party to the litigation also means that the assignor has the opportunity to dispute the validity of the assignment.

5.45   However, if the equitable assignee fails to join the assignor in proceedings to enforce the assignment, that does not mean that the proceedings are a nullity. This flows from the preponderance of authority to the effect that the need to join the assignor is a procedural matter only and not a substantive component of the cause of action against the debtor: *Thomas v National Australia Bank Limited* [2000] 2 Qd R 448 at 456–8; *Alma Hill Constructions Pty Ltd v Onal* (2007) 16 VR 190 at 194–202. Although the proceedings in such circumstances are not a nullity, the cases are divided over whether the assignor must nevertheless be joined after proceedings have been commenced and before the case goes to final judgment. The decisions in *Thomas v National Australia Bank* at 458, and *Alma Hill Constructions v Onal* at 194–5 and 202, suggest that it is not always necessary, although it would only be in exceptional circumstances that the assignor would not be required to be joined to the proceedings. However, in *Equuscorp Pty Ltd v Haxton* at 37–8, Gummow and Bell JJ said:

> [A]n action by an equitable assignee without joining the assignor is not a nullity; the action may be liable to be stayed pending joinder, but no such application for a stay has been made in the present litigation … [A]ny outstanding assignor must be joined before final judgment can be obtained by the assignee, but that has been held not to be necessary where the assignee is seeking interlocutory relief.

Similar views were voiced by the United Kingdom Supreme Court in *Roberts v Gill & Co Solicitors* [2011] 1 AC 240 at 263; [2010] 4 All ER 367 at 388, by Nettle JA in *Westbourne Grammar School v Sanget Pty Ltd* [2007] VSCA 39 at [9], and by Barrett J in *Treadwell v Hickey* [2009] NSWSC 1395 at [98].[17]

5.46   On the other hand, in some circumstances, such as with a winding up petition, the need to join the assignor is unnecessary. In *Re Steel Wing Company, Limited* [1921] 1 Ch 349 at 357, Lawrence J said:

---

15.   M Smith, *The Law of Assignment: The Creation and Transfer of Choses in Action*, Oxford University Press, Oxford, 2007, pp 128–33.

16.   Smith, *The Law of Assignment*, note 15 above, pp 144–6.

17.   See also Smith, *The Law of Assignment*, note 15 above, pp 148–57.

The main reason why an assignee of a part of a debt is required to join all the parties interested in the debt in an action to recover the part assigned to him is in my opinion because the Court cannot adjudicate completely and finally without having such parties before it. The absence of such parties might result in the debtor being subjected to future actions in respect of the same debt, and moreover might result in conflicting decisions being arrived at concerning such debt. In my opinion, however, this reasoning does not apply to a winding up petition. After a winding up order has been made the Court in all cases when it is necessary will investigate, adjudicate upon, and settle the petitioner's debt as well as the debts of the other creditors. In the case of an assignee of part of a debt the Court in adjudicating upon his claim can and will do so in the presence of the persons entitled to the remainder of the debt, and the rights of all parties interested in the debt will be completely and finally settled once and for all.

5.47   Another example of where the assignor did not need to be joined to the proceedings occurred in *Tolhurst v Associated Portland Cement Manufacturers Ltd* (see 5.29), where the assignor clearly had no interest in the chose in action and had ceased to exist. The assignee was not denied its right to enforce the chose in action because of a failure to join the assignor to the enforcement proceedings.

5.48   By the nineteenth century the common law's prohibition on assignments of debts and choses in action had been modified. The common law came to recognise that the assignee was able to sue in the assignor's name on the debt or chose in action: *Norman v Federal Commissioner of Taxation* (1963) 109 CLR 9 at 26–7.

5.49   In England, in 1873, legislation was passed governing the legal assignment of debts and choses in action: *Judicature Act 1873* (UK) s 25(6). In New South Wales similar legislation is set out in s 12 of the *Conveyancing Act 1919* (NSW) which stipulates:

> Any absolute assignment by writing under the hand of the assignor (not purporting to be by way of charge only) of any debt or other legal chose in action, of which express notice in writing has been given to the debtor, trustee, or other person from whom the assignor would have been entitled to receive or claim such debt or chose in action, shall be, and be deemed to have been effectual in law (subject to all equities which would have been entitled to priority over the right of the assignee if this Act had not passed) to pass and transfer the legal right to such debt or chose in action from the date of such notice, and all legal and other remedies for the same, and the power to give a good discharge for the same without the concurrence of the assignor: Provided always that if the debtor, trustee, or other person liable in respect of such debt or chose in action has had notice that such assignment is disputed by the assignor or anyone claiming under the assignor, or of any other opposing or conflicting claims to such debt or chose in action, the debtor, trustee or other person liable shall be entitled, if he or she thinks fit, to call upon the several persons making claim thereto to interplead concerning the same, or he or she may, if he or she thinks fit, pay the same into court under and in conformity with the provisions of the Acts for the relief of trustees.

The effect of s 12 is that 'a debt must be regarded as a piece of property capable of legal assignment in the same sense as a bale of goods': *Fitzroy v Cave* at 373.

5.50   Provisions that are essentially the same as s 12 can be found in other Australian jurisdictions.[18] The only significant variations in these provisions are in the Australian Capital Territory and Western

---

18.   *Civil Law (Property) Act 2006* (ACT) s 205; *Law of Property Act 2000* (NT) s 182; *Property Law Act 1974* (Qld) s 199; *Law of Property Act 1936* (SA) s 15; *Conveyancing and Law of Property Act 1884* (Tas) s 86; *Property Law Act 1958* (Vic) s 134; *Property Law Act 1969* (WA) s 20.

Australia. In the Australian Capital Territory, a note to the relevant provision states that a chose in action is not confined to legal choses in action and includes, inter alia, 'rights under a trust'.[19] In Western Australia a debt or other chose in action is deemed to include part of a debt or other chose in action.[20] The effect of provisions such as s 12 is that 'a debt must be regarded as a piece of property capable of legal assignment in the same sense as a bale of goods': *Fitzroy v Cave* at 373.

5.51   Legislation such as s 12 does not prohibit or invalidate assignments of debts and choses in action according to the traditional rules of equity: *William Brandt's Sons & Co v Dunlop Rubber Company Limited* [1905] AC 454 at 461. The purpose of s 12 is not to change the equitable rules as to the assignment of choses in action, but rather to enable the assignee to sue the debtor without having to join the assignor to the proceedings: *Re Westerton* [1919] 2 Ch 104 at 133. In *Equuscorp Pty Ltd v Haxton* at 33, French CJ, Crennan and Kiefel JJ, speaking of s 25(6) of the *Judicature Act 1873* (UK) said:

> Section 25(6) operated as a 'machinery' provision which rendered debts and other legal causes of action directly assignable. A cause of action assigned under the subsection could therefore be brought by an assignee in its own name. The substantive law relating to assignments was not altered. A chose in action not assignable at common law prior to the enactment of s 25(6) was not rendered assignable by its enactment. Equitable assignments were not affected.

5.52   If there has been a valid assignment pursuant to s 12, the assignor will not be able to sue the debtor or other person. In *Read v Brown* (1888) 22 QBD 128 at 132, Lord Esher MR said:

> The debt is transferred to the assignee and becomes as though it had been his from the beginning; it is no longer to be the debt of the assignor at all, who cannot sue for it, the right to sue being taken from him; the assignee becomes the assignee of a legal debt and is not merely an assignee in equity, and the debt being his, he can sue for it, and sue in his own name. We must give that meaning to the language of the subsection; and, that being so, an assignee in order to shew that the debt is his and that he may sue upon it must prove the assignment; he must, if suing, prove the assignment to himself in order to recover judgment, and the fact of the assignment is therefore part of his cause of action.

Thus, in enforcing the debt, an assignee has available to it all legal means of enforcement, including garnishee proceedings and, in the case of a corporation, winding up the corporation: *Equuscorp Pty Ltd v Haxton* at 34–5.

5.53   Not all legal choses in action are assignable under s 12. In *Torkington v Magee*, at 430, Channell J said:

> I think the words 'debt or other legal chose in action' mean 'debt or right which the common law looks on as not assignable by reason of its being a chose in action, but which a Court of Equity deals with as being assignable'.

---

19. *Civil Law (Property) Act 2006* (ACT) s 205(1).
20. *Property Law Act 1969* (WA) s 20(3). A part of a debt or chose in action is also assignable pursuant to relevant legislation in New Zealand: *Property Law Act 2007* (NZ) s 48. Furthermore, the New Zealand legislation states that a chose in action includes 'an amount that will or may be payable in the future under a right already possessed': *Property Law Act 2007* (NZ) s 53.

5.54   Channell J's statement follows logically from the fact that s 12 has its origins in the English judicature system reforms of the 1870s which were designed only to reform the administration of the legal system: see 3.4–3.6. Section 25(6) of the *Judicature Act 1873* (UK) did not permit the assignment at law of what was not previously unassignable in equity. On the other hand, s 12 does not govern the assignment of other choses in action such as patents, copyright, trade marks, life insurance policies and marine insurance policies. They are covered by separate legislative provisions.[21]

5.55   For those debts and choses in action that are assignable pursuant to s 12, the following conditions must be satisfied:

1. There must be a clear intention to make 'an immediate and irrevocable transfer' of the debt or chose in action to the assignee: *Norman v FCT* at 32. It is not sufficient to merely authorise the debtor or other person to pay someone else.

2. The assignment must be absolute. It cannot be conditional: *Clyne v Deputy Commissioner of Taxation* (1981) 150 CLR 1 at 20; 35 ALR 567 at 580. The reason why the assignment must be absolute is to ensure that the debtor or other person is protected in that at all times he or she knows to whom payment must be made. Thus, an assignment can only be absolute if it enables the assignee to give a good discharge for the debt. Furthermore, the requirement that the assignment must be absolute enables the assignee to sue on the debt or chose in action in his or her name because an absolute assignment means that the assignor no longer has any interest at all in the debt or chose in action. In *Durham Bros v Robertson* [1898] 1 QB 765, there was an assignment of a book debt which was expressed to endure until money lent by the assignee to the assignor was repaid. The assignee sought to recover the book debt from the debtor. The Court of Appeal held that the assignee's action failed because the assignment was not absolute as required by s 12. The court held the assignment to be conditional only. Chitty LJ, at 773, said:

   > Where the Act applies it does not leave the original debtor in uncertainty as to the person to whom the legal right is transferred; it does not involve him in the question as to the state of the accounts between the mortgagor and the mortgagee. The legal right is transferred, and is vested in the assignee. There is no machinery provided by the Act for the reverter of the legal right to the assignor dependent on the performance of a condition; the only method within the provisions of the Act for revesting in the assignor the legal right is by a retransfer to the assignor followed by a notice in writing to the debtor, as in the case of the first transfer of the right. The question is not one of mere technicality or of form: it is one of substance, relating to the protection of the original debtor and placing him in an assured position.

   However, the requirement of an absolute assignment does not preclude there being a valid assignment pursuant to s 12 where the assignment provides for, or implies, the need for a re-assignment back to the assignor: *Clyne v Deputy Commissioner of Taxation* at CLR 20; ALR at 580. Furthermore, in *One.Tel (in liq) v Watson* [2009] NSWCA 282 at [107], Sackville AJA said:

   > [I]f an assignment unconditionally transfers all the rights of the assignor in the chose in action to the assignee, the fact that in certain circumstances, which may or may not occur, a resulting trust will be implied in favour of the assignor does not prevent the assignment being absolute.

---

21.   *Patents Act 1990* (Cth) s 14; *Copyright Act 1968* (Cth) ss 196–197; *Trade Marks Act 1995* (Cth) ss 106–111; *Life Insurance Act 1999* (Cth) ss 200–203; *Marine Insurance Act 1909* (Cth) ss 56–57.

Thus, in *Burlinson v Hall* (1884) 12 QBD 347, the facts concerned a situation where A owed money to C, but was owed money by B. A assigned the debt with B to C on the basis that, out of the funds recovered from B, C pay himself the amount owed by A and hold any surplus on trust for A.

Because an assignee can sue in his or her own name if the assignment is absolute, a logical consequence of this is that part of a debt or chose in action cannot be assigned pursuant to s 12 (*Deposit Protection Board v Dalia* [1994] 2 AC 367 at 380–1, 392; [1994] 2 All ER 577 at 580), although the relevant legislation in Western Australian does permit assignment of part of a debt or chose in action: see 5.50. This is because the assignor still has an interest in the debt or chose in action and thus must usually be joined in any proceedings instituted against the debtor by the assignee: see 5.44–5.47. Thus, part of a debt or chose in action can only be assigned in equity: see 5.123–5.125. In enforcing an equitable assignment of part of a debt or chose in action, the assignee needs to join the assignor to the proceedings: *Re Steel Wing Company, Limited* at 357. Furthermore, if the assignor of part of a debt or chose in action sues to enforce the part of the debt or chose retained, he or she must join the assignee to the proceedings: *Walter & Sullivan Ltd v J Murphy & Sons Ltd* [1955] 2 QB 584 at 588–9; [1955] 1 All ER 843 at 845.

3. The assignment must be in writing and signed by the assignor. The use of the words 'under the hand of the assignor' in s 12 means that the assignment cannot be signed by another person, even if that person has the authority of the assignor: *Technocrats International v Fredic Ltd* [2004] EWHC 692 (QB) at [53]; *Trustee Solutions Ltd v Dubery* [2007] 1 All ER 308 at 316. No particular form of words is necessary. So long as it is clear that the debt or chose in action has been assigned, this requirement of the statute will be satisfied: *William Brandt's Sons & Co v Dunlop Rubber Company Limited* at 462.

4. Express notice in writing must be given to the debtor or other person by either the assignor or assignee: *Norman v FCT* at 29.[22] Notice by implication or by operation of law or by the equitable doctrine of constructive notice is not sufficient: *Consolidated Trust Co Ltd v Naylor* (1936) 55 CLR 423 at 438–9. Notice can only be given at the time of, or after, the assignment: *Bishop v Financial Trust Limited* [2008] NZCA 170 at [35]. There are no formal requirements as to the notice and it need not even state the date of the assignment. Notice can be given by post if it is properly addressed and posted. Receipt of the notice in such cases is presumed in the absence of evidence to the contrary: *Australian Trade Commission v Solarex Pty Ltd* (1987) 78 ALR 439 at 443, 446. In *Leveraged Equities Limited v Goodridge* (2011) 274 ALR 655 at 703 it was held that compliance with statutory provisions relating to the giving of notice set out in s 170 of the *Conveyancing Act 1919* (NSW) and its equivalents in other Australian jurisdictions[23] would satisfy the requirements for the giving of notice under s 12. The debtor or other person can sight the assignment to check its validity before paying: *Grey v Australian Motorists & General Insurance Co Pty Ltd* [1976] 1 NSWLR 669 at 681. Notice to the assignee is not required: *Grey v Australian Motorists & General Insurance Co Pty Ltd* at 675–6, 678–9. The effect of giving notice is that the legal right to the debt or chose in action passes to the assignee: *Bateman v Hunt* [1904] 2 KB 530 at 538. The significance of the notice is that the debtor or other person is advised as to whom he or she must pay: *Consolidated Trust Company Ltd v Naylor* (1936) 55 CLR 423 at 439.

---

22. In New Zealand the requirement to give notice has been abolished as of the start of 2008: *Property Law Act 2007* (NZ) ss 50–51.

23. *Law of Property Act 2000* (NT) s 219; *Property Law Act 1974* (Qld) s 347; *Law of Property Act 1936* (SA) s 112.

The giving of notice means that the debtor or other person should pay the debt to, or perform for, the assignee. If, however, the debtor or other person fulfils his or her obligation in favour of the assignor in disregard of the notice, the assignee will, nevertheless, be entitled to enforce his or her claim against the debtor or other person, notwithstanding that the latter has already paid the assignor: *McIntyre v Gye* (1994) 51 FCR 472 at 479–80; 122 ALR 289 at 295.

5.56 With respect to s 12, the following further points should be noted:

1. The section cannot be used to assign future choses in action. A future chose in action can be described as only the prospect or possibility of becoming entitled in the future to some right or interest. Because it is not a presently existing right or interest, a future chose in action cannot be assigned at law: *Norman v FCT* at 26.
2. An assignment under s 12 is subject to equities having priority over the rights of the assignee: see 7.49.
3. Section 12 permits the voluntary assignment of debts or choses in action by means of a deed or gift: *Re Westerton* at 110–14.

5.57 A final aspect of s 12 is the issue of whether it applies to the assignment of an equitable chose in action, such as an interest in a partnership. The wording of the section is unclear on this issue. The section applies to 'any debt or other *legal* thing in action' but refers to notice being given to the 'debtor, *trustee*, or other person'. The effect of the section is stated to be to pass the '*legal* right to such debt or thing in action' and 'all other *legal* and other remedies' for it.

5.58 In *Everett v Commissioner of Taxation* (1980) 143 CLR 440; 28 ALR 179, the High Court of Australia dealt with the validity of an assignment of part of a partnership interest. Because the assignment was not absolute it could not be assigned pursuant to s 12. However, the court indicated that if it had been absolute it could have been assigned pursuant to s 12. The court's majority joint judgment at CLR 447; ALR 182–3, said:

> [T]hough the interest of a partner is an equitable interest, it may be assigned under s 12 of the Conveyancing Act 1919 (NSW), as amended … The interest, being a chose in action, falls within the expression 'debt or other legal thing in action' because the section, in providing that notice shall be given to a trustee 'as a person liable in respect of such debt or other legal chose in action', appears to contemplate the assignment by a beneficiary of an equitable chose in action against a trustee. There would be no point in referring to a trustee if the section made provision only for the assignment by strangers to the trust of debts owing by, and choses against, persons who happen to be trustees. The expression 'legal chose in action' may be read as 'lawfully assignable chose in action'.

5.59 However, Austin[24] has argued that s 12 does not apply to the assignment of equitable choses in action for the following reasons:

1. Equitable rights were never the concern of common law courts simply because they were not recognised, nor was jurisdiction asserted over them by the courts of common law. Since s 25 of the *Judicature Act 1873* (UK) was designed to resolve differences between the common law and equitable rules, s 25(6) could have no application with regard to equitable choses in action

---

24. R P Austin, 'The Conveyancing Act, 1919 (As Amended), Section 12 and Equitable Choses in Action' (1976) 7 *Sydney Law Review* 394.

because there were no differences to be resolved between the rules of common law and equity on this issue, since the common law had no rules for purely equitable rights.

2. Section 12 was designed to permit the assignee under an absolute assignment to sue the debtor without joining the assignor as a party to the proceedings. Before 1873 the assignee of an equitable chose in action under an absolute assignment could sue without joining the assignor to such proceedings. Therefore, s 12 offers no assistance to such an assignee. Accordingly, the section was not intended to cover the assignment of equitable choses in action.

5.60   The reality of the matter is that s 12 is poorly drafted legislation. Austin suggests that the word 'trustee' in s 12 be confined to the trustee in bankruptcy. Such an interpretation would, he suggests, render s 12 as being consistent with established equitable principles.

5.61   However, if s 12 does apply to the assignment of equitable choses in action, it is suggested that the section's provisions are *not* mandatory, and that the section merely provides a method by which such choses in action may be assigned. This view is supported by the decision in *Everett v Commissioner of Taxation* itself where, in the already quoted extract from the majority's judgment (see **5.58**), it is said that an equitable chose in action 'may be assigned under s 12'.

ASSIGNMENTS IN EQUITY

5.62   An assignment in equity can arise in the following circumstances:
- where the assignment is of future property; or
- where there has been a failure to comply with the requirements of a legal assignment of the property; or
- where the assignment is of equitable property.

In all these circumstances, for an assignment to be effective in equity, the assignor must display an intention to assign. The assignor must show that he or she is parting with dominion over the property. No particular form of words is necessary to establish consent. In *William Brandt's Sons & Co v Dunlop Rubber Company Limited* at 462, Lord Macnaghten said:

> But, says the Lord Chief Justice, 'the document does not, on the face of it, purport to be an assignment nor use the language of an assignment'. An equitable assignment does not always take that form. It may be addressed to the debtor. It may be couched in the language of command. It may be a courteous request. It may assume the form of mere permission. The language is immaterial if the meaning is plain. All that is necessary is that the debtor should be given to understand that the debt has been made over by the creditor to some third person.

5.63   Thus, in *Bell v The London North-Western Railway Company* (1852) 51 ER 651, a letter from a contractor to his employer contained a request to pass the cheques due on his account 'to my account' with a particular branch of a named bank. The court held that the letter did not constitute an equitable assignment to the bank but rather that it constituted the bank as the contractor's agent to receive the money. Sir John Romilly MR, at 652–3, indicated that if the contractor's letter had invited the employer to pass the cheques to the bank, rather than to his account with the bank, it would have constituted an equitable assignment. In *Burridge v MPH Soccer Management Ltd* [2011] EWCA Civ 835, the Court of Appeal had to determine whether the following words amounted to an intention to assign: 'The fee due to [Harrison] is to be sent to the Football Association for onward transmission to the agent … [at] Lloyds TSB … Sort code 30-93-71 … account number …

03717572 MPH Soccer Management Ltd'. The court unanimously held that there was an equitable assignment of the fee.

On the other hand, an intention to grant a revocable mandate, while retaining ownership of the property, will not qualify as an equitable assignment of the property: *Comptroller of Stamps (Victoria) v Howard-Smith* (1936) 54 CLR 614 at 619–20.

THE ASSIGNMENT OF FUTURE PROPERTY

5.64   The expression 'future property' refers to property that may come into existence at some future date. The word 'expectancy' is also used to convey this concept. Thus, dividends, prior to being declared and becoming payable as debts by the company to shareholders, are an example of future property or an expectancy. In *Ansett Australia Limited v Travel Software Solutions Pty Ltd* (2007) 214 FLR 203 at 213, Hargrave J observed that '[i]t is not strictly possible to assign a mere expectancy or possibility, because it is not an existing chose in action'. However, an assignment of future property will be recognised and enforced in equity if it is for valuable consideration. Although the agreement to assign need not be in any particular form of words, there must be a sufficiently clear expression of intention to assign or else the purported assignment will, as was the case in *Ansett Australia v Travel Software Solutions* at 215, not be enforced. When the future property comes into existence, it does not vest in the assignor. Rather the assignor automatically becomes a bare trustee (see 4.20–4.22) of it for the assignee: *RIL Aviation HL 7740 and HL 7741 Pty Ltd v Alliance & Leicester plc* [2011] NSWCA 423 at [206]–[207].

5.65   The law relating to the assignment of future property is underpinned by the maxim that equity looks on that as done which ought to be done (see 2.47–2.50): *Federal Commissioner of Taxation v Everett* (1978) 38 FLR 26 at 51; 21 ALR 625 at 644. This is so 'because the assignor [having] received the consideration, his conscience is bound to recognise that an assignment has occurred as soon as the property comes into existence': *Porters v Cessnock City Council* [2005] NSWSC 1275 at [25].

5.66   The basis of the equitable rule relating to assignments of future property is found in *Holroyd v Marshall* (1862) 11 ER 999 at 1007, where Lord Westbury said:

> [I]f a vendor or mortgagor agrees to sell or mortgage property, real or personal, of which he is not possessed at the time, and he receives the consideration for the contract, and afterwards becomes possessed of property answering the description in the contract, there is no doubt that a Court of Equity would compel him to perform the contract, and that the contract would, in equity, transfer the beneficial interest to the mortgagee or purchaser immediately on the property being acquired. This, of course, assumes that the supposed contract is one of that class of which a Court of Equity would decree specific performance. If it be so, then immediately on the acquisition of the property described the vendor or mortgagor would hold it on trust for the purchaser or mortgagee, according to the terms of the contract.

5.67   In *Norman v FCT*, at 24, Windeyer J said:

> In equity a would-be present assignment of something to be acquired in the future is, when made for value, construed as an agreement to assign the thing when it is acquired. A court of equity will ensure that the would-be assignor performs this agreement, his conscience being bound by the consideration. The purported assignee thus gets an equitable interest in the property immediately

the legal ownership of it is acquired by the assignor, assuming it to have been sufficiently described to be then identifiable. The prospective interest of the assignee is in the meantime protected by equity.

5.68   In relation to the requirement of consideration, *Holroyd v Marshall* makes it clear that the requirement is for valuable consideration: see 2.38–2.39. Furthermore, the consideration must have been paid or executed by the assignee. If it has not, as occurred in *JT Nominees Pty Ltd v Macks* (2007) 97 SASR 471 at 500, there can be no assignment of future property in equity.

5.69   In considering the equitable rule as to the assignment of future property, a number of issues need to be analysed. These are:

- whether the property in question is present or future property;
- how certain the description of the property in the assignment must be;
- whether the contract of assignment must be capable of being specifically enforced for the assignment to be valid; and
- the nature of the assignee's right as a result of such an assignment.

Present or future property

5.70   In most cases it is easy to ascertain if the property assigned is future or present property. A simple illustration of future property is a beneficiary's expectancy under a will in the period before the death of the maker of the will. All the beneficiary has in such a case is the hope or prospect of acquiring some interest in property should the maker of the will die before the beneficiary without revoking or altering the terms of the will: *Re Ellenborough, Towry Law v Burne* [1903] 1 Ch 697 at 699. Another example of future property is a beneficiary's expectancy of receiving income and/or capital under a discretionary trust: *Lygon Nominees Pty Ltd v Commissioner of State Revenue* (2007) 23 VR 474 at 495.

5.71   However, in some cases there are difficulties in determining whether the property assigned is present or future property. All the cases analysed below involved purported voluntary assignments of property by a taxpayer with the aim of transferring property that would attract a higher liability for income tax in the hands of the assignor than in the hands of the assignee. Because the assignments were voluntary they could only be valid if they did *not* involve future property.

5.72   In *Norman v FCT*, the facts involved a voluntary deed between a husband and wife whereby the husband purported to assign to the wife two items of property. First, there was interest on a loan, which the borrower was entitled to repay to the assignor at any time and without notice. Second, there were dividends on certain shares owned by the assignor. The Commissioner of Taxation argued that, because the assignments were voluntary, they were ineffective on the basis that they involved future property. The High Court of Australia found for the Commissioner with the result that the interest and dividends were both taxable in the hands of the husband.

5.73   In relation to the dividends the High Court was unanimous. The dividends were future property because they would only come into existence if, and when, the company declared dividends. It was only at that point of time that the dividends would become present property. Windeyer J, at 40, said:

> Is a dividend that may become payable in the future upon shares presently held something that can be assigned in equity? Is it a present chose in action or a mere possibility? Is it property in existence, or something not in existence and therefore not capable of being assigned in the

absence of consideration? I think it is the latter. The court will not compel directors to declare a dividend … A dividend is not a debt until it is declared. Until then it is in the eye of the law a possibility only. When it is declared it becomes a debt for which the shareholder who is on the register at that date of declaration may sue.

5.74   In relation to the interest on the loan a bare majority found in favour of the Commissioner. For the majority, Menzies J, at 21, said:

I regard interest which may accrue in the future upon an existing loan repayable without notice as having the character of a right to come into existence rather than a right already in existence.

5.75   For the minority, Windeyer J, at 37, said:

It is true too that the interest … that the deed assigned was not due and payable at the date of the deed. But a contract to pay a sum of money on a future day, call it interest or what you will, calculable in amount according to conditions presently agreed, is in my view a presently existing chose in action.

5.76   In relation to what the husband had done, Windeyer J, at 38, went on to say:

What he assigns is not, it seems to me, a right to arise in the future but a present contractual right to be paid at a future date a sum of money, to be calculated in the agreed manner.

5.77   The judgment of Windeyer J in *Norman v FCT* makes a significant point about the question of whether any given property is present or future property. His Honour draws a distinction between an existing contractual obligation to pay a sum of money in the future, which is characterised as present property, and the sum of money itself, which is characterised as future property. This distinction lies at the heart of the issue of whether property is present or future property. The fact that the present right does not result in any income being received in the future is irrelevant. Thus, had the taxpayer in *Norman v FCT* assigned his presently existing right to receive dividends, as opposed to dividends as future property, the assignment would have been valid. If the company declined to declare any dividends that fact would be irrelevant to the validity of the assignment.

5.78   In *Shepherd v Commissioner of Taxation of the Commonwealth of Australia* (1965) 113 CLR 385, the facts involved a taxpayer who was entitled to royalties in relation to the manufacture of castors. By a voluntary deed he assigned 'all [his] right title and interest in and to an amount equal to ninety per centum of the income which may accrue during a period of three years … from [the] royalties'. The Commissioner of Taxation argued that the property assigned was future property and that the assignment was ineffective because it was for no consideration. The majority of the High Court of Australia found in favour of the taxpayer on the ground that the assignment involved present property. Because the deed sought to assign only part of the royalties, the assignment could only be effective in equity: see 5.123–5.125. In this respect, Barwick CJ, at 392, said that the language of the voluntary deed 'expressed indications of an intent presently to assign portions of [the assignor's] right to royalties'. Accordingly, the assignment was valid in equity.

5.79   Barwick CJ noted that the question of whether the purported assignment dealt with present or future property was very much a question of construing the deed of assignment. His Honour, at 390, then observed that the taxpayer in this case assigned 'the right to the royalties rather than the royalties as after acquired property'. His Honour, at 392, went on to say:

No doubt to speak of the subject matter of the gift as an amount of income to accrue from royalties would seem to support the conclusion that what is to be given is the property in the form of money produced by the promise to pay royalties. But the full description of the subject matter of the assignment is of 'the right' to such amounts — an unlikely expression to describe the money itself. In my opinion, it indicates that the taxpayer was not intending to promise that he would pay money measured by the amount of royalties accrued or that he was intending to assign the royalties themselves. Its use rather suggests, to my mind, that he was intending to place the persons he wished to benefit in the position of being able themselves to assert a right to receive the appropriate amounts from the licensee.

5.80   In *Everett v Commissioner of Taxation*, a taxpayer purported to assign a fraction of his share in a partnership together with the right to receive a corresponding share of partnership profits. The majority of the High Court of Australia held that the assignment involved present property. In *Booth v Federal Commissioner of Taxation* (1987) 164 CLR 159; 76 ALR 375, the High Court of Australia ruled that the assignment by a landlord of a percentage of the right to receive rent payable in respect of particular premises involved present property, holding that the assignment was analogous to the facts of *Shepherd v Commissioner of Taxation* and not *Norman v FCT*.

5.81   In *Booth v FCT*, at CLR 175; ALR 385, Toohey and Gaudron JJ observed that it was 'necessary to look … closely at the language of the assignments' and 'that much depend[ed] upon the way in which an assignment is drafted'. The facts of decided cases will be of little relevance, as was pointed out in *Shepherd v Commissioner of Taxation*, at 393, by Barwick CJ when he said:

> [*Norman v FCT*] … in my opinion, has no relevance to the problem raised by the language of the deed poll as applied to the facts of this case.

Description of the property

5.82   For a valid assignment of future property the property must be described with sufficient particularity to permit its identification when it comes into existence or into the possession of the assignor. In *Tailby v Official Receiver* (1888) 13 App Cas 523 at 533, Lord Watson said:

> There is but one condition which must be fulfilled in order to make the assignee's right to a future chose in action, which is, that, on its coming into existence, it shall answer the description in the assignment, or in other words that it shall be capable of being identified as the thing or one of the very things assigned. When there is no uncertainty as to its identification, the beneficial interest will immediately vest in the assignee.

5.83   *Tailby v Official Receiver* makes it clear that one looks at the particular future property when it comes into existence and sees if it fits the terms of the assignment, rather than seeing if the future property is specifically determinable from the terms of the assignment alone.

Assignment of future property and specific performance

5.84   Considerable discussion has been provoked by Lord Westbury in *Holroyd v Marshall* as to what he meant when he said that equity would compel the performance of an assignor's promise to assign future property provided the contract was 'one of that class of which a Court of Equity would decree specific performance'. This passage suggests that the assignment is not valid if, as at the date upon which the subject matter of the assignment comes into the hands of the assignor, the court would decline an order for specific performance of the contract to assign.

5.85 This interpretation of Lord Westbury's statement was rejected by Lord Macnaghten in *Tailby v Official Receiver* at 547–8, where his Lordship said:

> Greater confusion still, I think, would be caused by transferring considerations applicable to suits for specific performance — involving as they do, some of the nicest distinctions and most difficult questions that come before a court — to cases of equitable assignment or specific lien where nothing remains to be done in order to define the rights of the parties, but the court is merely asked to protect rights completely defined as between the parties to the contract, or to give effect to such rights either by granting an injunction or by appointing a receiver, or by adjudicating on questions between rival claimants … The doctrines relating to specific performance do not, I think, afford a test or measure of the rights accrued.

5.86 Whether or not the assignment is bound up with the availability of specific performance can be crucial. As Lord Macnaghten observed, the remedy of specific performance involves matters of fine distinction and it would be odd that such matters should have a bearing on the validity of an assignment of future property. A court has no jurisdiction to order specific performance if damages at common law are an adequate remedy. Furthermore, even if damages are an inadequate remedy, specific performance can be refused on a variety of discretionary grounds: see Chapter 23. On Lord Westbury's view, equity would not compel an assignor to perform his or her promise if the assignee could, for instance, be adequately compensated by an order for damages at common law.

5.87 However, on the approach of the House of Lords in *Tailby v Official Receiver*, the following proposition emerges: If A, for valuable consideration agrees to assign future property to B, and the consideration has been paid or executed by B, when A acquires property that falls within the description of that which A agreed to assign, then, in equity, the property vests in B as soon as it is acquired by A and can be identified: *JT Nominees Pty Ltd v Macks* at 499–500. There is no need for any further assurance by A or action to be taken by B.

5.88 If the views expressed in *Tailby v Official Receiver* and *JT Nominees Pty Ltd v Macks* are correct then the question remains as to what Lord Westbury meant in *Holroyd v Marshall*. Keeler[25] has suggested that Lord Westbury was merely making the point that the property assigned must be sufficiently identifiable to be the subject matter of a decree of specific performance.

Nature of the assignee's right

5.89 The issue raised here is the nature of the assignee's interest in the assignment. This raises the question of whether the right is more than merely a personal contractual right. The issue is of considerable significance in certain circumstances dealing with the position of the assignee in the period between the assignment of the future property and the time when the property comes into existence or is acquired by the assignor.

5.90 In *Palette Shoes Pty Ltd v Krohn* (1937) 58 CLR 1 at 27, Dixon J said:

---

25. J F Keeler, 'Some Reflections on *Holroyd v Marshall*' (1967–70) 3 *Adelaide Law Review* 361.

As the subject to be made over does not exist, the matter primarily rests in contract. Because value has been given on one side, the conscience of the other party is bound when the subject comes into existence, that is, when as is generally the case, the legal property vests in him. Because his conscience is bound in respect of a subject of property, equity fastens upon the property itself and makes him a trustee of the legal rights or ownership for the assignee.

5.91 This passage suggests that an assignee's rights are essentially contractual and protected by equity. In most cases such an analysis is adequate. However, in other cases the analysis is inadequate. For example, if an assignor assigns an expectancy by way of mortgage, but before the property comes into existence or into the possession of the assignor, the assignor is both declared a bankrupt and discharged from bankruptcy, does the assignee still have his or her security in the property when it comes into existence or into the possession of the assignor?

5.92 In addressing this situation it could be said that the assignee does not have security over the property because, if the assignee's rights are merely contractual, so too are the assignor's obligations. The assignor's obligation is to pay and as such is an item provable in the assignor's bankruptcy. If so proved, a discharge from bankruptcy will operate to discharge the assignor from his or her obligations. Thus, when the property comes into existence or into the assignor's possession he or she owes no obligations to the assignee. It can also be said that if the assignor's obligation to pay is in essence a debt and the obligation to pay is ancillary to the debt, then, upon discharge from bankruptcy, s 153(1) of the *Bankruptcy Act 1966* (Cth) releases the assignor from the debt and the ancillary obligation to pay. Thus, the assignee does not have his or her security right when the property comes into existence or the possession of the assignor.

5.93 This interpretation finds support in *Collyer v Isaacs* (1881) 19 Ch D 342 at 351–3, where Jessel MR observed that, in the period until the property the subject of the assignment comes into existence or into the assignor's possession, an assignee's rights are merely contractual with the consequence that a discharged bankrupt is not bound by the assignment. However, subsequent cases reject the analysis upon which the decision in *Collyer v Isaacs* is based.

5.94 In *Re Lind, Industrials Finance Syndicate Limited v Lind* [1915] 2 Ch 345, Lind had an expectancy under his mother's will. Prior to her death he borrowed from two separate sources, in each case assigning the expectancy as security for the loan. Lind was declared bankrupt, but was subsequently discharged. He then borrowed money from a third source and again assigned his expectancy as security for the loan. His mother then died. The issue before the Court of Appeal was whether the third assignee's interest in the property inherited by Lind under his mother's will had priority over the interests of the first two assignees. On the basis of *Collyer v Isaacs*, the first two assignees would have had no interest in the property because Lind's discharge from bankruptcy would have released him from his obligations to them.

5.95 However, the Court of Appeal unanimously ruled in favour of the first two assignees. The court found that the pre-bankruptcy assignments survived Lind's bankruptcy. All three judges rejected the notion that an assignee's rights rested only in contract. There was a higher right. The crucial factor establishing this higher right was the fact that an assignee of future property obtains an equitable interest in the property immediately it comes into existence or into the possession of the assignor. This equitable interest arises without any intervention by either the assignor or assignee. It arises automatically. If an assignee's rights were merely contractual, some act would need to be undertaken by the assignor to give effect to the assignment and create the assignee's equitable interest. Bankes LJ, at 373–4, said:

> It appears to me to be manifest … that equity regarded an assignment for value of future acquired property as containing an enforceable security as against the property assigned quite independent of the personal obligation of the assignor out of his imported covenant to assign. It is true that the security was not enforceable until the property came into existence, but nevertheless the security was there, the assignor was the bare trustee of the assignee to receive and hold the property for him when it came into existence.

5.96 Swinfen Eady LJ, at 360, said:

> [A]n assignment for value of future property actually binds the property itself directly it is acquired automatically on the happening of the event, and without any further act on the part of assignor and does not merely rest in, and amount to, a right in contract, giving rise to an action. The assignor, having received the consideration, becomes in equity, on the happening of the event, trustee for the assignee of the property devolving upon or acquired by him, and which he had previously sold and been paid for.

5.97 The practical implication of *Re Lind* is that an assignee of an expectancy taken as security for a loan has the right not to prove his or her debt in the assignor's subsequent bankruptcy, and can simply rely on the security, in much the same way as an ordinary secured creditor can upon the bankruptcy of a debtor. This means that the assignee obtains more than merely contractual rights as a result of the assignment, and further, that the right is proprietary in nature. This is clearly the result of *Re Lind* where the rights of the first two assignees were of a sufficiently proprietary nature to attract the rules determining priority between competing equitable interests: see 7.6.

5.98 The decision in *Re Lind* has been approved in a number of High Court decisions in Australia: *Palette Shoes Pty Ltd v Krohn* at 27; *Norman v FCT* at 24; *Everett v Commissioner of Taxation* at CLR 450; ALR 185; *Booth v FCT* at CLR 165, 178; ALR 377–8, 387.

THE EQUITABLE ASSIGNMENT OF LEGAL PROPERTY

5.99 An equitable assignment of a legal interest in property can arise if the requirements for a legal assignment of that property have not been complied with. To ascertain if the property has been assigned in equity one must first ask whether the assignment is for valuable consideration or voluntary. Furthermore, if the assignment is voluntary then one must also ask the question of whether or not the property was capable of being assigned at law.

Equitable assignment of legal property for consideration

5.100 An assignment of legal property for consideration takes effect in equity immediately upon the consideration being paid or executed: *Holroyd v Marshall* at 1006. The rule here is an application of the equitable maxim that equity looks on that as done which ought to be done: see 2.47–2.50; *Norman v FCT* at 33. In *Everett v Commissioner of Taxation*, at CLR 450; ALR 185, the majority of the High Court of Australia said:

> [A]n equitable assignment of, or a contract to assign, present property for value takes effect immediately and passes the beneficial interest to the assignee.

5.101   The meaning of consideration in this context is generally the same as consideration that is sufficient to support a simple contract at common law.[26]

5.102   In *Holroyd v Marshall*, Lord Westbury stated that this principle depended upon the contract to assign being specifically enforceable. However, for much the same reasons, as with the assignment of future property (see 5.84–5.88), it is questionable whether this is in fact a requirement for the validity of the equitable assignment. This was specifically held to be the case in the context of an assignment or agreement to assign an equitable interest in trust property: *Reef & Rainforest Travel Pty Ltd v Commissioner of Stamp Duties* [2002] 1 Qd R 683 at 687.

5.103   In addition to the above, statute may impose a requirement of writing in relation to particular types of property. For example, dispositions of interests in land must be in writing: see 6.8–6.9. However, if an insistence on compliance with such a statutory requirement would be tantamount to allowing it to be used as an instrument of fraud, an assignment of legal property for consideration will be valid in equity notwithstanding the absence of writing: *Last v Rosenfeld* [1972] 2 NSWLR 923.

The voluntary assignment of legal property assignable at law

5.104   If no consideration has been given for the assignment of legal property the question that must be asked is whether the property involved is property that is or is not assignable at law.

5.105   In relation to the equitable assignment of legal property capable of being assigned at law it could be thought that such assignments were not possible because of the equitable maxims that equity will not assist a volunteer and that equity will not perfect an imperfect gift. However, this is not the case. The validity of such equitable assignments stems from the principles set out in *Milroy v Lord* (1862) 45 ER 1185 at 1189, where Turner LJ said:

> I take the law of this court to be well settled, that, in order to render a voluntary settlement valid and effectual, the settlor must have done everything which, according to the nature of the property comprised in the settlement, was necessary to be done in order to transfer the property and render the settlement binding upon him.

5.106   The statement by Turner LJ contains two limbs. The first limb concerns the requirement that an assignor do all that is necessary to be done to transfer the property. The second limb concerns the requirement that the assignor do all that is necessary to be done to render the assignment binding upon the assignor.

5.107   The rationale for the principles in *Milroy v Lord* was explained in *Corin v Patton* (1990) 169 CLR 540 at 580; 92 ALR 1 at 29, by Deane J as follows:

> [A]n intended gift under such a voluntary assignment will be effective in equity only if the overall circumstances of the case are such that the stage is reached where equity regards the gift as complete, that is to say, as having been actually made. Until that stage is reached, equity will neither recognize the existence of a trust nor protect the donee from the exercise by the donor of any legal rights remaining in him. The reason why that is so is that, in the absence of special

---

26.   R P Meagher, J D Heydon & M J Leeming, *Meagher, Gummow and Lehane's Equity: Doctrines and Remedies*, 4th ed, LexisNexis Butterworths, Sydney, 2002, p 227.

circumstances giving rise to particular doctrines such as the doctrine of equitable estoppel, equity does not recognize an obligation in conscience that requires a person who remains the owner of property to adhere to or to give effect to an intention to give it away ... However, if the stage is reached where equity regards a gift of specific property as having been already made, it will necessarily treat the beneficial interest in that property as having passed to the donee.

The first limb of Milroy v Lord

5.108   In relation to the first limb of the statement by Turner LJ, there has been considerable debate as to what it actually means. What did he mean when he said that an assignor had to do everything that was 'necessary to be done'? Before discussing this question it must first be appreciated that irrespective of what one takes to be the meaning of the statement by Turner LJ, one must know what is required for a valid legal assignment of the property in question before one can ascertain if there has been an assignment of the property in equity. As to the requirements for the legal assignment of various forms of legal property see 5.36–5.56.

5.109   In *Anning v Anning* (1907) 4 CLR 1049, each of the three members of the High Court of Australia offered different interpretations of this aspect of *Milroy v Lord*. Griffith CJ, at 1057, tendered the view that a voluntary assignment of legal property would be effective in equity if the assignor had performed those steps that only the assignor could perform for the legal assignment of the property. Isaacs J, at 1069, was of the view that unless all the steps that were necessary for a legal assignment had been performed there could be no assignment in equity unless it was for consideration. Higgins J, at 1082, took the view that, if the assignor had performed those steps that the assignor could perform for the assignment of the property at law, the assignment would be valid in equity.

5.110   The difference in these views can be illustrated by the example of a voluntary assignment of a debt where there has been compliance with all of the requirements of s 12 of the *Conveyancing Act 1919* (NSW) or its equivalents in other Australian jurisdictions (see 5.49), except that notice of the assignment has not been given to the debtor. On the view of Griffith CJ the assignment would be effective in equity because the giving of notice is not a step that only the assignor can do. It can be given by the assignee. On the view of Isaacs J the assignment would be ineffective because, in the absence of consideration, it can only be effective if all the steps for a valid legal assignment have been carried out. On the view of Higgins J the assignment would be ineffective because the assignor had not given notice of the assignment, a step that the assignor could have performed.

5.111   In the wake of *Anning v Anning* (1907) 4 CLR 1049, no clear consensus emerged as to which of the views expressed in that case was correct until the High Court decision in *Corin v Patton*, although in Queensland the view of Griffith CJ was adopted by legislation.[27] In *Corin v Patton* the majority of the High Court adopted the view of Griffith CJ.

5.112   In *Corin v Patton*, the facts concerned Torrens title land owned by Mr and Mrs Patton as joint tenants. Mrs Patton was terminally ill and, on the assumption that she would die before her husband, the land would have passed to her husband automatically upon her death in accordance with the principle of survivorship that applies to property held as joint tenants. Mrs Patton did not want this to happen upon her death. She wanted her share of the property to go to her children. To

---

27. *Property Law Act 1974* (Qld) s 200.

achieve this result she wanted to sever the joint tenancy and thereby exclude the operation of the principle of survivorship upon her death. One way in which a joint tenancy can be severed is if a joint tenant assigns his or her interest in the property to another person. With this in mind Mrs Patton executed three documents. The first was a memorandum of transfer of her interest in the property to her brother, Mr Corin. The transfer was stated as being subject to a mortgage to the State Bank of New South Wales, which held the relevant certificate of title. The second document was a trust deed by which Mr Corin declared that he held the interest transferred to him by Mrs Patton on trust for her. The third document was a will by which Mrs Patton left her estate to her children in equal shares. At the time of her death the transfer to Mr Corin had not been registered. Nor had any steps been undertaken to have the State Bank produce the certificate of title so that the transfer could be registered. The issue before the High Court was whether Mrs Patton had, before her death, assigned, either at law or in equity, her interest in the property to Mr Corin. If she had, the joint tenancy with Mr Patton would have been severed with the consequence that Mrs Patton's interest in the property would have passed, in accordance with the terms of her will, to her children. If Mrs Patton had not assigned her interest in the property before her death then the joint tenancy would not have been severed and Mr Patton would become the sole owner of the property in accordance with the principle of survivorship.

5.113 The High Court ruled that there had been no assignment of the property, that the joint tenancy had not been severed, and, therefore, that Mr Patton became the sole owner of the property upon the death of his wife. In coming to that conclusion it was clear that there had not been a legal assignment of the property to Mr Corin on the basis that the memorandum of transfer had not been registered: see **5.38**. Furthermore, the court held that there had been no assignment in equity. Because no effort had been made to produce the certificate of title to enable registration of the transfer, there was no equitable assignment of the property on any of the three views in *Anning v Anning*. The most liberal view, that of Griffith CJ, would have required production of the title documents, because that was an act that only Mrs Patton, as assignor, could compel the State Bank to do. Although it was, strictly speaking, not necessary for the court to express a considered view as to which of the three views in *Anning v Anning* was correct, a majority of the court (Mason CJ, McHugh and Deane JJ) endorsed the view of Griffith CJ. Deane J, at CLR 582; ALR 30, said:

> The test [for a voluntary equitable assignment of Torrens title land] is a twofold one. It is whether the donor has done all that is necessary to place the vesting of the legal title within the control of the donee and beyond the recall and intervention of the donor. Once that stage is reached and the gift is complete and effective in equity, the equitable interest in the land vests in the donee and, that being so, the donor is bound in conscience to hold the property as trustee for the donee pending the vesting of the legal title.

5.114 Since the decision in *Corin v Patton*, New South Wales, the Northern Territory, Queensland and Tasmania have enacted legislation permitting the unilateral severance of a joint tenancy.[28] The essence of this legislation is that a joint tenant can execute an instrument in prescribed form transferring his or her interest to himself or herself and lodge it for registration. The instrument can be lodged without production of the relevant certificate of title. Upon registration the joint

---

28. *Real Property Act 1900* (NSW) s 97; *Land Title Act 2000* (NT) s 59; *Land Title Act 1980* (Qld) s 59; *Land Titles Act 1980* (SA) s 63.

tenancy is severed. The New South Wales legislation, set out in s 97 of the *Real Property Act 1900*, was considered in *McCoy v Estate of Caelli* [2008] NSWSC 986. In that case, Caelli executed the relevant instrument just prior to his death. A few days after his death it was lodged for registration. Upon receiving notice of its lodgment, McCoy, who was Caelli's mother and registered as joint tenant on the title to the land, sought an injunction to prevent the Registrar-General registering the instrument. The issue before the court was whether the execution of the instrument effected a severance of the joint tenancy in equity. In essence the issue was whether there had been an effective assignment of Caelli's interest in equity. Brereton J, at [27], said that s 97 'does not contemplate or support any pre-existing equitable severance upon lodgment, let alone execution, of a unilateral transfer' and that '[a]n unregistered unilateral transfer effects no equitable severance'. His Honour, at [31], went on to say that, even if an equitable severance was possible, it had not been achieved in this case. Caelli had not done everything that was necessary to be done in accordance with the principles in *Corin v Patton* because he 'had not lodged the transfer before he died, and as it remained in the control of [Caelli] it was revocable up until the moment of his death, so that ... there was no perfected transfer such as might arguably have effected a severance in equity'.

The second limb of Milroy v Lord

5.115　The requirement in the second limb of the statement by Turner LJ in *Milroy v Lord* that the assignor has done all that is necessary to be done to render the assignment binding on the assignor was discussed by the Court of Appeal in New South Wales in *Costin v Costin* (1997) NSW Conv R 55–811. This case dealt with the issue of whether an assignor had done enough to render a gift of property binding upon the assignor, or in the words of Deane J in *Corin v Patton* whether the gift was 'beyond the recall and intervention of the donor'. *Costin v Costin* concerned a case where there was an initial attempt to sever a joint tenancy in relation to Torrens title land by an assignment by one joint tenant of his interest to his son. The assignor handed over an appropriate transfer document as well as giving written instructions to the solicitors who held the certificate of title to release it to the assignee. The solicitors refused to do so because they believed that they needed the authority of both the joint tenants to release the certificate of title to the assignee. The assignor later changed his mind and assigned his interest to a second son and the second son was duly registered as co-owner of the property. The first son argued that there had been an effective equitable assignment to him and that the second son held the interest in the property on trust for the first son. The court held the assignment to the first son was ineffective. Although the assignor satisfied the requirements of the first limb of the statement of Turner LJ in *Milroy v Lord*, he had not complied with the second limb. The assignor had not put the transfer beyond his recall. He had not done everything that had to be done to render the assignment binding upon him. In the context of Torrens title land and the second limb of *Milroy v Lord*, in *Stone v Registrar of Titles* [2012] WASC 21 at [120], Simmonds J said the following:

> [W]here a certificate of title has been issued, and is held by or for the donor and the non-assigning joint tenant, the donor has not done all that is necessary for him to have done to effect a transfer of legal title simply by executing the transfer of his interest and delivering it to the donee/transferee while also requiring the non-assigning joint tenant to deliver the certificate of title to the transferee, and notwithstanding that the non-assigning joint tenant is compellable for this purpose. The incompleteness lies in the revocability of the requirement to deliver ... The gift is not perfect until the non-assigning joint tenant produces the certificate of title to the donee/transferee.

In practical terms this means that where there is a direction to a third party to produce a certificate of title to an assignee, the assignment in equity 'is not binding on the donor and the gift is incomplete, unless the duplicate certificate of title is in fact produced to the donee/transferee': *Stone v Registrar of Titles* at [127]. It is only at that stage that the assignor has put the transfer beyond recall and thereby satisfied the requirements of the second limb of the statement of Turner LJ in *Milroy v Lord*.

5.116   The decision in *Costin v Costin* gives rise to an illogical distinction which can be illustrated in circumstances where A and B are joint tenants of Torrens title land and A hands over a memorandum of transfer assigning his or her interest to C for no consideration. If A also gives D, the custodian of the certificate of title, a direction to produce it so that the transfer can be registered there is, on the basis of *Costin v Costin*, no equitable assignment of the property until the certificate of title is produced. However, if B is the custodian of the certificate of title and A directs B to produce the certificate of title to enable the transfer to be registered, B would not be permitted to retain possession of the certificate of title and thereby frustrate registration of the transfer: *Motor Auction Pty Ltd v John Joyce Wholesale Cars Pty Ltd* (1997) CCH Conv R 55–818. In this case there is an effective equitable assignment of the property. In this situation the direction to produce the certificate of title renders the assignment effective in equity because it is beyond recall and binding upon the assignor. In the former case the direction to produce the certificate of title does not effect an effective equitable assignment because it is not beyond recall and binding upon the assignor. There seems to be little logic in the distinction between the two cases.

5.117   In *Corin v Patton*, if the requirements of *Milroy v Lord* had been satisfied before Mrs Patton's death — in other words, if the certificate of title had been delivered to Mrs Patton's brother — her death before registration of the transfer would not have rendered the assignment ineffective: *Stone v Registrar of Titles* at [119]. This is because her brother would have had, before Mrs Patton died, a transfer that could have been registered immediately. In *Watt v Lord* (2005) 62 NSWLR 495 at 505–7, it was held that, where a memorandum of transfer in registrable form is delivered to the assignee together with the certificate of title, the death of the assignor does not preclude subsequent registration of the transfer. This principle is given statutory force in the Northern Territory and Queensland.[29]

Equitable assignment of debts and choses in action

5.118   In *Olsson v Dyson* (1969) 120 CLR 365, the facts concerned a purported oral assignment of a debt. Following the death of the assignor, the issue before the High Court of Australia was whether the debt had been validly assigned to the assignee or formed part of the assignor's estate. Given that the assignment was oral, there was clearly no valid assignment at law as required by statute: see 5.55–5.56. The court also held that there was no equitable assignment of the debt. Windeyer J, at 387, observed that, because the assignor had not executed a written assignment of the debt, the requirements set out in *Milroy v Lord* had not been satisfied and therefore there was no equitable assignment of the debt.

5.119   Thus, where the debt or chose in action is one that is capable of being assigned pursuant to s 12, for an assignment to be effective in equity it will need to be in writing and signed by the assignor. However, notice to the debtor or obligor does not have to be given: *McIntyre v Gye* at FCR 479–80; ALR 295. In enforcing the debt or chose in action, the assignee will generally need to join the assignor to the enforcement proceedings (see 5.44–5.47).

---

29. *Land Title Act 2000* (NT) s 187; *Land Title Act 1994* (Qld) s 183.

5.120 Smith contests the validity of the decision in *Olsson v Dyson* on the basis that, prior to the enactment of s 12 of the *Conveyancing Act 1919* (NSW) and its equivalents in other jurisdictions, there would have been a valid equitable assignment of the debt, there being no requirement in equity that the assignment be in writing. He argues that, as the purpose of s 12 was not substantive but rather facilitative (see **5.51**), '[i]t would be odd if a requirement not intended to impose additional formalities, but rather to do away with them, was nevertheless treated in equity as effectively imposing such formalities'.[30]

Equitable assignments based upon unconscientiousness

5.121 The above discussion on voluntary assignments of legal property capable of being assigned at law is focused on the examination of the steps required to be undertaken for the assignment of the property at law and whether the steps actually undertaken render the assignment effective in equity, notwithstanding that all the steps required for a legal assignment have not been carried out. However, in the light of the English Court of Appeal decision in *Pennington v Waine* [2002] 4 All ER 215, it appears that an equitable assignment of property is possible irrespective of what steps have been taken by the assignor. In that case the assignor of shares in a particular company wanted the assignee to qualify as a director of the company. The only way in which that could be done was if the assignee had a sufficient number of shares in the company. The assignor signed but did not, before his death, deliver to the assignee the transfer of shares. The court ruled that there was an effective equitable assignment of the shares irrespective of the steps, if any, that the assignor had undertaken to effect a legal assignment of the property. The court based its decision on the principle that, in the circumstances of the case, it would have been unconscientious if the assignment was not binding upon the assignor.

5.122 The decision in *Pennington v Waine* has been welcomed by Hepburn who suggests that the decision 'represents a fundamental shift in equitable ideology' which she urges Australian courts to adopt.[31] In the light of the recognition by the courts that the principle of unconscientiousness underpins principles of equity (see **2.4–2.5**), Australian courts may well follow the approach heralded by *Pennington v Waine*, notwithstanding spirited criticism of the decision by Meagher, Heydon and Leeming.[32]

The voluntary assignment of legal property not assignable at law

5.123 In relation to the equitable assignment of legal property that is *not* assignable at law, arguably the only example of such property is part of a debt or chose in action. Except in Western Australia such property can only be assigned in equity. In Western Australia, s 20(3) of the *Property Law Act 1969* (WA) permits the legal assignment at law of part of a debt or chose in action.

5.124 If the legal property cannot be assigned at law the assignment will be effective in equity if the assignor has manifested an intention to make an immediate and irrevocable transfer: *Shepherd v Commissioner of Taxation* at 391. In ascertaining whether there is the requisite intention the assignment need not purport to be an assignment. What is important is that the language used

---

30. Smith, *The Law of Assignment*, note 15 above, p 188.
31. S Hepburn, 'The Discourse of Conscience in the Assessment of Voluntary Assignments in Equity' (2006) 1 *Journal of Equity* 117, p 133.
32. Meagher et al, *Equity: Doctrines and Remedies*, note 26 above, p 232.

clearly establishes that the assignor intended to assign the property irrespective of whether it was expressed in the form of a command, courteous request or mere permission: *William Brandt's Sons & Company Limited v Dunlop Rubber Co Ltd* at 462.

5.125 The principles set out in *Milroy v Lord* do not apply. Nor is consideration required. In *Norman v FCT*, at 34, Windeyer J said:

> To say that the donor must do everything that according to the nature of the property is necessary to transfer it means little when it is in law not transferable. These considerations have added weight in the case of part of a debt: for a part of a debt was never assignable so as to be recoverable at law even in an indirect way … The whole of a debt being now voluntarily assignable under the statute, it would be a strange anomaly if a part could not be the subject of voluntary equitable assignment.

THE EQUITABLE ASSIGNMENT OF EQUITABLE PROPERTY

5.126 The assignment of equitable property can only be achieved in equity. Because equitable property is not recognised at common law it cannot be the subject of a legal assignment. For a voluntary assignment of equitable property the assignment must be absolute. Apart from any statutory requirement of writing, all that is necessary for a valid equitable assignment is 'a clear expression of an intention to make an immediate disposition': *Norman v FCT* at 30. As to ascertaining the assignor's intention, the principles noted in 5.124 are equally applicable in this context.

5.127 The requirement of writing for equitable assignments of equitable property is set out in legislative provisions that require an assignment of an equitable interest or trust subsisting at the time of the assignment to be in writing.[33] These sections apply to equitable interests in both realty and personalty: *PT Ltd v Maradona Pty Ltd (No 2)* (1992) 27 NSWLR 241 at 250–2.

5.128 An absolute equitable assignment of equitable property does not require consideration: *Kekewich v Manning* (1851) 42 ER 519 at 524. However, if the assignment of equitable property is not absolute, but merely by way of charge as security for the payment of money or the performance of an obligation, it will be invalid unless made for consideration: *Re Earl of Lucan* (1890) 45 Ch D 615.

5.129 In the case of the assignment of a whole equitable chose in action, the equitable assignee is entitled to sue in his or her own name without joining the assignor. This is so because the result of the assignment is that the assignor retains no interest at all in the property (in contrast to the equitable assignment of a legal chose in action where, as discussed at 5.44, the assignor becomes the bare trustee of the property). Therefore, there is no substantive reason for requiring the assignor to be joined to the proceedings initiated by the assignee: *Redman v The Permanent Trustee Co of New South Wales Ltd* (1916) 22 CLR 84 at 95.

---

33. *Civil Law (Property) Act 2006* (ACT) s 201(3); *Conveyancing Act 1919* (NSW) s 23C(1)(c); *Law of Property Act 2000* (NT) s 10(1)(c); *Property Law Act 1974* (Qld) s 11(1)(c); *Law of Property Act 1936* (SA) s 29(1)(c); *Conveyancing and Law of Property Act 1884* (Tas) s 60(2)(c); *Property Law Act 1958* (Vic) s 53(1)(c); *Property Law Act 1969* (WA) s 34(1)(c).

6

DISPOSITIONS OF EQUITABLE INTERESTS AND THE REQUIREMENT OF WRITING

INTRODUCTION

6.1   This chapter is concerned with the statutory requirement of writing as it affects the disposition of equitable interests. In Chapter 5 the requirements for the valid assignment of equitable interests were analysed and it was noted that s 23C(1)(c) of the *Conveyancing Act 1919* (NSW) (and its equivalents in other Australian jurisdictions) was the most important statutory provision imposing a writing requirement for the validity of such assignments: see 5.127. However, the requirements of s 23C(1)(c) are not confined to dealings with equitable interests in property by way of assignment.

6.2   Section 23C(1)(c) is concerned with 'dispositions' of equitable interests in property. In relation to the purpose of s 23C(1)(c), Green has written:

> A principal reason for singling out subsisting equitable interests for protection is because evidence of their movement will often be the only indicator of where a particular right resides at any given time. There is no documentary paper title, nor generally is there physical possession: two indicia which facilitate the identification of a legal proprietor. In general there is only an invisible entitlement to certain rights perceived by courts of equity behind the veil of legal title.[1]

In *Pascoe v Boensch* (2008) 250 ALR 24 at 28, it was said that the purposes of s 23C(1)(c) are: (i) to prevent hidden oral transactions in equitable interests; and (ii) to enable a trustee to ascertain who are the beneficiaries of a trust.

6.3   Whether the requirements of s 23C(1)(c) catch any particular transaction involving equitable interests in property is the focal concern of this chapter. This is not a topic without difficulty. In *Vandervell v Inland Revenue Commissioners* [1967] 2 AC 291 at 329; [1967] 1 All ER 1 at 18, Lord Wilberforce observed that s 23C(1)(c) 'is not easy to apply to the varied transactions in equitable interests which now occur'.

6.4   It is clear from the legislative definitions[2] of 'disposition' and their judicial interpretation that a 'disposition' includes, but goes beyond, an assignment. In *PT Ltd v Maradona Pty Ltd (No 2)* (1992)

---

1.   B Green, 'Grey, Oughtred and Vandervell — A Contextual Reappraisal' (1984) 47 *Modern Law Review* 385, p 386.
2.   *Civil Law (Property) Act 2006* (ACT) s 3; *Conveyancing Act 1919* (NSW) s 7(1); *Law of Property Act 2000* (NT) s 4; *Property Law Act 1974* (Qld) s 3(1); *Law of Property Act 1936* (SA) s 7(1); *Property Law Act 1958* (Vic) s 18(1); *Property Law Act 1969* (WA) s 7(1).

27 NSWLR 241 at 249–50, Giles J, after considering relevant authorities, concluded that a disposition 'points to a wide concept, extending to any form of assurance, disclaimer or release of property'. A disposition of property can be broadly defined as including any acts taken by an owner of property that result in that owner ceasing to be the owner of the property. According to Giles J, a critical aspect of such a definition is 'the intention and the result, not the mechanism by which the intention is fulfilled'.

6.5 Judicial pronouncements make it clear that a disposition includes a declaration of trust: *Comptroller of Stamps (Vic) v Howard-Smith* (1936) 54 CLR 614 at 621–2. The legislative definitions of 'disposition' in the Australian Capital Territory, the Northern Territory, New South Wales and Queensland,[3] but not in other Australian jurisdictions, include a declaration of trust within the meaning of 'disposition'.

6.6 In *Timpson's Executors v Yerbury* [1936] 1 KB 645 at 664; [1936] 1 All ER 186 at 194, Romer LJ confirmed the varied nature of acts that could amount to a disposition of an equitable interest in property. According to his Honour, equitable interests in property can be disposed of by four different methods:

1. assignments;
2. directions by beneficiaries to trustees;
3. agreements to assign; and
4. declarations of trust.

6.7 Although there are other types of dealings that would come within the meaning of a disposition, this chapter will focus on those mentioned by Romer LJ. However, before analysing these four modes of disposition some comments need to be made about s 23C of the *Conveyancing Act 1919* (NSW).

THE PROVISIONS OF S 23C OF THE CONVEYANCING ACT 1919 (NSW)

6.8 Section 23C of the *Conveyancing Act 1919* (NSW)[4] stipulates as follows:

23C Instruments required to be in writing

(1) Subject to the provisions of this Act with respect to the creation of interests in land by parol:

    (a) no interest in land can be created or disposed of except by writing signed by the person creating or conveying the same, or by the person's agent thereunto lawfully authorised in writing, or by will, or by operation of law,

    (b) a declaration of trust respecting any land or any interest therein must be manifested and proved by some writing signed by some person who is able to declare such trust or by the person's will,

---

3.   *Civil Law (Property) Act 2006* (ACT) s 3; *Conveyancing Act 1919* (NSW) s 7(1); *Law of Property Act 2000* (NT) s 4; *Property Law Act 1974* (Qld) s 3(1).

4.   The equivalents of s 23C in other Australian jurisdictions are: *Civil Law (Property) Act 2006* (ACT) s 201; *Law of Property Act 2000* (NT) s 10; *Property Law Act 1974* (Qld) s 11; *Law of Property Act 1936* (SA) s 29; *Conveyancing and Law of Property Act 1884* (Tas) s 60(2); *Property Law Act 1958* (Vic) s 53; *Property Law Act 1969* (WA) s 34.

(c) a disposition of an equitable interest or trust subsisting at the time of the disposition, must be in writing signed by the person disposing of the same or by the person's will, or by the person's agent thereunto lawfully authorised in writing.

(2) This section does not affect the creation or operation of resulting, implied, or constructive trusts.

6.9 The following points should be made about s 23C:

- The writing requirements within s 23C(1) can be satisfied by more than one document provided they are obviously interconnected: *Australia and New Zealand Banking Group Ltd v Widin* (1990) 102 ALR 289 at 297–300.
- Section 23C(1)(b) does not require the trust of land to be created in writing. It merely requires evidence in writing in relation to a declaration of trust of land: *Byrnes v Kendle* (2011) 243 CLR 253 at 272; 279 ALR 212 at 226–7. However, the disposition or creation of an interest pursuant to s 23C(1)(a) must *itself* be in writing. Similarly, in all Australian jurisdictions except Queensland, the disposition of a subsisting interest pursuant to s 23C(1)(c) or its equivalents must also be in writing. In Queensland s 11(1)(c) of the *Property Law Act 1974* (Qld) only requires dispositions of subsisting equitable interests to be evidenced in writing.
- Section 23C(1)(a) and s 23C(1)(b) apply to the creation or disposition of interests, whereas s 23C(1)(c) only applies to the disposition of subsisting interests.
- Section 23C(1)(a) applies to the disposition of legal and equitable interests in land: *Adamson v Hayes* (1973) 130 CLR 276 at 297, 304, 318–19.
- Section 23C(1)(a) and s 23C(1)(b) apply only to land, whereas it has been held that, despite the references to land in the opening sentence of the section, s 23C(1)(c) applies to interests in land and personalty: *PT Ltd v Maradona Pty Ltd (No 2)* at 250–2; *Warner v Hung, in the matter of Bellpac Pty Limited (Receivers and Managers Appointed) (In Liquidation) (No 2)* [2011] FCA 1123 at [129].

DISPOSITIONS BY WAY OF ASSIGNMENT

6.10 The assignment of equitable interests in property has already been analysed: see 5.126–5.129. It was noted there (see 5.127) that s 23C(1)(c)[5] required assignments of equitable interests to be in writing.

6.11 It must be stressed that s 23C(1)(c) only applies in cases of subsisting equitable interests in property. If the assignor has both the legal and equitable interest in property s 23C(1)(c) does *not* apply. This is a consequence of the decision in *Commissioner of Stamp Duties (Queensland) v Livingston* [1965] AC 694; [1964] 3 All ER 692, in which the Privy Council ruled that where a person owns property legally and beneficially there is no distinction between the legal and equitable interests. As discussed in Chapter 4 (see 4.25–4.29), this case concerned the nature of the interest of a residuary beneficiary in the assets of an unadministered estate. The Privy Council ruled that while the estate was in the process of administration, the whole of the interest or right of property in the

---

5. The equivalents to s 23C(1)(c) in other Australian jurisdictions are *Civil Law (Property) Act 2006* (ACT) s 201(3); *Law of Property Act 2000* (NT) s 10(1)(c); *Property Law Act 1974* (Qld) s 11(1)(c); *Law of Property Act 1936* (SA) s 29(1)(c); *Conveyancing and Law of Property Act 1884* (Tas) s 60(2)(c); *Property Law Act 1958* (Vic) s 53(1)(c); *Property Law Act 1969* (WA) s 34(1)(c).

assets of the estate vested in the executor as full owner. In particular, Viscount Radcliffe, at AC 712; All ER 699, said:

> A ... criticism has occasionally been expressed to the effect that it is incredible ... to deny a residuary legatee all beneficial interest in the assets of an unadministered estate. Where, it is asked, is the beneficial interest in those assets during the period of administration? It is not, ex hypothesi, in the executor: where else can it be but in the residuary legatee? This dilemma is founded on a fallacy, for it assumes mistakenly that for all purposes and at every moment of time the law requires the separate existence of two different kinds of estate, the legal and the equitable. There is no need to make this assumption. When the whole right of property is in a person, as it is in an executor, there is no need to distinguish between the legal and equitable interest in that property, any more than there is for the property of a full beneficial owner.

6.12 In *Westdeutsche Landesbank Girozentrale v Islington London Borough Council* [1996] AC 669 at 706; [1996] 2 All ER 961 at 989, Lord Browne-Wilkinson made the same point when he said:

> A person solely entitled to the full beneficial ownership of money or property, both at law and in equity, does not enjoy an equitable interest in that property. The legal title carries with it all rights. Unless and until there is a separation of the legal and equitable estates, there is no separate equitable title.

6.13 The consequence of the reasoning in *Commissioner of Stamp Duties (Queensland) v Livingston* and *Westdeutsche Landesbank Girozentrale v Islington London Borough Council* is that where an absolute owner of property grants an equitable interest in that property to another person or effects an equitable assignment of that property, there is no disposition of a *subsisting* equitable interest to that person. Rather, in both cases there is the creation of an equitable interest which is quite distinct from the disposition of a subsisting equitable interest. As a result, s 23C(1)(c) does not apply to such dispositions: *Baloglow v Konstanidis* [2001] NSWCA 451 at [116]–[117]; *Warner v Hung* at [137].

6.14 If the grant of an equitable interest in property or the equitable assignment of property involves land, a writing requirement arises pursuant to either s 23C(1)(a) or s 23C(1)(b). However, these two subsections will not apply to such dispositions of personal property. As already noted, s 23C(1)(a) and s 23C(1)(b) only apply to dispositions relating to land: see 6.9.

DISPOSITIONS BY WAY OF A DIRECTION BY A BENEFICIARY TO A TRUSTEE

6.15 A direction by a beneficiary to a trustee of property in relation to the equitable interest in that property can take various forms. Two forms of such direction are, first, a direction to hold trust property for a third party and, second, a direction to transfer trust property in its entirety to a third party.

Direction to hold property on trust for a third party

6.16 The situation envisaged here is where a beneficiary instructs his or her trustee to hold the equitable interest in property the subject of the trust on trust for a third party and no longer for the beneficiary. The question that arises is whether an oral direction in such circumstances is effective to dispose of the property. In *Grey v Inland Revenue Commissioners* [1960] AC 1; [1959] 3 All ER 603, the House of Lords ruled that such an oral direction was ineffective to dispose of the equitable interest in the face of the requirement of writing set out in s 23C(1)(c).

6.17   In *Grey v IRC*, Hunter was the beneficiary under a bare trust of 18,000 shares. Grey and Randolph were the trustees. On 18 February 1955 Hunter orally and irrevocably directed the trustees to hold those shares on various trusts for Hunter's grandchildren with the intention that such direction should result in Hunter ceasing to have any equitable interest in the shares. One week later Hunter executed various declarations of trust confirming the effect of the oral direction given to the trustees. Stamp duty was payable on these documents and the issue before the House of Lords was whether the amount of stamp duty payable was to be assessed according to the value of the shares (*ad valorem* duty) or whether only nominal duty was payable. The taxing authorities assessed the documents as being liable to *ad valorem* stamp duty on the basis that the executed declarations of trust, and not the earlier oral direction, effected the disposition of the equitable interest in the shares. The trustees contested this assessment on the basis that the earlier oral direction was effective to dispose of the equitable interest in the shares and that the later written declarations merely confirmed what had taken place earlier. On this basis, the trustees argued that the later written declarations did not effect the disposition of the equitable interest in the shares and were thus only liable to nominal stamp duty. The trustees' argument could only succeed if Hunter's oral direction to them was *not* a disposition within the meaning of s 23C(1)(c). If Hunter's oral direction to the trustees was a disposition within the meaning of s 23C(1)(c) it was ineffective because of non-compliance with that subsection's writing requirement. In such a case the written declarations executed by Hunter one week later would have disposed of Hunter's equitable interest in the shares and would accordingly have been liable to *ad valorem* stamp duty.

6.18   The House of Lords ruled against the trustees and upheld the assessment of *ad valorem* stamp duty on the written declarations of trust. Viscount Simonds, at AC 12–13; All ER 605, said:

> If the word 'disposition' is given its natural meaning, it cannot, I think, be denied that a direction given by Mr Hunter, whereby the beneficial interest in the shares theretofore vested in him became vested in another or others, is a disposition … [T]here is no justification for giving the word 'disposition' a narrower meaning than it ordinarily bears.

6.19   The facts of *Grey v IRC* dealt with personal property. If the direction given by Hunter had dealt with real property, compliance with s 23C(1)(c) would still have been necessary because the subsection deals with equitable interests in real and personal property. In these circumstances s 23C(1)(a) would have imposed a similar writing requirement because that subsection deals with the disposition of legal and equitable interests in land: see 6.9.

6.20   If the facts of *Grey v IRC* had been decided upon the basis of Queensland's legislative provision dealing with the disposition of a subsisting equitable interest, *ad valorem* stamp duty would not have been payable on the declarations of trust executed by Hunter. This is because s 11(1)(c) of the *Property Law Act 1974* (Qld) only requires that the disposition of subsisting equitable interests be *evidenced* in writing. Nothing in s 11(1)(c) requires such dispositions to be in writing. Thus, Hunter's earlier oral direction would have been valid. The later declarations of trusts would have only been evidence of an earlier oral transaction and would have had no dispositive effect. As such, the declarations would only have attracted *nominal* stamp duty.

Direction to transfer property to a third party

6.21   The situation envisaged here is where a beneficiary directs his or her trustee to transfer both the legal and equitable interests in the trust property to the third party so that the third party becomes the absolute owner of the property. If the direction to the trustee is oral, there is nothing in s 23C(1) that requires writing in relation to the legal title where the trust property is personal property. (As to the position in cases where there is an oral direction relating to trust property that is real property see 6.26.) The issue that requires analysis is whether such an oral direction is effective in relation to the equitable interest in the personal property. The House of Lords, in *Vandervell v IRC*, ruled that such an oral declaration was effective and that s 23C(1)(c) did not impose a requirement of writing in relation to such directions relating to trusts of personal property.

6.22 In *Vandervell v IRC*, a bank was a bare trustee of shares for Vandervell. He orally directed the bank to transfer the shares to the Royal College of Surgeons. His intention was that the college acquire both the legal and equitable interests in the shares. Vandervell was assessed as liable for surtax on the shares pursuant to relevant income tax legislation, on the basis that his oral direction to the bank did not result in a disposition of the shares to the college. If the oral direction was an effective disposition of the shares to the college, Vandervell was not liable for the surtax. On this issue the House of Lords unanimously ruled in favour of Vandervell, holding that his direction to the trustee was not a disposition within the parameters of s 23C(1)(c). Vandervell's oral direction was therefore effective and did not have to be in writing. However, on other grounds not relevant to the issues discussed in this chapter, the House of Lords, by a bare majority, held that Vandervell was liable for the surtax.

6.23 Lord Upjohn, at AC 311–12; All ER 7, stated that *Grey v IRC* was distinguishable from the present case because in *Grey v IRC* the transaction was one that dealt only with the equitable interest, whereas in the present case the transaction involved dealing with both the legal and equitable interests. His Lordship opined that there is no justification for invoking the provisions of s 23C(1)(c) 'where the beneficial owner wants to deal with the legal estate as well as the equitable estate'. Lord Upjohn noted further that in cases where the legal and beneficial estates are vested in the legal owner and the legal owner desires to transfer the whole of the legal and beneficial interests to another person, no more than a transfer of the legal estate is required. There is no need for compliance with s 23C(1)(c). The same principle applied to the facts of the present case where the legal and equitable interests were vested in different persons, but in circumstances where the equitable interest owner was in a position to give directions to the bare trustee with regard to that legal interest. Lord Upjohn was of the view that to require separate assignments in express terms of both the legal and equitable interests would make for unnecessary complications and make s 23C(1)(c) 'more productive of injustice than the supposed evils it was intended to prevent'.

6.24 Lord Donovan, at AC 317–18; All ER 11, observed that Vandervell's direction 'achieved the same result as if there had been no separation of the [legal and equitable] interests'. His Lordship further noted that the disposition to the college 'was a disposition not of the equitable interest alone, but of the entire estate in the shares'. Accordingly, s 23C(1)(c) was of no relevance.

6.25 In *Vandervell v IRC*, at AC 330; All ER 18, Lord Wilberforce said that, if Vandervell had died before his direction to the trustee had been carried out, the gift would nevertheless have been valid on the basis that Vandervell had done everything within his power to transfer the property to the college. However, in *Parker & Parker v Ledsham* [1988] WAR 32 at 37, Rowland J held that in such circumstances the direction to the trustee would be revoked by the death of the person making the direction.

6.26 The facts of *Vandervell v IRC* dealt with an oral direction to a trustee of personal property. Had Vandervell's oral direction related to a trust of real property writing would have been required pursuant to the provisions of s 23C(1)(a), which deals with dispositions of legal and equitable interests in land.

DISPOSITION BY WAY OF CONTRACT TO ASSIGN AN EQUITABLE INTEREST

6.27 The situation envisaged here is a contract for valuable consideration to assign an equitable interest in property. The question that arises is whether such a contract must be in writing pursuant to the provisions of s 23C(1)(c). At the heart of this question lies the relationship between s 23C(1)(c) and s 23C(2). On the ordinary meaning of the words used in s 23C(1)(c), a contract for valuable consideration to assign an equitable interest in property would be a 'disposition' within the meaning of the legislation, and would therefore have to be in writing. However, s 23C(2) effectively dispenses with the requirement of writing in the context of the creation of, inter alia, constructive trusts. It is a well-settled principle of law that a contract for valuable consideration to assign property of any kind gives rise to a constructive trust whereby the vendor is a constructive trustee of the property for the purchaser, provided it is specifically enforceable: *Bunny Industries Ltd v FSW Enterprises Pty Ltd* [1982] Qd R 712 at 713–16.[6] Section 23C(2) would therefore indicate that such a contract does not need to meet the requirement of writing mandated by s 23C(1)(c).

6.28 An important authority on this question is the decision of the House of Lords in *Oughtred v Inland Revenue Commissioners* [1960] AC 206; [1959] 3 All ER 623. In this case, Mrs Oughtred held a beneficial life estate in certain shares. Her son Peter held the equitable reversionary interest in those shares. Mrs Oughtred also owned absolutely a number of other shares in the same company. By an oral agreement of 18 June 1956 Mrs Oughtred and her son agreed that on 26 June 1956 she would transfer to him the shares in the company that she owned absolutely and in return Peter would surrender to her his equitable reversionary interest in the shares in which Mrs Oughtred had an equitable life estate, thereby making her the absolute beneficial owner of those shares. On 26 June 1956 three documents were executed to effectuate the oral agreement of 18 June 1956. The first document was a deed of release which noted that the shares formerly held by trustees on trust for Mrs Oughtred for life with an equitable reversionary interest to Peter, were now held on trust for Mrs Oughtred absolutely and that it was intended to transfer legal title to her whereupon the trustees would be released from their trusteeship. The second document transferred, for nominal consideration, the shares formerly owned absolutely by Mrs Oughtred to Peter. The third document was a transfer, for nominal consideration, of the legal title from the trustees to Mrs Oughtred in relation to the shares referred to in the first document. The third document was assessed by the taxing authorities as liable for the payment of *ad valorem* stamp duty on the basis that the earlier oral contract was ineffectual in transferring Peter's equitable reversionary interest to Mrs Oughtred because such a transaction amounted to a disposition within the meaning of s 23C(1)(c) and had to be in writing. The taxing authorities argued that it was the third document which effected the disposition in favour of Mrs Oughtred and was therefore liable to *ad valorem* stamp duty. A bare majority in the House of Lords found in favour of the taxing authorities.

6.29 For the majority, Lord Jenkins, at AC 239–40; All ER 632–3 (Lord Keith concurring, at AC 232; All ER 628), took the view that *ad valorem* stamp duty was payable because the transfer

---

6. For an analysis of the nature of the obligations of a vendor to a purchaser in these circumstances see *Englewood Properties Ltd v Patel* [2005] 3 All ER 307.

from the trustees to Mrs Oughtred related to a dealing in property and as such attracted *ad valorem* stamp duty under the relevant stamp duty legislation. This approach made it unnecessary for his Lordship to determine whether or not s 23C(1)(c) or s 23C(2) applied. However, Lord Jenkins opined that, even if the earlier oral agreement created a constructive trust, the later transfer to Mrs Oughtred from the trustees would have conferred upon her rights superior to those gained on the creation of the constructive trust. In such circumstances the transfer would be dutiable at *ad valorem* rates under the stamp duty legislation.

6.30 Lord Denning, at AC 233; All ER 628–9, took the view that even if the oral agreement of 18 June 1956 was effective to dispose of Peter's equitable reversionary interest to his mother, the subsequent transfer from the trustees to Mrs Oughtred attracted *ad valorem* stamp duty. However, Lord Denning also was of the view that the oral agreement was ineffective to dispose of Peter's equitable reversionary interest because of the requirement of writing in s 23C(1)(c). In his Lordship's view s 23C(2) did not do away with that requirement.

6.31 For the minority, Lord Radcliffe, at AC 227–8; All ER 625–6, accepted the view that the oral agreement of 18 June 1956 gave rise to a constructive trust and that the disposition was effected by the oral agreement. In such a situation s 23C(2) dispensed with the need for writing. The transfer from the trustees to Mrs Oughtred of 26 June 1956 did not dispose of Peter's reversionary interest and accordingly was only liable to nominal stamp duty. Lord Cohen, at AC 230–2; All ER 627–8, accepted the view that Peter became constructive trustee of his equitable reversionary interest as a result of the oral agreement of 18 June 1956. He also conceded that if the transfer from the trustees to Mrs Oughtred of 26 June 1956 had transferred an equitable interest in the shares to Mrs Oughtred, it would have been liable to *ad valorem* stamp duty. However, he took the view that the documentation did not do this. Mrs Oughtred was absolutely entitled to the shares as at 26 June 1956, not because the documentation of 26 June 1956 transferred an equitable interest to her, but because Peter, having become constructive trustee of his equitable reversionary interest by virtue of the earlier oral agreement, could not dispute Mrs Oughtred's title to the shares. Accordingly, no *ad valorem* stamp duty was payable.

6.32 The decision in *Oughtred v IRC* contains no clear majority opinion on the question of whether an agreement for valuable consideration for the transfer of an equitable interest in personal property must be in writing. The decisions of Lords Jenkins and Keith were based upon the terms of relevant stamp duty legislation, which made it unnecessary for them to express a decided view on the relationship between s 23C(1)(c) and s 23C(2). In their view, if there was a written document relating to an earlier oral agreement it was liable to *ad valorem* stamp duty pursuant to relevant stamp duty legislation, irrespective of whether a constructive trust arose as a result of the earlier oral agreement.

6.33 Lord Cohen's decision in *Oughtred v IRC* was ultimately also based upon considerations relating to the interpretation of stamp duty legislation rather than the provisions of s 23C(1)(c) and s 23C(2). Because the relevant documentation in the case was not, in his Lordship's opinion, an instrument transferring an equitable interest, it was not liable to *ad valorem* stamp duty. However, Lord Cohen did address the relationship between s 23C(1)(c) and s 23C(2) and expressed the view that even if an oral agreement for valuable consideration to transfer an equitable interest created a constructive trust, s 23C(1)(c) had to be complied with for the assignment of the equitable interest by the vendor to the purchaser. No explanation of this reasoning was given by Lord Cohen.

6.34   Of the other two Lords in *Oughtred v IRC*, only Lord Radcliffe was unambiguously of the view that the oral agreement for valuable consideration to transfer an equitable interest created a constructive trust with the consequence that the writing requirement of s 23C(1)(c) did not apply because of the provisions of s 23C(2). Lord Denning expressed a view diametrically opposed to that of Lord Radcliffe. His Lordship said that an oral agreement for valuable consideration would be ineffective to dispose of an equitable interest because of the requirement of writing in s 23C(1)(c), and that nothing in s 23C(2) changed this requirement.

6.35   In *Neville v Wilson* [1997] Ch 144; [1996] 3 All ER 171, the Court of Appeal in England, when confronted with this diversity of opinion in *Oughtred v IRC*, unanimously endorsed Lord Radcliffe's view. The court, at Ch 158; All ER 182, said:

> So far as is material to the present case, what subsection (2) says is that subsection (1)(c) does not affect the creation or operation of implied or constructive trusts. Just as in *Oughtred v Inland Revenue Commissioners* … the son's oral agreement created a constructive trust in favour of the mother, so here each shareholder's oral or implied agreement created an implied or constructive trust in favour of the other shareholders. Why then should subsection (2) not apply? No convincing reason was suggested in argument and none has occurred to us since. Moreover, to deny its application in this case would be to restrict the effect of general words when no restriction is called for, and to lay the ground for fine distinctions in the future … [W]e hold that subsection (2) applies to an agreement such as we have in this case.

6.36   The decision in *Neville v Wilson* was endorsed by the Court of Appeal in New South Wales in *Baloglow v Konstanidis*, at [120]–[125], by Priestley JA (Mason P concurring) and in the High Court by Heydon J in *Halloran v Minister Administering National Parks and Wildlife Act 1974* (2006) 229 CLR 545 at 573–4; 224 ALR 79 at 100. Furthermore, the Court of Appeal in Queensland, in *Reef & Rainforest Travel Pty Ltd v Commissioner of Stamp Duties* [2002] 1 Qd R 683 at 688, referred to *Neville v Wilson*, as the basis for its conclusion that, in relation to a written agreement to assign, for consideration, 88 units in a unit trust, '[t]he result probably was, at the very least, to constitute [the seller] a constructive trustee for the 88 units for the transferee'.

6.37   If the views of Lord Radcliffe in *Oughtred v IRC* and the Court of Appeal in *Neville v Wilson* are accepted and a constructive trust arises following an oral agreement for consideration to transfer an equitable interest in personal property, the nature of the trust that arises bears further analysis. If a constructive trust arises in these circumstances, the transferor becomes the trustee of the equitable interest. In cases of constructive trusts the trustee is not involved in transferring property or interests in property. Rather, the prospective constructive trustee retains the relevant property but holds it as trustee and not absolutely. Thus, in cases of oral agreements for consideration to transfer an equitable interest in property, the transferor retains the property but continues to hold it as trustee. In such cases it can legitimately be argued that there can be no question of s 23C(1)(c) being at all relevant because there is no disposition of a subsisting equitable interest in property. However, if this approach is correct, one is left with the absurd consequence of there being no requirement of writing in relation to the creation of the constructive trust, whereas if the trustee were to subsequently assign his or her, usually valueless, equitable interest held as trustee, writing would be required pursuant to s 23C(1)(c) as this would amount to a disposition of a subsisting equitable interest.

6.38   On the other hand, it could be argued that the factual circumstances of *Oughtred v IRC* and *Neville v Wilson* do not give rise to a constructive trust of an existing equitable interest, but rather the creation of a new interest that is carved out of the subsisting equitable interest. It could be argued that the creation of such a new interest is in effect a declaration of trust with respect to relevant equitable property that is the subject of the agreement. Because a declaration of trust is within the definition of 'disposition' as used in s 23C(1)(c) (see 6.5), an agreement of the kind under discussion would need to be in writing. Section 23C(2) would not remove the writing requirement because that subsection only relates to implied and constructive trusts. The advantage of such an interpretation would be that it avoids the absurdity of the kind discussed in the previous paragraph that arises if agreements of the kind under discussion give rise to constructive trusts.

6.39   The facts of *Oughtred v IRC* dealt with an oral agreement for valuable consideration to transfer a subsisting equitable interest in personal property. If the case had concerned real property, the issues it would have raised in relation to s 23C would be the same as those that arose in *Oughtred v IRC*. This is because s 23C(1)(c) applies to both real and personal property: see 6.9. In a case concerning real property s 23C(1)(a) would also be relevant because it applies to the disposition of legal and equitable interests in land: see 6.9. However, the writing requirements in both s 23C(1)(a) and s 23C(1)(c) are for all intents and purposes identical when considered in this context. Thus, s 23C(1)(a) does not raise any issues not already raised by s 23C(1)(c).

DISPOSITIONS BY WAY OF DECLARATION OF TRUST

6.40   As already noted, a disposition includes a declaration of trust for the purposes of s 23C(1)(c): see 6.5. In *Comptroller of Stamps (Vic) v Howard-Smith* at 621–2, Dixon J observed that in a declaration of trust of an equitable interest the declarant 'retains the title to the equitable interest, but constitutes himself trustee thereof, and, by his declaration, imposes upon himself an obligation to hold it for the benefit of others, namely the donees'.

6.41   Given that a disposition includes a declaration of trust for the purposes of s 23C, it follows that 'a declaration of trust of an equitable interest or trust subsisting at the time of the declaration of trust, must be in writing' pursuant to s 23C(1)(c). Such a view flows from a natural interpretation of the subsection. However, academic opinion suggests that declarations of trust of subsisting equitable interests are not bound by the requirements of s 23C(1)(c). Meagher, Heydon and Leeming[7] suggest that s 23C(1)(c) does not apply because a declaration of trust of an equitable interest is not an outright assignment of that interest and therefore not a 'disposition' for the purposes of the subsection. A consequence of this view, as Green observes, leads to the absurd result of 'permitting [an] oral declaration of trust which shifts the valuable beneficial rights out of a subsisting equitable interest, but requiring written assignment if at a later stage the declarant decides to part with the valueless equitable interest retained by him'.[8] Such a result is avoided if a declaration of trust of personalty must be in writing.

6.42   Ong[9] suggests other reasons for supporting the view that declarations of trust of subsisting equitable interests are not bound by the requirements of s 23C(1)(c). He argues that to suggest otherwise leads to incongruous results when the subsection is read together with s 23C(1)(b), which

---

7.   R Meagher, J D Heydon and M Leeming, *Meagher, Gummow and Lehane's Equity: Doctrines and Remedies*, 4th ed, LexisNexis Butterworths, Sydney, 2002, p 304.

8.   Green, 'Grey, Oughtred and Vandervell — A Contextual Reappraisal', note 1 above, p 387.

9.   D S K Ong, *Trusts Law in Australia*, 4th ed, Federation Press, Sydney, 2012, pp 154–5.

stipulates that declarations of trust in relation to land must be evidenced in writing. First, Ong argues that if declarations of trust of subsisting equitable interests in real and personal property have to be *made* in writing pursuant to s 23C(1)(c), it is odd that a declaration of trust with respect to real property only has to be *evidenced* in writing pursuant to s 23C(1)(b). Second, Ong suggests that, because s 23C(1)(b) applies only to real property, it impliedly exempts declarations of trust of personal property from the need to be either created or evidenced in writing. To hold otherwise, he suggests, results in the incongruous position of declarations of trust over *legal* interests in personal property being outside the scope of s 23C, but declarations of trust over *equitable* interests in personal property having to comply with s 23C(1)(c). Ong states that both of the problems that he suggests arise by requiring writing for declarations of trust of subsisting equitable interests would be removed if s 23C(1)(c) is held not to apply to such declarations.

6.43　Although there is merit in Ong's arguments, they, as well as the views of Meagher, Heydon and Leeming, should be rejected, given that a 'disposition' for the purposes of s 23C(1)(c) includes a declaration of trust and further, because of the fact that s 23C(1)(c) applies to both real and personal property: see 6.9.

7

PRIORITIES

INTRODUCTION

7.1 The topic of priorities is concerned with the principles that apply to the resolution of disputes between parties who have competing interests in property. A simple illustration of such a dispute would be the situation where a landowner grants consecutive mortgages over his or her land and then defaults in making the prescribed repayments under those mortgages. If the land is subsequently sold so as to repay the mortgagees, but the sum realised on sale is insufficient to repay both of them, a priority dispute arises between the two mortgagees as to who is entitled to be paid first.

7.2 In resolving any priority dispute the first critical step is to identify the nature of the proprietary interests held by the parties to the dispute and, in particular, whether they are legal or equitable interests. Once the nature of the interest is ascertained the dispute will then fit into one of four contexts. These contexts are:

1. Competing legal interests.
2. Competing equitable interests.
3. A prior legal interest competing with a later equitable interest.
4. A prior equitable interest competing with a later legal interest.

7.3 General law rules exist that are applied to resolve the priority dispute depending upon which of these four contexts arises. In some cases these general law rules are modified by statute, especially in the context of priority disputes involving land. This chapter will first explore the general law rules and then look at significant modifications to such rules by statutory provisions involving land. However, priority issues between security interests over personal property which are determined according to the provisions of the *Personal Property Securities Act 2009* (Cth) are beyond the scope of this book.[1]

COMPETING LEGAL INTERESTS

7.4 The rule in the context of competing legal interests is that priority is given to the legal interest that is created first in time. For example, in the context of old system title land, if A creates a legal lease in favour of B and then conveys the land in fee simple to C, B's legal lease prevails over C's conveyance, with the result that C takes the fee simple in the land subject to B's lease.

---

1. For a brief discussion of priority issues in this context see N Mirzai, 'The Personal Property Securities Act 2009 — A Personal Property Torrens Register? An Analysis of the Priority Afforded to Interests Perfected by Registration' (2012) 20 *Australian Property Law Journal* 102.

7.5   In the above example the competing interests of B and C are only partially inconsistent. Where the competing interests are totally inconsistent there is an issue of whether there is a priority dispute at all. For example, if A, the owner of old system land, executes consecutive conveyances of the fee simple in the land to B and then to C, it could be said that B takes his or her interest to the total exclusion of C in accordance with the first in time rule. However, it could equally be argued that B prevails simply because C gains no interest in the property at all. This latter argument is based upon an application of the principle of *nemo dat quod non habet* (a person cannot convey an interest which he or she does not have). Pursuant to this principle, A, having already conveyed the fee simple to B, has nothing left that can be conveyed to C. The conveyance to C is thus a nullity and no priority issue arises.

COMPETING EQUITABLE INTERESTS

7.6   In *Moffett v Dillon* [1999] 2 VR 480 at 491, it was stated by Brooking JA (Buchanan JA, at 506, concurring) that the resolution of priority disputes in the context of competing equitable interests in property could be resolved by applying either of two distinct rules. The first rule is that, generally, if the holder of the second equitable interest takes with notice of the first equitable interest, he or she takes that interest subject to the first equitable interest. The second rule is that, prima facie, the equitable interest first created prevails. However, this prima facie rule can be displaced if the holder of the second equitable interest has a 'better equity'. The onus of proof in such cases is upon the holder of the second equitable interest to displace the prima facie priority of the first equitable interest holder: *Platzer v Commonwealth Bank of Australia* [1997] 1 Qd R 266 at 279.

7.7   In *Moffett v Dillon* at 504, Ormiston JA left open the question of whether there were two distinct rules that can be applied in the resolution of priority disputes between competing equitable interests as stated by Brooking JA. His Honour suggested that it may be that the question of notice is but one of the factors to be taken into account in assessing where the 'better equity' lies as between the holders of the competing equitable interests. In the discussion that follows, the approach of Brooking JA will be followed and the two rules will be separately analysed.

The notice rule

7.8   The first of the rules referred to by Brooking JA in *Moffett v Dillon* is that, generally, if the holder of the second equitable interest takes his or her interest with notice of the first equitable interest, he or she takes that interest subject to the first interest. In other words, in such circumstances the holder of the first equitable interest has priority over the second equitable interest holder.

7.9   Notice, for the purposes of this rule, includes actual or constructive notice. In *Barclay's Bank plc v O'Brien* [1994] 1 AC 180 at 195–6; [1993] 4 All ER 417 at 429, Lord Browne-Wilkinson said:

> The doctrine of notice lies at the heart of equity. Given that there are two innocent parties, each enjoying rights, the earlier right prevails against the later right if the acquirer of the later right knows of the earlier right (actual notice) or would have discovered it had he taken proper steps (constructive notice). In particular, if the party asserting that he takes free of the earlier rights of another knows of certain facts which put him on inquiry as to the possible existence of the rights of that other and he fails to make such inquiry or take such other steps as are reasonable to verify whether such earlier right does or does not exist, he will have constructive notice of the earlier right and take subject to it.

7.10   In *JNJ Investments Pty Ltd v Sunnyville Pty Ltd* [2006] QSC 138, a vendor of Torrens title land contracted to sell property to a purchaser. On the day of settlement of this contract, the vendor completed a sale of the property to a second purchaser for a higher price. The first purchaser, upon becoming aware of what had happened, lodged a caveat to prevent registration of the second purchaser's transfer. The second purchaser commenced proceedings to have the caveat removed. The issue before the court was whether the first purchaser had priority over the second purchaser. Mullins J, at [70], held that the first purchaser had priority because the second purchaser 'had notice of the first [purchaser's] equitable interest at the time of the acquisition of its interests'.

7.11   The general rule on notice is subject to exceptions. One such exception is where the holder of the first equitable interest is guilty of conduct that induces a belief on the part of the second equitable interest holder at the time the second interest is obtained that the first equitable interest no longer exists: *Moffett v Dillon* at 492. Another is where the holder of the first interest agrees to the postponement or waiver of his or her priority: *Platzer v Commonwealth Bank* at 273.

The 'better equity' rule

7.12   The second of the rules referred to by Brooking JA in *Moffett v Dillon* is that, prima facie, priority goes to the holder of the equitable interest that was first created. However, the prima facie rule can be displaced if the holder of the second equitable interest has a 'better equity' or, to put it another way, the two interests are not equal. In this context equality means 'the non-existence of any circumstance which affects the conduct of one of the rival claimants, and makes it less meritorious than that of the other': *Bailey v Barnes* [1894] 1 Ch 25 at 36. This displacement arises due to the nature of equitable doctrines being rooted in the notion of precluding unconscientious conduct: see 2.4–2.5. Thus, if it would be unconscientious for the holder of the first equitable interest to prevail over the holder of the second equitable interest, the latter prevails because he or she has the 'better equity'.

7.13   This rule is an application of the maxim 'where the equities are equal the first in time shall prevail'. The general principle of priority in the context of competing equitable interest is reflected in the Latin phrase *qui prior est tempore potior est jure* (he or she who is first in time takes precedence).

7.14   The correct formulation of this rule is a matter that has been debated in the courts. According to the formulation by Brooking JA in *Moffett v Dillon*, prima facie priority goes to the holder of the equitable interest first created with such priority only displaced if the holder of the subsequently created equitable interest has a better claim to priority on the basis that he or she has a 'better equity'. This approach is also reflected in the judgment of Gibbs CJ in *Heid v Reliance Finance Corporation Pty Ltd* (1983) 154 CLR 326 at 333; 49 ALR 229 at 233, where his Honour said:

> In the present case the interest of the appellant was first in time. The question therefore is whether his conduct … has the consequence that [the holder of the second equitable interest] has the better equity, and the appellant's interest should be postponed to that of [the holder of the second equitable interest].

7.15   The other approach to formulating the rule is to award priority to the equitable interest holder that has the 'better equity', but if the merits are equal then, as a last resort, award priority to the first in time. Thus, in *Latec Investments Ltd v Hotel Terrigal Pty Ltd* (1965) 113 CLR 265 at 276, Kitto J stated the rule as follows:

> In all cases where a claim to enforce an equitable interest in property is opposed on the ground that after the interest is said to have arisen a third party innocently acquired an equitable interest in the same property, the problem … is to determine where the better equity lies. If the merits are equal, priority in time of creation is considered to give the better equity … But where the merits are unequal, as for instance where conduct on the part of the owner of the earlier interest has led the other to acquire his interest on the assumption that the earlier did not exist the maxim [*qui prior est tempore potior est jure*] may be displaced and priority accorded to the latter interest.

Support for this approach is also found in the considered decision of the Queensland Court of Appeal in *AG(CQ) Pty Ltd v A & T Promotions* [2011] 1 Qd R 306 at 319–22 and *Barlin Investments Pty Ltd v Westpac Banking Corporation* [2012] NSWSC 699 at [31].

7.16   The difference between these competing formulations of the rule does not have any practical consequences for the resolution of individual priority cases. In all cases the result will be the same irrespective of which formulation of the rule is adopted. In each case it will be a question of whether the equities are equal. In *Heid v Reliance Finance Corporation*, Mason and Deane JJ, at CLR 341; ALR 239, observed:

> It will always be necessary to characterize the conduct of the holder of the earlier interest in order to determine whether, in all the circumstances, that conduct is such that, in fairness and in justice, the earlier interest should be postponed to the later interest.

7.17   On the question of where the 'better equity' lies, the onus of proof lies upon the holder of the later equitable interest to show that the equities are not equal and are in his or her favour, thereby justifying priority over the holder of the earlier equitable interest: *Moffett v Dillon* at 501–4. In *Rice v Rice* (1853) 61 ER 646 at 648, Kindersley V-C was of the view that, in assessing where the 'better equity' resides, a court had to have reference to the following three matters:

1. The nature and condition of the respective equitable interests.
2. The circumstances and manner of acquisition of these interests.
3. The whole conduct of the parties.

7.18   Cases since *Rice v Rice* have demonstrated that the third of the matters is the vital one. In relation to the first matter, the nature and condition of the equitable interests is only important where an interest is defined as a mere equity: see 4.39. Where a priority issue involves a mere equity and an equitable interest, the equitable interest will always prevail. This is because 'a mere equity … does not participate in competitions of priorities with equitable interests which have been acquired in good faith, for valuable consideration and in a manner which can be clearly shown without obtaining any decision of the court upholding them': *Double Bay Newspapers Pty Ltd v A W Holdings Pty Ltd* (1996) 42 NSWLR 409 at 425. This is illustrated by the facts of *Latec Investments Ltd v Hotel Terrigal Pty Ltd* (1965) 113 CLR 265: see 4.44–4.46. In that case the right of MLC was characterised as an equitable interest in property and, because its interest had that status, it prevailed over the right of Hotel Terrigal, which was characterised as a mere equity. In such circumstances Kitto J, at 278, observed that 'the maxim *qui prior est tempore* [*potior est jure*] is not applicable, for it applies only as between equitable interests'.

7.19   However, apart from cases involving mere equities, the characteristics and attributes of the relevant equitable interest have not been held to be relevant in cases of priority disputes. As was noted in Chapter 4, equitable interests in property are not uniform in terms of the attributes and qualities they possess. As long as the interests are of a proprietary nature, notwithstanding differences in their respective attributes, they will be treated as equal for the purposes of priority disputes.

7.20   As to the second matter referred to in *Rice v Rice*, the cases demonstrate that the manner and circumstances surrounding the creation of competing equitable interests are of negligible weight in resolving priority disputes. Thus, in *Moffett v Dillon* at 491 and 499–501, it was held that the holder of the second equitable interest in relation to Torrens title land did not have the 'better equity' simply because the interest was in registrable form whereas the first equitable interest holder's interest was not in registrable form.

7.21   As to the third matter referred to in *Rice v Rice*, although the conduct of both parties to a priority dispute is relevant, the major focus is on the conduct of the holder of the first equitable interest. This is because, in the absence of conduct by the holder of the first equitable interest warranting postponement of his or her equitable interest in favour of the second equitable interest, priority will go to the holder of the first equitable interest. The conduct of the holder of the second equitable interest will be relevant where there has been postponing conduct by the holder of the first equitable interest and the second interest holder has committed acts or omissions that are of equal weight or significance to the postponing conduct of the holder of the first equitable interest. In such cases the two lots of conduct effectively cancel each other out and the holder of the first equitable interest will prevail in the priority dispute because of the conduct of the holder of the second equitable interest.

7.22   One of the major forms of postponing conduct by the holder of the first equitable interest is conduct that leads the second equitable interest holder to acquire his or her interest on the supposition that the earlier equitable interest did not exist: *Latec Investments v Hotel Terrigal* at 276.

7.23   A leading illustration of such conduct is found in *Abigail v Lapin* (1934) 51 CLR 58. In this case Lapin owed money to Mr Heavener, Lapin's solicitor. As security for the loan Mr and Mrs Lapin transferred their Torrens title land to Mrs Heavener as her husband's nominee. The transfer document was in absolute form and was accompanied by the certificate of title. Mrs Heavener became registered and then executed a mortgage, which remained unregistered, in favour of Abigail as security for a loan. The issue before the court was whether Lapin's equitable interest of an equity of redemption prevailed over Abigail's subsequent equitable mortgage. The Privy Council found in Abigail's favour on the basis of the conduct by Lapin which enabled Mrs Heavener to present herself as having power to deal with the property as absolute owner. Such conduct displaced Lapin's priority according to the time of the creation of the respective equitable interests in the land.

7.24   The decision in *Abigail v Lapin* was endorsed and followed by the High Court of Australia in *Breskvar v Wall* (1971) 126 CLR 376. In this case Mr and Mrs Breskvar borrowed money from Petrie. As security for the loan they gave Petrie an executed memorandum of transfer and certificate of title in relation to their Torrens title land. The memorandum had left blank the space in which the name of the transferee would normally have been inserted. Such an incomplete transfer was void under relevant legislation in Queensland. Petrie inserted the name of his grandson, Wall, into the blank space and Wall was registered as proprietor of the land. Wall then contracted to sell the land to Alban Pty Ltd. Before any transfer to Alban was registered, the Breskvars became aware of what had happened and lodged a caveat on the title to the land protecting their interest in the property and preventing any transfer of it being registered. The caveat had to be removed for the transfer from

Wall to Alban to proceed. For the caveat to be removed, Alban's equitable interest in the land, which arose pursuant to its contract with Wall, had to have priority over the Breskvars' interest in the land based upon the right to set aside the fraudulent registration of Wall as registered proprietor. Thus, the issue before the High Court was whether Alban's later equitable interest prevailed over the earlier equitable interest of the Breskvars. The High Court unanimously decided in favour of Alban.

7.25   The first point to note about the High Court decision is that Barwick CJ, at 387–8, Windeyer J, at 399, Owen J, at 400 and Gibbs J, at 413, were prepared to consider the Breskvars' interest as an equitable interest in the property. On that basis, they ruled that the Breskvars were guilty of postponing conduct and that Alban's later interest was therefore entitled to priority. McTiernan J, at 393–4 and Menzies J, at 399 based their decisions on the Breskvars' postponing conduct, thereby implicitly treating their interest as an equitable interest in property. Walsh J, at 408–9, made no determination as to whether the Breskvars' interest was an equitable interest in the property or a mere equity. In his view, in either case Alban was entitled to succeed, either because the Breskvars were guilty of postponing conduct if they were considered to be holders of an equitable interest in the property, or because there was no priority issue between the parties if the Breskvars' interest was only a mere equity: see 7.18. On the issue of why the Breskvars were guilty of postponing conduct Barwick CJ, at 388–9, said:

> The priority of the [Breskvars] will only be lost by some conduct on the part of the [Breskvars] which must have contributed to the assumption, false as the event proved, upon which the holder of the competing equity acted when that equity was created. Here the [Breskvars] armed [Petrie] with the means of placing himself or his nominee on the register. They executed a memorandum of transfer, without inserting therein the name of a purchaser; they handed over the relevant duplicate certificate of title and they authorised [Petrie], if the occasion arose for the exercise of his powers as a mortgagee, to complete and register the memorandum of transfer … Here … it can properly be said that 'the case … becomes one of an agent exceeding the limits of his authority but acting within its apparent indicia'. The [Breskvars] therefore, lose the priority to which the prior creation of their interest in the land would otherwise have entitled them.

7.26   In a similar vein Gibbs J, at 413, said:

> The interest of the [Breskvars] was created first in point of time but the [Breskvars] have lost their priority by their conduct which had the effect of inducing Alban Pty Ltd to act to its prejudice. The [Breskvars] had armed Petrie with the power to deal with the land as owner, by entrusting him with a certificate of title and a signed memorandum of transfer in blank, and thus enabled Wall to sell to Alban Pty Ltd as owner of the land. In these circumstances … the equitable interest of the [Breskvars] is postponed to that of Alban Pty Ltd.

7.27   The decision of the High Court in *Heid v Reliance Finance Corporation* is a further illustration of postponing conduct on the part of the holder of the first equitable interest in property. In this case Heid sold Torrens title land to Connell Investments. An employee of Connell Investments did the paperwork for this transaction. Part of the proceeds of sale to be received by Heid was to be applied to a particular investment by Connell Investments on behalf of Heid. The balance of the proceeds of sale was to be secured by a mortgage over the land from Connell Investments in favour of Heid. To facilitate these arrangements Heid executed a contract for the sale of the land to Connell Investments, a memorandum of transfer and a mortgage. These documents were handed to Connell Investments. Connell Investments never invested part of the sale proceeds as it had agreed to do, nor were the transfer and mortgage in favour of Heid registered. In these circumstances Heid had two equitable interests in the land, namely, a vendor's lien in relation to the money that was not invested as instructed, and an equitable mortgage. Connell Investments borrowed money from Reliance Finance Corporation. Connell Investments executed a mortgage in favour of Reliance Finance and handed it to Reliance Finance together with the certificate of title and memorandum of transfer from Heid to Connell Investments. Reliance had the transfer registered, and lodged a caveat in relation to the mortgage. Thus, Reliance gained an equitable interest in the land. Connell Investments then executed a mortgage in favour of Alexander in relation to a loan from Alexander. Alexander lodged a caveat in relation to the mortgage. Subsequently Heid lodged a caveat in relation to his equitable mortgage. At the time Reliance Finance and Alexander made their loans to Connell Investments they had no notice of Heid's equitable interests in the land. The issue before the High Court was whether Heid's earlier equitable interests had priority over the subsequent equitable interests of Reliance Finance and Alexander. The court unanimously ruled in favour of Reliance Finance and Alexander. In relation to Heid's conduct, Mason and Deane JJ, at CLR 345; ALR 242, said:

> The delivery of the documents to the employee armed the purchaser with the capacity to represent itself to be the true owner of the property and to engage in fraudulent and deceptive conduct of the kind that took place.

7.28 In *Heid v Reliance Finance Corporation* there was a division of opinion as to the theoretical basis upon which Reliance Finance and Alexander gained priority over Heid, despite Heid's equitable interests being the first in time of creation. Gibbs CJ, at CLR 335– 6; ALR 234–5, stated that the priority principle in such cases was based upon principles of estoppel. The essential elements of estoppel are a representation upon which the representee acts to his or her detriment. The fact that no direct representation is made in priority cases by the holder of the first equitable interest is, according to his Honour, immaterial. It is sufficient that such a holder enables a third party to act as an absolute owner and that such a holder's conduct contributed to that situation arising. In such cases the holder of the first equitable interest is, according to Gibbs CJ, estopped from denying the existence of the subsequent equitable interest.

7.29 The alternative view in *Heid v Reliance Finance Corporation* on this issue was put by Mason and Deane JJ. Their Honours, at CLR 339–42; ALR 238–40, took the view that estoppel was an inadequate explanation. In particular, they disagreed with the view of Gibbs CJ to the effect that there was no need for a direct representation to be made by the holder of the first equitable interest to the holder of the second equitable interest. In their view priority was determined upon a theoretical basis that combined elements of negligence and estoppel. Their Honours, at CLR 342; ALR 239, said:

> Fairness and justice demand that we are primarily concerned with acts of a certain kind — those acts during the carrying out of which it is reasonably foreseeable that a later equitable interest will be created and that the holder of that later interest will assume the non-existence of the earlier interest.

7.30 On the facts of *Heid v Reliance Finance Corporation*, Mason and Deane JJ held that it was reasonably foreseeable that some such deception as actually took place would occur. The two crucial aspects of Heid's conduct that led to the finding against him were: (i) the issuing of an acknowledgment on the memorandum of transfer that the full sale price for the land had been paid by Connell Investments; and (ii) handing over the memorandum of transfer and certificate of title to the employee of Connell Investments.

7.31   The approach of Mason and Deane JJ in *Heid v Reliance Finance Corporation* has received the support of later cases, including *Jacobs v Platt Nominees Pty Ltd* [1990] VR 146 at 151–4, and *Elderly Citizens Homes of SA Inc v Balnaves* (1998) 72 SASR 210 at 225. Furthermore, in *Mercury Geotherm Ltd (In Receivership) v McLachlan* [2006] 1 NZLR 258 at 272, Potter J said:

> In New Zealand the postponement of the first to the second equitable interest is not based exclusively on the doctrine of estoppel, but on a general and flexible principle that preference should be given to what is the better equity in an examination of the relevant circumstances. The question involves general considerations of fairness and justice.

The special position of beneficiaries under trusts

7.32   In cases where the holder of the first equitable interest has the interest of a beneficiary under a trust, the priority rules are differently applied. In essence, a beneficiary's interest under a trust is not postponed because of the *trustee's* abuse of his or her position as trustee: *Shropshire Union Railways and Canal Company v R* (1875) LR 7 HL 496. If the later equitable interest holder obtains his or her interest as the result of some conduct by the *beneficiary* that allows the later interest to arise in the belief that the beneficiary's interest does not exist, the interest of the beneficiary will be postponed to that of the second interest holder: *Shropshire* at 509–10, 513 and 514.

7.33   *Shropshire* is a leading illustration of these principles. In that case Holyoake, as trustee of shares for Shropshire, held all title documents relating to the shares. In breach of trust Holyoake borrowed from Robson and gave Robson the share certificate as security for the loan. Robson held the shares but did not have them registered into his name on the company register. The issue before the court was whether Shropshire's earlier equitable interest as beneficiary under the trust of the shares was defeated by Robson's later equitable mortgage over the shares. The House of Lords ruled that Shropshire's earlier equitable interest had priority. Holyoake's conduct was of the type that results in the holder of the first equitable interest being defeated in priority disputes in cases such as *Abigail v Lapin* (see 7.23) and *Heid v Reliance Finance Corporation*: see 7.27–7.30. However, the critical distinction here is that the conduct in question in *Shropshire* was not that of the holder of the first equitable interest in property, as in *Abigail v Lapin* and *Heid v Reliance Finance Corporation*, but the holder of the legal interest in that property. It was pointed out in *Shropshire* at 512–13, that Holyoake, as trustee, was the proper person to have possession of title documents to trust property and that, accordingly, it was up to Robson to satisfy himself that Holyoake was not a trustee. The underlying rationale for the rule in relation to beneficiaries under a trust is that, were it otherwise, the efficacy and utility of trusts as an institution would be severely curtailed: *Shropshire* at 507–8.

7.34   The principles in *Shropshire* do not apply if the later equitable interest is obtained in circumstances where the trustee of the beneficiary's equitable interest neglects to obtain title documents to the property and, as a result, subsequent equitable interests are created. In such circumstances, the beneficiary's interest will be no better than that of the trustee in any priority dispute, and the holder of the subsequent equitable interest will have priority over the trustee's legal interest. If the holder of the subsequent equitable interest has priority over that of the trustee, the holder of the subsequent equitable interest will also have priority over the beneficiary's earlier equitable interest.

7.35 The rationale for this proposition was explained in *Walker v Linom* [1907] 2 Ch 104 at 118–19, by Parker J, who said:

> I have to ask myself … whether … there is any real ground for drawing a distinction between the wrongful conduct of trustees in relation to title deeds in their possession as trustees and the wrongful conduct in relation to title deeds which as a fact never came into their possession, and are therefore never held by them upon trust at all. In my opinion there is such a real ground of distinction. In the former case the trustees hold the deeds for their [beneficiaries], and are bound to deal with them in accordance with the trusts upon which they are held. In the latter case the trustees never held the deeds for their [beneficiaries], and their breach of duty lies in not obtaining them. In the former case the trusteeship, so far as the deeds are concerned, is complete, and the deeds cannot be dealt with improperly if the trustees do their duty, and the [beneficiaries] may fairly assume that they will do their duty. In the latter case the trusteeship, so far as the deeds are concerned, is incomplete, and the person who retains them is in a position to deal with them without reference to the trustees, so that the [beneficiaries] have no one on whose possession of the deeds they are entitled to rely as standing between them and the perpetration of a fraud.

7.36 In *Walker v Linom*, Walker created an equitable interest in certain property he owned in favour of his wife pursuant to a marriage settlement. The trustees of the marriage settlement failed to get title documents to that property from Walker who was therefore able to hold himself out as being the absolute owner of the property. Walker subsequently mortgaged the property and defaulted under the mortgage. The mortgagee, in exercise of its power of sale under the mortgage, sold the property to Linom. Neither the mortgagee nor Linom had any notice of Mrs Walker's equitable interest. Linom's equitable interest as purchaser of the property had priority over both the trustee's legal interest and Mrs Walker's equitable interest as beneficiary under the trust.

The exception to the 'better equity' rule in Dearle v Hall

7.37 A significant exception to the 'better equity' rule relates to competing interests in personalty pursuant to the rule in *Dearle v Hall* (1828) 38 ER 475. In accordance with the rule, if there are competing assignees of personalty, priority is granted to the later assignee if:

1. The assignment was for valuable consideration.
2. The assignee took the assignment without notice of the earlier assignment at the time of giving consideration.
3. The assignee was the first to give notice of the assignment to the trustee, debtor or fundholder as the case may be.

7.38 The basis of the rule is that, by failing to give notice first, the first assignee has left the assignor in apparent possession of the interest and has enabled the assignor to make the subsequent assignment. The result is that the first assignee has facilitated the commission of a fraud upon the second assignee and, accordingly, it is only fair that the second assignee have priority over the first assignee.

7.39 The rule in *Dearle v Hall* is strictly applied and the assignee who gives notice first is guaranteed priority even if the other assignee is not at fault in terms of giving notice. This is forcefully illustrated by the decision in *Re Dallas* [1904] 2 Ch 385, where Dallas was the appointed executor and beneficiary of a legacy under his father's will. Prior to his father's death Dallas assigned his expectancy by way of security for certain loans, first from Stuart and then from Brooks. Following his father's death Dallas renounced probate and his sister, Beedell, applied successfully for letters of administration in relation to her deceased father's estate. The day after the grant of letters of administration to Beedell, Brooks gave her notice of his assignment. Six days later Stuart became aware for the first time that Beedell had been granted letters of administration. Stuart gave notice of his assignment to her the following day. The Court of Appeal held that Brooks had the prior claim to the legacy because he had given notice of his assignment to Beedell first. This was so despite the facts that Stuart had given notice as soon as he discovered that Beedell had been granted letters of administration, and Stuart's failure to give notice earlier in no way contributed to the creation of Brooks' equitable interest that arose pursuant to the second assignment from Dallas.

7.40   Vaughan Williams LJ, at 414, affirmed that the operation of the rule in *Dearle v Hall* was in no way dependent upon any assessment of the conduct of the assignees. Furthermore, his Lordship, at 410–13, pointed out that the earliest that notice could have been given by either of the assignees was from the date Beedell was granted letters of administration because notice could only be given when: (i) the expectancy came into existence; and (ii) there was a person in proper control of the property to whom notice could be given. The first condition was met with the death of the testator. The second condition was satisfied with the grant of letters of administration to Beedell. The judgments of the other two members of the Court of Appeal were of similar effect.

7.41   It can be noted that in *Re Dallas*, if Beedell had been the appointed executrix in the testator's will, notice could have been given to her immediately following the testator's death. This is because, as executrix, Beedell would have been authorised to deal with estate property as from the date of death and would not have had to wait until probate was granted. However, this point does not resolve the notice rule where an executor appointed by the will renounces the position but is given notice in the period before so renouncing. In *Re Dallas*, Stirling LJ, at 417, and Cozens-Hardy LJ, at 418, while not expressing a considered opinion on the issue, indicated that such notice would be ineffective for the purposes of the rule in *Dearle v Hall*. On the other hand, if the renouncing executor was also to be the assignor, as was the case in *Re Dallas*, notice to such an executor would in all cases be ineffective.

7.42   In relation to the rule in *Dearle v Hall* the following points can be made:

1. The second assignee will not gain priority under the rule, even if he or she gives notice first, unless he or she gives valuable consideration for the assignment. The rationale for this requirement is that if the second assignee is a volunteer he or she cannot be said to be defrauded by the first assignee being given priority. Nevertheless, the second assignee should give notice because, for the reason noted in point 2 below, such notice would protect the second assignee against a subsequent and third assignee, even if the third assignee gave valuable consideration for the assignment.
2. The first assignee does not need to give valuable consideration for his or her assignment. If the first assignee gives notice first, he or she will have priority over the second assignee even if the second assignee gave valuable consideration for the assignment.
3. The rule applies to personalty only, but for the purposes of the rule personalty includes realty, which is notionally treated as personalty pursuant to the doctrine of conversion: *Gresham Life Assurance Society v Crowther* [1915] 1 Ch 214.
4. The rule applies to equitable assignments of equitable interests and legal interests in personalty: *Marchant v Morton Downs & Co* [1901] 2 KB 829. If s 12 of the *Conveyancing Act 1919* (NSW) and its equivalent provisions in other Australian jurisdictions apply to the assignment of equitable choses in action (see 5.57–5.61), presumably the rule in *Dearle v Hall* applies where

one of the competing assignees gains their equitable interest pursuant to an assignment of an equitable chose in action in accordance with the provisions of s 12.

5. Notice has to be given to the trustee, debtor or other fundholder as the case may be. The person to whom notice is given is the person from whom the assignor was, before the assignment, and the assignee is, after the assignment, entitled to expect performance, of the legal or equitable obligation that has been the subject of the assignment. Notice to one of a number of trustees is effective even if that trustee does not communicate the fact of notice to his or her co-trustees. Such notice will enable the relevant assignee to assert priority over the assignee who later gives notice to all the trustees. This rule applies even if the trustee who received the first notice dies or retires as trustee without having communicated the fact of notice to his or her co-trustees: *Ward v Duncombe* [1893] AC 369.

6. Notice need not take any special form and may be oral: *Re Dallas* [1904] 2 Ch 385 at 399. If both assignees give notice on the same day, they are regarded as having given notice simultaneously, in which case the first assignee will gain priority: *Re Dallas* at 395. However, notice is not required to perfect the equitable assignee's title. Notice is not part of the equitable assignment: *Ward v Duncombe* at 392.

7. The rule only applies to competing equitable *assignees*. It thus follows that it would not apply as between a person who has equitable tracing rights and an equitable assignee.[2]

8. For the rule to apply, the *assignor* must *beneficially* own the personal property that is assigned: *B S Lyle v Rosher* [1958] 3 All ER 597. According to the reasoning of the majority in *Lyle v Rosher*, the rule in *Dearle v Hall* cannot be used to resolve a priority dispute between competing equitable assignees of personal property who gained their interests pursuant to assignments from the trustee where the assignor is the trustee. This is because the assignor has no beneficial interest at the time of the assignment. Indeed, it would appear that this reasoning applies if it is only at the time of the *second* assignment that the assignor has no beneficial interest in the property assigned: *Lyle v Rosher* at 602. The ruling in *Lyle v Rosher* has been criticised by Meagher, Heydon and Leeming on two grounds. First, they point to contrary earlier authority involving the application of the rule in *Dearle v Hall* to cases where the assignor has either never, or at the time of the second assignment, had a beneficial interest in the property assigned. Second, they point to the fact that a priority dispute between competing equitable assignees of future personal property is subject to the rule in *Dearle v Hall*, as is demonstrated by *Re Dallas*: see 7.39–7.40. However, at the time of the equitable assignment of future property there can be no beneficial interest in the assignor because in so far as the assignor is concerned, the property has not yet come into existence.[3]

COMPETING PRIOR LEGAL AND LATER EQUITABLE INTERESTS

7.43   In a priority dispute between the holder of an earlier legal interest and the holder of a later equitable interest, the general rule is that the holder of the earlier legal interest will have priority. This general rule is subject to four exceptions, all of them relating to circumstances in which the holder of the later equitable interest obtains priority because of the conduct of the earlier legal interest

---

2. D W McLauchlan, 'Priorities — Equitable Tracing Rights and Assignment of Book Debts' (1980) 96 *Law Quarterly Review* 90, pp 95–8.

3. R Meagher, J D Heydon & M Leeming, *Meagher, Gummow and Lehane's Equity: Doctrines and Remedies*, 4th ed, LexisNexis Butterworths, Sydney, 2002, pp 333–4.

holder. The first two exceptions examined below are based upon the principle that the holder of the later equitable interest is an innocent person who is entitled, in the circumstances, to priority over the holder of the earlier legal interest. It is also arguable that these two exceptions are based upon principles of estoppel. The third and fourth exceptions examined below are clearly applications of principles of estoppel.

7.44   The first exception relates to circumstances where the earlier legal interest holder has been a party to fraud that leads to the creation of the later equitable interest. In *Northern Counties of England Fire Insurance Company v Whipp* (1884) 26 Ch D 482, Crabtree gave a legal mortgage of old system title land to Northern Counties. Crabtree was the manager of that company and was also entrusted with a key to a safe that housed the documents of title relating to the mortgage. Crabtree removed the title documents from the safe and executed a second mortgage to Whipp. Because of the earlier legal mortgage, the only property interest that Crabtree had in relation to the land at the time of the mortgage to Whipp was an equity of redemption. Thus, the mortgage to Whipp could only be an equitable mortgage. In a priority dispute between Northern Counties and Whipp it was argued that Northern Counties' legal interest should be postponed on the ground of fraud. Fry LJ, at 494–5, speaking on behalf of the Court of Appeal, ruled that there was no fraud on the part of Northern Counties because Northern Counties 'never combined with Crabtree to induce [Whipp] to lend her money'. His Lordship said that fraud would arise 'where the owner of the legal estate has assisted in or connived at the fraud which has led to the creation of a subsequent equitable interest, without notice of the prior legal interest'. Fry LJ, at 490, also pointed out that it was irrelevant if the fraudulent purpose that was achieved was not the one intended and if the intended victim of the fraud differed from the actual victim.

7.45   The second exception to the general principle that the holder of a prior legal interest has priority over the holder of a later equitable interest is where the holder of the legal estate fails to obtain or retain possession of the title documents, thereby enabling another person to hold himself or herself out as the legal owner of the property. In such cases it would be inequitable for the holder of the legal interest to have priority over the holder of a subsequently created equitable interest. It was on this basis that Linom gained priority over the trustee in *Walker v Linom*: see 7.36. Mere carelessness on the part of the holder of the legal interest is not enough to constitute postponing conduct: *Evans v Bickell* (1801) 31 ER 908 at 1005–6. 'Gross negligence' in the sense of a special degree of lack of care or prudence is needed for this exception to arise.

7.46   The third exception to the general principle that the holder of a prior legal interest has priority over the holder of a later equitable interest is where the legal interest holder has entrusted title documents to an agent for the limited purpose of raising money and the agent, acting in excess of his or her authority, fraudulently creates a security for a larger sum in favour of a person who is unaware of the agent's limited authority. Thus, in *Brocklesby v Temperance Permanent Building Society* [1895] AC 175, a father authorised his son to raise a loan on the security of certain property in the sum of £2250. The son actually raised £3500. The father was held liable for the full amount raised by the son.

7.47   The final exception to the general principle that the holder of a prior legal interest has priority over the holder of a later equitable interest is where the holder of the legal interest, although not parting with title documents, gives another person a document that confers upon that person an equitable interest or a right to acquire a legal interest. Thus, in *Barry v Heider* (1914) 19 CLR 197, Barry executed a transfer of Torrens title land to Schmidt. The transfer could not be registered because the Land Titles Office was in the process of issuing a new certificate of title covering the land that was the subject of the transfer. Barry authorised the Land Titles Office to issue the new certificate of title to Schmidt. Schmidt mortgaged the land to Heider. Before either the transfer to Schmidt or the mortgage to Heider were registered, Barry sought an injunction to restrain the registration of the transfer to Schmidt on the grounds that it was executed due to fraud. Barry also sought a declaration that the land was free from the mortgage. The High Court upheld Barry's claim in relation to the transfer to Schmidt. However, Heider's equitable mortgage had priority over Barry's legal title because Barry had enabled Schmidt to represent himself as having a good title and was thus able to mortgage the property to Heider.

COMPETING PRIOR EQUITABLE AND LATER LEGAL INTERESTS

7.48   The rule in the context of a holder of a prior equitable interest competing with the holder of a later legal interest is that the latter will prevail only if the legal interest is acquired for valuable consideration, in good faith (bona fide) and without notice of the earlier equitable interest: *Pilcher v Rawlins* (1872) LR 7 Ch 259 at 268. The bona fide purchaser is in a superior position because, in the memorable words of Maitland, '[e]quity cannot touch him, because, to use the old phrase, his conscience is unaffected [by the earlier equitable interest]'.[4] If the acquisition of the legal estate is not in accordance with the rule, the purchaser of the legal interest will take that interest subject to the earlier equitable interest. The rule is an application of the maxim 'where there is equal equity the law shall prevail'. The purchaser of the legal estate bears the onus of proof in relation to the three elements of the rule: *Attorney-General v Biphosphated Guano Company* (1879) 11 Ch D 327 at 337.

7.49   Before examining the three elements of the rule, the one exception to the rule must be noted. Pursuant to s 12 of the *Conveyancing Act 1919* (NSW) and its equivalent provisions in other Australian jurisdictions (see 5.49–5.56), an assignment under the section is 'subject to all equities which would have been entitled to priority over the right of the assignee if this Act had not passed'. This means that an assignment complying with s 12 is, for priority purposes, viewed as an equitable assignment and thus, any priority dispute between an assignee pursuant to s 12 and the holder of an earlier equitable interest in the property will be determined by the rules that apply as to competing equitable interests: *Lawrence v Hayes* [1927] 2 KB 111 at 120–1. The word 'equities', as used in s 12, is broadly interpreted: *Re Harry Simpson and Co Pty Ltd v The Companies Act* (1964) 81 WN (NSW) 207 at 209. It includes an equitable set-off that could have been asserted against the assignor: *Muscat v Smith* [2003] 1 WLR 2853. It also extends to cross-claims and counter-claims that can be established against the assignor: *Franks v Equitiloan Securities Pty Ltd* [2007] NSWSC 812.

Valuable consideration

7.50   For the holder of the legal interest to prevail over the holder of an earlier equitable interest, the former must have given valuable consideration. Nominal consideration will not suffice. However, the consideration need not equal the full value of the property: *Bassett v Nosworthy* (1673) 23 ER 55 at 56. This element is a reflection of the maxim that 'equity will not assist a volunteer': see 2.34–2.42.

---

4.   F W Maitland, *Equity and the Forms of Action at Common Law*, Cambridge University Press, Cambridge, 1929, p 119.

Good faith

7.51   In addition to the requirement of valuable consideration, the holder of the legal interest must have obtained it in good faith (bona fide). By this it is meant that he or she cannot have acted unconscientiously in acquiring the legal interest. In many cases the lack of good faith is established by the purchaser of the legal estate acquiring the legal estate with notice of an earlier equitable interest. However, this requirement is distinct from the requirement as to notice, and a purchaser of the legal estate for valuable consideration and without notice of an earlier equitable interest will still need to establish the element of good faith to gain priority over the holder of the earlier equitable interest: *Midland Bank Trust Co Ltd v Green* [1981] AC 513 at 528; [1981] 1 All ER 153 at 157; *Pilcher v Rawlins* at 269.

Notice

7.52   The requirement that the holder of the legal interest acquires it without notice of the existence of any earlier equitable interest is the most significant issue in relation to the rule. The relevant time at which there must be no notice is the time the purchaser furnishes consideration. If the lack of notice continues until the acquisition of the legal interest takes place, the purchaser will gain priority even if the legal interest was purchased from a trustee who sold the property in breach of trust: *Pilcher v Rawlins* at 267.

7.53   If the purchaser of the legal interest acquires notice after furnishing consideration but before acquiring the legal interest, then the question of priority will depend upon whether the earlier equitable interest was that of a beneficiary under a trust. If the earlier equitable interest is that of a beneficiary under a trust, the purchaser of the later legal interest will not prevail over the beneficiary under the trust because in equity one cannot improve one's position by acquiring property where the acquisition is known to involve a breach of trust. However, in all other cases where the purchaser of the legal interest receives notice of an earlier equitable interest after furnishing consideration, he or she will have priority over that equitable interest notwithstanding that such notice was received before actually acquiring the legal interest: *Pilcher v Rawlins* at 267–8.

7.54   In cases where a purchaser of the legal interest complies with the bona fide purchaser rule set out above (see 7.48) and then resells the property to a second purchaser who has notice of the earlier equitable interest, the second purchaser has priority over the holder of the earlier equitable interest, despite the fact that the second purchaser had notice of that interest. In *Wilkes v Spooner* [1911] 2 KB 473 at 487, Farwell LJ gave the rationale for this result when he said:

> [I]n justice to the owner of the land who had no notice when he acquired the land, it would not be right to hamper his power of dealing with his own land, because certain persons, who possibly would be the only customers for the land likely to pay the best price, have such notice.

7.55   The principle in *Wilkes v Spooner* does not apply in circumstances where a trustee in breach of trust or some other fraudulent purpose, having sold the property to a purchaser taking the legal interest in good faith, for valuable consideration and without notice of the trust, then reacquires the property from that purchaser. In such circumstances the trustee cannot take advantage of his or her wrongdoing by reacquiring from the person to whom he or she has previously sold the property.

7.56   Notice for the purposes of the rule means actual, constructive or imputed notice. These forms of notice at common law are now set out in statutory provisions in all Australian states with the exception of Western Australia.[5]

7.57   Actual notice means actual knowledge of the existence of the earlier equitable interest. The source of the notice needs to be someone with an interest in the property. A purchaser does not have actual notice based upon statements by persons who have no interest in the property.

7.58   Constructive notice means knowledge of the existence of the earlier equitable interest that would have come to a person's attention had that person made inquiries that a reasonably prudent person would have made in the circumstances: *Barclay's Bank v O'Brien* at AC 195–6; All ER 429. A person with actual knowledge of a document that affects title to land has constructive knowledge of its contents: *Cosser v Collinge* (1832) 40 ER 108.

7.59   In the context of old system title land, a purchaser acquiring the legal interest in the land has constructive knowledge of any equitable interest that would be discovered by a search of the register: *Mills v Renwick* (1901) 1 SR (Eq) 173. However, in New South Wales, Victoria, Queensland and Tasmania, legislative provisions stipulate that constructive notice does not extend to equitable interests that would have been discovered by a search of the register that goes back in time beyond a good root of title that is at least 30 years old, except in Tasmania where the time period is 20 years.[6] Similarly, a purchaser of old system title land has constructive notice of equitable interests in the land that would be revealed by a physical inspection of the land. Thus, if an inspection of the property would have revealed that someone other than the vendor of the land was in occupation of the land and further inquiry would have revealed that the occupier had an equitable lease over the land, the purchaser of the legal interest will have constructive notice of the equitable interest and thus take the legal interest subject to the earlier equitable lease: *Marsden v Campbell* (1897) 18 LR (NSW) (Eq) 33.

7.60   Imputed notice is actual or constructive notice that an agent of the purchaser has received or should have received. The purchaser is bound by the agent's notice. In many cases the agent is a solicitor acting on behalf of the purchaser. Under the general law imputed notice extends, in some cases, to all matters known by the agent whether or not they have come to the attention of the agent in the course of his or her agency with the purchaser: *Hargreaves v Rothwell* (1836) 48 ER 265 at 267–8. In all states except Western Australia, legislative provisions make it clear that the doctrine of imputed notice extends only to an agent's actual or constructive knowledge acquired in the course of the agency with the purchaser.[7]

PRIORITIES AND OLD SYSTEM TITLE LAND

7.61   In the context of priority disputes involving old system title land, the general law principles are often not applicable because of the operation of legislation relating to the registration of

---

5.   *Conveyancing Act 1919* (NSW) s 164; *Property Law Act 1974* (Qld) s 256; *Law of Property Act 1936* (SA) s 117; *Conveyancing and Law of Property Act 1884* (Tas) s 5; *Property Law Act 1958* (Vic) s 199.

6.   *Conveyancing Act 1919* (NSW) s 53(3); *Property Law Act 1974* (Qld) s 256; *Conveyancing and Law of Property Act 1884* (Tas) s 35(5); *Property Law Act 1958* (Vic) s 44(6).

7.   *Conveyancing Act 1919* (NSW) s 164(1)(b); *Property Law Act 1974* (Qld) s 256(1)(b); *Law of Property Act 1936* (SA) s 117(1)(b); *Conveyancing and Law of Property Act 1884* (Tas) s 5(1)(b); *Property Law Act 1958* (Vic) s 199(1)(b).

instruments by which persons acquire interests in the land. In the Australian Capital Territory and the Northern Territory this issue does not arise because there is no old system title land in either territory. In Australia's six states steps are being undertaken to have old system land converted to Torrens title so that eventually old system title land will be eliminated completely in Australia. Indeed, in Queensland and South Australia the process is almost complete. These two states have legislative provisions dealing with registration of instruments relating to old system title land that affect priority disputes.[8] However, because of the virtual elimination of old system title land in Queensland and South Australia, their provisions will not be analysed. The discussion here will focus on the relevant statutory provisions in New South Wales, Victoria, Tasmania and Western Australia.

New South Wales, Victoria and Tasmania

7.62   The central proposition in the relevant statutory provisions in New South Wales, Victoria and Tasmania is that priority between holders of competing interests in old system title land goes to the interest holder who registers his or her interest first.[9] For an interest holder to gain priority by registering his or her interest first, the interest must have been acquired in good faith (bona fide) and for valuable consideration.

7.63   Before examining the requirements of valuable consideration and good faith, two important points need to be noted as to the operation of these statutory provisions. First, they only apply if the priority dispute relates to competing interests created by instruments. Thus, if the competing interests are equitable mortgages, one of which is created by a written instrument and the other is created by deposit of title documents with the mortgagee, registration of the written instrument will not give its holder priority. Rather, priority will be determined according to the relevant general law rules as to competing equitable interests.

7.64   Second, the legislative provisions do not differentiate between legal and equitable interests. Irrespective of whether the competing interests are legal or equitable, priority will go to the holder of the interest first registered: *Darbyshire v Darbyshire* (1905) 2 CLR 787 at 800–2, 813–17 and 820–2.

Good faith

7.65   To claim priority by registration, the instrument under which the interest arises must have been executed in good faith (bona fide). The requirement of good faith must be on the part of the person taking under the instrument even though he or she may not have actually executed the instrument. Thus, in a deed of conveyance it is only the vendor that usually executes it whereas it will be the purchaser who seeks priority by registering the instrument. In New South Wales and Tasmania the legislation explicitly states that bad faith on the part of the party from whom an interest is taken will not deprive the party taking the interest from priority based upon registration of the instrument.[10] The onus of proving good faith is upon the person asserting priority based upon registration of his or her instrument: *Jones v Collins* (1891) 12 LR (NSW) L 247 at 250.

---

8.   *Property Law Act 1974* (Qld) s 246; *Registration of Deeds Act 1935* (SA).
9.   *Conveyancing Act 1919* (NSW) s 184G; *Registration of Deeds Act 1935* (Tas) s 9; *Property Law Act 1958* (Vic) s 6.
10.   *Conveyancing Act 1919* (NSW) s 184G(2); *Registration of Deeds Act 1935* (Tas) s 9(2).

7.66   The most significant example of a lack of good faith for the purposes of the legislation is where a person takes an interest with notice of a prior interest in the land. Notice includes actual, constructive or imputed notice.[11] The meaning of these forms of notice is discussed at 7.56–7.60.

7.67   The crucial issue concerning notice relates to the question of timing. Notice received before the *execution* of the instrument upon which priority by registration is based precludes priority based upon registration of that instrument: *Scholes v Blunt* (1917) 17 SR (NSW) 36. Notice received after execution of the instrument but before its registration does not preclude priority based upon registration of that instrument: *Burrows v Crimp* (1887) LR (NSW) L 198 at 210.

Valuable consideration

7.68   For priority to be gained by registration the interest in the instrument must be acquired for valuable consideration: see 2.38–2.39. Thus, in *Bullen v a'Beckett* (1863) 15 ER 684, a conveyance for 10 shillings was held to be for nominal consideration and thus not entitled to the benefits of the legislation.

7.69   An interest acquired for no, or only nominal, consideration should nevertheless be registered because such registration will preserve the interest holder's priority against interests in the land created after registration. For example, if A acquires an interest in land for nominal consideration and registers it, he or she will not be able to claim priority by registration. However, if after A's registration B, for valuable consideration, acquires an interest in the same land, B will not be able to assert priority over A by registering his or her interest. This is because B's interest will have been acquired with notice of A's interest and thus B will have failed to satisfy the legislative requirement of good faith: see 7.65–7.67. Any priority dispute between A and B will therefore be determined by the general law rules relating to priority disputes.

Western Australia

7.70   In Western Australia, s 3 of the *Registration of Deeds Act 1856* (WA) states that instruments relating to old system title land have priority according to the date of registration. However, the section has no requirements as to good faith and valuable consideration in the acquisition of interests. Furthermore, the section declares 'absolutely null and void' any unregistered interest as against any later registered interest, provided that the later interest was acquired in good faith (bona fide) and for valuable consideration. This part of the section makes no requirement that the later interest acquired in good faith and for valuable consideration has to be registered. Thus, if A acquires an interest in the land and does not proceed to registration, and then B acquires an interest in the land in good faith and for valuable consideration, A's interest is null and void as against B's interest, even though B has not registered his or her instrument. However, B should register his or her instrument, because if C acquires an interest in the land and registers the instrument by which that interest was acquired, C will have priority over B, even if C's interest was not acquired in good faith and for valuable consideration. To avoid this result B must register his or her instrument before C registers his or her instrument.

---

11. *Conveyancing Act 1919* (NSW) s 164; *Conveyancing and Law of Property Act 1884* (Tas) s 5; *Property Law Act 1958* (Vic) s 199.

PRIORITIES AND TORRENS TITLE LAND

7.71   In *Breskvar v Wall* at 381, Barwick CJ said that 'the Torrens system … is not a system of registration of title but a system of title by registration'. This statement confirms that, in the context of Torrens title land, the question of priorities is properly couched in the terminology of registered and unregistered interests. This is a consequence of the fact that Torrens title legislation throughout Australia stipulates that no interest in Torrens title land is acquired until registration of the instrument by which such an interest is acquired.[12] The practical significance of registration is 'to provide third parties with the information necessary to comprehend the extent or state of the registered title to the land in question': *Westfield Management Ltd v Perpetual Trustee Co Ltd* (2007) 233 CLR 528 at 531; 239 ALR 75 at 77.

7.72   It is common, as a matter of convenience, to refer to registered and unregistered interests under the Torrens system as legal and equitable interests respectively. However, in *Halloran v Minister Administering National Parks and Wildlife Act 1974* (2006) 229 CLR 545 at 559–60; 224 ALR 79 at 88, Gleeson CJ, Gummow, Kirby and Hayne JJ made the following apt observation:

> With respect to the land registered under the provisions of [the Torrens system], references to vesting at law and vesting in equity are apt to mislead. The Torrens system is one of title by registration, not of registered title. The assimilation of the registered title to a legal title may be convenient so long as it is appreciated what is involved. It is likewise with respect to the use of the term 'equitable' to describe interests recognised in accordance with the principles of equity but not found on the Register.

7.73   Any priority dispute in the context of Torrens title land will fall into one of the following three contexts:

1.   Competing registered interests.
2.   A registered interest competing with an unregistered interest.
3.   Competing unregistered interests.

Competing registered interests

7.74   Torrens title legislation in all Australian jurisdictions stipulates that upon registration of an interest, the registered proprietor of that interest acquires it subject to interests previously registered on the folio of the register for the land in question.[13] The consequence of these provisions is that, in all Australian jurisdictions except Queensland and Tasmania, priority between holders of competing registered interests in land goes to the holder whose interest was registered first, irrespective of when the competing interests were created.[14] In Queensland and Tasmania provisions to this effect[15]

---

12.   *Land Titles Act 1925* (ACT) s 57(1); *Real Property Act 1900* (NSW) s 41; *Land Title Act 2000* (NT) s 184; *Land Title Act 1994* (Qld) s 181; *Real Property Act 1886* (SA) s 67; *Land Titles Act 1980* (Tas) s 49(1); *Transfer of Land Act 1958* (Vic) s 40(1); *Transfer of Land Act 1893* (WA) s 58.

13.   *Land Titles Act 1925* (ACT) s 58(1); *Real Property Act 1900* (NSW) s 42(1); *Land Title Act 2000* (NT) s 188(1); *Land Title Act 1994* (Qld) s 184(1); *Real Property Act 1886* (SA) s 69; *Land Titles Act 1980* (Tas) s 40(1); *Transfer of Land Act 1958* (Vic) s 42; *Transfer of Land Act 1893* (WA) s 68(2)(a).

14.   *Land Titles Act 1925* (ACT) s 48(6); *Real Property Act 1900* (NSW) s 36(9); *Land Title Act 2000* (NT) s 181; *Real Property Act 1886* (SA) s 56(1); *Transfer of Land Act 1958* (Vic) s 34(1); *Transfer of Land Act 1893* (WA) s 53.

15.   *Land Title Act 1994* (Qld) s 178(1); *Land Titles Act 1980* (Tas) s 48(5).

are qualified by others dealing with, in Queensland, settlement notices,[16] and in Tasmania, priority notices.[17] These provisions enable the purchaser of an interest in land to lodge a notice on the title to the relevant land. The notice has the effect of giving the purchaser priority against any other interest that has been lodged for registration between the date that the purchaser lodged the notice and the date that he or she lodges the instrument for registration of the interest being purchased. The benefit of these notice provisions is confined to a maximum of two months in Queensland and 60 days in Tasmania after the date on which the notice is lodged. Thereafter, priority is accorded to the person whose interest is first registered.

Competing registered and unregistered interests

7.75   The effect of registration of an interest in Torrens title land is to give the registered proprietor an indefeasible title to that interest. The expression 'indefeasible title' means that the registered proprietor's interest is held free of any other interest not registered on the folio of the register for the land in question: *Frazer v Walker* [1967] 1 AC 569 at 580–1; [1967] 1 All ER 649 at 652. Torrens title legislation in all Australian jurisdictions confirms that upon registration the registered proprietor acquires his or her interest free of unregistered interests.[18] This is so even if the registered proprietor, prior to registration, has notice of such unregistered interests.[19]

7.76   However, the concept of indefeasible title is not absolute. Exceptions to indefeasibility exist in all Australian jurisdictions. Where there is an exception to indefeasibility the effect is that the registered proprietor acquires his or her interest subject to the unregistered interest that arises pursuant to the relevant exception. The effect of the exceptions to indefeasibility is to confer priority to holders of unregistered interests over the holders of registered interests in Torrens title land.

7.77   The majority of exceptions to indefeasibility are created by statute, the most important of which is fraud by the registered proprietor in obtaining registration of his or her interest.[20] In addition to statutory exceptions there exists the so-called '*in personam* exception' to indefeasibility.

Fraud

7.78   The essence of the fraud exception is that the fraud must relate to the circumstances in which the registered proprietor obtained his or her registered interest: *Breskvar v Wall* at 384. The fraud must relate to the current state of the title. Fraud by predecessors in title will not affect the current registered proprietor.

---

16. *Land Title Act 1994* (Qld) ss 138–152.
17. *Land Titles Act 1980* (Tas) s 52.
18. *Land Titles Act 1925* (ACT) s 58(1); *Real Property Act 1900* (NSW) s 42(1); *Land Title Act 2000* (NT) s 188(1); *Land Title Act 1994* (Qld) s 184(1); *Real Property Act 1886* (SA) s 70; *Land Titles Act 1980* (Tas) s 40(2); *Transfer of Land Act 1958* (Vic) s 42; *Transfer of Land Act 1893* (WA) s 68(1).
19. *Land Titles Act 1925* (ACT) s 59; *Real Property Act 1900* (NSW) s 43; *Land Title Act 2000* (NT) s 188(2); *Land Title Act 1994* (Qld) s 184(2); *Real Property Act 1886* (SA) s 72; *Land Titles Act 1980* (Tas) s 41; *Transfer of Land Act 1958* (Vic) s 43; *Transfer of Land Act 1893* (WA) s 134.
20. *Land Titles Act 1925* (ACT) s 58(1); *Real Property Act 1900* (NSW) s 42(1); *Land Title Act 2000* (NT) s 188(3)(b); *Land Title Act 1994* (Qld) s 184(3); *Real Property Act 1886* (SA) s 69; *Land Titles Act 1980* (Tas) s 40(3); *Transfer of Land Act 1958* (Vic) s 42; *Transfer of Land Act 1893* (WA) s 68.

7.79   In *Assets Co Ltd v Mere Roihi* [1905] AC 176 at 210, the Privy Council defined fraud as follows:

> [B]y fraud in [the legislation] is meant actual fraud, that is dishonesty of some sort, not what is
> called constructive or equitable fraud … [T]he fraud which must be proved in order to invalidate
> the title of the registered proprietor for value … must be brought home to the person whose
> registered title is impeached or to his agents. Fraud by persons from whom he claims does not
> affect him unless knowledge of it is brought home to him or his agents. The mere fact that he
> might have found out fraud if he had been more vigilant, and had made further inquiries which
> he omitted to make, does not of itself prove fraud on his part. But if it be shown that his suspicions
> were aroused, and that he abstained from making inquiries for fear of learning the truth, the case
> is very different and fraud may properly be ascribed to him.

7.80   The High Court has accepted this definition of fraud. Thus, in *Butler v Fairclough* (1917)
23 CLR 78 at 97, Isaacs J defined fraud as 'actual fraud, moral turpitude'. In *Wicks v Bennett* (1921)
30 CLR 80 at 91, Knox CJ and Rich J referred to fraud as 'something more than mere disregard of
rights of which the person sought to be affected had notice'. However, more recently the High Court
has expanded this quite strict interpretation of fraud to include, without specifying, some forms of
equitable fraud: *Bank of South Australia Limited v Ferguson* (1998) 192 CLR 248 at 255; 151 ALR 729
at 732. This approach was endorsed by the Court of Appeal in Victoria in *Russo v Bendigo Bank Ltd*
[1999] 3 VR 376 at 382–5, and by the Court of Appeal in New South Wales in *Grgic v ANZ Banking
Group Ltd* (1994) 33 NSWLR 202 at 221, where Powell JA said:

> [T]hose species of 'equitable fraud' which are regarded as falling within the concept of 'fraud' for
> the purposes of s 42 of the Act are those … in which there has been an element of dishonesty or
> moral turpitude on the part of the registered proprietor of the subject interest or on the part of
> his or its agent.

7.81   Thus, for equitable fraud to come within the statutory definition of fraud, proof of
dishonesty is necessary: *Gerard Cassegrain & Co Pty Limited v Cassegrain* [2011] NSWSC 1156 at
[169]. Furthermore, 'the mere fact that a person might have discovered fraud if further enquiries
had been made does not of itself prove fraud. The enquiry is an enquiry for actual dishonesty not
for want of due care': *Pyramid Building Society (in liq) v Scorpion Hotels Pty Ltd* [1998] 1 VR 188
at 194. In *Grgic*, Powell JA cited, as an example, a collusive or colourable sale by a mortgagee to a
subsidiary company such as occurred in *Latec Investments Ltd v Hotel Terrigal Pty Ltd* (1965) 113
CLR 265: see 4.44–4.45.

7.82   In *Assets Co Ltd v Mere Roihi*, Assets became the registered proprietor of certain lands
formerly owned by certain Maoris. There were allegations of fraud against predecessors to Assets
and from whom Assets purchased the land. However, there was no fraud committed by Assets itself.
The Privy Council ruled that there was no fraudulent statement made by the company's agents nor
any bribery, corruption or dishonesty. Nor had Assets refrained from making inquiries which an
honest purchaser would have made.

7.83   Mere prior knowledge of an unregistered interest is not of itself fraud: *Mills v Stockman*
(1967) 116 CLR 61 at 78. It is also the case that knowledge that the earlier unregistered interest will
be defeated by registration is insufficient of itself to amount to fraud by the registered proprietor:
Bahr v Nicolay (No 2) (1988) 164 CLR 605 at 653; 78 ALR 1 at 35. This point is in fact confirmed by

the provisions of the Torrens legislation in all Australian jurisdictions.[21] However, with respect to these legislative provisions, the courts have interpreted them in such a way that they only become operative upon registration: *IAC (Finance) Pty Ltd v Courtenay* (1963) 110 CLR 550 at 572. Until that time a purchaser is affected by notice of unregistered interests. However, once registered, the fact of mere notice of an unregistered interest will not affect the indefeasible title of the purchaser.

7.84   In *Loke Yew v Port Swettenham Rubber Co Ltd* [1913] AC 491, Port Swettenham purchased land from Eusope. Loke Yew was part owner of the land but was not registered. Eusope only agreed to transfer the land to Port Swettenham when given an assurance that Port Swettenham would not disturb Loke Yew's possession of the land. Upon registration, Port Swettenham asserted title to the whole of the land to the exclusion of Loke Yew. The issue before the court was whether Port Swettenham's title was obtained by fraud and thus defeasible to the interest of Loke Yew. The Privy Council found for Loke Yew and held that Port Swettenham acquired its title through fraud. Port Swettenham had more than mere knowledge of Loke Yew's unregistered interest. The assurances it made to Eusope had been made to induce Eusope to execute the transfer of the land and amounted to a deliberate plan to deprive Loke Yew of his interest.

7.85   The decision in *Loke Yew v Port Swettenham* can be contrasted to *R M Hosking Properties Pty Ltd v Barnes* [1971] SASR 100, where Barnes had an unregistered interest in a two-year lease with an option to renew it for a further term of two years. During the term of the lease Hosking purchased the property from the original landlord. Hosking knew of the lease and agreed to accept title subject to the occupation of the land by Barnes. When Barnes sought to exercise the option Hosking gave him a notice to quit the property, stating that he (Hosking) was not bound by the unregistered lease. Hosking prevailed in court. The court ruled that, although Hosking knew of the unregistered interest, that knowledge was not enough to establish fraud. Unlike the case of *Loke Yew v Port Swettenham*, there was no proven plan of dishonesty or fraud, and no evidence that the original landlord had been induced to sign the transfer to Hosking on the basis of Hosking's statements.

7.86   As to the time when fraud must be present for the exception to arise, the generally accepted view is that it is up to the time of registration: *Bahr v Nicolay (No 2)* at CLR 633; ALR 20. Thus, any conduct after registration could not be considered as constituting fraud. However, in *Bahr v Nicolay (No 2)* at CLR 615–16; ALR 7, Mason CJ and Dawson J suggested that post-registration conduct by the registered proprietor may be considered on the issue of whether there is fraud by the registered proprietor. This approach has been endorsed by Wood J in *Snowlong Pty Ltd v Choe* (1991) 23 NSWLR 198 at 212, but rejected by Owen J in *Conlan v Registrar of Titles* (2001) 24 WAR 299 at 328–9. However, whether post-registration conduct is relevant for the fraud exception is to a large extent an academic question. This is so because post-registration conduct that would amount to fraud will be caught under the *in personam* exception to indefeasibility: see 7.88–7.102.

7.87   A final aspect of fraud to be noted relates to fraud by the agent of the registered proprietor. If the fraud by the agent is within the scope of the agent's actual or apparent authority, on ordinary agency principles that fraud binds the registered proprietor, even if the registered proprietor was innocent and the agent was acting for his or her own fraudulent purposes. If the agent's fraud is

---

21.   *Land Titles Act 1925* (ACT) s 59; *Real Property Act 1900* (NSW) s 43; *Land Title Act 2000* (NT) s 188(2); *Land Title Act 1994* (Qld) s 184(2); *Real Property Act 1886* (SA) s 72; *Land Titles Act 1980* (Tas) s 41; *Transfer of Land Act 1958* (Vic) s 43; *Transfer of Land Act 1893* (WA) s 134.

not within his or her actual authority then the registered proprietor is not affected by that fraud: *Schultz v Corwill Properties Pty Ltd* (1969) 90 WN (NSW) (Pt 1) 529. Thus, in *Dollars & Sense Finance Ltd v Nathan* [2008] 2 NZLR 557, a mortgage was registered in favour of a lender as security for a loan that it had made to a borrower. The borrower had forged the signature of the mortgagor, in circumstances where the lender had forwarded the relevant documentation to the borrower to obtain the signature of the mortgagor. In these circumstances, the New Zealand Supreme Court held that the borrower had acted as agent for the lender and that the forgery was an act done within the scope of the agency, even though the lender had no knowledge of the forgery and the forgery was done exclusively for the benefit of the lender.

In personam rights

7.88 In addition to statutory exceptions there exists the so-called '*in personam* exception' to indefeasibility. The *in personam* exception is based upon personal claims against a registered proprietor of an interest which, if successfully prosecuted before the court, will lead to orders being made requiring the registered proprietor to divest himself or herself of his or her interest, either in whole or part, in favour of the claimant: *Hillpalm Pty Ltd v Heaven's Door Pty Ltd* (2004) 220 CLR 472 at 491; 211 ALR 588 at 601. However, until the register has been amended in accordance with orders made by the court, the register remains conclusive vis-à-vis third parties.

7.89 The existence of *in personam* rights was referred to in *Barry v Heider* (1914) 19 CLR 197 at 213, where it was said that the Torrens system in no way destroyed 'the fundamental doctrines by which Courts of Equity have enforced, as against registered proprietors, conscientious obligations entered into by them'. In the Northern Territory and Queensland, legislation gives statutory form to such rights by stipulating that the benefits of indefeasibility do not apply in relation to 'an equity arising from the act of the registered proprietor'.[22]

7.90 The personal rights enforced here are not confined to those based upon equitable claims. Common law claims are also recognised. In *Grgic v ANZ Banking Group Ltd* at 222, the New South Wales Court of Appeal ruled that *in personam* claims could only be based upon 'known legal causes of action or equitable causes of action'. Although many of the equitable causes of action require an element of unconscientiousness to be established, there is no superadded requirement to establish unconscientiousness in order to establish an *in personam* claim: *White v Tomasel* [2004] 2 Qd R 438 at 455–6; *Harris v Smith* [2008] NSWSC 545 at [66]–[67].

7.91 Two simple illustrations of the *in personam* exception can be briefly noted. First, if a registered proprietor contracts to sell land and the contract is capable of being specifically enforced, the registered proprietor cannot defend the action for specific performance on the basis that his or her title is indefeasible and not subject to rights or interests not recorded on the register: *Paradise Constructors & Co Pty Ltd v Poyser* (2007) 20 VR 294 at 304. Second, if the registered proprietor is a trustee, the trust can be enforced against the trustee for the benefit of the beneficiaries. The trustee cannot deny the beneficiaries' rights by simply claiming that he or she has an indefeasible title free of all interests other than those recorded on the register: *Ciaglia v Ciaglia* (2010) 269 ALR 175 at 200.

---

22. *Land Title Act 2000* (NT) s 189(1)(a); *Land Title Act 1994* (Qld) s 185(1)(a).

7.92   Other examples of successful *in personam* claims include: (i) the equity to order rectification of a contract for the sale of land and the retransfer of land in situations where a person becomes a registered proprietor of land due to a mistake (*Tutt v Doyle* (1997) 42 NSWLR 10 at 14; *Harris v Smith* at [53]–[54]);[23] (ii) where a registered proprietor gains registration in breach of his or her fiduciary duties (*TatAurangi Tairuakena v Mua Carr* [1927] NZLR 688); and (iii) where a registered proprietor obtains registration as the result of unconscionable or unconscientious conduct: *Permanent Mortgages Pty Ltd v Vandenbergh* [2010] WASC 10 at [375]–[379]; (iv) where a discharge of mortgage has been registered as the result of a mistake: *Dixon v Barton* [2011] NSWSC 1525 at [74]–[81].

7.93   Although the scope of the principle of *in personam* rights has not been precisely defined, it is clear that it does not encompass all known legal or equitable causes of action: *Farah Constructions Pty Ltd v Say-Dee Pty Ltd* (2007) 230 CLR 90 at 169; 236 ALR 209 at 267. In *Bahr v Nicolay (No 2)*, at CLR 638; ALR 23–4, it was made clear that the principle of *in personam* rights could not be used so as to circumvent the principle of indefeasibility. Furthermore, the principle 'do[es] not supply a canvas on which a plaintiff can paint any picture': *LHK Nominees Pty Ltd v Kenworthy* (2002) 26 WALR 517 at 556.

7.94   In recent times the question of whether violations of the principles set out in *Barnes v Addy* (1874) 9 Ch App 244 (see Chapter 28) give rise to *in personam* claims has been considered in a number of cases. In relation to the situations where the registered proprietor knowingly receives trust property following a trustee's breach of fiduciary duty in violation of the 'knowing receipt' principle set out in *Barnes v Addy*, the beneficiary under the trust has no *in personam* claim against the registered proprietor. The *in personam* exception to indefeasibility does not arise merely because the registered proprietor had notice of an earlier interest or notice of third party fraud: *Farah Constructions Pty Ltd v Say-Dee Pty Ltd* (2007) 230 CLR 89 at 169–71; 236 ALR 209 at 267–9. However, if a person knowing of a dishonest and fraudulent design on the part of a fiduciary or trustee assists in the furthering of that design in violation of the 'knowing assistance' principle set out in *Barnes v Addy*, and, as a result, becomes a registered proprietor of land, that person's conduct comes within the fraud exception to indefeasibility noted above: see 7.78–7.87.

7.95   The conduct of the registered proprietor giving rise to an *in personam* exception can be before or after he or she becomes registered, as is illustrated by the decision in *Bahr v Nicolay (No 2)*. In that case, the Bahrs were registered proprietors of land who contracted to sell it to Nicolay. The contract stipulated that Nicolay would lease the land back to the Bahrs for three years and then resell it back to them. Nicolay became registered proprietor and then sold the land to the Thompsons. The Thompsons knew of the arrangement between the Bahrs and Nicolay and in the contract of purchase from Nicolay expressly acknowledged it. After the Thompsons became registered they confirmed in writing to the Bahrs that they were required to sell back the land to them. Later the Thompsons changed their minds and sought to rely on the register to defeat the Bahrs' claims to the land. Any dishonest conduct by the Thompsons was found to have occurred after they became registered proprietors. The issue before the High Court was whether the Thompsons had an indefeasible title. The High Court unanimously ruled against the Thompsons. The case was argued on behalf of the Bahrs on two grounds: namely, the fraud and *in personam* exceptions to indefeasibility.

---

23.   The extent to which mistake gives rise to *in personam* claims is fully explored in L Griggs, 'Indefeasibility and Mistake — the Utilitarianism of Torrens' (2003) 10 *Australian Property Law Journal* 1.

7.96   As to fraud, Mason CJ and Dawson J held that fraud was established because post-registration conduct by a registered proprietor was within the fraud exception. Referring to *Loke Yew v Port Swettenham*, they were of the view that there was no difference between giving an undertaking which induces a transfer of property to be executed and an undertaking honestly given but subsequently repudiated. Wilson and Toohey JJ adopted the more traditional view of fraud as excluding post-registration conduct and thus found no fraud on the part of the Thompsons. Brennan J did not make any determination based upon fraud.

7.97   As to the *in personam* exception, all members of the High Court found in favour of the Bahrs. The fact that the Thompsons had expressly acknowledged the Bahrs' rights in the contract and in the written letter to them after registration gave rise to an *in personam* claim against him. There was, however, some difference of opinion as to the precise nature of the Bahrs' *in personam* right. Wilson, Toohey and Brennan JJ took the view that the Thompsons' undertaking with respect to the Bahrs' right to repurchase the land gave rise to a constructive trust. Mason CJ and Dawson J said that the 'matrix of circumstances' was sufficient to establish that there was an intention to create an express trust.

7.98   A number of subsequent decisions further illustrate the potency of the *in personam* exception. In *Mercantile Mutual Life Insurance Co Ltd v Gosper* (1991) 25 NSWLR 32, Mrs Gosper was the registered proprietor of land subject to a mortgage to Mercantile Mutual. Mr Gosper borrowed money from Mercantile Mutual and it was agreed that the loan would be secured by a variation of the existing mortgage over Mrs Gosper's property. Mr Gosper forged his wife's signature to the variation and it was registered. After her husband's death Mrs Gosper discovered what had happened. She sought orders removing the variation of the mortgage from her title. The issue before the court was whether Mercantile Mutual had an indefeasible title in so far as the variation was concerned or whether it was defeated on the basis of an *in personam* claim by Mrs Gosper. The majority of the New South Wales Court of Appeal held in favour of Mrs Gosper. Mahoney JA at 47–8 (Kirby P agreeing at 37), held that the variation was a forgery and that the only way it could be removed from the register was if there were *in personam* rights against Mercantile Mutual. The mere fact of the variation being a forgery was not enough. However, there were other factors, the main one being that, in producing the title to have the variation registered, Mercantile Mutual had acted without the authority of Mrs Gosper. Mercantile Mutual used the title deed in breach of its obligations to Mrs Gosper and its use of the title deed was a necessary step in securing the registration of the variation. The majority concluded that Mercantile Mutual should not be permitted to retain a benefit that had been procured by an act which constituted a breach of its obligations to Mrs Gosper. In effect, Mercantile Mutual's unauthorised use of the certificate of title constituted unconscientious conduct on its part: *Vella v Permanent Mortgages Pty Ltd* [2008] NSWSC 505 at [379]–[380].

7.99   In his dissent, Meagher JA, at 52, argued that, if the loan to Mr Gosper had proceeded simply by means of discharging the existing mortgage over Mrs Gosper's land and was replaced by a new, albeit forged, mortgage to Mercantile Mutual in an amount to cover the original loan and the loan to Mr Gosper, Mercantile Mutual would have obtained, pursuant to *Frazer v Walker*, an indefeasible title. His Honour ruled that the same result should follow where, in effect, the same situation eventuates by variation of the existing mortgage.

7.100   In *Story v Advance Bank of Australia* (1993) 31 NSWLR 722, the Court of Appeal in New South Wales had to consider *in personam* exceptions in the context of a mortgage granted by a corporation to a bank, where the corporation was a 'family' company operated by Mr and Mrs Story. The loan was to Mr Story only with the mortgage being over land owned by the corporation. Mr Story forged his wife's signature on the mortgage documents. Mrs Story claimed an *in personam* exception against the bank on the basis that the bank had failed to make appropriate inquiries to determine whether Mrs Story had indeed executed the mortgage. The Court of Appeal ruled against Mrs Story. Gleeson CJ, at 737 (Cripps J, at 742, agreeing), held that even if the bank had not made adequate inquiries of what was going on in the corporation 'that does not produce the result that it is against conscience for the bank to rely upon its statutory rights' to an indefeasible title as to the mortgage. Mahoney JA agreed, but also elaborated more fully on the *in personam* exception to indefeasibility. His Honour, at 739–41, made the following points:

(a) not all interests that a person has under the general law or would have against a registered proprietor are personal equities within the *in personam* exception;

(b) merely to show that an instrument is a forgery will not of itself give rise to an *in personam* exception;

(c) in some cases it could be that an *in personam* exception may arise by the failure of the registered proprietor to make inquiries as to the execution of an instrument, but the mere failure to make such inquiries does not have this effect;

(d) under corporations legislation, provisions are set out which prevent a corporation from contending that a document was not validly executed, with the effect that the person relying on that document is relieved from the obligation to make any inquiries as to its execution.

In light of these observations no *in personam* exception arose against the bank.

7.101 In *Vassos v State Bank of South Australia* [1993] 2 VR 316, the bank obtained a mortgage over land owned by three tenants in common. One of the tenants in common subsequently obtained a substitute mortgage for a greater sum by forging the signatures of the other two tenants in common. In this case the bank's mortgage was not obtained as the result of fraud, nor was the *in personam* exception applicable. In relation to the latter, Hayne J, in distinguishing this case from *Mercantile Mutual v Gosper*, reaffirmed that more than a mere forgery was required. His Honour, at 333, observed that, even though the bank was negligent in the manner in which it took the forged mortgage, there was 'no misrepresentation by it, no misuse of power, no improper attempt to rely on its legal rights, no knowledge of wrongdoing by any other party … Even if by making reasonable enquiries the bank could have discovered the fact of the forgery I do not consider that that fact alone renders its conduct unconscionable'.

7.102 In *Macquarie Bank Ltd v Sixty-Fourth Throne Pty Ltd* [1998] 3 VR 133, a bank's carelessness in failing to check the attesting signatures affixed to a forged mortgage from a trust company was held not to give the trust company an *in personam* right to have the mortgage set aside. In reaching that conclusion Winneke P, at 136, said:

> It is, I concede, logically attractive to argue that legitimate equitable claims should not be emasculated by setting the threshold level of conduct, short of statutory fraud, too high; on the other hand it is, in my view, an argument of equally compelling force that the threshold should not be set so low as to defeat the concept of indefeasibility which is entrenched in and central to the Torrens system of registration of interests in land; a system which itself recognises that the register is paramount and that, save in exceptional circumstances, those who have suffered loss, without any fault on their own part, will have to content themselves with compensation out of the fund made available for the purpose.

On the basis of the decision in this case, the Victorian Court of Appeal expressed doubts, in *Paradise Constructors v Poyser* at 304, as to whether *Mercantile Mutual Life Insurance v Gosper* would be followed in Victoria.

Volunteers and the Torrens system

7.103   In light of the relevance of the equitable maxim that 'equity will not assist a volunteer' it is interesting to note that, in all but two Australian jurisdictions, the issue of whether a volunteer obtains an indefeasible title is not explicitly dealt with by legislation. In the Northern Territory and Queensland, legislation stipulates that no exception to indefeasibility arises merely because the registered proprietor obtained his or her interest as a volunteer.[24]

7.104   In other Australian jurisdictions the position is less clear. In Victoria, cases such as *King v Smail* [1958] VR 273 and *Rasmussen v Rasmussen* [1995] 1 VR 613 have stated that a volunteer does not, on registration of his or her interest, obtain an indefeasible title and takes subject to unregistered interests. The rationale for these decisions lies in the view that it was never the intention of the Torrens title legislators to confer indefeasibility upon volunteers. On the other hand, in New South Wales, the Court of Appeal in *Bogdanovic v Koteff* (1988) 12 NSWLR 472 held that a volunteer who obtained registration of his interest without notice of any unregistered interest obtained an indefeasible title. This decision was based upon the view that the only exceptions to indefeasibility are those expressly created by statute. Because the legislation created no express exception in relation to volunteers, they obtained an indefeasible title upon registration of their interests. In Western Australia, in *Conlan v Registrar of Titles* (2001) 24 WAR 299 at 330–7, following a detailed analysis of the cases, Owen J came to a similar conclusion. Furthermore, as was observed by Tipping J in *Regal Castings Ltd v Lightboy* [2009] 2 NZLR 433 at 480, it would 'seem illogical' if a forged instrument could give an innocent registered proprietor an indefeasible title but a volunteer could not get an indefeasible title upon registration. Finally, in *Farah Constructions v Say-Dee* at CLR 172; ALR 269, the High Court, without analysing the issue, stated that a registered proprietor obtains priority even if he or she is a volunteer.

Competing unregistered interests

7.105   Priority disputes between competing unregistered interests in Torrens title land are resolved by the same rules that apply under general law principles about disputes between holders of competing equitable interests. The holder of the unregistered interest created first will have priority over a holder of a subsequently created unregistered interest unless the first in time is guilty of postponing conduct. The application of this rule has already been illustrated in cases involving Torrens title land such as *Breskvar v Wall* (see 7.24–7.26) and *Heid v Reliance Finance Corporation*: see 7.27–7.30.

7.106   An important factor in applying the rule in the context of Torrens title priority disputes relates to the issue of whether a failure by the holder of the first unregistered interest to lodge a caveat amounts to postponing conduct. In neither *Breskvar v Wall* nor *Heid v Reliance Finance Corporation* did this issue directly affect the priority dispute. Had the holders of the first unregistered interest in both cases lodged caveats they would have preserved their positions against subsequent unregistered interest holders. However, the failure to lodge caveats was not what constituted postponing conduct. Rather, it was the fact that, by handing over title documents to another person, they enabled those

---

24.   *Land Title Act 2000* (NT) s 183; *Land Title Act 1994* (Qld) s 180.

persons to hold themselves out as being entitled to deal with the property in a manner that led subsequent interest holders to believe no subsisting unregistered interests existed.

7.107 Failure to lodge a caveat by the holder of an unregistered interest in Torrens title land will constitute postponing conduct when, in the light of all the circumstances, it leads subsequent holders of unregistered interests to acquire them on the mistaken assumption that the earlier unregistered interest does not exist: *Heid v Reliance Finance Corporation* at CLR 342; ALR 239.

7.108 In determining whether a failure to caveat constitutes postponing conduct, it must first be appreciated that the purpose of a caveat is to protect an unregistered interest and not to give notice of it, although it does have that effect: *J & H Just (Holdings) Pty Ltd v Bank of New South Wales* (1971) 125 CLR 546 at 552. A caveat achieves this purpose by preventing registration of subsequent interests that are inconsistent with the interest that is the subject of the caveat.

7.109 Given the protective function of a caveat, if the holder of the first unregistered interest in a priority dispute also has possession of the relevant certificate of title, failure to lodge a caveat will not amount to postponing conduct: *Barlin Investments Pty Ltd v Westpac Banking Corporation* at [32]. Lodgment of a caveat is unnecessary to protect that interest as it would not give the interest holder any greater protection than he or she already has by virtue of possession of the relevant certificate of title. This protection flows from the fact that possession of the certificate of title precludes any other interest holder from registering his or her interest because such registration requires the lodgment of the certificate of title together with the instrument by which the interest is acquired.

7.110 The facts and result of *J & H Just (Holdings) v Bank of New South Wales* illustrate and confirm this point. In that case, the bank loaned money to Josephson. The bank obtained a mortgage in registrable form as well as the certificate of title but did not register the mortgage. Later, J & H Just (Holdings) advanced further money to Josephson on the security of the land. They asked Josephson about the certificate of title and accepted his statement that it was with the bank for safekeeping. J & H Just (Holdings) lodged a caveat. A priority dispute in relation to the two unregistered mortgages was resolved, by the High Court, in favour of the bank. In coming to this conclusion, the court ruled that the bank would have priority because its interest was the first in time, unless it could be established that the bank was guilty of some act or default sufficient to make it inequitable for it to maintain such priority. The court reaffirmed that the failure to lodge a caveat would not, of itself, lead to a displacement of priority gained according to time. By receiving the title documents, the bank had taken adequate precautions to protect itself. It had no duty to register the mortgage or lodge a caveat. The bank's conduct did not mislead J & H Just (Holdings) or arm Josephson in the same sense as had occurred in the holding out cases such as *Abigail v Lapin*: see 7.23.

7.111 In *Avco Financial Services v Fishman* [1993] 1 VR 90, Fishman mortgaged land to the State Bank. The mortgage was registered. A second mortgage between the bank and Fishman was entered into, but was not registered. Nor was a caveat lodged by the bank. Fishman entered into a third mortgage with Avco, which had no notice of the second unregistered mortgage to the bank. They wrote to the bank seeking details of the amount owing under the first (registered) mortgage. The bank responded, but said nothing about having an unregistered second mortgage. The issue was whether Avco had priority over the bank's second mortgage due to the bank's failure to lodge a caveat. Tadgell J ruled in favour of the bank, finding that it had not done anything justifying postponement of its priority according to time. He reaffirmed that the purpose of a caveat was protective and not to give notice.

Having possession of the title documents meant that the bank did not need the protection gained by lodgment of a caveat. Citing *J & H Just (Holdings) v Bank of New South Wales*, Tadgell J, at 95, said:

> The Bank was not to be expected to lodge a caveat to give notice of its second mortgage to persons who might be induced to lend to the mortgagors by their false statements or representations that no second mortgage had been taken by them.

7.112   It can be noted that the ruling in *J & H Just (Holdings) v Bank of New South Wales* — that the purpose of a caveat is to protect an unregistered interest and not to give notice of it — was subsequently rejected by Callinan J in his judgment in the High Court decision in *Black v Garnock* (2007) 230 CLR 438 at 463–70; 237 ALR 1 at 21–6. His Honour, at CLR 470; ALR 26, took the view that it would be subversive of the Torrens system if 'a person interested in, or entitled to deal with, land, who has not acted fraudulently, might suddenly and unexpectedly be saddled with, or postponed to, an equitable estate or interest in land which could have been, but was not made the subject of protection by prompt lodgment of an instrument or the filing of a caveat pending the lodgment'. Furthermore, in *Capital Finance Australia Ltd v Struthers* [2008] NSWSC 440 at [44], Hamilton J said that, although he was bound to follow the law as set out in *J & H Just (Holdings) v Bank of New South Wales*, there was 'considerable force' in Callinan J's comments in *Black v Garnock*.

7.113   In cases where the holder of the first unregistered interest does not also have possession of the certificate of title, the question of whether his or her failure to lodge a caveat amounts to postponing conduct will, as already noted, depend upon whether that failure, in the light of all the circumstances, leads subsequent holders of unregistered interests to acquire them on the mistaken assumption that the earlier unregistered interest does not exist. It is clear that, if the second unregistered interest holder has *not* searched the register, a failure by the first unregistered interest holder to lodge a caveat will not be viewed as postponing conduct. The second unregistered interest holder, not having searched the register, cannot be said to have been misled by the failure to lodge the caveat: *Newcastle City Council v Kern Land Pty Ltd* (1997) 42 NSWLR 273 at 284.

7.114   However, in cases where the second unregistered interest holder has relied upon a search of the register prior to obtaining his or her interest, courts in the various Australian jurisidictions have not addressed in a consistent manner whether the failure to lodge a caveat by the first unregistered interest holder amounts to postponing conduct.

7.115   In New South Wales, it is reasonably clear that such a failure to lodge a caveat will generally amount to postponing conduct. In *Person-to-Person Finances Pty Ltd v Sharari* [1984] 1 NSWLR 745, Tredgolde had a registered mortgage over Torrens title land. As a registered mortgagee he also held the certificate of title. Sharari took a subsequent mortgage over the property, but his solicitor failed to have that mortgage registered and Sharari did not lodge a caveat to protect his unregistered mortgage. Subsequently, Person-to-Person took a mortgage over the property after being told by the owner of the land that Tredgolde had the only other mortgage over the property. Person-to-Person's search of the register revealed only Tredgolde's mortgage. Person-to-Person lodged a caveat in respect of its unregistered mortgage. The issue before the court was whether Sharari's failure to lodge a caveat amounted to postponing conduct. McLelland J ruled that Sharari was guilty of postponing conduct and that, therefore, Person-to Person had priority over Sharari. His Honour, at 738, said:

[I]t is the settled practice of competent solicitors … acting for second or subsequent mortgagees, to ensure either the prompt registration of the mortgage or lodgment of a caveat. The failure by [Sharari] through his solicitor to conform to this practice would lead naturally to those who searched, such as [Person-to-Person], to believe that there was no such outstanding second mortgage, and it is my opinion that the failure of [Sharari], in the absence of registration of his mortgage, to lodge a caveat led [Person-to-Person] to acquire its mortgage on the supposition that no unregistered second mortgage already existed, in circumstances which make it inequitable as between the parties that [Sharari's] mortgage should have priority over that of [Person-to-Person].

7.116   In Victoria, the failure to lodge a caveat in these circumstances has been found to constitute postponing conduct in some, but not all, cases. *Osmanoski v Rose* [1974] VR 523 is a case where the failure to lodge a caveat was held to constitute postponing conduct. In that case, A contracted to sell land to B and then again to C. When C contracted he searched the register and saw that A was the registered proprietor. B had not lodged a caveat in relation to his unregistered interest at that time but did lodge one before C lodged a transfer for registration. The court held that B's failure to lodge a caveat before C contracted with A was postponing conduct as it led to C contracting with A in the belief that there was no other interest such as B's in existence.

7.117   On the other hand, in *Jacobs v Platt Nominees Pty Ltd* [1990] VR 146, the Victorian Full Court held that the failure to lodge a caveat did not amount to postponing conduct. In this case the first unregistered interest was that of an option to purchase land. The holder of the option, the daughter of the registered proprietors, had reason to believe that her parents would not sell the land to anybody else and, therefore, decided not to lodge a caveat. The registered proprietors then contracted to sell the land to another purchaser. The issue before the court was whether the daughter's failure to caveat meant that her interest was postponed to that of the subsequent purchaser. The Full Court, at 160, in ruling that the failure to caveat did not amount to postponing conduct, said:

[The daughter] had secured the option from her parents in such a way that it was inconceivable that her father and mother would join together to sell the motel in breach of the option. It was, in short, not reasonably foreseeable that her failure to lodge a caveat exposed herself or others to a risk of a later sale. In this setting her explanation that she did not want to upset her father by lodging a caveat was entirely consistent.

7.118   A final view on this matter is that expressed by Debelle J in *Elderly Citizens Homes of SA Inc v Balnaves* (1998) 72 SASR 210 at 227, where his Honour stated that the effect of the failure to lodge a caveat will largely be determined by whether or not it is general conveyancing practice to lodge a caveat and search the register when the interest in question is created. In this respect, it can be noted that lodgment of caveats and searching the register is common conveyancing practice in relation to unregistered mortgages. However, although searching the register is common in relation to contracts for the purchase of property, lodgment of caveats after entry into the contract is not common conveyancing practice.

The Torrens system and the special position of beneficiaries under trusts

7.119   It has already been noted that, on the authority of *Shropshire Union Railways and Canal Company v R*, under general law principles relating to competing equitable interests, a beneficiary's interest under a trust is not postponed because of the *trustee's* abuse of his or her position as trustee:

see 7.32–7.36. The issue that arises is whether the *Shropshire* rule applies in the context of Torrens title land. The question to be answered can be raised in the context of the following circumstances. Suppose that A is a trustee of Torrens title land for B. In breach of his or her trust obligations, A creates an unregistered interest, such as a mortgage, in favour of C who has no knowledge of the trust as B has not lodged a caveat with respect to his or her beneficial interest in the land.

7.120 In *Abigail v Lapin* at 69, Lord Wright stated that the question did not arise on the facts of that case (see 7.23) because Mrs Heavener was not a trustee for Lapin, and therefore Lapin could not invoke the *Shropshire* rule to preserve his priority over Abigail. His Lordship left unanswered the question of whether the *Shropshire* rule applied in the context of the Torrens system with its provisions for 'the protection of equitable interests by caveats'. This comment may well suggest that the failure by B to lodge a caveat would amount to postponing conduct, entitling C's unregistered interest to prevail over B's interest as beneficiary under a trust, thereby negating the application of the *Shropshire* rule in the context of Torrens title land. However, such a conclusion would have the effect of undermining the special position afforded to beneficiaries that is the rationale for the *Shropshire* rule. The fact that the Torrens system does provide for 'the protection of equitable interests by caveats', is not, it is suggested, a sufficient basis to exclude Torrens title land from the scope of the operation of the *Shropshire* rule.

Section 43A of the Real Property Act 1900 (NSW)

7.121 In New South Wales s 43A of the *Real Property Act 1900* (NSW) is also relevant in the context of priority disputes between holders of competing unregistered interests. The section stipulates as follows:

> **43A Protection as to notice of person contracting or dealing in respect of land under this Act before registration**
>
> (1) For the purpose only of protection against notice, the estate or interest in land under the provisions of this Act, taken by a person under a dealing registrable, or which when appropriately signed by or on behalf of that person would be registrable under this Act shall, before registration of that dealing, be deemed to be a legal estate.
> (2) No person contracting or dealing in respect of an estate or interest in land under the provisions of this Act shall be affected by notice of any instrument, fact, or thing merely by omission to search in a register not kept under this Act.
> (3) Registration under Division 1 of Part 23 of the Conveyancing Act 1919 shall not of itself affect the rights of any person contracting or dealing in respect of estates or interests in land under the provisions of this Act.
> (4) Nothing in subsection (2) or (3) operates to defeat any claim based on a subsisting interest, within the meaning of Part 4A, affecting land comprised in a qualified folio of the Register.

7.122 Section 43A deals with the position of a purchaser of a registered interest in Torrens title land in the period between completion of the transaction and actual registration. With old system title land a purchaser on completion of the transaction acquires the legal interest and is not bound by any equitable interest unless he or she had notice of it as at completion. However, with Torrens title land, it is only upon registration that the purchaser acquires a registered interest: see 5.38. Prior to that point of time, and notwithstanding that the purchase has been completed, his or her interest is still an unregistered interest. Section 43A is designed to give such a purchaser protection against earlier unregistered interests in the period between completion of the purchase and the registration of the interest that has been acquired. Section 43 of the *Real Property Act 1900* (NSW) is not of any assistance to such a purchaser because the protection against notice of unregistered interests afforded by s 43 only arises upon registration, not before it: see 7.83. In *Nabeth Taleb v National Australia Bank Ltd* [2011] NSWSC 1562 at [40], Bryson AJ said that '[t]he effect of section 43A is to advance the time when the purchaser has protection against notice to a time earlier than obtaining legal title by registration under the *Real Property Act*'.

7.123   The effect of s 43A(1) is that, if the holder of an unregistered interest satisfies the requirements of the section, from the time of settlement of a contract by which that holder acquires his or her interest, he or she has a 'deemed … legal estate'. In *IAC (Finance) Pty Ltd v Courtenay* at 584, Taylor J noted that the holder of an unregistered interest who fulfilled the requirements of s 43A was, in relation to any priority dispute with the holder of an earlier unregistered interest in the same land, in the same position as a bona fide purchaser of the legal estate taking the same for value and without notice of an earlier equitable interest in relation to a priority dispute with the holder of that earlier equitable interest under general law principles. As previously noted, such a purchaser of the legal estate has priority over the holder of the earlier equitable interest: see 7.48. Thus, a holder of an unregistered interest who complies with the requirements of s 43A has priority over the holder of earlier unregistered interests. This understanding of the effect of s 43A was confirmed in *John Alexander's Clubs Pty Ltd (ACN 097 896 109) v White City Tennis Club Ltd* (2010) 241CLR 1 at 42; 266 ALR 462 at 489–90, where, in a unanimous joint judgment, the High Court said:

> [I]t is now settled that [s 43A] is directed to the protection before registration of an interest under a registrable instrument and confers upon the holder of that interest the same protection against notice of an earlier unregistered interest as that which is achieved by a purchaser who acquires the legal estate at common law. By this means there is introduced into the administration in New South Wales of the Torrens system an analogy to the doctrine of bona fide purchaser as a means of regulating priorities between competing claimants to registration of unregistered dealings.

7.124   Given that the effect of s 43A is to incorporate the general law doctrine of the bona fide purchaser taking for value and without notice, one must have given valuable consideration for the interest acquired at settlement to get the section's protection. Section 43A makes no explicit reference to consideration, but in *IAC (Finance) v Courtenay* the court talked in terms of a 'purchaser' getting s 43A protection, clearly implying the necessity of valuable consideration.

7.125   However, s 43A does not protect a purchaser who has notice, actual or constructive, of an earlier unregistered interest prior to completion of his or her purchase: *Barlin Investments Pty Ltd v Westpac Banking Corporation* [2012] NSWSC 699 at [37]. But, if that purchaser actually does get registered, he or she obtains an indefeasible title at the expense of the earlier unregistered interest pursuant to ss 42–43 of the *Real Property Act*.

7.126   The principal requirement of s 43A is that the holder of the unregistered interest has a 'dealing registrable' in relation to his or her interest. This means that the holder must have acquired his or her interest directly from the registered proprietor of the land: *Weller v Williams* [2010] NSWSC 716 at [18]. However, if registration of the instrument setting out that interest is prevented by a caveat on the title, the instrument is not a 'dealing registrable' for the purposes of s 43A: *Nabeth Taleb v National Australia Bank Ltd* at [43]–[49]. Furthermore, in *Nabeth Taleb v National Australia*

Bank Ltd at [41], Bryson AJ held that if the holder of an unregistered instrument has not, at the time of settlement of the transaction, paid the relevant stamp duty and had the instrument stamped by the Office of State Revenue he or she does not hold a dealing registrable and therefore does not have the protection afforded by s 43A. In coming to this conclusion on this point his Honour disagreed with an earlier decision of Windeyer J in *Diemasters Pty Ltd v Meadowcorp Pty Ltd* (2001) 52 NSWLR 572 at 581.

7.127 A person who obtains an interest by fraud cannot gain the protection afforded by s 43A: *Diemasters Pty Ltd v Meadowcorp Pty Ltd* at 580–1. Furthermore, a void dealing, such as a forged dealing, is not a dealing registrable and does not attract the protection given by s 43A.[25] However, if a forged dealing is actually registered, the registered proprietor obtains an indefeasible title if he or she is not a party to any fraud. The fact that the instrument was a forgery means that, prior to registration, the unregistered interest would be defeated in a priority dispute with an earlier unregistered interest. In both *Jonray (Sydney) Pty Ltd v Partridge Bros Pty Ltd* (1969) 89 WN (NSW) Pt 1) 568 and *Mayer v Coe* (1968) 88 WN (NSW) (Pt 1) 549, it was suggested that if notice of a void instrument was received after completion of the transaction but before its registration, the true proprietor could prevent registration of it by obtaining an injunction to prevent registration.

7.128 A final aspect of s 43A protection is that the protection is not everlasting. In *Diemasters Pty Ltd v Meadowcorp Pty Ltd* at 581, Windeyer J said:

> [Section 43A] envisages that a dealing will be lodged for registration. Its purpose is to assist a party who lodges a dealing for registration, not to assist one who makes no effort to get protection of registration.

In that case his Honour held that s 43A protection was not available to a person who had taken no steps to get registered within a period of 14 months after settlement of the transaction.

7.129 The application of s 43A can be illustrated by the following example. B, a purchaser, takes a transfer of unencumbered property from A, the registered proprietor. If B has no notice of unregistered interests at the time of completion, B has the protection of s 43A in relation to any existing unregistered interests. Before registration of the transfer, B sells the land to C, a subsequent purchaser. On completion of the sale, B hands to C the transfer from A to B and the transfer from B to C. C does not have the benefit of s 43A, as he or she is not dealing directly with the registered proprietor, who is still A. C's transfer from B can only be registered after B's transfer from A is registered.

7.130 Thus, successive transfers do not extend the protection of s 43A to the ultimate purchaser — C in the above example. However, C could get s 43A protection if, instead of receiving two transfers from B, C received on completion of his or her purchase from B a transfer of the property from A. This is referred to as a transfer by direction, and involves A transferring the land to C at the direction of B. In such a case, C's transfer by direction does get s 43A protection because C is taking his or her interest directly from A and no intervening instruments need to be registered before C's transfer can be registered.

7.131 The application of s 43A to transfers by direction was confirmed in *Jonray (Sydney) v Partridge Bros* where the court held that a person in C's position must accept a transfer by direction. C could take steps to ensure that that transfer was properly executed by A and that A was properly

---

25. P Butt, *Land Law*, 6th ed, Lawbook Co, Sydney, 2010, p 795.

identified. If the transfer by direction was a forgery, C could not get s 43A protection, but if it was registered and there was no fraud on C's part, C would gain an indefeasible title. Thus, the position of a transferee in a transfer by direction is the same as a transferee in an ordinary transfer. In the above example, if C wants to avoid accepting a transfer by direction and its associated obligations of establishing the identity of A, C can do so by insisting on a clause in the contract of purchase from B to the effect that C will only accept a transfer from B as registered proprietor. In such a case, B will have had to register his or her transfer from A before settlement of the sale to C.

7.132   However, the problem associated with having successive transfers from A to B and from B to C can be overcome by the so-called successive effect of s 43A pursuant to the rule in *Wilkes v Spooner*: see 7.54. The application of the rule in *Wilkes v Spooner* in the context of s 43A was confirmed in *Jonray (Sydney) v Partridge Bros* and *Barlin Investments Pty Ltd v Westpac Banking Corporation* [2012] NSWSC 699 at [39].

7.133   In the context of competing prior equitable and later legal interests, the rule in *Wilkes v Spooner* stipulates that if X has a prior equitable interest and Y is a purchaser of the legal interest, taking it in good faith, for valuable consideration and without notice of X's interest, Y's interest gains priority over X's interest. If Y then sells the legal estate to Z, Z's interest has priority over X's interest, even if Z had notice of X's interest.

7.134   If the rule in *Wilkes v Spooner* is applied to the first example above (see 7.129), B gains the benefit of s 43A in relation to his or her transfer from A. As was stated in *IAC (Finance) v Courtenay*, B acquires on completion a deemed legal estate. B's subsequent transfer to C is one where the protection B acquired passes on to C in the same way as Y's legal estate, and priority over X, passed to Z in the example in the previous paragraph pursuant to the rule in *Wilkes v Spooner*. Indeed, C's position is better than B's because C gets the benefit of s 43A even if C had notice of some unregistered interest. What is critical from the perspective of C is that, when B obtained his or her transfer from A, B complied with the requirements of s 43A. If B does not acquire s 43A protection, then neither does C: *Diemasters Pty Ltd v Meadowcorp Pty Ltd* at 580. A consequence of the rule in *Wilkes v Spooner* in this context is that, in the absence of some contractual provision to the contrary in the contract between B and C, C is not entitled to demand that B register his or her transfer from A before completion of the contract between B and C. However, C can insist that both A and B are represented at completion so that C can be satisfied that the transfer from A to B is not subject to some equity or unregistered interest. If A does not oblige in this respect, C is entitled to insist upon A's transfer to B being registered before completion of the sale from B to C: *Neeta (Epping) Pty Ltd v Phillips* (1974) 131 CLR 286 at 303–4; 3 ALR 151 at 165.

7.135   The type of transaction in the example discussed in the previous paragraph is not a common occurrence. However, a more common occurrence in which the problems with s 43A do arise is illustrated in the following example. P owns Torrens title land and contracts to sell it to R. P's property is subject to a mortgage to Q, which is to be discharged on completion of the sale. On completion, R will receive a discharge of the mortgage between P and Q and a transfer from P to R. It used to be thought that the transfer did not get the direct protection of s 43A because it was not a dealing which was immediately registrable because the discharge of the mortgage had to be registered before the transfer was registered. This was said to be so because R did not take an interest under the discharge of the mortgage. Rather, it was P who did. However, R does get s 43A protection by the successive effect of s 43A pursuant to the rule in *Wilkes v Spooner* [1911] 2 KB 473.

7.136   However, following the decision in *Weller v Williams*, R no longer needs to rely upon the *Wilkes v Spooner* principle in this context. In that case, involving facts essentially the same as in the example in the previous paragraph, Ball J, at [18], said:

> The transfer is immediately registrable because the interest that is sought to be registered is derived immediately from the person who is entitled to grant it. It is true that, if it is registered in that form without a discharge of the mortgage ... , then [the purchasers] would take their interest subject to that mortgage. But that does not mean that the transfer is not immediately registrable. Nor does the fact that [the purchasers] may not be prepared for the transfer to take place in those circumstances; or that a transfer in those circumstances may be a breach by the [vendors] of their obligations under that mortgage. The requirement that the interest be in registrable form goes to the characteristics of the instrument, not whether or not the parties would want it to take effect in certain circumstances.

The consequence of the decision in *Weller v Williams* is that an earlier unregistered interest holder would not be able to prevent R from getting registered.

7.137   Furthermore, if R had borrowed money from S and on settlement of R's purchase S was to have a mortgage registered over the property, the earlier unregistered interest holder would not be able to prevent S getting the mortgage registered. In such circumstances S would not have the protection afforded by s 43A. However, R would have the protection afforded by s 43A and thus could not have his or her transfer stopped by the earlier unregistered interest holder. Such registration would extinguish the earlier unregistered interest and leave the way open for S to have the mortgage registered: *Weller v Williams* at [19]. The reasoning of Ball J in *Weller v Williams* was endorsed by Hodgson JA when his Honour refused to grant an application to grant a stay of the orders made by Ball J: *Weller v Williams* [2010] NSWCA 201 at [9].

Part III:
Relationships of Trust

8

CONFIDENTIAL INFORMATION

INTRODUCTION

8.1   In the course of everyday dealings it is common for people to disclose information to others, with the intention that the information only be used for particular purposes. Equity will prevent the unauthorised use of information by recipients in those circumstances and may hold them to account for any wrongful use. Such claims are generally referred to as actions for 'breach of confidence'.

8.2   The disclosure of confidential information can occur in all the myriad types of relationships that exist in a society: from governmental, through business and commercial relationships and into private, domestic relationships. Equity has fashioned a number of broad principles of confidence in response to the need to protect the multifarious forms of confidential relationship. But the cases all stem from the basic proposition stated by Lord Greene MR in *Saltman Engineering Co Ltd v Campbell Engineering Co Ltd* (1948) 65 RPC 203 at 213:

> If a defendant is proved to have used confidential information, directly or indirectly obtained from a plaintiff, without the consent, express or implied, of the plaintiff, he will be guilty of an infringement of the plaintiff's rights.

WHAT IS CONFIDENTIAL INFORMATION?

8.3   Because of the myriad ways obligations of confidence arise it has proven impossible to provide a strict definition of the phrase 'confidential information': *Corrs Pavey Whiting & Byrne v Collector of Customs (Vic)* (1987) 14 FCR 434 at 449–50. The phrase is best viewed as a term that covers information that is subject to an obligation of confidentiality.

8.4   The better approach is therefore to ask: What sorts of relationships give rise to obligations of confidence? Confidences arise in three sorts of relationships: private confidences, confidences relating to government secrets, and commercial confidences. This chapter will examine these confidential relationships from the perspective of the modern action for breach of confidence. The doctrine will be examined in terms of its origins and elements. In more recent times the doctrine has been developed to include protections for privacy. The extension of the doctrine will also be examined.

THE ORIGINS OF BREACH OF CONFIDENCE

8.5   The origins of the obligation of confidence are not easy to pigeonhole.[1] There are various claims to its parentage. In *Morison v Moat* (1851) 68 ER 492 at 498, Turner VC said:

> Different grounds have indeed been assigned for the exercise of that jurisdiction. In some cases it has been referred to property, in others to contract, and in others, again, it has been treated as founded upon trust or confidence, meaning, as I conceive, that the court fastens the obligation on the conscience of the party, and enforces it against him in the same manner as it enforces against a party to whom a benefit is given the obligation of performing a promise on the faith on which the benefit has been conferred; but, upon whatever ground the jurisdiction is founded, the authorities leave no doubt as to the exercise of it.

Property origins

8.6   In one respect the action for breach of confidence is property-based. In many cases the information has taken the form of property, such as written (but unpublished) descriptions of inventions, which may be protected by copyright. But it is also clear that the exercise of the jurisdiction is not dependent upon the information being characterised as property (rights *in rem*).

8.7   Many trade secrets or processes will be protected by the obligation of confidence even though they may lack the essential elements of novelty or inventiveness necessary for registration as a patent or other form of intellectual property: *Krueger Transport Equipment Pty Ltd v Glen Cameron Storage* [2008] FCA 803. For example, in *Franklin v Giddins* [1978] Qd R 72, the plaintiff was unable to rely on statutory protection of his newly bred fruit tree as it was not a patentable invention or process, and yet it was protected by equity's obligation of confidence.

8.8   Many people may wish to rely on equity instead of statutory registration schemes because the latter are costly, time consuming or inconvenient, and the protection that they provide is normally limited to a term of years.[2] The equitable action for breach of confidence suffers from none of these drawbacks.

8.9   Stuckey has argued that the interest protected in actions of breach of confidence is, in its purest form, a right *in personam* and hence not property in either legal or equitable senses.[3] This was the approach adopted by Lord Upjohn in *Phipps v Boardman* [1967] 2 AC 46 at 127–8; [1966] 3 All ER 721 at 759, where his Lordship said:

> The true test is to determine in what circumstances the information has been acquired. If it has been acquired in such circumstances that it would be a breach of confidence to disclose it to another then courts of equity will restrain the recipient from communicating it to another. In such cases such confidential information is often and for many years has been described as the property

---

1.   For an historical account of the origins and development of breach of confidence see M Richardson, M Bryan, M Vranken & K Barnett, *Breach of Confidence, Social Origins and Modern Developments* Edward Elgar, Cheltenham (UK), 2012.

2.   R P Meagher, D Heydon & M Leeming, *Meagher, Gummow and Lehane's Equity: Doctrines and Remedies*, 4th ed, LexisNexis Butterworths, Sydney, 2002, p 1109.

3.   J Stuckey, 'The Equitable Action for Breach of Confidence: Is Information Property?' (1981) 9 *Sydney Law Review* 402.

of the donor, the books of authority are full of such references: knowledge of secret processes, 'know-how', confidential information as to the prospects of a company or of someone's intention or the expected results of some horse race based on stable or other confidential information. But in the end the real truth is that it is not property in any normal sense but equity will restrain its transmission to another if in breach of some confidential relationship.

8.10 In *OBG Ltd v Allan* [2008] 1 AC 1 at 77; [2007] 4 All ER 545 at 611, Lord Walker (who was in dissent but perhaps not on this point) said that confidential information cannot be regarded as a form of property. The High Court has also doubted that property provides a basis for the action: *Moorgate Tobacco Co Ltd v Philip Morris Ltd (No 2)* (1984) 156 CLR 414; 56 ALR 193; *Brent v Federal Commissioner of Taxation* (1971) 125 CLR 418. A consequence of this view is that confidential information cannot be assigned.

8.11 However, as noted below, while obligations of confidence operate personally, confidential information will also be protected in cases where it lies in the hands of innocent third parties: *Butler v Board of Trade* [1971] Ch 680; [1970] 3 All ER 593. This suggests that there are dimensions to the right of confidence that operate against the world (*in rem*): *Elecon Australia Pty Ltd v Brevini Australia Pty Ltd* [2009] FCA 1327 at [262]–[269]; *Coogan v News Group Newspapers Ltd* [2012] EWCA Civ 48 at [50].

8.12 Additionally, trade secrets are often sold in commercial transactions: *TS & B Retail Systems Pty Ltd v 3Fold Resources Pty Ltd (No 3)* (2007) 158 FCR 444; 239 ALR 117; *O'Mustad & Son v S Allcock & Co Ltd* (1928) 1B IPR 773. Trade secrets can be held by a trustee in bankruptcy: *Re Keene* (1922) 2 Ch 475. They can be devised by will: *Morison v Moat* (1851) 68 ER 492. The fact that one can transfer bundles of rights concerning trade secrets indicates that they have property characteristics: *DPC Estates Pty Ltd v Grey* [1974] 1 NSWLR 443 at 460; *Smith Kline & French Laboratories (Aust) Ltd v Secretary, Department of Community Services & Health* (1990) 22 FCR 73 at 121–2; 95 ALR 87 at 136. Finally, many of the remedies for breach of confidence are proprietary in the way that the court can order that information be delivered up, or that it be held on constructive trust. In *Farah Constructions Pty Ltd v Say-Dee Pty Ltd* (2007) 230 CLR 89 at 143–4; 236 ALR 209 at 246, the High Court said:

> The protection given by equitable doctrines and remedies causes confidential information sometimes to be described as having a proprietary character, 'not because property is the basis upon which that protection is given, but because of the effect of that protection'. Certain types of confidential information share characteristics with standard instances of property. Thus trade secrets may be transferred, held in trust and charged.

8.13 One way to resolve these conflicting positions is to split the doctrine into two distinct causes of action, one for commercial/proprietorial confidences and the other for personal confidences.[4] Another, more nuanced approach is to treat the equitable right of action, and not the information itself, as property: *Smith Kline & French Laboratories v Secretary, Department of Community Services and Health* at FCR 121; ALR 136. Therefore, if a third party purchased a right to keep information confidential, that person would not have acquired property but instead an equity, which would

---

4.   J Birch, 'Breach of confidence: Dividing the cause of action along proprietary lines' (2007) 81 *Australian Law Journal* 338.

then be enforceable against others seeking to use the information in breach of the obligation of confidence: *TS & B Retail Systems Pty Ltd v 3Fold Resources Pty Ltd (No 3)*. In *Painaway Australia Pty Ltd (in prov liq) (admin apptd) — Painaway Australia Pty Ltd v JAKL Group Pty Ltd* [2011] NSWSC 205 at [308], Ward J said:

> Overall, although there is still uncertainty surrounding this area, it is generally accepted that it is not possible for equity to assign confidential information, as confidential information is not 'property' capable of being assigned. There is authority, however, for the proposition that it is possible to assign the right to enforce an obligation to keep information confidential.

8.14   Such an assignment of the right to enforce confidences is subject to the rules regarding the assignment of personal obligations: see 5.28–5.29. Personal obligations will not be assignable if they amount to slavery or forced labour. In *Mid-City Skin Cancer & Laser Centre v Zahedi-Anarak* (2006) 67 NSWLR 569 a doctor was found to owe obligations of confidence to an assignee as the duty was characterised as being negative in nature and could be complied with by doing nothing. Because of that it was not analogous to an assignment of personal services that offended public policy (see 5.30).

Contract origins

8.15   Many obligations of confidence will arise between parties who are in a contractual relationship. Indeed, many contractual relationships will impose duties of confidence expressly, and in such cases the extent of those obligations is determined by the contract: *Deta Nominees Pty Ltd v Viscount Plastic Products Pty Ltd* [1979] VR 167 at 190.

8.16   Express covenants are often used restrictively in employment contexts to prevent use of confidential information after the termination of employment. While there were earlier doubts, it now appears that an express clause can extend contractual obligations of confidence beyond what would be imposed by equity: *Wright v Gasweld Pty Ltd* (1991) 22 NSWLR 317. However, it should be remembered that restrictive clauses are read subject to the doctrine against restraint of trade (*Twenty-First Australia Inc v Shade* [1998] NSWSC 325), so it is unlikely that such a clause would be upheld should it seek to protect frivolous or trivial information: *Wright v Gasweld* at 333. Contractual obligations may also be enforceable against individuals after the information has already been released into the public domain: *Brand v Monks* [2009] NSWSC 1454 at [180]. Contracts which provide for unqualified or unclear prohibitions are less likely to be upheld (*Caterpillar Logistics Services (UK) Ltd v de Crean* [2011] EWHC 3154), whereas contracts which provide for a process of obtaining express permission to communicate are less likely to be struck down: *Ministry of Defence v Griffin* [2008] EWHC 1542.

8.17   Obligations of confidence can also be implied into contracts: *Deta Nominees v Viscount Plastic Products* at 190. When the contractual duty of confidence is implied it will mirror the equitable duty of confidence: *Mid-City Skin Cancer & Laser Centre v Zahedi-Anarak* at 602.

8.18   However, duties of confidence are not dependent on contractual relationships. The equitable duty will lie dormant and unaffected by contractual obligations and may spring into effect should the contractual obligation fail to eventuate. In *Seager v Copydex Ltd* [1967] 2 All ER 415, the plaintiff entered into negotiations with the defendant company, who sought to market the plaintiff's patented invention known as the 'Klent' grip. In the course of negotiating a marketing agreement, the plaintiff unexpectedly told the defendant about a new invention, which he had not yet patented, called the 'Invisigrip'. The defendant's agents told the plaintiff that they were only interested in marketing the Klent grip. Negotiations eventually broke down. After that time agents of the defendant sought to patent a new design that was substantially similar to the Invisigrip. The plaintiff sought an injunction to prevent the defendant company from marketing the new grip. The plaintiff also sought damages or an account of profits in the alternative.

8.19   The defendant company was found to have breached the plaintiff's confidence. Lord Denning MR, at 417, found that the jurisdiction of the court did not depend on any implied contract. Rather, equity would intervene on the basis that people who have received information in confidence should not be allowed to take unfair advantage of it. Lord Denning MR also stated that in cases where part of the information was publicly available (such as the parts of the design contained in the Klent patent specification), and partly private (such as the amendments made in the Invisigrip design), the recipient of the information must be careful to only use that part of the information which is public.

8.20   Both Salmon and Winn LJJ, at 418–19, agreed with Lord Denning MR. They also found that the defendant was liable for breaching confidence even though the defendant's agents had unconsciously copied the Invisigrip design. An injunction was refused. Instead, damages were ordered to be assessed on the basis of reasonable compensation.

Tort basis

8.21   Breach of confidence has sometimes been characterised as a tort. While this characterisation has been around for a long time, in the United Kingdom the tendency to describe the action as a tort has been accelerated by the application of the *Human Rights Act 1998* (UK). In *Campbell v Mirror Group Newspapers Ltd* [2004] 2 AC 457 at 465; [2004] 2 All ER 995 at 1002–3, Lord Nicholls found that breach of confidence had changed its nature and said the following:

> The continuing use of the phrase 'duty of confidence' and the description of the information as 'confidential' is not altogether comfortable. Information about an individual's private life would not, in ordinary usage, be called 'confidential'. The more natural description today is that such information is private. The essence of the tort is better encapsulated now as misuse of private information.

New Zealand has also expressly recognised a privacy tort: see 8.136. There remain some doubts in the English and Welsh jurisdictions as to whether the action has become completely 'fused' with common law. In *Mosley v News Group Newspapers Ltd* [2008] EWHC 1777, Eady J expressed doubts about tort taking over the action. In Australia, the action has remained firmly entrenched in equity. This will be discussed further below.

Human rights origins

8.22   Following on from these tortious developments in England and Wales and spurred on by the *Human Rights Act 1998* (UK), some English and Welsh judges have now characterised breach of confidence as being based in human rights jurisprudence. In *Campbell v Mirror Group Newspapers*, at AC 473; All ER 1010, Lord Hoffmann stated that in England the law of private confidence has moved away from being based on duties of good faith and has moved to the protection of human autonomy and dignity. In *Mosley v News Group Newspapers Ltd*, at [7], Eady J found that the law afforded protection to information when there was a reasonable expectation of privacy, primarily because the law is concerned to prevent the violation of a citizen's autonomy, dignity and self-esteem. This adaptation of breach of confidence into the human rights jurisprudence will be discussed at 8.138–8.151.

Unjust enrichment

8.23 An alternative basis for the protection of confidential information lies in unjust enrichment. Professor Gareth Jones has stated that breach of confidence is a restitutionary claim to make good profits obtained from the wrongful use of confidential material.[5] This argument is strengthened by the tendency of some judges to calculate equitable compensation in a restitutionary way: *Attorney-General v Observer Ltd* [1990] 1 AC 109 at 262; [1988] 3 All ER 545 at 644–5; *Minister for Mineral Resources v Newcastle Newspaper Pty Ltd* (1997) 40 IPR 403.

8.24 However, as argued by Richardson, the principle of restitution appears unable to explain equity's protection of personal information, which has little or no commercial value and from which no real account can be made.[6] The restitutionary basis of the account of profits remedy is often difficult to employ and, as a result, relief is more often based on equitable compensation (what was lost by the plaintiff) rather than unjust enrichment (what was gained by the defendant).

Equitable origins in conscience

8.25 It is now well established that equity has its own jurisdiction to protect obligations of confidence which is independent of contract, tort and property: *Commonwealth v John Fairfax & Sons Ltd* (1980) 147 CLR 39 at 50; 32 ALR 485 at 491.

8.26 This jurisdiction appears to have grown out of the earlier line of cases concerning common law copyright in unpublished manuscripts. Alternatively, it can be viewed as an expression of equity's protection of contractual obligations and good faith: *Abernethy v Hutchinson* (1825) 47 ER 1313.

8.27 In *Moorgate Tobacco Co Ltd v Philip Morris Ltd (No 2)* at CLR 437–8; ALR 208, Deane J said:

> It is unnecessary, for the purposes of the present appeal, to attempt to define the precise scope of the equitable jurisdiction to grant relief against an actual or threatened abuse of confidential information not involving any tort or any breach of some express or implied contractual provision, some wider fiduciary duty or some copyright or trade mark right. A general equitable jurisdiction to grant such relief has long been asserted and should, in my view, now be accepted … Like most heads of exclusive equitable jurisdiction, its rational basis does not lie in proprietary right. It lies in the notion of an obligation of conscience arising from the circumstances in or through which the information was communicated or obtained. Relief under the jurisdiction is not available, however, unless it appears that the information in question has 'the necessary quality of confidence about it' (per Lord Greene MR, *Saltman* (1948) 65 RPC, at 215) and that it is significant, not necessarily in the sense of commercially valuable (see *Argyll v Argyll* [1967] Ch 302 at 329) but in the sense that the preservation of its confidentiality or secrecy is of substantial concern to the plaintiff.

---

5. G Jones, 'Restitution of Benefits Obtained in Breach of Another's Confidence' (1970) 86 *Law Quarterly Review* 463.
6. M Richardson, 'Breach of Confidence, Surreptitiously or Accidentally Obtained Information and Privacy: Theory vs Law' (1994) *Melbourne University Law Review* 673.

Therefore the traditional essence of the equitable obligation is unconscientious conduct: *R v Dept of Health; Ex parte Source Informatics Ltd* [2000] 1 All ER 786 at 796; *Australian Broadcasting Corporation v Lenah Game Meats Pty Ltd* (2001) 208 CLR 199 at 227; 185 ALR 1 at 14. The notion of unconscientiousness obviously attaches to situations where the parties have an established relationship of trust (in the broad sense). However, as we shall see below, the notion of unconscientiousness is not limited to these types of situations. Equity will also view the actions of a thief or industrial spy as unconscientious, even though they have no prior relationship with the plaintiff.

THE MODERN DOCTRINE OF BREACH OF CONFIDENCE

8.28   In *Coco v A N Clark (Engineers) Ltd* [1969] RPC 41 at 47, Megarry J clearly set out the elements of the modern action as follows:

> In my judgment, three elements are normally required if, apart from contract, a case of breach of confidence is to succeed. First, the information itself, in the words of Lord Greene MR in the *Saltman* case on page 215, must 'have the necessary quality of confidence about it'. Secondly, that information must have been imparted in circumstances importing an obligation of confidence. Thirdly, there must be an unauthorised use of that information to the detriment of the party communicating it.

Each of these three elements will be analysed in turn.

Information that has a quality of confidence

8.29   The primary and most essential characteristic of confidential information is that it be information which has not entered the public domain and become common knowledge: *Saltman Engineering Co Ltd v Campbell Engineering Co* at 215. All three types of confidential information (see 8.4) are subject to this requirement. However, each protects different subject matter. The discussion will first centre on the concepts of secrecy and the public domain and then move on to consider the different categories of confidences.

Secrecy and the public domain

8.30   Where information has been published on a non-confidential basis, it cannot be treated as confidential. The question of whether the information has entered the public domain is a question of fact: *Missingham v Shamin* [2012] NSWSC 288. For example, in the area of trade secrets, the publication of a patent can be fatal to a claim of confidence if it can be shown that there is no ancillary secret surrounding the patent: *O'Mustad & Son v S Allcock & Co Ltd* [1963] 3 All ER 416; *Maggbury Pty Ltd v Hafele Australia Pty Ltd* (2001) 210 CLR 181; 185 ALR 152. Publication of patent specifications in other jurisdictions may also destroy duties of confidence if it can be shown that regular reference is made to foreign patent specifications by people within the jurisdiction: *Franchi v Franchi* [1967] RPC 149. However, if the patent specifications do not cover the entirety of the trade secret, duties of confidence will survive in relation to the unpublished information: *Castrol Australia Pty Ltd v Emtech Associates Pty Ltd* (1980) 33 ALR 31; *Seager v Copydex*.

8.31   Copyrighted designs may also lose the quality of confidence when they become shown to the public. In *Lucasfilm Ltd v Ainsworth* [2008] EWHC 1878 (Ch) (overturned on other grounds in *Lucasfilm Ltd v Ainsworth* [2012] 1 AC 208; [2011] 4 All ER 817), the original prop designer from *Star Wars* who created the Stormtrooper helmets and other props had gone into the business of making helmets and costumes for the public. Lucasfilm Ltd attempted to stop the prop designer by arguing (amongst other things) that the designs were confidential but Mann J found that the designs lost their confidential nature when the films were released.

8.32 Publication of information subject to a personal confidence will usually destroy any duties of confidentiality. In *Lennon v News Group Newspapers Ltd* [1978] FSR 573, John Lennon failed to prevent his former wife from publishing secrets of their married life, on the basis that he had himself published information on the topic. In *British Broadcasting Corporation v Harpercollins Publishers Ltd* [2010] EWHC 2424 (Ch), the BBC failed to injunct the publication of a book by Ben Collins, who intended to use the book to reveal his identity as the 'White Stig' from the *Top Gear* television show. The BBC argued that this information was confidential but Morgan J had found that numerous papers had published the information in the weeks preceding the release of the book.

8.33 However, publications that are transitory and unlikely to be remembered will not destroy duties of confidentiality. For example, a television broadcast of an informant's identity did not destroy confidentiality in *G v Day* [1982] 1 NSWLR 24. Similarly, a Chinese pop star was successful in restraining the publication of an embarrassing video tape on the internet, even after a verbal account of the contents had been published in a Hong Kong newspaper: *Kwok v Thang* [1999] NSWSC 1034. In *Australian Football League v Age Company Ltd* (2006) 15 VR 419, the names of three AFL players who had tested positive to drugs were published on an internet discussion forum. An electronic newspaper article had also named the players to a limited group of subscribers for about five hours. A further publication of one of the player's names had occurred when a telephone caller named the player on the *Fox Footy* television program. Regardless, Kellam J found that the information had still not yet fully entered the public domain and remained confidential. A permanent injunction was ordered on the release of the players' identities.

8.34 Nor will publications of differing versions of similar information destroy confidence. The publication of authorised photos of the wedding of Catherine Zeta-Jones and Michael Douglas by a magazine did not mean that a rival, unapproved publisher could publish different, unauthorised images in breach of confidence: *OBG Ltd v Allan*.

8.35 Publication to a small group of recipients, who understand that the information is to remain confidential, will not destroy the information's quality of confidence. Thus, Prince Charles was able to prevent the publication of his diaries, even though he regularly gave copies of them to a select group of between 45 and 75 people: *Prince of Wales v Associated Newspapers Ltd* [2008] Ch 57; [2007] 2 All ER 139.

8.36 An issue that arises is whether defendants can rely on their own breaches of confidence to argue that the information is no longer secretive. Information will lose its confidentiality when published by a defendant, particularly if published widely: *Attorney-General v Observer*, discussed at 8.67–8.68. This does not mean that the defendant's breach of obligation will be without remedy. Rather, it means that remedies for that breach may be limited to an account of profits or compensation, as injunctive relief may be futile.

Personal information

8.37 The jurisdiction to protect personal and private information developed out of a series of cases which upheld the right of authors and artists to prevent unauthorised publication of works that they wished to keep secret: *Crowder v Hilton* [1902] SALR 82; *Millar v Taylor* (1769) 98 ER 201; *Turner v Robinson* (1860) 10 Ir Ch 121. The most famous of these cases is *Prince Albert v Strange* (1849) 47 ER 1302; 41 ER 1171. In this case, Queen Victoria's consort sought to restrain publication of private etchings made by him and the Queen. The Prince had given the etchings to the Royal printer. An employee was presumed to have sold extra copies to a third party after which the prints went through a variety of hands until they landed with the defendant. The defendant sought to display the etchings and publish a catalogue describing them. The plans to display the etchings were dropped at trial but the defendant maintained that he had a right to do so if he wished.

8.38 At trial, the defendant's right to display the etchings or publish the catalogue was denied. On appeal Lord Cottenham LC found that the jurisdiction to prevent unauthorised use was based both in property (in what the modern reader might regard as copyright in unpublished works) and in equity's power to restrain breaches of trust, confidence or contract. As the etchings had come to Strange via a breach of contract, trust or confidence, equity could prevent the unauthorised use of the materials. Since the decision in *Prince Albert v Strange*, equity has come to protect a variety of types of personal and private information that has been relayed in confidence.

Sexual relationship, preferences and activity

8.39 Equity will intervene to protect privacy in a number of situations. The clearest examples are those cases concerning exposure of the personal information that arose in marriage or de facto relationships. For example, in *Argyll v Argyll* [1967] Ch 302; [1965] 1 All ER 611, the Duchess of Argyll was able to prevent her ex-husband from publishing intimate details of her marital behaviour in a Sunday newspaper.

8.40 Equity will also protect the details of a person's sexual preference and activity if such details have been communicated in confidence, but outside of marriage: *Goodwin v NGN Ltd* [2011] EWHC 1437 (QB); *Contostavlos v Mendahun* [2012] EWHC 850 (QB). For example, in *Stephens v Avery* [1988] Ch 449; [1988] 2 All ER 477, the plaintiff succeeded in restraining the defendant from publishing an account of her affair with another woman (who was later murdered by the plaintiff's husband). Browne-Wilkinson VC, at Ch 454; All ER 481, said that 'to most people the details of their sexual lives are high on their list of those matters which they regard as confidential'. In *Giller v Procopets* (2008) 24 VR 1, the videotaped sexual activities of a couple which had been taped after their de facto relationship had come to an end, were also said to be confidential. In *Ntuli v Donald* [2010] EWCA Civ 1276, Ntuli, the ex-girlfriend of Howard Donald (a singer from the boy band 'Take That'), was enjoined from disclosing intimate, personal or sexually explicit details regarding the relationship. Similarly, in *Mosley v News Group Newspapers Ltd*, the sado-masochistic activities of a group of S & M practitioners were found to have been confidential as the group met regularly and with an understanding that the group's activities be based on trust and discretion. Some of the women in the group were paid for their services but the group members were also friends, and on this basis the relationships in the group were said to be confidential.

8.41 While the details of a sexual relationship are confidential that does not necessarily mean that the bare fact of the existence of a sexual or familial relationship is confidential: *SKA v CRH* [2012] EWHC 766 (QB) at [26]; *Goodwin v NGN Ltd* at [90]. In *Hutcheson (Formerly Known As 'KGM') v News Group Newspapers Ltd* [2011] EWCA Civ 808, the plaintiff (who was chef Gordon Ramsey's father-in-law) failed to prevent the publication of the fact that he had a second 'secret' family. At trial Eady J found that there could be no expectation of privacy over such a bare fact and, on appeal, Gross LJ expressed sympathy with this position.

8.42 The courts will also look at the depth and length of the relationship. Communication of the details of casual, transient sexual relationships may be harder to restrain. In *A v B plc* [2003] QB 195, an English Premier League footballer was unsuccessful in preventing publication of stories by two women he had had affairs with. Lord Woolf CJ felt the relationships did not possess the same requirements of confidentiality as a long-term relationship such as marriage. Similarly, in *Theakston v Mirror Group Newspapers Ltd* [2002] EWHC 137 (QB) at [60], information pertaining to a television presenter's visit to a brothel was not confidential given the fact that the relationship was a 'fleeting transaction for money' (although a photograph of him at the brothel was held to be confidential). Neither will all the information imparted in the course of a personal relationship be confidential. In *Lord Browne of Madingley v Associated Newspapers Ltd* [2008] QB 103, the fact that the confidant had been in a long-term homosexual relationship with the plaintiff (a high-ranking businessman in a large multinational corporation) did not mean that all the information imparted in that relationship was confidential. The ex-lover wished to publish details of the plaintiff's allegedly improper use of company resources and the Court of Appeal found that the plaintiff did not have a reasonable expectation of privacy in relation to these issues.

Private journals and reminiscences

8.43 Journals containing personal thoughts and recollections will also be protected as confidential. In a modern version of *Prince Albert v Strange*, Prince Charles was able to claim breach of confidence over the publication of extracts from his personal diaries by a former employee. The diaries were circulated amongst a select group of readers on the understanding that they not be published. The employee had also been under a contractual obligation of confidence: *Prince of Wales v Associated Newspapers*.

8.44 In *McKennitt v Ash* [2008] QB 73, the Court of Appeal upheld a decision not to allow the publication of parts of a memoir on the grounds that the memoir contained personal information of a confidential nature. The memoir had been written by the friend of Loreena McKennitt, a renowned folk musician, and recounted their friendship of many years. The book contained a number of personal and private details including facts relating to McKennitt's relationship with her fiancé (who died in tragic circumstances), her grieving process, her home in Ireland, her record contract and McKennitt's state of health. All of these issues were found to have been confidential.

Medical information

8.45 A person's medical history, including information on infectious diseases, mental health and drug addiction, will be the subject of protection, especially when the disclosure of the patient's medical condition would subject the patient to ridicule or embarrassment: *X v Y* [1988] 2 All ER 648; *W v Edgell* [1990] 1 All ER 835. For example, supermodel Naomi Campbell was able to claim damages for the publication of details of her group therapy for narcotics addiction and photographs of her attendance at meetings: *Campbell v Mirror Group Newspapers*. Positive drugs results of three AFL players were also found to be confidential in *Australian Football League v Age Company Ltd*. However, the protection of medical information is subject to the defence of public interest (see 8.97–8.108), which may justify publication: *Spelman v Express Newspapers* [2012]

EWHC 355 (QB). Also, if medical information has been anonymised there will be no breach if the information is published: *R v Dept of Health; Ex parte Source Informatics Ltd* [2000] 1 All ER 786. The court will judge whether information has been sufficiently anonymised: *Local Authority v Health Authority (disclosure: restriction on publication)* [2004] 1 All ER 480.

Witnesses, informants, suspects and released prisoners

8.46   The identity of witnesses and informants will also be protected by equity in circumstances where assurances of confidence were given to them, and they would suffer prejudice from being identified, with no resulting benefit to the public: *G v Day*. This is the case even where photographs may have been shown in the public domain for a short period: *Falconer v Australian Broadcasting Corporation* [1992] 1 VR 662. In *Venables v News Group Newspapers Ltd* [2001] 1 All ER 908, released prisoners, who had been convicted of killing a child when they were themselves children, were also protected by confidence. The protection of confidence was afforded to them because of the risk of serious injury or death should the public become aware of their identity and whereabouts. A similar protection was afforded in Northern Ireland to a convicted killer to prevent publication of his image, personal details and address, after he had served his sentence: *Callaghan v Independent News and Media Ltd* [2009] NIQB 1. On the other hand, a majority of the New Zealand Supreme Court allowed the publication of a video in which an accused person (who had been acquitted of the murder), confessed to killing the victim. While the court dealt with the issue under the New Zealand privacy tort (see 8.136–8.137), the majority stated that there could be no expectation of confidence if the person was being interviewed by police and knowingly videotaped: *Television New Zealand Ltd v Rogers* [2007] 1 NZLR 156.

Cultural information

8.47   On a wider level, cultural and religious information that is of a highly sensitive nature can be protected by equity. In *Foster v Mountford & Rigby Ltd* (1976) 14 ALR 71, Muirhead J enjoined the publication of a scholarly text on the lives of the Pitjantjatjara People in the Northern Territory. The information had been imparted to the author in the greatest of confidence. The author had been accepted into the community and been given access to the people's sacred rites and law. The information had an enormous potential to harm the social fabric of the Aboriginal community should it have become available to the uninitiated. Given that damages were inadequate, an injunction was granted. However, if the courts view the cultural or religious practices as harmful to the public they will not be afforded protection: *Church of Scientology of California v Kaufman* [1973] RPC 635. *Foster v Mountford & Rigby Ltd* was referred to positively in *Wyman on behalf of the Bidjara People v State of Queensland* [2012] FCA 397, a case concerning an application to prevent an anthropologist from sharing data taken from one anthropological study with another, for the purpose of a native title claim. The application for injunction failed in this case because the judge could not find evidence that there was any inappropriate sharing of confidential information.

Commercial information

8.48   Equity protects a variety of sorts of confidential commercial information. These are generally referred to as 'trade secrets'. A distinction can be made at the outset between trade secrets, which will be vigorously protected by equity, and other forms of commercial knowledge that are considered to be too general or obvious to justify protection. Claims that lack detail or seek to protect information that is common knowledge will fail: *Amway Corporation v Eurway International Ltd* [1974] RPC 82. Additionally, a global claim that fails to particularise the specific pieces of confidential information will also fail: *O'Brien v Komesaroff* (1982) 150 CLR 310; 41 ALR 255.

8.49   Information is more likely to be classed as a trade secret when it is of a detailed nature and acquired with effort: *Robb v Green* [1895] 2 QB 1. Additionally, if the information was the product of a special relationship with the plaintiff's clients, it is more likely to be protected: *Westminster Chemical New Zealand Ltd v McKinley & Tasman Machinery & Services Ltd* [1973] 1 NZLR 659 at 666.

8.50   In *Ansell Rubber Co Pty Ltd v Allied Rubber Industries Pty Ltd* [1967] VR 37 at 50, Gowans J said:

> Some factors to be considered in determining whether given information is one's trade secret are: (1) the extent to which the information is known outside of his business; (2) the extent to which it is known by employees and others involved in his business; (3) the extent of measures taken by him to guard the secrecy of the information; (4) the value of the information to him and to his competitors; (5) the amount of effort or money expended by him in developing the information; (6) the ease or difficulty with which the information could be properly acquired or duplicated by others.

8.51   Some specific examples of trade secrets include:

1. Designs for machinery: *Ansell Rubber Co v Allied Rubber Industries*; clothing: *Peter Pan Manufacturing Corp v Corsets Silhouette Ltd* [1963] 3 All ER 402; film costumes: *Lucasfilm Ltd v Ainsworth*; methods of construction: *Cranleigh Precision Engineering Ltd v Bryant* [1966] RPC 81; and tools: *Seager v Copydex*.
2. Chemical formulae: *Weston v Hemmons* (1876) 2 VLR (Eq) 121; the results of experiments: *Smith Kline & French Laboratories v Secretary, Department of Community Services & Health*; and recipes: *Crowder v Hilton*.
3. Ideas for entertainment, such as TV shows or exhibitions, which have been developed to the stage that they could become realised in actuality: *Fraser v Thames Television Ltd* [1984] QB 44; *Talbot v General Television Corp Pty Ltd* [1980] VR 224; *Darvall McCutcheon (a firm) v HK Frost Holdings P/L (in liq)* (2002) 4 VR 570. However, a bare idea that is obvious and undeveloped will not be protected: *De Maudsley v Palumbo* [1996] FSR 447 (an idea for a nightclub).

Trade secret or employee 'know-how'? 6/4/14

8.52   Difficulties arise in the employment context when employees seek to leave their jobs and set up businesses in competition with their former employers. In these cases the courts are guided by the principle that an employee should be free to use his or her accumulated knowledge, skill and experience ('know-how'). By the same token, there is an implied term in every employment contract that an employee 'shall honestly and faithfully serve his master; that he shall not abuse his confidence in matters pertaining to his service, and that he shall, by all reasonable means in his power, protect his master's interests in respect to matters confided to him in the course of his service': *Robb v Green* at 10–11. These interests must be balanced out: *Manildra Laboratories Pty Ltd v Campbell* [2009] NSWSC 987; *Labelmakers Group Pty Ltd v LL Force Pty Ltd* [2012] FCA 512 at [291]. As a starting point it has been observed that the more that information can be understood as part of the general knowledge of the employee, the less likely it will be protected by equity: the 'more that information can be identified as part of the general stock of knowledge which the former employee must use in carrying on his occupation, the less likely it is that the alleged confidentiality of the information will be protected': *Freedom Motors Australia Pty Ltd v Vaupotic* [2003] NSWSC 506 at [13].

8.53   To aid this process of balancing, the courts have adopted a three-tiered classification of employment information: *Faccenda Chicken Ltd v Fowler* [1985] 1 All ER 724. Information can be classed in the following categories:

1.   trivial information, which is publicly available or so obvious that it cannot be protected;
2.   information that must be treated confidentially until the termination of employment, whereupon it becomes part of the ex-employee's collective skill, knowledge and ability; or
3.   highly confidential trade secrets, which will be protected by the courts even after the termination of employment.

In *Faccenda* it was said that only the last category could be protected by an action for breach of confidence. This was rejected in *Wright v Gasweld*, where the New South Wales Court of Appeal held that the second category may also be protected by a valid restraint of trade clause in an employment contract.

8.54   The difficulty with using the *Faccenda* classification can be illustrated by the example of the employee who, after leaving the employ of the employer, approaches the employer's customers. If ex-employees have done this with the aid of stolen or copied customer lists they will be found to have breached their obligation of confidence: *AIIB Pty Ltd v Beard* [2009] NSWSC 1001 at [157]; *Riteway Express Pty Ltd v Clayton* (1987) 10 NSWLR 238; *Print Investments Pty Ltd v Art-vue Printing Ltd* (1983) 1 IPR 149; *Metrans Pty Ltd v Courtney-Smith* (1983) 8 IR 379; *Thomas Marshall (Exports) Ltd v Guinle* [1979] Ch 227; [1978] 3 All ER 193; *Helmore v Smith (No 2)* (1886) 35 Ch D 449. Records of dealings with individual clients have also been classified as confidential: *Williams Summers & Co Ltd v Boyce & Kimmond & Co* (1907) 97 LT 505.

8.55   However, if an ex-employee approaches clients in circumstances where knowledge regarding the clients is public and easily obtainable this will be treated as trivial information, not to be protected: *NP Generations Pty Ltd v Feneley* (2001) 80 SASR 151; *TV Shopping Network Ltd v Scutt* (1998) 43 IPR 451. This is, of course, subject to any valid restraint of trade clause in the employment contract: *Bluescope Steel Ltd v Kelly* (2007) 72 IPR 289 at 309.

8.56   To complicate matters further, information taken dishonestly will be protected by the courts even when it relates to know-how: *Halliday & Nicholas Insurance Brokers Pty Ltd v Corsiatto* [2001] NSWCA 188 at [16]–[17]; *Roger Bullivant Ltd v Ellis* [1987] FSR 172. Ex-employees are not entitled to approach customers if they have dishonestly removed or deliberately memorised lists of the ex-employer's clients: *Wessex Dairies Ltd v Smith* [1935] 2 KB 80. Of course, the idea of 'dishonest' or 'deliberate' memorisation is an extremely slippery one and hard to distinguish from the employees' ordinary memories: *SSC&B: Lintas New Zealand Ltd v Murphy* [1986] 2 NZLR 436. Nevertheless, the distinction between deliberate memorisation and ordinary memories remains the law: *Weldon & Co v Harbinson* [2000] NSWSC 272 at [70]; *Commercial & Accounting Services (Camden) Pty Ltd v Cummins* [2011] NSWSC 843 at [40]–[41].

8.57   These difficult issues were canvassed by the New South Wales Court of Appeal in *Del Casale v Artedomus (Aust) Pty Limited* (2007) 73 IPR 326. The appellants were former employees and directors of the respondent company (Artedomus). The company had discovered and sourced a supply of Italian modica stone from the Ragusa region which was highly sought after. When they left the company the directors agreed that they would keep confidential any sensitive commercial information they had obtained from the company for three years. The appellants then established a competitor which began to import the same stone. Artedomus argued that the information concerning the source of the stone was a trade secret and the appellants' actions were a breach of confidence. The trial judge agreed, ordering a permanent injunction on the use of the information about the source of the supply of the modica stone. On appeal, the New South Wales Court of Appeal overturned the finding of confidentiality. Following Dean,[7] Hodgson JA, at 335–6, said that the following list would help in determining whether information was a trade secret:

1. The extent to which the information is known outside the business.
2. The extent to which the trade secret was known by employees and others involved in the plaintiff's business.
3. The extent of measures taken to guard the secrecy of the information.
4. The value of the information to the plaintiffs and their competitors.
5. The amount of effort or money expended by the plaintiffs in developing the information.
6. The ease or difficulty with which the information could be properly acquired or duplicated by others.
7. Whether it was plainly made known to the employee that the material was [held] by the employer as confidential.
8. The fact that the usages and practices of the industry support the assertions of confidentiality.
9. The fact that the employee has been permitted to share the information only by reason of his or her seniority or high responsibility.
10. That the owner believes these things to be true and that belief is reasonable.
11. The greater the extent to which the 'confidential' material is habitually handled by an employee, the greater the obligation of the confidentiality imposed.
12. That the information can be readily identified.

8.58   Hodgson JA found that in cases where it is difficult to separate out the trade secret from the know-how of the ex-employee, the courts will err in favour of allowing the employee to use the information. This is particularly the case when the secret could have been discovered by the defendant using their know-how and a process of experimentation. Hodgson JA, at 336, said:

> [W]here the confidential information is something that is ascertainable by enquiry or experiment, albeit perhaps substantial enquiry or experiment, and the knowhow which the ex-employee is clearly entitled to use extends to knowledge of the question which the confidential information answers, it becomes artificial to treat the confidential information as severable and distinguishable from that know-how; and in that kind of case, courts have tended not to grant relief.

Government secrets

8.59   The government is also able to call upon the intervention of equity to protect information that it believes should be kept secret. However, the government occupies a special position as a confider and is subject to a greater deal of scrutiny, given the significant importance of the public's

---

7.   R Dean, *The Law of Trade Secrets and Personal Secrets*, 2nd ed, Law Book Co, Sydney, 2002, p 190.

right to discuss, review and criticise government action: *Commonwealth v John Fairfax & Sons* at CLR 51; ALR 492–3. The government's confidence will only be protected when it can be shown to be in the public interest: *Trevorrow v State of South Australia (No 4)* (2006) 94 SASR 64; *State of Victoria v Nine Network* [2007] VSC 431.

8.60   This involves the court in a balancing act where the public's need to know is weighed against whatever public interests there are in maintaining secrecy (such as national security): *Commonwealth v John Fairfax & Sons Ltd*; *Minister for Mineral Resources v Newcastle Newspaper Pty Ltd*. The public interest has been defined as 'something which is of serious concern and benefit to the public': *British Steel Corp v Granada Television Ltd* [1981] AC 1096 at 1113; [1981] 1 All ER 417 at 429–30; *Attorney-General (UK) v Heinemann Publishers Australia Pty Ltd* (1987) 10 NSWLR 86 at 170. Any restriction on the use of confidential information will be limited to what is strictly necessary to protect the public interest: *Attorney-General (UK) v Jonathan Cape Ltd* [1976] 1 QB 752.

8.61   While there is some authority to the contrary in *British Steel Corp v Granada Television Ltd*, it appears that in Australia, semi-government authorities and statutory corporations are treated as being part of the government for the purposes of the law of breach of confidence, and subject to the same balancing test of public interest: *Esso Resources Ltd v Plowman* (1995) 183 CLR 10 at 32; 128 ALR 391 at 403.

8.62   The most (in)famous cases of a government attempting to protect confidential information are the *Spycatcher* cases. In *Attorney-General (UK) v Heinemann Publishers Australia Pty Ltd* (1988) 165 CLR 30, Peter Wright had published details of his life as a spy for the United Kingdom in a book entitled *Spycatcher*. The United Kingdom alleged that the publication of the book was a breach of contract, confidence and fiduciary duty and sought to restrain its publication.

8.63   At first instance, *Attorney-General (UK) v Heinemann Publishers Australia Pty Ltd* (1987) 8 NSWLR 341 at 373–4, Powell J refused to grant the injunction on the basis that the book concerned facts and details that were decades old and hence of little import to the current government of the United Kingdom. Additionally, much of the information contained in the book had already been published by others, sometimes with the approval of the British government.

8.64   The New South Wales Court of Appeal upheld Powell J's decision: *Attorney-General (UK) v Heinemann Publishers Australia Pty Ltd* (1987) 10 NSWLR 86. Street CJ dissented, by finding that while the application could be classified as the enforcement of a foreign law, it could be justified on the grounds that the local sovereign supported the interests of the foreign sovereign. Kirby P and McHugh JA agreed with Street CJ's conclusion that the action was the enforcement of a foreign public law, but found that the court would not support such an action.

8.65   When commenting on the claim for breach of confidence McHugh JA, at 191, said:

> [R]ules worked out to govern the contractual, property, commercial and private confidences of citizens are not fully applicable where the plaintiff is a government or one of its agencies. Private citizens are entitled to protect or further their own interests, no matter how selfish they are in doing so. Consequently, the publication of confidential information which is detrimental to the private interest of a citizen is a legitimate concern of a Court of Equity. But governments act, or at all events are constitutionally required to act, in the public interest. Information is held, received and

imparted by governments, their departments and agencies to further the public interest. Public and not private interest, therefore, must be the criterion by which equity determines whether it will protect information which a government or governmental body claims is confidential.

Kirby P, at 164–5, agreed with the findings of Powell J that the information had already been placed in the public domain. Moreover, Kirby P found that the duty alleged by the United Kingdom government was far too wide as it was not limited in time or to content. On this point Kirby P, at 163, observed:

> I cannot accept that a person living in Australia would be so imprisoned by an equitable duty of confidence or by his duty as a fiduciary. Such duties do not extend so far. They must be reconciled with the freedom to speak which is such a precious feature of our society.

8.66 By the time the High Court heard the matter, the book had been widely published in the United States and Australia. The High Court (Mason CJ, Wilson, Brennan, Deane, Dawson, Toohey and Gaudron JJ) held that there should be no restraint on publication, given that they had no jurisdiction to enforce the interests of a foreign state.

8.67 In England, attempts to prevent publication were also unsuccessful. By the time the matter was decided by the House of Lords the book was available in Ireland, Canada, Australia and the United States. Parts of the book had been serialised and reported by English newspapers and the action concerned injunctions against those newspapers, preventing further publication of the details in Wright's book: *Attorney-General v Observer*. The House of Lords found that the worldwide publication of *Spycatcher* had destroyed secrecy so that injunctions would be futile. However, an action for account of profits was made against one of the newspapers, which had published a serialised extract prior to the widespread availability.

8.68 Interestingly, members of the House of Lords appeared upset that Wright (who was not a party to the action) was able to avoid liability given that he was outside the jurisdiction. Lord Goff, at AC 288; All ER 663–4, said:

> Certainly, the prospect of Peter Wright, safe in his Australian haven, reaping further profits from the sale of his book in this country is most unattractive … If within the jurisdiction of the English court he would be held liable to account for any profits made by him from his wrongful disclosure.

8.69 Since *Spycatcher* there have been cases involving members of the special forces in the armed services who have been held to confidences and prevented from publishing their experiences. '*R' v Attorney-General* [2004] 2 NZLR 577 concerned a former member of the SAS who was a member of patrol Bravo Two Zero, which was dropped into Iraq during the first Gulf War to find and destroy Scud missiles. Other members of that patrol had published accounts of their mission, which had sold well as books and films. The accounts were not popular with serving members of the SAS who saw them as being one-sided and unfair to the patrol member who was killed on the mission. At the request of the majority of the members of the SAS the Ministry of Defence required all serving members to sign confidentiality agreements, or leave the SAS and be returned to their units. The agreement forbade the disclosure of information relating to the SAS without the approval of the Ministry of Defence. R signed an agreement but only after being pressured into doing so. R later left the SAS and returned home to New Zealand. He went on to write his own account of the Bravo

Two Zero incident and after courting publishers a copy was provided to the Ministry of Defence. The Minister successfully sought to restrain the publication on the basis of the agreement. The Privy Council found that the pressure brought to bear on the soldier was legitimate and hence not unconscientious nor undue, even though he was not given independent legal advice: see 10.36–10.39.

8.70   The same contract was considered again in *Ministry of Defence v Griffin* [2008] EWHC 1542 (QB), where a former member of the United Kingdom Special Forces (who had signed the confidentiality agreement when joining) had made a number of public disclosures regarding his experiences. The ex-member had not sought the Ministry of Defence's approval for these disclosures. Even though the judge believed that the disclosures were largely anodyne, the judge was prepared to enforce the contractual provisions requiring that the ex-member seek permission from the Ministry. As stated in **8.16**, a contractual agreement can expand on the categories of information that can be considered confidential.

The duty or obligation of confidence

8.71   *Coco v A N Clark (Engineers)* is the leading case on the question of whether there exists a duty of confidence. In this case, the plaintiff entered into negotiations with the defendant regarding a joint venture to manufacture a moped that had been designed by the plaintiff. During the course of negotiations access to the designs had been granted to the plaintiff. After the negotiations broke down the defendant began to manufacture mopeds that incorporated some of the plaintiff's design elements. The plaintiff sought an interlocutory injunction to prevent the manufacture and sale of the moped.

8.72   Megarry J set down the three necessary elements of the modern action for breach of confidence. In particular, Megarry J, at 48, said that the question of whether information had been communicated under an obligation of confidence was objective:

> [I]f the circumstances are such that any reasonable man standing in the shoes of the recipient of the information would have realized that upon reasonable grounds the information was being given to him in confidence, then this should suffice to impose upon him the equitable obligation of confidence.

On the balance of convenience the injunction was not granted although undertakings were accepted by Megarry J that a notional royalty should be accounted for per sale should the plaintiff succeed at trial.

8.73   Megarry J's objective test has been accepted on numerous occasions: *Mense v Milenkovic* [1973] VR 784; *Castrol Australia v Emtech Associates*; *Telstra Corp Ltd v First Netcom Pty Ltd* (1997) 148 ALR 202 at 208. Meagher, Heydon and Leeming[8] have questioned whether reasonableness is an appropriate standard for equity to impose given that equity may require a person to conduct their affairs according to higher standards than those of the general populace. In *Deta Nominees v Viscount Plastic Products*, at 191, Fullagar J proposed that the test should be referenced to whether an equity lawyer would recognise the information as the plaintiff's property. However, later in the judgment, Fullagar J stated that the relevant question was whether a person of ordinary intelligence, in all the circumstances of the case, including (1) the relationship of the parties; (2) the nature of the information; and (3) the circumstances of the communication, would recognise that the information

---

8.   Meagher et al, *Equity: Doctrines and Remedies*, note 2 above, pp 1112–13.

was imparted in confidence. It should therefore be accepted that an objective, 'reasonableness' test is appropriate for determining whether communication was confidential.

Types of situations importing an obligation of confidence

8.74 Duties of confidence will be readily imported in situations where the confider has expressly stated that the proposed communication is to be confidential: *Attorney-General (UK) v Heinemann Publishers Australia Pty Ltd* (1987) 10 NSWLR 86 at 189–90; *Stephens v Avery* at Ch 456; All ER 482.

8.75 In other situations, confidentiality will be inferred from the relationship between the parties, for example, where the parties are married or in a de facto relationship, or close friends: *Argyll v Argyll*; *Giller v Procopets*. Duties of confidence are also commonly found in fiduciary relationships (*Phipps v Boardman*), or where the parties are engaged in a joint enterprise: *Coco v A N Clark (Engineers)* at 48. Professional relationships such as those between solicitors and clients, priests and devotees and doctors and patients can also be ones of confidence, primarily because of their fiduciary dimensions.

8.76 It is also clear that the relationship between an employer and employee is one that can generate such obligations. However, much will turn on the type of duties of employment and it should not be assumed that all relationships of employment import duties of confidence: *Hivac Ltd v Park Royal Scientific Instruments Ltd* [1946] Ch 169; [1946] 1 All ER 350; *Hitchcock v TCN Channel Nine Pty Ltd (No 2)* [2000] NSWCA 82. As discussed above, even in circumstances where a duty of confidence is established, the employee will generally only be bound to preserve trade secrets rather than general know-how: see 8.52–8.57.

Unsolicited and accidental communications

8.77 In some circumstances a confider will volunteer information without warning the confidant that the information is confidential. A difficult question then arises as to whether the circumstances of the receipt were confidential because it may be unfair to force duties of confidence on unsuspecting parties. In *Fractionated Cane Technology Pty Ltd v Ruiz-Avila* [1988] 2 Qd R 610; (1988) 13 IPR 609, the defendants were not held to have received information in confidence when they (along with others) attended a test-run of the plaintiff's machine which proceeded to produce unexpected results. Given there was no prior agreement about confidentiality and since the results had surprised everyone, the court refused to find that the circumstances attracted duties of confidence.

8.78 However, much turns on the objective assessment of the circumstances. For example, in *Seager v Copydex* (see 8.18–8.20), even though the plaintiff unexpectedly volunteered information about the Invisigrip, the circumstances of the negotiations (which occurred over a period of a year) were treated as confidential.

8.79 Accidental disclosures may also impart a duty of confidence if it is clear that the information has a confidential quality and has been mistakenly imparted: *Attorney-General v Guardian Newspapers (No 2)* [1988] 2 All ER 620 at 658–9. In *Trevorrow v State of South Australia*, documents including legal advice had been provided accidentally to the plaintiff by the Office of State Records. The plaintiff was suing the State of South Australia for damage he suffered during his upbringing as an Aboriginal state ward and his solicitors had accessed historical records concerning the decision to make him a ward. Legal documents were accidentally disclosed which discussed the legality of the Aboriginal Protection Board's exercise of power. These documents were arguably privileged and certainly had a confidential quality. Nevertheless, the Full Court of the South Australian Supreme Court found that the information had not been imparted in circumstances where a reasonable person would have thought the documents were confidential. The Crown had a policy of making the documents available and there was nothing in the circumstances which would have made a reasonable person aware that the information was to be kept confidential.

Misappropriation of information

8.80   A difficulty arises when the information has not been acquired in confidential circumstances, for example, when it has been stolen via an act of industrial espionage. Technically one could argue that such information cannot be protected because it has not been communicated in circumstances importing duties of confidence.

8.81   Such an argument was rejected in *Franklin v Giddins* where the defendant stole cuttings of a new strain of nectarine developed by the plaintiff. Dunn J, at 79–80, said:

> I find myself quite unable to accept that a thief who steals a trade secret, knowing it to be a trade secret, with the intention of using it in commercial competition with its owner, to the detriment of the latter, and so uses it, is less unconscionable than a traitorous servant. The thief is unconscionable because he plans to use and does use his own wrong conduct to better his position in competition with the owner, and also to place himself in a better position than that of a person who deals consensually with the owner.

8.82   Older authority supports Dunn J's view. In *Exchange Telegraph Co Ltd v Central News Ltd* [1897] 2 Ch 48 at 54, an injunction was granted preventing the defendant from 'surreptitiously obtaining or copying from sheets of letterpress, tapes or other documents'. In *Crowder v Hilton* the defendant was liable for stealing the plaintiff's recipe book and publishing the recipes. Other early cases protected unpublished manuscripts or artistic works that had been reproduced without permission: *Millar v Taylor* (1769) 98 ER 201; *Turner v Robinson* (1860) 10 Ir Ch 121; *Prince Albert v Strange*. Newer authority also accepts the principle. In *Australian Broadcasting Corp v Lenah Game Meats*, the majority accepted that equity would protect personal information collected surreptitiously. In *Imerman v Tchenguiz* [2011] 1 All ER 555 at 578, a unanimous Court of Appeal in England said:

> If confidence applies to a defendant who adventitiously, but without authorisation, obtains information in respect of which he must have appreciated that the claimant had an expectation of privacy, it must, a fortiori, extend to a defendant who intentionally, and without authorisation, takes steps to obtain such information. It would seem to us to follow that intentionally obtaining such information, secretly and knowing that the claimant reasonably expects it to be private, is itself a breach of confidence … In our view, it would be a breach of confidence for a defendant, without the authority of the claimant, to examine, or to make, retain, or supply copies to a third party of, a document whose contents are, and were (or ought to have been) appreciated by the defendant to be, confidential to the claimant. It is of the essence of the claimant's right to confidentiality that he can choose whether, and, if so, to whom and in what circumstances and on what terms, to reveal the information which has the protection of the confidence.

Eavesdroppers

8.83   But what of intermeddling third parties who receive information via eavesdropping or legal forms of espionage? In *Malone v Metropolitan Police Commissioner* [1979] Ch 344 at 376, Megarry V-C said that those who communicate confidential information to others accept the risks of third parties being able to overhear that communication. As a result, telephone conversations that had been tapped by the police were not the subject of confidence because 'the speaker is taking such risks of being overheard as are inherent in the system'. According to Megarry V-C, the question of whether there is an obligation of confidence depends on the method of communication.

8.84   But as Meagher, Heydon and Leeming[9] point out, this focus on the risks of eavesdropping is misplaced. The focus of investigation should be whether the actions of the defendant are unconscientious. Eavesdroppers will be bound if they intercept information in circumstances where it is clearly not meant for them, regardless of the ease with which eavesdropping may be committed. The case of *Francome v Mirror Group Newspapers Ltd* [1984] 2 All ER 408, appears to support this approach. In this case illegal phone tapping was said to be a breach of confidence, even though the risks of illegal phone tapping would appear to be as high (or low) as legal tapping by authorities.

Liability for the actions of agents and employees

8.85   It appears that the actions of agents and employees can be imputed to their principals and employers respectively: *Seager v Copydex*. Such a finding was made in *Coulthard v South Australia* (1995) 63 SASR 531 at 535, where King CJ made the following observation:

> It is to be expected that equity would follow the law in such circumstances and that the common law doctrine of the vicarious liability in tort of an employer for the acts of employees in the course of their employment would apply in equity to breaches of confidence. It is to be expected that equity would act upon the conscience of the employer by requiring the employer to accept responsibility for the employee's breach of confidence.

Third parties

8.86   What action can be taken against third parties who come into possession of confidential information? As is made clear by early authorities, equity will not hesitate to act against third parties who receive information knowing that it was the subject of a breach of obligation: *Prince Albert v Strange*. In *Wheatley v Bell* [1982] 2 NSWLR 544 at 555, Helsham CJ in Eq said that an injunction can be obtained against any third party who knowingly obtained the confidential information in breach of confidence or in any other fraudulent manner.

8.87   All that is necessary for liability is that the third party have actual or constructive notice of the breach: *Ansell Rubber Co Pty Ltd v Allied Rubber Industries Pty Ltd* at 45–6. Some have suggested that the defence of a bona fide purchaser without notice should apply to an innocent purchaser of confidential information who later becomes aware of the breach. However, this was rejected by Helsham CJ in Eq in *Wheatley v Bell*, because his Honour found that confidential information was not property, and hence, not subject to the rule. However, his Honour did mention the possibility of the third party raising the defence of change of position.

---

9.   Meagher et al, *Equity: Doctrines and Remedies*, note 2 above, p 1119.

8.88   The problem with the view of Helsham CJ is that it ignores the obvious fact that sometimes the information will be property. Evans has suggested that an alternative way to understand the position of third parties in receipt of confidential information is to treat them as coming under the second limb of *Barnes v Addy* (1874) 9 LR Ch App 244: see Chapter 18.[10] Under this principle strangers who participate with knowledge in a breach of trust are treated as constructive trustees of the property. However, this principle requires actual notice (*Consul Development Pty Ltd v DPC Estates Pty Ltd* (1975) 132 CLR 373; 5 ALR 231), and would therefore appear to be more restrictive than the current approach to third parties in receipt of confidential information. Moreover, in *Farah Constructions Pty Ltd v Say-Dee Pty Ltd*, the High Court refused to employ the second limb of *Barnes v Addy* in a case where it was alleged that a fiduciary had misapplied confidential information. The claim failed for a number of reasons, one of which was that the information was publicly available and therefore not confidential. But the majority, at CLR 143–4; ALR 246, found that even if the information had been confidential it did not have characteristics of property that would have enabled the rule in *Barnes v Addy* to apply.

Breach of the duty of confidence

Establishing a breach

8.89   Once a plaintiff has established a duty of confidence owed by the defendant, the plaintiff must prove that the defendant's actions were in breach of that duty. Gurry[11] has argued that this question can be asked by examining the purpose of the confider in communicating the information to the defendant:

> The test which has found widespread acceptance is whether or not the information was disclosed for a limited purpose. If the information was disclosed for a limited purpose, the confidence crystallises around that limited purpose. The confidant will be bound by an obligation the content of which is not to use or disclose the information for any purpose other than the limited one for which the information was imparted.

8.90   However, Australia's Full Court of the Federal Court rejected the blanket imposition of this test in *Smith Kline & French Laboratories (Australia) Ltd v Secretary, Department of Community Services & Health* (1991) 28 FCR 291; 99 ALR 679. In this case the plaintiff, a drugs company, had supplied detailed information relating to the performance of one of its drugs to the government, for the purpose of extending its patent. Another drug company opposed the extension of the patent and sought approval to market a generic version of the drug. The plaintiff sought an injunction to prevent the government from using the information it supplied to assess the competitor's application. Both at trial before Gummow J (*Smith Kline & French Laboratories (Australia) Ltd v Secretary, Department of Community Services and Health* (1990) 22 FCR 73; 95 ALR 87) and on appeal the application failed. The Full Court, at FCR 303; ALR 691, found that, while the information was confidential, there was no breach of duty. The confider's purpose test was not appropriate in cases where each party's interest was different and known to be so. Rather, the question of breach should be answered

---

10.   M Evans, *Equity and Trusts*, 3rd ed, LexisNexis Butterworths, Sydney, 2012, pp 199–200.

11.   F Gurry, 'Breach of Confidence', in P D Finn (ed), *Essays in Equity*, Law Book Company, Sydney, 1985, p 118.

by seeing whether unfair advantage had been taken of the information. The Full Court, at FCR 304; ALR 692, said:

> Whether one adopts the 'reasonable man' test suggested by Megarry J or some other, there can be no breach of the equitable obligation unless the court concludes that a confidence reposed has been abused, that unconscientious use has been made of the information.

In the circumstances it was reasonable for the plaintiff to expect the government to use the information in the interests of public health. This had wider implications than the confider's purpose of extending the patent. The test of breach therefore entails an 'enquiry into the extent and limits of the obligation of confidentiality that may be imposed on an individual in regard to particular pieces of confidential information in his or her possession': *NRMA Ltd v Geeson* (2001) 40 ACSR 1 at 6.

8.91 The test of breach in *Smith Kline & French Laboratories* was adopted by the English Court of Appeal in *R v Department of Health; Ex parte Source Informatics Ltd* [2000] 1 All ER 786. In this case drug prescriptions were provided by patients to pharmacists for the sole purpose of allowing the pharmacists to dispense drugs. The pharmacists wished to supply their prescription records to a company so it could conduct research into prescription practices. All information that identified patients was to be removed. The government department refused to give its permission to the pharmacists on the grounds that it would be a breach of confidence.

8.92 The Court of Appeal found that the pharmacists would not breach confidence if they supplied anonymised information, even though this went beyond the confider's purpose in supplying the information. The confider's purpose was said to be irrelevant when the information was anonymous.

Detriment

8.93 It is an open question as to whether or not there is a requirement of detriment in the action for breach of confidence: *Holyoake Industries (Vic) Pty Ltd v V-Flow Pty Ltd* [2011] FCA 1154 at [187]. In *Smith Kline & French Laboratories v Secretary, Department of Community Services & Health* (1990) 22 FCR 73 at 112; 95 ALR 87 at 126, Gummow J said:

> The basis of the equitable jurisdiction to protect obligations of confidence lies, as the present case illustrates, in an obligation of conscience arising from the circumstances in or through which the information, the subject of the obligation, was communicated or obtained: *Moorgate Tobacco Co Ltd v Philip Morris Ltd (No 2)* (1984) 156 CLR 414 at 438; 56 ALR 193 at 209. The obligation of conscience is to respect the confidence, not merely to refrain from causing detriment to the plaintiff. The plaintiff comes to equity to vindicate his right to observance of the obligation, not necessarily to recover loss or to restrain infliction of apprehended loss. To look into a related field, when has equity said that the only breaches of trust to be restrained are those that would prove detrimental to the beneficiaries?

8.94 This view was supported in *Hitchcock v TCN Channel Nine Pty Ltd (No 2)* at [29]; *NRMA Ltd v Geeson* and *NP Generations Pty Ltd v Feneley* (2001) 80 SASR 151.

8.95 In England a similar attitude was adopted in *Attorney-General v Observer*, where four members of the House of Lords stated that financial or economic detriment was not a necessary feature. Lord Keith, at AC 256; All ER 640, said:

I would think it a sufficient detriment to the confider that information given in confidence is to be disclosed to persons to whom he would prefer not to know of it, even though the disclosure would not be harmful in any positive way.

8.96 On the other hand, in *Commonwealth v John Fairfax & Sons*, Mason J concluded that detriment was an essential ingredient. However, it may be that his Honour's requirement for detriment is set at a low level. His Honour, at CLR 51; ALR 492, said:

It may be a sufficient detriment to the citizen that disclosure of information relating to his affairs will expose his actions to public discussion and criticism.

His Honour was adamant, on the other hand, that the government must show more than mere embarrassment for it to be successful in claiming breach of confidence, given the importance of freedom of speech.

DEFENCES

The public interest defence

8.97 The impact of public interest on the government's ability to protect confidential information has already been discussed above: see 8.59–8.70. A defence is available to private citizens whereby a breach of confidence can be excused if it can be proven to be in the public interest. Early authorities established that there was no confidence in an 'iniquity': *Gartside v Outram* (1856) LJ Ch 113 at 114; *Minister for Immigration and Citizenship v Kumar* (2009) 253 ALR 219 at 225. This early concept of iniquity included criminal and fraudulent conduct but was later expanded to include misconduct which ought to be disclosed in the public interest: *Initial Services Ltd v Putterill* [1968] 1 QB 396; [1967] 3 All ER 145.

8.98 Relatively trivial matters in which a claimant may have acted below a recognised standard of behaviour will not automatically trigger the defence, as normally a high degree of misbehaviour must be demonstrated: *McKennitt v Ash* [2005] EWHC 3003 (QB) at [97] (upheld on appeal: *McKennitt v Ash* [2008] QB 73).

8.99 While there was some authority to the contrary (*Allied Mills Industries Pty Ltd v Trade Practices Commission* (1981) 34 ALR 105), a recognised public interest will not automatically trump the public interest in preserving private confidences: *A v Hayden* (1984) 156 CLR 532: 56 ALR 82. Instead, it is a process whereby the respective public interests in keeping the confidence and making the information public are weighed and compared: *Spelman v Express Newspapers* at [44]–[52]. In *Prince of Wales v Associated Newspapers*, at Ch 124–5; All ER 156, Lord Phillips CJ said:

[T]he test to be applied when considering whether it is necessary to restrict freedom of expression in order to prevent disclosure of information received in confidence is not simply whether the information is a matter of public interest but whether, in all the circumstances, it is in the public interest that the duty of confidence should be breached. The court will need to consider whether, having regard to the circumstances, it is legitimate for the owner of the information to seek to keep it confidential or whether it is in the public interest that the information be made public.

8.100 While this statement was made in the context of the privacy developments in England and Wales, it still appears to be a correct statement on the balancing process that needs to be undertaken in equity.

Danger to individuals or the public

8.101 The defence can be used by private citizens to expose dangers to public safety or health: *Church of Scientology of California v Kaufman*. For example, in *W v Edgell* [1990] 1 All ER 835, a doctor was employed to provide a psychiatric assessment of an inpatient who had killed five people. The report was originally sought to secure the patient's release but the findings in the report were so adverse that the application for release was not pursued. At the doctor's direction a copy of his report was forwarded to the Secretary of State. In assessing whether this breach of confidence was excusable, the Court of Appeal found that the public interest in disclosing the report to the authorities outweighed the public interest in the patient's confidentiality, given the serious concerns for the safety of the public.

8.102 Similarly, in *Hubbard v Vosper* [1972] 2 QB 84; [1972] 1 All ER 1023, Lord Denning MR stated (at an interlocutory stage) that the publication of a book on Scientology by an ex-member of that religion could be justified via a public interest in exposing the secrets of Scientology, which was at the time viewed by some as a dangerous practice.

The public interest and the administration of justice

8.103 The public interest in the administration of justice can also justify a breach of confidence, although the extent to which such a defence is available in Australia is open to question. In *Lion Laboratories Ltd v Evans* [1985] QB 526; [1984] 2 All ER 417, employees of the manufacturer of breath testers were not liable for leaking information which questioned the accuracy of the breath testers. This was because the breath testers were used to convict people of driving offences and as such there was a public interest in making sure the tests were accurate. In *Campbell v Tameside Metropolitan Borough Council* [1982] QB 1065; [1982] 2 All ER 791, a teacher brought an action in negligence against an education authority after she was beaten by a student. In pursuance of her claim she sought access to the authority's psychological assessment records to prove that the authority had been aware of the student's mental instability. The Court of Appeal found that the public interest in allowing the teacher to properly litigate her claim was of enough weight to override the authority's duty of confidence to the student. However, this approach has not always found favour in Australia: *AG Australia Holdings Ltd v Burton* (2002) 58 NSWLR 464. In *Richards v Kadian* [2005] NSWCA 328, the New South Wales Court of Appeal refused to follow this line of thought. The child plaintiff had brought proceedings against his doctor, alleging that the doctor had been negligent in failing to diagnose a congenital heart condition. In preparing a defence to the claim, the doctor sought to interview the child's treating specialists. Access had been granted to the specialists' records but the plaintiff refused to give the specialists permission to be interviewed. It was argued by the defendant doctor that the obligations of confidence had been waived by the plaintiff when the action had commenced. The court found that in order for confidence to have been waived, there had to be an identifiable public interest which went beyond the effects on the private rights of the parties. As no other public interests were affected by the confidentiality apart from those of the parties, the court refused to find that the obligations of confidence had been waived.

Public interest and sexual activity

8.104 Breaches of confidence in relation to sexual conduct might also be justified in the public interest. In *Stephens v Avery*, at Ch 453–4; All ER 480–1, Brown-Wilkinson V-C said that the courts would not enforce a duty of confidence relating to matters which had a gross immoral tendency, although his Lordship stated that it may be too difficult to apply this principle in modern times, as (some might argue) there is no generally accepted code of sexual morality. These issues again came to the fore in *Mosley v News Group Newspapers Ltd*, where the plaintiff (the President of Federation Internationale de l'Automobile) belonged to a group of practising sado-masochists who acted out prison roles, including the wearing of uniforms, dominating behaviour and the shaving of the plaintiff's bottom. The defendant newspaper convinced a member of the group to covertly film its activities. The newspaper argued that the breach of confidence was justified because the sexual role play was 'Nazi'-themed. Eady J accepted that if there had been such activity it may have been in the public interest for it to have been reported. However, after reviewing the evidence the judge found that the group activities were not inspired by Nazism or intended to deride the Holocaust. Moreover, the judge refused to find that publication was justified on the basis that the activity was adulterous and depraved. Eady J, at [127], said:

> [I]t is not for the state or for the media to expose sexual conduct which does not involve any significant breach of the criminal law. That is so whether the motive for such intrusion is merely prurience or a moral crusade. It is not for journalists to undermine human rights, or for judges to refuse to enforce them, merely on grounds of taste or moral disapproval. Everyone is naturally entitled to espouse moral or religious beliefs to the effect that certain types of sexual behaviour are wrong or demeaning to those participating. That does not mean that they are entitled to hound those who practise them or to detract from their right to live life as they choose.

Public figures and the Woodward defence

8.105 In *Woodward v Hutchins* [1977] 2 All ER 751, a number of pop stars, including Tom Jones and Engelbert Humperdinck, attempted to prevent their former public relations agent from publishing 'tell all' stories about their sexual encounters. Lord Denning MR found that, as the pop stars had created favourable but false images of their private lives, there was a public interest in the truth being told. More recently, it has been said in *A v B plc* [2003] QB 195 that public figures who court public attention about an issue will have less ground to object if the public have an understandable and legitimate interest in being told the information. Thus, in *Campbell v Mirror Group Newspapers*, there was no confidence preventing the press from publicising Naomi Campbell's narcotics addiction, given her continued public statements that she had not taken drugs (although the details of her treatment were confidential). However, the converse is also true. In *McKennitt v Ash*, the folk singer's aversion to publicity and concern with privacy was a factor in finding against any defence based on *Woodward*.

8.106 Australian courts have retreated from Lord Denning MR's far-reaching position on public interest. It has been said in Australia that a public interest must be more weighty and precise than a broad public interest in the truth being told: *Castrol Australia v Emtech Associates*; *Bacich v Australian Broadcasting Corp* (1992) 29 NSWLR 1; *NRMA v Yates* [1999] NSWSC 701. This line of cases shows that there is a difference between the concept of the public interest and what the public may be interested in: *Sullivan v Sclanders* (2000) 77 SASR 419; *Australian Football League v Age Company Ltd* at 440; *Jameel v Wall Street Journal Europe Sprl* [2007] 1 AC 359 at 408; [2006] 4 All ER 1279 at 1321.

Public interest or clean hands?

8.107   In *Corrs Pavey Whiting & Byrne v Collector of Customs (Vic)* (1987) 14 FCR 434 at 445–52, Gummow J went so far as to doubt whether the public interest defence was truly a defence at all and believed it was better understood as an expression of equitable principles based on conscience, such as clean hands or iniquity. This approach was adopted in *Sullivan v Sclanders* (2000) 77 SASR 419, and commented on favourably in *AG Australia Holdings Ltd v Burton* (2002) 58 NSWLR 464. It was also adopted in *Australian Football League v Age Company Ltd*, at 436, where Kellam J said that the defence required that:

(a) The proposed disclosure will in fact disclose the existence of or the real likelihood of the existence of an iniquity that is a crime, civil wrong or serious misdeed of public importance;

(b) that the iniquity is of a character of public importance in the sense that what is to be disclosed affects the community as a whole, or affects the public welfare; and

(c) that the person who is seeking to protect the confidence is doing so in order to prevent disclosure to a third party with a real and direct interest in redressing the alleged crime, wrong or misdeed.

Motives behind disclosure and threats of blackmail

8.108   In *Lion Laboratories v Evans*, Stevenson LJ, at 536–7, said:

> There is confidential information which the public may have a right to receive and others, in particular the press, now extended to the media, may have a right and even a duty to publish, even if the information has been unlawfully obtained in flagrant breach of confidence and irrespective of the motive of the informer.

However this approach can be contrasted with more recent British cases which have involved personal confidence where a confidant has allegedly attempted to blackmail the confider. In these cases the courts have taken a more cautious approach to disclosure because the public interest has to be balanced against a disclosure fulfilling a blackmailer's demands: *DFT v TFD* [2010] EWHC 2335 (QB) at [23]; *AMM v HXW* [2010] EWHC 2457 (QB) at [38]. In *WXY v Gewanter* [2012] EWHC 496 (QB) the claimant was a woman with close ties to a foreign head of state. She sought an injunction preventing the publication of various allegations including that she had had sexual relations with a person and then lied under oath about the relationship, and that she knew the foreign head of state was financing terrorism. The defendants had allegedly threatened to publish this information, unless WXY provided assistance in convincing the head of state to pay his outstanding debts to companies related to the defendants. Slade J refused to recognise a defence of public interest. The allegations were mere threats of iniquity. Slade J, at [64], held that '... the public interest asserted is based on an allegation of wrongdoing, the credibility of the allegation and the reliability of the source of information are material to the balancing exercise'. The danger to the public only required disclosure to the authorities, not to the public at large.

Change of position

8.109   The defence of change of position is a defence to an action for unjust enrichment. The defence is generally made available to innocent third parties who mistakenly receive money and act to their detriment, for example, by making substantial investments with it: *David Securities Pty Ltd v Commonwealth Bank of Australia* (1992) 175 CLR 353; 109 ALR 57; *Gertsch v Atsas* [1999] NSWSC 898; *K and S Corporation Ltd v Sportingbet Australia Pty Ltd* [2003] SASC 96. In such circumstances the defendant is not held liable to account for money expended.

8.110   Some commentators have suggested that the defence should also be available to innocent third parties who receive confidential information.[12] As yet there is no Australian authority that is directly on point, although theoretically the defence should be available, particularly in cases where the plaintiff seeks restitutionary relief.

Forced disclosure

8.111   A confidant may be forced to disclose information by legal compulsion. For example, public health statutes often require the mandatory reporting of infectious diseases, and often provide for the disclosure of infected persons' names and addresses, for example, under s 18 of the *Public Health Act 1991* (NSW). In such cases the defendant is not liable for breach of confidence.

8.112   Similarly, courts may order that confidential documents be provided in the discovery process: *Campbell v Tameside Metropolitan Borough Council*. This will often involve the court in the balancing of the public interests: *D v National Society for the Prevention of Cruelty to Children* [1978] AC 171; [1977] 1 All ER 589.

8.113   Quasi-judicial bodies may also have powers to call on documents. In *Royal Women's Hospital v Medical Practitioners Board of Victoria* (2006) 15 VR 22, a hospital refused to supply health records to the Medical Practitioners Board of Victoria. The Board had sought the records as part of an investigation, sparked by Senator Julian McGauran, into a late-term abortion that had been performed in the hospital. The abortion had been performed as the child had been diagnosed with dwarfism and the pregnant woman had threatened self-harm should an abortion not be performed. The Senator alleged that the child had been misdiagnosed and made a complaint to the Medical Board. The main thrust of the hospital's argument was that there was a public interest immunity which protected it from the Board's power of investigation. Public interest immunity is normally claimed by government officials and members of the executive to keep sensitive governmental information secret. The Victorian Court of Appeal found that the hospital had no right to claim such an immunity and that the Board's powers of investigation could not be resisted. The doctors were later cleared of misconduct by the Board.[13]

Laches

8.114   The general equitable defence of laches or delay (see 31.13–31.22) is available to actions for breach of confidence: *Attorney-General (UK) v Heinemann Publishers Australia Pty Ltd* (1988) 10 NSWLR 86.

Unclean hands

8.115   It can be argued in some cases that relief should not be granted because of the way in which the confider has conducted himself or herself and the means chosen to protect the information:

---

12. Evans, *Equity and Trusts*, note 10 above, pp 204–5.
13. C Stewart, 'Victorian Doctors Cleared of Late Term Abortion' (2007) 4 *Journal of Bioethical Inquiry* 4.

Hubbard v Vosper. For example, in *Campbell v Mirror Group Newspapers Ltd*, the newspapers were free to contradict Campbell's claim that she had never used drugs (but not by publishing details and photographs of her attendance at therapy meetings). As with all cases concerning the unclean hands defence (see 31.8–31.12), the improper behaviour must be shown to be directly related to the relief sought: *Talbot v General Television Corp Pty Ltd* at 240.

REMEDIES

Injunctions

8.116 The primary remedy for breach of confidence is an injunction. It should be noted that if the breach of duty stems from a purely equitable duty of confidence it could be argued that the injunction would stem from equity's exclusive jurisdiction and hence there need be no reference to the adequacy of damages: see 24.11–24.12.

8.117 However, in *Foster v Mountford & Rigby*, the fact that the potential injury to the Aboriginal community was not possible to compensate was used to justify an injunction. Similarly, compensation may be more equitable in situations where the breach was committed innocently: *Seager v Copydex*.

8.118 Subject to what will be said below about the springboard doctrine, injunctions will not be granted in cases where the information has moved into the public domain: *Attorney-General v Observer*. In such cases, an account of profits or equitable compensation may still be ordered.

The springboard doctrine

8.119 It has been said that a confidant must not be in a better position for having breached a commercial confidence by getting a 'head start' on competitors: *Seager v Copydex* at 417. Equity will prevent a defaulting confidant from being able to use information even after it has entered the public domain. This idea is known as the 'springboard' doctrine: *Austral Ships Pty Ltd v Incat Australia Pty Ltd* [2009] FCA 368; *Dart Industries Inc v David Bryar & Associates Pty Ltd* (1997) 38 IPR 389.

8.120 In *Terrapin Limited v Builders' Supply Co (Hayes) Ltd* [1967] RPC 375 at 391, Roxburgh J introduced the concept of a 'springboard' when he said:

> As I understand it, the essence of this branch of the law, whatever the origin of it may be, is that a person who has obtained information in confidence is not allowed to use it as a spring-board for activities detrimental to the person who made the confidential communication, and spring-board it remains even when all the features have been published or can be ascertained by actual inspection by any member of the public.

The facts of *Terrapin* concerned the manufacture of a pre-fabricated structure. The structure had been put on the market and was thus susceptible to reverse engineering. However, the defendants breached confidence by using the designs of the plaintiff, and by doing so got a head start on other competitors in the field. To counter this unfair advantage the court ordered that the defendant be placed under a special disability, in the form of an injunction preventing it from entering the market, which lasted until the information had fully reached the public domain.

8.121 The purpose of the springboard order is to prevent the defendant from taking unfair advantage of their wrongdoing: *Bullivant v Ellis* [1987] ICR 464. The order must be sought during the period when the unfair advantage is still being enjoyed: *Sun Valley Foods Ltd v Vincent* [2000] FCR 825. The burden of proving the exact nature of the unfair advantage is on the claimant: *QBE Management Services (UK) Ltd v Dymoke* [2012] EWHC 80 at [247].

Delivery-up

8.122   The court can order a defendant to deliver up property in the defendant's possession which has been created, compiled or manufactured as a result of a breach of confidence: *Blockbuster Australia Pty Ltd v Karioi Pty Ltd* [2009] NSWSC 1089; *Ansell Rubber Co v Allied Rubber Industries*.

Equitable damages and equitable compensation

8.123   A competent court can order equitable damages under what is commonly referred to as Lord Cairns' Act: see Chapter 26. The calculation of damages must be a compensatory basis. In commercial confidences, it will be easier to calculate damages based on the damages to business interests. There is no strict formula for how damages should be calculated. In *Talbot v General Television Corp Pty Ltd* the defendant was ordered to pay damages for breach of confidence in relation to the unauthorised use of an idea for a television show. The Victorian Full Court ordered damages assessed by reference to the depreciation of the idea's value caused by the breach.

8.124   Breaches of private confidences have proven more difficult to compensate, especially in the absence of the plaintiff suffering some recognisable psychiatric injury. In *Giller v Procopets*, Neave JA ordered equitable damages for the breach of a personal confidence on the basis that an injunction would have been granted, and damages should be available in lieu of specific relief: see 26.55–26.63.

8.125   Exemplary damages are not available because they are punitive: *Harris v Digital Pulse Pty Ltd* (2003) 56 NSWLR 298: see 26.30–26.37. However, aggravated damages, which relate to damage to the plaintiff's dignity, have been found to be available: *Giller v Procopets*: see 26.38. There is some dispute in the United Kingdom about the availability of aggravated and exemplary damages. Naomi Campbell was able to get general damages and aggravated damages (modest though they were) in *Campbell v Mirror Group Newspapers*. In *Douglas v Hello! Ltd* [2003] 3 All ER 996, the judge thought himself able to order aggravated and exemplary damages but declined to do so. But in *Mosley v News Group Newspapers*, Eady J found that there was not yet sufficient authority to suggest that exemplary damages were available. Perhaps this is a result of the fusion of equitable and human rights principles which is currently under way in the United Kingdom: see 8.136.

8.126   Another option would be to allow equitable compensation to be ordered from the inherent jurisdiction in the same way that it is available for breaches of fiduciary duty: see 26.2–26.5. Neave JA accepted this in *Giller v Procopets*. In this case the defendant had shown (or attempted to show) photographs and video of the plaintiff having sex, to the plaintiff's family, friends and co-workers. The trial judge found that while the plaintiff had been greatly distressed by the defendant's actions, she was not suffering any recognised psychiatric condition which could be compensated for. On appeal, all the three judges found that damages for mental distress could be ordered in the inherent jurisdiction of equity and under Lord Cairns' Act, even in cases where the plaintiff had not suffered recognised psychiatric injury. The main argument was that damages should be available, as it would be strange for equity to offer injunctive relief but then fail to offer a remedy to the plaintiff in cases when an injunction would be too late to stop the damage. Again, all three judges agreed that aggravated damages should be available to compensate for the manner in which the confidence had been abused. Aggravated damages were said to be compensatory and not punitive in nature.

8.127   More recently in *Force India Formula One Team Ltd v 1 Malaysia Racing Team SDN BHD* [2012] EWHC 616 (Ch), Arnold J also accepted that both equitable damages and equitable compensation were available for breaches of confidence. This case concerned breaches of confidence that resulted in no unfair advantage or financial gain. In calculating the amount of monetary relief Arnold J referred to *Wrotham Park* damages, where damages are available for a breach of contract where there is no financial loss. In *Wrotham Park Estate Company Limited v Parkside Homes Limited* [1974] 2 All ER 321, it was found that damages for such a breach could be calculated by assessing how much it would have hypothetically cost the defendant to be released from the contractual obligation. Arnold J used these so-called 'negotiation damages' as a measure for working out the compensation available for a breach of confidence where there was no commercial gain or advantage arising from the breach: see 26.71–26.75.

Account of profits

8.128   As an alternative to equitable compensation, the defendant may be made to account for the profits (see 30.25–30.31) made from a breach of duty: *Peter Pan Manufacturing Corp v Corsets Silhouette Ltd* [1963] 3 All ER 402.

8.129   Account of profits can be a difficult remedy to provide, especially given the problems of isolating the relevant profits from a defendant's income stream. An allowance can be awarded to the defendant for their time, effort and skill but the onus for establishing the allowance falls on the defendant: *Bluescope Steel Ltd v Kelly* [2007] FCA 517 at [166]; *Harris v Digital Pulse Pty Ltd* (2003) 56 NSWLR 298 at 372–5, 384.

8.130   In the United Kingdom, it now appears that an account of profits can be ordered for a breach of confidence which is purely contractual and which has not resulted in damage. In *Attorney-General (UK) v Blake* [2001] 1 AC 268; [2000] 4 All ER 385, the defendant was a convicted double agent who had escaped to Russia in the 1960s. He published a memoir of his adventures long after the events in the memoir had entered the public domain. However, this was considered to be a breach of his contractual duties not to disclose government secrets. The House of Lords found that the defendant's profits from publication could be claimed by the Crown, even though the equitable duty of confidence had ceased. Moreover, there was no actual damage suffered by the Crown given that the information was already public. Nevertheless, a majority found that an account could be ordered because of the exceptional circumstances of the case. Lord Nicholls, at AC 285; All ER 397, said:

> If confidential information is wrongfully divulged in breach of a non-disclosure agreement, it would be nothing short of sophistry to say that an account of profits may be ordered in respect of the equitable wrong but not in respect of the breach of contract which governs the relationship between the parties.

Australian courts have, to date, declined to follow *Blake*: *Hospitality Group Pty Ltd v Australian Rugby Union* (2001) 110 FCR 157 at 195–6.

Constructive trusts

8.131   Constructive trusts are available as a remedy for breach of confidence: *LAC Minerals Ltd v International Corona Resources Ltd* [1989] 2 SCR 574. The remedy will be most clearly available when the confidential information is property. This is because the imposition of a trust requires that there is property to be held on trust: see Chapter 21.

8.132   However, the Supreme Court of Canada has held that a constructive trust can be imposed for breach of confidence, regardless of whether the information has taken a proprietorial form: *Cadbury Schweppes Inc v FBI Foods* (1999) 167 DLR (4th) 577. The decision can perhaps be explained by the distinction which Gummow J made in *Smith Kline & French Laboratories v Secretary, Department of Community Services & Health*. As discussed above (see 8.13), his Honour stated that in cases where the information is not property, the equity that arises from breach might itself be considered as property.

THE EMERGENCE OF PRIVACY RIGHTS

The traditional approach to privacy protection

8.133   The early decisions on breach of confidence gave rise to the American common law right of privacy. However, in Australian jurisprudence it has been said that there is no common law right to privacy: *Victoria Park Racing & Recreation Grounds Co Ltd v Taylor* (1937) 58 CLR 479; *Cruise v Southdown Press Pty Ltd* (1993) 26 IPR 125; *Australian Consolidated Press Ltd v Ettingshausen* (1995) 38 NSWLR 404.

8.134   Generally speaking, privacy 'rights' can only be enforced when they have been incidentally affected by the commission of some other tort.[14] Nuisance has been used as a basis in England and in Australia: *Khorasandjian v Bush* [1993] 3 All ER 669; but see *Hunter v Canary Wharf Ltd* [1997] AC 655; [1997] 2 All ER 426; *Raciti v Hughes* (1995) 7 BPR 14,837. Alternatively, trespass to land has also been used to prevent the broadcasting of videotaped images: *Lincoln Hunt Australia Pty Ltd v Willesee* (1986) 4 NSWLR 457; *TCN Channel Nine Pty Ltd v Inning* (2002) 54 NSWLR 333. However, an injunction will not issue unless it can be shown that damages, including exemplary damages, are inadequate to compensate the plaintiff.

8.135   The limitations of this approach lay in the requirement that the claimant have an interest in the land upon which the interference occurred. This was illustrated in *Kaye v Robertson* (1991) FSR 62. The plaintiff, a television personality, was seriously injured and convalescing in a closed hospital ward when he was photographed by the defendant. The plaintiff sought to restrain the publication of a photograph because of its embarrassing nature. However, the plaintiff was unable to prove an actionable trespass to the person (the flash of the camera was not a battery), nor a trespass to land (the plaintiff had no proprietary interest in the hospital ward, only a licence to occupy). As such, his claim of privacy failed.

---

14.   For an excellent review of privacy issues, see P Loughlan, B McDonald and R van Krieken, *Celebrity and the Law*, Federation Press, Sydney, 2010, pp 90–169 and B McDonald, 'Tort's Role in Protecting Privacy: Current and Future Directions' in S Degeling, J Edelman & J Goudkamp (eds), *Torts in Commercial Law*, Thomson Reuters, Sydney, 2011, pp 63–86.

Developments in New Zealand

8.136   While New Zealand has a Bill of Rights, there is no specific protection of privacy contained within it: *Lange v Atkinson* [2000] 3 NZLR 385. New Zealand courts have therefore looked to developing a tort of privacy to fill in the gap left by the common law: *Bradley v Wingnut Films* [1993] 1 NZLR 415; *P v D* [2000] NZLR 591. The tort has many elements which have been borrowed from breach of confidence, but the main requirement is that there be a disclosure of private facts which is highly objectionable to a reasonable person. In *Hosking v Runting* [2004] NZCA 34, the publication of photographs of children of a television celebrity, taken when they were in a public space, was not said to be offensive. Interestingly, this test is taken from Gleeson CJ's judgment in *Australian Broadcasting Corp v Lenah Game Meats*: see 8.158.

8.137   In *Television New Zealand Ltd v Rogers*, a majority of the New Zealand Supreme Court allowed the publication of a video where an accused person, who had been acquitted of killing a woman, confessed to her murder. The video had been excluded from the evidence at the trial and had been released by the police to the media. Blanchard, Tipping and McGrath JJ held that there could be no reasonable expectation of privacy when a person was being interviewed by police and knowingly videotaped.

Developments in the United Kingdom

8.138   English and Welsh courts have also looked to expanding the protection of privacy interests. However, they have decided not to depart from the old rule that there is no general action for breach of privacy: *Wainwright v Home Office* [2002] QB 1334; [2003] 3 All ER 943. Instead, they have combined the law of confidential information with the human rights jurisprudence of the European Union, under the *Human Rights Act 1998* (UK). The two relevant articles to cases of breach of confidence are Article 8 (the right to respect for private and family life) and Article 10 (the right to freedom of expression).

8.139   In *Douglas v Hello! Ltd* [2001] QB 967; [2001] 2 All ER 289, Catherine Zeta-Jones and Michael Douglas, a married couple, and the publisher of the magazine *OK!* sought to enjoin publication of photographs that had been taken at the couple's wedding without their approval. The couple had entered into a contract with *OK!* magazine for the publication of wedding photographs (for a considerable sum after a bidding war with *Hello!* magazine). All guests were made aware that photography was forbidden and that *OK!* had the rights to images. Staff members were made to sign confidentiality agreements. In spite of these precautions and very tight security, a freelance photographer had managed to take photographs and supply them to the rival publisher of *Hello!* magazine. The initial issue before the Court of Appeal of England and Wales was whether an injunction should be granted to prevent *Hello!* from publishing the unauthorised photographs.

8.140   At trial, an injunction was granted, but the decision was quickly overturned by the Court of Appeal. It was found that the balance of convenience lay against the granting of an injunction. This was primarily because the Douglas/Zeta-Jones family had traded their rights as commodities, and, as such, damages would be an adequate remedy for any proved breach, as well as for any breach of the rights of *OK!*. In so finding the Court of Appeal emphasised the role that breach of confidence could play in protecting rights to privacy, especially given the requirement of the *Human Rights Act 1998* (UK) to bring English law into line with the law of the European Union. The doctrine of confidential information was said to be available to protect the right to respect for private life, under Article 8 of the *European Convention on Human Rights and Fundamental Freedoms 1950*. In discussing the role of confidential information in protecting privacy, Sedley LJ, at QB 1001; All ER 320, said:

> The law no longer needs to construct an artificial relationship of confidentiality between the intruder and victim: it can recognise privacy itself as a legal principle drawn from the fundamental value of personal autonomy.

8.141 *OK!* magazine managed to publish its wedding images some hours prior to *Hello!* magazine and the matter went back to trial. After an unsuccessful attempt to strike out the defence in *Douglas v Hello! Ltd (No 2)* [2003] 1 All ER 1087, the matter went to trial in *Douglas v Hello! Ltd (No 3)* [2003] 3 All ER 996. Douglas and Zeta-Jones were successful in gaining modest damages of £14,600 under breach of confidence: *Douglas v Hello! Ltd (No 6)* [2004] EMLR 13. The photographs were treated as akin to trade secrets, given their commercial value. The fact that the defendants had acted surreptitiously to obtain the photographs meant that they had acted unconscientiously, with resulting detriment to the married couple. Interestingly, Lindsay J stated that aggravated and exemplary damages could be awarded but he declined to do so. *OK!* were also successful in gaining damages for breach of confidence. Lindsay J found the images to be confidential, that *Hello!* had acted unconscientiously by purchasing photographs that they knew had been taken in breach of confidence, and that *OK!* magazine had suffered a detriment of over £1,000,000.

8.142 The trial decision was appealed: *Douglas v Hello! Ltd* [2006] QB 125; [2005] 4 All ER 128. The Court of Appeal upheld the finding of breach of confidence for the Douglases but overturned the decision to award damages to *OK!* magazine, finding that no obligation of confidence arose in the magazine's favour. It was said that any confidence owed to *OK!* only related to the authorised images taken by the magazine.

8.143 This decision was then appealed by *OK!* magazine as one of the three cases decided in *OBG Ltd v Allan*. This appeal fused a number of appeals on questions of unfair competition. The majority of the House of Lords (Lord Hoffmann, Baroness Hale and Lord Brown) restored the trial judge's finding in favour of *OK!*. Lord Hoffmann could find no legal or policy reason for denying the rights of *OK!* as they had paid consideration for the right to exclusive images from the Douglases who were in control of their wedding images. Lord Hoffmann found that the security arrangements at the wedding were not only for the benefit of the Douglases but also for *OK!* magazine in respect of any photographic images taken, not just the authorised ones. Both Baroness Hale and Lord Brown agreed with Lord Hoffmann. Lord Brown also found that *OK!*'s rights related to the prevention of publication of the unauthorised photographs rather than limiting those rights to the authorised ones.

8.144 In dissent, Lord Nicholls disputed that the information contained in the unauthorised photographs was in any way substantially different from the authorised ones. His Lordship found that the publication by *OK!* of its own images was enough to destroy the confidence in the approved photographs. Lord Walker argued that there was nothing confidential about the images. His Lordship, at AC 83; All ER 616, found that the law did not allow people to complain about being photographed, unless the photograph was either embarrassing, had been procured through the misuse of official powers or was a trade secret. His Lordship doubted that the images were a trade secret and said that the fact that security was in place could not automatically invest the images with the quality of confidence.

8.145 Since the *Douglas* litigation, the doctrine of breach of confidence has continued to push into the privacy realm. Some have seen the use of Article 8 as splitting the doctrine of confidence into two arms: a traditional arm which is regulated under the old principles, and a new arm which is characterised primarily as a privacy tort, which is dictated by a balancing exercise between Article 8 and 10 interests: *Goodwin v NGN Ltd* [2011] EWHC 1437 (QB) at [61]. The starting point for this 'tort' is to inquire whether the claimant had a reasonable expectation of privacy which should be protected by Article 8. This is in turn answered by asking whether the disclosure of information would offend a reasonable person of ordinary sensibilities, when placed in the same position as the claimant: *Campbell v Mirror Group Newspapers*. A number of factors are relevant to this inquiry including 'the attributes of the claimant, the nature of the activity in which the claimant was engaged, the place at which it was happening, the nature and purpose of the intrusion, the absence of consent and whether it was known or could be inferred, the effect on the claimant and the circumstances in which and the purposes for which the information came into the hands of the publisher': *Murray v Express Newspapers plc* [2009] Ch 481 at 502.

8.146 To illustrate, Sir Elton John failed to enjoin the publication of a photograph of him walking down the street because the photograph contained no embarrassing information: *Sir Elton John v Associated Newspapers* [2006] EWHC 1611 (QB). Similarly Rio Ferdinand, the English football captain, failed to prevent the publication of details of his relationship with an old girlfriend, including an innocuous photo of him speaking on a mobile phone: *Ferdinand v MGN Ltd* [2011] EWHC 2454 (QB). Contrastingly, in *Murray v Express Newspapers plc*, J K Rowling (acting on her infant son's behalf) successfully sued a provider of photographic images for providing photos of her son to the media. The photos were of the son in a pram with his family walking down the street. Given the child's age, he was not upset or distressed by the publication of the image but his mother nevertheless brought the action on his behalf to provide some privacy. The trial judge struck out the action. He refused to find that the photographs were private as they had been taken in the street and did not reveal any information which would have caused embarrassment. However, the Court of Appeal overturned that finding and held that the child had a reasonable expectation of privacy to be able to go to a café with his parents, as this was part of his recreation time, and photography during that time was intrusive. The matter was remitted for retrial.

8.147 If the information can be classed as protected by Article 8 then the court must move to consider whether the Article 8 interests are outweighed by Article 10: *McKennitt v Ash*. In that context the defences of public interest may be considered and a test of proportionality must be applied: *Prince of Wales v Associated Newspapers* at Ch 79; All ER 156. In *Hutcheson (Formerly Known As 'KGM') v News Group Newspapers Ltd* [2011] EWCA Civ 808, the plaintiff's right to keep details of a second secret family were balanced against the rights of the public to know about the second family, coupled with other claims that were being made about the plaintiff's alleged misdirection of corporate funds. Another case in contrast is *AMP v Persons Unknown* [2011] EWHC 3454 (TCC), where the plaintiff's mobile phone was stolen. The thief downloaded photographs off the phone which were of an explicit nature, taken by the plaintiff's boyfriend. The thief attempted to blackmail the plaintiff and uploaded the files onto BitTorrent. The court ordered an injunction as the plaintiff had a reasonable expectation of privacy in the photographs, and given the material was not journalistic, it was hard to see how its disclosure would be supported by Article 10. In *ETK v News Group Newspapers Ltd* [2011] EWCA Civ 439, ETK was a famous person in the entertainment industry who had had an affair in the past with a co-worker, X. The affair was known to ETK's wife and colleagues, but not his children. Later X was sacked and the *News of the World* wished to publish the story of her sacking. The Court of Appeal found that the information had not entered the public domain even though it was known by ETK's colleagues. Moreover the balancing exercised with Article 10, was in favour of an injunction, as while there was value in freedom of speech it had to be weighed against the rights of privacy of ETK, his wife and X, and the rights of ETK's children not to be subject to teasing and ridicule. In the instant case, the Court of Appeal found that the benefits of free speech were wholly outweighed by the harm that would be done through the interference with the rights of privacy of all those affected.

8.148 The use of injunctions to protect these confidences in the UK has now given birth to the so-called 'super-injunction', which prevents not only publication of the details of a confidence but also the claimant's identity and even the existence of the proceedings. The use of super-injunctions has caused considerable controversy because of the gagging effect such use has on free speech. Many of these are based on preventing publication of allegations of the sexual affairs of the rich and famous: *JIH v News Group Newspapers Ltd* [2011] EWCA Civ 42; *MNB v News Group Newspapers Ltd* [2011] EWHC 528 (QB); *Goodwin v News Group Newspapers Ltd* [2011] EWHC 1309 (QB). For example, in *OPQ v BJM* [2011] EWHC 1059 (QB), an unnamed TV personality was able to seek an injunction *contra mundum* ('against the world') to prevent publication of photographs of him/her having sex that were being used to blackmail him/her. Jeremy Clarkson successfully, for a time, gagged his ex-wife's claims that they had had an affair after he was remarried: *AMM v HXW* [2010] EWHC 2457 (QB). In *TSE v News Group Newspapers Ltd* [2011] EWHC 1308 (QB), an English professional footballer gagged publication of details of an extramarital affair. In *Terry v Persons Unknown* [2010] EWHC 119 (QB), Premier League footballer and English captain John Terry unsuccessfully sought a super-injunction to prevent publication of allegations that he had a sexual relationship with the wife of teammate and fellow international, Wayne Bridge. Tugendhat J held that there was insufficient evidence of a threat to publish the information. Manchester United's living legend Ryan Giggs sought a super-injunction to prevent publication of details of his affair with model Imogen Thomas, after he alleged that she asked for money to keep her story quiet . Justice Eady granted an injunction in *CTB v NGN Ltd* [2011] EWHC 1232 (QB). Eady found that Giggs did have an expectation of privacy given the details were of an intimate and sexual nature. Eady J found that there was no public interest in 'kiss and tell stories'. His Lordship, at [33], said:

> It will rarely be the case that the privacy rights of an individual or of his family will have to yield in priority to another's right to publish what has been described in the House of Lords as 'tittle-tattle about the activities of footballers' wives and girlfriends': see eg *Jameel v Wall Street Journal Europe SPRL* [2007] 1 AC 359 at [147].

8.149 The injunction was largely ignored and many comments were posted on the social media website Twitter revealing Giggs' identity. A Scottish newspaper also published a thinly disguised photograph of Giggs. Other newspapers published stories regarding the super-injunction, often next to unnamed photographs of Giggs. The defendant sought an application to reveal Giggs' identity but this was refused by Eady J in *CTB v News Group Newspapers Ltd* [2011] EWHC 1326 (QB). The same day, John Hemming MP used parliamentary privilege to identify Giggs as the claimant in the case. The defendants again sought an application to name Giggs but were refused by Tugendhat J: *CTB v News Group Newspapers Ltd* [2011] EWHC 1334 (QB). Later Giggs stated that Thomas had not requested money and when Giggs failed to comply with directions the matter lapsed and was automatically struck out. In *CTB v News Group Newspapers Ltd* [2011] EWHC 3099 (QB), Giggs failed to have the matter reinstated. Tugendhat J, at [91], observed that 'the way that this case has been conducted by the parties has done much to undermine confidence in the administration of justice'.

8.150   As a response to these problems, Lord Neuberger chaired a Parliamentary Committee on super-injunctions which made a number of recommendations regarding the procedure for making such applications but rejected calls for specialised judges or courts to deal with these issues.[15] The Committee also found that it would not be constitutionally possible to issue a 'hyper-injunction' which could gag parliamentary privilege. Unfortunately, the Committee refrained from making a statement that it might be good for professional people in the sport and entertainment industry to stop having illicit affairs.

8.151   Given that the UK courts have moved so far into integrating the European human rights into their doctrine, it could be argued that the English cases are now of decreasing relevance to Australian conditions. Caution should be exercised in reliance on these decisions, but it should also be said that the differences are not as great as some would make out. First, the traditional doctrine and categories still apply in the United Kingdom, and resort may not need to be had to the articles for the resolution of commercial confidences: *OBG Ltd v Allan*. Second, even in cases of personal and governmental confidences, the gulf between Australian and English authorities is not so wide. English judges have tended to overemphasise the difference between the new 'tort' approach and the traditional doctrine. It is claimed that the tort approach is radically different because it allows judges to enforce confidences in circumstances where there is no pre-existing relationship giving rise to an enforceable duty of confidence: *Mosley v News Group Newspapers Ltd* at [7]. But as *Franklin v Giddins* demonstrates, this is possible under the traditional doctrine: see 8.79–8.80. Equity does not require a pre-existing relationship before imposing a duty of confidence. What is needed is a form of unconscientious conduct. Finally, as more Australian jurisdictions adopt human rights legislation akin to the UK model, there may well be reconvergence between the Australian and English approaches.

Australian approaches to privacy protection

8.152   Privacy rights are created under statutory schemes in Australia, such as under the *Privacy Act 1988* (Cth). However, these schemes generally relate to access and control of personal records rather than protection of wider privacy interests. Additionally, Australian jurisdictions (apart from the Australian Capital Territory and Victoria) lack domestic protection of human rights.[16] These factors may have led to one thinking that Australian courts would be slow to follow the jurisprudence currently developing in England and New Zealand.

8.153   Initially, it was said that equity may restrain the publication of photographs even when they have been taken in public spaces surreptitiously, if they are embarrassing or offensive: *Bathurst City*

---

15. Lord Neuberger, *Report of the Committee on Super-Injunctions: Super-Injunctions, Anonymised Injunctions and Open Justice* 2011, http://www.judiciary.gov.uk/Resources/JCO/Documents/Reports/super-injunction-report-20052011.pdf (accessed 29 May 2012).
16. *Human Rights Act 2004* (ACT) s 12; *Charter of Human Rights and Responsibilities Act 2006* (Vic) s 13.

Council v Saban (1985) 2 NSWLR 704 at 708; *Hellewell v Chief Constable of Derbyshire* [1995] 4 All ER 473 at 476. Hodgson CJ in Eq adopted this principle in *Kwok v Thang*. This case concerned the contents of a video tape taken of the plaintiff in a passionate encounter with one of the defendants. The plaintiff was a Chinese pop star and had come to Australia on tour. While on tour he was befriended by the defendants. The defendants had filmed the encounter in a hotel room as a way of extorting money from the plaintiff. An account of the contents of the tape had been published in a Hong Kong newspaper. The plaintiff sought an injunction to prevent further publication. Hodgson CJ in Eq found that the balance of convenience required that the defendants be restrained from publishing the contents of the video tape. The prior publication in Hong Kong was transitory and unlikely to be remembered and hence did not destroy confidentiality. There was a serious question to be tried as to whether the defendants had breached confidence given that they had only been friends for a short period of time. Hodgson CJ in Eq stated that one need not have a longstanding friendship before equity would find an obligation of confidence.

8.154   In *Donnelly v Amalgamated Television Services Pty Limited* (1998) 45 NSWLR 570, Hodgson CJ in Eq restrained the publication of a video taken of the plaintiff in his underpants during a legal search of his house. The plaintiff was convicted of the charges relating to the search. The tape was not used in the prosecution and police had given the tape to a television station. This was considered by Hodgson CJ in Eq to be an abuse of police power, which triggered the plaintiff's right to equitable relief. The risk of public humiliation could not be overcome by the availability of exemplary damages. Hence, an injunction was ordered even though there was no trespass.

8.155   The above cases all illustrate that if the defendant is directly responsible for some unconscientious act leading to publication they can be restrained either via an action for breach of confidence or through some inherent equitable jurisdiction. However, as shown in *Donnelly v Amalgamated Television Services*, equity will also be able to take action against third parties who were not responsible for the recording of the information but who seek to publish it in the knowledge that it was recorded unconscionably.

8.156   This extension of the equitable jurisdiction was discussed in *Australian Broadcasting Corp v Lenah Game Meats*. A majority of the High Court refused to restrain the publication of video footage by the ABC which had been taken of the slaughtering processes employed by the plaintiff when butchering possum meat. The film had been recorded by hidden cameras that had been placed by animal liberationists inside the plaintiff's building. It was assumed that the liberationists had trespassed when placing the cameras in the building. The footage was then supplied to the broadcaster who aired it after the plaintiff's original attempts to bring an injunction failed. The plaintiff sought an injunction to prevent further broadcasts of the footage.

8.157   The primary issue was whether the broadcaster could be restrained via an injunction, given that it had not committed an actionable wrong in obtaining the footage. A claim was made that further publication would be unconscientious (because the broadcaster knew that the footage had been obtained via a trespass) and unconscientiousness on its own would allow for an injunction.

8.158   However, a majority of the High Court (Gleeson CJ, Gaudron, Gummow, Hayne and Kirby JJ; Callinan J in dissent) disagreed. In doing so the majority judges gave the most detailed consideration to date in Australia of the use of equity to protect privacy. The main issue related to whether the tape contained confidential or private information. Gleeson CJ supported the general principle that equity could act to restrain publication of photographic material surreptitiously obtained. However, the act recorded must be of a 'private' nature before equity should intervene because only then would it be unconscientious to publish the footage. The issue of what was 'private' was therefore central. His Honour, at CLR 226; ALR 13, said:

> There is no bright line which can be drawn between what is private and what is not. Use of the term 'public' is often a convenient method of contrast, but there is a large area in between what is necessarily public and what is necessarily private. An activity is not private simply because it is not done in public. It does not suffice to make an act private that, because it occurs on private property, it has such measure of protection from the public gaze as the characteristics of the property, the nature of the activity, the locality, and the disposition of the property owner combine to afford. Certain kinds of information about a person, such as information relating to health, personal relationships, or finances, may be easy to identify as private; as may certain kinds of activity, which a reasonable person, applying contemporary standards of morals and behaviour, would understand to be meant to be unobserved. The requirement that disclosure or observation of information or conduct would be highly offensive to a reasonable person of ordinary sensibilities is in many circumstances a useful practical test of what is private.

Applying this test, Gleeson CJ, at CLR 227; ALR 13–14, found that the footage was not of a private act:

> The problem for the respondent is that the activities secretly observed and filmed were not relevantly private. Of course, the premises on which those activities took place were private in a proprietorial sense. And, by virtue of its proprietary right to exclusive possession of the premises, the respondent had the capacity (subject to the possibility of trespass or other surveillance) to grant or refuse permission to anyone who wanted to observe, and record, its operations. The same can be said of any landowner, but it does not make everything that the owner does on the land a private act. Nor does an act become private simply because the owner of land would prefer that it were unobserved. The reasons for such preference might be personal, or financial. They might be good or bad. An owner of land does not have to justify refusal of entry to a member of the public, or of the press. The right to choose who may enter, and who will be excluded, is an aspect of ownership. It may mean that a person who enters without permission is a trespasser; but that does not mean that every activity observed by the trespasser is private.

8.159 Gleeson CJ's finding that the footage was not private meant it was not unconscientious for the ABC to publish the footage. Gleeson CJ said that his decision would have been different had the ABC been the trespasser. In such a case he said he would have followed the line of authority, beginning with *Lincoln Hunt Australia Pty Ltd v Willesee*, to find the actions of the trespasser as unconscientious. Gleeson CJ also opined that had the footage been of a private nature, such as the footage in *Donnelly*, it would have been unconscientious for the ABC to televise it.

8.160 Gummow and Hayne JJ dealt with the claim that the respondent company had a right to privacy. Their Honours believed that *Victoria Park Racing & Recreation Grounds Co v Taylor* was no longer a bar to the creation of a new tort of privacy, but they cautioned that a preferable course would be to adapt recognised forms of action to meet new situations and circumstances. They accepted the analysis of Sedley LJ in *Douglas v Hello! Ltd* (see 8.140) that privacy was based on the fundamental value of personal autonomy. As such, Gummow and Hayne JJ queried whether any generalised tort of privacy should be available to corporations. Their Honours felt that the company had not sufficiently made out a cause of action and, as such, an injunction could not be granted. Gaudron J agreed with their reasons.

8.161   Kirby J disagreed with the views of Gaudron, Gummow and Hayne JJ on the ability of the court to grant an injunction but he nevertheless agreed that an injunction should not be granted. Kirby J believed that equity did have the power to prevent the media from broadcasting improperly obtained information even when the media was not directly involved in the improper activities. His Honour also believed that a tort of privacy might be developed, but thought that the question did not need to be decided in the extant case. Nevertheless, Kirby J still refused to order an injunction because he thought that it would improperly interfere with the implied freedom of political communication, described in *Lange v Australian Broadcasting Corporation* (1997) 189 CLR 520; 145 ALR 96. The discussion of animal welfare was a legitimate matter of governmental and political concern and should not be prevented by an injunction.

8.162   Callinan J (in dissent) found that the ABC's use of the footage was a breach of confidence and that equity should intervene, given the clear violation of the company's right of possession over the land. His Honour was also prepared to go the next step and recognise a tort of privacy and he believed that the implied constitutional right of political communication was not implicated in the case. Given these findings, he believed the injunction should have been ordered.

8.163   *Lenah Game Meats* may have opened the door to privacy-based claims but the Australian courts have generally been reticent to rush in.[17] The District Court of Queensland has accepted a tort in *Grosse v Purvis* [2003] QDC 151, but the Victorian Full Court and the Federal Court have so far declined to create a tort of privacy: *Giller v Procopets*; *Kalaba v Commonwealth* [2004] FCA 763. The Australian Law Reform Commission, the NSW Law Reform Commission and the Victorian Law Reform Commission have all argued that a statutory tort needs to be created but as yet no legislation has been introduced.[18]

8.164   To that extent, the doctrine of confidential information remains the main source of protection for privacy in Australia. Gleeson CJ's requirements, first, that information is private and, second, that disclosure is highly offensive to a reasonable person of ordinary sensibilities, now appear to be the key requirements. The fact that the information has been obtained via trespass is a factor to consider, but it is not determinative of the issue of breach of privacy, nor of unconscientiousness: *Pillay T/As West Corp Mortgage Market v Nine Network Australia Pty Ltd* [2002] NSWSC 983; *Windridge Farm Pty Ltd v Grassi* [2011] NSWSC 196.

---

17.   M Johnston, 'Should Australia Force the Square Peg of Privacy into the Round Hole of Confidence or Look to a New Tort?' (2007) 12 *Media and Arts Law Review* 44.

18.   ALRC, 'For Your Information: Australian Privacy Law and Practice', Report 108, 2008; NSWLRC, 'Invasion of Privacy', Report 120, 2009; VLRC, 'Surveillance in Public Places', Final Report 18, 2010. For a discussion see N Witzleb, 'Statutory cause of action for privacy? A critical appraisal of three recent Australian law reform proposals' (2011) 19 *Torts Law Journal* 104.

9

FIDUCIARY OBLIGATIONS

INTRODUCTION

9.1 The word 'fiduciary' has its roots in the Latin word *fiducia*, which means confidence. A fiduciary relationship is therefore a relationship of confidence. The person in whom confidence is reposed within that relationship is referred to as the fiduciary. The person to whom fiduciary obligations are owed is called the beneficiary (or principal).[1] If a fiduciary abuses his or her position to obtain an advantage or benefit at the expense of the beneficiary, the latter will be able to seek relief from a court of equity to prevent such advantage accruing to the fiduciary. The rationale for equity's intervention on behalf of the confiding party was set out in the High Court of Australia in *Maguire v Makaronis* (1997) 188 CLR 449 at 465; 144 ALR 729 at 738, by Brennan CJ, Gaudron, McHugh and Gummow JJ when they said:

> Equity intervenes ... not so much to recoup a loss suffered by the plaintiff as to hold the fiduciary to, and vindicate, the high duty owed to the plaintiff ... [T]hose in a fiduciary position who enter into transactions with those to whom they owe fiduciary duties labour under a heavy duty to show the righteousness of the transactions.

9.2 Unfortunately, there is no universally accepted definition of a fiduciary relationship. Nor is there a universally acknowledged test for determining when a fiduciary relationship exists.[2] This has made the study and development of fiduciary duties difficult. Sir Anthony Mason, speaking extra-judicially, has said that fiduciary relationships are 'a concept in search of a principle'.[3]

9.3 Additionally, while judges and authors often describe relationships as being 'fiduciary', not all aspects of such a relationship will be governed by fiduciary principles. In *The Bell Group Ltd (in liq) v Westpac Banking Corporation (No 9)* (2008) 225 FLR 1 at 493, Owen J said:

> In my view the state of the law is this. Where a person has undertaken to act in the interests of another and where the nature of that relationship, its surrounding circumstances and the obligations attaching to it so require, it will be held to be fiduciary. But the fact that it is categorised as fiduciary does not mean that all of the obligations arising from it are themselves fiduciary. Unless there are some special circumstances in the relationship, the duties that equity demands

---

1. S Worthington, *Equity*, 2nd ed, Oxford University Press, Oxford, p 129.
2. J Glover, *Equity, Restitution and Fraud*, LexisNexis Butterworths, Sydney, 2004, p 26; G E Dal Pont, *Equity and Trusts in Australia*, 5th ed, Law Book Co, Sydney, 2011, p 106; M Conaglen, *Fiduciary Loyalty: Protecting the Due Performance of Non-Fiduciary Duties*, Hart Publishing, Oxford, 2010.
3. A Mason, 'Themes and Prospects' in P D Finn (ed), *Essays in Equity*, Law Book Co, Sydney, 1985, p 246.

from the fiduciary will be limited to what I have described as the core obligations: not to obtain any unauthorised benefit from the relationship and not to be in a position of conflict. They stem from the fundamental obligation of loyalty.

On from this case, in *Westpac Banking Corporation v The Bell Group Ltd (In Liq) (No 3)* [2012] WASCA 157 at [886], Lee AJA said:

> The fiduciary principle was developed to monitor and redress 'abuse of a loyalty reposed' in a relationship where one party occupies a position of influence, ascendancy or power in relation to the other and has undertaken to use that position for the welfare of the other.

9.4   As shall be discussed below, equity uses the relationship to determine whether any fiduciary duties have arisen, but equity will not usually override any existing legal obligations that exist between the parties in tort and contract. Fiduciary duties will then only arise in the parts of the relationship which are not captured by contract and tort. As Dal Pont explains, it is 'better to speak of the relevant fiduciary duties to avoid perpetuating the incorrect impression that a "fiduciary" relationship encompasses every aspect of the parties' relationship': *Canberra Residential Developments Pty Ltd v Brendas* (2010) 188 FCR 140 at 147; 273 ALR 601 at 608; *Re Coomber* [1911] 1 Ch 723 at 728–729.[4]

9.5   This chapter begins by examining the nature and character of fiduciary duties, the relationships that are presumed to carry such duties, other situations in which fiduciary duties may arise and the extent of fiduciary obligations.

THE NATURE OF FIDUCIARY OBLIGATIONS

Strict horizontal and vertical duties

9.6   Fiduciary obligations are strict.[5] The essence of fiduciary obligations is that the fiduciary is precluded from acting in any other way than in the interests of the person to whom the duty to so act is owed. In short, the fiduciary obligation is one of 'undivided loyalty': *Beach Petroleum NL v Kennedy* (1999) 48 NSWLR 1 at 46–7.

9.7   The fact that there was no intent to defraud on the part of the fiduciary is irrelevant: *Nocton v Lord Ashburton* [1919] AC 492. The liability of the fiduciary does not depend on establishing that the person to whom fiduciary duties are owed suffered loss or injury: *Birtchnell v Equity Trustees, Executors and Agency Co Ltd* (1929) 42 CLR 384 at 408–9. A fiduciary's liability arises even if the person to whom the duty is owed was unlikely or even unable to have made a profit from an opportunity exploited by the fiduciary: *Warman International Ltd v Dwyer* (1995) 182 CLR 544 at 558; 128 ALR 201 at 209. Nor will it matter that the beneficiary would have consented to the fiduciary making a profit had the beneficiary been properly informed, if informed consent was never obtained: *Murad v Al-Saraj* [2005] EWCA Civ 959.

9.8   Glover has shown that fiduciary obligations can be owed in two ways: horizontally and vertically.[6] In a horizontal situation the duties are owed by both parties to each other. Each is both

---

4.   Dal Pont, *Equity and Trusts in Australia*, note 2 above, p 99.
5.   R Flannigan, 'The Strict Character of Fiduciary Liability' (2006) *New Zealand Law Review* 209.
6.   J Glover, *Equity, Restitution and Fraud*, note 2 above, pp 26–27.

a fiduciary for the other and both benefit from the obligations. An example of this situation is with a partnership. Contrastingly, in vertical situations the fiduciary duties are only owed by one party to the other and this duty is not reciprocated. An example of such a vertical duty is that between a guardian and ward. Horizontal and vertical duties will have a differing emphasis on the characteristics of fiduciary duties.

Prohibitive (negative) duties rather than prescriptive (positive) duties

9.9   While fiduciary obligations are strict, it is important to appreciate that a fiduciary's obligation 'does … not impose positive legal duties on the fiduciary to act in the interests of the person to whom the duty is owed': *Breen v Williams* (1996) 186 CLR 71 at 113; 138 ALR 259 at 289. Fiduciary obligations are therefore said to be limited to negative or proscriptive duties, where fiduciaries are forbidden from acting in ways that conflict with their duties: *Wilden Pty Ltd v Green* (2009) 38 WAR 429. Fiduciary obligations tell fiduciaries 'what not to do, not what they have to do'.[7] Equity does not require the fiduciaries to act positively in the interests of their beneficiaries: *Groeneveld Australia Pty Ltd v Nolten (No 3)* (2010) 80 ACSR 562 at 574. It is therefore fallacious to claim that a fiduciary must 'act' in the best interests of the principal. Such positive duties are better regulated by contract, tort or other equitable doctrines: *Pilmer v Duke Group Ltd (in liq)* (2001) 207 CLR 165 at 198; 180 ALR 249 at 270–1. It is still possible for fiduciaries to owe positive duties, not pursuant to their fiduciary obligations, but under principles that include breaches of contractual or tortious obligations.

9.10   The only exception to the negative nature of fiduciary duties is the duty to disclose possible conflicts of interests and seek the informed consent of the beneficiary of the relationship: see 9.120–9.124. However this is more commonly seen as a defence to a claim of breach than a positive obligation: *Blackmagic Design Pty Ltd v Overliese* (2011) 191 FCR 1 at 22; *National Mutual Property Services (Australia) Pty Ltd v Citibank Savings Ltd* [1998] FCA 564. In *Fitzwood Pty Ltd v Unique Goal Pty Ltd (in liq)* (2001) 188 ALR 566 at 576, Finkelstein J refused to describe the obligation to seek informed consent as a positive duty but instead described it as a 'means by which the fiduciary obtains the release or forgiveness of a negative duty'. In *Maguire v Makaronis* at CLR 467; ALR 739, Brennan CJ, Gaudron, McHugh and Gummow J said that a fiduciary has no *duty* to obtain an informed consent but rather 'the existence of an informed consent would have gone to negate what otherwise was a breach of duty'.

9.11   These issues are illustrated by *Westpac Banking Corporation v The Bell Group Ltd (In Liq) (No 3)*, where it was argued that the directors had breached their duties to act in the best interests of their companies and to exercise their powers properly, when they had authorised loans which were in the overall interests of the corporate group, but not in the interests of some of the individual companies within that group. At trial (*The Bell Group Ltd (in liq) v Westpac Banking Corporation (No 9)*), Owen J found that the directors' duties to act in the companies' best interests and to exercise powers properly were fiduciary duties. In so finding, Owen J argued that these duties were, in substance, negative or proscriptive duties because directors' powers cannot be exercised in the interests of someone other than the company and (or) in a way that is not in the best interests of the

---

7.   G Dempsey & A Greinke, 'Proscriptive Fiduciary Duties in Australia' (2004) *Australian Bar Review* 1, p 2.

company. But, as Langford makes clear, there are problems with framing these duties as negative.[8] The duties require directors to take positive steps to investigate and consider options as well as consider action to prevent transactions from taking place. Owen J, at 499, was clearly conscious of these difficulties, but nevertheless felt that '[t]he integrity of the language emerges relatively unscathed'.

9.12   On appeal (*Westpac Banking Corporation v The Bell Group Ltd (In Liq) (No 3)*), Lee AJA appeared willing to discard the notion that fiduciary duties were only negative (at least when they concerned a director's duty to act in the company's best interests). At [897]–[898], Lee AJA said:

> Prescriptive obligations that arise in a fiduciary relationship may have particular connection with the fiduciary nature of the relationship… The disloyalty of a fiduciary manifested by the repudiation of such an obligation, that results in detriment to the party to whom the obligation is owed, is as offensive to good conscience and equity as an act by a fiduciary that is in breach of a proscriptive fiduciary obligation, and entitlement to appropriate relief in equity should follow.

Drummond AJA also seemed willing to reject the notion that the director's fiduciary duty to act in the company's best interests was negative, on the basis that directors were in a special position as fiduciaries. At [1978], Drummond AJA said:

> In my opinion, until the High Court declares the law to be otherwise, long established authority requires the duties of company directors to act bona fide in the interests of the company and to exercise their powers for proper purposes to be accepted as fiduciary ones even though they may require the directors to take positive action. Further, that the directors' own interests may be involved or that they may be in a situation of conflict will not necessarily mean that they have breached their fiduciary obligations in taking such action, if their actions have benefited the company.

Carr AJA did not expressly find that the duty was a positive one. However, his Honour, at [2733], referred with approval to *Kalls Enterprises Pty Ltd (in liq) v Baloglow* [2007] NSWCA 191 at [159], where Giles JA said that these duties should be viewed as fiduciary, 'until the High Court says otherwise'.

9.13   In *Friend v Brooker* (2009) 239 CLR 129 at 160; 255 ALR 601 at 620, the High Court endorsed the view that fiduciary duties are only negative in nature. However, it is suggested that there is a level of unreality in any dichotomy which rests on acts and omissions. The distinction is a slippery one and it is arguably dangerous for the limits of fiduciary principles to be based on such a shifting principle. Thus, in *Pilmer v Duke Group Ltd (in liq)* at CLR 214; ALR at 284, Kirby J, questioned the viability of the distinction on the basis that omissions frequently shade into commissions. Furthermore, as *Westpac Banking Corporation v The Bell Group Ltd (In Liq) (No 3)* illustrates, there are many obligations owed by fiduciaries which seem to be positive, or, at the very least, could be constructed as positive.[9] Equally difficult are attempts by some to preclude positive duties on the basis that they are not ones which correspond with the fiduciary's obligation of loyalty.[10] It is not

---

8.   R T Langford, 'The Fiduciary Nature of the Bona Fide and Proper Purposes Duties of Company Directors: *Bell Group Ltd (in liq) v Westpac Banking Corp (No 9)*' (2009) 31 *Australian Bar Review* 326, pp 339–40.
9.   J D Heydon, 'Are the Duties of Company Directors to Exercise Skill and Care Fiduciary?' in S Degeling & J Edelman (eds), *Equity In Commercial Law*, Law Book Co, Sydney, 2005; P Parkinson, 'Fiduciary Obligations' in P Parkinson (ed), *The Principles of Equity*, 2nd ed, Law Book Co, Sydney, 2003, p 347.
10.   G Dempsey & A Greinke, 'Proscriptive Fiduciary Duties in Australia', note 7 above, p 2.

clear why positive duties would be unable to secure loyalty in the same manner as negative ones. There may be good reasons for keeping tort and contract law claims separate from fiduciary claims, but one should not need the artificiality of positive/negative duties to maintain that separation.

Interests which are protected by fiduciary duties

9.14 Fiduciary duties are primarily used to protect economic and proprietorial interests.[11] Australian courts have been reluctant to expand protected interests to include non-economic interests, for example, personal injury damages and damages for mental distress, because of a fear that such interests are better served by other areas of law, such as tort law. It has also been said that equity would find it difficult to value such non-economic interests, although in cases like *Giller v Procopets* (2008) 24 VR 1, Australian equity has begun to recognise damages for mental distress and aggravated damages (at least in cases of breach of confidence).

9.15 Joyce has argued that this fear of non-economic injuries is unfounded and that non-economic interests should be protected by fiduciary duties where a breach has occurred which embodies forms of exploitation and betrayal.[12] In such cases, Joyce argues, fiduciary principles can address conflicts of interests in ways that tort law cannot. But the underlying question should be: what does fiduciary duty add to the issue of how the legal system responds to cases of non-economic loss? If tort law can deal with abuses of trust and betrayal via the use of aggravated and exemplary damages, what is it that equity can add? This is discussed further below in the area of child abuse at 9.81–9.87.

The search for a unifying principle: loyalty, trust and confidence, vulnerability or undertaking?

9.16 The lack of a uniform test for the existence of fiduciary duties has led some to search for a unifying principle of fiduciary law.[13] In *Bristol and West Building Society v Mothew* [1998] Ch 1 at 18; [1996] 4 All ER 698 at 711–12, Millett LJ stated that the 'distinguishing obligation of a fiduciary is loyalty'. While loyalty is a key touchstone of fiduciary duty, there are a number of other factors which courts have drawn upon to determine the existence and content of fiduciary obligations. In *Breen v Williams* at CLR 107; ALR 284, Gaudron and McHugh JJ stated that other relevant factors include 'the existence of a relation of confidence; inequality of bargaining power; an undertaking by one party to perform a task or fulfil a duty in the interests of another party; the scope for one party to unilaterally exercise a discretion or power which may affect the rights or interests of another; and a dependency or vulnerability on the part of one party that causes that party to rely on another'.

9.17 Trust and confidence are ordinarily features of fiduciary duties: *LAC Minerals Ltd v International Corona Resources Ltd* [1989] 2 SCR 574 at 597. But as Meagher, Heydon and Leeming[14] suggest, actual trust and confidence is not always needed to be shown, for example in cases of trusts where a beneficiary has never met the trustee.

---

11. Dal Pont, *Equity and Trusts in Australia*, note 2 above, p 102.
12. R Joyce, 'Fiduciary Law and Non-economic Interests' (2002) *Monash Law Review* 239.
13. See R Flannigan, 'The Core Nature of Fiduciary Accountability' (2009) *New Zealand Law Review* 375.
14. R Meagher, D Heydon & M Leeming, *Meagher, Gummow and Lehane's Equity: Doctrines and Remedies*, 4th ed, LexisNexis Butterworths, Sydney, 2002, p 157.

9.18 Vulnerability may be another factor relevant to the imposition of fiduciary duties, particularly vertical fiduciary duties: *Fast Financial Solutions Pty Ltd v Crawford* [2012] NSWSC 40 at [117]. In *Hospital Products Ltd v United States Surgical Corporation* (1984) 156 CLR 41 at 142; 55 ALR 417 at 488, Dawson J thought it relevant to examine the 'position of disadvantage or vulnerability on the part of one of the parties which causes him to place reliance upon the other and requires the protection of equity in acting on the conscience of that other'. But the issue becomes whether vulnerability is a characteristic or a consequence of the fiduciary obligation. In the same case Mason J, at CLR 96–97; ALR 454, said that '[t]he relationship between the parties is therefore one which gives the fiduciary a special opportunity to exercise the power or discretion to the detriment of that other person who is accordingly vulnerable to abuse by the fiduciary of his position'. In *C-Shirt Pty Ltd v Barnett Marketing and Management Pty Ltd* (1996) 37 IPR 315 at 316, Lehane J said:

> I do not think that in Australian law 'vulnerability', though it may be a characteristic of some of those to whom fiduciary duties are owed, is the touchstone of fiduciary obligation: the fundamental question is for what purpose, and for the promotion of whose interests, are powers held?

In *Pilmer v Duke Group Ltd (in liq)* at CLR 217–18; ALR 286–7, Kirby J also doubted the sufficiency of vulnerability and said that more was needed to call up a fiduciary obligation.

9.19 It can also be relevant to ask whether one party has undertaken to act for the other party's interests, particularly in horizontal relationships, such as in partnerships and joint ventures: *Di Russo v Butkovic* [2011] WASC 156. Edelman J (writing before his elevation to the judiciary) said that voluntary undertakings are the key to modern understandings of fiduciary relationships:

> [I]f we persist in seeing fiduciary obligations as imposed by law, and dependent upon conceptions of status, the quest to understand and explain why different fiduciaries owe different duties will remain an impossible task. In contrast, by understanding fiduciary duties as terms which are expressed or implied into manifested undertakings to another, it is much easier to understand why the nature of fiduciary duties will always depend upon the circumstances. This explanation illuminates the reason why exactly the same analysis is undertaken by courts when determining, on the one hand, whether fiduciary duties have arisen and, on the other hand, in determining whether such duties should be implied into contracts or other voluntary undertakings. The analyses are the same because fiduciary duties *are* terms expressed or implied in voluntary undertakings.[15]

In *Hospital Products Ltd v United States Surgical Corporation* at CLR 96–7; ALR 454, Mason J argued that the critical feature of a fiduciary relationship was:

> … that the fiduciary undertakes or agrees to act for or on behalf of or in the interests of another person in the exercise of a power or discretion which will affect the interests of that person in a legal or practical sense.

9.20 Mason J's theory of undertaking seems to presuppose some form of agreement or contract. Oftentimes the existence of an agreement is central to the finding of fiduciary duty (particularly in commercial relationships), but there are many types of fiduciary obligations which do not arise out

---

15. J Edleman, 'When do fiduciary duties arise?' (2010) 126 *Law Quarterly Review* 302 at 327.

of agreements, and the undertaking theory does not seem to provide a basis for understanding these duties, unless some form of implied undertaking is assumed.[16]

9.21   Professor (now Justice) Finn argued that all of these issues could be embodied in a doctrine of 'reasonable expectations', where the imposition of a fiduciary duty would be dependent on whether the principal had an objectively reasonable expectation that the fiduciary would act in the beneficiary's interest to the exclusion of their own personal interests.[17] This test has been used in Australian cases: *Hadid v Lenfest Communications Inc* [1999] FCA 1798; *Brunninghausen v Glavanics* (1999) 46 NSWLR 538. But, as Glover points out, the question of what is 'reasonable' just replaces the older characteristics within an empty normative shell, which the judges will have to fill in with the old characteristics and/or other values they hold dear. In that sense, reasonable expectations is a limitation device rather than a rational test, much as is 'reasonable foreseeability' in negligence.[18]

9.22   Each characteristic therefore is dominant in some forms of fiduciary obligation, but none is sufficient on its own to describe the totality of fiduciary experience. Conaglen has argued that the concept of fiduciary loyalty encapsulates a series of principles that provide a form of 'prophylactic' protection for non-fiduciaries, duties.[19] In that sense fiduciary loyalty serves like a form of immunisation which protects a fiduciary from the temptation to depart from their broader non-fiduciary obligations to act in the best interests of their principles. Fiduciary duties remove fiduciaries from situations of conflict, and this makes the fiduciary's compliance with their other duties more likely.

CONFLICTS BETWEEN INTEREST AND DUTY

9.23   At its heart, the duty imposed upon a fiduciary operates in circumstances where there is a conflict between the fiduciary's 'duty' and his or her 'interest'. In *Aberdeen Railway Co v Blaikie Brothers* [1843–60] All ER Rep 249 at 252, Lord Cranworth said:

> [A fiduciary will not be permitted] to enter into engagements in which he has, or can have, a personal interest conflicting, or which possibly may conflict, with the interests of those whom he is bound to protect.

9.24   The word 'duty' in this context does not have a technical meaning. It does not refer to legally imposed obligations. Rather, it refers to the actions undertaken by a fiduciary on behalf of another person. These actions are not confined to those undertaken in the performance of a fiduciary's mandatory or discretionary functions. These actions also include voluntary acts.

9.25   The word 'interest', in this context, signifies the presence of some personal concern on the part of a fiduciary or of some possible significant pecuniary value in a decision to be taken by the fiduciary. Finn notes:

16. See generally, M Leeming, 'The scope of fiduciary obligations: How contract informs, but does not determine, the scope of fiduciary obligations' (2009) 3 *Journal of Equity* 181.

17. P D Finn, 'The Fiduciary Principle' in T G Youdan (ed), *Equity, Fiduciaries and Trusts*, Carswell, Toronto, 1989.

18. Glover, *Equity, Restitution and Fraud*, note 2 above, pp 32–33. See also P Parkinson, 'Fiduciary Obligations', note 9 above, p 391.

19. Conaglen, *Fiduciary Loyalty: Protecting the Due Performance of Non-Fiduciary Duties*, note 2 above, pp 4, 269–276.

The pecuniary dimension of the fiduciary's concern may take the form of an actual, prospective, or possible profit to be made in, or as a result of, the decision he takes or the transaction he effects. Or it may take the form of an actual, prospective, or possible saving, or a diminution of a personal liability.[20]

In *Settlement Agents Supervisory Board v Property Settlement Services Pty Ltd* [2009] WASCA 143 at [72], McLure JA said:

> Not all interests are within the conflict rule. The interest must give rise to a conflict or a real or substantial possibility of a conflict: *Hospital Products* (103) (Mason J). There are other formulations of the required connection such as 'a sensible, real or substantial possibility' (*Clay v Clay* (2001) 202 CLR 410) and 'a significant possibility' (*Chan v Zacharia* (1984) 154 CLR 178 at 198). The extension to cover a real or substantial possibility of a conflict serves at least two functions. First, it is intended to signify that not all personal interests come within the conflict rule. An interest will not fall within the conflict rule if it is too remote or insubstantial: *Hospital Products* (103) (Mason J). Secondly, an anticipatory breach of the conflict rule can be restrained: *Re Thomson; Thomson v Allen* [1930] 1 Ch 203.

In the *Grimaldi v Chameleon Mining Pty Ltd (ACN 098 773 785) (No 2)* (2012) 200 FCR 296 at 346; 287 ALR 22 at 68, the Full Court of the Federal Court said:

> One comment should be made about the term 'interest' as used in the conflict formula. Put compendiously, the term signifies the presence of some personal concern of possible pecuniary value in a decision taken, or a transaction effected, within the scope of a fiduciary's duties. Importantly for present purposes, it may be a contingent or expectant one, as where a trustee uses a trust's shareholding in a company to vote himself onto the company's board from which position he will be likely to derive directors' fees: see for example *Re Macadam; Dallow v Codd* [1946] Ch 73 at 81; or where a dealing with an agent proceeds on the assumption that a success fee is to be paid if a transaction is effected: *McCann v Switzerland Insurance Australia Ltd* (2000) 203 CLR 579.

9.26   The rationale of the rule against conflicts was stated in *Bray v Ford* [1896] AC 55 at 51–2, where Lord Herschell said:

> It does not appear to me that this rule is, as has been said, founded upon principles of morality. I regard it rather as based upon the consideration that, human nature being what it is, there is a danger, in such circumstances, of the person holding a fiduciary position being swayed by interest rather than by duty, and thus prejudicing those whom he was bound to protect. It has, therefore, been deemed expedient to lay down this positive rule.

9.27   This passage was cited with approval by Gaudron and McHugh JJ in *Breen v Williams* at CLR 108; ALR 285. In that case the High Court held that it was impossible to establish any conflict of interest and duty, unauthorised profit or loss in relation to a doctor denying a patient access to the doctor's medical records. Accordingly, the court held that the doctor's refusal to give such access did not amount to a breach of any fiduciary obligation.

9.28   A fiduciary's obligation not to allow his or her duty to conflict with his or her interest can be examined under the following three headings:

---

20. P D Finn, *Fiduciary Obligations*, Law Book Co, Sydney, 1977, p 204.

1. unauthorised remuneration;
2. assuming a double character; and
3. benefits derived to the exclusion of the person to whom the fiduciary obligation is owed.

Unauthorised remuneration

9.29 Cases within this category cover situations in which a fiduciary, in the actual performance of his or her duties, obtains financial benefits beyond those that are authorised. The purpose of the rule in these cases is not to prevent a fiduciary obtaining fair remuneration for services performed, but rather to prevent secret or unauthorised profits being made: *Dale v IRC* [1954] AC 11 at 27; [1953] 2 All ER 671 at 674. Cases involving the payment of bribes or secret commissions serve as typical examples.

9.30 In *Reading v R* [1949] 2 KB 232; [1949] 2 All ER 68 (Court of Appeal); [1951] AC 507; [1951] 1 All ER 617 (House of Lords), Reading was a sergeant in the English army stationed in Egypt. He accompanied civilian trucks through security checkpoints in order to assist them in transporting contraband goods. In return he was paid for his assistance. The court ruled that Reading owed fiduciary duties to the Crown and the amount recoverable by the Crown was the full amount that Reading had received for his services.

9.31 The payment of tips or gratuities is another form of payment beyond agreed remuneration. However, in this situation, if the payment is small and made after the performance of services as an acknowledgment that they were very well performed, the fiduciary is entitled to keep the payment: *The Parkdale* [1897] P 53 at 58–9. On the other hand, if the payment is made before or during the performance of services, the fiduciary will have to account for it on the basis that it would be seen as a bribe. If the payment to the fiduciary is ostensibly made for past services, he or she will have to account for it if it can be shown that it would likely influence future dealings. In such cases the size of the payment will be indicative of the intent behind its payment.

Assuming a double character

9.32 Cases in this category involve transactions in which a fiduciary acts in that capacity on the one hand and as an undisclosed principal on the other. In *Armstrong v Jackson* [1917] 2 KB 822, Armstrong instructed Jackson, a stockbroker, to buy shares in a certain company. Jackson transferred his own shares in that company to Armstrong. The court ruled that Jackson had breached his fiduciary duties to Armstrong. McCardie J, at 823–4, said:

> A broker who is employed to buy shares cannot sell his own shares unless he makes a full disclosure of the fact to his principal, and the principal, with a full knowledge, gives his assent to the changed position of the broker ... [A] broker who secretly sells his own shares is in a wholly false position. As a vendor it is to his interest to sell his shares at the highest price. As broker it is his clear duty to the principal to buy at the lowest price and to give unbiased and independent advice ... as to the time when and the price at which shares shall be bought, or whether they shall be bought at all. The law has ever required a high measure of good faith from an agent. He departs from good faith when he secretly sells his own property to the principal ... It matters not that the broker sells at the market price, or that he acts without intent to defraud. The prohibition of the law is absolute. It will not allow an agent to place himself in a situation which, under ordinary circumstances, would tempt a man to do that which is not best for his principal. The Court will not enter into

discussion as to the propriety of the price charged by the broker, nor is it material to inquire whether the principal has or has not suffered a loss. If the breach of duty by the broker be shown, the Court will set aside the transaction.

Benefits derived by fiduciary to the exclusion of the beneficiary

9.33   Cases in this category involve a fiduciary, acting within the scope of his or her undertaking, deriving a profit or benefit that should have gone to the person to whom the fiduciary duties were owed. It is in this area that the breaches of fiduciary duty cases most commonly arise. In the context of this type of case, in *Chan v Zacharia* (1984) 154 CLR 178 at 199; 53 ALR 417 at 433, Deane J said:

> Stated comprehensively in terms of the liability to account, the principle of equity is that a person who is under a fiduciary obligation must account to the person to whom the obligation is owed for any benefit or gain (i) which has been obtained or received in circumstances where a conflict or significant possibility of conflict existed between his fiduciary duty and his personal interest in the pursuit or possible receipt of such a benefit or gain or (ii) which was obtained or received by use or by reason of his fiduciary position or of opportunity or knowledge resulting from it.

9.34   Deane J's statement divides this category of case into two interlocking sub-rules, namely:

1. cases in which a fiduciary is not to derive a profit or benefit that should have gone to the person to whom fiduciary duties are owed (the breach of undertaking sub-rule); and
2. cases in which a fiduciary is not to gain a profit or benefit through the misuse of his or her position as a fiduciary (the misuse of position sub-rule).

   Each of the sub-rules will be analysed in turn.

The breach of undertaking sub-rule

9.35   The purpose of this sub-rule is to prevent a fiduciary acting for his or her own benefit in a transaction undertaken for the benefit of the person to whom he or she stands in a fiduciary relationship. Critical to determining if there has been a breach of fiduciary duties is the determination of the scope of the fiduciary's undertaking. The relationship between the parties must be examined to ascertain the scope of the fiduciary's duties before any question of breaches of fiduciary duties can be entertained: *Phipps v Boardman* [1967] 2 AC 46 at 127; [1966] 3 All ER 721 at 758; *Hospital Products Ltd v United States Surgical Corporation* at CLR 102; ALR 458. The existence of a fiduciary obligation does not determine the scope of the fiduciary's duties. That comes from the circumstances surrounding the relationship: *News Ltd v Australian Rugby Football League Ltd* (1996) 139 ALR 193 at 312. Whether or not what a fiduciary does is within the scope of his or her undertaking is a question of fact in each case. Conduct that may fall within the fiduciary component of a relationship in one case may not do so in another case: *Beach Petroleum NL v Kennedy* at 45. In *Omnilab Media Pty Limited v Digital Cinema Network Pty Ltd* (2011) 285 ALR 63 at 89, Jacobson J said:

> [T]he subject matter over which the fiduciary obligations extend is determined by the character of the venture or undertaking for which the relationship exists … [T]his is to be ascertained not merely from the express agreement of the parties, whether embodied in a written instrument or not, but also from the course of dealing actually pursued by the entity to whom the duties are owed.

Similarly, in *Canberra Residential Developments Pty Ltd v Brendas* (2010) 188 FCR 140 at 147; 273 ALR 601 at 608, the Full Court of the Federal Court said:

> [T]he mere existence of a fiduciary relationship does not define the nature of the duties that arise for three reasons. First, it is wrong to assume that the duty owed by a fiduciary attaches to every aspect of the fiduciary's conduct, however irrelevant that conduct is to the relationship that is the source of the duty. Second, the scope of the duty is very much dependent upon the facts of the particular case. In most cases the duty will be determined in large part by reference to the nature of the activities of the principal ... Third, defining the scope of the duty must be approached with commonsense and with an appreciation of the sort of circumstances in which it has been applied in the past. It should only be applied to a state of affairs which discloses a real conflict of duty and interest and not just some theoretical or rhetorical conflict.

9.36 In *Clark Boyce v Mouat* [1994] 1 AC 428; [1994] 4 All ER 268, solicitors acted for a woman who mortgaged her property to cover her son's debt to a finance company. The same solicitors acted for the son. The solicitors had disclosed the potential conflict between their respective duties to the woman and her son on a number of occasions. The solicitors' advice to the woman that she obtain independent legal advice was never acted upon by the woman. The woman claimed a breach of fiduciary duties by the solicitors, arguing that they should have advised her on the wisdom of the transaction and investigated the son's financial position before she executed the mortgage. In the circumstances, the Privy Council rejected the woman's claim on the ground that the solicitors' undertaking to the woman extended only to giving *legal* advice.

9.37 If it is determined that a fiduciary's actions are within the scope of his or her undertaking, the fiduciary cannot enter into arrangements in which his or her interests conflict, or possibly conflict, with the interests of those the fiduciary is bound to protect. In *Phipps v Boardman* at AC 124; All ER 756, Lord Upjohn was of the view that the possibility of conflict must be a 'real sensible possibility' before the fiduciary will be held accountable. However, in the same case, Lord Hodson, at AC 111; All ER 748, appears to be of the view that even remote possibilities of conflict will result in a finding against the fiduciary. The views of Lord Upjohn were endorsed by Gibbs J in *Consul Developments Pty Ltd v DPC Estates Pty Ltd* (1975) 132 CLR 373 at 394; 5 ALR 231 at 248; Mason J in *Hospital Products v USSC* at CLR 103; ALR 459; Deane J in *Chan v Zacharia* at CLR 198; ALR 433; Gummow J in *Breen v Williams* at CLR 135; ALR 306–7; the Court of Appeal in New South Wales in *Beach Petroleum NL v Kennedy* at 89; and the Full Court of the Federal Court in *Blackmagic Design Pty Ltd v Overliese* at 21.

9.38 Once the scope of a fiduciary's undertaking is defined and it is established that an action on his or her part amounts to a conflict between his or her interest and duty, the only way in which the fiduciary can escape liability is by making a full and proper disclosure to the person whom he or she is bound to protect, and obtain that person's consent to the action; see 9.120–9.124.

9.39 Similar considerations apply to cases in which a fiduciary has a conflict of duty and duty (see 9.46–9.47). As with conflict of duty and interest cases, these also involve 'breach[es] of the same over-riding duty of undivided loyalty': *Beach Petroleum v Kennedy* at 46. An example would be a solicitor acting for two clients in the same matter. In such cases 'the fiduciary ... may be unable to discharge adequately the one obligation without conflicting with the requirement for observance of the other obligation': *Breen v Williams* at CLR 135; ALR 306. Thus, in *Farrington v Rowe McBride*

& Partners [1985] 1 NZLR 83, clients A and B had the one solicitor acting for them. Client A's verdict in a personal injuries claim was, on the advice of the solicitor, invested in client B's development company which subsequently went into liquidation. Client A successfully sued the solicitor for breach of fiduciary duty under the conflict of duty and duty principle. In the Court of Appeal, Richardson J, at 90, said:

> A solicitor's loyalty to his client must be undivided. He cannot properly discharge his duties to one whose interests are in opposition to those of another client. If there is a conflict in his responsibilities to one or both he must ensure that he fully discloses the material facts to both clients and obtains their informed consent to his so acting … And there will be some circumstances in which it is impossible, notwithstanding such disclosure, for any solicitor to act fairly and adequately for both. But the acceptance of multiple engagements is not necessarily fatal. There may be an identity of interests or the separate clients may have unrelated interests. In some circumstances they may even be able and prepared to look after their own interests. Such cases seem straightforward so long as it is apparent that there is no actual conflict between duties owed in each relationship. However, the difficulty lies in determining in particular cases that there is no such conflict.

9.40   A leading case illustrating the above principles is *Phipps v Boardman*. In this case Boardman acted as a solicitor for a trust. He attended the annual general meeting of Lester & Harris Ltd, a company in which the trust had a substantial shareholding. Boardman and Tom Phipps, one of the beneficiaries under the trust, were unhappy with the state of the company. Together they planned to acquire shares in the company to take it over. Boardman was able to assess the viability of the takeover because of information about the company he gained whilst acting as solicitor for the trust. Boardman advised the beneficiaries of the trust of these plans and no objection was made by any of them. He also had the consent of two of the three trustees; the third, being senile, was not advised of these plans. The takeover was successful and resulted in profits to the trust in relation to its shareholding in the company as well as for Boardman and Tom Phipps in relation to the shares they had personally acquired. John Phipps, one of the beneficiaries under the trust, sought an account of the profits made by Boardman and Tom Phipps on the grounds of breach of fiduciary duties.

9.41   By a bare majority the House of Lords held in favour of John Phipps. An initial issue before the House of Lords was whether Tom Phipps could be sued. This was not fully analysed because Tom Phipps chose to be treated the same as Boardman. However, four Law Lords considered Tom Phipps was properly sued: Lord Cohen at AC 104; All ER 744; Lord Hodson at AC 106; All ER 745; Lord Guest at AC 114; All ER 750; Lord Upjohn at AC 125; All ER 757. The majority Law Lords (Lord Cohen at AC 100–3; All ER 741–3; Lord Hodson at AC 109–11; All ER 747–8; Lord Guest at AC 114–17; All ER 750–2) all held that the information obtained by Boardman was trust property and that it was irrelevant that the trustees of the trust were in no position to acquire the shares in the company for the trust. Because there was a conflict, or at least a possibility of a conflict, between Boardman's duty and interest, the informed consent of the trustees was needed before the purchase of shares by Boardman and Tom Phipps could be upheld. On the other hand, as Lord Hodson noted, at AC 112; All ER 749, Boardman was entitled to 'payment … on a liberal scale in respect of the work and skill employed in obtaining the shares and the profits therefrom': see 9.129–9.130.

9.42   The minority Law Lords (Viscount Dilhorne at AC 912; All ER 735–6; Lord Upjohn at AC 129–33; All ER 760–2) held that the information gained by Boardman was of no use to the trustees because they could not make any use of it to purchase the shares acquired by Boardman and Tom Phipps. Both of their Lordships were of the view that had there been a breach of fiduciary duties, on the facts of the case there had not been a consent because the senile trustee had neither been informed, nor asked, about the purchase of shares by Boardman and Tom Phipps.

Misuse of fiduciary position sub-rule

9.43 The purpose of this sub-rule is to prevent a fiduciary using his or her position to secure or assist in exploiting a profit-making opportunity. If a fiduciary acts in such a way he or she must account for any profit or benefit derived as a result. The applicable rule here was reaffirmed in *Towers v Premier Waste Management Ltd* [2011] EWCA Civ 923 at [10] by Mummery LJ when he said:

> If a director obtains the opportunity for himself, he will be liable to the company for breach of duty regardless of the fact that he acted in good faith or that the company could not, or would not, take advantage of the opportunity.

In *Cook v Deeks* [1916] 1 AC 554, a construction company had for some time gained contracts to lay tracks for the Canadian Pacific Railway Co. Two of the construction company directors formed a new private company of their own, which negotiated another contract with Canadian Pacific Railway. The construction company argued that this amounted to a breach of fiduciary duty on the part of the directors. The Privy Council agreed, holding that the directors deliberately used their position to exclude the construction company whose interest it was their duty to protect.

9.44 Perhaps the leading authority in this line of cases is *Regal (Hastings) Ltd v Gulliver* [1967] 2 AC 134; [1942] 1 All ER 378. In that case, the directors of Regal formed a subsidiary company with the intention that Regal own all the shares in the subsidiary company. The directors sought a lease of two cinemas for the subsidiary company. However, the landlord was not prepared to grant the lease unless the subsidiary company had a paid-up capital of £5000. Because Regal did not have the necessary capital to invest £5000 in the subsidiary, the directors decided that Regal would invest £2000 and that they would invest the balance themselves. From the shares issued to them in the subsidiary, the directors made a profit. The House of Lords unanimously ruled that irrespective of whether or not Regal could have purchased the shares, the directors were liable to Regal for the profit they made. Lord Macmillan, at AC 153; All ER 391, said:

> The sole ground on which it was sought to render them accountable was that, being directors of the plaintiff company and therefore in a fiduciary relation to it, they entered in the course of their management into a transaction in which they utilised the position and knowledge possessed by them in virtue of their office as directors, and that the transaction resulted in a profit to themselves. The point was not whether the directors had a duty to acquire the shares in question for the company and failed in that duty. They had no such duty. We must take it that they entered into the transaction lawfully, in good faith and indeed avowedly in the interests of the company. However, that does not absolve them for accountability for any profit which they made, if it was by reason and in virtue of their fiduciary office as directors that they entered into the transaction.

9.45 In *Phipps v Boardman* at AC 124; All ER 757, Lord Upjohn commented on *Regal (Hastings) v Gulliver* as follows:

> That was an obvious case where the duty of the director and his interest conflicted. The scheme had been that Regal would make a profit, in fact its directors did.

CONFLICTS OF DUTY AND DUTY

9.46 Fiduciaries are also obliged to avoid conflicts of competing fiduciary duties. A conflict will exist if the duties are inconsistent or irreconcilable: *Settlement Agents Supervisory Board v Property Settlement Services Pty Ltd* at [76]. A classic example of such conflicts exists where lawyers act simultaneously for two competing clients, without informing them of his or her conflicting duties: *Eiszele v Hurburgh* [2011] TASSC 65 at [35]. It is no defence to an allegation of breach of fiduciary duty in such circumstances for lawyers to argue that the breach of duty was caused by their maintenance of duty to another client: *Hilton v Barker Booth & Eastwood (a firm)* [2005] 1 WLR 567. However, in *Dominic v Riz* [2009] NSWCA 216, a solicitor who acted for two clients on a transaction was not found to have breached her fiduciary duty when she advised the client to seek separate and independent financial and legal advice.

9.47 Another example is that of directors who hold simultaneous directorships in competing companies. There is a rule that allows such directors to hold office in competing companies until a real conflict arises: *London and Mashonaland Exploration Co Ltd v New Mashonaland Exploration Co Ltd* [1891] WN 165.

PRESUMED RELATIONSHIPS THAT CARRY FIDUCIARY DUTIES

9.48 In *Breen v Williams* at CLR 92; ALR 273, Dawson and Toohey JJ observed that the law has not formulated 'any precise or comprehensive definition of the circumstances in which a person is constituted a fiduciary in his or her relations with another'. Nevertheless, some relationships are presumed to give rise to fiduciary obligations. In other cases the factual circumstances of the relationship may give rise to a finding of a fiduciary relationship. In this context a critical question that has confronted the courts in recent times is the degree to which they will make findings that fiduciary duties are owed in the context of commercial relationships.

Trustee–beneficiary

9.49 The quintessential fiduciary relationship is that between a trustee and beneficiary. In *Hospital Products Ltd v United States Surgical Corporation* at CLR 68; ALR 432, Gibbs CJ said that '[t]he archetype of a fiduciary is of course the trustee'. Executors bearing trust powers will also be subject to fiduciary duties: *Goldie v Getley (No 3)* [2011] WASC 132 at [177].

Director–company

9.50 Directors (and other corporate officers) are fiduciaries for their companies and must avoid conflicts of interest and duty, as well as not use information that they receive in their capacity as directors for personal gain: *Regal (Hastings) Ltd v Gulliver; Omnilab Media Pty Limited v Digital Cinema Network Pty Ltd* at 89.[21] In *Consul Developments v DPC Estates* at CLR 394; ALR 249, Gibbs CJ said:

> It is well settled that a director stands in a fiduciary position in relation to his company and in my judgment a person who though irregularly appointed assumes the position of director and on behalf of the company performs the tasks of finding, investigating and reporting upon properties

---

21. J Svehla, 'Director's Fiduciary Duties' (2006) 27 *Australian Bar Review* 192.

suitable for purchase by the company owes a fiduciary duty to the company with which his private interests cannot be allowed to conflict.

9.51   But interestingly the courts have not applied the conflict rule as strictly as in other areas and it is recognised that a director may take up a directorship with a competing company or set up a business in competition: *Bell v Lever Brothers Ltd* [1932] AC 161 at 195; *London and Mashonaland Exploration Co Ltd v New Mashonaland Exploration Co Ltd* [1891] WN 165; *Mills v Mills* (1938) 60 CLR 150. In *Riteway Express Pty Ltd v Clayton* (1987) 10 NSWLR 238, McLelland J felt that a director rights to use company information should be limited in the same way as an employee's right to use confidential information. After reviewing the authorities Jessup J in *Links Golf Tasmania Pty Ltd v Sattler* [2012] FCA 634 at [562], said:

> It is, in my view, a striking feature of the authorities referred to above how rare have been the circumstances in which a court has been called on to deal with the pure case of a director's involvement in a competing business, without any additional or complicating factor. However, as a Judge sitting at first instance, I must accept that, in Australia, *Bell v Lever Bros* is good law to the extent that it stands for the proposition that *merely* by acting as a director of a competing company, or carrying on a competitive business on his or her own behalf, a company director will not be regarded as being in breach of his or her fiduciary obligations ... Stated in its highest form, the proposition for which *Bell v Lever Bros* stands is, as put by McLure P in *Streeter* (278 ALR at 303 [69]), 'a director is permitted to occupy board positions in competing companies.' That is to say, merely by occupying such positions, the director will not be regarded as placing himself or herself in a position of conflict. But, it must be accepted, Lord Blanesburgh's words in *Bell v Lever Bros* extended also to the permissibility of a director conducting a business on his or her own account in competition with the company on the board of which he or she sat. That would, presumably, involve the performance of active, executive, functions in a competitive business, and would not be analogous to a situation in which the director held non-executive positions on the boards of two companies.

9.52   These issues were discussed in *Streeter v Western Areas Exploration Pty Ltd* (2011) 278 ALR 291 where two directors of a mining company (WAE) had been approached regarding a new nickel mining venture. They proposed to use WAE as the corporate vehicle for the venture but this was not acceptable to the other parties and they set up a new company (WANL). WANL also came to purchase mining rights from WAE which were unrelated to the nickel venture and the sale was conducted when the directors were directors of both WAE and WANL.

9.53   Later WANL became a successful venture and WAE claimed that the directors had breached their fiduciary duties by diverting the nickel opportunity away from WAE. The sale of the mining rights from WAE to WANL was also said to be a breach of fiduciary duty. At trial Hennan J ordered a constructive trust over the shares held by the directors in WANL. This was reversed on appeal. McLure found that there was no breach of fiduciary duty on the part of the directors in setting up WANL as directors were entitled to pursue other business ventures. The directors had breached fiduciary duties in relation to the sale of the mining rights (given their conflicting duties) but these breaches had no causal relationship with the profits flowing to the directors from the success of WANL. Buss JA agreed with this finding but Murphy JA dissented, finding that there was a sufficient causal connection. The Court unanimously found that the claims were barred by laches: see 9.129.

9.54 A director's fiduciary obligations will usually continue for an appropriate or reasonable time after he or she ceases to be a director: *Southern Real Estate Pty Ltd v Dellow & Arnold* (2003) 87 SASR 1 at 10–11. What amounts to a reasonable time will depend upon the facts and circumstances of the case. However, the resignation will not sever the fiduciary duties if it is shown that the resignation was prompted by the wish to personally pursue a business opportunity that arose during the directorship: *Streeter v Western Areas Exploration Pty Ltd* at 350–1; *Vadori v AAV Plumbing* [2010] NSWSC 274 at [201]–[202]; *Canadian Aero Service Ltd v O'Malley* [1974] SCR 592; 40 DLR (3d) 371.

9.55 As *Regal (Hastings) v Gulliver* shows, the obligations are strict, and the fact that the director may be acting bona fide and taking up an investment opportunity which is also in the interests of the company, is irrelevant to the question of breach. Informed consent is the only option for the director seeking to take up corporate opportunities.

9.56 Directors also owe duties under statute to act in the company's best interests and to properly exercise their powers.[22] Questions arise as to whether these duties are fiduciary in nature, as both duties are arguably positive and therefore outside the fiduciary ambit. In *The Bell Group Ltd (in liq) v Westpac Banking Corporation (No 9)* at 498–9, Owen J said:

> In my view the duty to act in the interests of the company and the duty to exercise powers properly stem from a fundamental requirement for loyalty. Directors undertake to act on behalf of the company and to manage the business of the company. A company does not exist other than by virtue of a legal fiction. In this respect the company is in a similar position to a beneficiary who is an infant or a person with a mental disability: it simply cannot exercise its own powers and must do so through the good graces of the persons who have undertaken to act on its behalf. All (or at least most) of the classic indicia of the fiduciary relationship are present. The directors act in a representative capacity. There is a dependency of the company on its directors. And there is scope for the directors to exercise a discretion or power that may affect the rights or interests of the company. If, as I believe is the case, loyalty is the keystone of a fiduciary relationship, it applies in abundance to the association between a director and the company.

9.57 On this issue of whether such duties were positive in nature Owen J found that they were not, as they did not prescribe what a director should do but rather forbade the director from acting otherwise than in the company's best interests, for proper purposes and in ways that avoided conflicts of interest: *The Bell Group Ltd (in liq) v Westpac Banking Corporation (No 9)* at 500. As noted above (see 9.11–9.12), the decisions of Lee and Drummond AJJA in *Westpac Banking Corporation v The Bell Group Ltd (In Liq) (No 3)* expressly disagree with this duty as being negative and with the necessity for the fiduciary duties of directors to be treated as proscriptive. But regardless of their characterisation there is no doubt that the director's duty to act in the company's best interests has, for a long time, been accepted by judges as fiduciary in nature. Most modern cases take this approach and treat the fiduciary duties and the statutory duties which impose positive obligations as synonymous: *Hydrocool Pty Ltd v Hepburn* (2011) 279 ALR 646; *Westpac Banking Corporation v The Bell Group Ltd (In Liq) (No 3)* at [855]–[870].

---

22. For example, *Corporations Act 2001*(Cth), ss 182, 183.

9.58   English courts have found that directors must disclose past wrongdoing to their companies, even where that wrongdoing had no negative effect on the company's position: *Item Software (UK) Ltd v Fassihi* [2004] EWCA 1244. This argument was rejected in Australia by Hollingworth J in *P & V Industries v Porto* (2006) 14 VR 1 at 4–10 where his Honour found that such a duty was prescriptive and outside fiduciary principles. Later cases have found similarly: *Levy v Bablis* [2007] NSWSC 565 at [15]–[18].

Duties owed by directors to shareholders?

9.59   Directors do not ordinarily owe fiduciary duties to shareholders: *Freitag v Bruderle* [2011] QCA 313 at [27]; *Joinery Products Pty Ltd v Imlach* [2008] TASSC 40 at [10].[23] However, if 'a special factual relationship between the directors and the shareholders' exists, the directors may also owe fiduciary duties to shareholders: *Peskin v Anderson* [2000] EWCA Civ 326 at [33]; *St George Soccer Football Association Inc v Soccer NSW Ltd* [2005] NSWSC 1288 at [51]; *Crawley v Short* [2009] NSWCA 410 at [102].

The rationale for directors having fiduciary obligations to shareholders in special circumstances was explained by Biscoe AJ in *McClymont v Critchley* [2011] NSWSC 493 at [163], as follows:

> The general rule is that a director of a company owes a fiduciary duty to the company as a whole and not to individual shareholders. The bare relationship between a director and shareholder cannot without more give rise to a fiduciary relationship. However, in some circumstances a director of a proprietary company may owe a fiduciary duty to a shareholder so long as it does not compete with the director's duty to the company as a whole. This principle is sensitive to, and requires close examination of the circumstances of the particular case. Circumstances which may point to the existence of a fiduciary obligation include the shareholder's dependence upon information known to the director; the existence of a relationship of confidence, reliance or trust; the vulnerability of the shareholder; the significance of any positive action taken by or on behalf of the director to promote the transaction; the structure of the shareholdings; and the significance of the particular transaction to the parties. This is consistent with the seminal principle that 'Rules of equity have to be applied to such a great diversity of circumstances that they can be stated in only the most general terms and applied with particular attention to the exact circumstances of each case': *Boardman v Phipps* [1967] 2 AC 46 at 123.

Thus, where directors conduct negotiations for a takeover or an acquisition of the company's business, they are obliged to loyally promote the interests of all shareholders: *Jones v Jones* [2009] VSC 292; *Silversides Superfunds Pty Limited v Silverstate Developments Pty Limited* [2008] NSWSC 904; *Coleman v Myers* [1977] 2 NZLR 225 at 234; *Brunninghausen v Glavanics*.

9.60   Directors owe a fiduciary duty to shareholders to advise them fully and frankly of relevant information necessary to make an informed decision at a general meeting: *Chequepoint Securities Ltd v Claremont Petroleum NL* (1986) 11 ACLR 94. This obligation to make full and fair disclosure does not oblige the directors to give shareholders every piece of information that might conceivably affect their voting. The adequacy of the information must be assessed in a practical, realistic way, having regard to the complexity of the proposal: *ENT Pty Ltd v Sunraysia Television Ltd* [2007] NSWSC 270.

---

23. B Nosworthy, 'Directors' fiduciary obligations: is the shareholder an appropriate beneficiary?' (2010) 24 *Australian Journal of Corporate Law* 282.

Duties owed by directors to creditors?

9.61   In contrast to shareholders, there do not appear to be fiduciary obligations owed by directors to creditors: *R v Spies* (2000) 201 CLR 603; 173 ALR 529. Fiduciary obligations may arise in cases where the company has become insolvent, as the interests of the creditors begin to take over the interests of the shareholders, as the assets of the company effectively become the assets of the creditors as the company lurches into liquidation: *Angas Law Services Pty Ltd (in liq) v Carabelas* (2005) 226 CLR 507; 215 ALR 110.

Legal practitioner–client

9.62   Legal practitioners owe fiduciary duties to their clients when acting for them in matters. A practitioner cannot make unauthorised profits, or act in a way that puts their own interests, or those of others, into conflict with the interests of their clients: *Hilton v Barker Booth* [2005] 1 All ER 561. This rule forbids the lawyer from entering into dealings with their clients without the clients' fully informed consent. For example, in *Maguire v Makaronis*, the High Court found that solicitors breached their fiduciary duties when they both acted as solicitors for the purchasers of a poultry farm and financed the sale with a secured mortgage over their client's property. Fiduciary duties also prevent lawyers from acting for third parties, when the interests of those third parties conflict with the interest of the client: see 9.46. Such conflicts can be avoided as long as all parties know that the same practitioner is acting for different parties to the transaction and no actual conflict of interest arises: *Rigg v Sheridan* [2008] NSWCA 79.

9.63   Should a conflict arise, the lawyer can be restrained by an injunction from acting for a party: *Commissioner for Consumer Protection v Robinson* [2012] WASC 105; *Kyriackou v Commonwealth Bank of Australia* [2009] VSCA 241 at [22]; *Newman v Phillips Fox* (1999) 21 WAR 309. The foundation of this form of intervention is the court's jurisdiction over fiduciary duties: *Kallinicos v Hunt* (2005) 64 NSWLR 561 at 582; *Grieves v Tully* [2011] FamCA 617 at [73].

9.64   In determining whether a legal practitioner has taken up the responsibility to act for a client, regard must be first had to the written retainer and then any possible implied retainer. A fiduciary duty may arise independent of a retainer but this must be determined by the existence of a relationship of trust and confidence: *Watson v Ebsworth & Ebsworth* (2010) 278 ALR 487 at 525–7.

9.65   There are differing views as to whether the fiduciary duties survive the termination of the retainer.[24] It is clear that duties of confidentiality will still be owed to a client, even after the solicitor–client relationship has ended. In *Prince Jefri Bolkiah v KPMG (a firm)* [1999] 2 AC 222 at 235; [1999] 1 All ER 517 at 527, Lord Millett found that the duty of confidence survived the end of retainer but the other fiduciary duties did not. Australian cases have found similarly: *PhotoCure ASA v Queen's University at Kingston* [2002] FCA 905; *Kallinicos v Hunt* (2005) 64 NSWLR 561; *Pacific Telecommunications Ltd v Optus Networks Pty Ltd* [2005] NSWSC 550.

9.66   On the other hand, in *Spincode Pty Ltd v Look Software Pty Ltd* (2001) 4 VR 501, Brooking JA found that the duty of loyalty survived beyond the retainer, and later Victorian cases have followed

---

24.   M Bender, 'Taking Up the Cudgels: Will a Notion of Ongoing Loyalty Prevent a Lawyer from Acting Against a Former Client?' (2006) 13 *eLaw Journal: Murdoch University Electronic Journal of Law* 113.

this trend: *Sent v John Fairfax Publication Pty Ltd and Hills* [2002] VSC 429; *Village Roadshow Ltd v Blake Dawson Waldron* [2003] VSC 505; *Commonwealth Bank of Australia v Kyriackou* [2008] VSC 146; *Connell v Pistorino* [2009] VSC 289. There has also been recognition in Tasmania and Western Australia: *Gugiatti v City of Stirling* (2002) 25 WAR 349 at [8]–[13]; *Holborow v Macdonald Rudder* [2002] WASC 265 at [23], [25]; *Wagdy Hanna & Associates Pty Ltd v National Library of Australia* (2004) 155 ACTR 39 at [55].

9.67   In reality, whether the duty not to act against the interests of former clients is fiduciary or not, will probably be of no moment. Even if there is no fiduciary duty, duties of confidence and the court's power to control the due administration of justice may fill in any apparent void left by fiduciary duty, so that threatened breaches may be restrained: *Allison v Tuna Tasmania Pty Ltd* [2011] TASSC 52 at [1]; *Ismail-Zai v the State of Western Australia* [2007] WASCA 150 at [24]. In *Kyriackou v Commonwealth Bank of Australia* [2009] VSCA 241 at [22], the Court of Appeal of Victoria cited the trial judge with approval when he stated:

1. The Court will restrain a legal practitioner from continuing to act for a party to litigation if a reasonable person informed of the facts might reasonably anticipate danger of misuse of confidential information of a former client, and that there is a real and sensible possibility that the interest of the practitioner in advancing the case in litigation might conflict with the practitioner's duty to keep the information confidential and to refrain from using that information to the detriment of the former client.
2. The danger of misuse of confidential information is not the sole touchstone for curial intervention where a solicitor acts against a former client. There is also an independent equitable obligation of loyalty which forbids a solicitor acting against a former client in the same or a closely related matter. Intervention may also be justified on this ground in the exercise of a Court's supervisory jurisdiction over its own officers.
3. There is an overriding jurisdiction to intervene so as to protect the due administration of justice arising where a reasonably informed member of the public would conclude that solicitors should be prevented from acting.

Agent–principal

9.68   Agents are presumed to be fiduciaries for their principals. Agency can appear in many types of legal relationship, including real estate agency, powers of attorney and commercial agency. Agents are obliged to communicate information they have in their possession to their principal: *Premium Real Estate Ltd v Stevens* [2009] 2 NZLR 384 at 398. The failure to do this will be a breach of fiduciary duty if non-disclosure amounts to a preference in favour of the agent's own interests: *Chen v Marcolongo* (2009) 260 ALR 353 at 375. In *McKenzie v McDonald* [1927] VLR 134, a real estate agent advised a woman to exchange her farm for his property in the city. The agent knowingly offered a lesser price for the farm than its market value and inflated the price of his own property. The agent was found to owe fiduciary duties which were breached by his dishonest conduct. In *Pedersen v Larcombe* [2008] NSWSC 1362, a real estate agent bought the plaintiff's property in breach of fiduciary duty. The agent failed to seek the advice of other agents as to the property's market price, failed to advertise the property, and failed to seek other prospective buyers. In *Premium Real Estate Ltd v Stevens*, the agent both failed to inform the principals about the fact that the purchaser was a known property speculator and misled them into thinking he was buying it as a residence. Consequently, the New Zealand Supreme Court found a breach of duty when the principals settled for a price lower than what the property was worth and where it later sold for considerably more after a relatively short period of time.[25]

9.69 If a principal appoints an agent knowing that the agent already works for another principal, any potential conflict can be regarded as being of the later principal's own making, and the later principal will be unable to complain: *Beach Petroleum NL v Kennedy*. But even in such a situation the agent must act in good faith and cannot deliberately prejudice the interests of one principal over another: *Bristol and West Building Society v Mothew*. If an actual conflict arises the agent should cease acting for one, or both, of the principals. In *McCourt v Cranston* [2009] WASC 56 (affirmed on other grounds *McCourt v Cranston* [2012] WASCA 60), an agent was found to have breached her fiduciary duties by acting for both the vendor and the purchaser of land. The purchaser believed that the contract was conditional on the sale of her home (which was also being sold by the agent) but the vendor believed that the sale was unconditional. The agent gave advice to the vendor that the sale should be treated as unconditional, but failed to give such advice to the purchaser. The court found that the agent had acted in breach of her fiduciary duty, and that, should the contract be unconditional, the agent should indemnify the purchaser for any loss.

9.70 In cases where an agency arises from a contract, the scope of fiduciary obligations will be determined by the contract. In *Hospital Products Ltd v United States Surgical Corporation* at CLR 97; ALR 454–5, Mason J said:

> That contractual and fiduciary relationships may co-exist between the same parties has never been doubted. Indeed, the existence of a basic contractual relationship has in many situations provided a foundation for the erection of a fiduciary relationship. In these situations it is the contractual foundation which is all-important because it is the contract that regulates the basic rights and liabilities of the parties. The fiduciary relationship, if it is to exist at all, must accommodate itself to the terms of the contract so that it is consistent with, and conforms to, them. The fiduciary relationship cannot be superimposed upon the contract in such a way as to alter the operation which the contract was intended to have according to its true construction.

9.71 In *John Alexander's Clubs Pty Limited v White City Tennis Club Limited* (2010) 241 CLR 1 at 36; 266 ALR 462 at 484, the High Court observed that the terms of the contract governing the scope of fiduciary obligations included implied terms. This meant that if there was no implied term imposing some fiduciary obligation 'it will be very difficult to superimpose the suggested fiduciary obligation upon that limited contract'.

Partner–partner

9.72 Partnership also gives rise to presumed fiduciary duties: *Barescape Pty Limited v Bacchus Holdings Pty Limited (No 9)* [2012] NSWSC 984 at [131]. Partnership exists when people work together in an enterprise for the purpose of making a profit. In *Re Agriculturist Cattle Insurance Co* (1870) LR 5 Ch App 725 at 733, James LJ said:

> Ordinary partnerships are by the law assumed and presumed to be based on the mutual trust and confidence of each partner in the skill, knowledge and integrity of every other partner.

---

25. See J Glister, 'Breach of fiduciary duty: *Brickenden* lives on (*Premium Real Estate v Stevens*)' (2011) 5 *Journal of Equity* 59.

As between the partners and the outside world (whatever may be their private arrangements between themselves), each partner is the unlimited agent of every other in every manner connected with the partnership business, and not being in its nature beyond the scope of the partnership.

9.73 There does not need to be a formal partnership for fiduciary obligations to arise. In *United Dominions Corporation Ltd v Brian Pty Ltd* (1985) 157 CLR 1 at 12; 60 ALR 741 at 747, Mason, Brennan and Deane JJ said:

A fiduciary relationship can arise and fiduciary duties can exist between parties who have not reached, and who may never reach, agreement upon the consensual terms which are to govern the arrangement between them. In particular, a fiduciary relationship with attendant fiduciary obligations may, and ordinarily will, exist between prospective partners who have embarked upon the conduct of the partnership business or venture before the precise terms of any partnership agreement have been settled. Indeed, in such circumstances, the mutual confidence and trust which underlie most consensual fiduciary relationships are likely to be more readily apparent than in the case where mutual rights and obligations have been expressly defined in some formal agreement. Likewise, the relationship between prospective partners or participants in a proposed partnership to carry out a single joint undertaking or endeavour will ordinarily be fiduciary if the prospective partners have reached an informal arrangement to assume such a relationship and have proceeded to take steps involved in its establishment or implementation.

9.74 Fiduciary duties can exist beyond the partnership, at least until the assets of the partnership have been fully wound up. In *Chan v Zacharia*, the partnership had been determined but it was still not open to one of the partners to exercise an option to renew the business's lease in his own name. However, in *Friend v Brooker,* the High Court refused to find that any fiduciary duties remained between individuals in a partnership, after that partnership had been converted into a corporate structure, leaving the previous partners as directors. As directors they owed fiduciary duties to the company but not to each other.

Guardian–ward

9.75 Guardianship is another presumed category of fiduciary duty. Guardians are appointed by courts or tribunals to care for adults who have become incapable of making decisions for themselves. Guardians can also be appointed for children, and parents are ordinarily the natural guardians of children. The fact that a guardian has been appointed via a statutory mechanism is no bar to the imposition of fiduciary duties: *State of South Australia v Lampard-Trevorrow* (2010) SASR 331 at 399.

9.76 A guardian must provide independent legal advice to a ward, if the ward has a possible right of action and the ward's interests conflict with those of the guardian. In *Bennett v Minister of Community Welfare* (1992) 176 CLR 408, the High Court recognised that there was a fiduciary duty to inform a ward that he may have a cause of action in personal injury, after losing four fingers of his left hand when in the defendant's care.

9.77 The duty to provide independent legal advice to the ward appears to be a positive duty but perhaps can be explained as part of the general duty of disclosure of conflicts. However, such a duty may fail if it is cast too widely. In *State of South Australia v Lampard-Trevorrow*, the plaintiff was an Aboriginal ward of the state and was illegally removed from his family. At trial, the court, at 346, found (amongst other things) that the Aboriginal Protection Board (APB) had breached a fiduciary duty to:

> ... take steps to see that the plaintiff was armed with all relevant information concerning the circumstances of his removal, fostering and return to his natural family, and in particular, a disclosure to him of the APB's view that it had knowingly acted without legal authority. The APB also had a duty to see that the plaintiff obtained independent legal advice. The APB breached these duties and as an emanation of the State, legal responsibility falls on the State with respect to these breaches.

The Full Court of South Australia overturned this finding, and stated that the trial judge's finding on fiduciary duty were too wide-ranging and imposed positive duties. The Full Court, at 402–3, also found against a duty to inform the plaintiff of a breach of statutory power:

> While not decisive, we are struck by the novelty of the concept that a person or entity exercising statutory powers, who might be in a fiduciary relationship with a person affected by those powers, is under a duty to bring to the attention of that person the fact of a possible exceeding of those powers and under a duty to ensure that the person obtains proper legal advice.

> There is another oddity about the proposed duty. The duty identified by the judge could have been discharged meaningfully only by bringing to the attention of someone other than Bruce Trevorrow the possible excess of power, and by arranging for that person to obtain legal advice. Until he was getting towards adulthood, there would have been little point in discussing these things with Bruce Trevorrow. Moreover, if the APB discharged the duty identified, how could it possibly sit back and leave Bruce Trevorrow in Mrs Davies' custody, having informed someone on Bruce Trevorrow's behalf that it has acted unlawfully and that they should ensure that they get legal advice about obtaining redress for that?

9.78 Guardians, while owing fiduciary duties, are not trustees of the property of their charges: *Jodrell v Jodrell* (1851) 51 ER 339; *Guardianship and Administration Tribunal v Perpetual Trustees Qld Ltd* [2008] QSC 49; *Crossingham v Crossingham* [2012] NSWSC 95 at [19]–[25]. In *Countess of Bective v Federal Commissioner of Taxation* (1932) 47 CLR 417 at 420–21, Dixon J said:

> It is a general rule that guardians of infants, committees of the person of lunatics, and others who are entrusted with funds to be expended in the maintenance and support of persons under their care are not liable to account as trustees. They need not vouch the items of their expenditure, and, if they fulfil the obligation of maintenance in a manner commensurate with the income available to them for the purpose, an account will not be taken. Often the person to be maintained is a member of a family enjoying the advantages of a common establishment; always the end in view is to supply the daily wants of an individual, to provide for his comfort, edification and amusement, and to promote his happiness. It would defeat the very purpose for which the fund is provided, if its administration were hampered by the necessity of identifying, distinguishing, apportioning and recording every item of expenditure and vindicating its propriety ... Courts of equity have not disguised the fact that the general rule gives to a parent or guardian dispensing the fund an opportunity of gaining incidental benefits, but the nature and extent of the advantages permitted must depend peculiarly upon the intention ascribed to the instrument.

9.79   In *Clay v Clay* (2001) 202 CLR 410; 178 ALR 193, a widow purchased the house of her late husband for market value, even though she was guardian of his children and that under his will the children had equal beneficial interests in his estate when they reached the age of 25 years. The High Court found that there was no breach of fiduciary duty as there was no conflict between the widow's interests and her duty as guardian of the children. As stated above, guardians are not trustees and the widow had purchased the property at market value. Moreover, the money went into the fund to pay for the children's maintenance and advancement. Nor did the children have an immediate beneficial interest in the property at the time it was sold.

9.80   Cases of breaches of fiduciary duty in guardianship often raise difficult issues of lengthy delays in the bringing of claims. Claims often involve facts that occurred decades before trial and may then run afoul of problems with evidence and laches: *The Salvation Army (South Australia Property Trust) v Rundle* [2008] NSWCA 347. For example, in *Arthur v State of Qld* [2004] QSC 456, a woman claimed breach of fiduciary duty for being forced to adopt out her child when she was 17 and a ward of the state. The child had been born nearly 40 years before the trial, many of the key witnesses were dead and the claim failed for lack of evidence. Even had the evidence supported her claim (it did not) the judge believed that laches (see 9.126) was an appropriate defence.

9.81   One of the major issues that has arisen in relationship to guardianship concerns cases of child abuse, where plaintiffs have claimed breach of fiduciary duty for physical and sexual abuse. These developments were encouraged by Canadian case law which recognises that parents, guardians and priests owe fiduciary duties to children not to abuse them physically and sexually: *M(K) v M(H)* [1992] 3 SCR 6; *KLB v British Columbia* (2001) 197 DLR (4th) 431; *VB v Cairns* (2003) 65 Ont R (3d) 343; *Doe v O'Dell* (2003) 230 DLR (4th) 383; *Kraus v Joao* 2008 CanLII 25057; *RD v GS* 2011 BCSC 1118. The duty has even been extended to the non-abusing parent who knowingly fails to step in and prevent the abuse from occurring: *J(LA) v J(H)* (1993) 102 DLR (4th) 177. However, attempts to prove the existence of fiduciary duties owed by the state have been less successful except where children were under the guardianship of the state: *Reference re Broome v Prince Edward Island* [2010] 1 SCR 360. Initially the duty was cast as a duty to act in the child's best interests: *M(M) v F(R)* (1997) 52 BCLR (3d) 127. But more recently the Supreme Court of Canada has rejected the 'best interests of the child' as the basis for liability and instead returned to breaches of trust and loyalty as the basis of the fiduciary liability of those in the position of parental authority: *KLB v British Columbia* [2003] 2 SCR 403; *EDG v Hammer* [2003] 2 SCR 459.

9.82   In contrast, Australian courts have consistently denied that a guardian's fiduciary duty includes a duty to take reasonable care for the ward's physical safety, on the basis that the interests protected are not economic or proprietorial: *Tusyn v State of Tasmania* (2004) 13 Tas R 51. Initially, actions were not struck out by judges on the grounds that fiduciary claims could possibly succeed: *Johnson v Department of Community Services* [1999] NSWSC 1156; *Carter v Corporation of the Sisters of Mercy of the Diocese of Rockhampton* [2001] QCA 335. In *Williams v Minister, Aboriginal Land Rights Act 1983* (1994) 35 NSWLR 497 at 511, Kirby P was prepared to recognise the possibility of fiduciary duties being used to regulate want of proper care, but by the time of trial in the matter, Abadee J refused to entertain the fiduciary claim on the grounds that the claim was just being used to circumvent time limitations: *Williams v Minister, Aboriginal Land Rights Act 1983* (1999) 25 Fam LR 86. In *Paramasivam v Flynn* (1998) 90 FCR 489; 160 ALR 203, the Full Court of the Federal Court also refused to recognise a breach of fiduciary claim. The duty to refrain from inflicting personal injury was recognised but the court did not see why the duty should be described as fiduciary. In *Cubillo v Commonwealth* (2001) 112 FCR 455 at 576–8; 183 ALR 249 at 368–70, the Full Court of the Federal Court again found that the appropriate laws were that of tort and that there was no room for the superimposition of fiduciary duties on common law duties simply to improve the nature and extent of the remedies available to an aggrieved party.

9.83   Much also centres on the way that some of these claims are framed by judges as involving prescriptive duties. Claims for breach of fiduciary duty failed in *Webber v State of New South Wales* [2003] NSWSC 1263, *SB v State of New South Wales* [2004] VSC 514, and *TB v State of New South Wales* [2009] NSWSC 326, because the judges viewed the claims as alleging the breach of positive duties rather than the traditional negative ones.

9.84   The reluctance of Australian judges to find a fiduciary duty not to physically and sexually injure wards is therefore based on two objections: first, a duty to refrain from physical and sexual abuse is a positive duty and not fiduciary in nature; and second, such injuries are non-economic and non-recoverable according to fiduciary doctrine. On examination of the first objection, even if one accepts the general reduction of fiduciary duties to proscriptive dimensions (as described by the Supreme Court of Canada in *KLB v British Columbia*), it is hard to see how a duty not to physically and sexually injure a ward could be framed as a positive duty. The earlier Canadian cases which cast the duty as being to act in the ward's best interests approach do offend the rule against positive duties as they are too prescriptive (and vague). However, if the duty is cast back to the negative requirements of loyalty and fidelity, why should a duty to refrain from sexual and physical abuse fall outside the guardian's proscriptive duties?

9.85   The second objection is clearly stronger. Tort law obviously has a better capacity to deal with such claims. If people are resorting to fiduciary claims because the limitation periods for tortious claims are too harsh, the better response would be a legislative one that recognises the unique difficulties of claims for child abuse and which remedies the shortcoming of the current limitation schemes.

9.86   Failing that, the question should be asked as to why fiduciary principles should not accommodate non-economic loss, particularly in cases where the tortious remedies are no longer available. Equity has begun to recognise non-economic losses in cases of confidential information: *Giller v Procopets*. As stated above, Joyce has argued that non-economic interests should be protected by fiduciary duties where a breach has occurred which embodies forms of exploitation and betrayal.[26]

9.87   Regardless of these arguments, the current Australian case law suggests that fiduciary duties will remain unavailable for addressing claims of child abuse. If we come to accept this point, perhaps it is time to stop saying that equity is not beyond childbearing. She clearly is barren in this area. Equity no longer appears to be concerned with not letting a wrong be without a remedy: see 2.15–2.20.

---

26.   R Joyce, 'Fiduciary Law and Non-economic Interests', note 12 above.

FIDUCIARY RELATIONS OUTSIDE OF THE PRESUMED RELATIONSHIPS

Commercial relationships

9.88   Outside of the presumed fiduciary relationships, the factual circumstances of a particular case may give rise to a finding that a fiduciary relationship exists, depending on findings relating to undertaking, vulnerability and dependence: *Hodgson v Amcor Ltd* [2012] VSC 94 at [1343]. A critical area in which this question arises is in the context of commercial relationships. The major arguments against equitable intervention in commercial relations are based upon grounds of the certainty and security of commercial transactions. Thus, in *Hospital Products Ltd v United States Surgical Corporation* at CLR 149; ALR 494, Dawson J said:

> To invoke the equitable remedies sought in this case would, in my view, be to distort the doctrine and weaken the [fiduciary] principle upon which those remedies are based. It would be to introduce confusion and uncertainty into the commercial dealings of those who occupy an equal bargaining position in place of the clear obligations which the law now imposes upon them.

9.89   If parties in a commercial setting are sophisticated and intelligent people, negotiating at arm's length with legal assistance, there is little scope for the imposition of a fiduciary duty: *Jireh International Pty Ltd t/as Gloria Jean's Coffee v Western Exports Services Inc* [2011] NSWCA 137 at [107]. In *John Alexander's Clubs Pty Ltd v White City Tennis Club Ltd* at CLR 35–6; ALR 483–4, the High Court said:

> [T]he reason why commercial transactions falling outside the accepted traditional categories of fiduciary relationship often do not give rise to fiduciary duties is not that they are 'commercial' in nature, but that they do not meet the criteria for characterisation as fiduciary in nature. The point is illustrated in the *Hospital Products* case [at CLR 122–3] by Deane J's treatment of the distributorship contract between USSC and Mr Blackman's company as follows:

>> The express term of the contract in the present case requiring the distributor to use its 'best efforts' to build up the market for, and distribute, the products in Australia 'to the common benefit' of both manufacturer and distributor did not, of itself, impose a general fiduciary duty on the distributor to seek no profit or benefit for itself or to disregard its own interests where they conflicted with the manufacturer's. In the context of the term precluding the distributor from dealing in any competing product, the reference to 'the common benefit' was no more than a reflection of the commercial fact that, while the distributorship subsisted, it was in the interests of both manufacturer and distributor that, consistently with ordinary economic restraints on pricing, the market for the manufacturer's product in the relevant area be maximized.

Furthermore, in *Rawley Pty Ltd v Bell (No 2)* [2007] FCA 583 at [261], Finn J said:

> [O]utside of commercial agency, partnership and trust relationships, care needs to be taken in concluding that commercial parties are in a fiduciary relationship for some or all purposes — not because a commercial relationship cannot be fiduciary, but because such a relationship, commonly, possesses characteristics (eg known adversarial interests, the reasonable expectation of self-reliance, etc) which negative a fiduciary finding.

9.90 However, despite this oft-expressed reluctance on the part of courts to intrude into commercial matters by the imposition of equitable duties and obligations, 'business relationships ... clearly can attract fiduciary obligations': *News Ltd v Australian Rugby Football League Ltd* (1996) 139 ALR 193 at 311. This is more likely if the parties are acting in reliance on one another for a common end, akin to a partnership: *Mulvaney Holdings Pty Ltd v Thorne* [2012] QSC 127 at [25].[27]

9.91 The High Court decision in *United Dominions Corporation v Brian* is a case in which a fiduciary relationship was found to exist in a commercial context. The facts concerned a joint venture agreement for the development of land between United Dominions Corporation (UDC), Security Projects Ltd (SPL) and Brian Pty Ltd (Brian). The land in question was owned by SPL. The joint venture was largely financed by funds from UDC secured by a mortgage signed by SPL. The joint venturers provided the balance of funds for the development. The development realised a significant profit. However, UDC retained the profit. No distribution of profit was made to Brian. UDC's claim to what would otherwise have been Brian's share of profits was based upon a provision in the mortgage to SPL, referred to as the 'collateralisation clause', to the effect that the mortgage was security for *any* money that had been advanced to SPL. SPL was indebted to UDC in respect of other projects apart from the joint venture. Brian was never informed of the existence of the collateralisation clause. Brian claimed that the clause breached fiduciary obligations owed to it by UDC and SPL.

9.92 The High Court found in Brian's favour. It held that SPL and UDC owed fiduciary duties to Brian and that the collateralisation clause in the mortgage was obtained in breach of such duties. Dawson J, at CLR 16; ALR 750–1, said:

> [I]t is quite clear that a fiduciary relationship may arise during negotiations for a partnership or, for that matter, a joint venture, before any partnership or joint venture agreement has been finally concluded if the parties have acted upon the proposed agreement as they had in this case. Whilst a concluded agreement may establish a relationship of confidence, it is nevertheless the relationship itself which gives rise to fiduciary obligations. That relationship may arise from the circumstances leading to the final agreement as much as from the fact of the final agreement itself.

9.93 By way of contrast to *United Dominions Corp v Brian* one can examine the High Court decision in *Hospital Products Ltd v United States Surgical Corporation*. In this case, Blackman negotiated an exclusive distributorship arrangement for Australia in relation to products manufactured by United States Surgical Corporation (USSC). Blackman was to use his best efforts to promote USSC products within Australia. Blackman's company, Hospital Products Ltd (HPL), was soon after substituted as the distributor. Subsequently, HPL, using USSC products as models, began to manufacture products that were essentially identical to those manufactured by USSC. HPL then terminated its arrangement with USSC and began to sell its own products to USSC customers. USSC argued that HPL owed it fiduciary obligations and that HPL's conduct amounted to a breach of fiduciary duties owed to it.

---

27. See, J Knowler and C Rickett, 'The fiduciary duties of joint venture parties: when do they arise and what do they comprise?' (2011) 42 *University of Wellington Law Review* 117.

9.94 By a bare majority the High Court held that there was no fiduciary relationship between the parties and that USSC's right to relief rested in a claim for damages for breach of contract. The majority considered that because the relationship between the parties was a commercial one entered into by equal parties at arm's length with the intention that both parties would gain a profit, it was inappropriate to find a fiduciary relationship between the parties. USSC had rights against HPL for breach of an implied contractual term that the distributor would use its best efforts to promote USSC products within Australia. In relation to USSC's claim based upon breach of fiduciary obligations, Gibbs CJ, at CLR 734; ALR 436, said:

> What is attempted in this case is to visit a fraudulent course of conduct and a gross breach of contract with equitable sanctions. It is not necessary to do so in order to vindicate commercial morality, for the ordinary remedies for damages for fraud and breach of contract were available to USSC.

9.95 The High Court considered the issue of joint ventures again in *John Alexander's Clubs Pty Limited v White City Tennis Club Limited*. This case concerned an option to purchase part of the land at the famous White City tennis grounds from NSW Tennis Association (NSW Tennis). NSW Tennis wished to sell the land after alternative facilities had been built for the Sydney Olympics. Various parties ran tennis activities on the land, including the White City Tennis Club (the Club). John Alexander's Clubs Pty Ltd (JACS) was interested in purchasing the land and entered into an agreement with the Club called a 'memorandum of understanding (MOU)' which formalised their intention to work together to create a new tennis club. The MOU noted that JACS promised that it would seek to obtain an option to purchase the land (or part of it) from NSW Tennis. Later, the land ownership changed hands. The new owners granted JACS an option to purchase which allows JACS or another nominate entity the right to exercise the option (the Third White City Agreement). The Club was a party to this agreement and agreed to JACS's option being unconditional. Soon after, disputes arose between JACS and the Club. JACS sought to terminate the MOU on the grounds that the Club had repudiated it. JACS nominated a company called Poplar Holdings Pty Ltd (Poplar) to exercise the option and it became the owner of the land. The Club argued that JACS had breached its fiduciary obligation to the Club and that Poplar held the land on constructive trust for the Club.

9.96 The High Court found that JACS did not owe any fiduciary duties to the Club. French CJ, Gummow, Hayne, Heydon and Kiefel JJ, at CLR 33; ALR 482, said:

> Here the contracts to which JACS and the Club were parties are important in assessing whether JACS was bound by a fiduciary duty in relation to its exercise of the cl 8 option. The MOU obliged JACS to obtain an option, and exercise it in a certain way and on certain conditions. Before the First White City Agreement, JACS had not been able to obtain an option to buy part of the White City Land. By that agreement, and the Second and Third White City Agreements, it obtained an option, and the Club obtained an additional option after the JACS option expired. The Club, as party to the Third White City Agreement, consented to the unconditional nature of JACS's option. The Club could have bargained for more precision in cl 8, using its ability to refuse to agree to surrender the lease. It apparently did not. The Club was not relying on representations by JACS. It was not overborne by some greater strength possessed by JACS. It was not depending on JACS to carry out dealings of which the Club was necessarily ignorant. It was not trusting JACS to do

anything. What JACS and the Club did in relation to the Third White City Agreement and the exercise of JACS's option under cl 8(a), they did consulting their own interests, with knowledge of what the other was doing.

9.97 It is clear that no express agreement is necessary in a commercial relationship for a fiduciary duty to arise: *United Dominions Corp v Brian*. In cases where fiduciary duties have arisen in such informality, the fiduciary should be able to withdraw after giving appropriate notice. Notice will bring the fiduciary duties to an end, but obligations of confidence may continue: *Chirnside v Fay* [2007] 1 NZLR 433.

Employee–employer

9.98 Employees may be fiduciaries for their employers, depending on the level of trust, confidence and vulnerability implicit in the employment relationship: *C & K A Flanagan Sailmakers Pty Ltd v Walker* [2002] NSWSC 1125.[28] In *Michael Wilson and Partners Ltd v Nicholls* [2009] NSWSC 1033 at [69], Einstein J said:

i.   fiduciary duties arise not as result of the mere fact that there is an employment relationship, but rather from the fact that within a particular contractual relationship, there are specific contractual obligations which the employee has undertaken which have placed him/her in a situation where equity imposes fiduciary duties in addition to the contractual obligations;

ii. an implied contractual term is not to be equated with a fiduciary obligation;

iii. the critical feature of fiduciary relationships is that the fiduciary undertakes or agrees to act for or on behalf of or in the interests of another person in the exercise of a power or discretion which will affect in a legal or practical sense the interests of that other person …

iv. it is necessary to consider with precision the precise activity agreed to be undertaken by a particular employee and to ask if that employee had agreed to perform that activity solely in the interests of the employer to the exclusion of his/her own interests.[29]

9.99 Even though an employee may be a fiduciary, this will not be so in all cases, and there is some judicial opinion that they will be rare. In *Nottingham University v Fishel* [2000] EWHC 221 (QB), Elias J observed that 'the essence of the employment relationship is not typically fiduciary at all' and that '[i]ts purpose is not to place the employee in a position where he is obliged to pursue his employer's interests at the expense of his own'. In *Ranson v Customer Systems Plc* [2012] EWCA Civ 841 at [41], Lewison LJ, speaking for a unanimous Court of Appeal, said:

> [T]he hallmark of a fiduciary is a *single-minded* duty of loyalty. The duty of loyalty in that context has a precise meaning: 'namely the duty to act in the interests of another' … [T]his is not a feature of an employment relationship. In the employment context the duty of loyalty, although given the same label, 'is one where each party must have regard to the interests of the other, but not that either must subjugate his interests to those of the other'. Again it is, perhaps, unfortunate that conceptually different things have been given the same label.

---

28. See D Brodie, 'The employment relationship and fiduciary obligations' (2012) 16 *Edinburgh Law Review* 198.
29. This decision was appealed, on other grounds, to the Court of Appeal: *Nicholls v Michael Wilson & Partners Ltd* (2010) 243 FLR 177; and the High Court: *Michael Wilson & Partners Ltd v Nicholls* (2011) 282 ALR 685.

9.100   A fiduciary duty will arise if the relationship requires a standard of behaviour higher than the contractual standard.[30] In *Victoria University of Technology v Wilson* [2004] VSC 33, academics working at a university exploited for themselves an opportunity to develop certain computer programs in circumstances where they were approached, by a former student of the university, for help with such a project while employed by the university. The court held that the academics breached fiduciary obligations owed to the university in that they should not have exploited the opportunity for themselves as the opportunity was one presented to the university which the university would have exploited for itself. In contrast, in *University of Western Australia v Gray* (2009) 179 FCR 346; 259 ALR 224, a university professor, who had patented treatments for liver tumours in his own name, was not found to have breached fiduciary duties to his former university employer. The professor had not exploited any 'opportunity' to the exclusion of his employer, as had the employees in *Victoria University of Technology v Wilson*. Nor was there any implied duty to 'invent' in the employment contract which gave property rights to the university over the professor's inventions. The duty of the professor was to research and the professor was free to publish his findings, even though that might destroy patentability. On that basis it was not a breach of fiduciary duty for the professor to later exploit the research and take out intellectual property for himself.

9.101   In *Lonmar Global Risks Ltd v West* [2010] EWHC 2878 (QB), the question arose as to whether employees employed in the international brokering market had a duty to report to their employer that they or other employees had been approached by a competitor. Hickinbottom J, at [151]–[152], held that an employee's contractual duty of good faith did not encompass such a duty of disclosure, but that such a duty did arise if the employee owed fiduciary obligations to the employer. On the facts of the case, his Honour, at [213]–[215], ruled that fiduciary obligations did not arise. This was so in this case because the particular employees did not have any management responsibilities or board level involvement.

9.102   The fiduciary duties owed by employees will normally cease with the termination of employment: *Hodgson v Amcor Ltd* at [1370]. However, other equitable obligations such as obligations of confidence may continue. During employment, the duties will apply to employees even outside of office hours but it will not be a breach for an employee to seek alternative employment, at least in the absence of an express contractual clause to the contrary: *Holyoake Industries (Vic) Pty Ltd v V-Flow Pty Ltd* [2011] FCA 1154 at [109]–[111].

Financial adviser–client

9.103   Financial and investment advisers may owe fiduciary duties: *Calvo v Sweeney* [2009] NSWSC 719 at [219]; *L T King v Besser* (2002) 172 FLR 140. In *Daly v Sydney Stock Exchange* (1986) 160 CLR 371 at 377; 65 ALR 193 at 196, Gibbs CJ said:

> It was right to say that Patrick Partners owed a fiduciary duty to Dr Daly and acted in breach of that duty. The firm, which held itself out as an adviser on matters of investment, undertook to advise Dr Daly, and Dr Daly relied on the advice which the firm gave him. In those circumstances the firm had a duty to disclose to Dr Daly the information in its possession which would have revealed that the transaction was likely to be a most disadvantageous one from his point of view. Normally, the relation between a stockbroker and his client will be one of a fiduciary nature and

---

30.   Dal Pont, *Equity and Trusts in Australia*, see note 2, p 142.

such as to place on the broker an obligation to make to the client a full and accurate disclosure of the broker's own interest in the transaction.

Brennan J, at CLR 385; ALR 202, said:

> The duty of an investment adviser who is approached by a client for advice and undertakes to give it, and who proposes to offer the client an investment in which the adviser has a financial interest, is a heavy one. His duty is to furnish the client with all the relevant knowledge which the adviser possesses, concealing nothing that might reasonably be regarded as relevant to the making of the investment decision including the identity of the buyer or seller of the investment when that identity is relevant, to give the best advice which the adviser could give if he did not have but a third party did have a financial interest in the investment to be offered, to reveal fully the adviser's financial interest, and to obtain for the client the best terms which the client would obtain from a third party if the adviser were to exercise due diligence on behalf of his client in such a transaction.

9.104 In *Aequitas Ltd v AEFC Ltd* [2001] NSWSC 14 at [307], Austin J said:

> The advisory fiduciary relationship may arise whether or not there is an anterior fiduciary relationship between the parties, such as the relationship of broker and client. The relationship can arise even where parties are dealing with one another in a transaction in which the adviser has an obvious commercial self-interest.

9.105 But the fiduciary duties will not arise purely because there was a reliance on the skills of the defendant. In *Pilmer v Duke Group Ltd (in liq)*, a financial adviser had prepared a valuation report which was then relied upon by the plaintiff. The plaintiff invested in a company which the defendant had advised had a reasonable and fair share price. After investing in the company the share price fell dramatically. The plaintiff alleged breach of contract, negligence and breach of fiduciary duty. The High Court found that there was no fiduciary obligations owed by the defendant. The plaintiff had relied on the defendant to competently value the shares but the defendant did not guide or influence the plaintiff into investing.

Banks–customers

9.106 Banks are not ordinarily fiduciaries for their clients and their relationships are determined by contract and tort law. However, a banker–client relationship may become fiduciary if the bank takes on a role of investment adviser, where the customer comes to rely on the impartial advice of the bank: *Commonwealth Bank v Smith* (1993) 42 FCR 390 at 391; *Territory Sheet Metal Pty Ltd v Australia and New Zealand Banking Group Ltd* [2009] NTSC 31 at [1434].[31] The key issue appears to be the nature of the adviser's undertaking, namely whether 'the banker undertakes or agrees to act for or on behalf of or in the interests of its customer in the exercise of some power or discretion affecting the interests of the customer in a legal or practical sense': *Fletcher (as trustee of the Brian Fletcher Family Trust) v St George Bank Ltd (No 2)* [2011] WASC 277 at [116]. Conversely, if the bank does not assume the role of an adviser and no reliance is apparent there will be no fiduciary duty: *Commonwealth Bank v Finding* [2001] 1 Qd R 168.

---

31. A Tuch, 'Investment Banks as Fiduciaries: Implications for Conflicts of Interest' (2005) 29 *Melbourne University Law Review* 478.

Doctor–patient

9.107   There is Canadian authority which recognises the existence of fiduciary duties in the doctor–patient relationship: *McInerney v MacDonald* [1992] 2 SCR 138. In *Norberg v Wynrib* [1992] 2 SCR 226, the Canadian Supreme Court found that a doctor breached his fiduciary obligations by pressuring his drug-addicted patient to provide him with sexual favours in exchange for drugs.

9.108   The High Court rejected these authorities in *Breen v Williams*. In this case, a patient sought the medical records of her treating doctor, which she believed may have been useful for her claim against a supplier of breast implants. The doctor agreed to provide the records but on the basis that the woman grant him an indemnity from any claims being made against him. The woman refused and argued (amongst other things) that the doctor owed her a fiduciary duty to provide her with the medical records. The High Court refused to find that there was a fiduciary duty to provide medical records, as this would have imposed a positive obligation. The relationship between doctor and patient was said to be primarily contractual and there was no express or implied term that the doctor would provide his medical records to the patient.

9.109   Some have viewed *Breen* as denying the possibility of fiduciary duties existing in doctor–patient relationships. However, Dawson, Toohey JJ, at 92, and Gaudron and McHugh JJ, at 107, all saw the possibility of fiduciary duties arising in some circumstances. Gummow J was of the belief that the relationship was fiduciary in character, because of the reliance that patients place on their doctors' level of skill. His Honour, at CLR 134; ALR 297, said:

> [T]he relationship between medical practitioner and patient who seeks skilled and confidential advice and treatment is a fiduciary one. That will be so regardless of whether it is because the relationship between the parties is one which gives the medical practitioner a special opportunity to affect the interests of the patient who is vulnerable to abuse by the fiduciary of his position, or because the medical practitioner undertakes to exercise professional skill for the benefit of the patient, and particular reliance is placed upon the medical practitioner by the patient.

> Advice given by the physician to the patient involves specialised knowledge and matters of skill and judgment, which render the advice difficult, if not impossible, of objective and unassisted assessment by the patient. Hence the particular reliance placed upon the physician. In a real sense, especially if invasive procedures upon the person of the patient are involved, the patient has delegated control to the person providing health care. Further, for the patient to obtain the benefit sought from the relationship the patient often must reveal confidential and intimate information of a personal nature to the medical practitioner. Finally, the efforts of the medical practitioner may have a significant impact not merely on the economic but upon the fundamental personal interests of the patient.

9.110   After *Breen* it has been said that the impact of fiduciary relationships on doctors is of limited possibility.[32] The main areas of potential appear to be in situations where the doctor is making secret profits from the treatment of the patient, such as being paid for patient recruitment in clinical trials. There are no Australian cases on this issue. In *Bateley v Land* [2001] NSWSC 64, an interlocutory

---

32.   T M Carlin, 'Doctors as Fiduciaries — Revisiting the Past with an Eye on the Future' (2001) 9(1) *Journal of Law and Medicine* 95, p 102.

decision concerned with an amendment of a statement of claim, the plaintiff wished to add a claim that a drug company had breached a fiduciary duty to inform the plaintiff (who was a participant in the trial) that another patient had experienced an adverse event from the drug. The amendment was allowed. In the Californian case of *Moore v Regents of the University of California* 793 P 2d 479 (1990), the Supreme Court of California found a doctor had breached fiduciary duties by using the patient's excised tissue to develop an immortal cell line. The cell line was patented and was being used to manufacture new proteins which had an enormously profitable potential.

9.111 Another possible ground for breach of fiduciary duty is in the area of open disclosure of medical error. Faunce and Bolsin have argued that there is a fiduciary duty on doctors to disclose their medical errors to their patients.[33] There are two main problems with these arguments. First, both tort and contract law have recognised similar duties, and it may prove redundant to add fiduciary duties to the mix: *Naylor v Preston Area Health Authority* [1987] 2 All ER 353; *Wighton v Arnott* [2005] NSWSC 637.[34] Second, the duty to provide information appears to be a positive requirement, which would fall foul of the rule requiring fiduciary duties to be negative. Perhaps a possible way around this second problem is to view the admission of mistakes as part of the duty of disclosure of a possible conflict. Again, there are no cases directly on point. In *Kite v Malycha* (1998) 71 SASR 321, it was found that there was no fiduciary duty on the part of the doctor to inform the patient that he had contacted his medical indemnity provider, after suspecting that he may have been responsible for worsening the patient's condition. The judge found that the notification to the insurer was in the patient's best interests in any case.

Crown–indigenous peoples

9.112 Governments do not ordinarily owe fiduciary obligations to their citizens, even when they are overseas and at risk of torture: *Habib v Commonwealth (No 2)* (2009) 175 FCR 350 at 360–6; 254 ALR 250 at 261–6.[35] However, courts in a number of jurisdictions have discussed the existence of fiduciary duties owed by the Crown to indigenous peoples.[36] The existence of such fiduciary duties stems from the recognition that aboriginal peoples, as the original occupiers of land, have special rights that are protected by the imposition of fiduciary duties upon the Crown in the way government power affecting the interests of aboriginal peoples is exercised. The notion of the Crown's fiduciary duties to its aboriginal peoples is most developed in Canada.

9.113 In Canada, aboriginal rights arose from the occupation of lands before French and British colonisation.[37] Following colonisation, special provisions protecting aboriginal rights were found in various Canadian constitutional documents starting with the Royal Proclamation of 1763 issued by King George III and culminating in s 35(1) of the Constitution Act 1982 which stipulates:

---

33. T A Faunce & S N Bolsin, 'Fiduciary Disclosure of Medical Mistakes: The Duty to Promptly Notify Patients of Adverse Health Care Events' (2005) 12 *Journal of Law and Medicine* 478.
34. B Madden & T Cockburn, 'Bundaberg and Beyond: Duty to Disclose Adverse Events to Patients' (2007) 14 *Journal of Law and Medicine* 501.
35. See P Finn, 'Public Trusts, Public Fiduciaries' (2010) 38 *Federal Law Review* 335.
36. E Fox-Decent, 'Fashioning Legal Authority from Power: The Crown–Native Fiduciary Relationship' (2006) 4 *New Zealand Journal of Public International Law* 91.
37. J I Reynolds, *A Breach of Duty: Fiduciary Obligations and Aboriginal Peoples*, Purich Publishers, Saskatoon, 2005.

The existing aboriginal and treaty rights of the aboriginal peoples of Canada are hereby recognized and affirmed.

9.114   In the Canadian Supreme Court decision of *Guerin v R* (1984) 13 DLR (4th) 321 at 334, Dickson J set out the essence of the Crown's fiduciary duties to Canada's aboriginal peoples as follows:

> [T]he nature of Indian title and the framework of the statutory scheme established for disposing Indian land places upon the Crown an equitable obligation, enforceable by the courts, to deal with the land for the benefit of the Indians … [The obligation] is a fiduciary duty … The fiduciary relationship between the Crown and the Indians has its roots in the concept of aboriginal, native or Indian title. The fact that Indian bands have a certain interest in lands does not, however, in itself give rise to a fiduciary relationship between the Indians and the Crown. The conclusion that the Crown is a fiduciary depends upon the further proposition that the Indian interest in the land is inalienable except upon surrender to the Crown. An Indian band is prohibited from directly transferring its interest to a third party. Any sale or lease of land can only be carried out after a surrender has taken place, with the Crown acting on behalf of the band's behalf. … The surrender requirement, and the responsibility it entails, are the source of a distinct fiduciary obligation owed by the Crown to the Indians.

His Honour, at 343, further observed that 'given the unique character of both the Indians' interest in land and of their historical relationship with the Crown', the Crown's fiduciary relationship with aboriginal peoples is *sui generis*.

9.115   The consequence of constitutionalising indigenous rights in s 35(1) of the *Constitution Act 1982* is that the exercise of government power over aboriginal rights must be reconciled with the Crown's fiduciary duties. In *R v Sparrow* (1990) 70 DLR (4th) 385 at 409–10, the Supreme Court ruled that such reconciliation requires the government to justify any regulation that infringes or affects aboriginal rights, with the Supreme Court being the ultimate arbiter of whether any such government action is justified. In *Delgamuukw v British Columbia* (1997) 153 DLR (4th) 193 at 260–3, Lamer CJ indicated that in justifying an infringement of aboriginal rights, the Crown has to establish that the infringement is in furtherance of a legislative objective that is compelling and substantial. Furthermore, the infringement has to be assessed as being consistent with the special fiduciary relationship between the Crown and aboriginal peoples. In this process of assessment the Crown must take into account the existence and importance of aboriginal rights.

9.116   In *R v Marshall* (1999) 177 DLR (4th) 513 Marshall, a Mi'kmaq Indian was charged with violations of restrictive fishing legislation. However, the Supreme Court of Canada found that, pursuant to Treaties of 1760–1761, the Mi'kmaq people were entitled to unqualified rights to fish and trade for sustenance. The court ruled that, in the absence of any justification of the legislation's infringement of Marshall's treaty rights to fish, he was entitled to acquittals on all charges against him.

9.117   In Australia the development of the notion of the Crown having fiduciary duties to aboriginal peoples has not attracted judicial support to the same extent as in Canada. The most prominent judicial support for the concept is found in the decision of Toohey J in *Mabo v Queensland (No 2)* (1992) 175 CLR 1; 107 ALR 1. In that case the Meriam people of the Murray Islands argued, inter alia, that the Crown owed them a fiduciary duty to the extent of being required to protect their rights and interests in the Murray Islands. Although the High Court ruled in favour of the Meriam people, only Toohey J, at 199–205; ALR 156–61, was prepared to accept that the Crown stood in a fiduciary relationship with the Meriam people. However, his Honour observed that the existence of this fiduciary relationship does not preclude the use of the legislative power of the Crown to extinguish aboriginal rights, even though any such legislation would constitute a breach of the Crown's fiduciary duties.

9.118   Since Toohey J's judgment in *Mabo* there has been little consideration of fiduciary duties owed to aboriginal peoples in Australia. In *Wik Peoples v Queensland* (1996) 187 CLR 1; 141 ALR 129, the matter was raised but not dealt with by any of the majority judges. Brennan CJ, in dissent, found that the Crown's power to extinguish native title did not, by itself, give rise to fiduciary duties. Brennan CJ believed that it was necessary for the exercise of the Crown's power to be for the benefit of aboriginal peoples before the Crown could be found to owe fiduciary duties to them. In *Thorpe v Commonwealth (No 3)* (1997) 144 ALR 677 at 688, Kirby J stated that the question of whether the Crown owed fiduciary duties to aboriginal peoples in Australia remained open. However, in *Bodney v Westralia Airports Corporation Pty Ltd* (2000) 180 ALR 91 at 109–16, Lehane J rejected the view that fiduciary duties were owed to aboriginal peoples. Professor Bartlett has argued that, with the passage of the *Native Title Act 1993* (Cth), any possible fiduciary duties which may have existed were replaced by the statutory schemes for surrender and extinguishment.[38]

9.119   Toohey J's analysis of the Crown's fiduciary duties to aboriginal peoples in *Mabo* reflects the legal position in Canada before the introduction of s 35(1) of the *Constitution Act 1982*. Prior to the introduction of s 35(1), aboriginal rights in Canada could be extinguished by government legislation under the doctrine of parliamentary supremacy. It was only with the constitutional entrenchment of aboriginal rights that the situation changed with the recognition that the Crown owed fiduciary duties to aboriginal peoples in the context of legislation that infringed their rights. On the Canadian experience, constitutional entrenchment of aboriginal rights by Australia is necessary before these rights can be afforded meaningful legal recognition and protection. In the meantime, aboriginal rights remain the objects of political whim and opportunism.

DEFENCES

Informed consent

9.120   As stated above, the duty imposed upon the fiduciary is strict. The primary way a fiduciary is able to escape liability for conduct that amounts to a breach of fiduciary duty is if the conduct was undertaken with the fully informed consent of the person to whom the fiduciary obligations are owed. The question of whether fully informed consent has been given is 'a question of fact to be determined having regard to all the circumstances of each particular case': *Maguire v Makaronis* at CLR 466; ALR 739; *Diamond Hill Mining Pty Ltd v Huang Jin Mining Pty Ltd* [2011] VSC 288 at [95]; *Barescape Pty Limited v Bacchus Holdings Pty Limited (No 9)* at [154]–[160]. The burden of proving informed consent rests with the fiduciary: *Macquarie v Makaronis* at CLR 466; ALR 739.

---

38.   R H Bartlett, *Native Title in Australia*, 2nd ed, LexisNexis Butterworths, Sydney, 2004, p 598.

9.121 The disclosure must be a full and frank disclosure of all material facts: *New Zealand Netherlands Society 'Oranje' Inc v Kuys* [1973] 2 NZLR 163 at 166; [1973] 2 All ER 1222 at 1225; *Blackmagic Design Pty Ltd v Overliese* at 23. 'Material facts' include all relevant information which is necessary for the beneficiary to make a proper judgment as to whether to give consent to the activity which would otherwise be a breach of duty: *Diamond Hill Mining Pty Ltd v Huang Jin Mining Pty Ltd* at [95]. Material facts extend to facts which might have affected the decision of the person to whom fiduciary duties are owed and is not confined to facts which would have affected that decision: *FHR European Ventures LLP v Mankarious* [2011] EWHC 2308 (Ch) at [79]. The disclosure requirement extends to facts known to the fiduciary and to those that he or she has deliberately refrained from acquiring. However, there is no requirement that the fiduciary disclose things he or she is unaware of but which a prudent person would have discovered as the result of making inquiries: *BLB Corporation of Australia v Jacobsen* (1974) 48 ALJR 372 at 378.

9.122 In some cases, it may be necessary that the beneficiary or principal obtain independent, skilled advice: *Maguire v Makaronis* at CLR 466–7; ALR 739. It is no defence by a fiduciary to show that, had there been a disclosure, it would have made no difference as to how a client would have acted: *Commonwealth Bank v Smith* (1991) 102 ALR 453 at 479. In *Consul Developments Pty Ltd v DPC Estates Pty Ltd* at CLR 399–400; ALR 253, Gibbs J noted that the fiduciary cannot in any way induce the decision to grant such consent.

9.123 In *Phipps v Boardman*, the House of Lords made comments on the question of consent to a transaction involving a solicitor who owes fiduciary duties to clients who are trustees of a trust. In such cases there is no doubt that the unanimous consent of the trustees is necessary: Lord Upjohn in *Phipps v Boardman* at AC 128; All ER 759. However, in that case, Viscount Dilhorne, at AC 93; All ER 737, and Lord Cohen, at AC 104; All ER 744, suggested that the consent of the beneficiaries to the trust is also necessary. Lord Hodson, at AC 112; All ER 749, implied the same when he observed that the solicitor in that case was in a fiduciary position in relation to the trustees and through them in relation to the beneficiaries. It is, however, suggested that these views are mistaken and that a solicitor in such a case owes fiduciary duties to the trustees only. The interests of the beneficiaries are adequately protected by the fiduciary duties owed to them by the trustees of the trust.

9.124 In the context of the director–company relationship, the House of Lords in *Regal (Hastings) Ltd v Gulliver*, held that, for a director to escape liability for breach of fiduciary duties, the consent of the company through a resolution of shareholders at a general meeting of the company was required. However, in *Queensland Mines Ltd v Hudson* (1978) 18 ALR 1, the Privy Council upheld the validity of the consent of a company given by its board of directors. In *Whitehouse v Carlton Hotel Pty Ltd* (1987) 162 CLR 285 at 295; 70 ALR 251 at 258, the High Court stated that it *may* be that in *some* cases the directors only can give the consent. On one level it can be argued that the *Queensland Mines v Hudson* approach is correct given that a director usually stands in a fiduciary relationship with the company and not its shareholders, and thus the consent of the shareholders is unnecessary. However, the problem with this approach is illustrated by the facts of *Queensland Mines v Hudson* itself. In that case, the director of the company seeking the consent of the company participated in the decision of the board of directors that granted the consent. Although the director was only one of a number of directors, it is difficult to see how the board's decision can be said to have been in conformity with Gibbs J's dictum in *Consul Developments v DPC Estates*.

Contractual exclusion or variation of fiduciary duties

9.125 Because many of the relationships which contain fiduciary duties are often sourced in contract, it is possible for contractual terms to impose or vary fiduciary duties: *Hospital Products*; *MacIntosh v Fortex Group Ltd* [1997] NZLR 711. The nature of the fiduciary duty is determined examining the contract as a whole in the light of the surrounding circumstances known to the parties and the purpose and object of the transaction: *Pacific Carriers Limited v BNP Paribas* (2004) 218 CLR 451 at 461–2; 208 ALR 213 at 221; *Toll (FGCT) Pty Limited v Alphapharm Pty Limited* (2004) 219 CLR 165 at 179; 211 ALR 342 at 341–2.

9.126 It may even be possible to exclude the operation of fiduciary duties in their entirety: *Hodgson v Amcor Ltd* at [1348]. In the banking environment it is possible to exclude fiduciary duties by express agreement in a contract. In *Australian Securities and Investments Commission v Citigroup Global Markets Australia Pty Limited (No 4)* (2007) 160 FCR 35, Citigroup had been contracted to advise Toll Holdings on a takeover bid for Patrick Corporation, but on the basis that the relationship would not be fiduciary. Meanwhile, the investment arm of Citigroup (which was separated from the advising section by a Chinese wall) had bought a large number of shares in Patrick Corporation. When the takeover bid was made public, the investment arm dumped the shares. ASIC argued that this amounted to a conflict of interest. Jacobsen J found that there was no conflict because the parties had agreed that there would be no fiduciary duty.

9.127 In coming to his decision, Jacobson J, at 77, said:

> It may well be that a fiduciary cannot exclude liability for fraud or deliberate dereliction of duty but beyond that there appears to be no restriction in the law to prevent a fiduciary from contracting out of, or modifying, his or her fiduciary duties, particularly where no prior fiduciary relationship existed and the contract defines the rights and duties of the parties.

In that case, Citigroup had been contracted to advise Toll Holdings on a takeover bid for Patrick Corporation, but on the basis that the relationship would not be fiduciary. Meanwhile, the investment arm of Citigroup (which was separated from the advising section by a Chinese wall) had bought a large number of shares in Patrick Corporation. When the takeover bid was made public, the investment arm dumped the shares. ASIC argued that this amounted to a conflict of interest. Jacobsen J found that there was no conflict because the parties had agreed that there would be no fiduciary duty.

Unclean hands

9.128 In *Caratinos v Magafas* [2008] NSWCA 304, the New South Wales Court of Appeal found that a clean hands defence (see 31.8–31.12) could be applied to breach of fiduciary duty. In the particular case, the defendant partner was accused of breaching fiduciary duties on property developments but numerous false statements had been lodged by the plaintiff to taxation authorities in relation to the developments. The court found that this disentitling conduct should have been taken into account by the trial judge when fashioning relief, and that relief should only have been provided where the plaintiff was able to demonstrate full and frank disclosure of the illegal and fraudulent conduct to the relevant authorities. Additionally, the plaintiff should have made arrangements to pay any additional tax and penalties that were owed.

Laches

9.129 Laches is also available as a defence to a claim of breach of fiduciary duty: see 31.13–31.22. In *Streeter v Western Areas Exploration Pty Ltd* (2011) 278 ALR 291 at 303, the defence of laches was raised to bar a claim of breach of fiduciary duty made by a company, Western Areas Explorations Pty Ltd, against two former directors. The directors had invested in a mining venture after having been introduced to that venture by another officer of the company. The shareholders knew of this behaviour in 2000 but took six years to bring an action, after which time the venture had grown to be worth over $900 million. The shareholders could have chosen to remove both directors in 2000 but nothing was done, seemingly because they were content to let the directors take the risks associated with the investment. Only after it was successful did they seek to bring a claim. On this basis, the Court of Appeal of Western Australia found it unjust to allow a claim, and stated that the claim was barred by laches.

REMEDIES

9.130 Typical remedies (which are discussed in more detail in later chapters) for breaches of fiduciary duties include:[39]

- an account for profits: *Warman International Ltd v Dwyer* (see 30.25–30.31); [40]
- equitable compensation: *O'Halloran v R T Thomas & Family Pty Ltd* (1998) 45 NSWLR 262 (see 26.2–26.38);
- the imposition of a constructive trust: *Furs Ltd v Tomkies* (1936) 54 CLR 583 (see 28.93–28.107); *Chan v Zacharia*; and
- rescission: *Armstrong v Jackson* (see 9.32 and Chapter 27).

9.131 In relation to the remedy of a constructive trust, in *John Alexander's Clubs Pty Ltd v White City Tennis Club Ltd* at CLR 45; ALR at 492, the High Court said:

> A constructive trust ought not to be imposed if there are other orders capable of doing full justice … [C]are must be taken to avoid granting equitable relief which goes beyond the necessities of the case. Another point … is that third party interests must be borne in mind in deciding whether a constructive trust should be granted. [Legal authority] does not permit a constructive trust to be declared in a manner injurious to third parties merely because the plaintiff has no other useful remedy against a defendant.

Furthermore, according to Gibbs CJ in *Daly v The Sydney Stock Exchange Limited* at CLR 379, where the benefit which is obtained by a fiduciary as a consequence of its breach of duty is a loan of money, it may be 'contrary to principle' to impose a constructive trust over the money and thereby transforming the creditor's personal claim into a proprietary remedy.

9.132 Although a fiduciary will be held liable for breaches of his or her duty, a court will, in an appropriate case, make some allowance for remuneration of the fiduciary in recognition of

---

39. See M Conaglen, 'Remedial ramifications of conflicts between a fiduciary's duties' (2010) 126 *Law Quarterly Review* 72.
40. See P Devonshire, 'Account of profits for breach of fiduciary duty' (2010) 32 *Sydney Law Review* 389; M Conaglen, 'The extent of fiduciary accounting and the importance of authorisation mechanisms' (2011) 70 *Cambridge Law Journal* 548.

the fiduciary's work and effort: *Keppel v Wheeler* [1927] 1 KB 577; *Phipps v Boardman; Imageview Management Limited v Jack* [2009] EWCA Civ 63; *Bank of Ireland v Jaffrey* [2012] EWHC 1377 (Ch). The current position in relation to such allowances was summed up in *Chirnside v Fay* [2007] 1 NZLR 433 at 470, where Blanchard and Tipping JJ observed:

> The principle which has developed from *Boardman v Phipps* and subsequent cases is that there is a presumptive requirement that the errant fiduciary disgorge all profits made by dint of the breach. There is room, however, for the Court to exercise its discretion to allow the errant fiduciary some measure of allowance or recompense for effort, skill and enterprise in making those profits, if it would be unjust not to do so. All the relevant circumstances must be taken into account. The more reprehensible the fiduciary's conduct, the less inclined the Court may be to make any allowance or to be liberal in the amount awarded. The essence of the exercise is to define fairly the profit for which the fiduciary is required to account.

9.133   In *Guinness Plc v Saunders* [1990] 2 AC at 663 at 701; [1990] 1 All ER 652 at 667, Lord Goff noted that such allowances should be confined to 'cases where it cannot have the effect of encouraging trustees in any way to put themselves in a position where their interests conflict with their duties as trustees'. For a discussion of these principles in relation to trustees see 21.82–21.84.

10

UNDUE INFLUENCE

INTRODUCTION

10.1 Whereas the common law generally assumes that the parties to particular transactions have equal bargaining power, equity recognises that often this may not be the case and it may enable a party to set aside a transaction where it can be shown that the relationship between the parties was tainted by inequality, unfairness or actual abuse.

10.2 There are two main equitable rules which aim to examine the circumstances in which a transaction is made for the purpose of assessing whether it offends equity's insistence on good conscience. Those rules are:

1. the doctrine against unconscionable conduct; and
2. the doctrine of undue influence.

The broader of the two, and the more significant in Australian law, is the doctrine against unconscionable conduct, which is discussed in Chapter 11. Closely related, yet quite distinct, is the narrower doctrine of undue influence. At the conclusion to Chapter 11, the relationship between these two branches of equity will be considered. However, at this point a brief note on the distinction between the two principles can be made.

10.3 Unconscionable conduct refers to a situation where one party to a transaction is under a special disadvantage that was knowingly exploited by the other in securing the deal. Undue influence is similar in that it also acts to prevent the unconscientious effects of inequality. However, rather than looking to the actions of the stronger party, undue influence focuses upon the relationship that existed between the parties and asks whether the nature of that relationship impaired the quality of the consent that was given. In particular, what excites equity's involvement is a powerful ascendancy by one party over the other. In *Johnson v Smith* [2010] NSWCA 306 at [2], Allsop P summarised the distinction as follows:

> [T]he equitable doctrines of undue influence and unconscionable dealing or conduct are distinct. The former (undue influence) looks to the quality of consent or assent of the weaker party and the latter (unconscionable dealing or conduct) looks to the attempted enforcement, or retention of a benefit, of a dealing with a person under a special disability.

10.4 It should also be noted that the material in this chapter and Chapter 11 is considered in the context of *inter vivos* transactions (including gifts) rather than testamentary dispositions. Undue influence and unconscionability are conceptually quite different in the context of wills.

THE NATURE OF UNDUE INFLUENCE

10.5   At common law there are various principles upon which the quality of the consent given by one party to a transaction is called into question that will enable the affected party to seek relief. Thus, a written contract will be void if it is radically different in nature to that which the party signing the contract believed he or she was signing (*non est factum*) and a contract can be set aside if procured as the result of duress. It is easy to appreciate that real consent is absent in such transactions. In equity, the principle of undue influence also focuses on the quality of consent given to the transaction. This was made clear by Deane J in *Commercial Bank of Australia Ltd v Amadio* (1983) 151 CLR 447 at 474; 46 ALR 402 at 423, when he said that '[u]ndue influence, like common law duress, looks to the quality of the consent or assent of the weaker party'. The purpose of the doctrine of undue influence is 'to protect people from being forced, tricked or misled in any way by others into parting with their property': *Allcard v Skinner* (1887) 36 Ch D 145 at 182–3. The fact that the proposal to enter a contract or make a gift came from the weaker party does not preclude a finding of undue influence: *Spong v Spong* (1914) 18 CLR 544 at 549.

10.6   However, two points need to be made in relation to the principle of undue influence. First, while it is acknowledged that a relationship of influence need not be characterised by anything so obvious as outright domination, the influence must still be 'undue'. To speak merely of 'influence' is to fail to appreciate the high level of ascendancy that is required in order for a party to obtain relief. In *Anderson v McPherson (No 2)* [2012] WASC 19 at [247]–[248], Edelman J said:

> The party seeking to set aside a transaction for undue influence must prove … a relationship going beyond mere confidence and influence. It must be a relationship involving dominion and ascendancy by one person over the will of the other, and correlative dependence by the other.

Edelman J cited with approval the case of *Tufton v Sperni* [1952] 2 TLR 516 at 532, where Morris LJ said that the domination by the defendant of the mind and will of the plaintiff must be such that 'the mind of the latter became a mere channel through which the wishes of the former flowed'.

10.7   Second, even if, as a matter of analogy, the setting aside of a transaction on the basis of undue influence seems less demanding than more compelling examples available at common law, such a perception ignores the fundamental and historical focus of equity to inquire into situations where there is an abuse of inequality offending 'good conscience', without the need for more. In fact, the very need for equitable doctrines such as undue influence is demonstrated by the very strict requirements that must be satisfied if a weaker party is to obtain relief under common law principles such as *non est factum* and duress.

CATEGORIES OF UNDUE INFLUENCE

10.8   Traditionally there have existed two distinct categories of transactions that attract equitable intervention on the basis of the principles of undue influence. The distinguishing characteristic between the two categories is whether there is, or is not, a special relationship between the parties to the transaction. Cases in which there is no special relationship between the parties are generally referred to as ones of *actual* or *express* undue influence. Cases in which a special relationship exists between the parties are generally referred to as ones of *presumed* undue influence, and can be subcategorised according to the basis upon which the existence of the special relationship is established. In *Allcard v Skinner* at 171, Cotton LJ said the following in relation to the two categories of undue influence:

> First, where the Court has been satisfied that the gift was the result of influence expressly used by the donee for the purpose; second, where the relations between the donor and donee have at or shortly before the execution of the gift been such as to raise a presumption that the donee had influence over the donor. In such a case the Court sets aside the voluntary gift, unless it is proved that in fact the gift was the spontaneous act of the donor acting under circumstances which enabled him to exercise an independent will and which justifies the Court in holding that the gift was the result of a free exercise of the donor's will. The first class of cases may be considered as depending on the principle that no one shall be allowed to retain any benefit arising from his own fraud or wrongful act. In the second class of cases the Court interferes, not on the ground that any wrongful act has in fact been committed by the donee, but on the ground of public policy, and to prevent the relations which existed between the parties and the influence arising therefrom being abused.

10.9   Each of the two categories of undue influence must be considered separately. This is so because, in cases of actual undue influence, the focus of attention is on the nature and extent of influence that must be established, whereas in cases of presumed undue influence, a rebuttable presumption arises that undue influence existed where the presumed relationship is found to arise.

ACTUAL UNDUE INFLUENCE

10.10   In cases where there is no special relationship between the parties to the transaction, a person seeking equitable relief on the basis of the principles of undue influence must establish that actual undue influence was exerted by the other party to the transaction. Following the House of Lords decision in *Barclays Bank Plc v O'Brien* [1994] 1 AC 180 at 189; [1993] 4 All ER 417 at 423, cases of actual undue influence are also often referred to as 'Class 1 undue influence' cases. In *Johnson v Buttress* (1936) 56 CLR 113 at 134, in discussing such cases, Dixon J said:

> The source of power to practise such a domination may be found in no antecedent relation but in a particular situation, or in the deliberate contrivance of the party. If this be so, facts must be proved showing that the transaction was the outcome of such an actual influence over the mind of the alienor that it cannot be considered his free act.

10.11   In *Allcard v Skinner* at 171, Cotton LJ indicated that a case of actual undue influence could be established if 'there has been some unfair and improper conduct, some coercion from outside, some overreaching, some form of cheating, and generally, though not always, some personal advantage by a donee in some close and confidential relation to the donor'.

10.12   Once actual undue influence has been established, the onus is upon the party exerting the influence to rebut the presumption that the transaction was entered into by the other party as a result of the influence: see 10.34–10.44.

10.13   Cases of actual undue influence are uncommon. They are also difficult to prove. In *Frederick v State of South Australia* (2006) 94 SASR 545, a South Australian magistrate resigned from his position during a meeting with the Chief Magistrate. The magistrate had been recently convicted of two criminal offences. However, the convictions were subsequently set aside. The magistrate argued that the resignation was ineffective on the basis that it was procured by the exertion of actual undue influence by the Chief Magistrate. The Supreme Court rejected the claim on the basis that the magistrate, as a person who had had a long career as a lawyer and magistrate, was not in a position of being the victim of actual undue influence. White J, at 580, said the following in relation to the magistrate's decision to resign:

> I accept that [he] valued his position as a magistrate both for the honour which the office entailed, his satisfaction with the work and because it was his source of livelihood. I accept that [he] wished to maintain his position as long as practicable and that he signed the resignation letter reluctantly. I accept that immediately before signing the resignation letter he said words to the effect that he felt that he did not really have any choice but to resign with dignity, and that that statement reflected his state of mind at that time. However, that evidence falls short, in my opinion, of establishing that [his] will was overborne or that his agreement to resign was procured by undue influence. The fact that the choices apparently open to him were unpalatable does not indicate that his will was overborne. It is an unfortunate fact that often people are called upon to make difficult decisions and, in particular, to make decisions which they would prefer very much to not have to make. Where a person confronts the circumstance, and makes the difficult decision, it will often be inappropriate to speak of their will having been overborne. In my opinion, that is the position in the present case.

PRESUMED UNDUE INFLUENCE

10.14   Cases dealing with presumed undue influence involve the existence of a special relationship between the parties to the transaction. The existence of the special relationship gives rise to a presumption that the transaction was obtained as a result of undue influence by the stronger party in the relationship over the weaker party. The presumption of undue influence only arises upon proof of the existence of a special relationship. The effect of the presumption is that the weaker party will be able to seek equitable relief, unless the presumption of undue influence is rebutted by the stronger party. In *Johnson v Buttress* at 134, Dixon J set out the relevant principles as follows:

> But the parties may antecedently stand in a relation that gives to one an authority or influence over the other from the abuse of which it is proper that he should be protected. When they stand in such a relation, the party in the position of influence cannot maintain his beneficial title to property of substantial value made over to him by the other as a gift, unless he satisfies the court that he took no advantage of the donor, but that the gift was the independent and well-understood act of a man in a position to exercise a free judgment based on information as full as that of the donee.

10.15   In recent decades there has been debate in the cases as to whether, in cases of presumed undue influence, it also had to be shown that the transaction was manifestly disadvantageous to the weaker party. In *National Westminster Bank Plc v Morgan* [1985] AC 686 at 707; [1985] 1 All ER 821 at 829, the House of Lords indicated that it had to be a manifestly disadvantageous transaction before equitable relief could be granted. In Australia, this view was accepted in *Farmer's Co-operative Executors & Trustees Ltd v Perks* (1989) 52 SASR 399 at 404, but rejected in *Baburin v Baburin* [1990] 2 Qd R 101 at 109. Subsequent House of Lords decisions in *CIBC Mortgages Plc v Pitt* [1994] 1 AC 200 at 209; [1993] 4 All ER 433 at 439 and *Royal Bank of Scotland v Etridge (No 2)* [2002] 2 AC 773 at 799, 821, 841; [2001] 4 All ER 449 at 461, 482, 501, have effectively overruled the decision in *National Westminster Bank v Morgan*. While a 'manifest disadvantage' provides a factual inference of abuse of the relationship, its use should not extend beyond that, and a plaintiff who is able to establish undue influence should be entitled to equitable relief regardless of the nature of the transaction itself.

10.16   In analysing cases of presumed undue influence the two critical matters to be discussed are:

(i) establishing the special relationship; and

(ii) rebutting the presumption of undue influence.

Establishing the special relationship

10.17   There are two ways in which the special relationship in presumed undue influence cases can be established. The first relates to cases where the relationship falls into one of the traditionally accepted relationships of influence. The second relates to cases where a relationship of influence has to be proved on the individual facts of any given case. Following the decision in *Barclays Bank v O'Brien* at AC 189; All ER 423, these two groups of cases have been respectively referred to as 'Class 2A undue influence' and 'Class 2B undue influence'.

Class 2A undue influence

10.18   The relationships that the courts have repeatedly recognised as being in a special class are those where it can be presumed any transaction made favouring the stronger party was brought about by the undue exercise of that party's influence. They include those existing between:

- parent and child: *Lancashire Loans Ltd v Black* [1934] 1 KB 380;
- guardian and ward: *Hylton v Hylton* (1754) 28 ER 349;
- solicitor and client: *Westmelton (Vic) Pty Ltd v Archer & Shulman* [1982] VR 305;
- doctor and patient: *Bar-Mordecai v Hillston* [2004] NSWCA 65; and
- religious leader and follower: *Allcard v Skinner*.

10.19   In *Royal Bank of Scotland v Etridge* at AC 797; All ER 460, Lord Nicholls asserted that a presumption arising by virtue of a recognised class of relationship is 'irrebuttable'. This approach has been rejected in Australia: *Janson v Janson* [2007] NSWSC 1344 at [93]. However, it is difficult to rebut such a presumption, and even being able to explain the relationship in some other way, such as that the parties were also in a de facto relationship, will not guarantee success: *Bar-Mordecai v Hillston* at [149].

10.20   An important feature of the use of these relationships is that the presumption does not apply to the mere conferral of a benefit by one party to the other — in order to attract the equitable presumption, the benefit must flow from the 'weaker' party to the 'stronger'. This requirement can be easily appreciated in the last three of the relationships listed above: see 10.18. It is fair to assume that the solicitor, doctor and religious leader will have far more influence over their clients, patients and followers respectively, so that a significant gift or transaction from members of the latter group to their stronger counterpart among the first group would raise suspicions which one would not have if the gift or transaction flowed from the stronger party to the weaker. The direction of the presumption is, of course, particularly clear in the case of a gift. However, in cases of contracts where the obligations or benefits flow from both parties, the same principle will still apply — it is the undue influence of the recognised stronger party over the weaker that will set aside the transaction.

10.21   Yet the presumption in cases of parent/guardian and child/ward might seem less obvious than those where there is a particular relationship of trust and reliance flowing from the weaker party to the stronger. Are not the relationships between parent/guardian and child/ward much more mutual than the other recognised categories, especially when the child is no longer a minor? Why is 'child and parent' not also a special relationship? Certainly, these familial relationships appear distinct from those arising elsewhere. However, it should be borne in mind that all that is established by the relationship is a presumption that can be rebutted if not truly reflective of the parties' positions. Thus, while a benefit conferred by a parent to a child will not automatically raise a presumption of undue influence (*Brown v New South Wales Trustee & Guardian* [2011] NSWSC 1203 at [46]) and one from a child to a parent will, evidence may be produced in both instances to show the contrary: *Stone v Registrar of Titles* [2012] WASC 21 at [207]. The most obvious reason for not admitting the reverse of the 'parent and child' relationship to the special class would seem to be the traditional view of parental authority and control over a child, which was particularly strong throughout the Victorian era when the special categories were consolidated by the courts. It is also seen as entirely natural for parents to bestow benefits on their offspring out of a desire to assist them to get on in life: *Wilby v St George Bank Ltd* (2001) 80 SASR 404 at 414.

10.22   Some clarification of the scope of the presumption arising in religious circumstances is warranted. While the category of 'religious leader and follower' clearly refers to a situation where a religious minister or leader receives a personal benefit from a follower, such as occurred in *McCulloch v Fern* [2001] NSWSC 406, the influence bearing upon the donor will not always be so individualised. Instead, it will often be the case that the donor's free will is overcome simply as a result of subscribing to the beliefs and doctrines of the religious order. Thus, in *Hartigan v International Society for Krishna Consciousness Inc* [2002] NSWSC 810, the court set aside a gift of land made by Hartigan to the Hare Krishna movement, despite admitting that no one person could be identified by evidence as a spiritual adviser who, directly or indirectly, suggested that she make the donation. Bryson J, at [28], said:

> The court's approach, in cases of gifts influenced by religious advisers or religious beliefs, is more exacting than ordinary community standards and goes well beyond overcoming deliberate exploitation. It may be unconscionable to accept and rely on a gift which was fully intended and understood by the donor and originated in the donor's own mind, where the intention to make the gift was produced by religious belief.

10.23   There are suggestions that the trustee–beneficiary relationship is a Class 2A relationship: *Union Fidelity Trustee Co of Australia Ltd v Gibson* [1971] VR 573 at 577, and *Johnson v Buttress* at 119. However, as Meagher, Heydon and Leeming[1] observe, there is no justification, in the absence of special circumstances, for suggesting that there is a relationship of undue influence between a trustee and beneficiary, and that unless the transaction is one involving trust property, there should be no presumption invalidating the transaction. In cases where trust property is involved, a beneficiary is already protected by the rules relating to fiduciary obligations: see Chapter 9.

10.24   Another controversial relationship is that of 'man and fiancée': *Tillet v Varnell Holdings Pty Ltd* [2009] NSWSC 1040 at [77]. While there is no doubt that 'husband and wife' is not included in the class (*Yerkey v Jones* (1939) 63 CLR 649 at 675), there are several old authorities, such as *In re Lloyd's Bank; Bomze v Momze* [1931] 1 Ch 289 at 302, recognising a man's influence over a

---

1.   R Meagher, D Heydon & M Leeming, *Meagher Gummow & Lehane's Equity: Doctrines and Remedies*, 4th ed, LexisNexis Butterworths, Sydney, 2002, pp 513–4.

woman to whom he is engaged. To find this as a matter of presumption would seem at odds with a modern appreciation of gender equality, and later cases have suggested that the relationship of a man and his fiancée is no longer a Class 2A relationship: *Zamet v Hyman* [1963] 3 All ER 933 at 937–8; *Louth v Diprose* (1992) 175 CLR 621 at 630; 110 ALR 1 at 7. However, in the recent English decision of *Leeder v Stevens* [2005] EWCA Civ 50, the Court of Appeal assumed that it was still a Class 2A relationship. The court even extended it by analogy to a relationship between a married man and a woman with whom he was having an affair where the couple had talked about getting married at some time in the future. Enonchong argues that the decision 'is insecure in judicial as well as academic authority and is not well-founded in principle' and should 'be treated with considerable caution'.[2] Nevertheless, in *Grace v Grace* [2012] NSWSC 976 at [86], Brereton J said that the relationship between a man and his fiancée was 'arguably' one of presumed undue influence.

Class 2B undue influence

10.25   If the parties to the transaction do not fall within a Class 2A relationship, a special relationship can nevertheless be established on the particular facts and circumstances of their relationship. These Class 2B relationships arise 'where it is proved that the party benefiting from the transaction occupies or assumes towards another a position naturally involving an ascendancy or influence over that other, or a dependency or trust on the latter's part': *Janson v Janson* [2007] NSWSC 1344 at [72].

10.26   In *Royal Bank of Scotland v Etridge* at AC 797, 822, 842–3; All ER 449, 483, 503, a number of the members of the House of Lords made strong statements against the usefulness of identifying Class 2B relationships as a separate category for the purposes of the doctrine of undue influence. However, this approach has not, to date, been accepted by the High Court. Thus, Class 2B relationships operate as a separate category of relationships for the purpose of the doctrine of undue influence in Australia.

10.27   The range of evidence that may be adduced in order to show that the relationship gives rise to a presumption of undue influence is unlimited. While evidence directly relevant to the transaction at issue is not required, as is the case with actual undue influence (see 10.10–10.11), the applicant will be seeking to draw the court's attention to any number of factors that frame the relationship as appropriately influential. Extreme age (young or old), mental or physical disability, illiteracy, poor education, lack of business knowledge and experience are all important in this regard, but it is how these matters colour the relationship that is crucial. The nature of such factors is that they place the applicant in a weak and dependent position vis-à-vis the other party. This will be particularly so when the applicant can show that he or she has relied upon the other in the past and places a high level of trust in that party. If the 'stronger' party is a family member or old friend, the presumption will arise more readily.

10.28   In *Johnson v Buttress*, the facts involved Buttress, a man of 67 years of age, and Johnson, a distant relative by marriage. Buttress had limited capabilities — he was entirely illiterate, inexperienced in business and possessed less than average intelligence. He was regarded as unstable in his affections and in forming his intentions. He had difficult relations with his children.

---

2.   N Enonchong, 'The Irrebuttable Presumption of Influence and the Relationship Between Fiancé and Fiancée' (2005) 121 *Law Quarterly Review* 567, p 572.

His relationship with Johnson became closer after the death of his wife. Johnson cared for Buttress and he often stayed at her home with her family for periods of time. It was while he was living with Johnson that he and she went to a solicitor's office and executed a transfer of his property at Maroubra to her entirely. The rent paid by tenants of this property was Buttress's sole source of income. Buttress understood, at that time, that he was dealing, and parting, with his property. But nothing was said to direct his attention to the fact that he was in effect divesting himself of the whole of his property without obtaining any equivalent benefit, and it was not suggested that the advice he received in the office of Johnson's solicitor was independent advice. Soon after the transfer, Buttress moved to Johnson's block of land in the Blue Mountains where he lived in a tent. After his death, the administrator of his estate brought an action to set aside the gift to Johnson on the ground that it was tainted by undue influence.

10.29   The High Court unanimously set aside the transaction on the grounds of undue influence. Although there was clearly no question of the relationship between Buttress and Johnson being a Class 2A relationship, the majority of the High Court took the view that such a presumption did arise in light of the nature of the particular relationship between the parties. In explaining how this conclusion was reached, Dixon J, at 136–7, made clear the role of factors indicating weakness:

> The first and most important consideration affecting the question is the standard of intelligence, the equipment and character of Buttress. No doubt, once it is established that a relation of influence exists, the presumption arises independently of these matters. It has been said that it is an error to treat the subjects of capacity and of influence as if they were separate elements. But, in any case, in this peculiar case it is the man's illiteracy, his ignorance of affairs, and his strangeness in disposition and manner that provide the foundation for the suggested relation.

Later, Dixon J, at 138, said:

> I think that when the circumstances of the case are considered with the character and capacity of Buttress they lead to the conclusion that an antecedent relation of influence existed which throws upon Mrs Johnson the burden of justifying the transfer by showing that it was the result of the free exercise of the donor's independent will. This, in my opinion, she has quite failed to do.

10.30   Latham CJ, Evatt and McTiernan JJ were in agreement that the case was one where the relationship brought about a presumption of undue influence. However, Starke J, at 126, found that the evidence indicated that the case was more properly viewed as one of actual undue influence:

> Now I feel some difficulty in assenting to the learned judge's view that the facts disclose a peculiar relationship of trust and confidence between [Buttress] and [Johnson] which brings [Buttress] within the 'protected class' in respect of which there is a presumption of undue influence. But the age and capacity of [Buttress], the improvident and unfair nature of the transaction, the want of proper advice, the retention of the rents of the property transferred, the various testamentary dispositions, and the other circumstances mentioned, afford evidence from which the learned judge might justly infer that the transfer was not the result of the free and deliberate judgment of [Buttress], but the result of unfair and undue pressure on the part of [Johnson].

10.31   The reasoning of both Starke J and the rest of the High Court in *Johnson v Buttress* is a sound demonstration of the fluid relationship between actual undue influence and the influence said to be presumed upon evidence of the strength of the particular relationship. Which of these two classes of undue influence is likely to be established in any given case is really a matter of degree. As such, it is not surprising that there will be occasional disagreement between judges as to which class more accurately describes the situation before them. The classification of undue influence cases as either Class 1, Class 2A or Class 2B has a limited function — each class is a means of establishing undue influence. Thus, the disagreement between Starke J and the rest of the court in *Johnson v Buttress* resulted in no disparity upon the outcome that all the judges reached. Once the court is satisfied as to the existence of undue influence, the focus shifts from the classes and moves squarely on to the stronger party who has the onus of rebutting the presumption of influence in order to uphold the relevant transaction.

10.32 In *Bester v Perpetual Trustee Co Ltd* [1970] 3 NSWR 30, Bester, as a young woman, was encouraged to make a settlement of a substantial inheritance received from her father. The effect of this irrevocable document was to put the assets, which comprised her inheritance, beyond her control and provide her with only a modest annual income from the property. At the time of settlement, Bester was 21 years of age, without parental guidance and possessed of extremely limited business experience. She was influenced by three much older men — the representative from her trustee company, and her two uncles, one of whom was the solicitor who drafted the deed of settlement. In these circumstances, Street J had little difficulty in finding that undue influence was raised successfully by Bester who was, after many years, seeking to rescind the settlement. His Honour, at 34–5, said:

> The present relationship is very close to, if not indeed, within, the scope of the traditional relations. But whether within or without the traditional relations, the present facts involve a degree of confidence equivalent thereto … Indeed, the very presence, in the circumstances surrounding this deed, of the paternal element that pervades the discussions between all concerned is consistent with, and corroborates, the existence of the special relationship of influence.

UNDUE INFLUENCE AND THIRD PARTIES

10.33 It is well established that operative undue influence can arise in a situation where the dominant party to a relationship of undue influence is not a direct recipient of some benefit or property from the weaker party, but rather through the involvement of a third party. Undue influence involving third parties arises in the following situations:

(i) where there is a relationship of undue influence between A (the dominant party) and B (the weaker party) which results in a transfer of property or conferral of some benefit from B to C (a third party); or

(ii) where there is a relationship of undue influence between A (the dominant party) and B (the weaker party) which results in B undertaking obligations to C (a third party) which will be for the benefit of A, an example being where B acts as a guarantor of A's loan from C.

An illustration of the first situation is the case of *Verduci v Golotta* [2010] NSWSC 506 at [67]–[74], where the court set aside a loan and mortgage in circumstances involving a solicitor-client relationship where the client borrowed money from the solicitor's father. Illustrations of the second situation are discussed below: see 10.48–10.76.

REBUTTAL OF UNDUE INFLUENCE

10.34   Once the applicant has satisfied the court that there is a case of actual undue influence or the existence of a special relationship of influence, the stronger party to the transaction has the task of rebutting the presumption that the transaction was the result of undue influence. The aim of the stronger party is not necessarily to rebut the nature of the relationship but rather to focus upon proving that 'the gift was the independent and well-understood act of a man in a position to exercise a free judgment based on information as full as that of the donee': *Johnson v Buttress* at 134. This test is not satisfied simply by establishing that the donor understood the transaction: *Bar-Mordecai v Hillston* [2004] NSWCA 65 at [167], [183]. As was pointed out by Lord Eldon in *Huguenin v Baseley* (1807) 33 ER 526 at 636, the question is not whether the applicant knew what he or she was doing but how the intention to do it was produced.

10.35   In relation to the rebuttal of undue influence in the parent–child relationship, in *Lamotte v Lamotte* (1942) 42 SR (NSW) 99 at 102–03, Roper J said:

> I have some doubt whether a presumption of influence arises as between parent and child when the child is 43 years of age and the parent 75, or if it arises whether it is not rebutted by the mere proof of the ages. The cases dealing with the presumption of parental influence are almost all cases when the transaction was affected shortly after the child attained its majority and the consequent capacity to make a binding gift and the relationship giving rise to the presumption is frequently spoken of as that between parent and *young* child. On the whole, however, I think that the parental influence is presumed to continue until the 'emancipation' of the child: that emancipation is not presumed merely from the attainment of any particular age, and that the onus of establishing it is on the parent … [T]he ages of the parties is simply one of the matters to be taken into consideration in dealing with the question of emancipation. If emancipation is established then the gift has to be dealt with on the same footing as any other gift. 'A child may make a gift to a parent, and such a gift is good if it is not tainted by parental influence. A child is presumed to be under the exercise of parental influence as long as the domination of the parent lasts. Whilst that domination lasts, it lies on the parent maintaining the gift to disprove the exercise of parental influence, by showing that the child had independent advice, or in some other way. When the parental influence is disproved, or that influence has ceased, a gift from a child stands on the same footing as any other gift; and the question to be determined is, whether there was a deliberate, unbiased intention on the part of the child to give to the parent': *Wright v Vanderplank* (1856) 44 ER 340 at 345. The existence of a proper feeling of respect and regard for the parent does not necessarily indicate the continued existence of the parental influence which gives rise to the presumption in question. 'A man of mature age and experience can make a gift to his father or mother because he stands free of all overriding influence except such as may spring from what I may call filial piety': *Powell v Powell* [1900] 1 Ch 243 at 245–6.

More recently, in *Tillett v Varnell Holdings Pty Ltd* at [80], Brereton J said:

> The relationship between parent and child is one of presumed influence, but only for so long as the child is yet to be 'emancipated' from the control of their parent. At what point a child becomes emancipated is not fixed. While some authorities have focused on the age of the child, and assumed that a child becomes emancipated in the years shortly after attaining majority [*Lamotte v Lamotte* (1942) 42 SR (NSW) 99 at 102–3], the better view is that emancipation is to be determined by reference to the ongoing nature of the relationship between parent and child … How long the

influence can be regarded as continuing depends upon each particular case. However, where the parent is elderly and the child is in middle age — having left home years before — it is unlikely that there will be an ongoing relationship of undue influence.

Independent advice

10.36   The single most important feature of the transaction that can assist the stronger party in trying to save it is the receipt by the weaker party of independent advice. For independent advice to have the effect of rebutting the presumption of undue influence, the independent advice should be particularly thorough and address all aspects of the transaction at hand, including advice as to the propriety of the transaction: *Janson v Janson* [2007] NSWSC 1344 at [82]–[83]. Furthermore, the adviser must be fully informed of all material facts relevant to the transaction: *Brusewitz v Brown* [1923] NZLR 1106 at 1116–7.

10.37   The giving of independent advice is not required by law: *Inche Noriah v Shaik Allie Bin Omar* [1921] AC 127 at 135–6. However, it is of particular importance in many cases. In *Goldie v Getley [No 3]* [2011] WASC 132 at [140], Simmonds J summed up the position as follows:

> Although there is no rule of law that where such a relationship exists the donor should have independent advice at the time of making the gift in order to rebut the presumption, and, particularly if the court is of opinion that independent advice would not have had any effect on the transaction, or that the gift was trifling or of a simple character, nevertheless independent advice is an important factor in determining whether the gift is the pure voluntary and well-understood act of the donor. This is particularly so if the gift should be of a large sum of money, or the circumstances of the relationship, however proper the court may regard them, strongly suggest that the donor was in a position of grave inequality in relation to the donee, or where the transaction may be of a complicated character … [I]t is undoubtedly true that in many authorities the presence or absence of independent advice has had a great influence on the court's decision on this vital question. If the donor, however, should receive independent advice, and either misunderstands the advice or is given possibly erroneous advice whereby he fails to appreciate or realize the financial implications and the detriment to himself involved in the gift, a court of equity will not set aside the gift if the donor otherwise understood the nature of the transaction and acted therein in the full exercise of his will.

10.38   In relation to evidence of independent legal advice and the weight to be attached to it, in *Royal Bank of Scotland v Etridge* at AC 798; All ER 460, Lord Nicholls said:

> Proof that the complainant received advice from a third party before entering into the impugned transaction is one of the matters a court takes into account when weighing all the evidence. The weight, or importance, to be attached to such advice depends on all the circumstances. In the normal course, advice from a solicitor or other outside adviser can be expected to bring home to a complainant a proper understanding of what he or she is about to do. But a person may understand fully the implications of a proposed transaction, for instance, a substantial gift, and yet still be acting under the undue influence of another. Proof of outside advice does not, of itself, necessarily show that the subsequent completion of the transaction was free from the exercise of undue influence. Whether it will be proper to infer that outside advice had an emancipating effect,

so that the transaction was not brought about by the exercise of undue influence, is a question of fact to be decided having regard to all the evidence in the case.

10.39 Thus, in *Bester v Perpetual Trustee* (see 10.32), the onus was upon the trustee company to show that the influence had not hindered Bester in the free exercise of her own will in making the settlement. It sought to do so on the basis that she had received advice from a disinterested solicitor prior to signing the deed. The solicitor had read the document to Bester and asked if she had any questions about it, to which she answered 'No'. Street J found that response to be a powerful indicator to the solicitor that Bester had no real understanding of the effect of the transaction at all. His Honour, at 35, questioned the value of the independent advice received in this case and its ability to offset the presumption:

> I am of the view, however, that such part as he played in connexion with this settlement could not fairly be described as meeting that degree of independent advice that [Bester], as a person subject to a relationship of influence, was entitled to receive. [The solicitor] was, I accept, most careful to read the document through, and to invite questions of [Bester]. But it was not textual advice upon the engrossment which was of prime importance in this regard: rather, it was advice upon the more general topic of whether a settlement should be entered into at all, and, if so, the general nature of the settlement, which in my view ought to have been provided for [Bester].

For this, and other reasons which shall be discussed below (see 10.41), Street J found for Bester and allowed the settlement deed to be set aside.

Lack of improvidence

10.40 Another indicator that undue influence has not been brought to bear upon the transaction is that it is not improvident for the applicant. If the stronger party can show that the transaction does not cause excessive loss to the other, then it is more plausible that it was entered into freely. Obviously, the situation differs between instances where the applicant has made a gift and those where they have formed a contract with the stronger party. In the former case, the making of a gift will always be a loss to the applicant, so the courts examine the extent of that gift vis-à-vis his or her total holdings in order to assess providence. For example, in the case of *Union Fidelity Trustee Co of Australia Ltd v Gibson*, the applicant was an executor seeking to set aside the discharge of a mortgage made by the deceased that effectively forgave a £15,000 debt owed by her business advisers. In setting aside the discharge of mortgage, Gillard J, at 580, said:

> [T]he alleged gift was of a very substantial sum of money, even for a woman of means … It was a sum far greater than any set aside by her in trust for her brother or given to him by will … . Although it was urged, with some justification, that she was grateful to the defendant … the size of the amount, in my view, make[s] it very difficult to accept this as being the explanation.

10.41 Similarly, in *Bester v Perpetual Trustee*, Street J found that the settlement was improvident as it tied up Bester's property and effectively removed any control she might have over it. His Honour, at 35, said:

> [T]he absence of any power of revocation, absolute or qualified, the absence of any right to have resort to the corpus, absolute or qualified, the absence of any right to intervene in the activities

of the trustees, either in particular matters or in point of the selection of trustees, are all factors which go, in my view, to justify this transaction being categorized as in some respects improvident.

10.42   Contractual dealings are perhaps slightly easier, as the focus of the court is turned upon the adequacy of consideration. It may be recalled that at contract law, the courts will only inquire into whether consideration is sufficient rather than adequate. That is, it must be recognisably present, but the courts will not decide whether consideration is fair for what is received in return. The court will not help parties avoid bad bargains. However, at equity, a closer look at consideration is warranted for the purpose of examining whether the transaction is made in good conscience. Thus, if it can be seen that the consideration provided by the stronger party in return for the benefit conferred by the weaker is adequate, then that may be used to help rebut the weaker party's case of undue influence.

10.43   Two additional points need to be made in regard to establishing the providence of contracts as a means of rebuttal. First, there is no corresponding requirement upon the weaker party that he or she must show improvidence when making out the grounds for relief. The weaker party must simply establish undue influence of any class. The actual effect of the undue influence is not relevant — and so a transaction can be set aside using this equitable doctrine even when it is a contract that provides very real benefits to the weaker party.

10.44   Second, special problems are posed by contracts of guarantee where no direct benefit flows to the guarantor, who has merely acted as surety for a loan from the other party to a third party — the borrower. In this way, it seems that an applicant who has acted as guarantor is in a position similar to one who has bestowed a gift and that improvidence must be viewed accordingly. But the situation is in fact more complex as it is recognised that often the guarantor will receive indirect benefits from his or her part in the transaction — particularly when he or she is related to the person receiving the loan. Duggan[3] suggests that the main factors relevant to the improvidence or otherwise of a contract of guarantee are, first, the nature and extent of any indirect benefits, and, second, the risk of loss to the guarantor. This risk factor is assessed by reference to the extent of the guarantee relative to the guarantor's wealth and the probability that he or she will be called upon to pay in accordance with the guarantee. Thus, what is required is a combination of the approaches taken in regard to gifts and non-guarantee contracts. The size of the benefit provided by the applicant and also what he or she may expect in return are both relevant in evaluating providence. It is to be appreciated that such an exercise is not straightforward and the motivations of guarantors are not always clear. The problems which arise in respect of contracts of guarantee where the undue influence is actually exercised by a third party are addressed below: see 10.48–10.76.

GENERAL EQUITABLE DEFENCES

10.45   Although not strictly a means of rebutting the applicant's case, the point can be made that the other party may resist the action on more general equitable grounds. In particular, the doctrine of laches or delay (see 31.13–31.22) may prevent relief being given where it appears that, after the influence has been removed, the weaker party has not taken any steps to set aside the

---

3.   A J Duggan, 'Undue Influence' in P Parkinson (ed), *The Principles of Equity*, 2nd ed, Lawbook Co, Sydney 2003, 393, p 411.

transaction. Does this indicate that he or she, in the independent exercise of his or her free will, accepts the transaction?

10.46 In *Allcard v Skinner*, Allcard had entered a Protestant religious order which required a vow of poverty to be taken by members of its sisterhood. Thus, she had transferred substantial property holdings to the mother superior of the order for her to hold on trust for the general purposes of the sisterhood. She also made a will leaving all her property to the sisterhood. After eight years as a sister, Allcard left the sisterhood and soon thereafter joined the Roman Catholic Church. She revoked her will but made no demand for the return of property from the sisterhood until a further five years had elapsed. The evidence established that soon after leaving the sisterhood she had a conversation with her brother, a barrister, about getting her money back. He said she did not need the trouble and had better leave it alone. She also consulted a solicitor about making a new will and discussed with him the gifts she had made to the sisterhood. He told her it was too large a sum to leave behind without asking for it back. Despite that advice, she did nothing about it for a further four years. Although the gift to the sisterhood was the result of undue influence, the Court of Appeal held that Allcard's claim to have it returned was defeated by confirmation, estoppel, acquiescence and or laches. Lindley LJ said that it was not necessary to decide whether or not delay alone would be a sufficient defence, because the case did not rest on mere lapse of time. His Lordship, at 186, said:

> There is far more than inactivity and delay on the part of [Allcard]. There is conduct amounting to confirmation of her gift.

His Lordship, at 189, concluded:

> Whether the Plaintiff's conduct amounts in point of law to acquiescence or laches, or whether it amounts to an election not to avoid a voidable transaction, or whether it amounts to a ratification or a confirmation of her gifts, are questions of mere words which it is needless to discuss. In my judgment, it would not be fair or right to the Defendant to compel her now to restore the money sought to be recovered by this appeal. Nor, in my opinion, would such a result be in conformity with sound, legal, or equitable principles.

Bowen LJ, at 192–3, said:

> Five years is a long time in the life of anybody, and is a long time in the life of a person who has passed her life in seclusion like [Allcard]. Every day and every hour during those five years she has had the opportunity of reflecting upon her past life and upon what she has done … Having belonged to the Church of *England* she at once entered the Church of *Rome*. The influence, therefore, ceased completely. She was surrounded by persons perfectly competent to give her proper advice. She had her solicitor. She had her brother, a barrister himself, and she had the directors of the consciences of the community which she had entered … In my view, [Allcard's claim] ought to be dismissed, and dismissed on the ground that the time which has elapsed, though not a bar in itself, though not accurately to be described as mere laches which disentitles [Allcard] to relief, is nevertheless, coupled with other facts of the case, a matter from which but one reasonable inference ought to be drawn by men of the world — namely, that the lady considered her position at the time, and elected and chose not to disturb the gift which she then at that moment felt, if she had the will, she had the power to disturb.

10.47 The crucial determinant of whether laches will apply to block relief is not the length of the delay per se. While that is obviously highly significant, it is the delay after the applicant is freed from the influence and is aware of the possibilities of setting aside the transaction that really matters. Thus, in *Bester v Perpetual Trustee*, a delay of much more than five years — 20 in fact — was held as no bar to the weaker party's suit for undue influence. Street J, at 37, made it clear that what is required for laches to be found is 'an act or a course of conduct subsequent to becoming aware of the initial invalidity of the transaction, which act or course of conduct has such significance as in law or in equity to amount to a conscious and deliberate affirmation of the original transaction'. So, a delay of many years while the plaintiff seeks resources in order to bring his or her action will not constitute a bar to relief — especially when those financial difficulties stem from the improvidence of the gift: *Hartigan v International Society for Krishna Consciousness Inc*.

UNDUE INFLUENCE AND THIRD PARTY GUARANTEES

10.48 Reference was made earlier (see 10.44) to the difficulty of assessing the improvidence of a contract of guarantee. Such contracts are generally problematical because the guarantor is much more likely to be influenced by the third party for whom they are acting as surety than the party with whom they are actually transacting — the creditor. How then can the contract of guarantee be set aside when the other party to it has exercised no undue influence personally but the guarantor's entrance into the agreement has been coloured by influence from another source?

10.49 Unsurprisingly, the approach is to see whether the undue influence of the third party can be sufficiently connected to the contracting party. In instances where the creditor has appointed an agent to bring about the contract and have the relevant documents executed by the guarantor, then of course no real third party exists. Any undue influence the agent has over the guarantor is sheeted home to the creditor under basic agency principles. An agency may be applied in cases where the party charged with obtaining the guarantor's agreement and signature is actually appointed as an agent, or where there is sufficient investiture in such person of ostensible authority, so that to external eyes it seems that the creditor holds that person out as its agent.

10.50 Regardless of whether an agency situation exists or not — and in many cases that may be difficult to establish — the creditor will be tainted by the undue influence of any third party of which it has actual or constructive notice.

10.51 In *Bank of New South Wales v Rogers* (1941) 65 CLR 42, Rogers, a mature woman of sound intelligence, although lacking in business experience, had, since the death of her parents, lived with her uncle (Gardiner) and relied upon his advice in commercial matters. In order to assist his business venture, which was in trouble, Rogers put forward the bulk of her property as security for a loan from the Bank of New South Wales. In fact, her uncle was on the brink of bankruptcy and the guarantee was unlikely to save him. When his business did indeed collapse, the bank moved to recover from Rogers under the contract of guarantee she had made with it. She sought to set aside the contract on the ground of undue influence. The High Court found that a presumption of undue influence arose from the relationship which existed between the uncle and his niece and that finding was not successfully rebutted. The transaction was blatantly improvident to Rogers and she had received no independent advice prior to making it. The court found unanimously in favour of Rogers as the bank was unable to rebut the presumption by pointing to any independent advice she had received.

10.52   As for the bank's knowledge of what was occurring, Starke J found that it knew that Rogers lived with Gardiner, even if it was unaware that they were niece and uncle respectively. His Honour, at 55, said:

> [T]he bank knew that some special relationship existed between Gardiner and [Rogers], some relationship that was not merely one of business but of confidence and trust, which enabled Gardiner to exercise influence over her. And if this is so, then it was for the bank to establish that the security given to it by [Rogers] was free from any undue influence and was the voluntary and well-understood act of her mind.

10.53   McTiernan J, at 61, was even clearer in setting forth the approach in third party cases:

> The proof of [Rogers'] claim to relief is twofold. It is necessary for her to prove that Gardiner procured the securities to be given to the bank by undue influence or other fraudulent means, and that the [bank] through [its manager] … had notice either actual or constructive that the securities were obtained by such means. If this state of circumstances is established, the bank has the onus of justifying the retention of the securities. It must show that the giving of them was the free and well-understood act of [Rogers].

10.54   Additionally, the High Court found that the bank itself had been less than forthcoming to her. As was noted by Starke J, at 55, Rogers 'was not told that Gardiner's position was hopeless and that her securities would be engulfed in his ruin'.

10.55   Thus, the undue influence attaches to a creditor if it merely has constructive notice of it. Once that is established to the court's satisfaction, the creditor is given the task of rebutting the presumption. The basic approach to rebuttal has already been examined (see 10.34–10.44) but it should be recalled that providence is generally an uncertain indicator in contracts of guarantee and, if anything, even more store is placed upon the receipt by the guarantor of independent advice than is usual.

The Yerkey v Jones principle

10.56   The principles discussed above are treated somewhat differently in cases where the guarantor is the wife of the debtor and the latter has used his influence over his wife to procure her agreement to the contract with the creditor. Following Dixon J's judgment in *Yerkey v Jones* (1939) 63 CLR 649, where, in such a situation, the creditor relies upon the husband to procure the wife's consent to the agreement, she need not prove actual or constructive notice of the undue influence. In short, she is relieved of compliance with the second stage of what McTiernan J, in *Bank of New South Wales v Rogers*, identified as a 'twofold' process. The behaviour of the husband is sheeted home to the bank independent of agency or notice.

10.57   In *Yerkey v Jones*, Mr and Mrs Yerkey brought a claim against Mr and Mrs Jones that arose out of a mortgage over real property. Mr Jones entered into a contract for the purchase of a poultry farm at Payneham near Adelaide from Mr and Mrs Yerkey. The purchase price was to be paid in instalments. However, it was a condition that part of the purchase price be secured by way of a second mortgage over another property owned by Mrs Jones. Mr Jones negotiated the sale conditions with Mr Yerkey and it was not until a week after agreeing to buy the property that

Mr Jones advised Mrs Jones that he had agreed to buy the Payneham property and that he might get into trouble if Mrs Jones did not provide a mortgage over her property. Shortly thereafter Mrs Jones gave a second mortgage as was requested. Mr and Mrs Jones received advice from Mr Yerkey's solicitors. Subsequently, Mrs Jones took proceedings to have the mortgage set aside.

10.58   Although the High Court denied Mrs Jones any equitable relief, the judgment of Dixon J is important in that it articulates the existence of a special equity that protects the position of a wife acting as a guarantor in relation to her husband's debts. Dixon J, at 678, said:

> Although the relation of husband to wife is not one of influence, yet the opportunities it gives are such that if the husband procures his wife to become surety for his debt a creditor who accepts her suretyship obtained through her husband has been treated as taking it subject to any invalidating conduct on the part of her husband even if the creditor be not actually privy to such conduct.

10.59   Later, Dixon J, at 683, said:

> [I]f a married woman's consent to become a surety for her husband's debt is procured by the husband and without understanding its effect in essential respects she executes an instrument of suretyship which the creditor accepts without dealing with her personally she has a prima-facie right to have it set aside.

10.60   The special equity referred to by Dixon J in *Yerkey v Jones* has been mired in controversy. It is hard to reconcile it with equity's refusal to admit spousal relationships into the special class of relationships giving rise to a presumption of undue influence. If such a presumption cannot automatically arise from a spousal relationship, then why should creditors be automatically responsible for undue influence that can only be subsequently proven, and of which they had no means of knowing? It has been argued that the principle reflects a sexist and paternalistic attitude towards women. It has also been asked, if it applies in favour of a wife, why it should not also apply to situations where a husband becomes a guarantor for loans taken out by his wife. By the early 1990s it was assumed by many that the *Yerkey v Jones* principle had become anachronistic, and therefore no longer binding upon the courts: *Akins v National Australia Bank* (1994) 34 NSWLR 155 at 168–73.

10.61   However, in *Garcia v National Australia Bank* (1998) 194 CLR 395; 155 ALR 614, the majority of the High Court dramatically reaffirmed the principle in *Yerkey v Jones*. In that case a married woman and her husband executed a mortgage in 1979 in favour of the National Australia Bank that was secured over their matrimonial home. The mortgage not only secured all money owing under the mortgage, it also secured any money owing pursuant to future guarantees given by either the husband or the wife to the bank. Between 1985 and 1987, the wife signed several guarantees relating to loans made to businesses conducted by the husband. There was no explanation of the precise extent of these transactions by the bank to the wife. Although she was a capable and professional woman who had her own business as a physiotherapist, she did not realise that the guarantees were also linked to the mortgage entered into in 1979. Importantly, the wife obtained no personal benefit from the transactions. In 1989, the woman and her husband were divorced and she commenced proceedings to have the guarantees set aside.

10.62   The High Court majority, in setting aside the guarantees, found that, despite there being no actual undue influence by the husband, it was nevertheless unconscientious for the bank to enforce a guarantee in such circumstances. The High Court majority noted that there were two possible ways in which a wife in such circumstances could seek equitable relief. The first is where there is actual undue influence by a husband over a wife and the second is where, in the absence of actual undue influence, the *Yerkey v Jones* principle applies. In relation to these two situations the High Court majority, at CLR 405; ALR 620, said:

> The former kind of case is one concerning what today is seen as an imbalance of power. In point of legal principle, however, it is actual undue influence in that the wife, lacking economic or other power, is overborne by her husband and goes surety for her husband's debts when she does not bring a free mind and will to that decision. The latter case is not so much concerned with imbalances of power as with lack of proper information about the purport and effect of the transaction.

10.63   In relation to the *Yerkey v Jones* principle, the High Court majority, at CLR 408; ALR 622, noted that the principle was an equitable one distinct from, and not subsumed by, the rules that applied in relation to unconscionable transactions (see Chapter 11) as set out in cases such as *Commercial Bank of Australia v Amadio* (1983) 151 CLR 447; 46 ALR 402. The majority, at CLR 409; ALR 623, then said that, pursuant to this principle, the enforcement of a guarantee against the wife would be unconscientious where:

> (a) in fact the surety did not understand the purport and effect of the transaction; (b) the transaction was voluntary (in the sense that the surety obtained no gain from the contract the performance of which was guaranteed); (c) the lender is to be taken to have understood that, as a wife, the surety may repose trust and confidence in her husband in matters of business and therefore to have understood that the husband may not fully and accurately explain the purport and effect of the transaction to his wife; and yet (d) the lender did not itself take steps to explain the transaction to the wife or find out that a stranger had explained it to her.

The majority, at CLR 411; ALR 625, noted that for the principle to apply, the lender had to have notice 'at the time of taking the guarantee that the surety was then married to the creditor'. It can be noted that the *Yerkey v Jones* principle only operates in the context of guarantees. It does not apply to other instruments or transactions: *Narain v Euroasia (Pacific) Pty Ltd* (2009) VR 387 at 393–6.

10.64   It should be noted that the majority in *Garcia v National Australia Bank*, at CLR 404; ALR 620, recognised that the principle in *Yerkey v Jones* could extend to other close relationships, such as 'to long term and publicly declared relationships short of marriage between members of the same or of opposite sex'. However, this suggestion, and the issue of whether the *Yerkey v Jones* principle extends to other relationships such as elderly parent and child and friends sharing an ethnic background, has received a mixed reception from the courts and commentators.[4] In *Australian Regional Credit v Mula* [2009] NSWSC 325 at [138], McCallum J said that '[t]he principle in *Garcia* is premised on an assumption as to what lenders are "taken to have understood" about the ways in which wives and husbands are disposed to deal with each other. An equally well-founded assumption can be made as to a lender's understanding of the likely conduct of, at least, elderly parents towards their adult children.' In *Agripay Pty Limited v Byrne* [2011] 2 Qd R 501 at 507, Margaret McMurdo P took a broader view and said:

---

4.   A Stavrianou, 'Expanding the Equitable Doctrine of Wife's Special Equity' (2007) 18 *Journal of Banking and Finance Law and Practice* 105, pp 115–7.

There seems to be no sound reason why these principles should be limited to wives entering into guarantees of their husbands' liabilities. Human weaknesses and unconscionable conduct are not limited to heterosexual marriage relationships. These legal principles should apply equally to all vulnerable parties in personal relationships.

10.65 In *Permanent Mortgages Pty Ltd v Vandenbergh* [2010] WASC 10 at [197], Murphy J said: 'I would not see the burden of current authority as supporting an extension of the *Garcia* principles enunciated in the High Court by treating the relationship of aged parent/child as, in itself, synonymous with the husband/wife relationship for the purposes of the application of those principles'.

10.66 Whatever the position may be, it may well be that guarantees in the context of such relationships are adequately covered by the equitable principles relating to unconscionable transactions and statutory unconscionability provisions such as those in the *Australian Consumer Law* (see Chapter 11).

10.67 In relation to the requirement that the wife understand the import and effect of the transaction, in *State Bank of New South Wales Ltd v Chia* (2000) 50 NSWLR 587 at 599, Einstein J said that this includes, at a minimum, 'an understanding of the fact of liability, the general extent of liability and the possible consequences of default'. As to the issue of the transaction being voluntary, the wife/guarantor will be held to be a volunteer unless the benefit of gain is direct or immediate. In *Agripay Pty Limited v Byrne*, on facts not substantially dissimilar to those in *Garcia v National Australia Bank*, the husband used the guaranteed loan funds to invest in a joint superannuation fund and managed agricultural investment. Margaret McMurdo P, at 508, observed that, even though, at best, there was some prospect of eventual profits that may have benefited the wife, this did not mean that the wife was not a volunteer. Furthermore, even if there was to be some eventual modest benefit in the future, the same result would apply, because the benefit would be 'neither direct or immediate'. In *State Bank of New South Wales Ltd v Chia* at 601, Einstein J observed that '[i]ncidental benefit which accrues generally to the family of which the wife is a member is not sufficient benefit to render a transaction which does not otherwise contain a "real benefit", non-voluntary'.

10.68 In the case of a wife acting as guarantor for her husband's loans where the guarantee was entered into as the result of actual undue influence by the husband, the lender must rebut the presumption that the transaction was the result of the husband's influence in order to enforce the guarantee. This requires the lender to show that the wife received independent advice that freed her from the husband's influence: *Yerkey v Jones* at 684. The meaning of independent advice in this context is the same as discussed above: see 10.36–10.39.

10.69 In cases where the *Yerkey v Jones* principle applies in relation to a wife's guarantee, the High Court majority in *Garcia v National Australia Bank*, at CLR 409; ALR 623, said that it is enough if the lender or 'stranger' had explained the transaction to her. This requirement is less stringent than that which is required in cases of actual undue influence.

10.70 In so far as the lender explaining the transaction to the wife is concerned, Dixon J said in *Yerkey v Jones* at 685, in a passage approved by the High Court majority in *Garcia v National Australia Bank* at CLR 407; ALR 621–2:

If the creditor takes adequate steps to inform [the wife] and reasonably supposes that she has an adequate comprehension of the obligations she is undertaking and an understanding of the effect of the transaction, the fact that she has failed to grasp some material part of the document, or, indeed, the significance of what she is doing, cannot … in itself give her an equity to set [the guarantee] aside.

10.71 The same principle would, it is suggested, apply to advice given by the lender's solicitor, as it would be viewed as an explanation by the lender, rather than by an independent solicitor.

10.72 If an explanation of the transaction was given to the wife by the husband's solicitor, the cases are divided as to whether such an explanation would be sufficient to allow the lender to enforce the guarantee. In *State Bank of New South Wales Ltd v Chia* [2000] NSWSC 552 at [233],[5] an explanation provided by the husband's solicitor was held, in the circumstances of that case, to be sufficient. However, in *ANZ Banking Group v Fuller* [2004] NSWSC 305 at [115], it was stated that an explanation by a solicitor acting for both the wife and her husband would not be sufficient on the basis of the solicitor's conflict of interest.

10.73 In England, the *Yerkey v Jones* principle is not recognised and the question of the enforcement of a guarantee given by a wife for her husband's debt is a matter determined under undue influence principles. However, the question of a wife's consent to the guarantee in such circumstances was considered by the House of Lords in *Royal Bank of Scotland v Etridge*. This was a case which was heard together with seven other unrelated cases all of which involved allegations of undue influence being brought to bear on individual wives who had entered into mortgage transactions with different banks as security for their husbands' indebtedness, or to secure the indebtedness of a company through which their husbands carried on business. Each of the wives asserted that she signed the mortgage under the undue influence of her husband and in each case the bank sought to enforce the mortgage signed by the wife. In each case the bank claimed an order for possession of the matrimonial home.

10.74 During the course of argument each of the wives raised a defence that the respective bank was on notice that her concurrence in the transaction had been procured by her husband's undue influence. However, as the circumstances differed in each of the eight cases, the court acknowledged that some of the wives had made out a case of undue influence while some had not. Importantly, the House of Lords did not apply a presumption of undue influence; rather, it assessed the evidence tendered by each of the wives in support of their allegation that undue influence was the inducement to their entry into the transactions. In those circumstances, the House of Lords allowed the appeals by five of the wives and dismissed the appeals in the remainder of the cases.

10.75 In discussing what a lender would need to do to ensure that the guarantee could be enforced against a wife, the House of Lords recognised that, although advice from a completely independent solicitor would be ideal, '[t]he advantages attendant upon the employment of a solicitor acting solely for the wife do not justify the additional expense this would involve for the husband': *Royal Bank of Scotland v Etridge* at AC 810; All ER 471–2. However, if 'there are any facts known to the bank which increase the inherent risk that the wife's consent to the transaction may have been procured by the husband's undue influence or misrepresentation, it may be necessary for the bank to be satisfied

---

5. This part of the decision in this case was not reported in the New South Wales Law Reports citation referred to in 10.67 above.

that the wife has received advice about the transaction from a solicitor independent of the husband before the bank can reasonably rely on the wife's apparent consent': *Royal Bank of Scotland v Etridge* at AC 850; All ER 510.

10.76 Ogilvie has summarised the effect of the House of Lords decision as follows:

> [T]o be relieved from potential tainting by the husband's conduct, all the bank need do is require a certificate that independent legal advice has been given. Where the advice is poor, or the wife signs nevertheless, either the lawyer or the wife, respectively, must bear the loss.[6]

As Dal Pont suggests, '*Etridge* may herald a shift in focus from creditors, whose duties are clear, to solicitors, whose task is potentially more complex, thus making solicitors more likely targets for litigation'.[7]

REMEDIES

10.77 The principal remedy for undue influence is that of rescinding the contract or transaction and for the defendant to account for any profits (see 30.25–30.31) gained from the transaction: *Mahoney v Purnell* [1996] 3 All ER 61 at 88. However, rescission will not always be available: see 27.24–27.43. In some cases equitable compensation (see 26.2–26.38) will be ordered (*Hartigan v International Society for Krishna Consciousness* at [98]), or a remedial constructive trust (see Chapter 28) imposed: *McCulloch v Fern* [2001] NSWSC 406 at [118]. If the contract or transaction is yet to be performed, then specific performance will not be available: see 23.60.

RELATED DOCTRINES

10.78 It would be remiss not to acknowledge the place of undue influence in the wider context of equitable doctrine generally. Undue influence also has a strong connection to the principles relevant to fiduciary obligations: see Chapter 9. The importance of relationships to each is the cause of significant overlap, despite the fact that 'trustee and beneficiary' is better viewed as not being a special relationship for the purpose of presuming undue influence: see 10.23.

10.79 The doctrine of undue influence may seem to be a rather old-fashioned legal device, often overshadowed in Australia by fiduciary duties and the strides made in the area of unconscionable transactions: see Chapter 11. The latter's focus upon the transaction at hand rather than the relationship that surrounds it has meant that, by comparison, undue influence is perceived as difficult for an applicant to make out, despite any assistance provided by the presumptions which may be made in his or her favour. When one considers the doctrine alongside the statutory remedies provided by the *Australian Consumer Law* and in particular, in New South Wales, the far-ranging *Contracts Review Act 1980*, its usefulness seems yet more limited.

---

6. M H Ogilvie, 'The Reception of Etridge (No 2) in Canada' [2008] *Journal of Business Law* 191, p 194.
7. G E Dal Pont, *Equity and Trusts in Australia*, 5th ed, Lawbook Co, Sydney, 2011, p 250. For a discussion on the issue of the lender being able to rely on explanations of guarantee entered into by a wife see M Brown, 'The Bank, the Wife and the Husband's Solicitor' (2007) 14 *Australian Property Law Journal* 147.

Part IV:
Unconscientious Dealings

11

UNCONSCIONABLE TRANSACTIONS

INTRODUCTION

11.1   The doctrine of unconscionable transactions has acquired great significance in Australian law and acts as a powerful bulwark against injustices that can arise under the formalist approach of the common law. Pursuant to the doctrine of unconscionability, equitable relief is given where there has been 'an abuse of power possessed by one party over the other by virtue of the other's position of special disadvantage': *Australian Competition and Consumer Commission v Radio Rentals Ltd* (2005) 146 FCR 292 at 297. In *Johnson v Smith* [2010] NSWCA 306 at [5], Allsop J said that such an abuse of power could occur 'because of the unconscientious use of power arising or existing in the circumstances or … the unconscientious attempt to retain the benefit obtained from the person with the special disadvantage'. In *Louth v Diprose* (1992) 175 CLR 621 at 638; 110 ALR 1 at 14, Deane J observed that 'the intervention of equity is not merely to relieve the plaintiff from the consequences of his own foolishness. It is to prevent victimisation'. In exercising its jurisdiction here, an equity court looks beyond the fiction of equality of bargaining power that the common law takes for granted.

11.2   The growth of the doctrine of unconscionability has been significant since the High Court decision of *Commercial Bank of Australia v Amadio* (1983) 151 CLR 447; 46 ALR 402, and it is suitably flexible to apply to all transactions regardless of the length of dealing or relationship which exists between the parties. The doctrine is thus much more accessible than that relating to undue influence. Nevertheless, there is a distinct connection between the two doctrines and they may both arise from the same facts. The Australian courts' propensity to offer relief using this equitable doctrine has also been matched by the introduction of several legislative enactments giving wide powers to the courts to respond to contracts made with an absence of good conscience.

11.3   It is important to appreciate the subtleties of terminology if confusion is to be avoided. It has often been said that the very nature of equity is founded upon good conscience and that the notion of unconscionability is a theme that runs throughout its entire jurisdiction and exists in numerous forms and contexts. However, in *Tanwar Enterprises Pty Ltd v Cauchi* (2003) 217 CLR 315 at 324–5; 201 ALR 359 at 364–5, the High Court held that 'unconscientious' is a more accurate term than 'unconscionable' in this context: see 2.5. For the purposes of this chapter unconscionability is used in the specific sense relating to transactions involving the knowing exploitation by one party of a special disadvantage of another.

ELEMENTS OF UNCONSCIONABLE TRANSACTIONS

11.4   Equity's ability to strike down transactions tainted by unconscionability has existed for, and been developed over, many years, but the significance of the High Court's recent work in this area is that it has given a definite framework to the application of the doctrine. In *CBA v Amadio*, at CLR 474; ALR 422, Deane J said:

> The jurisdiction is long established as extending generally to circumstances in which (i) a party to a transaction was under a special disability in dealing with the other party with the consequence that there was an absence of any reasonable degree of equality between them and (ii) that disability was sufficiently evident to the stronger party to make it prima facie unfair or 'unconscientious' that he procure, or accept, the weaker party's assent to the impugned transaction in the circumstances in which he procured or accepted it. Where such circumstances are shown to have existed, an onus is cast upon the stronger party to show that the transaction was fair, just and reasonable.

11.5   Other judges have given expression to the doctrine but the variations between formulations are not substantial. The essential elements are, as Deane J identifies:

1. A is under a special disadvantage or disability;
2. B knew, or is likely to have known, about that disadvantage; and
3. B proceeds to use that disadvantage unconscientiously in order to obtain A's consent to the transaction.

In many cases of unconscionable transactions, there is an inadequacy of consideration. In relation to this situation, in *Blomley v Ryan* (1956) 99 CLR 362 at 405, Fullagar J said:

> [I]nadequacy of consideration, while never of itself a ground for resisting enforcement, will often be a specially important element in cases of this type. It may be important in either or both of two ways — firstly as supporting the inference that a position of disadvantage existed, and secondly as tending to show that an unfair use was made of the occasion.

11.6   Before analysing each of these elements, it is appropriate to note the following general observations in relation to unconscionability made by Spigelman CJ in *Attorney General (NSW) v World Best Holdings Ltd* (2005) 63 NSWLR 557 at 583:

> Unconscionability is a well-established but narrow principle in equitable doctrine. It has been applied over the centuries with considerable restraint and in a manner which is consistent with the maintenance of the basic principles of freedom of contract. It is not a principle of what 'fairness' or 'justice' or 'good conscience' requires in the particular circumstances of the case … [R]estraint in decision-making remains appropriate. Unconscionability is a concept which requires a high level of moral obloquy. If it were to be applied as if it were equivalent to what was 'fair' or 'just', it could transform commercial relationships … The principle of 'unconscionability' would not be a doctrine of occasional application, when the circumstances are highly unethical, it would be transformed into the first and easiest port of call when any dispute … arises.

As was pointed out by Edelman J in *Anderson v McPherson (No 2)* [2012] WASC 19 at [255], '[t]he object of the doctrine [of unconscionability] is not to protect people from the consequences of their own mistakes'. Thus, in *Kakavas v Crown Melbourne Limited* [2012] VSCA 95, a casino was held not to be liable on principles of unconscionability in relation to losses incurred by a problem gambler.

11.7 Practical recognition of these observations can be seen in the fact that mere inequality of bargaining power between parties does not give rise to a situation of unconscionability. In *Australian Competition and Consumer Commission v C G Berbatis Holdings Pty Ltd* (2003) 214 CLR 51 at 64; 197 ALR 153 at 157, Gleeson CJ said:

> A person is not in a position of relevant disadvantage ... simply because of inequality of bargaining power. Many, perhaps even most, contracts are made between parties of unequal bargaining power, and good conscience does not require parties to contractual negotiations to forfeit their advantages, or neglect their own interests ... Unconscientious exploitation of another's inability, or diminished ability, to conserve his or her own interests is not to be confused with taking advantage of a superior bargaining position.

11.8 Furthermore, in commercial contracts, the availability of relief on the basis of principles of unconscionable transactions is limited. In *FMT Aircraft Gate Support Systems v Sydney Ports Corporation* [2010] NSWSC 1108 at [35], Pembroke J said:

> Caution is required when equitable principles are sought to be imposed on well resourced and well advised commercial parties. In any given case, there might possibly be a proper basis to put submissions based on the equitable doctrine of unconscionability ... However, the opportunities will be limited. That is because the state of affairs on which the application of equitable doctrines is usually predicated — vulnerability, dependence, mistaken assumption or inducement — will rarely exist in such circumstances.

11.9 In assessing whether any transaction is unconscionable, the relevant time frame is when the transaction was entered into. This is of particular importance in relation to conditional contracts. In *Gustav & Co Ltd v Macfield Limited* [2008] 2 NZLR 735 at 741, the New Zealand Supreme Court held that the appropriate time to assess whether a conditional contract was unconscionable was when the contract was entered into and not when it became, or was declared, unconditional. However, the court, at 745, went on to note that 'material variations to a contract should be examined for unconscionability as at the date upon which they are agreed'.

Special disadvantage or disability

11.10 There is no fixed list of what constitutes a special disadvantage. What is required is some characteristic 'which seriously affects the ability of the innocent party to make a judgment as to his own best interests': *CBA v Amadio* at CLR 462; ALR 413.

11.11 In *Australian Competition and Consumer Commission v Samton Holdings Pty Ltd* (2002) 117 FCR 301 at 318; 189 ALR 76 at 92, the Full Court of the Federal Court stated that factors going to establishing a special disadvantage fell into one of two categories: 'constitutional' and 'situational'. The court said:

> The special disadvantage may be constitutional, deriving from age, illness, poverty, inexperience or lack of education. Or it may be situational, deriving from particular features of a relationship between actors in the transaction such as the emotional dependence of one on the other.

11.12 However, as was pointed out by Gleeson CJ in *ACCC v Berbatis Holdings*, at CLR 63; ALR 157, as useful as such categorisation of special disadvantage may be, '[t]here is a risk that categories, adopted as a convenient method of exposition of an underlying principle, might be misunderstood, and come to supplant the principle. The stream of judicial exposition of principle cannot rise above the source'.

11.13 Bearing in mind Gleeson CJ's caveat, examples of constitutional factors that can lead to establishing a special constitutional disadvantage were set out by Fullagar J in *Blomley v Ryan* at 405, as follows:

> The circumstances adversely affecting a party, which may induce a court of equity either to refuse its aid or to set a transaction aside, are of great variety and can hardly be satisfactorily classified. Among them are poverty or need of any kind, sickness, age, sex, infirmity of body or mind, drunkenness, illiteracy or lack of education, lack of assistance or explanation where assistance or explanation is necessary. The common characteristic is that they have the effect of placing one party at a disadvantage vis-à-vis the other.

The mere presence of one or more of these characteristics in a party to a transaction will not automatically amount to a special disadvantage in all cases. As Fullagar J states, what is required is that the characteristic amounts to a position of disadvantage as against the other party. Thus, as was pointed out by Edelman J in *Anderson v McPherson (No 2)* at [265]:

> It is clear that a person could be ill, or poor, or even 'affected by delusions' but still be perfectly capable of making a judgment as to his or her own best interests. Nor will a person even in a greatly inferior bargaining position necessarily lack capacity to make a judgment about that person's own best interests.

In *Hampton v BHP Billiton Minerals Pty Ltd (No 2)* [2012] WASC 285 at [179], Edelman J also noted that '[l]eaving school at an early age is not an established special disability'.

11.14 The personal circumstances of two guarantors in the cornerstone case of *CBA v Amadio* involved a number of characteristics that amounted to placing them in a position of special disadvantage. The facts of this case concerned a son's failing building business. He arranged to obtain further finance from the Commercial Bank of Australia to a total value of $270,000. In order to receive this increase on his company's overdraft, the son was required by the bank to arrange for a guarantee. The son approached his parents (the Amadios) who were elderly Italian migrants with a limited grasp of English. He told them that he needed them to execute a contract of guarantee in favour of the bank that would be limited to $50,000 and six months' operation. The Amadios agreed to this. In fact, when the bank manager arrived at their home in order for them to execute a deed of mortgage over that property, its terms were not limited to any amount or time period. Although the issue of time length was discussed at this meeting, there was no doubt that the Amadios were unsure as to the nature and extent of their liability under the contract. The bank manager was aware of the virtually hopeless state of the son's business but did not make inquiries as to whether his parents also appreciated this situation. Nor did he or the son suggest that the Amadios receive independent advice about the providence of the transaction. The Amadios executed the deed and the bank sought to recover against them when their son's business collapsed. They sought to avoid the contract on the basis of unconscionability.

11.15 The High Court found for the Amadios, with a majority (Mason, Wilson and Deane JJ) basing their decision upon principles of unconscionability. Their Honours viewed the Amadios as being at a special disadvantage for a number of reasons. In this respect, Deane J, at CLR 476; ALR 424, said:

> The bank ... was a major national financial institution. It was privy to the business affairs and financial instability of Amadio Builders ... It had actually suggested, through Mr Statton, that Mr and Mrs Amadio enter into the mortgage transaction to secure Amadio Builders' indebtedness to it. It was aware of the contents of its own document which Mr Virgo presented to Mr and Mrs Amadio for their signature. In contrast was the position of Mr and Mrs Amadio. Their personal circumstances have already been mentioned. They were advanced in years. Their grasp of written English was limited. They relied on [their son] for the management of their business affairs and believed that he and Amadio Builders were prosperous and successful. They were approached in their kitchen by the bank, acting through Mr Virgo, at a time when Mr Amadio was reading the newspaper after lunch and Mrs Amadio was washing dishes. They were presented with a complicated and lengthy document for their immediate signature. They had received no independent advice in relation to the transaction which that document embodied and about which they had learned only hours earlier from [their son] who ... had misled them as regards the extent and duration of their potential liability under it. Apart from indicating that the guarantee/mortgage was unlimited in point of time, Mr Virgo made no personal attempt to explain it to them.

11.16 It should be noted that the circumstances of the Amadios went beyond mere inequality of position. It will be rare for both parties to a transaction to come to the negotiating table in a state of perfect equality. Special circumstances are required to warrant equitable intervention. This was emphasised by Mason J in *CBA v Amadio*, at CLR 462; ALR 413, when he said that the purpose of qualifying 'disadvantage' by the adjective 'special' was to 'disavow any suggestion that the principle applies whenever there is some difference in the bargaining power of the parties'. Thus, the High Court rejected the suggestion made by Lord Denning MR in the English case of *Lloyds Bank Ltd v Bundy* [1975] QB 326; [1974] 3 All ER 757 that such inequality may be a basis for equitable relief. The House of Lords has also dismissed such a fluid and unworkable role for equity: *National Westminster Bank Plc v Morgan* [1985] 1 AC 686; [1985] 1 All ER 821.

11.17 The situation of the Amadios was not simply one of inequality — though that description was clearly apt. However, most individuals suffer from a power imbalance when contracting with financial institutions. In requiring something stronger, Mason J, at CLR 462; ALR 413, insisted that 'the disabling condition or circumstance [be] one which seriously affects the ability of the innocent party to make a judgment as to his own best interests'. The combination of factors present in the case had that effect.

11.18 In relation to situational special disadvantage, the decision of the High Court in *Louth v Diprose* is instructive. In that case, the transaction under review was a gift of $58,000 from Diprose to Louth in order that she could purchase a house in which to live with her children. Diprose was romantically infatuated with Louth and despite her disinterest they maintained contact over the course of seven years. During that time they had sexual intercourse only twice in the early months. Louth made it clear she was not possessed of similar feelings for Diprose and in fact had relationships with other men. The parties did not live together but when Louth moved to Adelaide, he followed her. Diprose spent time at Louth's house and provided financial assistance and help to her generally. She rented a house at a reduced rate from her sister and brother-in-law. When that couple announced an intention to separate, the brother-in-law suggested to Louth that she might have to pay a more realistic amount of rent or look for alternative accommodation. Louth was unsettled by this development and told Diprose that if she were forced to move from the house she would commit suicide. It was after this conversation that Diprose made the gift of money to her, despite the fact that the sum comprised most of his own holdings and he had children of his own to support. Diprose subsequently brought an action to claim the beneficial interest in the property that Louth had purchased with the money he gave her. The High Court found in his favour on the ground that the transaction should be set aside as unconscionable.

11.19   A bare assessment of the parties' positions did not portray Diprose as being specially disadvantaged. On the contrary, he seemed to be the stronger of the two, as Toohey J, at CLR 651; ALR 24, was keen to highlight in his vigorous dissent:

> It was [Diprose] who continued to seek her out. She did not mislead him in regard to her position; she did not hold out any false hopes to him. They were both adults; each had been married before … and [Diprose] was a practising solicitor who must have appreciated fully the consequences that the law would ordinarily attach to the gifts he made to [Louth] including the money involved in the purchase of the Tranmere house. It was [Diprose's] idea to buy the house, not [Louth's].

11.20   However, the majority did not look at the facts in the same light as Toohey J, but rather focused upon Diprose's infatuation, as the lower courts had done before them. Deane J, at CLR 638; ALR 14, described the situation as follows:

> [The] special disability arose not merely from [Diprose's] infatuation. It extended to the extraordinary vulnerability of [Diprose] in the false 'atmosphere of crisis' in which he believed that the woman with whom he was 'completely in love' and upon whom he was emotionally dependent was facing eviction from her home and suicide unless he provided the money for the purchase of the house. [Louth] was aware of that special disability. Indeed, to a significant extent, she had deliberately created it. She manipulated it to her advantage to influence [Diprose] to make the gift of the money to purchase the house.

11.21   Throughout the case, reference is repeatedly made to the 'emotional dependence' and 'infatuation' of Diprose, but it is clear from many judgments (as it is from the above quote) that it was the 'manipulation' of this situation by Louth that gave Diprose's unrequited love its status as a 'special disadvantage'. While the other party's behaviour is obviously relevant to the later elements of the unconscionability doctrine, reference to it at the initial stage of determining the 'special disadvantage' of a plaintiff would seem to be at odds with the previous case law. However, where the special disadvantage derives from a relationship, such considerations would seem to be necessary and valid.

Knowledge

11.22   It is clear that the defendant must have known or ought to have known of the special disadvantage of the other party. The requirement of knowledge is necessary because the defendant cannot be said to have acted unconscientiously if he or she had no knowledge of the plaintiff's special disadvantage. In *CBA v Amadio*, at CLR 467; ALR 417, Mason J said:

[I]f A having actual knowledge that B occupies a situation of special disadvantage in relation to an intended transaction, so that B cannot make a judgment as to what is in his own interests, takes unfair advantage of his (A's) superior bargaining power or position by entering into that transaction, his conduct in so doing is unconscionable. And if, instead of having actual knowledge of that situation, A is aware of the possibility that that situation may exist or is aware of facts that would raise that possibility in the mind of any reasonable person, the result will be the same.

In the same case, Deane J, at CLR 474; ALR 422, said:

[Was the] disability … sufficiently evident to the stronger party to make it prima facie unfair or 'unconscientious' that he procure, or accept, the weaker party's assent to the impugned transaction in the circumstances in which he procured or accepted it.

11.23   In relation to the subject of the required knowledge, in *ACCC v Radio Rentals*, at 298, Finn J said:

It is knowledge of a particular state of affairs which itself embodies a judgment as to the disabled party's ability to conserve his or her own affairs in the parties' dealing. It is that state of affairs which is to be 'sufficiently evident' to the stronger party. If that person does not actually know of that state of affairs and is not 'wilfully ignorant' of it (in the sense that he or she is intent on not knowing it despite what is evident to him or her: cf *Owen and Gutch v Homan* (1853) 4 HLC 997 at 1035), that person must at least be aware of circumstances that would cause him or her or a reasonable person in his or her position to suspect from what is evident that that state of affairs may exist.

11.24   It is rare for knowledge to pose much difficulty for an applicant, as the circumstances will normally be so clear that the constructive knowledge of the other party is easily established. The facts of *CBA v Amadio* (see 11.14) are a good example of the stronger party having sufficient awareness of the various weaknesses present in the other. The bank in that case had actual knowledge of the commercial risk that the guarantee posed to the Amadios. It also had constructive knowledge of their inability to fully comprehend this risk due to their poor language skills, advanced age, and misrepresentations by their son in whom they clearly reposed a high level of trust.

11.25   The facts of *Louth v Diprose* (see 11.18) were more pronounced — there, it was beyond doubt that Louth was aware of the infatuation of Diprose. His dogged persistence in pursuit of her affections for seven years made that only too plain. The finding of actual knowledge in this case led the court to its acceptance of the portrayal of Louth as a woman who 'manipulated' the situation by the creation of an 'atmosphere of crisis'.

11.26   In this vein, the facts of *Blomley v Ryan* demonstrate another instance of actual knowledge. Ryan was an elderly sheep farmer who sold his property at a significant undervalue to Blomley, a neighbouring grazier. The negotiations with Ryan were conducted by Blomley and his agent, the manager of the area's stock and station store. The court found that Ryan had a well-known fondness for liquor and both Blomley and his agent knew of his regular indulgence in drinking bouts. Indeed, the agent sold him his rum through his store. At the time Ryan was called upon to negotiate with the others, he had been drinking heavily for days. He looked extremely old and sick according to most witnesses. Yet, neither Blomley nor the agent claimed to have noticed anything untoward. The court greeted their ignorance with extreme disbelief and readily found that they did, in fact, have actual knowledge of Ryan's disadvantage. Of particular significance in reaching this conclusion was the fact that Blomley and his agent had produced a bottle of rum at the negotiations, which took place during the afternoon on the relevant day. Thus, they had indicated their knowledge of Ryan's fondness for drink and had actually assisted him to reach the intoxicated state under which he made the unfavourable transaction. The High Court refused to grant specific performance to Blomley on the ground that the contract was unconscionable. Ryan's drunkenness was not viewed as an incapacity to contract but rather as a characteristic causing weakness, which was known and exploited by Blomley. This exploitation was apparent from the highly favourable terms received by Blomley and the corresponding improvidence of the transaction for Ryan.

11.27 In the case of *Elkofairi v Permanent Trustee Co Ltd* [2002] NSWCA 413, the issue of the defendant's knowledge arose in the context of a case involving the practice commonly known as asset lending. Asset lending was described by Basten JA in *Perpetual Trustee Company Ltd v Khoshaba* [2006] NSWCA 41 at [128] as being 'to lend money without regard to the ability of the borrower to repay by instalments under the contract, in the knowledge that adequate security is available in the event of default'. In *Elkofairi v Permanent Trustee Co Ltd*, the lender was found to be aware that Mrs Elkofairi had no income and that the loan was for a large amount and secured over her only asset. The lender had made virtually no enquiries relating to the purpose of the loan. The lender, who knew that Mrs Elkofairi had not received any legal advice about the loan, did not make any enquiries of Mrs Elkofairi's income or capacity to service the loan. Speaking for the Court of Appeal, Beazley JA, at [55], noted that these circumstances should have 'sounded a warning bell' to the lender. Her Honour, at [56], in finding that the lender had knowledge of Mrs Elkofairi's special disadvantage, said:

> In my opinion, notwithstanding that the [lender] did not have knowledge of the [Mrs Elkofairi's] lack of education and her language and domestic difficulties, her lack of income, in the circumstances of this transaction — that is a large borrowing secured over her only asset, in circumstances where the application form failed to disclose any income for either husband or wife — placed her in a special position of disadvantage. Though the full extent of that special position of disadvantage was not known to the [lender], nonetheless the absence of any relevant financial information was sufficient to put the respondent on notice of [Mrs Elkofairi's] lack of capacity to meet the repayment obligations under the mortgage. That left as the only source of repayment the selling of her only asset, as again the [lender] must be taken to have known.

Although the court found that the loan was unconscionable, the courts have made it clear that asset lending *per se* does not give rise to an unconscionable transaction. Other factors have to be present: *Kowalczuk v Accom Finance Pty Ltd* (2008) 77 NSWLR 205 at 227; 252 ALR 55 at 76–7. Furthermore, in cases where asset lending is found to constitute an unconscionable transaction 'relief setting aside a mortgage … will usually be granted only on condition that the mortgagor do equity by paying or securing to the mortgagee the amount of any benefit obtained by the mortgagor from the relevant mortgage advance': *Butler v Vavladelis* [2012] VSC 186 at [17].

Unconscionable exploitation of the disadvantage

11.28 A special disadvantage, and the other party's knowledge of it, does not make a transaction unconscionable. It is the third element which crystallises these two factors into a situation where equitable relief is merited. The stronger party must exploit the weakness that he or she knows to exist in the other in order to procure consent to a transaction. Inequality of bargaining power will often be a factor to be taken into account in assessing whether the stronger party has taken advantage of the weaker party's special disability.

11.29 In cases where the elements of special disadvantage and knowledge have been established, and the transaction is shown to be improvident, there arises 'an equitable presumption to the effect that the improvident transaction was a consequence of the special disadvantage, and that the defendant has unconscientiously taken advantage of the opportunity presented by the disadvantage': *Turner v Windever* [2003] NSWSC 1147 at [106] (a decision upheld on appeal: *Turner v Windever* [2005] NSWCA 73). However, a transaction may still be unconscionable even if it is not improvident.

11.30 The three cases discussed so far amply demonstrate the requirement of unconscionable exploitation of the disadvantage. In *CBA v Amadio* (see 11.14) the Amadios' special disadvantage was knowingly used to procure them into signing a contract of guarantee, which was not limited by time or extent of liability, to secure a loan to their son who was in serious financial trouble. In *Louth v Diprose* (see 11.18) the infatuated Diprose made a gift of $58,000 to Louth so that she could purchase a house. In *Blomley v Ryan* (see 11.26), the drunken Ryan sold his entire landholding to Blomley at a price described by McTiernan J, at 392, as 'strikingly disproportionate' to the estimated market value.

11.31 In none of these cases did the weaker party agree to a transaction that was in their best interests. In all of them, the courts found that the stronger party had used his or her position of strength to gain the agreement of the other. This is the kernel of the doctrine of unconscionability and what attracts equity's intervention.

DEFENCES

11.32 As always, a successful defence will challenge one or more of the assertions made by the party seeking relief. The most likely ground for defence is to rebut the argument that the transaction was unfair or that the special disadvantage was exploited. However, the defence need not focus solely upon the third element. It will be recalled that the most contentious issue in *Louth v Diprose* (see 11.18) was whether an unrequited romantic infatuation was a 'special disadvantage', and it was in fact on this point, more than any other, that Toohey J's dissent would seem to rest. In regard to knowledge, the suggestion was made above that it would be difficult to reject the proposition that this has been made out by the applicant simply because the court will consider whether the circumstances demonstrate constructive knowledge.

11.33 In rejecting the element of unconscionability, the stronger party may point to a number of things in his or her defence. In showing that the special disadvantage was not exploited, the provision of assistance to the weaker party will be crucial. In the case of the Amadios, for example, the language assistance that an interpreter would have provided would have helped in rebuttal. The provision of independent advice generally will be the most significant defence in any case. That is not to say that independent advice will always exonerate the stronger party. Although in *Blomley v Ryan* the same solicitor acted for both vendor and purchaser in executing the unfavourable contract, the state of Ryan, the behaviour of Blomley up to that point and the improvidence of the deal would be unlikely to be of no consequence, even if independent advice had been given. Just as with instances of undue influence, independent advice will go a long way to showing freedom of consent and lack of exploitation, but ultimately the outcome of any given case will depend upon the quality of the advice given in the light all the surrounding circumstances: *Bester v Perpetual Trustee Co Ltd* [1970] 3 NSWR 30: see 10.39.

11.34   The improvidence or otherwise of the transaction will also be of importance. In the case of a non-guarantee contract this factor raises the question of adequacy of consideration. Where the transaction is a gift, or a guarantee contract, then there is no obvious benefit to the party giving, so improvidence must be looked at against their total interests. In both *CBA v Amadio* (see 11.14) and *Louth v Diprose* (see 11.18) the weaker party could ill afford the benefit they were seeking to transfer, by guarantee and gift respectively. Thus, the other party in each case failed to establish a defence of lack of unconscionable exploitation — all the evidence pointed in that direction.

11.35   Finally, as with all other equitable remedies, relief may be denied if a party can raise an equitable defence such as laches (see 31.13–31.22) or other equitable misconduct that amounts to a failure to come to equity with clean hands: see 31.8–31.12.

REMEDIES

11.36   A party who successfully raises the doctrine of unconscionability will usually seek to avoid the transaction. This may occur in a number of ways. He or she may do so by means of resisting the stronger party's action for specific performance of the contract, as occurred in *Blomley v Ryan*: see 11.25–11.26. Alternatively, he or she may seek the return of property by rescission of the impugned transaction: see Chapter 27.

11.37   However, in some situations other equitable remedies will be available. Thus, in *CBA v Amadio* at CLR 481; ALR 428 the option of imposing conditions upon an order for rescission was discussed and, in *Schipp v Cameron* [1998] NSWSC 997, equitable compensation was ordered.

STATUTORY UNCONSCIONABILITY PURSUANT TO THE AUSTRALIAN CONSUMER LAW

11.38   The area of unconscionability is one in which statute meets and complements the judge-made law to dramatic effect. The federal, state and territory legislatures have all enacted legislation which covers unconscionable conduct and/or related concepts dealing with what might generally be referred to as unfair conduct. This chapter will only discuss the unconscionability provisions set out in the *Australian Consumer Law* (ACL).[1] The provisions of the ACL are set out in Schedule 2 of the *Competition and Consumer Act 2010* (Cth) (CCA).[2] The unconscionability provisions of the ACL are found in ss 20, 21 and 22. These sections were previously enacted as s 51AA, s 51AB and s 51AC of the *Trade Practices Act 1974* (Cth) (TPA). Section 131A(1) of the CCA stipulates that the provision of financial services or products are not subject to the ACL. However, financial services and products are regulated by ss 12CA, 12CB and 12CC of the *Australian Securities and Investments Commission Act 2001* (Cth) (ASIC Act) which mirror the provisions of ss 20–21 of the ACL. In *Tonto*

---

1.   Examples of other relevant legislation include the *Independent Contractors Act 2006* (Cth); the *Contracts Review Act 1980* (NSW); s 106 of the *Industrial Relations Act 1996* (NSW). Furthermore, consumer credit legislation in all states and territories contain provisions dealing with unjust transactions, 'unjust' being defined to include 'unconscionable, harsh or oppressive'.

2.   Prior to 2010 the *Competition and Consumer Act 2010* (Cth) was known as the *Trade Practices Act 1974* (Cth).

Home Loans Australia Pty Ltd v Tavares [2011] NSWCA 389 at [290], Allsop P observed that 'the context of "unconscionable" in the *ASIC Act* does not give it a distinct or different meaning from its equivalent provisions in the [ACL]. All [these] ... provisions have similar purposes in the protection of consumers and the promotion of just and fair markets'.

11.39 The unconscionability provisions of the ACL relate to the actions of persons. Pursuant to Australian constitutional law, the Commonwealth government's competence to legislate in relation to unconscionable conduct is confined to doing so in relation to persons who are corporations. In relation to persons who are not corporations such legislative competence rests with the various States and Territories. Although the provisions of the ACL do effectively cover unconscionable conduct by any person, s 131(1) of the CCA confines the application of the ACL as a law of the Commonwealth to the activities of corporations. In relation to unconscionable conduct by persons who are not corporations, the provisions of the ACL are enforced as a law of the State or Territory where such conduct occurred. This stems from the fact that all States and Territories have passed legislation adopting the provisions of the ACL as part of their law. Thus, depending upon the nature of the person engaged in unconscionable conduct, the provisions of the ACL will be enforced either as a law of the Commonwealth or as a law of the relevant State or Territory.

11.40 As noted above, ss 20–22 of the ACL relate to the conduct of persons 'in trade or commerce'. Section 2 of the ACL defines 'trade or commerce' as meaning '(a) trade or commerce within Australia or (b) between Australia and places outside Australia; and includes any business or professional activity (whether or not carried on for profit)'.

11.41 In *Concrete Constructions (NSW) Pty Ltd v Nelson* (1990) 169 CLR 594 at 603–4; 92 ALR 193 at 197, the majority of the High Court gave the following interpretation to the meaning of the words 'in trade or commerce':

> [T]he reference to conduct 'in trade or commerce' ... can be construed as referring only to conduct which is itself an aspect or element of activities or transactions which, of their nature, bear a trading or commercial character. So construed, to borrow and adapt words used by Dixon J ... in *Bank of NSW v The Commonwealth* (1948) 76 CLR 1, at p 381, the words 'in trade or commerce' refer to 'the central conception' of trade or commerce and not to the 'immense field of activities' in which [persons] may engage in the course of, or for the purposes of, carrying on some overall trading or commercial business ... [The words relate to] the conduct of a [person] towards persons, be they consumers or not, with whom it ... has or may have dealings in the course of those activities or transactions which, of their nature, bear a trading or commercial character ... In some areas, the dividing line between what is and what is not conduct 'in trade or commerce' may be less clear and may require the identification of what imports a trading or commercial character to an activity which is not, without more, of that character.

11.42 The major purpose of unconscionability provisions of the ACL is to provide a greater and more flexible range of remedies to aggrieved parties than is available pursuant to general law principles: *ACCC v Berbatis Holdings* at CLR 83; ALR 173. It is important to note that the legislative initiatives in this area do not render the equitable doctrine of unconscionable conduct redundant. While litigants may prefer the remedial flexibility of the various statutes, they still have the option of pursuing relief under the equitable principles.

11.43   The critical issue, however, with the three statutory unconscionability sections is to what extent, if any, the meaning of unconscionable conduct in each of them is broader than that pursuant to equitable principles. In relation to s 20, this is a matter of some dispute. However, it is clear that the notion of unconscionable conduct under ss 21 and 22 is broader than unconscionable conduct in equity: *Australian Competition and Consumer Commission v Simply No-Knead (Franchising) Pty Ltd* (2000) 104 FCR 253 at 265; 178 ALR 304 at 315; *Canon Australia Pty Ltd v Patton* (2007) 244 ALR 759 at 767–9.

11.44   It should also be noted that s 20(2) of the ACL states that the prohibition set out in s 20(1) does not apply to conduct prohibited by ss 21 or 22. Thus, if conduct is caught by either ss 21 or 22, no action can be pursued under s 20.

Unconscionable conduct pursuant to the unwritten law — s 20

11.45   Section 20(1) stipulates as follows:

> A person must not, in trade or commerce, engage in conduct that is unconscionable, within the meaning of the unwritten law from time to time.

11.46   The reference to 'unwritten law' is a reference to the judge-made law of unconscionability, which the Commonwealth seeks to harness to the section without the risk of modifying it in any way through an attempt at expressing what it might mean. The Explanatory Memorandum to s 20 when originally enacted as s 51AA of the TPA states that the section 'embodies the equitable concept of unconscionable conduct as recognised by the High Court in *Blomley v Ryan* and *Commercial Bank of Australia v Amadio*'.

11.47   The critical question in relation to s 20 relates to whether or not its reference to unconscionable conduct extends beyond that associated with the conduct caught by the equitable principle of unconscionability discussed above.

11.48   In *ACCC v Samton Holdings* at FCR 317; ALR 91, the court identified the following four ways in which unconscionable conduct has been used in the case law:

1. As an organising idea informing specific equitable rules and doctrines which do not in terms refer to, or require, an explicit finding of unconscionable conduct — eg rules on stipulations as to time and notices to complete.
2. In relation to specific equitable doctrines of which estoppel, unilateral mistake, relief against forfeiture and undue influence are examples. They are united by the idea that equity will prevent an unconscionable insistence on strict legal rights and are conditioned upon the explicit finding of unconscionable conduct in the persons against whom they are invoked.
3. In relation to the discrete doctrine of unconscionable dealing which concerns one species of unconscionable conduct.
4. In relation to unconscionable conduct founding a cause of action not mediated by any discrete doctrine.

11.49   The first category is simply a reflection of the general nature of equity (see 2.4), and it has no relevance as to the meaning of unconscionable conduct in s 20. In relation to the fourth category, it too is not a basis for defining unconscionable conduct in the context of s 20. As the court in *Samton*, at FCR 319; ALR 93, observed, 'equitable doctrine does not presently provide a remedy against conduct simply on the basis that it is unfair in the opinion of a judge. It cannot be applied to unconscionable conduct at large'. The court held that the second and third ways in which unconscionability has been used in the case law come under the 'rubric of unconscionable conduct' caught by s 20. The court, at FCR 318; ALR 92, held that, at the very least, under this rubric of unconscionable conduct, equity will:

(i) Set aside a contract or disposition resulting from the knowing exploitation by one party of the special disadvantage of another. The special disadvantage may be constitutional, deriving from age, illness, poverty, inexperience or lack of education. Or it may be situational, deriving from particular features of a relationship between actors in the transaction such as the emotional dependence of one on the other. (ii) Set aside as against third parties a transaction entered into as the result of the defective comprehension by a party to the transaction, the influence of another and the want of any independent explanation to the complaining party. (iii) Prevent a party from exercising a legal right in a way that involves unconscionable departure from a representation relied upon by another to his or her detriment. (iv) Relieve against forfeiture and penalty. (v) Rescind contracts entered into under the influence of unilateral mistake.

11.50 The first category refers to the traditional equitable understanding of unconscionability discussed above and there is no doubt that it comes within the meaning of unconscionable conduct in s 20. This is confirmed by the High Court decision in *ACCC v Berbatis Holdings*. However, in that case the High Court, at CLR 74, 114; ALR 165, 199, left open the question whether unconscionable conduct in s 20 extended to four other categories of conduct listed in *ACCC v Samton Holdings*.

11.51 The facts of *ACCC v Berbatis Holdings* concerned the desire by lessees (Mr and Mrs Roberts) of premises in a shopping centre to renew or extend their lease in order that they could make an advantageous sale of their business. The lessees were keen to do so, as their daughter suffered from a serious illness and they felt unable to keep their business going and provide her with sufficient care. Their existing lease made no provision for renewal or extension and so the Roberts were required to negotiate with the lessors to this end. The lessors agreed to the granting of a new lease, enabling the sale of the business by the Roberts, but as a condition of doing so, required the Roberts to abandon a legal claim against the lessors based upon overcharging of centre management fees. The Roberts were uncomfortable about surrendering this claim, which other tenants in the centre were also making, believing it entitled them to approximately $50,000. However, they did so, secured the new lease and sold their business. Although settlement of the tenants' claim subsequently showed that the Roberts would have received only a little under $3000 had they continued participation, the Australian Competition and Consumer Commission (ACCC) sought orders alleging that the conduct on the part of the lessors, in insisting that the claim be abandoned if a new lease was to be granted, amounted to unconscionable conduct under s 20.

11.52 At first instance, French J found for the ACCC, saying that the Roberts were at a 'special disadvantage' of a 'situational', rather than 'constitutional' nature; that is, their disability was not due to any particular personal characteristics of the kind observed in *Blomley v Ryan* or *CBC v Amadio*, but rather, it arose from the position they were in and their keen desire to be rid of the business. In doing so, however, French J did not rely upon the daughter's illness as a factor. French J took the view that the provision of independent advice to Mrs Roberts was of little impact in overcoming the unconscionability arising from the Roberts' 'situational disadvantage'. On appeal, the Full Federal Court reversed French J's findings. The majority of the High Court, while disagreeing with some of the reasoning of the Full Federal Court, ultimately decided that unconscionability under s 20 had not been made out and denied relief to the Roberts.

11.53 The High Court majority found that there was no 'special disability' under which the Roberts could be said to have been operating when they negotiated the new lease with the lessors. In explaining the reasoning of the majority, it is worth quoting at some length the words of Gleeson CJ, at CLR 64–5; ALR 157–8, on the nature of 'special disability':

> In the present case, there was neither a special disadvantage on the part of the lessees, nor unconscientious conduct on the part of the lessors. All the people involved in the transaction were business people, concerned to advance or protect their own financial interests. The critical disadvantage from which the lessees suffered was that they had no legal entitlement to a renewal or extension of their lease; and they depended upon the lessors' willingness to grant such an extension or renewal for their capacity to sell the goodwill of their business for a substantial price. They were thus compelled to approach the lessors, seeking their agreement to such an extension or renewal, against a background of current claims and litigation in which they were involved. They were at a distinct disadvantage, but there was nothing 'special' about it. They had two forms of financial interest at stake: their claims, and the sale of their business. The second was large; as things turned out, the first was shown to be relatively small. They had the benefit of legal advice. They made a rational decision, and took the course of preferring the second interest. They suffered from no lack of ability to judge or protect their financial interests … In truth, there was no lack of ability on their part to make a judgment about anything. Rather, there was a lack of ability to get their own way. That is a disability that affects people in many circumstances in commerce, and in life. It is not one against which the law ordinarily provides relief.

11.54 As to the scope of s 20, the ACCC conceded that this case could have been decided on an understanding of the section that represented simply the equitable doctrine relating to unconscionable transactions. Nevertheless, the High Court majority was clearly aware of the emerging rival interpretations of s 20, and that it would need to be addressed at some future point. In this respect Gummow and Hayne JJ, at CLR 72; ALR 163–4, acknowledged:

> [T]he question as to which particular manifestations of equity's concern with unconscientious or unconscionable conduct are reached by [s 20] … is an important one because [s 20] does more than re-enact for application in trade and commerce the general law principles concerned. Contravention of [s 20] attracts particular remedies under the Act which may not otherwise be available and provides, as this case illustrates, for litigation to be instituted and conducted by a public body, the ACCC.

11.55 In *ACCC v Berbatis Holdings* in the High Court, only Kirby J, at CLR 84; ALR 174, in dissent, was prepared to say that the reach of the s 20 went further than the principles of unconscionable dealing set out in *Blomley v Ryan* or *CBC v Amadio*. Although his Honour, at CLR 96; ALR 183, referred to 'the place of [s 20] in the Act, its history and its educative and deterrent purposes' in support of a wider view, it was left unclear how those considerations could square with the very clear words of the Explanatory Memorandum. However, cases such as *GPG (Australia Trading) Pty Ltd v GIO Australia Holdings Ltd* (2001) FCR 23 at 76; 191 ALR 342 at 389 and *Hampton v BHP Billiton Minerals Pty Ltd (No 2)* [2012] WASC 285 at [189]–[190], strongly suggest that the broader interpretation of s 20 as suggested by *ACCC v Samton Holdings* (see 11.49) does not reflect a proper interpretation of that section.

Unconscionable conduct and consumers — s 21

11.56   Section 21 applies to consumer contracts made between persons for the supply of goods and services of a kind ordinarily acquired for personal, domestic or household use or consumption. Section 21(1) stipulates as follows:

> A person must not, in trade or commerce, in connection with the supply or possible supply of goods or services to another person, engage in conduct that is, in all the circumstances, unconscionable.

The operation of this provision is confined to consumer transactions, as is made clear in sub-sections (5) and (6), which stipulate:

> (5) A reference in this section to goods or services is a reference to goods or services of a kind ordinarily acquired for personal, domestic or household use or consumption.
>
> (6) A reference in this section to the supply or possible supply of goods does not include a reference to the supply or possible supply of goods for the purpose of re-supply or for the purpose of using them up or transforming them in trade or commerce.

11.57   The meaning of unconscionability in s 21 is broader than under equitable principles. Although s 21(2) states that, in determining whether a person (the supplier) has acted unconscionably, the court may consider any matters, the subsection goes on to list the following relevant matters:

> (a) the relative strengths of the bargaining positions of the supplier and the consumer; and
>
> (b) whether, as a result of conduct engaged in by the person, the consumer was required to comply with conditions that were not reasonably necessary for the protection of the legitimate interests of the supplier; and
>
> (c) whether the consumer was able to understand any documents relating to the supply or possible supply of the goods or services; and
>
> (d) whether any undue influence or pressure was exerted on, or any unfair tactics were used against, the consumer or a person acting on behalf of the consumer by the supplier or a person acting on behalf of the supplier in relation to the supply or possible supply of the goods or services; and
>
> (e) the amount for which, and the circumstances under which, the consumer could have acquired identical or equivalent goods or services from a person other than the supplier.

11.58   Furthermore, s 21(4) stipulates that in determining whether there is unconscionability pursuant to the section:

> (a) the court must not have regard to any circumstances that were not reasonably foreseeable at the time of the alleged contravention; and
>
> (b) the court may have regard to conduct engaged in, or circumstances existing, before the commencement of this section.

11.59   In *Australian Competition and Consumer Commission v Keshow* [2005] FCA 558, the court ruled that s 21 had been breached in relation to the sale of educational materials and household goods to members of an indigenous community in the Northern Territory. Mansfield J, at [3], summarised the basis upon which he reached his decision as follows:

> The overall picture which the evidence presents is that the respondent is what is sometimes called a 'humbugger'. ... He took advantage of the lack of education and commercial experience of those in the communities ... In many instances, the educational materials were not needed or useful

259

having regard to the age of the child or children of the consumer. The products he contracted to provide were most commonly not supplied, or not supplied in their entirety. Whether a contract to provide educational materials was met was haphazard. The payment arrangements in each instance involved an open-ended periodic payment authority, procured at the instance of the respondent, and authorising payment on the day which Centrelink or like benefits were regularly received by the particular complainant or other community resident. The respondent in a number of instances continued to receive periodic payments well after the value of the goods to be provided by him (whether or not they had been provided) had been received. In fact, there is no evidence to show that the respondent maintained adequate records of what products had been sold to which consumers, whether the products had been provided, as agreed, or what had been paid for them.

Unconscionable conduct and small business — s 22

11.60 Section 22 aims to protect small businesses, especially lessees and franchisees, in relation to unconscionable conduct by big business: *Jefferson Ford Pty Ltd v Ford Motor Company of Australia Ltd* (2008) 167 FCR 372 at 403; 246 ALR 465 at 492. Thus, it has been said that one purpose of the section 'was to set a norm of conduct [that] had the purpose of protecting the legal rights of small businesses and ensuring that they could confidently deal with large firms': *Hoy Mobile Pty Ltd v Allphones Retail Pty Ltd (No 2)* [2008] FCA 810 at [414].

11.61 Section 22(1) states that a person must not, in trade or commerce, 'engage in conduct that is, in all the circumstances, unconscionable' in connection with:

(a) the supply or possible supply of goods or services to a person (other than a listed public company); or

(b) the acquisition or possible acquisition of goods or services from a person (other than a listed public company).

11.62 In determining whether a person, as a 'supplier', has engaged in unconscionable conduct in breach of s 22(1) in relation to the supply of goods or services to a person or corporation, as a 'business consumer', s 22(2) sets out the following non-exhaustive list of circumstances that can be taken into account by a court:

(a) the relative strengths of the bargaining positions of the supplier and the business consumer; and

(b) whether, as a result of conduct engaged in by the supplier, the business consumer was required to comply with conditions that were not reasonably necessary for the protection of the legitimate interests of the supplier; and

(c) whether the business consumer was able to understand any documents relating to the supply or possible supply of the goods or services; and

(d) whether any undue influence or pressure was exerted on, or any unfair tactics were used against, the business consumer or a person acting on behalf of the business consumer by the supplier or a person acting on behalf of the supplier in relation to the supply or possible supply of the goods or services; and

(e) the amount for which, and the circumstances under which, the business consumer could have acquired identical or equivalent goods or services from a person other than the supplier; and

(f) the extent to which the supplier's conduct towards the business consumer was consistent with the supplier's conduct in similar transactions between the supplier and other like business consumers; and

(g) the requirements of any applicable industry code; and

(h) the requirements of any other industry code, if the business consumer acted on the reasonable belief that the supplier would comply with that code; and

(i) the extent to which the supplier unreasonably failed to disclose to the business consumer:

  (i) any intended conduct of the supplier that might affect the interests of the business consumer; and

  (ii) any risks to the business consumer arising from the supplier's intended conduct (being risks that the supplier should have foreseen would not be apparent to the business consumer); and

(j) if there is a contract between the supplier and the business consumer for the supply of the goods or services:

  (i) the extent to which the supplier was willing to negotiate the terms and conditions of any contract for supply of the goods or services with the business consumer; and

  (ii) the terms and conditions of the contract; and

  (iii) the conduct of the supplier and the business consumer in complying with the terms and conditions of the contract; and

  (iv) any conduct that the supplier or the business consumer engaged in, in connection with their commercial relationship, after they entered into the contract; and

(k) without limiting paragraph (j), whether the supplier has a contractual right to vary unilaterally a term or condition of the contract between the supplier and the business consumer for the supply of the goods or services; and

(l) the extent to which the supplier and the business consumer acted in good faith.

In considering the potential application of these criteria, the Full Court of the Federal Court in *Australian Securities and Investments Commission v National Exchange Pty Ltd* (2005) FCR 132 at 142, said:

> The starting point in making [a] determination as to unconscionability is the list of factors to which the Court's attention is drawn by [s 22(2)]. These factors should be considered and weighed as a whole. Some may weigh in favour of a characterisation of the conduct as unconscionable and others may not. It is not appropriate to approach this list as exhaustive. This list is indicative of some of 'the relevant circumstances'.

Thus, in considering the potential application of the criteria noted in s 22(2), it is not permissible to go through those listed, find one that fits the case before the court and then conclude that there has been unconscionable conduct. All the circumstances of the case must be considered: *Australian Competition and Consumer Commission v Oceana Commercial Pty Ltd* [2004] FCAFC 174 at [181].

11.63 A similar list of factors is set out in s 22(3) to assist the court in determining whether a person, as an 'acquirer', has contravened s 22(1) in connection with the acquisition or possible acquisition of goods or services from a person, as a 'small business supplier'. In determining whether there is unconscionability pursuant to either s 22(1), s 22(5) stipulates that:

(a) the court must not have regard to any circumstances that were not reasonably foreseeable at the time of the alleged contravention; and

(b) the court have regard to circumstances existing before the commencement of this section but not to conduct engaged in before that commencement.

11.64   In *Australian Competition and Consumer Commission v Allphones Retail Pty Ltd (No 2)* (2009) 253 ALR 324 at 347, Foster J made the following comments as a guide to the meaning of the word unconscionable in the context of s 22:

> The scope of [s 22] is wider than that of [s 20]. The meaning of *unconscionable* for the purposes of [s 22] is not limited to the meaning of the word according to established principles of common law and equity … The ordinary or dictionary meaning of *unconscionable*, which involves notions of serious misconduct or something which is clearly unfair or unreasonable, is picked up by the use of the word in [s 22]. When used in that section, the expression requires that the actions of the alleged contravenor show no regard for conscience, and be irreconcilable with what is right or reasonable. Inevitably the expression imports a pejorative moral judgment … Normally, some moral fault or moral responsibility would be involved. This would not ordinarily be present if the critical actions are merely negligent. There would ordinarily need to be a deliberate (in the sense of intentional) act or at least a reckless act.

In *Canon Australia Pty Ltd v Patton* (2007) 244 ALR 759 at 768 it was said that unconscionability in this context required 'a high level of moral obloquy'.

11.65   These statements of principle were approved by the Court of Appeal in Victoria in *Body Bronze International Pty Ltd v Fehcorp Pty Ltd* (2011) 282 ALR 571 at 588. In relation to their application to cases of breach of contract, Macauley AJA, at 589, said:

> [I]t should be recognised that not every breach of contract, even a deliberate breach, necessarily involves the moral obloquy that the authorities suggest needs be present for unconscionable conduct in breach of [s 22] to be made out. Although it may be true that for an act to have that moral character it will usually be conduct that is intentional or at least reckless, it does not follow that any breach that is intentional necessarily has that moral character … A decision may be taken to break a contract because, upon rational commercial considerations, the burden of performance may be greater and more onerous than the liability to be incurred if the conduct amounts to breach. The party committing the breach may know that it will deliver to the opposite party an opportunity to exercise rights both under and outside the contract that flow from the breach, and that the opposite party has the means to exercise and enforce those rights. Those rights may include seeking injunctive relief to restrain the breach, accepting a repudiation of the contract so as to terminate executory obligations and seeking damages, or keeping the contract on foot and merely seeking damages. There may be nothing offensive to conscience in a commercial participant taking such a commercial decision in given circumstances. Whether or not it amounts to unconscionable conduct does not simply flow from it being a deliberate breach; it must be evaluated in 'all the circumstances'. The real question is what 'more' is required than conscious breach to convert it into unconscionable conduct. The answer to that question must, at least in part, lie in the value judgment of the particular decision-maker. It means, of course, that minds can reasonably differ. However some guidance in the exercise of that judgment is to be found in the list of matters to which [s 22(2)] directs the court to have regard. That judgment is not to be informed merely by a sense of distaste for the impugned conduct.

11.66   In *Tonto Home Loans Australia Pty Ltd v Tavares* at [291], Allsop P, speaking for the Court of Appeal in New South Wales, said:

> It is neither possible nor desirable to provide a comprehensive definition. The range of conduct is wide and can include bullying and thuggish behaviour, undue pressure and unfair tactics, taking advantage of vulnerability or lack of understanding, trickery or misleading conduct. A finding requires an examination of all the circumstances.

11.67   In *Australian Competition and Consumer Commission v Dukemaster Pty Ltd* [2009] FCA 682, in a case involving renewals of retail leases, Gordon J held that a landlord was in breach of s 22 in circumstances where the landlord had set an inflated figure for the rent, required a quick response from a tenant who spoke little or no English and threatened eviction if the terms of the new lease were not accepted. His Honour also found that the landlord had engaged in misleading or deceptive conduct in violation of s 18 of the *Australian Consumer Law*. What is clear from this decision is that misleading or deceptive conduct can be utilized in ascertaining whether there has been a breach of s 22.[3]

11.68   Another example of a successful claim pursuant to s 22 is *Australian Competition and Consumer Commission v Dataline.Net.au Pty Ltd* [2006] FCA 1427, in which a wholesale internet provider acted unconscionably in relation to its dealings with particular internet service providers. The conduct included refusing to permit the providers to obtain independent legal advice and threats of disconnection if the providers did not sign further agreements.

Remedies

11.69   The remedies available for breaches of ss 20–22 are set out in Chapter 5 of the ACL. First, s 232 allows for injunctions to be ordered to restrain breaches of any of the three sections. Injunctive relief can be sought by the relevant Minister, the ACCC, or by any person who has suffered loss or is likely to suffer loss as a result of any such breach.

11.70   Second, damages can be recovered pursuant to s 236 for loss or damage suffered as the result of a breach of any of the three sections.

11.71   Third, s 243 is particularly significant as it enables a range of ancillary orders to be made, including voiding or variation of the contract, return of money or property, repair of property and payment of money to compensate for loss or damage suffered. The ability to void a contract is especially important as this is a stronger remedy than that of rescission under the equitable doctrine and may be used despite the existence of a bona fide third party who has provided valuable consideration, although the courts will be very cautious in affecting such a person's rights. Any person who has suffered, or is likely to suffer, loss as a result of a breach of any of the three sections can seek an order under s 243. Furthermore, the ACCC can seek s 243 orders on behalf of persons who have suffered loss as a result of breaches of any of the three sections.

11.72   Finally, the ACCC is able to institute proceedings seeking the imposition of a civil pecuniary penalty under s 224(1)(a)(i).

---

3.   For a discussion of this case see E Webb, 'Unconscionable Conduct in *Australian Competition and Consumer Commission v Dukemaster Pty Ltd* — A Recognition of "Acoustic Segregation" in Retail Leasing Transactions?' (2010) 18 *Australian Property Law Journal* 48.

UNCONSCIONABILITY AND UNDUE INFLUENCE

11.73 It is clear that the doctrines relating to unconscionable transactions and undue influence are closely related. But just how closely is a matter of some debate. Hardingham, while making it clear that he was not advocating a 'general unifying principle of universal application', made the following statement:

> [T]he boundaries between traditional heads of intervention against unconscionable behaviour — specifically between common law duress and actual undue influence or pressure, between presumed undue influence and unconscionable dealing as such — are shifting. Lines of demarcation are not now as clearly defined as they may have been in the past. As a consequence, the traditional heads themselves may be ready for some redefinition or rationalisation.[4]

11.74 In spite of this sentiment, the judicial approach has repeatedly been to recognise the strong connection between the two doctrines, yet deny that their operation is really quite similar. In *Bridgewater v Leahy* (1998) 194 CLR 457 at 478; 158 ALR 66 at 80, Gaudron, Gummow and Kirby JJ said:

> [E]ach doctrine may be seen as a species of that genus of equitable intervention to refuse enforcement of or to set aside transactions which, if allowed to stand, would offend equity and good conscience. However, there are conceptual and practical distinctions between them.

11.75 What are these distinctions? The classic statements in this regard are both derived from *Commercial Bank of Australia v Amadio* (1983) 151 CLR 447; 46 ALR 402. In that case, Deane J, at CLR 474; ALR 423, said:

> Undue influence, like common law duress, looks to the quality of the consent or assent of the weaker party … Unconscionable dealing looks to the conduct of the stronger party in attempting to enforce, or retain the benefit of, a dealing with a person under a special disability in circumstances where it is not consistent with equity or good conscience that he should do so.

11.76 In the same case, Mason J, at CLR 461; ALR 412, said:

> Although unconscionable conduct in this narrow sense bears some resemblance to the doctrine of undue influence, there is a difference between the two. In the latter the will of the innocent party is not independent and voluntary because it is overborne. In the former the will of the innocent party, even if independent and voluntary, is the result of the disadvantageous position in which he is placed and of the other party unconscientiously taking advantage of that position.

11.77 The distinctions between undue influence and unconscionable transactions were referred to by Austin J in *Turner v Windever* [2003] NSWSC 1147 at [131], as follows:

> The similarities in operation of the two doctrines can engender false assumptions about similarity of scope. It is essential for a judge at first instance to bear in mind the different evidentiary foundations of cases invoking the doctrines, the one focusing on evidence of the prior relationship and the domination and dependence said to have been engendered, and the other focusing on the position of special disadvantage of one party and the other party's knowledge of it at the

---

4. I Hardingham, 'Unconscionable Dealing' in P D Finn (ed), *Essays in Equity*, Law Book Co, Sydney, 1985, 1, p 2.

point of transaction. Thus, if a plaintiff is permitted to shift from reliance on one doctrine to reliance on the other at the trial, the defendant's evidentiary preparation for the hearing could be undermined. On the other hand, if a plaintiff has prepared its case with a view to invoking one doctrine, the evidence is unlikely to be sufficient to warrant relief under the other.

11.78 However, the fine line between undue influence and unconscionability has been blurred further with the recognition that relationships may constitute a special disadvantage. This was a novel development from the decision of *Louth v Diprose*, at CLR 638; ALR 14, where the majority of the High Court were satisfied that Louth had manipulated the situation through the creation of an 'atmosphere of crisis' (see 11.18–11.21).

11.79 *Louth v Diprose* pales in comparison with the decision in *Bridgewater v Leahy*. In that case the High Court heard an appeal by the daughters and widow of a deceased man (York) who had made a will significantly advantaging his nephew by bequeathing him an option to purchase a pastoral property for $200,000. The land was worth almost $700,000. It was clear that York wished to reward his nephew for many years of hard work on the property. He also was not as close to his daughters, had made provision for them at various points of their lives, and wished his landholdings to remain intact rather than be broken up upon his death. Three years after making this will, York made an *inter vivos* sale of a substantial part of the property to his nephew and forgave a large part of the balance of the purchase price so that the nephew effectively paid $150,000. This transaction was suggested by the nephew about a year beforehand and in fact was an improvement to the daughters' position as, without it, the nephew could simply have purchased the entire property for $200,000 under the terms of the option granted by the will. York died not long after this sale.

11.80 Describing the basis of the daughters' claim is complicated by the fact that parts of the action fell by the wayside as the matter progressed through the courts. They initially challenged both the will and the *inter vivos* transaction as tainted by undue influence and unconscionability. Much of their subsequent success rested upon the High Court's finding that the trial judge applied stricter tests, which were appropriate in the testamentary context, to the *inter vivos* transaction. By the time the matter was heard by the High Court, the only remaining issue was that of unconscionability in respect of the *inter vivos* transaction. A majority of three found this was made out while a minority consisting of Gleeson CJ and Callinan J was in dissent on many issues.

11.81 The majority based their finding of unconscionability upon the view that York was specially disadvantaged by the relationship he had with his nephew. Gaudron, Gummow and Kirby JJ, at CLR 493; ALR 92, said:

> The relationship between Bill [York] and Neil meant that, when Neil raised the question of using the proceeds of sale of the Injune Land [to buy a portion of the Yorks' pastoral property], they were meeting on unequal terms. Neil took advantage of this position to obtain a benefit through a grossly improvident transaction on the part of his uncle.

11.82 The minority's finding could not be more at variance with this view. Gleeson CJ and Callinan J found no special disability. York was of clear mind and he knew the effect of the *inter vivos* transaction. Indeed, their Honours, at CLR 469; ALR 73, said it was entirely in accord with his 'long standing and firmly held wishes', and reiterated that the disadvantage must be 'special'. There were none of the characteristics that had constituted a 'special disadvantage' in previous cases.

11.83   The majority ordered that the amount stipulated by the forgiveness of debt be invalidated but not the purchase of the land, which was the other part of the *inter vivos* transaction. The matter was remitted to the Supreme Court of Queensland for determination of an appropriate amount to be forgiven from the purchase debt after taking account of the adequate provision of the daughters and widow from that property. The minority's condemnation of this order was based upon the view that it would not have been possible for York, while still living, to bring an action of unconscionability. According to Gleeson CJ and Callinan J, at CLR 473; ALR 76, the 'proper relief would have been to set aside the entire transaction and make an order for accounts'.

11.84   The decision and result in *Bridgewater v Leahy* is the subject of much criticism from a variety of angles. If a close and influential relationship is so easily characterised as a 'special disadvantage', what separate justification can be made for the retention of undue influence, apart from the evidential convenience of classes of presumption? Finlay has summed up the effect of *Bridgewater v Leahy* thus:

> [W]hile in cases such as *Amadio* and *Blomley v Ryan* it is possible to discern clear distinctions between the doctrines of unconscionability and undue influence, the distinctions are blurred in cases where the 'disability' is the fact of a relationship which is abused. *Bridgewater v Leahy* in particular demonstrates how the lines are blurred. But it also demonstrates how unconscionability can be what a court wants it to be … This is the very difficulty which critics of unconscionability as a separate doctrine have feared.[5]

11.85   An example of this heightened flexibility of unconscionability in the wake of *Bridgewater v Leahy* may be seen in the finding by Palmer J, in *McCulloch v Fern* [2001] NSWSC 406, that a dying wife, already under the undue influence of her religious leader, was used as a tool of unconscionability by the latter in securing the agreement of her husband to a substantial financial gift of money held by them jointly. The husband's 'vulnerability to persuasion' by his wife, under such circumstances, constituted the special disadvantage which the religious leader had exploited unconscionably.

11.86   However, there are signs that the width of the doctrine applied in *Bridgewater v Leahy* has not been wholeheartedly adopted by the courts. Foremost in this respect are the words of the High Court majority in *ACCC v CG Berbatis Holdings*, which insist, while not rejecting the Federal Court's recognition of 'situational disadvantage' (see 11.11), that it must be significantly 'special': see 11.12–11.13. But additionally, the Victorian Court of Appeal rejected any hint of finding a special disadvantage on the basis of the relationship between the parties in *Mitchell v 700 Young Street Pty Ltd* [2003] VSCA 42 at [2], with Ormiston JA saying that 'it would be a sad state of affairs if courts interfered as of course with gifts and beneficial transactions effected to children in circumstances where it could truly be said that they were entered into "in consideration of the natural love and affection" that parents have for their offspring'.

---

5.   A Finlay, 'Can We See the Chancellor's Footprint: *Bridgewater v Leahy*' (1999) 14 *Journal of Contract Law* 265, pp 271–2.

12

EQUITABLE ESTOPPEL

INTRODUCTION

12.1   In simple terms, an estoppel is an equitable claim that prevents someone from denying the existence of a state of affairs in circumstances where such denial would be unconscientious. The word 'estopped' means 'precluded' or 'prevented'.[1] This necessarily has an impact upon those legal rights which would otherwise be exercisable by the person estopped. A simple example would be a situation where A has induced B to believe that A will not insist upon his or her strict legal rights under a contract that exists between them. If B relies upon the assumption that B will not be exposed to liability should B fail to perform his or her obligations exactly, the law recognises that it is unconscientious to allow A to subsequently sue B for breach of contract.

12.2   In *The Bell Group Ltd (in liq) v Westpac Banking Corporation (No 9) (2008) 225 FLR 1 at 393,* Owen J said:

> Put in general terms, [estoppel] is a doctrine designed to protect a party from the detriment that would flow from that party's change of position if the assumption or expectation that led to it were to be rendered groundless by another.

12.3   While fairly simple to discuss in terms of broad principle, it must be understood that the word 'estoppel' raises a multiplicity of more precise meanings dependent upon the circumstances of the case. As the title of this chapter implies, estoppel exists under both the common law *and* equity. Within both jurisdictions, the concept has a number of specific forms so that one will come across references to estoppel by deed, estoppel by judgment, estoppel in pais, estoppel by conduct, estoppel by representation, *High Trees* estoppel, promissory estoppel and proprietary estoppel among others. There is a considerable degree of overlap between some of these forms of estoppel and confusion can arise.

COMMON LAW ESTOPPEL

12.4   While the basic notion of preventing parties from insisting on their actual legal rights is central to all forms of estoppel, the major difference between them is determined by the nature of the belief which has led to the compromise of those rights. Although it was originally not so

---

1.   In relation to the word 'estoppel', in *Seven Network (Operations) Ltd v Warburton (No 2)* [2011] NSWSC 386 at [41], Pembroke J noted that '[i]n broad terms, estoppel, a word of Old French derivation that has become enshrined in our law, refers to a bar or impediment preventing a party from asserting a fact or a claim that is inconsistent with a position previously taken'.

confined, at common law the focus has been upon assumptions of fact. These could arise by means of judicial decision (estoppel by record or issue estoppel), agreement by both parties (estoppel by deed or estoppel by convention), and also by representation made by one to the other (estoppel by representation). The general principle of common law estoppel was stated by Dixon J in *Grundt v Great Boulder Pty Gold Mines Ltd* (1937) 59 CLR 641 at 674 as being that, 'the law should not permit an unjust departure by a party from an assumption of fact which he has caused another party to adopt or accept for the purpose of their legal relations'.

12.5   It was due to the decision of the House of Lords in *Jorden v Money* [1843–60] All ER Rep 350 that common law estoppel was confined to assumptions and representations of existing fact. This limitation was intended by their Lordships to apply to all forms of estoppel and should be understood in light of the development of contract law during this time. Representations of future intention (that is, promises) were to be governed by the presence of a contractual relationship between representor and representee with a price being paid for the promise in the form of sufficient consideration.

12.6   Estoppel in equity, however, never really laboured under the restriction imposed by *Jorden v Money*. Parties who made representations of future intention were estopped from denying them in situations where they had been reasonably relied upon by others. This inconsistency with *Jorden v Money* was more covert than blatant at first but the distinction between existing fact and future intention came to be that which defined the realms of estoppel under the common law and equity respectively.

12.7   The second distinction between estoppel under the two jurisdictions is that it is commonly said of common law estoppel that it is a rule of evidence, while estoppel in equity may confer substantive rights. By this it is meant that common law estoppel is a device used merely to determine the facts upon which the legal rights of the parties will then be determined by the court, whereas, in equity, rights flow directly from the operation of estoppel in equity. This classification is a natural consequence of the first distinction — if the scope of common law estoppel is confined to representations of fact, its true role is to establish which facts the court will adjudge. If the estoppel is successfully raised, then the representor will be precluded from denying the facts assumed by the representee.

12.8   The idea of common law estoppel as an evidentiary rule derives from the judgment of Bowen LJ in *Low v Bouverie* [1891] 3 Ch 82 at 105, and is a significant barrier to attempts by some recent members of the High Court to fuse equitable and common law estoppel into one doctrine, despite their otherwise quite high level of similarity: see 12.66–12.70. The limited role of estoppel at common law was well conveyed by the metaphor that it was a shield but not a sword. Conversely, when estoppel in equity conferred substantive rights it was said to be a sword as well as a shield. However, it would be a mistake to see the analogy of common law estoppel as a shield as implying that its use was defensive only. As Mason CJ and Wilson J said in *Waltons Stores (Interstate) Ltd v Maher* (1988) 164 CLR 387 at 400; 76 ALR 513 at 521, 'this does not mean that a plaintiff cannot rely on an estoppel. Even according to traditional orthodoxy, a plaintiff may rely on an estoppel if he has an independent cause of action'. The role of the estoppel in such a case is to establish the state of affairs from which the action arises.

12.9   In *Silovi Pty Ltd v Barbaro* (1988) 13 NSWLR 466 at 472, Priestley JA set out a series of enumerated points in order to clarify the law on estoppel. The first three offer a concise summary of the ideas presented so far:

> (1) Common law and equitable estoppel are separate categories, although they have many ideas in common. (2) Common law estoppel operates upon a representation of existing fact, and when certain conditions are fulfilled, establishes a state of affairs by reference to which the legal relation between the parties is to be decided. This estoppel does not itself create a right against the party estopped. The right flows from the court's decision on the state of affairs established by the estoppel. (3) Equitable estoppel operates upon representations or promises as to future conduct, including promises about legal relations. When certain conditions are fulfilled, this kind of estoppel is itself an equity, a source of legal obligation.

THE DEVELOPMENT OF EQUITABLE ESTOPPEL

12.10   Equitable estoppel is the result of bringing together the two significant forms of estoppel that existed in equity — promissory estoppel and proprietary estoppel. The essential difference between the two forms of estoppel was described by Brennan J in *Waltons Stores (Interstate) Ltd v Maher* at CLR 420; ALR 535–6, as follows:

> In cases of promissory estoppel, the equity binds the holder of a legal right who induces another to expect that that right will not be exercised against him … In cases of proprietary estoppel, the equity binds the owner of property who induces another to expect that an interest in the property will be conferred on him.

Unlike the situation at common law since *Jorden v Money*, neither of these estoppels were limited to assumptions of existing fact but operated so as to hold a representor to a statement of future intention. The bringing together of these two estoppels reflects the high incidence of doctrinal similarity between them.

12.11   Before considering equitable estoppel in its modern form, it is worth noting the former roles of both promissory and proprietary estoppel and their attendant differences.

Promissory estoppel

12.12   The doctrine of consideration has often been seen as leading to injustices. The equitable doctrine of promissory estoppel evolved to overcome many of these injustices. The very essence of promissory estoppel is that a promisor is precluded from going back on his or her promise even though the promise is not supported by consideration moving from the promisee. In *Equititrust Ltd (formerly Equitiloan Ltd) v Franks* (2009) 259 ALR 388 at 401, Handley AJA, noted that promissory estoppel 'is based on a non-contractual promise or assurance which, in its orthodox form, becomes binding in equity, so as to restrain the promisor from enforcing his strict legal rights'. In *DHJPM Pty Limited v Blackthorn Resources Limited* (2011) 285 ALR 311 at 323, Meagher JA said that 'a promissory estoppel operates as an equitable restraint on the exercise or enforcement of contractual and other rights and is negative in substance'.

12.13   Although the initial impact of promissory estoppel on the law of contract was to provide equitable relief where a contractual remedy was not available due to the absence of consideration, the modern doctrine of equitable estoppel can provide relief in various other areas where contractual remedies are unavailable. Some of these areas include:

* where, during negotiations to enter into a contract, an offeree, believing that the offer will not be revoked proceeds to act to his or her detriment upon that belief;
* where there has been non-compliance with the statutory requirement of writing with respect to a contract involving land;
* where the rule in *Hoyt's Pty Ltd v Spencer* (1919) 27 CLR 133 precludes the finding of a collateral contract: *Wright v Hamilton Island Enterprises Ltd* [2003] QCA 36;
* where the doctrine of privity prevents a third party to the contract from enforcing it: *Trident General Insurance Co Ltd v McNiece Bros Pty Ltd* (1988) 165 CLR 107 at 145; 80 ALR 574 at 601.

12.14   The principles which underlie promissory estoppel were present in nineteenth century case law, but they were given a more contemporary formulation by Denning J in the case of *Central London Property Trust Ltd v High Trees House Ltd* [1947] 1 KB 130. In that case Central London Property Trust (CLPT) leased a block of flats to High Trees House (HTH) for a period of 99 years. In 1940, CLPT agreed to accept a reduced rent, which was paid for the next five years by HTH. CLPT accepted the reduction because of the low occupancy rate for the flats during World War II. In 1945, with the flats all fully let, CLPT asserted a claim for the full rent thereafter. Denning J said that CLPT was entitled to the full rent as claimed, on the basis that the agreement for a reduced rent was only for as long as the flats were not fully let. The critical aspect of the case was the statement by Denning J that, if CLPT had claimed the full rent for the years 1940–45, it would have failed. Even though the promise to accept a reduced rent was not supported by consideration, the principle of promissory estoppel would have been raised against CLPT, preventing recovery of the forgone rent.

12.15   For many years the operation of promissory estoppel principles was subject to two important limitations:

1. The promise had to be in the context of one intended to affect a pre-existing legal relationship between the parties: *Combe v Combe* [1951] 2 KB 215 at 220. In *High Trees*, this was satisfied in that the parties were in a lease relationship and the promise was in relation to terms agreed under that lease.
2. Promissory estoppel could only be used as a defence to an action brought by the promisor against the promisee. It was said that it could only be used as a 'shield' and not as a 'sword': *Combe v Combe* at 220. In *High Trees*, this was satisfied as it was HTH, the defendant/promisee, that would have used promissory estoppel as a defence to a claim for the forgone rent by CLPT, the plaintiff/promisor.

12.16   In Australia, the doctrine of promissory estoppel was first authoritatively accepted by the High Court in *Legione v Hateley* (1983) 152 CLR 406; 46 ALR 1.

Proprietary estoppel

12.17   In relation to proprietary estoppel, it always was able to act as a sword as well as a shield and it is this feature that it has brought to equitable estoppel generally. Proprietary estoppel's other major difference from promissory estoppel is its operation in the realm of real property law. This estoppel operates to restrict the legal rights of landowners if they have encouraged the belief in another, or at least acquiesced in that other's belief, that he or she has some entitlement over the property and that belief has been acted upon; for example, by some alteration or improvement having been made to the land. However, no proprietary estoppel claim is available if the plaintiff and defendant have a legally enforceable contract relating to the property: *Giumelli v Giumelli* (1999) 196 CLR 101 at 121; 161 ALR 473 at 482; *Riches v Hogben* [1985] 2 Qd R 292 at 301. As Young CJ in Eq observed in *Barnes v Alderton* [2008] NSWSC 107 at [55], 'contract and proprietary estoppel are mutually exclusive'.

12.18   Due to the two methods by which the assumption of an interest could arise, proprietary estoppel was recognised as comprising two streams. The first is estoppel by encouragement, which was described by Handley JA in *Delaforce v Simpson-Cook* (2010) 78 NSWLR 483 at 488, as follows:

> Such an estoppel comes into existence when an owner of property has encouraged another to alter his or her position in the expectation of obtaining a proprietary interest and that other, in reliance on the expectation created or encouraged by the property owner, has changed his or her position to their detriment. If these matters are established equity may compel the owner to give effect to that expectation in whole or in part.

12.19   *Dillwyn v Llewelyn* [1862] All ER 384 is the classic example of estoppel by encouragement. In that case a father put his son into possession of land which he purported to voluntarily convey to his son. The conveyance was ineffective. With his father's assent and approval, the son built and occupied a house on the land. After the father's death, the son sought a declaration that he was the owner of the land in equity and that the trustees of the land be ordered to convey the land to him absolutely. The House of Lords made these orders.

12.20   The other stream of proprietary estoppel is estoppel by acquiescence, which was succinctly explained by Cranworth LJ in *Ramsden v Dyson* (1866) LR 1 HL 129 at 140–1, as follows:

> If a stranger begins to build on my land supposing it to be his own, and I, perceiving his mistake, abstain from setting him right, and leave him to persevere in his error, a Court of equity will not allow me afterwards to assert my title to the land on which he had expended money on the supposition that the land was his own. It considers that, when I saw the mistake into which he had fallen, it was my duty to be active and to state my adverse title; and that it would be dishonest in me to remain wilfully passive on such an occasion, in order afterwards to profit by the mistake which I might have prevented.
>
> But it will be observed that to raise such an equity two things are required, first, that the person expending the money supposes himself to be building on his own land; and, secondly, that the real owner at the time of the expenditure knows that the land belongs to him and not to the person expending the money in the belief that he is the owner. For if a stranger builds on my land knowing it to be mine, there is no principle of equity which would prevent my claiming the land with the benefit of all the expenditure made on it. There would be nothing in my conduct, active or passive, making it inequitable in me to assert my legal rights.

12.21   For a proprietary estoppel claim to be successful, the plaintiff must have suffered some detriment. In *Barnes v Alderton* at [42], Young CJ in Eq put it as follows:

> No equity arises to raise a proprietary estoppel unless the person in whose favour it is being raised, has acted to their prejudice or detriment in some way whether in terms of direct expenditure or on some other basis. However, the detriment may not necessarily be expenditure of money, commonly a claimant leaves her job, moves in with the promisor and does his housekeeping for many years … However, … minor expenditure such as day to day living expenses or minor repairs will not qualify.

12.22 It is to be noted that there is not a great difference between the two streams of proprietary estoppel. Rather, they simply reflect differing levels of passivity on the part of the landowner. The actions of the landowner, in either encouraging expenditure or acquiescing in expenditure, constitute fraud in equity. In *Ward v Kirkland* [1967] Ch 194 at 239, Ungoed-Thomas J observed as follows:

> It was suggested before me that there was a distinction between an act which is acquiescing or encouraging a person in such circumstances to expend money and merely standing aside with the knowledge that such money was being expended in reliance on having the right which is claimed. I, for my part, fail to see any substance in this distinction. The fundamental principle of the equity is unconscionable behaviour, and unconscionable behaviour can arise where there is knowledge by the legal owner of the circumstances in which the claimant is incurring the expenditure as much as if he himself were requesting or inciting that expenditure. It seems to me that abstention as well as request or incitement can fall within the principle from which the recognition of the claimant's equity arises.

12.23 A commonly cited statement of the relevant elements of proprietary estoppel is that of Fry J in *Willmott v Barber* (1880) 15 Ch D 96 at 105–6, where his Honour said:

> A man is not to be deprived of his legal rights unless he has acted in such a way as would make it fraudulent for him to set up those rights. What, then, are the elements or requisites necessary to constitute fraud of that description? In the first place the plaintiff must have made a mistake as to his legal rights. Secondly, the plaintiff must have expended some money or must have done some act (not necessarily upon the defendant's land) on the faith of his mistaken belief. Thirdly, the defendant, the possessor of the legal right, must know of the existence of his own right which is inconsistent with the right claimed by the plaintiff. If he does not know of it he is in the same position as the plaintiff, and the doctrine of acquiescence is founded upon conduct with a knowledge of your legal rights. Fourthly, the defendant, the possessor of the legal right, must know of the plaintiff's mistaken belief of his rights. If he does not, there is nothing which calls upon him to assert his own rights. Lastly, the defendant, the possessor of the legal right, must have encouraged the plaintiff in his expenditure of money or in the other acts which he has done, either directly or by abstaining from asserting his legal right.

12.24 Later cases indicated that one did not have to establish all these elements to succeed in a proprietary estoppel claim, with the 'real test' being, as Buckley LJ said in *Shaw v Applegate* [1978] 1 All ER 123 at 131, 'whether on the facts of the particular case the situation has become such that it would be dishonest, or unconscionable, for the plaintiff, or for the person having the right sought to be enforced, to continue to seek to enforce it'. More recently, in *Thorner v Major* (2009) 3 All ER 945 at 957, Lord Walker of Gestingthorpe said that 'the doctrine [of proprietary estoppel] is based on three main elements: … a representation or assurance made to the claimant; reliance on it by the claimant; and detriment to the claimant in consequence of his (reasonable) reliance'.

The consolidation of promissory and proprietary estoppels

12.25 In *Waltons Stores v Maher,* the High Court handed down its most significant decision on the topic of estoppel. The significance of this case was that it consolidated promissory and proprietary estoppels into the single, and broader, principle of equitable estoppel.

12.26   In *Waltons Stores v Maher*, the Mahers owned commercial premises in Nowra which Waltons was interested in leasing. Waltons wanted to relocate its business in Nowra to new premises and the Mahers' site was available. The agreement that was reached was that the Mahers would demolish the existing premises and erect a new building to meet the specifications of Waltons. A draft agreement for lease was sent to the solicitors for the Mahers. Some amendments were discussed. Waltons' solicitors indicated that they expected their client's agreement to the alterations and said they would let the Mahers know if the amendments were not acceptable. The Mahers' solicitors sent the amended lease, duly executed by the Mahers, to Waltons' solicitors 'by way of exchange'. The letter was not acknowledged by Waltons' solicitors until two months later. The Mahers began to demolish the existing premises, as time was critical if they were to complete the demolition and rebuilding in time for the start of the lease agreement. Waltons was found to know what the Mahers were doing. However, after receiving the letter and executed lease, Waltons reconsidered its position and a few months later wrote to the Mahers' solicitors saying that the lease had not been executed by Waltons and that Waltons was not proceeding with it. The Mahers sued Waltons for damages for breach of contract on the basis that Waltons was estopped from denying the existence of the lease.

12.27   The majority of the High Court (Mason CJ, Wilson and Brennan JJ) found for the Mahers on the basis of equitable estoppel. (The minority of Deane and Gaudron JJ found for the Mahers on the basis of common law estoppel.) In finding in favour of the Mahers on the basis of equitable estoppel, the majority did so in circumstances where there was no pre-existing contract between the parties and on the basis that the Mahers used estoppel as the basis for a cause of action and not merely as a defensive mechanism. In so doing, the High majority removed the already noted (see 12.15) limitations on the operation of promissory estoppel. In coming to their decision, the majority made it clear that promissory estoppel was but a species of the broader principle of equitable estoppel — the other major species being proprietary estoppel. The underlying rationale for equitable estoppel was firmly based in the notion of unconscionability or unconscientiousness: see 2.4–2.5. Mason CJ and Wilson J, at CLR 404; ALR 524, said:

> One may therefore discern in the cases a common thread which links them together, namely, the principle that equity will come to the relief of a plaintiff who has acted to his detriment on the basis of a basic assumption in relation to which the other party to the transaction has 'played such a part in the adoption of the assumption that it would be unfair or unjust if he were left free to ignore it': per Dixon J in *Grundt v Great Boulder Pty Gold Mines Ltd* (1937) 59 CLR 641 at 675 … Equity comes to the relief of such a plaintiff on the footing that it would be unconscionable conduct on the part of the other party to ignore the assumption.

ELEMENTS OF EQUITABLE ESTOPPEL

12.28   The essence of the principle of equitable estoppel is equity's concern with circumstances in which a plaintiff has acted to its detriment on the basis of a fundamental assumption where the defendant's role in the adoption of that assumption by the plaintiff is such that it would be unconscientious to deny the plaintiff equitable relief. It is the defendant's failure, having induced or acquiesced in the adoption or maintenance of the assumption, with knowledge that it would be relied upon, to fulfil the assumption or otherwise permit the plaintiff to avoid the detriment to which he or she has been exposed that makes the conduct of the defendant unconscientious and which attracts the intervention of equity.

12.29 However, the courts have cautioned against the 'undisciplined recourse to the principle [of equitable estoppel] as a ready panacea for real or imagined grievances arising from negotiations between parties': *Capron v Government of Turks & Caicos Islands* [2010] UKPC 2 at [34]. Thus, in *Yeoman's Row Management Ltd v Cobbe* [2008] 4 All ER 713 at 737–8, in the context of a property development agreement between sophisticated commercial parties, Lord Walker of Gestingthorpe said:

> [E]quitable estoppel is a flexible doctrine which the court can use, in appropriate circumstances, to prevent injustice caused by the vagaries and inconstancy of human nature. But it is not a sort of joker or wild card to be used whenever the court disapproves of the conduct of a litigant who seems to have the law on his side. Flexible though it is, the doctrine must be formulated and applied in a disciplined and principled way. Certainty is important in property transactions. As Deane J said in the High Court of Australia in *Muschinski v Dodds* (1985) 62 ALR 429 at 452:
>
> > Under the law of [Australia] — as, I venture to think, under the present law of England … proprietary rights fall to be governed by principles of law and not by some mix of judicial discretion … subjective views about which party 'ought to win' … and 'the formless void of individual moral opinion'.[2]

It is thus generally difficult to establish an equitable estoppel in a legal relationship between commercial parties operating at arms length and where their rights and obligations are carefully and extensively set out in formal documents: *Austotel Pty Ltd v Franklins Selfserve Pty Ltd* (1989) 16 NSWLR 582 at 585–6.

Clear and unambiguous representation

12.30 To establish a case based upon principles of equitable estoppel there needs to be a promise or a sufficiently clear and unambiguous representation. In relation to this requirement, in *Tadrous v Tadrous* [2012] NSWCA 16 at [39], Meagher JA observed that 'an equitable estoppel can be established notwithstanding that the expectation contains elements that would not be sufficiently certain to amount to a valid contract or is formed on the basis of vague assurance'. The rationale for this requirement of certainty stems from the fact that equitable estoppel is founded on the principle of unconscientiousness and unconscientiousness is difficult to establish if the representation is ambiguous or unclear: *Australian Crime Commission v Gray* [2003] NSWCA 318 at [200].

12.31 The promise or representation can be either express or implied. In *Legione v Hateley* at CLR 438–9; ALR 1 at 23–4, Mason and Deane JJ said:

> The requirement that a representation as to existing fact or future conduct must be clear … does not mean that the representation must be express. Such a clear representation may properly be seen as implied by the words used or to be adduced from either the failure to speak where there was a duty to speak or from conduct. Nor is it necessary that a representation be clear in its

---

2. Writing extra-judicially about this case, Lord Neuberger of Abbotsbury said: 'The message from the House of Lords in *Cobbe v YRML* is that it is simply not for the courts to go galumphing in, wielding some Denningesque sword of justice to rescue a miscalculating, improvident or optimistic property developer from the commercially unattractive, or even ruthless, actions of a property owner, which are lawful in common law': Lord Neuberger of Abbotsbury, 'Thoughts on the Law of Equitable Estoppel' (2010) 84 *Australian Law Journal* 225, p 230.

entirety. It will suffice if so much of the representation as is necessary to found the propounded estoppel satisfies the requirement.

12.32   In relation to the statement by Mason and Deane JJ that the representation does not have to be totally clear and unambiguous or free of any uncertainty, in *Australian Crime Commission v Gray* at [205], Ipp JA proffered the following example:

> Say, for example, a non-contractual representation was made whereby the representor orally promised to deliver a large quantity of produce specified by a nominated tonnage. Assume that the promise did not specify imperial tons or metric tonnes in circumstances where it was not reasonably possible to infer whether tons or tonnes were promised. Assume that the [relying party] relied on the promise and altered its position to its detriment. Assume further that the representor made no delivery whatever and repudiated its promise. If, in these circumstances, the [relying party] sued on the grounds of a promissory estoppel, I suggest that it would be self-evident that the representor would be liable to pay equitable compensation even though it was not possible to determine whether the quantity promised was in metric or imperial quantities. The unconscionability of the situation would not be negated by the ambiguity. Equity would intervene by fashioning relief based on the concept of 'minimum detriment'.

However, in *Westpac Banking Corporation v the Bell Group Ltd (in liq) (No 3)* [2012] WASCA 157 at [1748]–[1751], Drummond AJA expressed the view that ambiguity or lack of clarity will be fatal to any promissory estoppel case. However, this was not necessarily so in proprietary estoppel cases where 'vague and imprecise conduct is often enough to give rise to an equitable proprietary estoppel'. His Honour, at [1753], observed that this was so because, unlike promissory estoppel cases, proprietary estoppel cases 'do not depend on proof of clear representations or promises but on conduct with respect to property of the parties said to be estopped that is often diffuse and ambiguous, but which is sufficient, in the circumstances of the particular case, to attract the intervention of equity'.

12.33   Furthermore, whether the relevant representation is sufficiently clear and unambiguous is, as Lord Walker of Gestingthorpe observed in *Thorner v Major* at 964, 'hugely dependent on context'. Thus, in *Accurate Financial Consultants Pty Ltd v Koko Black Pty Ltd* [2008] VSCA 86 at [178], Dodds-Streeton JA said:

> A representation which is insufficiently certain or complete to create a contract may found proprietary estoppel. Where necessary to inhibit unconscionability, equity will construe a representation robustly in context, to determine its meaning as reasonably understood by the addressee. In my opinion, the standard of certainty, clarity and completeness required of the representation cannot sensibly be determined in isolation from other elements of proprietary estoppel in the circumstances of each particular case. Moreover, ambiguity or indeterminacy generated by the representor in the context of unconscionable conduct should not confer immunity from equity's 'long arm'.

12.34   In light of the above, it is understandable that in *Yeoman's Row Management Ltd v Cobbe* at 726, Lord Scott of Foscote said that, in the context of an arm's length negotiation between experienced businessmen, '[a]n expectation dependent upon the conclusion of a successful negotiation is not an expectation of an interest having [sufficient] certainty' to ground a claim in equitable estoppel. However, in *Thorner v Major*, in the context of a family relationship, an expectation generated by somewhat oblique remarks was sufficiently clear and certain to establish a proprietary estoppel claim.

12.35 For the sufficiently clear and unambiguous promise or representation to lead to a claim based upon equitable estoppel, in *Waltons Stores v Maher* at CLR 428–9; ALR 542, Brennan J set out what he saw as the elements that had to be satisfied, as follows:

> In my opinion, to establish an equitable estoppel, it is necessary for a plaintiff to prove that (1) the plaintiff assumed that a particular legal relationship then existed between the plaintiff and the defendant or expected that a particular legal relationship would exist between them and, in the latter case, that the defendant would not be free to withdraw from the expected legal relationship; (2) the defendant has induced the plaintiff to adopt that assumption or expectation; (3) the plaintiff acts or abstains from acting in reliance on the assumption or expectation; (4) the defendant knew or intended him to do so; (5) the plaintiff's action or inaction will occasion detriment if the assumption or expectation is not fulfilled; and (6) the defendant has failed to act to avoid that detriment whether by fulfilling the assumption or expectation or otherwise.

12.36 Although Brennan J's statement has not been approved by the High Court as a whole, it has been the formulation of principle most commonly cited and applied by lower courts in Australia and has been described as the 'seminal description' of the elements of equitable estoppel: *The Bell Group Ltd v Westpac Banking Corporation* at 409. A closer examination of the six elements is therefore warranted. In this discussion, for convenience, the party making the promise or representation will be referred to as 'the representor' and the party to whom the promise or representation is made will be referred to as 'the relying party'.

Assumption or expectation

12.37 In relation to the first element Brennan J said that the relying party must have 'assumed that a particular legal relationship then existed between the [relying party] and the [representor] or expected that a particular legal relationship would exist between them and, in the latter case, that the [representor] would not be free to withdraw from the expected legal relationship'. However, there is some doubt as to the need for the requirement that the representor would not be free to withdraw from the expected legal relationship: *EK Nominees Pty Ltd v Woolworths Ltd* [2006] NSWSC 1172 at [259]; *Alstom Ltd v Yokogawa Australia Pty Ltd (No 7)* [2012] SASC 49 at [1526]. In the subsequent High Court decision of *Commonwealth v Verwayen* (1990) 170 CLR 394; 95 ALR 321, no mention of this requirement is made in any of the judgments of Mason CJ, Deane, Dawson or McHugh JJ when dealing with the general principles of estoppel.

12.38 The nature of the relying party's assumption is important in relation to the type of estoppel that arises. If the assumption is one of an existing fact, a case of common law estoppel arises. (In *Waltons Stores v Maher* the minority found for the Mahers on this basis, viewing the evidence as establishing that the Mahers believed that Waltons had completed the exchange of the lease.) Equitable estoppel will arise if the assumption is that the representor will act in a particular way in the future. According to Brennan J, the relying party needs to show that he or she assumed that a particular legal relationship existed or would exist between the parties. According to the majority in *Waltons Stores v Maher*, this was established on the facts of that case. A similar approach is detected in *Mobil Oil Australia Ltd v Lyndel Nominees Pty Ltd* (1998) 153 ALR 198 at 235, where the Full Court of the Federal Court said that 'it is a necessary element of the principle that the [representor] has created or encouraged an assumption that "a particular legal relationship" or "interest" would arise or be granted'.

12.39   However, Brennan J's requirement of a legal relationship would exclude equitable estoppel from a promise or representation made where the relying party assumes that the representor will behave in a manner outside the context of a legal relationship. A broader view was taken by Priestley JA in *Austotel Pty Ltd v Franklins Selfserve Pty Ltd* at 610, where his Honour indicated that it was enough if the relying party assumed that 'a promise [would] be performed'. An example where the representor's behaviour is outside any existing or expected legal relationship, and which might come within Priestley JA's formulation, is where A promises to pay B $200 within 10 days. The approach of Priestley JA was seemingly approved by Meagher JA (Macfarlan JA agreeing) in the New South Wales Court of Appeal in *DHJPM Pty Limited v Blackthorn Resources Limited* at 324–5.

12.40   It also appears to be the case that, in all the circumstances, the relying party's assumption must be reasonable. A claim based upon equitable estoppel can fail if it is not reasonable for the relying party to have adopted the assumption. In *Salienta Pty Ltd v Clancy* [1999] NSWSC 916, a proposed purchaser of land had been in possession of the property and had had a contract to purchase it that was subsequently terminated by the vendor following the purchaser's breach. The purchaser had spent money on improvements to the property on the assumption that the expenditure would be credited to the purchase price in a contract to be entered into at a price lower than that which had been set out in the earlier contract. Bryson J held that the assumption was unreasonable given that, at all relevant times, the terms upon which the vendor would sell the land had clearly been made out in writing. Thus, it was not unconscientious for the vendor to assert its title to, and possession of, the land.

Inducement

12.41   Initially, it needs to be stressed that it is the assumption that is induced by the promise or representation, rather than the promise or representation itself, that forms the basis for a claim based upon equitable estoppel: *Waltons Stores v Maher* at CLR 413–14, 428–9, 458–9; ALR 531, 542, 564–5; *Commonwealth v Verwayen* at CLR 412–13, 444–5, 453–6, 500–2; at ALR 332–3, 356–7, 363–4, 396–8.

12.42   The assumption adopted by the relying party must have been induced by the conduct of the representor. In most cases the conduct will be the making of the promise or representation. As already noted (see 12.31), the promise or representation can be express or implied. Silence can give rise to an implication of a promise, as is illustrated by *Waltons Stores v Maher*, where the silence and acquiescence on the part of Waltons gave rise to an implication that it had promised to complete its transaction with the Mahers. In this context, in *Waltons Stores v Maher* at CLR 429; ALR 542, Brennan J said:

> For the purposes of the second element, a defendant who has not actively induced the plaintiff to adopt an assumption or expectation will nevertheless be held to have done so if the assumption or expectation can be fulfilled only by a transfer of the defendant's property, a diminution of his rights or an increase in his obligations and he, knowing that the plaintiff's reliance on the assumption or expectation may cause detriment to the plaintiff if it is not fulfilled, fails to deny to the plaintiff the correctness of the assumption or expectation on which the plaintiff is conducting his affairs.

12.43 In relation to the types of conduct by the representor that could be said to induce the assumption, in *Commonwealth v Verwayen*, at CLR 444; ALR 356, Deane J said the following:

> The cases indicate four main, but not exhaustive, categories in which an affirmative answer to that question may be justified, namely, where that party:
>
> (a) has induced the assumption by express or implied representation;
> (b) has entered into contractual or other material relations with the other party on the conventional basis of the assumption;
> (c) has exercised against the other party rights which would exist only if the assumption were correct;
> (d) knew that the other party laboured under the assumption and refrained from correcting him when it was his duty in conscience to do so.

Reliance

12.44 The relying party must act, or refrain from acting, in reliance on the assumption. A causal link between the assumption and the action or conduct by the relying party must be established. It is not necessary that the assumption be the only reason that the relying party acted or refrained from acting. It is sufficient if it was a reason: *Flinn v Flinn* [1999] 3 VR 712 at 749. The action or conduct undertaken must be reasonable in all the circumstances: *Waltons Stores v Maher* at CLR 406; ALR 525. In *Commonwealth Bank of Australia v Carotino (Australia) Pty Ltd* [2011] SASC 42 at [145], Kelly J said:

> [R]eliance on the assumption must be reasonable in two ways. First, it must be reasonable for the [relying party] to adopt the assumption in question on the strength of the representation made. Secondly, the action taken by the [relying party] in reliance upon the representation must be itself reasonable.

12.45 An important factor in assessing reasonableness here will be the characteristics of the relying party, including whether he or she is advised by lawyers, and whether he or she is well resourced and used to dealing in commercial transactions. In cases of substantial commercial enterprises that are legally represented, the court will carefully scrutinise whether the relying party's actions are reasonable. If not, an estoppel claim will be denied: *Austotel Pty Ltd v Franklins Selfserve Pty Ltd* at 585. In *Waltons Stores v Maher*, although the Mahers were legally represented, the facts were such that both the Mahers and their solicitors were encouraged and induced to make the same mistake, thereby not precluding the finding of an estoppel.

Knowledge or intention

12.46 According to Brennan J in *Waltons Stores v Maher*, the representor must actually know, or intend, that the relying party will act or refrain from acting in reliance on the assumption or expectation. In cases of assumptions based upon a promise or representation, knowledge is 'easily inferred'. In cases where the assumption arises outside the context of a promise or representation, the requirement of knowledge or intention is more difficult to establish: *Waltons Stores v Maher* at CLR 423; ALR 538. However, it can be established, as was the case in *Waltons Stores v Maher*, in cases where 'the defendant encourages a plaintiff to adhere to an assumption or expectation already formed, or acquiesces in an assumption or expectation when, in conscience, objection ought to be stated': *Pazta Company Pty Ltd v Idelake Pty Ltd* [2008] NSWSC 941 at [26].

12.47   Furthermore, according to Brennan J, it is not enough that the representor *ought* to have known that the relying party would act or refrain from acting in reliance on the assumption or expectation. A contrary view was suggested by Deane J in *Commonwealth v Verwayen* at CLR 445; ALR at 356. In relation to the difference of views between Brennan J and Deane J, in *New Zealand Pelt Export Company Limited v Trade Indemnity New Zealand Limited* [2004] VSCA 163 at [99], Nettle JA, speaking for a unanimous Court of Appeal in Victoria, said:

> [I]f it were necessary to make a choice, there are at least three reasons to prefer Deane J's formulation. In the first place, it is more consistent with the observations of Mason CJ and Wilson J in *Waltons Stores v Maher,* that the principle which underlies *High Trees* estoppel is that the courts will grant relief to a plaintiff who has acted to his detriment on the basis of a basic assumption in relation to which the other party has played such a part in the adoption of the assumption that it would be unfair or unjust if left free to ignore it. That view accords with the broad general ground of estoppel that where one of two innocent parties must suffer, the loss should fall on him by whose indiscretion it was occasioned. Secondly, as the joint judgment of Mason CJ and Wilson J in *Waltons Stores v Maher* demonstrates, the principle which underlies *High Trees* estoppel is the same principle as underlies the kind of estoppel exemplified in *Ramsden v Dyson*; and the better view is that in such a case the party to be estopped need not know of the full extent of his or her legal rights — it is sufficient that he or she ought to have appreciated what they were. Parity of reasoning suggests that it may be sufficient in a case of *High Trees* estoppel that the party to be estopped ought to have known that the other party would be induced by the estopped party's conduct to adopt and act on the basis of an assumption or expectation. Thirdly, the source of the idea that actual knowledge is an essential requirement seems to be the judgment of Lord Denning in *Crabb v Arun District Council* [[1976] Ch 179 at 188], and while his Lordship did say in that case that it was necessary that the party to be estopped know and intend that the other party act on the basis of the relevant assumption, his Lordship based his judgment on the speech of Lord Cairns in *Hughes v Metropolitan Railway Co* [(1877) 2 App Cas 439 at 448], and Lord Cairns did not speak in terms of knowledge or intent. The crucial passage of his speech was as follows:
>
> > … if parties who have entered into definite and distinct terms involving certain legal results — certain penalties or legal forfeiture — afterwards by their own act or with their own consent enter upon a course of negotiation which has the effect of leading one of the parties to suppose that the strict rights arising under the contract will not be enforced, or will be kept in suspense, or held in abeyance, the person who otherwise might have enforced those rights will not be allowed to enforce them where it would be inequitable having regard to the dealings which have thus taken place between the parties. My Lords, I repeat that I attribute to the Appellant no intention here to take advantage of, to lay a trap, but it appears to me that both parties by entering upon the negotiation which they entered upon, made it an inequitable thing that the exact period of six months dating from the month of October should afterwards be measured out as against the Respondent as the period during which the repairs must be executed.

The approach of Nettle JA was endorsed by Macaulay J in *Leading Synthetics Pty Ltd v Adroit Insurance Group Pty Ltd* [2011] VSC 467 at [69].

Detriment

12.48   The relying party must suffer, or stand to suffer, detriment if the assumption made by it is not fulfilled. In *Grundt v Great Boulder Pty Gold Mines Ltd* at 674–5, Dixon J said:

[T]he basal purpose of the doctrine [of estoppel] … is to avoid or prevent a detriment to the party asserting the estoppel by compelling the opposite party to adhere to the assumption upon which the [relying party] acted or abstained from acting. This means that the real detriment or harm from which the law seeks to give protection is that which would flow from the change of position if the assumption were deserted that led to it. So long as the assumption is adhered to, the party who altered his situation upon the faith of it cannot complain. His complaint is that when afterwards the other party makes a different state of affairs the basis of an assertion of right against him then, if it is allowed, his own original change of position will operate as a detriment.

The principle enunciated by Dixon J applies to both promissory and proprietary estoppels: *Delaforce v Simpson-Cook* at 491.

12.49   There must be a link between the detriment and the assumption or expectation. In *Thompson v Palmer* (1933) 49 CLR 507 at 547, Dixon J said that the relying party must suffer detriment in the sense that, 'as a result of adopting [the assumption or expectation] as the basis of action or inaction, [the relying party] will have placed himself in a position of material disadvantage if departure from the assumption is permitted'.

12.50   The notion of detriment conjures up the idea that the relying party will be worse off in some way. It is not enough that the relying party merely acted upon the representor's promise. In *Je Maintiendrai Pty Ltd v Quaglia* (1980) 26 SASR 101 at 106, the Full Court in South Australia held that it was necessary that the going back on the promise or representation would 'result in some detriment and therefore some injustice' to the relying party.

12.51   In *Walsh v Walsh* [2012] NSWCA 57 at 14, Meagher JA, speaking for a unanimous Court of Appeal, said that '[t]he detriment which can support an estoppel by encouragement need not be financial and it is not necessary, where that detriment is the expenditure of money, that the expenditure have been on the property in respect of which the estoppel is sought to be enforced'. The detriment suffered cannot be minor. It has been variously described as needing to be material or significant or substantial. In *Sullivan v Sullivan* [2006] NSWCA 312 at [20], Handley JA said:

> The object of the exercise is to do equity and for that purpose 'detriment' is no narrow or technical concept. It need not consist of expenditure of money or other quantifiable financial disadvantage so long as it is something substantial. The requirement must be approached as part of a broad inquiry as to whether departure from a promise would be unconscionable in all the circumstances.

In *Hawker Pacific Pty Ltd v Helicopter Charter Pty Ltd* (1991) 22 NSWLR 298 at 307–8, Handley JA said:

> While a single peppercorn may constitute valuable consideration which can support a simple contract it seems to me that the loss of such an item would not constitute a 'material detriment', 'material disadvantage', or a 'significant disadvantage' for the purposes of the law of estoppel. It may seem strange that there should be such a distinction. However in the first case the consideration has been accepted as the price of a bargain which the law strives to uphold. Promissory estoppels and estoppels by representation lack this element of mutuality, and the relevant detriment has not been accepted by the party estopped as the price for binding himself to the representation or promise.

12.52   In assessing the existence of detriment one must distinguish between expectation and reliance loss. It is clear that it is the reliance loss, and not expectation loss, that goes to establishing detriment. In *Delaforce v Simpson-Cook* at 491, Handley AJA summarised the position as follows:

> The relevant detriment is not the loss flowing from non-fulfilment of the promise or assurance. The detriment that makes an estoppel enforceable is that which the [relying party] would suffer, as a result of his or her original change of position, if the assumption which induced it was repudiated by the [representor].

In the context of the facts of *Waltons Stores v Maher*, the expectation loss suffered by the Mahers was the loss of rent they expected Waltons to pay during the term of the anticipated lease. The reliance loss was the wasted expenditure incurred in demolishing and rebuilding the premises. It was the reliance loss, and not the expectation loss, that established detriment in that case.

12.53   The significance of detriment is that it is this factor which makes it unconscientious or unjust for the representor to depart from the promise or representation. In *Waltons Stores v Maher*, at CLR 404; ALR 524, Mason CJ and Wilson J said:

> [E]quity will come to the relief of a [relying party] who has acted to his detriment on the basis of a basic assumption in relation to which the other party has 'played such a part in the adoption of the assumption that it would be unfair or unjust if he were left free to ignore it': per Dixon J in *Grundt* [at 675]… Equity comes to the relief of such a [relying party] on the footing that it would be unconscionable conduct on the part of the other party to ignore the assumption.

Failure to avoid detriment

12.54   The representor must have failed to act to avoid the relying party suffering detriment. One way in which action could be taken to avoid the detriment is by simply fulfilling the assumption or expectation.

12.55   However, it must be understood that the object of equitable estoppel is not to compel the representor to fulfil the assumption or expectation, but rather to avoid detriment if the assumption or expectation goes unfulfilled. Thus, this might be done by the representor advising the relying party that the assumption is mistaken before irreversible detriment has been incurred. In this respect, in *Vella v Wah Lai Investment (Australia) Pty Ltd* [2004] NSWSC 748 at [169], in a passage subsequently approved by the Victorian Court of Appeal in *ACN 074 971 109 (as trustee for the Argot Unit Trust) v The National Mutual Life Association of Australasia Ltd* (2008) 21 VR 351 at 391, Campbell J said:

> If one party, who has encouraged another to act on the basis that a particular state of affairs exists, gives notice that that state of affairs should no longer be regarded as existing then, unless the other party has already irretrievably prejudiced himself by acting on the assumption that that state of affairs exists, the estoppel will cease to bind, either immediately or after the other party has been given reasonable notice. This is the result of the principle that the relief which is appropriate to give effect to an estoppel is the minimum relief which would prevent the injustice arising by the person estopped departing from the assumption or expectation which has been induced.

Entire agreement clauses and equitable estoppel

12.56 A question with respect to equitable estoppel is whether a clause in a contract which denies any legal effect to previous negotiations and representations can prevent a relying party from pleading a case based upon equitable estoppel. In relation to such entire agreement clauses, in *Franklins Pty Ltd v Metcash Trading Ltd* (2009) 76 NSWLR 603 at 734; 264 ALR 15 at 141, Campbell JA, speaking for the Court of Appeal on this point, said:

> I would accept that an entire agreement clause … that … specifically denies efficacy to all previous negotiations and representations, could not overcome an equitable estoppel, once established. An 'entire agreement clause' might create a factual difficulty in the way of proof of the elements of equitable estoppel, most obviously, proof of inducement or reliance, and I would not want to rule out the possibility that it might be relevant to any precise remedy granted (though I cannot at present think of an example of when that might occur). However, it does not create an insuperable obstacle of principle. Consistently with the equitable principle that it will not allow a contract to be an instrument of fraud, equity would not permit an entire agreement clause to stultify the operation of its doctrines.

RELIEF BASED UPON EQUITABLE ESTOPPEL

12.57 Establishing the elements of equitable estoppel gives rise to an equity in favour of the relying party. This means that the relying party is entitled to some equitable relief. The relief is not based upon there being a promise or representation, but rather upon the expectation that the promise or representation generated: *Giumelli v Giumelli* at CLR 121; ALR 482.

12.58 It has often be said that there needs to be proportionality between the relief ordered and the detriment suffered, or that the court will, in making its orders, determine the minimum equity required to do justice to the relying party: *Waltons Stores v Maher* at CLR 419; ALR 535; *Commonwealth v Verwayen* at CLR 417, 429–30, 441–2; ALR 336, 345–6, 354. However, this is no longer the case. In *Walsh v Walsh* at [31], Meagher JA stated the current position as follows:

> There is no governing principle that requires that the relief granted be that which is the minimum necessary to do justice. To the extent that there is a prima facie entitlement to relief on the basis that the adopted expectation is to be made good, that entitlement must be weighed against any injustice to the estopped party in doing so and the detriment suffered by the party who has acted upon the induced expectation. Consideration should also be given to whether the proposed relief has any adverse effects on the interests of third parties.

12.59 In exercising its discretion to make an order in favour of the relying party, in promissory estoppel cases the courts have made it clear that the orders to be granted are generally reliance based in the sense that they are designed to prevent the relying party from suffering detriment: *Waltons Stores v Maher* at CLR 427; ALR 540; *Commonwealth v Verwayen* at CLR 411–12, 429, 501; ALR 331–2, 345, 397–8. This is because, satisfying the relying party's equity will not usually require going beyond preventing that party from suffering detriment.

12.60 Thus, in *Mobil Oil v Lyndel Nominees* at 238, the court concluded that relief in such cases 'is intended to relieve against detriment suffered and not to make good an expectation'. Similarly, in *ACN 074 971 109 v The National Mutual Life Association of Australasia* at 394, Dodds-Streeton JA said:

[The] doctrine [of equitable estoppel] … permits the court to do what is required in order to avoid detriment to the party who has been induced to act upon an assumed state of affairs … [T]hus … according to the circumstances of any given case, the relief required may be less than making good the assumption on the basis of which the plaintiff was encouraged to deal … [W]hat is required to satisfy the equity which arises against an estopped party depends on the circumstances.

12.61 However, it is clear that, in proprietary estoppel cases, a court will usually frame an expectation based order in the sense of making good the assumption or expectation relied upon by the relying party, rather than on the avoidance of detriment: *Delaforce v Simpson-Cook* at 492–7. In *Ramsden v Dyson*, at 170, Lord Kingsdown said:

If a man … under an expectation created or encouraged by the landlord that he shall have a certain interest [acts to his detriment] upon the faith of such expectation … a Court of equity will compel the landlord to give effect to such … expectation.

12.62 Similarly, in *Donis v Donis* (2007) 19 VR 577 at 582–3, Nettle JA said the following:

As the … decision in *Giumelli v Giumelli* shows … there is no such restriction in cases where the expectation which is encouraged is the acquisition of an interest in property. In such cases the remedy relates to the understanding of the parties and the expectation that has been encouraged. *Prima facie* the estopped party can only fulfil his or her equitable obligation by making good the expectation which he or she has encouraged. The estopped party, having promised to confer a proprietary interest on the party entitled to the benefit of the estoppel, and the latter having acted upon the promise to his or her detriment, is bound in conscience to make good the expectation … The *prima facie* position will yield to individual circumstances. Principle and authority compel the view that where a plaintiff's expectation or assumption is uncertain or extravagant or out of all proportion to the detriment which the plaintiff has suffered, the court should recognise that the claimant's equity may be better satisfied in another and possibly more limited way … [B]efore granting relief the court is required to consider all of the circumstances of the case, including the possible effects on third parties, and to avoid going beyond what is required for conscientious conduct or would do injustice to others. But that does not mean that the court is required to be 'constitutionally parsimonious' or that it is necessary for there to be substantial correspondence between expectation and the monetary value of the detriment suffered, or which but for the relief to be accorded would be suffered.

12.63 In *Giumelli v Giumelli* the High Court said there was nothing in earlier cases that precluded a court from granting relief in equitable estoppel cases on the basis of making good the relying party's assumption or expectation. In *Giumelli v Giumelli* at CLR 123; ALR 484, Gleeson CJ, McHugh, Gummow and Callinan JJ cited with approval a statement by Deane J in *Commonwealth v Verwayen* at CLR 445; ALR 356, where his Honour said:

[T]he question whether departure from the assumption would be unconscionable must be resolved not by reference to some preconceived formula framed to serve as a universal yardstick but by reference to all the circumstances of the case, including the reasonableness of the conduct of the [relying] party in acting upon the assumption and the nature and extent of the detriment which he would sustain by acting upon the assumption if departure from the assumed state of affairs were permitted.

The types of orders that can be made in fulfilling the expectation include ordering a transfer of the property to the relying party, the imposition of a trust, or granting a charge or lien over the property. Ultimately it is a question of what is appropriate in the circumstances: *Tadrous v Tadrous* at [43]–[49].

12.64   In *Giumelli v Giumelli*, parents promised their son that, if he continued to live on a property owned by them, they would subdivide it and give him the portion containing the house in which he lived. On the basis of this the son stayed and gave up a career opportunity that would have taken him away from the property. The relationship between the parents and son broke down when the son married a woman of whom his parents did not approve, and they refused to transfer the property to the son. The High Court granted the son monetary relief to the value of the property that should have been transferred to him by his parents. The High Court did not order a transfer of the property to the son. However, the monetary compensation was nevertheless a remedy based upon the son's lost expectation rather than reliance loss or any actual detriment suffered by the son.

12.65   Thus, generally relief in promissory estoppel cases will be reliance based whereas in proprietary estoppel cases it will be expectation based. In *ACN 074 971 109 v The National Mutual Life Association of Australasia* at 394, Dodds-Streeton JA summarised the current state of the law on relief for equitable estoppel as follows:

> It is true that in *Giumelli v Giumelli*, Gleeson CJ and McHugh, Gummow and Callinan JJ said that *Verwayen* did not foreclose as a matter of doctrine relief making good the assumption in an appropriate case. But nothing which their Honours said in *Giumelli* suggests that there was any change from the view expressed in *Verwayen* that the doctrine of equitable estoppel enables a court to do what is required to avoid detriment to the party who has been induced to act upon an assumed state of affairs, and thus that the relief required in a given case may be less than making good the assumption. Accordingly, since *Giumelli*, in the majority of commercial cases not involving the acquisition of an interest in real property in which the doctrine of equitable estoppel had been invoked, the relief accorded it has been no more than was necessary to avoid detriment.

FUSION OF EQUITABLE AND COMMON LAW ESTOPPELS?

12.66   The complexity attendant upon having so many varieties of estoppel makes unification an attractive prospect. The successful merger of promissory and proprietary estoppels in *Waltons Stores v Maher* has fuelled speculation as to the possibility of an even more challenging simplification — the joining of common law and equitable estoppels. The leading advocates of this were Mason CJ and Deane J, neither of whom agreed with the model designed by the other and both of whom have now vacated the High Court bench. While the present members of the High Court have not dismissed the possibility of unification they are yet to find a suitable occasion for the implementation of such an innovation. It is clear, however, that the legacy left them by Mason CJ and Deane J is far from uncomplicated.

12.67   The principal difficulty in fusing common law and equitable estoppel lies in reconciling their very different origins and purposes so as to decide upon the form that a single doctrine would ultimately take. The different functions of the estoppels in the two jurisdictions are most apparent in the remedies they provide. The contrary positions adopted by Mason CJ and Deane J in *Commonwealth v Verwayen* reflect the differing emphasis they placed upon the two jurisdictions when formulating their own particular model. Deane J's unified estoppel reflected common law roots at the expense of equitable influences. He denied that it could act as a sword and limited its role to establishing the state of affairs by which the court was to resolve the dispute — in other words, his estoppel was to have the evidentiary quality so often referred to at common law. Consequently, his view that the 'prima facie entitlement' of a successful claimant is simply to have the assumption made good is a logical conclusion. However, he did admit that the availability of that remedy should be qualified if such 'relief would exceed what could be justified by the requirements of conscientious conduct and would be unjust to the estopped party': *Commonwealth v Verwayen* at CLR 442; ALR 354. For a number of reasons, Deane J's view has not attracted much support from commentators or his fellow judges. Its chief failure would seem to be the rejection of estoppel as a source of substantive rights — a position to which it would now seem quite difficult to return.

12.68 The proposal by Mason CJ is very different from that of Deane J. In *Commonwealth v Verwayen*, at CLR 413; ALR 333, Mason CJ said:

> [I]t would confound principle and common sense to maintain that estoppel by conduct occupies a special field which has as its hallmark function the making good of assumptions. There is no longer any purpose to be served in recognising an evidentiary form of estoppel operating in the same circumstances as the emergent rules of substantive estoppel. The result is that it should be accepted that there is but one doctrine of estoppel, which provides that a court of common law or equity may do what is required, but not more, to prevent a person who has relied upon an assumption as to a present, past or future state of affairs (including a legal state of affairs), which assumption the party estopped has induced him to hold, from suffering detriment in reliance upon the assumption as a result of the denial of its correctness. A central element of that doctrine is that there must be a proportionality between the remedy and the detriment which is its purpose to avoid. It would be wholly inequitable and unjust to insist upon a disproportionate making good of the relevant assumption.

12.69 The impetus for unification seems to have lessened since the decision in *Commonwealth v Verwayen*. Writing extra-judicially in 2006, Justice Handley of the New South Wales Court of Appeal said:

> Any single overarching doctrine [of estoppel] would be at such a high level of abstraction that it would serve no useful purpose. Each form of estoppel has its own elements, although some are common to others. The similarities warrant their recognition as a form of estoppel but the differences make each a distinct form with its own history and requirements. There is no more need for a single overarching doctrine for estoppel than there is for torts. Estoppel by deed, by grant, and by convention are common law doctrines which preclude contradiction but do not require a change of position induced by belief in the truth of facts. Estoppel by representation, developed in equity and borrowed by law, precludes contradiction if the representee's belief in the truth of the representation induced a detrimental change of position and the rights of the parties are governed by the facts as represented. Proprietary and promissory estoppels are equitable. Proprietary estoppel by encouragement enforces proprietary expectations which the person estopped has created or encouraged when their repudiation would be unconscionable. Proprietary estoppel by standing by enforces an equity against the fraud of an owner who seeks to rely on his property rights to profit from the known mistake of another. Promissory estoppel is a defensive equity which restrains the enforcement of positive rights by a person whose promise induced a change of position which makes such enforcement inequitable. The distinctly equitable

estoppels change the rights of the parties, while the others change them indirectly by changing the facts. Each form has a separate history and a distinct source in law or in equity. The various rationales — recital, grant, convention, representation, positive promise or encouragement, fraud and mistake, and negative promise — are different. There is no single overarching principle.[3]

12.70 In a similar vein, also writing extra-judicially in 2007, Justice Brereton of the Supreme Court of New South Wales said:

That there is no overarching doctrine of common principle is reflected in the disparate operation of the different estoppels: some estoppels are founded on unconscionability, which is irrelevant to others; some estoppels alter the rights of the parties, others alter only the facts; some, once raised, are permanent, whereas others may be only temporary.[4]

3. K R Handley, *Estoppel by Conduct and Election*, Thomson, Sweet & Maxwell, London, 2006, pp 20–21.
4. P L G Brereton, 'Equitable Estoppel in Australia: The Court of Conscience in the Antipodes' (2007) 81 *Australian Law Journal* 638, p 643.

13

RELIEF AGAINST FORFEITURE

INTRODUCTION

13.1 In certain circumstances where a person stands to lose some interest in property because of his or her breach of contract or as a result of the contract being terminated for some other reason, that interest may be protected by a court pursuant to principles relating to relief against forfeiture. In *Hyman v Rose* [1912] AC 623 at 631, Lord Loreburn LC said that equity's jurisdiction here was 'to prevent one man from forfeiting what in fair dealings belongs to someone else, by taking advantage of a breach from which he is not commensurately and irreparably damaged'.

13.2 The jurisdiction to relieve against forfeiture is underpinned by the principle of unconscientiousness. Relief will be granted if it would be unconscientious to allow forfeiture to occur: *Stern v McArthur* (1988) 165 CLR 489 at 526–7; 81 ALR 463 at 488. The extent of this jurisdiction was outlined in Lord Wilberforce's speech in *Shiloh Spinners Ltd v Harding* [1973] AC 691 at 723–4; [1973] 1 All ER 90 at 101, where he said:

> [E]quity expects men to carry out their bargains and will not let them buy their way out by uncovenanted payment. But it is consistent with these principles that we should reaffirm the right of courts of equity in appropriate and limited cases to relieve against forfeiture for breach of covenant or condition where the primary object of the bargain is to secure a stated result which can effectively be attained when the matter comes before the court, and where the forfeiture provision is added by way of security for the production of that result. The word 'appropriate' involves consideration of the conduct of the applicant for relief, in particular whether his default was wilful, of the gravity of the breaches, and of the disparity between the value of the property of which forfeiture is claimed as compared with the damage caused by the breach.

The doctrine only applies where the relief is sought from the exercise of some power by the other party to the transaction, such as termination of a contract. It does apply where, for example, termination of a contract is automatic: *Hampton v BHP Billiton Minerals Pty Ltd (No 2)* [2012] WASC 285 at [233]–[240]. Thus, if the termination of contract A, leads to the automatic termination of contract B, there can be no relief against forfeiture in the context of contract B.

13.3 Typical illustrations of what Lord Wilberforce was referring to include provisions in leases that entitle the landlord to re-enter the premises and forfeit the lease in the event of the tenant not paying rent and clauses in mortgages that enable the mortgagee to determine the mortgage if the mortgagor fails to make loan repayments.

13.4 In broad terms, equitable intervention on the basis of these principles relates to circumstances involving fraud, accident, mistake or surprise: *Shiloh Spinners Ltd v Harding* at AC 723; All ER at 101. In cases other than those involving accident or mistake, one must establish that the conduct of the party seeking to enforce the right of forfeiture has 'in some significant respect caused or contributed' to the breach of contract by the other party: *Tanwar Enterprises Pty Ltd v Cauchi* (2003) 217 CLR 315 at 335; 201 ALR 359 at 373.

13.5 In *RHG Mortgage Securities v BNY Trusts Company* [2009] NSWSC 1432 at [137], McDougall J observed that, in order to establish a case for relief against forfeiture, a plaintiff needs to do the following:

(i)   identify the right or rights that would be forfeited;
(ii) identify the legal rights, the exercise of which would effect the forfeiture; and
(iii) identify the reasons why the exercise of those legal rights would be unconscientious.

13.6 In ascertaining whether the exercise of legal rights is unconscientious, the court does not confine its enquiry only to the conduct of the person exercising the legal right. In *ING Bank (Australia) Ltd v O'Shea* [2010] NSWCA 71 at [19], Giles JA said:

> Unconscientiousness does not mean attention is given only to the conduct of the person exercising the right, and regard is had to the conduct of the party seeking relief and to other matters providing the circumstances in which the unconscientiousness of the exercise of the right must be judged. But it remains the ultimate question.

13.7 Because the granting of relief against forfeiture is consistent with ordering specific performance of the contract, most cases involving relief against forfeiture involve interests in land. This is because contracts for the sale of land or interests in land are generally specifically enforceable (see 23.23–23.29), whereas the opposite is generally the case with respect to contracts involving personal property (see 23.19–23.22) or personal services: see 23.41–23.43. Thus, in *Scandinavian Trading Tanker Co AB v Flota Petrolera Ecuatoriana* [1983] 2 AC 694; [1983] 2 All ER 763, relief against forfeiture was refused in circumstances where, pursuant to a time charter, a shipowner withdrew the vessel from the service of the charterer when the charterer failed to make relevant payments in accordance with an essential time stipulation because it would have been tantamount to specific performance of a contract for personal services. However, if a contract relating to personal property or personal services is specifically enforceable, relief against forfeiture will be available: *Federal Airports Corporation v Makucha Developments Pty Ltd* (1993) 115 ALR 679 at 700; *BICC plc v Burndy Corporation* [1985] Ch 232 at 251–2; [1985] 1 All ER 417 at 427–8.

13.8 The willingness of courts to exercise their jurisdiction to relieve against forfeiture fluctuates from time to time. In the wake of the most recent High Court decision on the matter in *Tanwar Enterprises Pty Ltd v Cauchi* at CLR 328; ALR 368, in *Damco Nominees Pty Ltd v Moxham* [2012] VSC 79 at [76], Mukhtar AsJ observed that '*Tanwar* does not favour an expansive view of the equitable jurisdiction to relieve against forfeiture'. In *Tanwar Enterprises Pty Ltd v Cauchi* the High Court made it clear that a court should be reluctant to interfere with deliberately negotiated contractual rights and that the jurisdiction to relieve against forfeiture does not authorise it to remake a contract into a form that it thinks is more reasonable or fair. Furthermore, the High Court stated that a court will not intervene where some supervening event operates more to the advantage of one party than the other, and the event was one for which the parties might have made, but did not make, some express provision. The High Court went on to approve a comment made by Mason CJ in *Stern v McArthur*, at CLR 503; ALR 471, where his Honour said that 'the jurisdiction to grant relief against forfeiture does not authorize a court to reshape contractual relations into a form the court thinks more reasonable or fair where subsequent events have rendered one side's situation more favourable'. On the other hand, the parties to a contract cannot oust the jurisdiction to relieve against forfeiture by including an express term to that effect in their contract: *Federal Airports Corporation v Makucha Developments Pty Ltd* at 700.

13.9   There are various types of cases where relief against forfeiture issues typically arise, including: (i) contracts for the sale of land; and (ii) contracts for the lease of land. Each of these two broad categories will be considered in turn. This will be followed by a brief discussion of the issue of relief against forfeiture in the context of option contracts.

CONTRACTS FOR THE SALE OF LAND

13.10   Relief against forfeiture can arise in a number of different situations involving the sale of land. These include: (i) forfeiture of payments made under a contract; (ii) forfeiture of a purchaser's interest under a contract for the sale of land; and (iii) forfeiture of the deposit.

Forfeiture of payments made under a contract

13.11   At common law a defaulting purchaser can recover instalment payments, apart from the deposit (see 13.21–13.28), made under a contract for the sale of land, unless the contract provides that the vendor is entitled to forfeit such payments. However, in the latter case equity provides relief against forfeiture of those payments. The principles here were expressed by Dixon J in *McDonald v Dennys Lascelles Ltd* (1933) 48 CLR 457 at 678–9, as follows:

> It is now beyond question that instalments already paid may be recovered by a defaulting purchaser when the vendor elects to discharge the contract … Although the parties might by express agreement give the vendor an absolute right at law to retain the instalments in the event of the contract going off, yet in equity such a contract is considered to involve a forfeiture from which the purchaser is entitled to be relieved … But, where there is no express agreement excluding the implication made at law, by which the instalments become repayable upon the discharge of the obligation to convey and the purchaser has a legal right to the return of the purchase money already paid which makes it needless to resort to equity and submit to equity as a condition of obtaining relief, the vendor appears to be unable to deduct from the amount of the instalments the amount of his loss occasioned by the purchaser's abandonment of the contract. A vendor may, of course, counterclaim for damages in the action in which the purchaser seeks to recover the instalments.

13.12   As an alternative to the above, a purchaser can seek relief against forfeiture of his or her interest in land under the contract pursuant to principles discussed below: see 13.13–13.20.

Forfeiture of a purchaser's interest under a contract of sale

13.13   Relief against forfeiture principles can also arise in circumstances where it would be unconscientious for the defaulting purchaser to lose his or her interest in land as a result of the termination of the contract by the vendor. In such cases the defaulting purchaser will seek the remedy of specific performance rather than relief against forfeiture, because at that time, the contract having been validly terminated by the vendor, the purchaser no longer has any interest — the vendor has already forfeited the interest. The logical consequence is that the purchaser cannot seek relief against forfeiture of a non-existent interest. He or she must seek specific performance of the contract: *Tanwar Enterprises v Cauchi* at CLR 334–5; ALR 372–3. In determining whether the contract should be specifically enforced, the court will need to ascertain whether it was, in all the circumstances, unconscientious for the vendor to have forfeited the purchaser's interest.

13.14   A common example of the operation of these principles arises in cases where the purchaser fails to complete a transaction in accordance with an essential time stipulation (see 2.24–2.25) and the vendor subsequently terminates the contract. In *Union Eagle Ltd v Golden Achievement Ltd* [1997] AC 514; [1997] 2 All ER 215, the Privy Council rejected a purchaser's application for specific performance in circumstances where the vendor had terminated the contract after the purchaser was late by 10 minutes in seeking to tender the balance of the purchase price where time was the essence of the contract. This aspect of the decision has been criticised by Stevens as follows:

> It seems unconscionable that a failure to comply with a time stipulation by a mere 10 minutes should entitle the vendor to *both* the benefit of the substantial deposit and immediate resale at a higher price. The degree of fault on the part of the purchaser is slight compared to the detriment he will suffer ... In such circumstances the only reason why a vendor would want to [terminate], rather than accept performance tendered almost immediately after the appointed time, is that he anticipates obtaining an increased price by reselling his asset, and the breach is exploited to escape the bargain originally entered ... It is suggested that a purchaser who has tendered performance a *de minimis* period of time after it was due should be entitled to seek equitable relief against forfeiture of his deposit if it can be shown that the vendor has not in fact suffered any loss as a result of the failure to perform on time, which would prima facie be the case if he resold the property at a profit.[1]

Nevertheless, in very similar circumstances in *Rick Dees Ltd v Larsen* [2007] 3 NZLR 577, the New Zealand Supreme Court followed the approach of the House of Lords in *Union Eagle v Golden Achievement*.

13.15   The leading Australian authority in this context is *Tanwar Enterprises v Cauchi*. In that case, a purchaser of land pursuant to three separate contracts was granted two lengthy extensions of time to complete the transactions. A further date was agreed upon for completion with time being of the essence. The purchaser failed to complete on this date and the vendors terminated the contracts. The purchaser's failure to complete was due to delay in getting finance in place to complete the transactions. The purchaser was, however, in a position to complete the contracts on the next day. The purchaser sought specific performance of the contracts. The High Court unanimously ruled against the purchaser. In the joint judgment of Gleeson CJ, McHugh, Gummow, Hayne and Heydon JJ, at CLR 336; ALR 373, their Honours said that there was nothing unconscientious in the vendors being able to terminate the contract for the purchaser's failure to comply with an essential time stipulation. They also noted that, in broad terms, such unconscientious conduct arose in circumstances involving fraud, accident, mistake or surprise, and that in cases other than those

---

1.   J Stevens, 'Having Your Cake and Eating it? *Union Eagle Ltd v Golden Achievement Ltd*' (1998) 61 *Modern Law Review* 255, p 260.

involving accident or mistake, the conduct of the vendor had to have 'in some significant respect caused or contributed' to the breach of contract by the other party. On the facts of the case there was no such conduct by the vendors.

13.16 Their Honours, at CLR 328; ALR 368, noted that 'the court will not readily intervene against the loss of a contract for sale validly [terminated] by the vendor for breach of an essential condition'. In this respect their Honours referred to the outcome of the earlier case of *Union Eagle v Golden Achievement*. Although their Honours recognised that the English courts were less flexible in applying relevant principles in this area of the law, they were in agreement with the sentiments expressed by Lord Hoffmann, at AC 519; All ER 218–9, where his Lordship observed that it was a 'beguiling heresy' to suggest that the jurisdiction to relieve against forfeiture was 'unlimited and unfettered' and then continued as follows:

> It is worth pausing to notice why it continues to beguile and why it is a heresy. It has the obvious merit of allowing the court to impose what it considers to be a fair solution in the individual case. The principle that equity will restrain the enforcement of legal rights when it would be unconscionable to insist upon them has an attractive breadth. But the reasons why the courts have rejected such generalisations are founded ... upon practical considerations of business. These are, in summary, that in many forms of transaction it is of great importance that if something happens for which the contract has made express provision, the parties should know with certainty that the terms of the contract will be enforced. The existence of an undefined discretion to refuse to enforce the contract on the ground that this would be 'unconscionable' is sufficient to create uncertainty. Even if it is most unlikely that a discretion to grant relief will be exercised, its mere existence enables litigation to be employed as a negotiating tactic. The realities of commercial life are that this may cause injustice which cannot be fully compensated by the ultimate decision in the case.

13.17 Lord Hoffmann, at AC 520; All ER 220, then said the following in relation to the vendor's right to terminate a contract for breach of an essential term:

> Its purpose is ... to restore to the vendor his freedom to deal with his land as he pleases. In a rising market, such a right may be valuable but volatile. Their Lordships think that in such circumstances a vendor should be able to know with reasonable certainty whether he may resell the land or not.

13.18 Finally, in *Tanwar Enterprises v Cauchi*, their Honours, at CLR 328; ALR 369, observed that mere supervening events and changes in circumstances are insufficient to render forfeiture by a vendor unconscientious.

13.19 As already noted, in cases where fraud or surprise are the grounds upon which unconscientiousness is based, the vendor must have caused or contributed to the purchaser's breach. In *Tanwar Enterprises v Cauchi*, at CLR 335–6; ALR 374, the High Court referred to and explained the decision in the earlier case of *Legione v Hateley* (1983) 152 CLR 406; 46 ALR 1, as being an instance of surprise. In that case, on the basis of somewhat uncertain statements made by the office of the vendors' solicitors, the purchasers were lulled into a belief that the vendors would accept completion of the contract if it occurred within a couple of days of the due date for completion, time being of the essence in respect of that date. In these circumstances the High Court ruled that the forfeiture by the vendors was unconscientious.

13.20 In establishing unconscientiousness based upon fraud or surprise the conduct by the vendor will in many cases give rise to a separate cause of action in favour of the purchaser. For example, it may constitute a vitiating factor such as a mistake, misrepresentation, undue influence (see Chapter 10) and so on. Or it may give rise to a claim based upon the principles of equitable estoppel: see Chapter 12. However, it is clear from the decision in *Legione v Hateley* that the conduct of the vendor does not of itself have to give rise to a cause of action. In that case, notwithstanding that the vendors' conduct did not give rise to an estoppel, the purchasers succeeded in establishing that the vendors' forfeiture was unconscientious.

Forfeiture of the deposit

Equitable jurisdiction

13.21 The deposit paid by a purchaser in a contract for the sale of land is treated differently to other payments of the purchase price. In addition to being a part payment of the purchase price, a deposit is seen as a guarantee of the purchaser's bona fides. In *Howe v Smith* (1884) 27 Ch D 89 at 101, Fry LJ said that the deposit is 'an earnest to bind the bargain so entered into, and creates by fear of its forfeiture a motive in the payer to perform the rest of the contract'. Thus, a vendor is entitled to forfeit the deposit if the purchaser fails to complete the purchase. The principles set out in *Howe v Smith* apply with equal vigour in relation to contracts which do not involve land: *Fiorelli Properties Pty Ltd v Professional Fencemakers Pty Ltd* [2011] VSC 661 at [32]–[39]. If the vendor brings an action against the purchaser for damages for breach of contract, the vendor must give credit for the deposit that has been forfeited in reduction of the damages that are otherwise recoverable against the purchaser: *Commissioner of Taxation of the Commonwealth of Australia v Reliance Carpet Co Pty Limited* (2008) 236 CLR 342 at 350; 246 ALR 448 at 454; *Ng v Ashley King (Developments) Ltd* [2010] 4 All ER 914 at 922–8.

13.22 The vendor's right to forfeit the deposit is not, however, absolute. In some cases equity will grant the purchaser relief against forfeiture of the deposit. If the deposit is in the nature of a penalty (see Chapter 14), equity will grant such relief. However, the application of the law on penalties to deposits is not rigorous. As Butt has noted, 'most deposits … exceed the amount of damage a vendor is likely to suffer from the purchaser's default, and if strictly measured by this test should be characterised as "penalties"'.[2]

13.23 For relief against forfeiture of a deposit, the purchaser needs to establish two points. First, the amount of the deposit must be excessive. Second, the conduct of the vendor in demanding to retain such a deposit must be, in all the circumstances, unconscientious.

13.24 In relation to the amount of the deposit, it is generally accepted that a deposit of 10 per cent of the purchase price is reasonable and not excessive: *Mehmet v Benson* (1963) 81 WN (Pt 1) (NSW) 188 at 191; *Lexane Pty Ltd v Highfern Pty Ltd* [1985] 1 Qd R 446 at 455. There are no Australian authorities where relief against forfeiture has been granted in relation to deposits of 10 per cent, or less, of the purchase price. This approach was confirmed by the Privy Council decision in *Union Eagle v Golden Achievement* where the vendor was held as entitled to terminate the contract and forfeit the deposit of 10 per cent of the purchase price.

---

2.   P Butt, *The Standard Contract for the Sale of Land in New South Wales*, 2nd ed, LBC Information Services, Sydney, 1998, p 454.

13.25   Where the deposit exceeds 10 per cent of the purchase price, whether it is unconscientious for the vendor to forfeit the deposit will depend upon all the facts and circumstances of the case. In this respect, Dal Pont makes the following observations:

> A mere comparison of percentages is not decisive; also potentially relevant are 'the nature of the property sold and the circumstances of the case generally', including prevailing practice and market conditions. An important factor is the risk to which the vendor is exposed by virtue of the terms of the contract, which in turn is a function of matters such as the length of the settlement period, whether the purchaser is given possession or other benefits before the date of completion, the subject matter of the contract, and the nature of the breaches alleged.[3]

13.26   In *Re Hoobin (dec'd)* [1957] VR 341, a deposit of 25 per cent was upheld in circumstances where the contract dealt with the sale of a hotel with a completion date some eight years after contracts were entered into and where the purchaser had possession of the property during that period of time. In *Coates v Sarich* [1964] WAR 2, another case of extended time to complete where the purchaser was allowed into possession in the meantime, a deposit of 30 per cent was upheld in relation to a contract for the sale of a farm. The Full Court in this case observed that a higher deposit was justified because the long period of time to completion — 16 years — exposed the vendor to significant risk. The risk was that, if the purchaser defaulted and the vendor had to terminate the contract, the farm might no longer be as profitable and valuable because it had been run down by the way in which it was managed by the purchaser while in possession.

13.27   However, in the absence of special circumstances such as those outlined in *Re Hoobin* and *Coates v Sarich*, a deposit in excess of 10 per cent will normally be viewed as a penalty and relief against forfeiture will be granted to the purchaser: *Ng v Ashley King (Developments) Ltd* at 922. Thus, in *Smyth v Jessup* [1956] VLR 230, and *Saunders v Leonardi* (1976) 1 BPR 9409, deposits of 40 per cent and 27 per cent respectively were held to be excessive.

13.28   In exercising its jurisdiction to relieve against forfeiture of the deposit the court grants relief in relation to the whole of the deposit. However, there is some authority to suggest that a court can grant relief as to part only of the deposit. Thus, in *Mehmet v Benson*, the trial judge indicated that relief would apply to only that part of the deposit above 10 per cent of the purchase price. The matter was not discussed when the case went to the High Court, but dicta there indicate that the court agreed with the trial judge's approach: *Mehmet v Benson* (1965) 113 CLR 295 at 309, 315. Similarly, in *Freedom v AHR Constructions Pty Ltd* [1987] 1 Qd R 59 at 66, McPherson J took the view, without discussing it, that equity will 'relieve wholly or in part against forfeiture of the sum paid'. Such an approach is not problematical as equity can, as a condition of granting relief, do so on terms that the amount forfeited is subject to a set-off (see 31.32–31.41) for the actual loss suffered by the vendor. Alternatively, it can be justified on the basis that other forms of equitable relief can be partial, an example being partial rescission: see 27.14–27.17.

---

3.   G E Dal Pont, *Equity and Trusts in Australia*, 5th ed, Law Book Co, Sydney, 2011, p 386. In England, the law is that 'if the deposit exceeds the customary 10%, it will be an invalid penalty'.

Statutory jurisdiction

13.29 In New South Wales and Victoria the courts are given statutory jurisdiction to order a vendor to refund a deposit to a defaulting purchaser if the court thinks it is fit to do so.[4] Contractual provisions attempting to exclude this statutory jurisdiction have been held to be attempts to oust the jurisdiction of the courts and are therefore void on public policy grounds: *Aribisala v St James Homes (Grosvenor Dock) Ltd* [2007] EWHC 1694 (Ch) at [33]. The court's jurisdiction under these sections is unfettered. However, in practice, the courts have exercised the jurisdiction in such a way that the refund of the deposit will be ordered only when it would be 'unjust and inequitable' for the vendor to forfeit it: *Lucas & Tait (Investments) Pty Ltd v Victoria Securities Ltd* [1973] 2 NSWLR 268 at 272–3; *Romanos v Pentagold Investments Pty Limited* (2003) 217 CLR 367 at 376; 201 ALR 399 at 404.

13.30 In *Nassif v Caminer* (2009) 74 NSWLR 276 at 289–90, in a case dealing with s 55(2A) of the *Conveyancing Act 1919* (NSW), the Court of Appeal approved of the following principles in relation to the statutory jurisdiction to order a refund of a deposit set out by Santow JA in *Havyn Pty Ltd v Webster* [2005] NSWCA 182 at [173]:

(a) Section 55(2A) confers upon the Court a statutory jurisdiction to return forfeited deposits which was not previously available either at common law or in equity. Therefore, it would be wrong to seek to confine the jurisdiction conferred by the words of the statute by analogy with the jurisdiction of common law and equity to relieve against penalties or forfeiture.

(b) Notwithstanding this, it is important for a Court in considering the scope of the discretion conferred by s 55(2A) to bear in mind that a deposit is an earnest of performance. That fact forms part of the context in which the discretion falls to be exercised, and means that a Court will not lightly be moved to order the return of a deposit paid as an earnest of performance, and forfeited in accordance with the express terms of the contract when performance does not occur.

(c) That context is significant when considering the justice and equity of the case, and whether the Court 'sees fit' to order the deposit to be returned. It does not involve putting a gloss on the words of the statute requiring the applicant to show 'special circumstances' (or satisfy any like test) before a deposit will be returned.

(d) In particular, this principle mandates against characterising a forfeited deposit as a windfall to the vendor, merely because it is forfeited.

(e) In considering an application under s 55(2A), it will often be material for the Court to consider a number of factors, including (though not exhaustively) the nature of a deposit, the terms of the contract providing for its forfeiture and the circumstances in which the deposit was forfeited.

13.31 It can be noted that the fact that the vendor forfeits a deposit in a rising market and then sells the property for a profit does not of itself make it unjust that the vendor retains the deposit. It is but a factor to be taken into account in the court's decision to order a refund of the deposit and may be decisive, as it was in *Nelson v Bellamy* [2000] NSWSC 182. However, in other cases where the property was sold at a profit or at a higher price the court did not order a refund of the deposit: *Borda v Burgess* [2003] NSWSC 1171; *Midill (97PL) Ltd v Park Lane Estates Ltd* (2009) 2 All ER 1067; *Baird v Chambers* [2010] NSWSC 272. On the other hand, the resale of the property at a loss

---

4. *Conveyancing Act 1919* (NSW) s 55(2A); *Property Law Act 1958* (Vic) s 49(2).

will 'normally provide a strong reason for refusing to make an order under [these sections]': *Baird v Chambers* at [16].

CONTRACTS FOR THE LEASE OF LAND

13.32   At common law a landlord may forfeit the lease if the tenant breaches any term of the lease. Historically, the common law did not permit forfeiture and forfeiture was only permitted if the lease expressly or impliedly granted the landlord such a right.[5] However, legislation in all Australian jurisdictions now allows for a landlord to forfeit for breaches of the lease.[6]

13.33   Equity's jurisdiction to relieve against forfeiture was historically generally only exercised in relation to the failure to pay rent. Relief here is conditional upon the tenant paying outstanding rent and the landlord's costs: *Gill v Lewis* [1956] 2 QB 1 at 13. In *Twinside Pty Ltd v Venetian Nominees Pty Ltd* [2008] WASC 110 at [37], the court approved the following summary of relevant principles on this issue:

> Courts normally relieve against forfeiture for non-payment of rent. Provided the landlord is compensated for all arrears of rent and any loss arising from the non-payment, the tenant will generally succeed in having the lease restored ... In line with this principle, a history of tardy payments is not of itself grounds for refusing relief against forfeiture. Nevertheless, the tenant is not entitled to relief as of right ... Relief generally will be refused where the tenant is hopelessly insolvent, for in such a case an order re-instating the lease would be futile. This is so even though the tenant is able to pay the arrears of rent at the time of the proceedings, because the court is entitled to take into account the improbability that rent will be paid in the future, or that its payment may be a preference for creditors. But where the tenant's financial position was not 'hopeless', and the tenant had entered into a scheme of arrangement with creditors to try to trade out of its difficulties, relief was granted on payment of arrears to date.[7]

13.34   Thus, it is clear that 'the starting point is a general rule that relief against forfeiture for non-payment of rent will be granted to a lessee who has remedied its defaults in payment of rent. However, the remedy is discretionary and in exceptional circumstances relief may be refused for reasons arising from the lessee's poor financial position': *Twinside v Venetian Nominees* at [40]. An illustration of such circumstances is the decision in *Direct Food Supplies (Vic) Pty Ltd v DLV Pty Ltd* [1975] VR 358, where relief against forfeiture was refused in circumstances where the tenant conceded that it was insolvent and not in a position to pay its debts, including rent. To have granted relief would have exposed the landlord to having to disgorge those payments if the tenant went into liquidation. However, the fact that there are serious grounds for concern as to whether the tenant is able to make future rental payments is not a sufficient reason to refuse relief. That is because any subsequent breach of the lease will lead to a future termination by the landlord from which relief against forfeiture is most unlikely to be granted: *Old Papa's Franchise Systems Pty Ltd v Camisa Nominees Pty Ltd* [2003] WASCA 11 at [132].

---

5.   P Butt, *Land Law*, 6th ed, Law Book Co, Sydney, 2010, pp 399–400.

6.   *Land Titles Act 1925* (ACT) s 120(1)(d); *Conveyancing Act 1919* (NSW) s 85(1); *Law of Property Act 2000* (NT) s 119(1)(d); *Property Law Act 1974* (Qld) s 107(d); *Real Property Act 1886* (SA) s 125(3); *Land Titles Act 1980* (Tas) s 67(b); *Transfer of Land Act 1958* (Vic) s 67(1)(d); *Transfer of Land Act 1893* (WA) s 93(2).

7.   As stated in P Butt, *Land Law*, 5th ed, Law Book Co, Sydney, 2006, pp 395–6.

13.35 Legislation setting out a court's jurisdiction to relieve against forfeiture in relation to breaches of the covenant to pay rent is found in all Australian jurisdictions except the Australian Capital Territory and Western Australia.[8] Furthermore, legislation permitting courts to grant relief against forfeiture for breach of covenants other than those dealing with rent exists in all Australian jurisdictions.[9] These various statutory provisions do not displace equity's inherent jurisdiction to relieve against forfeiture. Furthermore, they are applied by the courts in general conformity with established equitable principles, so that relief will only be granted if, in all the circumstances, it would be unconscientious for the landlord to forfeit the lease.

OPTIONS

13.36 There is some uncertainty as to whether an option to acquire an interest in property attracts equity's jurisdiction relating to relief against forfeiture in circumstances where the grantor of the option refuses to transfer the property interest to the grantee. Common examples of options where the issue of relief against forfeiture has been raised are in leases which grant the tenant an option for a further lease upon the expiration of the initial lease and/or an option for the tenant to purchase the leased property.

13.37 If the grantor's refusal to transfer the interest to the grantee is because the grantee has failed to exercise the option in accordance with its terms it has been held that relief against forfeiture is not available. An example would be a failure by the grantee to exercise the option on time. In *Buildev Development Pty Ltd v Pic Sales Pty Ltd* [2003] NSWSC 1245 at [22], a case concerned with the failure to comply strictly with the manner in which an option was to be exercised, Campbell J said:

> [T]here is a more fundamental problem with the availability of relief against forfeiture [in this case]. That problem is that there simply has not been a forfeiture. A forfeiture arises when, by reason of a breach by one party (or perhaps a third party), the other party becomes entitled to bring to an end the property right of the first, and does so. In the present case the property right of the Grantee, in the form of the option, has simply expired by effluxion of time. The Grantee has breached no obligation which it had concerning the land, and the Grantor has done nothing which has in law brought about the ending of the Grantee's property right in the land. There is no scope for relief against forfeiture to operate.

13.38 If the grantor's refusal to transfer the interest to the grantee is based upon a failure by the grantee to perform some condition precedent to the exercise of the option, the state of authorities is somewhat unclear. A common example of such a condition precedent in the context of a lease which contains an option for a further term is that the tenant duly performs and complies with the obligations under the initial lease. In *Finch v Underwood* (1875) 2 Ch D 310 at 314, James LJ

---

8. *Landlord and Tenant Act 1899* (NSW) ss 8–10; *Landlord and Tenant Act 1936* (SA) ss 4, 5, 7, 9; *Supreme Court Civil Procedure Act 1932* (Tas) s 11(14) and (14A); *Supreme Court Act 1986* (Vic) ss 79, 80, 85. In the Northern Territory and Queensland, provisions permitting the court to grant relief against forfeiture of lease cover breaches of other covenants as well: *Law of Property Act 2000* (NT) ss 137–138; *Property Law Act 1974* (Qld) s 124.
9. *Civil Law (Property) Act 2006* (ACT) s 426(5); *Conveyancing Act 1919* (NSW) s 129; *Law of Property Act 2000* (NT) ss 137–138; *Property Law Act* (Qld) s 124; *Landlord and Tenant Act 1936* (SA) s 12; *Conveyancing and Law of Property Act 1884* (Tas) s 15; *Property Law Act 1958* (Vic) s 146; *Property Law Act 1969* (WA) s 81. The provisions in the Northern Territory and Queensland include breaches of the covenant to pay rent.

opined that such a case 'is one of condition precedent; it is not a case of forfeiture, and none of the considerations applicable to forfeiture apply to it'. This traditional approach to the matter was recently confirmed in Canada by the Court of Appeal in British Columbia in *Clark Auto Body Ltd v Integra Custom Collision Ltd* (2007), 277 DLR (4th) 201 at 209, where Kirkpatrick J, speaking for the court, said:

> In my opinion, it is essential to distinguish between the court's equitable jurisdiction to grant relief from forfeiture for the non-observance of covenants in an existing lease ... from the failure to comply with conditions precedent to the exercise of an option to renew a lease. In the former, equity recognizes that a tenant may be permitted to cure its default and be relieved from forfeiture to allow it to retain the balance of the term of the lease. In the latter, there is no compulsion on the tenant to exercise the renewal option, but if it does so, the tenant must comply with the conditions precedent. If the tenant fails to comply, it does not suffer a penalty or forfeiture of an existing tenancy. Equity will not intervene.

13.39 In Australia the approach exemplified in *Finch v Underwood* has been accepted in *Kim v Abbey Orchid Property Investments Pty Ltd* (1981) NSW Conv R 55-039, *Flagstaff Investments Pty Ltd v Cross Street Investments Pty Ltd* [1999] NSWSC 999 at [33], *Wallville Pty Ltd v Liristis Holdings Pty Limited* [2001] NSWSC 894 at [29], and *Century Yuasa Batteries Pty Ltd v Martin* [2002] TASSC 91 at [26].

13.40 However, there are indications of support for a more flexible approach in some Australian cases. Thus, in *Leads Plus Pty Ltd v Kowho Intercontinental Pty Ltd* [2000] NSWSC at [19]–[20], Young J took the view that 'only in exceptional circumstances ... equity does have jurisdiction to make ... an order [for relief against forfeiture in relation to an option] but one must find that there is unconscionable conduct before one can exercise that discretion'. In this case a tenant sought such relief in relation to the landlord's refusal to grant a new lease where the tenant was a day late in exercising the option. Young J, at [23], in refusing to make the order, said:

> The tenant did not look at the lease until just before the last day the option could be exercised, and at the very least slack office procedures were the reason why the option was not exercised in time. These are matters involving failure to act with reasonable diligence or prudence rather than pure accident or surprise.

13.41 A similar approach was adopted in *Beamer Pty Ltd v Star Lodge Supported Residential Services Pty Ltd* [2005] VSC 236 at [439]–[444], and *Xiao v Perpetual Trustee Company Ltd* [2008] VSC 412 at [100]–[106]. In support of this approach Rossiter has pointed out that an option gives rise to an interest in land and, as such, it ought to be amenable to protection pursuant to the relief against forfeiture principles, on the basis that:

> Failure to exercise the option in time or failure to observe other conditions attaching to exercise may be overlooked by equity if the grantor's insistence on his legal entitlement to deny the continued existence of the option is, in all the circumstances, unconscionable.[10]

13.42 However, statute has been enacted in the Northern Territory, New South Wales, Queensland and Western Australia which, in the context of an option in a lease, permits a court to grant relief

---

10. C J Rossiter, *Penalties and Forfeiture*, Law Book Co Ltd, Sydney, 1992, p 196.

against forfeiture to a tenant who has not complied with a condition precedent to the exercise of the option. Such relief includes an order that the grantor comply with the option agreement.[11] However, the legislation does not permit relief in circumstances where the grantee has failed to comply with the requirements for a valid exercise of the option.

REMEDIES

13.43   The usual form of remedy in relief against forfeiture cases of the type that arise in cases such as *Legione v Hateley* and *Tanwar Enterprises v Cauchi* is an order for specific performance or, in cases of negative contractual stipulations, an injunction. In cases involving forfeiture of money, the usual order is for repayment of the money that has been forfeited. In appropriate cases it has been held that other remedies can be ordered. Thus, in *On Demand Information plc v Michael Gerson (Finance) plc* [2003] 1 AC 368, at 381–2, 383; [2002] 2 All ER 949 at 959, 960, it was said that, where the property in dispute has been sold to a third party and relief against forfeiture cannot be ordered, a court can grant whatever is the most appropriate other remedy in the plaintiff's favour, provided that relief against forfeiture would have been ordered prior to the property being passed on to the third party.

13.44   In the context of relief against forfeiture of a lease, the position in equity in relation to remedies was described in *Janos v Chama Motors Pty Ltd* [2011] NSWCA 238 at [6], by Young JA as follows:

> In equity, if relief against forfeiture is granted and the lease has been determined by re-entry, the proper order is that the landlord, at the tenant's expense, execute and deliver a new lease for the balance of the term of the determined lease. This is to be contrasted with the proper order where the tenant obtains relief against forfeiture after forfeiture but before the landlord has acted upon the forfeiture and determined the lease. In such a case, the court grants an injunction to prevent the landlord acting on the forfeiture. Of course the term 'forfeiture' in this connection means merely 'liable to be forfeited'.

His Honour, at [7], went on to note that this position may be affected to some extent by legislation, including the unresolved question of 'whether or not a registered Torrens System lease continues to exist, despite re-entry, until the Registrar-General extinguishes it under s 55 of the *Real Property Act 1900*,[12] a section which notes that such a lease, after re-entry, determines upon the Registrar-General's entry on the register'.

---

11. *Conveyancing Act 1919* (NSW) ss 133C–133G; *Law of Property Act 2000* (NT) s 143; *Property Law Act 1974* (Qld) s 128; *Property Law Act 1969* (WA) ss 83A–83E.

12. Equivalent provisions in other Australian jurisdictions are *Land Titles Act 1925* (ACT) s 87; *Land Title Act 2000* (NT) s 70; *Real Property Act 1886* (SA) s 126; *Land Titles Act 1980* (Tas) s 71; *Transfer of Land Act 1958* (Vic) s 70; *Transfer of Land Act 1893* (WA) s 104.

14

PENALTIES

INTRODUCTION

14.1   In many contracts the parties to it will include a clause that sets out what their obligations to each other will be in the event that one of them breaches the contract. In the paradigm case, there will be a clause that stipulates the sum of money to be paid by the contract breaker to the other party as compensation for the breach of contract. Less frequently, the clause will stipulate the sum to be paid if the contract is terminated pursuant to a contractual right to terminate even if the contractual right can be exercised in the absence of a breach of contract: *O'Dea v Allstates Leasing System (WA) Pty Ltd* (1983) 152 CLR 359; 45 ALR 632. In either case, such a clause is generally referred to as a 'liquidated damages clause' or an 'agreed damages clause'. In *Environmental Systems Pty Ltd v Peerless Holdings Pty Ltd* [2008] VSCA 26 at [79], Nettle JA said that '[t]he ordinary meaning of "liquidated damages" is a sum fixed by the parties to a contract as a genuine pre-estimate of damage in the event of breach, whether as a pre-determined lump sum, or by means of a specified calculation or scale of charges or other positive data'.

14.2   The advantage of such a clause is that, subject to the power of the court in appropriate cases to grant relief against forfeiture (see Chapter 13), the plaintiff does not have to prove any loss or damage in relation to the breach of contract, as the obligation cast upon the defendant is enforceable against the defendant upon the plaintiff's termination of the contract for the defendant's breach: *Boucaut Pay Co Ltd v The Commonwealth* (1927) 40 CLR 98 at 106–7. Thus, the plaintiff recovers the sum stipulated as a debt. In relation to the advantages of such clauses, in *AMEV-UDC Finance Ltd v Austin* (1986) 162 CLR 170 at 193; 68 ALR 185 at 201, Mason and Wilson JJ said:

> In the case of provisions for agreed compensation and, perhaps, provisions limiting liability, that latitude is mutually beneficial to the parties. It makes for greater certainty by allowing the parties to determine more precisely their rights and liabilities consequent upon breach or termination, and thus enables them to provide for compensation in situations where loss may be difficult or impossible to quantify or, if quantifiable, may not be recoverable at common law. And they may do so in a way that avoids costly and time-consuming litigation.

Thus, in *J-Corp Pty Ltd v Mladenis* [2009] WASCA 157 at [7], Buss JA observed that it was common in building contracts to include liquidated damages clauses setting sums to be paid by builders who do not complete the building works on time.

14.3   However, such a clause will not always be enforceable. If such a clause is not enforceable, it is because it is a 'penalty'. The jurisdiction to relieve against penalties is historically rooted in the practice of equity, although by the end of the seventeenth century the common law courts also had established a similar jurisdiction which was then regulated by legislation enacted in 1696 and 1705. By the time the modern law relating to penalties was settled in the seminal decision of *Dunlop Pneumatic Tyre Co Ltd v New Garage & Motor Co Ltd* [1915] AC 79, the issue of whether the law on penalties had its origin in equity or the common law was viewed as being immaterial: *Austin v United Dominions Corporation Ltd* [1984] 2 NSWLR 612 at 625–6.[1]

14.4 Relief against penalties is based upon 'the underlying principle of equity that effect will not be given to a contractual provision which produces unconscientious results': *Killarney Investments Pty Ltd v Macedonian Community of WA (Inc)* [2007] WASCA 180 at [90]. In *AMEV-UDC Finance Ltd v Austin* at CLR 193; ALR 201, Mason and Wilson JJ said:

> The test to be applied in drawing that distinction is one of degree and will depend on a number of circumstances, including (1) the degree of disproportion between the stipulated sum and the loss likely to be suffered by the plaintiff, a factor relevant to the oppressiveness of the term to the defendant, and (2) the nature of the relationship between the contracting parties, a factor relevant to the unconscionability of the plaintiff's conduct in seeking to enforce the term.

14.5 In ascertaining whether any contractual term is a penalty, this chapter will focus upon the paradigm case of a liquidated damages clause as defined in 14.1 above. However, the penalty rule applies to other clauses that stipulate what is to occur upon breach of a contract. Examples of such clauses include:

(i) clauses requiring the contract breaker to transfer property, such as shares, in the event of a breach of contract, rather than pay a sum of money: *Wollondilly Shire Council v Picton Power Lines Pty Limited* (1994) 33 NSWLR 551 at 555;

(ii) clauses authorising the innocent party, following a breach of contract, to retain, withhold or extinguish payments due to the contract breaker, but not yet paid. Thus, in *Gilbert-Ash (Northern) Ltd v Modern Engineering (Bristol) Ltd* [1974] AC 689; [1973] 3 All ER 195, the provision enabled contractors to suspend or withhold payment of large sums of money payable by them to subcontractors in the event of the subcontractors committing a breach of contract;

(iii) clauses 'entitling the innocent party to the retransfer of property which had previously been transferred to the contract breaker': *General Trading Company (Holdings) Ltd v Richmond Corporation Ltd* [2008] 2 Lloyd's Rep 475 at 496;

(iv) clauses 'requir[ing] a contract breaker to forfeit a deposit or sum of money due or to become due to the other party in the event of breach': *General Trading Company (Holdings) Ltd v Richmond Corporation Ltd* at 496.

On the other hand, 'if a sum of money is payable by instalments, and it is provided that in the event of one instalment not being punctually paid the whole sum shall immediately become payable, the acceleration of payment is not a penalty': *O'Dea v Allstates Leasing System (WA) Pty Ltd*, at CLR 366; ALR 635. However, the principle in *O'Dea v Allstates Leasing Systems* is contingent upon the original sum of money to be paid being a presently existing debt. The principle does not apply if the sum is merely one that the plaintiff claims is owed. Thus, if A claims that he or she is owed $X by B and the

---

1. On the historical development of the jurisdiction with respect to penalties see C J Rossiter, *Penalties and Forfeiture*, Law Book Co Ltd, Sydney, 1992, pp 1–20; *Andrews v Australian and New Zealand Banking Group Limited* [2011] FCA 1376 at [7]–[81].

claim is settled out of court on the basis that B will pay, by agreed instalments, the lesser sum of $Y, if the settlement agreement also stipulates that a breach by B in paying any of the instalments will mean that B must pay the full amount claimed ($X), such a stipulation will be viewed as a penalty: *Zenith Engineering Pty Ltd v Qld Crane and Machinery Pty Ltd* [2000] QCA 221 at [4], [9], [13].

THE BASIS OF THE INTERVENTION AGAINST PENALTIES

14.6   In *Ringrow Pty Ltd v BP Australia Pty Ltd* (2005) 224 CLR 656 at 669; 222 ALR 306 at 314, a unanimous High Court observed that the 'law of contract normally upholds the freedom of parties, with no relevant disability, to agree upon the terms of their future relationships' and that the law on penalties was an exception to that principle that 'require[d] good reason to attract judicial intervention to set aside the bargains upon which parties of full capacity have agreed'. This exception to the principle of freedom of contract has attracted considerable criticism. In this respect, Hachem notes the following:

> Today, criticism is voiced in a sharper manner, with Judge Posner in the USA often at the forefront. In his view [set out in *XCO International Inc v Pacific Scientific Company*, 369 F3d 998 at 1001–2 (2004)] the current state of the law on agreed sums payable on breach of an obligation is an anomaly, the underlying rationale 'mysterious' and 'one of the abiding mysteries of the common law' which in the end turns out to be an 'anachronism, especially in cases in which commercial enterprises are on both sides of the contract'.[2]

14.7   Critics of the law against penalties argue that the enforceability of agreed damages clauses should not be determined by the principles relating to penalties. Rather, these clauses should be upheld subject to relief being granted pursuant to principles related to vitiating factors under the general law, especially duress and unconscionability, as well as related legislative provisions. Indeed, this approach has, to some extent, been adopted in Canada where an agreed damages clause will not be a penalty in the absence of oppression: *Elsey v J G Collins Insurance Agencies Ltd* [1978] 2 SCR 916 at 937.

14.8   The criticism of the law against penalties is reflected in the cautious approach the courts take in determining whether a particular agreed damages clause is a penalty. Thus, in *Alfred McAlpine Capital Projects Ltd v Tilebox Ltd* [2005] EWHC 281 (TCC) at [48], Jackson J said:

> Because the rule about penalties is an anomaly within the law of contract, the courts are predisposed, where possible, to uphold contractual terms which fix the level of damages for breach. This predisposition is even stronger in the case of commercial contracts freely entered into between parties of comparable bargaining power.

14.9   Similar comments were made in *AMEV-UDC Finance Ltd v Austin* at CLR 193–4; ALR 201–2, where Mason and Wilson JJ said:

> The courts should not, however, be too ready to find [a penalty] lest they impinge on the parties' freedom to settle for themselves the rights and liabilities following a breach of contract. The doctrine of penalties answers ... an important aspect of the criticism often levelled against unqualified freedom of contract, namely the possible inequality of bargaining power. In this way

---

2.   P Hachem, *Agreed Sums Payable Upon Breach of an Obligation*, Eleven International Publishing, The Hague, 2011, pp 84–5.

the courts strike a balance between the competing interests of freedom of contract and protection of weak contracting parties.

ESTABLISHING THE EXISTENCE OF A PENALTY

14.10   The critical feature that distinguishes an enforceable liquidated damages clause from a penalty was described in *Dunlop Pneumatic Tyre Co Ltd v New Garage & Motor Co Ltd* [1915] AC 79 at 86, where Lord Dunedin said:

> The essence of a penalty is a payment of money stipulated as in terrorem of the offending party; the essence of liquidated damages is a genuine covenanted pre-estimate of damage.

Thus, the critical question in determining whether a clause is a penalty or not is whether the sum stipulated in the clause is a genuine pre-estimate of the loss likely to be suffered by the plaintiff: *Zachariadis v Allforks Australia Pty Ltd* (2009) 26 VR 47 at 67. A clause will not be a genuine pre-estimate of the likely loss to be suffered if the sum stipulated amounts to a threat designed to induce the debtor to perform the contract. Hachem notes that '[t]he reasoning behind this approach is that parties are not allowed to compel each other to perform the contract by threatening what is perceived as punishment, ie the payment of the agreed sum'.[3]

14.11   In *Bridge v Campbell Discount Co Ltd* [1962] AC 600 at 622; [1962] 1 All ER 385 at 395, Lord Radcliffe indicated that the words 'in terrorem' did not add anything to the idea conveyed by the word 'penalty'. It is clear that the words do not refer to an obligation to make a payment extracted as the result of duress or unconscionability. Thus, the critical issue that a court has to determine is 'whether at the time the contract was entered into the predominant contractual function of the provision was to deter a party from breaking the contract or to compensate the innocent party for breach': *PSAL Ltd v Kellas-Sharpe* [2012] QSC 31 at [71].

14.12   Because the power to strike down a penalty constitutes an interference with the parties' freedom to contract, the burden of proof in establishing that the clause is a penalty lies with the party seeking to escape liability under it, that is, the party claiming that the clause is a penalty: *Multiplex Constructions Pty Ltd v Abgarus Pty Ltd* (1992) 33 NSWLR 504 at 527.

14.13   As to the frequency with which courts will find that a liquidated damages clause is a penalty, in *Lansat Shipping Co Ltd v Glencore Grain BV* [2009] EWCA Civ 855 at [33], Lord Clarke of Stone-cum-Ebony MR, speaking for the English Court of Appeal, said:

> [T]he court has to be careful not to set too stringent a standard and bear in mind that what the parties have agreed should normally be upheld. Any other approach, he said, would lead to undesirable uncertainty especially in commercial contracts. On the other hand, … the circumspection that the courts show before striking down a clause when the parties are of equal bargaining power does not displace the rule that the clause must be a genuine pre-estimate of damage.

---

3.   Hachem, *Agreed Sums Payable Upon Breach of an Obligation*, note 2 above, p 36.

PENALTIES AND BREACH OF CONTRACT

14.14   It has traditionally been accepted that the law on penalties is confined to clauses stipulating the payment of money in relation to a breach of contract, and that it does not apply to clauses in a contract relating to the payment of money on the occurrence of an event other than a breach of contract: *Export Credits Guarantee Department v Universal Oil Products Co* [1983] 2 All ER 205 at 223. This rule has been widely criticised.[4] For example, if a contract between X and Y states that it can be terminated in the case of Y's breach or bankruptcy, the loss to X is the same in both cases. There seems to be no reason why a liquidated damages clause in the contract is capable of being classified as a penalty in the first case but not in the second.

14.15   With this in mind, a different approach was suggested in *Integral Home Loans Pty Ltd v Interstar Wholesale Finance Pty Ltd* [2007] NSWSC 406 at [71]–[74], where Brereton J said:

> Insofar as it has been suggested that the doctrine relating to the unenforceability of penalties is confined to payments (and transfers, retentions or withholdings) conditioned on a breach of obligation by one party — and thus that a provision in a contract providing for payment of money by one party on the occurrence of a specified event, rather than on breach of a contractual duty, cannot be a penalty — this must be judged according to substance and not form. It is clear that where the right to terminate and receive a payment arises on the happening of any number of events, only some of which are breaches of contract, the doctrine of penalty applies where in fact the termination is by reason of a breach. In this context, it would be extraordinary ... if whether a provision was void as a penalty depended upon whether it was conditioned on a breach of contract as distinct from being a consequence of an election to terminate pursuant to an event entitling a party to terminate — often called an 'event of default' — that did not involve a breach of contract. It would be wholly inconsistent with the maxim that equity looks to the intent, rather than to the form ... Accordingly, I would hold that a penalty is a contractual liability to pay or forfeit or suffer the retention of a sum of money or property which is agreed in advance to be payable (or forfeited or retainable), by one party to the other, upon or in default of the occurrence of an event which can be seen, as a matter of substance, to have been treated by the parties as lying within the area of obligation of the first party, in the sense that it is his or her responsibility to see that the specified event does or does not occur, and where the stipulated payment is out of all proportion or unrelated to the damage which might be sustained by the other party by reason of the particular occurrence or default.

14.16   On appeal, a unanimous Court of Appeal held that the current state of authority meant that it was not open for a judge at first instance to take the approach that Brereton J took: *Interstar Wholesale Finance Pty Ltd v Integral Home Loans Pty Ltd* (2008) 257 ALR 292. However, the views of Brereton J were endorsed by the High Court in *Andrews v Australia and New Zealand Banking Group Ltd* [2012] HCA 30 at [78], where, after an analysis of the history of penalties, the unanimous joint judgment of the Court concluded 'that the restrictions upon the penalty doctrine urged by the Court of Appeal in *Interstar* should not be accepted'. In this case, the High Court was concerned with whether certain fees payable by a bank's customers were capable of being classified as penalties even though those fees did not require a breach of contract to occur before being payable. An example of such fees included over the limit and late payment fees charged by the bank in relation to credit card

---

4.   Rossiter, *Penalties and Forfeiture*, note 1 above, pp 66–70.

accounts. The High Court held that such fees could be classified as penalties and remitted the matter to the trial judge for determination as to whether they were in fact penalties.

14.17 On the other hand, in the context of a loan contract, a clause that stipulates that interest on the loan is, for example, to be 50 per cent per annum but that only 10 per cent per annum is payable if regular loan repayments are made on particular dates, is not construed as a penalty in relation to the amount of interest payable if loan repayments are not paid on those dates: *PSAL Ltd v Kellas-Sharpe* at [61]–[67]. This is so because the higher interest payment is not payable because of a breach of contract; it is in fact payment in accordance with the contractual obligation, and the payment of the reduced rate of interest is merely a concession and not penal in nature. However, if the loan document is differently drafted and stipulates that interest at the rate of 10 per cent per annum was payable, but that interest at the rate of 50 per cent per annum would apply to loan repayments that were not paid on the stipulated dates, the clause could be classified as a penalty if the payment of interest at 50 per cent per annum was not a genuine pre-estimate of the lender's loss in such circumstances. *Yarra Capital Group Pty Ltd v Sklash Pty Ltd* [2006] VSCA 109 is an example of a case of this type, although the court held that the higher interest payable for late payments on a loan was not, in all the circumstances, a penalty. This approach has been criticised on the basis that 'the distinction [between them] depends upon form and has nothing whatever to do with substance'.[5] On the other hand, even though a clause in a mortgage 'that imposes higher and lower rates of interest is able to avoid the application of the law concerning penalties, by making the lower rate a bonus for compliance rather than a penalty for breach, a mortgage so drafted can still be looked at for its substantial commercial effect when one is considering whether it is unjust within the meaning of the *Contracts Review Act* [1980 (NSW)]': *Kowalczuk v Accom Finance* (2008) 77 NSWLR 205 at 244. Furthermore, such clauses may be found to be unconscionable under the statutory unconscionability provisions of the *Australian Consumer Law* or the *Australian Securities and Investments Commission Act 2001* (Cth): *PSAL Ltd v Kellas-Sharpe* at [84]–[120].

THE PRINCIPLES IN THE DUNLOP CASE

14.18 In *Dunlop Pneumatic Tyre v New Garage & Motor* at 86–8, Lord Dunedin summarised the basic principles governing the distinction between liquidated damages clauses and penalties. They are as follows:

(i) The operation of the clause as either a liquidated damages clause or penalty is determined by construing the clause with reference to the circumstances as they existed at the time the contract was entered into. The nature and purpose of the contract, together with the relative positions of the parties are often weighty factors to be taken into account in the process of construction. Thus, where the contracting parties are well equipped to protect their respective commercial interests, it is less likely that a liquidated damages clause will be classified as a penalty: *Tullett Prebon Group Ltd v El-Hajjali* [2008] EWHC 1924 (QB) at [32].

(ii) The use of the words 'penalty' or 'liquidated damages' in the clause is not conclusive as to the effect of the clause. The court is concerned with the substance of the clause, rather than its mere form. Thus, in *Clydebank Engineering and Shipbuilding Co Ltd v Don Jose Ramos Yzquierdo y Castaneda* [1905] AC 6, a clause used the word 'penalty' but was construed as a liquidated damages clause.

---

6.   Rossiter, *Penalties and Forfeiture*, note 1 above, p 120.

(iii) A clause will be a penalty if the sum stipulated 'is extravagant and unconscionable in amount in comparison with the greatest loss that could conceivably be proved to have followed from the breach'. In *AMEV-UDC Finance v Austin*, at CLR 190; ALR 199, it was said that a clause would be a penalty if the sum stipulated was 'out of all proportion to damage likely to be suffered as a result of the breach'. More recently, in *Ringrow v BP Australia*, at CLR 669; ALR 312, the High Court said that what was required was 'a "degree of disproportion" sufficient to point to oppressiveness'. But, as was observed by Colman J in *Lordsvale Finance Plc v Bank of Zambia*, [1996] QB 752 at 763–4; [1996] 3 All ER 156 at 167:

> [T]he jurisdiction in relation to penalty clauses is concerned not primarily with the enforcement of inoffensive liquidated damages clauses but rather with protection against the effect of penalty clauses. There would therefore seem to be no reason in principle why a contractual provision the effect of which was to increase the consideration payable under an executory contract upon the happening of a default should be struck down as a penalty if the increase could in the circumstances be explained as commercially justifiable, provided always that its dominant purpose was not to deter the other party from breach.

In *State of Tasmania v Leighton Contractors Pty Ltd* (2005) 15 Tas R 243 at 251–2, the Tasmanian Full Court of the Supreme Court said:

> The learned primary judge used the terms 'extravagant', 'exorbitant', 'totally disproportionate', 'not a genuine pre-estimate' and 'unconscionable' to characterise [the relevant clause] as a penalty. … [These] words are often used as an aggregate and, allowing for changes of usage, describe differing conceptual approaches to the test. Those conceptual approaches have been made more complex by the addition of terms such as 'in relation to any possible amount … within the contemplation of the parties', 'greater and unreasonably or inequitably so', and 'true damages reasonably assessed'. The terms encapsulate the following propositions: (i) A comparison between the sum provided for in the event of a breach and the greatest loss which could conceivably be proven in the light of the total amount of the contract as a whole; (ii) Comparison between the sum provided and the nature of the breach. If any breach activates the operation of a 'damages' term, irrespective of its import, then it might more readily be regarded as penalty; (iii) Equivalence of bargaining power at the time of agreement or whether one party was subject to unreasonable pressure in performance; (iv) The potential outcomes to which the clause was directed; (v) The means, if any, used in the compilation of the sum provided; (vi) The import of the contract provision for 'damage' is to be considered at the time of the making of the contract, not as at the time of the breach.

In making the comparison between the amount stipulated in the clause and the likely loss to be suffered by the plaintiff, a court should not compare the actual loss occasioned by breach and the amount provided for in the contract. Rather, the question is whether, at the date of the contact, the amount stipulated was out of all proportion to the likely loss to be suffered: *Zachariadis v Allforks Pty Ltd* at 79.

(iv) If, however, the defendant's breach is of an obligation to pay a sum of money, a clause that stipulates a sum that is merely greater than the sum which ought to have been paid is a penalty. Although this principle has subsequently often been cited with approval, Peden[6] contests

---

7. E Peden, 'Liquidated Damages' in G Tolhurst & E Peden (eds), *Commercial Issues in Contract Law*, Ross Parsons Centre of Commercial, Corporate and Taxation Law Monograph Series, Sydney, 2008, p 81.

its validity and suggests that '[t]oday it is not possible to say that a sum is "extravagant and unconscionable in amount" merely because it is "a sum greater than the sum which ought to have been paid" ... [This] test is best seen as reflection of the law current at the time of *Dunlop*. It cannot be taken at face value today'.

(v) There is a rebuttable presumption that the clause is a penalty if it stipulates that the same sum is to be paid for breaches of any of a number of different obligations, some of which may result in serious, and others only trifling, losses.

(vi) [I]t is no obstacle to the sum stipulated being a genuine pre-estimate of damage in circumstances where the consequences of the breach are such as precise pre-estimation of damages is almost impossible. Indeed, that is just the situation when it is probable that pre-estimated damage is the true bargain between the parties.

14.19   In *Ringrow v BP Australia*, at CLR 663; ALR 309, the High Court, although reaffirming the principles in *Dunlop Pneumatic Tyre v New Garage & Motor*, hinted that perhaps these principles may need to be reformulated in the light of either some specific features of Australian conditions or elements of the contemporary marketplace. However, the High Court left consideration of that question and reformulation of principles, if any, to a future case where such matters were issues before the court.

14.20   In *Dunlop Pneumatic Tyre v New Garage & Motor*, Dunlop sold tyres, covers and tubes to New Garage, which then sold these items to the public. New Garage agreed not to alter, remove or tamper with the markings on the tyres and tubes, not to resell the goods below prices stipulated in the contract, not to supply goods to certain customers and not to export the goods. Clause 5 of the contract stipulated that New Garage would pay £5 for each tyre, cover or tube that was sold below the stipulated price. New Garage breached the terms of Clause 5 by selling tyres and tubes below the stipulated prices. Dunlop sought to enforce Clause 5. The question to be determined was whether Clause 5 was a penalty. The House of Lords held that it was not a penalty. In coming to that conclusion, the House of Lords focused on the difficulty in assessing damages for the possible breaches of the contract by New Garage. This was a key factor in upholding the amount of £5 as a genuine pre-estimate of the loss and for rebutting the presumption set out in the fifth of Lord Dunedin's points noted above: see 14.18.

14.21   In *Zachariadis v Allforks Australia Pty Ltd*, Zachariadis, was the guarantor for Priority Road Express Pty Ltd (PRE), which entered into four 60-month agreements with Allforks Australia Pty Ltd (Allforks) to hire forklift trucks. Clause 2.1 of each agreement provided that the agreement could be terminated upon any breach of it by PRE. Clause 14.1 of each hire agreement provided that, upon termination, PRE was to return the equipment to Allforks and to pay to it all charges that would otherwise have been payable from the date of termination of the agreement to its expiry date. The issue before the court was whether Clause 14.1 was a penalty or whether it was enforceable against Zachariadis as PRE's guarantor. Neave JA, at 79–80, speaking for the Victorian Court of Appeal held that the clause was a penalty because (i) it did not provide a means of calculating the net loss which PRE would suffer if the hire agreement was terminated early; (ii) it would not have been difficult to produce a formula that projected any such loss; and (iii) many of the breaches of the hire agreement which could occur would produce little or no loss.

14.22   In *AMEV-UDC Finance v Austin*, a lessee of printing equipment defaulted on the lease. The lessor exercised a contractual power to terminate the lease. Pursuant to Clause 12 of the lease, the lessee was required, upon such termination, to pay the remaining instalments due under the unexpired term of the lease. The High Court held this to be a penalty on the grounds that: (i) Clause 12 required payment of the lease payments in full with no rebate given for the acceleration in payments; and, (ii) the lessor did not have to account to the lessee for the proceeds of sale of the printing equipment. On the other hand, in *Esanda Finance Corporation Ltd v Plessnig* (1989) 166 CLR 131; 84 ALR 99, on facts somewhat similar to *AMEV-UDC Finance v Austin*, the relevant clause was found not to be a penalty because it did take into account the benefits that flowed to the lessor by the acceleration of payments that was triggered by the lessee's default.

14.23 The case of *Esanda Finance v Plessnig* gives rise to a problematical situation that flows from the High Court's decision to permit, pursuant to the agreed damages clause, the recovery by the lessor of what was, in effect, the recovery of expectation damages by the lessor. However, pursuant to *Shevill v Builders Licensing Board* (1982) 149 CLR 620; 42 ALR 305, such damages are not available to a plaintiff who terminates a contract pursuant to a contractual right to terminate for a breach which would not be a terminating breach at common law. In *Esanda Finance v Plessnig*, at CLR 147; ALR 109, Brennan J noted that this was a matter that would need to be resolved by the High Court in the future.

EFFECT OF AN ENFORCEABLE LIQUIDATED DAMAGES CLAUSE

14.24 An enforceable liquidated damages clause entitles the plaintiff to recover the sum stipulated without the need to prove any loss: *Pigram v Attorney General for the State of New South Wales* (1975) 132 CLR 216; 6 ALR 15. If damages for actual loss sustained by the plaintiff would have exceeded the sum stipulated, decisions in *Diestal v Stevenson* [1906] 2 KB 345 and *Cellulose Acetate Silk Co Ltd v Widnes Foundry (1925) Ltd* [1933] AC 20 support the view that the plaintiff is nevertheless confined to recovering the sum stipulated. This view is also supported by the majority of academic[7] and other judicial opinions, such as the recent decision of the Court of Appeal in Western Australia in *J-Corp Pty Ltd v Mladenis* at [35]–[37]. Similarly, if the sum stipulated merely exceeds the damages that the plaintiff could have recovered had there been no liquidated damages clause, the plaintiff is entitled to recover the sum stipulated: *Bartercard Ltd v Myallhurst Pty Ltd* [2000] QCA 445 at [24]; *Alfred McAlpine Capital Projects Ltd v Tilebox Ltd* at [45].

14.25 However, an interesting question that arises is: what is the effect of a clause where the sum stipulated is grossly insufficient when compared to the real loss suffered by the plaintiff? It is suggested that such a clause can be held unenforceable, thereby permitting the plaintiff to recover unliquidated damages. Thus, in *Silent Vector Pty Ltd v Squarcini* [2008] WASC 246 at [63], Jenkins J said:

> [I]t is interesting to note that [the law of penalties] entirely relates to the circumstances in which a contractor alleges that the terms of the relevant clause amount to a penalty because the amount of, so called, liquidated damages is 'extravagant and unconscionable'. It does not address the issue as to when, if at all, such a clause would be struck down because it did not amount to a genuine pre-estimate of damages because the stipulated amount in the clause was grossly insufficient and unconscionable to the principal. Whether such a clause would be struck down on this basis is not a matter I have to consider [in this case] … [However], the breadth of, or the severe consequences

8. Rossiter, *Penalties and Forfeiture*, note 1 above, pp 75–7.

of the relevant clause to the principal, is one matter which may emphasise the need of the court to find clear and unmistakeable words in the Contract denying the principal the right to claim unliquidated damages: *Decor Ceilings Pty Ltd v Cox Constructions Pty Ltd (No 2)* [2005] SASC 483 at [81].

14.26 This issue has arisen in the context of building contracts where '$nil' has been inserted into a standard form liquidated damages clause in a building contract in relation to a principal's rights if the building contractor is late in completing the contract work. In such cases it appears that the enforcement of such a liquidated damages clause depends upon whether, on a proper construction of the contract, the operation of its provisions is mandatory or discretionary. In this context, in *J-Corp Pty Ltd v Mladenis* at [3], Buss JA observed that 'an intention to exclude the common law right to damages for breach of contract must be expressed in clear and unambiguous terms'.[8]

EFFECT OF A PENALTY

14.27 A liquidated damages clause that is classified as a penalty is unenforceable. However, this does not mean that the plaintiff is unable to be compensated for his or her loss. The plaintiff is able to recover damages according to the principles governing the assessment of damages at common law for breach of contract: *W & J Investments Ltd v Bunting* [1984] 1 NSWLR 331 at 335–6.

14.28 In assessing the plaintiff's damages, it is an unresolved question as to whether the sum stipulated in such a clause operates to put a cap on the sum of damages that a court can award to the plaintiff: *AMEV-UDC Finance v Austin* at CLR 192–3; ALR 200–1. In support of the proposition that the sum stipulated in such a clause does set a ceiling on the level of damages recoverable by the plaintiff, Rossiter has written as follows:

> [A]n agreed damages clause … in fact contains two promises. One is a promise by the promisor made to the promisee that he or she will pay to the promisee the agreed sum upon the specified breach. The other is a promise by the promisee made to the promisor that he or she undertakes not to seek recovery of an amount exceeding the agreed sum for the specified breach. If the agreed sum is penal in that it did not amount to a genuine pre-estimate of the loss flowing from the breach, only the former promise is affected by the penalty. The promisee's failure to pre-estimate the loss does not negate the consideration received from the promisor regarding the upper limit on liability.[9]

---

9. For a discussion of this issue see T Thomas, '$Nil Liquidated Damages: An Exhaustive Remedy for Delay Under a Construction Contract?' (2008) 24 *Building & Construction Law Journal* 82.

10. Rossiter, *Penalties and Forfeiture*, note 1 above, p 71.

Part V:
Trusts

15

INTRODUCTION TO TRUSTS

INTRODUCTION

15.1 In its most simple form, a trust exists when the beneficial ownership of property is separated from the legal ownership of the property. The notion of separating title from beneficial ownership is the beating heart of the trust relationship. However, it is merely a starting point, for trust law has become extremely complicated over the centuries. The trust remains equity's greatest gift to the Western legal system (see 1.18).

15.2 The obligation of the titleholder in the trust has its origins in equity, for in the beginning, such a relationship was only enforceable in Chancery.[1] The development of the trust and its relationship with the medieval use has already been discussed at 1.17–1.29. Common law was, and remains, uninterested in the way that a titleholder deals with beneficial interests in his or her property. In contrast, equity has always been concerned with whether the titleholder has any obligation to use the property for the benefit of others. In this, and the following chapters, we will analyse the situations in which equity imposes such obligations of trust.

THE ELEMENTS OF A TRUST

15.3 Subject to what will be said in following chapters about charitable and constructive trusts, there are three essential elements to any trust relation ship. These three elements are:

1. *the trustee* — a legal person who holds a vested legal title (or a vested equitable title) in the property, subject to fiduciary duties;
2. *trust property* — property in real or personal form which is identified or ascertainable and capable of being held on trust. The trust property can be legal or equitable property; and
3. *the beneficiary* (sometimes referred to as the *cestui que trust* in older cases, or the *object* of the trust in modern cases) — a person, or group of persons, who hold a beneficial equitable estate in the property and on whose behalf the trustee must act.

15.4 It should be noted that the person who creates the trust during their lifetime is usually referred to as a *settlor*. Such a trust is often described as an *inter vivos* trust or a *settlement*. When the trust has been created in a will, the creator is the author of the will, namely the *testator* (if male), or *testatrix* (if female). A trust created in a will is referred to as a *post mortem* trust. In this and following chapters, the word *creator* will be used as a collective noun to cover both a settlor and a testator/testatrix.

---

1. M Leeming, 'What is a Trust?' (2008) 31 *Australian Bar Review* 211.

15.5   Significantly, the creation of a trust also creates (or separates out) the legal and equitable estates in the property: *Commissioner of State Revenue v Lend Lease Funds Management Ltd* [2011] VSCA 182. In the New South Wales Court of Appeal decision in *DKLR Holding Co (No 2) Pty Ltd v Commissioner of Stamp Duties (NSW)* [1980] 1 NSWLR 510 at 518–9, Hope JA said (in relation to trusts of land):

> An unconditional legal estate in fee simple is the largest estate which a person may hold in land. Subject to qualifications arising under the general law, and to the manifold restrictions now imposed by or under statutes, the person seised of land for an estate in fee simple has full and direct rights to possession and use of the land and its profits, as well as full rights of disposition. An equitable estate in land, even where its owner is absolutely entitled and the trustee is a bare trustee, is significantly different. What is, perhaps, its essential character is to be traced to the origin of equitable estates in the enforcement by Chancellors of 'uses' or 'trusts'... [A]lthough the equitable estate is an interest in property, its essential character still bears the stamp which its origin placed upon it. Where the trustee is the owner of the legal fee simple, the right of the beneficiary, although annexed to the land, is a right to compel the legal owner to hold and use the rights which the law gives him in accordance with the obligation which equity has imposed upon him. The trustee, in such a case, has at law all the rights of the absolute owner in fee simple, but he is not free to use those rights for his own benefit in the way he could if no trust existed. Equitable obligations require him to use them in some particular way for the benefit of other persons.

15.6   A common way to create a trust would be for a creator to transfer title to a trustee on the basis that the trustee is to use the property for a beneficiary. As we shall see, this is not the only way that trusts are created, but it illustrates the point that in many cases there will be three actors in the life of a trust relationship: creator, trustee and beneficiary.

15.7   The three actors need not always be different legal persons. It is possible for a creator and a trustee to be the same person, for example, when a trust is created by declaration of trust: see Chapter 16. Similarly, it is possible for a creator to be a beneficiary, in cases where the creator instructs the trustee to hold the property for his or her benefit. Finally, a trustee might also be a beneficiary, but only in situations where the trustee is one of a number of beneficiaries. However, it is impossible to be the sole trustee and sole beneficiary because once a person owns complete legal and equitable estates they are said to merge together, leaving no distinction between them: *DKLR Holding Co (No 2) Pty Ltd v Commissioner of Stamp Duties (NSW)* (1982) 149 CLR 431 (see 4.7). The merger of the estates will only come about when the legal and equitable estates are equal and co-extensive: *Goodright v Wells* (1781) 99 ER 491 at 495; *Harmood v Oglander* (1803) 32 ER 293 at 301; *Adamstoun Holdings Pty Ltd v Brogue Tableau Pty Ltd* [2007] WASCA 43.

THE THREE SPECIES OF A TRUST

15.8   There are three species of trust: express trusts, resulting (or sometimes referred to as implied) trusts, and constructive trusts.

Express trusts

15.9   Express trusts are created intentionally by a creator via express declarations, transfers or directions. Chapter 16 will discuss the ways in which express trusts can be created and

Chapter 17 will look at ways they can be terminated and varied. There are myriad types of express trust, including:

- fixed and discretionary trusts;
- bare trusts;
- charitable trusts;
- commercial trusts; and
- family trusts.

Fixed and discretionary trusts

15.10   Express trusts can be characterised by the nature of the beneficiaries' entitlement. In cases where each beneficiary has a set quantum of interest in the trust property the trust is described as a 'fixed' trust. In a fixed trust the beneficiaries have substantial rights to enforce the proper administration of the trust as they are said to have an equitable property interest in the trust. These rights are discussed in detail in Chapter 21.

15.11   In cases where the beneficiaries' entitlements are subject to the trustees' discretion the trust is referred to as a 'discretionary' trust. Caution should be exercised in using this phrase as discretionary trusts can take myriad forms and the term has 'no fixed meaning': *Chief Commissioner of Stamp Duties (NSW) v Buckle* (1998) 192 CLR 226 at 234; 151 ALR 1 at 3–4; *Scaffidi v Montevento Holdings Pty Ltd* [2011] WASCA 146 at [24]. Trustees may have a discretion relating to the size of the beneficiaries' entitlements or to whether a person should even be chosen as a beneficiary. In situations where the trustee can choose beneficiaries from a class, the beneficiaries only have an expectancy that they may be chosen to be a beneficiary. This is a weaker, non-proprietary form of equitable interest and, as a result, such beneficiaries have fewer rights, which are primarily limited to enforcing the proper administration of the trust. For this reason the discretionary trust is often referred to as a 'trust power' because the trustee's discretion is a form of power of appointment.

15.12   Discretionary trusts can also be classed as 'exhaustive' or 'non-exhaustive': *Re Richstar Enterprises Pty Ltd; Australian Securities and Investments Commission v Carey (No 6)* (2006) 153 FCR 509. In an exhaustive trust, the trustees must distribute the income earned by the trust capital. In a non-exhaustive trust they are permitted to accumulate such income: *Secretary, Department of Families, Housing, Community Services and Indigenous Affairs v Elliott* [2009] FCAFC 37 at [22]. The rights of beneficiaries in discretionary trusts are discussed further in Chapter 21.

Bare trusts

15.13   The simplest form of express trust is a bare trust: see 4.19. In bare trusts trustees only have an obligation to hold the trust property until such times as the beneficiaries demand it be transferred to them: *Thorpe v Bristile Ltd* (1996) 16 WAR 500; *Jessup v Lawyers Private Mortgages Ltd* [2006] QCA 432 at [42]; *Wade v Wade* [2009] WASC 118. In *Herdegen v Federal Commissioner of Taxation* (1988) 84 ALR 271 at 281, Gummow J defined a bare trust as follows:

> Today the usually accepted meaning of 'bare' trust is a trust under which the trustee or trustees hold property without any interest therein, other than that existing by reason of the office and the legal title as trustee, and without any duty or further duty to perform, except to convey it upon demand to the beneficiary or beneficiaries or as directed by them, for example, on sale to a third party.

15.14 As to what his Honour meant by the expression 'without any duty or further duty to perform', in *Chief Commissioner of Stamp Duties v ISPT Pty Ltd* (1998) 45 NSWLR 639 at 651, Mason P said:

> It is … clear that some active duties, though not of management, are imposed on some, but not all, bare trustees. Meagher JA, referring to a bare trust, observed in *Corumo Holdings Pty Ltd v C Itoh Ltd* (1991) 24 NSWLR 370 at 398 that 'as a matter of strict logic, almost no situation can be postulated where a trustee cannot in some circumstances have active duties to perform'.

15.15 A bare trustee certainly has a duty to preserve trust property. In *CGU Insurance Limited v One.Tel Limited (in liq)* (2010) 242 CLR 174 at 182–3; 268 ALR 439 at 446, the High Court said:

> The trustee of a bare trust has no interests in the trust assets other than those which exist by reason of the office of trustee and the holding of legal title. Further, the trustee of a bare trust has no active duties to perform other than those which exist by virtue of the office of the trustee, with the result that the property awaits transfer to the beneficiaries or awaits some other disposition at their direction. One obligation of a trustee which exists by virtue of the very office is the obligation to get the trust property in, protect it, and vindicate the rights attaching to it. That obligation exists even if no provision of any statute or trust instrument creates it. It exists unless it is negated by a provision of any statute or trust instrument.

However, the presence of duties which go beyond preservation, such as a requirement for the trustee to carry on a business, would indicate that the trustee is more than a bare trustee: *Old Papa's Franchise Systems Pty Ltd v Camisa Nominees Pty Ltd* [2003] WASCA 11 at [57].

15.16 Finally, the fact that a trust can be terminated pursuant to the rule in *Saunders v Vautier* (1841) 49 ER 282 does not mean that the trustee is a bare trustee, unless the beneficiaries have, pursuant to the rule in *Saunders v Vautier*, called upon the trustee to terminate the trust: *Chief Commissioner of Stamp Duties v ISPT Pty Ltd* at 651–2: see 21.48.

15.17 Bare trusts arise in various circumstances. These include (i) the assignor of future property becomes a bare trustee of the property for the assignee when the property comes into existence (see 5.64); (ii) the vendor of land, upon payment of the purchase price by the purchaser becomes a bare trustee of the land for the purchaser (*Stern v McArthur* (1988) 165 CLR 489 at 523; 81 ALR 463 at 485); and (iii) a person who holds legal title to property where the purchase price has been provided by another person is, applying the principles of resulting trusts (see Chapter 18), a bare trustee of the property for the person providing the purchase price: *Herdegen v Federal Commissioner of Taxation* at 281.

15.18 In terms of the rights of a beneficiary of a bare trust, Meagher, Heydon and Leeming observe that:

> … a sole beneficiary under a bare trust inter vivos (i) may demand transfer of the legal title from the trustee, so rendering himself legal and beneficial owner; (ii) may, subject to s 23C(1) of the *Conveyancing Act 1919* (NSW) and its equivalents in other States … dispose of his beneficial interest to others whether by transfer or sub-trust; (iii) may pursue the property the subject of the

trust by the tracing remedies into the hands of third parties; (iv) but may not assert his interest against a bona fide purchaser for value of the legal title without notice.[2]

Charitable trusts

15.19   Trusts for charitable purposes are usually express trusts, which are created for a particular purpose. These trusts are peculiar because they have no beneficiaries. They are discussed in Chapter 18.

Commercial trusts

15.20   The mechanism of trust is amenable to several forms of commercial venture. Trading trusts are often used to operate businesses because they are subject to different tax regimes and reporting mechanisms. Unit trusts are a particularly popular form of commercial trust whereby a corporate trustee invests trust funds for beneficiaries. The beneficiaries' entitlements to the funds are based on the number of 'units' they have purchased to enter the scheme. This is a general account of unit trusts and they may vary greatly as to their nature. For this reason it has been said that the phrase 'unit trust' 'does not have a constant, fixed normative meaning': *CPT Custodian Pty Ltd v Commissioner of State Revenue* (2005) 224 CLR 98 at 110; 221 ALR 196 at 200; *Kent v SS 'Maria Luisa' (No 2)* (2003) 130 FCR 12 at 33.

15.21   Perhaps the most socially important form of commercial trust is the superannuation trust. Superannuation trusts provide retirement and other benefits to their members. The payment of superannuation contributions by employers is now compulsory in Australia and this has had an enormous impact on the number, size and social significance of superannuation trusts. Unfortunately there has been a corresponding increase in the complexity of regulation of these trusts. A discussion of these trusts is beyond the scope of this work.

Family trusts

15.22   The tax implications of the trust relationship have also made the trust popular in the family context. Family trusts, mainly in the form of discretionary trusts with corporate trustees, are used extensively to lessen the impact of income tax, via the ability to split income between family members.

Resulting trusts

15.23   Resulting trusts are imposed by equity in circumstances where it is presumed that a trust was intended, but for some reason it was never properly constituted. For example, a resulting trust will be automatically imposed by a court in circumstances where an express trust has failed to eventuate for want of proper disposition of the trust property. In another case, courts may impose a resulting trust on a volunteer who has received the legal title to property after another person has provided the purchase price. This is because the courts will presume that there was an intention in such circumstances that the property be held on trust for the purchaser. Resulting trusts are discussed in detail in Chapter 19.

---

2.   R Meagher, D Heydon & M Leeming, *Meagher, Gummow & Lehane's Equity: Doctrines and Remedies*, 4th ed, LexisNexis Butterworths, Sydney, 2002, p 127.

Constructive trusts

15.24   Constructive trusts are imposed by the court and are not necessarily dependent upon the intentions of the parties: *Allen v Snyder [1977] 2 NSWLR 685 at 690*. In that sense constructive trusts often have a remedial function, in that they can be used to remedy breaches of equitable obligation. Constructive trusts are discussed in Chapter 28.

TRUSTS IN THE FAMILY OF LEGAL RELATIONSHIPS

Contracts and trusts

15.25   Because of their diversity, trusts have similarities with many other types of legal and equitable relationships. For example, there is a great deal of crossover between the relationships of trust and contract. In *Gosper v Sawyer* (1985) 160 CLR 548 at 568–9; 58 ALR 13 at 26, Mason and Deane JJ said:

> The origins and nature of contract and trust are, of course, quite different. There is however no dichotomy between the two. The contractual relation ship provides one of the most common bases for the establishment or implication and for the definition of a trust.

15.26   Express trusts are often created by contracts under seal (deeds). But there remain fundamental differences between the two relationships. The first of these relates to the source of their obligations. The source of contractual obligations is always the agreement expressed in the contract. Contrastingly, the source of obligation in a trust is conscience, as recognised and enforced in equity. To the extent that a trust deed may alter the rights and duties of the parties to a trust, it can be said that equity will recognise the altered moral obligations between the parties and enforce them.

15.27   The second major difference between trusts and contract is in the area of consideration. Simple contracts require consideration to be passed between the parties for them to be legally effective. Trusts do not require consideration for them to be valid. Most trusts are the result of unilateral action by creators.

15.28   The other major difference between contracts and trusts lies in the disputed area of privity of contract.[3] The common law concept of privity states that a third party beneficiary to a contract has no right to sue for its breach if he or she is not a party to the contract: *Dunlop Pneumatic Tyre Co Ltd v Selfridge & Co* [1915] AC 847 at 853; *Coulls v Bagot's Executor & Trustee Co Ltd* (1967) 119 CLR 460 at 478. In contrast, beneficiaries of a trust can compel its performance and may seek relief for any breach even though they have not provided consideration and are not parties to any instrument that may have created the trust: *Corin v Patton* (1990) 169 CLR 540 at 557; 92 ALR 1 at 12 (see 2.41).

15.29   Characteristics of contracts and trusts merge in contracts created by the parties for the benefit of a third person. According to the doctrine of privity, only the contracting parties can sue for breach of such a contract. Third party beneficiaries are unable to sue on the contract: *Woodar Investment Development Ltd v Wimpey Construction UK Ltd* [1980] 1 All ER 571. If a party sues for

---

3.   C H Tham, 'Trust, not Contract: Restoring Trust in the *Contracts (Rights of Third Parties) Act*' (2005) 21 *Journal of Contract Law* 107.

breach, and damage has only been suffered by the third party, the contracting party will usually only recover nominal damages: *Coulls v Bagot's Executor and Trustee Co Ltd* at 501–2.

15.30   However, if it can be shown that the contract included an agreement for the contractual rights to be held on trust for a third party, then the contracting party may sue on behalf of the third party and recover substantial losses: *Les Affreteurs Reunis SA v Leopold Walford (London) Ltd* [1919] AC 801; *Wilson v Darling Island Stevedoring and Lighterage Co Ltd* (1956) 95 CLR 43. This exception to the doctrine of privity was discussed by Deane J in *Trident General Insurance Co Ltd v McNiece Bros Pty Ltd* (1988) 165 CLR 107; 80 ALR 574. In this case a majority of the High Court held that a third party beneficiary of an insurance contract could sue on its own behalf even though it was not a party. The reasons of the majority all differ as to the basis of the third party's capacity to sue. Only Deane J dealt with the issue as a trust of a contractual obligation. His Honour, at CLR 147–8; ALR 602–3, said:

> A trust can attach to the benefit of the whole contract or of the whole or part of some particular contractual obligation. In the case of a policy of liability insurance under which the insurer agrees to indemnify both a party to the contract and others, there is no reason in principle or in common sense why the party to the contract should not hold the benefit of the insurer's promise to indemnify him on his own behalf and the benefit of the promise to indemnify others respectively upon trust for those others. Where the benefit of a contractual promise is held by the promisee as trustee for another, an action for enforcement of the promise or damages for its breach can be brought by the trustee. In such an action, the trustee can recover, on behalf of the beneficiary, the damages sustained by the beneficiary by reason of breach. If the trustee of the promise declines to institute such proceedings, the beneficiary can bring proceedings against the promisor in his own name, joining the trustee as defendant.

15.31   Therefore, the general principle is that if A makes a promise to B for the benefit of C, the promise could then be enforced against A by C, if B can be considered the trustee of A's promise: *Winterton Constructions Pty Ltd v Hambros Australia Ltd* (1991) 101 ALR 363 at 370; *Enervite Export Pty Ltd v Carsten Pty Ltd* (1997) 26 ACSR 433; *Fluor v ASC Engineering* [2007] VSC 262; *Re Australian Property Custodian Holdings Limited (in liquidation)* [2012] NSWSC 679 at [23]–[24]. The question of whether contractual rights are held on trust is answered by examining the words of the agreement: *McLellan v Sharantelli Pty Ltd* [2000] VSC 174; *Berry v Questor Financial Services Ltd* [2009] NSWSC 1402 at [62]–[79]. The intention must be to create a trust, and not just an intention to benefit a third party: *Dalton v Ellis; Estate of Bristow* [2005] NSWSC 1252. If it is clear that there was no intention to create a trust of the promise, or if there is no intention to benefit the third party, then no trust will be found: *Specialist Diagnostic Services Pty Ltd v Healthscope Ltd* [2010] VSC 443; *Marks v CCH Australia Ltd* [1999] 3 VR 513. However, if there is an intention to benefit a third party and a trust is an effective mechanism then a trust can be implied: *Re Emilco Pty Ltd* [2001] NSWSC 1035. In that sense, in *Kowalski v MMAL Staff Superannuation Fund Pty Ltd (ACN 064 829 616) (No 3)* [2009] FCA 53 at [92], Finn J, said that it is:

> … not necessary that the contracting parties know and understand that they are creating a trust. It is sufficient that they intend to create a relationship which, in equity, conforms to that of a trust.

15.32   The relevant intention is ordinarily that of the promisee of the contract, although there may be cases where the intention of the promisor is relevant. It has been said that courts should not be reluctant to infer a trust in cases where parties make a contract for the benefit of the third party: *Mizzi v Reliance Financial Services Pty Ltd* [2007] NSWSC 37 at [72].

Fiduciary relationships and trusts

15.33   Fiduciary relationships are discussed in Chapter 9. It is true, if perhaps trite, to say that every trustee is a fiduciary but not all fiduciaries are trustees: *Visnic v Sywak* (2009) 257 ALR 517 at 524, 527. Trusts are a subset of fiduciary relationships and the duties owed by trustees to their beneficiaries are fiduciary in character. However, not all fiduciary relationships will be ones of trust as not all fiduciary relationships concern the holding of property by one person for another.[4] Even in cases where funds are being held in a fiduciary capacity, it does not necessitate the existence of a trust: *DP Mann v Coutts & Co* [2003] EWHC 2138 (Comm).

15.34   Fiduciary duties and obligations of trust are not mutually exclusive. A person can owe separate and co-existing fiduciary and trustee obligations: *Chan v Zacharia* (1984) 154 CLR 178; 53 ALR 417. In *Visnic v Sywak*, the Court of Appeal drew a distinction between breach of fiduciary duty and a breach of a trustee's duty to transfer the legal ownership of trust property back to a beneficiary. It was found at trial that the defendant held shares on trust and the defendant was ordered to return those shares to the plaintiff. In addition to these orders the plaintiff sought an account of profits and/or equitable damages for the breach of fiduciary duty and the plaintiff appealed the trial judge's decision to refuse such relief. The Court of Appeal upheld the trial judge's decision not to order an account of profits and equitable compensation. While there was a breach of trust, it was not clear that there was a breach of fiduciary duty in relation to a conflict of interest and duty; nor could it be said that any profit made by the defendant was sufficiently connected (in a causal sense) to the refusal to hand back the shares.

Deceased estates and trusts

15.35   Executors of deceased estates occupy a similar role and perform a similar function to trustees. Executors, like trustees, are fiduciaries: *Johnson v Trotter* [2006] NSWSC 67. However, an executor's duties exist in relation to the proper administration of the deceased's estate. The primary functions are to collect the assets of the deceased, to pay off any debts owed by the estate and to distribute the assets in accordance with the will: *Williams v Williams* [2005] 1 Qd R 105. Executors can become trustees if they have completed their duties but still retain possession of the property of the estate: *Pagels v MacDonald* (1936) 54 CLR 519 at 526; *Porteous v Rinehart* (1998) 19 WAR 495 at 503. Additionally, wills commonly contain express trusts. These will often appoint executors as trustees, giving them a trustee role in addition to their role as personal representatives of the deceased.

15.36   There are differences between the interests held by beneficiaries of a trust and beneficiaries of an estate. Unlike the beneficiaries of a trust, the beneficiaries of a deceased estate gain no proprietary interest in the estate until it is administered (unless the estate is being held on trust): *Commissioner of Stamp Duties (Qld) v Livingston* [1965] AC 694; [1964] 3 All ER 692: see 4.25–4.29.

---

4.   J D Heydon & M J Leeming, *Jacobs' Law of Trusts in Australia*, LexisNexis Butterworths, Sydney, 2006, p 6.

Bailments and trust

15.37   A bailment consists of the delivery of goods (choses in possession) from one person (the bailor) to another (the bailee). In a bailment the goods are held by the bailee on the basis of a number of conditions that might be express or implied. The primary condition of all bailments is that the goods will be delivered up according to the bailor's instructions. Bailment is therefore a contractual relationship, the breach of which gives rise to common law contractual remedies.

15.38   Bailment is similar to trust, in the sense that the bailee (like the trustee) has duties to care for the goods and not use them for his or her own purposes, unless permitted to do so under the contract for bailment. Relationships of bailment may also be fiduciary in character: *Hospital Products Ltd v United States Surgical Corporation* (1984) 156 CLR 41; 55 ALR 417. However, unlike the position of a trustee, a bailee is only conferred a weak possessory title by a bailment. A bailment does not create a trust as the bailee does not take a vested title in the property: *Davis v Hueber* (1923) 31 CLR 583.

15.39   These issues are illustrated by *Olma v Amendola* [2004] SASC 274. The dispute that arose between the plaintiffs and the defendant in this case concerned an amount of money that was provided to the defendant by the plaintiffs. The money had come into the plaintiffs' hands through a compensation claim and the defendant had offered to take the money and invest it for the plaintiffs. The plaintiffs argued that the money was held by the defendant on trust and that interest earned over the period should be accounted for by the defendant. The defendant argued that she was a gratuitous bailee and that, although she had to repay the original amount, she was not bound, as a bailee, to pay back any interest. She argued alternatively that the agreement was a form of *mutuum* or quasi-bailment, where a person borrows personalty for consumption, with an obligation to later replace the personalty with an equivalent amount in quantity and quality. The trial judge found that the evidence of the parties' intention was that the money was to be held on trust and that the plaintiffs retained their beneficial ownership of the funds. The plaintiffs were therefore entitled to interest on the original amount. These findings were upheld on appeal.

Agency and trust

15.40   An agency exists where one person (the principal) authorises another person (the agent) to act as the principal's representative. The actions of an agent bind the principal. Like bailments, agency agreements are based in contract.

15.41   While agents are usually fiduciaries, they are not trustees as they do not have title in the property of the principal. An agent is also subject to the directions of the principal, unlike a trustee who is free to manage the day-to-day affairs of the trust: *Re Brockbank; Ward v Bates* [1948] Ch 206; [1948] 1 All ER 287.

15.42   Agency and trust can exist in the same relationship, as is common in cases of professional relationships like solicitor–client. Agency and trust co-exist where the trustee can be directed to administer the trust in certain ways by the settlor or beneficiary, or where an agent purchases property in his or her own name on behalf of the principal: *R v Hopkins* (1915) 20 CLR 446. If an agent receives money on behalf of the principal, he or she may be treated as holding that money on trust if he or she is duty bound to keep the money in a separate account. However, if the agent is allowed to mix funds with his or her own money then the money will be more likely to be treated as a debt owed to the principal: *Walker v Corboy* (1990) 19 NSWLR 382; *Grapecorp Management Pty Ltd (in liq) v Grape Exchange Management Euston Pty Ltd* [2012] VSC 112 at [46]–[50].

15.43   An illustration of these issues can be found in *Loughran v Perpetual Trustees WA Ltd* [2007] VSC 50, where an application was made to order the production of documents which related to a film investment scheme. The plaintiffs argued that the scheme was a trust and they were entitled to these documents as beneficiaries. The agreement for the scheme expressly stated that the scheme was a unit trust, but it also provided that once units were allocated, the relationship would become that of principal and agent. The trustee's agency powers included the power to enter into contracts, make claims, and bring, defend or compromise legal proceedings. The trust funds were said to be held in credit by the trustee as agent. For these reasons, Harper J, at [20], said:

> It is clear, then, that by the Second Multiple Prospectus Deed, the trustee is, in the discharge of many of its responsibilities, clothed with the mantle of an agent rather than that of a trustee. It is therefore not helpful or accurate to speak of the 'Trust' or the Second Multiple Prospectus Trust Deed (a name that the Deed itself does not adopt). Indeed, one might ask in these circumstances whether the defendant's designation throughout as 'trustee' was appropriate; or whether that designation was anything more than a marketing tool rather than an accurate representation of its role under the Deed. For the defendant itself has argued, in support of its position on the two questions I must answer, that when (for example) the Second Multiple Prospectus Deed authorises 'the trustee' to receive fees on behalf of production contractors, it receives those fees not as trustee at all, but in the quite different capacity of agent.

Unsecured debts and trusts

15.44   Debtors are not normally trustees for their creditors, as debtors do not hold identifiable funds in which creditors have an equitable interest.[5] A debt is not a specific piece of property in which a creditor has an interest as a beneficiary. Rather, debts are rights (choses in action, which are contractual in origin) which give creditors the power to demand payment. If the demand is not satisfied then the creditor has the right to sue the debtor to recover the owed amount. The position of creditors is therefore very different from that of beneficiaries. Beneficiaries have equitable interests in the property held by the trustee. Creditors do not have an interest in their creditor's property. A creditor only has access to common law remedies to pursue the debt. In *Caruana v DPP* [2011] VSC 658 at [69], Kyrou J said:

> The indicators that may be taken into account in distinguishing between an amount owed as a debt and an amount held on trust include the following:
>
> (a) If it is proved on the facts that the parties' intention was that the payee was entitled to use the money as his or her own, and was only under an obligation to repay the same amount of money either on demand or at a specified time in the future, then there is no trust and the amount owed is a debt [*Re Broad; Ex parte Neck* (1884) 13 QBD 740 at 746].
>
> (b) If it is proved on the facts that the parties' intention was that the payee would hold the money for the benefit of the payer, would deal with the money as a separate fund on behalf of the payer and would not be free to use the money as his or her own, then a trust will arise [*Cohen v Cohen* (1929) 42 CLR 91 at 101].

---

5.   D Heydon & M Leeming, *Jacobs' Law of Trusts in Australia*, note 4 above, pp 12–13.

(c) The absence of a prohibition on the payee depositing the money into a general account (or the absence of a requirement that the payee deposit the money into a separate account) is significant [*Re Australian Elizabethan Theatre Trust* (1991) 30 FCR 491 at 498] but not determinative in distinguishing between an amount owed as a debt and an amount held on trust. Where the intention to create a trust emerges from other facts, the payee can still be a trustee [*Associated Alloys Pty Ltd v ACN 001 452 106 Pty Ltd (in liq)* (2000) 202 CLR 588 at 604]].

(d) A requirement that the payee is to keep the money received from the payer separate from the payee's own funds is generally indicative of a trust. However, the fact that the payee deposits the money into a separate bank account is not conclusive of an intention to establish a trust [*Re Kayford Ltd (in liq)* [1975] 1 WLR 279 at 282].

(e) If the trustee and the beneficiary agree that the money can be paid into a general account maintained by the trustee, then the trustee must retain sufficient funds in that account to fulfill his or her obligations as trustee [*Stephens Travel Service International Pty Ltd v Qantas Airways Ltd* (1988) 13 NSWLR 331 at 348–9] (footnotes inserted).

15.45   Questions arise concerning trusts when funds are received by businesses from creditors and placed into special accounts which are not mixed with the businesses' own funds. If the business is bound to keep the funds separate then it is possible that the funds are held on trust, rather than simply representing a debt: *Cohen v Cohen* (1929) 42 CLR 91. In *Henry v Hammond* [1913] 2 KB 515 at 521, Channel J said:

> It is clear that if the terms upon which the person receives the money are that he is bound to keep it separate, either in a bank or elsewhere, and hand that money so kept as a separate fund to the person entitled to it, then he is a trustee of that money and must hand it over to the person who is his cestui que trust. If on the other hand he is not bound to keep the money separate, but is entitled to mix it with his own money and deal with it as he pleases, and when called upon to hand over an equivalent sum of money, then in my opinion he is not a trustee … but merely a debtor.

15.46   The distinction is crucial if the business later becomes insolvent as trust funds will not ordinarily form part of the assets of the business in the insolvency. In *Re Kayford Ltd (in liq)* [1975] 1 All ER 604, a mail order company received funds from customer orders and placed them in a special account. After the company went into liquidation it was held that the funds were intended to be held on trust for its customers. The evidence suggested that the company had always intended to protect the customers' funds. This intention, when coupled with the fact that the funds were placed in a separate account, was enough to establish a trust. A similar result occurred in *Stephens Travel Service International Pty Ltd (receivers and managers appointed) v Qantas Airways Ltd* (1988) 13 NSWLR 331, where the New South Wales Court of Appeal found an express trust where a travel agency collected airfares for an air line from customers and paid them into a separate account.

15.47   In other cases the evidence may not be strong enough to support an intention to create a trust: *Re Fada (Australia) Ltd* [1927] SASR 590. In *Walker v Corboy*, the lack of separate accounts and the absence of any use of the term 'trust' meant that the court could not find a trust.

15.48   One of the issues that arises from the *Kayford*-style trust concerns the interests of beneficiaries in the funds when the funds prove to be inadequate for satisfying all the interests that were intended to be protected. Ordinarily the funds will be divided up on a proportionate basis, which is referred to as a *pari passu* approach: *Re Australian Home Finance Ltd* [1956] VLR 1. In *OT*

Computers Ltd (in administration) v First National Tricity Finance Ltd [2003] EWHC 1010 (Ch), Pumfrey J was faced with an insolvent computing company which had created two accounts: one for customers' deposits for customers who had not received their goods, and the other for payments set aside for 'urgent suppliers'. Pumfrey J, at [15], said:

> The trusts alleged to have been created are necessarily express trusts, and for such trusts to be created there must be certainty of words, certainty of subject matter, and certainty of objects. Certainty of words requires that the words used are sufficient to demonstrate an intention to create a trust, and, so far as necessary, the terms of that trust. Second, the property to be comprised within the trust must itself be identified with sufficient clarity. Finally, the class of persons who are beneficiaries of the trust have to be sufficiently ascertained.

15.49 Difficulties arose for customers in relation to the first trust because the company received customer funds into its general account and only transferred them into the trust account from time to time. In the event of a shortfall, Pumfrey J stated that it was intended that each customer was entitled to a proportionate amount of the funds, rather than an amount relevant to what had actually been deposited. While this would cause some difficulties in accounting, Pumfrey J said that each customer and the proportionate amount of his or her payment could be ascertained. In relation to the urgent suppliers trust, Pumfrey J found that the term 'urgent suppliers' was too vague and failed the 'list certainty' test: see 16.55.

15.50 The issue arose again in *Brazzill v Willoughby* [2009] EWHC 1633 (Ch), where a bank called Kaupthing Singer & Friedlander Limited (KSF), which was owned by Icelandic interests, went into severe financial distress during the Global Financial Crisis. The UK Financial Services Authority ordered that KSF open a segregated account with the Bank of England which was to be credited with deposits from customers made on 2–3 October 2008. While the order was made to protect depositors should KSF become insolvent, the order was not publicly known and people continued to make deposits with the bank. Amounts were deposited into the Bank of England by KSF's employees, who made decisions about whether a deposit received during the period was from a 'customer' or not. Decisions were made under great pressure and in an ad hoc fashion. In the end, not all customers who made deposits after the order had their deposits transferred into the segregated account. Some days later, the Treasurer ordered that KSF's accounts be transferred to two other banks via a statutory order, which was effectively an involuntary novation of KSF's accounts. KSF went into administration the next day.

15.51 Arguments arose as to the nature of the segregated account and whether it had been created as a trust, and who the beneficiaries of that trust were meant to be. One party, representing trade creditors of KSF, argued that the funds held could not be a trust as the beneficiaries were not certain at the time the trust was created. The other parties accepted that there was a trust but argued that the beneficiaries should only be those account holders whose funds were deposited by the employees. Alternatively, it was argued that the beneficiaries should be all the depositors who made deposits after the order, regardless of whether their money was transferred into the segregated account.

15.52 Peter Smith J found that a trust was intended, and that, based on the notice, the intended beneficiaries were all the depositors who made deposits after the order, less any sum that they withdrew from their accounts over that time. Following *OT Computers Ltd*, the funds and the shortfall were ordered to be shared on a proportionate basis by all the depositors, including depositors who had not been initially recognised by the KSF staff as 'customers' depositing into a customer account. Of course, the difficulty with this finding is that if the KSF staff did not intend for a depositor's fund to be protected by an amount in the Bank of England trust, it is hard to see how the requirement for certainty of intention has been satisfied: see 16.4. Perhaps the explanation rests on the fact that this trust was created under a statutory scheme, and the effect of the statute was to manufacture certainty of intention, given its purpose was to protect depositors.

15.53 Problems might also exist in the insolvency context if the creation of the trust is seen as a voidable preference under insolvency legislation: *Corporations Act 2001* (Cth) s 533FA; *Bankruptcy Act 1966* (Cth) s 122: see Chapter 17. A trust can be set aside as a voidable preference if it can be shown that:

1. the business (if a company) was insolvent when the trust was created; or if the business was a natural person in sole tradership, the trust was created within six months of the commencement of bankruptcy; and
2. the creditor received more from the trust than they would have received if the trust were set aside and the creditor had to prove the debt.

15.54 On one view, if the funds were business funds which were then declared to be held on trust, this could be viewed as a voidable preference. Alternatively, if the funds were received by the business but never beneficially owned by the business, then the trust property will have never been an asset of the company and the trust could not be viewed as a voidable preference. As stated by Dal Pont, there has yet to be a definitive Australian judicial pronouncement about the way in which *Kayford* trusts are affected by these rules against voidable preferences.[6]

Quistclose trusts

15.55 The institutions of debt and trust can co-exist in the one transaction if there is a common (or 'mutual') intention that funds will be held for specific purposes, and if those purposes cannot be met, the money will be repaid: *Bieber v Teathers Limited* [2012] EWHC 190 (Ch); *Brown v InnovatorOne Plc* [2012] EWHC 1321 (Comm) at [947]. This is known as a *Quistclose* trust.[7] In *Barclays Bank Ltd v Quistclose Investments Ltd* [1970] AC 567; [1968] 3 All ER 651, Rolls Razor Pty Ltd (Rolls Razor) borrowed a large amount of money from Quistclose Investments Ltd (Quistclose). Quistclose lent the money on the basis that it was to be used for the specific purpose of paying Rolls Razor's shareholders their dividends. Rolls Razor deposited the money in a special account with Barclays Bank. Barclays were informed that the money was only to be used to pay the dividend. Before the dividend was paid, Rolls Razor went into liquidation. The bank sought to use the money in the account to set off the debts which were owed to it by Rolls Razor. Quistclose sought to retrieve the money and claimed that the bank had no right to use the funds in a set-off.

15.56 Lord Wilberforce found that the mutual intention of Rolls Razor and Quistclose was relevant to determining whether a trust existed. The mutual intention of the parties, as evidenced by the terms of the loan, showed that the sum advanced was not intended to become part of the assets of the borrower. Moreover, the sum would be used exclusively for the purpose for which it was lent.

---

6. G E Dal Pont, *Equity and Trusts in Australia*, 6th ed, Lawbook Co, Sydney, 2011, p 780.
7. See generally, W Swadling (ed), *The Quisclose Trust – Critical Essays*, Hart Publishing, Oxford, 2004.

15.57   In these circumstances Lord Wilberforce found that the agreement between Quistclose and Rolls Razor created a primary trust for the shareholders. When that trust could not proceed (due to Rolls Razor's insolvency) the loan became subject to a secondary trust in favour of Quistclose in the event of the money not being used for its dedicated purpose. Finally, given that the bank had notice of the mutual intention of the parties to create a trust, it was bound to respect that trust and could not use the funds to set off debts owed to it by Rolls Razor.

15.58   The *Quistclose* trust has been accepted as part of Australian law on numerous occasions: *Australasian Conference Assoc Ltd v Mainline Constructions Pty Ltd (in liq)* (1978) 141 CLR 335 at 353; *Austintel Investments Australia Pty Ltd v Lam* (1990) 19 NSWLR 637; *Educational Resources Pty Ltd (in liq) v Poteri* (1996) 20 ACSR 628; *Australian Receivables Ltd v Tekitu Pty Ltd* [2011] NSWSC 1306 at [109]–[116]. It has become popular because it allows a creditor to gain a priority over other creditors in insolvency. Unlike unsecured creditors, creditors who are also beneficiaries are able to call on the specific property of the trust to satisfy their debts. Because of the significant mischief that can occur through the overuse of *Quistclose* trusts some judges have attempted to limit their operation to situations where money is lent to discharge the debts of the borrower: *Re Miles; Ex parte National Australia Bank v Official Receiver* (1988) 20 FCR 194 at 199. However, authorities have approved of *Quistclose* trusts for other purposes, such as the purchase of equipment (*Re EVTR* [1987] BCLC 646), the payment of legal fees (*Legal Services Board v Gillespie-Jones* [2012] VSCA 68) the subscription of shares (*Re Associated Securities Ltd & the Companies Act* [1981] 1 NSWLR 742), or trusts for the payment of creditors of the lender: *Carreras Rothmans Ltd v Freeman Mathews Treasure Ltd* [1985] Ch 207; [1985] 1 All ER 155. This broader application of *Quistclose* trusts found support in *George v Webb* [2011] NSWSC 1608 at [199]–[200], where Ward J said:

> The *Quistclose* principle is not limited in its application to money paid for the purpose of discharging debts but can apply where the funds are to be applied for other purposes. In *Re EVTR* [1987] BCLC 646, for example, money was lent to buy equipment and in *Re Associated Securities Ltd and the Companies Act* [1981] 1 NSWLR 742, the money was lent to subscribe for shares. Nor does it seem necessarily to be limited to cases where the money was lent to the recipient as opposed to money paid to the recipient for particular purposes (say, as is the case on my view of the evidence in this case, in anticipation of a proposed acquisition). In *EVTR*, where funds were advanced for the sole purpose of purchasing equipment and the company was placed into receivership before the equipment arrived (but after part of the money had been used to pay the deposit), the court held that the receiver could not retain the returned deposit money and those funds were required to be returned to the lender. Dillon J said 'On *Quistclose* principles, a resulting trust in favour of the provider of the money arises when money is provided for a particular purpose only, and that purpose fails'.

15.59   A case which illustrates a wide concept of purpose is *Shepard v Mladenis* [2011] NSWSC 1431. This case concerned Dr Wallman, a recently divorced obstetrician and gynaecologist, who was defrauded by an introduction agency, called Hearts United. Wallman paid $200,000 for personal relationships counseling. Hearts United arranged for Wallman to be introduced to 'Lily', who was described as being Australian/Chinese with blonde hair with a surname 'Bolivique'. She may or not have been a fictitious person. Hearts United convinced Wallman to pay large sums of money to facilitate his marriage to Lily. Lily (or someone pretending to be her) then requested larger sums ($200,000) that she could borrow from Wallman to help her organise the release of her father's estate in Croatia. Further amounts were requested which totaled over two million dollars. All the moneys were paid to Hearts United. No marriage eventuated and Wallman was made bankrupt. Mladenis, the director and owner of Hearts United, used the funds to purchase a number of items including real estate, a Porsche, a Lexus, a BMW, and a Lamborghini. Pembroke J found that the money was held on a *Quistclose* trust and that the funds could be traced into the purchases. Pembroke J, at [56]–[58], said:

> The terms of the conversations between Dr Wallman and Mr Mladenis made it plain that the payments made to Hearts United up until late 2009, were made for the sole purpose of being paid to Lily to enable her to recover property from her father's estate. Similarly, the terms of the conversations between Dr Wallman and Mr Mladenis made it plain that the payments made to Hearts United and Mrs Mladenis after late 2009, were made for the sole purpose of funding the fictional attempts brought against Lily to recover the payments made to her. In these circumstances, those monies in the hands of the recipients were impressed with a trust that they would only be paid in accordance with the stated purposes.

15.60   The mutual intention of the parties can be discerned from the language employed by the parties, the nature of the transaction and the relevant circumstances attending the relationship between them: *Re Australian Elizabethan Theatre Trust; Lord v Commonwealth Bank of Australia* (1991) 30 FCR 491 at 502–3; 102 ALR 681 at 693. Nor is the presence of an intention to lend money for a purpose enough to establish a trust. It must also be intended that the moneys be used exclusively for the purpose or repaid on the failure of the purpose: *Compass Resources Ltd v Sherman* [2010] WASC 41 at [67]; *Legal Services Commissioner v Brereton* [2011] VSCA 241 at [96]. In some cases it has been held that the intention of the borrower or recipient of the funds alone is enough to constitute a *Quistclose* trust: see 16.28–16.31.

15.61   A significant factor to consider is the way that the moneys are held in account. If they are banked into a general account and mixed with other moneys it will be harder to infer a mutual intention that the moneys are held on trust and to be used exclusively for the intended purpose: *Salvo v New Tel Ltd* [2005] NSWCA 281 at [79]; *Gliderol International Pty Ltd v Hall* (2001) 80 SASR 541. However, in *Cook v Alto Prestige Pty Ltd* [2010] NSWSC 92 at [148], Bergin CJ in Eq said:

> Whilst the establishment of a separate account may be an indicator of the existence of a trust the fact that a separate physical account was not established in the circumstances of this case does not mean that there is no trust property.

In this particular case careful records had been taken of the amounts owed and how they had been employed. This evidence was enough to support the existence of a trust.

15.62   However in most cases the lack of a separate bank account is fatal to the *Quistclose* claim. For example, in *McManus RE Pty Ltd v Ward* [2009] NSWSC 440, a deposit for the purchase of a hotel was paid directly into the vendor's personal account. Absent any other indication that the money was to be held on trust, Palmer J found that the money was simply a debt and no trust had been created. McKechnie J found similarly in *Smith v Western Australia* [2009] WASC 189, where the mother and sister of a drug dealer were unable to establish a mutual intention to create a trust for funds which they provided to the drug dealer to help him pay his legal costs and mortgage. The drug dealer's house was being confiscated as part of proceeds of crime legislation and the mother and sister claimed an interest in the house arising from their loans. This claim failed as there was no intention that they were to be given an interest in the house in response to their provision of funds. In *Raulfs v Fishy Bite Pty Ltd* [2012] NSWCA 135, money paid by one partner to fund a partnership was not found to have been paid with any objective intention that the money would be held on trust and repaid if the partnership failed. An intention to hold the funds on trust would have cut across the underlying assumption that partners had a right in every asset of the partnership: *Canny Gabriel Castle Jackson Advertising Pty Ltd v Volume Sales (Finance) Pty Ltd* (1974) 131 CLR 321 at 327–8; 3 ALR 409 at 412; *Federal Commissioner of Taxation v Everett* (1980) 143 CLR 440 at 446–7; 28 ALR 179 at 182.

15.63   Reference to the 'purpose' of the trust in *Quistclose* should not be understood as creating a new type of non-charitable purpose trust: *Australian Elizabethan Trust* at FCR 502; ALR 692–3; *Salvo v New Tel* at [38]. Rather, the purpose behind the loan is relevant to the determination of the parties' mutual intention.

15.64   Questions arise as to the exact nature of the *Quistclose* trust. Some commentators have suggested that the trust is actually two trusts: an express trust in favour of creditors and a resulting trust in favour of the lender in circumstances when the express trust has failed.[8] In *Twinsectra Ltd v Yardley* [2002] 2 AC 164; [2002] 2 All ER 377, Lord Millett rejected the primary-secondary trust analysis of *Quistclose*. He found that no beneficial interest was conferred to the creditors. The beneficial interest always remained with the lender because the funds would be returned to the lender should the purpose of the loan not be satisfied. To that extent the arrangement was akin to a retention of title clause. Lord Millett, at AC 186; All ER 403, believed that the best trust model to use in those circumstances was not a two-limbed trust but a resulting trust:

> I … hold the *Quistclose* trust to be an entirely orthodox example of the kind of default trust known as a resulting trust. The lender pays the money to the borrower by way of loan, but he does not part with the entire beneficial interest in the money, and insofar as he does not it is held on a resulting trust for the lender from the outset. … [T]he borrower … has a very limited use of the money, being obliged to apply it for the stated purpose or return it. He has no beneficial interest in the money, which remains throughout in the lender subject only to the borrower's power or duty to apply the money in accordance with the lender's instructions. When the purpose fails, the money is returnable to the lender, not under some new trust in his favour which only comes into being on the failure of the purpose, but because the resulting trust in his favour is no longer subject to any power on the part of the borrower to make use of the money.

In *Bieber v Teathers Ltd* at [20], Norris J, in referring to *Twinsectra Ltd v Yardley*, said:

> It is a resulting trust in favour of the payer with a mandate granted to the recipient to apply the money paid for the purpose stated. The key feature of the arrangement is that the recipient is precluded from misapplying the money paid to him. The recipient has no beneficial interest in the money: generally the beneficial interest remains vested in the payer subject only to the recipient's power to apply the money in accordance with the stated purpose. If the stated purpose cannot be achieved then the mandate ceases to be effective, the recipient simply holds the money paid on resulting trust for the payer, and the recipient must repay it.

---

8.   M Evans, *Equity and Trusts*, 3rd ed, LexisNexis Butterworths, Sydney, 2012, p 428–9.

15.65   The classification of the *Quistclose* trust as a resulting trust has gained some adherents in Australia, or has at least been quoted favourably on occasion, but it is not yet in clear ascendancy: *Drakeford v Bromhead* [2003] NSWSC 296; *Rahnam Investments Pty Ltd v Esplin* [2004] NSWSC 529; *Frontier Touring Co Pty Ltd v Rodgers* (2005) 223 ALR 433; *Cook v Alto Prestige Pty Ltd* at [151]–[154]. In *Re Australian Elizabethan Theatre Trust* at FCR 501; ALR 691, Gummow J preferred to describe the *Quistclose* trust as a single express trust with two limbs rather than a combination of express trust and resulting trust.

15.66   Later Australian cases have continued to treat *Quistclose* trusts as orthodox examples of express trusts: *Raulfs v Fishy Bite Pty Ltd* at [51]; *Compass Resources Ltd v Sherman* [2010] WASC 41 at [69]. In *Quince v Varga* [2009] 1 Qd R 359 at [38], the Queensland Court of Appeal read Lord Millett's passage favourably and found that the potential difference in the classification of the trust as an express trust or a resulting trust was not a practical problem (at least in the case at hand). The Court of Appeal, at [40], held that the trust was an express trust, or a resulting trust that arose after the failure of the purpose of a loan. In *Salvo v New Tel Ltd*, Spigelman CJ noted the resulting trust theory but felt that it was not necessary to decide whether it was valid in Australia, as he believed the facts before him proved the existence of an express trust for the lender (of one of the two funds being claimed). Young CJ in Eq clearly stated that he thought that the better analysis was that *Quistclose* trusts were express trusts, given the uncertainty in the meaning of the term 'resulting trust'. Handley JA, in dissent on this point (but not on the result), believed that Lord Millett's decision in *Twinsectra* should be followed. In *Ying v Song* [2010] NSWSC 1500 at [249], Ward J felt that the matter was still unsettled but later in *George v Webb* at [266]–[283], after an exhaustive review of the authorities and academic commentary, Ward J found that the *Quistclose* trust was an express trust, the breach of which could give rise to accessorial liability under the rule in *Barnes v Addy* (1874) LR 9 Ch App 244: see 28.109–28.160. In *Pearson v Western Australia* [2012] WASC 102 at [4], Simmonds J felt it would not matter whether it was an express or resulting trust. This is probably correct for all practical purposes. Either way of looking at the *Quistclose* trust yields the same result; namely, that the creditor retains a beneficial interest in the loan moneys which can be enforced should the primary purpose fail: *Re Australian Elizabethan Theatre Trust* at FCR 501; ALR 691.

15.67   It is difficult to understand *Quistclose* trusts when viewed through the prism of traditional trust principles. The problems relate primarily to the nature of the shareholder's interest in the trust. If the mutual intention had created a primary trust for the shareholders, then logically it should follow that the shareholders should have an enforceable beneficial interest, which remains enforceable regardless of the insolvency of the trustee. An insolvent trustee remains liable to beneficiaries and trust assets cannot form part of the estate in insolvency. Why then is there a need for a secondary trust? Ford and Lee have suggested that the mutual intention in *Quistclose* may have been that the dividends should only be paid if the company was an ongoing concern.[9]

15.68   Perhaps the answer is that the creditors in a *Quistclose* trust do not receive a beneficial equitable interest at all: *Mercantile Mutual Insurance (Australia) Ltd v Farrington* (1996) 44 NSWLR 634 at 646. In *Re Northern Development (Holdings) Ltd* (unreported, UK, High Court (Chancery Div), 1978) Megarry V-C stated that the creditor's beneficial interest was 'in suspense' until payment. However,

---

9.   H A J Ford and W A Lee, *Principles of the law of trusts* (Online), Thomson Reuters, Sydney, [1390].

this would mean that only the lender would have a beneficial interest in the property and this could not explain how the creditors could be allowed to take the property under the primary trust.

15.69   Lord Millett's resulting trust analysis does not resolve these difficulties. In *Quistclose* trusts the court's inquiry into the *actual* intention of the lender to create the trust does not match the rationale of resulting trusts, which exist where there are *presumptions* as to intention to create a trust. The actual intention of the creator is examined to rebut the existence of a resulting trust, not to establish it: see Chapter 19.

Securities and trusts

15.70   Debts will often be secured. This means that the debtor has agreed to give the creditor a proprietary interest in one or more of his or her assets. Should the debtor not pay, the creditor can realise the security by taking possession of the secured property or by ordering that it be sold and the proceeds be used to satisfy the debt.

15.71   Securities come in many forms. Examples include mortgages, bills of sale, equitable charges and equitable liens. In mortgages and bills of sale (mortgages over personalty), the property is legally transferred to the lender (mortgagee), with a promise that it will be reconveyed back to the borrower (mortgagor) when the money is repaid. A mortgagee is not a trustee of the property and, while there are some duties of good faith owed by mortgagees to their mortgagors (see, for example, at 3.24–3.26), these are not ordinarily of a fiduciary character: *Warner v Jacob* (1882) 20 Ch D 220.

15.72   The equitable charge is very similar to a trust. In *Weston v Metro Apartments Pty Ltd* [2002] NSWSC 876 at [18]–[19], Einstein J described an equitable charge as follows:

> A charge involves the notion of a monetary obligation due from one party to another, where the chargee may have recourse to some asset of the chargor to obtain satisfaction in the event of non-payment of an obligation. A charge typically involves some item of property or fund being available to answer an obligation, such that, at least to the extent that the court's assistance can be obtained, the chargee will have an 'interest' in the charged property, and so become entitled to the protection of a court of equity to prevent dissipation of that property, and to compel its realisation for the agreed or identified purpose.

15.73   Thus, an equitable charge is a form of security that allows the creditor (chargee) to order the sale of the property after a triggering event, like default of payment. To contrast the equitable charge with a trust we can examine the following examples:

(i) A devises Blackacre to B charged with the payment of a debt owed to C;

(ii) A devises Blackacre to B on trust to pay debt owed to C.

15.74   In situation (i) no trust is created because B has no personal obligation to hold Blackacre for the benefit of C. C's interest in Blackacre is an equitable interest but only of a security nature. If B does not pay the debt, C has no remedy against B personally, but must proceed in equity to have Blackacre sold and to have his debt paid out of the proceeds: *In re Bank of Credit and Commerce International SA (No 8)* [1998] AC 214 at 226; [1997] 4 All ER 568 at 576. If a surplus remains after the repayment of the debt it belongs to B. If B does pay out the debt he holds the property for his own benefit.

15.75   In (ii) a trust is created. B must pay the debt to C and if he does not C's remedy is against B personally for performance or for administration of the trust and not against the property itself. If Blackacre is sold and the proceeds are more than sufficient to pay C then the surplus will be held on trust by B for the residuary beneficiary or next-of-kin as the case may be: *King v Denison* (1813) 35 ER 102 at 106–7. B will not be entitled to the surplus.

15.76   Whether a charge or trust is created depends on the intention of the transferor. This is not always an easy matter to ascertain, although words such as 'charged with' or 'subject to' are generally indicative of an equitable charge, not a trust.

15.77   The equitable lien is related to the charge, and is an equitable remedy used to protect a party against an inequitable loss: *Re Stephenson Nominees v Official Receiver* (1987) 76 ALR 485 at 504; *Smith v The State of Western Australia* [2009] WASC 189 at [31]–[34]. In *Hewett v Court* (1982) 149 CLR 639 at 663; 46 ALR 87 at 104–5, Deane J said:

> An equitable lien is a right against property which arises automatically by implication of equity to secure the discharge of an actual or potential indebtedness ... Though called a lien, it is, in truth, a form of equitable charge over the subject property ... in that it does not depend upon possession and may, in general, be enforced in the same way as any other equitable charge, namely, by sale in pursuance of court order or, where the lien is over a fund, by an order for payment thereout. ... Equitable lien differs from traditional mortgage in that it does not transfer any title to the property and therefore cannot be enforced by foreclosure. While it arises by implication of some equitable doctrine applicable to the circumstances, its implication can be precluded or qualified by express or implied agreement of the parties ... It can exist over land or personalty or both.

15.78   Trusts and these securities are quite different from each other. The equitable property interests of beneficiaries are always in existence and are always enforceable. The interests of secured creditors, while in existence from the formation of the agreement, are usually only enforceable after a triggering event. The remedies for breach of trust are also different, as beneficiaries can seek the proper performance of the trust at all times. The interest of a secured creditor in property is only enforceable after breach.

15.79   Beneficiaries can access the several remedies for breach of trust, unlike secured creditors who need to sell trust property to satisfy their needs: *Associated Alloys Pty Limited v ACN 001 452 106 Pty Limited* (2000) 202 CLR 588; 171 ALR 568. Finally, the equitable property rights generated by securities are unlike the interest of a beneficiary because they come without any fiduciary obligations.

15.80   It is not always easy to distinguish between trusts and security interests. This is especially the case when the security has taken the form of an equitable charge. The answer will always lie in the intention of the person transferring the property.[10] This is determined by examination of the language of the instrument: *Boral Bricks v Davey* [2010] QSC 131; *Boral Resources (Qld) Pty Ltd v Andrews* [2010] QSC 491; *Allen's Asphalt Pty Ltd v SPM Group Ltd* [2009] QCA 134 at [47]; *Craddock v Scottish Provident Institution* (1893) 69 LT 380 at 382. If the transferor intends that the title be transferred, 'subject to' payments being made to another, then it will be construed as

---

10.   Heydon & Leeming, *Jacobs' Law of Trusts*, note 4 above, p 30.

a charge. For example, property might be given 'to A subject to A paying B $1000'. This transfer evidences an intention that the obligation to pay is annexed to property as opposed to being a fiduciary obligation imposed on the transferee. The obligation is of a finite nature. It is satisfied after compliance. As such, it is not of the same extent and duration as the trustee's fiduciary obligations to care for the beneficiaries' interest in a trust: *Countess of Bective v Federal Commissioner of Taxation* (1932) 47 CLR 417.

Conditional dispositions and trusts

15.81   Transfers of property which are subject to obligations being fulfilled to third parties will ordinarily be viewed as equitable charges. However, it is also possible to place conditions on dispositions of property that do not create a charge or confer a proprietary interest on the third party. Such conditions might be viewed as merely unenforceable 'precatory' obligations, enforceable conditions precedent or subsequent, or equitable personal obligations. These types of conditions are all distinguishable from trusts and charges.

Precatory words

15.82   If a transferor of property indicates a motive, hope or expectation that the property will be used in a particular way, the condition will be viewed as precatory and import no legal or equitable obligations: *Re Williams* [1897] 2 Ch 12. For example, gifts made in the belief that 'justice will be done to my relatives' will impose a moral obligation which has no force: *In the Will of Warren; Verga v Taylor* [1907] VLR 325. Similarly, in *Re Singh (dec'd)* [1995] 2 NZLR 487, a disposition worded 'without however creating a binding trust in that regard' clearly indicated that the stipulations were not binding. The language of these 'conditions' is not imperative and hence non-binding either as a trust, condition subsequent or precedent, or as a personal equitable obligation.

Conditions precedent and subsequent

15.83   If the transfer is made subject to a binding condition precedent, the transfer will not take place until the condition precedent is satisfied: *Re Gardiner (dec'd)* [1971] 2 NSWLR 494. If the condition is a condition subsequent, the property will be forfeited if the condition is not fulfilled. If the disposition states that the obligation is to be fulfilled within a time period it is viewed as a condition precedent: *Re Gardiner (dec'd)* at 498. In reality, it makes little difference whether the condition is precedent or subsequent as the effect will be the same; that is, the transfer will not be successful and the donee will be divested of the property: *Re Gardiner (dec'd)* at 498. However, the courts are generally reluctant to interpret a condition so that it requires forfeiture, and a high degree of certainty concerning the donor's intention will be required before a forfeiture condition is found: *Re Boning* [1997] 2 Qd R 12.

Personal equitable obligations

15.84   In some circumstances the courts will interpret a conditional disposition as imposing a personal equitable obligation on the donee, such as the payment of an amount of money — for example, an annuity — to a third party: *O'Sullivan Partners (Advisory) Pty Ltd v Foggo* [2012] NSWCA 40 at [93]–[99]; *Re Hodge* [1940] Ch 260; *Re Williams; Williams v Williams* [1897] 2 Ch 12 at 19; *Rees v Engelbach* (1871) LR 12 Eq 225. Sometimes the obligation to the third party will be less definite, such as an obligation to 'support' or 'take care' of a third party, or make sure they 'want for nothing': *Re Moore* (1886) 55 LJ Ch 418; *Broad v Bevan* (1823) 38 ER 198; *Hammond* *v Hammond* [2007] NSWSC 106. Such a personal equitable obligation does not create a property right in the third party beneficiary. Nor will the breach of the obligation give rise to a forfeiture of the gift. However, the personal obligation is enforceable and the breach of it may give rise to orders of specific performance, injunctions or equitable compensation: *Kauter v Kauter* [2003] NSWSC 741; *Messenger v Andrews* (1828) 38 ER 885; *Gregg v Coates* (1856) 53 ER 13.

15.85 For example, in *Gill v Gill* (1921) 21 SR(NSW) 400, a disposition of a farm to the testator's son was made on the condition that the son pay the testator's debts and allow the testator's three daughters to live in part of the farmhouse for as long as they remained unmarried. Harvey J found that the conditions were not conditions subsequent. Nor did they create a trust in favour of the sisters. Rather, the conditions were said to impose a personal equitable obligation on the son to provide appropriate accommodation to his remaining unmarried sisters. Importantly, his Honour, at 407, said:

> In some cases the court may see that what the testator intended was to attach a charge or a trust upon the property, in other cases it may conclude a personal liability alone is intended. The view taken would depend partly on the language used to describe the obligation, partly on the nature of the property given to the obligee, and partly on the nature of the obligation. In cases where the obligation is merely personal in its nature, calling for the personal activity of the obligee, it may be the court could not effectively order specific performance; I see no reason why, in such cases the court should not mould the remedy so as to give a remedy by way of damages for the breach of the quasi contract.

15.86 The primary reason for enforcing the obligation is that the donee has accepted the property and, by accepting the benefit of the property, must accept the condition. Harvey J, at 406, described the obligation as arising from the equitable doctrine that a person cannot 'approbate and reprobate' under the same instrument.

Determining construction

15.87 The question of how one should characterise a disposition is therefore a question of construction. If the disposition is worded in such a way as to impose a direct obligation on the donee to take care of the third party in some way, but without giving the third party a proprietary interest, the condition will be viewed as creating a personal equitable obligation. If the disposition is created with a condition that leads to forfeiture, but without reference to personal obligations being owed to the third party, it is more likely to be viewed as a charge, condition precedent or condition subsequent.

15.88 In cases where the conditional disposition is possibly a charge, condition precedent or condition subsequent, courts prefer to view the disposition as imposing a charge. It has been said that a conditional disposition will be treated as taking effect as a charge even where words of condition are used: *Re Gardiner (dec'd)*. The courts prefer to treat the disposition as imposing a charge because this will give the third party a proprietary interest in the property. If the disposition was treated as a condition subsequent or precedent and if, for some reason, the donee failed to take the gift (for example, if they refused, or died before transfer), the third party would receive nothing as the gift would fail. However, by construing the disposition as imposing a charge, the third party receives a proprietary interest which is independent of the actions of the donee: *Re Oliver; Newbold v Beckett* (1890) 62 LT 533. Even if the donee rejects the gift, the interest created by the charge will survive.

15.89   It should also be noted that a condition may impose personal equitable obligations and a charge at the same time: *In re Cowley* (1885) 53 LT 494; *Re Lester; Lester v Lester* [1943] Ch 324; [1942] 1 All ER 646.

Retention of title clauses and trusts

15.90   Retention of title clauses, or *Romalpa* clauses, are contractual clauses used in the sale of goods.[11] They allow suppliers to retain title in delivered goods until such time as full payment has been made: *Aluminium Industrie Vaassen BV v Romalpa Aluminium Ltd* [1976] 2 All ER 552. Should the buyer become insolvent, the goods do not form part of the buyer's estate in insolvency and the supplier is able to repossess them.

15.91   In *Associated Alloys Pty Limited v ACN 001 452 106 Pty Limited (in liq)* (2000) 202 CLR 588 at 617; 171 ALR 568 at 588, Kirby J summarised the general approach to *Romalpa* clauses and said that they will not generally be effective unless:

> (1) they are clearly accepted as part of the agreement between the parties; and (2) they can be applied to the original goods that were sold where such goods may be readily identified, retrieved intact, reconstituted, separated and returned to the seller; or (3) a separate financial account or fund has been established, as proper to a fiduciary relationship between the parties, in order to receive the proceeds of the sale of the goods possessed by one but still purportedly owned by another.

15.92   In cases where the goods have not been transformed by the manufacturing process and remain in their original state, *Romalpa* clauses operate very much like a bailment and are therefore quite distinguishable from a trust relationship.[12] However, where the goods have been mixed with other goods or used in a manufacturing process or sold, *Romalpa* clauses can operate like a trust or a charge. For example, some *Romalpa* clauses require that the proceeds from any sale of the goods be held in separate accounts. Failure to do so may leave the buyer liable to account as a trustee: *Puma Australia Pty Ltd v Sportsman's Australia Ltd (No 2)* [1994] Qd R 159. However, if the alleged beneficiary acquiesces in the 'trustee's' failure to hold separate accounts it might be impossible to say that a trust was ever constituted: *Rondo Building Services Pty Ltd v Casaron Pty Ltd* [2003] 2 Qd R 558. Alternatively, if there is no intention for the proceeds to be held and accounted for separately, it is more likely that the funds will be treated as an unsecured debt: *Dwyer v Chicago Boot Co Pty Ltd* [2011] SASC 27 at [111]–[116]; *Chattis Nominees Pty Ltd v Norman Ross Home Works Pty Ltd (Receivers appointed) (in liq)* (1992) 28 NSWLR 338 at 346–7. It will be very difficult to imply that proceeds were to be held on trust in the absence of express terms: *Toveill Pty Ltd v Australian Quality Plus Pty Ltd* [2010] NSWSC 1003.

15.93   The similarities between trusts, charges and *Romalpa* clauses were discussed by the High Court in *Associated Alloys Pty Limited v ACN 001 452 106 Pty Limited (in liq)*. The High Court was asked to decide whether a particular *Romalpa* clause had created a charge or a trust. The seller had supplied steel to the buyer on terms that contained a *Romalpa* clause. The clause stated that if the

---

11.   For a discussion of these clauses, trusts and the new *Personal Property Securities Act 2009* (Cth) see J Glister, 'Trusts and the PPSA' (2011) 34 *University of New South Wales Law Journal* 628.

12.   Dal Pont, *Equity and Trusts in Australia*, note 6 above, p 491.

steel was sold before full payment, the buyer was required to hold in a separate account an amount of the proceeds that was equal to the amount owing on the steel 'at the time of the receipt of such proceeds'. The buyer had used the steel in the manufacturing process and sold the steel products to a third party. The third party had paid some, but not all, of the purchase price of the products. The buyer then went into liquidation.

15.94 The question for the High Court was whether the proceeds clause created a trust or a statutory charge. Statutory charges are charges coming within the definition of 'charge' under s 262(1)(f) of the *Corporations Law*. This definition included charges over book debts. If the clause created a statutory charge the agreement was invalid as it had not been registered under the *Corporations Law*. Section 266 of the *Corporations Law* requires all charges to be registered. However, if the agreement created a trust, it was valid as there is no need to register trusts under the *Corporations Law*.

15.95 The answer to the question hinged on the meaning of the word 'proceeds' in the proceeds clause. If the buyer was obliged to keep both the money and the book debts as 'proceeds' for the seller, then the clause would come under the definition of 'charge' under the *Corporations Law*, and be invalidated for want of registration. If the word 'proceeds' could be confined to the actual moneys paid by the third party, the clause could be considered to come under the definition of trust.

15.96 A majority of the High Court (Gaudron, McHugh, Gummow and Hayne JJ) found that the clause had created a trust of the amounts that had been paid by the third party. The majority, at CLR 602; ALR 576–7, read the reference to 'proceeds' in the clause to refer only to the amounts that had actually been paid by the third party and not to the book debts, and said:

> The proper construction of the phrase 'the proceeds' is revealed by a consideration of the proceeds subclause as a whole … The phrase 'the proceeds' is to be construed as referring to moneys received by the buyer and not debts which may be set out in the buyer's books (or computer records) from time to time … The concluding sentence of the proceeds subclause would be strained if the phrase 'the proceeds' were to include book debts. In the event that a debt were subject to conditions, it may prove to be difficult to determine when the buyer is in 'receipt' of that intangible obligation. Moreover, to attempt to equate a chose in action, 'in dollar terms', to a sum of money, namely 'the amount owing by the [buyer] to the [seller] at the time of the receipt of such proceeds', is, at the very least, conceptually problematic. In contrast, limiting the phrase 'the proceeds' to refer to payments made to the Buyer results in this equation operating with certainty.

15.97 Given the buyer was only obliged to hold actually received moneys on behalf of the seller, the agreement was outside the *Corporations Law*'s definition of charge. It could be treated as a trust given the parties had manifested the appropriate intention to create a trust.

15.98 However, the majority found that the seller could not be given relief for breach of trust. The seller had failed to prove that the proceeds received by the buyer were received in relation to the steel that was subject to the *Romalpa* clause. This lack of evidence was fatal to the seller's claims of relief.

15.99 Kirby J also dismissed the seller's appeal but disagreed with the majority as to the reason. He found that the word 'proceeds' included book debts. As such, the clause created a charge that was void for registration. His Honour, at CLR 625; ALR 594–5, said:

Once a retention of title clause is purportedly expressed to cover debts, goods manufactured from the goods supplied, or the proceeds of on-sales, the approach to be taken is one that looks beyond legal technique and form to the substance and reality ... This was recognised by Mummery J in *Compaq Computer Ltd v Abercorn Group Ltd* [1991] BCC 484 at 493 when he said:

> In determining whether any given agreement creates a charge, equity looks to the substance and reality of the transaction. What on the face of it may appear to be an out-and-out disposition of a legal or equitable interest in property by way of assignment or conveyance or an out-and-out disposition of a beneficial interest in property by way of trust, may in fact be by way of security only, with a right of redemption and, therefore, in the nature of a charge.

This is the approach which I would also take. I would do so because [the seller] is relying on the law of equity to impose on [the buyer] an obligation, once the goods are changed by manufacture, to hold the proceeds of their sale in trust for [the seller]. Mummery J was not, of course, asserting that trusts are, of their nature, securities. But he was cautioning against exclusive concentration on the terms of an instrument purporting to create a trust, to the neglect of an examination of the purpose and effect of that instrument when considered for its substance and not merely its form.

Powers of appointment and trusts

15.100   In a power of appointment, the titleholder of property (the *donor*) gives another person (the *donee*) the power to deal with, or dispose of, the property that is the subject of the power. Normally the power will allow the donee to transfer the property to a third party who can be chosen from a class of people specified in the power (the *objects* of the power). Unlike a trustee, the donee of a power is not usually given the title to the property: *Re in the Will of McCracken; Webb v McCracken* (1906) 3 CLR 1018. Nor is a donee necessarily subjected to any fiduciary duties.

15.101   Powers contain instructions to the donee as to how to exercise them. Powers may confer a discretion on the donee to choose who is to receive an interest in the property. The different types of discretion give rise to the following four types of power (*R & I Bank of Western Australia Ltd v Anchorage Investments Pty Ltd* (1993) 10 WAR 59 at 81; *Scaffidi v Montevento Holdings Pty Ltd* [2011] WASCA 146 at [77]):

1. *general powers*, where the donee is empowered to appoint the property to anyone including himself or herself;
2. *special powers*, which are powers to appoint the property to specific individuals or classes of objects, not including the donee;
3. *hybrid powers*, where the donee can give the property to anyone in the world except for a particular group or class or individual; and
4. *intermediate powers*, where the donee can add to the specified class of objects in the power.

15.102   Just because a donee has been granted the power to dispose of property this does not necessarily mean that the donee is obliged to exercise that power. In cases where the donee is under no obligation to exercise the power, the donee is said to have a *mere power* or *bare power*.

15.103   Mere powers are unlike trusts because they confer a wide discretion, which is incompatible with the fiduciary nature of the trust relationship. The donee can choose to act whereas the trustee must always act in the interest of the beneficiaries. Similarly, a general power of appointment cannot be a trust as it allows the donee to choose anyone, including himself or herself, to be the object of the power. Trustees, in contrast, cannot use their station for their own betterment. In situations where a trustee is granted a general power, the power will be read down to preclude the trustee from appointing himself or herself. Finally, another major distinction between powers and trusts relates to title. Trustees must have vested title in the trust property, whereas a donee need not have title to have the authority to deal with the property subject to the power.[13]

15.104   However, powers are normally conferred in wills and in trusts. This creates complexities because, in most circumstances, the donee of the power will be obliged to use it to transfer the property among a class of objects. In cases where the donee is obliged to exercise the power, and where the power is also in either special or hybrid form, the power is called a *trust power*.

15.105   Trust powers are the essential mechanisms of discretionary trusts. They are the means by which the power is given to a discretionary trustee to choose beneficiaries and the scope of their entitlements. If the power is a trustee power, fiduciary obligations are imposed and the donee cannot use the power for his or her own benefit: *Smith v Glegg* [2005] 1 Qd R 561.

15.106   The task of identifying the nature and effect of a power is a matter of interpretation: *Hourigan v Trustees Executors and Agency Co Ltd* (1934) 51 CLR 619. Some basic principles of construction exist. For example, words which convey an obligation to use the power will indicate it is a trust power. Contrastingly, if the power states that if it is not exercised the property should be given to a specified person (sometimes referred to as 'a gift over in contemplation'), it will be treated as a mere power: *Breadner v Granville-Grossman* [2001] Ch 523; [2000] 4 All ER 705. This is because the inclusion of the gift indicates that there is an implied discretion not to exercise the power.

15.107   Similarly, if a power is granted to someone who is a trustee, it will be presumed that the power will be treated as a special power and not a general power. Trustees should not be able to exercise powers for their own benefit (in the absence of express provisions to the contrary): *Metropolitan Gas Company v Federal Commissioner of Taxation* (1932) 47 CLR 621.

15.108   Why does the distinction between trust powers and mere powers matter? Both mere and trust powers are required to describe their objects with sufficient certainty. It used to be the case that trust powers and mere powers were subjected to different tests of certainty. This now appears to have changed: *Re Baden's Deed Trusts; McPhail v Doulton* [1971] AC 424; [1970] 2 All ER 228. This will be discussed in greater detail at 16.67–16.75, 16.92–16.100.

15.109   More importantly, an object of a mere power has no right to demand that it be exercised, whereas the objects of a trust power have the right to be considered and can compel proper administration of the trust: *Gartside v IRC* [1968] AC 553; [1968] 1 All ER 121.

---

13.   Dal Pont, *Equity and Trusts in Australia*, see note 6 above, p 505.

16

CREATION OF EXPRESS TRUSTS

INTRODUCTION

16.1 Express trusts can be created in three main ways:

1. by *declaration*, where a title holder expresses his or her intention to hold their property on trust for another;
2. by *transfer*, where title is transferred to a person with instructions that it be held on trust for another; the transfer can occur either via an *inter vivos* transaction (which is generally referred to as a 'settlement') or *post mortem* (by will); and
3. by *direction*, where the beneficiary of an existing trust directs the trustee to hold his or her interest on trust for another.

16.2 The success of the trust's creation depends on a number of factors. The trust must be sufficiently certain with respect to the creator's intention, the trust property and the description of beneficiaries. The trust must be properly constituted, meaning there must be a complete transfer of the title of the property to the trustee. Depending on the nature of the property, there may also be requirements of writing. These issues will be discussed in turn.

THE THREE CERTAINTIES

16.3 Express trusts must satisfy the three requirements of certainty of intention, subject matter and beneficiaries (or objects): *Knight v Knight* (1840) 49 ER 58 at 68; *Varma v Varma* [2010] NSWSC 786 at [474]; *Ying v Song* [2010] NSWSC 1500 at [239]. If the trust is uncertain it will fail and the property will be held on resulting trust for the creator, or his or her representatives: see Chapter 19.

Certainty of intention

16.4 An express trust will not be valid unless it is clear that the creator has intended to create a trust: *Australian Receivables Ltd v Tekitu Pty Ltd* [2011] NSWSC 1306 at [103]–[104]. This will rarely be an issue in cases where the trust is evidenced by a deed: *Hyhonie Holdings Pty Ltd v Leroy* [2004] NSWCA 72 at [40]. However, in many other situations questions can arise as to whether there was an intention for the trust property to be held for the benefit of another.

16.5 It should be noted from the outset that resulting and constructive trusts do not have to satisfy certainty of intention. As we shall see, an intention to create a trust is presumed in resulting trusts and generally irrelevant to constructive trusts.

The nature of intention

16.6 The requirement of certainty of intention does not mean that the creator has to be fully aware of the law of trusts before they can be found to have intended to create a trust: *Re Armstrong (dec'd)* [1960] VR 202. Ford and Lee point out that:

> What in fact happens is that the creator of a trust evinces an intention to create in others the kind of interests which can be validly created more effectively by a trust than some other legal apparatus or to impose on somebody the kind of fiduciary obligations which the legal system will enforce in a distinctive way … If a person has shown an intention that another should be entitled to benefit out of specific property and a trust is, in the circumstances, the appropriate legal mechanism for giving effect to that intention, an inference will be made that the person intended to create a trust.[1]

16.7 We have already seen that there are similarities between trusts and other legal relationships, such as charges and personal equitable obligations. As was discussed in Chapter 15, the courts will examine the evidence, particularly the words employed by the transferor, to determine what sort of interest was intended to be created. If it can be shown that a full-blown equitable interest is granted in the property, with correspondingly wide fiduciary duties being owed by the legal title holder, it can be said that a trust was intended: *Bahr v Nicolay (No 2)* (1988) 164 CLR 605 at 618; 78 ALR 1 at 9.

16.8 Because of the focus on the creator's intention it is possible to create a trust without using the words 'trust' or 'trustee': *Registrar of the Accident Compensation Tribunal (Vic) v Federal Commissioner of Taxation* (1993) 178 CLR 145 at 165; 117 ALR 27 at 39. There is no required formula: *Sheikholeslami v Tolcher* [2011] FCA 1050 at [151]–[156]; *Pascoe v Boensch* (2008) 250 ALR 24 at 29. The intention to create a trust can also be inferred from conduct: *Commonwealth v Booker International Pty Ltd* [2002] NSWSC 292. The intention to create a trust must be an intention to create a relationship in respect to property that the law characterises as a trust: *Re Armstrong (dec'd)*. In *Valeress Pty Ltd v Valenest Pty Ltd (in liquidation)* [2011] NSWSC 465 at [63]–[64], Sackar J said:

> In relation to establishing certainty of intention to create a trust, it is clear that an intention to create a trust may be established without the use of technical language such as the word 'trust' itself. Likewise, in the situation where the term 'trust' is not used, this will not necessarily be determinative of whether or not there is a trust; in both situations the conduct of the alleged creator of the trust must be construed in context to determine their overall intention … With regards to inferring intention, the court will consider the language of the parties with reference to the factual matrix of events and the circumstances of the parties. Further, in inferring intention a court will look to the nature of the transaction and the circumstances of the matter, including commercial necessity.

16.9 In *Saunders v Deputy Commissioner of Taxation* [2010] WASC 261 at [22], Kenneth Martin J summarised the principles relating to intention as follows:

---

1. H A J Ford & W A Lee, *Principles of the law of trusts* (Online), Thomson Reuters, Sydney, [2010].

1. The existence of a trust is to be determined with reference to a declaration of trust by the subjective intention of the settlor, although that intention may be inferred from objective circumstances.

2. Because it is a subjective intention which is at issue, the parole evidence rule does not limit the evidence which may be taken into account in determining whether a trust was validly declared.

3. Subjective intention may be inferred from language employed in the written instrument.

4. Subjective intent may also be inferred from the conduct of the parties as well as from the surrounding circumstances in a particular case.

5. Generally speaking, the legal onus of establishing that the intention to create a trust existed at the relevant time remains with the person asserting the existence of the trust.

6. Where there is an unambiguous use of language in a written instrument establishing a trust, the evidentiary onus will shift to a contradicting party to show that a trust does not exist through the establishment, if possible, of a contrary intention.

7. The evidentiary onus falls upon the party seeking to show the contrary intention and strong evidence is required to do so.

8. The evidence as to a contrary intention may be circumstantial. All relevant circumstances may be examined to determine whether there actually was the intention to create a trust.

9. Subsequent events may be proved to negate a finding as to an intention to create a trust. Circumstantial evidence that will be admissible to be weighed in this process may include the circumstance where an ostensible declarant of a trust nevertheless continues to exercise personal dominion over the property the subject of the declaration of trust.

10. Evaluations of subjective intention towards the establishment of a trust raise issues of fact which are to be determined by reference to the particular circumstances of each individual case.

11. The word 'sham' is an expression carrying a well understood legal meaning: see *Equuscorp Pty Ltd v Glengallan Investments Pty Ltd* (2004) 218 CLR 471 at [46], where it was observed that a sham 'refers to steps which take the form of a legally effective transaction but which the parties intend should not have the apparent, or any, legal consequences'.

As we shall see below (see 16.16–16.23), the reference in the above quote to 'subjective' intention needs to be read in light of more recent decisions, but as a general statement, the above passage is a useful summary of the principles. Some recent case examples will illustrate these points.

16.10 *Shah v Shah* [2010] EWCA Civ 1408 shows that the word 'trust' is not necessary to evidence an intention to create a trust. The Court of Appeal found that a statement in a letter which said, 'I am as from today holding 4,000 shares in the above company for you', was enough to evidence an intention to create a trust. Although legal ownership of the shares had not changed, the statement evidenced an intention to create a beneficial interest by way of a trust.

16.11 In *La Housse v Counsel* [2008] WASCA 207, the deceased had set up two accounts in his daughters' names, where he expressed himself to be trustee of the accounts. Later the deceased used the moneys to purchase a house which, in his will, he gifted to his ex-girlfriend. The will named the girlfriend as the executrix of his estate. The daughters claimed ownership of the house on constructive trust. The executrix denied that the accounts were trust accounts and claimed that the deceased's actions indicated that he had no intention to create a trust. The Court of Appeal of Western Australia found that the evidence overwhelmingly showed an intention to create a trust of the moneys. The creation of the accounts and his statements to third parties indicated that he had intended for two trusts to be created. The use of the funds was a breach of trust which could be remedied via the imposition of a constructive trust over the house.

16.12 Being silent will not ordinarily indicate an intention to create a trust. In *Foley v Foley* [2006] QSC 347, an allegation that grandparents had agreed to hold the beneficial title of land on trust for their grandson was rejected. Statements were made by the grandmother which indicated that the grandson would be given a beneficial interest, and the grandfather did not contradict those statements. After the grandmother's death, the property was transferred into the grandfather's sole ownership and the grandfather refused to be bound by any agreement concerning an *inter vivos* trust. Mullins J could not find evidence that the grandfather had ever intended to hold the property on trust for his grandson. The fact that he did not remonstrate with his wife when she made statements about giving the child the property did not prove that the grandfather had agreed to create a beneficial interest for the grandson while the grandfather was still alive.

16.13 In some cases it will be possible to prove an intention to create a trust, but the terms of the trust may be less extensive than what is alleged. In *Kauter v Hilton* (1953) 90 CLR 86, a woman claimed the entire beneficial estate in a bank account; namely, both principal and interest. While she succeeded in proving an intention to create a trust, the High Court found that the intention was to grant her a beneficial estate that was subject to the creator's reservation of a life interest in the account. This had the effect of postponing her beneficial interest until the creator's death.

Was there an intention to create a trust immediately or at a later time?

16.14 The intention must also be to create a trust at that time so that it becomes operative at that time. A party may express an intention to create a trust at a later time but if the trust is not created the purported beneficiaries cannot force the person to constitute the trust, as they are volunteers. In *Harpur v Levy* (2007) 16 VR 587, a deceased person had attempted to create a trust prior to death, but the trust was not intended to commence until a later time. Death unkindly intervened. The Victorian Court of Appeal found that the deceased's intentions meant that the trust had never been constituted.

16.15 A distinction can be drawn between the intention in *Harper v Levy* to create a trust at a later time and cases where the creator intends to create a trust immediately, but wishes to postpone the beneficiaries' rights of entitlement to a later date. In *Re Armstrong (dec'd)*, two investment accounts had been deposited by the settlor in a bank for two years. The bank manager was instructed to give the principal sums to the settlor's sons when the investments matured. Interest was to be paid to the creator. The court found that there was an intention to create a trust for the sons over the capital amounts, even though those beneficial rights were postponed until the investments matured.

Can an expressed intention be rebutted by evidence of subjective intention?

16.16 In older cases the use of the word 'trust' did not always satisfy the requirement for certainty of intention, if a trust was not actually intended by the purported settlor. In *Commissioner of Stamp Duties v Jolliffe* (1920) 28 CLR 178, a husband opened a bank account, purportedly on trust, for his wife. Later his wife died and death duties became payable on the proceeds of the account. The husband denied that his real intention was to create a trust. A majority of the High Court found that words of declaration could not create a trust contrary to the true intention of the creator. As such, the trust was not valid even though express words of trust were used.

16.17   The decision in *Jolliffe* contained a very strong dissent from Isaacs J. His Honour, at 187, said:

> An open declaration of trust is … an expression of intention that is final and beyond recall.

16.18   Later, Isaacs J, at 191, went on and said:

> I cannot believe that, for instance, a solemn deed of trust or a will can be open to the reception of parol evidence, not of mistake as to its nature, or as to any condition of execution, or as to undue influence or other well understood causes of ineffectiveness, but merely of personal secret intention not to do what the document purports to effect.

16.19   In later cases it was held that even though a declaration of trust was made, the creator's subsequent actions could be used to contraindicate an intention to create a trust: *Re Lamshed* [1970] SASR 224 at 239. In *Arthur v Public Trustee* (1988) 90 FLR 203 at 209, Asche CJ said:

> [E]quity will only enforce a trust to the extent that the intention to create a trust is clear … Words alone may suffice but where those words are at odds with the donor's action proof may be lacking.

16.20   In *Strang v Strang* [2009] NSWSC 760 at [68], Nicholas J said:

> The crucial question is whether there was the requisite intention at the time the declaration was made. In order to determine the true position it may be necessary to consider the circumstances which existed at the time of execution of the instrument, and also subsequent events which may negate the expression of intention to create a trust …. However, it must be kept in mind that strong evidence of a contrary intention is required to rebut the unambiguous words of a declaration of trust … The question is one of fact in all cases.

16.21   However, in *Shortall v White* [2007] NSWCA 372 at [24]–[29], Handley JA found that the subjective test should only be applied when the trust is claimed to have been created unilaterally, without consideration and without the beneficiaries being informed. In cases where the trust is created as part of a contract with consideration, the appropriate test is the objective test of intention and the purported trustee will not be able to later disclaim the trust by alleging that he or she never intended to create one if there is objective evidence that a trust was intended.

16.22   These issues of intention were extensively re-examined by the High Court in *Byrnes v Kendle* (2009) 243 CLR 253; 279 ALR 212. This case concerned a house in Murray Bridge, South Australia. The house was registered under the Torrens system to Clifford Kendle. Clifford was married to Joan Byrnes. In 1997 Clifford signed an 'acknowledgment of trust' which declared that he held one undivided half interest in the property as tenant in common for Joan. The couple separated in 2007. Later in that year Joan assigned her interest under the trust to her son Martin. Clifford argued that he did not have a real intention to create a trust and that he could bring evidence to show his true intention. The High Court disagreed and found that there was an intention to create a trust and that intention could be proven by the objective evidence contained in the acknowledgment. Heydon and Crennan JJ, at CLR 290; ALR 241–2, summed up the essence of the High Court's thinking on the matter when they said:

[T]he 'intention' [to create a trust] is an intention to be extracted from the words used, not a subjective intention which may have existed but which cannot be extracted from those words. This is as true of unilateral declarations of alleged trust as it is of bilateral covenants to create an alleged trust. It is as true of alleged trusts which are not wholly in writing as it is of alleged trusts which are wholly in writing. In relation to alleged trusts which are not wholly in writing, the need to draw inferences from circumstances in construing the terms of conversations may in practice widen the extent of the inquiry, but it does not alter its nature ... [S]ubjective intention is irrelevant both to the question of whether a trust exists and to the question of what its terms are.

16.23   French CJ, at CLR 262; ALR 218, said the following of the decision in *Jolliffe*:

Given its statutory and factual setting, *Jolliffe* should not be taken as authority for the general proposition that where there has been an explicit written declaration of trust, unaffected by vitiating factors, evidence is admissible to contradict the intention to create a trust manifested by the declaration ... What Isaacs J said in *Jolliffe* was entirely consistent with the principle that a trust cannot be created unless the person creating it intends to do so.

Gummow and Hayne JJ, at CLR 277; ALR 231, said the following of *Jolliffe*:

Jolliffe should not be regarded as retaining any authority it otherwise may have had for the proposition that where the creation of an express trust is in issue, regard may be had to all the relevant circumstances not merely to show the intention manifested by the words and actions comprising those circumstances, but to show what the relevant actor meant to convey as a matter of 'real intention'.

Finally, Heydon and Crennan JJ, at CLR 291; ALR 242, ruled as follows:

[Isaacs J's] dissent is indeed powerful, and as a statement of trusts law generally it is to be preferred in Australia ... to the majority's statement in *Jolliffe's* case and the cases which have followed it.

16.24   It is not yet known what effect *Byrnes v Kendle* will have on situations where there has been an express declaration of trust which is a sham. For example, if a declaration of trust is alleged to have been made and the settlor/trustee later becomes insolvent, the settlor will ordinarily face a high burden in proving that the trust was intended and properly constituted as there is a natural suspicion against the existence of a trust. In *Owens v Lofthouse* [2007] FCA 1968, a bankrupt failed to prove that she had declared a trust of four properties prior to her bankruptcy as the trust document did not appear to be genuine and the bankrupt had previously claimed outright ownership of the titles, which raised sufficient questions over her real intentions.

The burden of proof

16.25   In cases where the intention of the creator is questioned, the burden of proof lies on the person who alleges that a trust was intended: *Herdegen v Federal Commissioner of Taxation* (1988)

84 ALR 271. In cases of *inter vivos* trusts, evidence may consist of oral or written statements: *Hyhonie Holdings Pty Ltd v Leroy*.

Precatory words

16.26 As was stated at 15.82, if the creator transfers property and expresses a motive, hope or expectation that the property will be used in a particular way, the condition will be viewed as precatory and impose no obligation: *Re Adams and the Kensington Vestry* (1884) 27 Ch D 394; *Re Hill, Public Trustee v O'Donnell* [1923] 2 Ch 259; *S v S* [2010] NIMaster 7. A mere intention to create a trust which is not acted upon will not satisfy the requirement of certainty of intention: *Atwell v Atwell* [2002] TASSC 119 at [25]. Professionally drawn clauses that contain precatory words are unlikely to be interpreted as creating trusts: *Re Will of Logan* [1993] 1 Qd R 395.

16.27 These issues were canvassed in *Chang v Tjiong* [2009] NSWSC 122, where a home unit had been held on trust by a son for his father and mother. The father had provided the purchase moneys (with his own funds and gifts from his children) but the property had been put into the name of his son, George. After George died a dispute arose as to whether George's estate was entitled to keep the moneys from the sale. It was argued by other family members that the property was held on trust for the father and that when he died intestate the interest in the unit should have passed to the mother and then through her estate. The issue revolved around whether a trust had been created by the father or whether his disposition was merely precatory. The intention to create a trust was said to be based on a number of old letters that had been found which were written by the father to George. In one of the letters, the father stated:

> My ways have offended and upset Mum. Look after her after I am gone. It is better that she live with a child. Use the money from the home unit for her. If there is any left over after she is gone, use it for Roy if he still needs it. There are also others in the family who need the money for their studies.

Roy was the father's illegitimate son who had been born to the father's mistress in Japan. Palmer J found that the letters evidenced an intention to create a trust that was not precatory. The letters showed it was the father's intention to create a trust for himself, with a life estate to his wife, with a remainder to be held in a discretionary trust for the remaining family members, including the illegitimate son.

Mutual intention of the creator and trustee to create a trust

16.28 While in the majority of cases the intention of the creator is paramount, in a limited number of cases the mutual intention of the creator and the trustee will be relevant for the determination of intention to create a trust. A *Quistclose* trust is an example of mutual intention: see 15.55–15-69.

The sole intention of the trustee

16.29 While *Quistclose* trusts make the creator's (lender's) and the trustee's (borrower's) mutual intention relevant, in some cases it appears to have been held that the trustee's sole intention can be relevant to the question of whether a trust was intended. These cases ordinarily concern businesses under stress where amounts received on behalf of creditors are placed in special accounts, with the intention that they will be protected if the business becomes insolvent. In *Re Kayford Ltd (in liq)* [1975] 1 All ER 604, a mail order company received funds from customer orders and placed them in a special account. The company went into liquidation and it was held that the funds were intended to be held on trust for its customers. The company's anxiety about protecting customers, coupled with the fact that the funds were placed in a separate account, indicated an intention to hold the funds on trust. This was the case, even though the customers were completely unaware of the company's actions. If we treat the customers as being creators and the company as a trustee, one can understand *Re Kayford* as supporting the proposition that a trustee's unilateral decision to create a trust will be binding.

16.30 In *Stephens Travel Service International Pty Ltd (receivers and managers appointed) v Qantas Airways Ltd* (1988) 13 NSWLR 331, the New South Wales Court of Appeal upheld an express arrangement whereby a travel agency collected airfares for an airline, paid them into an account and then made periodic remittances to the airline. The customers of the airline had no intention to create a trust, yet the court found that the agreement between the agency and the airline created an express trust for the funds.

16.31 At first glance, *Re Kayford* and *Stephens Travel Service* offend the requirement that mutual intention comes from both the creator and the trustee, as in these cases the intention appears to have been based solely on the intentions of the trustee. Later cases have refused to find a trust in cases where clients are ignorant of the way their purchase moneys are being held. In *Peter Cox Investments Pty Ltd (in liq) v International Air Transport Association* (1999) 161 ALR 105 at 118, O'Loughlin J refused to find a trust, in similar circum stances to *Stephens Travel Service International*, on the basis that '[t]here was no evidence before the court of any directions having been given by clients to the company as to how and in what manner the moneys were to be held or applied'.

16.32 Perhaps the better way to interpret *Re Kayford* and *Stephens Travel Service* is to understand the person who receives funds as both settlor and trustee. On receipt of the funds the company takes legal title and then manifests an intention to hold that title on trust for the creditors.[2] This interpretation is questionable for *Kayford*, as it is clear from Megarry J's judgment that he treated the money as never belonging to the company.[3] However, *Stephens Travel Service* is more amenable to it, given there was an express agreement between the travel agent and the airline that any funds received by the agent would be held on trust for the airline. A secondary problem does arise with this interpretation. If the business receiving the money takes the title and then declares a trust, it may well be viewed as a voidable preference under insolvency legislation: see 17.40–17.47.

The knowledge of the beneficiaries

16.33 The beneficiaries need not know of the trust for it to be valid: *Moriarty v Various Customers of BA Peters Plc (in administration)* [2008] EWHC 2205 (Ch) at [18]. The requirement for certainty of intention is not affected by the beneficiary being unaware of his or her interest in the trust: *Rose v Rose* (1986) 7 NSWLR 679 at 686.

Nominating beneficiaries for life insurance policies

16.34 Problems also arise in respect of funds for life insurance which are held by associations on the death of their members. Questions can arise as to whether the funds are intended to be held

---

2. G E Dal Pont, *Equity and Trusts in Australia*, 5th ed, Lawbook Co, Sydney, 2011, p 497.
3. J D Heydon & M J Leeming, *Jacobs' Law of Trusts in Australia*, LexisNexis Butterworths, Sydney, 2006, p 16.

on trust and who the beneficiaries are intended to be. This was discussed in *In the Matter of An Application By Police Association of South Australia* [2008] SASC 299, where a de facto couple, who were both members of the Police Association, died together in a car crash. Association members were automatically given life insurance cover. Members had been encouraged to tell the Association who they wished payouts to be made to, should the member die. The woman had been previously married and had completed her nomination form during that relationship. She had indicated that she wished for the insurance moneys to be paid to her husband, and if he predeceased her, to future children, or, if there were no children, to her parents. The man had a son to a prior relationship. When he filled in the form he indicated that he wished for the payout to go to his brother. The couple entered into a relationship in 2003 and they had a child together. No further forms were completed by the couple to reflect their new domestic arrangements.

16.35   It was argued by the Public Trustee that the life insurance funds were being held on trust by the Association but that the Association was not bound to follow the nominations. The brother of the man argued that the money was held on trust by the Association for the nominated person as beneficiary. It was also possible that the nominations were direct assignments which immediately transferred the couple's rights under the insurance policy to the nominated persons (the ex-husband and the brother).

16.36   Doyle J first dealt with the assignment issue. His Honour found that there was no direct assignment of the rights to the insurance moneys. This was because the nomination could be changed by the member until death, which indicated that no rights were being transferred to the named beneficiaries in the nomination.

16.37   Instead, Doyle J found that the effect of the intention of the parties had to be read against the background of the rules of the Association and the insurance scheme, the Association's communication with members and the forms. On that basis Doyle J found that the intention was to create a trust for beneficiaries named by the deceased couple. Doyle J also found that if he was incorrect about there being an express trust then he would find that there was a constructive trust based on the parties' intentions. The effect of this interpretation was that the deceased man's brother, who was named in the form, took the moneys as a beneficiary. In terms of the woman, her declaration appointing her husband of the time was said to have been overturned by their subsequent divorce. Her failure to send in a new form could not be taken as an approval for the ex-husband retaining an interest. As Doyle J, at [110], said, people were 'notoriously inattentive' to such matters. Her moneys were found then to go to the child of the relationship.

The parol evidence rule

16.38   If the disposition was made in writing it may be subject to the parol evidence rule which prevents the admission of evidence which is extrinsic to the written document. The parol evidence rule will *not* apply in situations where:

1. the disposition of the property that constitutes the trust is not required to be in writing (for example, where the disposition was of personal property): *Boccalatte v Bushelle* [1980] Qd R 180;
2. the document was not intended to be a complete expression of the transferor's intention: *Star v Star* [1935] SASR 263;
3. parol evidence is needed to establish the actual intent of the settlor at the time of the purported creation of the trust: *Owens v Lofthouse* [2007] FCA 1968 at [66]; *B & M Property Enterprises Pty Ltd (in liq) v Pettingill* [2001] SASC 75;

4. the document is ambiguous: *Lutheran Church of Australia v Farmers Cooperative Executors & Trustees Ltd* (1970) 121 CLR 628; *Boranga v Flintoff* (1997) 19 WAR 1;

5. the document was created in circumstances of alleged fraud, duress or mistake: *Rochefoucauld v Boustead* [1897] 1 Ch 196; *Last v Rosenfeld* (1972) 2 NSWLR 923; *Menezes v Salmon* [2009] NSWSC 2.

16.39   In cases of *post mortem* trusts, the law restricting extrinsic evidence in the interpretation of a will also applies in addition to the parol evidence rule.

What if the trust document is lost or destroyed?

16.40   If the trust document is destroyed it may be possible to admit oral evidence regarding its existence: *Mack v Lenton* (1993) 32 NSWLR 259 at 261. In *Maks v Maks* (1986) 6 NSWLR 34, the plaintiff sought to establish the contents of a trust through oral secondary evidence. McLelland J, at 36, said:

> It has been held, in relation to the *Statute of Frauds*, s 7, first that it is not necessary for the purposes of the section that the writing be contemporaneous with the creation of the trust, and, secondly, that the writing must show not only that there is a trust, but also what are the terms and conditions of that trust: see *Smith v Matthews* (1861) 45 ER 831. It has also been held in relation to the *Law of Property Act* 1925 (UK), s 40, and in relation to the *Instruments Act 1958* (Vic), s 126, (each re-enacting in substance that portion of the *Statute of Frauds*, s 4, dealing with contracts for the sale of land) that the statutory requirement may be satisfied by secondary evidence of the existence and contents of the writing when the original has been lost or destroyed: see *Barber v Rowe* [1948] 2 All ER 1050 and *Giasoumi v Hutton* [1977] VR 294. The same principle must I think apply to the *Conveyancing Act*, s 23C(1)(b). Nevertheless, bearing in mind the object of these statutory requirements ('for prevention of frauds and perjuries' — see the title and preamble to the *Statute of Frauds*) I am of opinion that where the original writing is not produced and secondary evidence is relied on, there must be clear and convincing proof not only of the existence, but also of the relevant contents, of the writing, of the same order as the proof required to establish an entitlement to the rectification of a written instrument (see *Pukallus v Cameron* (1982) 43 ALR 243 at 247, 250–251), the two classes of case being to my mind in relevant respects analogous.

16.41   In *Minassian v Minassian* [2010] NSWSC 708 at [43], Ball J found that s 48 of the *Evidence Act 1995* (NSW) allows a party to prove the contents of a document (like a trust) by adducing evidence of an admission made by another party to the proceeding as to the contents of the document (s 48(1)(a)) or, in cases where the document in question is not available, by 'adducing from a witness evidence of the contents of the document in question': s 48(4).

Certainty of subject matter

16.42   An express trust cannot exist without trust property. The trust property must therefore be reasonably identifiable or ascertainable at the time the trust is created. This requirement is known as 'certainty of subject matter'.

16.43   Vague dispositions that do not identify the property will fail: *Re Appleby's Estate* (1930) 25 Tas LR 126. Examples of vague dispositions include directions to 'consider my near relations' in

Sale v Moore (1827) 57 ER 678, or to 'make ample provision' in *Winch v Brutton* (1844) 60 ER 404. Additionally, the quantum of interest must be specified if various beneficial interests are intended. For example, in *Boyce v Boyce* (1849) 60 ER 959, it was not clear which of the houses a beneficiary was intended to receive. In both *Perpetual Trustee WA Ltd v Roverwest Pty Ltd* [2004] WASC 81 and *Bakranich v Robertson* [2005] WASC 12, trusts of land failed because they did not clearly state what land was to be the subject of the failed trusts.

16.44   One of the equitable maxims that is used here is 'that which is not certain is capable of being rendered certain'. As long as it is possible to piece together the clues to determine the identity and quantum of the property it will be sufficiently certain. In *Re Golay's Will Trusts* [1965] 2 All ER 660, a gift of 'reasonable income' was upheld because the words 'reasonable income' were, in the circumstances, capable of objective determination. In *Estate of Chau (dec'd)* [2008] QSC 156, 'a trust over any money that I may have including any bank accounts' was held to include a wealth management account which contained units in a unit trust with a bank.

16.45   Problems can occur when the trust property is part of a number of identical items, for example, '5% of 950 shares'. If the shares have not been specifically identified the trust subject matter may be uncertain: *Federal Commissioner of Taxation v Clarke* (1927) 40 CLR 246. In modern times this may be difficult as companies no longer need to individually number their shares.

16.46   This issue was discussed in *Herdegen v Federal Commissioner of Taxation* (1988) 84 ALR 271, where Mr and Mrs Herdegen held all the shares in Onedin Investments Pty Ltd. Mr Herdegen was the registered holder of 59 shares and Mrs Herdegen was the registered holder of 41 shares. The shares were numbered. After selling the shares they were assessed as subject to taxation but they claimed they were exempt as 'bare trustees'. The trust allegedly arose when Mr Herdegen promised that either he or his wife would hold 37 shares on behalf of Mr Boyden and 38 shares for Mr Allen. The rest was to be held between Mr and Mrs Herdegen, but the evidence was unsatisfactory and confused. Gummow J found that an express trust had not been created because it was not certain whether a trust had really been intended. It was unclear which bundle of shares was to be used to create the trusts and it was also unclear who was intended to be the beneficiaries of which bundle. His Honour also raised the issue of whether the shares the subject of the trusts needed to be identified. Gummow J, at 279, said:

> I should add that with respect to the 38 shares allegedly held on trust by Mr Herdegen, no attempt was made to indicate how they were selected from among the parcel of 59 shares numbered 1–10 and 52–100. The same is true of Mrs Herdegen's shares. As to whether such specific identification was essential to establish certainty of subject matter, or whether the shares might be treated as fungible for this purpose, the authorities appear to be unsettled: *Rollestone v National Bank of Commerce* (1923) 252 SW 394 at 398; *Busch v Truitt* (1945) 160 P 2d 925 at 928; affd 163 P 2d 739.

16.47   The authors of *Jacob's Law of Trusts* have argued that *Herdegen* is authority for not allowing a trust where the shares are not specifically identified.[4] However, the Court of Appeal of England and Wales upheld a disposition of this sort in circumstances where the shares all came from the same company: *Hunter v Moss* [1994] 3 All ER 215. Here, the gift was of 50 of 950 shares which were all of the same class.

---

4.   Heydon & Leeming, *Jacobs' Law of Trusts in Australia*, note 3 above, p 64.

16.48   *Hunter v Moss* was thoroughly examined by Campbell J in *White v Shortall* [2006] NSWSC 1379. This case concerned a declaration of trust over a total of 1.5 million shares of which 222,000 shares were to be held for the plaintiff with the remaining shares being held for the defendant. The defendant had promised in writing to hold the shares on trust but he later refused to recognise the disposition. It was argued by the defendant that the declaration of trust was ineffective because the declaration offended the rule of certainty of subject matter. Importantly, the company's shares were not numbered so it was not possible to directly identify each share being transferred by reference to a number.

16.49   After reviewing English and American authorities Campbell J found that a gift of part of a shareholding was not uncertain as to subject matter. Campbell J, at [212], said:

> A trust of this kind is not analogous to a simple trust, where a single and discrete item of property is held on a bare trust for a single beneficiary. Rather, it is a trust of a fund (the entire shareholding of 1.5 million shares) for two different beneficiaries (the plaintiff and the defendant himself), where powers of management are necessarily involved in the trust (to sell or encumber, within limits that such dealings do not impinge on the plaintiff's rights), and where duties on the trustee would arise as a matter of law (eg to deal with any dividends and capital distributions by distributing them in the appropriate proportions). It is because the trust is construed as being of the entire shareholding that it is not necessary for the plaintiff to be able to point to some particular share and be able to say 'That share is mine'. It is because of this feature of the trust that the defendant declared that an attempt to draw an analogy with cases concerning whether property passes in items of goods when the goods are not appropriated to the contract … fails — because in those cases, identification of the individual items in which property has passed is essential if the property in them is to pass. The construction that is needed … does not require there to be identification of particular shares in which the beneficiary has the beneficial interest. Given the nature of shares in a company, it is perfectly sensible to talk about an individual having a beneficial interest in 222,000 shares out of a parcel of 1.5 million, even if it is not possible to identify individual shares that are held on trust.

The decision was upheld on appeal: *Shortall v White*. It has also been referred to favourably by English courts (*Pearson v Lehman Brothers Finance SA* [2010] EWHC 2914 (Ch) at [231]–[232]) and on appeal: *Pearson v Lehman Brothers Finance SA* [2011] EWCA Civ 1544 at [71].

The notion of 'trust property'

16.50   The subject matter must be property in either legal or equitable form for it to be held on trust. Therefore, the concept of 'trust property' includes real property in tangible and intangible forms, choses in action and choses in possession (goods): *Comptroller of Stamps (Vic) v Howard-Smith* (1936) 54 CLR 614 at 621–2; *Secure Parking (WA) Pty Ltd v Wilson* (2008) 38 WAR 350 at 377. These issues were discussed in *St Vincent de Paul Society Qld v Ozcare Ltd* [2011] 1 Qd R 47, a case which concerned a dispute between the St Vincent de Paul Society and a company which had been created by the society. It was alleged that land had been transferred to the company in breach of trust and it was argued that the members of the company held their membership in the company on trust for St Vincent de Paul. The trial judge had struck out this pleading on the basis that it was not possible for the members to hold their rights on trust as they were not property. The trial judge found that because members had to accept the philosophy of the society or the Catholic ethos meant that membership was personal and not proprietorial. The Court of Appeal disagreed. The rights of members were choses in action. They were substantial and there was no prohibition on assignment of members' rights in the articles of association. The fact that members had to ascribe to the values of the society or Catholicism left membership open to millions of people in Australia and was not any more restrictive than the personal membership requirements of many proprietary companies.

16.51   Legislative definitions are also available for 'trust property'. For example, s 3 of the *Trustee Act 1958* (Vic)[5] stipulates:

> 'property' includes real and personal property, and any estate share and interest in any property, real or personal, and any debt, and any thing in action, and any other right or interest, whether in possession or not.

16.52   Future property cannot be held on trust: *Re Rule's Settlement* [1915] VLR 670. The distinction between future property and present property was discussed at 5.70–5.80. A creator cannot transfer title in property in which he or she does not have an interest. As such, a mere expectancy, like the interests of a discretionary beneficiary, or of an intended beneficiary under a will, cannot be held on trust.

Certainty of objects

16.53   A trust will fail if the beneficiaries are not identified with sufficient certainty. This is known as 'the beneficiary principle'. The leading statement of the beneficiary principle comes from *Morice v Bishop of Durham* (1804) 32 ER 656 at 658, where Sir William Grant MR said:

> There can be no trust over the exercise of which this court will not assume a control; for an uncontrollable power of disposition would be ownership, and not trust. If there be a clear trust, but for uncertain objects, the property, that is the subject of the trust, is undisposed of, and the benefit of such trust must result in those, to whom the law gives ownership in default of disposition by the former owner. But this doctrine does not hold good with respect to trusts for charity. Every other trust must have a definite object. There must be somebody, in whose favour the court can decree performance.

16.54   The underlying rationale of the beneficiary principle is that the courts would be unable to properly enforce trusts if there were no beneficiaries to complain about breach of trust: *Pascoe v Boensch* at 29.

16.55   The beneficiary principle operates to strike down trusts that are created for purposes rather than for specific beneficiaries: *Re Astor's Settlement Trusts* [1952] Ch 534. There are two exceptions to this rule. The first exception is charitable trusts, which are discussed in Chapter 18. The second exception is a particular anomalous group of trusts for animals and tombs, which will also be discussed in Chapter 18.

16.56   The beneficiary principle will not strike down a trust that has a purpose as long as the trust has certain beneficiaries. *Quistclose* trusts illustrate this principle as they are created for a purpose, but they do not fall foul of the beneficiary principle because they have certain beneficiaries. Another

---

5.   See also *Trustee Act 1925* (NSW) s 5; *Trustee Act 1907* (NT) s 82; *Trustee Act 1936* (SA) s 4; *Trustee Act 1898* (Tas) s 4; *Trustees Act 1962* (WA) s 6.

possible example is a trust for a purpose that also directly or indirectly benefits an ascertained group of beneficiaries. For example, in *Re Denley's Trust Deed* [1969] 1 Ch 373, a trust for the creation and maintenance of a sports ground was upheld, as the ground was to be used by the employees of a company and other people given permission by the trustees. These people were treated by the judge as being ascertainable beneficiaries with standing to enforce the trust. The decision in *Re Denley's Trust Deed* has not met with much success in Australia: *Strathalbyn Show Jumping Club Inc v Mayes* (2001) 79 SASR 54. There is a history of Australian courts treating such dispositions as valid non-charitable purpose trusts: see 18.168–18.170. But there are some examples of acceptance. In *Yeomans v Yeomans* [2005] QSC 085, a trust to 'establish a fund for the indigenous and intercultural education of my grandchildren within the Asia-Pacific and Indian Sub-Continent region' was upheld as being a purpose trust with defined beneficiaries, as the grandchildren were ascertainable.

Certainty of beneficiaries in fixed trusts

16.57 The level of certainty required by the beneficiary principle changes depending upon whether the trust is a fixed trust or a discretionary trust. In a fixed trust the beneficiaries must be identifiable in such a way as to allow the court to draw up a complete list of the beneficiaries at the time their beneficial interests come into effect: *Kinsela v Caldwell* (1975) 132 CLR 458; 5 ALR 337; *Commissioner of State Revenue v Viewbank Properties Pty Ltd* [2004] VSC 127. This is known as 'list certainty'.

16.58 Trusts will not fall foul of the rule if they misdescribe the identity of the beneficiary in circumstances where the identity of the intended beneficiary can be otherwise discerned: *Andrew v Dobson* (1788) 29 ER 1232; *O'Brien (as Executor of the Will of Hogan) v Warburton* [2012] WASC 82 at [191].

16.59 Gifts to identifiable individuals will clearly satisfy the rule but problems can arise when the gift is made to a class. For example, difficulties have often arisen with fixed trusts for 'friends'. In *Re Gulbenkian's Settlement Trusts* [1970] AC 508 at 524; [1968] 3 All ER 785 at 792, Lord Upjohn said:

> That class must be as defined as the individual; the court cannot guess at it. Suppose the donor directs that a fund be divided equally between 'my old friends', then unless there is some admissible evidence that the donor has given some special 'dictionary' meaning to that phrase which enables the trustees to identify the class with sufficient certainty, it is plainly bad as being too uncertain. Suppose that there appeared before the trustees (or the court) two or three individuals who plainly satisfied the test of being among 'my old friends', the trustees could not consistently with the donor's intentions accept them as claiming the whole or any defined part of the fund. They cannot claim the whole fund for they can show no title to it unless they prove they are the only members of the class, which of course they cannot do, and so, too, by parity of reasoning they cannot claim any defined part of the fund and there is no authority in the trustees or the court to make any distribution among a smaller class than that pointed out by the donor. The principle is, in my opinion, that the donor must make his intentions sufficiently plain as to the objects of his trust and the court cannot give effect to it by misinterpreting his intentions by dividing the fund merely among those present. Secondly, and perhaps it is the most hallowed principle, the Court of Chancery, which acts in default of trustees, must know with sufficient certainty the objects of the beneficence of the donor so as to execute the trust.

16.60   In *Lempens v Reid* [2009] SASC 179, a gift to 'such of them my friends who resided with me from overseas' failed as the deceased had not provided any information as to who these people were and all attempts at finding them had failed.

16.61   Some rules of construction have been adopted by the courts to save dispositions from uncertainty. For example, the term 'relations' will, in the absence of a contrary intention, be restricted to those blood relations who would have taken under intestacy rules: *Re Fox* [1997] 1 Qd R 43 at 46; *Re Gansloser's Will Trusts* [1952] 1 Ch 30; *Re Bridgen; Chaytor v Edwin* [1938] Ch 205.

16.62   Ordinarily, the question of certainty is timed at the date the trust instrument becomes effective, meaning that list certainty needs to be satisfied at the time that the trust or will comes into force: *Kinsela v Caldwell; Re Leverhulme* [1943] 2 All ER 274. A trust will not fail for want of list certainty if at the time of the creation of the trust the beneficiaries were ascertainable, but later some of the class of beneficiaries have disappeared, been forgotten or become impossible to find: *Re Hain's Settlement; Tooth v Hain* [1961] 1 All ER 848.

16.63   In *Prosper v Wojtowicz* [2005] QSC 177, the testator made a gift on trust to 'persons who attend my funeral and who are not (and were not) at any time related to me'. Unfortunately, a complete and accurate list of attendees had not been kept at the funeral. Wilson J, at [31], said:

> In the present case, when the testator died the class was sufficiently defined to be ascertainable at the date of distribution: it would have been possible to have a complete list of funeral attendees compiled. That such a complete list was not in fact compiled does not invalidate the trust (although it does give rise to administrative problems for the applicant).

16.64   Problems can occur when the list of possible beneficiaries is extremely long and the job of discerning the identity of the beneficiaries cannot be completed at the time the trust comes into effect. In *Re Saxone Shoe Co Ltd's Trust Deed* [1962] 2 All ER 904 at 912, Cross J said that the task of identifying beneficiaries depended on what was 'probable rather and not on what was theoretically possible'.

16.65   The problem of identifying a large number of beneficiaries was discussed in *West v Weston* (1998) 44 NSWLR 657. In this case a testator had created a trust for 'the living issue at the time of my death of my four grandparents ... as attain 21 years'. The executrix had made every effort to discern the identities of the beneficiaries, which numbered over 1600 people. However, the executrix was unable to be certain as to the identity of any further beneficiaries. If the trust failed the entire estate would go to the Crown as *bona vacantia*. Young J held that strict list certainty should not be applied given that, in modern times, it was difficult to trace lineages because people no longer automatically took their father's family name as their own. Moreover, the rule against perpetuities had been relaxed, taking off the pressure to ascertain beneficiaries so that their interests could vest within the perpetuity period: see Chapter 17. For these reasons, Young J, at 664, thought the list certainty rule should be restated as follows:

> The rule will be satisfied if, within a reasonable time after the gift comes into effect, the court can be satisfied on the balance of probabilities that the substantial majority of beneficiaries have been ascertained and that no reasonable inquiries could be made which would improve the situation.

16.66 Young J's reformulation has not been the subject of much judicial scrutiny, although it can be noted that a similar disposition to a wide family class failed for uncertainty, when it might have been saved using the *West v Weston* formulation: *Mustard as Executrix of Thanas (dec'd) v Oikonomov* (unreported, SC(WA), Owen J, 19 August 1998). It should, however, be noted that the decision was handed down a number of days before the *Weston* case. In *Prosper v Wojtowicz* [2005] QSC 177, Wilson J distinguished *Weston* and declined to comment on its force. However, in *Re Meyerstein (dec'd)* [2009] VSC 564 at [22], Ross J applied the *West v Weston* formulation to an intestate estate where it had been difficult to discern who were the next of kin.

16.67 In academic circles, Creighton[6] has criticised *Weston* because of the impossibility of measuring a 'substantial majority' of beneficiaries when one does not know the total number. Creighton is also critical of the fact that it is not possible to ascertain the size of the beneficiaries' shares, which defeats the whole purpose of having a fixed trust. Finally, Creighton argues that Young J's test effectively authorises a breach of trust because distribution to the identified beneficiaries means that the shares will not be distributed equally among *all* the beneficiaries.[7] Dal Pont[8] is less critical of the decision and suggests that the effect of the decision is not unlike the situation where trustees or beneficiaries are allowed to terminate trusts when not all the beneficiaries have come into existence: see Chapter 21.

16.68 Once the identity of the beneficiaries has been ascertained, the fact that it is difficult to find the whereabouts or continued existence of the beneficiaries does not affect the certainty of the disposition. In *Lempens v Reid* [2009] SASC 179 at [21], Gray J stressed that 'it is important to distinguish conceptual uncertainty from the difficulty of ascertainment'. Trustees can always apply to the court for directions or pay the missing beneficiary's share into court: *Re Gulbenkian Settlement Trusts* at AC 524; All ER 793. For example, in *Re Benjamin; Neville v Benjamin* [1902] 1 Ch 723, the court found that once the criteria was found to be certain, an order could be made to distribute the estate to those members of the class which have been ascertained. If a person entitled to a portion of the estate appeared later, the executor would be protected against the claims of a newly discovered beneficiary. The beneficiary retains a right to pursue a claim against the beneficiaries who had been paid incorrectly, but he or she cannot pursue the trustee. Such a court order is now referred to as a '*Benjamin* order'.

Certainty of beneficiaries in discretionary trusts

16.69 It should be recalled that discretionary trusts, or trust powers, are forms of trust whereby the trustee is given the discretion to choose the beneficiaries: see 15.11. In cases where the trustee's discretion is unfettered, the power of the trustee is called a general power. Note, however, that in such circumstances the trustee will be unable to use the power for his or her benefit. If the trustee is permitted to appoint himself or herself under a general power then there will be no trust, as such a power is tantamount to ownership. Where the trustee is allowed to choose from beneficiaries of a particular class, the power is referred to as a special power. The trustee's power might also be an

---

6. P Creighton, 'Certainty of Object of Trusts and Power: the Impact of *McPhail v Doulton* in Australia' (2000) 22 *Sydney Law Review* 91 at 97.

7. Creighton, 'Certainty of Object of Trusts and Power: the Impact of *McPhail v Doulton* in Australia', note 6 above, p 98.

8. Dal Pont, *Equity and Trusts in Australia*, note 2 above, p 523.

intermediate or hybrid power, in which case the trustee is allowed to choose beneficiaries as long as they are not part of a particular class.

16.70 Until 1971, the list certainty rule was also applied to discretionary trusts, regardless of the form of the power. This changed with *In Re Baden's Deed Trusts; McPhail v Doulton* [1971] AC 424; [1970] 2 All ER 228. In this case a creator created a trust that gave his trustees the discretion to use the net income of the trust for the benefit of the staff of a company, their relatives and dependants. The executors of the creator's estate argued that the trust was void because it was a trust power where the beneficiaries could not be ascertained with list certainty. They requested that the funds become part of the creator's estate. The trustees argued that the disposition was in fact a mere power and hence not subject to the requirements of list certainty.

16.71 The House of Lords unanimously found that the disposition was a trust power, given the mandatory language employed by the creator. The case was then remitted back to trial to determine whether the trust was void for uncertainty.

16.72 The House was divided on the issue of what the test for certainty should be for trust powers. A majority (Lord Reid, Viscount Dilhorne and Lord Wilberforce) found that the test for certainty should be whether or not it was possible to say with certainty whether any given individual is or is not a member of the class. This test is known as 'criterion certainty'.

16.73 Lord Wilberforce gave the leading speech. In his speech his Lordship drew distinctions between the different types of uncertainty that can arise in relation to a trust power. His Lordship, at AC 457; All ER 247, contrasted 'linguistic or semantic uncertainty' with 'evidential uncertainty'. If the class of beneficiaries was uncertain because of the language employed in the disposition, the trust will be void for criterion uncertainty. If, however, the uncertainty relates to the gathering of evidence of the beneficiaries' identity, the trust should be upheld.

16.74 In addition to the requirement of criterion certainty, Lord Wilberforce, at AC 457; All ER 247, said that a trust power may also fail because it is administratively unworkable. A trust that is administratively unworkable would be one with criteria:

> ... so hopelessly wide as not to form 'anything like a class' so that the class is administratively unworkable or ... one that cannot be executed ... I hesitate to give examples for they may prejudice future cases, but perhaps 'all the residents of Greater London' will serve.

16.75 By accepting criterion certainty as the test, Lord Wilberforce brought the requirement of certainty for trust powers in line with the certainty requirements for mere powers. In the earlier case of *Re Gulbenkian Settlement Trusts*, the House of Lords found that a mere power of appointment would be valid if it could be said with certainty whether any given individual was or was not a member of the class of objects. However, in *McPhail v Doulton* Lord Wilberforce, at AC 457; All ER 247, stressed that the assimilation of the certainty tests did not indicate that there should be a complete assimilation of trust powers and mere powers. The essential differences between the two, discussed at 15.100–15.109, remain.

16.76 After the decision in *McPhail v Doulton* the matter was remitted back to trial where, on appeal, it was argued that the use of the words 'relatives' and 'dependants' was semantically uncertain: *Re Baden's Deed Trusts (No 2)* [1973] Ch 9. However, the judges of the Court of Appeal upheld the trust, but for different reasons. Sachs LJ believed that it was not necessary to be able to disprove that a person was in the class of beneficiaries. It was only necessary to prove that a person met the criteria. If they did not they were not in the class. Megaw LJ stated that criterion certainty would be satisfied if a substantial number of beneficiaries were ascertained, even if there remained a substantial number of others whose status was uncertain. This indicates that if only one person was able to satisfy the criteria it would not be sufficient. The criteria would have to be shown to be workable over a number of objects. Stamp LJ believed that the trustee had to be able to say definitely whether a person *was* or *was not* in the class. In the circumstances, the word 'dependants' was easy to apply with certainty, but the word 'relatives', if understood widely, would have been uncertain given the impossibility of the trustees being able to check genealogies. However, the trust could be rendered certain by understanding 'relatives' to mean 'next of kin'.

16.77   The rule in *McPhail v Doulton* has been favourably received in Australia, although the High Court has yet to rule on its validity. Cases include *Spotlight Stores Pty Ltd v Commissioner of Taxation* [2004] FCA 650; *Hyde v Holland* [2003] NSWSC 733; *Re Blyth* [1997] 2 Qd R 567; *Horan v James* [1982] 2 NSWLR 376 at 379; and *Herdegen v Federal Commissioner of Taxation* (1988) 84 ALR 271. These authorities indicate that the decision is good law for Australia.[9] The decision was also reaffirmed by the Privy Council: *Schmidt v Rosewood Trust Ltd* [2003] 2 AC 709; [2003] 3 All ER 76.

Trusts for unincorporated associations

16.78   In *Kibby v Registrar of Titles* [1999] 1 VR 861 at 870–1, the court approved the following statement of the key features of an unincorporated association set out in *Conservative & Unionist Central Office v Burrell* [1980] 3 All ER 42 at 58:

(i) there must be members of the association;
(ii) there must be a contract binding the members inter se;
(iii) there will normally be some constitutional arrangement for meetings of members and for the appointment of committees and officers;
(iv) a member will normally be free to join or leave the association at will;
(v) the association will normally continue in existence independently of any change that may occur in the composition of the association;
(vi) there must as a matter of history have been a moment in time when a number of persons combined or banded together to form the association.

16.79   Unincorporated associations are not legal persons and have no separate legal identity from their members: *Benbrika v R* [2010] VSCA 28 at [70]. Problems occur when people, particularly testators, wish to leave property to unincorporated associations, because such dispositions will often offend the beneficiary principle by not describing their objects with sufficient certainty. Alternatively, these dispositions may fail because they will be deemed to be trusts for non-charitable purposes. Such dispositions can also fall foul of the rule against perpetuities if the disposition includes gifts to future members which will vest beyond the perpetuity period: see Chapter 17.

16.80   Dispositions to unincorporated associations can be construed in three main ways: (i) as an absolute gift to members to hold as joint tenants; (ii) as a gift to existing members, subject to the

---

9.   P Creighton, 'Certainty of Object of Trusts and Power: the Impact of *McPhail v Doulton* in Australia', note 6 above, p 103.

rules of the association; or (iii) as a trust to be held to further the purposes of the association: *Neville Estates Ltd v Madden* [1962] Ch 832; *Radmanovich v Nedeljkovic* (2001) 52 NSWLR 641.

16.81   Courts begin from the presumption that the donor intended the disposition to take as an absolute gift to the members of the association as joint tenants at the date of the disposition. This presumption can be rebutted if the evidence suggests that the donor intended for the property to be held on trust or according to the rules of the association: *Hunt v McLaren* [2006] EWHC 2386 (Ch) at [94]. Evidence sufficient to rebut the presumption includes the form of the gift, the numbers and identity of the membership, the subject matter of the gift and the capacity of the members to end their relationship with the association and recover their interests in the property: *Bacon v Pianta* (1966) 114 CLR 634 at 638.

16.82   If the disposition is interpreted as an absolute gift it will not be subject to the law of trusts: *Re Goodson* [1971] VR 801; *McCraken v Attorney-General (Vic)* [1995] 1 VR 67 at 70. Nor will it offend the rule against perpetuities, as long as the ascertained members can take their interests in the gift during the perpetuity period: *Re Smith* [1914] 1 Ch 937; *Re McAuliffe (dec'd)* [1944] St R Qd 167.

16.83   When the disposition is read as being a gift to existing members, the constitution of the unincorporated association becomes relevant: *Re Bucks Constabulary Widows' and Orphans' Fund Friendly Society (No 2)* [1979] 1 WLR 936. In some cases the gift to the members is read as being a gift subject to the rules of the association. Some associations forbid the members from dividing up the property and taking their shares. In such associations new members take an interest in the shares of retiring members and the property cannot simply be divided up among the members. Members are bound by these rules, as the rules operate as a contract between the members. In these circumstances, the disposition may fail because it breaches the requirements of certainty and the rule against perpetuities: *Neville Estates Ltd v Madden*.

16.84   What happens if the association comes to an end? In *Re GKN Bolts & Nuts Ltd etc Works Sports and Social Club* [1982] 1 WLR 774, a social club had come to an end and sold its sports ground. Megarry V-C, at 776, said that the court's approach should be based on reasonableness, fairness and common sense. Given the club's rules were silent on distribution, Megarry V-C found that distribution of the assets should be on the basis of equality among the members, irrespective of the length of membership or the amount of subscriptions paid. The club rules did recognise various classes of membership but Megarry V-C found that only full members should be entitled to shares in the distribution. A similar approach was adopted in *Hunt v McLaren*, where Lawrence Collins J found that beneficial ownership belonged to members entitled to vote at the club's annual general meeting.

16.85   A change of name or address will not mean that an association has ceased to exist. In *In The Estate of Dulcie Edna Rand (decd)* [2009] NSWSC 48, Harrison J investigated a gift held on trust to the 'Philippines and Australia Episcopal Church'. Unfortunately, no such organisation existed. It was discovered that the testatrix had a connection with a church congregation that now referred to itself as St Paul's Multicultural Filipino-Anglican Ministry. This was found to be the same organisation even though its name and address had changed.

16.86   What happens to the property if the membership of the association is reduced to one member? In *Re Bucks Constabulary Widows' and Orphans' Fund Friendly Society (No 2)*, Walton J found that associations were not 'tontine societies', meaning that if only one member existed the association had come to an end and the property should go to the state, *bona vacantia*. However, in *Hanchett-Stamford v Attorney-General* [2009] Ch 173; [2008] 4 All ER 323, the court found that the last remaining member could retain absolute ownership of association assets. This case concerned the Performing and Captive Animals Defence League, which was established in 1914 to prevent cruelty to performing animals and which also sought the banning of their performance and the closure of municipal zoos. It was not incorporated. The League had become less active into the 1970s but had accumulated enough funds to purchase Sid Abbey, which was the principal wing of a Gothic house with several rooms, extensive grounds and a swimming pool. The land was registered in the name of Mr Hanchett-Stanford and Mr Hervey as trustees for the League. The League also had a portfolio of shares worth over £1.77m. By the time of the litigation the only surviving member was Mrs Hanchett-Stanford, who wished to have the League declared to be charitable, so that the properties could then be directed to the Born Free Foundation, a charity with similar objects. After advertising for existing members to come forth, a group called the Captive Animals Protection Trust appeared. This organisation had split from the League in its earlier days. It sought to be given the funds.

16.87   Because the League's purpose was to change the law, it was found not to be charitable. The judge was unable to apply a *cy-près* scheme to give the property to similar associations. The question then arose as to who owned the assets. Either the property would go to the last surviving member (Mrs Hanchett-Stanford) or it would go to the state. Lewison J found that there was no reason to take away the surviving member's property rights and that Mrs Hanchett-Stanford could become the owner of the Abbey and shares absolutely.

16.88   When the disposition takes the form of a trust for the purposes of the association, the trust can only be valid if the purposes of the association are charitable: *Re Recher's Will Trusts* [1972] Ch 529. However, such an interpretation hinges on evidence of the creator's intention when creating the trust. The trust will be interpreted to be for the purposes of the association in the absence of evidence to benefit the individual members of the association.

16.89   These principles were illustrated by *Leahy v Attorney-General (NSW)* [1959] AC 457; (1959) 101 CLR 611. Here, a testator created a *post mortem* trust under which the trustees had the discretion to select an order of nuns or Christian Brothers to take the beneficial ownership of his farm. The trustees argued that the trust was in fact an absolute gift of the property to the members of the order that they would select, rather than a charitable trust. The trustees preferred this construction of the will, as it gave them the freedom to select contemplative orders of nuns, which were outside the range of religious orders that equity treats as having a charitable purpose: see 18.12.

16.90   The Privy Council accepted that there was a prima facie presumption that a trust in favour of an unincorporated association was an absolute gift to its members. However, they found that in this case the presumption had been rebutted. The fact that the objects of the trust were widespread and difficult to discern, coupled with the fact that the trust property was not easily divisible, indicated that the testator did not intend to make a gift to the individual members of any selected order. As such, it was a trust for a charitable purpose, or, more correctly, a trust with mixed charitable and non-charitable purposes.

16.91   If it is found that a trust is intended and the class of beneficiaries includes present and future members of the association, the trust may offend the rule against perpetuities. This is because the class of beneficiaries is not closed and beneficial interests may come into existence at times beyond the perpetuity period: see Chapter 17.

16.92   Alternatively, if the intention of the donor is that the trust is to be used to further the purposes of the association and not the members, it will run foul of the beneficiary principle, unless the purpose is charitable. For example, in *Bacon v Pianta* (1966) 114 CLR 634, a disposition to the Communist Party of Australia 'for its sole use and enjoyment' was found to be a trust for the Party and not for its individual members. The language of the testator rebutted the presumption of there being a gift in favour of the members. The disposition failed as a trust as it was for a non-charitable purpose. Contrast this case with the decision in *McLean v Attorney-General* [2002] NSWSC 377, where a gift to the Cessnock District Crippled Children's Association, an unincorporated association which no longer existed, was found to have a charitable purpose.

16.93   As stated by Evans, it is unfortunate that such an important area of law is so obscure.[10] Fortunately, it is now very easy for associations to take up a legal personality under numerous schemes for incorporation.[11] If an association takes up a legal personality, it is possible to bypass the entire sorry morass of the above rules because the disposition will be a simple gift to the legal person. Additionally, in New South Wales, the Northern Territory, Queensland and Victoria, the legislatures have been wise enough to amend their succession laws to allow gifts to unincorporated associations to be effective regardless of whether the members are ascertainable.[12]

The rule against delegation of testamentary power

16.94   In Australia, a more restrictive approach is applied to trusts under wills than in relation to trusts *inter vivos*. Even in cases where a testamentary disposition is perfectly certain under the rule in *McPhail v Doulton* it may be struck down if it offends the rule against delegation of testamentary power. The rule was discussed in *Tatham v Huxtable* (1950) 81 CLR 639, where the High Court struck out a power of appointment in a will on the basis that the testators are not allowed to delegate their will-making power. The executor was given power to distribute the balance of an estate to people the executor believed had 'rendered service meriting consideration by the testator'. This disposition offended the cardinal rule against non-delegation. Later decisions of the High Court have left the rule undisturbed: *Lutheran Church of Australia v Farmers Cooperative Executors & Trustees Ltd* (1970) 121 CLR 628.

16.95   However, English decisions have accepted that such testamentary trust powers should not offend the rule, as long as the beneficiaries are described with certainty, which, after *McPhail v Doulton*, means criterion certainty: *Re Beatty's Will Trusts* [1990] 3 All ER 844.

---

10.   M Evans, *Equity and Trusts*, 3rd ed, LexisNexis Butterworths, Sydney, 2012, p 438.

11.   *Associations Incorporation Act 1991* (ACT); *Associations Incorporation Act 1984* (NSW) (but see also *Associations Incorporation Act 2009* (NSW) which has been passed but not yet commenced at time of writing); *Associations Act 2003* (NT); *Associations Incorporation Act 1981* (Qld); *Associations Incorporation Act 1985* (SA); *Associations Incorporation Act 1964* (Tas); *Associations Incorporation Act 1981* (Vic); *Associations Incorporation Act 1987* (WA).

12.   *Succession Act 2006* (NSW) s 43; *Wills Act 2000* (NT) s 42; *Succession Act 1981* (Qld) s 63; *Wills Act 1997* (Vic) s 47 (applies only to non-charitable unincorporated associations).

16.96   There are four exceptions to the rule. First, general powers of appointment are not subject to the rule as they are practically equivalent to an absolute gift and therefore treated as a disposition of the property by the testator: *Tatham v Huxtable* at 653–4.

16.97   Second, special powers will not be subject to the rule if the special power can satisfy list certainty. In such a case the testator is treated as having already disposed of his or her interest in the property among the beneficiaries. The donee merely allocates the respective shares: *Re Blyth* [1997] 2 Qd R 567.

16.98   Third, a hybrid or intermediate power will not offend the rule, if the disposition includes a gift or a trust in default or appointment: *Lutheran Church of Australia v Farmers Cooperative Executors & Trustees Ltd* at 644. However, if the hybrid power is not coupled with a gift or trust over in default, the power will fall foul of the rule against delegation, even if it is criteria certain. For example, in *Horan v James* [1982] 2 NSWLR 376, the New South Wales Court of Appeal struck down a disposition that gave the residue of an estate to trustees with the power to choose anybody to be a beneficiary, barring the testator's wife. The disposition was found to be completely certain under the rule in *McPhail v Doulton*, but nevertheless invalid as it was an attempt by the testator to leave the beneficial distribution of the residue to the executors: *Horan v James* at 381.

16.99   The authority of *Horan v James* was doubted by Sheller JA in *Gregory v Hudson* (1998) 45 NSWLR 300. In that case a testator had left the residue of his estate to the trustee of a trust that was already in existence. After reviewing the authorities, Sheller JA, at 310, said that the finding of certainty in *Horan v James* was doubtful, as certainty is achieved by an exclusive definition but may not be achieved by 'the mere exclusion of one person or some persons in a class'. Sheller JA's comments suggest that a hybrid power will never be valid under a will, because it cannot satisfy list certainty. These comments are confusing because they seem to place doubt over the status of *McPhail v Doulton* in the context of wills. Thankfully, the comments are strictly obiter, as Sheller JA eventually found the disposition to be valid. Given the disposition was to an existing trustee under a valid trust there was no uncertainty, and no delegation of testamentary power.

16.100   The fourth exception to the rule against delegation relates to charitable trusts. These trusts are not subject to the rule: *Horan v James* at 386.

16.101   The rule against delegation of testamentary power has been subject to vociferous criticism by academics and judicial officers alike, but it remains the law: *Lines v Lines* [2003] SASC 173; *Nabainivalu v Hopkins* [2006] NSWSC 215; *Re The Full Board of The Guardianship and Administration Board* [2003] WASCA 268. In *Kam v HSBC International Trustee Ltd* [2008] HKCFI 496, the Hong Kong Court of First Instance, when faced with the choice of adopting the rule, declined to do so. In *Horan v James*, at 381, Hutley JA said that the rule was 'arbitrary and confusing'. With respect, Hutley JA's comments are correct. As stated by Thomas J in *Re Blyth* [1997] 2 Qd R 567 at 575:

> It is difficult to see why a person should not be able to dispose of property by will in the same way as he or she may dispose of it in his or her lifetime.

16.102   The rule in *Tatham v Huxtable* has been removed by legislation in the Australian Capital Territory, New South Wales, the Northern Territory, Queensland and Victoria.[13] It is hoped that eventually sanity will prevail in this area and similar reforms will occur in other jurisdictions. Barring statutory intervention, it appears that a review by the High Court will be the only way that the principle can be overturned: *Gregory v Hudson* (1998) 45 NSWLR 300 at 304. Even in those jurisdictions that have been reformed, there may still be dispositions which will remain subject to the rule as reform will ordinarily apply only to estates arising after the passage of the law: *Klemke v Lustig* [2010] VSC 502 at [20].

COMPLETE CONSTITUTION OF AN EXPRESS TRUST

16.103   In addition to the requirements of the three certainties, a trust must be completely constituted for it to be valid. 'Complete constitution' generally refers to the irrevocable transfer of the trust property and the creation of the beneficial interest. The laws of assignment and disposition have already been discussed in detail in Chapters 5 and 6.

16.104   As stated at 16.1, there are three ways of creating a trust: by declaration, by transfer and by direction: *Commissioner of State Revenue v Lam & Kym Pty Ltd* (2004) 10 VR 420. The rules regarding constituting a trust will change depending on a number of factors including: (i) how the trust is created; (ii) whether the trust is voluntary; and (iii) whether the transfer of title needs to be in writing.

Declarations of trust

16.105   In cases where the creator declares himself or herself to be a trustee, the legal transfer of property does not need to occur as the creator and trustee are the same legal person. However, as discussed at 6.5, declarations of trust are treated as 'dispositions' for the purposes of legislation that deals with the requirements for writing: *Comptroller of Stamps (Vic) v Howard-Smith* (1936) 54 CLR 614 at 621–2. Questions, therefore, need to be answered about which parts of s 23C(1) of the *Conveyancing Act 1919* (NSW) and its equivalents are relevant to the creation of trusts.[14]

Declarations of trusts over realty

16.106   If the trust is one for real property it is necessary that the trust be evidenced in writing, as s 23C(1)(b) of the *Conveyancing Act 1919* (NSW) and its equivalents clearly cover a declaration of trust 'respecting any land or interest therein': see 6.8–6.9. In *Kauter v Hilton* at 98, the High Court said:

> [The legislation] does not require that a trust of land should be created by writing. The trust may be created orally. All that the section requires is that the trust so created should be manifested and proved by writing.

---

13. *Wills Act 1968* (ACT) s 14A; *Succession Act 2006* (NSW) s 44; *Wills Act 2000* (NT) s 43; *Succession Act 1981* (Qld) s 64; *Wills Act 1997* (Vic) s 48.
14. The equivalents of s 23C in other Australian jurisdictions are: *Civil Law (Property) Act 2006* (ACT) s 201; *Law of Property Act 2000* (NT) s 10; *Property Law Act 1974* (Qld) s 11; *Law of Property Act 1936* (SA) s 29; *Conveyancing and Law of Property Act 1884* (Tas) s 60(2); *Property Law Act 1958* (Vic) s 53; *Property Law Act 1969* (WA) s 34.

16.107 But are declarations of trusts over land also covered by s 23C(1)(a) and its equivalents? The question is important as s 23C(1)(a) requires more than evidence in writing. It prevents the creation or disposition of an interest in land unless the creation or disposition is in writing by the creator (or by their agent who must also be authorised in writing). If only s 23C(1)(b) applies to trusts of land, it would be possible, as stated in *Kauter v Hilton*, to create a trust orally and later evidence it in writing. However, if s 23C(1)(a) also applies it would not be possible to create the trust orally. It would only come into being on the satisfaction of the writing requirements of s 23C(1)(a).

16.108 Valuable consideration is not required for a declaration of trust: *Robson v Robson* [2011] QSC 234 at [165].

16.109 High Court authority concerning the applicability of s 23C(1)(a) to the creation and disposition of equitable interests is not overly helpful. In *Adamson v Hayes* (1973) 130 CLR 276, the High Court was split on whether s 23C(1)(a) and its equivalents applied to the creation and disposition of equitable interests in land. Menzies J, at 292, felt that it should only apply to legal interests, which would mean that the declaration of trusts would not be covered by the section. However, both Walsh J, at 297, and Gibbs J, at 304, felt that it applied to both legal and equitable interests. Subsequent decisions support the reasoning of Walsh and Gibbs JJ: *Theodore v Mistford* [2003] QCA 580 at [5] and [51].[15]

16.110 Regardless of the majority view in *Adamson v Hayes*, it has been argued that s 23C(1)(a) does not apply to declarations of trust over interests in land, as the more onerous requirements imposed by para (a) would otherwise render s 23C(1)(b) redundant. In *Secretary, Department of Social Security v James* (1990) 95 ALR 615, an applicant for the age pension was given reduced benefits because she held a unit in her name. The applicant argued that she held the unit on trust for her disabled daughter and that the unit should not be considered as her asset. It was found that the applicant had declared a trust at the time of acquisition and that the trust could be evidenced in writing at any later time. Lee J, at 622, found that declarations of trust were not covered by s 23C(1)(a) and its equivalents as it would mean that s 23C(1)(b) was either 'an odd exception or otiose'. Later cases from other jurisdictions have followed Lee J's decision and not applied s 23C(1)(a) to declarations of trusts over realty: *Hagan v Waterhouse* (1992) 34 NSWLR 308; *Low v Dykgraaf* [2001] WASC 332 at [10]; *Equuscorp Pty Ltd v Jimenez* [2002] SASC 225 at [119]; *Gentsis v Forty-first Advocate Management Pty Ltd* [2004] VSC 398 at [90]; *Yard v Yardoo Pty Ltd* [2006] VSC 109 at [352]; *Thompson v White* [2006] NSWCA 350 at [134].

Declarations of trust over legal personalty

16.111 Declarations of trust over legal interests in personal property are not required to be in writing as they are not concerned with realty or with subsisting equitable interests: *Re Allco Securities Pty Ltd* [2011] NSWSC 1250 at [11]. Nor is valuable consideration required for such a declaration of trust: *Robson v Robson* at [165]. In *Jones v Lock* (1865) LR 1 Ch App 25 at 28, Lord Cranworth LC said:

> If I give any chattel that, of course, passes by delivery, and if I say, expressly or impliedly, that I constitute myself a trustee of personalty, that is a trust executed, and capable of being enforced without consideration. I do not think it necessary to go into any of the authorities cited before

---

15. Heydon & Leeming, *Jacobs' Law of Trusts*, note 2 above, pp 291–2.

me; they all turn upon the question, whether what has been said was a declaration of trust or an imperfect gift. In the latter case the parties would receive no aid from a Court of equity if they claimed as volunteers. But when there has been a declaration of trust, then it will be enforced, whether there has been consideration or not.

Declaration of trust over equitable interests of realty and personalty

16.112 A declaration of trust of a subsisting equitable interest (whether it be realty or personalty) does need to be in writing because s 23C(1)(c) covers dispositions of subsisting equitable interests: see 6.40–6.43 and *Mills v Sportsdirect.Com Retail Ltd* [2010] EWHC 1072 (Ch) at [70].

How can a trust be 'manifested and proved in writing'?

16.113 In *Secretary, Department of Social Security v James* at 622, Lee J said:

> The requirements of s 34(1)(b) [of the *Property Law Act 1969* (WA)] may be satisfied by a combination of documents capable of being read together. Any informal writing may stand as evidence of the existence of a trust including correspondence from third parties, a telegram, an affidavit or an answer to interrogatories … The date of creation of the writing is not material. It may come into existence at any time after the declaration of the trust.

16.114 In *Pascoe v Boensch*, a married couple, who had become divorced, agreed that the woman would transfer her joint tenancy to her ex-husband if he would declare that the property was held on trust for their children. The man and woman declared in writing in 1999 that the property was being held for the benefit of the 'Boensch family' and that the woman would transfer her interest in the property to the man so that it could be held on trust. The transfer was signed by the woman but never registered as the mortgagee bank would not agree to its registration unless the man agreed to refinance his mortgage. The man became bankrupt in 2005 and the trustee in bankruptcy argued that the memorandum had been ineffective to create a trust as it did not satisfy s 23C(1)(b). Finn, Dowsett and Edmonds JJ disagreed with the trustee in bankruptcy and found that the requirements for writing had been satisfied. In their joint judgment, their Honours, at 27–8, said:

> Section 23C(1)(b) of that Act requires (inter alia) any declaration of trust respecting any interest in land to be manifest and proved by some writing signed by the declarant. This subparagraph — which imposes an evidentiary requirement — clearly applies to the memorandum, if it is to be an effective declaration of trust. What it requires is that the writing admits the trust and satisfies the 'three certainties' of intention, subject-matter and object (to which we refer below): see *Hagan v Waterhouse* (1991) 34 NSWLR 308 at 385–6. Additionally, though, because the memorandum, if effective, disposed of an existing equitable interest, it needed as well to satisfy the requirements of s 23C(1)(c) of the Conveyancing Act. The writing requirement of that subparagraph — which deals with the disposition of an equitable interest or a subsisting trust and which imposes a validity requirement — has the objects of preventing hidden oral transactions in equitable interests and of enabling trustees to ascertain who in truth are the beneficiaries: *Vandervell v Inland Revenue Cmrs* [1967] 2 AC 291 at 311; [1967] 1 All ER 1 at 7. But the subparagraph does not require the writing to set out the terms of the trust or the fact that a trust exists: compare *Re Tyler, Graves v King* [1967] 3 All ER 389 at 392; [1967] 1 WLR 1269 at 1275.

Creation by transfer

16.115   Trusts created by transfer will be executed when the title of the trust property has been completely and irrevocably transferred to the trustee. As stated at 16.1, this can occur in two contexts: in *inter vivos* trusts and *post mortem* trusts.

16.116   For *inter vivos* trusts, it may be necessary for the disposition to be evidenced in writing if the trust property consists of realty or a subsisting equitable interest: *Equuscorp Pty Ltd v Jimenez* [2002] SASC 225. However, executory trusts may be enforceable if everything necessary to transfer title has been done by the creator. The rule in *Milroy v Lord* (1862) 45 ER 1185 applies to trusts created by voluntary transfer: see 5.104–5.117. In *Corin v Patton* (1990) 169 CLR 540; 92 ALR 1, the purported transfer of title to create a trust of Torrens land was ineffective under the first limb of *Milroy v Lord*, as the settlor had not requested the certificate of title to be produced, and in that sense she had not 'done everything necessary to be done': see 5.112–5.113. In *Marchesi v Apostoulou* [2006] FCA 1122, a declaration of trust by a bankrupt made prior to bankruptcy was ineffective as the bankrupt had not gained permission from registered mortgagees over the titles and the transfer to the trust company would not have been able to be registered without their permission.

16.117   *Post mortem* trusts must satisfy the general requirements for the creation of a valid will. Primarily, such trusts must be in writing and signed by the testator in the presence of two or more witnesses.[16] The major exception to this is the secret trust, which is discussed at 16.145–16.165.

Creation by direction

16.118   A trust is created when the beneficiary of an existing trust directs the trustee to hold his or her interest on trust for another. This is a disposition of a subsisting equitable interest and, as such, must be in writing: *Grey v Inland Revenue Commissioners* [1960] AC 1; [1959] 3 All ER 603, and see 6.16–6.20.

An agreement to create a trust at a later time

16.119   Should a contract to create a trust of land on a future date be in writing? In Queensland, the Court of Appeal has held that executory contracts for interests in land are covered by the requirements for writing in the *Property Law Act 1974* (Qld) s 11(1)(b); *Riches v Hogben* [1986] 1 Qd R 315; *Theodore v Mistford*.

16.120   However, it has been argued by some judges that s 23C does not apply to contracts to create interests in land in the future as an agreement to create a trust in the future does not 'dispose' of an interest in land: *ISPT Nominees Pty Ltd v Chief Commissioner of State Revenue* (2003) 59 NSWLR 196. This logic is based on the fact that s 23C is concerned with dispositions rather than agreements: *Halloran v Minister Administering National Parks and Wildlife Act 1974* (2006) 229 CLR 545; 224 ALR 79; *Sorna Pty Ltd v Flint* [2000] WASCA 22 at [7]; *Abjornson v Urban Newspapers Ltd* [1989] WAR 191 at 200. In *Thompson v White*, a joint venture agreement involved the purchase of property in the name of one of the parties with a view to renovating it and selling it. The profits were to

---

16.   *Wills Act 1968* (ACT) s 9; *Succession Act 2006* (NSW) s 7; *Wills Act 2000* (NT) s 8; *Succession Act 1981* (Qld) s 9; *Wills Act 1936* (SA) s 8; *Wills Act 1992* (Tas) s 10; *Wills Act 1997* (Vic) s 7; *Wills Act 1970* (WA) s 8.

be split between the parties. The agreement did not purport to immediately create any legal or equitable interest in the property in favour of the other parties to the joint venture. On that basis, the New South Wales Court of Appeal found that there was no requirement for the agreement to be in writing.

16.121 Nevertheless, it may be that an agreement to create a trust of land in the future is covered by other Statute of Frauds provisions. Section 54A(1) of the *Conveyancing Act 1919* (NSW)[17] states:

> No action or proceedings may be brought upon any contract for the sale or other disposition of land or any interest in land, unless the agreement upon which such action or proceedings is brought, or some memorandum or note thereof, is in writing, and signed by the party to be charged or by some other person thereunto lawfully authorised by the party to be charged.

16.122 In *Baloglow v Konstanidis* [2001] NSWCA 451, Giles JA found that s 54A applies to the initial stage of an agreement to create or dispose of an interest in land. Section 23C then arises at the later stage during which the agreement is performed and the disposition becomes effective. Does s 54A and its equivalents apply to agreements to create a trust at a later time? In *ISPT Nominees Pty Ltd v Chief Commissioner of State Revenue*, Barrett J found that a contract for a declaration of a trust did not fall within the ambit of the section as a declaration was neither a sale nor a disposition of an interest in land. Barrett J repeated that finding in *Khouri v Khoury* [2004] NSWSC 770, but that decision was overturned on appeal in *Khoury v Khouri* (2006) 66 NSWLR 241, where the New South Wales Court of Appeal unanimously found that an agreement to create a trust at a future time was an agreement concerning the disposition of an interest in land which was required by s 54A to be in writing. The case concerned a claim by one brother (Bechara) that his brother (Peter) had promised to declare that he held a one-half share in a house on trust for Bechara. The promise was allegedly made on the basis of an agreement that Bechara would pay Peter $30,000 and then pay Peter's share of the loan repayments on the mortgage over the house. Bryson JA disputed Barrett J's classification of the agreement as an agreement to create a trust in the future. Bryson JA saw the facts as supporting an agreement to create an interest in the land immediately and on that basis found that it was subject to s 23C. Nevertheless, his Honour felt that even if the agreement were one to create an interest in the future it would still be subject to s 54A. Handley JA, at 243, agreed and said:

> A declaration of trust of land creates an equitable interest in the land in favour of the beneficiary and does not convey an existing interest to him. A contract for the creation of a new interest, legal or equitable, in land is nevertheless a contract for the disposition of that interest.

16.123 Hodgson JA, at 244, said in agreement:

> If it could take effect at all, it was as an agreement to create a trust. The primary judge held that such an agreement was not affected by s 54A of the Conveyancing Act. In my opinion, he was in error. Although a declaration of trust in respect of land is a creation of an interest in that land rather than

---

17. *Civil Law (Property) Act 2006* (ACT) s 204; *Law of Property Act 2000* (NT) s 62; *Property Law Act 1974* (Qld) s 59; *Law of Property Act 1936* (SA) s 26; *Conveyancing and Law of Property Act 1884* (Tas) s 36; *Instruments Act 1958* (Vic) s 126. In Western Australia the *Statute of Frauds 1677* (UK) s 4 applies by virtue of the *Law Reform (Statute of Frauds) Act 1962*.

a transfer or assignment of such an interest, it is in my opinion plainly a disposition of an interest in land, within the meaning of s 54A. The grant of a lease is a creation of an interest in land rather than a transfer or assignment of such an interest; and I do not think it could be said that it is not a disposition of an interest in land. In my view, a declaration of trust is not relevantly different.

16.124   In *Ciaglia v Ciaglia* (2010) 269 ALR 175, White J, following Bryson JA's decision in *Khoury*, found that s 54A applied to executed and executory contracts over land.

The effect of the non-compliance with the requirements of writing

16.125   If the settlor seeks to revoke a trust of realty he or she will be able to do so if the trust is not evidenced in writing. In *Wratten v Hunter* [1978] 2 NSWLR 367, a son was given land by his dying father. At the funeral of the father the son declared that he was going to hold the land on trust for the other members of the family. However, his brother and sister later were unsuccessful in enforcing the trust as the trust was not evidenced in writing. Nor could they seek remedies in part performance as they were volunteers.

16.126   If a trust does not comply with the requirements for writing and the purported trustee seeks to rely on this failure, it may be fraud for the trustee to deny the trust: *Barnes v Alderton* [2008] NSWSC 107; *Bloch v Bloch* (1981) 180 CLR 390; (1981) 37 ALR 55; *Bannister v Bannister* [1948] 2 All ER 133. In *Rochefoucauld v Boustead* [1897] 1 Ch 196 at 206, Lindley LJ said:

> It is further established by a series of cases, the propriety of which cannot now be questioned, that the Statute of Frauds does not prevent the proof of a fraud; and that it is a fraud on the part of a person to whom land is conveyed as a trustee, and who knows it was so conveyed, to deny the trust and claim the land himself. Consequently, notwithstanding the statute, it is competent for a person claiming land conveyed to another to prove by parol evidence that it was so conveyed upon trust for the claimant, and that the grantee, knowing the facts, is denying the trust and relying upon the form of conveyance and the statute, in order to keep the land himself.

16.127   This notion is supported by the maxim that equity will not permit a statute to be used as an instrument of fraud: *Yard v Yardoo Pty Ltd* [2006] VSC 109 at [352]–[354]; *Last v Rosenfeld* at 927–8; *Ciaglia v Ciaglia* at 190–4. In *Schweitzer v Schweitzer* [2010] VSC 543 at [18], Cavanough J said:

> A clearly established category of case to which the maxim applies is a transfer of land on trust where the transferee knows that the land was transferred on trust. If such a transaction is established, the transferee will not be able to rely on the absence of evidence in writing to resist the enforcement of the trust. It is not necessary to decide here whether the trust so enforced is the original express trust or some other kind of trust that arises concurrently with the express trust and is exempt from the operation of s 53 by sub-s (2) [of the *Property Law Act 1958* (Vic)].

16.128   The quote from Cavanough J raises the issue of the nature of this trust. Is the trust a constructive trust or an express trust? In older cases these trusts have been described as constructive trusts: *Bannister v Bannister* at 136. This analysis allows the trust to survive its lack of formality because of the exception provided to constructive trusts in the *Statute of Frauds* provisions. However, it could be argued in the alternative that the existence of fraud prevents the fraudulent defendant from being able to raise the *Statute of Frauds* provisions as a defence. This allows the trust to remain as an express trust. In recent Australian cases, judges have voiced agreement with the express trust analysis: *Equuscorp Pty Ltd v Jimenez* at [128]; *Wade v Wade* [2009] WASC 118 at [83].

16.129   The beneficiary may also be able to employ an equitable doctrine such as part performance, estoppel, or resulting trusts to circumvent the requirements for writing. These doctrines would ordinarily require the passing of some form of consideration or detriment arising from the purported beneficiary which is referenced to or reliant upon the agreement. In *Khoury v Khouri* the purported beneficiary was unable to claim part performance because he could not show that the payments he made were unequivocally referable to the contract to create a trust, as required by the doctrine of part performance: see 23.77–23.89. On that basis the requirements for writing applied and the oral agreement was unenforceable. A similar claim made by an uncle over properties held by his nephew failed in *Faraday v Rappaport* [2007] NSWSC 34, where White J could find no acts of part performance or circumstances that would give rise to estoppel and, on that basis, any agreement that the nephew would hold the land on trust failed for lack of writing.

VOLUNTEERS AND INCOMPLETELY CONSTITUTED TRUSTS

16.130   Once a trust has been completely constituted it can be enforced by a beneficiary, even if the beneficiary is a volunteer: *Paul v Paul* (1882) 20 Ch D 742. However, if a trust is not completely constituted it cannot be enforced by a volunteer. This is an application of the maxim that 'equity will not assist a volunteer': see 2.34–2.42. At best there may be an agreement to create a trust; for example, a contract in which A agrees to transfer property to B to hold the same on trust for C. This contract is only enforceable in equity by the parties to that agreement that have provided valuable consideration.

16.131   If the intended beneficiary, C in the above example, has given valuable consideration for the agreement to create a trust, he or she can enforce the agreement by seeking a decree of specific performance: *Pullan v Koe* [1913] 1 Ch 9. A trust arises when the decree of specific performance has been carried out and the trust has been completely constituted. The remedy is available to the intended beneficiary because valuable consideration has been given. The intended beneficiary is not a volunteer.

16.132   It must be noted that if the intended beneficiary is within marriage consideration he or she is not a volunteer. The use of marriage settlements is not common in the contemporary world, but was in times gone by, and many of the cases in this area of the law were ones involving trusts arising under so-called marriage settlements; see 1.27–1.28.

16.133   The position of an intended beneficiary under an incompletely constituted trust needs to be looked in more detail. This will be done in a series of examples where:
* A is the settlor;
* B is the intended trustee;
* C is the intended beneficiary.

Situation 1

16.134   A promises to convey Blackacre to B to be held on trust for C. Neither B nor C provides valuable consideration and the agreement is not in deed form.

(a) Is the trust properly constituted? No, as there has been no conveyance.

(b) What remedy is needed against A to constitute the trust? Specific performance.

(c) Can B obtain specific performance? No, as he or she is a volunteer.

(d) Can C obtain specific performance? No, as he or she is a volunteer.

Situation 2

16.135 A promises to convey Blackacre to B to be held on trust for C. B provides valuable consideration, but C does not.

(a) Is the trust properly constituted? No, as there has been no conveyance.

(b) What remedy is needed against A to constitute the trust? Specific performance.

(c) Can B obtain specific performance? Yes, because he or she has provided valuable consideration. Once the decree is carried out and Blackacre is in B's name, the trust is completely constituted.

(d) What other remedy could B seek? Damages at common law, and this may be his or her only remedy if specific performance is not available for some reason.

(e) What would B's measure of damages be? They would be either substantial or nominal depending upon whether or not the contract has constituted B as a trustee of A's promise to convey Blackacre. If B is a trustee of A's promise, damages will be substantial because B will be recovering the loss to the trust (in effect the loss to C): see 15.29. The damages that are recovered are also recovered for the trust and thus B holds those damages on trust for C: *Dalton v Ellis; Estate of Bristow* [2005] NSWSC 1252 at [53]; *Lloyds v Harper* (1880) 16 Ch D 290. If B is not a trustee of A's promise then the damages recovered are B's to keep for himself or herself and reflect the loss suffered by B. In most cases B suffers no loss and his or her damages will thus be nominal. Usually B has suffered no loss and will, thus, recover only nominal damages: *Coulls v Bagot's Executor & Trustee Co Ltd* (1966) 119 CLR 460 at 501–2.

(f) If B does nothing, what are C's rights? If there is trust of A's promise, then there is a completely constituted trust of the promise and C has the rights of a beneficiary under that trust to enforce it: see 15.30–15.32. In such circumstances C could effectively force B to take action against A. C can bring an action against B, the trustee, that has the effect of compelling B to sue A for breach of contract. However, C can only initiate such proceedings if B refuses to sue A: *Stanley v Layne Christensen Company* [2006] WASCA 56 at [30]. In formal procedural terms, C sues in an action in which B and A are joined as defendants. This was explained by Brereton J in *Mizzi v Reliance Financial Services Pty Ltd* [2007] NSWSC 37 at [79], as follows:

> At law, the beneficiary of a trust could not sue an obligor to the trust, the proper plaintiff being the trustee. However, in equity, the beneficiary may sue in its own name, joining the trustee and other beneficiaries as defendants. In the case of a trust of a contractual promise, the beneficiary can sue the promisor if the trustee refuses, joining the trustee as a defendant … In substance, the action involves the beneficiary compelling the reluctant trustee to sue by joining it as a defendant.

The remedies obtained are as discussed above when looking at B's options in suing A for breach of contract. If there is no trust of A's promise then C, being a volunteer, has no rights at all. Equally, C could be said to have no action as C is not privy to the contract.

Situation 3

16.136 A agrees to transfer Blackacre to B to be held on trust for C. The agreement between A and B is set out in a deed in which B has not provided valuable consideration.

(a) Is the trust properly constituted? No, as there has been no conveyance.

(b) What remedy is needed against A to constitute the trust? Specific performance.

(c) Can B obtain specific performance? No, as he or she is a volunteer.

(d) What other remedy could B seek? Damages at common law, because the use of a deed is an exception, at common law, to the requirement of consideration.

(e) What would B's measure of damages be? The same situation applies here as with situation 2, depending upon whether B is or is not a trustee of A's promise.

(f) If B does nothing, what are C's rights? The same situation applies here as with situation 2, depending upon whether B is or is not a trustee of A's promise.

16.137 In Situations 2 and 3 the critical issue is whether there is a trust of a promise, so that the chose in action that B has against A to enforce the promise made by A constitutes trust property held by B on trust for C: see 15.29–15.32.

16.138 A number of cases are relevant to this idea. In *Fletcher v Fletcher* (1844) 67 ER 564, a settlor by voluntary deed covenanted with a trustee that if either or both of the settlor's two sons survived him, the settlor's legal personal representative would pay a certain sum of money to the trustees for the trustees to hold on trust for the sons. After the settlor's death the trustee refused to sue on the deed. One son survived the settlor and sought recovery out of the settlor's estate of the money. The son's action was successful.

16.139 In ascertaining whether a promisee in the type of case such as *Fletcher v Fletcher* is a trustee of a promise it is usual to inquire whether both promisor and promisee intended to contract on the basis that the promisee (B in the situations above) contracted as trustee. However, in *Trident General Insurance Co Ltd v McNiece Bros Pty Ltd* (1988) 165 CLR 107 at 148, Deane J said that the intention of the promisee (B in the situations above) alone could be sufficient. If an implication of intention is relied upon, that is to be ascertained primarily by construing the contract in the light of surrounding circumstances and the nature of the contract.

16.140 Another important case in this context is that of *Cannon v Hartley* [1949] Ch 213. In that case a husband and wife entered into a separation deed whereby the husband covenanted that if he became entitled to his parents' estate he would give half of it to his wife for life with remainder to go to their daughter. The daughter was also a party to the deed but gave no consideration. The husband inherited his parents' estate. The wife died, but the husband refused to settle the half share of his parents' estate in favour of his daughter. The daughter sued for damages at common law. As a volunteer she was not entitled to seek specific performance. It was argued that she should also be denied damages at common law because that would have been tantamount to obtaining a decree of specific performance. Romer J refused to accept that argument and awarded damages in favour of the daughter. What this case stands for is the proposition that, although equity will not assist a volunteer, it will not frustrate one.

16.141 The importance of *Fletcher v Fletcher* and *Cannon v Hartley* is as follows: *Fletcher v Fletcher* establishes the idea that in our examples in situations 2 and 3 above there is the concept of B being a trustee of a promise. *Cannon v Hartley* is important because it shows that even if C is a volunteer, equity will not frustrate him or her in seeking a remedy of damages at common law where there is a trust of a promise.

16.142   However, the views just put have been challenged by a number of cases. In *Re Pryce* [1917] 1 Ch 234, a case which was essentially the same as situation 3 above, except that the property in question at the time of the voluntary deed being executed was future property. The issue before the judge was whether he could direct B to sue A. Eve J said that he could not do so because that would have the effect of giving C a remedy that C could not obtain directly. This decision effectively rejected the concept of a trust of a promise and the underlying principle in *Cannon v Hartley* that equity will not frustrate a volunteer.

16.143   *Re Pryce* was followed in *Re Cook's Settlement Trust* [1965] Ch 902. The essence of this case was that in a voluntary deed, A agreed with B that, if paintings owned by A were subsequently sold, the proceeds would be held by B on trust for C. The paintings were subsequently sold and A refused to carry out his agreement. B sought the court's advice as to whether or not he could sue A. Buckley J ruled that B ought not to sue A. Buckley J, at 913–4, said:

> The covenant with which I am concerned did not, in my opinion create a debt enforceable at law, that is to say, a property right, which, although to bear fruit only in the future and upon a contingency, was capable of being made the subject of an immediate trust, as was held to be the case in *Fletcher v Fletcher* ... [T]his covenant upon its true construction is, in my opinion, an executory contract to settle a particular fund or particular funds of money which at the date of the covenant did not exist and which never came into existence.

16.144   *Re Cook's Settlement* offers a basis of distinguishing *Fletcher v Fletcher* and supporting *Re Pryce* on its facts. Both *Re Pryce* and *Re Cook's Settlement* concern a voluntary deed to settle future property. Given that future property cannot be trust property, it is argued that nor can a promise relating to future property be trust property. On the other hand, those who reject *Re Pryce* and *Re Cook's Settlement* argue that the promise, although it deals with future property, is itself presently existing property, and as such, capable of being trust property.

SECRET TRUSTS

16.145   In certain circumstances a testator may wish to make gifts secretly. This can only be possible if the gift can be made outside or parallel to the will, as the will is a public document. A secret trust occurs when the testator leaves property to a donee in a will, but communicates his or her intention that the donee is to hold the property on trust for another person. Secret trusts can take two forms: *fully secret trusts*, where there is no record of the testator's intention to create a trust in the will, and *half secret trusts*, where the testator indicates his or her intention that the donee is not to take the gift beneficially, but is to hold subject to some private instruction that has been communicated by the testator: *Howell v Hyde* [2003] NSWSC 732 at [39].

16.146   The cases of *Ledgerwood v Perpetual Trustee Co Ltd* (1997) 41 NSWLR 532 at 535; *Ottaway v Norman* [1972] 1 Ch 698 at 711, indicates that the following three steps are necessary to create a secret trust:

1. the testator must intend to subject the donee to an obligation of trust;
2. the testator must communicate the intention to the donee; and
3. the donee must accept the obligation before the testator's death.

16.147   Before we consider these three steps, it should be noted that secret trusts are valid regardless of whether the requirements for creating a valid will have been satisfied. In *Ledgerwood v Perpetual Trustee Co Ltd* at 536, Young J said:

> Because the trust flows from the effect on the conscience of the fiduciary, it matters not that there are problems with the formalities under the Wills Act or delegation of testamentary power or that there is a technical problem such as the beneficiary of the half secret trust witnessing the will.

Intention of the testator

16.148   Secret trusts are subject to the requirement of certainty of intention. This can cause evidential problems, especially for fully secret trusts where there is no record in the will of the testator's intentions. Inquiries as to the testator's intention can therefore be wide-ranging and extrinsic evidence can be led. For example, in *Voges v Monaghan* (1954) 94 CLR 231, the testator had left his entire estate to the appellant. The testator had two dependants at the time of his death: his niece and a domestic servant. There was circumstantial evidence that the testator had given written instructions to the appellant to pay the two dependants the sum of £3 per week. The appellant made half-yearly payments to the dependants, but stopped after being called to pay estate taxes. The appellant argued that the payments were discretionary. However, at trial the judge disbelieved the appellant's claims. A majority of the High Court (McTiernan, Webb, Fullagar and Kitto JJ) upheld the trial decision and found that circumstantial evidence, including a number of conversations between the testator and the parties to the case, evidenced the testator's intention to provide for the dependants. *Howell v Hyde* is another example, where evidence existed of conversations and statements that had been made by the testatrix over a long period of time that she would leave her company shares and investments to her de facto partner, but that he would be required to pass those shares and investments on to the plaintiff.

Communication of the intention to the donee

16.149   It is necessary for the testator to communicate his or her intention to the donee before death. In the case of a fully secret trust the communication can occur at any time up until death. If the trust is a half secret trust, it has been said that the communication must occur before, or at the time of, the making of the will: *Guest v Webb* [1965] VR 427; *Re Keen; Evershed v Griffiths* [1937] Ch 236; [1937] 1 All ER 452; *In re Karsten (dec'd); Edwards v Moore* [1953] NZLR 456. However, the most recent Australian decision which had to consider this point directly found that there should be no difference between half and fully secret trusts, and that communication can occur at any time up until death.

16.150   In *Ledgerwood v Perpetual Trustee Co Ltd*, the testatrix made the following disposition in clause 3 of her will:

> I GIVE free of all duties all my articles and effects of personal or domestic or household use of ornament, furniture and jewellery and any motor car belonging to me to my Trustees with respect

that they will dispose of the same in accordance with any existing or future Memorandum written or signed by me but the foregoing expression of my wishes shall not create any trust or legal obligation even if communicated to any person in my lifetime.

Sometime after the will was made the testatrix made the following memorandum:

TO: MY TRUSTEES This is the written Memorandum referred to in Clause 3 of my Will dated 15 August, 1988. I GIVE (free of all duties) my contents contained in Unit 21 'Murilla' Double Bay, 2028, my jewellery and other articles and my effects of household domestic personal use or ornament to MY FRIEND SHIRLEY MINELL and if she should not survive me THEN for her daughter CHARMAINE LEDGERWOOD absolutely.

Shirley Minell predeceased the testatrix. Charmaine Ledgerwood sought to enforce the trust. The parties sought a declaration in relation to the proper construction of the will.

16.151   Young J found that the trust was valid and in doing so declined to follow the cases that had held that communication must occur prior to the making of the will. His Honour preferred the approach of the Irish cases of *Re Browne; Ward v Lawler* [1944] Ir R 90 and *Re Prendeville (dec'd); Prendeville v Prendeville* (unreported, High Court of Ireland, Baron J, 5 December 1990), which had found that the timing of the communication was immaterial as long as it occurred before death. Young J, at 540, said that the enforceability of the trusts depended upon the conscience of the donee and for that reason the timing of communication was irrelevant, as long as the trustee had accepted the obligations before the testator's death.

16.152   In relation to what is required to meet the requirements of communication, it must be noted that the fact and terms of the trust must be communicated. If only the fact of the trust has been communicated, but not its terms, the secret trust fails. In such cases the legatee then holds on resulting trust for the residuary beneficiary or next-of-kin as the case may be. This is because the legatee's conscience is bound by knowledge of the fact of the intended trust. In *Re Boyes; Boyes v Carritt* (1884) 26 Ch D 531, the testator advised his solicitor/legatee that the property was to be held on trust, but died before telling the solicitor the terms of the trust. Two letters were found amongst the testator's papers after his death setting out the intended beneficiary. Because the terms of the trust were not communicated prior to death the secret trust failed, and the solicitor held on resulting trust for the testator's next-of-kin. The same result would apply if the solicitor had accepted the fact of trust and knew of, but refused to accept, the terms of the trust before the testator's death. Kay J, at 536, said:

If the trust was not declared when the will was made, it is essential in order to make it binding, that it should be communicated to the devisee or legatee in the testator's lifetime and that he should accept that particular trust. It may possibly be that he would be bound if the trust had been put in writing and placed in his hands in a sealed envelope, and he had engaged that he would hold the property given to him by the will upon the trust so declared although he did not know the actual terms of the trust: *McCormick v Grogan* (1869) LR 4 HL 82. But the reason is that it must be assumed if he had not so accepted the will would be revoked. Suppose the case of an engagement to hold the property not upon the terms of any paper communicated to the legatee or put into his hands, but of any paper that might be found after the testator's death.

16.153   As the quote suggests it may be sufficient for the terms to be communicated in a sealed envelope. In *In Re Keen; Evershed v Griffiths*, suggests that if a sealed envelope with the terms of the trust is given to the legatee with instructions that it not be opened until after the testator's death, communication of the terms of the trust has been satisfied. Lord Wright MR, at Ch 242–3; All ER at 456–7, in response to the suggestion that a sealed envelope was not a notification of the trust, said:

> I am unable to accept this conclusion, which appears to me to put too narrow a construction on the word 'notified' ... To take a parallel, a ship which sails under sealed orders, is sailing under orders though the exact terms are not ascertained by the captain till later. I note that the case of a trust put into writing which is placed in the trustees' hands in a sealed envelope, was hypothetically treated by Kay J as possibly constituting a communication in a case of this nature: *In re Boyes*. This, so far as it goes, seems to support my conclusion. The trustees had the means of knowledge available whenever it became necessary and proper to open the envelope. I think Mr Evershed was right in understanding that the giving of the sealed envelope was a notification.

16.154   As these cases illustrate, the communication can be oral or by informal writing. However, if the property involved is land, there may be a requirement of writing, depending upon how secret trusts are classified. This is a matter discussed at 16.164–16.165.

Acceptance by the donee

16.155   A donee can accept the obligations of the trust expressly or by acquiescence: *In Re Williams; Williams v Parochial Church Council of the Parish of All Souls, Hastings* [1933] Ch 244; *Ottaway v Norman* [1972] Ch 698; [1971] 3 All ER 1325. The donee must, in some way, encourage the testator to believe that the testator's intentions will be carried out. It is the acceptance of the trust that binds the conscience of the donee: *Blackwell v Blackwell* [1929] AC 318 at 324. Acceptance can be very informal. For example, in *Howell v Hyde* at [10]–[30], [50], the donee's comments of 'yes, mate' and 'she'll be right, mate' were viewed as evidencing his acceptance. In cases of silence by the donee, equity has taken the view that the donee is positively bound to say something if he or she rejects the notion that he or she is not to enjoy the property beneficially: *Brown v Pourau* [1995] 1 NZLR 352 at 367; *Aljaro Pty Ltd v Weidmann* [2001] NSWSC 206 at [14].

16.156   If the gift is made to more than one donee jointly, it is enough that one of the donees has accepted the obligation. Acceptance by one will bind the others: *Moss v Copper* (1861) 70 ER 782; *Re Young; Young v Young* [1951] Ch 344; [1950] 2 All ER 1245; *Ledgerwood v Perpetual Trustee Co Ltd* at 537. However, Dal Pont states that if the donees take the gift as tenants in common, acceptance by one will not bind the others.[18] On the issue of communication to, and acceptance by, one only of two joint donees the principles were summarised as follows in *Re Stead; Witham v Andrew* [1900] 1 Ch 237 at 241:

> If A induces B either to make, or to leave unrevoked, a will leaving property to A and C as tenants in common, by expressly promising, or tacitly consenting, that he and C will carry out the testator's wishes, and C knows nothing of the matter until after A's death, A is bound, but C is not bound; the reason stated being, that to hold otherwise would enable one beneficiary to deprive the rest of their benefits by setting up a secret trust. If, however, the gift were to A and C as joint tenants, the authorities have established a distinction between those cases in which the will is made on the faith of an antecedent promise by A and those in which the will is left unrevoked on the faith of a subsequent promise. In the former case, the trust binds both A and C, the reason stated being

---

18.   Dal Pont, *Equity and Trusts in Australia*, note 2 above, p 546.

that no person can claim an interest under a fraud committed by another; in the latter case A and not C is bound, the reason stated being that the gift is not tainted with any fraud in procuring the execution of the will.

16.157   Earlier authorities suggested that if the trustee of a secret trust renounces the obligation after acceptance, the secret trust would fail: *Re Maddock; Llewelyn v Washington* [1902] 2 Ch 220 at 231. However, later authorities have stated that a trustee's disclaimer would not invalidate the trust as it would be an equitable fraud to allow a defaulting trustee to take the beneficial interest in the trust property: *Blackwell v Blackwell* at 328; *Ledgerwood v Perpetual Trustee Co Ltd* at 535–6.

Proof

16.158   It can be exceptionally difficult to prove the existence of a secret trust: *Skinner v Frappell* [2008] NSWCA 296; *Brown v Willoughby* [2012] WASC 20. The onus of proving the secret trust lies with the person claiming that it exists. The standard of proof is the balance of probabilities: *Re Snowden (dec'd)* [1979] Ch 528 at 537; [1979] 2 All ER 172 at 179. It is not always necessary to prove that the donee/secret trustee was guilty of fraud, in the sense of deliberate and conscious wrongdoing: *Howell v Hyde* at [43]–[45].

The nature of the secret trust

16.159   The nature of the secret trust has been subject to long debate. One view is that they are testamentary trusts and even though all the legislative requirements relating to the making of a will have not been complied with, equity enforces the trusts on the grounds that not to do so would allow the donee/secret trustee to use the statute as an instrument of fraud. Because the donee has accepted the trust obligation it would be unconscionable if he or she were able to plead the statute and thus negate his or her trust responsibility: *Jones v Badley* (1868) 3 Ch App 362 at 363–4. On this view the secret trust arises at the date of death of the testator which is the date that the will is operative.

16.160   An alternative view is that the secret trust arises outside of the context of wills legislation and has nothing to do with such legislation. This argument has it that it is the communication of the trust and its acceptance by the legatee that removes the matter from the scope of the succession legislation: *Blackwell v Blackwell* at 339–40, 342. On this view the secret trust arises when the requirements of secret trusts have been satisfied. In *Re Snowden (dec'd)* at Ch 535; All ER 177, Megarry V-C said:

> [T]he whole basis of secret trusts … is that they operate outside the will, changing nothing that is written in it, and allowing it to operate according to its tenor, but then fastening a trust to the property in the hands of the recipient.

16.161   Which of these two views is correct is of practical significance for two reasons. First, if the intended beneficiary is a witness to the will, on the first theory, then he or she will not be able to take the interest beneficially because of the statutory rule that a witness to a will cannot also take any interest in property pursuant to the will. This would mean that there would be a trust for the residuary beneficiary or next-of-kin as the case may be. On the second theory, the intended beneficiary, even though he or she witnessed the will, would not be affected at all and would take a beneficial interest pursuant to the secret trust, as was the case in such circumstances in *Re Young; Young v Young* [1951] Ch 344 at 350–1; [1950] 2 All ER 1245 at 1250–1.

16.162   Second, if the intended beneficiary dies before the testator, on the first theory, the beneficial interest passes to the testator's residuary beneficiary or next-of-kin as the case may be, on the principle that this happens to any interests left to a person under a will where that person pre-deceases the testator. On the second theory, the earlier death of the intended beneficiary under the secret trust means that the beneficial interest under the secret trust forms part of the deceased's intended beneficiary's estate and passes according to that intended beneficiary's will or on intestacy. This was held to be the case in *Re Gardner; Huey v Cunningham* [1923] 2 Ch 230 at 233. In that case a testatrix left her husband all her property in her will 'knowing that he will carry out my wishes'. Four days after the will was executed she signed an unattested memorandum which gave her husband a life interest with instructions that, after his death, it should be divided equally among a number of named beneficiaries. The husband had been told of the testatrix's wishes and had agreed to the conditions shortly after the will was executed. Ten years later the testatrix died leaving only personal property. Her husband died soon after. One of the named beneficiaries (a niece) had died after the will and memorandum were executed but before the testatrix had died. Questions were raised as to whether the niece's interest failed or whether it would pass to her legal personal representative. Romer J, at 233, said:

> I should without hesitation say that in the present case the husband held the corpus of the property upon trust for the two nieces and the nephew, notwithstanding the fact that the niece predeceased the testatrix. The rights of the parties appear to me to be exactly the same as though the husband, after the memorandum had been communicated to him by the testatrix in the year 1909, had executed a declaration of trust binding himself to hold any property that should come to him upon his wife's partial intestacy upon trust as specified in the memorandum.

16.163   The second theory appears to be the more favoured in modern times. It is also the view accepted in the New South Wales decision of *Ledgerwood v Perpetual Trustee Co Ltd* at 536–7, in which case, if accepted, the secret trust is an *inter vivos* trust.

16.164   The issue then arises as to whether the secret trust is an express trust or a constructive trust. On one view it can be seen as an express trust given the clear intentions of the testator that property be held by the donee/secret trustee on trust for the intended beneficiary. It is just the non-compliance with formalities that differentiates it from the usual express trust created by a will. On the other hand, it is suggested that it is a constructive trust because the trust is enforced notwithstanding a lack of compliance with the statutory requirements of wills legislation. Such a view is suggested in *obiter* comments of the High Court in *Bathurst City Council v PWC Properties Pty Ltd* (1998) 195 CLR 566 at 583; 157 ALR 414 at 424. Academic opinion and earlier authority also supports this view: *Dixon v White* (unreported, SC (NSW), Holland J, 14 April 1982).[19]

16.165   The issue is of practical significance in cases where the property is land. If it is a constructive trust the statutory requirements of writing are not applicable: s 23C(2) of the *Conveyancing Act 1919*

---

19. Ford & Lee, *Principles of the law of trusts* (Online), note 1 above, [6350].

(NSW) and its equivalents in other Australian jurisdictions.[20] If it is an express trust writing would be required in cases of land: s 23C(1) of the *Conveyancing Act 1919* (NSW) and its equivalents in other Australian jurisdictions.[21] However, it could then be argued that the writing requirement would not be required on the basis that equity would not allow the requirements of s 23C(1) to be used to perpetrate a fraud.

20. *Civil Law (Property) Act 2006* (ACT) s 201(4); *Law of Property Act 2000* (NT) s 10(2); *Property Law Act 1974* (Qld) s 11(2); *Law of Property Act 1936* (SA) s 29(2); *Conveyancing and Law of Property Act 1884* (Tas) s 60(2); *Property Law Act 1958* (Vic) s 53(2); *Property Law Act 1969* (WA) s 34(2).
21. *Civil Law (Property) Act 2006* (ACT) s 201(1); *Law of Property Act 2000* (NT) s 10(1); *Property Law Act 1974* (Qld) s 11(1); *Law of Property Act 1936* (SA) s 29(1); *Conveyancing and Law of Property Act 1884* (Tas) s 60(2); *Property Law Act 1958* (Vic) s 53(1); *Property Law Act 1969* (WA) s 34(1).

17

VARIATION AND TERMINATION OF TRUSTS

VARIATION OF EXPRESS TRUSTS

17.1   There may be several reasons why it may prove expedient to vary a trust instrument. For example, if the trust instrument has been drafted in a restrictive fashion it may severely limit the power of the trustee to structure funds so as to limit the impact of taxation. Express trusts can be varied in three main ways:

1. via a provision contained in the trust document itself;
2. via the inherent power of the court; or
3. via a statutory power bestowed on the courts.

Powers to vary contained in express trusts

17.2   A trust instrument can contain express provisions that give the trustee the power to make certain amendments to the trust arrangement. For example, it is common for discretionary trusts to grant a power to the trustee to add beneficiaries to the class of objects.[1] In *Kearns v Hill* (1990) 21 NSWLR 107, the New South Wales Court of Appeal found that the power of variation contained in a trust instrument was to be given its natural and ordinary meaning even where it included a power to vary the identity of the beneficiaries of the trust.

17.3   An express power to vary must be exercised bona fide and in a way that benefits the trust overall: *Wilson v Metro Goldwyn Mayer* (1980) 18 NSWLR 730.

Inherent power to vary trusts

17.4   In England it has been held that the court has no general power to change the terms of an express trust: *Re New* [1901] 2 Ch 534 at 544–5. However, the court may declare that a trustee can deviate from the terms of the trust if it can be shown that there is an emergency and variation is necessary to salvage the trust property. In *Chapman v Chapman* [1954] AC 429; [1954] 1 All ER 798, the House of Lords stated that there were four types of emergency that could be remedied by the courts' inherent jurisdiction:

1. changes in the nature of investments for infants from personalty to realty: *Lord Ashburton v Lady Ashburton* (1801) 31 ER 910; *Re Jackson* (1882) 21 Ch D 786;

---

1.   H A J Ford & W A Lee, *Principles of the law of trusts* (Online), Thomson Reuters, Sydney, [15,260].

2. investments in business transactions not authorised by a trust of settled land: *Re Collins* (1886) 32 Ch D 229; *Havelock v Havelock* (1881) 17 Ch D 807;

3. payment of maintenance out of income, even where there is a direction to accumulate income: *Re New* [1901] 2 Ch 534; *Re Tollemache* [1903] 1 Ch 955; and

4. compromises in favour of unborn children: *Re Trenchard* [1902] Ch 378; *Salkeld v Salkeld (No 2)* [2000] SASC 296.

17.5 In *Tickle v Tickle* (1987) 10 NSWLR 581, Young J decided not to follow the restrictions placed on the courts' power as set down by *Chapman v Chapman*. Instead, his Honour, at 586, found that the inherent power might embrace circumstances where there was 'an element of salvage and a flavour of compromise and the combination of these factors may make it a proper case for the court to exercise jurisdiction to vary'. As such, Young J thought it wise to add a fifth category where the power to vary should be exercised when circumstances have occurred that have tended to thwart the creator's intention and where the parties have consented to a course which will effect an alternative scheme in line with the creator's intention.

17.6 The inherent power must only be used in cases of emergency. In *Re Langford (dec'd) Equity Trustees Ltd v Langford* [2005] VSC 84 at [31] (decision varied on appeal but not on this point), Byrne J found that the sale of settled land to pay outstanding land tax was not an emergency, as it was possible that the beneficiaries could all agree to the sale, even though they had not all done so by the date of hearing.

17.7 The power cannot be used to salvage charitable trusts. In *James N Kirby Foundation v Attorney-General (NSW)* (2004) 62 NSWLR 276; (2004) 213 ALR 366, White J found that there was no inherent power to vary a trust deed for a charitable trust and distinguished *Tickle v Tickle* on the basis that it was concerned with a trust for infants and did not apply to charities. Courts are bound to follow charitable trusts which are capable of being executed and can only create schemes when the execution of the charitable trust has become impossible: *Ku-ring-gai Municipal Council v Attorney-General* (1954) 55 SR (NSW) 65.

Statutory power to vary trusts when expedient

17.8 After the Second World War, the taxation of family trusts in Great Britain led to political pressure to allow variation of express trusts in ways that would lessen the impact of taxation.[2] That pressure was heightened by the decision in *Chapman v Chapman*, the result being that several legislative provisions were passed in Great Britain to expand the power of courts to vary trust instruments. These changes were mirrored in several Australian jurisdictions and take various forms.

17.9 The most common form of statutory power allows the court to vary a trust when it is expedient to do so and where there is no power contained in the trust document to take part in an advantageous dealing. For example, s 63(1) of the *Trustee Act 1958* (Vic) stipulates:[3]

> Where in the management or administration of any property vested in trustees, any sale, lease, mortgage, surrender, release or other disposition, or any purchase, investment, acquisition,

---

2. Ford & Lee, note 1 above, [15,000].

3. For other statutes on this matter see *Trustee Act 1925* (NSW) s 81; *Trustee Act 1925* (ACT) s 81; *Trustee Act 1936* (SA) s 59B; *Trustee Act 1898* (Tas) s 47; *Trustees Act 1962* (WA) s 89.

expenditure or other transaction, is in the opinion of the court expedient, but the same cannot be effected by reason of the absence of any power for that purpose vested in the trustees by the trust instrument (if any) or by law, the court may by order confer upon the trustees, either generally or in any particular instance, the necessary power for the purpose on such terms and subject to such provisions and conditions (if any) as the court thinks fit and may direct in what manner any money authorized to be expended, and the costs of any transaction are to be paid or borne as between capital and income.

17.10 These sections apply to both private and charitable trusts: *Freeman v Attorney-General* [1973] 1 NSWLR 729; *James N Kirby Foundation v Attorney-General (NSW)*. However, the sections are not to be used in the variation of charitable trusts as a substitute for a *cy-près* application: *Trustees of the Kean Memorial Trust Fund v Attorney-General for South Australia* (2003) 86 SASR 449; and see Chapter 18. Each of the major components of these sections will be examined.

Management or administration

17.11 A variation of trust will not be permitted under these sections unless it is expedient in the management or administration of the property: *Re Gaydon* [2001] NSWSC 473; *Perpetual Trustee v Godsall* [1979] 2 NSWLR 785; *Ku-Ring-Gai Municipal Council v The Attorney-General* (1954) 55 SR (NSW) 65 at 74. The words 'management or administration' have been said to be of 'wide import' and 'pick up everything that a trustee may need to do in practical or legal terms in respect of trust property': *Royal Melbourne Hospital v Equity Trustees Ltd* (2007) 18 VR 469 at 500. The phrase concerns both 'the manner in which trust property is managed, administered, handled, directed or controlled and the actual carrying out of those functions': *Arakella Pty Ltd v Paton* (2004) 60 NSWLR 334 at 354. In *Ballard v Attorney-General for the State of Victoria* [2010] VSC 525 at [32], Kyrou J said:

> Although their meanings may largely overlap, the disjunctive use of the words ['management' and 'administration'] indicates that they are not necessarily synonymous and that an unduly narrow interpretation should be avoided. This Court [in *Hornsby v Playoust* (2005) 11 VR 522 at 527] has held that 'management' refers to 'the management of trust property in the commercial or practical sense', whereas 'administration' encompasses 'all of the legal powers and duties which might be possessed by a trustee in respect of trust property'.

Expedient

17.12 The word 'expedient' is given a flexible meaning, but should be read to mean expedient for the beneficiaries: *Riddle v Riddle* (1952) 85 CLR 202 at 214. The term means 'advantageous', 'desirable', 'suitable to the circumstances of the case' and includes 'expediency created by sound practical business considerations': *Trust Company Fiduciary Services Ltd v Challenger Managed Investments Ltd* [2008] NSWSC 1155 at [24]; *Application of NSFT Pty Ltd* [2010] NSWSC 380 at [17]. The court may refuse to order a variation if not all the beneficial interests have been represented on the question of expediency: *Feeney v Feeney* [2008] NSWSC 298.

17.13 In the Northern Territory, s 50A of the *Trustee Act 1893* (NT) does not limit the court's power to expedient or advantageous dealings. The court can make orders as it 'thinks fit and for which the trustee has no power under the trust instrument or a law in force in the Territory'.

17.14 Examples of expedient variations include *Arakella Pty Ltd v Paton*, where Hamilton J used the power to change the nature of the beneficiaries' interest in a unit trust from units to shares, on the basis that it did not subvert the beneficial interests but accommodated them to the commercial needs of the trust. In *Colonial Foundation Ltd v The Attorney-General* [2007] VSC 344, the deletion of otiose clauses which had been rendered redundant was found to be expedient, as were changes to the trustee's power to vary the trust deed and distribute capital and income, so that investment could be targeted to more capital growth.

The intention of the creator of the trust

17.15   The intention of the creator of the trust is a relevant consideration in discovering what is expedient: *Riddle v Riddle* at 224. The exercise of the court's discretion should be informed, but not governed by, the intention of the settlor or testator/trix: *Royal Melbourne Hospital v Equity Trustees Ltd* at 493–4; *Alexander v Alexander* [2011] EWHC 2721 (Ch) at [22]. In *Stein v Sybmore Holdings* [2006] NSWSC 1004 at [53], Campbell J, having observed that the search for the creator's intention can go beyond the language used in the trust, said:

> [T]here is a more general sense in which one can tell, from the terms of the trust deed and the sort of context of social institutions and laws within which it was made, whether the conferring of power to carry out a particular dealing or type of dealing will involve a departure from the spirit of the settlor's intention. It has some analogy to the way in which the court, in deciding whether to settle a *cy près* scheme, decides whether there was a general charitable intention. It involves trying to ascertain whether a departure from the strict letter of administering the trust is a departure in some respect that is an important part of the settlor's intention, or a departure in a matter of inessential detail. The type of trust that is involved could be relevant here. A simple trust, to invest and pay income to or for the benefit of a nominated person, could probably not be altered, by the making of an order under s 81, to the same extent as could a more complex trust, like a family discretionary trust, or a superannuation trust. In the latter type of trusts, it is within the spirit of the settlor's intention that there can be changes, within a certain ambit, in the beneficial interests in the trust property — whether by the exercise of a trustee's discretion, or by conferring discretions on someone other than a trustee, as happens with the opportunity for a member of a superannuation fund to nominate, from time to time, who will receive benefits. In the latter type of trusts, there is a well-understood context of law (often tax law) which the trusts are clearly intended to take advantage of — it is often not difficult to conclude that keeping advantages of that type is within the spirit of the settlor's intentions, or if that context of law were to change, it might be possible to conclude that it was within the spirit of the settlor's intention the trust should accommodate itself to whatever the new law was.

Adverse impact on beneficial interests?

17.16   It is clear that a variation will not be expedient if it adversely affects the interests of all the beneficiaries. In *Re Ansett Australia Ltd* (2006) 151 FCR 41, the court refused a variation which would have allowed a resolution to be put to a meeting which was adverse to the interests of the beneficiaries. But variations may be expedient if they adversely affect some of the beneficiaries as an incidental effect of management and administration. It has been said that 'expediency' requires that the variation be expedient for the trust 'as a whole': *Re Craven's Estate* [1937] Ch 431 at 436; *Re Sykes* [1974] 1 NSWLR 597 at 600. In *Riddle v Riddle*, at 222, Williams J said that, '[t]he sole question is whether it is expedient in the interests of the trust property as a whole'. This might be one reason for not allowing a variation which negatively alters some of the beneficial interests.

17.17   However, it would be wrong to suggest that the court can never vary a trust where the variation will alter some of the beneficial interests, even negatively: *Re Dawson* [1959] NZLR 1360. In *Arakella Pty Ltd v Paton* it was found that beneficial interests could be altered and affected by variation as long as the variation was for the purpose of advancing the expedient management of the trust, and not solely to subvert the beneficial interests. To that extent, the effect on the beneficial interests may only be incidental or consequential to the variation: *Westfield Queensland No 1 Pty Ltd v Lend Lease Real Estate Investments Ltd* [2008] NSWSC 516 at [53]; *NM Superannuation Pty Ltd v Hughes* (Supreme Court of New South Wales, McLelland CJ in Eq, 5 March 1996, unreported).

17.18   In *Stein v Sybmore Holdings*, Campbell J went so far as to say that s 81 of the *Trustee Act 1925* (NSW) did not contain a requirement for the variation to be expedient for the trust 'as a whole'. His Honour found that the section did allow for beneficial interests to be altered. Campbell J approved of a postponement of the vesting date of the beneficial interests under a trust, in circumstances where the delay might have caused potential beneficiaries to be added to a class (watering down other interests), or caused some classes of beneficiaries to miss out altogether. The change nevertheless was asked for by the beneficiaries (and granted), given the large tax liabilities they would have faced had the property vested when originally intended.

17.19   Both *Arakella Pty Ltd* and *Stein v Sybmore Holdings* may be explicable on the basis that the New South Wales section expressly recognises the court's power to include 'adjustment of the respective rights of the beneficiaries'. But the power to vary beneficial interests has also been found to exist even in jurisdictions without this express recognition. In *Royal Melbourne Hospital v Equity Trustees Ltd*, the Victorian Court of Appeal had to consider whether to give trustees a power to sell portions of a large estate of settled land to create a managed fund so that mounting land taxes could be paid. If the land taxes were not paid the estate would be sold in portions by the state government to meet the debts. The grandchildren, who were entitled to the use of the land for life, were in favour of doing nothing as this left their rights least affected. But by doing nothing, eventually all the property would have to be sold to meet the tax debts and nothing would be left for residuary beneficiaries (a number of charities). The variation to create a managed fund would avoid this eventuality as larger amounts could be sold to create a fund which could then meet the debt. However, the immediate impact of such sales would be to accelerate the reduction of the grandchildren's rights. It was argued that such a variation was not in the interests of the trust as a whole, because the grandchildren would be adversely affected earlier than what they would otherwise be. The Court of Appeal rejected those arguments and found in favour of the creation of a managed fund. Bell AJA, at 504, said:

> The submissions of the minority (but not the majority) grandchildren would deny the court any capacity to bring a sense of proportion to the exercise of the expedience power. No matter how clear the settlor's intention to create several beneficial interests, how inimical the consequences of inaction for the trust property or the interests of one class of beneficiaries, how great the sphere of beneficial enjoyment preserved, how small the degree of beneficial enjoyment reduced, how fairly the scales are held between the various beneficial interests and how expedient the power is in all other respects, if conferring the power would disadvantage some or even a single beneficiary, that, it is submitted, is the end of it. Those submissions must be rejected. This 'large and important' [quoting *Riddle v Riddle* at 214] power is not exercised by the principle of the dog in the manger. The true position is that a power, otherwise expedient for the management or administration of the trust property and in the interests of the trust or beneficiaries as a whole, may be conferred

even if its impact may be relatively positive for some beneficiaries and relatively negative for others. A power does not necessarily lose its character of being expedient for that purpose because it may impact differentially on the beneficiaries.

The absence of any power

17.20   The statutory power cannot be used when the trustees have the power to conduct the transaction in question, either because it is contained in the trust deed or is conferred by another statute: *Royal Melbourne Hospital v Equity Trustees Ltd*; *Trust Company Fiduciary Services Ltd v Challenger Managed Investments Ltd* at 363.

Any transaction

17.21   The word 'transaction' has been read to include an amendment of a trust deed: *James N Kirby Foundation v Attorney-General (NSW)* at NSWLR 280; ALR 370; *Re Bowmil Nominees Pty Ltd* [2004] NSWSC 161 at [16]; *Re Philips New Zealand Ltd* [1997] 1 NZLR 93. 'Transactions' do not include requests for advice from the court on how the trustees should exercise their powers: *Re Ansett Australia Ltd* at 64.

Statutory power to vary on behalf of infants, the unborn and incompetent beneficiaries

17.22   Some jurisdictions also provide for variation of the beneficial interests of infants, incompetent persons and unborn beneficiaries.[4] In Queensland, Victoria and Tasmania it is possible to vary a trust when the beneficiary is unable to consent to such variation as long as it is for the benefit of the beneficiaries.[5] In Western Australia it is not possible to vary the trust if it is to the detriment of the beneficiaries.[6] In South Australia, under s 59C(3) of the *Trustee Act 1936* (SA), the power cannot be exercised if:

(a) application to vary is substantially motivated by a desire to avoid, or reduce the incidence of tax;

(b) the proposed exercise of powers would be in the interests of beneficiaries of the trust and would not result in one class of beneficiaries being unfairly advantaged to the prejudice of some other class;

(c) the proposed exercise of powers would not disturb the trusts beyond what is necessary to give effect to the reasons justifying the exercise of the powers; and

(d) the proposed exercise of powers accords as far as reasonably practicable with the spirit of the trust.

17.23   These powers are commonly used to extend the vesting date on trusts to prevent distribution of funds that will terminate the trust and bring on tax liabilities: *Thomas Hare Investments Ltd v Hare* [2012] VSC 200; *Re Plator Nominees Pty Ltd* [2012] VSC 284. The statutory powers can be used to vary trusts which operate outside of the jurisdiction of the court: *Re McDonald Family*

---

4.   *Trusts Act 1973* (Qld) s 95; *Trustee Act 1936* (SA) s 59C; *Variation of Trusts Act 1994* (Tas) ss 13, 14; *Trustee Act 1958* (Vic) s 63A; *Trustees Act 1962* (WA) s 90.

5.   *Trusts Act 1973* (Qld) s 95; *Variation of Trusts Act 1994* (Tas) ss 13, 14; *Trustee Act 1958* (Vic) s 63A.

6.   *Trustees Act 1962* (WA) s 90.

Trust (No 1) [2010] VSC 324; *Re Ker's Settlement Trust* [1963] 1 Ch 553; *Re Paget's Settlement* [1965] 1 WLR 1046.

17.24   These statutory powers can be illustrated by *Perpetual Trustees Victoria Ltd v Barns* [2012] VSCA 77. The case concerned Ms Barns, who was born with autism. Both her mother and father had died. Under her father's will, she was entitled to the income of a trust managed by the trustee, Perpetual Trustees Victoria Limited. The will also empowered the trustees to pay excess income not needed by Ms Barns to a number of charitable institutions. Any residue left after the death of the testator's wife and Ms Barns was to be given to the Lord Mayor's Fund. The trust allowed advances of capital to be made to the testator's wife but it was silent about such advances to the daughter. Unfortunately, the income was no longer sufficient to support Ms Barns' needs. The trustees brought an application to allow the sum of $50,000 per annum to be taken from the trust's capital to help cover the costs of caring for Ms Barns. The Attorney General did not oppose, but did not consent, to these orders. Robson J, at [48]–[50], ruled that the trustee's application was one that involved a distribution of the trust property that went beyond management or administration of the trust and that, consequently, s 63 of the *Trustee Act 1958* (Vic) did not authorise the court to grant the trustee's application. Robson J also declined to vary the trust under s 63A, finding that it could not be ordered without the consent of the other organisations who might be entitled to some distribution of the funds. The Court of Appeal overturned these findings. Focusing solely on s 63A, William AJA found that the power in s 63A was not dependent on the consent of those who might be beneficially entitled. The proposed arrangement was fair and proper overall and it matched the general intention of the testator.

17.25   While there is no corresponding provision in New South Wales, in *Tickle v Tickle* (1987) 10 NSWLR 581 at 584, Young J held that s 50 of the *Minors (Property and Contracts) Act 1970* (NSW) empowered the court to transfer the trust property of minors, as long as it was for the minors' benefit.

17.26   However, the New South Wales courts' general statutory vesting powers cannot be used to vary trusts and extinguish the interests of unborn beneficiaries. In *Estate of McCready* [2004] NSWSC 887, the testator created a gift of a house on trust, with the income to the deceased son for life and the remainder to the son's children. The son was aged 60 and had no children. The trustees sought to extinguish the interests of unborn children so that the property could be given absolutely to the deceased's son. The plaintiff requested that the court exercise its powers under s 72 of the Trustee Act, which states:

> Where any property is subject to a contingent right in an unborn person or class of unborn persons, who, on coming into existence, would in respect thereof become entitled to or possessed of the property on any trust, the Court may make a vesting order releasing the property from the contingent right, or vesting in any person the estate or interest to or of which the unborn person or class of unborn persons would, on coming into existence, be entitled or possessed in the property.

17.27   Barrett J denied the application. Section 72 was not intended to be a species of independent variation of trusts provision. Barrett J found that, unlike the provisions in other states, s 72 did not allow the rights of unborn persons to be extinguished except as may be necessary or desirable to carry into effect some separately existing requirement of equity. Because the son had no existing equitable right to the whole property, there could be no basis for the exercise of the power.

TERMINATION OF TRUSTS

Illegality

17.28   A trust for an illegal purpose will be void, regardless of whether the trust is express or resulting. This is primarily because equity will not assist a person who has acted with an illegal intent. Any estate involved will be allowed to lie where it falls, meaning that equity will not upset the legal title of the property by imposing a trust: *Holman v Johnson* (1775) 98 ER 1120; *Muckleston v Brown* (1801) 31 ER 934. For example, a trust fund dedicated to paying the fines of poachers who had been imprisoned for non-payment was invalid because it encouraged illegal activity: *Thrupp v Collett (No 1)* (1858) 43 ER 844.

17.29   The court's finding of illegality depends on whether the party has to rely on evidence of his or her own fraud to prove their title — equity will not assist them: *Tinsley v Milligan* [1994] 1 AC 340; [1993] 3 All ER 65. However, if it is possible to prove title without the need to rely on evidence of illegality, the title can be upheld in equity. For example, in *Tinsley v Milligan*, a house had been purchased jointly by the parties but registered in the name of one party, so as to allow the other to continue to get social security. Given that one party had provided part of the proceeds, an automatic presumption arose of a resulting trust. The resulting trust was found to be valid because it arose without the necessity to bring evidence of the illegal purpose behind the transaction.

17.30   In Australia, the *Tinsley v Milligan* approach has been rejected and a more flexible test adopted that requires the court to examine the policy behind the law that has been breached: *Edmunds v Pickering* (1999) 75 SASR 407 (app'd and aff'd on other grounds: *Pickering v Smoothpool Nominees Pty Ltd* (2001) 81 SASR 175). Moreover, it is necessary to bring evidence of what the law is which has allegedly been breached (*Robson v Robson* [2011] QSC 234), especially if it is the law of a foreign jurisdiction: *Damberg v Damberg* (2001) 52 NSWLR 492.

17.31   The leading Australian authority is *Nelson v Nelson* (1995) 184 CLR 538; 132 ALR 133. In this case a mother paid the purchase price of a house which was registered in her son's and daughter's names. The purpose behind the transaction was to allow the mother to purchase another home at some future time, with the benefit of a subsidy under the *Defence Service Homes Act 1918* (Cth). The subsidy was only available for one house. Sometime later the mother purchased another house with the use of the subsidy, making false declarations that she did not own any other property. The house in the children's names was later sold. The daughter argued that she had a beneficial interest in the proceeds, whereas the mother and the son claimed a beneficial interest for the mother.

17.32   Deane and Gummow JJ, at CLR 546; ALR 139, stated that there were three relevant doctrines in the case. The first concerned the presumption of resulting trust in favour of the mother. The second concerned the presumption of advancement that arose in favour of the daughter. The third doctrine was that of illegality on the mother's ability to rebut the presumption of advancement.

17.33   On the issue of illegality, Deane and Gummow JJ found that there should be no general policy of letting the loss fall where it lies. Instead, equity should look at the specific circumstances of the case and the particular policy behind the law that had been breached. After analysing the Act, Deane and Gummow JJ, at CLR 570; ALR 158, found that the policy was to help eligible persons purchase dwellings. It was not to prevent them from owning more than one house. As such, the policy did not require the court to automatically refuse equitable relief. Additionally, given that the mother was seeking equitable relief, she was obliged to make good the amounts that she had defrauded from the government, before a resulting trust would be enforced.

17.34   McHugh J came to similar conclusions and found that, given that the Act contained its own penalties for making false declarations, the policy of the Act would not be defeated by the provision of equitable relief. McHugh J, at CLR 613; ALR 193, said:

> [C]ourts should not refuse to enforce legal or equitable rights simply because they arose out of or were associated with an unlawful purpose unless: (a) the statute discloses an intention that those rights should be unenforceable in all circumstances; or (b) (i) the sanction of refusing to enforce those rights is not disproportionate to the seriousness of the unlawful conduct; (ii) the imposition of the sanction is necessary, having regard to the terms of the statute, to protect its objects or policies; and (iii) the statute does not disclose an intention that the sanctions and remedies contained in the statute are to be the only legal consequences of a breach of the statute or the frustration of its policies.

McHugh J also required that the wrongdoer take all necessary steps to remedy the wrongdoing before equity provided relief.

17.35   Toohey J, at CLR 592–3; ALR 176, also rejected the *Tinsley v Milligan* approach as a 'triumph of procedure over substance'. His Honour, at CLR at 595; ALR 178, observed that universal application of the principle of illegality would lead to 'unjust and capricious results'. However, Toohey J, at CLR 597–8; ALR 180, did not require the mother to pay back the subsidy as that was a matter for the government.

17.36   Dawson J took a different path and found that the false declaration was not sufficiently related to the circumstances giving rise to the resulting trust. The purchase of the home occurred a substantial period before the false declaration was made. His Honour, at CLR 581; ALR 166, rejected, the distinction drawn in *Tinsley v Milligan* between cases where the illegality needs to be relied upon and those where it does not. Like Toohey J, Dawson J did not require the mother to repay the subsidy, given that the government had the power to recall it.

17.37   *Nelson v Nelson* shows that the primary issue is whether the statute is intended to make trusts unenforceable. Since *Nelson v Nelson* the courts have upheld transactions which concealed beneficial interests to gain access to the first home buyers grant, and to avoid land tax and minimise capital gains tax: *Robins v Robins* [2006] WASC 301; *Tesoriero v Tesoriero* [2007] NSWSC 54. Neither of these transactions were struck down for illegality as the grant and taxation schemes were not aimed at making such trusts unenforceable. In *Strang v Strang* [2009] NSWSC 760, a trust of a weekend lease held under the *Crown Lands Consolidation Act 1913* (NSW) was upheld. While the Act required interests in Crown lands to be created in accordance with the Act, there was nothing in the Act which made trusts of such interests illegal. Nor was there any underlying policy in the Act which required such trusts to be unenforceable.

17.38   As *Nelson v Nelson* shows, if it can be shown that the legislation contains its own penalties for breach which do not render the trust void, it is possible that the court can uphold the trust as being in accordance with the policy of the Act. *Menezes v Salmon* [2009] NSWSC 2 concerned a trust of land where the beneficiary was a foreign national. This trust was not approved under s 21A of the *Foreign Acquisitions and Takeovers Act 1975* (Cth), but Macready AsJ found that the imposition of a trust would not be inconsistent with the Act, as the Act did not make it illegal for a foreign national to own land in Australia. Penalties could be imposed for failing to notify the Treasurer of an intention to buy land. Because of this the court would not strike down the trust as that would effectively impose additional sanctions on the plaintiff. Other courts have found similarly: *Huang v Fu* [2011] NSWSC 316; *Fan v Tang* [2010] NSWSC 11; *Ikeuchi v Liu* [2001] QSC 54. In *Sheikholeslami v Tolcher* [2011] FCA 1050, Yates J found similarly and said that the defence of unclean hands would only require the foreign national to notify the Treasurer of the beneficial interest.

17.39   If a trust is created with the intention that it will serve an illegal purpose and the purpose never eventuates, the trust is unlikely to be struck down: *White v O'Neill* [2010] NSWSC 1193 at [35]. In *Day v Couch* [2000] NSWSC 230, the plaintiff was in a car accident and believed that he was liable for a large claim of damages. He transferred properties to his father for the purpose of making them unavailable to any possible creditors. However, no claim was brought against him. After his father's death he sought a declaration that he was the beneficial owner of the properties on resulting trust. There was no breach of any statute as the consequences of the illegal intent did not occur. As such, Bryson J upheld the imposition of a resulting trust.

Trusts and bankruptcy

17.40   The *Bankruptcy Act 1966* (Cth) provides for the striking down of trusts which are either undervalued transactions or transactions which are aimed at defeating creditors.

Undervalued transactions

17.41   Section 120 renders void any transfer of property for less than market value which occurs within five years of the commencement of the bankruptcy. Declarations of trust are clearly within the provisions of the section: *Ambrose (Trustee) in the matter of Poumako (Bankrupt) v Poumako* [2012] FCA 889. There are a number of exceptions, such as payments of tax, maintenance, and debt agreements: s 120(2). Transfers will not be void if they took place more than two years prior to the commencement of bankruptcy and the transferee can prove that at that time the transferor was solvent: s 120(3). However, if the transfer occurred less than two years prior to the commencement of bankruptcy, the provision is activated and it will not matter that the transferee had acted in good faith and paid valuable consideration, if that consideration was less than market value: *Anscor Pty Ltd v Clout* (2004) 135 FCR 469. If the transfer was to a related entity, the transfer has to have taken place more than four years prior to the commencement of bankruptcy. There is a rebuttable presumption that a person who had not kept books, records and accounts was insolvent: s 120(3A).

Transactions to defeat creditors

17.42   Section 121 of the *Bankruptcy Act 1966* (Cth) stipulates:

(1) A transfer of property by a person who later becomes a bankrupt (the transferor) to another person (the transferee) is void against the trustee in the transferor's bankruptcy if:
   (a) the property would probably have become part of the transferor's estate or would probably have been available to creditors if the property had not been transferred; and
   (b) the transferor's main purpose in making the transfer was:
      (i) to prevent the transferred property from becoming divisible among the transferor's creditors; or
      (ii) to hinder or delay the process of making property available for division among the transferor's creditors.

17.43 An exception is spelt out in s 121(4), where a transfer will not be void if:

(a) the consideration that the transferee gave for the transfer was at least as valuable as the market value of the property; and

(b) the transferee did not know, and could not reasonably have inferred, that the transferor's main purpose in making the transfer was the purpose described in paragraph (1)(b); and

(c) the transferee could not reasonably have inferred that, at the time of the transfer, the transferor was, or was about to become, insolvent.

17.44 Section 121 was considered in *Trustees of the Property of Cummins (a bankrupt) v Cummins* (2006) 227 CLR 278; 224 ALR 280. The case concerned Cummins, a barrister, who had become bankrupt after failing to pay income tax for nearly 45 years. In 1987 he had transferred his legal and beneficial interests in his matrimonial home to his wife, and he also transferred his shares in his chambers to a trustee, where the trust was set up to benefit his family. The barrister argued that his main purpose for doing this was to limit his exposure to professional negligence liability, as he claimed to fear the possibility that barristers would lose their immunity from negligence. The trustee in bankruptcy argued that the main purpose in transferring the assets was to avoid the Commonwealth Government's considerable claims for unpaid income tax.

17.45 Gleeson CJ, Gummow, Hayne, Heydon and Crennan JJ, in a joint judgment, found for the Commonwealth. Their Honours found, at CLR 292; ALR 288, that to satisfy the 'main purpose' test, the trustees in bankruptcy had to show that the circumstances appearing in the evidence gave rise to a reasonable and definite inference that the main purpose was to avoid creditors. On the facts, the inference was open to be found. Their Honours based their decision on the findings of the trial judge that:

- [Mr Cummins] was well aware in August 1987 that he had incurred very substantial liabilities to [the ATO], contingent only on [the ATO] issuing assessments in respect of past income years;
- [Mr Cummins] was well aware at that time that [the ATO] would issue assessments once [his] longstanding tax delinquency became known, an event that could occur at any time;
- [Mr Cummins] divested himself voluntarily of virtually all his substantial assets in August 1987;
- in any event, the assets retained by [Mr Cummins] were not sufficient to meet his taxation liabilities, if [the ATO] decided to issue assessments; and
- [Mr Cummins] saw the transfers as increasing the chances that his assets would be protected from any claims made by [the ATO].

17.46 The term 'creditors' is not limited to creditors who later prove their debt in the bankruptcy: *Nelson v Mathai* (2011) 253 FLR 139 at 141–6.

Trusts and corporate insolvency

17.47 Similar powers to those in the Bankruptcy Act discussed above can be found in Part 5.7 of the *Corporations Act 2001* (Cth). The main provision is s 588FE. The section describes a number of situations where transactions by corporations will be voidable:

- Section 588FE(2) states that insolvent transactions are voidable where the transaction occurred during either the six months ending on the relation-back day, or, if it occurred after that date, up to the date of the company's winding up. Transactions will be voidable if the transaction was uncommercial, an unfair preference, an unfair loan or an unreasonable director-related transaction, which occurred during the relation-back period;

- Section 588FE(3) states that a transaction will be voidable if it was both an insolvent transaction and uncommercial and it was entered into within two years ending on the relation-back day.
- Section 588FE(4) states that a transaction will be voidable if it was an insolvent transaction with a related entity and it was entered into within four years ending on the relation-back day; and
- Section 588FE(5) states that a transaction will be voidable if it was an insolvent transaction entered into for the purpose of defeating, delaying or interfering with the rights of creditors and it was entered into within 10 years ending on the relation-back day.

Trusts which are fraudulent conveyances

17.48   The *Fraudulent Conveyances Act 1571* (13 Eliz 1, c 5) made conveyances voidable when they were made with intent to defraud creditors. Modern versions of this Act can be found in most Australian jurisdictions.[7] For example, ss 172 and 173 of the *Property Law Act 1958* (Vic), state:

172 Voluntary conveyances to defraud creditors
(1) Save as provided in this section, every alienation of property made, whether before or after the commencement of this Act, with intent to defraud creditors, shall be voidable, at the instance of any person thereby prejudiced.
(2) This section shall not affect the operation of a disentailing assurance, or the law of bankruptcy or insolvency for the time being in force.
(3) This section shall not extend to any estate or interest in property alienated for valuable consideration and in good faith or upon good consideration and in good faith to any person not having, at the time of the alienation, notice of the intent to defraud creditors.

173 Voluntary disposition with intent to defraud
Every voluntary disposition of land made with intent to defraud a subsequent purchaser is voidable at the instance of that purchaser.

17.49   In *Marcolongo v Chen* (2011) 242 CLR 546; (2011) 274 ALR 634, French CJ, Gummow, Crennan and Bell JJ found that an 'intent to defraud' included attempts to delay, hinder and defeat creditors. The majority also found that it was sufficient of the section to prove an intent to hinder, delay or defeat creditors without also showing that the debtor wanted creditors to suffer loss or had a purpose of causing loss. Nor does the intent to defraud need to be the sole or dominant intent. The expression 'an intent to defraud creditor' should therefore be given a liberal interpretation: *Cassegrain v Gerard Cassegrain & Co Pty Ltd* [2012] NSWSC 403 at [255].

17.50   The onus of proving the intent to defraud, and the lack of good faith and consideration, rests with the person seeking to have the transfer set aside: *Huynh v Helleh Holdings Pty Ltd* (2001) NSWSC 1162 at [18]; *PT Garuda Indonesia Ltd v Grellman* (1992) 35 FCR 515 at 527–8. The alienation need not affect all creditors, as long as some are affected: *Singh v Kaur Bal* [2011] WASC 303 at [37]. Persons who are prejudiced by the transaction have standing to sue under the section: *Silvera v Slavic* (1999) 46 NSWLR 124; *Langdon v Gruber* [2001] NSWSC 276.

---

7. *Civil Law (Property Act) 2006* (ACT) ss 239–240; *Conveyancing Act 1919* (NSW) ss 37A, 37B; *Law of Property Act 2000* (NT) ss 208–209; *Property Law Act 1974* (Qld) ss 228–229; *Law of Property Act 1936* (SA) ss 86–87; *Conveyancing and Law of Property Act 1884* (Tas) ss 40–41; *Property Law Act 1958* (Vic) ss 173–174; *Property Law Act 1969* (WA) ss 90–91.

17.51   The term 'every alienation' encompasses every conceivable means whereby property might be removed from the reach of a person's creditors: *Hall v Poolman* (2007) 215 FLR 243 at 361. Declaration of trusts fall within the ambit of the section: *Dueeasy Pty Ltd v D & M Hughes Civil Engineering Pty Ltd (in liq)* [2006] NSWSC 333.

17.52   The benefit of these sections is that, unlike s 121 of the Bankruptcy Act, they only require an intent to defraud creditors, not proof that the sole or principal intention was to defraud creditors: *The Bell Group Ltd (in liq) v Westpac Banking Corporation (No 9)* (2008) 225 FLR 1 at 735–6; *Andrew v Zant Pty Ltd* (2004) 213 ALR 812.

17.53   If it can be shown that the transaction creates no barrier to the creditor's rights of satisfaction, it may be difficult to prove an intent to defraud in the absence of specific evidence of such an intent. In *Agusta Pty Ltd v Provident Capital Ltd* [2012] NSWCA 26, Agusta incurred fees to Provident, when it was acting as a trustee. Agusta had a right to be indemnified out of the trust assets for those fees: see 20.34. Later, Agusta was replaced as trustee by Riva and trust assets were transferred to Riva. Provident argued that the transfer of trust property to Riva was void because the transfer was intended to delay or hinder its rights to be paid. There was no direct evidence of any intention to defraud Provident. An intention could only be inferred from the nature of the transaction and the effect that it had on Provident's rights to be paid. The Court of Appeal found that Provident could still seek payment from the assets even though they had passed to Riva. The transfer of trustee rights to Riva included Agusta's right to be indemnified for the fees. Provident was the only creditor of the trust. There was, therefore, no equitable reason, preventing Provident from subrogating its rights with Riva's right to be indemnified for those costs. Barrett JA, at [83], said:

> In summary, the alienation by Agusta to Riva did not alter the steps that Provident could effectively have taken to enforce against the Kings Park land the money judgment it had obtained against Agusta. Both before and after the alienation, execution at law was not open to trust creditors but they were entitled to assert Agusta's preferred beneficial interest and thereby to obtain equitable execution through the sale of trust property by a receiver appointed by the court. The fact that Agusta's preferred beneficial interest and the creditors' rights of subrogation in relation to it subsisted in the trust assets after they became vested in the new trustee meant that it was not incumbent upon Agusta to obtain from Riva any particular undertaking to protect those creditors. The trust assets, when received by the new trustee, continued to have imposed upon them the entitlements derived by creditors from the former trustee's preferred beneficial interest and this was so whether or not any such undertaking was sought from or given by the new trustee.

17.54   Because there was no evidence of a specific intention to defraud and the trust assets were still available to satisfy the debt, it could not be argued that there was an attempt to delay or hinder Provident.

Trusts and the powers of the Family Court

17.55   The Family Court has the power to declare the rights and titles that parties to a marriage have to property and it has the power to make alterations to those rights: *Family Law Act 1975* (Cth) ss 78, 79. Section 85A of the Family Law Act also allows the courts to make orders it thinks are just and equitable in relation to property dealt with by ante-nuptial and post-nuptial settlements which are made in relation to the marriage.

17.56   Section 106B(1) of the Act stipulates:

> In proceedings under this Act, the court may set aside or restrain the making of an instrument or disposition by or on behalf of, or by direction or in the interest of, a party, which is made or proposed to be made to defeat an existing or anticipated order in those proceedings or which, irrespective of intention, is likely to defeat any such order.

17.57   The word 'disposition' is defined to include 'the issue, grant, creation, transfer or cancellation of, or a variation of the rights attaching to, an interest in a company or a trust': *Family Law Act 1975* (Cth) s 106B(5). In exercising the power the court is required to have regard to the protection of a bona fide purchaser or other person interested. A 'person interested' includes a person with an interest in a trust including a beneficial interest, the interests of a settlor, a power of appointment, a power to rescind or vary a power in a trust and an interest that is conditional, contingent or deferred. The court's power extends to bankruptcy proceedings and agreements created therein and creditors may also seek an order under s 106B. In *Coventry v Smith* (2004) 181 FLR 220; 31 Fam LR 608, the Full Court of the Family Court employed the section to overturn a variation of trust that removed the husband's right to appoint new trustees (and effectively control the trust). The variation of trust was overturned on the basis that it was aimed at putting the beneficial interests of the husband beyond the court's reach and the husband was found to be the principal beneficiary of the trust with a vested interest. As such, his beneficial rights were considered to be assets available for distribution on divorce.

17.58   These provisions were examined by the High Court in *Kennon v Spry* (2008) 238 CLR 366; 251 ALR 257. The case concerned a family trust which had been created orally by famous equity barrister Dr ICF Spry in 1968, and later recorded in writing in 1981. Dr Spry was the settlor and trustee. The trust was a discretionary trust where the beneficiaries were all the issue of Dr Spry's father and their spouses. In 1983 Dr Spry removed himself as a beneficiary. When his marriage came into difficulties in 1998 he executed a document which removed himself and his wife as capital beneficiaries. Dr Spry and his wife separated in 2001. In 2002, he created four trusts for his daughters and he exercised his discretion as trustee to apply all the income and capital from the primary trust into the trusts for his daughters. He also transferred a number of shares into the daughters' trusts. Later that year he appointed Kennon as joint trustee, with himself, of the four trusts for the daughters. Mrs Spry made an application to the Family Court seeking to set aside the 1998 document which had removed her as a beneficiary, and the later transactions which had benefited the daughters. At trial, Strickland J found in favour of Mrs Spry and set aside the transactions using s 106B. Strickland J ordered that Dr Spry pay the wife a sum of over $2 million. The Full Court dismissed an appeal and the matter then proceeded to the High Court.

17.59   The High Court upheld the finding that the trustee powers of Dr Spry constituted property for the purposes of s 79 of the Family Law Act: see Chapter 21. The High Court also upheld the use of s 106B to void the removal of Mrs Spry as a beneficiary and the transfer of the capital and income to the daughters' trusts. French CJ reiterated Strickland J's finding that Dr Spry had made the 1998 instrument knowing the marriage was in trouble and with the intention to move the assets of the trust away from the reach of the Family Court. The transfer of the trust moneys into the daughters' trusts was likewise an attempt to defeat future Family Court proceedings. French CJ, at CLR 395; ALR 278, found that:

> Because the 1998 instrument effectively disposed of Mrs Spry's equitable right to be considered in the application of the Trust fund, and having regard to the trial judge's conclusions about the

purpose of the instrument, the order setting it aside was an appropriate exercise of the Family Court's power under s 106B.

17.60   Gummow and Hayne JJ found similarly. Their Honours, at CLR 411; ALR 291, stated:

> What matters in this case is that once the 1998 instrument and the 2002 instrument were set aside by the s 106B orders, the property of the parties to the marriage or either of them was to be identified as including the right of the wife to due administration of the Trust, accompanied by the fiduciary duty of the husband, as trustee, to consider whether and in what way the power should be exercised. And because, during the marriage, the husband could have appointed the whole of the Trust fund to the wife, the potential enjoyment of the *whole* of that fund was 'property of the parties to the marriage or either of them'.

17.61   Kiefel J dealt with the issues according to s 85A. She found that the original trust was a settlement for the purposes of the section (even though it had been created in 1968, many years before the marriage), and that each further contribution could be viewed as a new trust created at that time, for the purposes of the section. Her Honour, at CLR 443; ALR 317–8, said:

> Section 85A(1) is intended to have a wide operation, to property held for the benefit of the parties on a settlement and to which they have contributed. It is intended to apply to settlements whether they occur before or during marriage. The essential requirement of the section is that there be a sufficient association between the property the subject of a settlement and the marriage the subject of proceedings. It does not require that a settlement made prior to marriage be directed to the particular marriage at the point it is made. It is sufficient for the purposes of the section that the association of which it speaks (made in relation to) be present when the Court comes to determine the application of the property settled under s 85A(1). In the present case the Trust was used to hold property for the benefit of the parties to the marriage upon the terms of the Trust. It thereby acquired the nuptial element. Section 85A(1) applies.

17.62   According to Keifel J, the fact that the trust also concerned people outside of the marriage did not rob it of the connection to the marriage and the connection to s 85A. The question of whether a trust has the requisite nuptial element has to be answered by the contributions made by the married parties and the holding of property of their benefit.

17.63   Heydon J gave a rigorous dissent. His Honour did not view the interests of Dr Spry as proprietorial and therefore saw no reason for the employment of s 106B. On the issue of whether s 85A was relevant, Heydon J, at CLR [186]; ALR 306, stated:

> But can the Trust be said to be ante-nuptial? For a settlement to be an ante-nuptial or post-nuptial settlement, it must have a nuptial character: it must have been 'made in relation to the marriage'. That is, it must have been made in contemplation of the particular marriage in relation to which s 85A is invoked. There is nothing in the 'recitals or substance' of the Trust to suggest that it was. The fact that there are persons who are not connected with the marriage to which the settlement is said to relate who are 'substantial potential beneficiaries' prevents it being ante-nuptial or post-nuptial. At the time of the trial, apart from the four children of the husband and wife, the beneficiaries included the husband's sister, her three children and the daughter of the husband's deceased sister. The beneficiaries in future would include any person who married those five people, together with the issue of those marriages. In 1968 it was foreseeable that the beneficiaries would in due course be as numerous as they have turned out to be, and are likely

to be in future. Further, however wide the words 'made in relation to the marriage' in s 85A(1) are, and their breadth can vary from statute to statute, they cannot be stretched to establish the necessary relationship between the making of the Trust in 1968 and the marriage in 1978. The relevant settlement must be made in relation to *the* marriage, not simply in relation to marriage.

17.64   After the High Court's decision Dr Spry liquidated his assets and those in his daughter's trusts realising over $4.4m. In a restaurant conversation with two of his daughters he threatened to disappear and said that he would burn the money and go to gaol rather than comply with the court orders. One of the daughters went to Dr Spry's house and discovered the $4.4m in cash. She rang Mrs Spry and they removed the money and had it deposited in the trust account of Mrs Spry's solicitor. Enforcement proceedinsg were commenced. After Dr Spry agreed to the release of some of the funds to his wife (in exchange for some funds being released to him to pay his legal expenses) Coleman J ordered that the amount in the trust account be used to satisfy the outstanding sums owed to Mrs Spry (plus interest) with the remainder being released to Dr Spry (apart from a sum to be used to pay costs). Dr Spry appealed that decision on the basis that the money was trust money belonging beneficially to his daughters. The Full Family Court upheld the orders of Coleman J: *Stephens v Stephens (Enforcement)* (2009) 42 Fam LR 423.

Trusts which offend public policy

Trusts promoting immorality

17.65   Trusts can also be struck down because they offend public policy. For example, a trust that promotes immorality will be invalid. Under this heading, trusts in favour of future illegitimate children have been struck down: *Re Ayles' Trusts* (1875) 1 Ch D 282. However, it would seem highly unlikely that this would be the case in modern times.

17.66   Agreements can also be struck down when they are sexually immoral, such as when they enable prostitutes to carry on their trade: *Upfill v Wright* [1911] 1 KB 506; *Pearce v Brooks* (1866) LR 1 Exch 213; *Girardy v Richardson* (1793) 170 ER 275. In *Fender v St John-Mildmay* [1938] AC 1 at 42, Lord Wright said:

> The law will not enforce an immoral promise, such as a promise between a man and woman to live together without being married, or to pay a sum of money or to give some other consideration in return for immoral association.

17.67   However, cases concerning agreements to live in a de facto relationship now need to be viewed against the background of social and legal changes in the late twentieth–early twenty-first centuries. In *Andrews v Parker* [1973] Qd R 93, an agreement that a woman would return property should she forsake her de facto relationship and go back to her husband was upheld as it had not brought about the immoral relationship. Similarly, in *Seidler v Schallhofer* [1982] 2 NSWLR 80, an agreement to continue a de facto relationship for a period (wherafter the relationship would be abandoned or lead to marriage) was not void because the state of 'immorality' of the relationship was already in existence when the agreement was struck.

17.68   One might have argued that with the decriminalisation and/or legalisation of prostitution in most Australian jurisdictions that these public policy arguments may have lost their force. However, in *Ashton v Pratt (No 2)* [2012] NSWSC 3, Brereton J struck down an agreement for provisions of 'escort services' because, amongst other things, it promoted sexual immorality. The case concerned an escort,

Madison Ashton, who provided escort services to the late billionaire, Richard Pratt. Ashton alleged that she had contracted with Pratt to provide him with services as his mistress in exchange for him settling $5 million of trust for her two children, paying her $500,000 per annum, $36,000 per annum for rental accommodation and $30,000 per annum for travel expenses. Brereton J, at [52], said:

> The arrangements between Ms Ashton and Mr Pratt involved none of the saving graces which enabled a different result to be reached in the cases to which I have referred [including *Andrews v Parker* and *Seidler v Schallhofer*]. Those arrangements were not made to facilitate continuation of an existing cohabitation, but to establish the 'mistress relationship'. The evidence does not reveal a relationship, or consideration, beyond 'meretricious sexual services'. In my view, on the current state of the authorities, the arrangements were contrary to public policy and illegal in the relevant sense. Had they otherwise constituted a contract, it would have been void as contrary to public policy.

Trusts restraining marriage

17.69   Trusts that completely restrain a person from marrying, or which encourage a person to divorce, are also void: *Re Johnson's Will Trusts* [1967] 1 All ER 553.

17.70   Confusingly, a number of exceptions exist. A trust for one's widow or widower which ceases on their remarriage is valid: *Lloyd v Lloyd* (1852) 61 ER 338. Partial restraints on marriage, such as preventing marriage to a person of a particular religious denomination, race, ethnicity or class, have also been upheld: *Duggan v Kelly* (1847) 10 Ir Eq R 295; *Jenner v Turner* (1880) 16 Ch D 188. For example, a trust set up for a Baronet on the condition that he marry an approved wife, who had to be a woman of 'Jewish blood' who worshipped according to the Jewish faith, was upheld in *Re Tuck's Settlement* [1978] Ch 49; [1978] 1 All ER 1047. However, if a partial restraint is worded in such a way that it forces the beneficiary to divorce or prevents them from marrying it will be struck down: *Trustees of Church Property of the Diocese of Newcastle v Ebbeck* (1960) 104 CLR 394; [1961] ALR 339.

17.71   In *Ramsay v Trustees Executors & Agency Co Ltd* (1948) 77 CLR 321, a gift of income to the testator's son with an absolute gift to take effect at the end of the marriage with his present wife was also upheld. The intention of the testator was not to separate the married couple but merely to prevent the wife from receiving any interest in the funds. The son still got the benefit of the income from the trust while married, which indicated that there was no intention to encourage divorce.

17.72   In *Ellaway v Lawson* [2006] QSC 170, the testatrix left a gift in her will to her two daughters but required the interest of one daughter to be conditional on her divorcing her current husband or his death. Unlike *Ramsay*, there were no other gifts to this daughter. It was argued that the conditions were against public policy as they encouraged divorce and wished the husband dead. Douglas J rejected these arguments and upheld the condition. There did not appear to be an obligation imposed on the daughter to divorce. While troubled by the lack of any other gift, Douglas J thought that there were other means for ameliorating this problem (namely through a family maintenance application). Douglas J also opined that society's changing attitude to divorce may suggest that the public policy issue is no longer as prominent as it had been in the past, although his Honour declined to decide on that issue.

17.73   In *Jones v Krawczyk* [2011] NSWSC 139 at [38], White J discussed these issues and said:

> It does not logically follow that because the *Family Law Act* provides ready means for dissolving marriages that have broken down that there has been a change in public policy that marriages should be preserved and protected. In my view Parliament's recognition in s 43(1)(a) [of the

Family Law Act 1975] of the need to preserve and protect the institution of marriage cannot be dismissed as mere propaganda. It is a deliberate statement by the Commonwealth Parliament of public policy.

Nevertheless, White J upheld a testamentary condition that the deceased daughter was not be able take to control of the trust whilst married to, or living with, her husband. White J found that it was the deceased's intention to protect the daughter rather than to encourage her to divorce. White J, at [44], also found that:

> If the plaintiff receives adequate provision out of the estate for her proper maintenance, education and advancement in life, even if that provision is less than that which she would have received had she exercised a power of appointment of income or capital to herself as beneficiary, it is not likely that she would divorce and separate herself from her husband in order to obtain that power of appointment.

Trusts which separate parent and child

17.74   Trusts which have the effect of separating parent and child will also offend public policy: *Re Boulter* [1922] 1 Ch 75. If a gift is conditional on the children only living with their father this will offend public policy and the condition will be struck down: *Re Piper* [1946] 2 All ER 503.

17.75   In *Penfold v Perpetual Trustee* [2002] NSWSC 648, the testator had created a will where the children would get no capital benefits until the death and burial or cremation of their mother (who had been divorced from the testator). The children argued that the requirement was void against public policy because it had a tendency to wish their mother dead and engender hatred for her being alive. It was argued that the condition was calculated to cause family disharmony. Windeyer J disagreed and found that the fact that the children's interests were delayed was not an encouragement to hatred or murder. The intention of the testator was to ensure that his ex-wife would not benefit from his estate.

Trusts which demand the adherence to, or forbearance from, a religious faith

17.76   Conditional gifts which require the adherence to religious practice are not void against public policy, unless they have a secondary effect of creating strife between married partners or parents and children, or possibly interfere with the parents' capacity to raise a child (such as choosing whether they can go to a Catholic school): *Trustees of Church Property of the Diocese of Newcastle v Ebbeck*; *Re Tegg* [1936] 2 All ER 878.

17.77   Similarly, conditions which forbid adherence to particular faiths are also upheld on similar bases, such as forfeiture on the person's adherence to Roman Catholicism: *Blathwayt v Lord Cawley* [1976] AC 397; [1975] 3 All ER 625.

Trusts which discriminate on the basis of race

17.78   As the partial restraints on marriage demonstrate, there is no general prohibition on the imposition of racially discriminatory conditions being part of a trust. In *Kay v South Eastern Sydney Area Health Service* [2003] NSWSC 292, the testatrix (who wrote her own will) gave a gift on trust as follows:

> I give The Children's Hospital at Randwick $10,000 for treatment of White [underlined twice] babies.

It was argued that the condition was against public policy and that the condition could be struck off leaving the disposition free of it. Young J disagreed and found that the condition was an integral part of the gift which could not be removed. Both s 8 of the *Racial Discrimination Act 1975* (Cth) and s 55 of the *Anti-Discrimination Act 1977* (Cth), expressly provide that any charitable disposition is not subject to the Act. On that basis Young J found that there was no public policy against a racist condition. The gift was a valid charitable gift and on that basis was upheld.

17.79 There are issues that remain unresolved after *Kay v South Eastern Sydney Area Health Service*. The first relates to non-charitable gifts which contain racist or religious conditions. It might be argued, using Young J's logic, that non-charitable trusts and gifts offend public policy as these are not specifically exempted from the provisions of the legislation at the state and federal level.[8]

17.80 Additionally, s 12 of the *Racial Discrimination Act 1975* (Cth) expressly prohibits a person from refusing to dispose of an interest in land to another by reason of race, colour or national or ethnic origin. State-based anti-discrimination laws have similar prohibitions but exclude testamentary dispositions from the prohibition.[9]

17.81 Another issue is whether the institutions which receive such gifts should employ them in the fashion dictated by the gift. In *Kay v South Eastern Sydney Area Health Service* Young J stated that the hospital could either refuse the gift or take the gift and then set aside more of its general funds for the treatment of non-white babies. The danger of such an approach is that it may cause the donee to fall foul of the legislative prohibitions on racially based service provision.

17.82 The final issue relates to the problem of uncertainty in the racial categories used in some of these gifts. As Young J recognised in *Kay v South Eastern Sydney Area Health Service*, the general phrases commonly used in such dispositions often fail for want of certainty. In *In re Tarnpolsk* [1958] 1 WLR 1157, the phrase 'a person of the Jewish race' was found to be uncertain. Similarly, in *Clayton v Ramsden* [1943] 1 All ER 16 at 19, the phrase 'not of Jewish parentage' was found to be uncertain as it did not stipulate 'what percentage or proportion of Jewish blood' would satisfy the condition. In *Re Allen; Faith v Allen* [1953] Ch 810 at 817; [1953] 2 All ER 898 at 902, Lord Evershed MR gave the example of 'pure blooded Englishman' as an uncertain term. In *Kay v South Eastern Sydney Area Health Service* a further gift of a house with a condition that it could be sold to a 'young white Australian couple' was found to be completely valueless, as it was not clear what was meant by the word 'white', or 'Australian', or 'couple'.

17.83 It should be said here that the present state of the law with regard to racist conditions is entirely unsatisfactory and there is need for reform. Many of the older cases were decided at times when racism was an accepted part of life. It is difficult to see how such concepts can continue to be employed in an age when the very concept of race is questioned. That is not to say that the wishes of donors should be afforded no respect, but it is time to reopen the question of whether such categories of condition clearly harm the public interest.

---

8. J D Heydon & M J Leeming, *Jacobs' Law of Trusts in Australia*, LexisNexis Butterworths, Sydney, 2006, p 120.
9. *Discrimination Act 1991* (ACT) s 21; *Anti-Discrimination Act 1991* (Qld) ss 76–80; *Equal Opportunity Act 1984* (SA) s 38; *Equal Opportunity Act 1995* (Vic) ss 47–48; *Equal Opportunity Act 1984* (WA) ss 21A, 35AN, 47A, 66ZH.

Mistake, misrepresentation, undue influence and incapacity

17.84   A trust will be set aside when it has been created by a settlor who has laboured under a fundamental mistake as to the nature of the transaction. Such a settlor can plead that the trust was not created by his or her action (*non est factum*): *Saunders v Anglia Building Society* [1971] AC 1004. Less serious cases of mistake concerning terms of the trust might be cured by rectification of the trust document: *Re Butlin's Settlement Trusts* [1976] Ch 251.

17.85   If the settlor has been induced to create a trust by misrepresentation, or has been pressured into creating a trust via undue influence, the trust will be voidable: *Johnston v Johnston* (1884) 52 LT 76; *Williams v Bayley* (1866) LR 1 HL 200. A recent example of fraudulent misrepresentation in the creation of a trust is *Tjiong v Tjiong* [2012] NSWCA 201. This case involved the estate of the late George Tjiong. Two of George's children, Katrina and Lindsay, sought to set aside a discretionary trust which had been created by George's brother and executor, Richard Tjiong, who was also trustee of the discretionary trust. The court held that the daughters had been fraudulently deceived into giving their consent to the creation of the trust. They were falsely told that they would avoid a large tax liability and therefore be better off financially by settling a trust. The court also found that Richard had made payments in breach of trust and had fabricated a claim against the deceased estate.

17.86   Similarly, a trust, whether created *inter vivos* or by will, will be set aside if the person lacked the mental capacity to understand the nature and effect of the transaction. The person's capacity must be disproven, as the law presumes that all adults have capacity: *Hawkes v Wilkie* [2012] NSWSC 1039 at [15]; *Owners of Strata Plan No 23007 v Cross* (2006) 153 FCR 398 at 414; *Szoda v Szoda* [2010] NSWSC 804 at [20]–[26]. The settlor will lack capacity when he or she understands the transaction but has delusions about other aspects relating to the disposition and is thus incapable of making a rational decision in relation to the trust property: *Crago v McIntyre* [1976] 1 NSWLR 729. Such a trust is voidable at the option of the settlor (or his or her representative). Trusts made by minors, or by those affected by drugs, are voidable.[10]

Restraints on alienation

17.87   Once property has been given absolutely on trust, any restraint that is inconsistent or repugnant to that absolute gift will be invalid. For example, a restraint purporting to prevent the sale of the property after it has been given absolutely will be void: *Public Trustee v Donoghue* [1999] TASSC 147. Similarly, in *Brandon v Robinson* (1811) 34 ER 379, a trust which granted a life interest was given on the basis that the life interest was not transferable. This restraint was void because the life interest contained a power to alienate, which was offended by the condition subsequent.

17.88   A partial restraint may not be void if it does not hamper the enjoyment of the property. A restraint that limits transfer of the property to family members might be upheld if the family is large: *Re Macleay* (1875) LR 20 Eq 186. However, in *Re Brown (dec'd); District Bank v Brown* [1954] Ch 39, a restraint that allowed sale only to one or more of three brothers was found to be too restrictive.

17.89   A distinction must be drawn between an absolute gift that is subject to a restraint, and a determinable interest that automatically ends on the happening of some event. The absolute gift,

---

10.   Heydon & Leeming, note 8 above, pp 52–3.

which is subject to a condition subsequent, in effect grants a complete interest, that is then divested on the satisfaction of the condition. As such, this type of condition subsequent is void as a restraint on alienation. If, however, the interest transferred in trust is determinable, the interest is considered to have ended naturally on the occurrence of the event: *Hood v Oglander* (1865) 55 ER 733 at 737. The difference relates purely to the form and wording of the disposition: *In re Scientific Investment Pension Plan Trusts* [1999] Ch 53; [1998] 3 All ER 154.

17.90   For example, a trust 'to A on trust for B for life, but if B ceases to use the property as a hotel, then to C' is considered to contain a restraint on alienation. The life interest is granted to B, but can be artificially cut short by the event of B no longer using the property as a hotel. Such a condition subsequent is a restraint on alienation. However, if the trust was worded 'to A on trust for B for life until B ceases to use the property as a hotel', B's life interest is always limited in time to the event of the property no longer being used as a hotel. If and when the property is no longer used as a hotel, B's estate comes naturally to an end. This disposition is not considered to be an absolute gift with a limitation, as the interest contains the limitation within itself. As such, there is no restraint on the interest granted.

17.91   Ford and Lee state some examples of words that are usually treated as conferring a defeasible interest subject to a condition subsequent.[11] They are 'but if', 'provided that' or 'on the condition that'. Words that are commonly taken to create a determinable interest include 'until', 'during' and 'so long as'.

17.92   If a condition subsequent is treated as being an invalid restraint on alienation it is struck out, leaving the disposition free of it: *Yates v University College London* (1875) LR 7 HL 438.

The rule against indestructible trusts

17.93   A trust instrument that seeks to prevent beneficiaries from eventually using and exhausting the capital of the trust funds will be void. Such a trust is objectionable because it prevents the trust property from being alienable: *Re Cain* [1950] VR 382 at 391. Such a trust also offends the rights of beneficiaries under the rule in *Saunders v Vautier* (1841) 49 ER 282: see Chapter 23. The rule against indestructible trusts does not apply to charitable trusts as they are for purposes and not for beneficiaries.

A perpetual gift of income or a gift of capital and income?

17.94   If a trust gives an unlimited and perpetual gift of income, the courts may adopt a rule of construction which reads the gift as one of the capital of the fund as well as the income. This allows such trusts to avoid the rule against indestructibility. There is English authority which allows this presumptive rule of construction to only be used in cases of private (non-charitable) trusts, because only private trusts are affected by the rule against indestructibility: *Re Levy* [1960] Ch 346. However, in *Congregational Union of New South Wales v Thistlethwayte* (1952) 87 CLR 375, the High Court found that the rule of construction may be applied to both charitable and non-charitable trusts. As the rule is one of construction it can be rebutted by evidence of the creator's actual intention.

---

11.   Ford & Lee, note 1 above, [7160].

17.95   The Australian cases show the rule of construction has been relatively easy to rebut in cases of charitable trusts: *Re Denheart (dec'd)* [1973] VR 449; *Re Williams (dec'd)* [1955] VLR 65. The effect of rebutting the rule of construction in cases of charitable trusts is to limit the rights of the charitable beneficiary to call upon the capital of the fund for distribution: *Melbourne Jewish Orphan & Children's Aid Society Inc v ANZ Executors & Trustee Company Ltd* [2007] VSC 26.

THE RULE AGAINST PERPETUITIES

17.96   The rule against perpetuities, which is sometimes referred to as the rule against remoteness of vesting, prevents interests in property becoming vested at times too remote in the future. The purpose behind the rule is to place time limits on the creation of interests in property that prevent testators from being able to forever control property from the grave via the use of infinite successive interests.[12]

17.97   The rule applies to both private and charitable trusts: *National Tourism Development Authority v Coughlan* [2009] IEHC 53. In charitable trusts the property must vest in the trustee within the perpetuity period. If there is a gift for charitable purposes with a gift over to a non-charitable purpose, the rule of perpetuities will apply to both. Should the gift be based on the satisfaction of a condition subsequent and the event occur outside the perpetuity period, the gift over is void, and the initial gift for charitable purposes is taken absolutely: *The Cram Foundation v Corbett-Jones* [2006] NSWSC 495; *Re Bowen, Lloyd Phillips v Davis* [1893] 2 Ch 491; *Re Baillie, Faithful v Sydney Industrial Blind Institution* (1907) 7 SR (NSW) 265. If however the charitable gift is a determinable condition or dedication, the disposition is not subject to the rule against perpetuities, as the reverter interest is considered already vested: *Freemasons Hospital v Attorney General of Victoria* [2010] VSC 373 at [107]; *The Cram Foundation v Corbett-Jones* at [42]. For the differences between conditions subsequent and determinable conditions see 17.89.

17.98   The rule does not apply to general powers of appointment, because under a general power of appointment the donee can become the owner of the property. However, the rule does apply to special powers of appointment and hybrid and intermediate powers where the trustee cannot appoint himself or herself: *Nemesis Australia Pty Ltd v Commissioner of Taxation* (2005) 150 FCR 152; 225 ALR 576.

17.99   The rule is arguably the most hated and obscure of the property laws handed down from our English forebears. However, as McCrimmon observes:

> While strong arguments can be made for the abolition of the Rule, that fact remains that it is part of our law and legal practitioners and law students should have an understanding of its application.[13]

17.100   There are three versions of the rule:

1. the old rule against perpetuities;
2. the modern rule against perpetuities; and
3. the modern rule as modified by statute.

---

12. L McCrimmon, 'Understanding the Rule Against Perpetuities: Adopting a Five Step Approach to a Perpetuities Problem' (1997) 5 *Australian Property Law Journal* 130 at 131.
13. McCrimmon, note 12 above, p 130.

The old rule against perpetuities

17.101   The old rule against perpetuities stated that a gift to an unborn person with a remainder to the unborn person's children was void: *Whitby v Mitchell* (1890) 44 Ch D 85. For example, a gift of a life estate to A, with the remainder to his unborn daughter for life, with remainder to her children was void. Such a gift would take as a contingent gift to the unborn daughter, free of the successive remainders. This version of the rule has been abolished.[14]

The modern rule against perpetuities

17.102   The modern rule against perpetuities can be stated as follows: an interest that is created to vest some time in the future, must vest within a life in being plus 21 years from the date the instrument becomes effective: *Cadell v Palmer* (1883) 6 ER 956; *Air Jamaica Ltd v Charlton* [1999] 1 WLR 1399 at 1408–9. If it is possible that the interest will vest outside this period it will be void, even if it is probable that the interest will vest within the period. The slightest chance of the interest vesting outside the period will be enough for the interest to be struck down. Note that the rule is *not* concerned with how long an interest will last. It is only concerned that the interest *vest* within the perpetuity period.

17.103   Importantly, the issue of vesting is determined at the date the instrument takes effect. For example, if the instrument is a will, the issue of vesting is examined at the date of the testator's death. Alternatively, if the trust is created *inter vivos*, the issue of vesting is determined at the date the trust instrument becomes effective. An interest that is uncertain at this time will breach the rule even where it has, through the passage of time, actually vested within the period.

Vested and contingent interests

17.104   A 'vested interest' is an interest in property that has taken effect in possession, or one that *will* take effect in possession through the natural determination of prior estates: *Austin v Wells* [2008] NSWSC 1266 at [12]. To illustrate, consider a gift 'to A on trust for B for life, and then to C'. This disposition contains three separate interests: the legal title of A as trustee, the equitable life estate in B and the remainder to C. All of these interests are considered to be vested. A's interest has taken effect in possession. A is a trustee and has legal title from the instant the instrument comes into effect. Similarly, B has an interest in possession because the equitable right is enforceable from the moment the trust is constituted. C's interest in remainder has not yet taken effect in possession, but we know that it will because eventually B will die and the remainder will automatically pass to C. Additionally, C is an ascertained person and there is no question about his or her identity nor any contingency that must be satisfied before C can take his or her interest. In that sense, C is said to be 'vested in interest'.

17.105   To contrast, consider a gift of property 'to A on trust for B for life, then to C if C attains 21 years'. Unlike the previous example, C's interest will not automatically come into possession on B's death. C's interest is subject to a contingency, and is referred to as a 'contingent remainder'. C's interest will only vest if C attains the age of 21.

---

14.   *Conveyancing Act 1919* (NSW) s 23A; *Perpetuities Act 1994* (NT) s 21; *Property Law Act 1974* (Qld) s 216; *Law of Property Act 1936* (SA) s 61; *Perpetuities and Accumulations Act 1992* (Tas) s 21; *Perpetuities and Accumulations Act 1968* (Vic) s 12; *Property Law Act 1969* (WA) s 114.

Rules of construction

17.106   There are a number of rules of construction which can be applied by judges to discern whether interests are vested or contingent. Generally speaking, the courts will adopt an interpretation that favours the creation of vested interests rather than contingent ones. There are three main examples of rules of construction which are relevant here:

- A gift which grants an interest but then postpones that interest until the beneficiary reaches a certain age is considered to be a vested interest. For example, a gift 'to B, to be payable when B reaches 25 years' creates a vested interest in B which is subject to a condition subsequent: *Re Croser* (1973) 6 SASR 420. If B doesn't reach 25 years of age then the gift will be divested. Such a gift is unlike a gift 'to B if A attains 25 years' because it grants an interest immediately but then postpones the enjoyment of the gift, whereas the gift 'to B if B attains 25 years' gives B nothing until he or she reaches 25.
- A gift which includes a right to income will be treated as a vested interest even if the gift is conditional on reaching a certain age. For example, a gift of a fund to 'B if B attains 25 years' is contingent but if trustees are directed to pay income to B prior to reaching 25 years, the courts will find B's interest is vested, as beneficial rights have been bestowed on B prior to reaching the stipulated age.
- A conditional gift which includes a gift over to another if the condition is not satisfied is presumed to create a vested interest in the first donee. For example, a gift 'to the eldest son of X living at my death if he attains 25 years, but if he dies under 25, to Y', is interpreted to give the eldest son of X under 25 a vested interest which is subject to divesting should he not reach the age of 25.[15] This is known as the rule in *Phipps v Ackers* (1842) 8 ER 539. It applies to both personalty and realty: *Collins v Equity Trustees* [1997] 2 VR 166 at 169; *Re Heath* [1936] Ch 259. The rule was applied by the Full Court of the Family Court in *Coventry v Smith* where the relevant gift was held on trust for the husband but on the condition that he survive to the distribution date of the trust. The disposition also provided for a gift over should the husband not survive to the distribution date. The husband's interest was found to be vested and, as such, his beneficial interests were assets available for distribution on divorce.

The perpetuity period: a life in being plus 21 years

17.107   To satisfy the modern rule against perpetuities the interest must be certain to vest within the perpetuity period. The perpetuity period is equivalent to a life in being plus an additional 21 years. The phrase 'a life in being' is usually a reference to the life of someone mentioned expressly in the disposition. The life in being must be human and the person must be alive at the date of the creation of the interest: *Re Kelly; Cleary v Dillon* [1932] IR (Irish) 255 at 260. For example, in a gift to 'B for life and then to any children of B who attain 18 years' the life in being is taken to be B. The contingent interests of the unborn children must vest within 21 years after the death of B.

17.108   More than one person can be employed in a disposition as 'lives in being'. When a class is used, the 21 years runs from the death of the last survivor in the class. Classes will only be valid if the class is not capable of increasing in number when the instrument takes effect. Moreover, the class must be capable of ascertainment at the date the instrument comes into effect. Classes

---

15.   Ford & Lee, note 1 above, [7,300].

that are impossible to ascertain will not be able to constitute lives in being. However, where ascertainment is merely difficult, as opposed to impossible, the class will be upheld. For example, a gift that shall not vest until '21 years after the death of the last survivor of all persons living at my death' is invalid because the lives in being are uncertain and impossible to ascertain: *Re Moore* [1901] 1 Ch 936.

17.109 Lives in being can also be implied from the wording of the disposition. For example, in a gift in a will 'to A on trust for such of my grandchildren as attain 21 years' the lives in being are implied to be the children of the settlor, even though they are not expressly mentioned in the disposition: *Yeomans v Yeomans* [2005] QSC 085 at [21]. This is because the disposition is effective upon the death of the settlor and at this stage the class of grandchildren is still capable of increase. Therefore, the grandchildren cannot be employed as the lives in being. In contrast, it is not possible for the testator to have further children, meaning that the class of children is closed. Hence, the children of the testator will be the lives in being, as opposed to the grandchildren.

17.110 The lives in being need not be the lives of those who are taking an interest in the property. A disposition can expressly define the lives in being to be another class of person, as long as the class is ascertainable at the time of the instrument coming into effect. A popular example of this principle is the 'royal lives' clause where the lives in being are defined to be the descendants of a particular member of the royal family. For example, in *Clay v Karlson* (1998) 19 WAR 287, the life in being was defined to be the last living survivor of King George V.

17.111 If no lives are stipulated then the length of the perpetuity period will be 21 years. If the life in being is an unborn child (*en ventre sa mere* — 'in the belly of the mother') the length of gestation is added to the perpetuity period.

Some examples of the workings of the rule

17.112 Below are some classic examples that illustrate the workings of the modern rule against perpetuities:

- An inter vivos gift *'to A on trust for B for life, and then to any of B's children that marry'*. In this disposition the life in being is taken to be B. If B is alive at the time of the creation of the trust, the gift to the children is void. B's interest is vested but the children's interest is contingent on them marrying. B may have children after the trust is created and those children might marry more than 21 years after B's death.
- A gift of a gravel pit *on trust to A to use until the pit is exhausted, and then to be sold and divided equally among the testator's living issue*. Assume that the pit is actually exhausted after six years. This gift will still be void because at the date the gift becomes effective it may take longer than a life in being and 21 years for the pit to be exhausted. This is known as an example of the magic gravel pit: *Re Wood* [1894] 2 Ch 394; *Longtom Pty Ltd v Oberon Shire Council* (1996) 7 BPR 14,799.
- A gift *'to A on trust for B for life, then to anyone who may become B's wife for life, then for B's eldest son then living'*. B is the life in being. B's life interest is vested. The interest of any wife he marries will be vested from the time of the marriage as it will come into effect on the natural determination of B's interest, that being his death. The vesting occurs within the perpetuity period as she must marry B within his lifetime. However, the remainder to the eldest son will fail. B might marry a very young person who has not been born at the time of the creation of the

instrument. She could survive him by more than 21 years. The interest of the son is contingent on the son being the eldest living son at the time of his mother's death. As such, the son's interest might vest outside the perpetuity period. This is known as the example of the unborn widow: *Harris v King* (1936) 56 CLR 177.

• *A testamentary gift 'to A, my wife, for life, then to A's children for life, then for such of any children of my brother and sister who attain 21'.* In this example, the wife is treated as the life in being. Assume that at the death of the testator his parents were both aged 66. Regardless of this fact, it is presumed under the modern rule that both parents were fertile and could produce more children. Therefore, the gift over to the nephews and nieces is too remote as it was possible that the parents of the testator could have more children who might then also have children and add to the class more than 21 years after the death of the wife. This is known as the example of the fertile octogenarian: *Ward v Van der Loeff* [1924] AC 653.

• *A testamentary gift to 'A for life, then for such of A's grandchildren that are alive at my death, or born within five years after, who attain the age of 21'.* In this example, assume that A was aged 65 at the time the will came into operation. She also had two surviving children and one grandchild. This disposition is also invalid under the modern rule. In this example, A must be the life in being. A is presumed to be fertile, so the implied class of A's children is capable of increase. Additionally, the class of A's grandchildren is also capable of increase. It is theoretically possible that A might have another child after the testator's death. That child might theoretically be able to give birth within five years of being born. Hence, a grandchild might be born within the five-year period but not reach 21 years within the perpetuity period. This is known as the example of the precocious toddler: *Re Gaite's Will Trusts; Banks v Gaite* [1949] 1 All ER 459.

These examples illustrate some of the more absurd workings of the rule. The presumptions of fertility, when coupled with the requirement of initial certainty, result in conclusions that are logical but senseless.

Class gifts and class closing rules

17.113   As the above examples illustrate, a gift that is made to an indeterminate class can only be valid if the exact nature of each member's interest is ascertained within the perpetuity period. For example, in a gift to 'A on trust for B for life and then such of B's children that attain 25 years', the disposition to the children will be wholly invalid. B is the life in being. It is possible that B could have children who will not turn 25 within 21 years after his or her death. The entire gift to the children will fail even for those children who do turn 25 within the perpetuity period.

17.114   The class closing rules, which are sometimes referred to as the rule in *Andrews v Partington* (1791) 29 ER 610, can operate to save such dispositions. Class closing rules come into effect where a person disposes an interest upon an identified class of persons who must attain a certain age before they will receive their interest, for example, 'to A on trust for all my children who attain the age of 18 years'. Under the rule the class closes when the first member of the class becomes entitled to the distribution of his or her share: *Bassett v Bassett* [2003] NSWSC 691. As soon as a child attains 18 years the class will close and only children who are alive at that time will qualify as coming within it. If the class closes before the perpetuity period it will not offend the modern rule: *Lehmann v Haskard* (unreported, SC(NSW), Young J, No 2335/96, 29 August 1996).

17.115   The class closing rules, while related to the rule against perpetuities, are separate from them, and as such they have survived the statutory modifications of perpetuities rules set out below: *Napper v Miller* [2002] NSWSC 1122.

Statutory modification of the rule

17.116   The rule against perpetuities has been abolished in South Australia: *Law of Property Act 1936* (SA) s 61. In other states a number of reforms have been introduced that lessen the harshest and most ludicrous incidents of the modern rule. Those reforms generally effect instruments created after their enactment, except in the Northern Territory and South Australia, where reforms have retrospective effect.

17.117   The primary reform has been the introduction of wait-and-see provisions.[16] This has reversed the initial certainty rule so that an interest will not infringe the rule merely because it appears to have the potential to. Rather, the courts are required to postpone the invalidation of any infringing trust to see if the interests actually vest within the perpetuity period: *Yeomans v Yeomans*. In *Nemesis Australia Pty Ltd v Commissioner of Taxation*, there were a number of dispositions which could possibly have vested outside the perpetuity period. The court refused to invalidate the dispositions as it was possible that the interests could vest prior to the expiry of the period. Tamberlin J, at 586, found that the wait-and-see provisions applied so that the disposition must be treated as if it were not subject to the rule until such time as it becomes established that the vesting must occur outside the perpetuity period. Similarly, in *Public Trustee v Bennett* [2004] NSWSC 955 at [14], Gzell J said, in relation to the New South Wales Act:

> The *Perpetuities Act 1984*, s 8(1) provided that where a provision of a settlement that created an interest would infringe the rule against perpetuities, the interest should be treated, until such time (if any) as it became certain that it must vest, if at all, after the end of the perpetuity period, as if the provision did not infringe that rule and its becoming so certain did not affect the validity of any thing previously done in relation to the interest. Section 9(1) provided that where a provision of a settlement created an interest and the vesting of the interest depended on the attainment by any person of a specified age and it became apparent that the provision would infringe the rule against perpetuities, but that it would not infringe that rule if the specified age had been a lesser age, the interest should, for all purposes, be treated as if, instead of its vesting depending on the attainment by the person of the specified age, its vesting depended on the attainment by the person of the greatest age that, if put in place of the specified age, would save the provision from infringing the rule.

17.118   The second major reform is in relation to the calculation of the perpetuity period. In some jurisdictions the period is set at 80 years automatically.[17] In other jurisdictions it is possible to select a period not more than 80 years in duration.[18] Failure to select a period in these jurisdictions will leave the traditional perpetuity period in place. In *Yeomans v Yeomans*, a case concerning a

---

16. *Perpetuities and Accumulations Act 1985* (ACT) s 9; *Perpetuities Act 1984* (NSW) s 8(1); *Law of Property Act 2000* (NT) s 184; *Property Law Act 1974* (Qld) s 210; *Perpetuities and Accumulations Act 1992* (Tas) s 9; *Perpetuities and Accumulations Act 1968* (Vic) s 6; *Property Law Act 1969* (WA) s 103.
17. *Perpetuities and Accumulations Act 1985* (ACT) s 8; *Perpetuities Act 1984* (NSW) s 7.
18. *Law of Property Act 2000* (NT) s 187; *Property Law Act 1974* (Qld) s 209; *Perpetuities and Accumulations Act 1992* (Tas) s 6; *Perpetuities and Accumulations Act 1968* (Vic) s 5; *Property Law Act 1969* (WA) s 101.

Queensland will, the testator had not selected an alternative perpetuity period and the common law period applied.

17.119   The third reform consists of an automatic reduction in age for beneficial interests that would fail because they are stipulated to take effect upon the beneficiaries reaching a specified age beyond 21 years plus a life in being. In some jurisdictions the age can be read down to an age that would not infringe the modern rule.[19]

TERMINATION BY BENEFICIARIES

17.120   The rule in *Saunders v Vautier* (1841) 49 ER 282 allows beneficiaries to terminate a trust when they are absolutely entitled, of the age of majority and in agreement. This rule and its exceptions are discussed in detail in Chapter 21.

---

19. *Perpetuities and Accumulations Act 1985* (ACT) s 10; *Perpetuities Act 1984* (NSW) s 9(1); *Law of Property Act 2000* (NT) s 191(1); *Property Law Act 1974* (Qld) s 213; *Perpetuities and Accumulations Act 1992* (Tas) s 11; *Perpetuities and Accumulations Act 1968* (Vic) s 9; *Property Law Act 1969* (WA) ss 105, 107.

18

CHARITABLE TRUSTS

INTRODUCTION

18.1 Charitable trusts are express trusts, which exist for a purpose rather than for identifiable beneficiaries. In *Attorney-General (NSW) v Perpetual Trustee Co Ltd* (1940) 63 CLR 209 at 222, Dixon and Evatt JJ said:

> A charitable trust is a trust for a purpose, not for a person. The objects of ordinary trusts are individuals, either named or answering a description, whether presently or at some future time. To dispose of property for the fulfilment of ends considered beneficial to the community is an entirely different thing from creating equitable estates and interests and limiting them to beneficiaries. In this fundamental distinction sufficient reason may be found for many of the differences in treatment of charitable and ordinary trusts.

18.2 In that sense the major difference between charitable and other express trusts is that charitable trusts are not subject to the beneficiary principle: *Commissioner of Taxation (Cth) v Bargwanna* (2012) 286 ALR 206 at 208. In other respects charitable trusts exhibit the same characteristics and are subject to the same rules regarding certainty, constitution and fiduciary duties as other express trusts. In this chapter we will examine the particular rules that apply to the identification and validity of charitable trusts. This chapter will also examine the small category of non-charitable purpose trusts that have also been found to be valid even though they offend the beneficiary principle.

18.3 Other differences between charitable trusts and express trusts should be noted. First, charitable trusts are often referred to as 'public' trusts because of the requirement that they confer a benefit on the general public.[1] Because of their public nature both the courts and the Attorneys-General of the states have power to supervise the operation of charitable trusts: *Num-Hoi, Pon Yu, Soon-Duc Society Inc v Num Pon Soon Inc* (2001) 4 VR 527. In relation to the role of the Attorney-General in disputes concerning charitable trusts, in *Tomasevic v Jovetic* [2011] VSC 131 at [6], Pagone J said:

> It is clear that there are some cases where the Attorney-General's 'presence' as a party is required to proceedings where there is a dispute concerning a charitable trust. The necessity for the Attorney-General to be a party depends upon the nature of the dispute … The necessity for the Attorney-General to be a party derives from the role of the Attorney-General as the guardian of charities. The Attorney-General also represents the Crown and is the legal protector of all persons

---

1. G E Dal Pont. *Equity and Trusts in Australia*, 5th ed, Lawbook Co, Sydney, 2011, p 841.

interested in charity funds. As representative of those holding a beneficial interest the role of the Attorney-General to a proceeding also binds all beneficiaries to the outcome of the proceeding.

In *Hum-Hoi, Pon-Yu, Soon-Duc Society Inc v Num Pon Soon Inc* at 534–5, it was held that the presence of the Attorney-General was required in proceedings involving the identity of the trustees, because the case was one concerning the conduct and management of a charity and only the Attorney-General had power to institute such proceedings.

18.4   Second, a charitable trust is not subject to the rule against indestructible trusts. A charitable trust can therefore be structured in such a way as to exist indefinitely: *Monds v Stackhouse* (1948) 77 CLR 232 at 247–8. However, charitable trusts are subject to the rule against perpetuities in that the trustee's interest must vest within the perpetuity period: *Re Goode (dec'd)* [1960] VR 117.

18.5   The third major difference between charitable and other express trusts is that the court has the inherent power to enforce and extensively vary the terms of charitable trusts, whereas it lacks such an extensive jurisdiction in relation to other express trusts. Because of those extensive powers it is impossible for a charitable trust to fail because of administrative unworkability: *Commissioner of Stamp Duties (NSW) v Way* (1951) 83 CLR 570.

THE MEANING OF 'CHARITABLE' PURPOSE

18.6   There is no exhaustive definition of the term 'charitable purpose'. Rather, the courts begin from the position established by the *Statute of Charitable Uses 1601* (43 Eliz I, c 4), which is sometimes referred to as the *Statute of Elizabeth*. The Preamble to the *Statute of Charitable Uses* contained a statement as to the types of charitable purpose that would be recognised at law. They include, in rough translation:

- the relief of poverty;
- care of aged persons and the sick;
- care of soldiers and mariners;
- advancement of education through universities and schools;
- repair of bridges, havens, ports, churches and highways;
- the care of orphans;
- the maintenance of prisons;
- the marriage of poor maids;
- support for young tradesmen and persons decayed;
- the relief or redemption of prisoners or captives; and
- relief for poor persons concerning the payment of taxes.

18.7   The statute has been repealed in some jurisdictions.[2] However, the Preamble is employed by judges as a tool for determining whether a purpose is charitable: *Royal National Agricultural and Industrial Association v Chester* (1974) 3 ALR 486 at 487. In New South Wales, the Australian Capital Territory and Queensland the continued use of the Preamble is given statutory recognition.[3] The

---

2.   *Legislation Act 2001* (ACT) s 17, Sch 1; *Imperial Acts Application Act 1969* (NSW) s 8; *Trusts Act 1973* (Qld) s 103(1).

3.   *Trustee Act 1925* (ACT) s 104, Sch 1; *Imperial Acts Application Act 1969* (NSW) s 9(2); *Trusts Act 1973* (Qld) s 103(1).

process employed by the court was described by Lord Simonds in *Gilmour v Coates* [1949] AC 426 at 442–3; [1949] 1 All ER 848 at 852, as follows:

> [F]rom the beginning it was the practice of the court to refer to the preamble of the statute in order to determine whether or not it was charitable. The objects there enumerated and all other objects which by analogy are 'deemed within its spirit and intendment' and no other objects are in law charitable. That is settled and familiar law.

18.8   The question of whether a purpose falls within the 'spirit and intendment' of the Preamble is a difficult one. By necessity the courts are required to reason by analogy and the analogies have widened over time. In *Scottish Burial Reform and Cremation Society v Glasgow Corp* [1968] AC 138 at 147, Lord Reid said:

> The courts appear to have proceeded first by seeking some analogy between an object mentioned in the preamble and the object with respect to which they had to reach a decision. And they then appear to have gone further and to have been satisfied if they could find an analogy between an object already held to be charitable and the new object claimed to be charitable. And this gradual extension has proceeded so far that there are few modern reported cases where a bequest or donation was made or an institution was being carried on for a clearly specified object which was for the benefit of the public at large and not of individuals, and yet the object was held not to be within the spirit and intendment of the Statute of Elizabeth I.

18.9   To illustrate the principle, in *Royal National Agricultural and Industrial Association v Chester*, a trust for the breeding and racing of pigeons failed because there was no analogous charitable purpose in the Preamble. Contrastingly, a trust for the not-for-profit publication of law reports was found to be charitable in *Incorporated Council of Law Reporting (Qld) v Federal Commissioner of Taxation* (1971) 125 CLR 659, on the grounds that the reporting of cases was fundamental to society in the same way that the maintenance of roads and the promotion of agriculture were fundamental and within the spirit of the Preamble. The examples show that the process of reasoning by analogy has not always provided strictly logical results. By the same token, the flexibility of the process has allowed judges to evolve the concept of charity over time: *Scottish Burial Reform and Cremation Society v Glasgow Corp* at 154.

18.10   A significant collation of the types of charitable purpose was accomplished by Lord Macnaughten in *Commissioner for Special Purposes of Income Tax v Pemsel* [1891] AC 531 at 583, where his Lordship said:

> 'Charity' in its legal sense comprises four principal divisions: trusts for the relief of poverty; trusts for the advancement of education; trusts for the advancement of religion; and trusts for other purposes beneficial to the community, not falling under the preceding heads.

Lord Macnaughten's four divisions proved popular and have been the starting point for the discussion of what is charitable for more than 100 years.

PUBLIC BENEFIT

18.11   In addition to the requirement that a purpose comes within the spirit and intendment of the Preamble, a charitable trust must provide a benefit to the public. The benefit must be for the entire public or for a significant proportion of it. In relation to the different meanings of 'benefit', in *Helena*

Partnerships Ltd v Commissioner for Her Majesty's Revenue and Customs [2012] EWCA Civ 569 at [78], Lloyd LJ said:

> Without attempting to lay down any rigid distinctions, there are charities which provide direct benefits to individuals, whether by way (for example) of the relief of the poor, the elderly or the infirm, education of students at schools or universities, or medical treatment in hospitals. These are the charities that provide direct benefits [to individuals]. They are justified as being for the public benefit on the basis that it is desirable that there should be such provision for those in particular need or, in the case of education, that it is a good thing that the population should receive education. There are other charities which provide less, or nothing, in the way of identifiable benefits to individuals, where the benefit is either entirely general (animal welfare, as instanced above, which is justified as promoting the moral improvement of the public generally) — these are cases of wider benefit as classified above — or the benefit is general although some individuals may obtain more benefit than others, such as bridges, sea-walls or fire brigades, again only by way of example — these provide indirect benefits as classified above. In the case of the first category of charities, it is seen as for the public benefit that the direct benefit to individuals should be available for, and provided to, those in need. In the latter cases, which include various examples of public works, the carrying out of the works is seen as for the public benefit, because of the public or general need, and the indirect benefit to individuals is incidental to that of the public, because of the nature of the operations in question and the way in which their benefits are experienced.

18.12   There may be two reasons why a trust for a charitable purpose will fail for want of public benefit. First, a charitable trust will fail if it confers no public benefit at all. For example, trusts established to stop the practice of vivisection have failed because there would be an overall detrimental effect to the public should such experimentation cease: *National Anti-Vivisection Society v Inland Revenue Commissioners* [1948] AC 31 at 46–9. Furthermore, trusts for the advancement of religion have failed where they have the object of favouring cloistered or contemplative orders who have little contact with the outside world: *Gilmour v Coats* [1949] AC 426. However, *Gilmour v Coats* was doubted in *Crowther v Brophy* [1992] 2 VR 97 at 100, where Gobbo J said:

> It is at least open to doubt whether *Gilmour v Coats* represents the law in Australia where there has been a number of decisions recognising that the contemplative life may convey sufficient elements of public benefit to make assistance for the pursuit of such life charitable within the traditional definition of charity … [I]t may be that the test of the success of intercessory prayer [in *Gilmour v Coats*] is an inappropriate test and that the enhancement in the life, both religious and otherwise, of those who found comfort and peace of mind in their resort to intercessory prayer was a more appropriate consideration to adopt.

It should also be noted that, in relation to charities subject to federal jurisdiction the decision in *Gilmour v Coats* has been overruled by legislation: see 18.50.

18.13   Second, a charitable trust will fail where benefit is provided to a group or class whose membership excludes other members of the public, based on inherent personal characteristics. For example, a trust for the descendants of three children failed in *Re Compton* [1945] Ch 123. Lord Greene MR, at 131, said:

> [A] gift under which the beneficiaries are defined by reference to a purely personal relationship to a named propositus cannot on principle be a valid charitable gift. And this, I think, must be

the case whether the relationship be near or distant, whether it is limited to one generation or is extended to two or three or in perpetuity. The inherent vice of the personal element is present however long the chain and the claimant cannot avoid basing his claim on it.

18.14 The *Compton* test has been used to strike down charitable trusts when the potential recipients of the trust funds have been defined by reference to blood relation, employment or contract: *Re Mills (dec'd)* (1981) 27 SASR 200. For example, a gift to a school exclusively for the children of Masons was found to be non-charitable in *Thompson v Federal Commissioner of Taxation* (1959) 102 CLR 315.

18.15 Similarly, trusts for the employees of a company and their relatives are also non-charitable: *Davies v Perpetual Trustee Co Ltd* [1959] AC 439; [1959] 2 All ER 128. In *Oppenheim v Tobacco Securities Co Ltd* [1951] AC 297; [1951] 1 All ER 31, a trust had been created to provide for the educational needs of children of the employees and former employees of a company and its subsidiaries. The total number of employees of the group of companies exceeded 110,000. Nevertheless, the trust was not said to be of benefit to a section of the public. Lord Simonds, at AC 306; All ER 34, said:

> These words 'section of the community' have no special sanctity, but they conveniently indicate first, the possible (I emphasise the word 'possible') beneficiaries must not be numerically negligible, and secondly, that the quality which distinguishes them from other members of the community, so that they form by themselves a section of it, must be a quality which does not depend on their relationship to a particular individual ... A group of persons may be numerous but, if the nexus between them is their personal relationship to a single propositus or to several propositi, they are neither the community or a section of the community for charitable purposes.

18.16 Some qualifications on the operation of the *Compton* test should be noted. First, the requirement for public benefit does not apply to trusts for the relief of poverty: *Dingle v Turner* [1972] AC 601; [1972] 1 All ER 878. For example, and as a point of contrast to *Thompson v Federal Commissioner of Taxation*, a trust for the relief of poverty for the children of Freemasons was upheld in *NSW Masonic Youth Property Trust v Attorney-General of NSW* [2009] NSWSC 1301 at [177]–[216].

18.17 Secondly, trusts for people from particular geographic locales do not offend the rule, as they can be applied regardless of inherent personal characteristics: *Re Tree* [1948] Ch 325; 2 All ER 65.

18.18 Thirdly, a request by the creator that family members, or others connected by association or contract, be given preference in the administration of the charity, will not invalidate the trust: *Public Trustee v Young* (1980) 24 SASR 407. For example, in *Permanent Trustee Co (NSW) Ltd v Presbyterian Church (NSW) Property Trust* (1946) 64 WN (NSW) 8, a trust which established educational scholarships was upheld, even though the testator had directed that preference be given to his lineal descendants. Roper J, at 10, said:

> The principle underlying in these cases appears to be that provided the paramount purpose of the foundation or endowment is to benefit the public or a section of it, the requirement that a private class of person be preferred is effective and does not affect the validity of the gift.

18.19 The purpose of the trust need not be effected in the jurisdiction for it to be of benefit to the public, so that gifts to benefit people overseas will be charitable: *Kytherian Association of Qld v Sklavos* (1958) 101 CLR 56; *Public Trustee of Queensland v Neale* [2008] QSC 343.

Presuming public benefit

18.20 It has long been said that there is a rebuttable presumption that trusts for relief of poverty, advancement of religion and advancement of education are of benefit to the public: *National Anti-Vivisection Society v Inland Revenue Commissioners* at 42. Trusts that fall into the fourth category of *Pemsel's* case must be proven to be beneficial.

18.21 This approach was doubted by the Upper Tribunal (Tax and Chancery Chamber) in *Independent Schools Council v Charity Commission for England and Wales* [2012] 1 All ER 127 at 148–53. The tribunal, at 152, found against a presumption of public benefit and said:

> We think that Lord Wright's approach [in *National Anti-Vivisection Society*] was simply a recognition of how a judge would deal practically with a particular case before him. He would start with a predisposition that an educational gift was for the benefit of the community; but he would look at the terms of the trust critically and if it appeared to him that the trust might not have the requisite element, his predisposition would be displaced so that evidence would be needed to establish public benefit. But if there was nothing to cause the judge to doubt his predisposition, he would be satisfied that the public element was present. This would not, however, be because of a presumption as that word is ordinarily understood; rather, it would be because the terms of the trust would speak for themselves, enabling the judge to conclude, as a matter of fact, that the purpose was for the public benefit.

Frankly, the move to describing the presumption as a 'predisposition' adds little of any value. In any event, s 3(2) of the *Charities Act 2006* (UK) removes the presumption in English law, with the result that English authorities on this point have less utility in Australian jurisprudence than in earlier times. On that basis it is suggested that the rebuttable presumption of public benfit in the first three categories of *Pemsel's* case remains good law in Australia.

Political purposes trusts

18.22 A trust that has a political purpose will not be charitable. In *Bowman v Secular Society Ltd* [1917] AC 406 at 442, Lord Parker, in finding that the Secular Society's objects were non-charitable, said:

> The abolition of religious tests, the disestablishment of the Church, the secularization of education, the alteration of the law touching religion or marriage, or the observation of the Sabbath, are purely political objects. Equity has always refused to recognise such objects as charitable... [A] *trust for the attainment of political objects has always been held invalid*, not because it is illegal, for every one is at liberty to advocate or promote by any lawful means a change in the law, but *because the Court has no means of judging whether a proposed change in the law will or will not be for the public benefit, and therefore cannot say that a gift to secure the change is a charitable gift.* (Emphasis added.)

18.23 A trust will be deemed to be political when it has the purpose of changing the law: *Anti-Vivisection Society v Inland Revenue Commissioners*. Examples include a trust to establish a nationalised health service (*Re Bushell (dec'd)* [1975] 1 All ER 721), or to reform the alphabet (*Re Shaw* [1957] 1 All ER 745), or a trust to prevent the use of performing animals: *Hanchett-Stamford v Attorney-General* [2008] 4 All ER 323.

18.24   A gift to an organisation will be deemed political when the dominant purpose of the organisation can only be effectuated through legal change: *Re Cripps* [1941] Tas SR 19. For example, a gift to Amnesty International failed because the primary purpose of the organisation was to effect the release of political prisoners: *McGovern v Attorney-General* [1982] Ch 321; [1981] 3 All ER 493. It matters not that the legal changes may occur outside the jurisdiction. A gift to the Free Papua Movement was said to be political as the movement's aim was to wrest control of Irian Jaya from Indonesia: *Application of Van Campen-Beekman* [2007] NSWSC 916. If the dominant purpose is to maintain a law, for example, the prohibition of abortion, it will also be deemed to be non-charitable: *Molloy v Commissioner of Inland Revenue* [1981] 1 NZLR 688.

18.25   However, if changing or maintaining a law is only an incidental part of the purpose of the association, the gift may succeed: *Royal North Shore Hospital of Sydney v Attorney-General (NSW)* (1938) 60 CLR 396. Alternatively, if the purposes of the association include mixed charitable and political purposes, it may be possible to save the gift using legislation which prevents mixed gifts from failing: *Public Trustee v Attorney-General of New South Wales* (1997) 42 NSWLR 600 (see 18.114–18.120).

18.26   Writing extra-judicially, the late Justice Santow argued that the rule against political trusts should be varied. Not all changes to the law should be viewed as political, nor should all trusts which advocate such change be struck down. His Honour said:

> There is a crucial distinction, inhering in *McGovern*, between permissibly changing the law within the framework of its established policy and impermissibly reversing the law along with its established policy. Incremental change to the law consistent with its established direction may indeed be permitted today.[4]

Following Justice Santow's lead, Young CJ in Eq was equally critical of the *Bowman* principle in *Attorney-General (NSW) v The NSW Henry George Foundation Ltd* [2002] NSWSC 1128. That case concerned a trust to further the study of Henry George's ideas about a unitary land tax system, and pursuing them via legislative change. His Honour, at [63]–[64], said:

> There is a feeling of what I might call 'judicial cop out' in the policy that the court cannot judge the public benefit of proposals to amend the law. Indeed, in many instances, the fact that diverse arguments are presented to the public on issues of importance may itself be important to the community. Indeed, it is clear that when considering what is of benefit to the community, the court rules on what is beneficial at the date of the trust or at the hearing. Courts are well equipped to do this.

In any event, Young J found that the trust was intended to educate people about the works of Henry George and that the non-charitable parts of the trust, which sought legal change, could be severed: see 18.114–18.120.

18.27   Finally, the High Court considered the issue of charity and political activity in *Aid/Watch Incorporated v Commissioner of Taxation of the Commonwealth of Australia* (2010) 241 CLR 539; 272 ALR 417. This case concerned Aid/Watch which was an organisation that sought to promote

---

4.   G F K Santow, 'Charity in its Political Voice — a Tinkling Cymbal or a Sounding Brass?' (1999) 18 *Australian Bar Review* 225, p 247.

the more efficient use of Australian and multinational foreign aid directed to the relief of poverty. Its activities included research and public campaigns intended to generate public debate and to bring about changes in government policy and activity relating to the provision of foreign aid. By s 50-5 of the *Income Tax Assessment Act 1997* (Cth), ss 65J(1)(baa) and 123E of the *Fringe Benefits Tax Assessment Act 1986* (Cth) and s 176-1 of the *A New Tax System (Goods and Services Tax) Act 1999* (Cth), an entity which has been endorsed as a 'charitable institution' by the Commissioner is exempt from liability to taxation under those Acts. The term 'charitable institution' is not defined in the legislation. The issue before the High Court was whether Aid/Watch was a charitable institution.

18.28   The majority of the High Court (French CJ, Gummow, Hayne, Crennan and Bell JJ; Heydon and Kiefel JJ dissenting) held that Aid/Watch was a charitable institution. The majority held that the generation by lawful means of public debate concerning the efficiency of foreign aid directed to the relief of poverty was a purpose beneficial to the community and apt to contribute to the public welfare and, further, the fact that Aid/Watch's purposes and activities involved agitation for legislative and political change did not disqualify it from being found to be a charitable institution. Accordingly, the objects and activities of Aid/Watch qualified as charitable under the fourth category of charitable purposes recognised in *Pemsel's* case.

18.29   The High Court decision was subsequently distinguished in *Re Greenpeace New Zealand Inc* [2011] 2 NZLR 815. In that case Greenpeace had as one of its objects the promotion of a philosophy in support of protection of the environment. It also had as an object political activity in the form of promoting disarmament and peace. In determining whether Greenpeace's activities were charitable or not, Heath J, at 833, ruled that it was necessary to make both a qualitative and quantitative assessment of these political activities in order to determine whether or not they were merely ancillary to Greenpeace's charitable purposes. From a qualitative perspective, Greenpeace's political objectives were quite independent of its otherwise charitable purposes. This was in contrast to *Aid/Watch Incorporated v Commissioner of Taxation of the Commonwealth of Australia* where the activity was ancillary to its primary charitable purpose. In this respect, Heath J, at 836, observed that Greenpeace's 'political activities [were] not necessary to educate members of the public on the issues of concern to Greenpeace'. In relation to the quantitative assessment of Greenpeace's political activities, Heath J, at 836, concluded that 'the extent to which Greenpeace relies on its political activities to advance its causes means that the political element cannot be regarded as "merely ancillary" to [its] charitable purposes'.

CHARITABLE TRUSTS AND GOVERNMENTAL FUNCTIONS

18.30   Gifts to the government to carry out its ordinary functions are not charitable. The case of *Re Cain* [1950] VLR 382 concerned a gift to the Children's Welfare Department of Victoria. Dean J, at 138, said:

> In my opinion, if the present gift be construed as a gift for carrying on the ordinary activities of a Government department pursuant to a statute, the gift is not a gift for charitable purposes, even if the activities are such that if carried on by private persons they would be charitable. Such activities are simply part of the government of the country.

Neverthless, Dean J found the gift to be charitable as it was not to go into general revenue, but would rather be used for the benefit of the children in the government's care, in ways which had not otherwise been provided for by the government.

18.31 As Dean J's judgment illustrates, the problem with the rule against charitable gifts to government lies in the massive expansion of the role of government into the lives of the citizenry that occurred in the twentieth century. The birth of the welfare state and the governmental provision of health and education services has meant that government functions have swept up many of the areas which had in the past been the provision of charities.

18.32 The courts have attempted to draw distinctions between bodies that carry out the policies of the government, paid for by the government's revenue (which are not charitable), and bodies which provide services which are totally or partially funded by the government, but which are nevertheless not part of the government, and therefore charitable. These issues were considered by the High Court in *Central Bayside General Practice Association Ltd v Commissioner of State Revenue (Vic)* (2006) 228 CLR 168; 229 ALR 1. The case concerned a medical practice which was fully funded by the Commonwealth Government, and whose purposes included providing health care to the residents of the Bayside area, improving communications between patients and general practitioners, and meeting the special health needs of Aboriginal and Torres Strait Islanders and non-English speaking patients. While the objects of the practice were clearly charitable, the Victorian Commissioner for State Revenue had refused to classify the practice as charitable because it received the entirety of its funds from the Commonwealth Government. Nearly half of those funds had been granted under conditions that the practice had agreed to comply with. On that basis the Commissioner argued that the practice was so much under the control of the government that it should be treated as acting as an arm of the government.

18.33 The High Court found against the Commissioner. Gleeson CJ, Heydon and Crennan JJ found that the conditions of the grant were negotiated by the practice and not merely dictated by the government. There was not ongoing management and control by the government and, while donors were permitted to place conditions on the receipt of charitable funds, that did not render the practice an arm of government. Nor did the fact that the practice's purposes matched those of the government mean that the practice's charitable status had been lost. Gleeson CJ, Heydon and Crennan JJ, at CLR 184–5; ALR 12, said:

> The [practice] had a certain charitable purpose. The government wanted to advance the very same purpose. The [practice] decided to advance its purpose by receiving funds from the government and spending them in the manner it did. These events did not cause the [practice] to cease to be a charitable body merely by reason of the fact that the government is not a charitable body. Many charities implement government policy in the sense that their goals — providing education, aiding the sick and the poor — are the same as those of the government ... The mere fact that the [practice] and the government both have a purpose of improving patient care and health does not establish that the [practice] has the purpose of giving effect to government purposes, abdicating any independent fulfilment of its own. The [practice]'s purpose is charitable. It remains charitable even though the government is the source of the funds it uses to carry out that purpose. Its consent to the attachment by the government of conditions to the employment of those funds does not establish that the [practice] is not independently carrying out its purpose.

18.34   Kirby and Callinan JJ agreed. Kirby J, at CLR 210; ALR 33, who followed the analysis of Dean J in *Re Cain*, said:

> The reasoning behind this analysis suggests a bifurcation between bodies that carry out governmental policy, using funds derived from Consolidated Revenue; and bodies that receive public funds but are not part of the machinery of government. For bodies that are part of such machinery, the charitable 'purposes' necessary to attract characterisation as a 'charitable body' are absent. Their purposes are governmental. Such bodies are therefore no more than an agent of government. Their activities may be beneficial to individuals and to the community, but they are still performing activities decreed by government. They lack the spark of altruism and benevolence that is essential to characterisation as 'charitable'. They are, in Dean J's words, 'simply part of the Government of the country'.

CHARITABLE TRUSTS AND PROFITS

18.35   A charitable institution may make a profit, as long as that profit is reinvested back into the charitable purpose: *The Incorporated Council of Law Reporting of the State of Queensland v FCT* (1971) 125 CLR 659 at 669–70; *Crystal Palace Trustees v Minister of Town and Country Planning* [1951] 2 Ch 132; [1950] 2 All ER 857; *Re Tennant* [1996] 2 NZLR 633 at 640.

18.36   In *In re Resch's Will Trusts; Le Cras v Perpetual Trustee Co Ltd* [1969] 1 AC 514; [1967] 3 All ER 915, the charitable nature of a gift of income to the Sisters of Charity who operated for St Vincent's Private Hospital was questioned as the hospital charged for its services. The Privy Council ruled that the hospital was charitable. In delivering the judgment of the Privy Council, Lord Wilberforce, at AC 540–1; All ER 921, after noting that the purpose of a hospital was prima facie charitable, said the following as to what circumstances might lead to a hospital not being charitable:

> [T]here may be certain hospitals, or categories of hospitals, which are not charitable institutions. Disqualifying indicia may be either that the hospital is carried on commercially, ie, with a view to making profits for private individuals, or that the benefits it provides are not for the public, or a sufficiently large class of the public to satisfy the necessary tests of public character.

18.37   In relation to whether St Vincent's Private Hospital was run for profit, Lord Wilberforce, at AC 541; All ER 921, said:

> [I]t is accepted that [St Vincent's Private Hospital] is not run for the profit, in any ordinary sense, of individuals. Moreover, if the purposes of the hospital are otherwise charitable, they do not lose this character merely because charges are made to the recipients of benefits. But what is said is that surpluses are made and are used for the general purposes of the Sisters of Charity. This association, while in a broad sense philanthropic, has objects which may not be charitable in the legal sense. Furthermore its purposes, though stated in its 'constitutions' are not limited by law, other than the canon law of the Roman Catholic Church, and under this, they are empowered, and may be obliged, to alter their purposes so as to include other objects which, may not be strictly charitable. Their Lordships do not consider it necessary to enter on these latter considerations. For whatever the Sisters of Charity may be empowered to do with regard to their general property, as regards the … [gift of] income …, given to them as trustees, they are bound by the trusts declared in the will under which any money received by them must be applied exclusively for

the general purposes of the private hospital as above defined. As regards these purposes ... the making of profits for the benefit of individuals is not among them. The most that is shown is that, on a cash basis, and without making such adjustments as would be required for commercial accounting, a net surplus is produced over the years which in fact has been applied largely, though not exclusively for hospital purposes. The share of income given by the will must be devoted entirely to the purposes of the private hospital. The character, charitable or otherwise, of the general activities of the sisters, is not therefore a material consideration.

18.38   In relation to the issue of whether the hospital serviced 'a sufficiently large class of the public to satisfy the necessary tests of public character', it was argued that the hospital failed the test here because it excluded the poor from its benefits. In response to this argument, Lord Wilberforce, at AC 544; All ER 923, said:

> It would be a wrong ... to state that a trust for the provision of medical facilities would necessarily fail to be charitable merely because by reason of expense they could only be made use of by persons of some means. To provide, in response to public need, medical treatment otherwise inaccessible but in its nature expensive, without any profit motive, might well be charitable: on the other hand to limit admission to a nursing home to the rich would not be so. The test is essentially one of public benefit, and indirect as well as direct benefit enters into the account. In the present case, the element of public benefit is strongly present. It is not disputed that a need exists to provide accommodation and medical treatment in conditions of greater privacy and relaxation than would be possible in a general hospital and as a supplement to the facilities of a general hospital. This is what the private hospital does and it does so at, approximately, cost price. The service is needed by all, not only by the well-to-do. So far as its nature permits it is open to all: the charges are not low, but the evidence shows that it cannot be said that the poor are excluded: such exclusion as there is, is of some of the poor — namely those who have (a) not contributed sufficiently to a medical benefit scheme or (b) need to stay longer in the hospital than their benefit will cover or (c) cannot get a reduction of or exemption from the charges. The general benefit to the community of such facilities results from the relief to the beds and medical staff of the general hospital, the availability of a particular type of nursing and treatment which supplements that provided by the general hospital and the benefit to the standard of medical care in the general hospital which arises from the juxtaposition of the two institutions.

18.39   Property owned by charitable institutions may be let to businesses if those businesses conduct activities which are incidental to the charitable purpose: *Salvation Army (Vic) Property Trust v Fern Tree Gully Corporation* (1952) 85 CLR 159. In *Ryde Municipal Council v Macquarie University* (1978) 139 CLR 633; 178 ALR 41, it was found that the lease of a building at the university to businesses such as banks, book shops and food outlets was not a breach of the charitable purpose of the university (in the context of levying council rates). Gibbs CJ, at CLR 643; ALR 49, stated:

> Ordinarily speaking, one would not say that the purpose of the University was to provide shops or other commercial establishments for the use of staff or students. However, it is now well settled that when an exemption from rates or taxes is given in respect of land used for the purposes of a charity, the exemption is not confined to land used for those purposes the pursuit of which make the body a charity, ie, which give it its character as such. If the land is used for purposes which are merely a means to the fulfilment 'of the charitable purposes and incidental thereto' it is within the exemption.

However, the extent of the use of trust land for purposes outside of the charitable purpose is dependent on the terms of the trust, and if the use of trust land is restricted to purely charitable purposes, commercial usages may be breaches of trust. In *James Cook University v Townsville City Council* [2011] QSC 209, the court agreed that land dedicated to the functions of the university could be used for usages incidental to the charitable purposes of a university (such as retail and banking services for staff and students) but the court remained unconvinced that the land could be used for unrestricted commercial leasing.

18.40 In *Tasmanian Electronic Commerce Centre Pty Ltd v Commissioner of Taxation* (2005) 142 FCR 371; 219 ALR 647, the promotion of digital commerce and the provision of aid to businesses for that purpose was deemed to be charitable. Heerey J, at FCR 389; ALR 663, said:

> Once it is accepted that assistance to business and industry can provide a public benefit of the kind which the law recognises as charitable, a proposition which does not seem to be in dispute in the present case, I do not see how the fact that individual businesses may benefit can be a disqualifying factor. On the contrary, if business in general is assisted, it seems inevitable that some firms at least will become profitable, or more profitable, as a result of that assistance. There would be no point in the exercise if this were not the case. It would be an odd result if an institution established to benefit business could only qualify as a charity if the recipients of its benefits made losses or did no more than break even.

18.41 The cases above considered situations where the charity itself made a profit and reinvested that profit into its charitable purposes. But what if the charity owned separate businesses which were for profit, but those profits were paid back to the charity? In earlier cases, such separate entities were not considered to be charitable: *Darkinjung Pty Ltd v Darkinjung Local Aboriginal Land Council* (2006) FLR 394 at 446. In *Shire of Derby-West Kimberley v Yungngora Association Inc* [2007] WASCA 233, a cattle station which was owned by an Aboriginal association and whose profits were dispersed back into the local indigenous community, was not found to be charitable. Newnes AJA, at [84], said:

> The fact that the activities on the Land are a source of funds or other resources used by the Association for charitable purposes, or that the object of the pastoral business is to provide the resources by which those purposes might be achieved, does not, in my view, alter the nature of the use to which the Land is currently put. The Land is not, except to a small degree, used for charitable purposes; rather it is used essentially for the non-charitable purpose of operating a pastoral business, albeit with the object of providing resources which may be used for charitable purposes. Indeed, even if that non-charitable purpose were not the main purpose for which the Land were used, it would nevertheless be a distinct purpose so that, at the least, the Land would be used for a dual purpose.

18.42 The High Court considered these issues in *Commissioner of Taxation v Word Investments* (2008) 236 CLR 204; 251 ALR 206. The Wycliffe Bible Translators (Wycliffe) were a charitable group who sought to spread Christianity through the translation of the Bible into other languages. The organisation had been endorsed as a tax-exempt charity. Wycliffe had set up a separate company called Word Investments Ltd (Word) which operated a funeral home business and an investment scheme. Word operated on a profit basis but all profits were paid to the charitable purposes of Wycliffe. The Federal Commissioner of Taxation refused to classify Word as an exempt charity.

18.43 The majority of the High Court overturned the Commissioner's decision and found that Word was a charitable institution. Gummow, Hayne, Heydon and Crennan JJ held that the objects of Word were expressly charitable as they were aimed at advancing the spread of religion. On the issue of profit, their Honours, at CLR 220; ALR 214, said:

> It is … necessary to reject the Commissioner's arguments so far as they submitted that Word had a 'commercial object of profit from the conduct of its business' which was 'an end in itself' and was not merely incidental or ancillary to Word's religious purposes. Word endeavoured to make a profit, but only in aid of its charitable purposes. To point to the goal of profit and isolate it as the relevant purpose is to create a false dichotomy between characterisation of an institution as commercial and characterisation of it as charitable.

Their Honours did note that it would not be enough for Word to have stated purposes which were charitable. It had to carry out those purposes.

18.44 Kirby J dissented. His Honour, at CLR 248; ALR 238, raised the issue that the recognition of religious charities needs to be conservatively construed and said:

> Charitable and religious institutions contribute to society in various ways. However, such institutions sometimes perform functions that are offensive to the beliefs, values and consciences of other taxpayers. This is especially so in the case of charitable institutions with religious purposes or religious institutions. These institutions can undertake activities that are offensive to many taxpayers who subscribe to different religious beliefs or who have no religious beliefs. Although the parliament may provide specific exemptions, as a generally applicable principle it is important to spare general taxpayers from the obligation to pay income tax effectively to support or underwrite the activities of religious (and also political) organisations with which they disagree. This states a reason of constitutional principle for ensuring that any exemption of a 'charitable institution' with religious purposes or any specific 'religious institution' does not extend beyond an exemption that is clearly provided by law.

18.45 Kirby J, at CLR 250; ALR 239, was also concerned by the economic and competition aspects of the majority's decision and said:

> A taxation exemption for religious institutions, so far as it applies, inevitably affords effective economic support from the consolidated revenue fund to particular religious beliefs and activities of some individuals. This is effectively paid for by others. It involves a cross-transference of economic support.

18.46 With respect, his Honour was right to call into question the economic consequences of expanding the definition of charity to profit-making businesses. These businesses will invariably compete with non-charitable businesses, but will have a significant comparative advantage. That advantage could well cripple competitors and cause a consequential reduction of providers in the market. The result of such a decrease in competition will invariably be higher prices for consumers. This could result in significant public detriment.

18.47 There may be other serious consequences. Murray has stated:

If commercial fundraising by charities does increase, then, as emphasised by Kirby J, there may be important policy implications for government — for instance, the erosion of the tax base or a loss of competitive neutrality. In addition to those identified by Kirby J, potential issues include:

- as a corollary to the competitive neutrality concern, whether differential tax treatment of charitable and for-profit businesses might cause 'economic inefficiency';
- a potential increase in the risk of loss of an entity's charitable assets if commercial liabilities are not quarantined;
- the 'diversion' of the efforts of the controllers of an entity away from its charitable purpose and towards its commercial activities; and
- that individuals may view charities as less altruistic if they expand their commercial activities.[5]

18.48 The Federal Government considered these issues as part of the Henry Review of taxation.[6] The government also commissioned the Productivity Commission to review the not-for-profit sector. The review examined, among other things, the recent changes in the relationships between government, business and community organisations and whether there is scope to enhance these relationships so as to improve outcomes delivered by the not-for-profit sector.[7] The government responded in the 2011–12 Federal Budget with the creation of the Australian Charities and Not-for-profits Commission (ACNC). The ACNC will be responsible for determining charitable, public benevolent institution, and other not-for-profit status for all Australian Government purposes. It will also be responsible for providing education and support to the sector, implementing a 'report-once, use-often' general reporting framework for charities, and implementing a public information portal by 1 July 2013. None of these reforms appear to deal with the problem of reforming the meaning of 'charity'.

REFORMING THE LAW OF CHARITY

18.49 In Australia, a substantial review of the definition of charity occurred in the 'Report of Inquiry Into the Definition of Charities and Related Organisations 2001', a report commissioned by the Federal Government.[8] That report recommended the abandonment of the Preamble and the creation of a legislative definition of charity. That definition of charitable purpose included:

1. the advancement of health, which includes the prevention and relief of sickness, disease or of human suffering;
2. the advancement of education;
3. the advancement of social and community welfare, which includes the prevention and relief of poverty, distress or disadvantage of individuals or families; the care, support and protection of the aged and people with a disability; the care, support and protection of children and young people; the promotion of community development to enhance social and economic participation; and the care and support of members or former members of the armed forces and the civil defence forces and their families;

---

5. I Murray, 'Charity Means Business' (2009) 31 *Sydney Law Review* 309 at 326.
6. Commonwealth of Australia, *Australia's Future Tax System Consultation Paper*, Treasury, Canberra, 2008.
7. Productivity Commission, *Contribution of the Not for Profit Sector* <http://www.pc.gov.au/projects/study/not-for-profit> (last accessed 15 August 2012).
8. R F Sheppard, I R Fitzgerald & D Gonski, 'Report of Inquiry Into the Definition of Charities and Related Organisations, 2001' <www.cdi.gov.au> (last accessed 15 August 2012).

4. the advancement of religion;
5. the advancement of culture, which includes the promotion and fostering of culture and the care, preservation and protection of the Australian heritage;
6. the advancement of the natural environment; and
7. other purposes beneficial to the community, which without limitation include the promotion and protection of civil and human rights; and the prevention and relief of suffering of animals.

18.50   The recommendations were included in an exposure draft of a proposed Charities Bill in 2003, but the Bill was never introduced into Federal Parliament. Instead, a less ambitious change was introduced via the *Extension of Charitable Purpose Act 2004* (Cth). That Act included the provision of non-profit child care as a charitable purpose within the federal jurisdiction. It also stated that open and non-discriminatory self-help groups for the disadvantaged, and closed religious orders, provide a public benefit: see 18.78. Outside of these changes, the Preamble and the four categories of *Pemsel's* case still apply in Australian jurisdictions.

18.51   Other countries have also considered the legislative reform route. The New Zealand Government adopted a new definition of charity in the *Charity Act 2005*, which is based on the four *Pemsel's* case categories but expanded to include trusts for where the beneficiaries are related by blood, and trusts for marae (sacred clearings and meeting places of the Māori).

18.52   The United Kingdom passed its *Charities Act 2006*, which replaced the Preamble with a statutory definition of charitable purpose in s 2. Section 2(2) lists the following charitable purposes:

(a) the prevention or relief of poverty;
(b) the advancement of education;
(c) the advancement of religion;
(d) the advancement of health or the saving of lives;
(e) the advancement of citizenship or community development;
(f) the advancement of the arts, culture, heritage or science;
(g) the advancement of amateur sport;
(h) the advancement of human rights, conflict resolution or reconciliation or the promotion of religious or racial harmony or equality and diversity;
(i) the advancement of environmental protection or improvement;
(j) the relief of those in need by reason of youth, age, ill-health, disability, financial hardship or other disadvantage;
(k) the advancement of animal welfare;
(l) the promotion of the efficiency of the armed forces of the Crown, or of the efficiency of the police, fire and rescue services or ambulance services.

Section 2(4) also includes within the definition purposes recognised as being charitable by the *Recreational Charities Act 1958* (UK) and other purposes which are analogous or within the spirit and intendment of the other purposes.

18.53   It is regrettable that the Australian Government has failed to fully embrace reform of the definition of charity. Although the courts have done much to update the definition for modern times there are anomalies that have necessarily crept into the law from its reliance on the Preamble to a statute that is more than 400 years old. In *Central Bayside General Practice Association Ltd v Commissioner of State Revenue (Vic)*, at CLR 201; ALR 26, Kirby J, after noting these deficiencies, said that the continued use of the Preamble represented the 'irrational surrender to the pull of history over contemporary understandings of language'. Nevertheless, his Honour, at CLR 207; ALR 31, felt bound to follow *Pemsel's* case primarily because the risk of re-opening the question of the meaning of charity 'might produce a more restrictive and deleterious policy outcome than is represented by persistence with the approach that *Pemsel* mandates'.

TRUSTS FOR THE RELIEF OF POVERTY

The poor

18.54 'Poverty' is given a relative meaning in the law of trusts. In order to be valid as a gift for the relief of poverty the law does not require that the persons to be benefited should be destitute, or even on the border of destitution: *Re Gillespie (dec'd)* [1965] VR 402 at 406. Rather, a trust will relieve poverty when it provides money to those who would have to 'go short' because of their financial status: *Re Coulthurst (dec'd)* [1951] Ch 661 at 666. The concept of 'going short' in Australia has been taken to mean that the person is in necessitous circumstances which have prevented them from obtaining a modest standard of living: *Ballarat Trustees Executors & Agency Co v Federal Commissioner of Taxation* (1950) 80 CLR 350 at 355. Trusts for the 'distressed' have been viewed as relating to people who suffer economic pressure and impecuniousness: *Northern Sydney and Central Coast Area Health Service v Attorney-General* [2008] NSWSC 1223; *Re Pieper (dec'd)* [1951] VLR 42.

18.55 An intention to create a trust for the relief of poverty need not be evidenced by a direct statement, as long as there appears a general intention that the trust be used to benefit someone in necessitous circumstances: *Muir v Open Brethren* (1956) 96 CLR 166.

18.56 As noted at 18.16 above, the requirement of public benefit, contained in the *Compton* test, does not apply to trusts for the relief of poverty: *Dingle v Turner*. Trusts have been held to be charitable when they have the purpose of relieving poverty among poor relations, among poor employees, or among the children of Freemasons: *Re Scarisbrick's Will Trusts* [1951] 1 Ch 622 at 649; [1951] 1 All ER 822; *NSW Masonic Youth Property Trust v Attorney-General of NSW* at [177]–[216]. The main difficulty in such situations is determining whether the trust is a charitable trust or an express trust for identifiable beneficiaries. The determination rests on the intention of the testator as evidenced in the wording of the trust: *Re Segelman (dec'd)* [1996] Ch 17; [1995] 3 All ER 676.

The aged

18.57 While there is some earlier authority which suggests that a trust for the aged requires some added element for it to be charitable, it is now established that a trust for the aged is prima facie charitable: *City of Hawthorn v Victorian Welfare Association* [1970] VR 205 at 209.

18.58 However, if the trust is confined in an inappropriate way it will lose its charitable nature. For example, if the trust is confined to the wealthy aged then the trust will be non-charitable: *Hilder v Church of England Deaconess' Institution* [1973] 1 NSWLR 506 at 510.

The 'impotent'

18.59 The term 'impotent' has been taken as referring to those who suffer from an illness or disability, and those who are without family support networks. Examples of such trusts include, trusts for orphans (*Attorney-General (NSW) v Perpetual Trustee Co Ltd* (1940) 63 CLR 209), trusts for 'crippled children' (*The Cram Foundation v Corbett-Jones* [2006] NSWSC 495), trusts for 'retarded' or 'sub-normal' children (*Eurella Community Services Inc v Attorney General for the State of NSW* [2010] NSWSC 566), trusts for the blind (*Re Inman (dec'd)* [1965] VR 238), and trusts for single mothers ('who have erred once but not twice'): *Re Wyld* [1932] SASR 298. As charitable trusts may have existed for some time, there is a danger that the original language used may be considered offensive to modern ears, because of the common tendency for medical terms to come to be used derogatively. In *Eurella Community Services Inc v Attorney General for the State of NSW* at [7], Slattery J said:

> Some of the language from the first half of that sixty-year period now sounds quite foreign to modern ears but it must be used to assist in discovering the purposes of those who used it.

18.60 Gifts to hospitals and related institutions will also be charitable under this heading. Such gifts may also be included under the fourth category in *Pemsel's* case: *Perpetual Trustee Co Ltd v St Luke's Hospital* (1939) 39 SR (NSW) 408. As noted at 18.36–18.37 above, the charitable status of gifts to hospitals is not affected by the hospital charging for its services if the fees are put back into the running of the hospital.

TRUSTS FOR THE ADVANCEMENT OF EDUCATION

18.61 The word 'education' has a wide meaning in the law of trusts. It includes gifts to particular educational institutions, such as schools and universities, which, coming under the Preamble, are prima facie charitable: *Lankry v Clairvision School Limited* [2005] NSWSC 1094. It also includes gifts that are unrelated to institutions and stated in the broadest of terms. For example, in *Permanent Trustee Co (NSW) Ltd v Presbyterian Church (NSW) Property Trust* (1946) 64 WN (NSW) 8, a gift for 'the promotion and encouragement of education in New South Wales' was upheld as an educational trust.

18.62 Educational trusts can embrace specific purposes that are related, sometimes loosely, to education. Trusts for scholarships, buildings and the dramatic arts are all examples of valid educational trusts: *Re Leitch (dec'd)* [1965] VR 204; *Re Queensland State and Municipal Orchestra Endowment Fund* (1999) BC9905299; *Perpetual Trustee Co Ltd v Commissioner of Stamp Duties (NSW)* [1976] 1 NSWLR 127. Thus, in *McGrath v Cohen* [1978] 1 NSWLR 621, a gift to the Hebrew University of Jerusalem for the establishment of a rose garden in its grounds was upheld as a valid charitable trust for the advancement of education. A trust for establishing boys in employment on the land was found to be charitable in *Trustees of the Christian Brothers in Western Australia (Inc) v Attorney-General* [2006] WASC 191. Trusts for art and music competitions are also charitable: *Tantau v MacFarlane* [2010] NSWSC 224; *Corish v Attorney-General of NSW* [2006] NSWSC 1219; *Perpetual Trustee Co Ltd v Groth* (1985) 2 NSWLR 278; *Re Lowin: Perpetual Trustee Co Ltd v Robins* (1967) 2 NSWR 140.

18.63 Gifts to sporting associations will be held to be educational if they take effect within an educational setting: *Kearin v Kearins* (1956) 57 SR(NSW) 286. However, a trust to promote a sport that is unassociated with an educational purpose or general health and welfare is not charitable: *Re Nottage* [1895] 2 Ch 649; *Strathalbyn Show Jumping Club Inc v Mayes* [2001] SASC 73: see 18.105–18.107.

Research and education

18.64 The term 'education' has been taken to require the dissemination of knowledge. It has therefore been said that a trust to further pure research would not be educational because it would merely acquire knowledge: *Whicker v Hume* (1858) 7 HLC 124; 11 ER 50. However, in *Taylor v Taylor* (1910) 10 CLR 218 at 224, Griffith CJ said:

> I confess my inability to apprehend how the stock of available knowledge can be increased without diffusion of the addition to the existing stock ... In these days scientific research is recognised as one of the most efficient means of adding to the knowledge of mankind. We are all familiar with the fact that research scholarships are granted by universities and other institutions for this purpose. It is true that the holder of such a scholarship may, in breach of the honourable obligations incumbent upon him, fail to disclose the result of his researches, but the existence of that necessary risk cannot alter the character of an endowment granted for such a purpose.

18.65   Since *Taylor v Taylor*, courts in Australia have held a number of research trusts to be charitable, such as trusts for the study of natural history, trusts for research into disease, and trusts for cancer research: *Re Benham* [1939] SASR 450; *Estate of Schultz* [1961] SASR 377; *Re Simpson (dec'd)* [1961] QWN 50.

Trusts with no educational value

18.66   Trusts for education may be struck down on the basis of public benefit, if the knowledge that is being disseminated is considered to be worthless. For example, a trust to establish a training school for psychic mediums was found not to be valid in *Re Hummeltenberg* [1923] 1 Ch 237 at 242, where Russell J said:

> If a testator by stating or indicating his view that a trust is beneficial to the public can establish this fact beyond question, trusts might be established in perpetuity for all kinds of fantastic (though not unlawful) objects, of which the training of poodles to dance might be a mild example ... In my opinion the question, whether a gift is or may be operative for the public benefit is a question to be answered by the court forming an opinion upon the evidence before it.

18.67   In a similar fashion, the trust which gave the testator's studio as a museum failed in *Re Pinion (dec'd)* [1965] Ch 85; [1964] 1 All ER 890, because the contents contained nothing of value. In *Re Elmore (dec'd)* [1968] VR 390, a trust to prepare and publish the testator's writings was found to confer no public benefit when the writings were found to have no literary value.

TRUSTS FOR THE ADVANCEMENT OF RELIGION

The definition of religion

18.68   The Preamble did not make express reference to the advancement of religion because of Tudor concerns with church power. Over time, the concerns over religious charity diminished and trusts were accepted as being charitable when they sought the advancement of religion.[9] In *Roman Catholic Archbishop of Melbourne v Lawlor* (1934) 51 CLR 1 at 33, Dixon J said that 'advancement of religion' was a charitable purpose because '[t]he law has found a public benefit in the promotion of religion as an influence upon human conduct'.

18.69   In *Church of the New Faith v Commissioner of Pay-roll Tax (Vic)* (1983) 154 CLR 120 at 136; 49 ALR 65 at 74, Mason CJ and Brennan J defined 'religion' as follows:

---

9.   H A J Ford & W A Lee, *Principles of the law of trusts* (Online), Thomson Reuters, Sydney, [19050], [19250].

[F]or the purposes of the law, the criteria of religion are twofold: first, belief in a super-natural Being, Thing or Principle; and second, the acceptance of canons of conduct in order to give effect to that belief, though canons of conduct which offend against ordinary laws are outside the area of immunity, privilege or right conferred on the grounds of religion.

Advancement of religion generally

18.70 Trusts under this category must seek to advance religious purposes. In *United Grand Lodge of Ancient Free & Accepted Masons of England v Holborn Borough Council* [1957] 3 All ER 281 at 285, Donovan J said:

> To advance religion means to promote it, to spread its message, even wider among mankind; to take some positive steps to sustain and increase religious belief; and these things are done in a variety of ways which may be comprehensively described as pastoral and missionary.

18.71 In *Liberty Trust v Charities Commission* [2011] 3 NZLR 68 at 91–2, Mallon J said:

> [A]dvancing religion can include activities in the community rather than being confined to praying, preaching and building churches or looking after priests, ministers, nuns and the like … If charitable status is appropriate for churches and their public ceremonies or rituals it seems logical that this status should also apply to their other activities which are carried out as part of the faith to which the church subscribes. For example if a religious order believes that worship is best done through deeds rather than silent prayer, and if those deeds reaffirm and sustain that order's faith and lead to others ascribing to that religion, then their religion is advanced. The mere fact that others may carry out the same activities without ascribing to the religion, does not mean that those that are doing the activities for religious purposes are not advancing religion by carrying out that activity.

18.72 In this case the Liberty Trust engaged in a mortgage lending scheme which made interest-free loans to its donors and others. The lending scheme was based upon biblical principles and accompanied by significant biblical teachings. In ruling that the lending scheme entailed the advancement of religion, Mallon J, at 92–3, said:

> [A] mortgage scheme in and of itself is not an obvious candidate for the 'advancement of religion' category of charitable purposes … To advance religion the scheme must do more than have a connection with religion, be motivated by it or be conducive to it. Here it is said that the scheme advances religion because it 'teaches' the Bible's financial principles (such teachings include that money should not be a god or end in itself and that Christians should not burden themselves with heavy debt) and that by joining the scheme contributors help many others. Teaching religion through a lending scheme intended to be operated in accordance with Scripture, and which is promoted as being such, is to spread the message of the religion or is to take positive steps to sustain and increase religious beliefs … Liberty Trust exists [as was stated in *Re Banfield* [1968] 2 All ER 276 at 279] 'to do the will of God in practical Christianity'. While the activities will overlap with secular activities, it is the overt connection with the Christian faith and with the two churches under which Liberty Trust operates that in this case give Liberty Trust's activities their religious purpose. The overwhelming message promoted by Liberty Trust is a religious one. Throughout its website there are references to the Bible and to God. This religious message is reinforced with the newsletters that go out to those who have signed up to the scheme. Participants in the scheme would struggle not to notice the constant religious message Liberty Trust promotes.

18.73 Any general expression that reflects some concern with religious purposes will be enough to satisfy the test, as long as it can be shown to come with public benefit. For example, trusts for the 'work of the Lord' have been found to be charitable (*Re Brooks* (1969) 4 DLR (3d) 694), as have trusts for the independent study of the Bible: *Re Flatman* [1953] VLR 33. Other examples include trusts for missionary work, which are charitable regardless of whether the work is engaged in in Australia or overseas: *Hardey v Tory* (1923) 32 CLR 592.

Gifts to named churches or congregations

18.74 A gift to a named church, denomination, congregation or church body will be presumed to be limited to the religious purposes of those organisations: *Green v Third Church of Christ, Scientist* [2006] VSC 39; *Hardey v Tory* (1923) 32 CLR 592 at 595; *Presbyterian Church (NSW) Property Trust v Ryde Municipal Council* (1978) 2 NSWLR 387 at 404.

Trusts for buildings, grounds and cemeteries

18.75 Express reference is made in the Preamble to the repair of churches. As such, trusts for the repair or building of churches and related buildings, and the maintenance of church grounds, are valid charitable trusts: *Re Tyrie (dec'd)* [1970] VR 264; *Re Findlay's Estate* (1995) 5 Tas R 333. Trusts for graveyards in church grounds are also charitable: *Re Michner* [1922] QSR 39. Trusts for monuments or tombs that are not part of a church are not charitable, but may come under the heading of a recognised non-charitable purpose trust: *Re Spehr (dec'd)* [1965] VR 770. If the trust is for a private chapel it will not satisfy the test of public benefit: *Power v Tabain* [2006] WASC 59; *Hoare v Hoare* (1896) 56 LT 147.

18.76 In *Uniting Church in Australia Property Trust (Q) v Attorney-General* [2007] QSC 318, a gift of land for a holiday camp for youth of the Uniting Church was found to be for the advancement of religion, although it was recognised that the gift contained a mixture of charitable and non-charitable purposes. Other similar gifts have not been found to be charitable: see 18.108.

Trusts for prayers, masses and ceremonies

18.77 Trusts for public prayer and the saying of public masses and ceremonies are valid charitable purposes: *Nelan v Downes* (1917) 23 CLR 546; *Crowther v Brophy* [1992] VR 97. The reason for this is because such ceremonies reinforce and enhance religious beliefs. Trusts for private prayer or contemplation are of no public benefit and, as such, are not charitable: *Gilmour v Coats* [1949] AC 426; [1949] 1 All ER 848.

18.78 Some doubt has been expressed over the different treatment meted out to private prayer. The primary reason for the failure of private prayer has been the impossibility of proving that such prayer confers a benefit on society: *Gilmour v Coats* at AC 447; All ER 854. Some Australian judges have doubted the validity of the distinction on the grounds that private prayer enhances the lives of those involved and as such confers a benefit commensurate with public prayer: *Crowther v Brophy* at 100. The changes in the federal law brought about by the *Extension of Charitable Purpose Act 2004* (Cth) seem to reflect these concerns: see 18.50.

Gifts to religious office bearers or parishes

18.79 A gift to a religious office bearer will take the form of a trust when it is intended to bestow a benefit on the office rather than on the individual: *Re Hannah's Will* (1939) 34 Tas LR 45. Under this heading trusts to supplement the stipend of an office holder are said to be charitable: *Re Fall* [1944] Tas SR 41. Trusts for supporting retired ministers have also been found to be charitable: *Presbyterian Church of New Zealand Beneficiary Fund v Commissioner of Inland Revenue* [1994] 3 NZLR 363. Such trusts may also provide for the families of ministers: *Baptist Union of Ireland (Northern) Corporation Ltd v Commissioners of Inland Revenue* (1945) 26 TC 335. Questions arise as to whether gifts can include those to lay members of churches. In *Melbourne Anglican Trust Corp v Attorney-General* [2005] VSC 481, a trust for providing holiday homes for Anglican ministers was expanded to include lay members of the church who were licensed to perform church functions. However, in *Hester v Commissioner of Inland Revenue* [2005] 2 NZLR 172, a superannuation trust which provided benefits not only to ministers and their families, but also to all church employees, was not charitable. The distinction most probably lies in the fact that church ministry functions were being performed by the lay members in the first case, whereas ordinary employees were included in the latter.

18.80 Problems can occur if the trust is given to an office holder or to a parish where the tasks performed may further non-charitable purposes; for example, a trust for 'parish work'. Given the wide-ranging nature of parish work, such a gift may contain mixed charitable and non-charitable elements and hence be invalid: *Re Ashton (decd); Siddall v Gordon* [1955] NZLR 192. In *Farley v Westminster Bank Ltd* [1939] AC 430 at 435, Lord Atkin said:

> The expression covers the whole of the ordinary activities of the parish, some of which no doubt fall within the definition of religious purposes, and all of which, no doubt, are religious from the point of view of the person who is responsible for the spiritual care of the parish in the sense that they are conducive, perhaps, to the moral and spiritual good of the congregation. But that, I think, quite plainly is not enough; and that the words are so wide that I am afraid that on no construction can they be brought within the limited meaning of 'charitable' as used in the law.

18.81 Other examples of invalid trusts include gifts to office bearers which give them absolute and uncontrolled discretion to use the property as they think fit: *Union Trustee Co of Australia Ltd v Church of England Property Trust, Diocese of Sydney* (1946) 46 SR (NSW) 298; *Queensland Trustees Ltd v Halse* [1949] St R Qd 270; *Anglican Trusts Corporation of the Diocese of Gippsland v Attorney-General* [2008] VSC 352. These decisions can be compared with *Re Macgregor; Thompson v Ashton* (1932) 32 SR (NSW) 483, where a gift to the Anglican bishop for the time being 'for diocesan purposes' and 'for diocesan purposes generally' was found to be a gift for a charitable purpose. A further contrast can be made with *Re Rumball (decd); Sherlock v Allan* [1956] Ch 105, where a gift to 'the Bishop for the time being of the diocese of the Windward Islands … to be used by him as he thinks fit in his diocese' was found to be charitable.

18.82 The law on this point is in a poor state, primarily because of inconsistent findings about the purposes embraced by particular phrases. In *Synod of the Anglican Catholic Church in Australia v Tee* [2012] WASC 46 at [44], McKechnie J observed that '[t]he authorities … are not immediately easy to reconcile and there are sometimes fine distinctions which determine validity or invalidity'. In *Green v Trustees of the Property of the Church of England in Tasmania* [1992] TASSC 41 at [24], Crawford J said:

> The particular terms of a trust must be considered, together with the surrounding circumstances which may be taken into account, when construing the trust and its effect. Courts should take great care not to give undue weight to the decisions of other courts which depend to a significant

extent on the specific terms of particular trusts. When determining whether the gifts for the new diocese are valid charitable trusts it is first necessary to construe and interpret the words used by the testator and testatrix and the constitution and organisation of the Church at the time.

Public benefit and trusts for religion

18.83 The test of public benefit is difficult to apply to religious trusts because of the danger that the bigotry of the bench may manifest itself in judgments. For example, in earlier times, a trust for the instruction of people in the Jewish faith failed for being superstitious: *Da Costa v De Pas* (1754) 27 ER 150. Catholic orders of contemplative orders were said to have no public benefit, although this has now been changed in the federal jurisdiction: see 18.50. However, in more modern times the courts have been more open to alternative religions. For example, a trust to promote the mediocre religious writings of a builder was held to be charitable in *Re Watson (dec'd)* [1973] 3 All ER 678. However, there is still the possibility, even in these more enlightened times, that a purpose will be found to be so subversive of established morality that it ought not to be supported: *Re Jones* [1907] SALR 190.

18.84 Another deeper problem relates to whether trusts for the advancement of religion actually provide public benefit. Originally, the advancement of religion (independent of other charitable purposes such as the relief of poverty) was not considered to be charitable, primarily because of the Elizabethan suppression of religious diversity. Modern secular societies, like Australia, have the reverse policy of religious freedom and pluralism. But, ironically, this may lead to a similar rejection of advancement of religion as being charitable. In *Liberty Trust v Charities Commission* at 82–3, Mallon J said:

> The charitable status for trusts which advance religion is not without its critics. In a case commentary[10] on *Centrepoint Community Growth Trust v Commissioner of Inland Revenue* [1985] 1 NZLR 673 the point is made that whether there is social utility in the advancement of religion is 'a very much more doubtful proposition'. This is because the effect of religion is difficult to define and measure and any effect 'is usually of a very personal nature'. The question is asked 'why should some members of the community bear a heavier burden of taxation merely because the beliefs of others entitle their organisations to exemption from taxation?' A little more recently, in *Hester v Commissioner of Inland Revenue* [2005] 2 NZLR 172 at 174, it was said 'given the very considerable concessions made to charities, and given contemporary agnosticism and even seeming indifference in many quarters to religion, what is it that today supports the concession in favour of religious charities, and more particularly, where are the edges of this head of charity to be drawn?'

18.85 Nevertheless, Mallon J felt bound to recognise the advancement of religion as charitable, but her Honour's comments raise the issue starkly. There is no doubt that religious organisations play an enormously important role in the delivery of charitable services in the relief of poverty and sickness and in the advancement of education. But the assumption that the furtherance of religious beliefs, independently from other charitable purposes, is for the public benefit is far more difficult to accept, especially in a society which has refrained from adopting a singular system of religious

---

10. A W Lockhart, '*Centrepoint Community Growth Trust v Commissioner of Inland Revenue*' (1984–1987) 5 *Auckland University Law Review* 244.

beliefs. As cases like *Commissioner of Taxation v Word Investments* have expanded the capacity for religions to compete in markets for goods and services, it may now be worth examining the question of what effect the recognition of the advancement of religion is having on taxation, competition and prices in Australian markets, and whether, in light of these social costs, it is worth maintaining a presumption of public benefit.

TRUSTS FOR PURPOSES THAT ARE BENEFICIAL TO THE COMMUNITY

18.86 Trusts coming within the fourth category of *Pemsel's* case must be both beneficial to the community and be within the spirit and intendment of the *Statute of Charitable Uses*: *Incorporated Council of Law Reporting (Qld) v Federal Commissioner of Taxation* (1971) 125 CLR 659 at 667. It cannot be presumed that a trust which provides public benefit automatically falls within the spirit and intendment of that statute's Preamble. In *Partnerships Ltd v Commissioner for Her Majesty's Revenue and Customs*, a company providing housing accommodation was not said to have a charitable purpose, because the general provision of housing accommodation (without reference to special classes of need) was found by the Court of Appeal not to fall within the Preamble, even though the Court recognised that there would be indirect benefit to the public.

18.87 Because of the 'catch all' nature of the fourth category it is hard to summarise the types of trusts that fall under this grouping. In *Barby v Perpetual Trustee Co Ltd* (1937) 58 CLR 316 at 324, Dixon J said of the fourth category:

> In this now familiar classification of charitable gifts, the fourth class, as has often been pointed out, does not attempt to define a charitable object. It is no more than a final class into which various objects fall that are not comprised in the first three classes, but are nevertheless charitable. It has been found impossible to give an exhaustive definition of what amounts to a charitable purpose, but the authorities indicate the attributes that are to be looked for. The gift must proceed from altruistic motives or from benevolent or philanthropic motives. It must be directed to purposes that are for the benefit of the community or a considerable section or class of the community. The purposes must tend to the improvement of society from some point of view which may reasonably be adopted by the donor. The manner in which this tendency may be manifested is not defined by any closed category. It is capable of great, if not infinite, variation. It may be by the relief of misfortune; by raising moral standards or outlook; by arousing intellectual or aesthetic interests; by general or special education; by promoting religion; or by aiming at some other betterment of the community. The purposes must be lawful and must be consonant with the received notions of morality and propriety.

Gifts to a community

18.88 A gift to the general, or a specific, community will be a valid charitable purpose. For example, a gift to the 'community of Australia' was found to be valid in *Commissioner of Stamp Duties (NSW) v Way* (1951) 83 CLR 570. A gift to the 'Government of Bengal to be applied to charitable, beneficial and public works' was found to be charitable in *Midford v Reynolds* (1842) 41 ER 602, as was a gift of 'All the rest and residue of my property to charities nominated by the Govt' in *Ryder v the Attorney-General* [2004] NSWSC 1171.

18.89   Gifts may also be made under this heading to smaller locales and districts: *Re Baynes* [1944] 2 All ER 597. However, in *Attorney-General (Cayman Islands) v Wahr-Hansen* [2001] 1 AC 75; [2000] 3 All ER 642, a gift to 'benefit mankind in general' was found to be so wide as to include non-charitable elements.

Gifts to indigenous Australians

18.90   Gifts to indigenous Australians have been upheld as charitable: *Cant v Kirby* [2011] NSWSC 1193 at [46]–[47]; *Shire of Ashburton v Bindibindi Community Aboriginal Corporation* [1999] WASC 108; *Re Mathew (dec'd)* [1951] VLR 226; *Re Bryning* [1976] VR 100. In *Dareton Local Aboriginal Land Council v Wentworth Council* (1995) 89 LGERA 120 at 125, Bignold J said that the fourth category would cover such gifts given 'the widespread recognition in the common law of Australia of the plight of Aborigines in the Australian community in terms of their socio-economic status, opportunities for advancement, and the legacy of dispossession that was the inevitable result of British settlement in this country'. In *Public Trustee v Attorney-General of New South Wales* (1997) 42 NSWLR 600 at 609–12, Santow J opined that a gift to help race relations and improve the lot of Aborigines and Torres Strait Islanders would be charitable.

18.91   More specific gifts to provide accommodation and housing to Aboriginal Australians have also been found to be charitable: *Aboriginal Hostels Ltd v Darwin City Council* (1985) 55 LGRA 414; *Alice Springs Town Council v Mpweteyerre Aboriginal Corporation* (1997) 139 FLR 236; *Toomelah Co-operative Ltd v Moree Plains Shire Council* (1996) 90 LGERA 48.

Gifts to cultural and ethnic groups

18.92   Gifts to significant ethnic communities not related to geography have been upheld. Thus, in *Latimer v Commissioner for Inland Revenue* [2002] 3 NZLR 195, a gift to a defined class of Māori communities was upheld as charitable. A gift to the 'Black community of Hackney, Haringey, Islington and Tower Hamlet' was likewise upheld as charitable in *Re Harding (dec'd)* [2007] 1 All ER 747.

18.93   In *Radmanovich v Nedeljkovic* (2001) 52 NSWLR 641 at 665–6, Young CJ in Eq said that trusts to help ethnic community members settle in Australia were not yet charitable, but might be recognised as such in the future.

Trusts to aid the status of women

18.94   In *Victorian Women Lawyers' Association Inc v Commissioner of Taxation* (2008) 170 FCR 318; 250 ALR 516, it was held that the Victorian Women Lawyers' Association was charitable as its primary purpose was to remove barriers against, and increase opportunities for, women in the legal profession. The fact that society recognised the advancement of women in legislation and in international treaties, meant that there was community recognition of historical and persisting gender-based discrimination and the need to take positive steps to overcome it. Such a purpose was for the benefit of the community.

Public works and beautification trusts

18.95   The reference in the Preamble to repair of highways, havens, ports etc, has been used to justify trusts for the beautification of particular local areas and trusts for public works. For example, trusts have been upheld for 'the improvement of the city of Ballarat' (*Re Bones* [1930] VLR 346), and for the building of a public concert hall in Launceston: *Monds v Stackhouse*. Gifts of land for public parks are charitable, such as a trust for the establishment of an agricultural showground: *Brisbane City Council v Attorney-General (Qld)* [1979] AC 411; 19 ALR 681.

Gifts for improving agriculture, industry and commerce

18.96   Gifts to improve agriculture fall within the Preamble and are charitable. In *Inland Revenue Commissioners v Yorkshire Agricultural Society* [1928] 1 KB 611, a society which ran an agricultural show for the improvement and advancement of agriculture was found to be charitable.

18.97   Gifts may also be charitable if they are aimed at improving industry and commerce, either at large or in a specific locality. In *Commissioner of Taxation v The Triton Foundation* (2005) 147 FCR 362; 226 ALR 293, a charitable foundation was tasked with the 'promotion of a culture of innovation and entrepreneurship in Australia ... by visibly assisting innovators to commercialise their ideas'. In *Crystal Palace Trustees v Minister of Town and Country Planning* [1951] 2 Ch 132 at 142; [1950] 2 All ER 857, the charitable trust consisted of a leisure centre and park of some 200 acres for the purposes of education and recreation and the promotion 'of industry, commerce and art'. Dankwerts J, at Ch 142; All ER 858–9, said:

> In those circumstances, it seems to me that the intention of the Act in including in the objects the promotion of industry, commerce and art, is the benefit of the public, that is, the community, and is not the furtherance of the interests of individuals engaging in trade or industry or commerce by the trustees. It appears to me that the promotion of industry or commerce in general in such circumstances is a public purpose of a charitable nature within the fourth class in the enumeration of charitable purposes contained in *Pemsel*'s case [1891] AC 531, 583.

18.98   Another Australian example is *Tasmanian Electronic Commerce Centre Pty Ltd v Commissioner of Taxation*, where the promotion and funding of digital commerce in Tasmania was said to be charitable. In this case a crucial factor was that Tasmania was a relatively disadvantaged part of Australia. In relation to the benefit to the community of the promotion and funding of digital commerce in that state, Heerey J, at FCR 389; ALR 663, said:

> It seems to me self-evident that benefits to Tasmania's economy resulting in long-term economic advantage to Tasmania will be a benefit to the Tasmanian public, and indeed to the wider national public. In a capitalist economy like Australia, a prosperous and productive private sector generates profits and creates employment which in turn raises incomes which individuals can either spend, creating demand, or save, creating capital for further investment. Either way, people can make a better life for themselves and their families. In a prosperous economy, more money can be raised by taxes to improve education, health and other essential public services.

18.99   By way of contrast to this decision, in *Canterbury Development Corporation v Charities Commission* [2010] 2 NZLR 707, the Canterbury Development Corporation (CDC) sought to promote economic development in the Canterbury region in New Zealand by providing technical and financial assistance for the establishment and development of new businesses. Ronald Young J distinguished this case on the facts from the decision in *Tasmanian Electronic Commerce Centre Pty Ltd v Commissioner of Taxation*, and ruled that the CDC's activities were not for the benefit of the public or a significant section of it. This was so because the central focus of its activities was to assist and increase the profitability of particular businesses in the hope that it would improve the economic circumstances in the Canterbury region. It was also held that while relief of unemployment could be a charitable purpose under trust for the relief of poverty, this outcome was too remote from CDC's purposes, whose principal aim was to facilitate increased profitability of individual businesses. His Honour, at 720, said:

> Any public benefit therefore from CDC's purpose and operations is in my view too remote to establish CDC as a charity. Public benefit is not the primary purpose of CDC's objects or operation. Its primary purpose is the assistance of individual businesses. The creation of jobs for the unemployed, as opposed to jobs for those who are employed and not in need, is the hoped for, but remote and uncertain, result of the way in which CDC approaches its task. The relief of unemployment is certainly not a direct object or purpose of CDC's function. The public benefit is hoped for but ancillary. In the same way the general economic lift for the Canterbury region from CDC's work is the hoped for result of helping individual businesses. It is remote from the purpose and operation of CDC. Public benefit is not at the core of CDC's operation.

18.100   The promotion of tourism has been found not to be charitable: *Travel Just v Canada (Canada Revenue Agency)* 2006 FCA 343; [2007] 1 CTC 294. In *National Tourism Development Authority v Coughlan* [2009] IEHC 53, the Irish High Court refused to recognise as charitable a trust of golf courses in Killarney which aimed to preserve a small stretch of countryside and to promote tourism.

Animals and wildlife

18.101   Trusts for the 'benefit of animals generally' are not charitable: *Murdoch v Attorney-General (Tas)* (1992) 1 Tas R 117. This is because such a trust is viewed as being for the benefit of animals rather than the public. Contrastingly, trusts for animal shelters and for the prevention of cruelty to animals are charitable as they promote personal and public morality: *Perpetual Trustees Tasmania Ltd v Tasmania* [2000] TASSC 68; *Attorney-General (SA) v Bray* (1964) 111 CLR 402. However, if the primary purpose of the trust is to change the law, the fact that animal welfare is also an aim will not save the trust from being struck down as political: *Anti-Vivisection Society v Inland Revenue Commissioners*; *Re Inman, deceased* [1965] VR 238.

18.102   Trusts that create areas for animals, free of human contact, have been set aside on the basis that they do nothing to elevate the standard of human conduct: *Re Grove-Grady* [1929] 1 Ch 557; [1929] All ER Rep 158; *Re Green (dec'd)* [1970] VR 442. However, more recent judgments that reflect the concern with conservation have found that such reserves are valid charitable purposes, as the public can be said to benefit from the protection of rare or endangered species: *Attorney-General (NSW) v Satwell* [1978] 2 NSWLR 200.

Protection from war and disaster

18.103   Trusts with the purpose of protecting people from the effects of war or disaster are charitable: *Re Darwin Cyclone Tracy Relief Fund Trust* (1979) 39 FLR 260. Examples include trusts for fire engines (*Attorney-General v Walker* (1914) 31 WN (NSW) 59); rehabilitation after war (*Muir v Open Brethren* (1956) 96 CLR 166); and 'for the elimination of war': *Re Blyth* [1997] 2 Qd R 567.

Relief of taxes

18.104   Gifts for the payment of taxes or debts are charitable as they are expressly referred to in the Preamble. An example is a gift for the reduction of national debt: *Newland v Attorney-General* (1809) 36 ER 262.

Public sport and recreation

18.105   A trust that merely promotes sport is not charitable: *Royal National Agricultural & Industrial Association v Chester* (1974) 3 ALR 486; *AYSA Amateur Youth Soccer Association v Canada (Revenue Agency)* (2007) 287 DLR (4th) 4. In *Re Nottage* [1895] 2 Ch 649, a trust to encourage yacht racing was found to be non-charitable. Lindley LJ, at 655, said:

> It is a prize for a mere game ... Now, I should say that every healthy sport is good for the nation
> — cricket, football, fencing, yachting, or any other healthy exercise and recreation; but if it had
> been the idea of lawyers that a gift for the encouragement of such exercises is therefore charitable,
> we should have heard of it before now.

Lopes LJ, at 656, said:

> It is most difficult to draw a line separating charitable gifts from gifts not charitable; and the only
> safe course is to say that a particular class of gifts do not come within the definition of a charitable
> gift. I am of opinion that a gift, the object of which is the encouragement of a mere sport or game
> primarily calculated to amuse individuals apart from the community at large, cannot upon the
> authorities be held to be charitable, though such sport or game is to some extent beneficial to the
> public. If we were to hold the gift before us to be charitable we should open a very wide door, for
> it would then be difficult to say that gifts for promoting bicycling, cricket, football, lawn-tennis,
> or any outdoor game, were not charitable, for they promote the health and bodily well being of
> the community.

18.106   The decision in *Re Nottage* (and other such cases) was recently reaffirmed in *Northern NSW Football Ltd v Chief Commissioner of State Revenue* (2011) 281 ALR 147. A submission to the court that *Re Nottage* was no longer good law, was rejected. Speaking for the Court of Appeal, Gzell J, at 152–3, said:

> A formal submission was put that *Nottage* and *Chester* were wrongly decided and should no longer
> be part of the law of Australia. It was put that times have changed and this court should follow
> the Canadian decision in *Re Laidlaw Foundation* (1984) 13 DLR (4th) 491. The purposes of the
> foundation were to apply its property for the benefit of charitable organisations. It made gifts to
> organisations promoting amateur sports in Canada and promoting participation in international
> sporting events by Canadian amateur athletes. A surrogate court judge concluded that the
> recipients were charitable and an appeal to the Divisional Court was dismissed. It was pointed
> out that it was no longer necessary in Ontario to refer to the preamble to the *Charitable Uses
> Act* in order to determine whether or not a purpose was charitable. The preamble was replaced
> by a statutory provision. The Divisional Court held that the surrogate court judge reached the
> correct decision on correct principles. She had taken the view that while a purpose which had as
> its object the promotion of mere sport had traditionally been held to be non-charitable, this was
> not so if the purpose had as its object the promotion of a sport for a wider purpose beneficial to
> the community or for the public benefit. It was no longer necessary, she said, that the purpose be

associated with, or incidental to, an otherwise charitable purpose such as education. Rather, the promotion of amateur athletic sports under controlled conditions was itself a charitable purpose falling under the fourth head of charity in that it promoted health and was akin to cases holding that the promotion of health was a charitable object. The surrogate court judge went on to hold, in any event, that participation in organised amateur sports was educational and would thus fall under the second head of charity in that it provided training in discipline and promoted interaction between individuals.

Laidlaw is not part of the law in Australia. Furthermore, the Supreme Court of Canada in *AYSA Amateur Youth Soccer Association v Canada* (2007) 287 DLR (4th) 4 at 21 said that *Laidlaw* appeared to be an anomalous case based on a statutory provision that adopted only part of the common law test and was inconsistent with that court's holding that public benefit alone does not equal charity.

18.107 Inroads have been made into this principle when the trust can be considered to have an educational purpose. In *Internal Revenue Commissioners v McMullen* [1981] AC 1; [1980] 1 All ER 884, the House of Lords found that a trust to promote physical education and development in schools and universities as a supplement to educational development was charitable. In *Strathalbyn Show Jumping Club Inc v Mayes* [2001] SASC 73, Bleby J found that a trust for the promotion of a sport where it can be seen as but part of a broader educational purpose, or for the promotion of the general health and welfare of a sector of the community, may be a valid charitable trust. A similar result occurred in *Re Bicycle Victoria Inc and Commissioner of Taxation* [2011] AATA 444, where an organisation that promoted cycling as transport and recreation was found to benefit the community in ways beyond mere sport or recreation. Trusts that promote sport in the armed services and police force have also been upheld as trusts for defence and public safety when they have the primary purpose of enhancing the efficiency of those services: *Re Gray* [1925] Ch 362; *Inland Revenue Commissioners v City of Glasgow Police Athletic Association* [1953] AC 380; [1953] 1 All ER 747. However, in *Travis Trust v Charities Commission* [2008] NZHC 1912, a trust promoting horse racing failed as a charity. Williams J, at [59] said:

> A trust to promote racing could only be charitable in nature if its deeper purpose was the pursuit of some other objective, either in principle or, in accordance with charities jurisprudence, a charitable purpose in its own right within the spirit and intendment of the Statute of Elizabeth. Thus, if it could have been established that the true intention of the support for this race was the promotion of health, education or perhaps even animal welfare, it might have satisfied the test. But it is clear that none of these purposes is the deep reason for this Trust, and counsel for the appellant quite rightly did not pitch his case on that basis.

18.108 Trusts for recreation have also failed. For example, trusts for the creation of community centres for the purpose of promoting cultural welfare have failed (*Internal Revenue Commissioners v Baddeley* [1955] AC 572) as have trusts for clubs: *Re Wilson's Grant* [1960] VR 514 (Girls Friendly Society); *Attorney-General (NSW) v Cahill* [1969] 1 NSWR 85 (Catholic Boys Club); *Anglican Trusts Corporation of the Diocese of Gippsland v Attorney-General* [2008] VSC 352 (trust for a girls' camp for girls of the Gippsland Diocese of the Church of England). Confusingly, a trust for public recreational facilities will be valid when it can be said to be a gift to a community for public works: *Monds v Stackhouse*.

18.109   Legislation in Queensland, South Australia, Western Australia and Tasmania has expanded the definition of charity to include the provision of facilities for recreation. In Queensland, South Australia and Western Australia, the legislation requires that the facilities be provided in the interests of social welfare, with the object of improving the conditions of life for the persons for whom the facilities are intended. Moreover, it is necessary in these states for the facilities to be made available to both sexes, or, as an alternative, that the facilities are being made to persons because of youth, age, disability or other social and economic factors.[11] In Tasmania, the legislation imposes no such qualifications. The trust merely needs to be for recreation.[12]

Members of the armed services, ex-members and their families

18.110   Trusts for the benefit of members of the armed services are charitable: *Attorney-General for New South Wales Fred Fulham* [2002] NSWSC 629 at [51]; *Somerville v Attorney-General* (1921) 21 SR (NSW) 450. For example, in *Re Good* [1905] 2 Ch 60, a valid charitable gift consisted of a library for an officer's mess. In *Re Gray* [1925] Ch 362, the gift was of a fund to promote sport, including shooting, fishing, cricket, football and polo, being played in a regiment. Both gifts were said to be charitable as they enhanced the mental and physical abilities of the soldiers.

18.111   In *Navy Health Limited v Deputy Commissioner of Taxation* (2007) 163 FCR 1, the provision of health insurance to members, ex-members of the armed services and their family members was said to be charitable (although the particular insurance company could not be deemed a charitable institution for the purposes of fringe benefits tax as it provided insurance to others outside these classes).

18.112   Trusts for ex-members and returned servicemen and servicewomen are also charitable. In *Verge v Somerville* [1924] AC 496, a repatriation fund for returned soldiers was upheld as being of benefit to the community. Charitable status will also be extended to trusts for the children of returned soldiers: *Re Elgar (dec'd)* [1957] NZLR 1221. In *Downing v Federal Commissioner of Taxation* (1971) 125 CLR 185, Walsh J, at 199, said:

> I am of opinion that there is no justification for laying down a rule that either a trust for the benefit of ex-servicemen or a trust for the benefit of the dependants of ex-servicemen cannot be a valid charitable trust … A trust of either of those kinds may tend to promote the efficiency of the armed forces and to promote the security of the country and may be held for that reason to be charitable.

The notion that there can be a charitable trust for the families of soldiers therefore seems to be an exception to the *Compton* rule against naming a propositus by reference to blood relation.

Public safety and defence

18.113   Trusts that seek to promote public safety or defence are also charitable. Examples include trusts for the teaching of shooting (*Re Stephens* (1892) 8 TLR 792); the training of police or members of the armed services (*Lloyd v Federal Commissioner of Taxation* (1955) 93 CLR 645); and gifts to ambulance services: *Public Trustee of Queensland v State of Queensland* [2004] QSC 360.

---

11.   *Trusts Act 1973* (Qld) s 103(2); *Trustee Act 1936* (SA) s 69C; *Charitable Trusts Act 1962* (WA) s 5.
12.   *Variation of Trusts Act 1994* (Tas) s 4(1).

TRUSTS WITH MIXED CHARITABLE AND NON-CHARITABLE PURPOSES

18.114   A trust with mixed charitable and non-charitable purposes will ordinarily fail: *Morice v Bishop of Durham* (1804) 32 ER 656; *McCraken v Attorney-General (Vic)* [1995] VR 56. Such gifts are described as 'compendious' because it is not possible to separate the charitable from the non-charitable objects. Examples of compendious gifts include gifts for 'objects of benevolence and liberality': *Morice v Bishop of Durham*. Additionally, if the gift is worded to give the trustee a discretion to choose between charitable and non-charitable purposes, the gift will fail. An example of such a gift is a gift for 'charitable or benevolent purposes': *Attorney-General v Metcalfe* (1904) 1 CLR 421.

18.115   The gift may survive if the charitable and non-charitable purposes are severable. For example, a trust that has been created to apportion funds between the charitable and non-charitable purposes will be upheld: *Muir v Archdall* (1918) 10 SR (NSW) 10. If the quantities to apportion are uncertain, the court will apportion them in equal shares. Shares will be split between the charitable and non-charitable purposes, on the proviso that valid private trusts have been created for the non-charitable purposes.

18.116   If the charitable and non-charitable purposes can be read cumulatively, the gift will survive. For example, in a gift to 'charitable institutions bodies and organisations', the terms 'bodies' and 'organisations' are read consistently with the prior words to give them charitable meaning: *Smith v WA Trustee Executor & Agency Co Ltd* (1950) 81 CLR 320.

Gifts to associations

18.117   A gift to an association will be examined to see whether the association has charitable objectives and engages in charitable activities: *Inland Revenue Commissioners v City of Glasgow Police Athletic Association* [1953] AC 380; [1953] 1 All ER 747. If an association has incidental purposes that are non-charitable, the gift will be upheld but the trustees will be prevented from using the funds for the non-charitable objectives of the association: *Re Lloyd (dec'd)* [1958] VR 523. For example, in *Congregational Union of New South Wales v Thiselwayte* (1952) 87 CLR 375, the High Court upheld a gift to an association which included among its objects the furtherance of philanthropy and the preservation of religious liberty. The principles were held to be non-charitable, but were ancillary to the association's mission. The gift was upheld but the trustees were limited in applying the funds to philanthropic agencies that were religious in nature.

Statutory reform

18.118   Most jurisdictions have enacted statutory reforms to save trusts that have mixed charitable and non-charitable purposes.[13] Section 131 of the *Property Law Act 1958* (Vic) is typical when it states:

> (1) No trust shall be held to be invalid by reason of some non-charitable and invalid as well as some charitable purpose or purposes is or are or could be deemed to be included in any of

---

13. *Charitable Trusts Act 1993* (NSW) s 23; *Trusts Act 1973* (Qld) s 104; *Trustee Act 1936* (SA) s 69A; *Variation of Trusts Act 1994* (Tas) s 4(2), (3); *Property Law Act 1958* (Vic) s 131, *Charitable Trusts Act 1962* (WA) s 102.

the purposes to or for which an application of the trust funds or part thereof is by such trust directed or allowed.

(2) Any such trust shall be construed and given effect to in the same manner in all respects as if no application of the trust funds or any part thereof to or for any such non-charitable and invalid purpose had been or should be deemed to have been so directed or allowed.

The section saves compendious gifts by reading them down and restricting them to the purely charitable elements. For example, in *Leahy v Attorney-General (NSW)* [1959] AC 457; (1959) 101 CLR 611, a testator created a *post mortem* trust under which the trustees had the discretion to select an order of nuns or Christian Brothers to take the beneficial ownership of his farm. Problems arose because the phrase 'order of nuns' could be read to include contemplative orders that were non-charitable. The Privy Council held that the gift could be saved by the legislation because the predominant purpose of the gift was charitable.

18.119 The charitable intention must be clear to invoke the restorative power of the section. If there is no evidence, or weak evidence, of charitable intention then the legislation cannot save the provisions. Gifts for 'deserving journalists', 'raising the standard of life', and for a 'Catholic daily newspaper' all failed to attract the protection of the section because they were not found to contain a general charitable intention: *Perpetual Trustee Co Ltd v John Fairfax & Sons Pty Ltd* (1959) 76 WN (NSW) 226; *Re Blyth*; *Roman Catholic Archbishop of Melbourne v Lawlor*.

18.120 In cases where the trust gives the trustee a discretion to choose between charitable and non-charitable purposes, the gift can be saved as the legislation allows the court to 'apply a blue pencil' and strike out the non-charitable alternative: *Stratton v Simpson* (1970) 125 CLR 138; *Manns v Attorney General of New South Wales* [2010] NSWSC 12 at [50]–[54].

THE ENFORCEMENT OF CHARITABLE TRUSTS

18.121 The Crown, acting through the Attorney-General, is the only competent authority to protect and enforce charitable trusts: *Australian Incentive Plan Pty Ltd v Babcock & Brown International Pty Ltd (No 2)* [2011] VSC 43 at [7]. The jurisdiction originates from the ancient *parens patriae* jurisdiction, which gives the Crown and the courts the power to care for infants and the mentally disabled (who were traditionally classed *idiots* and *natural fools*, or *lunatics*): *Hunter Region SLSA Helicopter Rescue Service Ltd v Attorney-General (NSW)* [2000] NSWSC 456. The Attorneys-General of each jurisdiction represent the Crown's interests in matters of charitable trusts and have standing to appear. Indeed, the Attorney-General is a necessary party to any proceedings regarding a gift to charity that is made generally or for undefined charitable purposes, or for any proceedings concerning the alteration of a charity's rules. The representatives of charitable institutions can also appear when they are involved in the administration of the trust. A statutory right to appear has been granted in some jurisdictions to persons who have an interest in the charitable trust.[14]

---

14. See *Charities Procedure Act 1812*, 52 Geo III c 101, which appears to still apply in the Northern Territory; *Trustee Act 1925* (ACT) s 94A; *Charitable Trusts Act 1993* (NSW) s 6 (proceedings to be brought with the Attorney-General's permission or with the leave of the court); *Trusts Act 1973* (Qld) s 106(2), *Trustee Act 1936* (SA) ss 60(2), 66; *Religious Successory and Charitable Trusts Act 1958* (Vic) s 61 (two or more persons with the consent of a law officer); *Charitable Trusts Act 1962* (WA) s 21(1).

GENERAL ADMINISTRATIVE SCHEMES

18.122   In some cases the creator may have indicated a general charitable intention but not provided a description of the workings of the trust with sufficient detail. In *Corish v Attorney-General's Department of NSW* [2006] NSWSC 1219 at [9], Campbell J said:

> An administrative scheme supplements and/or clarifies any provisions the settlor has stipulated concerning the manner in which the objects of the trust are to be pursued, when practical circumstances show that the settlor's stipulation (if any) of the means is inadequate or impractical.

For example, an administrative scheme may be ordered when the creator neglected to name a trustee, or the trustee may have died before the gift takes effect: *Re Flatman* [1953] VLR 33. In *Rowe v Attorney General of New South Wales* [2012] NSWSC 371, a scheme was ordered when the trust instrument contained scant administrative conditions. In *College of Law Pty Ltd v Attorney General of NSW* [2009] NSWSC 1474, a scheme was ordered over trust property which was held under constructive trust, obviously lacking written instructions and a trust instrument.

18.123   When creating such a scheme the court can have regard to evidence of the creator's intention, which may take the form of religious beliefs, interests, and precatory directions: *Re Ashton's Charity* (1859) 54 ER 45; *Re Mann; Hardy v Attorney-General* [1903] 1 Ch 232.

CY-PRÈS SCHEMES

18.124   A *cy-près* scheme, unlike an administrative scheme, involves the variation of the creator's intended charitable purpose when it is impossible or impractical to carry out the objects of the trust in the way the creator of the trust intended: *Corish v Attorney-General's Department of NSW* at [9]. *Cy-près* schemes are only employed by the court in cases where there is a charitable intention but the charitable purpose is impossible to perform. In *Attorney-General (NSW) v Adams* (1908) 7 CLR 100 at 125, Isaacs J accepted the earlier definition of *cy-près* from *Re Taylor* (1888) 58 LT 538, by stating that the role of the court is to make orders that 'carry out the general paramount intention in some way as nearly as possible the same as that which the testator has particularly indicated without which his intention itself cannot be effectuated'.

18.125   Heydon and Leeming state:

> [I]n order for the court to order a cy-près scheme, one of the following has to occur:
>
> (1) there is
>   (a) a case of initial impossibility, and
>   (b) either an out-and-out intention to benefit charity or a general charitable intention plus a possible mode of effectuating that intention; or
> (2) there is a case of a supervening impossibility (whether the intention be general or merely particular); or
> (3) there is a case where a trust has exhausted its original purpose (whether the original purpose be particular or general in intent) and a surplus remains.[15]

---

15.   J D Heydon & M J Leeming, *Jacobs' Law of Trusts in Australia*, LexisNexis Butterworths, Sydney, 2006, p 208.

18.126   It should be emphasised that in cases of *initial impossibility* a *cy-près* scheme cannot be ordered where the creator has expressed a *specific* or *particular* intention, as opposed to a *general* charitable intention. If the creator has expressed particular and specific instructions as to how the trust is to function, the creator may have intended that the trust should fail completely if it could not be carried out exactly as expressed: *Good's Will Trusts v Batten* [1950] 2 All ER 653. Such a gift will fail completely if it is impossible to perform: *Uniting Church in Australia Property Trust (Victoria) v Royal Victorian Institute for the Blind* [1999] VSC 485. On the issue of whether there is a general or particular charitable intention, in *Attorney General for New South Wales v Perpetual Trustee Company (Limited)* (1940) 63 CLR 209 at 225, Dixon and Evatt JJ said:

> A distinction in trusts declared for charitable purposes has thus come to exist which, however clear in conception, has proved anything but easy of application. It is the distinction between, on the one hand, cases in which every element in the description of the trust is indispensable to the validity and operation of the disposition and, on the other hand, cases where a further and more general purpose is disclosed as the true and substantial object of the trust, which may therefore be carried into effect at the expense of some part of the particular directions given by the trust instrument. If there are insuperable objections, either of fact or of law, to a literal execution of a charitable trust it at once becomes a question whether the desires or directions of the author of the trust, with which it is found impracticable to comply, are essential to his purpose. If a wider purpose forms his substantial object and the directions or desires which cannot be fulfilled are but a means chosen by him for the attainment of that object, the court will execute the trust by decreeing some other application of the trust property to the furtherance of the substantial purpose, some application which departs from the original plan in particulars held not essential and, otherwise, keeps as near thereto as may be. The question is often stated to be whether the trust instrument discloses a general intention of charity or a particular intention only. But, in its application to cases where some particular direction or directions have proved impracticable, the doctrine requires no more than a purpose wider than the execution of a specific plan involving the particular direction that has failed. In other words 'general intention of charity' means only an intention which while not going beyond the bounds of legal conception of charity is more general than a bare intention that the impracticable direction be carried into execution as an indispensable part of the trust declared.

18.127   In New South Wales, s 10(2) of the *Charitable Trusts Act 1993* (NSW), provides that 'a general charitable intention is to be presumed unless there is evidence to the contrary in the instrument establishing the charitable trust'. In *Attorney General for New South Wales v Fred Fulham* at [22], Bryson J noted that 'when a general intention of charity is required it is an undemanding requirement and is supported by the presumption in s 10(2)'.

Initial impossibility

Trustee not specified or refuses to carry out the trust

18.128   There may be numerous reasons why a charitable trust is initially impossible to perform. A trustee may not have been specified, or, alternatively, the trustee may refuse to carry out the purpose of the trust: *Re Dominion Student's Hall Trust* [1947] Ch 183. For example, in *Re Lysaght* [1966] Ch 191, a trust for scholarships to the Royal College of Surgeons was created on the proviso that the scholarships were limited to non-Jewish and non-Catholic males. The trustees refused to accept the condition. The court found a general charitable intention that was frustrated by an impossibility. The impossibility was mended by a *cy-près* scheme that removed the offending conditions.

Charitable beneficiary never existed

18.129 If a donor has merely made a trivial misdescription of a donee the courts are free to direct that the gifts must go to the intended beneficiary and there is no need to resort to a scheme: *Re Wedgwood* [1914] 2 Ch 245. If there is uncertainty as to for whom the gift was intended, the court can call upon evidence of the donor's previous actions in making donations or their involvement with charities to discern which donee was intended: *Re Tharp* [1943] 1 All ER 257; *Hood v the Attorney-General for Western Australia* [2006] WASC 157.

18.130 Problems can arise if the charitable institution that the creator intends to benefit never existed at all. For example, in *Gray v Australian Cancer Foundation for Medical Research* [1999] NSWSC 492, trusts for the 'Cancer Research Foundation', 'Victorian Cancer Research Foundation', proved impossible because such institutions never existed. In such cases, courts will prefer to find a general charitable intention and then apply a *cy-près* scheme, by applying the funds to institutions that most closely resemble the creator's intention: *Public Trustee v Attorney-General* [2005] NSWSC 1267 at [19]; *Re Davis; Hannen v Hillyer* [1902] 1 Ch 876.

18.131 A similar problem exists for institutions without juristic personality, such as a 'home'. In *Executor Trustee Australia Ltd v Jamestown District Homes for the Aged Inc* [2007] SASC 262, the testatrix made a gift to the Belalie Home for the Aged, but this home was not incorporated and had been owned and operated by different corporations over time. Anderson J, at [35], found that:

> It is accepted that where a gift, and in particular a residuary gift, is made by a testator to a non-existent body, but from the description of the body set out by the testator in his will, it may be assumed that the testator intended it to be a body carrying on a charitable activity, then a Court of Equity will lean in favour of finding a general charitable intention to save the gift from lapse.

Anderson J found that the gift was a gift to the purposes of the lodge, and on that basis the gift should go to its current owner and operator, not the corporation who owned the lodge at the time the will was made.

Charitable beneficiary has ceased to exist

18.132 Ordinarily, in testamentary trusts, where a named beneficiary has ceased to exist at the date of the death of the testator, the gift to that beneficiary lapses. This is known as the 'lapse rule'. In cases of charitable gifts to beneficiaries who have ceased to exist by the time of the gift, the courts are more reticent to apply a *cy-près* scheme, as a gift to a specific institution is more likely to represent a particular, rather than a general, charitable purpose: *Re Tyrie (dec'd) (No 1)* [1972] VR 168 at 177–8; *Australian Executor Trustees Ltd v Attorney-General for the State of South Australia* [2010] SASC 348 at [50]. If there is a particular charitable intention which can no longer be satisfied, the gift will fail: *Re Ovey; Broadbent v Barrow* (1885) 29 Ch D 560; *Re Rymer; Rymer v Stanfield* [1895] 1 Ch 19; *Re Stemson's Will Trusts; Carpenter v Treasury Solicitor* [1970] 1 Ch 16.

18.133 There are 'exceptions' to the lapse rule which enable the courts to navigate around it: *Public Trustee of Queensland v Attorney-General for the State of Queensland* [2009] QSC 353. In *Australian Executor Trustees Ltd v Attorney-General for the State of South Australia* at [53], Kourakis J found that these techniques are not 'true exceptions to the general rule that a gift simpliciter to a non existent named "institution" fails. They are, instead, examples of the discernment of a wider charitable intention than that nominally expressed by the testator, which displaces the prima facie intention.'

18.134   First, if the named institution has a clear successor with almost identical objects then it may be possible for the gift to pass to that successor, without the institution being considered to have ceased to exist in a practical sense: *The Cram Foundation v Corbett-Jones* at [27]; *Re Faraker* [1912] 2 Ch 488; *Re Vernon's Will Trusts* [1972] Ch 300; [1971] 3 All ER 1061; *The Public Trustee of Queensland v State of Queensland* [2009] 2 Qd R 327. An example of these problems is *Public Trustee v Cerebral Palsy Association of Western Australia Ltd* (2004) 28 WAR 496, where the named beneficiary was the Spastic Welfare Association of Western Australia, a charitable association incorporated under the *Associations Incorporation Act 1987* (WA). The association had been dissolved by the Acting Commissioner of Corporate Affairs and its assets were transferred to the Cerebral Palsy Association of Western Australia, an incorporated company which had almost identical objects. The judge found that for practical purposes the institution had not ceased to exist and had continued to provide the same charitable undertakings and operations, albeit by a different corporate shell. Similar findings arose in *Estate of Rand (dec'd)* [2009] NSWSC 48, where a gift was made to an unincorporated church congregation which had changed its name but which was clearly the same congregation. Another example is *Davis v Adventist Development and Relief Agency* [2006] NSWSC 876, where an unincorporated association had since taken corporate form, but was nevertheless the same organisation.

18.135   Second, the lapse rule can be avoided where the gift indicates a dominant intention to give property to the purposes of the named beneficiary, so that a successor institution with the same purposes can be given the trust property. In *Sir Moses Montefiore Jewish Home v Howell & Co (No 7) Pty Ltd* [1984] 2 NSWLR 406 at 416, Kearney J said:

> In my view a disposition to a charitable corporation is to be treated as having presumptively the necessary elements creating a trust, so that the disposition to such a charitable corporation takes effect as a trust for the purposes of the corporation rather than as a gift to it to be applied as it sees fit.

18.136   In such cases the courts will assess the purposes of the alleged successor to see if they match those of the intended beneficiary: *Public Trustee of Queensland v Rutledge* [2010] QSC 379 at [18]–[22]. For example, in *ANZ Trustees Limited v Attorney-General of New South Wales* [2008] NSWSC 1081, a testamentary trust created by a Catholic priest who died in 1938 made a number of charitable gifts to various organisations. Advice was sought from the court about administration in 1943 but nothing had proceeded with the matter until it was returned to the court over 50 years later in 2007. In the course of that time, many of the organisations had changed their names or ceased to exist. Windeyer J made orders effecting gifts to successor organisations which had taken over the charitable purposes of the named beneficiaries.

18.137   In *Maher v Attorney-General for the State of Queensland* [2011] QSC 61, a gift to the trustees of the Order of the Sisters of Mercy for the religious charitable purposes of St Vincent's Orphanage at Nudgee had lapsed prior to the testator's death. The orphanage's work was taken over by Mercy Family Services. In ordering a *cy-près* scheme in favour of Mercy Family Services, Philippides J, at [13], said:

As mentioned, St Vincent's Orphanage no longer existed at the time the testator signed his will. The successor institution Mercy Family Services conducts its operations from the site of the former operations of the orphanage site at Nudgee. I am satisfied ... that it delivers the services formerly offered by St Vincent's Home for Children, together with a further range of services designed to meet the needs of children, young people and families. Mercy Family Services also provides assistance to former residents of St Vincent's Home for Children. It is thus apparent that the Mercy Family Services operates similar and expanded care and housing services from the site as well as other sites around Brisbane.

18.138   By way of contrast to *Maher v Attorney-General for the State of Queensland*, in *Australian Executor Trustees Ltd v Ceduna District Health Services Inc* [2006] SASC 286, a corporation running a retirement village was dissolved and taken over by a larger health and aged service. The health service was not found to be a successor organisation as its purposes were much broader and significantly different from the original beneficiary and the gift failed.

18.139   In earlier cases it was said that if the gift were made to an unincorporated association then it would be construed as a gift to the purposes of that association, whereas if it were a gift to a corporate beneficiary it would be construed as a gift to that body and hence subject to lapsing should the corporation have ceased to exist: *Re Vernon's Will Trust* [1972] Ch 300; [1971] 3 All ER 1061; *Re Finger's Will Trusts* [1972] Ch 286; [1971] 3 All ER 1050. However, Australian authorities downplay the importance of whether the beneficiary is incorporated or not. In *Sir Moses Montefiore Jewish Home v Howell & Co (No 7) Pty Ltd* Kerney J rejected any rule based on the corporate status of the intended beneficiary, and found that the presumption should be that the gift is given for the purposes of the organisation regardless of whether it is incorporated or not.

18.140   The third exception to the lapse rule exists when the gift is intended to be a gift to funds and/or assets of an organisation rather than to the named beneficiary. In *Re Tyrie (dec'd) (No 1)* at 178, Newton J said:

> If upon the true interpretation of the will the testator intended that the gift should operate simply as an accretion to the assets of the named institution so as to become subject to whatever charitable trusts were from time to time applicable to those assets, and if after the named institution itself ceased to exist its assets remained subject to charitable trusts which were still on foot at the testator's death, then the gift will be treated as taking effect as an accretion to any property which was at his death subject to those trusts.

18.141   An example of this is *In Re Lucas* [1948] Ch 424; [1948] 2 All ER 22, which involved a gift to a home for 'poor, crippled children'. By the time of the gift the home had been closed and a scheme was created for the assets, whereby they would be used to send 'poor, crippled children' to holiday homes. The gift was interpreted as being a gift to augment the charity's funds. Given that the funds had survived the closure of the home, the gift could pass to the scheme. A contrasting example is *In re Slatter's Will Trusts* [1964] Ch 512; [1964] 2 All ER 469. Here, the testatrix had made a gift of money to a tuberculosis hospital run by the Red Cross which had closed prior to her death. The hospital had been sold and the proceeds were not devoted to a continued charitable purpose but rather given back to the Red Cross. Because there was no surviving fund there was no way for the gift to be construed as a gift to augment the funds for the treatment of tuberculosis. There was no intention for the gift to go to the Red Cross. Nor was there a general charitable intention. The gift then fell subject to the lapse rule.

18.142 Finally, if the court can find that the gift contained a general charitable intention (as opposed to a particular intention) then the court can order the institution of a *cy-près* scheme: *Public Trustee of Queensland v State of Queensland* [2009] QSC 174; *Public Trustee of Queensland v Neale*. Unfortunately, the cases do not lend themselves to clear criteria as to when there is a general charitable intention rather than a particular one and 'it is at least arguable that every gift to a particular charitable institution must of necessity be a gift for its purpose'.[16]

18.143 A case in which this exception to the lapse rule was successfully argued was the decision in *Public Trustee of Queensland v Rutledge*. In that case the charitable purpose was to find homes for homeless and unwanted dogs. A testatrix left a gift to a named charitable organisation 'for the general purposes thereof'. At the date of her death, that organisation had ceased to exist. Philippides J, at [15], held that the wording of the clause in the will 'provides a clear indication that what was uppermost in the deceased's mind was not [the organisation] itself, but [its] purposes (the welfare of dogs)'. His Honour found that the gift exhibited a general charitable intent and ordered that the property that was the subject of the gift be applied *cy-près* by having it forwarded to a specified organisation that provided shelter for abandoned and unwanted dogs.

18.144 It should be noted that, in New South Wales, the provisions of s 10(2) of the *Charitable Trusts Act 1993* (NSW) (see 18.127) enables the court to presume a general charitable intention.

Charitable purpose impractical

18.145 Alternatively, a charitable trust can fail at the outset because the purpose is impractical: *Rechtman v Attorney-General for the State of Victoria* [2005] VSC 507. In *Attorney-General (NSW) v Perpetual Trustee Co Ltd* (1940) 63 CLR 209, the testatrix had left her farm, 'Milly Milly', for the training of 'orphan lads'. Unfortunately, the farm could not be used as a training farm, as it was too small and rundown. Nor were there enough funds available to properly equip the farm. The issue then became whether a general charitable intention had been evidenced that would allow the court to order the sale of the property and the use of the funds *cy-près*.

18.146 Dixon and Evatt JJ, at 227, said that although the issue of whether there was a general or particular charitable intention was primarily one of construction, 'the nature of the charitable trust itself and what is involved in the author's plan or project' also had to be examined. Their Honours, at 228, held that this required a distinction to be made between the *ends* of the testatrix's purpose and the *means* to which that purpose could be fulfilled. If the use of 'Milly Milly' was merely a means then the impossibility of using that farm for training was not a bar to the ordering of a *cy-près* scheme, because a general charitable intention survived the impossibility. If, however, the use of 'Milly Milly' was an end, the testatrix's intention was particular and no scheme could be ordered.

18.147 The High Court found that the testatrix had evidenced a general charitable intention and that a *cy-près* scheme could be ordered. Dixon and Evatt JJ, at 229, said:

> [T]here is nothing either in the language of the will or in the surrounding circumstances to suggest that the testatrix chose Milly Milly for any better reason than that, of the assets she was disposing by will, Milly Milly provided the most suitable means of giving effect to her intentions. The failure of her issue and the presence in her will of other charitable bequests form a sufficient foundation

---

16. Heydon & Leeming, note 15, p 221.

for the inference that her testamentary dispositions were based on a desire to devote much of her property to the general benefit of the community and to negative any idea that she may have been actuated less by a wish to advance the useful end to which she devoted the property, than by some desire to conserve Milly Milly intact, a desire to suppose for example, that it might continue as an enduring memorial to herself or her husband.

Supervening impossibility

18.148 A charitable purpose may become impossible after the trust has taken effect. In such cases a general charitable intention is not necessary as the property had already been effectively dedicated to charity. No question of lapse can arise: *The Cram Foundation v Corbett-Jones* at [49]; *Re Slevin, Slevin v Hepburn* [1891] 2 Ch 236.

18.149 For example, gifts may be given to hospitals, care units or schools that later close: *Warley Hospital Inc v Attorney-General for the State of Victoria* [2011] VSC 145; *In the Matter of Bianco (dec'd); Cox v Attorney-General (Vic)* (unreported, SC(Vic), No 5727/97, 23 September 1997). In *RSL Veterans' Retirement Villages Ltd v NSW Minister for Lands* [2006] NSWSC 1161, a trust for a retirement village for veterans was unable to maintain enough numbers of veterans to be sustainable. The court ordered a scheme whereby the village could offer places to others, while retaining a preference for current serving members of the Australian Defence Forces or associated Forces.

18.150 *Cy-près* can also be applied in supervening impossibility cases where the original terms have ceased to provide a suitable and effective method of using the trust property: *Attorney-General for New South Wales v Fred Fulham* at [12]–[17]. In *The Cram Foundation v Corbett-Jones* a *cy-près* was ordered for the use of a home which had been originally intended for the care of 'crippled' children. Changes in government policy to shift towards de-institutionalisation meant that the original terms were no longer a suitable and effective means of carrying out the donor's intention.

Satisfaction of original purpose

18.151 *Cy-près* schemes are also employed in situations where the original charitable purpose has been satisfied and a surplus of trust property remains: *Hickling v Lebsanft* [1999] QSC 362. In *Re Anzac Cottages Trust* [2000] QSC 175, a trust had been established to provide homes for the dependants of servicemen killed in World War I. That purpose had been fulfilled and all the homes bar one had been sold and the proceeds retained. The court was asked to order a *cy-près* scheme whereby the last cottage could be sold and then the proceeds distributed. The judge, in applying a *cy-près* scheme, had regard to the social and historical changes that had taken place and ordered the fund to be applied to various organisations that provided housing to needy family members whose spouse or parent had died in active service.

Statutory powers to create schemes

18.152 All Australian states have legislated to simplify *cy-près* mechanisms.[17] Neither the Australian Capital Territory nor the Northern Territory have made any legislative changes. The Queensland,

---

17. *Charitable Trusts Act 1993* (NSW) ss 9–10; *Trusts Act 1973* (Qld) s 105; *Trustee Act 1936* (SA) s 69B; *Charities Act 1978* (Vic) s 2; *Charitable Trusts Act 1962* (WA) s 7.

South Australian, Tasmanian and Victorian legislation is similar. Section 105 of the *Trusts Act 1973* (Qld) states:

(1) Subject to subsection (2), the circumstances in which the original purposes of a charitable trust can be altered to allow the property given or part of it to be applied cy-près shall be as follows—
   (a) where the original purposes, in whole or in part—
      (i)   have been as far as may be fulfilled; or
      (ii) can not be carried out; or
      (iii) cannot be carried out according to the directions given and to the spirit of the trust;
   (b) where the original purposes provide a use for part only of the property available by virtue of the trust;
   (c) where the property available by virtue of the trust and other property applicable for similar purposes can be more effectively used in conjunction, and to that end can suitably, regard being had to the spirit of the trust, be made applicable to common purposes;
   (d) where the original purposes were laid down by reference to an area which then was but has since ceased to be a unit for some other purpose, or by reference to a class of persons or to an area which has for any reason since ceased to be suitable, regard being had to the spirit of the trust, or to be practical in administering the trust;
   (e) where the original purposes, in whole or in part, have, since they were laid down—
      (i)   been adequately provided for by other means; or
      (ii) ceased, as being useless or harmful to the community or for other reasons, to be in law charitable; or
      (iii) ceased in any other way to provide a suitable and effective method of using the property available by virtue of the trust, regard being had to the spirit of the trust.
(2) Subsection (1) shall not affect the conditions which must be satisfied in order that property given for charitable purposes may be applied cy-près, except in so far as those conditions require a failure of the original purposes.

18.153   The effect of the legislation is to provide broader grounds for the application of *cy-près* schemes. The statutes in New South Wales, Queensland, Tasmania and Victoria do not do away with the requirement of a general charitable intention. However, in Western Australia, the legislation states that *cy-près* schemes can be applied 'whether or not there is any general charitable intention'.[18] In *Taylor v Princess Margaret Hospital for Children Foundation Inc* [2012] WASC 83 at [58], Edelman J felt that the Western Australian legislation had removed the traditional jurisdiction and said:

Where property is given on trust or to be applied for a charitable purpose, the *Charitable Trusts Act 1962* removes the requirement for a general charitable intention (see s 7(1)). And the *Charitable Trusts Act 1962* does not mention the previous equitable requirement that an application be 'as near as possible' to the charitable purposes of the bequest or trust. Instead it speaks of a disposition 'for some other charitable purpose' (s 7(1)). Nevertheless, it might be that 'a court would not readily approve a scheme which did not have that degree of resemblance, even though a cy-près approach is not mandatory': *Penny (as Executrix and Trustee of the Estate of Agnes Ann Wait Gaunce deceased) v Cancer and Pathalogical (Sic) Research Institute of Western Australia* (1994) 13 WAR 314 at 318.

---

18.   *Charitable Trusts Act 1962* (WA) s 7(1).

18.154   The New South Wales provisions are simpler in that s 9(1) of the *Charitable Trusts Act 1993* provides for the application of a *cy-près* scheme in 'circumstances in which the original purposes, wholly or in part, have since they were laid down ceased to provide a suitable and effective method of using the trust property, having regard to the spirit of the trust'. In *Attorney General for New South Wales v Fred Fulham* at [16]–[17], Bryson J said:

> [Section 9] of the *Charitable Trusts Act 1993* has widened the grounds on which the Court may act, in that it is no longer necessary that actual compliance with the original terms should be impossible. It is now enough that they have ceased to provide a suitable and effective method of using the trust property … The Court may alter the purposes of a charitable trust where the original purposes have ceased to provide a suitable and effective method of using the trust property; this is well short of a test requiring impossibility. Subsection 9(1) greatly widens the circumstances in which the Court may act and the influence which it may allow considerations of practicality to have.

In *Trust Company (Aust) Ltd v Attorney General* (NSW) [2011] NSWSC 323, White J applied the section to a trust to use a property as a convalescent home so that the land could be sold and the proceeds put into a fund. The trust of the home was no longer a suitable or effective way of giving effect to the spirit of the trust. In *Chartered Secretaries Australia Ltd v Attorney General of New South Wales* [2011] NSWSC 1274, Bryson AJ applied the section to a trust for the post-graduate studies in 'secretarial and administrative knowledge'. Since the creation of the trust in the 1970s the training and educational standards of such persons had changed, not making it impossible to administer the trust, but making it more difficult and less suited to the task of education. Bryson AJ approved a variation to allow the payment of post-graduate scholarships more generally on the basis that this would be a more suitable and effective method.

18.155   The Queensland statutory equivalent has been interpreted similarly. In *The Congregation of the Religious Sisters of Charity of Australia v The Attorney-General in and for the State of Qld* [2011] QSC 100, Martin J approved a *cy-près* scheme to change the purpose of a hospital from being a 'Hospice for the sick and the dying who were also poor' to a more general purpose to provide 'care for the sick or the dying'. The requirements of Medicare meant that hospital services needed to be provided to all Australians regardless of means, and the hospital could not survive financially if it had to limit its services to palliative care. Martin J approved of the change as the original terms had ceased to be a 'suitable and effective method of using the trust property'.

18.156   In some jurisdictions a limited power to settle *cy-près* schemes has also been bestowed on the Attorney-General.[19] For example, s 14 of the *Charitable Trusts Act 1993* (NSW), gives the Attorney-General power to establish schemes where the value of the trust property is less than $500,000, and where the Attorney-General is satisfied that the scheme is non-contentious.

Cy-près and conditional charitable gifts

18.157   A *cy-près* is available only if the gift is absolute. If the gift is conditional, the obligation or undertaking creates either a reverter or remainder, which a court cannot override with a *cy-près* scheme. If the gift stipulates what is to happen to the property on the triggering of the condition,

---

19.   *Charitable Trusts Act 1993* (NSW) Pt 4; *Trustee Act 1936* (SA) s 69B(3), (4); *Variation of Trusts Act 1994* (Tas) ss 7–9; *Charities Act 1978* (Vic) ss 4–5.

it creates a remainder and the property will pass on to that remainder-person: *Re Wilmott, Uniting Church in Australia Property Trust (Vic) v Royal Victorian Institute for the Blind* [1999] VSC 485. If the gift is silent on what is to happen to the property on the triggering of the condition, it creates a reversion, which will revert back to the donor on resulting trust.

18.158 Conditions can often be found to be void. The effect of a void condition will depend on whether the condition is 'determinable' or a 'condition subsequent': *Cabouche v Ramsay* (1993) 119 ALR 215. As discussed at 17.89, a determinable interest is created so that the condition is built into the gift, so that the gift is given until the triggering event occurs. If the donor uses the words 'while', 'during', 'so long as' or 'until', the courts will tend to construe the gift as being determinable. Importantly, because the determinable condition is built into the gift, the entire gift will fail if the determinable condition is found to be void: *Zapletal v Wright* [1957] Tas SR 211 at 218.

18.159 Contrastingly, if the gift is given and then a condition is attached, the condition will be described as a condition subsequent. Effectively, the property is given absolutely, but then a condition is fastened to it so that it will be cut short. Words such as 'provided that', 'on condition that', 'but if' or 'if it happen that' indicate the intention to create a condition subsequent. If the condition is found to be void, it is possible for the court to strike out the condition but leave the gift to stand so that it becomes an unconditional and absolute gift: *Perpetual Trustee Co Ltd v Gilmour* [1979] 2 NSWLR 716 at 720–721; *Hancock v Watson* [1902] AC 14 at 22.

18.160 These issues were discussed in *The Cram Foundation v Corbett-Jones*. The case concerned a charitable gift of a house for use by the Wollongong and District Society for Crippled Children as a home or hospital. The gift was 'subject to the proviso that should the property at any time cease to be used for these purposes it shall thereupon revert to my next-of-kin at that time'. The gift could no longer be used as a home or hospital and the organisation sought to have the power to sell, mortgage or lease the property to raise funds for providing accommodation, goods and services to people with disabilities in the Illawarra region. Brereton J could not order a *cy-près* scheme unless the condition was found to be a void condition subsequent. If the condition was a valid condition it would mean that the property would pass to the next of kin.

18.161 The wording was found to have created a condition subsequent. Even though the word 'revert' favoured the construction of a determinable interest, the phrase 'subject to the proviso that' and the fact that the gift would go on remainder to the next of kin indicated a condition subsequent and not a determinable interest.

18.162 The condition was subject to the common law rule against remoteness of vesting because the will had been created prior to the operation of the *Perpetuities Act 1984* (NSW) so the saving provisions in that Act were not available: see 17.117–17.119. Brereton J found that the condition was void because it could possibly vest outside the perpetuity period and on that basis he struck out the condition, which left the disposition as an absolute charitable gift. A *cy-près* scheme was then ordered. His Honour, at [80]–[83], set down the four principles for dealing with these situations as follows:

> First, property that is the subject of an absolute gift to charity, once vested, remains with charity forever. If the particular charity or purpose to which it is given subsequently fails, a cy pres scheme will be directed. In this context, cy pres is available regardless of whether or not the donor had a general charitable intention ... Secondly, property that is the subject of a limited or determinable gift

to charity reverts, upon termination of the gift, to the donor or his/her estate, unless there is a valid gift over ... Thirdly, however, property that is the subject of a conditional gift where the condition is void is regarded as the subject of an unconditional, or absolute, gift ... Fourthly, the true distinction ... is the distinction between a limited or determinable gift, and a conditional gift, and not between a limited or particular charitable intention and an 'out-and-out gift to charity'. If the gift is conditional and the condition is void, then it matters not that the testator might appear not only to have had no general charitable intention, but even to have had a plainly and solely particular one.

18.163   The reasoning in *Cram Foundation v Corbett-Jones* was followed in *Freemasons Hospital v Attorney-General for the State of Victoria* [2010] VSC 373. In this case the Freeemansons had sold a hospital which they had established and run since 1927. The sale had reaped nearly twenty million dollars and a dispute arose as to whether the funds should be used *cy-près* or whether they represented a determinable series of gifts which would revert back to the Freemasons when the charity failed. Gardiner AJ, at [107], ruled as follows:

> In my view, the evidence in these circumstances points to a conclusion that the Hospital, from its establishment, was the subject of a determinable gift ... From its foundation, the Hospital was administered under the auspices of freemasonry through a board of Grand Lodge and, subsequently, by the plaintiff through its board, which was intimately associated with freemasonry. An examination of the evidence ... reveals a very high degree of control exercised by freemasonry over the Hospital's activities and its financial affairs throughout the nearly 70 years it operated. I consider that when one has regard to the surrounding circumstances when one is trying to assess the intention here, it was intended that if freemasonry through Grand Lodge for one reason or another no longer operated the Hospital because it became impracticable to do so, the 'gifts' of freemasonry in Victoria which funded the Hospital's foundation and its continued expansion would revert to whence it came, ie Grand Lodge. Throughout the history of the Hospital, freemasonry maintained close control of its affairs and, until quite late in the piece was practically the sole source of finance for its capital and there was no intention to permanently relinquish the dedication ... While freemasonry has its philanthropic aspects, it is a closed organization with very prescriptive rules and codes and this was exemplified by the close superintendence by Grand Lodge over the years that the Hospital operated. This points in my view to an intention that should the Hospital venture cease operations and be wound down that the net proceeds should return to Grand Lodge.

18.164   Another case example is *Will of Meshakov-Korjakin (dec'd)* [2011] VSC 372. Here the testator had set out a charitable trust with its income being shared between a scholarship for the education of university students in Russian and the care of elderly. The trust stipulated that a suitable university chancellor must have accepted the scholarship in Russian within 12 months of the testator's death. If that did not happen the will stipulted that the gift would fail and the the fund would pass to the testator's friend. It was argued by the friend that the condition had been breached but Mukhtar AJ found that the University of Melbourne had accepted the gift within time. Payments had not yet been made but this was due to administrative problems (which could be amended through an administrative scheme) and because a family provisions claim had been lodged which prevented distribution. Mukhtar AJ also examined the gift over to the friend and found that it was valid and while there was uncertainty concerning when (or if) the gift would vest, the uncertainty was remedied by the wait and see provisions of the *Perpetuities and Accumulations Act 1968* (Vic): see 17.117.

Variation of charitable trusts outside of schemes of administration and cy-près

18.165   The general rules regarding variation of express trusts also apply to charitable trusts: see 17.1–17.21. As stated, trusts may contain an express power of variation or may be varied via the court's inherent or statutory powers.

18.166   In the absence of an express power to vary or the exercise of the court's powers, charitable trustees cannot alter the objects of a charitable trust: *Free Church of Scotland v Overtoun MacAlister v Young* [1904] AC 515. In *Attorney General for New South Wales v Fred Fulham* at [54], Bryson J said:

> The instrument creating a charitable trust may, in concept, confer power on some person to alter the charitable trust. It would not be enough that the rules of a voluntary association which conducted a charitable trust contained a power to amend the rules; the power must extend to alteration of the charitable trust, and it would be a question of construction of the rules to ascertain whether the power extended so far. It would also be for consideration whether some purported alteration fell within the power; there may be limits relating to the purposes for which the power may be exercised, or limits to the nature of the amendment authorised, arising from the limits, wide as they are, to the concept of an amendment or in some other way from limits in the terms in which the power was created.

18.167   In *NSW Masonic Youth Property Trust v Attorney-General of NSW*, Hall J found that the rules of a charitable trust established in 1923 had not been amended by changes, from over a 90-year period, to the rules of the unincorporated association which administered the fund.

VALID NON-CHARITABLE PURPOSE TRUSTS

18.168   As stated at 16.51–16.53, the beneficiary principle normally operates to strike down trusts that are created for non-charitable purposes: *Re Astor's Settlement Trusts* [1952] Ch 534. However, there exists a very small category of purpose trusts that have been upheld by courts, even though they are non-charitable. This odd and anomalous group is difficult to categorise. In *Taylor v Princess Margaret Hospital for Children Foundation Inc* at [2], Edelman J described these trusts as a 'category of purpose trust where "Homer nodded."' Some examples of the types of trust coming under this heading are trusts for the maintenance of pets (*Pettingall v Pettingall* (1842) 11 LJ Ch 176; *Re Dean* (1889) 41 Ch D 552) and trusts for the construction and maintenance of tombs unassociated with churchyards: *Re Hooper* [1932] 1 Ch 38. Another example was a trust for the promotion and furtherance of fox hunting: *Re Thompson* [1934] Ch 342.

18.169   These cases have not generally been followed in Australia, and there has been no support for expanding the recognised categories: *Public Trustee v Nolan* (1943) 43 SR (NSW) 169; *Pedulla v Nasti* (1990) 20 NSWLR 720. In *Grant v Yarra Glen & Lilydale Hunt Club Inc* [2006] VSC 482 a trust for fox hunting was found to be non-charitable. In *Re Hegarty* [2011] NSWSC 1194, Gzell J seemed to be prepared to recognise a trust for pets (a shelti, two cats and a budgie) but the trust failed from its inception when the trustee immediately surrendered the pets to the RSPCA.

18.170   These trusts must also satisfy the rule against indestructible trusts and the rule against perpetuities: see Chapter 17. In *South Eastern Sydney Area Health Service v Wallace* (2003) 59 NSWLR 259, a trust for the maintenance of a gravesite offended these rules because it was set up to continue forever, but the trust for the erection of the headstone and turf grave could survive and was upheld.

19

RESULTING TRUSTS

INTRODUCTION

19.1   In some circumstances, equity presumes that a trust was intended and will impose a trust relationship on the parties to a transaction. A resulting trust is a trust that arises by way of this presumed intention. Because resulting trusts arise in the absence of an expressed intention to create a trust they are often referred to as 'implied' trusts, although they should not be confused with express trusts where an intention to create the trust is implied from wording or surrounding circumstances. To avoid confusion, this chapter will only use the terminology of 'resulting trusts'.

19.2   Resulting trusts have traditionally been divided into two categories: *Yard v Yardoo Pty Ltd* [2006] VSC 109 at [297]; *Westdeutsche Landesbank Girozentrale v Islington Borough Council* [1996] AC 669 at 708; [1996] 2 All ER 961 at 990–1:

1.   Resulting trusts which arise when there has been a failure of an express trust, or, alternatively, where there is a surplus of trust property after a trust has been terminated. In these situations the remaining trust property is held on resulting trust for the creator of the trust because it is presumed that the creator intended to receive any leftover beneficial interest; and
2.   Resulting trusts which arise because contributions have been made to the purchase of property but the contributor has not been given a legal title that is equivalent to that contribution. In such a transaction, equity presumes that the equivalent legal title is held on trust for the contributor. This category of resulting trusts also includes trusts which arise when property has been voluntarily transferred to a person who has not provided consideration.

The first category of resulting trust has been referred to as an 'automatic resulting trust' and the second as a 'presumed resulting trust'. This distinction was made on the basis that equity presumes an intention to create a trust in the second category, but automatically imposes a trust in the first category, without reference to intention: *Re Vandervell's Trusts (No 2); White v Vandervell Trustees Ltd* [1974] 1 Ch 269 at 289; [1974] 1 All ER 47 at 64.

19.3   It has been said that the distinction between presumed and automatic resulting trusts is of little utility.[1] This is because even automatic resulting trusts involve an element of presumption about the creator's intention: *Westdeutsche Landesbank Girozentrale v Islington Borough Council* at AC 708; All ER 991; *Air Jamaica Ltd v Charlton* [1999] 1 WLR 1399.

---

1.   C E F Rickett & R Grantham, 'Resulting Trusts — The True Nature of the Failing Trust Cases' (2000) 116 *Law Quarterly Review* at 1519.

19.4 It should be noted from the outset that any presumption that equity makes about a person's intention can be rebutted by evidence of actual intention: *Calverley v Green* (1984) 155 CLR 242 at 270; 56 ALR 483 at 503; *Muschinski v Dodds* (1985) 160 CLR 583; 56 ALR 483. To that extent resulting trusts are still primarily concerned with the intention of the creator and can be distinguished from constructive trusts, which are not necessarily dependent on the intention of the parties for validity: see Chapter 28.

19.5 Equally important to note is that a resulting trust comes into existence from the date of the circumstances giving rise to its presumption. Once a presumption of resulting trust has arisen, which has not been disproved by evidence of actual intention or displaced by the presumption of advancement (see 19.46–19.47), the trust is considered to be in existence. In that sense the resulting trust is a *property institution* like an express trust, rather than a *remedy*, like some forms of constructive trust.[2] The beneficial interests under a resulting trust are, from the time of their creation, enforceable in the scheme of priorities: see Chapter 7.

19.6 However, there does appear to be some authority to the contrary. In *Westdeutsche Landesbank Girozentrale* at AC 705; All ER 987, Lord Browne-Wilkinson said that a person could not be a resulting trustee if he or she is ignorant of the facts giving rise to the trust. With respect, this statement is clearly wrong, as there are many examples which will be used below where resulting trusts are created despite the ignorance of the trustees.

19.7 Regardless of these disagreements about the institutional nature of resulting trusts, it can be agreed that they serve an important function. As stated by Rickett and Grantham:

> The resulting trust and its foundational presumptions operate as part of the law of property, simply as a series of default rules locating the beneficial interest in property when the transfer of the property is itself ambiguous as to the location of that interest, or ineffective to dispose of that interest.[3]

Some scholars have argued that beyond this basic, but fundamental, role lies an attempt by equity to prevent or reverse unjust enrichment on the part of those who have received legal title where there was no intention for them to obtain a beneficial interest.[4] However, the position that all resulting trusts are a form of restitution is debatable. In Australia there has been a reluctance on the part of the judiciary to recognise unjust enrichment as the remedial basis of trust law: *Muschinski v Dodds*. Additionally, while some forms of resulting trust have a restitutionary element, others are more concerned with providing clear rules as to how to pass property when there is a gap in knowledge about the parties' intention. A danger with the restitution approach is that it replaces intention as the foundation of resulting trusts with a remedial function. The remedial function of trusts is more properly dealt with in the context of constructive trusts. Any movement away from this threatens to merge resulting and constructive trusts.[5]

19.8 This chapter will concentrate on the role of resulting trusts in two areas:
1. where there has been an incomplete disposition of a beneficial interest in property; and

---

2. G E Dal Pont, *Equity and Trusts in Australia*, 5th ed, Lawbook Co, Sydney, 2011, p 746.
3. Rickett & Grantham, note 1 above, p 19.
4. R Chambers, *Resulting Trusts*, Clarendon Press, Oxford, 1997.
5. Rickett & Grantham, note 1 above, p 18.

2. where resulting trusts are presumed in property transfers, such as the purchase of property in the name of another or where contributions are made to the purchase price of property.

INCOMPLETE DISPOSITIONS OF A BENEFICIAL INTEREST

19.9   A resulting trust will be imposed when there has been an incomplete disposition of a beneficial interest in a trust. This can occur when an express trust fails, when the purpose of a trust fails or when a trust surplus exists after satisfaction of the purpose of a trust.

Failure of an express trust

19.10   A resulting trust will arise in cases when an attempt to create an express trust has failed. As discussed in previous chapters, there are numerous ways an express trust can fail. The trust may fail for not satisfying one of the three certainties. For example, a gift on trust to A will fail when it neglects to state who is to hold the beneficial interest. Alternatively, a trust may fail for want of proper constitution, or the requirements of writing: see Chapter 16. After an express trust fails, equity imposes a resulting trust by presuming an intention on the part of the creator for the trust property to revert back to the creator.

19.11   For example, in *Hodgson v Marks* [1971] Ch 892, A, the owner of a house, voluntarily transferred it to B, who in turn orally declared that the beneficial interest in the house remained with A. B subsequently sold the house to C. In the dispute between A and C as to ownership of the beneficial interest in the house, the English Court of Appeal held that the statutory requirement of writing set out in the s 53(1)(b) of the *Law of Property Act 1925* (UK) (the English counterpart to s 23C(1)(b) of the *Conveyancing Act 1919* (NSW) and its equivalents in other Australian jurisdictions: see 6.8) did not have the effect of making the declaration of trust unenforceable. Russell LJ, at 933, said:

> [T]he evidence is clear that [A's] transfer was not intended to operate as a gift, and, in those circumstances, I do not see why there was not a resulting trust of the beneficial interest to [A], which would not, of course, be affected by section 53(1). It was argued that a resulting trust is based upon implied intention, and that where there is an express trust for the transferor intended and declared – albeit ineffectively – there is no reason for such an implication. I do not accept that. If an attempted express trust fails, that seems to me just the occasion for implication of a resulting trust, whether the failure be due to uncertainty, or perpetuity, or lack of form.

19.12   If a trust fails for illegality, equity looks at the specific circumstances of the case and the particular policy behind the law that had been breached, before determining whether a resulting trust should be applied: *Nelson v Nelson* (1995) 184 CLR 538; 132 ALR 133. These principles are discussed in detail in Chapter 17.

Failure of the purpose of a loan

19.13   *Quistclose* trusts were discussed at 15.55–15.69. They arise when a lender loans money to a borrower for a particular purpose, such as paying third party creditors. In these transactions, the loan moneys are held to satisfy the purpose, but if the purpose fails to be satisfied a trust arises whereby the loan moneys are held on trust to return to the lender. This trust has been classified by Lord Millett, in *Twinsectra Ltd v Yardley* [2002] 2 AC 164; [2002] 2 All ER 377, as a resulting trust: see 15.63–15.64.

Trust surpluses after satisfaction of the purpose of a trust

19.14   A trust surplus might exist after the purpose of a trust has been satisfied, leaving a surplus, such as when beneficiaries in a fixed trust have taken all their entitlements or have died: *Australian Incentive Plan Pty Ltd v Babcock & Brown International Pty Ltd* [2010] VSC 564 at [17]–[18]. In such cases there will be a resulting trust of the surplus back to the creator of the trust. The treatment of any trust surplus depends on the intention of the creator as evidenced by the words of the trust. If the trust is worded to give the beneficiaries an absolute interest in the funds then no trust will result for the surplus. However, if the beneficiaries' interest is limited in entitlement, or limited by purpose, any trust surplus will be held on resulting trust: *Smith v Cooke* [1891] AC 297.

19.15   Charitable trusts that experience a trust surplus can often be saved *cy-près* with the surplus being employed for purposes as near as possible to that envisaged by the creator. However, *cy-près* schemes are dependent on the existence of a general charitable intention: see 18.126–18.127. If the trust lacks a general charitable intention any trust surplus will be held on resulting trust for the creator: *Re Abbott Fund Trust* [1900] 2 Ch 326. In some cases this will mean that the members of the public who made contributions to the trust will have to be tracked down before any surplus can be divided: *Re Gillingham Bus Disaster Fund* [1958] Ch 300; [1958] 2 All ER 749; affirmed [1959] Ch 62.

RESULTING TRUSTS THAT ARISE IN PROPERTY DISPUTES

Purchase of property in another person's name

19.16   If a purchaser buys property and voluntarily directs the transfer of the property into the name of another person, equity presumes that the owner holds that property on resulting trust for the purchaser: *Napier v Public Trustee (WA)* (1980) 32 ALR 158 at 158; *Turnbull v Gorgievski* [2000] NSWSC 365. Equity assumes, in the absence of any contrary intention or presumption of advancement (see 19.46–19.47 below), that it was intended that the owner hold that title on trust for the person who provided the purchase price: *Tesoriero v Tesoriero* [2007] NSWSC 54. For example, if A purchases property from B, and directs that B transfer the title into C's name, equity presumes that C holds the property on trust for A.

19.17   The presumption applies to both real and personal property. For example, in *Russell v Scott* (1936) 55 CLR 440, an aunt opened a joint account with her nephew. She supplied all of the funds for the account and during her lifetime the account was used solely for her support. When the account was opened, the aunt had told the nephew and others that the balance remaining in the account at her death would belong to him. The High Court found that the aunt intended the nephew to take beneficially whatever remained in the account at the date of her death.

19.18   The High Court held that the aunt had, during her lifetime, vested the legal right to the debt in the nephew including the legal right to take by survivorship on her death. Since however, she had provided all of the funds for the account, there arose a presumption of resulting trust in her favour. The real question was whether the presumption had been rebutted. The High Court held that, in relation to the balance of the account at her death, the presumption of resulting trust was rebutted and that, upon the aunt's death, the principle of survivorship meant that the whole of the beneficial interest in the account passed to the nephew.

Dixon and Evatt JJ, at 451, said:

> The right at law to the balance standing at the credit of the account on the death of the aunt was thus vested in the nephew. The claim that it forms part of her estate must depend upon equity. It must depend upon the existence of an equitable obligation making him a trustee for the estate. What makes him a trustee of the legal right which survives to him? It is true a presumption that he is a trustee is raised by the fact of his aunt's supplying the money that gave the legal right a value. As the relationship between them was not such as to raise a presumption of advancement, prima facie there is a resulting trust. But that is a mere question of onus of proof. The presumption of resulting trust does no more than call for proof of an intention to confer beneficial ownership; and in the present case satisfactory proof is forthcoming that one purpose of the transaction was to confer upon the nephew the beneficial ownership of the sum standing at the credit of the account when the aunt died.

Their Honours, at 454–4, continued and said:

> Doubtless a trustee [the nephew] was during her life-time, but the resulting trust upon which he held did not extend further than the donor intended; it did not exhaust the entire legal interest in every contingency. In the contingency of his surviving the donor and of the account then containing money, his legal interest was allowed to take effect unfettered by a trust. In respect of his *jus accescendi* his conscience could not be bound. For the resulting trust would be inconsistent with the true intention of that person whose presumed purpose it must depend.

19.19   The presumption of resulting trust will not arise in cases where the purchase moneys have been provided as a loan. The presumption only applies when the provider of the moneys acts as a purchaser or directs that the purchase take place.[6] The onus of proving that the moneys were provided as a loan and not a gift lies with the person claiming that it is a loan: *Heydon v Perpetual Executors & Agency Co (WA) Ltd* (1930) 45 CLR 111.

19.20   In *Buffrey v Buffrey* [2006] NSWSC 1349 at [14], Palmer J summarised the position as follows:

> [I]f a presumption of resulting trust or a presumption of advancement arises where one party has contributed the whole of the acquisition cost of the property but the title to the property is placed in the name of another party:
>
> (a) whether either presumption is rebutted depends upon the intention solely of the party who provided the money because the question is whether that person intended to make a gift of an interest in the property to the person who did not contribute to its acquisition;
>
> (b) evidence by the person making the payment as to his or her intentions at the time of the transaction is admissible but the Court will treat that evidence with caution as the evidence of an interested party;
>
> (c) the Court is more assisted in determining the subjective intention of the person making the payment by evidence of that person's contemporaneous statements of intention, subsequent admissions against interest, subsequent dealings with the property, and by evidence of other relevant surrounding circumstances.

---

6.   J D Heydon & M J Leeming, *Jacobs' Law of Trusts in Australia*, LexisNexis Butterworths, Sydney, 2006, p 241.

Contributions to the purchase of property

19.21 In cases where the purchase money is provided by two or more parties jointly, and the property is put into the name of one of the parties, equity will presume a resulting trust in favour of the other party or parties. In *Calverley v Green*, at CLR 245–7; ALR 485, Gibbs CJ said:

> Consistently with these principles it has been held that if two persons have contributed the purchase money in unequal shares, and the property is purchased in their joint names, there is, ... in the absence of a relationship that gives rise to a presumption of advancement, a presumption that the property is held by the purchasers in trust for themselves as tenants in common in the proportions in which they contributed the purchase money.

19.22 In *Buffrey v Buffrey* at [14], Palmer J said:

> [I]f the presumption of resulting trust arises where the joint tenants have made unequal contributions to the acquisition cost:
>
> (a) the presumption may be rebutted by evidence showing that the common intention of the parties at the time of acquisition was for equality of interests despite inequality of contributions;
> (b) evidence of the subjective and uncommunicated intention of one of the parties is inadmissible as going to prove the common intention;
> (c) the common intention of the parties may be ascertained from the evidence as to their contemporaneous communicated statements of intention, subsequent admissions against interest, subsequent mutual dealings with the property, and from evidence as to other relevant surrounding circumstances.

The meaning of purchase price

19.23 For the presumption of resulting trust to arise, contributions that are made by the parties must go towards the purchase price of the property during or immediatelythereafter as to constitute part of the transaction: *The Ship 'Gem of Safaga' v Euroceania (UK) Ltd* (2010) 265 ALR 88 at 93; *Haley v Perkins* [2010] NSWSC 1091 at [78]. Importantly, equity determines this by looking at what was provided by the parties at the *date of purchase*: *Calverley v Green* at CLR 252–3; ALR 490. If the circumstances justify the presumption of a resulting trust *at that time*, the trust will be considered to have existed from then onwards.

19.24 Several types of contribution can be recognised as contributions to purchase price. Obviously, direct payment of money towards purchase will be included: *Field v Loh* [2007] QSC 350.

19.25 If a party has incurred a mortgage liability to provide contributions to the purchase price, that mortgage liability counts as a contribution: *Fedorow v Federow* [2011] ACTCA 10 at [27]; *Schweitzer v Schweitzer* [2010] VSC 543 at [26]; *Brennan v Duncan* [2006] NSWSC 674 at [8]; *Bloch v Bloch* (1981) 180 CLR 390. Joint mortgage liability is treated as equal contribution: *Dinsdale v Arthur* [2006] NSWSC 809 at [14]; *Buffrey v Buffrey* at [14].

19.26 Legal fees, stamp duty and incidental costs associated with the costs of acquisition can also be included in the calculation of interest: *Currie v Hamilton* (1988) 15 NSWLR 687 at 691; *Ryan v Dries* [2002] NSWCA 3 at [52]–[53]; *Damberg v Damberg* at [121]. However, in *Sivritas v Sivritas*

[2008] VSC 374, Kyrou J opined such costs should only be accounted for if they were a necessary condition of obtaining registered ownership of the property. Kyrou J, at [126], said:

> On this basis, stamp duty and registration fees would be included but legal fees and bank fees would not be. Although legal fees and bank fees are normally incurred in the purchase of property, they are not always incurred, and where they are incurred, their amounts may vary significantly depending on the purchaser's circumstances and, more importantly, they may be incurred as debts that are paid after the registration of the interest which is to be held on trust.

19.27 However, Kyrou J's decision seems to go against established authority. While some of these costs are payable after the registration of interests, they are *incurred* prior to or at the point of registration, in the same way as mortgage liability. Indeed, in some contracts, payment of the totality of the purchase price might occur after settlement or registration, and be secured via a lien. It could not be suggested that these payments of purchase price after settlement would not be accounted for in the resulting trust.

19.28 The presumption of resulting trust will not arise when payments are made towards costs incurred *after* the property has been acquired. For example, while there is English authority to the contrary (*Gissing v Gissing* [1971] AC 886 at 903; [1970] 2 All ER 780 at 787–8), Australian courts have refused to recognise payments of mortgage instalments as contributions if they are made by a party who incurred no mortgage liability at the date of purchase: *Tabtill Pty Ltd v Creswick* [2011] QCA 381 at [159]; *Liakos v Zervos* [2011] FAMCA 547 at [205]; *Trustees of Sandor v Ramirez* [1999] NSWCA 261. Similarly, if both parties incur equal mortgage liability at the date of purchase but only one party actually contributes the repayments, the beneficial interests of the parties are calculated on the initial liability and not on the basis of who made the repayments. This is because the payment of mortgage instalments is not payment of the purchase price. Rather, such payment is for the release of the charge which is created by the mortgage: *Calverley v Green* at CLR at 257–8; ALR 493. However, if both parties incur a mortgage liability but, at the date of purchase, it was never the intention of the parties to both pay the mortgage, it is open to the court to find that no contribution was made by the 'passive' mortgagor: *Thornton v Hyde* [2004] NSWSC 125; *Carlton v Goodman* [2002] EWCA Civ 545 at [22]. Alternatively, it is open to the courts in such circumstances to find the actions of the passive mortgagor as unconscionable: *Thornton v Hyde* at [18].

19.29 Given that equity is limited to an examination of contributions made at the time of the acquisition of the property, it would seem logical that only direct contributions to the purchase should be factored into the calculation of beneficial interests. However, in the United Kingdom courts have recognised that some indirect financial contributions, which occur after purchase, may be considered in the calculation of the beneficial interests. Thus, in *Midland Bank v Cooke* [1995] 4 All ER 562, the Court of Appeal found that once some direct financial contribution had been made it was then open to the court to calculate the beneficial interests on the basis of all contributions, whether direct or indirect, whether prior to or after purchase. Such an approach is objectionable for many reasons, primarily because it confuses the role of resulting trusts with that of constructive trusts. Chapter 28 contains greater discussion of the English cases in this area because their impact, from the Australian perspective, is largely on the operation of constructive trusts.

19.30 A resulting trust will not arise in favour of a party who has upgraded the property or maintained it: *Pettitt v Pettitt* [1970] AC 777; [1969] 2 All ER 385. Upgrades and maintenance will not be considered as contributions unless there was a common intention or agreement between the parties that is enforceable or gives rise to an estoppel: *Patrick Jones Photographic Studios Pty Ltd v Catt* [1999] NSWSC 421; *Sivritas v Sivritas* at [127].

19.31   The main exception to this principle appears to be where the property is purchased in stages, or was developed as part of a single project of development. In *Trustees of the Property of Cummins (a bankrupt) v Cummins* (2006) 227 CLR 278; 224 ALR 280, the High Court allowed amounts to be accounted for in a resulting trust where undeveloped land had been purchased and then built upon. The High Court found that there was a single 'transaction' which included both the purchase of the land and the construction of the house on that land, so that contributions to both could be taken into account. This extension of the class of relevant contributions is most probably justifiable on the basis that it reflects the intention of the parties and the way they have approached their ownership of the property.

THE NATURE OF CO-OWNERSHIP IN RESULTING TRUSTS

19.32   Where two or more persons contribute to the purchase of property in unequal proportions and put the property into their joint names, ordinarily equity presumes that the legal title is held on resulting trust for the purchasers as tenants in common in proportions equivalent to the proportions they contributed to the purchase price: *Calverley v Green* at CLR 246–7; ALR 485. However, in cases where the parties made equal contributions, equity presumed that the interests were held as joint tenants and not as tenants in common. The difference between tenancy in common and joint tenancy is that co-owners in a joint tenancy have right of survivorship so that if one of them dies, his or her interest will be distributed equally among the surviving tenants. Tenancies in common lack a right of survivorship and upon the death of a tenant their interest will devolve via the laws of succession.

19.33   Why did equity prefer joint tenancy when the contributions were equal? In such circumstances it was said that 'equity followed the law' and the common law always presumed that co-owners took as joint tenants in the absence of an express declaration of tenancy in common: *Morley v Bird* (1798) 30 ER 1192.

19.34   Statutory reforms have reversed the common law presumption of joint tenancy in some jurisdictions and imposed a presumption of tenancy in common.[7] In *Delehunt v Carmody* (1986) 161 CLR 464; 68 ALR 253, the High Court found that equity still followed the law in these jurisdictions and, given that the law had changed, equity would now presume tenancy in common when the parties make equal contributions to the purchase price. The presumption can be rebutted with evidence of actual intention: *Rix v Mahony* [2011] NSWSC 1308.

19.35   There may remain circumstances when equity will not intervene and change an express joint tenancy into a tenancy in common. The High Court indicated in *Trustees of the Property of Cummins (a bankrupt) v Cummins*, at CLR 303; ALR 297, that if a married couple purchase a matrimonial home expressly as joint tenants, then there will not be a reason for equity to transform the joint tenancy into tenancy in common. This will be discussed further below: see 19.51–19.55.

---

7.   *Conveyancing Act 1919* (ACT) s 26; *Conveyancing Act 1919* (NSW) s 26; *Property Law Act 1974* (Qld) s 35.

REBUTTING THE PRESUMPTION OF RESULTING TRUSTS

19.36 When the presumption of resulting trusts arises, evidence can be admitted of the actual intention of the parties to prove that no such trust was intended.[8] Alternatively, the intention may be that the respective shares in the property reflect a different distribution than that arising from contribution. In *Shephard v Doolan* [2005] NSWSC 43 at [25], White J said:

> If the evidence establishes that it was the intention of the parties that their respective interests should be in accordance with something other than their contributions to the purchase price, such as their contributions to the purchase of the land and discharge of a mortgage, effect will be given to that intention so that although the trust will arise at the time of purchase, the quantum of their interests will fluctuate in accordance with that intention.

19.37 The relevant intention is that of the contributing parties: *Martech Energy Systems Pty Ltd (in liq) v Bell* [2005] VSC 198 at [15]. The whole body of evidence concerning intention must be examined, including evidence which supports the presumption of a resulting trust and evidence which refutes the presumption: *Black Uhlans Incorporated v New South Wales Crime Commission* [2002] NSWSC 1060 at [138].

19.38 Evidence of the circumstances surrounding transfers is admissible, whether it be written or parol evidence. In *Sivritas v Sivritas* at [122], Kyrou J said:

> A person's intention can be found or inferred from his or her contemporaneous words and conduct. From a consideration of a person's words and conduct, certain inferences may be drawn, having regard to the surrounding circumstances and context in which they were uttered or performed.

19.39 The evidence concerning intention must be convincing before the presumption is rebutted as the presumption of a resulting trust will not lightly be set aside: *Brennan v Duncan* [2006] NSWSC 674 at [13]; *Shephard v Cartwright* [1955] AC 431 at 455; *Charles Marshall Pty Ltd v Grimsley* (1956) 95 CLR 353 at 365; *Brown v Brown* (1993) 31 NSWLR 582 at 596; *Cone v Burch* [2010] NSWCA 168 at [30]. If the evidence of the parties' intention is confused and contradictory, the presumption will stand: *Thompson v Leigh* [2006] NSWSC 540 at [38].

Timing of evidence and admissions against interest

19.40 It is important to note that the evidence must relate to the intention of the parties at the time that the interests were created: *Calverley v Green* at CLR 251; ALR 488; *Little v Saunders* [2004] NSWSC 655 at [32].

19.41 The traditional approach is that statements regarding intention which are dated after the creation of the trust are inadmissible for proving the intention of the parties, unless they relate to circumstances arising in the immediate aftermath of the transaction: *Markoska v Markoska* [2011] FAMCA 572 at [63]; *Brennan v Duncan* at [14]; *Shephard v Cartwright*. In *Charles Marshall Pty Ltd v Grimsley*, at 365–6, the High Court said:

---

8.   Heydon & Leeming, note 6 above, p 246.

The presumption can be rebutted or qualified by evidence which manifests an intention to the contrary. Apart from admissions, the only evidence that is relevant and admissible comprises the acts and declarations of the parties before or at the time of the purchase … or so immediately thereafter as to constitute a part of the transaction … Subsequent statements or acts by the donor could only be evidence not for but against him so far as they were admissions that the plaintiffs were the beneficial owners of the shares. Subsequent statements or acts by the plaintiffs could only be evidence not for but against them so far as they were admissions that the shares were allotted to them as trustees for their father.

19.42 As this passage suggests, evidence may be admissible when it goes against the interest of the person deposing it: *Sivritas v Sivritas* at [121]; *Brennan v Duncan* at [14]; *Killen v Rennie* [2005] NSWCA 392 at [85]; *Martech Energy Systems Pty Ltd (in liq) v Bell* at [17]. In that sense the evidence works as an admission against interest: *La Housse v Counsel* [2008] WASCA 207.

19.43 This approach has been challenged on occasion: *Davies v The National Trustees Executors and Agency Co of Australasia Ltd* [1912] VLR 397 at 403. An exception to the inadmissibility rule was recognised in *Wilkins v Wilkins* [2007] VSC 100 at [15], where Kaye J said:

[E]vidence of subsequent declarations as to intention by the donor, unconnected in time with the purchase of the property, is inadmissible if it is adduced to prove the truth of those declarations. Of course, such evidence may be admissible on other bases, for example, to rebut evidence adduced by the party holding the legal interest and which opposes the implication of a resulting trust. Thus for example where, in a case such as this, the party claiming to own the property absolutely has adduced evidence as to acts or conduct of the purchaser which are said to be inconsistent with the existence of a resulting trust, the donor (or his or her representatives) is entitled to adduce evidence to rebut that testimony.

19.44 In *Australian Building and Technical Solutions Pty Ltd v Boumelhem* [2009] NSWSC 460 at [133], Ward J said:

Evidence of the acts or statements … prior to or at the time of the transaction may be used to rebut the presumption. There is some authority to suggest that evidence of subsequent acts or statements may only be used to support the presumption (essentially as admissions) (eg *La Housse v Counsel* [2008] WASCA 207). However, it is clear from the authorities extracted below that testimonial evidence by the party of his or her intention at the time of the transaction is admissible, though generally viewed with caution. Given that there are no especial rules governing admissibility in matters of the present kind (*Damberg* at [45]) (and though there is no question of such evidence in the present case) there appears no compelling reason why other evidence of subsequent acts or statements will necessarily be inadmissible unless against interest, though such evidence also would likely be viewed with caution.

19.45 Apart from statements of intention, other evidence of facts and dealings surrounding the transaction can be admitted even though it arose after the transaction: *Trustees of the Property of Cummins (a bankrupt) v Cummins* at CLR 300; ALR 295; *Draper v Official Trustee* (2006) 156 FCR 53; 236 ALR 499; *Neilson v Letch (No 2)* [2006] NSWCA 254 at [28].

THE PRESUMPTION OF ADVANCEMENT

19.46   In some cases equity refuses to presume an intention to create a resulting trust and instead presumes that any purchase or contribution was intended to be a gift by way of advancement: *Grey v Grey* (1677) 23 ER 185.[9] This presumption of advancement only arises in cases where purchase moneys or contributions are provided by a husband to a wife or by a parent to a child (not necessarily biological children but someone to whom the provider of funds stands in the position of a parent), because it is assumed that husbands and parents are 'under a species of natural obligation' to provide property to their wives and children, respectively: *Murless v Franklin* (1818) 36 ER 278 at 280. The underlying justification appears to be to enable dependants to live their lives and become economically independent.[10] It does not arise in other fiduciary relationships, like those between companies and directors: *SCE Building Constructions Pty Ltd (in liq) v Saad* [2003] NSWSC 796. The effect of a presumption of advancement is to override the presumption of resulting trust with the result that the legal and equitable estates will stay where they lie.

19.47   The presumption of advancement, like the presumption of resulting trust, can be rebutted by evidence of the intention of the parties *at the time of the transfer*. If it is shown that there was no actual intention to confer a beneficial interest on the legal title holder the presumption will not be effective and the normal presumption of resulting trust will apply: *Calverley v Green* CLR 251; ALR 488–9. The onus of rebutting the presumption of advancement lies on the person asserting a resulting trust: *Calverley v Green* at CLR 269–70; ALR 496.

Transfers from husband to wife

19.48   The presumption of advancement arises when a husband either provides the purchase price or makes contributions to the purchase price of property in which the wife is given a legal interest: *Kais v Turvey* (1994) 11 WAR 357 at 360. It does not arise in cases of transfers from a wife to her husband: *March v March* (1945) 62 WN (NSW) 111; *Trustees of the Property of Cummins (a bankrupt) v Cummins* at CLR 298; ALR 293; *Falloon v Madden* [2012] NSWSC 652 at [38]. In the past it has been assumed that the husband had a natural duty to provide for his wife (and children) and this gave rise to the presumption. In *Scott v Pauly* (1917) 24 CLR 274 at 282, Isaacs J said:

> [The presumption of advancement] is an inference which the courts of equity in practice drew from the mere fact of the purchaser being the father, and the head of the family, under the primary moral obligation to provide for the children of the marriage, and in that respect differing from the mother.

19.49   Why this reasoning should not be removed in modern times is hard to understand. The issue has not escaped judicial criticism. In *Calverley v Green* at CLR 268; ALR 501, Deane J advocated an adjustment of the doctrine to 'reflect modern conceptions of equality in status and obligations of a wife vis-a-vis a husband'.

---

9. For an excellent account of *Grey v Grey* case see J Glister, '*Grey v Grey* (1677)' in C Mitchell and P Mitchell (eds), *Landmark Cases in Equity*, Oxford, Hart Publishing, 2012, pp 63–85.
10. J Glister, 'The Presumption of Advancement' in C Mitchell (ed), *Constructive and Resulting Trusts*, Oxford, Hart Publishing, 2010.

19.50   The presumption can also arise in cases where a transfer occurs between a man and his intended wife or fiancee: *Wirth v Wirth* (1956) 98 CLR 228; *Bertei v Feher* [2000] WASCA 165. Such a transfer is considered to be a gift in contemplation of marriage. If the marriage does not occur, the gift should be returned. If the gift is not returned it will be then held on resulting trust: *Jenkins v Wynen* [1992] 1 Qd R 40. Alternatively, the gift may be recoverable either as a conditional gift or by way of a constructive trust: *Kais v Turvey* (1994) 11 WAR 357 at 362.

The joint purchase of a matrimonial home

19.51   In *Trustees of the Property of Cummins (a bankrupt) v Cummins*, Cummins, a barrister, was bankrupted after failing to pay income tax for nearly 45 years. He and his wife had purchased a house in 1970. Cummins had contributed 23.7 per cent to the purchase price and his wife had contributed 76.3 per cent. In 1987 Cummins transferred his legal and beneficial interests in the matrimonial home to his wife. Although Mrs Cummins gave no consideration for the transfer, she did pay stamp duty on the transfer as well as the fee for a necessary valuer's report. Cummins argued that the main purpose for doing this was to limit his exposure to professional negligence liability, as he claimed to fear the possibility that barristers would lose their immunity from negligence. The trustee in bankruptcy argued that the main purpose in transferring the assets was to avoid the Commonwealth Government's considerable claims for unpaid income tax.

19.52   The High Court found that the transaction had the main purpose of avoiding creditors and was hence void: see 17.42–17.46. That then left the question of how the shares in the property should be divided. Should one half go to the wife and the other to the trustee in bankruptcy, or should the proceeds of sale be divided up in accordance with the proportionate contributions made to the purchase of the home? The High Court found that where a husband and a wife purchase a matrimonial property it will generally be inferred that the property will be divided equally between them irrespective of the contributions that were made. Equally, if the property has been registered in joint names, equity will not interfere with that joint tenancy by creating disproportionate shares reflecting their contributions. The High Court, at CLR 302–3; ALR 296–7, quoted Professor Scott, who has argued that contributions to the purchase of the matrimonial home are done on an ad hoc basis, without a view as to who will be given an interest for what share if the home is purchased. Professor Scott said that when a house is purchased in the name of one of the married parties it could be inferred that both should be given a one-half share, regardless of their contributions.[11] In the light of these observations, the High Court, at CLR 302–3; ALR 296–7, said:

> That reasoning applies with added force in the present case where the title was taken in the joint names of the spouses. There is no occasion for equity to fasten upon the registered interest held by the joint tenants a trust obligation representing differently proportionate interests as tenants in common. The subsistence of the matrimonial relationship, as Mason and Brennan JJ emphasised in *Calverley v Green*, supports the choice of joint tenancy with the prospect of survivorship. That answers one of the two concerns of equity, indicated by Deane J in *Corin v Patton*, which founds a presumed intention in favour of tenancy in common. The range of financial considerations and accidental circumstances in the matrimonial relationship referred to by Professor Scott answers the second concern of equity, namely the disproportion between quantum of beneficial ownership and contribution to the acquisition of the matrimonial home.

---

11.   A W Scott, *The Law of Trusts*, 4th ed, Little Brown, Boston, 1989, vol 5, 454, p 239.

19.53   Later cases have employed the presumption of joint tenancy in matrimonial homes. In *Registrar General of NSW v Van Den Heuvel* [2010] NSWCA 171, the presumption was applied to a claim for compensation under the Torrens assurance fund. In this case, the wife had been defrauded by her husband when he had forged her signature to a registered mortgage. There was no evidence regarding what amounts she had contributed to the purchase of the property. On the basis of *Cummins*, the wife was presumed to have had an interest as a joint tenant and compensation was calculated on that basis.

19.54   The Full Federal Court discussed the *Cummins* presumption in *Sui Mei Huen v Official Receiver for Official Trustee in Bankruptcy* (2008) 248 ALR 1. This case concerned a divorced couple where the ex-husband had become bankrupt. Prior to the bankruptcy, the couple had owned a home as joint tenants, subject to a mortgage under which both parties were jointly liable. Due to marital difficulties the man had moved out of the home and later signed an agreement which stated that the whole property belonged to the wife. The surrender of his interest was on the condition that the wife paid all future outgoings, indemnified the husband against any liability in relation to the mortgage, and made no further claim on him under the *Family Law Act 1975* (Cth) or for maintenance and support. The husband was later made bankrupt and the trustee in bankruptcy challenged the agreement concerning ownership of the house. A federal magistrate found that the agreement was invalid as it was voluntary and that the husband retained his interest in the house as per the presumed *Cummins* joint tenancy.

19.55   The Full Federal Court overturned the federal magistrate's findings. They found that the *Cummins* presumption of joint tenancy was not irrebuttable. It could be displaced by an express or constructive agreement between a husband and wife concerning their interests. In this case the agreement between the parties had created a constructive trust of the husband's legal half-interest in the property in favour of the wife, which was conditional on the wife's obligations to pay the mortgage and to forbear from suing for maintenance. To that extent the *Cummins* presumption of joint tenancy had been rebutted and the agreement was enforceable against the ex-husband and, consequently, the trustee in bankruptcy.

The presumption of advancement and de facto relationships

19.56   The presumption of advancement does not arise in de facto relationships: *Napier v Public Trustee (WA)* at 158; *Pulham v Delaney* [2008] NSWSC 1231. This was confirmed in *Calverley v Green*, a case in which the parties had been in a longstanding de facto relationship and lived as husband and wife for more than 10 years. In the early years of the relationship the parties lived in the man's house but they eventually decided to buy a new house to live in. The man had difficulty in obtaining finance on his own, but finance was eventually approved on the basis that the man and the woman would be jointly and severally liable under a mortgage. However, it was agreed that the repayments of that mortgage would be made by the man. A deposit of $9000 was paid by the man from the proceeds of the sale of his house and the balance was raised from the mortgage. The parties were registered as joint tenants.

19.57   On dissolution of the relationship, the woman claimed her half-share in the house. It was held at first instance that the woman had no beneficial interest in the property because the sole reason for naming her a joint tenant was to obtain finance. The Court of Appeal reversed that decision and found that the parties were joint owners in both law and equity.

19.58 A majority of the High Court (Gibbs CJ, Mason, Brennan and Deane JJ; Murphy J dissenting) found that the woman's liability under the mortgage was a contribution to the purchase price of the house. As a result, equity presumed that the joint tenancy was held subject to a resulting trust of tenancies in common, which reflected the respective contributions to the purchase price.

19.59 Arguments were raised that the de facto relationship should give rise to a presumption of advancement. In response to this argument, Gibbs CJ was critical of earlier authority that explained the presumption as being founded in the moral duty of a husband. Instead, Gibbs CJ, at CLR 250–1; ALR 487–8, said:

> The presumption should be held to be raised when the relationship between the parties is such that it is more probable than not that a beneficial interest was intended to be conferred, whether or not the purchaser owed the other a legal or moral duty of support. It is true that this may require a reconsideration of the correctness of the actual results reached in some of the earlier cases, but to regard that as a barrier to acceptance of the principle would be to treat the established categories as frozen in time. As Dixon CJ said [in *Wirth v Wirth* (1956) 98 CLR 228 at 238], that would not be characteristic of the doctrines of equity … Once one rejects … any notion of moral disapproval … as inappropriate to the resolution of disputes as to property in the twentieth century, it seems natural to conclude that a man who puts property in the name of a woman with whom he is living in a de facto relationship does so because he intends her to have a beneficial interest, and that a presumption of advancement is raised.

19.60 However, as the evidence showed that the man had no intention of conferring an interest on the woman at the time of the purchase, Gibbs CJ, at CLR 251; ALR 488–9, found that the presumption of advancement was rebutted. As such, the presumption of resulting trust survived, as it was not rebutted by the evidence.

19.61 The other majority judges declined to recognise de facto relationships as giving rise to the presumption of advancement. Mason and Brennan JJ, at CLR 260; ALR 495, said:

> The term 'de facto husband and wife' embraces a wide variety of hetero sexual relationships; it is a term obfuscatory of any legal principle except in distinguishing the relationship from that of husband and wife. It would be wrong to apply … the presumption of advancement.

19.62 Because de facto relationships embraced a wide variety of relationships, and given that the parties had chosen not to be married, Mason and Brennan JJ, at CLR 261; ALR 496, thought it inappropriate to apply a similar presumption to that applied between married partners. In agreeing with the statements of Mason and Brennan JJ, Deane J, at CLR 268; ALR 501, said:

> The exceptional cases in which equity assumes an intention of 'advancement' and thereby precludes a presumption of a resulting trust are defined by reference to recognised categories of relationships rather than by the actual presence of love or affection … Any adjustment of those relationships must … be made by reference to logical necessity and analogy and not by reference to idiosyncratic notions of what is fair and appropriate.

Deane J then found that he was bound by the authority in *Napier v Public Trustee (WA)* which precluded de facto relationships from the presumption.

19.63   Murphy J gave a typically forthright dissent. His Honour, at CLR 264; ALR 498, took the view that both the presumption of resulting trusts and that of advancement were 'inappropriate to our times, and are opposed to a rational evaluation of property cases arising out of personal relationships'. According to Murphy J, at CLR 264; ALR 498, presumptions can only be made in law when they accord with common experience. If standards of behaviour change, so should the presumptions, 'otherwise the rationale for the presumptions is lost, and instead of assisting the evaluation of evidence, they may detract from it'. Murphy J, at CLR 265; ALR 498, said:

> The notion that such a deliberate act raised a presumption of a trust in favour of the transferor, would astonish an ordinary person.

19.64   As such, Murphy J, at CLR 265; ALR 498, believed that the legal title should be taken as indicating the correct division of the property, especially given that the property was land under the Torrens system. The Torrens system is based on the paramountcy of registration and any presumption that undermined registered interests was destructive of the system.

19.65   Since *Calverley v Green* there have been numerous changes to the regulation of de facto relationships, which require the courts to deal with their breakdown in exactly the same manner as they would a broken marriage: see 28.234–28.237. If, in the law of property, marriages are treated in exactly the same way as de facto relationships, it is time for *Calverley v Green* to be reexamined. In *Ryan v Ryan* [2012] NSWSC 636 at [69], Ward J said that:

> [W]hilst these legislative developments may invite reconsideration of established categories to which the presumption applies, they do not necessarily compel the extension of the presumption. (They may, in fact, invite consideration of whether the presumption is still relevant in any event.) Until *Calverley v Green* falls to be re-considered at an appellate level, in light of these legislative amendments and other relevant factors such as (perhaps) current views in society as to familial obligation, the decision would no doubt be accorded the appropriate precedential weight by a judge hearing the present case.

The position of resulting trusts in the United Kingdom after Stack v Dowden

19.66   Differences between Australian approaches and those taken in the United Kingdom have already been touched upon: see 19.29. The most far-reaching change occurred in *Stack v Dowden* [2007] 2 AC 432; [2007] 2 All ER 929, where the House of Lords decided to jettison the presumption of resulting trusts altogether, and to rely instead on the common intention constructive trust for the resolution of domestic property disputes. The parties to the dispute had lived in a de facto relationship since 1975 and had had four children. Over the years, the woman in the relationship had earned more money and had contributed nearly two-thirds to the costs of acquiring the home in which the family lived. The property was registered as jointly owned and on the breakdown of the relationship the man sought a half-share of the house.

19.67   Baroness Hale gave the leading speech in the House of Lords. The starting point, according to her Ladyship, was to follow the law, so that if the property was held jointly the beneficial interests will be similarly treated. If the parties seek to have a different distribution of the assets, the onus of proving a different beneficial ownership will rest on the person asserting it. Her Ladyship, at AC 454; All ER 949, then said:

> The question is, how, if at all, is the contrary to be proved? Is the starting point the presumption of resulting trust, under which shares are held in proportion to the parties' financial contributions to the acquisition of the property, unless the contributor or contributors can be shown to have had a contrary intention? Or is it that the contrary can be proved by looking at all the relevant circumstances in order to discern the parties' common intention?

19.68   In answer to that question, Baroness Hale, at AC 455; All ER 949, determined to discard the use of resulting trusts and to replace them with common intention constructive trusts:

> The presumption of resulting trust is not a rule of law. According to Lord Diplock in *Pettitt v Pettitt*, the equitable presumptions of intention are 'no more than a consensus of judicial opinion disclosed by reported cases as to the most likely inference of fact to be drawn in the absence of any evidence to the contrary'. Equity, being concerned with commercial realities, presumed against gifts and other windfalls (such as survivorship). But even equity was prepared to presume a gift where the recipient was the provider's wife or child. These days, the importance to be attached to who paid for what in a domestic context may be very different from its importance in other contexts or long ago … The law has indeed moved on in response to changing social and economic conditions. The search is to ascertain the parties' shared intentions, actual, inferred or imputed, with respect to the property in the light of their whole course of conduct in relation to it.

19.69   The decision of the House of Lords to discard the presumption of resulting trusts in domestic property cases marks a severe parting of the ways between English and Australian approaches. Baroness (now Lady) Hale's comment that the 'presumption of resulting trust is not a rule of law' is quite at odds with the picture of Australian law that emerges from the previous discussion. In *Jones v Kernott* [2012] 1 AC 776; [2012] 1 All ER 1265, the Supreme Court of the United Kingdom confirmed Lady Hale's approach. Lord Walker and Lady Hale SCJJ, at AC 786; All ER 1272–3, said:

> In the context of the acquisition of a family home, the presumption of a resulting trust made a great deal more sense when social and economic conditions were different and when it was tempered by the presumption of advancement. The breadwinner husband who provided the money to buy a house in his wife's name, or in their joint names, was presumed to be making her a gift of it, or of a joint interest in it. That simple assumption—which was itself an exercise in imputing an intention which the parties may never have had—was thought unrealistic in the modern world by three of their Lordships in *Pettitt v Pettitt* [1970] AC 777; [1969] 2 All ER 385. It was also discriminatory as between men and women and married and unmarried couples. That problem might have been solved had equity been able to extend the presumption of advancement to unmarried couples and remove the sex discrimination. Instead, the tool which equity has chosen to develop law is the 'common intention' constructive trust. Abandoning the presumption of advancement while retaining the presumption of resulting trust would place an even greater emphasis upon who paid for what, an emphasis which most commentators now agree to have been too narrow: hence the general welcome given to the 'more promising vehicle' of the constructive trust: see Gardner and Davidson, 'The Future of Stack v Dowden' (2011) 127 *Law Quarterly Review* 13, p 16 …

The time has come to make it clear, in line with *Stack v Dowden* (see also *Abbott v Abbott* [2007] UKPC 53), that in the case of the purchase of a house or flat in joint names for joint occupation by a married or unmarried couple, where both are responsible for any mortgage, there is no presumption of a resulting trust arising from their having contributed to the deposit (or indeed the rest of the purchase) in unequal shares. The presumption is that the parties intended a joint tenancy both in law and in equity. But that presumption can of course be rebutted by evidence of a contrary intention, which may more readily be shown where the parties did not share their financial resources.

This formulation of common intention constructive trusts will be discussed further in Chapter 28.

Transfers from parent to child

19.70   There is a presumption of advancement when purchase money is provided by a parent and the legal title is taken by a child: *Calverley v Green* at CLR 267; ALR 500. It is not necessary for the child to prove some financial need for support for the presumption to arise: *Callaghan v Callaghan* (1995) 64 SASR 396 at 405.

The position of a parent

19.71   The key requirement for the presumption of advancement is that the purchase price be provided by someone in *loco parentis* (in the position of a parent). As such, the presumption can also apply to illegitimate and adopted children, as well as to other forms of familial relationship, as long as one party has acted as the parent for the other: *National Executors & Agency Co of Australasia Ltd v Fenn* [1924] SASR 470; *Beecher v Major* (1865) 62 ER 684.

19.72   The following types of relationships have failed to raise a presumption of advancement because there was no relationship of parent and child between the parties:

- provision of deposit by son for mother: *McDermott v McDermott* [2001] WASC 184;
- purchase in the name of a sister: *Noack v Noack* [1959] VR 137;
- purchase in the name of a brother: *McGregor v Nicol* [2003] NSWSC 332;
- purchase in the name of a nephew: *Russell v Scott* (1936) 55 CLR 440;
- purchase in the name of a son-in-law (*Knight v Biss* [1954] NZLR 55), daughter-in-law (*Z v Z* (2005) 34 Fam LR 296; *Yoshino v Niddrie* [2003] NSWSC 57 at [45]; *Anderson v McPherson (No 2)* [2012] WASC 19 at [143]), or de facto daughter-in-law (*Tesoriero v Tesoriero*), or agreement with future daughter-in-law: *Townsend v Townsend* [2006] NTSC 7;
- purchase in the name of a stepchild (*Re Bulankoff* [1986] 1 Qd R 366), or de facto stepchild: *Oliveri v Oliveri* (1993) 38 NSWLR 665; and
- purchase in the name of a grandchild: *Soar v Foster* (1858) 70 ER 64.

19.73   Traditionally, it was thought that the presumption of advancement would only arise when a father provided funds for the purchase of property for his children: *Scott v Pauly* (1917) 24 CLR 274 at 282. It was assumed that women had no obligation to provide for their children, probably because the laws of *femme covert* would have made it impossible for them to hold property: *Bennet v Bennet* (1879) 10 Ch D 474 at 478. However, in more recent cases the presumption has been recognised as arising between a mother and her children: *Peterson v Hottes* [2012] QSC 50; *Wong v Wong* [2008] NSWSC 330; *Brown v Brown* (1993) 31 NSWLR 582; *Nelson v Nelson*.

The presumption and adult children

19.74   The presumption applies to adult children: *Brown v Brown; Sellers v Siemianowski* [2008] NSWSC 538; *Sleboda v Sleboda* [2008] NSWCA 122; *Dearing v Dearing* [2009] NSWSC 1394 at [32]. English authority suggests that the presumption gets weaker as the child gains more independence. In *Lasker v Lasker* [2008] 1 WLR 2695 at 2700, Lord Neuberger said:

> The presumption of advancement still exists, although it was said as long ago as 1970 to be a relatively weak presumption which can be rebutted on comparatively slight evidence: see per Lord Upjohn in *Pettit v Pettit* [1970] AC 777 at 814. I would add that it is even weaker where, as here, the child was over 18 years of age and managed her own affairs at the time of the transaction.

In *Paulet v Stewart* [2009] VSC 60, Habersberger J accepted these comments but found that the presumption of advancement was appropriate in a case where the adult child was deaf and a disability pensioner who had been highly dependent on her mother.

19.75   Canadian courts have for some time not applied the presumption of advancement to independent adult children: *McLear v McLear Estate* (2000) 33 ETR (2d) 272 (Ont SCJ); *Cooper v Cooper Estate* (1999) 27 ETR (2d) 170 (Sask QB). The Supreme Court of Canada has followed these cases but found further that, in transfers of property from parents to adult children, there should therefore be a rebuttable presumption that the adult child is holding the property in trust for the ageing parent to facilitate the free and efficient management of that parent's affairs: *Pecore v Pecore* [2007] 1 SCR 795. Australian courts have yet to consider this approach, but given the ageing of the Australian population and the growing danger of financial elder abuse, there is much to recommend it.

REBUTING THE PRESUMPTION OF ADVANCEMENT

19.76   The presumption of advancement can also be rebutted with evidence of intention: *Macquarie Bank Limited v Lin* [2005] QSC 221; *Australian Building and Technical Solutions Pty Ltd v Boumelhem* at [130]. In *Damberg v Damberg* [2001] NSWCA 87 at [42]–[43], Heydon JA said that the presumption could be rebutted:

> … by showing, on the balance of probabilities, that the parent or parents did not have that intention. In the present circumstances, where the husband alone transferred the property, it is his actual intention alone which is to be ascertained: *Calverley v Green* (1984) 155 CLR 242 at 246–251 … It has been said that although the presumption is rebuttable, it does 'not … give way to slight circumstances': *Shephard v Cartwright* [1955] AC 431 at 445 … quoted in *Charles Marshall Pty Ltd v Grimsley* (1956) 95 CLR 353 at 365 by Dixon CJ, McTiernan, Williams, Fullagar and Taylor JJ. According to Viscount Simonds, the quoted words were uttered by Lord Eldon LC in *Finch v Finch* (1808) 33 ER 671; in fact they were not, though they appear in the headnote, though the expression 'slight circumstances' was used by the losing counsel, Sir Samuel Romilly, in argument (at 673), and though Lord Eldon LC said that the 'presumption is not to be frittered away by nice refinements' (at 674).

Heydon JA also stated that the relevant standard of evidence is the balance of probabilities and not any higher standard.

Is the presumption a genuine presumption?

19.77   On one view, the presumption of advancement creates a situation where an intention to make a gift is presumed. That presumption can then be rebutted with evidence which would lead to the presumption of resulting trust arising which could, in turn, then be rebutted.[12] However, Australian courts have eschewed this approach. In *Martin v Martin* (1959) 110 CLR 297 at 303, the High Court said that the presumption is called a presumption but 'it is rather the absence of any reason for assuming that a trust arose'. In *Anderson v McPherson (No 2)* at [134], Edelman J said:

> In this sense, the presumption of advancement is not a presumption at all. It is simply a description of facts where the presumption of resulting trust (or, more accurately, the presumption of a declaration of trust) does not arise.

Professor Chambers has expressed the converse position. He has said:[13]

> The presumption of resulting trust is simply a situation in which there is no apparent reason (or consideration or basis) for the transfer of assets to the recipient at the expense of another. Evidence of a reason, such as an intention to give, rebuts the presumption because it fills a gap in the evidence and not because it displaces a presumed fact. The presumption of advancement, on the other hand, is a true presumption because it is an inference of the existence of a secondary fact, that the provider has an intention to give.

GIFTS AND RESULTING TRUSTS

19.78   Presumptions of resulting trust and of advancement can also arise in gifts (voluntary transfers of property). For example, if A makes a gift of property to B, a presumption of resulting trust may arise so that B holds the property on trust for A.

19.79   Equity treats gifts of realty differently to gifts of personalty. Unfortunately, the operation of the presumptions in gifts of land has been made problematic because of the operation of the English *Statute of Uses 1535*. Prior to that statute, equity presumed that any interest in land given without consideration to a stranger (meaning someone to whom a presumption of advancement would not arise) was held on resulting use.[14] After the statute the use was executed and the ownership reverted back to the grantor, leaving the transfer ineffectual. Contrastingly, if a donor had expressly declared that they held the land on use for the donee, the use would be executed and the land (both legal and equitable estates) would be transferred to the donee.[15] As was discussed in Chapter 1, in the seventeenth century the chancellor eventually came to recognise the 'double use' or trust. Questions then arose as to whether the old wording would be effective to give rise to a resulting trust.

19.80   The problem was never resolved in England (which perhaps indicates that the issue is not as earth-shattering as it appears). In *House v Caffyn* [1922] VLR 67, Cussen J found that a gift of

---

12.   See the discussion in J Glister 'Is there a presumption of advancement?' (2011) 33 *Sydney Law Review* 39.

13.   R Chambers, 'Is There a Presumption of Resulting Trust?' in C Mitchell (ed), *Constructive and Resulting Trusts*, Oxford, Hart Publishing, 2010, 267, pp 285–6.

14.   H A J Ford & W A Lee, *Principles of the law of trusts* (Online), Thomson Reuters, Sydney, [21080].

15.   J D Heydon & M J Leeming, *Jacobs' Law of Trusts in Australia*, 7th ed, LexisNexis Butterworths, Sydney, 2006, p 252.

old system land to a stranger would not give rise to the presumption of resulting, but that a gift of Torrens land to a stranger would. This was followed by Dixon CJ in *Wirth v Wirth* (1956) 98 CLR 228 at 236–7.

19.81   In some jurisdictions, legislation provides that no presumption of resulting trust will arise in a voluntary transfer of realty, unless the transferor expresses an intention to create a use or a trust.[16] In New South Wales, the relevant section is s 44 of the *Conveyancing Act 1919*, and there is conflicting authority as to the effect of that section on Torrens system land. In *Newcastle City Council v Kern Land Pty Ltd* (1997) 42 NSWLR 273, Windeyer J found that s 44 did apply to registered Torrens dealings as they were conveyances within the meaning of the section. However, in *Ryan v Hopkinson* (1990) 14 Fam LR 151 at 155, Bryson J, in ruling that s 44(1) did not so apply, said:

> In my opinion the whole subject of resulting trusts is not touched on in any way by s 44, which relates to the conveyance of legal estates by conveyances which purport to be or operate as conveyances to uses. The language used is technical and the text of s 44(1) shows that a distinction was drawn between resulting uses on the one hand and trusts on the other. The use referred to is the use of medieval and Tudor law which the Statute of Uses 1535 executed. It is very doubtful whether the Statute of Uses ever had the effect of executing a use in relation to land under the Torrens system, which is generally inconsistent with the continued operation of this part of the former conveyancing law. Further the Statute of Uses was repealed by the Imperial Acts Application Act 1969 (NSW), so that in 1983 there was no room for a use to result or pass in any other manner under that statute, hence no room for the operation of s 44(1). A resulting trust is an equitable interest; a resulting use prevents the legal estate from passing; the two inhabit different universes and s 44(1) has no operation on the present case.

Later cases have preferred the views expressed by Windeyer J: *Bhana v Bhana* [2002] NSWSC 117; *Singh v Singh* [2004] NSWSC 109 at [34]–[35]; *Drayson v Drayson* [2011] NSWSC 965 at [59].

19.82   With regards to personalty, if a gift of personalty which can produce income is made to a stranger, a resulting trust will be presumed: *Hendry v E F Hendry Pty Ltd* [2003] SASC 157. Otherwise, gifts of personalty will not give rise to a resulting trust. Any person claiming that a gift was not intended must prove their claim on the balance of probabilities: *Joaquin v Hall* [1976] Ch 181.

THE FUTURE OF RESULTING TRUSTS

19.83   While Murphy J is not normally regarded as a giant of equity, his criticisms in *Calverley v Green* of both the presumption of resulting trust and the presumption of advancement are cutting and have a degree of attractiveness. A critic might see the presumptions as outdated, anachronistic and sexist.

19.84   Other Australian judges agree. In *Dullow v Dullow* (1985) 3 NSWLR 531 at 535–6, Hope JA found it was ridiculous that the medieval law of uses, which developed in response to the particular concerns of that society, should have such an impact on fact finding in modern times:

---

16.   *Conveyancing Act 1919* (NSW) s 44; *Law of Property Act 2000* (NT) s 6; *Property Law Act* (Qld) s 7; *Property Law Act 1958* (Vic) s 19A(3); *Property Law Act 1969* (WA) s 38.

One would have thought that there could have developed principles which assumed that when land was transferred into the name of a person, whether with or without consideration, and no matter what consideration came from, that person was presumed to hold both the legal and beneficial ownership. This could be disproved and it could show that the intention of the person causing the land to be transferred was to have the beneficial ownership himself.

19.85 Unfortunately, the wholesale dismantling of the presumptions appears to be beyond legitimate judicial power, at least in Australia: *Anderson v McPherson (No 2)* at [115]. Resulting trusts have become barnacles of equity that only legislation can remove. In *Calverley v Green* at CLR 266; ALR 266, Deane J said:

> The relevant presumptions are, however, too well entrenched as 'land-marks' in the law of property ... to be simply discarded by judicial decision. Indeed, the law embodying them has been said in this court to be so clear that it 'can ... no longer be the subject of argument' (per Dixon CJ, McTiernan, Williams, Fullagar and Taylor JJ, *Charles Marshall Pty Ltd v Grimsley* [(1956) 95 CLR 353 at 364]). If they are to be modified to avoid prima facie assumptions that a person intends the opposite to that which he does, it must be by legislative intervention which will not disturb past transactions which may conceivably have been structured by reference to them.

19.86 In *Nelson v Nelson*, at CLR 602; ALR 183–4, McHugh J called upon the legislature to abolish the presumptions on the grounds that they could wreak significant injustice to parties who are unaware of their existence. Of course, these comments can be contrasted with the decision of the House of Lords in *Stack v Dowden* (see 19.65–19.67), but the discarding of resulting trusts in that case was only for the limited purpose of domestic property disputes, and cannot be seen as a wholesale removal of resulting trusts from English law.

19.87 To some extent the presumptions have already been abolished by legislation in Australia. The failure of the British parliament to create legislative solutions has perhaps pushed the British judges into their unenviable position. As we shall see in Chapter 28, legislative regimes, such as the *Family Law Act 1975* (Cth) and the *Property (Relationships) Act 1984* (NSW), override any presumption of trust and allow for distribution of property on grounds unconnected with traditional legal and equitable interests. However, these statutes are normally confined to domestic property relationships and do not usually affect the law of succession or insolvency.

19.88 In many cases constructive trusts will also be available to remedy injustices caused by the operation of the presumptions. As discussed in Chapter 28, the presumptions will not apply if reliance upon them would amount to unconscientious conduct, and equity will intervene to impose a constructive trust in such circumstances: *Baumgartner v Baumgartner* (1987) 164 CLR 137; (1987) 76 ALR 75.

19.89 But what of those cases where the presumptions still operate? Surely, if the presumptions have to remain, they should be modified and updated to accord with modern social beliefs about gender equality and freedom of cohabitation and the relationships between familial generations. The New South Wales Court of Appeal took this approach in *Brown v Brown*, where all three judges found that the presumption of advancement should be applied in a gender neutral fashion. Kirby P (who dissented on the issue of whether there was sufficient evidence to rebut the presumption of advancement), at 599, said that there was a:

… general desirability that the law should not be expressed in terms which differentiate between people on the ground of their gender unless the differentiation is firmly based upon rational grounds supported by fact, not mere prejudice stereotype or history received from earlier times when attitudes to women were different.

19.90   Some critics have suggested that, while the application of gender neutrality in this case helps to break down stereotypes, it may actually materially disadvantage women.[17] Issues concerning the structural inequalities facing women and others are beyond the scope of this work, but it should be noted that, until such times as the presumptions are removed altogether, there are good reasons for removing sexist and stereotypical visions of a woman's place in society, such as decreasing the arbitrary functioning of rules and strengthening the symbolic importance of generality in law. Having said that, there are good and bad ways of legislating for reform. In the United Kingdom, an attempt to abolish the presumption of advancement in the *Equality Act 2010* (UK) has been criticised because of the patchwork and incomplete manner in which it was implemented.[18]

19.91   Like the common law, equity has evolved over time in response to social reality. It should continue to do so. In *Wirth v Wirth* (1956) 98 CLR 228 at 238, in a case extending the presumption of advancement to a man's fiancée, Dixon J said that maintaining a distinction between a married woman and a man's fiancée in the context of the application of the presumption of advancement:

> … involves almost a paradoxical distinction that does not accord with reason and can find a justification only on the ground that the doctrine depends on categories closed for historical reasons. That is not characteristic of doctrines of equity.

In continuing to treat married couples differently from de facto couples in the context of the same presumption, the law has failed to address another instance of the same 'paradoxical distinction'.

---

17. L Sarmas, 'A Step in the Wrong Direction: The Emergence of Gender "Neutrality" in the Equitable Presumption of Advancement' (1994) 10 *Melbourne University Law Review* 759 at 765.
18. J Glister, 'Section 199 of the Equality Act 2010: How Not to Abolish the Presumption of Advancement' (2010) 73 *Modern Law Review* 785.

20

TRUSTEES

INTRODUCTION

20.1   This chapter examines the rights, powers and duties of trustees. These matters are extremely important in practice. However, this was not always so. In earlier times the nature of the role of a trustee was of lesser importance than today. This flowed from the fact that during this 'classical period' most trusts related to land owned by the aristocracy with trustees not being burdened by particularly onerous duties given that the beneficiaries were generally also the occupiers of the land. The trustee in this classical period has been described by one scholar as 'a name-lender, a human instrument, or mere stooge' whose 'main function … was to distribute assets in ways not allowed at common law'.[1] However, in modern times the trustee has obligations that are both more complex and burdensome than in earlier times. This is due to modern trusts being more concerned with property such as cash, bonds and shares. This form of property requires a trustee to be much more actively involved in terms of maximising the value of the property and dealing with tax and other considerations than is the case with land occupied by the beneficiary of the trust.[2] This has also resulted in the role of trustee being more commonly undertaken by professionals such as solicitors, accountants and trustee corporations (particular superannuation trustees).[3] We now live in the age of the 'professional trustee class'.

APPOINTMENT, RETIREMENT AND REMOVAL OF TRUSTEES

Appointment

20.2   Trustees are appointed in the original instrument. Additionally, the trust may contain a power to appoint new trustees. That power may be exercised by the trustee or a third party (usually referred to as an 'appointer'). Only a legal person (a natural person or corporation) with the capacity to hold and deal with property can be appointed as a trustee. For example, corporations are able to be appointed as trustees, as long as their constitutional documents allow them to be appointed: *Re Levin & Co Ltd* [1936] NZLR 558. In contrast, minors are generally unable to act as trustees, because they are presumed to lack the capacity to deal with the management of trust property. In New South Wales and the Australian Capital Territory, the appointment of a minor as trustee is void and the minor

---

1.   M W Lau, *The Economic Structure of Trusts*, Oxford University Press, Oxford, 2011, p 3.
2.   Lau, *The Economic Structure of Trusts*, note 1 above, p 3.
3.   G Moffat, *Trusts Law, Text and Materials*, 4th ed, Cambridge University Press, Cambridge, 2005, pp 405–11.

will not be reappointed after reaching majority.[4] In other jurisdictions the appointment of a minor is not automatically void, but given that a minor lacks capacity, the appointment is delayed until the minor reaches majority. In the interim, a replacement trustee can act in the minor's stead. The rule against minors acting as trustees does not affect the imposition of resulting and constructive trusts: *Sanofi-Aventis Australia Pty Ltd v Kartono* [2006] NSWSC 1284 at [7].

20.3   If, for whatever reason, a prospective trustee fails to take up the office of trustee, the trust will not fail: *Mallot v Wilson* [1903] 2 Ch 494. In the case of a testamentary trust, the trustee's office will fall on the legal personal representatives of the testator's estate until a new trustee is appointed: *Re Smirthwaite's Trusts* (1871) LR 11 Eq 251. In the case of an *inter vivos* trust, the trust property will divest back to the settlor, and will be held by the settlor as trustee until the appointment of a new trustee: *Pearce v Pearce* (1856) 52 ER 1103; *Jasmine Trustees Limited v Wells and Hind* [2008] Ch 194 at 209; [2007] 1 All ER 1142 at 1161; *Meier v Dorzan Pty Limited* [2010] NSWSC 664 at [46].

20.4   Most trusts will contain an express power of appointment. In the absence of an express power of appointment, most jurisdictions have granted powers of appointment to particular classes of individuals.[5] The appointees of the statutory power include any person named in the trust instrument or, in the absence of such a person, any continuing or surviving trustees or legal personal representatives of the last surviving or continuing trustee. The statutory power can be exercised when:

1.   a trustee dies: *Church of England Property Trust v Rossi* (1893) 14 LR (NSW) Eq 186;
2.   a trustee is out of the jurisdiction for 12 months or more: *Re Geelong Waterworks & Sewerage Trust* [1955] VLR 302;[6]
3.   a trustee refuses to act: *Re Birchall; Birchall v Ashton* (1889) 40 Ch D 435;
4.   a trustee is incapable (*Re East* (1873) 8 Ch App 735), or unfit to act: *Re Turner* [1923] VLR 189; or
5.   a trustee desires to be discharged: *Re Pearse* (1917) 34 WN (NSW) 97.

20.5   The appointment must be made in writing, and in New South Wales and the Australian Capital Territory may be made by registered deed.[7] In *Retravision (NSW) Ltd v Copeland* [1997] NSWSC 466, Young J found that the New South Wales section required that the deed be registered before it took effect. Later decisions have accepted this analysis: *Lubavitch Mazal Pty Ltd v Yeshiva Properties No 1 Pty Ltd* [2003] NSWSC 535 at [40]; *Attorney-General for New South Wales v Fred Fulham* [2002] NSWSC 629 at [59]; *Commonwealth Bank of Australia v Nick Frisina Pty Ltd* [1999] NSWSC 907 at [12]. However, in *Statewide Developments Pty Ltd (in liq) (Recs and Mgrs Appointed) v Azure Property Group (Holdings) Pty Ltd* [2012] NSWSC 616 at [16], Pembroke J felt that these decisions were incorrect and that a registered deed may not be necessary if the trust

---

4.   *Conveyancing Act 1919* (ACT) s 151A; *Conveyancing Act 1919* (NSW) s 151A; *Minors (Property and Contracts) Act 1970* (NSW) s 10.
5.   *Trustee Act 1925* (ACT) s 6; *Trustee Act 1925* (NSW) s 6; *Trustee Act 1907* (NT) s 11; *Trusts Act 1973* (Qld) s 12; *Trustee Act 1936* (SA) s 14; *Trustee Act 1898* (Tas) s 13; *Trustee Act 1958* (Vic) s 41; *Trustees Act 1962* (WA) s 7.
6.   In New South Wales (*Trustee Act 1925* s 6(2)(c)) and the Australian Capital Territory (*Trustee Act 1925* s 6(2)(c)) a trustee who has remained out of the jurisdiction for more than two years may be replaced even though the trusts have been properly delegated.
7.   *Trustee Act 1925* (ACT) s 6(1); *Trustee Act 1925* (NSW) s 6(1).

instrument provided for another mechanism of appointment. Indeed, in all jurisdictions, apart from Queensland, statutory powers of appointment are said to be subject to any express conditions in the trust regarding appointment.[8] For example, in *Kendell v Sweeney* [2005] QSC 64 at [40] (aff'd *Kendell v Kendell* [2005] QCA 390), an appointment made in New South Wales in accordance with a trust deed was valid even though it was not in a registered deed.

20.6 Equity does not limit the number of trustees that can be appointed but in some jurisdictions the number of trustees is limited by legislation to four persons.[9] Note also that some Acts limit the number of trustees that can be appointed using the statutory power of appointment discussed below.[10]

Inherent power

20.7 The court has an inherent power to appoint trustees on the basis that equity will not allow a trust to fail for want of a trustee. The power can be exercised when it is expedient and practical for the court to appoint a new trustee. The court will consider factors such as the wishes of the trust's creator, the views of the beneficiaries, and the best method of promoting the execution of the trust: *Re Tempest* (1866) LR 1 Ch App 485. Heydon and Leeming give some examples of situations where the court has found it expedient to exercise its power to appoint a new trustee. They include circumstances where:

1. an infant trustee has been appointed;
2. a trustee has become bankrupt;
3. a trustee has been convicted of a felony;
4. a corporate trustee has been dissolved;
5. a trustee has gone missing;
6. a trustee suffers from mental or physical incapacity; and
7. a trustee resides permanently outside the jurisdiction.[11]

Statutory power

20.8 In most jurisdictions this inherent power is mirrored in statute.[12] The court's inherent power will not be exercised in cases where an appointment can be made using an express or a statutory power of appointment: *Re Gibbons' Trust* (1882) 30 WR 287. The statutory power requires that the appointment of the new trustee is 'expedient'. 'Expediency' generally requires some advantage to the interests of the beneficiaries or the security of the trust: *Porteous v Rinehart* (1998) 19 WAR 495 at 507; *Trustees of the Daughters of Our Lady of the Sacred Heart v Registrar-General* [2008] NTSC 13. In *Smith v Smith* [2006] WASC 166 at [3], Murray J said:

---

8. *Trustee Act 1925* (ACT) s 6(11); *Trustee Act 1925* (NSW) s 6(13); *Trustee Act 1907* (NT) s 11(5); *Trusts Act 1973* (Qld) s 10; *Trustee Act 1936* (SA) s 71; *Trustee Act 1898* (Tas) s 13(5); *Trustee Act 1958* (Vic) s 41(10); *Trustees Act 1962* (WA) s 7(8).
9. *Trusts Act 1973* (Qld) s 11; *Trustee Act 1958* (Vic) s 40.
10. *Trustee Act 1925* (ACT) s 6(6); *Trustee Act 1925* (NSW) s 6(5)(b); *Trustees Act 1962* (WA) s 7.
11. J D Heydon & M J Leeming, *Jacobs' Law of Trusts in Australia*, LexisNexis Butterworths, Sydney, 2006, p 336-8.
12. *Trustee Act 1925* (ACT) s 70; *Trustee Act 1925* (NSW) s 70; *Trustee Act 1907* (NT) s 27; *Trusts Act 1973* (Qld) s 80; *Trustee Act 1936* (SA) s 36; *Trustee Act 1898* (Tas) s 32; *Trustee Act 1958* (Vic) s 48; *Trustees Act 1962* (WA) s 77.

It has been held that in the context the word 'expedient' is one which carries the meaning that the action of appointment would be fit, or proper, or suitable, having regard to the interests of the beneficiaries, to the security of the trust property and to an efficient and satisfactory execution of the trusts and a faithful and sound exercise of the powers conferred upon the trustee.

20.9   When exerising the power of appointment the court must have regard to whether the proposed trustee is a 'proper person': *Re Tempest* (1866) LR 1 Ch App 485; *Hobkirk v Ritchie* (1933) 29 Tas LR 14. In *Northwest Capital Management v Westate Capital Ltd* [2012] WASC 121 at [283], Edelman J described three 'rules of practice' which must be considered:

1. Regard for the wishes of the settlor as expressed in the trust instrument or clearly to be collected from it. This consideration was expressed in negative terms in the leading authority, *Re Tempest* at 487, 'if the author of the trust has in terms declared that a particular person … should not be the trustee of the instrument';

2. Ensuring that the appointment will not promote the interests of some of the beneficiaries in opposition to the interests of others. This will ordinarily mean that it is a 'very salutary rule' (*Re Friend's Trusts* (1904) 21 WN (NSW) 166 at 1672) that a beneficiary will not be appointed as trustee, even if the beneficiary is 'a person of the highest character' (*Re Friend's Trusts* at 167) and even if there is a 'community of interest' between the beneficiaries and the trustee (*Johnstone v Johnstone* (1902) 2 SR (NSW) Eq 90 at 93);

3. Consideration of whether the appointment of a particular person will promote or impede the execution of the trust.

20.10   The courts are not bound to follow the directions in the trust instrument about the appointment of a replacement trustee. In *Scaffidi v Montevento Holdings Pty Ltd* [2011] WASCA 146 at [176], Murphy and Anderson JJ said:

In an application for the administration of a trust by the court, where the court decrees that some 'proper person' be appointed as trustee, the decree does not take away from the donee of the power of appointment under the instrument, the power of nominating for appointment new trustees, but after the decree the power may only be exercised subject to the supervision of the court. If the donee of the power repeatedly nominated improper persons, that would amount to a refusal to exercise the power, and the court could then makes its own appointment: *In Re Gadd* (1883) 23 Ch D 134 at 136–137. In *Re Gadd*, the donee of the power had nominated a particular person whom the court, on appeal, considered was a fit and proper person, and the court thereupon confirmed the nomination of the donee and made an order for that person's appointment. A general administration action has been virtually superseded by other specific actions in more recent times, such as an application for orders of the kind available under s 77 of the *Trustees Act* [*1962* (WA)]: *Pope v DRP Nominees* [1999] SASC 337 at [41]. The power in the court under s 77(1) of the Act to 'make an order for the appointment of a new trustee' would, in our view, on its proper construction, include the power to order, in appropriate circumstances, the appointment of a 'proper person' as trustee, with the particular person to be nominated by the donee of the power under the supervision of the court in accordance with the decision of *Re Gadd*.

20.11   The court is generally reluctant to appoint a replacement trustee who is aligned to the interests of a beneficiary (*Australian Olympic Committee Inc v Big Fights Inc (No 2)* (2000) 176 ALR 124), or those with close family ties to the beneficiaries: *Saul v Lin (No 2)* (2004) 60 NSWLR 275.

Disclaimer

20.12   A person cannot be forced to be a trustee of an express trust and a proposed trustee can always disclaim the appointment: *Robinson v Pett* (1734) 24 ER 1049. However, disclaimer will be ineffective if the person has impliedly accepted the trust, for example, by dealing with the trust property: *Conyngham v Conyngham* (1750) 27 ER 74. Additionally, the disclaimer must relate to the entirety of the trust to be effective: *Re Lord & Fullerton's Contract* [1896] 1 Ch 226. Disclaimers should take the form of a deed (*Re Scar* [1951] Ch 280), but a disclaimer may be implied from oral declarations and refusals to act: *Re Clout and Frewer's Contract* [1924] 2 Ch 230.

Death of a trustee

20.13   If a trust has several trustees and one of them dies, the office is continued by the surviving trustees.[13] The death of a sole trustee leaves the office vacant and the trustee's heirs and assigns have no automatic right to take up the office.[14] Some jurisdictions have attempted to remedy this situation by investing the legal personal representatives of the dead trustee with the trustee's powers, at least until such time as a new trustee is appointed.[15] In Queensland, s 16(2) of the *Trusts Act 1973* (Qld) provides that the Public Trustee is given the trust powers until the legal personal representatives of the deceased trustee offer to take up the trustee's powers or until a new trustee is appointed.

20.14   If a corporate trustee is dissolved, the court can appoint a new trustee: *King of Hanover v Bank of England* (1869) LR 8 Eq 350; *Smith v Smith* [2006] WASC 166. In *Danich Pty Ltd Re Cenco Holdings Pty Ltd* [2005] NSWSC 293, a company that was reregistered after a period of deregistration was revested with the trust property after reregistration.

Retirement

20.15   Trust deeds normally make provision for the retirement of trustees. Most jurisdictions have provided for a statutory mechanism for retirement should the trust instrument be silent on the issue.[16] A trustee is normally required to retire with the consent of his or her co-trustees and must retire in writing or via deed. All things necessary to vest the trust property in continuing trustees must be done to give effect to the retirement.

20.16   A promise or covenant that a trustee will retire in certain situations does not bring about an automatic retirement when those situations arise: *Whitton v ACN 003 266 886 Pty Ltd (in liq)* (1996) 42 NSWLR 123; *Danich Pty Ltd Re Cenco Holdings Pty Ltd* at [14]–[15].

---

13.   *Trustee Act 1925* (ACT) s 57; *Trustee Act 1925* (NSW) s 57; *Trustee Act 1907* (NT) s 23; *Trusts Act 1973* (Qld) s 16(1); *Trustee Act 1936* (SA) s 32; *Trustee Act 1898* (Tas) s 25; *Trustee Act 1958* (Vic) s 22; *Trustees Act 1962* (WA) s 45.

14.   Heydon & Leeming, *Jacobs' Law of Trusts in Australia*, note 11 above, p 346.

15.   *Conveyancing Law and Property Act 1884* (Tas) s 34(1); *Trustee Act 1958* (Vic) s 22; *Trustees Act 1962* (WA) s 45(2).

16.   *Trustee Act 1925* (ACT) s 8; *Trustee Act 1925* (NSW) s 8; *Trustee Act 1907* (NT) s 12; *Trusts Act 1973* (Qld) s 14; *Trustee Act 1936* (SA) s 15; *Trustee Act 1898* (Tas) s 14; *Trustee Act 1958* (Vic) s 44; *Trustees Act 1962* (WA) s 9.

Removal

Express power in the instrument

20.17   Trustees may be removed by using express powers outlined in the trust instrument. If the procedures laid down for the exercise of the power have not been followed the attempted removal of the trustee will fail: *Northwest Capital Management v Westate Capital Ltd* [2012] WASC 121 at [218]–[225]. Courts will examine the proper construction of the language of the power to see that it is wide enough to allow for the removal of the trustee and the appointment of a replacement: *Montefiore v Guedalla* [1903] 2 Ch 723 at 725–726; *In Re Christina Brown* (1921) 22 SR (NSW) 90 at 93–94.

20.18   The express power to remove trustees and appoint new ones has often been described as a 'fiduciary power': *Re Skeats' Settlement; Skeats v Evans* (1889) 42 Ch D 522 at 526; *In Re Newen* (1894) 2 Ch 297 at 309; *Re Burton; Wily v Burton* (1994) 126 ALR 557 at 559–560; *Pope v DRP Nominees Pty Ltd* (1999) 74 SASR 78 at [46]–[48].

20.19   Other cases have put the power as being one to be exercised in good faith and for the benefit of the trust as a whole. In *Duke of Portland v Topham* (1864) 11 HLC 32 at 54, Lord Westbury LC said:

> I think we must all feel that the settled principles of the law upon this subject must be upheld, namely, that the donee, the appointor under the power, shall, at the time of the exercise of that power, and for any purpose for which it is used, act with good faith and sincerity, and with an entire and single view to the real purpose and object of the power, and not for the purpose of accomplishing or carrying into effect any bye or sinister object (I mean sinister in the sense of its being beyond the purpose and intent of the power) which he may desire to effect in the exercise of the power.

20.20   In *Hillcrest (Ilford) Pty Ltd v Kingsford (Ilford) Pty Ltd (No 2)* [2010] NSWSC 285 at [38], Biscoe AJ found that 'the removal and appointment power must be exercised for the benefit of beneficiaries, not for the benefit of the person upon whom the power is conferred'. Other cases have followed this formulation: *Berger v Lysteron Pty Ltd* [2012] VSC 95 at [84].

20.21   However, the express power conferred may be broad enough to allow appointors to remove and appoint trustees for their own benefit, which would seem incompatible with the power being fiduciary in nature. In *Scaffidi v Montevento Holdings Pty Ltd* at [151], Murphy JA and Hall J stated that in such cases 'the trust property may be regarded, at least for certain statutory purposes, as effectively owned by the appointor, or as property in which the appointor has a contingent interest.'

The court's power to remove trustees

20.22   If the trust instrument is silent on the issue of removal, only the court has the power to remove a trustee. There are two sources of the court's power to remove trustees: an inherent jurisdiction and the statutory power of appointment.[17]

---

17. *Trustee Act 1925* (ACT) s 70; *Trustee Act 1925* (NSW) s 70; *Trustee Act 1907* (NT) s 27; *Trusts Act 1973* (Qld) s 80; *Trustee Act 1936* (SA) s 36; *Trustee Act 1898* (Tas) s 32; *Trustee Act 1958* (Vic) s 48; *Trustees Act 1962* (WA) s 77.

20.23   For the inherent jurisdiction, the welfare of the beneficiaries is the dominant consideration in determining whether or not it is proper to remove a trustee: *Trojan v Nest Egg Nominees Pty Ltd* [2004] SASC 182; *Rosenberg v Fifteenth Eestin Nominees Pty Ltd* [2007] VSC 101 at [171]; *Deutsh v Deutsh* [2011] VSC 345 at [13]. In *Miller v Cameron* (1936) 54 CLR 572 at 575, Dixon J said:

> The jurisdiction to remove a trustee is exercised wit h a view to the interests of the beneficiaries, to the security of the trust property and to an efficient and satisfactory execution of the trusts and a faithful and sound exercise of the powers conferred upon the trustee. In deciding to remove a trustee the Court forms a judgment based upon considerations, possibly large in number and varied in character, which combine to show that the welfare of the beneficiaries is opposed to his continued occupation of the office. Such a judgment must be largely discretionary. A trustee is not to be removed unless circumstances exist which afford ground upon which the jurisdiction may be exercised. But in a case where enough appears to authorise the Court to act, the delicate question whether it should act and proceed to remove the trustee is one upon which the decision of a primary Judge is entitled to especial weight.

20.24   For the statutory jurisdiction, the main test is whether the removal of the trustee is 'expedient', as discussed above: see 20.7. The statutory power can be exercised even where there is an appointor who is willing and able to appoint: *Pope v DRP Nominees Pty Ltd* (1999) 74 SASR 78.

Reasons for removal

20.25   Trustees can be removed on the grounds that they are unfit for office. Trustees who act in ways inimical to the trust will be removed: *Officer v Haynes* (1877) 3 VLR (Eq) 115; *McLauchlan v Prince* [2002] WASC 274. Similarly, trustees who fundamentally misunderstand their duties and responsibilities will be removed (*Mansour v Mansour* (2009) 24 VR 498) as will be trustees who are hopelessly conflicted: *Hill v Fry* [2008] VSC 13. Trustees who have disappeared and become uncontactable may also be removed: *Kennedy v Kennedy* [2011] NSWSC 1619.

20.26   Trustees may also be removed when they have become incapable of acting, such as when they have been made bankrupt: *Miller v Cameron*. However, corporate trustees in liquidation will not automatically be replaced, as the liquidators in charge of such companies may be well placed to perform trustee functions, at least until the company has been dissolved: *Wells v Wily* [2004] NSWSC 607. A tardy trustee may not necessarily be removed (*Re Greif* [2005] VSC 266), but if the effective administration of the trust has broken down it may be necessary to replace the trustee: *Smith v Smith*.

20.27   The mere fact that the trustee and the beneficiaries are in disagreement is not a sufficient ground for removal: *Re Brockbank; Ward v Bates* [1948] Ch 206; [1948] 1 All ER 287. Nor will a trustee be removed merely because the beneficiaries wish to replace the trustee and appoint another: *Guazzini v Pateson* (1918) 18 SR (NSW) 275; *Colston v McMullen* [2010] QSC 292; *Kershaw v Micklethwaite* [2010] EWHC 506 (Ch). It may be necessary for inquiries to be made into why there is dissention between the trustee and the beneficiaries, otherwise there is a risk that the beneficiary might be able to manufacture a dispute and then use that as a reason for seeking the removal of a trustee: *Re Whitehouse* [1982] Qd R 196 at 206; *Forster v Davies* (1863) 55 ER 245. However, trustees will be removed if insoluble conflict between them and beneficiaries destroys the trustees' capacity to carry on their duties: *Craven-Sands v Koch* [2000] NSWSC 374; *Kain v Hutton* [2007]

3 NZLR 349; *The Thomas and Agnes Carvel Foundation v Carvel* [2007] EWHC 1314 (Ch); *Crowle Foundation v NSW Trustee & Guardian* [2010] NSWSC 657 at [178]; *Rayner v N J Sheaffe Pty Ltd* [2010] NSWSC 810; *Scott v Scott* [2012] EWHC 2397 (Ch). It is not therefore necessary to establish bad faith, misconduct or breach of trust before a trustee is removed: *Elovalis v Elovalis* [2008] WASCA 141 at [40].

20.28 If there are breaches of trust they will not automatically lead to removal unless there is positive misconduct: *Princess Anne of Hesse v Field* [1963] NSWR 998. In cases where the trustee has been negligent, the trustee will only be removed if the negligence endangered the trust property or showed a lack of honesty, capacity or fidelity: *Letterstedt v Broers* (1884) 9 App Cas 371 at 385–6.

20.29 In South Australia the court has power to remove and replace trustees in the interests of the beneficiaries and/or to advance the trust, without finding any fault or inadequacy on the part of the existing trustees.[18]

Are these disputes arbitrable?

20.30 The parties in a dispute concerning the removal of a trustee may agree to refer the matter to arbitration. In *Rinehart v Welker* [2012] NSWCA 95, mining magnate Gina Rinehart sought to enforce an agreement to the effect that her family would arbitrate any disputes concerning her trusteeship of her family's discretionary trust. Some of her children sought to have her removed as trustee and argued, amongst others things, that the agreement was against public policy as it ousted the court's jurisdiction over the removal of trustees. While the Court of Appeal found that the arbitration agreement did not apply to the dispute at hand (for reasons of drafting) Bathurst CJ (McColl JA agreeing), at [175], said:

> [I]t is my opinion that at least in circumstances where the trustee and each beneficiary have expressly agreed to their disputes being referred to arbitration, a court should give effect to that agreement. The supervisory jurisdiction of the court is not ousted. It continues to have the supervisory role conferred upon it by the relevant legislation … There may be powerful commercial or domestic reasons for parties to have disputes between a trustee and beneficiary settled privately. It does not seem to me that the matters to which I have referred above should preclude a court from giving effect to such an agreement provided the jurisdiction of the court is not ousted entirely.

In his dissenting judgment, Young JA, at [226], said:

> I consider that the difficulties in a court enforcing any decision of an arbitrator are so great (or could be so great if a party was uncooperative) that the opposite view is preferable. Whilst a court could make orders authorising a Registrar to sign transfers on behalf of the former trustee and direct the Registrar General to register them, removal and replacement of trustees usually involves the taking of accounts and an in personam order against the former trustee which if he or she disobeys it leads to imprisonment. It is stretching things to contemplate that an order for imprisonment would be an appropriate enforcement procedure to perfect an arbitrator's award.

---

18. *Trustee Act 1936* (SA) s 36.

Vesting

20.31 Trust property must be vested in trustees for the trust to be properly constituted. 'Vesting' refers to the process of securing the transfer of legal title to a trustee. When trusts are initially created this process occurs automatically, as one of the requirements of a trust is that the legal title be transferred and held by trustees. When new trustees take up their offices the legal title needs to be transferred to them, or 'vested' with them, for the appointment to be effective.

20.32 Most statutory provisions dealing with appointment and/or retirement state that once a new trustee is validly appointed, the trust property is vested automatically in him or her, as a joint tenant with any continuing trustee.[19] If the property is subject to a system of registered transfer, like Torrens system land, the property will not vest until that transfer is registered in accordance with that system. In *Statewide Developments Pty Ltd (In Liq) (Recs and Mgrs Appointed) v Azure Property Group (Holdings) Pty Ltd* at [24], Pembroke J found that this automatic vesting power did not require that the appointment of the new trustee be made via registered deed. As long as the appointment was valid according to the trust instrument, automatic vesting would occur.

20.33 The court can make vesting orders to overcome any problems associated with transferring title into the names of new trustees.[20] In the Northern Territory and South Australia the statutory power is limited to transfers of land, stocks and choses in action, but other jurisdictions are not limited by the nature of the trust property. The court's power should only be exercised when other methods of transferring title have failed or where they are inexpedient, difficult or impractical: *Bloomingdale Holdings v 87 Stevedore Street* [2010] VSC 268 at [26]; *Casella v Casella* [1969] VR 49. The power is not to be used as a substitute for normal methods of conveyancing (*Chang v Registrar of Titles* (1978) 137 CLR 177; (1976) 8 ALR 285) and the dominant considerations for the court are the preservation of the trust property and the welfare of the beneficiaries: *Re Dobrotwir* [2011] VSC 402 at [38].

RIGHTS OF TRUSTEES

The right to reimbursement and exoneration

20.34 Trustees have a right to be indemnified for costs and expenses incurred in the proper administration of the trust: *Southern Wine Corporation Pty Ltd (in liq) v Frankland River Olive Co Ltd* (2005) 31 WAR 162. In the exercise of this right the trustee can have recourse to the trust property: *JA Pty Ltd v Jonco Holdings Pty Ltd* [2000] NSWSC 147. If the trustee incurs a liability to a third party in tort arising from the proper administration of the trust, he or she is entitled to an indemnity: *Gatsios Holdings v Mick Kritharas Holdings (in liq)* [2002] NSWCA 29. The indemnity can be for past, present or future work and the amount of the indemnity need not be precisely known or quantified: *Re Application of Sutherland* [2004] NSWSC 798 at [11]–[15]; *Kennett v Charlton* [2007] NSWSC 190 at [16]; *Agusta Pty Ltd v Official Trustee in Bankruptcy* [2009] NSWCA 129.

---

19. *Trustee Act 1925* (ACT) s 9; *Trustee Act 1925* (NSW) s 9; *Trustee Act 1907* (NT) s 13; *Trusts Act 1973* (Qld) s 15 (not retirement); *Trustee Act 1936* (SA) s 16; *Trustee Act 1898* (Tas) s 15; *Trustee Act 1958* (Vic) s 45 (not retirement); *Trustees Act 1962* (WA) s 10 (not retirement).

20. *Trustee Act 1925* (ACT) ss 71, 78; *Trustee Act 1925* (NSW) ss 71, 78; *Trustee Act 1907* (NT) ss 28, 37; *Trusts Act 1973* (Qld) s 82; *Trustee Act 1936* (SA) ss 37, 41; *Trustee Act 1898* (Tas) ss 33–34; *Trustee Act 1958* (Vic) s 51; *Trustees Act 1962* (WA) s 78.

20.35   In *Savage v Union Bank of Australia Ltd* (1906) 3 CLR 1170, the High Court found that trustees have an additional right of exoneration that allows them to draw directly on trust assets to discharge their duties, as opposed to paying out of their own funds and seeking reimbursement.

Reasonable expenses

20.36   For the right of indemnity to arise, the trustee's expenses must have been reasonably incurred in the course of the trustee's duties.[21] If the expenses are unreasonable, or not associated with the exercise of trust duties, the indemnity may be reduced or completely denied: *Re O'Donoghue* [1998] 1 NZLR 116. In *RWG Management Ltd v Commissioner for Corporate Affairs* [1985] VR 385 at 396, Booking J said:

> A trustee's right to be indemnified out of the Trust property is limited to liabilities or expenses that have been properly incurred in the execution of the trust: *Stott v Milne* (1884) 25 Ch D 710, at p 715; *Re Beddoe* [1893] 1 Ch 547 at p 588. If, for example, a trustee incurs some liability by an act in relation to the trust property which is in excess of his powers, he has no right of indemnity: *Leedham v Chawner* (1858) 70 ER 191. The result is the same where a liability is incurred as the result of conduct on the part of the trustee which is in breach of his duty, not as being in excess of power, but as being in breach of his duty to execute the trust with reasonable diligence and care: *Ecclesiastical Commissioners v Pinney* [1900] 2 Ch 736 at pp 742–3, per Rigby LJ, a case of contract; *Benett v Wyndham* (1862) 45 ER 1183 and *Re Raybould* [1900] 1 Ch 199, cases of tort.

20.37   In *Gatsios Holdings v Nick Kritharas Holdings (in liq)*, the New South Wales Court of Appeal was seemingly critical of the term 'properly incurred'. Spigelman CJ, at [8], doubted whether the term was really a test and Meagher JA, at [47], doubted whether it meant anything more than 'non-criminal' or 'non-fraudulent'. The Victorian Court of Appeal was not as discouraging in *Nolan v Collie* (2003) 7 VR 287, where it was found that the test should be restated as 'not improperly incurred', meaning expenses incurred in circumstances of bad faith, without power or in the absence of reasonable care and diligence would not be indemnified.

20.38   Expenses which are incurred outside the terms of the trust or in the course of a breach of the trustee's core obligation will give rise to the right of indemnity: *Strang v Strang* [2009] NSWSC 760; *Holli Managed Investments Pty Ltd v Australian Securities Commission* (1998) 90 FCR 341; 160 ALR 409. In *Nolan v Collie* at 310, these core duties were said to include the duty to keep and render accounts, the duty to avoid conflicts, the duty to obtain an unauthorised benefit and the duty to adhere to and carry out the terms of the trust. But if it can be shown that the conduct was merely a 'slip' or a 'mere error of judgment' in the day to day management of the trust, which occurred in good faith, then it may still be open to the court to order remuneration: *Nolan v Collie* at 310.

Trustees' legal expenses

20.39   If trustees are sued in their capacity as trustees, the trustees are entitled to defend their conduct as an incident of administration and they can be indemnified for their legal costs: *In Re Llewellin; Llewellin v Williams* (1887) 37 Ch D 317 at 327; *National Trustees Executors and Agency Co of Australasia v Barnes* (1941) 64 CLR 268; *Bovaird v Frost* [2009] NSWSC 917 at [26]–[45]; *Drummond v Drummond* [1999] NSWSC 923 at [43]–[47]; *Fay v Moramba Services Pty Ltd* [2010]

---

21.   L Aitken, 'A liability "properly incurred"? — The trustee's right to indemnity, and exemption from liability for breach of trust' (2011) 35 *Australian Bar Review* 53 at 54.

NSWSC 725 at [4]. This is even when they are sued by the beneficiaries: *Re Application of Macedonian Orthodox Community Church St Petka Inc (No 3)* [2006] NSWSC 1247 at [49]. In *Metropolitan Petar v Mitreski* [2012] NSWSC 16 at [114], Brereton J said:

> I therefore do not accept that it can be said that there is a breach of trust in resorting to trust assets to fund the defence of litigation brought against the trustee. Upon incurring a liability in the course of its duties as such, the trustee is entitled to be indemnified out of the trust assets. If it is not improperly defending proceedings brought against it as trustee, the trustee is entitled to resort to the trust assets to fund its defence. Only if the trustee takes more than the proper limit of its right of indemnity would there be a breach of trust. What costs orders will be made, and to what extent the [trustee] will be held entitled or disentitled to indemnity out of the trust assets, will be known only following the outcome of these proceedings, and any consequential issues in respect of costs. It is not possible to say now that the [trustee] has, by resorting to trust assets to fund the defence of these proceedings and the associated litigation, thereby committed a breach of trust; it may have taken no more than it was entitled to take in exercise of its right of indemnity. If, when the question of costs is ultimately determined and quantified, it transpires that the [trustee] has helped itself to more than its legitimate entitlement, that will then be a different question.

The 'clear accounts' rule

20.40   Any claim for indemnity will be set-off against any loss caused by the trustee's breach. This is referred to as the 'clear accounts' rule: *Australian Securities and Investments Commission v Letten (No 17)* (2011) 286 ALR 346 at 352–3. In *RWG Management Ltd v Commissioner for Corporate Affairs* at 397–8, Brooking J said that the trustee may only claim an indemnity if there is a balance left over after compensation has been paid to the trust for losses for which the trustee is responsible.

Expanding or contracting the right under the express terms of the trust

20.41   Theoretically, the trustee's right to indemnity may be expanded by the trust deed so as to allow trustees to be reimbursed even in cases of breach of trust. Practically this will be difficult as such expansion will be treated as an exclusion clause and read as strictly as possible: *McLean v Burns Philp Trustee Co Ltd* (1985) 2 NSWLR 623; *Armitage v Nurse* [1998] Ch 241; [1997] 2 All ER 705. The effect of exclusion clauses is discussed at 21.85–21.87.

20.42   On the other side of the equation, there is conflicting authority as to whether the trustee's right to indemnity can be excluded by the trust.[22] It has been said that the right to indemnity is an inseparable incident of the office of the trustee which cannot be excluded: *Kemtron Industries Pty Ltd v Commissioner of Stamp Duties* [1984] 1 Qd R 576; *Jessup v Queensland Housing Commission* [2002] 2 Qd R 270 at 275; *JA Pty Ltd v Johnco Holdings Pty Ltd*. In Queensland, s 65 of the *Trusts Act 1973* (Qld) specifically states that the right to indemnity cannot be excluded. In other jurisdictions, it may still be considered a breach of public policy to have a clause which takes away the trustee's right to indemnity, as such a clause directly seeks to undermine the trustee's statutory rights: *Moyes v J and L Developments Pty Ltd (No 2)* [2007] SASC 261. However, there have been cases where the right to indemnity has been viewed as subject to provisions of the trust deed. In *RWG Management Ltd v Commissioner for Corporate Affairs (Vic)*, Brooking J found that if a trustee was willing to accept

---

22.   See the discussion in P Edmundson, 'Express limitation of a trustee's rights of indemnity' (2011) 5 *Journal of Equity* 77.

the office in a situation where the trust instrument ousted his or her indemnity, the trustee should be free to do so.

The proprietary nature of the trustee's right to reimbursement and exoneration

20.43 The trustee's right to indemnification has priority over the interests of the beneficiaries: *Chief Commissioner of Stamp Duties v Buckle* (1998) 192 CLR 226 at 245–6; 151 ALR 1 at 13–14. If the beneficiaries call for the distribution of trust assets, the trustee must be reimbursed before that distribution: *Octavo Investments Pty Ltd v Knight* (1979) 144 CLR 360; (1979) 27 ALR 129. If the beneficiaries are suing the trustee for breach of trust the trustee is entitled to retain trust funds as an indemnity for his or her legal costs in defending the claim: *Hayman v Equity Trustees Ltd* [2003] VSC 353.

20.44 The right to indemnification is an equitable property right, either in the form of a lien or a charge, that is effective against third parties in any priority dispute over the trust property: *Trim Perfect Australia v Albrook Constructions* [2006] NSWSC 153 at [20]. In *Octavo Investments Pty Ltd v Knight* at CLR 367; ALR 134, the trustee's right of indemnity was described by Stephen, Mason, Aickin and Wilson JJ as follows:

> It is common ground that a trustee who in discharge of his trust enters into business transactions is personally liable for any debts that are incurred in the course of those transactions: *Vacuum Oil Co Pty Ltd v Wiltshire* (1945) 72 CLR 319. However, he is entitled to be indemnified against those liabilities from the trust assets held by him and for the purpose of enforcing the indemnity the trustee possesses a charge or right of lien over those assets: *Vacuum Oil Co Pty Ltd v Wiltshire*. The charge is not capable of differential application to certain only of such assets. It applies to the whole range of trust assets in the trustee's possession except for those assets, if any, which under the terms of the trust deed the trustee is not authorised to use for the purposes of carrying on the business: *Dowse v Gorton* [1891] AC 190.

20.45 The trustee must seek a judicial sale or the appointment of a receiver to enforce this security and cannot resort to a foreclosure or sale out of court: *ANZ Banking Group Ltd v Intagro Projects Pty Ltd* [2004] NSWSC 1054. The trustee will ordinarily have to have possession or control of the trust assets, and is entitled to keep that possession until the lien has been satisfied: *Re Exhall Coal Co Ltd* (1866) 55 ER 970; *Re Enhill Pty Ltd* [1983] 1 VR 561. However, the security is not destroyed if possession is lost. In *Ronori Pty Ltd v ACN 101 071 998 Pty Ltd* [2008] NSWSC 246 at [15], Barrett J said:

> Although the trustee's right to resort to trust property is sometimes described as a lien, it is not essential for the enjoyment and effectuation of the right that possession of the trust property be retained. The right entails, as I have said, a beneficial interest in the property. It is not in the nature of a possessory security.

20.46 In *ANZ Banking Group Ltd v Intagro Projects Pty Ltd* at [15], White J, said that if third parties hold trust assets the trustee may obtain control of them, if necessary by invoking the assistance of the court.

20.47 If the trustee is replaced, the new trustee will take the property subject to the old trustee's lien, with the possible exception of a bona fide purchaser for value without notice: *Belar Pty Ltd (in* *liq) v Mahaffey* [2000] 1 Qd R 477. There are conflicting authorities as to whether the old trustee may retain possession of the trust property and refuse to transfer possession to the new trustee until satisfied. In *Re Suco Gold Pty Ltd (in liq)* (1983) 33 SASR 99 at 109, King CJ stated that '[t]he right of possession of the trustee, until his right of indemnity is exercised, is superior to those of a new trustee or the *cestuis que trust*'. However, in *Lemery Holdings Pty Ltd v Reliance Financial Services Pty Ltd* [2008] NSWSC 1344 at [50], Brereton J, after an extensive review of the authorities, said:

> [I]t follows in principle that a former trustee does not have a right to retain, as against a new trustee, the trust assets as security for an accrued right of indemnity, though the former trustee is entitled to ensure the new trustee does not take steps which will destroy, diminish or jeopardise the old trustee's right of security, which subsists in the trust assets after their transfer to the new trustee.

20.48   In *Prior v Simeon (No 2)* [2011] WASC 61 at [20], Corboy J disagreed and said:

> [I]t appears to me that the plaintiff is entitled to an order for possession of the Land in aid of his accrued right of indemnity and not merely pursuant to a direction of the court made ancillary to an order for judicial sale. First, that is the conclusion reached by the Full Court of the Supreme Court of South Australia in *Re Suco Gold* and I regard myself as bound by that decision unless I conclude that it is plainly wrong (and I do not consider the decision to be plainly wrong). Second, as between trustee and beneficiary, it appears to me that the right of a trustee to recover possession of property the subject of an equitable lien from the beneficiary is consistent with the nature of the proprietary interest recognised by the High Court in *Octavo Investments* and *Commissioner of Stamp Duties (NSW) v Buckle*. As between the trustee and the beneficiary, it is the trustee who is entitled to possession of the property that is subject to its lien where there is an accrued right of indemnity.

20.49   Creditors of the trustee have rights against the trustee's equitable property rights over the trust property. In cases where the trustee has become insolvent, the creditors may be subrogated to the rights of indemnification enjoyed by the trustee: *Arkmill Pty Ltd v Tippers Co Pty Ltd* [2006] QSC 248. Alternatively, the rights of the trustee will vest in the trustee in bankruptcy or liquidator: *Re Suco Gold Pty Ltd (in liq)* at 99; *Garra Water Investments Pty Ltd (in liq) v Ourback Yard Nursery Pty Ltd* [2012] SASC 44 at [31]. In *Federal Commissioner of Taxation v Bruton Holdings Pty Limited (in liq)* (2010) 188 FCR 516 at 525, Graham J said:

> Where a trustee company has a duty to incur debts for the purposes of the trust business, it also has a duty to pay those debts. If the company's obligation as trustee to pay the debts incurred in carrying out the trust cannot be performed unless the liquidation of the trustee company proceeds, the liquidator's costs, expenses and remuneration should be regarded as debts of the trustee company incurred in discharging the duties imposed by the trust and as covered by the trustee's right of indemnity.

20.50   The costs and expenses of the liquidator must relate to those incurred in the administration of the trust, such as the costs of identifying, recovering, realising, protecting and distributing trust assets: *Re Sutherland, French Caledonian Travel Service Pty Ltd (in liq)* (2003) 59 NSWLR 361; *Glazier Holdings Pty Ltd (in liq) v Australian Men's Health Pty Ltd (in liq)* [2006] NSWSC 1240 at [42]; *Dayroll Pty Ltd (in Liq) v Dayroll NSW Pty Ltd* [2009] NSWSC 895 at [5]; *Re Dalewon Pty Ltd (in liq)* [2010] QSC 311 at [13]–[18].

Bare trustees and the right to reimbursement and exoneration

20.51   It might be argued that bare trustees (see 15.13–15.18) should not enjoy a right to reimbursement or exoneration, as it is not part of their function to actively manage the trust property and any such costs in doing so would not be reasonably incurred. However, the High Court, in *CGU Insurance Limited v One.Tel Limited (in liq)* (2010) 242 CLR 174 at 182–3; 268 ALR 439 at 446, said that bare trustees have a duty to preserve the trust property. In both *Bruton Holdings Pty Limited (In Liq) v Commissioner of Taxation* (2011) 193 FCR 442 and *Caterpillar Financial Australia Limited v Ovens Nominees Pty Ltd* [2011] FCA 677, the costs of legal proceedings commenced by bare trustees were found to be recoverable because the costs were incurred in the protection of trust property.

Right to call upon beneficiaries to satisfy the right of indemnity

20.52   The right of a trustee to an indemnity also includes a right to pursue the beneficiaries personally for costs and expenses incurred by the trustee: *Ron Kingham Real Estate Pty Ltd v Edgar* [1999] 2 Qd R 439; *Balkin v Peck* (1998) 43 NSWLR 706. The basis of this right is that it would be unfair for the trustee to be burdened with costs while the beneficiaries receive their entitlements: *Hardoon v Belilios* [1901] AC 118; *Countryside (No 3) v Best* [2001] NSWSC 1152 at [39]. This aspect of the right to indemnity applies to beneficiaries who are of the age of majority (*sui juris*) and absolutely entitled to their beneficial interest: *Balkin v Peck*. In the majority of cases this right arises after the trust property has been exhausted and where the trustee has no other option but to pursue the beneficiaries personally to recoup costs. It does not apply to discretionary beneficiaries as they have no right to call upon the assets of the trust and are therefore without any real benefit. The trustee's right to pursue the beneficiaries personally survives the distribution of the trust assets and the termination of the trust relationship: *Grizonic v Ranken* [2011] NSWSC 471 at [62]. However a properly worded exclusion of the trustee's rights to indemnity will be binding: *Adams v Zen 28 Pty Ltd* [2010] QSC 36 at [34].

The right of contribution

20.53   Co-trustees are jointly and severally liable for losses occasioned by a breach of trust, even where one trustee is solely responsible for the loss: *Bahin v Hughes* (1886) 31 Ch D 390; *Cockburn v GIO Finance Ltd (No 2)* (2001) 51 NSWLR 624. Where two defendant trustees have committed a breach of trust each is liable to pay compensation to the beneficiary measured by the amount of loss attributable to their breach: *Fan v Tang* [2010] NSWSC 11. However, if only one trustee is available to be sued as a defendant that trustee will be liable. Even a passive trustee may be liable because their inactivity has allowed the co-trustees to breach the trust.

20.54   Innocent trustees may be entitled to an indemnity in circumstances where the active, defaulting trustee has retained trust property or personally benefited from the breach. In *Goodwin v Duggan* (1996) 41 NSWLR 158 at 166, Handley and Beazley JJA said:

> A trustee … has an equity to be indemnified by a co-trustee who personally received trust funds and converted them to his own use. Where the trust funds remain in the hands of the co-trustee the other trustee has an equity to follow such funds and require them to be repaid to the trust thereby securing a practical indemnity at least in part. The equity to relief in specie may be lost where the funds cannot be traced, but in our opinion there remains a personal equity against the trustee who received the funds which renders him primarily liable, as between the trustees, to make good the loss.

Indemnity may also arise in cases where the trustee, who is entitled to a right of indemnity, was misled by a co-trustee who was also a solicitor to the trust: *Re Partington* (1887) 57 LT 654.

20.55   The liability of co-trustees for breach of trust has been altered somewhat by statute.[23] Section 59(2) of the *Trustee Act 1925* (ACT) is a typical example of such alteration. It stipulates:

> A trustee shall be answerable and accountable only for the trustee's own acts, receipts, neglects, or defaults, and not for those of any other trustee, nor for any banker, broker, or other person with whom any trust moneys or securities may be deposited, nor for the insufficiency or deficiency of any securities, nor for any other loss, unless the same happens through the trustee's own wilful neglect or default.

The section applies to express trustees, resulting trustees, constructive trustees and personal representatives but it does not apply to other fiduciaries: *Metcalf & Kerr v Permanent Building Society (in liq)* (1993) 10 WAR 145.

20.56   The phrase 'willful neglect or default' in the legislation has been taken to mean a consciousness of wrongdoing or a reckless disregard for the trust's security: *In re City Equitable Fire Insurance Co* [1925] Ch 407. For example, in *In re Vickery* [1931] 1 Ch 572, an executor who was inexperienced with business affairs was fooled by a solicitor who managed to abscond with some of the funds of the estate. The plaintiffs claimed that the executor had breached the trust by retaining the solicitor and allowing him access to the funds. Maugham J, at 584, found that the trustee was not in 'wilful default' on the basis that the phrase required 'either a consciousness of negligence or breach of duty, or a recklessness in the performance of a duty'. His Honour found that the defendant was only guilty of an error of judgment and, as such, his actions did not amount to a wilful default.

20.57   In New South Wales, the leading case is *Dalrymple v Melville* (1932) 32 SR (NSW) 596. In this case a trustee had allowed his fellow trustee (a solicitor) to sell part of the estate of the trust in order to provide for the payment of some legacies. The trustee allowed the solicitor-trustee to be put in the position where he was able to misappropriate the proceeds of the sale of the trust property as well as two bearer cheques that were drawn from the trust funds to pay legatees. The trustee had always acted honestly and did not suspect that the solicitor-trustee was acting dishonestly. However, the court found that the trustee knew that it was his duty to safeguard the interests of the estate and that he failed to take simple precautions. Long Innes J found that the trustee was not relieved of liability by s 59(2) of the *Trustee Act 1925* (NSW). The conduct of the trustee was found to have been in wilful default as he took unnecessary risks. In other cases it has be found that a passive, though honest, trustee, who sits back and allows a co-trustee to breach the trust is in wilful default: *McLauchlan v Prince* [2001] WASC 43.

20.58   In other states, the trustee is required to have acted 'honestly and reasonably' before being excused. In *Green v Wilden Pty Ltd* [2005] WASC 83 at [508]–[511], Hasluck J said:

> It seems that the trustee allegedly in default bears the onus of proving that his or her conduct was honest and reasonable and that in all the circumstances of the case, he or she ought fairly to be

---

23.   *Trustee Act 1925* (ACT) s 59(2); *Trustee Act 1925* (NSW) s 59(2); *Trustee Act 1907* (NT) s 26; *Trusts Act 1973* (Qld) s 71; *Trustee Act 1936* (SA) s 35; *Trustee Act 1898* (Tas) s 27; *Trustee Act 1958* (Vic) s 36; *Trustees Act 1962* (WA) s 70.

excused: *Craven-Sands v Koch* (2000) 34 ACSR 341. The criterion of 'honestly' means the trustees must have acted in good faith and for the welfare of the Trust: *Cotton v Dempster* (1918) 20 WALR 14. 'Reasonably' means reasonably in the interests of the estate, not in the interest of the trustees themselves: *Re Morish* (1939) SASR 305 at 309. It also means acting with a degree of prudence that a person of ordinary intelligence and diligence can be expected to exhibit in the conduct of one's own affairs: *Fouche v Superannuation Fund Board* (1952) 88 CLR 609 at 641.

Conduct that has been held as unreasonable includes conduct that is negligent or careless, acting in an unauthorised manner without taking steps to ascertain whether the conduct was or was not authorised, doing nothing and simply accepting without enquiry what co-trustees have done and placing a co-trustee in a position to handle the Trust fund when he or she suspect that the co-trustee may misappropriate the Trust funds: *Dalrymple v Melville* (1932) 32 SR (NSW) 596.

Relief from breach of trust does not follow as a matter of course simply because the trustee proves that he or she has acted honestly and reasonably. The Court must look at all the circumstances to ascertain whether the trustee ought fairly to be excused for the breach. The term 'ought fairly be excused' means in fairness to the trustee and to the other persons who may be affected: *Marsden v Regan* [1954] 1 All ER 475 at 481.

This passage was approved on appeal by the Western Australian Court of Appeal in *Wilden Pty Ltd v Green* [2009] WASCA 38 at [160] and also in *Goldie v Getley (No 3)* [2011] WASC 132 at [275].

The right to impound a beneficial interest

20.59   If a breach of trust is committed by a trustee with the consent, advice or assistance of a beneficiary, the trustee may impound that beneficiary's interest and use it to satisfy the loss occasioned to the trust: *Fletcher v Collis* [1905] 2 Ch 24. This right is now included in legislation.[24]

The right to get directions from the court

20.60   Trustees have a right to seek advice and get directions from the court: *Re Permanent Trustee Australia Ltd* (1994) 33 NSWLR 547. A statutory right to seek advice and directions from the court has also been granted in all jurisdictions except the Northern Territory and Tasmania.[25]

20.61   Advice may be sought in relation to issues concerning the management or administration of the trust property, including advice as to the interpretation of the trust instrument, advice as to whether trust property can be made available for meeting the costs of litigation and advice as to whether to commence or defend proceedings: *In the Matter of Creditors' Trust of Jackgreen (International) Pty Ltd* [2011] NSWSC 748; *In the Matter of the Daquino Family Trust* [2009] NSWSC 429; *Re Saunders Nominees Pty Ltd; Ex Parte Saunders Nominees Pty Ltd* [2007] WASC 152; *The Kean Memorial Trust Inc v AG for SA (No 2)* [2007] SASC 133.

---

24.   *Trustee Act 1925* (ACT) s 86(1); *Trustee Act 1925* (NSW) s 86(1); *Trustee Act 1907* (NT) s 50; *Trusts Act 1973* (Qld) s 77; *Trustee Act 1936* (SA) s 57; *Trustee Act 1898* (Tas) s 53; *Trustee Act 1958* (Vic) s 68(1); *Trustees Act 1962* (WA) s 76.

25.   *Trustee Act 1925* (ACT) s 63; *Trustee Act 1925* (NSW) s 63; *Trusts Act 1973* (Qld) s 96; *Trustee Act 1936* (SA) s 91; *General Rules of Procedure in Civil Proceedings 1996* (Vic) r 54.02; *Trustees Act 1962* (WA) s 92.

20.62 It has been said that the procedure should not be used to resolve disputes between parties arising from breaches of trust: *Hartigan Nominees Pty Ltd v Rydge* (1992) 29 NSWLR 405. However, the fact that there is controversy between the parties, or even legal proceedings, does not bar the trustee from seeking advice: *Re Schneider* [2009] NSWSC 566 at [40]. In *Macedonian Orthodox Community Church St Petka Inc v His Eminence Petar The Diocesan Bishop of The Macedonian Orthodox Diocese of Australia and New Zealand* (2008) 237 CLR 66; 249 ALR 250, the High Court found that the legislative power to give advice in New South Wales was primarily to be used for determining the best interests of the trust estate, and in some cases that will necessarily involve answering questions which determine the rights of adversarial parties. If a beneficiary is opposed to the application as a party to litigation against the trustee, the beneficiary should be made a defendant to the trustee's application and any privileged material should be put in evidence as an exhibit to the trustee's witness statement that should not be served on the beneficiary: *Hargrave v Schumann; Application of Gnitekram Marketing Pty Ltd* [2010] NSWSC 1328 at [17].

20.63 If a trustee is advised by the court to act in a particular way, that trustee is protected from any claims arising from that conduct: *Re Grose* [1949] SASR 55. In this way the court's power is to give 'private advice' because 'its function is to give protection to the trustee': *Macedonian Orthodox Community Church St Petka Inc* at CLR 91; ALR 269; *Crnjanin v Ioos; Ioos v Crnjanin* [2010] NSWSC 750 at [27]. For example, a trustee can seek advice as to whether he or she can distribute the trust funds in circumstances where there may be outstanding claims on the funds from other creditors: *Re Yorke (dec'd): Stone v Chataway* [1997] 4 All ER 907. If the court gives its approval for distribution the trustees will be protected against those creditors by the court's sanction: *Thompson v Gamble* [2010] NSWSC 878 at [15]. Similarly, the court can give authorisation for an interim distribution of funds when there is pending litigation, and, by doing so, protect the trustee: *Re Estate of Blashild* [2009] NSWSC 566; *Blackman v Permanent Trustee Co Ltd* [2003] NSWSC 305.

20.64 The power to give advice is discretionary and courts may refuse to give advice when they see the advice as inappropriate or futile: *Re Atlantis Holdings Pty Limited* [2012] NSWSC 112; *Platypus Leasing Inc v Commissioner of Taxation* [2005] NSWCA 399.

POWERS OF TRUSTEES

20.65 Trustees' powers come from the trust instrument and legislation. Additional powers may be granted to trustees when a trust is varied: see Chapter 19. Any powers enjoyed by a trustee must be exercised in good faith and in accordance with the trustee's fiduciary duties.

Powers of sale

20.66 Trustees do not have a general power to sell the trust property and convert the proceeds, unless such a power is expressly or impliedly granted in the trust deed. This is because trustees are charged with the responsibility of preserving trust property.[26]

20.67 When the power of sale is conferred expressly in the trust document, the power is obviously limited to its terms. A power will be implied when it is necessary to give effect to the terms of the trust; for example, where there is a direction to distribute the trust property among beneficiaries

---

26. G E Dal Pont, *Equity and Trusts in Australia*, 5th ed, Lawbook Co, Sydney, 2011, p 672.

and the property is not divisible in its present state: *Altson v Equity Trustees, Executors & Agency Ltd* (1912) 14 CLR 341.

20.68   Statutory powers of sale also exist in all jurisdictions. These vary in scope. General powers to sell trust property are granted in Queensland and Western Australia.[27] In other jurisdictions more particular powers are granted; for example, a power to sell when the trustee has an express power to pay or apply capital moneys.[28]

Powers of management

20.69   In modern times, trusts are used as vehicles for several types of business enterprise. It is therefore necessary for modern trustees who are active in the control of trust businesses to be given sufficient power to manage trust estates. For example, active trustees have a general power to effect repairs to, and maintain, the trust property. However, if a trustee is inactive (for example, a bare trustee), that trustee will be without powers to repair and maintain trust property without the authority of the court: *Amos v Fraser* (1906) 4 CLR 78 at 84. At general law, even active trustees are without a power to effect improvements unless an express power is granted in the instrument.

20.70   In relation to the trustee's duty of management, in *Byrnes v Kendle* (2011) 243 CLR 253; 279 ALR 212, the High Court dealt with a case which raised questions regarding the duties of a trustee of a vacant residential property. Gummow and Hayne JJ, at CLR 277; ALR 231, noted that in such a case, 'as a general proposition … it is the duty of the trustee to render the land productive by leasing it, and this is so even if the trust instrument does not expressly so provide'. Heydon and Crennan JJ, at CLR 291–2; ALR 243, elaborated on this duty as follows:

> Even if there is no direction in the trust instrument that the trust property be invested, it is the duty of the trustee to invest the trust property subject to the limits permitted by the legislation in force under the proper law of the trust and subject to any limits stated in the trust document. If there are no limits of that kind, a trustee who receives a trust asset, like an executor of a deceased estate, must 'lay it out for the benefit of the estate' [*Rocke v Hart* (1805) 32 ER 1009 at 1010]. That is, it is the duty of a trustee to obtain income from the trust property if it is capable of yielding an income. If the property is money, it should be invested at interest or used to purchase income-yielding assets like shares. If the property consists of business assets, it should be employed in a business. If the property is lettable land, it should be let for rent. And if the intended means of gaining an income turn out to be unsatisfactory, those means must be abandoned and others found.

---

27. *Trusts Act 1973* (Qld) s 32(1)(a); *Trustees Act 1962* (WA) s 27.
28. *Trustee Act 1925* (ACT) s 38(1); *Trustee Act 1925* (NSW) s 38(1); *Trusts Act 1973* (Qld) s 45; *Trustee Act 1936* (SA) s 28B(1); *Trustee Act 1958* (Vic) s 20(1); *Trustees Act 1962* (WA) s 43(1). Another example is a power to sell so as to pay rates and charges on trust property: *Trustee Act 1925* (ACT) s 38(2); *Trustee Act 1925* (NSW) s 38(1A); *Trustee Act 1936* (SA) s 38(b)(2).

484

20.71   Legislation has been introduced to grant trustees wide powers of management. For example, most jurisdictions grant trustees the following powers:

1. powers to effect repairs and improvement of property;[29]
2. powers to insure the property;[30]
3. powers to carry on a business;[31] and
4. powers to settle claims made against the trust.[32]

20.72   While there is earlier authority to the contrary (*Re Irismay Holdings Pty Ltd* [1996] 1 Qd R 172), the power to settle claims made against the estate have been found to be subject to the consent of the beneficiaries: *Dowling v St Vincent De Paul Society of Victoria Inc* [2003] VSC 454.

Powers of maintenance and advancement

20.73   Trustees are often given powers to make payments to beneficiaries prior to the beneficiary obtaining an absolute right to his or her interest. Trust instruments often provide for the trustee to make payments from the income of the trust towards the *maintenance* of beneficiaries, or for payments out of the capital of the trust for the *advancement* of the beneficiaries. 'Maintenance' refers to periodic payments for such goods and services as food, clothes and medical treatment; whereas 'advancement' refers to lump sum payments for goods and services that establish the beneficiary in life, such as payments towards establishing a beneficiary in a trade or profession: *Public Trustee v Markham* (1999) 21 WAR 295. Prior to statutory reform, if the trust document was silent on maintenance and advancement, a trustee had to approach the court for approval of any payment of maintenance or advancement.

20.74   All jurisdictions barring Tasmania have now conferred statutory powers on trustees to make payments for the maintenance, education and benefit of beneficiaries out of income.[33] Statutory powers have also been conferred in some jurisdictions to make advancements out of capital.[34] Apart from Queensland, these statutory powers are subject to any contrary intention in the trust document.

20.75   The power to make payments for maintenance and advancement is subject to the duty to be impartial, discussed below: see 20.116–20.124.

---

29. *Trustee Act 1925* (ACT) ss 82, 83; *Trustee Act 1925* (NSW) ss 82, 82A; *Trustee Act 1907* (NT) s 18(2) (court-authorised expenditures); *Trusts Act 1973* (Qld) s 33; *Trustee Act 1936* (SA) ss 25A, 25B; *Trustee Act 1898* (Tas) s 47 (court-authorised expenditures); *Trustee Act 1958* (Vic) s 58; *Trustees Act 1962* (WA) s 30.
30. *Trustee Act 1925* (ACT) s 41; *Trustee Act 1925* (NSW) s 41; *Trustee Act 1907* (NT) s 14; *Trusts Act 1973* (Qld) s 47; *Trustee Act 1936* (SA) s 25; *Trustee Act 1898* (Tas) s 21; *Trustee Act 1958* (Vic) s 23; *Trustees Act 1962* (WA) s 46.
31. *Trusts Act 1973* (Qld) s 57; *Trustees Act 1962* (WA) s 55.
32. *Trustee Act 1925* (ACT) s 49; *Trustee Act 1925* (NSW) s 49; *Trustee Act 1907* (NT) s 21; *Trustee Act 1936* (SA) s 28; *Trustee Act 1898* (Tas) s 24; *Trustee Act 1958* (Vic) s 19; *Trustees Act 1962* (WA) s 42.
33. *Trustee Act 1925* (ACT) s 43; *Trustee Act 1925* (NSW) s 43; *Trustee Act 1907* (NT) s 24; *Trusts Act 1973* (Qld) s 61; *Trustee Act 1936* (SA) s 33; *Trustee Act 1958* (Vic) s 37; *Trustees Act 1962* (WA) s 58.
34. *Trustee Act 1925* (ACT) s 44; *Trustee Act 1925* (NSW) s 44; *Trustee Act 1907* (NT) s 24A; *Trusts Act 1973* (Qld) s 62; *Trustee Act 1936* (SA) s 33A; *Trustee Act 1898* (Tas) s 29; *Trustee Act 1958* (Vic) s 38; *Trustees Act 1962* (WA) s 59.

DUTIES OF TRUSTEES

20.76   Unlike trustee powers (which may or may not be exercised), trustee duties are always binding on a trustee. Trustees are fiduciaries and consequently subject to all the duties discussed in Chapter 9. The extent of the duties is largely determined by the trust instrument, although, as noted below, significant changes have been made by legislation. A general rule applies that trustees have to discharge their duties to the standard of what an *ordinary prudent person of business* would do in managing similar affairs: *Speight v Gaunt* (1883) 9 App Cas 1 at 19; *Austin v Austin* (1906) 3 CLR 516 at 525.

Duty to obey the terms of the trust

20.77   The High Court has stated that the trustee's most important duty is to obey the terms of the trust: *Youyang Pty Ltd v Minter Ellison Morris Fletcher* (2003) 212 CLR 484 at 498; 196 ALR 482 at 489. In *Cowan v Scargill* [1985] 1 Ch 270 at 288; [1984] 2 All ER 750 at 760, Megarry VC stated:

> This duty of the trustees towards their beneficiaries is paramount. They must, of course, obey the law; but subject to that, they must put the interests of their beneficiaries first.

As Heydon and Leeming state, the duty to obey the terms of the trust modifies all the other duties, given that the other duties are applied subject to their modification by the trust instrument.[35] Deviation from the strict terms of the trust may be sanctioned by the court if the deviation is proven to be necessary and beneficial: see Chapter 17.

Duty to inquire

20.78   Upon taking up their office, trustees are under a duty to inquire as to the state of the trust. This initially involves becoming familiar with the terms of the trust: *Hallows v Lloyd* (1888) 39 Ch D 686. Additionally, trustees must examine the trust property and relevant documentation to establish that title and control of the trust property is now under their control: *The Trustees of the Christian Brothers in Western Australia (Inc) v A-G (WA)* [2006] WASC 191 at [37]; *Reid v Hubbard* [2003] VSC 387; *Low v Bouverie* [1891] 3 Ch 82 at 99. These duties of inquiry are jointly and severally owed by co-trustees: *Guazzini v Pateson*. They also extend to resulting and constructive trustees: *Rob Evans of Robe Evans & Associates v European Bank Ltd* (2004) 61 NSWLR 75 at 100.

Duty to keep accounts and give information to beneficiaries

20.79   Trustees are obliged to keep records of the dealings of the trust, which must be produced to the beneficiaries when called for: *Re Whitehouse*. Accounts must be kept up to date and be accurate: *Struss v Wykes* [1916] VLR 200.

20.80   Accounts should not be mixed with the trustees' own funds or those of other parties: *Jessup v Queensland Housing Commission* [2002] 2 Qd R 270; *Lupton v White* (1808) 33 ER 817. In Victoria, a charitable trustee can apply to the court to approve a common investment fund.[36] The only guidance on the exercise of the power is that the court must be satisfied that intermingling is 'appropriate in the circumstances'. In *Charles Pearson Pty Ltd v A-G* [2006] VSC 260, Gillard J

---

35.   Heydon & Leeming, *Jacobs' Law of Trusts in Australia*, note 11 above, p 369.
36.   *Charities Act 1978* (Vic) Pt 1A.

ordered the creation of a common fund for a trustee company which administered over 77 different trust accounts. The court found it appropriate given the inefficiencies created with having to deal with so many different funds.

20.81 South Australia imposes a statutory duty on trustees to keep records.[37] Beneficiaries, the Public Trustee or co-trustees may request the production of trust records, so that they can be inspected and copied: *H Stanke and Sons Pty Ltd v Von Stanke* [2006] SASC 308 at [56]–[59]. Regulation 6(1) of the *Trustee Regulations 1996* (SA) provides a comprehensive list of records that must be kept, including authorising documents, letters received and sent by the trustee, copies of statutory declarations and affidavits, each deed, agreement or instrument, copies of tax returns, financial accounts, insurance policies, minutes of meetings, instructions for sale and investment records (amongst other things). Section 84C of the *Trustee Act 1936* (SA) provides the court with a wide discretionary power to appoint an inspector of the trust documents. The discretion under s 84C is to be exercised against the background of the equitable principles governing the obligations of trustees to their beneficiaries: *Oxer v Astec Paints Australia Pty Ltd* [2005] SASC 192. The administration of the trust should be the primary focus of the inspector's investigation rather than the conduct of particular trustees: *Hunter v Colton* [2009] SASC 129 at [9].

20.82 Trustees are duty bound to inform beneficiaries about their rights and entitlements when the beneficiaries reach the age of majority and become entitled to their interests: *Hawkesley v May* [1956] 1 QB 304; [1955] 3 All ER 353. While there is some authority to the contrary, it appears that the right to access this information is enjoyed by discretionary beneficiaries: *Colston v McMullen* at [45]; *Murphy v Murphy* [1999] 1 WLR 282; *Spellson v George* (1987) 11 NSWLR 300; *Nominees Pty Ltd v Rydge* at 409; *Walker v Symonds* (1818) 36 ER 751.

The nature of the beneficiaries' right to information

20.83 The beneficiaries' right to information has been said to have a proprietary dimension in the way that it grants a right akin to possession: *Re Simersall; Blackwell v Bray* (1992) 35 FCR 584; *Re Cowin* (1886) 33 Ch D 179. In *O'Rourke v Darbishire* [1920] AC 581 at 626; [1920] All ER Rep 1 at 17, Lord Wrenbury said:

> The beneficiary is entitled to see all trust documents because they are trust documents and because he is a beneficiary. They are in this sense his own.

20.84 Others have been critical of this view, given that the right stems more from the trustees' fiduciary obligation rather than from any species of equitable property: *Morris v Morris* (1993) 9 WAR 150. In *Spellson v George* (1987) 11 NSWLR 300, Powell J found that discretionary beneficiaries who only had a potential interest in the trust and no proprietary interest still had a right to information and to proper management and accounting. In *Hartigan Nominees Pty Ltd v Rydge*, a discretionary beneficiary wished to access a memorandum of wishes that the creator had written to the trustees. The majority felt that the document need not be disclosed, on the basis that the letter was not a trust document, nor was it confidential, and it was intended by the settlor to be kept from the beneficiaries. In the course of their judgments both Sheller JA and Kirby P (who was in dissent) questioned the proprietary nature of the beneficiaries' right to information. Sheller JA,

37. *Trustee Act 1936* (SA) ss 84A–84F.

at 444, felt it was an 'unhelpful trail' to follow, whereas Kirby P, at 421–26, felt that the better view was that a beneficiary's right stems from the trustee's fiduciary duty. Kirby P also believed that Australian society accepted a greater level of accountability now than in the past and, on that basis, proprietary rights to information may be sufficient rights, but they should no longer be necessary for a right to access information.

20.85   The better view, in light of these criticisms, is that the right to information is proprietary only in the way that it stems from a beneficiary's equitable interest in the trust property. If a beneficiary has a vested proprietary interest, their right to information will be proprietorial. If the beneficiary is discretionary, the right will not be proprietorial, but may stem from fiduciary duty: *Breen v Williams* (1996) 186 CLR 71 at 89; (1996) 138 ALR 259 at 270–1; *Rouse v IOOF Australia Trustees Ltd* (1999) 73 SASR 484; *Jacobson v Dafna Nominees Pty Ltd* [1999] VSC 529.

20.86   More recently, the English courts have eschewed property rights in favour of allowing access to trust information only when it was necessary as part of the court's inherent jurisdiction to supervise and intervene in the administration of trusts. There was said to be no general right to be given information but, rather, information may be provided if so ordered by the court. In *Schmidt v Rosewood Pty Ltd* [2003] 2 AC 709 at 734–5; [2003] 3 All ER 76 at 96–7, Lord Walker (giving the judgment of the Privy Council) said:

> Their Lordships have already indicated their view that a beneficiary's right to seek disclosure of trust documents, although sometimes not inappropriately described as a proprietary right, is best approached as one aspect of the court's inherent jurisdiction to supervise (and where appropriate intervene in) the administration of trusts. There is therefore in their Lordships' view no reason to draw any bright dividing-line either between transmissible and non-transmissible (that is, discretionary) interests, or between the rights of an object of a discretionary trust and those of the object of a mere power (of a fiduciary character). The differences in this context between trusts and powers are (as Lord Wilberforce demonstrated in *McPhail v Doulton* [1970] 2 All ER 228; [1971] AC 424) a good deal less significant than the similarities. The tide of Commonwealth authority, although not entirely uniform, appears to be flowing in that direction.

> However the recent cases also confirm (as had been stated as long ago as *Re Cowin* (1886) 33 Ch D 179) that no beneficiary (and least of all a discretionary object) has any entitlement as of right to disclosure of anything which can plausibly be described as a trust document. Especially when there are issues as to personal or commercial confidentiality, the court may have to balance the competing interests of different beneficiaries, the trustees themselves and third parties. Disclosure may have to be limited and safeguards may have to be put in place. Evaluation of the claims of a beneficiary (and especially of a discretionary object) may be an important part of the balancing exercise which the court has to perform on the materials placed before it. In many cases the court may have no difficulty in concluding that an applicant with no more than a theoretical possibility of benefit ought not to be granted any relief.

20.87   The decision in *Schmidt v Rosewood Pty Ltd* was concerned with a discretionary trust which had been set up on the Isle of Man by a Russian oil millionaire. The businessman died after having settled several million pounds on a discretionary trust in which he was a discretionary beneficiary. The deceased's son (on behalf of the estate) was seeking access to the trust documents to discover the nature of his father's entitlements. The son was concerned that millions of pounds previously held on trust had gone missing. The Privy Council ordered that the documents be provided, but in doing so they denied the proprietary nature of the rights of beneficiaries to information. While the decision was factually concerned with a discretionary trust, Lord Walker's comments are cast widely over all beneficiaries. The decision on the facts seems appropriate as the beneficiaries in *Schmidt v Rosewood Pty Ltd* were discretionary beneficiaries, without any proprietary rights. However, why should fixed beneficiaries with vested proprietary interests have their rights reduced so that information need only be produced on court order?

20.88   Australian authorities seemed to be split on whether *Schmidt v Rosewood Pty Ltd* should be followed. In *Avanes v Marshall* (2007) 68 NSWLR 595 at 599, Gzell J said:

> In my view, the approach in *Schmidt* should be adopted by Australian courts. The decision should not be regarded as abrogating the trustee's duty to keep accounts and to be ready to have them passed, nor the trustee's obligation to grant a beneficiary access to trust accounts. But when it comes to inspection of other documents there should no longer be an entitlement as of right to disclosure of any document. It should be for the court to determine to what extent information should be disclosed.

20.89   This case was concerned with whether beneficiaries could access correspondence between the barristers and solicitors for the trustees and correspondence between the trustees' solicitors and the trust's accountants: see 20.98–20.101. While the above quotation from *Avanes v Marshall* seems to suggest acceptance of *Schmidt v Rosewood Pty Ltd* it also qualifies its acceptance by stating that there is a duty to provide trust account information to beneficiaries. The quoted passage also suggests that only 'other documents' are subject to the *Schmidt v Rosewood Pty Ltd* approach, but these other documents are not defined.

20.90   In *Silkman v Shakespeare Haney Securities Limited* [2011] NSWSC 148 at [27], Hammerschlag J preferred the *Schmidt v Rosewood Pty Ltd* approach, and observed that:

> A consideration of the authorities reveals that the *Londonderry* approach has jurisprudential difficulties which the *Schmidt* approach does not have, including:
>
> (a) ascribing a workable and principled definition of the term 'trust documents';
>
> (b) divining the nature of the beneficiary's so-called proprietary interest in such documents. In *Hartigan Nominees v Rydge* ... Sheller JA articulated this difficulty by describing this 'trail' as unhelpful if not false;
>
> (c) that on the *Londonderry* approach a discretionary beneficiary who has no lesser interest in the due administration of the trust (but who has no proprietary interest in the assets) should, illogically, be denied disclosure;
>
> (d) that authorities which have taken the *Londonderry* approach have limited the beneficiary's right to disclosure by reference to the interests of third parties in maintaining confidentiality. It is difficult to reconcile this limitation with the principle for which *Londonderry* stands; and
>
> (e) reconciling a beneficiary's entitlement to documents such as a settlor's statement of intention or a constituent trust deed (which undoubtedly a beneficiary should properly have) with the fact that these instruments are themselves not assets or appurtenant to assets of the trust.

20.91   In *McDonald v Ellis* (2007) 72 NSWLR 605 at 619, Bryson AJ was critical of the *Schmidt v Rosewood Pty Ltd* approach and said:

> In *Avanes v Marshall* Gzell J after review of authorities, including recent authorities in Australia in which *Schmidt* reference has been made to, expressed the view that the approach in *Schmidt* should be adopted by Australian courts. I respectfully do not agree. It might be that the approach of *Schmidt* is appropriate where the interest of the beneficiary is no higher than those of the potential objects of a discretionary trust, although opinion in New South Wales is otherwise. However that may be, in the present case where the plaintiff's right is already vested in interest, it would be a departure from clearly established opinion in New South Wales not to treat the claim to information as based on a proprietary interest, or to withhold enforcement of it except so as to enforce some competing entitlement, such as that of the trustees considered in *In re Londonderry's Settlement*, which required such departure.

20.92   While *Schmidt v Rosewood Pty Ltd* has gained some support,[38] it has yet to be authoritatively approved. In *Schreuder v Murray (No 2)* (2009) 41 WAR 169, the Western Australian Court of Appeal declined to decide whether the *Schmidt v Rosewood Pty Ltd/Avanes v Marshall* approach or the *McDonald v Ellis* formula should be followed. In *Fay v Moramba Services Pty Ltd* at [99], Brereton J declined to express a view but decided the case on the assumption that discretionary beneficiaries had a right to see trust accounts.

20.93   Ultimately, the problem with an expansive interpretation of the *Schmidt v Rosewood Pty Ltd* approach is that, by removing the proprietary basis, there is reduced certainty for fixed beneficiaries, even though the intent was to have expanded remedies for discretionary beneficiaries. Regrettably, the *Schmidt v Rosewood Pty Ltd* line of authority throws doubt over a traditionally certain area of law for seemingly little advantage.[39] While some judges may be freer to pursue orders regarding disclosure that can be tailor-made to each complaint, trustees will be burdened with uncertainty when they are faced with requests for information from beneficiaries. Beneficiaries (particularly those vested under fixed trusts) will find that their rights to documents may have been significantly reduced. It is suggested that the better approach is to leave fixed beneficiaries with a proprietary right to information and then to pursue a *Schmidt v Rosewood Pty Ltd* approach in cases of requests by discretionary beneficiaries to access information. This certainly accords with the decisions in Australia like *Hartigan Nominees Pty Ltd v Ridge*, and it is an acceptable interpretation of *Schmidt v Rosewood Pty Ltd* given that it was focused on the rights of a discretionary beneficiary.

What is trust information?

20.94   The right to information does not mean that all documents should be handed over to any beneficiary: *Wentworth v de Montfort* (1988) 15 NSWLR 348 at 356. The duty to provide information is not absolute, as it needs to be measured alongside all the rights and obligations created by the trust instrument: *Rouse v IOOF Australia Trustees Ltd*. For example, one beneficiary's right to view these documents must be balanced against the rights of the other beneficiaries to have their identities remain confidential. In *Re Londonderry's Settlement; Peat v Walsh* [1965] Ch 918;

---

38.   J C Campbell, 'Access by trust beneficiaries to trustees' documents information and reasons' (2009) 3 *Journal of Equity* 97.

39.   G Dawson, 'A fork in the road for access to trust documents' (2009) 3 *Journal of Equity* 39.

[1964] 3 All ER 855, a trust had been established that granted the trustee a discretion to distribute the capital of the fund and thus terminate the trust. The trustees decided to exercise the power. A beneficiary, who was entitled to the residuary income if the discretionary power was not exercised, sought to examine documents such as the agenda and minutes of meetings of trustees as well as any documents prepared for the meetings. The trustees refused to provide this information. The Court of Appeal held that the beneficiary had no right to access the documents. Salmon LJ, at Ch 936–7; All ER 862, said:

> The settlement gave the absolute discretion to appoint to the trustees and not to the courts. So long as the trustees exercise this power with the consent of persons called appointors under the settlement, and exercise it bona fide with no improper motive, their exercise of power cannot be challenged in the courts and their reasons for acting as they did are, accordingly, immaterial. This is one ground for the rule that trustees are not obliged to disclose their reason for exercising a discretionary power. Another ground for this rule is that it would not be for the good of the beneficiaries as a whole, and yet another that it might make the lives of the trustees intolerable should such an obligation rest on them.

20.95   Salmon LJ then attempted to balance the right of beneficiaries to information with the above principles. His Lordship found that a balance could be struck by limiting the beneficiaries' right to access to 'trust documents'. His Lordship, at Ch 938; All ER 863, attempted to define these documents by stating that they had the following characteristics:

> (i) they are documents in the possession of trustees as trustees; (ii) they contain information about the trust which the beneficiaries are entitled to know; (iii) the beneficiaries have a proprietary interest in the documents and, accordingly, are entitled to see them. If any parts of a document contain information which the beneficiaries are not entitled to know, I doubt whether such parts can truly be said to be integral parts of a trust document. Accordingly, any part of a document that lacked the second characteristic to which I have referred would automatically be excluded from the document in its character as a trust document.

20.96   The major problem with Salmon LJ's definition of 'trust documents' is that it is circular: *Loughran v Perpetual Trustees WA Ltd* [2007] VSC 50 at [35]. The best that can be salvaged from the case is that beneficiaries have no right to reasons and that 'trust documents' are those documents that beneficiaries are entitled to inspect to protect an enforceable right (such as the right to review decisions made in bad faith). After *Re Londonderry's Settlement* it has been held that trust documents include financial accounts, profit and loss statements of investment companies and, on occasion, the names and addresses of other beneficiaries (although this is subject to issues of privacy): *Re Fairbairn* [1967] VR 633; *Attorney-General (Ont) v Ballard Estate* (1995) 119 DLR (4th) 750; *Slater v Global Finance Group Pty Ltd* (1999) 150 FLR 264; *Global Custodians Ltd v Mesh* [2002] NSWSC 47.

20.97   The position established in *Re Londonderry's Settlement* has been modified in Queensland and Western Australia so that aggrieved beneficiaries, or those who believe they are about to become aggrieved, can seek orders from the court requiring the trustees to give reasons for their decisions.[40]

---

40.   *Trusts Act 1973* (Qld) s 8; *Trustee Act 1962* (WA) s 94.

Legal advice as trust information

20.98 Legal advice given to trustees for the purpose of litigation may not necessarily be trust information. In *Talbot v Marshfield* (1865) 62 ER 728, a legal opinion given to trustees when they were being sued did not have to be produced to beneficiaries. In relation to the legal opinion, Kindersley VC, at 729, said:

> This was not to guide the trustees in the execution of their trust; but, after proceedings had been commenced against them, they took advice to know in what position they stood, and how they should defend themselves in the suit. It appears to me that the cestuis que trust have no right to see this case and opinion, unless they can make out that the trustees can charge the expense thereof on the trust funds. As to this there is no proof; the trustees may themselves have to bear the expense of this case and opinion, as having been stated and taken by them as litigant parties with the cestuis que trust.

20.99 Contrastingly, if the advice is paid for by trust funds, there is authority to suggest that the advice will be a trust document: *Brown v Oakshott* (1849) 50 ER 1058. However, in *Rollo Ventry Wakefield Gray v BNY Trust Co of Australia Ltd* [2009] NSWSC 789, Bergin CJ in Eq refused to order the production of documents that had been prepared in litigation against a beneficiary, where the trustee's legal costs were paid out of the trust estate. Bergin CJ found that the fact that the trustee's legal expenses were paid out of the estate did not convert the documents into trust documents. Her Honour, at [54], stated:

> The fact that an order was made that the plaintiff pay the defendant's costs coupled with an order of its entitlement to indemnification, does not in my view convert the privileged advice received by the defendant to defend itself into an advice for the benefit of the plaintiff and thus a trust document to which the plaintiff is entitled to access.

Bergin CJ did allow access to legal documents prepared during earlier proceedings when the beneficiary was suing a co-beneficiary and where the trustee was merely a nominal defendant. That advice was paid for out of the trust funds. It appears that the basis of allowing access was that the trustee was not an adversary during this part of the proceedings and the advice to the trustee was to assist it in acting for the plaintiff's benefit, at least as to half of the amounts to be repaid.

20.100 A case with similar issues arose in *Schreuder v Murray (No 2)*. The beneficiary sought to remove the trustee and during the course of proceedings wished to inspect documents held by the trustee regarding the administration of the estate, including legal advice. The trustee claimed legal professional privilege. The Court of Appeal of Western Australia found that the legal advice had been given for the administration of the estate and not to the trustee personally. The documents had not been created for the purpose of defending the trustee against any claims made by the beneficiary. On that basis the beneficiary was entitled to inspect the documents.

20.101 Following *Schreuder v Murray (No 2)*, Judd J, in *Krok v Szaintop Homes Pty Ltd (No 1)* [2011] VSC 16 at [14], said:

> In my opinion, a trustee's right to withhold, in the course of litigation, disclosure of a document from a beneficiary, on the ground of client legal privilege, is not to be determined by an analysis of the beneficiary's proprietary right to trust documents. The question is to be resolved by reference

to the ordinary principles applicable to the protection of privileged information and documents, and obligations of disclosure in litigation.

Paying the costs of production and copying

20.102 The costs of producing and copying documents that have been requested by the beneficiaries should be paid for by them. If the trustee needs to seek legal advice regarding the production of those documents they can be reimbursed from the estate for those costs: *Hatch v Harlekin Pty Ltd* [2008] WASC 167.

Creator's intention to keep documents confidential

20.103 If the creator of the trust intends that certain documents remain confidential, that intention may be enforced contrary to the beneficiaries' right to information. For example, in *Hartigan Nominees Pty Ltd v Rydge*, the settlor had created a document of instructions that he did not attach to the deed of settlement, with the intention that it remain confidential to the trustees. A majority of the New South Wales Court of Appeal found that the trustees were not obliged to make the document available. Kirby P dissented, as he believed the settlor's wishes were important for understanding the trust deed.

20.104 A similar result occurred in *Breakspear v Ackland* [2009] Ch 32, where the settlor had sent the trustees a non-binding 'wish' letter which contained instructions as to what factors should be included in the trustees' deliberations. The beneficiaries sought the production of the letter. Briggs J, adopting the *Schmidt v Rosewood Pty Ltd* approach, found that he had a discretion to order the disclosure of the document. Briggs J affirmed the general principle that trustees should not be forced to disclose their reasons and that the decision-making process of trustees should remain primarily confidential. Given that wish letters went to the process of the trustees' deliberations, they too could be considered confidential. However, Briggs J, at 53, said that the trustees or the courts may disclose such a letter:

> In the absence of special terms, the confidentiality in which a wish letter is enfolded is something given to the trustees for them to use, on a fiduciary basis, in accordance with their best judgment and as to the interests of the beneficiaries and the sound administration of the trust. Once the settlor has completely constituted the trust, and sent his wish letter, it seems to me that the preservation, judicious relaxation or abandonment of that confidence is a matter for the trustees or, in an appropriate case, for the court.

However, Briggs J, at 54, doubted whether the question of confidentiality should be answered completely by the wishes of the settlor:

> Trustees are fiduciaries exclusively for their beneficiaries and should not in my opinion be asked to accept, nor should they without good cause accept, restraints upon their use of relevant information which would prevent disclosure even where, in their view, disclosure was preferable to the continued maintenance of confidence.

20.105 The confidentiality of a wish letter may also be overriden by legal processes of discovery in family law proceedings. In the Family Court it has been held that wish letters may be produced under subpoena for the purposes of distributing marital property under s 75 of the *Family Law*

Act 1975 (Cth): *White and Tulloch v White* (1995) 19 Fam LR 696. In *Read v Chang* (2010) 44 Fam LR 198, a husband sought, via subpoena, the disclosure of a memorandum of wishes for a trust, of which his ex-wife was a discretionary beneficiary. Cohen J, distinguished *Hartigan Nominees Pty Ltd v Rydge* and *Breakspear v Ackland*, and found that the memorandum of wishes should be disclosed because it enlightened the court about the wife's future economic circumstances. Cohen J, at 203, said:

> In s 79 proceedings although the onus is on a party to prove the s 75(2) factors that party relies on, the court is not simply left to dismiss the party's case if it is unproven in whole or in part. The court continues, because of s 79(4)(e), to have the duty to take the matters listed in s 75(2) into account, 'so far as they are relevant.' As s 79(4) says 'the court shall take [them] into account' and, pursuant to s 79(2), 'shall not make an order under this section unless it is satisfied that, in all the circumstances, it is just and equitable to make the order.' Thus, it must be that the court has a duty which goes beyond the cases presented by the adversarial parties to reach a decision which is a proper exercise of discretion in the circumstances. Both parties are obliged to disclose their financial circumstances. Here, the wife as well as the husband really has the duty to seek to prove what she is likely to receive from the trust in future. Whereas the trustees were parties in the Supreme Court and as such were entitled to argue the issue of relevance, in the Family Court they are not parties in circumstances where both parties; that is the husband and wife, could not avoid the fact that the likely distributions to the wife from the trust is an issue so evidence which might reasonably tend to establish this must be regarded as relevant.

Is there a duty to provide information to potential beneficiaries?

20.106 Does the duty to provide information also require trustees to contact potential beneficiaries and inform them of their possible rights? In *SAS Trustee Corporation v Cox* (2011) 285 ALR 623; [2011] NSWCA 408, Cox, a policeman, was injured in the foot during duty. A year later he was seriously injured in a car accident while off-duty. After returning to work he was placed on restricted duties but later retired as medically unfit. He was paid a lump sum benefit. Over 17 years later he had recurring problems with his foot and applied for an allowance from the superannuation fund to help pay for the costs of treatment. He later discovered that he had been entitled to an allowance from the date that he retired but the superannuation trustee would only pay that allowance from the date of his application. Cox argued that the superannuation trustee had been duty bound to inform him of his rights to the allowance back in 1988 when he retired. Campbell JA, at 653–4, said:

> [T]he duty of any particular trustee depends on what is involved in faithfully carrying out the office of being trustee of that particular trust… There may be a core of duties that would always, or nearly always, be involved in faithfully carrying out a trust, regardless of its individual peculiarities. Beyond that, any additional duties of a particular trustee come to be understood through considering the practical exigencies of the types of decision that that particular trustee has to make, in the particular social or business environment in which that trustee is operating. To those factual matters one applies the standards of faithful performance of those duties that are laid down in the trust instrument, and of faithfully attempting to achieve the objectives articulated in the trust instrument. Because that is the way in which trustees' duties arise, one cannot say that trustees always are, or always are not, under a duty to inform a potential beneficiary of his or her entitlements under the trust.

On the facts, Campbell JA (McColl JA and Sackville AJA agreeing) found that there was no duty. While the trustee knew Cox was retiring it had no reason to think this was because of an injury sustained at work. Nor was there any positive duty set out in the trust instrument.

Duty to correctly pay beneficiaries

20.107   As part of the general duty to obey the terms of the trust, trustees must pay beneficiaries correctly. If a beneficiary has been overpaid, a trustee must reduce future payments to account for the overpayment: *Merriman v Perpetual Trustee Co Ltd* (1896) 17 LR (NSW) Eq 325. In the past it was said that trustees could not sue an overpaid beneficiary on grounds of fairness (*Re Aspinall* (1913) 30 WN (NSW) 215), but recent developments in the law of restitution may support an action for unjust enrichment: *David Securities Ltd v Commonwealth Bank of Australia* (1992) 175 CLR 353; 109 ALR 57. Statutory protection is now widely afforded to trustees who make mistaken payments in good faith.[41]

Duty not to profit from the trust

Remuneration

20.108   Fiduciaries are not entitled to profit from their office and, as a result, trustees are not permitted to receive remuneration: *Re Whitehead* [1958] VR 143. There are three exceptions to this general proposition.

20.109   The first is that remuneration is payable if authorised in the trust instrument: *Princess Anne of Hesse v Field*. The second is that an agreement can be entered into between trustees and beneficiaries to pay for services rendered by the trustees.[42]

20.110   The third exception is court-awarded remuneration. The court has an inherent and, in some jurisdictions, a statutory power, to award remuneration to ensure that the trust is properly administered, and that trustees are compensated for their efforts: *Will of Moore* (1896) 17 LR (NSW) B & P 78; *Re Duke of Norfolk's Settlement Trusts* [1982] Ch 61; [1981] 3 All ER 220.[43] That power can override the express terms of the trust and provide for additional remuneration, in exceptional circumstances, such as where the remuneration set out in the trust is completely inadequate: *Re White* (2003) 7 VR 219; *Parbery v ACT Superannuation Management Pty Ltd* [2010] NSWSC 941. The award can relate to past work or work to be done: *Re Creditors' Trust of Jackgreen (International) Pty Ltd* [2011] NSWSC 748 at [42]; *Tweedie v Attorney-General* (2003) 7 VR 219. In *Zevering v Callaghan* [2011] QCA 180 at [52], Daubney J said:

> It is for the applicant for further remuneration to show proper evidence of the quality and quantity of work done for which remuneration is sought. The court will adopt the role of an auditor when the remuneration charged is questioned and insist that proper accounts and records are kept.

---

41. *Trustee Act 1925* (ACT) ss 58, 60, 61A; *Trustee Act 1925* (NSW) ss 58, 60, 61A; *Trustee Act 1907* (NT) s 22; *Trusts Act 1973* (Qld) ss 66–68, 70, 75; *Trustee Act 1936* (SA) ss 29–31; *Trustee Act 1898* (Tas) s 26; *Trustee Act 1958* (Vic) ss 32–35; *Trustees Act 1962* (WA) ss 62–64, 67, 69.

42. Dal Pont, *Equity and Trusts in Australia*, note 26 above, p 643.

43. *Administration and Probate Act 1929* (ACT) s 70; *Probate and Administration Act 1898* (NSW) s 86; *Trustee Act 1907* (NT) s 78; *Trusts Act 1973* (Qld) s 101; *Administration and Probate Act 1919* (SA) s 70; *Trustee Act 1898* (Tas) s 58; *Trustee Act 1958* (Vic) s 77; *Trustees Act 1962* (WA) s 98.

20.111 Court-awarded remuneration may be refused or reduced by the court if the trustee has engaged in reprehensible misconduct. In *In the Will of Sherringham* (1901) 1 SR (NSW) (B&P) 48, the trustees had defaulted under a mortgage over the property and one of the trustees purchased the trust property at auction but at a much reduced price. The beneficiaries objected. It later was agreed between the beneficiaries and the trustees that the beneficiaries would not sue for breach of trust and that the property would be sold to one beneficiary (at a higher price), with the proceeds then distributed amongst the others. The trustees requested remuneration but the court refused it, primarily because the trustee had deliberately broken trust and purchased at a price the trustee knew was under value. A similar result occurred in *Will of Greer* (1911) 11 SR (NSW) 21, where executors had bought trust property at auction. Street J found the executors to have deliberately acted in a reprehensible manner and found them to be disentitled to commission. In *Atkins v Godfrey* [2006] WASC 83, the executor was entitled under the will to be paid usual professional fees for his work (the executor was a retired solicitor) but the beneficiaries argued that he had overcharged the estate for work performed by his firm and his son, a barrister. La Miere J, at [29], said:

> It seems to be established and accepted that where executors have been guilty of positive fraud or dishonesty in their office the courts will refuse them commission. As to acts or neglects falling short of fraud or dishonesty, whether the executor's commission should be refused or reduced will depend upon the severity of the breach, assessed according to its consequences and the culpability of the executor.

On that basis the remuneration was not completely refused, as there was no breach of trust, but it was reduced as the executor had not properly supervised the accumulation of fees and had not ensured that claims made against the estate were finalised earlier than they were.

20.112 There is discretion as to how the amount can be calculated. In New South Wales the general approach has been to order commission on a percentage basis on income and capital realisations rather than to order lump sums, although the court has power to order either or a combination of both: *Spence v Spence* [2003] NSWSC 1232. The range of percentage tends to vary between 0.4 per cent to 5.0 per cent, with lower percentages on the realisation of income (around 2.5 per cent) and higher on capital (around 5 per cent): *Re Estate of Ghidella* [2005] QSC 106. However, these are rules of thumb and courts are free to reduce rates where they see fit, especially given the fact that inflation has greatly increased the size of estates over the last 80 years, perhaps making higher percentages too generous. Earlier formulations of scales of percentages, as can be found in cases like *Re Barr Smith* [1920] SALR 380, have become less useful because of these increases in estate size. In *Watters; Re Estate of Dibbs* [2006] NSWSC 1277, Windeyer J, at [16], said:

> What is to be considered is the work done by the executors and what is a reasonable allowance for that work. It is not to be determined by rates of pay based on hourly rates for professional persons with large administrative offices to support. Neither, for that matter, is it to be determined by looking at hourly rates of pay of Registrars in this Court as was mentioned in the decision under review. It is true that values of assets, particularly real estate, and to some extent shares, have increased considerably over the past 20 or 30 years, but the value of money has decreased. Where the major asset in an estate is a home, sold for $2 million, commission of 2% on its realized value may be seen to be too high a figure for the executorial work done in bringing about the sale. It depends upon the facts of the particular case. The value to the estate of an executor's work may

to some extent be reflected in the price obtained for an asset. It is not possible to lay down any particular rule and I would not wish to be seen to be attempting to do so.

20.113   In *Re Will and Estate of Stone (dec'd); Patterson v Halliday* [2003] VSC 298, at [27], Smith J provided the following list of factors to be considered in exercising the court's discretion:

(a) the work and judgment involved in the realisation of assets and earning income,

(b) the extent of administrative activities,

(c) the responsibility generally,

(d) the amount of work done not reflected in financial terms,

(e) how long the estate was administered,

(f) the size of the estate and its capacity to pay,

(g) the work of a non-professional character not undertaken by the applicant and performed by professionals, and

(h) executors' pains and troubles relative to the result.

Self-dealing and trafficking

20.114   The duty not to profit from the trust also prevents trustees from taking a beneficial interest in trust property, or from borrowing from trust funds. This is sometimes referred to as 'trafficking' or 'self-dealing'. The underlying principle against self-dealing is that the trustee should not be placed in a position of conflict, where his or her interests compete with the interests of the beneficiaries.

20.115   The only exceptions to the rule against self-dealing are when the trustee purchases the trust property with the fully informed consent of the beneficiaries (who must be of age and full capacity): *Williams v Scott* [1900] AC 499. Alternatively, trustees may be able to purchase trust property if they are authorised to do so in the trust instrument (*Re Knowles' Will Trusts* [1948] 1 All ER 866), or if they are given permission by the court, exercising its inherent or statutory powers: *Union Trustee Co of Australia v Gorrie* [1962] Qd R 605 at 616; *Public Trustee v O'Donnell* [2008] SASC 181.[44] It may also be possible to use the court's powers to make orders for the expedient management of trusts to effect a transfer. In *Patros v Patros* [2007] VSC 83, the expediency power was used to order a sale to a trustee where the trustee was the widow of the sole registered proprietor of the family home. The purchase was for the benefit of the deceased's children.

Duty to act impartially between beneficiaries

20.116   It should be recalled that creators of trusts often grant successive interests in the trust instrument. The most common example of this is a trust that grants a beneficial life estate to one beneficiary ('the life tenant'), and a remaining beneficial interest ('the remainder') to another beneficiary, or group of beneficiaries ('remainderpersons'). In such a trust the life tenant is given the beneficial interest in any income from the trust property, leaving the capital for the remainderpersons. Trustees have a duty to avoid actions that benefit one set of beneficiaries at the expense of another: *Re Campbell* [1973] 2 NSWLR 146. In trusts that have life tenants and

---

44.   *Trustee Act 1925* (ACT), s 81; *Trustee Act 1925* (NSW), s 81; *Trustee Act 1907* (NT) ss 10A; *Trusts Act 1973* (Qld), s 94; *Trustee Act 1936* (SA) s 49; *Trustee Act 1898* (Tas) s 47; *Trustee Act 1958* (Vic), s 63; *Trusts Act 1962* (WA), s 89.

remainderpersons this means that the trustee must act in ways to protect both the income and capital of the trust.

20.117   The duty to act impartially has two major incidents. The first is that known as the rule in *Howe v Lord Dartmouth* (1802) 32 ER 56. This rule requires a trustee to convert certain types of trust property into forms of recognised investment within a year of the trust coming into being. It only applies when the trust property is granted to successive beneficiaries in a will and where the property consists of personalty that has a wasting, reversionary or hazardous nature. The duty of impartiality requires the property to be sold and the funds invested, because if the property remains as personalty it is possible that the remainderpersons will receive nothing after the life estate ceases. Conversion into permanent and secure investments allows the beneficial interests of remainderpersons to survive. The intention of the testator remains paramount in the rule in *Howe v Lord Dartmouth*. The rule only applies in the absence of a contrary intention expressed in the will.[45]

20.118   The second aspect of the duty to act impartially concerns apportionment. Apportionment is the process in which a trustee determines how to divide the profits and losses of the trust between life tenants and remainderpersons. For example, many trust estates consist of shares, leased real estate or profitable businesses. These types of trust property earn (or lose) income. The trustee must decide how to distribute the profits and losses between successive beneficiaries in a way that satisfies their duty of impartiality.

20.119   As a general starting point, it should be noted that a life tenant is entitled to all income earned after the trust becomes effective.[46] Remainderpersons only become entitled to profits before the trust becomes effective and after the life estate is finished; that is, upon the death of the life tenant. Difficulties arise in testamentary trusts when trust property bears income before the death of the testator which is not payable until after the testator's death.[47] Identical difficulties are faced when property bears income during the term of the life estate that is not payable until after the death of the life tenant.

20.120   The solution to the problem of apportionment is to treat all periodical payments to the trust from income-bearing sources as accruing from day to day: *Re Aspinall; Aspinall v Aspinall* [1961] 2 All ER 751.[48] Once this is done, an appropriate division of time, which allows for an apportionment of the income, can occur. Heydon and Leeming provide the following example.[49] Assume a testator died on 13 June leaving all of his property on trust for his wife for life with the remainder for his children. The major asset of the trust is a sum of $1000 borrowed at a fixed interest rate of 6 per cent per annum. The interest is payable half-yearly on 10 April and 10 October each year. In this example, an apportionment must be made of the amount paid on 10 October after the testator's death ($30).

---

45. Heydon & Leeming, *Jacobs' Law of Trusts in Australia*, note 11 above, p 445.

46. Dal Pont, *Equity and Trusts in Australia*, note 26 above, pp 649–54.

47. Heydon & Leeming, *Jacobs' Law of Trusts in Australia*, note 11 above, p 466.

48. *Conveyancing Act 1919* (ACT) s 144; *Conveyancing Act 1919* (NSW) s 144; *Property Law Act 1974* (Qld) s 232; *Law of Property Act 1936* (SA) s 64; *Apportionment Act 1871* (Tas) s 2; *Supreme Court Act 1986* (Vic) s 54; *Property Law Act 1969* (WA) s 131.

49. Heydon & Leeming, *Jacobs' Law of Trusts in Australia*, note 11 above, p 446.

20.121   The time from the last payment (10 April) to the death of the testator (13 June) is 64 days. The time from the death of the testator (13 June) to the next payment (10 October) is 119 days. The total amount of days is 183 days. The amount of $30 is then apportioned as follows:

64/183 by $30 = $10.49
119/183 by $30 = $19.51

The first amount belongs to capital because it forms part of the testator's estate prior to the life interest coming into being. The second amount is income going to the life estate, as it is income earned on the capital of the trust.

Capital or income?

20.122   Not all increases in the value of the trust property after the trust comes into force will be considered as income. Ordinary capital gain on assets is not income at all. If trust property appreciates and is sold, the entire amount is considered capital. Any resulting interest on the increased capital amount will be payable to the life estate as income.

20.123   If the property consists of shares, dividends are income that belongs to the life tenant: *Re Armitage; Armitage v Garnett* [1893] 3 Ch 337. Increase in the value of the shares is ordinarily treated as capital: *Scholefield v Redfern* (1863) 62 ER 587; *Hill v Permanent Trustee Co of NSW Ltd* [1930] AC 720. However, if shares are being bought and sold over a short-term period for the purpose of making profits, any capital gains may be treated as income: *Clark v Inglis* [2010] NSWCA 144; *Orr v Wendt* [2005] WASCA 199.

20.124   Bonus shares and dividends are more difficult to characterise. If the bonus shares are granted because the company is seeking to add capital to the company, the new shares are taken as capital of the trust. If a dividend is declared but the option is given to take the dividend in the form of extra shares, those shares are normally taken as income, unless the trustee is compelled to do so because to refuse would harm the interests of all the beneficiaries: *Mitchell v Hart* (1914) 19 CLR 33.

Duty to sell trust property

20.125   Trustees' powers of sale have already been discussed: see 20.66–20.68. In some circumstances trustees may be subject to a duty to exercise a power of sale, such as where the creator has intended that the trust property be sold and a fund be created for the purposes of the trust. In such circumstances the trust is referred to as a *trust for sale*. The duty to sell can be expressly stated in the trust or be implied from the intention of the creator, as expressed in the trust document: *Re Austin's Settlement* [1960] VR 532.

20.126   The duty to sell requires that the trustee sell the property for a fair price as soon as possible.[50] Trustees must exercise their power of sale within a reasonable time but are not obliged to sell 'at once, or at any precise, definite or particular time; they are entitled to use a reasonable discretion': *Cox v Archer* (1964) 110 CLR 1 at 7. Once the property is sold, the funds should be invested in authorised securities. If there are successive beneficiaries, interest earned on those funds is payable as income to life tenants.

---

50.   H A J Ford & W A Lee, *Principles of the law of trusts* (Online), Thomson Reuters, Sydney, [12180].

20.127 Some trusts contain a power to postpone sale or retain the property. Additionally, such powers are now implied in many jurisdictions by statute.[51] This power does not negate the duty to sell but it grants the trustee a greater discretion in choosing the most appropriate time to sell. A decision to postpone sale, made for sound economic reasons, will not be overturned by the courts even where it may negatively impact on an individual beneficiary's entitlements: *Perpetual Trustee Co Ltd v Noyes* (1925) 25 SR (NSW) 226.

Duty to invest

20.128 Trustees must act in the best interests of the beneficiaries, which in most cases means the beneficiaries' best financial interests: *Cowan v Scargill* at Ch 286–7; All ER 760; *Commissioner of Taxation v Interhealth Energies Pty Ltd as Trustee of the Interhealth Superannuation Fund* [2012] FCA 120 at [15]. In that sense, trustees are duty bound to invest trust funds in order to secure income for the beneficiaries: *Adamson v Reid* (1860) 6 VLR (E) 164. The duty is not of a fiduciary kind: *Iacullo v Remly Pty Ltd* [2012] NSWSC 190 at [55]. If a trustee fails to invest the funds he or she will be liable to pay interest: *Moyle v Moyle* (1831) 30 ER 565; *Pacella v Sherborne (No 2)* [2010] WASC 186.

20.129 It is common for the trust instrument to authorise particular investments. In cases where the trust instrument gives broad powers to invest, trustees must still act prudently and are forbidden from speculating with trust funds: *Fouche v Superannuation Fund Board* (1952) 88 CLR 609. The standard of care applicable to the trustee is to take as much care as an ordinary prudent person 'would take if he were minded to make an investment for the benefit of other people for whom he felt morally bound to provide': *Re Whiteley; Whiteley v Learoyd* (1886) 33 Ch D 347 at 355. Moreover, the word 'investment' has been read restrictively to exclude purchases of property for the enjoyment of the beneficiaries, and unsecured loans based on a promise to repay: *In the Will of Sherriff* [1971] 2 NSWLR 438; *Khoo Tek Keong v Ch'ng Joo Tuan Neoh* [1934] AC 529. In *Perpetual Trustee Company Ltd v Cheyne* [2011] WASC 225 at [52]–[56], Edelman J found that the word 'investment' would not cover the purchase by the trustee of membership rights in a superannuation fund which would then be legally owned by the beneficiary (a man with severe disabilities). The fact that the trustee would retain no legal right to the superannuation membership, nor receive anything back from the superannuation fund, meant that the purchase could not be classed as an 'investment'.

20.130 In earlier times, equity required that trustees invest in government stock: *Ex parte Lathorpe* (1785) 29 ER 119. Numerous legislative changes have since expanded the range of acceptable investments. Prior to the most recent reforms, the most common form of regulation involved a list of authorised investments contained in statute. However, all jurisdictions now have replaced such lists with a general power to invest in any form of investment.[52] A trustee exercising the power is to exercise it according to the standard of care, diligence and skill a prudent person of business would

---

51. *Trustee Act 1925* (ACT) s 27B; *Trustee Act 1925* (NSW) s 27B; *Trusts Act 1973* (Qld) s 31(1)(c); *Trustee Act 1958* (Vic) s 13(5); *Trustees Act 1962* (WA) s 27(1)(3).
52. *Trustee Act 1925* (ACT) s 14; *Trustee Act 1925* (NSW) s 14; *Trustee Act 1907* (NT) s 5; *Trusts Act 1973* (Qld) s 21; *Trustee Act 1936* (SA) s 6; *Trustee Act 1898* (Tas) s 6; *Trustee Act 1958* (Vic) s 5; *Trustees Act 1962* (WA) s 17.

exercise in managing the affairs of other persons.[53] The legislation requires trustees to have regard to a number of factors including:

- the purposes of the trust and the needs of the beneficiaries;
- the desirability of diversifying trust investments;
- the nature of and risk associated with investments;
- the need to maintain the real value of the capital or income of the trust;
- the risk of loss or depreciation;
- the potential for return;
- the length of the term of the proposed investment;
- the probable duration of the trust;
- the liquidity and marketability of the proposed investment during, and at the end of, the term of the proposed investment;
- the total value of the trust estate;
- the effect of the proposed investment for the tax liability of the trust;
- the likelihood of inflation affecting the value of the proposed investment;
- the cost (including commissions, fees, charges and duties payable) of making the proposed investment; and
- the results of a review of existing trust investments.

20.131   The legislation also empowers trustees to seek out independent investment advice and pay for it out of trust funds.[54] If a loss eventuates and a breach of trust is discovered, the court may take into account the nature of any independent advice given, as well as compare the trustee's investment strategy with the trustee's duty to invest when determining the extent of his or her liability.[55]

20.132   In New South Wales further guidance is provided to trustees of funds less than $50,000. The *Trustee Regulation 2005*, c 4, provides a list of investments (primarily with government) that may be considered appropriate.

Duty to act personally, unfettered and unanimously

20.133   Trustees have a duty to ensure that the trust is being carried out according to its terms and they cannot delegate their authority to others, including their co-trustees: *Re Flower & Metropolitan Board of Works* (1884) 27 Ch D 592. This duty is subject to three exceptions:

1. delegation permitted by the trust instrument: *Doyle v Blake* (1804) 2 Sch & Lef 231;
2. delegation permitted by statute;[56] and

---

53. *Trustee Act 1925* (ACT) s 14A; *Trustee Act 1925* (NSW) s 14A; *Trustee Act 1907* (NT) s 6; *Trusts Act 1973* (Qld) s 22; *Trustee Act 1936* (SA) s 7; *Trustee Act 1898* (Tas) s 7; *Trustee Act 1958* (Vic) s 6; *Trustees Act 1962* (WA) s 18.
54. *Trustee Act 1925* (ACT) s 14C(2); *Trustee Act 1925* (NSW) s 14C(2) (also in force in the ACT by virtue of Pt II of the *Trustee Act 1957* (ACT)); *Trustee Act 1907* (NT) s 8(2); *Trusts Act 1973* (Qld) s 24(2); *Trustee Act 1936* (SA) s 9(2); *Trustee Act 1898* (Tas) s 8(2); *Trustee Act 1958* (Vic) s 8(2); *Trustees Act 1962* (WA) s 20(2).
55. *Trustee Act 1925* (ACT) s 89; *Trustee Act 1925* (NSW) s 90; *Trustee Act 1907* (NT) s 10E; *Trusts Act 1973* (Qld) s 30B; *Trustee Act 1936* (SA) s 13C; *Trustee Act 1898* (Tas) s 12D; *Trustee Act 1958* (Vic) s 12C; *Trustees Act 1962* (WA) s 26B.
56. *Trustee Act 1925* (ACT) s 64; *Trustee Act 1925* (NSW) s 64; *Trustee Act 1907* (NT) s 3; *Trusts Act 1973* (Qld) s 56; *Trustee Act 1936* (SA) s 17; *Trustee Act 1958* (Vic) s 30; *Trustees Act 1962* (WA) s 54.

3. situations where delegation is a matter of necessity and the agency relates to ministerial acts unconnected with the trustee's exercise of discretion.[57]

20.134 Trustees may also appoint agents to act for them without infringing the rule against delegation, as long as the trustee retains the sole exercise of discretion. For practical reasons the appointment of agents is often necessary because trustees cannot do everything themselves: *Re Speight* (1883) 22 Ch D 727. Indeed, given the size of some trust estates, the trustee may be duty bound to appoint suitable agents to secure the proper administration of the trust. Many jurisdictions now recognise the right to appoint agents in legislation.[58] In the Northern Territory, South Australia and Tasmania, the power is circumscribed to the appointment of legal practitioners or bankers, as agents for the receipt or discharge of trust moneys.

20.135 When appointing agents and advisers to the trust, trustees must be careful to avoid fettering their discretion by committing themselves to a future course of conduct without considering all the factors that arise at the time the decision is to be made: *Re King* (1902) 29 VLR 793. The duty extends to resisting the dictation of beneficiaries: *Re Brockbank; Ward v Bates* [1948] Ch 206; [1948] 1 All ER 287. The duty to remain unfettered is related to the duty to consider: see 20.139–20.134.

20.136 Because co-trustees are all bound to act personally, they must also act unanimously: *Dulhunty v Dulhunty* [2010] NSWSC 1465 at [31]; *Sky v Body* (1970) 92 WN (NSW) 934 at 935–6; *Luke v South Kensington Hotel Co* (1879) 11 Ch D 121 at 125. Once a unanimous decision has been made, it is permitted for one trustee to implement it: *Re Billington (deceased); Union Trustee Company of Australia Ltd v Billington* [1949] St R Qd 102 at 155.

20.137 If co-trustees cannot agree on a course of action, one trustee cannot bind another and the status quo prevails, unless the trust instrument provides a mechanism for resolving such disputes or the court becomes involved: *Beath v Kousal* [2010] VSC 24. Trust instruments can provide for decisions by majority: *Re Butlin's Settlement Trusts; Butlin v Butlin* [1976] Ch 251. In cases where the court becomes involved, in *Estate of William Just (dec'd) (No 1)* (1973) 7 SASR 508 at 514, Jacobs J said:

> In these circumstances, it seems to me that the proper course is for the court to intervene upon principles analogous to those upon which a court acts when trustees of an imperative power by reason of disagreement among themselves as to the mode of execution, find it impossible to act. In such circumstances, the court will substitute itself in the place of the trustees and will exercise the power by the most reasonable rule. The court in such circumstances will take up the trust, for, if the trust can by any possibility be executed by the court, the non-execution by the trustee shall not prejudice the *cestui que trust* (see per Lord Kenyon in *Brown v Higgs* (1800) 31 ER 700 at 705). This is, in reality, an example of the equitable principle that a trust shall not fail for want of a trustee.

20.138 Charitable trusts are not subject to this duty and decisions can be made by majority: *Blacket v Blizard* (1829) 109 ER 317; *Re Whiteley; Bishop of London v Whiteley* [1910] 1 Ch 600.

---

57. Heydon & Leeming, *Jacobs' Law of Trusts in Australia*, note 11 above, pp 391–2.
58. *Trustee Act 1925* (ACT) s 53; *Trustee Act 1925* (NSW) s 53; *Trustee Act 1907* (NT) s 17; *Trusts Act 1973* (Qld) s 54; *Trustee Act 1936* (SA) s 24; *Trustee Act 1898* (Tas) s 20; *Trustee Act 1958* (Vic) s 28; *Trustees Act 1962* (WA) s 53.

Duty to consider the exercise of trust powers

20.139 Trustees are obliged to properly consider the use of their powers: *Re Gestetner Settlement; Barnell v Blumka* [1953] Ch 672; [1953] 1 All ER 1150. In cases where trustees are granted a discretion to choose when and how they will act, they are bound by fiduciary duty to give real and genuine consideration to the issue by examining the options and determining which one was an appropriate course of action, from time to time: *Fay v Moramba Services Pty Ltd* at [34]–[40]; *Re Baden's Deed Trusts; McPhail v Doulton* [1971] AC 424 at 449; [1970] 2 All ER 228 at 240. In *Elovalis v Elovalis* at [63] Buss JA said:

> Where a trust instrument confers on the trustee discretionary powers which are described as 'absolute' or 'uncontrolled', that description does not authorise the trustee to 'do what he likes' with the trust fund. Where the trust instrument confers on the trustee an 'absolute and uncontrolled' discretion in relation to the exercise of a power, the court will not compel the trustee to exercise it, but if the trustee proposes to exercise it, the court will ensure that it is not exercised improperly or unreasonably. Further, where the power is combined with a trust or duty, the court will enforce the proper and timely exercise of the power, but will not interfere with the trustee's discretion as to the particular time or manner of his or her bona fide exercise of it.

20.140 Trustees cannot fetter the exercise of their discretionary powers in advance: *Thacker v Key* (1869) LR 8 Eq 408; *In Re Vestey's Settlement* [1951] Ch D 209. If trustees make resolutions or agreements which fetter their discretion they will be unenforceable: *Moore v Clench* [1875] 1 Ch D 447; *Fitzwood Pty Ltd v Unique Goal Pty Ltd (in liq)* (2001) 188 ALR 566 (aff'd on appeal in *Fitzwood Pty Ltd v Unique Goal Pty Ltd (in liq)* [2002] FCAFC 285).

20.141 The duty to consider extends to bare and discretionary powers. In *Lutheran Church of Australia v Farmers' Co-operative Executors & Trustees Limited* (1970) 121 CLR 628 at 652, Windeyer J said:

> A discretionary power, given to a trustee as such, to act or not to act in a specified manner imposes a duty on the trustee at least to consider the matter and decide deliberately whether to exercise the power. Lord Reid recently said, in *In re Gulbenkian's Settlement* [1970] AC 508 at 518: 'A settlor or testator who entrusts a power to his trustees must be reliant on them in their fiduciary capacity so that they cannot simply put aside the power and refuse to consider whether it ought in their judgment be exercised'. If it is a mere power, the court cannot dictate to the trustees whether it should be exercised or not exercised. That discretion is committed to them. But, even in that case, the court is not entirely unconcerned; for if trustees having a purely discretionary power refuse to consider whether and how they will exercise their discretion, then the court will remove them and substitute new trustees — who will have the same discretion but who, it is hoped, will not be recalcitrant. That would not be a usurpation by the court of the discretion given to trustees. It would be merely a means of accomplishing its exercise one way or another by dutiful trustees.

20.142 In *Re Hay's Settlement Trust* [1981] 3 All ER 786 at 792, Megarry VC held that a trustee holding a bare power has certain duties:

> That brings me to … [discuss] the extent of the fiduciary obligations of trustees who have a mere power vested in them, and how far the court exercises control over them in relation to that power. In the case of a trust, of course, the trustee is bound to execute it, and if he does not, the court will

see to its execution. A mere power is very different. Normally the trustee is not bound to exercise it, and the court will not compel him to do so. That, however, does not mean that he can simply fold his hands and ignore it, for normally he must from time to time consider whether or not to exercise the power, and the court may direct him to do this. When he does exercise the power, he must, of course (as in the case of all trusts and powers) confine himself to what is authorised, and not go beyond it. But that is not the only restriction. Whereas a person who is not in the fiduciary position is free to exercise the power in any way that he wishes, unhampered by any fiduciary duties, a trustee to whom, as such, a power is given is bound by the duties of his office in exercising that power to do so in a responsible manner according to its purpose. It is not enough for him to refrain from acting capriciously; he must do more. He must 'make such a survey of the range of objects or possible beneficiaries' as will enable him to carry out his fiduciary duty. He must find out 'the permissible area of selection and then consider responsibly, in individual cases, whether a contemplated beneficiary was within the power and whether, in relation to the possible claimants, a particular grant was appropriate': per Lord Wilberforce in *Re Baden (No 1)* [1970] 2 All 228 at 240, 247; [1971] AC 424 at 449, 457.

20.143 The duty to consider also requires trustees to inform themselves of all relevant matters before making a decision. This might extend beyond simple matters of fact to include taking advice from appropriate experts, but not to the point of breaching the duty not to delegate: *Scott v National Trust* [1988] 2 All ER 705.

20.144 It may be possible for an agreement regarding the trustee's discretion to be viewed as a variation of the trust rather than a fetter on discretion. In *Dagenmont Pty Ltd v Lugton* [2007] QSC 272, a trust provided for a discretionary power to make payments out of income to two classes of beneficiaries. After a dispute arose between the directors of the trustee and a beneficiary, the trustee entered into an agreement to pay one of those beneficiaries an annual payment of $150,000 per year for the rest of the beneficiary's life out of either the capital or the income. The trustee later sought to have the agreement struck down as an illegal fetter on its discretionary power to make payments out of income. Chesterman J disagreed. He found that the agreement could be understood as a variation of the original deed, or, alternatively, as a form of release over the money in the agreement. The trust deed allowed the trustee to make both variations and give releases. On that basis the agreement was upheld.

Fraud on a power

20.145 'Fraud on a power' relates to situations where a trustee has exercised a discretionary power for an unauthorised or improper purpose.[59] The term 'fraud' does not necessarily connote dishonest or immoral behaviour in this context: *Vatcher v Paull* [1915] AC 372; *Medforth v Blake* [2000] Ch 86; [1999] 3 All ER 97; *Thoo v The Owners Strata Plan No 50276* [2011] NSWSC 657 at [180]. The primary issue is whether the trustee has acted with the intention to achieve an ulterior purpose: *Re Crawshay* [1948] 1 Ch 123.

20.146 Fraud on a power is commonly alleged in cases where a trustee makes a distribution to a person outside of the class of beneficiaries, or where a trustee exercises a discretion to exclude a class of beneficiaries, and the beneficiaries allege that this has been done capriciously: *Re Dick* [1953]

---

59. P Devonshire, 'Fraud on a Power: Patterns in the Mosaic' (2007) 22 *New Zealand Universities Law Review* 496, p 497.

1 Ch 343. The general principle is that the courts will not review a discretionary decision unless it was made in bad faith and/or without fair consideration. In *Karger v Paul* [1984] VR 161 at 164, McGarvie J outlined the principles as follows:

> It is an established general principle that unless trustees choose to give reasons for the exercise of a discretion, their exercise of the discretion can not be examined or reviewed by a court so long as they act in good faith and without an ulterior purpose: *Re Beloved Wilkes' Charity* (1851) 42 ER 330; *Duke of Portland v Topham* (1864) 11 ER 1242. For reasons given above, I would add the further requirement, so obvious that it is often not mentioned, that they act upon real and genuine consideration. In the context, it was in that sense that Lord Truro LC used the expression 'with a fair consideration' in *Re Beloved Wilkes' Charity*, [at 333]. In the case of an absolute and unrestricted discretion such as the discretion in the present case, the general principle is given unqualified operation: *Gisborne v Gisborne* (1877) 2 App Cas 300, at 305; *Tabor v Brooks* (1878) 10 Ch D 273; *Craig v National Trustees Executors and Agency Company of Australia Ltd* [1920] VLR 569.

20.147 *Karger v Paul* concerned a decision by trustees to transfer the entire capital of the trust to the deceased's husband, who died thereafter. The decision was challenged by a residuary beneficiary who was deprived of any entitlements by the trustee's decision. McGarvie J found that there had been no bad faith or failure to give genuine consideration to the decision.

20.148 In *Curwen v Vanbreck Pty Ltd* [2008] VSC 338, discretionary beneficiaries who were the grandchildren of the settlor had been excluded by the corporate trustee (which was controlled by their aunt) only after their parents had requested information about the trust. It was alleged that the aunt had exercised the power to exclude her nephews after she had realised that they were potential beneficiaries. Nevertheless, the claim of bad faith failed as the aunt had not been asked in cross-examination regarding her reasons for excluding the grandchildren. There was, therefore, no evidence upon which to base a claim of bad faith. In upholding these findings, the Court of Appeal, in *Curwen v Vanbreek Pty Ltd* (2009) 26 VR 335 at 354, said:

> The appellants rely upon circumstantial evidence to establish a fraudulent or improper purpose on the part of the trustee. A subjective intention or purpose may be inferred from objective or circumstantial matters which may include the exercise of a power of appointment. But the fact that an appointment is consistent with an improper purpose will not necessarily lead to the drawing of such an inference. So, in *Vatcher v Paull* [1915] AC 372 at 379 it was said that 'it is not enough that an appointor or some person not an object of power may conceivably derive some benefit.' An intention by an appointor to obtain an improper end is not necessarily to be inferred because the effect of an appointment is consistent with there having been an improper purpose in the making of the appointment. It will be a question of fact in each case.

20.149 Discretionary trustee are under no obligation to give reasons for their decision: *Tierney v King* [1983] 2 Qd R 580. There are no rules of natural justice which apply: *Tuftevski v Total Risks Management Pty Ltd* [2009] NSWSC 315. However, if the trustees do give reasons for their decision and those reasons evidence errors in the exercise of the trustees' discretion the court may then overturn the decision: *Hartigan Nominees Pty Ltd v Rydge* at 441–2.

The exercise of trustees' discretion and the rule in Re Hastings-Bass

20.150   The rule in *Re Hastings-Bass* [1975] Ch 25; [1974] 2 All ER 193 suggests that a decision of trustees to exercise their discretion may be overridden by the court if the trustees have failed to take matters into account which would have affected their decision. *Re Hastings-Bass* concerned trustees who had exercised their discretion to create a sub-trust with a life estate and remainders. It was later found that the remainders (but not the life estate) offended the rule against perpetuities. Questions arose as to whether the trustees' decision should be totally overturned (because of the unintended effects of the rule against perpetuities) or whether the part of the decision to award a life estate could stand. If the entire decision was overturned, all the property of the sub-settlement would have to be returned to the original trust. Conversely, if it failed in part, only that part would be returned. The difference was important as the original trust had become subject to estate tax, with the effect that the more that was returned to the original trust, the greater would be the tax liability. The trial judge overturned the decision of the trustees entirely. On appeal, the Court of Appeal found that the trustees' main intention had been to create a life estate and because this was unaffected by the rule of perpetuities, the exercise of the trustees' discretion in that respect should remain undisturbed, and that, to that extent, the decision of the trustees was allowed to stand. In making their decision, the Court of Appeal laid down a rule for when a trustee's exercise of discretion can be overturned by the courts.

20.151   Buckley LJ, at Ch 41; All ER 203, said:

> [W]here by the terms of a trust … a trustee is given a discretion as to some matter under which he acts in good faith, the court should not interfere with his action notwithstanding that it does not have the full effect which he intended, unless (1) what he has achieved is unauthorised by the power conferred upon him, or (2) it is clear that he would not have acted as he did (a) had he not taken into account considerations which he should not have taken into account, or (b) had he not failed to take into account considerations which he ought to have taken into account.

20.152   Other examples of where the rule has been employed to overturn the trustee's decision include *Green v Cobham* [2002] STC 820, where the settlement of new trusts and the appointment of new trustees was set aside on the grounds that the trustees had not taken into account the effect of the appointment on capital gains tax liability. Similarly, in *Burrell v Burrell* [2005] EWHC 245 (Ch), an appointment was set aside after it had been made by trustees without them considering the fact that it would attract a large inheritance tax penalty. In many cases where the rule has been relied upon to apply to have the decision of trustees set aside, the actions of the trustees were based upon professional advice that was subsequently found to be negligently given.

'Full legal effect' or 'full effect'?

20.153   *Re Hastings-Bass* would seem to suggest that the rule should only be applied when the trustees have failed to take into account the full *legal* effect of their decision. Nevertheless, the rule has not been confined to situations where the exercise of the trustees' discretion has been stymied because of their failure to consider some rule of law. In *Mettoy Pension Trustees Ltd v Evans* [1991] 2 All ER 513 at 555, it was said that the rule could be applied to all situations where trustees had neglected factors in the exercise of their discretion which would have changed the decision had the trustees taken such factors into account. Warner J, at 555, said:

If, as I believe, the reason for the application of the principle is the failure by the trustees to take into account considerations that they ought to have taken into account, it cannot matter whether that failure is due to their having overlooked (or to their legal advisers having overlooked) some relevant rule of law or limit on their discretion, or is due to some other cause.

'Would not have acted' or 'may not have acted'?

20.154   *Re Hastings-Bass* indicates that it is necessary for the court to be satisfied that the trustees would have acted differently had they taken into account that which they neglected. However, in *Sieff v Fox* [2005] 3 All ER 693, Lloyd LJ indicated that it might be sufficient to find that the trustees *might* have acted differently in cases where the trustees were under a duty to act, as opposed to situations where they exercise their powers voluntarily. Lloyd LJ, at 717, said:

> It seems to me that, for the purposes of a case where the trustees are not under a duty to act, the relevant test is still that stated in *Re Hastings-Bass*, namely whether, if they had not misunderstood the effect that their actual exercise of the discretionary power would have, they would have acted differently. In my judgment that is correct both on authority, starting with *Re Hastings-Bass* itself, and on principle. Only in a case where the beneficiary is entitled to require the trustees to act, such as *Kerr's case* [*Kerr v British Leyland (Staff) Trustees Ltd* (1986) [2001] WTLR 1071] or *Stannard's case* [*Stannard v Fisons Ltd* [1990] 1 PLR 179], should it suffice to vitiate the trustees' decision to show that they might have acted differently. The word 'might' has been used, as matter of decision, only in those two cases. In two cases it has been said (not as a matter of decision) that the 'might' test applies to a voluntary exercise of a power: *AMP (UK) Ltd v Barker* [2001] PLR 7 and *Hearn v Younger* [2002] WTLR 1317. I respectfully disagree with those observations, having had the benefit of what may have been fuller, and were no doubt different, submissions on the point. If an act by trustees is set aside, where the trustees have acted under an obligation, then the beneficiaries can require the trustees to start again, on the correct basis. It seems to me that the lower test of 'might' is appropriate in such cases … If the trustees' act was voluntary, so that they cannot be compelled to act again if the act is set aside, the more demanding test of 'would' is justified in order to decide whether the trustees' act can be set aside.

Does the rule require a breach of trust to have occurred?

20.155   In *Abacus Trust Company (Isle of Man) v Barr* [2003] Ch 405; [2003] 1 All ER 763, Lightman J introduced a new requirement for the operation of the rule. The case concerned a family trust based on the Isle of Man. The settlor requested that the trustees appoint 40 per cent of the trust on separate trusts for his sons. The message was poorly communicated and the trustees mistakenly appointed 60 per cent. The error was detected but no attempt had been made to remedy it for 10 years. The court was then asked to set aside the settlement. Lightman J, at Ch 417–8; All ER 770–1, said:

> In my view it is not sufficient to bring the Rule into play that the Trustee made a mistake or by reason of ignorance or a mistake did not take into account a relevant consideration or took into account an irrelevant consideration. What has to be established is that the Trustee in making his decision has … failed to consider what he was under a duty to consider. If the Trustee has in accordance with his duty identified the relevant considerations and used all proper care and diligence in obtaining the relevant information and advice relating to those considerations, the

Trustee can be in no breach of duty and its decision cannot be impugned merely because in fact that information turns out to be partial or incorrect.

20.156 Lightman J was clearly attempting to rein in the rule by adding the extra requirement of breach of duty. The added requirement seems to have had a short shelf-life. In *Sieff v Fox*, at 728–9, Lloyd LJ disagreed with Lightman J's decision to add this requirement. Its validity was also questioned (but not determined) in *Burrell v Burrell* at [21]. Edmundson has queried whether the additional requirement adds anything to the existing principle, as it does little to secure control of the rule.[60]

The whole or part of a decision?

20.157 The rule can also be applied to part of a decision, as well as an entire decision. In *Mettoy Pension Trustees Ltd v Evans* at 555, Warner J said:

> There may well be cases where the court, giving effect to the rule in *Hastings-Bass*, comes to the conclusion that, had the trustees not failed to take into account considerations which they ought to have taken into account, they would not have acted as they did at all, but would either have done nothing or done something quite different. In such a case the court must declare void the whole of the purported exercise of the trustees' discretion. There may however be cases where the court is satisfied that the trustees would have acted in the same way but with, for instance, the omission of a particular provision in a deed. I do not see why, in such a case, the court should not declare only that provision void. It seems to me that the remedy to be adopted by the court must depend on the circumstances of each case.

Failure to make a decision

20.158 The rule is not applicable to situations where the trustees have failed to exercise a discretion. In *Breadner v Granville-Grossman* [2000] 4 All ER 705, Park J refused to apply the rule in circumstances where trustees had failed to exercise a power of appointment before it expired. Park J found that part of the underlying reason for the rule was to remedy unconscientiousness and there was nothing unconscientious in the situation of the property falling to beneficiaries in default of the exercise of the discretionary power.

Effect on dealings with third parties

20.159 It has been argued that the rule should not be used to overturn contracts and other agreements with third parties.[61] Nolan and Conaglen have argued that the rule should only apply to the dispositive powers of trustees (the powers to dispose of the proprietary interests of the trust) and not to the trustee's administrative powers (to make contracts with third parties in pursuance of the management and administration of trust property). They argue that the trustee is a juristic person and, as such, should be bound by contract. The contract arises from the status of the trustee as a legal person and not from the trust. On that basis agreements with third parties should not be affected by the rule, at least to the extent that such agreements should not be rendered void *ab initio*.

---

60. P Edmundson, 'Setting aside trustees' decisions: How secure is the rule in Hastings-Bass?' (2008) 31 *Australian Bar Review* 36.
61. R Nolan & M Conaglen, '*Hastings-Bass* and Third Parties' (2006) *Cambridge Law Journal* 400.

Void or voidable?

20.160   The previous point raises the issue of the effect of a positive application of the rule on the trustee's decision. There are conflicting cases on whether the application of the rule renders the decision of the trustee void or voidable. In some cases the court has treated the decision as being voidable: *Donaldson v Smith* [2006] EWHC 1290 (Ch); *Sieff v Fox*; *Abacus Trust Co (Isle of Man) v Barr*. In others, the court treated the decision as void: *Turner v Turner* [1984] Ch 100; *Mettoy Pension Trustees Ltd v Evans*. The issue has a practical effect on other beneficiaries or third parties who have received trust property pursuant to the exercise of the trustee's discretion. If the transfer of property is void it must be returned to the trust. A voidable decision would at least provide the option of moulding relief in a less blunt fashion and allow the interests of third parties to be taken into account.

20.161   It has been argued that the better approach would be to find decisions which are made beyond the express terms of the trust as void, whereas decisions which are made incorrectly, but nevertheless within power, should be treated as voidable.[62]

Should the rule apply in Australia?

20.162   Most of the English decisions on the rule seemed to be initiated by concerns regarding taxation or pension schemes and it might be argued that *Re Hastings-Bass* has little relevance to Australia because of the great differences between English and Australian tax law and superannuation. Caution has been expressed by some commentators given the potential for the principle to expand.[63]

20.163   Earlier Australian authorities suggest a reticence to review the discretionary decisions of trustees and employ the rule. In *Karger v Paul*, McGarvie J refused to overturn the decision of trustees to transfer the entire capital of the trust to the deceased's husband, who died thereafter. The decision was challenged by a residuary beneficiary who was deprived of any entitlements by their decision. McGarvie J, at 163–4, said:

> As part of the process of, and solely for the purpose of, ascertaining whether there has been any such failure, it is relevant to look at evidence of the inquiries which were made by the trustees, the information they had and the reasons for, and manner of, their exercising their discretion. However, it is not open to the Court to look at those things for the independent purpose of impugning the exercise of discretion on the grounds that their inquiries, information or reasons or the manner of exercise of the discretion, fell short of what was appropriate and sufficient. Nor is it open to the Court to look at the factual situation established by the evidence, for the independent purpose of impugning the exercise of the discretion on the grounds the trustees were wrong in their appreciation of the facts or made an unwise or unjustified exercise of discretion in the circumstances. The issues which are examinable by the Court are limited to whether there has been a failure to exercise the discretion in good faith, upon real and genuine consideration and in accordance with the purposes for which the discretion was conferred. In short, the Court examines whether the discretion was exercised but does not examine how it was exercised.

---

62. Nolan & Conaglen, '*Hastings-Bass* and Third Parties', note 61 above, pp 17–18.
63. Edmundson, 'Setting aside trustees' decisions: How secure is the rule in Hastings-Bass?', note 60 above.

20.164 In *Asea Brown Boveri Superannuation Fund No 1 Pty Ltd v Asea Brown Boveri Pty Ltd* [1999] 1 VR 144 at 157, Beach J doubted that the rule would be applied in Australia:

> I know of no principle of law which permits a trustee to come to the court and say — 'Some time ago I made a decision concerning the trust fund of which I am a trustee in the mistaken belief that a certain state of affairs existed at that time. Had I then known what I now know I would not have made the decision I did but a totally different one. Because of my mistaken assumption I now ask the court to declare my earlier decision to be invalid.'

20.165 The rule has been applied on occasion in Australia. In *Sinclair v Moss* [2006] VSC 130, payments had been made to a discretionary beneficiary but the trustees' discretion had miscarried, as they had not properly taken into account the beneficiary's outside income, as required by the trust. Byrne J found that the decision should be overturned. In so finding, Byrne J found the trustee's determination to have been void rather than voidable. Twelve years of distribution (totalling over $500,000) were recalled from the beneficiary's estate. In *BMD v KWD* [2008] WASC 196, McKechnie J noted the rule but refused to overturn the decision of the Public Trustee to settle a dispute regarding the sale of land owned by a person under guardianship. In *Re CWK Nominees Pty Ltd* [2012] NSWSC 665 at [58], Ward J noted the rule but affirmed McGarvie J's statement in *Karger v Paul* that the court will not review the exercise of discretion if it has been in good faith upon genuine consideration and in accordance with the purposes for which the discretion is conferred and not some ulterior purpose.

20.166 The rule's popularity in England has also waned. In *Pitt v Holt* [2011] 2 All ER 450, the Court of Appeal undertook a detailed re-examination of the nature and scope of the rule in *Re Hastings-Bass* and concluded that the rule as promulgated and developed since the decision in *Mettoy Pension Trustees Ltd v Evans* was wrong and had to be corrected. In *Pitt v Holt* the detailed analysis was undertaken by Lloyd LJ, but a useful summary of his decision was set out by Mummery LJ, at 510, as follows:

> In his very fine comprehensive and clarifying judgment, with which I agree, Lloyd LJ convincingly demonstrates, by reference to principle and authority, that (a) the *ratio* in *Hastings-Bass* is not authority for the rule successfully invoked at first instance in the two cases under appeal and in a line of other cases since *Hastings-Bass*; (b) a disposition by a fiduciary is void if it is a misapplication of property outside the four corners of the discretion, a disposition of property to a non-object of the power, for instance, being *ultra vires* and without any legal or fiscal effect; (c) a disposition is not void if it is *intra vires*, even if the manner in which the discretion was exercised was 'legally flawed' by the fiduciary's failure to take into account a relevant consideration, such as the correct tax consequences of the disposition; (d) in proceedings to invalidate a disposition on the ground that the fiduciary has left a relevant consideration out of account or has taken an irrelevant consideration into account, a breach of fiduciary duty has to be established; (e) a claim for breach of fiduciary duty would not normally be made *by* a fiduciary (as has happened in practice under the *Hastings-Bass* rule), but rather *against* a fiduciary by a person claiming to be an object of the power; and (f) the court's jurisdiction to grant a discretionary remedy, such as rescission of the disposition, or other remedies for breach of trust, is subject to equitable defences.

Mummery LJ, at 511, observed that the wrong turn that had been taken in recent decades in relation to the rule in *Re Hastings-Bass* stemmed from the failure to take into account '[five] elementary distinctions and principles applicable to the validity of a disposition pursuant to a fiduciary power and to the discretionary remedy of rescission setting aside a disposition of property', which his Lordship, at 511–2, listed as follows:

> First, there is a fundamental distinction between, on the one hand, the *existence* and *extent* of a fiduciary power to make a disposition and, on the other hand, the *manner of exercise* of that power. In the case of a disposition to a non-object, the power does not exist. The purported disposition has no legal effect. It is void as against the whole world. If, however, the power to make the disposition exists, but there is a flaw in the manner in which the discretion has been exercised, the disposition will be valid, unless and until set aside as between the parties by order of the court.

> Secondly, a defect in the manner of making an *intra vires* decision to exercise a fiduciary power is not, and should not be treated as if it were, an excess of the power. The exercise of the discretion must, of course, be properly informed and considered. The discretion must be performed in an honest, fair and responsible manner, but those requirements of the way that a decision to exercise a discretion is made are not a sufficient basis for implying a legal limitation on the four corners of the power.

> Thirdly, analogies with judicial review in public law are unhelpful and unnecessary. There is an elementary distinction between, on the one hand, the liability in private law of a fiduciary for breach of duty and, on the other hand, the availability of judicial review for the control of abuses of public power … Judicial review in public law is concerned with the lawfulness of decisions and acts of public authorities to ensure that they are acting within the limits of a power usually set by statute. Breaches of duty in fiduciary law relate to discretionary dispositive powers privately entrusted to a fiduciary who has been selected to exercise the powers for the benefit of members within a designated class. The discretion of the fiduciary is not controlled by the court, which will not interfere with matters of judgment by the fiduciary. The only ground on which the court will review the exercise of the discretion is that of a breach of fiduciary duty. The underlying principles of fiduciary law and private property law are conceptually different from the public interest basis for reviewing the lawfulness of administrative action …

> [T]he correct basis of the court's jurisdiction to set aside a disposition by a fiduciary in purported exercise of a discretionary power is whether it was in breach of fiduciary duty. Talk of judicial review of the fiduciary discretion, or of interfering with the decision of a fiduciary decision-maker, and whether the flawed exercise of fiduciary discretion renders the disposition void or voidable does not grapple with the real point, which is whether there has been a breach of fiduciary duty. Once the focus is on breach of trust the rest should fall into place.

> Fourthly, if the disposition is a misapplication of property outside the scope of the power (e.g. a fraud on the power) that will be a breach of fiduciary duty and the disposition would be void. It would have no consequences, legal or fiscal. If, however, the disposition is made within the scope of the power, but pursuant to an exercise of discretion infected by a flawed process of decision-making (e.g. failure to take relevant factors into account or to leave relevant factors out of account), that may be a breach of duty but it is of a different kind of duty. The *intra vires* disposition will be valid unless and until the court, in its discretion, decides to grant rescission setting it aside or some other remedy, such as equitable compensation or an account.

Fifthly, whether or not there is a breach of fiduciary duty in a particular case will involve the court in an inquiry into the nature of the relevant duty, the nature of the breach, the basis of liability for breach, the applicability of any exceptions to, or exemptions from, a breach of duty and the availability of equitable defences to breach. Taking Lloyd LJ's example of a fiduciary taking into account and acting upon incorrect advice obtained from a professional adviser about the fiscal consequences of a disposition, there would be no breach of duty in such a case. *A fortiori* no question would arise of the court granting, either at the instance of the fiduciary or of an object of the power, the remedy of rescission setting aside the disposition so as to deprive it of fiscal effects on *Hastings-Bass* type grounds: e.g. that the adverse consequences were not intended or expected, that they were to the detriment of the beneficiaries and that the fiduciary would have acted differently and not made that disposition if he had received and taken into account the correct tax advice. The fact that a disposition by a fiduciary pursuant to a discretionary power had unintended tax consequences and did not achieve the desired effect, but without involving a departure from the terms of the trust or a breach of duty, is neither outside the scope of the power nor is it a ground for setting the disposition aside.

20.167 In *Pitt v Holt* the Court of Appeal heard two separate cases together. The first was that of *Pitt v Holt*, which concerned Pitt who had received a lump sum in relation to a personal injuries claim which had, upon professional advice, been put into a discretionary trust. It later became apparent that this transfer of funds had unintended adverse inheritance tax consequences that could have been avoided had the trust been drafted correctly. Pitt's personal representative sought a declaration from the court that the settlement into the trust should be set aside. The second case was that of *Futter v Futter* and involved the exercise by the trustees of powers of advancement under two discretionary trusts. The intention was to advance 'stockpiled gains' from offshore trusts to United Kingdom residents in such a way as to avoid incurring a charge to capital gains tax (CGT). The trustees had previously received legal advice to the effect that the losses incurred for CGT purposes by the recipient beneficiary could be off set against the stockpiled gains. The advice was incorrect. In both cases the trial judge set aside the transactions on the basis of the rule in *Re Hastings-Bass*. On appeal, the Court of Appeal over-ruled the decisions at first instance.

20.168 In coming to its decisions the Court of Appeal held that an act that is within the powers of the trustees but is said to be vitiated by the failure of the trustees to take into account a relevant factor such as, for example, a tax liability, is a potentially voidable act. Such an act will be voidable by a beneficiary if the beneficiary can show that it amounts to a breach of fiduciary duty. However, if trustees seek and follow apparently competent professional advice, they are not in breach of their fiduciary duty by failing to take into account relevant matters if the failure is a product of taking advice that turns out to be wrong. It thus follows that acts done in consequence of the advice are not vitiated by the error and are not voidable.

20.169 In *Pitt v Holt* it was clear on the facts that Pitt's personal representative did not have in mind and thus did not take into account the prospect of the inheritance tax consequences, but it was equally clear that the personal representative did seek proper professional advice and acted upon it. Thus, having sought professional advice that was believed to be correct, it could not be said that the personal representative had acted in breach of fiduciary duties. It followed that the transactions were neither void nor voidable. The Court of Appeal further held that the consequential tax liability was not a mistake as to the legal effect of the transaction but as to its consequences. Therefore, it was not a mistake that would attract the equitable jurisdiction to rescind a voluntary disposition for mistake.

20.170   In *Futter v Futter* the Court of Appeal ruled that the trustees' reliance on professional advice was entirely proper, and although they had failed to take into account the prospective charge to CGT on the advancements, they did so in reliance on the advice obtained. As a result, the advancements were not void because they were within the powers of the trustees. Nor were they voidable because no breach of fiduciary duty had been committed.

20.171   The practical impact of the decision in *Pitt v Holt* is that there are stricter limits on the rule in *Hastings-Bass* than previously was the case.[64] Trustees will now face a greater degree of difficulty when applying to the court to set aside actions which later turn out to have unforeseen and adverse consequences. It is likely that the trustees will seek to recover their losses in circumstances where the loss has been the product of poor professional advice.

---

64.   An appeal against the decision in *Pitt v Holt* is due to be heard by the Supreme Court of the United Kingdom in 2013.

21

BENEFICIARIES

INTRODUCTION

21.1   As the number and types of trusts has grown exponentially, so has the number and type of beneficial interests in trusts. This chapter firstly examines the increasingly complicated nature of beneficial interests, before examining the rights of beneficiaries and the personal remedies available to them for breach of trust.

THE NATURE OF BENEFICIAL INTERESTS

Beneficial rights in fixed trusts

21.2   The nature of beneficial interests is necessarily dependent upon the type of trust. Broadly speaking, fixed trusts with vested beneficial interests create a form of beneficial equitable ownership, which is highly protected by equity. In equity, the beneficiaries are the effective owners of the property.

Beneficial rights in discretionary trusts

21.3   In contrast, beneficiaries in discretionary trusts do not ordinarily have any proprietary interest in the trust property, although this should be said with caution as the terms 'discretionary beneficiary' and 'beneficial interests' are not fixed terms: *MSP Nominees Pty Ltd v Commissioner of Stamps (SA)* (1999) 198 CLR 494; (1999) 166 ALR 149. Caution should be exercised in making universal statements as each discretionary trust is different: see 15.11. Nevertheless, discretionary beneficiaries usually only enjoy a hope or expectation that they will be considered in the trustee's exercise of discretion. In *Gartside v Inland Revenue Commissioners* [1968] AC 553 at 607; [1968] 1 All ER 121 at 128, the House of Lords had to consider whether discretionary beneficiaries under a testamentary trust were liable for estate tax which was levied on interests in possession. Lord Reid, at AC 607; All ER 128, said:

> To have an interest in possession does not merely mean that you possess the interest. You also possess an interest in expectancy for you may be able to assign it and you can rely on it to prevent the trustees from dissipating the trust fund. 'In possession' must mean that your interest enables you to claim now whatever may be the subject of the interest. For instance, if it is the current income from a certain fund your claim may yield nothing if there is no income, but your claim is a valid claim, and if there is any income you are entitled to get it; but a right to require trustees

to consider whether they will pay you something does not enable you to claim anything. If the trustees do decide to pay you something, you do not get it by reason of having the right to have your case considered: you get it only because the trustees have decided to give it to you. Even if I had thought that objects of discretionary trusts have interests, I would not find any good reason for holding that they have interests in possession.

21.4   More recently, in *Cypjayne Pty Ltd v Rodskog* [2009] NSWSC 301 at [41], Brereton J said:

Thus a discretionary trust does not have beneficiaries in the traditional sense, whose interests together aggregate the beneficial ownership of the trust property. Instead, there is a class of persons, usually described in wide terms, who are the objects of a trust power to appoint either income or corpus or both to selected members of the class. The members of the class are objects of a trust power, rather than beneficiaries in the strict sense. They do not have a proprietary legal or equitable interest in the trust fund, though they have a right to due administration of the trust … They have no beneficial interest in the trust property; they are not persons for whose benefit the trust property is held by the trustee; at the highest they are members of a class of persons for the benefit of some one or more of whom the trustee may in due course hold property if it so determines. At best, they are potential beneficiaries, not beneficiaries.

Exhaustive and non-exhaustive trusts

21.5   Distinctions can be made between the rights of discretionary beneficiaries in exhaustive trusts (where income must be distributed) and non-exhaustive trusts (where income can be accumulated): see 15.12. In *Secretary, Department of Families, Housing, Community Services and Indigenous Affairs v Elliott* (2009) 174 FCR 387 at 394, a unanimous Full Federal Court drew distinction between four different categories of trust:

1.   An exhaustive trust with a closed class of beneficiaries;
2.   An exhaustive trust with an open class of beneficiaries;
3.   A non-exhaustive trust with a closed class of beneficiaries; and
4.   A non-exhaustive trust with an open class of beneficiaries.

The Full Federal Court found that it is impossible to measure the interests of individual beneficiaries in all four categories. However, in category 1 it may be possible to measure the collective interests of beneficiaries in relation to the capital. In categories 1 and 2 it was also possible to measure the collective interests of the beneficiaries to the income (because it must be distributed in an exhaustive trust). Finally, the interests of beneficiaries in categories 3 and 4 cannot be measured as there is no collective totality of interests.

21.6   The Full Federal Court relied on the judgment of Lord Reid in *Gartside v Inland Revenue Commissioners* at AC 606; All ER 127, where his Lordship said:

I think that this idea of a group or class right must have arisen in this way. Where the trustees are *bound* to distribute the whole income among the discretionary beneficiaries and have no power to retain any part of it or use any part of it for any other purposes, you cannot tell what any one of the beneficiaries will receive until the trustees have exercised their discretion. But you can say with absolute certainty that the individual rights of the beneficiaries when added up or taken together will extend to the whole income. You can have an equation $x + y + z = 100$ although you do not yet know the value of x or y or z. And that may lead to important results where the trust is of that character.

Rights to be considered

21.7 While not having proprietary rights in trust property, discretionary beneficiaries do have the right to be considered by the trustee in the exercise of the trustee's powers: *Re Smith* [1928] Ch 915; *Re Smith; Sainsbury v IRC* [1970] Ch 712 at 715; *Re Hay's Settlement Trusts* [1981] 3 All ER 786; *Wilkinson v Clerical Administrative and Related Employees Superannuation Pty Ltd* (1998) 79 FCR 469 at 480; *Fay v Moramba Services Pty Ltd* [2009] NSWSC 1428 at [39]. In *Lutheran Church of Australia South Australia District Inc v Farmers Co-operative Executives and Trustees Ltd* (1970) 121 CLR 628 at 652, Windeyer J said:

> A discretionary power, given to a trustee as such, to act or not to act in a specified manner imposes a duty on the trustee at least to consider the matter and decide deliberately whether to exercise the power. Lord Reid recently said, in *Re Gulbenkian's Settlement* [1970] AC 508 at 518: A settlor or testator who entrusts a power to his trustees must be reliant on them in their fiduciary capacity so that they cannot simply put aside the power and refuse to consider whether it ought in their judgment be exercised.

If it is a mere power, the Court cannot dictate to the trustees whether it should be exercised or not exercised. That discretion is committed to them. But, even in that case, the Court is not entirely unconcerned; for if trustees having a purely discretionary power refuse to consider whether and how they will exercise their discretion, then the Court will remove them and substitute new trustees — who will have the same discretion but who, it is hoped, will not be recalcitrant. That would not be a usurpation by the Court of the discretion given to trustees. It would be merely a means of accomplishing its exercise one way or another by dutiful trustees: *Inland Revenue Commissioners v Portway Colleges Trust* [1955] Ch 20 at 35.

Rights to termination

21.8 The fact that discretionary beneficiaries may be able to exercise their powers to terminate trusts and take legal ownership does not automatically mean that they have proprietary interests: *ING Life Ltd v Commissioner of State Revenue* [2008] QSC 248; *Kent v SS 'Maria Luisa'* (2003) 130 FCR 12 at 35–36. The beneficiaries' power to terminate the trust is discussed below: see 21.48–21.66.

Taxation and discretionary beneficiaries

21.9 Taxation is ordinarily levied on transactions or on ownership of property. The nature of beneficial interests is therefore an important issue for taxation because if a beneficiary does not enjoy a proprietary interest it may be argued that he or she should not be liable for taxation. Equally, if a trustee does not beneficially own property, it may argue that he or she is not liable to be taxed.

21.10 Taxation statutes often focus on whether a person has a 'beneficial interest' or 'beneficial entitlement'. A 'beneficial interest' usually denotes a proprietary interest held by one person for the benefit of another: *Commissioner of State Revenue v Serana Pty Ltd* (2008) 36 WAR 251 at 285. As a corollary, a 'beneficial entitlement' ordinarily requires a person to have taken an interest for their own enjoyment: *White v Commissioner of Stamp Duties* [1968] Qd R 140; *Ayerst (Inspector of Taxes) v C & K (Construction) Ltd* [1976] AC 167. In *Commissioner Of State Revenue v Landrow*

Properties Pty Ltd [2010] VSCA 197, a corporate trustee of a number of family trusts transferred units from a unit trust in which it owned property to itself in its capacity as trustee for another trust. The Commissioner of State Revenue assessed the transaction as being subject to the 'land rich provisions' of the *Duties Act 2000* (Vic). The trustee successfully argued that it should not be taxed as it was not beneficially entitled to the units. A later attempt to get the Victorian Court of Appeal to change its position in *Landrow* failed: *Commissioner of State Revenue v Challenger Listed Investments Ltd (as trustee for Challenger Di-versified Property Trust 1)* [2011] VSCA 272.

21.11   *Commissioner of State Revenue v Serana Pty Ltd* concerned the transfer of trust property from one, related, discretionary trust to another. The trustee argued that nominal stamp duty was payable on the transfer because no beneficial interest had passed in the conveyance. The Western Australia Court of Appeal agreed and found that, as the discretionary beneficiaries had no proprietary rights to the trust property, no beneficial interest had been passed. That decision can be contrasted with *Pharmos Nominees Pty Ltd v Commissioner of State Taxation* [2012] SASCFC 89. In that case the trustee of a discretionary trust which held substantial commercial properties transferred the control and ownership of the trustee to Pharmos for nearly seven million dollars. As part of the settlement the trustee granted an 'equity bond' which gave Pharmos rights to income and capital up to an amount of nearly three million dollars. The equity bond was assessed as being liable for stamp duty. The Full Court of the South Australian Supreme Court found that the effect of these transactions was to effectively remove the trustee's discretion as to the payment of income and capital and therefore convert Pharmos' interest from that of a discretionary beneficiary into a property interest, which could be taxed.

21.12   An alternative phrase which is sometimes employed in taxation legislation is 'present entitlement'. In *Pearson v Commissioner of Taxation* (2006) 232 ALR 55 at 62, Edmonds J said:

> A beneficiary is 'presently entitled' to a share of the income of the trust estate if, but only if: (a) the beneficiary has an interest in the income which is both vested in interest and vested in possession; and (b) the beneficiary has a present legal right to demand and receive payment of the income, whether or not the precise entitlement can be ascertained before the end of the relevant year of income and whether or not the trustee has the funds available for immediate payment.

21.13   The High Court considered some of these issues in *CPT Custodian Pty Ltd v Commissioner of State Revenue (Vic)* (2005) 224 CLR 98; (2005) 221 ALR 196. This case concerned unit trusts over land where the units were held by two companies. Under one of the trusts, the companies held half of the units. In the other trusts the companies effectively held all the units. The unit trust deeds conferred an equal interest in the trust property but dictated that the unit holders lacked any interest in any particular part of the trust fund. Unit holders were entitled to periodic distributions of income. Both the trustee and the manager were given a right to be paid fees and a right to be indemnified from the trust fund for those fees: see 20.34. The issue that arose was whether the companies should be treated as the owners of the land under s 3(1) of the *Land Tax Act 1958* (Vic). That section defined an 'owner' to be 'every person entitled to any land for any estate of freehold in possession'. The Commissioner argued that the individual units each provided fixed and ascertainable rights which conferred a proprietorial interest in the trust property which was akin to 'ownership'. Moreover, the Commissioner argued that if a unit holder held all the units of the trust then they were fully entitled to the beneficial interests of the trust and the trust property became vested in possession. The Commissioner also argued that in such a situation, the beneficiary was entitled to terminate the trust to perfect its title which, again, indicated a form of ownership: see 21.48.

21.14 The High Court did not agree with these arguments. Neither company was found to be entitled to 'freehold in possession'. The High Court found that the ownership of units did not necessarily confer an equitable interest in the property. The mere existence of a trust relationship did not automatically mean that a unit holder had to be vested with a proprietorial interest in the trust fund. The High Court, at CLR 112; ALR 202, rejected the:

> ...'dogma' that, where ownership is vested in a trustee, equitable ownership must necessarily be vested in someone else because it is an essential attribute of a trust that it confers upon individuals a complex of beneficial legal relations which may be called ownership.

21.15 The High Court also refused to recognise ownership where the unit holder held all of the units in the trust. The mere fact that a person may hold all the units in a trust did not mean that they were the 'owner' of the trust fund. Any beneficial rights in the unit trusts remained subject to the rights of the trustee and manager to be reimbursed and indemnified from the trust property and this prevented the beneficiary from terminating the trust. In any event, no termination had been attempted, so the trust remained on foot. The mere fact that such a power might be used did not mean that equity ought to regard as done that which might have been done: *CPT Custodian Pty Ltd v Commissioner of State Revenue (Vic)* at CLR 121; ALR 210.

21.16 Similar issues to those in *CPT Custodian Pty Ltd v Commissioner of State Revenue* arose in *Lygon Nominees Pty Ltd v Commissioner of State Revenue* (2007) 23 VR 474. Here, the trustee was the registered proprietor of land under 11 discretionary trusts and one unit trust. The trustee was assessed for tax on the total land value of all 12 trusts. The trustee argued that its liability should have been assessed separately on each trust in accordance with s 52 of the *Land Tax Act 1958* (Vic), which stipulated as follows:

> Every person in whom land is vested as a trustee, shall make returns and be assessed and liable in respect of the tax as if he were beneficially entitled to such land, save that when he is the owner of different lands in severalty in trust for different beneficial owners who are not, by reason of joint occupation or otherwise, liable to be jointly assessed for tax in respect of the same, the tax so payable by him shall be separately calculated and assessed in respect of each of those lands; and save also that when a trustee is also the beneficial owner of other land, he shall be separately assessed in respect of that land, and of the land of which he is a trustee, unless by reason of joint occupancy or for any other reason he is liable to be jointly assessed independently of this section.

21.17 The Commissioner argued that this section was not applicable as all the trusts were wholly discretionary and there were no beneficiaries with vested or contingent interests that were 'beneficial owners'. That expression was not defined by the Act. The Victorian Court of Appeal upheld the Commissioner's decision. The phrase 'beneficial owners' was taken to mean 'the owner of an equitable estate or interest'. The phrase could not be applied to the trusts in question as the discretionary beneficiaries had no proprietary rights over the trust property. Their rights were limited to a right to have the property properly administered. Redlich JA, at 495, speaking for the Court of Appeal, said:

The nature of a discretionary beneficiary's interest under a discretionary trust as a consequence of the objects' rights to have the trust properly administered, does not confer the required proprietary interest. The right of an object to take legal proceedings to prevent a disposal of income or capital by the trustee to persons outside the class of designated objects does not involve the assertion of a proprietary right by the object. While the objects of the power are able to enforce the fiduciary duties of the donee of such a power, the objects will acquire no direct interest in the property which is subject to the power until such time as the power may be exercised in their favour. Until the trustee elects to exercise the power of appointment in the object's favour, the interest of the object is no more than an expectancy to receive income or capital as a result of the exercise of the power by the trustee and is analogous to that of a beneficiary in the residue of an unadministered estate. While the discretionary beneficiary may enforce the terms of the trust, the beneficiary does not have an equitable proprietary interest in the trust assets which constitutes beneficial ownership of any of those trust assets.

21.18 In *Kafataris v The Deputy Commissioner of Taxation* (2008) 172 FCR 242, questions arose as to whether the applicants were the sole beneficiaries of separate self-managed superannuation trusts and 'absolutely entitled' to the trust assets for the purpose of capital gains tax legislation. The applicants were a married couple who jointly owned a property in Kings Cross, Sydney. In late June 2002 they declared in two separate deeds that they held their joint tenancies in superannuation trusts. Six days later, in the new financial year, the property was sold for a considerable capital gain. The question arose as to whether the transactions attracted capital gains tax. An exception existed in s 104-55 for situations where the asset was held in trust for a sole beneficiary who was absolutely entitled to the asset as against the trustee. Lindgren J found that the applicants were not 'sole' beneficiaries of their respective trusts as the couple's relatives were also listed as possible beneficiaries. Neither were the beneficiaries found to be absolutely entitled. Lindgren J, at 253–4, found that the phrase was 'intended to describe a situation in which the beneficiary of a trust has a vested, indefeasible and absolute entitlement in trust property and is entitled to require the trustee to deal with the trust property as the beneficiary directs'. That did not accurately reflect the interests of the applicants as they were not entitled to their half-interests in the property once they had been dedicated to the trust.

21.19 In *Commissioner of Taxation v Bamford* (2010) 240 CLR 481; 264 ALR 436, the High Court was asked to examine s 97(1) of the *Income Tax Assessment Act 1936* (Cth) which stipulated that a beneficiary's entitlement to a share in the income of a trust estate should be taken into account as part of the beneficiary's assessable income. Of particular importance was the meaning of the phrase 'presently entitled to a share of the income of the trust estate.' The High Court, at CLR 505; ALR 443–4 said:

> The opening words of s 97(1) speak of 'a beneficiary of a trust estate' who is 'presently entitled to a share of the income of the trust estate'. The language of present entitlement is that of the general law of trusts, but adapted to the operation of the 1936 Act upon distinct years of income. The effect of the authorities dealing with the phrase 'presently entitled' was considered in *Harmer v Federal Commissioner of Taxation* (1991) 173 CLR 264 at 271; 104 ALR 117 at 120–1, where it was accepted that a beneficiary would be so entitled if, and only if,
>
> > '(a) the beneficiary has an interest in the income which is both vested in interest and vested in possession; and (b) the beneficiary has a present legal right to demand and

receive payment of the income, whether or not the precise entitlement can be ascertained before the end of the relevant year of income and whether or not the trustee has the funds available for immediate payment.'

21.20   Finally, in *Colonial First State Investments Limited v Commissioner of Taxation* [2011] FCA 16 at [32], Stone J said that s 97(1) applied to beneficial interests which were derived during the tax years, not later when the income to be distributed was received by the trustee.

Insolvency and discretionary trusts

21.21   Traditionally, discretionary beneficiaries have not had to account for their interests in insolvency proceedings because they did not meet the definition of property in s 5 of the *Bankruptcy Act 1966* (Cth). However, orders to appoint a receiver under s 1323 of the *Corporations Act 2001* (Cth) have been found to include orders over the interests of a beneficiary in a discretionary trust. In *Re Richstar Enterprises Pty Ltd; Australian Securities and Investments Commission v Carey (No 6)* (2006) 153 FCR 509, French J opined that a receiver could be appointed in circumstances where a discretionary beneficiary controlled a trustee who was effectively the beneficiary's alter ego. In such circumstances the beneficiary could be treated as having an equitable interest because the beneficiary had practical control of the trustee's power of selection. French J felt that it was as good as certain that the beneficiary would have received the benefits of distribution of either income or capital or both.

21.22   The decision in *Re Richstar Enterprises Pty Ltd* has been criticised for assuming that trustees will misuse their power. Glover has argued that the decision impermissibly allows the court to assume that the trustee will abuse its position:

> No legal system which acknowledges the trust has ever managed to look through the discretionary trust consistently with the rule of law. Discretions of discretionary trustees are protected by the 'shield' of fiduciary duties and the law of powers. Even where legislatures go further than the Corporations Act and base courts' jurisdictions over discretionary trusts in abilities to 'control' or ' influence' trustees, there is still a problem. A constitutional principle stands in the way of making the 'proprietary inference' from control. Trustees and appointors, as well as other persons, cannot be assumed to act illegally before illegal acts are demonstrated. [1]

Family law and discretionary trusts

21.23   The Family Court has wide powers to deal with property rights on the dissolution of marriage. Section 4 of the *Family Law Act 1975* (Cth) stipulates that 'property' means:

   (a) in relation to the parties to a marriage or either of them — means property to which those parties are, or that party is, as the case may be, entitled, whether in possession or reversion; or

   (b) in relation to the parties to a de facto relationship or either of them — means property to which those parties are, or that party is, as the case may be, entitled, whether in possession or reversion.

---

1.   J Glover, 'A Challenge to Established Law on Discretionary Trusts? — *Re Richstar Enterprises*' (2007) 30 Australian Bar Review 70 at 89.

21.24   The court has found that the interests of a discretionary beneficiary are property of the marriage in situations where the beneficiary exercises de facto control over the trust. In *Marriage of Ashton* (1986) 11 Fam LR 457, the husband was found to enjoy property in circumstances where he was entitled to act as appointor of the family trust with the power to remove and appoint the trustee, and vary the terms of the trust. While not a beneficiary, the husband did receive income. Strauss J found that the husband's power of appointment amounted to a de facto ownership of the trust property. Similarly, in *Marriage of Goodwin* (1990) 101 FLR 386, the husband was found to have the only real interest in the trust property, when the trust conferred upon him a sole power of appointment.

21.25   The High Court dealt with these issues in *Kennon v Spry* (2008) 238 CLR 366; 251 ALR 257. The facts of this case are discussed at 17.58. For present purposes, Dr Spry (the husband) had created a discretionary trust for all of the issue of his father and their spouses. Both he and his wife were among the beneficiaries. When Dr Spry's marriage came into difficulties in 1998 he executed a document which removed himself and his wife as capital beneficiaries. Dr Spry and his wife separated in 2001. In 2002, he transferred all the income and capital from the trust into separate trusts for his daughters. He also transferred a number of shares into the daughters' trusts. Mrs Spry applied to the Family Court for an order to set aside both the 1998 document which had removed her as a beneficiary and the later transfers of funds to the trusts for the daughters. At trial, Strickland J ruled in favour of Mrs Spry and set aside the transactions and ordered that Dr Spry pay the wife a sum of over $2 million. These rulings were confirmed by the Full Court of the Family Court and by the High Court: see 17.59–17.63.

21.26   The relevant issue before the High Court was whether the rights of Dr Spry and Mrs Spry were property of the marriage within the meaning of s 79 of the *Family Law Act 1975* (Cth). French CJ found that Dr Spry's powers of appointment over the trustee meant that he had control of the trust property. His Honour found that trust property coupled with the trustee's power was property of the marriage. Equally, French CJ also found that Mrs Spry's right to be appointed, and her equitable right to due consideration, were property of the marriage. Gummow and Hayne JJ also found that the wife's right to be considered by the trustee was property of the marriage.

21.27   Heydon J's dissenting judgment followed the traditional characterisation of the interests of discretionary beneficiaries. His Honour found that neither Dr Spry nor Mrs Spry had any proprietary interest in the trust property as beneficiaries. Nor did Dr Spry enjoy any property when acting as trustee. The inclusion of the rights of discretionary beneficiaries and the powers of trustees within the definition of property was described by Heydon J as being wholly unreasonable. His Honour, at CLR 425; ALR 303, said:

> The definition of 'property' in s 4(1) contemplates interests in property either owned otherwise than as trustee, or owned as beneficial interests in a trust, so that those interests can be adjusted by orders made under s 79. The definition does not contemplate entitlements as trustee. The wife's submissions would enable a trustee who is not in law entitled to any personal enjoyment of the trust property, and who could never by his or her own act become entitled to any personal enjoyment of it, to be treated as though he or she were so entitled. The wife's submission would mean that if a husband (or a wife) were trustee of a discretionary trust having a bare power of appointment among persons who are not related to the trustee, and who did not include the trustee, the trustee would be, within the meaning of the definition of 'property' in s 4(1), 'entitled'

to the assets, and the 'interests' of the trustee reflected in that entitlement would be altered to the advantage of the other party to the marriage.

21.28   After the decision Dr Spry liquidated his assets and the assets of the daughters' trusts, realising over $4.4m. In a restaurant conversation with two of his daughters he threatened to 'disappear' and he said that as a last resort he would burn the money and go to gaol rather than give Mrs Spry her share. One of the daughters later went to Dr Spry's house and discovered over $4.4m in cash. She rang Mrs Spry and they removed the money whereafter it was deposited in the trust account of Mrs Spry's solicitor. Enforcement proceedings were commenced. After Dr Spry agreed to some of the money being released to the wife (in exchange for some funds being released to him for legal expenses) Coleman J in the Family Court ordered that the amounts in trust be used to satisfy the outstanding sums to Mrs Spry (plus interest), with the rest being released to Dr Spry (apart from a sum to be used to pay costs): *Stephens v Stephens* [2009] FAMCA 156. Dr Spry appealed that decision and said that the moneys were trust moneys which belonged beneficially to his daughters. The Full Court of the Family Court upheld the orders of Coleman J: *Stephens v Stephens* (2009) 42 Fam LR 423.

21.29   The decision in *Kennon v Spry* (like the decision in *Re Richstar Pty Ltd*) has been subject to criticism for favouring pragmatism over a principled approach to trusts law. Aitken has said:

> The judgment further dangerously muddies the waters with respect to the position of the object of a discretionary trust. The practical effect of the majority judgment is entirely unclear which is an unfortunate position for the litigants after a protracted and bitter dispute.[2]

21.30   Nevertheless, later cases have applied *Kennon v Spry* in the family law context. In *Simmons v Simmons* (2008) 40 Fam LR 520, the wife claimed that the husband's interest in the discretionary trust amounted to property for purposes of s 79 of the *Family Law Act 1975* (Cth). The trust was a non-exhaustive discretionary trust with an open class of beneficiaries. The wife conceded that the husband had no proprietary interest in the trust property. The husband applied to have her application struck out. The court found that it had the power to make orders with regard to the trust property even though those orders would affect third parties. There was a sufficient connection between the trust assets and the property of the marriage to make such orders. In *Allan v Allan* (2009) 41 Fam LR 565, the husband was a beneficiary under a discretionary trust. The husband was the appointor under the trust and had control over the corporate trustee. The court treated the trustee as being the alter ego of the husband, with the result that the trust property was property of the marriage. In *Essex v Essex* [2009] FAMCAFC 236, the Full Family Court found that a husband's right to income under a discretionary trust which was controlled by the husband's brother, was a financial resource of the husband. In *Pittman v Pittman* (2010) 43 Fam LR 121, the husband was found to have an irrevocable property right to capital and income in a discretionary family trust. The husband argued that his entitlements might be diluted over time if more beneficiaries were added to the trust but the Full Court of the Family Court felt that this was not an argument against the rights being considered as property. The fact that the value of property may vary over time was not a reason for refusing to categorise an item as property. In contrast, in *Harris v Harris* [2011]

---

2.   L Aitken, 'Muddying the Waters Further — *Kennon v Spry*: "Ownership", "Control" and the Discretionary Trust' (2009) 32 *Australian Bar Review* 173 at 175.

FAMCAFC 245 at [65], the Full Family Court, found that a husband did not have a proprietary interest as a discretionary beneficiary when he lacked any form of direct or indirect control over the trustee company. While the husband's mother was a director of the trustee company there was no evidence to suggest that the mother was a puppet of the husband or under his control. A new trial was ordered to examine these issues.

21.31 Legislation dealing with property adjustment for de facto relationships can also take into account the interests of discretionary beneficiaries: *C v B* [2007] 1 Qd R 212 at 220–21. In *WB v GSH* [2008] QSC 346, Applegarth J took into account the interests of the female de facto partner under a discretionary family trust in an application for property adjustment under the *Property Law Act 1974* (Qld). While the interests of the woman as a discretionary beneficiary in her father's family trust were taken into account, Appelgarth J ruled that the likelihood of the woman receiving substantial benefit under the trust was low, given that the father would probably exclude the daughter from receiving a distribution so as to prevent her ex-partner from receiving any benefit.

Social security and discretionary trusts

21.32 Discretionary beneficiaries have not traditionally been treated as 'owning' trust assets for the purpose of assessment for social security. This changed in 2002 when the *Social Security Act 1991* (Cth) was amended to take into account interests held under trusts. Where an individual, or an individual and their associates, holds more than 50 per cent of the beneficial interest in a trust, the trust is considered to be controlled by the individual, and its assets are taken into account in the calculation of benefits. In *Secretary, Department of Families, Housing, Community Services and Indigenous Affairs v Elliott*, the Full Federal Court found that beneficiaries under a particular discretionary trust did not have any right to income or capital until chosen by the trustee. As such, they had no legal or practical capacity to control the trust. Nor was there any interest which could be added to the interests of associates to equal more than 50 per cent of the beneficial interest. The decision by Centrelink to deny pensions to the beneficiaries was overturned.

Immigration and discretionary beneficiaries

21.33 An unusual combination of immigration law and trusts law arose in *Minister for Immigration and Citizenship v Hart* (2009) 179 FCR 212. This case was concerned with the nature of an established business skills visa, which allowed a person to stay in Australia when he or she had an 'ownership interest' in a qualifying business. The issue in the case was whether a discretionary beneficiary of a family trust had an 'ownership interest'. The visa applicant was a discretionary beneficiary in a trust and also owned 20 per cent of the shares in the corporate trustee. The trustee operated the qualifying business. It was argued by the Minister that neither the beneficiary's rights under the trust nor shares in the trustee amounted to an 'ownership interest' as neither discretionary beneficiaries nor shareholders enjoyed proprietorial interests in the assets of corporate trustees. A majority of the Full Federal Court found that they did. Both Spender and Grenwood JJ (Logan J in dissent), found that the definition of 'ownership interest' in the *Migration Act 1958* (Cth) was not to be read down to be consistent with the traditional understandings of ownership from other areas of law. The parliament was found to have intended a wider definition of ownership to apply to the visa scheme, which included businesses run through discretionary trusts with corporate trustees.

Discretionary beneficiaries, the problem of exceptionalism and the lack of unifying principles

21.34   The foregoing discussion has shown the difficulties faced by courts when trying to formulate a principled approach to defining the interests held by discretionary beneficiaries. It is perhaps time to recognise that there are now no unifying principles which help us to understand the nature of beneficial interests in discretionary trusts. Each decision turns on its own limited area of regulation. It has become impossible to draw up lines of principle which can apply across the board. If there are any surviving principles of broad application they are now so weak that they can effectively be ignored. The exceptions have become so numerous that they have killed the rules. The meaning of interests now depends on the peculiarities of individual legislative phrases and the underlying policies which drive the statute in question.

21.35   Does it really matter? For legislators, who are focused on resolving a particular problem or closing troublesome loopholes, the general cohesiveness of law is not a major concern. But for lawyers, whose primary task is to translate case law and statutes into language that guides the decisions of clients, it is a major issue. Because each statute is driven by its own forces the law is splintering to a morass of contradictory meanings. As a consequence, the law now lacks a principled and cohesive basis. The end result is that it is extremely difficult to advise clients on the consequences of different courses of action. The triumph of exceptionalism and pragmatism is leading to the death of certainty and predictability.

RIGHTS OF BENEFICIARIES

The right to compel performance

21.36   The beneficiaries, both individually and as a whole, have a right to seek the aid of the court in compelling the performance of the trust: *Bartlett v Bartlett* (1845) 67 ER 800. The right to compel performance embraces action against trustees for breach of trust.

The right to pursue third parties

21.37   Ordinarily, only the trustee can sue third parties who have caused damage to the trust property: *Alexander v Perpetual Trustees WA Ltd* (2003) 216 CLR 109; (2004) 204 ALR 417. However, the right to compel performance also embraces a right for beneficiaries to sue third parties but only in 'exceptional circumstances' where trustees refuse to perform their duty to protect the estate or the interests of the beneficiaries: *Hilliard v Eiffe* (1874) LR 7 HL 39 at 44; *Fried v National Australia Bank Ltd* [1999] FCA 737; *Shang v Zhang* [2007] NSWSC 856; *Wood v McLean* [2011] VSCA 37 at [7]. In such a case the beneficiary may sue the third party and join the trustee as a defendant: *Vandepitte v Preferred Accident Insurance Corporation of New York* [1933] AC 70. Earlier authority limited this right to equitable claims against third parties, but since the *Judicature Act* reforms courts have allowed beneficiaries to bring all claims that could have been brought by the trustee against third parties: *Lidden v Composit Buyers Ltd* (1996) 67 FCR 560 at 563–4; *Lamru Pty Ltd v Kation Pty Ltd* (1998) 44 NSWLR 432 at 436–7; *Mercedes Holdings Pty Ltd v Waters (No 2)* (2010) 186 FCR 450 at 474; *Davey v Herbst (No 2)* [2012] ACTCA 19 at [80].

21.38   In *Sharpe v San Paulo Railway Co* (1873) LR 8 Ch App 597 at 609–10, James LJ said:

[A] person interested in an estate or a trust fund could not sue a debtor to that trust fund, or sue for that trust fund, merely on the allegation that the trustee would not sue; but that if there was any difficulty of that kind, if the trustee would not take the proper steps to enforce the claim, the remedy of the cestui que trust was to file his bill against the trustee for the execution of the trust, or for the realization of the trust fund, and then to obtain the proper order for using the trustee's name, or for obtaining a receiver to use the trustee's name, who would, on behalf of the whole estate, institute the proper action, or the proper suit in this Court.

21.39   In *Hayim v Citibank NA* [1987] AC 730 at 748, Lord Templeman, giving the decision of the Privy Council, said:

A beneficiary has no cause of action against a third party save in special circumstances which embrace a failure, excusable or inexcusable, by the trustees in the performance of the duty owed by the trustees to the beneficiary to protect the trust estate or to protect the interests of the beneficiary in the trust estate.

21.40   Earlier cases defined exceptional circumstances to exist where the trustee and the third party had colluded together to injure the trust or where the trustee had become insolvent. In *Ramage v Waclaw* (1988) 12 NSWLR 84 at 91, Powell J found that the circumstances were not so limited. In *Chahwan v Euphoric Pty Ltd* [2009] NSWSC 805 at [17], Brereton J agreed and said:

[R]elevant exceptional circumstances seem to involve no more than a failure by the trustee — excusable or inexcusable — to sue on a cause of action against the third party in performance of the duties owed by the trustee to the beneficiary to protect the trust estate or to protect the interests of the beneficiary in the trust estate.

21.41   In *Deutsch v Deutsch* [2012] VSC 227 at [40], Hargrave J said:

Where a trustee refuses, fails or is unable to initiate proceedings involving the rights or property of the trust, beneficiaries of the trusts may in exceptional circumstances bring a claim in their own name to protect their beneficial interests in the property or right. For example, exceptional circumstances have been held to exist where:

(1)   the plaintiff is most materially interested in due enforcement of the claims, or would be most seriously prejudiced if they were abandoned or not duly prosecuted;
(2)   it is alleged that assets have been handed over to a third party 'hastily, improvidently, and not in conformity with their duty';
(3)   there exists a substantial impediment to the trustee prosecuting the proceedings;
(4)   it can be shown there exist recoverable assets which would 'probably be lost to the estate' but for such a suit;
(5)   the decision by the trustee not to institute proceedings was made by a party against whom the claim may lie; and
(6)   due to 'the nature of the assets or the position of the personal representative, it would be either impossible, or, at least, seriously inconvenient for the representatives to take proceedings'.

21.42   One obvious situation where exceptional circumstances apply is where the trustee has been declared bankrupt: *Duckworth v Water Corporation (No 2)* [2012] WASC 163 at [4]; *Roberts v Gill & Co* [2011] 1 AC 240 at 256; [2010] 4 All ER 367 at 381–2. Civil procedure rules may also apply different criteria for when a beneficiary can maintain an action: *Davies v Davies* [2009] WASCA 238 at [12].

21.43 When a beneficiary sues on behalf of the trust he or she brings the action that the trustee should have brought. The beneficiary does not sue for breach of duties owed to him or her directly: *Parker-Tweedle v Dunbar Bank plc (No 1)* [1991] Ch 12 at 19–20. The beneficiary must act on behalf of all the interests in the trust: *Financial Industry Complaints Service Ltd v Deakin Financial Services Pty Ltd* (2006) 238 ALR 616 at 634.

The right to restrain a breach of trust

21.44 Beneficiaries are entitled to injunctions to restrain threatened breaches of trust: *Howden v Yorkshire Miners Assoc* [1905] AC 256. The right stems from the exclusive jurisdiction of equity.

The right to possession of trust property

21.45 In cases where the trustee is passive (without active duties) and the beneficiaries are *sui juris* and absolutely entitled, the beneficiaries have a right to the possession of the property: *Turner v Noyles* (1903) 20 WN (NSW) 266. However, if the trustee is active in the management of the property, the right to possession does not arise.

The right to approach the court

21.46 Beneficiaries have a statutory right to approach the court which is similar to the trustee's right to seek directions.[3]

The right to information

21.47 Beneficiaries' right to information has been discussed at 20.79–20.106.

The right to extinguish the trust: the rule in Saunders v Vautier

21.48 A sole beneficiary of a trust, who is an adult (*sui juris*), legally capable and with a vested and indefeasible interest, may call for the trust assets, even though the trust instrument states that the assets are to be accumulated until a later date: *Saunders v Vautier* (1841) 49 ER 282; *Trustees of the Estate Mortgage Fighting Fund Trust v Commissioner of Taxation* (2000) 175 ALR 482. *Saunders v Vautier* concerned a beneficiary who was entitled to stock in the East India Company but the testator had directed the trustee to accumulate income until the beneficiary turned 25. The court held that he was vested and absolutely entitled to the stock and he was entitled to terminate the trust and have the stock transferred to him when he reached 21 (which was the age of majority at that time).

21.49 The rule is primarily used by beneficiaries to avoid age-based or time-based conditions. It is common, even in modern times, for conditions to be placed in trusts that grant a beneficial interest but then require it to accumulate income until the beneficiary reaches a certain age (for

---

3. *Trustee Act 1925* (ACT) s 63; *Trustee Act 1925* (NSW) s 63; *Rules of the Supreme Court 2009* (NT) r 54.02; *Trusts Act 1973* (Qld) ss 8, 96; *Trustee Act 1936* (SA) s 91; *Administration and Probate Act 1919* (SA) s 69; *Supreme Court Rules 2000* (Tas) r 604; *Supreme Court (General Civil Procedure) Rules 2005* (Vic) r 54.02; *Trustees Act 1962* (WA) ss 92, 94.

example 21 years, 25 years or 30 years). As long as beneficiaries have a vested interest they can terminate the trust prior to expiry of that term: *Wharton v Masterman* [1895] AC 186. For example, in *Austin v Wells* [2008] NSWSC 1266, the testator had created a trust for his niece for the balance of his estate which was conditional on her turning 30 years of age. The niece was 22 years of age and wished to take the trust funds. White J found that the gift had vested in interest and that the niece was entitled to exercise her rights to terminate the trust even though she was not yet 30 years of age. However, if there are contingencies that need to be satisfied in addition to any age requirement it may be harder to interpret the beneficiaries' interests as being vested. In *Simpson v Trust Co Fiduciary Services Ltd* [2009] NSWSC 912, a gift to the testator's grandchildren was conditional on them being 18 years of age but also conditional on them being alive at the death of their grandmother. Ward J found that their interests were not vested and they could not employ the rule in *Saunders v Vautier*.

21.50 Where there is more than one beneficiary and they are all *sui juris*, legally capable and absolutely entitled, they can all agree to terminate the trust and call for a distribution of trust property. In *Gosling v Gosling* (1859) 70 ER 423 at 426, Sir W Page Wood V-C said:

> The principle of this Court has always been to recognise the right of all persons who attain the age of twenty-one to enter upon the absolute use and enjoyment of the property given to them by a will, notwithstanding any directions by the testator to the effect that they are not to enjoy it until a later age — unless, during the interval, the property is given for the benefit of another. If the property is once theirs, it is useless for the testator to attempt to impose any fetter upon their enjoyment of it in full so soon as they attain 21.

21.51 Alternatively, the rule can be applied where there are successive beneficiaries, they all agree and are competent and of age. In *Kafataris v The Deputy Commissioner of Taxation* at 253, Lindgren J said:

> [T]he rule could be invoked by a life tenant and the remainder man: since their interests in combination exhaust the beneficial interest in the subject property, in combination they are entitled to direct the trustee to transfer the property as they will.

21.52 The rule can apply even if there are express provisions in the trust which prevent termination. The rule operates even where termination will defeat the intention of the trust: *Re Smith* (1928) Ch 915; *Re Coppel* (1950) VLR 328; *Trustees of Estate Mortgage Fighting Fund Trust v FCT* (2000) 175 ALR 482 at 497; *Koompahtoo Local Aboriginal Land Council v KLALC Property and Investment Pty Ltd* [2009] NSWSC 502.

21.53 The beneficiaries' right to terminate the trust is subject to the trustee's right of indemnity: *McKnight v Ice Skating Queensland (Inc)* [2007] QSC 273 at [35]; *Koompahtoo Local Aboriginal Land Council v KLALC Property and Investment Pty Ltd* at [42]. If there are arguments about the amount to be indemnified a provision can be made so that the transfer to the beneficiaries is not unduly delayed: *Kemtron Industries Pty Ltd v Commissioner of Stamp Duties* [1984] 1 Qd R 576 at 587.

Capacity

21.54 The rule in *Saunders v Vautier* requires that the beneficiary be legally competent. All adults are presumed to be competent but that capacity can be disproven with evidence that the beneficiary cannot understand the nature and effect of the transaction. In *Parkes-Linnegar v Watson* [2011] NSWSC 37, a trustee failed to establish that the beneficiary was mentally incapacitated. While the beneficiary did have Parkinson's disease there was no evidence that led to the conclusion that she did not understand the nature, quality and significance to her of the termination of the trust.

Contingent interests

21.55   The requirement for an absolute, vested interest means that the rule is not applicable where the beneficial interests are contingent and there are other beneficial interests which might take the gift on the contingency who have not consented, or cannot consent, to the termination of the trust: *Perpetual Trustee Co (Canberra) Ltd v Rasker* (1986) 84 FLR 268. In *Perpetual Trustee Company (Canberra) Ltd v Rasker*, the testator's son was given an interest which was contingent on the son surviving for 10 years after the death of the testator. If the son did not so survive there was a gift over to other beneficiaries. The court held that the son was not entitled to a transfer of the trust property prior to the expiration of the 10-year period, because of the contingency that the son may not survive that period and that the gift over would take effect. Similarly, in *Laycock v Ingram* [2008] VSC 113 at [14], beneficiaries were found not to have an absolute vested interest in a trust which was conditional on them surviving for a period of 21 years. If they did not survive, the property would go to the testatrix's then living issue who had reached 21 years of age. White J, at [14], said:

> [W]hat the rule in *Saunders v Vautier* requires, is that at the time the issue is considered, all beneficiaries participate in the termination of the trusts and for that to occur successfully, all must have between them absolute vested and indefeasible interests and be sui juris. Only then can the testatrix's wishes be defeated by an agreement between the beneficiaries. Those requirements are not satisfied by the proposal of the defendants. The proposed participants, while sui juris, do not have between them absolute vested indefeasible interests.

Discretionary beneficiaries and beneficiaries in unit trusts

21.56   The rule can be employed by all persons who are entitled to call for the due administration of the trust, and it does not require the beneficiaries to all have a defined proprietary interest: *Miskelly v Arnheim* [2008] NSWSC 1075 at [39]; *CPT Custodian Pty Ltd v Commissioner of State Revenue (Vic)* at CLR 118; ALR 207. In *Sir Moses Montefiore Jewish Home v Howell & Co (No 7)* [1984] 2 NSWLR 406, the beneficiaries were allowed to terminate a discretionary trust, but only after it was proven that all the beneficiaries were identified, the class of objects was closed and all the beneficiaries were in agreement. The trustee in this case was obliged to distribute the entire income every year, which strengthened the beneficiaries' claims regarding the application of the rule. The rule also applies to unit trusts but is again dependent on the agreement of all the unit holders, and is subject to the satisfaction of the trustee's right to indemnity: *Koompahtoo Local Aboriginal Land Council v KLALC Property and Investment Pty Ltd* at [17]; *Re Dobrotwir* [2011] VSC 402 at [49].

The rule in Saunders v Vautier and charitable trusts

21.57   The rule also applies to charitable trusts: *Wharton v Masterman* [1895] AC 186. In cases where a charitable beneficiary is given a perpetual right to income, it may prove difficult to show that the beneficiary is absolutely and indefeasibly entitled to the corpus of the trust. In *Melbourne Jewish Orphan & Children's Aid Society Inc v ANZ Executors & Trustee Company Ltd* [2007] VSC 26, two charitable beneficiaries were unable to employ the rule in *Saunders v Vautier* in a situation where the trust granted them the right to enjoy the income of a fund in perpetuity. Ordinarily a gift of income in perpetuity is subject to a rule of construction that presumes the creator intended such a gift to include the capital, so as to avoid the operation of the rule against indestructible trusts: see 17.93. However, that presumption can be rebutted with evidence of the creator's actual intention and in *Melbourne Jewish Orphan & Children's Aid Society Inc*, Gillard J found that the preponderance of evidence showed that the creator's intention was to set aside the corpus in perpetuity. It followed that the trust did not grant an absolute and indefeasible interest, so the charitable beneficiaries could not terminate the trust.

21.58 In Victoria, legislation prevents the rule in *Saunders v Vautier* from being applied to charitable trusts which grant the right to enjoy the income of a fund. Section 163 of the *Property Law Act 1958* (Vic) states:

> Where the will of any person who dies after the commencement of this Act contains a bequest to or a trust for the benefit of a charity or a number of charities or a class of charities and directs or purports to direct that the time of payment of the corpus bequeathed to or to be held in trust for the benefit of such charity charities or class of charities be postponed and that in the meantime the income arising from such corpus be paid to or distributed among such charity or charities or class of charities, such bequest trust and direction shall notwithstanding any rule of law or equity or any rule of construction be construed and take effect according to the tenor thereof.

21.59 The section was considered in *Norman v Australasian Conference Association Ltd* [2008] VSC 573, a case in which the Seventh Day Adventist Church had been given an entire estate, but the testator had limited the church's rights to income for 20 years only, after which the capital could be made available. The church wished to employ *Saunders v Vautier* to collapse the trust and call upon the capital immediately. Section 163 clearly prevented this from happening. Judd J reviewed the intention behind the section. It is clear from the parliamentary debates that there was a fear that testators would not make gifts of income to a charity (with a later gift of capital), if they knew that the charity could terminate the trust to shake off the testator's conditions. Nevertheless, Judd J found that s 163 did not prevent the court from ordering a variation under s 63 of the *Trustee Act 1958* (Vic) (see 17.9) which had the same effect as a termination under *Saunders v Vautier*.

Transfer of the property

21.60 The right pursuant to the rule in *Saunders v Vautier* has been taken as being a right to transfer the property *in specie*: *Seagar v Seagar* [1949] NZLR 812. The fact that the trust may dictate that the property must be sold and converted into funds is no bar to the rule applying to transfer the property *in specie*: *Feeney v Feeney* [2008] NSWSC 890; *Re Horsnaill* [1909] 1 Ch 631 at 635; *In re Tweedie and Miles* (1884) 27 Ch D 315 at 317. However, if the interests of other beneficiaries will be prejudiced, the right will be displaced and the monetary value will be transferred after the sale of trust assets: *Lloyd's Bank v Duker* [1987] 3 All ER 193.

21.61 If the property is transferred to the beneficiary and the beneficiary pays consideration to the trustee for the transfer, the transaction will be classified as a sale and not as an exercise of the beneficiaries' rights under the rule in *Saunders v Vautier*: *Shop, Distributive and Allied Employees Association (SDAEA) v Commissioner of State Revenue* [2005] VSC 484.

The exercise of the rule by some beneficiaries but not all

21.62   If some, but not all of the beneficiaries are of capacity and *sui juris*, it may be possible for the trustee to allow those who are of age and capacity to take their beneficial interest, leaving what remains as trust property. In *Whakatane Paper Mills Ltd v Public Trustee* (1939) SR (NSW) 426, Long Innes J recognised that the rule allowed a beneficiary to take his or her *aliquot* (divisible or proportionate) share of the trust property.

21.63   However, there are two provisos to this rule. The first is that the trust property must be divisible. If the trust property consists of real estate, mortgage debts, or shares in a private company it may be difficult to divide up the beneficiaries' shares until the property is converted: *Stephenson (Inspector of Taxes) v Barclays Bank Trust Co Ltd* [1975] 1 All ER 625 at 647; *Wilson v Wilson* (1951) 51 SR (NSW) 91.

21.64   The second proviso is that the proposed division must not have a detrimental effect on the remaining beneficial interests: *In re Horsnaill; Womersley v Horsnaill* [1909] 1 Ch 631. The question of detrimental effect involves considering the types of property and the interests of the beneficiaries: *Australian Olympic Committee Inc v Big Fights Inc (No 2)* (2000) 176 ALR 124 at 133. It does not include consideration of the interests of the trustees but it can take into account the wishes and intentions of the testator, although this, seemingly, has little weight. Even where property is easily divisible, the court may refuse to order conversion if the interests of the other beneficiaries are prejudiced. A pragmatic approach is adopted by the courts: *Manfred v Maddrell* (1951) 51 SR (NSW) 95 at 97.

21.65   For example, in *Lloyd's Bank v Duker* [1987] 3 All ER 193, a beneficiary was denied the right to convert her share of the trust property (shares) even though it was easily divisible, on the grounds that the division would have created an imbalance of control over the company. Similarly, the court will deny the beneficiaries' right to extinguish the trust so as to protect the interests of unborn beneficiaries or contingent beneficiaries: *Perpetual Trustee Company (Canberra) Ltd v Rasker*. In that sense, a creator may avoid the rule in *Saunders v Vautier* by creating a gift over to contingent beneficiaries.

Are there other ways to collapse the trust and distribute the trust property?

21.66   There may be other ways to collapse the trust and distribute the trust fund but such attempts will be dependent on the rights of the beneficiaries. In *Batt (as Trustees for the Gerard Batt Superannuation Fund) v Clipse (Caloundra) Pty Ltd* [2011] QSC 192, two unit holders in a unit trust sought to have the trust property sold via the appointment of statutory trustees under s 38 of the *Property Law Act 1974* (Qld). This mechanism is ordinarily employed as a way of dissolving co-ownership, either through sale of the co-owned property or through partition. Such applications can be made by 'co-owners in possession'. Ann Lyons J found that the unit holders were not co-owners. Her Honour, at [30], said:

> [I]t has been established that ownership of units in a unit trust does not give rise to rights in respect of individual property held within the unit trust if the unit trust deed:
>
> (a) grants to the trustee powers to deal with the unit trust property as if the trustee were the owner of the trust property at law and equity

(b) in priority to payment to unit holders:

(i) contemplates payment of debts or other obligations to persons employed to administer the trust;

(ii) grants to the trustee a right of remuneration and exoneration from the trust property; and

(c) affords no express right to any particular property held by the trust.

The right to trace

21.67   A beneficiary's right to pursue trust property is considered in Chapter 29.

THE BENEFICIARY'S PERSONAL REMEDIES FOR BREACH OF TRUST

Breach of trust

21.68   Chapter 20 outlined the duties of trustees. Any failure to carry out those duties, whether by act or omission, is a breach of trust. A breach of trust may be caused by conduct that is fraudulent, or by innocent conduct that falls below the standard of an ordinary prudent person of business.

21.69   If a trustee is found to have committed a breach of trust, the trustee is personally liable to return the trust to the state it would have been in had the breach not occurred: *Sinclair Investments (UK) Ltd v Versailles Trade Finance Ltd* [2011] EWCA Civ 347 at [40]–[42]. This restitutionary focus of trust remedies means that they are generally removed from considerations of foreseeability or remoteness: *Re Dawson (dec'd)* [1966] 2 NSWR 211 at 214.

21.70   Remedies for breach of trust fall into two sorts: personal remedies and proprietary remedies. Personal remedies can be used to pursue defaulting trustees who may be forced to compensate for any losses to the trust, or, alternatively, to account for any profits wrongfully made from the breach of trust. Proprietary remedies allow the beneficiaries to pursue trust property and recover it from the trustees, or from third parties who have received the property in bad faith or without consideration. These are discussed in Chapter 28.

Equitable compensation

21.71   Equitable compensation is discussed in detail at 26.2–26.38. Compensation is payable for any loss occasioned by a breach of trust: *Nocton v Lord Ashburton* [1914] AC 932.

21.72   As in other cases where equitable compensation is payable, the purpose of compensation in cases of breach of trust is to return the aggrieved parties to the positions they would have occupied had the equitable obligation not been breached. As such, compensation is calculated at the date of the judgment, 'with the full benefit of hindsight': *Canson Enterprises Ltd v Boughton & Co* [1991] 3 SCR 534.

21.73   Equitable compensation can be ordered to remedy losses caused by positive wrongdoing and fraudulent behaviour. Compensation is also payable for losses occasioned by the failure to act diligently. For example, when a trustee invests trust funds in unauthorised investments, the trustee is liable to compensate the fund to the full amount of the loss caused by the failed investments: *Knott v Cotte* (1852) 51 ER 588. If trustees negligently postpone the sale of a depreciating asset, compensation is payable to an amount equivalent to the difference between the current value of the asset and its value when it should have been sold: *Perpetual Executors, Trustees & Agency Co (WA) Ltd v West Australian Trustee, Executor and Agency Co Ltd* (1942) 44 WALR 29. A similar calculation is made for the unauthorised sale of an asset that later appreciates: *Re Bell's Indenture* [1980] 3 All ER 425. Trustees will also have to compensate the trust for any failure to purchase property the trustee was duty bound to purchase, where the loss is calculated by subtracting the price of the asset at the time the purchase should have been made from the value of the asset at the date of the termination of the trust: *Elder's Trustee and Executor Co Ltd v Higgins* (1963) 113 CLR 426.

Interest

21.74   Interest may be ordered payable on any award of equitable compensation: *Re Dawson (dec'd)* at 218. The court has discretion to award different rates of interest, as well as simple or compound interest: *Murdocca v Murdocca (No 2)* [2002] NSWSC 505.

21.75   The rate is determined by reference to two standards: the trustee rate and the mercantile rate. The trustee rate is calculated on the basis of what the trust would have earned in authorised investments.[4] In *Pateman v Heyen* (1993) 33 NSWLR 188, Cohen J found that the trustee rate was 4 per cent but more recently, in *Pistorino v Connell* [2010] VSC 511, Croft J found the rate to be 4.55 per cent. The mercantile rate is a higher rate, sometimes based on commercial rates, or at 1 per cent higher than the official bank rate or minimum lending rate: *Southern Cross Pty Ltd v Ewing* (1987) 91 FLR 271. The court retains a discretion to vary the rate to account for fluctuations in economic conditions and concerns for practical justice: *Re Tennant* (1942) 65 CLR 473.

21.76   The trustee rate is normally applied but the mercantile rate will be applied in three situations: *Re Dawson (dec'd)* at 218. The first is where the trustee ought to have received a higher rate of interest than the trustee rate because they were subject to a duty to invest in highly productive securities: *Nixon v Furphy* (1926) 26 SR (NSW) 408. The second situation exists where the trustee actually did receive a rate of interest higher than the trustee rate; for example, by using trust funds to reduce an overdraft: *Re Kearney* (1908) 8 SR (NSW) 87. The third situation arises where the trustee is presumed to have earned a mercantile rate in circumstances where trust funds have been misappropriated and the mercantile rate is necessary to recover fully any gains made from the misappropriation: *Hagan v Waterhouse* (1991) 34 NSWLR 308.

21.77   Simple interest is ordinarily ordered but the court retains a discretion to order compound interest in cases where the trustee has acted fraudulently or with gross negligence and an award of compound interest reduces the chance that any profit will remain in the trustee's hands: *Hagan v Waterhouse* at 393; *Alemite Lubrequip Pty Limited v Adams* (1996) 41 NSWLR 45; *Kation Pty Ltd v Lamru Pty Ltd* (2009) 257 ALR 336 at 365; *Harrison v Schipp* [2001] NSWCA 13 at [128]–[130].

21.78   Compound interest will also be awarded if it is shown that trust moneys were used in trade and speculation (*Ledger v Petagna Nominees Pty Ltd* (1989) 1 WAR 300), or that the trustee was obliged under the trust instrument to accumulate or reinvest income: *Mulleneux v Brennan* [2002] WASC 43.

---

4.   H A J Ford & W A Lee, *Principles of the Law of Trusts* (Online), Thomson Reuters, Sydney, [17140].

Set-off

21.79   Equity will allow a defaulting trustee, who has become liable to pay equitable compensation, to set off any gains made by the trustee through their default against the loss. However, any gains must arise from the same transaction as the default for a set-off to arise: *Bartlett v Barclays Bank Trust Co Ltd (No 1)* [1980] Ch 515; [1980] 2 All ER 92. Most jurisdictions have recognised a right to set off investment gains and losses in legislation.[5] The right to set-off in equity is more fully discussed at 31.32–31.41.

Account of profits

21.80   Trustees are not permitted to profit from their office and must account for any profits made. The remedy of account of profits is discussed at 30.25–30.31. In the context of breach of trust, an account of profits is ordered where the trustee has made an unauthorised profit from his or her office or where a breach of trust has allowed the trustee to make personal gain.

21.81   Account of profits and equitable compensation are mutually exclusive remedies: see 26.6. One cannot request an account of profits and equitable compensation to remedy the same breach of trust: *Heathcote v Hulme* (1819) 37 ER 322.

Just allowance

21.82   In cases where an account of profits is ordered, the court has the power to order a defaulting trustee to be paid a just allowance for their services and expenditures: *Phipps v Boardman* [1967] 2 AC 46 at 104; [1966] 3 All ER 721 at 744. In relation to just allowances, in *In re Jarvis* [1958] 2 All ER 336 at 341, Upjohn J said:

> Each case must depend on its own facts, and the form of inquiry which ought to be directed must vary according to the circumstances.

21.83   Just allowances are to be assessed on a liberal scale: *Paul A Davies (Aust) Pty Ltd v Davies* [1983] 1 NSWLR 440 at 448, 451. The court must examine what would be 'practically just' between the parties, when calculating just allowances: *O'Sullivan v Management Agency Ltd* [1985] 1 QB 428; [1985] 3 All ER 351.

21.84   Just allowances may be awarded even in cases where the conduct of the trustee has been fraudulent, although, given the width of the court's discretion, it may be unlikely that a generous allowance will be made, if at all: *Hagan v Waterhouse* (1991) 34 NSWLR 308. In *Australian Postal Corp v Lutak* (1991) 21 NSWLR 584 at 596, Bryson J said:

> The determination of what is a just allowance and whether it should include any share of profits or gains could not really be made on the basis of general rules, but could only be made by examining closely the facts of a particular case and the merits and claims of the trustee, and determining what would be just allowances in relation to those facts. Where the unauthorised investment has been a successful one and has produced a profit as well as enough to give back all monies

---

5.   *Trustee Act 1925* (ACT) s 89A; *Trustee Act 1925* (NSW) s 90A; *Trustee Act 1907* (NT) s 10F(1); *Trusts Act 1973* (Qld) s 30C; *Trustee Act 1936* (SA) s 13D(1); *Trustee Act 1898* (Tas) s 12E(1); *Trustee Act 1958* (Vic) s 12D(1); *Trustees Act 1962* (WA) s 26C(1).

laid out in the investment, there would often be a just claim for an allowance out of the profit. Interest, compensation for time and energy expended or a share of profits could, in my view, only be allowed after a close examination of the facts of a particular case. Cases vary widely, the claim of Tom Phipps in *Boardman v Phipps* to a liberal allowance being a very strong one while, at the other extreme, a claim by persons such as the Lutaks who applied stolen money to the purchase of a property with the apparent intention of owning it themselves and were later brought to account when their dishonest conduct was revealed is a very poor one. People who use stolen trust money, and are in effect laundering it and concealing what has happened to the money, and who are found out and have a constructive trust imposed upon them cannot expect much consideration. Where investments although unauthorised have proved successful it must often seem right to the parties involved and also to courts to divide the profits or gains in the same proportion as the contributions.

The effect of exclusion clauses

21.85   Trust deeds may contain exclusion clauses which protect or excuse the trustee from liability for breach of trust. In *McLean v Burns Philp Trustee Co Ltd* (1985) 2 NSWLR 623, it was said that such clauses will be read strictly. In *Walker v Stones* [2001] QB 902, the principle adopted was that an exclusion clause should be given its natural and ordinary meaning in the light of the contract as a whole, but that any ambiguity should be read against the person seeking to benefit from the exclusion.

21.86   Exclusion clauses which seek to remove all liability are inconsistent with the notion of the trust and clauses which seek to remove the trustee's liability for actual fraud will fail: *Wilden Pty Ltd v Green* [2009] WASCA 38 at [160]; *Scaffidi v Montevento Holdings Pty Ltd* [2011] WASCA 146 at [149]; *Rinehart v Welker* [2012] NSWCA 95 at [139]. It is not contrary to public policy to exclude a trustee's liability in negligence (even gross negligence) or equitable (constructive) fraud, but it will be against public policy to exclude liability for dishonesty or bad faith. In *Armitage v Nurse* [1998] Ch 241 at 254; [1997] 2 All ER 705 at 713, Millet LJ said:

> [T]here is an irreducible core of obligations owed by the trustees to the beneficiaries and enforceable by them which is fundamental to the concept of a trust. If the beneficiaries have no rights enforceable against the trustees there are no trusts. But I do not accept the further submission that these core obligations include the duties of skill and care, prudence and diligence. The duty of the trustees to perform the trusts honestly and in good faith for the benefit of the beneficiaries is the minimum necessary to give substance to the trusts, but in my opinion it is sufficient. … a trustee who relied on the presence of a trustee exemption clause to justify what he proposed to do would thereby lose its protection: he would be acting recklessly in the proper sense of the term.

21.87   Similarly, a clause which seeks to prevent beneficiaries from taking any proceedings against the trustee will be void for attempting to oust the jurisdiction of the court: *Permanent Trustee Co v Dougal* (1931) 34 SR (NSW) 83. However, a clause which merely discourages disputing the validity of the trust will not offend that rule: *Leerac Pty Ltd v Fay* [2008] NSWSC 1082 at [21].

PERSONAL CLAIMS AGAINST THIRD PARTIES

21.88   Trustees are duty bound to correctly pay beneficiaries: see 20.107. If beneficiaries are overpaid, or strangers receive trust property, the remaining beneficiaries are entitled to bring a personal action (an *in personam* claim) against them to recover the loss. In *Re Diplock* [1948] Ch 465; [1948] 2 All ER 318, the executors of a large estate innocently distributed a large sum to over a hundred charitable institutions in the mistaken belief that they were empowered to do so under the will. Unfortunately, the provision in the will failed, as it mixed charitable and non-charitable purposes, and a challenge to its validity was successfully brought by other beneficiaries of the estate. A settlement was reached with the executors but the beneficiaries decided to bring personal actions against the recipients who had been wrongfully paid.

21.89   The Court of Appeal, at Ch 476; All ER 324, upheld the bringing of the personal actions for recovery, even though the recipients were innocent of any wrongdoing. The court distinguished this sort of equitable claim from other common law claims like a claim for moneys paid under mistake of law. The Court of Appeal, at Ch 502; All ER 337, found that it did not matter that:

(a)   the deceased estate was not being administered by the court;
(b)   the mistake giving rise to the payment was one of law and not of fact; or
(c)   that the original recipient had no title and was a stranger to the estate.

However, the Court of Appeal, at Ch 503–4; All ER 338, found that a personal claim against third parties could only be brought by beneficiaries after all remedies had been pursued against the executors and exhausted.

21.90   The decision was appealed to the House of Lords and upheld: *Ministry of Health v Simpson* [1951] AC 251; [1950] 1 All ER 318. Lord Simonds, speaking for the House of Lords, indicated that the right to personally pursue third parties was limited to testamentary trusts. While there is some argument to the contrary, it appears that the majority of commentators accept that *Re Diplock* should not be limited to testamentary trusts and should be extended to all trusts.[6] In *Ron Kingham Real Estate Pty Ltd v Edgar* [1999] 2 Qd R 439 at 440, Davies JA seemed to indicate that this right was a general equitable right available to all beneficiaries. In *Blue Sky Private Equity Ltd v Crawford Giles Pty Ltd* [2012] SASC 28, Gray J applied the rule in a superannuation context without comment on the requirement that it be employed only for testamentary trusts. But in *Heperu Pty Ltd v Belle* (2009) 76 NSWLR 230 at 261; 258 ALR 727 at 758, the Court of Appeal of New South Wales said that *Ministry of Health v Simpson* was 'not authority for the wider proposition that equity permits a personal action against a volunteer receiving the traceable proceeds of misappropriated funds'.

21.91   The requirement that all remedies against the executors be exhausted has been removed in some jurisdictions that have introduced the rule in legislation and applied it to all types of trusts.[7]

---

6.   J D Heydon & M J Leeming, *Jacobs' Law of Trusts in Australia*, LexisNexis Butterworths, Sydney, 2006, pp 635–6; Ford & Lee, note 4 above, [17310]; G E Dal Pont, *Equity and Trusts in Australia*, 5th ed, Lawbook Co, Sydney, 2011, p 708.
7.   *Trusts Act 1973* (Qld) s 109; *Trustees Act 1962* (WA) s 65.

Part VI:
Remedies

22

DECLARATIONS

INTRODUCTION

22.1   A declaration is an order granted by a court that states with finality the true nature of the law or the rights, duties and interests of the applicant under it. The element of finality is important. Declaratory orders are non-coercive in the sense that there is no sanction built onto the order. This does not mean that it is of no legal consequence because it 'operates in law either as a res judicata or an issue estoppel and such an order is a final order for the purposes of appeal'.[1] In *Blackman v Gant* [2010] VSC 229 at [137] Vickery J said that 'a curial declaration says something about something. It has legal effect but otherwise does nothing'.

22.2   The circumstances in which the judicial power to grant declaratory relief are as outlined by Kitto J in *R v Trade Practices Tribunal, Ex parte Tasmanian Breweries Pty Ltd* (1969) 123 CLR 361 at 374:

> Judicial power involves, as a general rule, a decision settling for the future, as between defined persons or classes of persons, a question as to the existence of a right or obligation, so that an exercise of the power creates a new charter by reference to which that question is in future to be decided as between those persons or classes of persons ... [T]he process to be followed must generally be an enquiry concerning the law as it is and the facts as they are, followed by an application of the law as determined to the facts as determined; and the end to be reached must be an act which ... entitles and obliges the persons between whom it intervenes, to observance of the rights and obligations that the application of law to facts as shown to exist.

Thus, in *Nsi Group Pty Ltd v Mokas* [2006] NSWSC 976, the court refused to make an interim declaration of right as to the true construction of a contract, because the construction of a contract is something to be determined once and for all at the final hearing of the dispute. In *Re Elm* (2006) 69 NSWLR 145 at 153, Brereton J said that although a declaration cannot be granted on an interlocutory basis because a declaration 'is necessarily "final" in character', it can, in the appropriate case, be granted on an ex parte basis, that is, in the absence of the defendant at the hearing.

22.3   The declaration developed originally as an equitable remedy, though it has since become statutory in nature. The reason for this change in jurisdictional source was the restrictive practice of equity courts by which they would only grant a declaration as ancillary to some other form of relief. For example, a declaration that obligations were owed under the terms of a contract would

---

1.   P W Young, *Declaratory Orders*, 2nd ed, Butterworths, Sydney, 1984, p 213.

be granted only pursuant to an action seeking a further order, such as one compelling specific performance of those obligations. Parties could not seek the court's involvement to clarify their legal positions and then be left to resolve the matter themselves. It was said that equity would not grant 'naked' or mere declarations.

22.4 However, the usefulness of the declaration in its own right led to its recognition by statute as a form of relief capable of being granted by all courts and without the need for other remedies to be sought by, or even made available to, the parties: *Birkenfeld v Kendall and Yachting New Zealand Incorporated* [2008] NZCA 531 at [35]–[38].[2] This was accomplished as part of the reforms of the *Judicature Acts* in England and the subsequent adoption of that legislation in Australian jurisdictions. It is on the basis of this legislation that it has been said that declaratory relief is 'neither a legal nor an equitable remedy, but statutory': *Tito v Waddell (No 2)* [1977] Ch D 106 at 259; [1977] 3 All ER 129 at 256. However, the court's power to grant mere declaratory relief does not entitle the court to make 'general declarations concerning the conduct of a person in the absence of any relevant right power, privilege or immunity': *Northwest Capital Management v Westate Capital Ltd* [2012] WASC 121 at [317].

22.5 Despite its non-coercive nature, a declaration is a particularly useful form of relief. It enables the parties to clarify their legal obligations and rights and avoid further costly litigation. For example, in *Office of Fair Trading v Abbey National plc* [2008] EWHC 2325 (Comm), the court granted declarations on the question of whether certain terms and conditions used by banks in standard contracts between themselves and their customers amounted to penalties (on penalties see Chapter 14). Andrew Smith J, at [6], noted that the declarations would 'facilitate the expeditious, fair and orderly management of [any] cases brought by individual customers in county courts'. Alternatively, a declaration may establish that there are indeed rights to be enforced with the assistance of the courts, which may provide damages or some coercive remedy such as specific performance or injunction upon application.

DECLARATIONS AND THE REQUIREMENTS OF EVIDENCE AND A PROPER CONTRADICTOR

22.6 Although the making of a declaration order is very useful, there are two preliminary questions that need to be addressed in relation to whether the court should make a declaration. The first question is whether they can be made in the absence of evidence or whether the parties can consent to the making of the order. The second question is whether a declaration can be made in the absence of a proper contradictor.

22.7 In relation to the first question, it has been held in cases such as *Australian Competition and Consumer Commission v Grove & Edgar Pty Ltd* [2008] FCA 1956 at [18]–[21], that the fact that the parties may consent to the making of a declaration or provide assurances by way of admission or an agreed statement to the effect that asserted facts are true, is not enough. Such cases require the tendering of relevant evidence to establish a basis upon which the declaration can be made. However, in *Australian Competition and Consumer Commission v MSY Technology Pty Ltd (No 2)*

---

2. For an account of the reluctance by the courts to grant mere declaratory relief in New South Wales see P Radan, 'The Emergence of the Jurisdiction to Grant Mere Declaratory Relief in New South Wales' (2006) 1 *Journal of Equity* 41.

(2011) 279 ALR 609 at 616, Perram J, after a lengthy analysis of the relevant authorities, referred to the 'anaemic jurisprudential basis' upon which this proposition was based. His Honour, at 619–20, then concluded that the proposition was 'dubious in origin, insubstantial in its argument and is not required by [relevant higher case authority]' and that, 'even if it exists', it was in, federal courts, overcome by s 191 of the *Evidence Act 1995* (Cth) which stipulates that evidence is not required to prove the existence of agreed facts.[3] A similar conclusion was reached by Finkelstein J in *Australian Competition and Consumer Commission v Bridgestone Corporation* (2010) 186 FCR 214 at 217–8 and Tracey J in *Australian Competition and Consumer Commission v Sampson* [2011] FCA 116 at [16]–[18] and *Australian Competition and Consumer Commission v Turi Foods Pty Ltd (No 2)* [2012] FCA 19 at [17]–[18].

22.8   On the other hand, in *George Zoltan Ajkay v Hickey & Co Pty Limited* [2011] NSWSC 822 at [7]–[9], Pembroke J took another view when he said:

> Consent declarations without a hearing on the merits are a rarity. Courts will frequently not entertain them … It is perhaps stating the obvious to say that the making of a declaration is a judicial act determining and pronouncing a legal right: *Williams v Powell* [1894] 1 WN 141. It follows that a declaration that is not based on the court's review of the evidence but on the admissions of the parties may not always be satisfactory or prudent. As an order of the court, a declaration binds the parties to the proceedings before it. But the impact of a declaration may not be confined to the parties. Where the declaration 'will have effects on the community … that extend far beyond the interests of the original plaintiff and defendant' (*Myer Queenstown Garden Plaza Pty Ltd v Port Adelaide City Corporation* (1975) 33 LGRA 70 at 82), a declaration made based merely on the consent of the parties to the proceedings is inappropriate. If the declaration sought is confined to the private rights between the parties such as (to use the example proffered by Keely and Beaumont JJ in *BMI v Federated Clerks Union of Australia* (1983) 51 ALR 401 at 413–414) the respective rights of the parties under a contract — it may be appropriate to make a declaration by consent. However, where there is a risk that a declaration will have a wider effect than the respective rights of those parties, it must be based on evidence considered by the court.

22.9   In relation to the second question, it can be noted that a contradictor refers a person present before the court 'who has a true interest to oppose the declaration sought': *Russian Commercial and Industrial Bank v British Bank for Foreign Trade Ltd* [1921] 2 AC 438 at 448. In *Australian Competition and Consumer Commission v MSY Technology Pty Ltd (No 2)* at 620, Perram J was of the view that 'as a matter of correct legal doctrine a contradictor will be present when all proper defendants have been joined and so are bound to the result. They will not cease to be contradictors merely because they consent to the proposed declarations.' However, his Honour went on to say that he was unable to apply that principle because he was bound by the decision of the Full Court of the Federal Court in *BMI v Federated Clerks Union of Australia* (1983) 6 IR 416, which, according to his Honour, held that the requirement of a contradictor meant that there had to be a party arguing against the granting of the relief and that this requirement could not be satisfied where the matter proceeded by consent.

22.10   On an appeal from the decision of Perram J, the Full Court of the Federal Court in *Australian Competition and Consumer Commission v MSY Technology Pty Ltd* [2012] FCAFC 56 at [30],

---

3.   Equivalent statutory provisions in other jurisdictions are *Evidence Act 2011* (ACT) s 191; *Evidence Act 1995* (NSW) s 191; *Evidence Act 2001* (Tas) s 191; *Evidence Act 2008* (Vic) s 191.

approved the following statement of law in *IMF (Australia) Ltd v Sons Of Gwalia Ltd (Administrator Appointed)* (2004) 211 ALR 231 at 244, where French J said:

> A proper contradictor, for jurisdictional purposes, in my opinion cannot be confined to the class of party who comes to court ready to oppose the relief sought. There may be a case in which a party, whether a private person or body or a statutory regulator, expresses opposition to, and an intention to oppose, a proposed course of action by another party on the basis that it is in breach of some contractual or statutory prohibition. The party opposing the conduct may however decide for any one or more of a variety of reasons not to contest declaratory proceedings about the lawfulness of the proposed conduct.

In relation to the decision in *BMI v Federated Clerks Union of Australia*, the Full Court, at [30], said:

> In this case, the MSY parties had an interest to oppose the declaratory relief sought. That was sufficient to make them a proper contradictor. There was no want of power to grant declaratory relief. Rather, the question was whether, in light of the events which had transpired, which relevantly included a lack of any continued opposition to the declaratory relief sought, that relief ought still to be granted as a matter of discretion. *BMI* should be understood as a case where … that discretion had been exercised so as to refuse the declaratory relief sought.

Thus, as was noted by Perram J in *Secretary, Department of Health and Ageing v Export Corporation (Australia) Pty Ltd (No 2)* [2012] FCA 463 at [4], the effect of the Full Court decision in *Australian Competition and Consumer Commission v MSY Technology Pty Ltd* is that a court has 'power to make declarations by consent'.

NEGATIVE DECLARATIONS

22.11   Applications for declaratory relief are made, as was pointed out by Young JA in *Nicholls v Michael Wilson & Partners Limited* (2010) 243 FLR 177 at 208, 'almost entirely within the areas of public law, status, property law and trust or breach of contract' and will generally relate to some right that the applicant has against the defendant. However, in some cases a negative declaration can be obtained. A negative declaration is, in effect, a declaration that the defendant has no right against the applicant. For example, a negative declaration could declare that the applicant has not breached a contract or some specific statutory provision or committed a breach of trust.

22.12   Whether a negative declaration should be granted is a matter for the discretion of the court. In this respect, in *Messier-Dowty v Sabena SA (No 2)* [2001] 1 All ER 275 at 285–6, Lord Woolf MR said:

> The approach is pragmatic. It is not a matter of jurisdiction. It is a matter of discretion. The deployment of negative declarations should be scrutinised and their use rejected where it would serve no useful purpose. However, where a negative declaration would help to ensure that the aims of justice are achieved the courts should not be reluctant to grant such declarations. They can and do assist in achieving justice … While negative declarations can perform a positive role, they are an unusual remedy insofar as they reverse the more usual roles of the parties. The natural defendant becomes the claimant and *vice versa*. This can result in procedural complications and possible injustice to an unwilling 'defendant'. This in itself justifies caution in extending the circumstances where negative declarations are granted, but, subject to the exercise of appropriate circumspection, there should be no reluctance to their being granted when it is useful to do so.

JURISDICTION TO GRANT DECLARATIONS

22.13 Australia's superior courts have inherent power to grant declaratory relief: *Ainsworth v Criminal Justice Commission* (1992) 175 CLR 564 at 581; 106 ALR 11 at 22. This jurisdiction is reinforced in the legislation or rules establishing the relevant court.[4] For example, s 31 of the *Supreme Court Act 1935* (SA) stipulates:

> No action or proceeding shall be open to objection on the ground that a merely declaratory judgment or order is sought thereby, and the court shall have power to make binding declarations of right whether any consequential relief is or could be claimed or not.

It is widely acknowledged that there are very few real limits upon the power of courts to grant a declaration. Young has observed that 'what is often loosely referred to as matters of jurisdiction really are not so at all but merely situations where a court, having jurisdiction in the matter, refuses to exercise it'.[5] The consequence of this power is that declarations can be granted irrespective of whether other remedies are sought, and whether or not the rights are derived from the common law or equity.

22.14 Whether declarations are available in the context of statutory rights is dependent upon the relevant statute. However, for a statute to exclude declaratory relief, its provisions must be clear to that effect or there must be a necessary implication that declaratory relief is excluded: *Oil Basins Ltd v Commonwealth of Australia* (1993) 178 CLR 643 at 651; 117 ALR 338 at 343. In *Forster v Jododex Australia Pty Ltd* (1972) 127 CLR 421, Forster sought authority in accordance with the *Mining Act 1906* (NSW) to enter upon certain land for the purpose of mining exploration. Jododex Australia challenged Forster's application and the dispute was referred to the mining warden, whose office was created by the Act for the purpose of determining such disputes. While these proceedings were in place, Jododex Australia made an application to the Supreme Court of New South Wales for a declaration that Forster was not entitled to the exploration authority as it already held a similar licence over the same land. The court granted the declaration as sought, but discussed the possibility of its jurisdiction to do so being ousted by legislation conferring an exclusive responsibility upon some other body. This was not the case on these facts because, although the Mining Act did invest the mining warden with the ability to make a determination, it did not do so to the exclusion of the court's jurisdiction under s 75 of the *Supreme Court Act 1970* (NSW). Gibbs J, at 435–6, indicated that such a restriction upon the court's jurisdiction could not arise merely by virtue of an implication drawn from the creation of a specialised tribunal:

> The jurisdiction to make a declaration is a very wide one … However, the jurisdiction may be ousted by statute, although the right of a subject to apply to the court for a determination of his rights will not be held to be excluded except by clear words.

22.15 The principle enunciated by Gibbs J in *Forster v Jododex Australia* was applied not long after in *Law Society of NSW v Weaver* [1974] 1 NSWLR 271. In that case, the New South Wales

---

4. *High Court Rules* O 26 r 19; *Federal Court of Australia Act 1976* (Cth) s 21; *Supreme Court Rules* (ACT) O 29 r 5; *Supreme Court Act 1970* (NSW) s 75; *Supreme Court Act 1979* (NT) s 18; *Supreme Court Act 1995* (Qld) s 128; *Supreme Court Act 1935* (SA) s 31; *Supreme Court Rules 2000* (Tas) r 103; *Supreme Court Act 1986* (Vic) s 36; *Supreme Court Act 1935* (WA) s 25(6).

5. Young, *Declaratory Orders*, note 1 above, p 34.

Court of Appeal was quite prepared to grant a declaration that a solicitor had been engaged in professional misconduct, despite the existence of a specialist body to make such determinations. The court, at 272, said:

> It is a principle of statutory construction that a superior court of law will not be deprived of jurisdiction except by express words or necessary implication. The provision of another tribunal would not of itself ordinarily be sufficient to do so.

However, while the mere existence of another entity with power to deal with particular matters will not oust the jurisdiction of the court to grant a declaration, it is a significant factor for a court to consider in the exercise of its discretion: *Young v Public Service Board* [1982] 2 NSWLR 456.

22.16   While the jurisdiction to make declaratory orders is extremely wide and may only truly be said to be restricted by express ouster by parliament, it is also clear that the exercise of that jurisdiction is discretionary. As Hope and Priestley JJA said in *Rivers v Bondi Junction-Waverley RSL Sub-branch Ltd* (1986) 5 NSWLR 362 at 376, 'a plaintiff does not have an automatic right to a declaration because he can point to a failure by the defendant to comply with some requirement'. However, the range of factors a court may consider in deciding whether to exercise its discretion is incapable of precise definition due to very broad jurisdiction to issue declarations: *Forster v Jododex Australia* at 437; *Johnco Nominees Pty Ltd v Albury-Wodonga (NSW) Corp* [1977] 1 NSWLR 43 at 50–1.

22.17   That said, it is recognised that certain features of a case may point to it being an unsuitable occasion for the granting of the remedy. In *Ainsworth v Criminal Justice Commission*, a report prepared by the Commission, in breach of the rules of procedural fairness, made adverse recommendations concerning certain persons involved in the poker machine industry without any notice having been given to the persons concerned. The High Court held that, although prerogative relief was not available, the affected persons had a real interest in obtaining a declaration that there had been a failure to observe procedural fairness, because of the harm caused to their business or to their commercial reputation. The court observed that where a body such as the Commission, in exercising its statutory functions, breaches the rules of natural justice and causes damage to some person, that person is, prima facie, entitled to declaratory relief to the effect that the action of the relevant body occurred in breach of its duty to observe the rules of natural justice. In the course of their judgment in *Ainsworth v Criminal Justice Commission*, at CLR 581–2; ALR 22, Mason CJ, Dawson, Toohey and Gaudron JJ reaffirmed the breadth of a court's discretion to make an order for a declaration, but insisted that the discretion must be exercised within the 'boundaries of judicial power', that is, within the limits of the court's general jurisdiction. To that end, they identified the following three matters that should influence a court's decision to make such an order: (i) a declaration must be directed to the determination of legal controversies and not to the resolution of abstract or hypothetical questions; (ii) the person seeking relief must have a 'real interest'; and (iii) a declaration must produce foreseeable consequences for the parties.

Abstract or hypothetical questions

22.18   The court will not grant a declaration if, to do so, would result only in the court stating its opinion on an abstract or hypothetical question where there is no dispute relating to the facts of the case before the court: *Birkenfeld v Kendall and Yachting New Zealand Incorporated* at [41]–[42].

In a statement cited by Croft J in *ACN 004 443 627 (Southern Region) Ltd v Wallington Hardware & Timber Pty Ltd (No 2)* [2010] VSC 174 at [54], Tilbury[6] observes as follows:

> The courts will not generally grant declarations in respect of issues which are hypothetical or theoretical ... [A]n issue may warrant this description where: there is no dispute in existence; the dispute is not attached to the facts; the dispute is based on hypothetical facts; or, the dispute has ceased to be of practical significance. The justification of this consideration is a strong policy against advisory opinions. But, even in such cases justice may require the grant of a declaration in the light of the importance of the question and/or the practical utility of an answer.

22.19 Thus, in *Mellstrom v Garner* [1970] 1 WLR 603, Mellstrom and Garner were accountants who dissolved their partnership by an agreement which imposed a restraint upon the business activities of the former partners. The dissolution agreement was poorly drafted and the parties to it sought a declaration as to its true meaning. Harman LJ, at 604, said:

> [E]ach party seeks from the court a declaration as to the true interpretation of this nonsensical affair. It is not said that either of them has either broken any of its provisions or seeks to break them; it is not suggested that there are any facts whatever to be considered; and we are to make what in my younger days is to be called a declaration 'in the air'. That is against the principles of the Court of Chancery as I understand them.

22.20 Another example of this principle is found in *University of New South Wales v Moorhouse* (1975) 133 CLR 1; 6 ALR 193. Moorhouse, a successful author, applied for a declaration that the University of New South Wales had, by placing a photocopier in its library, authorised private individuals to infringe his copyright under the terms of relevant Commonwealth legislation. The trial judge granted the declaration, although he acknowledged a lack of factual evidence that Moorhouse's copyright had been infringed. On appeal, the High Court revoked the declaration. Gibbs J, at CLR 10; ALR 198, observed that 'as a general rule, the power to make a declaration will not be exercised when the court is called upon to answer a question that is purely hypothetical'. This was the case here as the basis for the declaration was not any proven fact, but rather an assumption that Moorehouse's copyright had indeed been infringed.

22.21 It may seem difficult to reconcile this generally accepted principle with the propensity of courts to make declarations concerning future rights and liabilities, even where those may be dependent upon the occurrence of some contingency. As was pointed out by Ward J in *In the matter of Painaway Australia Pty Ltd (in prov liq) (admin apptd) — Painaway Australia Pty Ltd v JAKL Group Pty Ltd* [2011] NSWSC 205 at [385], 'if the declaratory relief is for the purpose of defining a right or liability in anticipation of future events, then unless those future events are at least likely to occur the relief sought is arguably only in respect of a "purely hypothetical" question'. Thus, the fact that the court is asked to make a declaration order as to future legal rights when its purpose is to regulate the future conduct of parties does not necessarily render the question hypothetical. The following two cases are illustrative.

22.22 In *Russian Commercial and Industrial Bank v British Bank for Foreign Trade Ltd* [1921] 2 AC 438, the British bank had borrowed a substantial sum from the Russian bank upon the

---

6. M J Tilbury, *Civil Remedies, Vol 1, Principles of Remedies*, Butterworths, Sydney, 1990, p 350.

security of commercial bonds. The banks disagreed as to whether the borrower had to repay the loan in pounds sterling or in roubles which, as a result of the Russian Revolution, had dropped considerably in value. The British bank sought a declaration that it could pay in roubles, while the Russian bank argued that repayment had to be in pounds sterling. A majority of the House of Lords was prepared to make the declaration. In the context of the case before the court, Lord Dunedin, at 448, pointed out that the question for determination was 'in no sense … theoretical' but was 'a matter of real importance to the [English bank] as guiding their … conduct, to know whether the loan is … a rouble loan or a sterling loan. In the one case, they will probably redeem; in the other case, they will not'.

22.23   In *Commonwealth v Sterling Nicholas Duty Free Pty Ltd* (1972) 126 CLR 297, Sterling Nicholas sought a declaration that its proposed business operations would not be in breach of the customs laws of the Commonwealth. The High Court had no reservations about making a declaration in such circumstances and made reference to the usefulness of declaratory relief in assisting parties to determine their present rights to engage in particular conduct. The practical utility of the declaration to Sterling Nicholas meant that there was indeed a real question to be determined. Barwick CJ, at 305, said:

> The respondent undoubtedly desired and intended to do as he asked the court to declare he lawfully could do. The matter, in my opinion, was in no sense hypothetical, but in any case not hypothetical in a sense relevant to the exercise of this jurisdiction. Of its nature, the jurisdiction includes the power to declare that conduct which has not yet taken place will not be in breach of a contract or a law.

22.24   If the granting of a declaration will clarify rights that are the subject of a present or even potentially existing dispute, then the court is likely to exercise its discretion to do so. However, there are limits to this as the House of Lords demonstrated in *Regina (Rusbridger) v Attorney General* [2004] 1 AC 357; [2003] 3 All ER 784 when it declined to grant a declaration as to the likelihood of a criminal conviction, under an 1848 Act, for treason for advocating republicanism. Their Lordships' reason for refusal was that no prosecution under the legislation had been brought for over a hundred years; the Act had clearly been superseded by the *Human Rights Act 1998* (UK); and it had, in any case, not caused the applicant to desist from making calls for the abolition of the monarchy. According to Lord Hutton, at AC 372; All ER 797, 'the issue … brought before the courts [in this case] cannot be described as a live, practical question'. Thus, while in *Commonwealth v Sterling Nicholas Duty Free* the court was justified in granting a declaration because there clearly existed the essential elements of a dispute, if not at present, then certainly when Sterling Nicholas began its planned operations, declarations were not forthcoming in *University of New South Wales v Moorhouse* due to the absence of any established facts which affected rights and liabilities. Nor was this the case in *Rusbridger* because, although the facts were easily ascertainable, there was little possibility of their giving rise to a dispute.

22.25   The undesirability of making declarations on questions divorced from legal rights and consequences was starkly demonstrated by the facts of *Egan v Willis* (1998) 195 CLR 424; 158 ALR 527. In this case, the only form of relief sought was a declaration that a resolution of the Legislative Council of New South Wales was invalid. Egan was a Minister of the Crown and a member of the Legislative Council who refused to produce certain papers it had requested for tabling. The Council then passed a resolution (i) finding him guilty of a contempt of the House; (ii) suspending him from sitting in the House for the remainder of that day; and (iii) ordering him to attend at the House on the following day in order that he should explain his refusal to table the documents which had been requested. After refusing to depart from the House after this resolution was made, Egan was escorted from the premises on to the street by the Usher of the Black Rod. He then commenced an action in the Supreme Court of New South Wales seeking declarations that, first, the terms of the resolution were invalid, and second, that his removal to the footpath outside Parliament House constituted a trespass to his person. The matter was moved to the Court of Appeal, which found in favour of Egan only to the extent of finding a trespass to his person from the time he left the precincts of parliament and was deposited on the footpath. In dismissing the remainder of his claim, the Court of Appeal, in the words of Gaudron, Gummow and Hayne JJ, at CLR 438; ALR 529 in the High Court, 'dealt with the merits of the matter rather than on the footing that a bare declaration with respect to the validity of proceedings in the Legislative Council should not be made'. Their Honours, at CLR 438–9; ALR 529–30, indicated that this would not have been their preferred approach to such a matter, and said:

> Questions respecting the existence of the powers and privileges of a legislative chamber may present justiciable issues when they are elements in a controversy arising in the courts under the general law but they should not be entertained in the abstract and apart from a justiciable controversy. Declaratory relief should be directed to the determination of legal controversies concerning rights, liabilities and interests of a kind which are protected or enforced in the courts. This is so even though in the area of public law the ground of equitable intervention has not been limited to the protection of any particular proprietary or legal entitlement of the plaintiff.

22.26   McHugh J, at CLR 480; ALR 562, made it clear that he had stronger reservations about the use of declarations in cases of this kind and thought the central issue non-justiciable, and said:

> In the absence of a statutory requirement, a court should not entertain a claim for a declaration that a resolution of a House of Parliament is invalid. In the course of determining the legal rights of parties, it may be necessary for a court, as an incident of that determination, to hold that a resolution of a legislative chamber cannot affect a person's legal rights. But that is a different matter from directly entertaining a claim that a resolution of the chamber is invalid … [A]s a general rule, courts should eschew making such declarations even when the validity of the resolution is incidental to the determination of the plaintiff's legal rights. I would allow the appeal so that the Order of the Court of Appeal can be set aside. In lieu thereof, I would declare that the Supreme Court has no jurisdiction to make the declaration sought.

Need for a 'real interest' — locus standi

22.27   In order to obtain a declaration, the applicant must have a 'real interest' in the matter concerned. This is otherwise known as locus standi — the requirement that the applicant has standing to seek the relief sought. In respect of private rights such as those arising under a contract, it is easy to appreciate that persons whose rights are not at stake have no standing to ask the court to declare those of others. However, this does not mean that a person who is *not* a party to a contract cannot obtain declaratory relief in relation to the contract. Thus, a court can grant a declaration to a claimant who is not a party to a contract in relation to its construction, provided both parties to the proceedings have a sufficient or genuine and legitimate interest in the decision: *Milebush Properties Ltd v Tameside Metropolitan Borough Council* [2011] EWCA Civ 270 at [34]–[44], [71]–[88].

22.28   In relation to declarations in the area of public rights the issue of standing is more complex. When an individual seeks to raise a public right against the Crown, the first course of action should be to approach the Attorney-General who may bring the suit in his or her official capacity (ex officio) or in relation to the rights of the private individuals concerned (ex relatione). The Attorney-General has automatic standing, but cannot be compelled to exercise his or her office in this way. If the Attorney-General refuses to provide this assistance, then it is recognised that an individual may approach the court directly to assert the public right provided they meet at least one of the two threshold tests for standing. These were stated in *Boyce v Paddington Borough Council* [1903] 1 Ch 109 at 114, where Buckley J said:

> A plaintiff can sue without joining the Attorney-General in two cases: first, where the interference with the public right is such as that some private right of his is at the same time interfered with … and, secondly, where no private right is interfered with, but the plaintiff, in respect of his public right, suffers special damage peculiar to himself from the interference with the public right.

22.29   It is under the second limb of the test from *Boyce* that the courts are faced with difficult issues of standing. In *Australian Conservation Foundation Inc v Commonwealth* (1980) 146 CLR 493; 28 ALR 257, the High Court considered the standing of the Australian Conservation Foundation, an organisation dedicated to environmental protection, to challenge government decisions allowing a tourism development to proceed. Rather than insist upon the requirement from *Boyce* of 'special damage', the court said that the applicant need only show a 'special interest' in the matter. However, it was made clear that the interest must be one with tangible consequences. In this respect, Gibbs J, at CLR 530; ALR 270, said:

> [A]n interest, for present purposes, does not mean a mere intellectual or emotional concern. A person is not interested within the meaning of the rule, unless he is likely to gain some advantage, other than the satisfaction of righting a wrong, upholding a principle or winning a contest, if his action succeeds or to suffer some disadvantage, other than a sense of grievance or a debt for costs, if his action fails.

22.30   In this case the Australian Conservation Foundation was found not to have a 'special interest' in the sense required. However, Mason J, at CLR 547; ALR 284, pointed out that the requirement of one's interests being affected, could perhaps be satisfied in respect of social or political interests, as well as 'property or proprietary rights … business or economic interests'. This view of Mason J was demonstrated one year later in *Onus v Alcoa of Australia Ltd* (1981) 149 CLR 27; 36 ALR 425, in which members of an Aboriginal tribe were given standing to enforce provisions of the *Archaeological and Aboriginal Relics Prevention Act 1972* (Vic) in order to protect their relics from interference, damage or destruction. The tribe members held a 'special interest' in that they were custodians of the relics which they actually used and which were of cultural and spiritual importance to them. Thus, unlike the Australian Conservation Foundation in the earlier case, the applicants stood to suffer a palpable disadvantage or loss if their action failed.

Foreseeable consequences — utility

22.31   The final discretionary factor laid down in *Ainsworth v Criminal Justice Commission* is that a declaration should not be granted if it would produce 'no foreseeable consequences for the parties'. A declaration 'must have some effect on the rights and obligations of the parties to the proceeding in which the declaration is pronounced': *Australian Competition and Consumer Commission v Francis*

(2004) 142 FCR 1 at 32. Essentially, a court should not make the order where there is no practical utility in it doing so. As the Full Court of the Federal Court said in *Warramunda Village Inc v Pryde* (2001) 105 FCR 437 at 440:

> The remedy of a declaration of right is ordinarily granted as final relief in a proceeding. It is intended to state the rights of the parties with respect to a particular matter with precision, and in a binding way. The remedy of a declaration is not an appropriate way of recording in a summary form, conclusions reached by the Court in reasons for judgment. This is even more strongly the case when the conclusion is not one from which any right or liability necessarily flows.

22.32   This requirement was considered at length in the Federal Court in *Australian Competition and Consumer Commission v Francis*, at 33, where Gray J lamented that 'the fashion of seeking declarations has led, in many cases, to the Court granting them as a matter of course, and usually without discussion as to the adequacy of the terms of the declaration sought, or as to the necessity for one to be made'. The declaration sought by consent of both parties in this case pertained to conduct engaged in by Francis which was in breach of statutory provisions prohibiting misleading or deceptive conduct. His Honour, at 33, took the view that it was:

> … hard to see that a declaration that a person, by engaging in certain conduct, has contravened a provision of a statute can amount to a declaration of right. On its face, it does no more than to record something about the person's past conduct and its relationship with the statute concerned … [By contrast] a declaration of right will be as to a state of affairs, such as validity or invalidity, or the meaning of a particular provision in a particular factual context, so that the parties can resolve their controversies on the basis that the state of affairs exists.

22.33   However, despite the logic of this approach, the practice of making declarations confirming a past breach of statute seems to have been approved of by the High Court in *Rural Press Ltd v Australian Competition and Consumer Commission* (2003) 216 CLR 53; 203 ALR 217, and, as Gray J admitted in *ACCC v Francis*, at 36, is now 'established'. Despite his Honour's opinion that the requested declaration was 'pointless' in a situation such as this where the parties had already settled the matter, his Honour granted it just the same. In a case involving breaches of the *Workplace Relations Act 1996* (Cth), in *Cruse v Multiplex Ltd* (2008) 172 FCR 279 at 296, Goldberg and Jessup JJ said that courts, in exercising their discretion, could refuse declaratory relief in cases of this type in the following situations:

1. Where the dispute said to underlie the proceeding as a whole is entirely hypothetical …
2. Where … the underlying dispute has been settled, and it is part of the settlement that the court should be asked to make particular orders by consent.
3. As in situation 2, but where the parties are not agreed on the remedial orders which should be made (albeit that the facts and law are agreed or not controversial).
4. Where the terms of the declaration sought record the result of the case, but do not establish the content of the parties' ongoing rights or obligations.
5. Where the declarations sought are in the form of what Gummow, Hayne and Heydon JJ described as 'a bad precedent' in *Rural Press Limited v Australian Competition and Consumer Commission* [at CLR 91; ALR 245].

22.34   Many cases of lack of utility can also be seen to involve abstract or hypothetical questions. Indeed, there is a clear relationship between these two considerations. In situations where there is not a practical matter of rights to be determined, it logically follows that a declaration, even if made, would have no particular impact. This can be seen in the cases of *University of New South Wales v Moorhouse* (see 22.20) and *Egan v Willis* (see 22.25–22.26), in both of which a bare declaration was sought. In the former case, the lack of any factual proof of copyright infringement rendered the question one entirely abstract in nature. Consequently, the declaration granted by the trial court was of no assistance in clarifying the legal positions of the parties. Similarly, in *Egan v Willis*, the seeking, without more, of a declaration that the resolution of the Legislative Council was invalid, was also seen by some members of the bench as an abstract exercise. While such a question may need to be entertained in the context of a justiciable controversy, the court should resist doing so in relation to the powers and privileges of the legislature when that is not the case and there is no practical result to be gained by the making of a bare declaration.

22.35 Additionally, lack of utility can arise in respect of real legal controversies where the court is unsure what effect a declaratory order will have upon the dispute between the parties. The court will be particularly keen to ensure it does not grant a declaration that is ineffectual as a means of resolving the dispute, as to do so will damage its authority and may lead to further litigation. This was the basis for refusing a declaration in *Neeta (Epping) Pty Ltd v Phillips* (1974) 131 CLR 286; 3 ALR 151. It was unclear in that case whether the applicant, if successful in obtaining a declaration that a contract for sale of land had not been validly rescinded, would have proceeded to bring an action for specific performance. Thus, Barwick CJ and Jacobs J, at CLR 307; ALR 168, said:

> Unless the parties are agreed on the consequences which flow from a declaration that such a contract has not been validly rescinded it is generally undesirable that a court should so declare without any orders for consequential relief. If a party to such a contract claimed the Contract has not been validly rescinded such a judicial declaration is proper if that party continues ready and willing at the conclusion of the declaration to perform the Contract. A consequence of the declaration should be that the parties submit to the performance of the Contract on his part and for an order for specific performance of the Contract if that is appropriate. If such an order is not, or cannot be made, nor an inquiry into damages ordered then a declaration that on a certain day the Contract has not been validly rescinded serves no purpose in litigation.

22.36 More recently, in *Commonwealth of Australia v BIS Cleanaway Ltd* [2008] NSWCA 170, the Commonwealth government sought a declaration that its licence agreement with a company, allowing that company to deposit trade waste on Commonwealth land, had been novated to BIS Cleanaway. The issue of novation of the licence agreement was a preliminary matter to the question of whether BIS Cleanaway was liable to the Commonwealth in relation to certain terms of it. Declaratory relief was refused on the basis that there was no utility in granting such relief, as it would not finally resolve the issues between the parties. In refusing declaratory relief, Hodgson JA, at [8], speaking for the Court of Appeal, said:

> There would in my opinion be no practical consequences of the making of declarations of the kind sought, except such consequence as they may have in relation to a breach, claim or expense of the kind I have mentioned. And if and when the [Commonwealth] were to allege any such breach, claim or expense, this would almost certainly raise specific questions as to the interpretation of the licence, as to what, if there had been a novation, were the precise terms and effect of the novation (for example in relation to activities which had been undertaken prior to the novation), and what (if there had been a termination of the licence or some event affecting its operation

as from any particular time) was the effect of that termination, or that affectation, as to any application the licence had into the future from that time. Issues such as these would be issues that would best be dealt with together with determination of issues raised in connection with the orders actually sought in these proceedings, rather than separately from them in a piecemeal way.

22.37 It might be thought that this approach undermines the attractions of the declaration as a stand-alone form of relief, but in fact this is not so. In the New Zealand Court of Appeal case of *Countrywide Finance Ltd v State Insurance Ltd* [1993] 3 NZLR 745 at 751, Hammond J highlighted the usefulness of the remedy in the modern context of alternative dispute resolution, when he said:

> A declaration, after all, declares rights and then leaves it to parties to negotiate through (and around if they so desire) those rights. This is consistent with the more benign, and less paternalistic, approach of late twentieth century superior courts. Ultimately, party-based solutions are to be preferred.

22.38 The decision of Barwick CJ and Jacobs J in *Neeta (Epping) v Phillips* should not necessarily be seen to run contrary to this sentiment. Rather, what their Honours are saying is that they will not make a declaration in circumstances where the parties are unclear as to how they will react to the order. In particular, the courts will not make a declaration that serves only to fan the flames of further litigation.

DEFENCES

22.39 It should be noted that due to the jurisdiction to grant declaratory relief now being derived from statute, the role of traditional equitable defences such as unclean hands (see 31.8–31.12) and laches (see 31.13–31.2) have arguably been eliminated. However, in cases where a declaration is sought as ancillary to other equitable remedies such as an injunction, the usual equitable defences do apply: *Ambridge Investments Pty (in liq) v Baker* [2010] VSC 59 at [72]–[73].

22.40 Thus, in ruling that the unclean hands defence could be raised in relation to an application for a declaration that the plaintiffs were entitled to an equitable interest in certain land, the Full Court in South Australia said in *H Stanke & Sons Pty Ltd v O'Meara* (2007) 98 SASR 450 at 459:

> In these circumstances, the declaratory orders sought by the plaintiffs would simply express the result of the application of the relevant equitable principles. Whether or not this results in the declarations themselves being properly regarded as equitable, there is little doubt that the plaintiffs are seeking the aid of equity. Accordingly, there is no reason to exclude from the court's consideration other equitable principles such as the requirement as to clean hands.

Furthermore, in *Singh v Singh; Flora t/as Flora Constructions v Budget Demolition & Excavation Pty Ltd* [2008] NSWSC 386 at [153]–[164], declaratory relief was refused on the ground of laches.

DECLARATIONS IN CRIMINAL CASES

22.41 In *Gedeon v Commissioner of the New South Wales Crime Commission* (2008) 236 CLR 120 at 133; 249 ALR 398 at 404, the High Court noted that the 'power to make declaratory orders should be exercised sparingly where the declaration would touch the conduct of criminal proceedings'. The policy reasons for this approach relate to the fact that (i) with a declaration a lesser standard of proof applies than with criminal proceedings; (ii) the civil court may be usurping the functions of a jury in a criminal case; and (iii) seeking a declaration may amount to an abuse of process as a tactic for delaying the prosecution of a criminal trial: *Cousins v Merringtons Pty Ltd* [2007] VSC 542 at [31]. Thus, a declaration in respect of criminal conduct which has occurred has little practical utility and would usurp the jurisdiction and role of the criminal courts, and for those reasons, will not be made: *Brightwater Care Group (Inc) v Rossiter* [2009] WASC 229 at [19].

22.42   However, 'in particular circumstances the interests of justice may militate in favour of the making of a declaratory order': *Gedeon v Commissioner of the New South Wales Crime Commission* at CLR 134; ALR 404. Thus, in *Sankey v Whitlam* (1978) 142 CLR 1; 21 ALR 505, the Crown alleged that certain documents that were the subject of a subpoena in criminal proceedings were privileged and therefore did not need to be produced. The High Court granted declaratory relief to the effect that the documents were not privileged.

22.43   In *Gedeon v Commissioner of the New South Wales Crime Commission,* a declaration was sought in relation to 'controlled operation' authorities, issued pursuant to the *Law Enforcement (Controlled Operations) Act 1977* (NSW) (the Act), to obtain evidence of the sale to the applicants of cocaine that had been illegally imported into Australia. The applicants claimed that the issuance of the authorities was an act beyond the statutory power conferred upon the issuing officer by the Act. The High Court, at CLR 134; ALR 404, in granting declaratory relief, observed that '[t]here is a considerable public interest in the observance of due process by law enforcement authorities by putting beyond doubt important questions of the construction of the [Act]'. The significance of the result in this case was that the evidence obtained pursuant to the said controlled operations authorities was excluded from the trial of one of the applicants, and was the basis of an appeal against a criminal conviction for the other applicant.

22.44   On the other hand, if the declaration is sought as to possible or proposed future conduct, there is a greater prospect of the application being successful because it may amount to 'an inhibition against the commission of illegal acts in some instances, and an assurance of freedom of prosecution in others': *Re Tooth & Co* (1978) 31 FLR 314 at 333; 19 ALR 191 at 208. Thus, in *Tom & Bill Waterhouse Pty Ltd v Racing New South Wales* [2008] NSWSC 1013 at [74], Palmer J said that a court 'is less reluctant to make a declaration involving questions of criminal law where the facts are clear and undisputed, there are no criminal proceedings pending, and there is a pure question of law to be decided'. In that case, Waterhouse sought a declaration that the way it conducted its betting business did not constitute a criminal offence under certain legislation. In the circumstances of the case, his Honour found that all three of the factors mentioned were satisfied and granted the declaration.

23

SPECIFIC PERFORMANCE

INTRODUCTION

23.1 The remedy of specific performance is the principal means by which contractual obligations are enforced in equity. To a lesser extent the equitable remedy of an injunction can also be used to enforce a contract. Of course, contractual claims are also enforceable by an order for damages at common law. Whereas the common law remedy of damages is designed to provide monetary compensation to a plaintiff for losses resulting from a breach of contract by the defendant, the equitable remedies of specific performance and injunction are designed to force a defendant to perform his or her contractual obligation. These equitable remedies can be ordered even though a breach of contract has not yet occurred: *Turner v Bladin* (1951) 82 CLR 463 at 472. What is required is the mere existence of 'circumstances which will justify the intervention by a court of equity' to grant the decree: *Hasham v Zenab* [1960] AC 316 at 329. However, the mere existence of a contract, in the absence of a reasonable apprehension of it being breached, is not a basis for the court to order specific performance. In *Wolseley Investments Pty Ltd v Gillespie* [2007] NSWCA 358 at [33], Santow JA (Ipp and Tobias JJA agreeing) said that 'the trigger for the commencement of a specific performance suit will be some threat of refusal, express or at least implied, or some actual refusal, on the part of a contracting party to perform the contract in whole or part'. His Honour, at [19], also noted that, in cases of a threatened breach of a contract, the threat does not need to be explicit, but there must be more than merely a theoretical or remote possibility of a breach. However, in such cases, his Honour, at [47], also observed that a court has 'to consider the likelihood or degree of risk of non-performance before granting specific performance. Also to be considered is the discretionary factor of hardship and balance of convenience'.[1]

23.2 Where the contractual obligation is positive in substance, in that the defendant is required to perform some positive act, then specific performance is the appropriate remedy. Where the contractual obligation is negative in substance, in that the defendant is obliged not to do a certain act, then an injunction is the appropriate remedy. A common example of injunctive relief is the enforcement of valid restraints of trade. In practice, the need for specific performance is much greater than for an injunction. It should also be noted that specific performance is exclusively a remedy for the enforcement of contractual obligations. The injunction has applications beyond the field of contract law, and is an important enforcement order in various fields of law such as torts, trusts and

---

1. For a critique of this decision see K Dharmananda & N M Tan, 'Breach or Threatened Breach of Contract Before Specific Performance' (2008) 2 *Journal of Equity* 164.

other equitable obligations. Furthermore, many statutory rights and obligations are enforced by the injunction. The remedy of an injunction will be more closely scrutinised in Chapter 24.

NATURE OF SPECIFIC PERFORMANCE

23.3 Like most equitable remedies specific performance is *in personam* (see 2.52–2.57) in nature. This essentially means that the remedy attaches to the person of the defendant rather than to his or her property (*in rem*). This has the result that, provided the defendant is within the jurisdiction of the court, specific performance can be ordered even though the property that is the subject of the contract may be outside the court's jurisdiction. Thus, in *Richard West & Partners (Inverness) Ltd v Dick* [1969] 2 Ch 424, an English court ordered specific performance of a contract for the sale of land where the property was located beyond the court's jurisdiction in Scotland. Because of the *in personam* nature of specific performance, the sanction for non-compliance with an order for specific performance focuses on the person and not on the contract or property the subject of the contract. Thus, a defendant who fails to comply with the order will be guilty of contempt of court with the ultimate consequence of being imprisoned for such contempt (see 2.53).

23.4 The remedy of specific performance is applied in two distinct senses. First, there is specific performance in the proper sense, and second, relief analogous to specific performance. Specific performance in the proper sense presupposes an executory as opposed to an executed contract. Such contracts 'contemplate the execution of a formal document or other act in law under which the rights of the parties are to be governed': *Lighting By Design (Aust) Pty Ltd v Cannington Nominees Pty Ltd* (2008) 35 WAR 520 at 545. In *J C Williamson Ltd v Lukey & Mulholland* (1931) 45 CLR 287 at 297, Dixon J said:

> Specific performance, in the proper sense, is a remedy to compel the execution *in specie* of a contract which requires some definite thing to be done before the transaction is complete and the parties' rights are settled and defined in the manner intended.

23.5 In *Bridge Wholesale Acceptance Corporation (Australia) Ltd v Burnard* (1992) 27 NSWLR 415 at 423, Clarke JA explained that the order for specific performance in the proper sense is an order that the whole of the contract, and not individual obligations under it, be carried into effect. Thus, in a contract for the sale of land, upon a purchaser's application for specific performance in the proper sense, the court would order a vendor to execute a deed of conveyance or memorandum of transfer, as the case may be. Until the execution of such a document is achieved the rights of the parties have not been settled and defined as intended by the contract of sale.

23.6 Relief analogous to specific performance presupposes an executed contract, in the sense that nothing further needs to be done to settle or define the rights of the parties as intended by the contract. In fact, the contract itself fully establishes the parties' rights. The order for specific performance in such a case is 'to compel the [defendant] to perform its obligations according to the terms of the contract': *Bridge Wholesale Acceptance Corporation (Australia) Ltd v Burnard* at 423.

23.7 In *Waterways Authority of New South Wales v Coal & Allied (Operations) Pty Limited* [2007] NSWCA 276, the New South Wales Court of Appeal noted that the distinction between specific performance in the proper sense and relief analogous to specific performance 'lay in the underlying basis that attracted the intervention of equity'. Beazley JA, at [62], said that the equity that justifies the making of an order for specific performance in the proper sense is 'the need to place the parties in the relative legal positions contemplated by the contract'. In relation to relief analogous to specific performance, her Honour referred to the joint judgment of Isaacs and Rich JJ in *Pakenham Upper Fruit Company Limited v Crosby* (1924) 35 CLR 386 at 395, where their Honours observed that, in such cases, 'the equity must be sought in some other consideration appropriate to the actual legal relative situation of the parties'. In most such cases relief is given by way of mandatory injunction as was noted in *Fell v NSW Oil & Shale Co* (1889) 10 LR (NSW) Eq 255 at 259–60, where Owen CJ in Eq said:

> There arises not unfrequently some confusion between two classes of suits — both popularly described as suits for specific performance, though governed by very different principles — one, in which the contract is executory, and something remains to be done in order to complete the contract, where the contract is not intended to be the final instrument regulating the relations of the parties under the contract; the other in which the contract is executed, and the Court is asked to compel one of the parties to carry out the contract. To the former class only does the expression specific performance strictly apply. In the latter class the remedy is more frequently sought by way of injunction to prevent some breach of the contract, and so indirectly compelling the performance of the contract.

However, the significance of the distinction between the two senses of specific performance should not be overstated. In *Australian Hardwoods Pty Ltd v Commissioner for Railways* [1961] 1 All ER 737 at 743, the Privy Council held that the principles applicable to both were the same.

23.8 A fundamental distinction between damages at common law and the equitable order of specific performance is that, whereas a plaintiff will always get an award of damages if he or she establishes a breach of contract by the defendant, the same plaintiff will not automatically be entitled to equitable relief simply by establishing a breach of contract by the defendant. If a plaintiff's application for equitable relief is denied, he or she is confined to obtaining damages for breach of contract.

23.9 It is often said that common law damages for a breach of contract are available to a plaintiff 'as of right' but that equitable relief for the same breach is 'discretionary'. However, such a statement is, strictly speaking, not correct. It is correct that a damages award will always be made in favour of a plaintiff, who is ready, willing and able to perform the contract, upon proof of a breach by the defendant. With specific performance, it is only partially correct to say that it is discretionary. While the court can refuse such relief in the exercise of its discretion, the exercise of that discretion is subject to the court having the jurisdiction to entertain the application for specific performance. If the court does not have such jurisdiction the question of exercising its discretion does not arise. It is thus more accurate to say that specific performance will be denied on jurisdictional grounds and may be refused on discretionary grounds.

23.10 The distinction between jurisdictional and discretionary factors is of practical significance in relation to the damages that the plaintiff will be able to recover. In the case of a breach of contract, if specific performance is refused on discretionary grounds, so-called equitable damages (see Chapter 26) can be awarded. If specific performance is denied on jurisdictional grounds there is no power to award equitable damages, and a plaintiff is confined to recovering damages at common law for the breach of contract. Although the measure of damages recovered in either case is determined largely on the basis of the same principles (see 26.49), there are some circumstances that preclude the recovery of equitable damages that do not apply to common law damages: see 26.64. Thus, whether the plaintiff recovers equitable damages or common law damages can impact on the measure of damages awarded by the court.

23.11   Irrespective of whether jurisdictional or discretionary factors are involved in determining whether or not specific performance will be ordered in any given case, the basis of the court's decision is the principle of unconscientiousness. Therefore, when a court refuses to make an order for specific performance, be it on jurisdictional or discretionary grounds, it is effectively saying that it is *not* unconscientious for a plaintiff to be confined to recovering common law damages for breach of contract. On the other hand, when an order for specific performance is granted, the court is effectively saying that it would be unconscientious to confine the plaintiff to pursuing common law damages and that the justice of the case entitles him or her to pursue the equitable remedy of specific performance.

JURISDICTIONAL FACTORS PRECLUDING AN ORDER FOR SPECIFIC PERFORMANCE

Binding contract not for valuable consideration

23.12   As a rule, a court has no jurisdiction to grant specific performance of a promise not supported by valuable consideration: *Roxborough v Rothmans of Pall Mall Australia Ltd* (2001) 208 CLR 516 at 556; 185 ALR 335 at 364–5. In relation to a promise supported by nominal consideration only, Jones and Goodhart,[2] state that, in accordance with the equitable maxim 'Equity follows the law', equity will, like the common law, accept nominal consideration and thus specifically enforce such a promise. However, this view is inconsistent with the understanding of the meaning of 'valuable consideration' in the context of the maxim that 'equity will not assist a volunteer': see 2.38–2.39. Accordingly, Meagher, Heydon and Leeming[3] are correct in stating that 'a nominal sum of money such as $1 or £1 is not consideration' for the purposes of this rule.[4]

23.13   On the other hand, the inadequacy of consideration does not preclude a court entertaining an application for specific performance, although this may be a factor going towards refusing an application on discretionary grounds: see 23.58–23.59. Furthermore, although the court has no jurisdiction to order specific performance in (i) the case of a promise not supported by valuable consideration, but set out in a deed, and (ii) the case of a promise supported by nominal consideration only, in both cases damages at common law will be ordered for breach of such promises: *Cannon v Hartley* [1949] Ch 213 at 217; 1 All ER 50 at 53.

Inadequacy of damages at common law

23.14   If a plaintiff can be adequately compensated by an award of damages at common law the court has no jurisdiction to order specific performance: *Lucas Stuart Pty Ltd v Hemmes Hermitage Pty*

---

2.   G Jones & W Goodhart, *Specific Performance*, Butterworths, London, 1986, pp 15–16.

3.   R Meagher, D Heydon and M Leeming, *Meagher, Gummow and Lehane's Equity: Doctrines and Remedies*, 4th ed, LexisNexis Butterworths, Sydney, 2002, p 654.

4.   In New Zealand, legislation applying to deeds coming into operation after 1 January 2008 stipulates that the absence of valuable consideration in a deed is no longer a basis for refusing the remedy of specific performance: *Property Law Act 2007* (NZ) s 18(1).

Ltd [2010] NSWCA 283 at [5]. The adequacy or inadequacy of common law damages is determined by reference to the date of the order for specific performance and not the date of the contract: *ANZ Executors & Trustees Ltd v Humes Ltd* [1990] VR 615 at 632.[5] In England, in recent times, there has been a move towards regarding the issue of the adequacy of damages as a discretionary rather than a jurisdictional matter. However, this approach has not met with any support in Australia: *Waterways Authority of New South Wales v Coal & Allied (Operations) Pty Limited* at [95].

23.15   The question to be answered on the issue of the adequacy of damages has been framed in various ways. Thus, in *Adderley v Dixon* (1824) 57 ER 239 at 240 the Vice-Chancellor said that 'Courts of Equity decree the specific performance of contracts, not upon any distinction between realty and personalty, but because damages at law may not, in the particular case, afford a complete remedy'. In *International Advisor Systems Pty Limited v XYYX Pty Limited* [2008] NSWSC 2 at [41], the question asked was 'whether relegating the plaintiff to damages would leave it in as favourable a position in all respects as would exist if the defendant's obligation were specifically performed'. In *Wilson v Northampton and Banbury Junction Railway Company* (1874) LR 9 Ch App 279 at 284, Lord Selborne said that 'the Court gives specific performance instead of damages, only when it can by that means do more perfect and complete justice'. This statement was echoed by Lord Upjohn in *Beswick v Beswick* [1968] AC 58 at 102; [1967] 2 All ER 1197 at 1221, when his Lordship said that equitable relief will be available 'when damages are inadequate to meet the justice of the case'. Similarly, in *Araci v Fallon* [2011] EWCA Civ 668 at [42], Jackson LJ said the real question to be answered was 'whether it is just in all the circumstances that the claimant should be confined to his remedy in damages'.

23.16   Whatever the appropriate phrasing of the question is, it is clear that where there is significant difficulty in assessing the quantum of damages or in enforcing an award of damages, damages are inadequate: *Laemthong International Lines Co Ltd v Artis (The Laemthong Glory) (No 2)* [2005] 1 Lloyd's Rep 632 at 638. However, the mere fact that the defendant is threatened with insolvency and the contract would otherwise only attract the remedy of damages will not constitute inadequacy of damages, it being the view of the courts that ordering specific performance of contracts in such circumstances would unduly disrupt normal commercial activity: *Gilgandra Marketing Co-Operative Limited v Australian Commodities & Merchandise Pty Ltd* [2011] NSWSC 16 at [111].

23.17   In theory, the principle of inadequacy of damages at common law means that damages at common law is the primary remedy and specific performance is a secondary remedy. However, in practice it can be argued that the granting of an order for specific performance is not secondary in nature as compared to common law damages because the inadequacy of damages is increasingly easy to establish in many areas. This has led to specific performance being ordered routinely rather than in special circumstances. In support of this trend, Aitken has written:

> [W]hy should a contract breaker be able to disavow a solemn obligation when it no longer suits to carry it out, on the basis that at some stage in the future it will be mulcted of damages (which by definition may be hard to assess)? … It is little consolation to be told that the defendant is 'good' for the damages, and that after a protracted hearing (and possible delay in enforcement)

---

5.   See also I C F Spry, *Equitable Remedies*, 7th ed, Lawbook Co, Sydney, 2007, p 74.

a monetary sum which vaguely approximates to the 'damage' suffered (excluding the care and concern of litigating the matter) may at some point be payable by a recalcitrant defendant?[6]

23.18   The question of the inadequacy of damages at common law is one of fact in each case. Irrespective of the type of contract involved, the question to be determined by the court is whether damages will provide 'a complete remedy': *Adderley v Dixon* (1824) 57 ER 239 at 240. Each case ultimately depends on its own facts. If damages at common law are inadequate then the court has jurisdiction to grant an order for specific performance regardless of the type of contract that is involved: *Aristoc Industries Pty Ltd v R A Wenham (Builders) Pty Ltd* [1965] NSWR 581 at 588. Nevertheless, when looking at particular types of contract, general indications can be detected as to whether or not damages at common law are likely to be inadequate.

Contracts for the sale of personalty

23.19   In most cases common law damages will be an adequate remedy for contracts for the sale of personalty with the result that courts do not have jurisdiction to order specific performance of such contracts. Thus, contracts for the sale of shares or chattels will not be specifically enforced if substitute shares or chattels are readily available in an open market: *Duncuft v Albrecht* (1841) 59 ER 1104 at 1108. Damages at common law will be adequate, because if the plaintiff is required to pay more for the substitute shares or goods, that will be reflected in the amount of damages awarded at common law. The net result to the plaintiff will be that the shares or chattels will be ultimately acquired for the price at which they were contracted for with the defendant.

23.20   Although contracts involving personalty are generally ones in which damages at common law are an adequate remedy this is not an absolute rule. In *Aristoc Industries v RA Wenham (Builders)*, a case involving chattels, Jacobs J noted that there was a tendency to state that contracts involving chattels will not be specifically enforced unless the chattel is rare or unique. His Honour rejected this formulation and observed that the correct principle is that contracts involving chattels that are rare or unique will be enforced in equity because the rarity or uniqueness of the chattel is one aspect of the general question of the inadequacy of damages at common law. His Honour further observed that if damages at common law are an inadequate remedy, there is no principle which will prevent enforcement in equity simply because the subject matter of the contract is a chattel.

23.21   If the shares or chattels are not readily available on an open market, damages at common law will be inadequate and the court will have jurisdiction to specifically enforce the contract in question: *Dougan v Ley* (1946) 71 CLR 142 at 150. Thus, a purchaser of all of a company's shares has a particular interest in the due performance of the contract. Common law damages for breach of such a contract are inadequate and the court has jurisdiction to order specific performance of it: *Lionsgate Australia Pty Ltd v Macquarie Private Portfolio Management Ltd* [2007] NSWSC 371 at [64]–[65]. Similarly, contracts for the sale of chattels of unusual beauty or rarity or of special or sentimental significance to the purchaser are ones where damages at common law will usually be inadequate: *Falcke v Gray* (1859) 62 ER 250; see 23.58. Furthermore, damages at common law will usually be inadequate in cases where the item of personal property is the subject of great price fluctuations or if it would be difficult to establish the measure of damages at common law with any degree of accuracy, even though substitute items are available in an open market: *Adderley v Dixon*.

---

6.   L Aitken, 'When are Damages an Adequate Remedy?' (2004) 78 *Australian Law Journal* 544, pp 545–7.

Finally, if common law damages would otherwise be adequate, but the defendant is insolvent, damages will be held to be inadequate and specific performance will be granted: *Evans Marshall & Co Ltd v Bertola SA* [1973] 1 All ER 992 at 1006.

23.22 In *Dougan v Ley*, Dougan contracted to sell a taxi-cab, together with his registration and operator's licence issued by the Commissioner of Road Transport and Tramways, to Ley and Nash. Later, Dougan refused to go through with the sale and Ley and Nash sought an order for specific performance. Dougan argued that common law damages were an adequate remedy for the purchasers. The High Court granted the order. On the adequacy of damages arguments raised by Dougan, Dixon J, at 151, said:

> Where chattels are sold or otherwise disposed of by contract as part of the particular equipment of a business, there is ground for equity granting specific relief. ... In the present case I think we should have no difficulty in concluding that, because of the limited number of vehicles registered and licensed as taxi-cabs, because of the extent to which the price represents the value of the licence, and because of the essentiality to the purchasers' calling the chattel and the licence attached thereto, we should treat the contract as within the scope of the remedy of specific performance.

Land contracts

23.23 Damages at common law have almost invariably been seen as inadequate in contracts involving land. Thus, if a vendor in a contract for the sale of land refuses to convey title to a purchaser, the court has jurisdiction to order specific performance of the contract in favour of the purchaser on the basis that the purchaser cannot be adequately compensated by an award of damages at common law. A common justification for this practice is based upon the unique nature of each parcel of land. Thus, in *Loan Investment Corp of Australasia v Bonner* [1970] NZLR 724 at 745, Sir Garfield Barwick said:

> No two pieces of land can be identically situated on the surface of the earth. When a buyer purchases a parcel, no other piece of land, or the market value of the chosen land can be considered, in my opinion, a just substitute for the failure to convey the selected land.

23.24 Contracts involving land include contracts for the sale of land as well as contracts involving lesser interests in land such as leases. Although a licence to occupy land does not create an interest in land in the same way that a contract for the sale, or lease, of land does, such a licence has been held to come within the scope of contracts involving land for the purposes of the inadequacy of damages at common law principle: *Verrall v Great Yarmouth Borough Council* [1981] QB 202; [1980] 1 All ER 839.

23.25 The almost absolute nature of the principle that common law damages are inadequate in contracts involving the purchase of land is demonstrated by the decision in *Pianta v National Finance & Trustees Ltd* (1964) 180 CLR 146. In that case, the High Court ordered specific performance of a contract to a purchaser of land in circumstances where the purchaser was buying the land solely for the purpose of developing it for resale at a profit. The High Court held that, even in these circumstances, damages at common law were inadequate in so far as the purchaser was concerned.

23.26 In the case of a vendor seeking equitable relief against a defaulting purchaser, damages at common law has always been regarded as an inadequate remedy. This is so even where the vendor is entitled to receive a sum of money pursuant to the contract. Why this should be so is also not altogether clear. It has been said that the justification for this principle is that if common law damages are inadequate for a plaintiff/purchaser the same should apply to a plaintiff/vendor: *Turner v Bladin* at 473. However, a better explanation is that a vendor wants more than receipt of money on completion of a sale of land. He or she also wants to be legally divested of his or her interest in the land and that, consequentially, damages at common law would not be adequate compensation to the vendor: *Dougan v Ley* at 150.

23.27   The traditional approach of viewing common law damages as inadequate in cases of land contracts has been questioned. Thus, in *Union Eagle Ltd v Golden Achievement Ltd* [1997] AC 514 at 519; [1997] 2 All ER 215 at 219, the Privy Council observed that, in some circumstances, no distinction could be drawn between land sale contracts and other commercial contracts, because 'land can also be an article of commerce and a flat in Hong Hong is probably as good an example as one could find'. This observation clearly implies that damages could be an adequate remedy in contracts involving land.

23.28   In Canada, the Supreme Court rejected the traditional approach in *Semelhago v Paramadevan* [1996] 2 SCR 425 at 428–9; 136 DLR (4th) 1 at 9–11, where Sopinka J said:

> While at one time the common law regarded every piece of real estate to be unique, with the progress of modern real estate development this is no longer the case. Both residential, business and industrial properties are mass produced much in the same way as other consumer products. If a deal falls through for one property, another is frequently, though not always, readily available. It is no longer appropriate, therefore, to maintain a distinction in the approach to specific performance as between realty and personalty. It cannot be assumed that damages for breach of contract for the purchase and sale of real estate will be an inadequate remedy in all cases … Courts have tended, however, to simply treat all real estate as being unique and to decree specific performance unless there was some other reason for refusing equitable relief … Some courts, however, have begun to question the assumption that damages will afford an inadequate remedy for breach of contract for the purchase of land. In *Chaulk v Fairview Construction Ltd* (1977) 14 Nfld and PEIR 13, the Newfoundland Court of Appeal (per Gushue JA) … stated, at p 21:
>
> > The question here is whether damages would have afforded Chaulk an adequate remedy, and I have no doubt that they could, and would, have. There was nothing whatever unique or irreplaceable about the houses and lots bargained for. They were merely subdivision lots with houses all of the same general design, built on them, which the respondent was purchasing for investment or re-sale purposes only. He had sold the first two almost immediately at a profit, and intended to do the same with the remainder. It would be quite different if we were dealing with a house or houses which were of a particular architectural design or were situated in a particularly desirable location, but this was certainly not the case.
>
> Specific performance should, therefore, not be granted as a matter of course absent evidence that the property is unique to the extent that its substitute would not be readily available.[7]

---

7.   For a discussion and critique of this decision see R Chambers, 'The Importance of Specific Performance' in S Degeling & J Edelman, *Equity in Commercial Law*, Lawbook Co, Sydney, 2005, 431, pp 434–48.

23.29   Subsequent Canadian cases have indicated that the fundamental issue to be resolved by a court is whether the plaintiff seeking specific performance of a land contract has shown that the land rather than the money equivalent better serves the interests of justice. An important factor here relates to the uniqueness of the land being determined by consideration of matters such as the availability of similar land with comparable zoning, services, amenities and permissible density levels. There has also been a recognition that contracts for the purchase of investment properties, rather than contracts for the purchase of residential properties, are more likely to be ones where damages will be an adequate remedy: *United Gulf Developments Ltd v Iskandar* (2004) 235 DLR (4th) 609 at 615–17.

Contracts to pay or lend money

23.30   Generally, contracts to pay or lend money are ones where a plaintiff will be adequately compensated by an award of damages at common law. However, in some circumstances common law damages will not do justice to the plaintiff and the court will have jurisdiction to award equitable relief. In *Wight v Haberdan Pty Ltd* [1984] 2 NSWLR 280 at 290, Kearney J ordered specific performance of such a contract. Damages at common law were not an adequate remedy because of the complex questions that would have arisen, the delay and expense involved and the fact that damages would be extremely difficult, if not impossible, to assess with reasonable accuracy. On the other hand, even if specific performance is not available because of the adequacy of damages principle, in many cases the same practical result as specific performance is achieved by a plaintiff pursuing his or her claim in debt.

Contracts conferring a benefit on a third party

23.31   Contracts in which the promisor's obligation to be enforced is the conferral of a benefit upon a third party to the contract raise particular issues as to whether damages at common law are an adequate remedy. An important example of such a contract is where the promisor's obligation is to pay a sum of money to a third party. At first glance it could be surmised that damages would generally be an adequate remedy. However, this is not the case. The plaintiff's measure of damages in such a case will usually be nominal: *Coulls v Bagot's Executor & Trustee Co Ltd* (1967) 119 CLR 460 at 501–2. However, it is precisely because such damages are nominal that they will be seen as an inadequate remedy for a plaintiff. A court will have jurisdiction to order specific performance of such a contract because common law damages do not satisfy the demands of justice. In *Coulls v Bagot's Executor & Trustee Co*, at 503, Windeyer J said:

> Complete and perfect justice to a promisee may well require that a promisor perform his promise to pay money or transfer property to a third party.

23.32   In *Beswick v Beswick*, Peter Beswick contracted with his nephew John Beswick. By the terms of the contract Peter was to transfer his business to John and in return John agreed to employ Peter as a consultant for the rest of his life and after Peter's death to pay Ruth Beswick (Peter's wife) an annuity for the rest of her life. After Peter's death John refused to make the payments to Ruth. Ruth, in her capacity as the administratrix of Peter's estate, brought an action seeking specific performance of the obligation to pay the annuity. The House of Lords ruled in Ruth's favour holding that common law damages were an inadequate remedy. Lord Upjohn, at AC 102; All ER 1221, observed that in such a case, especially where the plaintiff has performed his or her contractual obligations and all that remained to be done was for the defendant to honour his or her obligation and pay money to the third party, equity would enforce the obligation as common law damages would be inadequate to meet the justice of the case. His Lordship observed that to deny equitable relief would 'fulfil no other object than that of aiding the wrongdoer'. In *Attorney General v Blake* [2001] 1 AC 268 at 282; [2000] 4 All ER 385 at 395, Lord Nicholls interpreted *Beswick v Beswick* as a case in which '[t]he law recognised that the innocent party to the breach of contract had a legitimate interest in having the contract performed even though he himself would suffer no financial loss from its breach'.

23.33   The inadequacy of damages in cases such as *Beswick v Beswick* stems from the fact that the plaintiff does not recover any damages in relation to losses suffered by the third party. This is because of the general rule that a plaintiff cannot recover damages for losses sustained by a third party to the contract: *The Albazero* [1977] AC 774 at 845; [1976] 3 All ER 129 at 136. However, if the plaintiff can recover damages for the third party's losses, then damages are an adequate remedy and a court has no jurisdiction to order specific performance.

23.34   The question of whether a plaintiff can recover damages in relation to losses suffered by a third party to a contract has been referred to as a 'legal black hole' and has troubled lawyers for some time. English cases have, through a series of decisions, come to the position that, as an exception to the general rule that a plaintiff can only recover damages for losses suffered by the plaintiff, the plaintiff can recover damages in relation to the loss suffered by a third party, but only if the third party has no claim of its own that can be pursued against the defendant who has breached his or her contract with the plaintiff.

23.35   The first of these cases arose in the context of contracts for the carriage of goods. In *The Albazero* at AC 847; All ER 137, Lord Diplock said:

> [I]n a commercial contract concerning goods where it is in the contemplation of the parties that the proprietary interests in the goods may be transferred from one owner to another after the contract has been entered into and before the breach which causes loss or damage to the goods, an original party to the contract, if such be the intention of them both, is to be treated in law as having entered into the contract for the benefit of all persons who have or may acquire an interest in the goods before they are lost or damaged, and is entitled to recover by way of damages for breach of contract the actual loss sustained by those for whose benefit the contract is entered into.

23.36   The second case effectively extended the principle in *The Albazero* to cases of the transfer of real property in the context of property development and construction. This meant that B, a contracting party, could bring an action to recover damages from A, the builder, for losses suffered by C, a third party, where under the building contract it was contemplated that the property would be purchased by C and there was a prohibition on the assignment of the benefit of the contract from B to C without the consent of A, thereby making it reasonably foreseeable that C would be unable to bring an action against A: *Linden Gardens Trust Ltd v Lenesta Sludge Disposals Ltd* [1994] 1 AC 85 at 114–5; [1993] 3 All ER 417 at 436–7.

23.37   More recently, in *Alfred McAlpine Construction Ltd v Panatown Ltd* [2001] 1 AC 518; [2000] 4 All ER 97, the House of Lords was faced with a situation in which A entered into a building contract with B for B to build commercial premises on land owned by C. B and C were part of a group of companies. As part of the arrangements made for the building work, A also executed a duty of care deed in favour of C in relation to the building work. This gave C a cause of action against A in relation to any defective building work on A's part. A's work was defective and the issue before the court was whether B could sue A to recover damages for losses incurred by C as a result of the defective building work. The majority of the House of Lords held that B could not recover damages for C's losses because C had a separate cause of action against A pursuant to the duty of care deed. The view of the minority was to the effect that if B was unable to recover for C's losses the law was defective in that B would be unable to get compensation in relation to not getting what B contracted for; that is, performance of the contract in favour of C.

23.38   The picture that emerges from the decision in *Alfred McAlpine Construction v Panatown* is that, in England, a plaintiff can sue the defendant and recover damages for losses suffered by the third party, but only if the third party has no cause of action of its own against the defendant. In Australia the approach signalled by *Alfred McAlpine Construction v Panatown* has attracted some support, although it is too early to state that it has clearly been accepted into Australian law. Thus, in *Stanley v Layne Christensen Company* [2006] WASCA 56 at [28], Wheeler JA, speaking for the Court of Appeal, noted that the law in this area may very well be changing in the way charted by the majority of the House of Lords in *Alfred McAlpine Construction v Panatown*. The consequence of these cases is that if a plaintiff does recover damages for losses suffered by a third party, damages would not be inadequate and a court would have no jurisdiction to order specific performance of the contract.

23.39   The situation encapsulated in cases such as *Beswick v Beswick* and *Alfred McAlpine Construction v Panatown* must be distinguished from situations where third parties are incidentally affected by a breach of a contract. In *Co-operative Insurance Society Ltd v Argyll Stores (Holdings) Ltd* [1996] 3 All ER 934 at 941, the Court of Appeal in England held that losses incurred by businesses as a result of a breach of a lease by the anchor tenant (a supermarket) in a shopping centre meant that damages at common law were inadequate because these businesses had no remedy against the anchor tenant. The court's ruling on the adequacy of damages issue is, with respect, misguided, because the lease did not contain any contractual obligation to confer any benefit upon these businesses. This is in contrast, for example, to *Beswick v Beswick* where the promisor (John Beswick) did promise to confer a benefit upon a third party (Ruth Beswick). The court's decision to order specific performance of the lease was reversed on appeal by the House of Lords, but on other grounds: see 23.49–23.51.

DISCRETIONARY FACTORS FOR REFUSING AN ORDER OF SPECIFIC PERFORMANCE

23.40   A variety of discretionary factors exist which enable a court to refuse to make an order for specific performance. Historically, some of them, such as the lack of mutuality, were treated as jurisdictional factors, but have since been transformed into discretionary factors. Some, but not all, of the discretionary factors are considered in the following pages. Other defences are detailed in Chapter 31.

Personal services contracts

23.41   Equity will not enforce a contract if to do so would result in compelling the defendant to maintain a personal relationship with the plaintiff. The underlying rationale for this principle lies in human nature and the undesirability of maintaining a personal relationship against the will of one of the parties to the contract. As was observed by Fry LJ in *De Francesco v Barnum* (1890) 45 Ch D 430 at 438, courts 'are bound to be jealous, lest they should turn contracts of service into contracts of slavery'. Typical examples include employment contracts and partnership agreements. However, this does not mean that the court will not enforce a contract which contains an obligation to enter into a contract for personal services. Specific performance of such an obligation would be an example of specific performance in the proper sense: see 23.4–23.5. In *Giles v Morris* [1972] 1 All ER 960, Megarry J observed that, even though a contract that has been entered into pursuant to a specific performance order may not be enforceable because it is a contract for personal services, this is no bar to ordering its execution. Although such a contract for personal services would usually not be specifically enforced, the plaintiff would nevertheless recover common law damages if it was breached. Megarry J further noted that simply because a contract contains an element of personal services does not automatically mean that it will not be enforced in equity. Similarly, in *Byrne v Australian Airlines Ltd* (1995) 185 CLR 410 at 428; 131 ALR 422 at 432, Brennan CJ and Dawson and Toohey JJ observed 'that a court will not, *save in exceptional circumstances*, order specific performance of a contract of personal service' (emphasis added).

23.42   In *Turner v Australasian Coal & Shale Employees Federation* (1984) 55 ALR 635, the Full Court of the Federal Court observed that in employment contracts specific performance had been traditionally denied on the ground that repudiation by one party destroyed the mutual confidence which must exist between an employer and employee, thereby making it undesirable to compel performance of an employment contract between them. However, the Full Court observed that this need not always be the case as not all employment relationships are ones where the relationship of mutual confidence must exist. Thus, in the situation of persons employed by large corporate enterprises, the Full Court, at 648, said:

> It is difficult to say that a relationship of mutual confidence must exist in the case of every person employed by a large corporate enterprise. There are many occupations in such enterprises where the precise identity of the employee performing a particular job is immaterial to the collective management of the corporation.

23.43   In *Downe v Sydney West Area Health Service (No 2)* (2008) 218 FLR 268 at 356–60, a contract of employment was enforced in circumstances where an employee had been suspended and there had not been any loss of trust or willingness to work between the employer and the employee. However, in *Tradition Australia Pty Ltd v Gunson* [2006] NSWSC 298, Barrett J, after consideration of the relevant authorities, indicated that specific performance of employment contracts would be an extremely rare occurrence. In that case, an employer sought specific performance of its contracts with three employees employed in a very specialised field within Australia's capital markets broking industry. The employees were engaged under fixed term contracts, but had, allegedly in breach of their contracts, commenced work with another employer at the time the employer sought relief. In denying equitable relief, Barrett J, at [26], suggested that earlier cases pointing to the theoretical possibility of specific performance of employment contracts were overwhelmingly ones in which the employer would have been compelled to maintain a relationship with an employee. In the case at hand, however, it would have been the employee being compelled to maintain a personal relationship with the employer. To grant specific performance in this case, according to his Honour, at [30], 'would be tantamount to making contracts of service into contracts of slavery'. Thus, it appears that in cases where specific performance of an employment contract is appropriate, it is more likely to be in favour of an employee against an employer, rather than in favour of an employer against an employee.

Constant court supervision

23.44   Contracts in which the parties' obligations are imprecisely defined will generally not be specifically enforced. The rationale for this principle stems from the fact that non-compliance with an order for specific performance is punishable as a contempt of court. Given the quasi-criminal consequence of contempt, it is entirely appropriate that the obligation to be specifically enforced must be sufficiently certain and precise so as to make the defendant's duty, in complying with the order, clear. In *Co-operative Insurance Society Ltd v Argyll Stores (Holdings) Ltd* [1998] AC 1 at 12–13; [1997] 3 All ER 297 at 1302–3, Lord Hoffmann said:

> It is the possibility of the court having to give an indefinite series of rulings to ensure the execution of the order which has been regarded as undesirable. Why should this be so? A principal reason is that … the only means available to the court to enforce its order is the quasi-criminal procedure of punishment for contempt … The prospect of committal or even a fine, with the damage to commercial reputation which will be caused by a finding of contempt of court, is likely to have at least two undesirable consequences. First, the defendant … has to make decisions under a sword of Damocles … Secondly, the seriousness of a finding of contempt for the defendant means that any application to enforce the order is likely … to be expensive in terms of cost to the parties and the resources of the judicial system.

23.45   This defence to an application for specific performance is usually phrased in terms of the principle that contracts requiring the constant supervision of the courts will not attract equitable relief. In *J C Williamson v Lukey & Mulholland* at 297–8, Dixon J said:

> Specific performance is inapplicable when the continued supervision of the court is necessary to ensure the fulfilment of the contract. It is not a form of relief which can be granted if the contract involves the performance by one party of services to the other or requires their continual co-operation.

23.46   In *Ryan v Mutual Tontine Westminster Chambers Association* [1893] 1 Ch 116, the facts involved an application for specific performance of a contract between a landlord and a tenant pursuant to which the landlord was obliged to employ a porter to perform certain services for the benefit of the tenant. The English Court of Appeal considered that the services to be performed by the porter would, for the long term of the contract, be required to be performed on a day-to-day basis and would require many and varied tasks to be performed, with the tasks changing from day to day. The court took the view that execution of the contract would require the constant supervision of the court and declined to order specific performance.

23.47   However, if the terms of the contract are sufficiently clearly defined, equitable relief will be granted. In *Tito v Waddell (No 2)* [1977] Ch 106 at 321; 3 All ER 129 at 308, Megarry V-C said:

> The real question is whether there is a sufficient definition of what has to be done to comply with the order of the court. That definition may be provided by the contract itself, or supplied by the terms

of the order, in which case there is the further question whether the court considers that the terms of the contract sufficiently support, by implication or otherwise, the terms of the proposed order.

23.48   An important area in which the constant court supervision principle arises is in the context of leases in modern shopping malls. Such malls invariably have one or more large retail shops such as supermarkets and department stores, commonly referred to as 'anchor tenants', and a larger number of smaller specialty shops. A common feature in leases for all tenants in the mall is that they will operate their businesses during normal business hours. Anchor tenants are vital to the success of shopping malls in that they tend to attract shoppers to the mall. Without the drawing power of anchor tenants, the smaller shops would not be able to survive. The question that has arisen in a number of cases is whether an anchor tenant who, in breach of its lease, shuts down its business, can be forced to continue to operate its business by an order for specific performance. The leading authority on this issue is *Co-operative Insurance Society v Argyll Stores*.

23.49   In *Co-operative Insurance Society v Argyll Stores*, Co-operative Insurance Society (CIS) was the owner of a shopping centre and Argyll Stores was the tenant of the centre's supermarket. With 19 years of the lease remaining, Argyll gave notice to CIS of its intention to close the supermarket. CIS, concerned that the closure would adversely affect other tenants, requested Argyll to keep operating the supermarket until a new supermarket operator could be found to take over the premises. Argyll refused to accede to this request and proceeded to close the supermarket. CIS sought specific performance of the lease obligation to operate the supermarket during normal business hours. A unanimous House of Lords refused the application. The principal basis for the decision was that enforcement of the obligation to carry on the supermarket business would require the constant supervision of the court.

23.50   Speaking for the House of Lords, Lord Hoffmann, at AC 13; All ER 303, drew a distinction between cases where the obligation that was the subject of an application for specific performance concerned the carrying on of activities and those where the obligation related to achieving a result. In the latter case, his Lordship said that if the result was defined with sufficient precision, specific performance would be ordered because the possibility of subsequent wasteful litigation would be minimised. The degree of precision in defining the obligation was of a higher order than that required to escape the consequences of a contract being void for uncertainty. However, with obligations of an ongoing nature, specific performance would not generally be ordered because of the threat of repeated litigation arising from disputes as to whether at any particular time the defendant was complying with the order. This was particularly important in this case because Argyll's obligation to keep the supermarket open was of an ongoing nature. However, Lord Hoffmann's speech on this point has been criticised by Radan as follows:

> If the obligation is defined with the requisite degree of precision it should be specifically enforced just as if the obligation is one concerned with producing a result. In the latter case specific performance is available because it is unlikely that there will be subsequent disputes requiring the court to determine whether the defendant has complied with the order. It is submitted that it would be equally unlikely that such disputes would arise if the precisely-defined obligation was one that required the carrying on of an activity on an ongoing basis.[8]

---

8.   P Radan, 'Specific Performance of a Lease Obligation to Operate a Business' (1997) 71 *Australian Law Journal* 740, p 743.

23.51 For Lord Hoffmann, a further reason against ordering specific performance in *Co-operative Insurance Society v Argyll Stores* was the fact that, if Argyll had to continue trading until the expiration of the lease, the effect of the order could very well be oppressive in that Argyll could have to carry on what was an unprofitable business for the remaining 19 years of the lease. Lord Hoffmann, at AC 18; All ER 307, rejected the argument put by CIS that an order for specific performance, once made, could subsequently be varied or set aside on the grounds of any actual oppression that resulted from complying with the order. However, decisions of the House of Lords and High Court of Australia clearly support the argument put forth by CIS. Although these cases deal with applications to set aside an order of specific performance on the grounds that compliance with the order is no longer possible (see 23.90), there is no reason in principle why such an application could not succeed in circumstances where the effect of the order is oppressive upon the defendant.

23.52 Although Lord Hoffmann's approach was generally endorsed by the High Court in *Patrick Stevedores Operations No 2 Pty Ltd v Maritime Union of Australia* (1998) 195 CLR 1 at 46–7; 153 ALR 643 at 670, it should not be assumed that obligations of an ongoing nature will never be specifically enforced. Lord Hoffmann, at AC 16; All ER 305, conceded this when he observed that the ordering of specific performance was ultimately a discretionary matter in which '[t]here are no binding rules' and that 'in exceptional circumstances' specific performance of an obligation to carry on a business could be specifically enforced. Indeed, in *Patrick Stevedores*, at CLR 46; ALR 670, the High Court said the following about the decision in *Co-operative Insurance Society v Argyll Stores*:

> What is significant is the acceptance by the House of Lords that the concept of 'constant supervision by the court' by itself is no longer an effective or useful criterion for refusing a decree of specific performance … Reference to constant court applications should not be misunderstood. The courts are well accustomed to the exercise of supervisory jurisdiction upon applications by trustees, receivers, provisional liquidators and others with the responsibility for the conduct of administrations. The reservation of liberty to apply to the Federal Court in respect of certain of the orders to be made is in no way out of the ordinary in the exercise of equitable jurisdiction.

23.53 The *Patrick Stevedores* decision signals a more flexible approach than that of Lord Hoffmann and has been embraced by subsequent Australian cases. Thus, in *Diagnostic X-Ray Services Pty Ltd v Jewel Food Stores Pty Ltd* [2001] 4 VR 632, *Co-operative Insurance Society v Argyll Stores* was distinguished on its facts and the tenant was ordered to carry on the business until such time as it found another tenant to take over the business. Furthermore, as discussed by Berryman,[9] a number of Canadian cases have shown a greater willingness to specifically enforce such obligations.

23.54 According to Meagher, Heydon and Leeming,[10] building contracts form a 'well-established exception' to the principle of constant court supervision as discussed above. In *Wolverhampton Corporation v Emmons* [1901] 1 KB 515, it was stated that a building contract could be specifically enforced in equity if three conditions were satisfied. First, the stipulations in the contract had to be stated with sufficient clarity to enable a court to ascertain whether there has been a breach by

---

9. J Berryman, 'Recent Developments in the Law of Equitable Remedies: What Canada Can do for You' (2002) *Victoria University of Wellington Law Review* 51, pp 85–7.
10. Meagher et al, *Equity: Doctrines and Remedies*, note 3 above, p 666.

the builder. Second, damages at common law had to be an inadequate remedy. Third, the builder had to be in possession of the building site by virtue of the contract. The following comments can be made in relation to these conditions. As to the first condition, the court in *Wolverhampton Corporation* was merely restating the general principle that applies to all contracts for which specific performance is sought. Unless contractual obligations are defined with sufficient clarity they will not be enforced in equity, and this applies equally to building contracts as to any other contract. The second condition simply states a rule that applies to all applications for the specific performance of a contract. The third condition is overstated. In *Thomas v Harper* (1935) 36 SR (NSW) 142, it was held that it was irrelevant as to how the builder came to be in possession of the building site. It is thus difficult to sustain the argument that *Wolverhampton Corporation* represents a 'well-established exception' to the general principle that contracts requiring constant court supervision will not attract equitable relief.

Hardship

23.55   An order for specific performance will be refused if it would result in unconscientious hardship upon the defendant. It is not any hardship to the defendant that will suffice. As was made clear in *Dowsett v Reid* (1912) 15 CLR 695, the court must balance the potential hardship to the defendant that would result if specific performance were granted with the potential hardship to the plaintiff if specific performance were refused. If the two cancel each other out, specific performance will be ordered despite the hardship to the defendant.

23.56   In *Patel v Ali* [1984] Ch 283, it was held that the fact that the defendant was under no hardship at the time of the contract, and that the hardship arose in the time between the date of the contract and the date of the hearing of the application for specific performance, did not mean that hardship could not be successfully raised by the defendant. However, as was also made clear in that case, circumstances giving rise to hardship after the date of contract, especially in cases of contracts for the sale of realty, would only arise in the most extraordinary and persuasive circumstances. Furthermore, if the circumstances arising after the contract were ones that were, or should reasonably have been, contemplated as matters that would occur after the contract was entered into, then it is less likely that these subsequent matters will be taken into account in establishing hardship: *ANZ Executors & Trustees v Humes* at 637.

23.57   The hardship principle extends to hardship to third parties to the contract, provided that the third party has a close connection to the defendant. An example is where the defendant has a moral or legal duty to the third party and the effect of ordering specific performance would be to actively prevent the defendant from discharging his or her duty to that third party: *Gall v Mitchell* (1925) 35 CLR 222.

23.58   The terms of a contract may, in special circumstances, establish hardship. In *Falcke v Gray* (1859) 62 ER 250, specific performance of an option to purchase rare China jars at a price 80 per cent below market value was declined on grounds of hardship to the defendant. Because the contract was for a rare and special chattel, the court had jurisdiction to award specific performance, as common law damages to the plaintiff would have been an inadequate remedy. However, the hardship to the defendant led the court to refuse the grant of relief in the exercise of its discretion.

23.59   Cases such as *Falcke v Gray*, where the inadequacy of consideration alone was sufficient to establish hardship, are rare. Simply because the terms of the contract are improvident, risky or unwise, will not be enough to establish hardship: *Axelsen v O'Brien* (1949) 80 CLR 219 at 226. Usually the inadequacy of consideration will be combined with one or more additional factors such as fraud, undue influence, mistake, intoxication, lack of independent legal or expert advice and the like. Thus, in *Kurth v McGavin* [2007] 3 NZLR 614, a purchaser of land was refused specific performance on the ground of hardship in circumstances where the vendor had entered into the contract in a state of intoxication and without the benefit of independent legal advice. Notwithstanding that adequate consideration was given by the purchaser, Priestley J, at 635, in refusing specific performance, said:

> The defendant's lack of independent legal advice and his state of mind during the formation of the contract, combined with the inherent uniqueness of his land and its significance to him, point to an order for specific performance being severe compared to the hardship faced by the plaintiff should damages be awarded instead.

Vitiating factors

23.60   Equitable relief will be refused if the contract is affected by vitiating factors due to the defendant's conduct or actions. Thus, contracts induced by a defendant's misrepresentation, mistake, duress, undue influence (see Chapter 10) or unconscionable transactions (see Chapter 11) will not be enforced in equity. Contracts that are unjust or unconscionable within the terms of any statutory principles such as unjust contracts pursuant to the *Contracts Review Act 1980* (NSW) will also not be specifically enforced.

Lack of mutuality

23.61   Specific performance is not available to a plaintiff unless the defendant could also have obtained relief against the plaintiff. This principle of mutuality cannot be raised by a defendant if the reason that the defendant could not get equitable relief against the plaintiff is to be found in the defendant's own conduct or default. Thus, if the defendant cannot get equitable relief because of some misrepresentation, unconscionable conduct, undue influence, laches and the like on his or her part, the plaintiff will not be denied relief on lack of mutuality grounds. The classic example of a lack of mutuality is a contract with a minor. The minor will be unable to receive an order for specific performance against the other party as that person will be unable to insist upon his or her rights against the minor. Thus, there is a lack of mutuality, which impairs the minor's own ability to seek the equitable remedy: *Boyd v Ryan* (1947) 48 SR (NSW) 163.

23.62   The critical aspect of the mutuality principle is the question of when mutuality must be present. In *Price v Strange* [1978] Ch 337; [1977] 3 All ER 371, it was held that the critical time for mutuality to be present is the date on which the court is to make the order for specific performance. The fact that mutuality may not have existed at an earlier time is irrelevant. In *Price v Strange*, mutuality was not present at the time of the breach of contract because the plaintiff's obligation to repair and renovate an apartment would have required the constant supervision of the court, thus precluding the defendant from obtaining specific performance: see 23.44–23.50. However, by the time of the hearing, the repairs and renovations had been completed, and thus there was no reason why the defendant would not have been able to obtain specific performance against the plaintiff.

Thus, mutuality was present at the date of hearing and the plaintiff obtained his order for specific performance.

23.63 An important exception to the requirement of mutuality concerns contracts for the sale of land or interests in land that are required by legislation to be evidenced in writing to be enforceable: see 23.67. If, for example, a vendor has the necessary written documentation signed by the purchaser, but the purchaser does not have written documentation signed by the vendor, mutuality clearly does not exist. The purchaser would be unable, due to the lack of documentation signed by the vendor, to seek specific performance against the vendor. This lack of mutuality would, on the application of the mutuality principle, mean that the vendor would be denied specific performance against the purchaser. However, it is clear that in this situation the vendor will be granted equitable relief, notwithstanding that the purchaser would be unable to obtain an order for specific performance.[11]

Plaintiff in substantial breach and/or not ready, willing and able to perform

23.64 A plaintiff will be denied equitable relief if he or she is in substantial breach of the contract. A substantial breach means a breach that would enable the other party to terminate the contract for that breach. Other breaches do not disqualify a plaintiff from obtaining relief in equity. In *Green v Sommerville* (1979) 141 CLR 594 at 610; 27 ALR 351 at 363, Mason J said:

> It is well settled that a plaintiff in a suit for specific performance is not required to show that he has strictly complied with all of his obligations under the contract; it is enough that he has performed and is ready and willing to perform the substance of the contract.

23.65 Even if the plaintiff has committed a substantial breach, the plaintiff will be entitled to equitable relief if the other party has affirmed the contract and elected not to terminate it: *Mehmet v Benson* (1965) 113 CLR 295. The court will make ancillary orders to compensate a defendant for any losses that result from the plaintiff's breach of contract.

23.66 A plaintiff must also be ready, willing and able to perform his or her own obligations before equitable relief will be ordered. This requirement can be established either by an admission on the pleadings, or by evidence: *Consolidated Credit Network v Illawarra Retirement Trust (No 2)* [2005] NSWSC 1007 at [76]. However, this does not mean that the plaintiff must have been ready, willing and able at all times. The requirement is that he or she be ready, willing and able at the time the equitable relief is sought. In *Mehmet v Benson*, the facts concerned a plaintiff who was a purchaser of land under an instalment contract, and who, during the currency of the contract, was declared bankrupt. While a bankrupt, the plaintiff, because of the limitations imposed upon a bankrupt to perform a contract, was not ready, willing and able to perform, and would thus not have been able to obtain an order for specific performance of the contract. However, the plaintiff obtained a discharge from bankruptcy and then sought an order for specific performance, and his application was successful before the High Court. Barwick CJ, at 307–9, said:

---

11. J D Heydon & M J Leeming, *Cases and Materials on Equity and Trusts*, 8th ed, LexisNexis Butterworths, Sydney 2011, pp 1175-6.

That the plaintiff was in default in payment of the instalments of the price and of the interest on the unpaid balance of it (time not being of the essence) though relevant to that question does not establish that he was not in the relevant sense ready and willing to perform the contract. If it were otherwise a purchaser in substantial default of inessential terms could never be granted specific performance. Indeed, the significance of the distinction between essential and inessential terms is derived from the fact that a person in breach of inessential terms may be granted specific performance …

The question as to whether or not the plaintiff has been and is ready and willing to perform the contract is one of substance not to be resolved in any technical or narrow sense. It is important to bear in mind what is the substantial thing for which the parties contract and what on the part of the plaintiff in a suit for specific performance are his essential obligations. Here the substantial thing for which the defendant bargained was the payment of the price: and, unless time be and remain of the essence, he obtains what he bargained for if by the decree he obtains his price with such ancillary orders as recompense him for the delay in its receipt. To order specific performance in this case would not involve the court in dispensing with anything for which the vendor essentially contracted.

Of course, the plaintiff must not by his unreadiness or unwillingness to perform have disowned his obligation to do so, or abandoned his rights to the benefit of the contract. But it is the essential terms of the contract which he must be ready and willing to perform. He seeks a transfer of the interest in land, the subject of the contract: the counterpart obligation is the payment of the price. In considering the question of the plaintiff's readiness and willingness in this respect in this case there are many factors. His default in paying the instalments of the price, whilst not conclusive, is amongst these factors …

In my opinion, notwithstanding the defaults of the plaintiff in the payment of the instalments of price, he was not unready or unwilling to perform the contract in its essential terms: specific performance ought to have been granted.

THE ENFORCEMENT IN EQUITY OF CONTRACTS UNENFORCEABLE AT LAW

23.67   This part of this chapter deals with the enforcement in equity of contracts required by statutory provisions to be evidenced in writing. These provisions do not deny the validity of oral contracts. Rather, they merely make them unenforceable. The most significant example of such legislative enactment relates to contracts for the sale of land or an interest in land. All Australian jurisdictions have statutory provisions, derived from the *Statute of Frauds* adopted by the English Parliament in 1677, in relation to such land contracts.[12] For example, s 54A(1) of the *Conveyancing Act 1919* in New South Wales stipulates as follows:

54A Contracts for sale etc of land to be in writing

---

12. *Civil Law (Property) Act* 2006 (ACT) s 204(1); *Conveyancing Act 1919* (NSW) s 54A(1); *Law of Property Act 2000* (NT) s 62; *Property Law Act 1974* (Qld) s 59; *Law of Property Act 1936* (SA) s 26(1); *Conveyancing and Law of Property Act 1884* (Tas) s 36(1); *Instruments Act 1958* (Vic) s 126(1) and *Property Law Act 1958* (Vic) s 53(1)(a); *Law Reform (Statute of Frauds) Act 1962* (WA) s 2 which stipulates that the *Statute of Frauds 1677* s 4 (UK) applies in Western Australia.

(1) No action or proceedings may be brought upon any contract for the sale or other disposition of land or any interest in land, unless the agreement upon which such action or proceedings is brought, or some memorandum or note thereof, is in writing, and signed by the party to be charged or by some other person thereunto lawfully authorised by the party to be charged.

23.68 The rationale and background to the English *Statute of Frauds* was explained in *Actionstrength Limited v International Glass Engineering In Gl En SpA* [2003] 2 AC 541 at 549; 2 All ER 615 at 621–2, where Lord Hoffmann said as follows:

> It is ... important to bear in mind that the purpose of the statute was precisely to avoid the need to decide which side was telling the truth about whether or not an oral promise had been made and exactly what had been promised. Parliament decided that there had been too many cases in which the wrong side had been believed. Hence the title, 'An Act for prevention of frauds and perjuries'. It is quite true ... that the system of civil procedure in 1677 was not very well adapted to discovering the truth. For one thing, the parties to the action were not competent witnesses ... The terms of the statute therefore show that Parliament, although obviously conscious that it would allow some people to break their promises, thought that this injustice was outweighed by the need to protect people from being held liable on the basis of oral utterances which were ill-considered, ambiguous or completely fictitious.

In *Golden Ocean Group Ltd v Salgaocar Mining Industries PVT Ltd* [2012] EWCA Civ 265 at [21]–[22], the Court of Appeal in England held that the legislation does not require that the agreement be contained in a single document, but can be met in a number of related documents.

23.69 That land contracts attracted this particular attention of the legislature reflects the political, economic, and social significance attached to land ownership. Through to the late nineteenth century England was predominantly a rural, agrarian society in which the ownership of land was at the core of political power and social prestige. Historically, the right to vote was dependant on the ownership of land. For example, in eighteenth-century England and Wales the franchise was dependant upon a man owning freehold property worth at least 40 shillings a year.[13] Furthermore, candidates for a seat in parliament were expected to have significant land holdings before being able to stand for election to parliament. Thus, the *Property Qualifications Act 1711* (UK) required members of parliament to possess real estate to the value of £600 in counties and £300 in boroughs.[14]

23.70 A failure to comply with the statutory requirement of writing renders the contract unenforceable. Thus, there can be no actions for remedies such as damages at common law and specific performance and injunction in equity. However, the consequence of unenforceability is not absolute. Equitable principles recognise two situations in which a contract that does not comply with the statutory writing requirement will, nevertheless, be enforced by an order for specific performance. First, the courts have long recognised that, if the reason for non-compliance with the statutory requirement is fraud on the part of the defendant, the contract will be specifically enforced. Second, equity will order the remedy of specific performance of a contract that does not comply with the statutory requirement if the elements of the doctrine of part performance are

---

13. W A Speck, *A Concise History of Britain 1707–1975*, Cambridge University Press, Cambridge, 1993, pp 7–8.
14. Speck, see note 13 above, p 10.

established. In both cases equitable principles prevent a party to the oral agreement from using the statute as a cloak for fraud.

23.71   The relief given in such cases was described by Young CJ in Eq in *Ciavarella v Polimeni* [2008] NSWSC 234 at [119], as follows:

> [I]f it would be fraudulent in the eyes of equity for the opposing party to rely on the statute, equity will order that that party execute a note or memorandum of the contract and will then proceed to grant specific performance. The plaintiff is not given relief because of the contract, rather the conduct of the parties subsequent to the contract raises an equity.

23.72   In some cases an injunction, rather than specific performance, may be the more appropriate order. However, given that the two exceptions noted above reflect equitable doctrines, only equitable remedies may be granted. Thus, even if, for example, the elements of part performance are established, this does allow a court to award damages at common law for breach of contract: *Penrith Whitewater Stadium Ltd v Lesvos Pty Ltd* [2007] NSWCA 196 at [40]; see 3.11.

23.73   It should also be observed that contracts that do not comply with a statutory requirement of writing may attract remedies that are entirely independent of the existence of the contract. Thus, the principles of equitable estoppel (*Tipperary Developments Pty Ltd v Western Australia* (2009) 38 WAR 488 at 521–2; 258 ALR 124 at 157–8 (see Chapter 12)), constructive trusts (see Chapter 28) and restitution may give a party to such a contract remedies relevant to those principles.

The statute cannot be used to perpetrate fraud

23.74   A defendant to an action for enforcement of an oral contract involving land will not be able to raise the absence of writing as a defence if the consequences of such a defence would be to perpetrate a fraud on the plaintiff. The courts have long recognised that, although the purpose of the statute is to prevent fraud, the statute itself cannot be relied upon if doing so will result in fraud: *Rochefoucauld v Boustead* (1897) 1 Ch 196 at 206; *Ciaglia v Ciaglia* (2010) 269 ALR 175 at 190–4. If the defendant were able to raise the statute as a defence to an application for specific performance in circumstances where the reason for the absence of writing was the fraud or dishonesty of the defendant, this would mean that the defendant would be using the statutory requirements of writing to perpetrate a fraud upon the plaintiff. The continued efficacy of this principle was recently reaffirmed by the High Court in *Halloran v Minister Administering National Parks and Wildlife Act* (2006) 229 CLR 545; 224 ALR 79, where the court used it as a basis for upholding the validity of an oral agreement to assign an equitable interest.

23.75   In *McCormick v Grogan* (1869) LR 4 HL 82 at 97, Lord Westbury said:

> The Court of Equity has, from a very early period, decided that even an Act of Parliament shall not be used as an instrument of fraud; and if in the machinery of perpetrating a fraud an Act of Parliament intervenes, the Court of Equity, it is true, does not set aside the Act of Parliament, but it fastens on the individual who gets a title under that Act, and imposes upon him a personal obligation, because he applies the Act as an instrument for accomplishing a fraud. In this way the Court of Equity has dealt with the Statute of Frauds.

23.76 In *Wakeham v MacKenzie* [1968] 2 All ER 783, Ball promised Wakeham that, if she moved in with him and looked after him, she would inherit the house when he died. Ball agreed to have this oral agreement reduced to a written form, but despite assurances to Wakeham that this had been done, he did not do so before he died. The court held that Ball's conduct amounted to equitable fraud, and made an order against Ball's estate enforcing the oral agreement and requiring the house to be transferred to Wakeham.

The doctrine of part performance

23.77 A second exception to the Statute of Frauds requirement of writing is the doctrine of part performance. The operation of the doctrine is confirmed by legislation in all Australian jurisdictions.[15] In *Actionstrength Limited v International Glass Engineering In Gl En SpA* at AC 549–50; All ER 622–3, Lord Hoffmann explained the emergence of, and rationale behind, this doctrine as follows:

> Very soon after the statute of 1677, the courts introduced the doctrine of part performance ... It was held that a contract, initially unenforceable because of the statute, could become enforceable by virtue of acts which the plaintiff did afterwards. The doctrine was justified by a combination of two reasons. The first was a form of estoppel: as Lord Reid said in *Steadman v Steadman* [1976] AC 536 [at] 540; [[1974] 2 All ER 977 at 980–1]:
>
>> If one party to an agreement stands by and lets the other party incur expense or prejudice his position on the faith of the agreement being valid he will not then be allowed to turn round and assert that the agreement is unenforceable.
>
> The second reason was that the acts done by the plaintiff could in themselves prove the existence of the contract in a way which could be an acceptable substitute for the note or memorandum required by the statute. These two reasons did not cover the same ground: acts which satisfied the first might fail to satisfy the second ... It was however still possible to adhere to the reconciliation of the statute and the part performance doctrine which the Earl of Selborne LC gave in *Maddison v Alderson* (1883) 8 App Cas 467 [at] 475–6:
>
>> In a suit founded on ... part performance, the defendant is really 'charged' upon the equities resulting from the acts done in execution of the contract, and not (within the meaning of the statute) upon the contract itself ... The matter has advanced beyond the stage of contract; and the equities which arise out of the stage which it has reached cannot be administered unless the contract is regarded.
>
> The reconciliation thus draws a distinction between the executory contract, not performed on either side, and the effect of subsequent acts of performance by the plaintiff. The former attracted the full force of the statute while the latter could create an equitable rather than purely contractual right to performance.

---

15. *Civil Law (Property) Act 2006* (ACT) s 204(2)(c); *Conveyancing Act 1919* (NSW) s 54A(2); *Law of Property Act 2000* (NT) s 5(c); *Property Law Act 1974* (Qld) s 6(d); *Law of Property Act 1936* (SA) s 26(2); *Conveyancing and Law of Property Act 1884* (Tas) s 36(2); *Property Law Act 1958* (Vic) s 55(d); *Property Law Act 1969* (WA) s 36(d).

23.78   Thus, in order to grant equitable relief based upon the doctrine of part performance a court will need to be satisfied that the 'acts of part performance are circumstances that make it unconscientious for a defendant to rely upon the statutory defence of a lack of writing': *Masterton Homes Pty Ltd v Palm Assets Pty Ltd* [2009] NSWCA 234 at [38].

23.79   An Australian formulation of the doctrine is found in *Waltons Stores (Interstate) Ltd v Maher* (1988) 164 CLR 387 at 432; 76 ALR 513 at 544, where Brennan J said:

> In order that acts may be relied on as part performance of an unwritten contract, they must be done under the terms and by the force of that contract and they must be unequivocally and in their nature referable to some contract of the general nature of that alleged.

23.80   For the doctrine of part performance to apply, three matters need to be established. First, the acts done must be done by the party to the contract seeking to rely on the doctrine, or his or her authorised agent: *McBride v Sandland* (1918) 25 CLR 69 at 79. Second, it must be shown that the acts done by the plaintiff were permitted, but not necessarily required, to be done by the terms of the oral agreement: *Regent v Millett* (1976) 133 CLR 679 at 683; 10 ALR 496 at 499. In *Khoury v Khouri* (2006) 66 NSWLR 241 at 268, Bryson JA, speaking for the Court of Appeal, in the context of an oral agreement relating to land, said:

> In the present case there are no acts of ownership such as taking possession, paying rates or paying for the upkeep or improvement of the property, or receipt of rent or profits, or any other act at all. Acts of part performance have been almost universally related to possession and use or tenure of the land itself, such as where a purchaser is put into possession by the vendor, or allowed to take possession by the vendor, or where the purchaser carries out improvements. They have not necessarily been acts which the contract requires to be done.

23.81   In *Regent v Millet* Regent purchased a property in the Sydney suburb of Sefton by providing $1000 of his own money and borrowing $3500. He orally agreed with the Milletts (his daughter and son-in-law) that, in return for payment of $1000 and an agreement to make the repayments on the $3500 loan, they could live in the house, treat it as their own and have it transferred into their names when all the payments had been made. The payments were made. However, Regent refused to uphold his part of the bargain. The Millets obtained an order for specific performance based upon the doctrine of part performance. The principal act relied upon by the High Court was the taking of possession of the Sefton property by the Milletts. The High Court held that this was an act permitted, but not required, to be performed by the oral contract. Nevertheless, it was, of itself, sufficient to attract the operation of the doctrine as an act in performance of the oral contract.

23.82   Acts done in *reliance* on the contract cannot be taken into account as acts in performance of the contract. Thus, in *TA Dellaca Pty Ltd v PDL Industries Ltd* [1992] 3 NZLR 88, it was held that, where a person who had agreed to take a lease of premises surrendered the lease on his former premises, the act of surrendering the lease was merely in reliance on the contract for lease and not in performance of it and did not qualify as an act of part performance.

23.83   The third matter to be established for the doctrine to apply is that the acts done must be unequivocally and in their own nature referable to a contract of the general nature of the alleged oral agreement: *McBride v Sandland* (1918) 25 CLR 69 at 78. Thus, if the acts were erecting improvements to a property, they would be consistent with an unconditional oral agreement to purchase the land, but would not be referable to an option agreement for the purchase of the land: *McBride v Sandland*. In establishing this element it is generally accepted that the court looks at the acts done and then judges to see if there is an implication of an agreement of the type alleged, rather than looking at the terms of the alleged oral agreement and judging if the acts are inconsistent with such an agreement: *McBride v Sandland* at 78; *Lighting By Design (Aust) Pty Ltd v Cannington Nominees Pty Ltd* (2008) 35 WAR 520 at 541.

23.84   A somewhat different view to that of *McBride v Sandland* is found in *Steadman v Steadman*, at AC 541–2; All ER 981–2, where Lord Reid said:

> I am aware that it has often been said that the acts relied upon must necessarily or unequivocally indicate the existence of a contract. It may well be that we should consider whether any prudent reasonable man would have done those acts if there had not been a contract but many people are neither prudent nor reasonable and they might often spend money or prejudice their position not in reliance on a contract but in the optimistic expectation that a contract would follow. So if there were a rule that acts relied on as part performance must of their own nature unequivocally show that there was a contract, it would be only in the rarest case that all other possible explanations could be excluded. In my view, unless the law is to be divorced from reason and principle, the rule must be that you take the whole circumstance, leaving aside the evidence about the oral contract, to see whether it is proved that the acts relied on were done in reliance on a contract: that will be proved if it is shown to be more probable than not.

23.85   As the High Court has not yet dealt with the issues raised by *Steadman v Steadman*, the law in Australia is that as set out in *McBride v Sandland*: *Lighting By Design (Aust) Pty Ltd v Cannington Nominees Pty Ltd* at 534–5, 538–41. In *Lighting By Design v Cannington Nominees* at 542–3, 558–66, it was held that the acts of tenants in staying on in possession of leased premises, coupled with payment of an increased rent, payment of water rates, council rates and land tax, and insuring the premises, were sufficient acts of part performance of an oral agreement for a new lease of the premises. In *Dixon v Barton* [2011] NSWSC 1525 at [144], it was confirmed that the deposit of title documents to land is prima facie an agreement to grant a mortgage over the land and that such conduct 'may be construed as a sufficient act of part performance of an implied agreement to give security so as to render the agreement capable of specific performance'.

23.86   A particular problem when considering whether particular acts amount to acts of part performance relates to the payments of money. The traditional view has been that a payment of money cannot, of itself, be an act of part performance, simply because the payment of money does not point to a particular type of contract: *Cooney v Burns* (1922) 30 CLR 216 at 222–3. Payments of money are characteristics of a wide variety of contracts. However, a payment of money combined with other factors can allow a court to find that part performance has been established: *Ciavarella v Polimeni* at [122]; *Dinh v Dang* [2007] QSC 3 at [20]. Thus, in *Francis v Francis* [1952] VLR 321 where there was an agreement for a loan, an advance of money, delivery of documents of title to the lender and an oral agreement made to give a legal mortgage as security, it was held that there were sufficient acts of part performance. The critical factor in this case was the delivery of documents of title. Without some act of that character there was nothing to give the transaction a semblance of a secured loan as opposed to an unsecured one.

23.87 Suggestions have been made in *Steadman v Steadman* that payments of money alone could amount to an act of part performance. For example, Lord Salmon, at AC 570; All ER 1006, said:

> It is no doubt true that often it is impossible to deduce even the existence of any contract from payment … Nevertheless the circumstances surrounding a payment may be such that the payment becomes evidence not only of the existence of the contract under which it was made but also of the nature of that contract. What the payment proves in the light of its surrounding circumstances is not a matter of law but a matter of fact.

23.88 However, Australian cases have consistently followed the traditional approach in relation to payments of money. Most recently, in the New South Wales Court of Appeal decision of *Khoury v Khouri* at 268, Bryson JA said:

> Acts on the land can much more readily be seen as unequivocally referable to the contract than payments of money. The anomaly of not recognising payment as an act of part performance is clear … Unless authoritatively directed to do otherwise, my view is that the Court of Appeal should apply the doctrine of part performance as it has received it, according to the terms in which it has been recognised in decisions of the High Court of Australia [in cases such as *McBride v Sandland* and *Regent v Millett*]. The unavailability of payments as acts of part performance is part of what has been so received.

23.89 In *Gerardis v Gerges* [2008] NSWSC 134, on completion of a contract for the sale of land, the vendor agreed to accept only part of the purchase price on the basis of an oral promise by the purchaser that he (the purchaser) would grant the vendor a mortgage over other land owned by the purchaser to secure eventual payment of the balance of the purchase price. The court, relying on the decision in *Khoury*, held that the vendor's completion of the sale contract was an act of part performance of the oral contract to grant a mortgage and ordered specific performance in relation to it.

THE EFFECT OF AN ORDER FOR SPECIFIC PERFORMANCE

23.90 The effect of the order for specific performance subjects the future exercise of the parties' contractual rights and obligations under the control of the court: *Singh (Sugadar) v Nazeer* [1979] Ch 474 at 480; [1978] 3 All ER 817 at 821–2. Thus, if equitable relief is actually ordered but compliance with it becomes impossible, and a party seeks alternative relief, that party must first have the order for specific performance vacated by the court. In *Sunbird Plaza Pty Ltd v Maloney* (1988) 166 CLR 245 at 258–60; 77 ALR 205 at 210–12, the High Court explained that a plaintiff for specific performance could not proceed to termination of a contract while an order for specific performance was still in force, simply because the defendant is, until the order is vacated, required to comply with the order and perform the relevant contractual obligation.

23.91 A dissenting voice on this issue is that of Meagher JA, who, in *Aarons v Advance Commercial Finance Ltd* (1995) NSWConvR 55–746 at 55,759, opined that the views of the High Court in *Sunbird Plaza* constituted a 'farouche proposition' for which there was no justification on the basis that an order for specific performance does not cause the contract to merge in the order, and that, therefore, the parties' contractual rights, including the right to terminate, remain unaffected. In *Dunworth v Mirvac Qld Pty Ltd* [2011] QCA 200, the Court of Appeal in Queensland unanimously followed the decision in *Sunbird Plaza Pty Ltd v Maloney*, although McMurdo J, at 57 (Dalton J agreeing), observed that there was 'particular force' in Meagher JA's criticism. However, in *Hamdan v Widodo [No 2]* [2010] WASC 6 at [121], following a lengthy and detailed analysis of cases on this issue, Johnson J said:

> In my view, there exists both binding and persuasive authority that, when an order has been made for specific performance, whether in general or specific terms, but the order has not been implemented, leave of the court is required if a party seeks to rescind the contract and also when a party seeks to implement that order in a way that is without the consent of the other party or is not the subject of a specific direction of the court. In my view, leave is required and the court must exercise its discretion taking into account the particular circumstances which apply.

24

INJUNCTIONS

INTRODUCTION

24.1 Injunctions are orders made by the courts either restraining or requiring performance of a specific act in order to give effect to the legal rights of the applicant. As such, they are 'practical tools in the administration of justice': *Orleans Investments Pty Ltd v Mindshare Communications Ltd* (2009) 254 ALR 81 at 110. An injunction that prevents a course of action is said to be prohibitive in nature, and this is the traditional essence of injunctive relief — it commands cessation of a wrongful act. Somewhat rarer, yet not too distant from this core principle, are mandatory injunctions that compel some behaviour of the person to whom they are directed. In cases where mandatory injunctions are granted it is clear that the defendant, while not positively engaged in wrongful conduct, has nevertheless, by a failure or omission to act, infringed upon the rights of the applicant. In commanding the doing of an act by such a defendant, the court is in effect commanding the harmful dormancy to cease. In this way, the two basic natures of injunctive relief — prohibitive and mandatory — may be seen as clearly related to a central principle.

24.2 A fundamental principle of the law relating to injunctions is that they should be expressed with precision. Thus, in *Attorney-General v Punch Ltd* [2003] 1 AC 1046 at 1055; [2003] 1 All ER 289 at 297–8, Lord Nicholls of Birkenhead said:

> An ... injunction, must be expressed in terms which are clear and certain. The injunction must define precisely what acts are prohibited. The court must ensure that the language of its order makes it plain what is permitted and what is prohibited. This is a well established, soundly based principle. A person should not be put at risk of being in contempt of court by an ambiguous prohibition, or a prohibition the scope of which is obviously open to dispute.

However, '[e]xcessively narrow formalism in framing the injunction may wreak its own injustice': *Maggbury Pty Ltd v Hafele Australia Pty Ltd* (2001) 210 CLR 181 at 220; 185 ALR 152 at 181. Thus, in *Orleans Investments v Mindshare Communications* at 110, Giles JA said:

> There are limits to the precision and clarity which can be attained ... [A plaintiff] should not suffer an injustice through undue insistence on precise statement of what the [defendant] must do or not do.

24.3 The origins of injunctive relief are found in equity's exclusive jurisdiction where it was used solely in support of equitable rights. But equity soon developed an auxiliary jurisdiction through which it offered more flexible forms of relief when those of the common law proved to be inadequate. Thus, in particular circumstances, injunctive relief is available to restrain breaches of contract, tortious wrongs and an array of other conduct that infringes upon rights recognised by the common law. In addition to the exclusive and auxiliary jurisdictions of equity to order injunctions, the common law courts were granted the ability to do the same through statutory reform enacted in the *Common Law Procedure Act 1854* (UK) which provided a distinct jurisdiction from both the exclusive and auxiliary operations of equity. It was narrower than the exclusive jurisdiction in that it did not enable the common law courts to issue injunctions in respect of equitable rights, nor did it enable the making of quia timet injunctions: see 24.54–24.58. At the same time, it was seen as wider than equity's auxiliary jurisdiction as there was no requirement of either a proprietary interest or inadequacy of damages: see 24.13–24.19.

24.4   With the introduction of the judicature system, the question arose as to the impact of the Australian equivalents of s 25(8) of the *Judicature Act 1873* (UK)[1] on these three jurisdictions to grant injunctive relief. Section 25(8) stipulated as follows:

> [A]n injunction may be granted or a receiver appointed by an interlocutory order of the court in all cases in which it shall appear to the court to be just or convenient that such order should be made; and any such order may be made either unconditionally or upon such terms and conditions as the court thinks just.

24.5   It will be recalled (see Chapter 3) that the widely acknowledged effect of the judicature system introduced in the 1870s was simply to enable a single court to administer both equity and common law. The reforms did not merge those two branches of the law into one contained body. However, the presence of s 25(8), with its simple criterion of justice or convenience, led some to the view that the previous jurisdictional boundaries had been eradicated by the reforming legislation: *Beddow v Beddow* (1878) 9 Ch D 89 at 92–3. This approach has been firmly rejected by a series of authoritative pronouncements commencing with *North London Railway Co v Great Northern Railway Co* (1883) 11 QBD 30. The High Court of Australia has shared in this rejection of any reading of s 25(8) that suggests that the courts have a general jurisdiction to order injunctions: *Mayfair Trading Co Pty Ltd v Dreyer* (1958) 101 CLR 428 at 454; *Australian Broadcasting Corporation v Lenah Game Meats Pty Ltd* (2001) 208 CLR 199 at 240, 269–70, 310–12; 185 ALR 1 at 24, 48, 81–3.

24.6   Thus, the fused administration generally, and the words of s 25(8) specifically, did not have the effect of abolishing the tripartite classification of jurisdiction to grant injunctions. This should not be seen as surprising — the arrival of the *Common Law Procedure Act 1854* (UK), granting the common law courts power to order injunctions, had not obliterated, in whole or part, the existence of the auxiliary jurisdiction at equity, nor lessened its ability to offer relief for common law wrongs where damages were inadequate. Indeed, Meagher, Heydon and Leeming[2] comment that the common law injunction has been surprisingly under-utilised in respect of actions such as breach

---

1.   *Supreme Court Act 1970* (NSW) s 66; *Supreme Court Act 1979* (NT) s 69; *Supreme Court Act 1995* (Qld) s 246; *Supreme Court Act 1935* (SA) s 29; *Supreme Court Civil Procedure Act 1932* (Tas) s 11(12); *Supreme Court Act 1986* (Vic) s 37; *Supreme Court Act 1935* (WA) s 25(9). In the Australian Capital Territory, the equivalent of s 25(8), set out in s 34 of the *Supreme Court Act 1933* (ACT), was repealed in 2006.
2.   R Meagher, J D Heydon & M Leeming, *Meaher, Gummow and Lehane's Equity: Doctrines and Remedies*, 4th ed, LexisNexis Butterworths, Sydney, 2002, p 715.

of contract, which have continued to be dealt with by equity in its auxiliary capacity. Thus, the three jurisdictions existed independently prior to 1873, and that situation was not altered by the ability after that time for a single court to exercise any one of them in granting injunctive relief that was most appropriate for the particular circumstances of the case before it.

INJUNCTIONS PROTECT RIGHTS

24.7   Injunctive relief will not be ordered if there has been no violation of the plaintiff's rights: *North London Railway Co v Great Northern Railway Co* (1883) 11 QBD 30 at 40. Thus, in the context of an application for an interlocutory injunction, in *Australian Broadcasting Corporation v O'Neill* (2006) 227 CLR 57 at 78; 229 ALR 457 at 475, Gummow and Hayne JJ said that 'where an interlocutory injunction is sought, it is necessary to identify the legal (including statutory) or equitable rights which are to be determined at the trial and in respect of which final relief is sought'. A number of cases demonstrate this essential point.

24.8   In *Victoria Park Racing and Recreation Grounds Company Ltd v Taylor* (1937) 58 CLR 479, the facts concerned the calling of horse races over the radio by a person who had erected a tower tall enough to observe the racecourse from an adjoining property. The racecourse owners sought an injunction to prevent the broadcasts, which they believed were affecting their attendance figures. The High Court denied the remedy on the basis that the defendant's actions, while they may have had the effect of reducing attendance figures, were not in any way illegal as they did not constitute a trespass. This decision was later echoed in *Australian Broadcasting Corporation v Lenah Game Meats Pty Ltd* (2001) 208 CLR 199; 185 ALR 1, where Lenah Game Meats was unable to obtain an injunction restraining the ABC from broadcasting potentially damaging images which it had obtained through a third party's trespass of Lenah Game Meats' 'brush tail possum processing facility'. Despite the illegal origins of the film footage, Lenah Game Meats was unable to point to any legal or equitable right which would be infringed by the broadcaster's transmission. Consequently, there was no jurisdiction for the court to make an order preventing the broadcast from taking place.

24.9   In *Thorne v British Broadcasting Corporation* [1967] 2 All ER 1225, Thorne was denied injunctive relief aimed at preventing the broadcasting by the BBC of what Thorne claimed were anti-German programs. The Court of Appeal held that no legal right of Thorne's had been infringed, and that the same result would follow even if the BBC's activities happened to constitute an offence under British anti-racial hatred legislation.

24.10   Finally, in *Paton v Trustees of British Pregnancy Advisory Service* [1979] QB 276; [1978] 2 All ER 987, an injunction was refused to a father who sought to prevent his wife having a legal abortion. The court made its ruling in this case on the basis that the father had no legal right at law or in equity to prevent the abortion and thus no rights of his would be violated by the wife having an abortion.

THE EXCLUSIVE AND AUXILIARY JURISDICTIONS

24.11   Injunctions granted in aid of equitable rights (such as the equitable obligation of confidence or a beneficiary's rights under a trust) are said to be awarded in equity's exclusive jurisdiction. Injunctions granted in aid of common law rights (such as the restraint of breaches of contract or tortious wrongs) or statutory rights are said to be awarded in equity's auxiliary jurisdiction. The distinction is important because with injunctions in the auxiliary jurisdiction, a plaintiff must first establish that damages at common law are an inadequate remedy, and, second, it may be the case in some situations that he or she must also show that the right being protected is a proprietary right.

24.12 However, in the exclusive jurisdiction, neither the inadequacy of damages nor the proprietary nature of the plaintiff's right are relevant in assessing whether the injunction should be granted.

Inadequacy of damages

24.13 As with the remedy of specific performance in relation to a contract, where the court has no jurisdiction to award the remedy unless damages at common law are inadequate (see 23.14–23.39), so too with injunctions in aid of common law rights in equity's auxiliary jurisdiction: *Lucas Stuart Pty Ltd v Hemmes Hermitage Pty Ltd* [2010] NSWCA 283 at [10]. The applicable guiding principles are the same here as with specific performance. In *Hatfield v TCN Channel Nine Pty Ltd* (2010) 77 NSWLR 506 at 536, Young JA observed that the modern formulation of the inadequacy of damages test was found in the judgment of Sachs LJ in *Evans Marshall & Co Ltd v Bertola SA* [1973] 1 All ER 992 at 1005, where his Lordship said that the question to be asked in this context is: '[I]s it just, in all the circumstances, that a plaintiff should be confined to his remedy in damages?'

24.14 Two cases illustrate the working of this principle in the context of injunctions. In *Aristoc Industries Pty Ltd v R A Wenham (Builders) Pty Ltd* [1965] NSWR 581, Aristoc, pursuant to a subcontract with a builder, delivered certain chairs that it had manufactured for installation at a new hall being built at the Royal Prince Alfred Hospital in Sydney. Before they were installed, it became clear that Aristoc would not be paid due to the builder's financial difficulties. Aristoc sought an injunction against Wenham, the assignee of the builder's contract, to restrain Wenham from in any way dealing with the chairs or obstructing Aristoc's attempt to recover possession of the chairs. Jacobs J held that damages at common law were inadequate in this case. Aristoc was more likely to be better off by recovering possession of and then disposing of the chairs than it was by pursuing any tortious remedy it might have had in relation to them. This was so because there would have been no remedy in detinue if the chairs had been fixed to the hall's floor, and, if the remedy of conversion had been pursued, damages would have been relatively low given that the chairs were custom made for the hospital hall.

24.15 In *Graham v K D Morris & Sons Pty Ltd* [1974] Qd R 1, Morris was building a significant construction on adjoining land owned by Graham. A crane on the building site was left to rotate freely and, when the wind blew in a certain direction, its jib encroached over Graham's property and was suspended over the roof of her house. Campbell J held that the invasion of Graham's airspace constituted a trespass and that damages at common law were inadequate because the danger of the jib suspended over Graham's house was very real and would last for 18 months until the construction work was completed. The trespass would also negatively impact on the sale price Graham could get if she wished to sell her home during that time. Morris argued that the grant of the injunction would constitute hardship because it would have to dismantle the crane at considerable expense. His Honour rejected this defence on the basis that the positioning of the crane stemmed from Morris's negligence and its cavalier attitude towards the building project.

The requirement of a proprietary right

24.16   In *Attorney-General v Sheffield Gas Consumers Co* (1853) 43 ER 119 at 125, Turner LJ, in refusing to grant an injunction, said that '[i]t is on the ground of injury to property that the injunction of this court must rest'. However, in *Cardile v LED Builders Pty Ltd* (1999) 198 CLR 380 at 395; 162 ALR 294 at 304, the High Court held that there is no general requirement that the right must be proprietary before injunctive relief can be granted.

24.17   It is clearly the case that injunctions are granted in various cases where it cannot be said that there is any proprietary right involved. Thus, in the context of statutory prohibitions (*Cooney v Council of the Municipality of Ku-ring-gai* (1963) 114 CLR 582) and statutory rights (*Bradley v The Commonwealth* (1973) 128 CLR 557; 1 ALR 241), there is no proprietary right requirement. Furthermore, injunctions in aid of contractual rights involving no proprietary rights have been granted in accordance with the seminal decision of *Lumley v Wagner* (1852) 42 ER 687: see 24.63.

24.18   It can be noted that the lack of a proprietary right in the plaintiff has been the traditional basis upon which injunctions have been denied in some situations, such as with the tort of trespass to the person. However, even in such situations the law is changing. Thus, in *Parry v Crooks* (1981) 27 SASR 1 at 7, Bray CJ, in the context of granting injunctive relief in relation to the tort of assault, noted that even though injunctive relief in torts was historically confined to cases affecting proprietary rights, there was now no principled reason why the power to grant an injunction should not be available with respect to all torts.

24.19   Most commentators now agree that the availability of injunctive relief in equity's auxiliary jurisdiction is not limited to the protection of legal rights that are proprietary in nature. A more accurate statement as to the relevance of the proprietary nature of the right in question is given by Spry when he writes as follows:

> [A]lthough it is incorrect to assert that an injunction can be obtained only in aid of property or in aid of a proprietary right, there are cases where in the particular circumstances the only possible reason for equitable intervention happens to lie in the support of what may be described as a proprietary right.[3]

What is meant by this is that in some cases the proprietary interest will indeed be crucial because without it there will simply be no right at all. For example, in the case of trespass to property, a plaintiff cannot obtain injunctive relief in the absence of a proprietary right in the property.

CLASSIFICATION OF INJUNCTIONS

24.20   There are a number of ways in which injunctions can be classified. First, they can be classified as mandatory or prohibitory injunctions, and, second, as interlocutory or perpetual injunctions. Furthermore, an injunction that is granted before there has been any infringement of the plaintiff's rights is classified as a quia timet injunction. It is necessary to examine each of these classifications in more detail.

---

3.   I C F Spry, *The Principles of Equitable Remedies*, 7th ed, Lawbook Co, Sydney, 2007, p 340.

MANDATORY AND PROHIBITORY INJUNCTIONS

24.21 The distinction between mandatory and prohibitory injunctions relates to whether the injunction commands some positive act to be done — the mandatory injunction — or whether it restrains or forbids conduct — the prohibitory injunction. In practice, the prohibitory injunction is the one most commonly sought.

Mandatory restorative injunctions

24.22 There are two types of mandatory injunctions. The first is the mandatory restorative injunction, which compels the defendant to repair the consequences of some wrongful act that he or she has committed. In order to obtain such an injunction, the plaintiff must show that, had the wrongful act not occurred but was merely threatened, he or she would have obtained a prohibitory injunction in relation to the apprehended wrong. For example, in a situation where a house has been built in contravention of statutory planning approval requirements, a mandatory restorative injunction will be granted requiring the defendant to demolish it, provided that the plaintiff can establish that he or she would have obtained a prohibitory injunction — before the house was built — preventing the defendant from building it.

24.23 Mandatory restorative injunctions were considered by the House of Lords in *Redland Bricks Ltd v Morris* [1970] AC 652; [1969] 2 All ER 576. In that case, Morris carried on a business as a market gardener. On adjoining land Redland Bricks conducted a quarrying business which caused subsidence to Morris's land. As part of his claim against Redland Bricks, Morris sought a mandatory injunction to have the land restored to its original state. The cost of doing so was £30,000, whereas the future damage to Morris, if no injunction was granted, amounted to £1500. The House of Lords declined to grant the injunction. Lord Upjohn, at AC 665–6; All ER 579–80, observed that in granting mandatory injunctions, each case depended very much on its own circumstances. With the facts of this case very much in mind, his Lordship then set out the principles to be applied. First, it must be shown that there is a 'very strong probability on the facts that grave damage will accrue to [the plaintiff] in the future'. Second, damages at common law have to be inadequate. Third, the cost to the defendant of preventing future occurrences needs to be taken into account, so that if he or she has acted 'wantonly' or 'unreasonably' the injunction can be granted even if the cost of remedial work is out of proportion to the actual gain flowing to the plaintiff from such expenditure being incurred. However, if the defendant has acted 'reasonably', the cost of complying with the injunction and the hardship it creates for the defendant must be weighed up against the loss suffered by the plaintiff. Fourth, the injunction, if granted, must be clearly worded so that 'the defendant knows exactly in fact what he has to do'.

24.24 Lord Upjohn's guidelines in *Redland Bricks v Morris* have not escaped critical analysis and the chief concern is that much of what is presented in the specific context of mandatory restorative injunctions is actually generic to all injunctions. While this is not true of his first principle — the need for a 'very strong probability of grave damage' — its accuracy, even in the context of mandatory restorative injunctions, may be doubted. As Meagher, Heydon and Leeming observe, such a requirement is not necessary where a mandatory injunction is granted ordering the defendant to remove trespassory hoardings.[4]

---

4. Meagher et al, *Equity: Doctrines and Remedies*, note 2 above, p 810.

24.25 In *Jessica Estates Pty Ltd v Lennard* [2007] NSWSC 1434 at [22], in the context of granting a mandatory restorative injunction where the defendant had almost completed the construction of a house in violation of a restrictive covenant, Brereton J said:

> Factors relevant to the exercise of the Court's discretion in this respect include the defendant's knowledge of the wrongful nature of his or her acts; whether the defendant has hastened the completion of the wrongful acts so as to steal a march on the Court (or the plaintiff); the hardship which would be caused to the plaintiff by the refusal of an injunction; the hardship which would be caused to the defendant by the grant of an injunction; and the extent to which the injuries suffered by the plaintiff are compensable by an award for damages.[5]

Mandatory enforcing injunctions

24.26 The second type of mandatory injunction is the mandatory enforcing injunction, which compels the defendant to do some positive act that he or she has promised to do for valuable consideration. In such cases the court will need to be satisfied that the agreement is specifically enforceable and that, in all the circumstances, it is just and equitable to grant the injunction: *Burns Philp Trust Co Pty Ltd v Kwikasair Freightlines Ltd* (1963) 63 SR (NSW) 492 at 496. In *Businessworld Computers Pty Ltd v Australasian Telecommunications Commission* (1988) 82 ALR 499 at 501, it was observed that courts will be extremely reluctant to grant a mandatory enforcing injunction if the agreement would not also have attracted the remedy of specific performance.

PERPETUAL AND INTERLOCUTORY INJUNCTIONS

Perpetual injunctions

24.27 Injunctions can also be classified according to the period of time for which the order is to remain in force. A perpetual injunction is the injunction granted after a full hearing of the claim on its merits. Because the merits of the case have been argued, the perpetual injunction is intended to finally settle relations between the parties. A perpetual injunction is not necessarily one that will remain permanently in place. In some cases it will of necessity be confined to a particular period of time. For example, with injunctions enforcing a valid restraint of trade, the maximum time that the injunction can remain in force is the term of the restraint.

Interlocutory injunctions

24.28 An interlocutory injunction is a provisional order made at an early stage in the proceedings before the court has had the opportunity to assess the merits of the application. Generally, interlocutory injunctions are expressed to be in force until the trial of the action or further order of the court. The term 'interim injunction' is often used interchangeably with interlocutory injunction. However, there is a technical difference between the two, in that an interim injunction is more temporary than an interlocutory injunction, and is usually expressed to remain in force until a specified date prior to the final hearing. Thus, in *Commonwealth of Australia v John Fairfax*

---

5. On appeal, the decision in this case was overruled on the ground that the restrictive covenant had not been breached. However, the Court of Appeal indicated that, had there been a breach of the restrictive covenant, the injunction had been properly granted: *Lennard v Jessica Estates Pty Ltd* (2008) 71 NSWLR 306.

& Sons Ltd (1980) 32 ALR 485, the plaintiff obtained an ex parte (see 24.30) interim injunction on 9 November 1980 that remained in force until 11 November 1980. On that date the defendant entered an appearance and the court granted an interlocutory injunction pending a final hearing of the matter.

24.29 An interlocutory injunction does not involve a trial on the merits of the case, since it is a temporary order that remains in effect until the merits of the case are fully argued and assessed by the court. It is here that the principal dilemma about interlocutory injunctions becomes apparent. In *Films Rover International Ltd v Cannon Film Sales Ltd* [1986] 3 All ER 772 at 780–1, Hoffmann J put it as follows:

> The principal dilemma about the grant of interlocutory injunctions, whether prohibitory or mandatory, is that there is by definition a risk that the court may make the 'wrong' decision, in the sense of granting an injunction to a party who fails to establish his right at the trial (or would fail if there was a trial) or alternatively, in failing to grant an injunction to a party who succeeds (or would succeed) at trial. A fundamental principle is therefore that the court should take whichever course appears to carry the lower risk of injustice if it should turn out to have been 'wrong' in the sense I have described.

24.30 In general, interlocutory injunctions will only be granted after notice of the application has been given to the defendant, so that the defendant has the opportunity to resist the claim. Thus, the hearing of such application is usually 'inter partes'. However, in urgent cases, interlocutory or interim injunctions can be granted in the absence of the defendant, or 'ex parte', as occurred initially in *Commonwealth of Australia v John Fairfax & Sons Ltd*. In *Orpen v Tarantello* [2009] VSC 143 at [27], Beach J listed the following principles that are applicable in relation to seeking an ex parte injunction:

(a) First, the duty owed by a plaintiff seeking an ex parte order is to place before the Court all material facts and matters.

(b) Secondly, the duty is an absolute one, owed to the Court.

(c) Thirdly, the disclosure of all material facts must be both full and fair.

(d) Fourthly, it is no excuse for a plaintiff to say he was not aware of the importance of a particular material fact.

(e) Fifthly, a party fails in this obligation 'unless he supplies the place of the absent party to the extent of bringing forward all the material facts which that party would presumably have brought forward in his defence to that application': *Thomas A. Edison Limited v Bullock* (1912) 12 CLR 679 at 681–2.

(f) Sixthly, materiality is to be decided by the Court, and not by the assessment of the plaintiff or his legal advisers.

24.31 The significance of interlocutory injunctions should not be underestimated. This is so because the fate of an application for interlocutory relief, more often than not, resolves the dispute between the parties. The vast majority of cases never proceed to a final hearing of the dispute. The parties usually accept the prima facie view of the court given at the interlocutory stage or settle their dispute: *Fellowes v Fisher* [1976] QB 122 at 129; [1975] 2 All ER 829 at 833. However, the very circumstances of a case will, in some instances, mean that it will, in practical terms, be resolved at the interlocutory stage. In this context, in *NWL Limited v Woods* [1979] 3 All ER 614 at 626, Lord Diplock said:

Where ... the grant or refusal of the interlocutory injunction will have the practical effect of putting an end to the action because the harm which will have been already caused to the losing party by its grant or its refusal is complete and of a kind for which money cannot constitute any worthwhile recompense, the degree of likelihood that the plaintiff would have succeeded in establishing his right to an injunction if the action had gone to trial is a factor to be brought into the balance by the judge in weighing the risks that injustice may result from his deciding the application one way rather than the other.

24.32 In considering whether an interlocutory injunction should be granted, the court must apply the test set out in *Beecham Group Ltd v Bristol Laboratories Pty Ltd* (1968) 118 CLR 618 at 622–3, where the High Court noted that the following two requirements had to be satisfied:

The first is whether the plaintiff has made out a prima facie case, in the sense that if the evidence remains as it is there is a probability that at the trial of the action the plaintiff will be held entitled to relief ... The second inquiry is ... whether the inconvenience or injury which the plaintiff would be likely to suffer if an injunction were refused outweighs or is outweighed by the injury which the defendant would suffer if an injunction were granted.

Prima facie case

24.33 In relation to the prima facie case requirement, the High Court in *Beecham Group v Bristol Laboratories*, at 622, said:

How strong the probability needs to be depends, no doubt, upon the nature of the rights [the plaintiff] asserts and the practical consequences likely to flow from the order he seeks.

24.34 The prima facie case requirement was discussed in *Shercliff v Engadine Acceptance Corporation Pty Ltd* [1978] 1 NSWLR 729 at 735–7, where Mahoney JA noted the following points: (i) it did not mean a finding that at trial the plaintiff would win; (ii) the term prima facie is used in the sense of 'likelihood', and does not refer to a prediction, but rather to the nature of the plaintiff's case; (iii) the term 'prima facie' may mean something less than 'more likely than not', and there is no requirement that the plaintiff must show a 'better than even' chance of ultimate success; and (iv) a prima facie case must always be established, irrespective of whether the second test of balance of convenience favours the grant of interlocutory relief.

24.35 In various cases judges use the expression 'serious question to be tried' rather than 'prima facie case'. Thus, in *Australian Broadcasting Corporation v O'Neill* (2006) at CLR 68; ALR 466, Gleeson CJ and Crennan J observed that a plaintiff had to establish 'that there is a serious question to be tried as to the plaintiff's entitlement to relief'. The use of the 'serious question to be tried' formulation stems from a passage in *American Cyanamid Co v Ethicon Ltd* [1975] AC 396 at 407; [1975] 1 All ER 504 at 510, where Lord Diplock said:

The use of such expressions as 'a probability', 'a prima facie case', or 'a strong prima facie case' in the context of the exercise of a discretionary power to grant an interlocutory injunction leads to confusion as to the object sought to be achieved by this form of temporary relief. The court no doubt must be satisfied that the claim is not frivolous or vexatious; in other words, that there is a serious question to be tried.

24.36   This passage suggests that the first requirement to be met for the grant of an interlocutory injunction will be satisfied if the plaintiff's claim is not frivolous or vexatious. This suggestion was emphatically rejected by Gummow and Hayne JJ in *Australian Broadcasting Corporation v O'Neill* at CLR 84; ALR 479. Earlier, their Honours, at CLR 83; ALR 479, said that there is no objection to the use of the 'serious question to be tried' formulation provided that it is understood as conveying the notion that the seriousness of the question, like the strength of the probability referred to in *Beecham v Bristol Laboratories*, depends upon the considerations emphasised in *Beecham Group v Bristol Laboratories*.

The balance of convenience

24.37   In relation to the 'balance of convenience' requirement, the court must weigh up the comparative injury that will arise from granting or withholding an injunction pending trial of the action, seeking out the major risk of damage and, in particular, of any irreparable damage, and, in some cases, evaluating the strength of the plaintiff's case for final relief: *Samsung Electronics Co Ltd v Apple Inc* (2011) 286 ALR 257 at 276–9. In *Cayne v Global Natural Resources plc* [1984] 1 All ER 225 at 237, this aspect was referred to as 'the balance of the risk of doing an injustice'. In assessing the risk of damage, it does not matter that, at the stage of the interlocutory application, the plaintiff has suffered no damage, provided that actual damage will reasonably result if the interlocutory injunction is not granted: *Swimsure (Laboratories) Pty Ltd v McDonald* [1979] 2 NSWLR 796.

24.38   The strength of the plaintiff's case will often be of importance in weighing up the balance of convenience. In *Kolback Securities Limited v Epoch Mining NL* (1987) 8 NSWLR 533 at 535–6, McClelland J said:

> [T]here are some kinds of case in which for the purpose of seeing where lies the balance of convenience … it is desirable for the Court to evaluate the strength of the plaintiff's case for final relief. One class of case to which this applies is where the decision to grant or refuse an interlocutory injunction will in a practical sense determine the substance of the matter in issue.

24.39   In *Hermescec v Carcagni* [2008] NSWSC 183, Hermescec purchased an Italian restaurant in Newcastle — the Benevenuti — from Carcagni. Soon thereafter, Carcagni opened up a competing Italian restaurant — the Grifone — a short distance away from the Benevenuti. Hermescec claimed that this constituted a breach of a covenant in restraint of trade that was agreed to when Carcagni sold his restaurant. He initiated proceedings for an injunction to enforce the restraint. Even though Hermescec established that he had a strong case against Carcagni, the application for an interlocutory injunction failed on the grounds of the balance of convenience. On this issue, Barrett J, at [21]–[23], said:

> If an interlocutory injunction is granted, Grifone would have to close down pending the court's final decision on the entitlement of [Hermescec] to relief by way of permanent injunction or damages or both. That would be a drastic result. If Grifone were able to stay open with an injunction in place, it could only be on the basis that the company of which [Carcagni] is sole shareholder and director was no longer the operator and [Carcagni] himself was no longer the manager. On [Carcagni's] evidence, such a situation would be impossible to achieve in any real sense, given that Grifone is in substance a one-man business operated by [Carcagni], albeit

with the assistance of employees. The practical result of an interlocutory injunction would be suspension of [Carcagni's] Grifone business … [T]his is a case in which any injunction pending trial would produce the very result to be put in issue at a final hearing. Such an interlocutory injunction would affect rights in a permanent fashion on evidence which may be supplemented and may be found to bear some different complexion at the trial. At this stage, therefore, 'the balance of the risk of doing injustice' favours [Carcagni], even though the prospects that he will in due course be subjected to a permanent injunction and also be ordered to pay damages and costs appear, at least at this stage, to be strong.

24.40   Particular note can be made of the granting of interlocutory mandatory injunctions and interlocutory injunctions in the context of defamation.

24.41   The concern with interlocutory mandatory injunctions is reflected in the following observations of Gummow J in *Businessworld Computers Pty Ltd v Australian Telecommunications Commission* at 502–3:

[M]andatory injunctions generally carry a higher risk of injustice if granted at the interlocutory stage [because]: they usually go further than the preservation of the status quo by requiring a party to take some new positive step or undo what he has done in the past; an order requiring a party to take positive steps usually causes more waste of time and money if it turns out to have been wrongly granted than an order which merely causes delay by restraining him from doing something which it appears at the trial he was entitled to do; a mandatory order usually gives a party the whole of the relief which he claims in the writ and makes it unlikely that there will be a trial … An order requiring someone to do something is usually perceived as a more intrusive exercise of the coercive power of the state than an order requiring him temporarily to refrain from action. The court is therefore more reluctant to make such an order against a party who has not had the protection of a full hearing at trial.

24.42   For some time it was said that a plaintiff seeking an interlocutory mandatory injunction would need to show that there was a 'high degree of assurance' that he or she would succeed at trial: *Shepherd Homes Ltd v Sandham* [1971] Ch 340 at 351; [1970] 3 All ER 402 at 412. This approach has been recently reaffirmed in England: *AMEC Group Ltd v Universal Steels (Scotland) Ltd* [2009] EWHC 560 (TCC) at [5]–[9]; *Assetco Plc v Shannon* [2011] EWHC 816 (Ch) at [15]. However, in Australia this requirement has been rejected. In *Tymbook Pty Ltd v State of Victoria* [2006] VSCA 89 at [33]–[35], after reviewing all the authorities, the Victorian Court of Appeal said:

In our view, it is desirable that a single test be applied in all cases where an interlocutory injunction is sought. There is nothing in the body of authority to which we have referred, nor any consideration of principle, which requires a special test to be applied to one sub-category of such injunction applications, namely, those where mandatory relief is sought … On the contrary … a mandatory interlocutory injunction may be justified in a particular case notwithstanding that the court does not feel the requisite 'high degree of assurance' … In our view … whether the relief sought is prohibitory or mandatory, the court should take whichever course appears to carry the lower risk of injustice if it should turn out to have been 'wrong', in the sense of granting an injunction to a party who fails to establish his right at the trial, or in failing to grant an injunction to a party who succeeds at trial.

24.43   In *Burke v Frasers Lorne Pty Ltd* [2008] NSWSC 988 at [4], Brereton J said that 'the same considerations apply to an interlocutory mandatory injunction as to any other interlocutory injunction, although the mandatory nature of the relief sought, and the potential consequences if it later be undone, is often telling on [the issue of] the balance of convenience'. In this case an interlocutory mandatory injunction was granted requiring the defendant to restore an asphalt surface to a driveway that had been removed by the defendant and replaced with reinforced turf. Brereton J held that the balance of convenience favoured the injunction being granted. A significant factor in the decision was the fact that the plaintiff had what his Honour, at [44], described as a 'very strongly arguable case for final relief'.

24.44   In defamation cases the principles applicable to interlocutory injunctions are exercised with exceptional caution: *Bonnard v Perryman* [1891] 2 Ch 269 at 284–5; *Hatfield v TCN Channel Nine Pty Ltd* at 522–3. Thus, in *Jakudo Pty Ltd v South Australian Telecasters Ltd* (1997) 69 SASR 440 at 442–443, Doyle CJ said:

> The reason why interlocutory injunctions are rarely granted in respect of defamatory material is … that the courts have recognised the substantial public interest in the free discussion of matters of public or general interest. That means that when the balance of convenience comes to be weighed, the public interest in free discussion of matters of public or general interest weighs heavily against the grant of an injunction. Particularly will this be so if the defendant puts forward material which shows that there are reasonable grounds to think that a defence of justification may succeed … When the real issue is not whether the words are defamatory, but that of justification, the plaintiff will have shown that there is a serious question to be tried as to the plaintiff's entitlement to relief. But, if there are reasonable grounds to suppose that a defence of justification may succeed that, coupled with the substantial public interest in the free discussion of matters of public and general interest, will usually mean that the balance of convenience is in favour of the refusal of a grant of an injunction.

24.45   In the High Court in *Australian Broadcasting Corporation v O'Neill* at CLR 68–9; ALR 466–7, Gleeson CJ and Crennan J, after approving of the above comments and referring to the basic principles governing the granting of interlocutory injunctions, said:

> In the context of a defamation case, the application of those organising principles will require particular attention to the considerations which courts have identified as dictating caution. Foremost among those considerations is the public interest in free speech. A further consideration is that, in the defamation context, the outcome of a trial is especially likely to turn upon issues that are, by hypothesis, unresolved. Where one such issue is justification, it is commonly an issue for jury decision. In addition, the plaintiff's general character may be found to be such that, even if the publication is defamatory, only nominal damages will be awarded.

24.46   In this case the ABC proposed to broadcast a television program which suggested that O'Neill was involved in the disappearance or possible murder of missing children and that he was a multiple murderer. His application for an interlocutory injunction to restrain the broadcasting of the program was rejected by a majority of the High Court.[6]

---

6.   For an analysis of this case and a discussion of interlocutory injunctions in defamation cases see D Rolph, 'Showing Restraint: Interlocutory Injunctions in Defamation Cases' (2009) 14 *Media and Arts Law Review* 255.

Undertaking as to damages

24.47   A usual condition of granting an interlocutory injunction is that the plaintiff gives an undertaking as to damages. The undertaking is given to and, where necessary, enforced by the court: *European Bank Limited v Evans* (2010) 240 CLR 432 at 438–9; 264 ALR 1 at 5.

24.48   The undertaking operates as a protection to the defendant or any other person affected by the operation of the injunction, should the court later rule that the interlocutory injunction should not have been granted. The undertaking binds the plaintiff to compensate the defendant or other person for any damage suffered by the defendant or other person on account of the granting of the interlocutory injunction. In relator proceedings (see 24.78–24.81), the undertaking is given by the relator, not the Attorney-General. In exceptional circumstances the court can dispense with the requirement of the undertaking as to damages: *Attorney-General v Albany Hotel Co* [1896] 2 Ch 696 at 700.

24.49   A critical issue with undertakings is their worth or value. Thus, in *Cambridge Credit Corporation Ltd v Surfers' Paradise Forests Ltd* [1977] Qd R 261, an undertaking given by an insolvent company that was in receivership was taken to be worthless and interlocutory relief was denied. However, the interlocutory injunction will be granted if a satisfactory third person provides the undertaking. It may be the case that the defendant or third party may also have to provide adequate security so as to ensure that the undertaking is not rendered worthless or less valuable by subsequent events leading up to the final hearing of the matter.

24.50   In enforcing the undertaking, the defendant must show that the granting of the interlocutory injunction was *the* cause, and not merely *a* cause, of the loss. In *Air Express Ltd v Ansett Transport Industries (Operations) Pty Ltd* (1981) 146 CLR 249, interlocutory injunctions were obtained restraining the issue of air freight permits to Air Express. The injunctions were subsequently discontinued after a hearing of the case on its merits. Air Express failed to recover damages for losses incurred by not having the permits issued. This was because the majority of the High Court held that the non-issue of the permits was not caused by the granting of the interlocutory injunctions but because the government would not have issued the permits until the dispute between the parties had been heard on its merits. Thus, it was the litigation itself, rather than the interlocutory injunction, that caused the loss. In effect, what the High Court was saying was that, even if the interlocutory injunction had not been granted, no permits would have been issued until such time as Ansett's challenge to the proposed government action was determined.

24.51   In adjudicating on a claim for compensation pursuant to an undertaking as to damages, 'the court is giving equitable relief. The undertaking is given to the court, not to the defendant and a defendant or third party has no right to compensation unless the court, in its discretion, considers it conscionable that there should be compensation': *Churnin v Pilot Developments Pty Ltd* [2007] NSWSC 1459 at [45]. Thus, delay on the part of the person seeking to enforce the undertaking is a ground for refusing to enforce the undertaking: *Smith v Day* (1882) 21 CH D 421 at 425–6, 427.

24.52   In relation to the assessment of damages pursuant to the undertaking, in *European Bank v Evans*, at CLR 439; ALR 5, where the High Court said:

> A party seeking an equitable remedy is required to 'do equity' and this is the origin of the requirement that the party giving an undertaking as to damages submit to such order for

payment of compensation as the court may consider to be just. Given its origin and application to varied circumstances in particular cases, the process of assessment of compensation cannot be constrained by a rigid formulation.

The High Court, at CLR 439; ALR 5–6, then approved the following statement by Aickin J in *Air Express v Ansett Transport Industries* at 266–7, where his Honour said:

> In a proceeding of an equitable nature it is generally proper to adopt a view which is just and equitable, or fair and reasonable, in all the circumstances rather than to apply a rigid rule. However the view that the damages should be those which flow directly from the injunction and which could have been foreseen when the injunction was granted, is one which will be just and equitable in the circumstances of most cases and certainly in the present case.

24.53   In order to have an interlocutory injunction varied or set aside once it has been granted, the defendant must show that there has been a 'material change of circumstances since the original application was heard, or the discovery of new material which could not reasonably have been put before the court on the hearing of the original application': *Brimaud v Honeysett Instant Print Pty Ltd* (1988) 217 ALR 44 at 46–7.

QUIA TIMET INJUNCTIONS

24.54   Generally, injunctive relief relates to some infringement or alleged infringement of the plaintiff's rights. However, injunctions can be granted in relation to circumstances where there has not yet been an infringement of rights, provided that the risk to the plaintiff's rights 'is both imminent and real': *London Borough of Islington v Elliott* [2012] EWCA Civ 56 at [29]. Injunctions granted on the basis that there is such a threat to the plaintiff's rights are known as quia timet injunctions. The expression 'quia timet' means 'since he fears'. The essential purpose of a quia timet injunction is to prevent a wrong being committed: *Proctor v Bayley* (1889) 42 Ch D 390 at 398. Traditionally, the quia timet injunction was only available in relation to equitable rights, but is now seemingly available in respect of all matters by virtue of the injunction provisions of legislation implementing the judicature system: see 24.4–24.6.

24.55   In *Redland Bricks v Morris*, at AC 665; All ER 579, Lord Upjohn observed that a quia timet injunction arises in the following two types of case: (i) where, as yet, no harm to the defendant has occurred but it is threatened or intended; and (ii) where harm has been done by the earlier actions of the defendant, and the plaintiff has been compensated, but the plaintiff fears that future wrongs may be committed by the defendant.

24.56   The question of hardship to the defendant in quia timet injunction cases is a particularly important factor for the court to take into account, especially if the conduct of the defendant is not wanton. This is so because the plaintiff has not, as yet, suffered loss or damage and, in any event, the plaintiff will be able to be compensated by an award of common law damages or equitable compensation, as the case may be, if and when loss or damage does occur. In this context, in *Jessica Estates v Lennard* at [50], [58], Brereton J said:

> While hardship is a relevant consideration in the exercise of the discretion to grant or withhold injunctive relief, the mere circumstance that the grant of final relief will occasion great hardship to the defendant is insufficient reason to decline to enforce a plaintiff's rights ... It is not mere

hardship, but unnecessarily disproportionate hardship, that may inform the discretion to decline relief: usually hardship will justify refusal of a final injunction only if the benefit of an injunction to the plaintiff is so slight as not to justify the hardship that an injunction would inflict on the defendant. But it is necessary to remember that *prima facie* the plaintiff is entitled to have its rights enforced against the defendant which has been established to be a wrongdoer … [However], hardship is usually entitled to little weight where the defendant has taken a calculated risk, knowing of the other party's opposition, and lost.[7]

24.57   In assessing whether to grant a quia timet injunction, the courts have framed the test for the likelihood of an infringement of the plaintiff's rights with expressions such as 'reasonably certain' in *FCA Finance Pty Ltd v Moreton Central Sugar Mill Co Ltd* [1975] Qd R 250 at 253, and 'very strong probability' in *Redland Bricks v Morris* at AC 665; All ER 579. As to the necessary loss or damage that is threatened, it has been said by the courts that it must be 'grave damage' in *Thynne v Petrie* [1975] Qd R 260 at 262, 'substantial' in *FCA Finance v Moreton Central Sugar Mill* at 253, and 'very substantial' in *Hooper v Rogers* [1975] Ch 43 at 50; [1974] 3 All ER 417 at 421.

24.58   Spry sums up the position in relation to quia timet injunctions as follows:

> [A]lthough it is … true that a quia timet injunction will not issue unless the plaintiff is able to show a substantial risk of a breach of his rights, in the sense that he must be able to show more than an insignificant or illusory risk … the degree of probability that the material injury will occur must be weighed together with its gravity and likely consequences, as well as with other matters that may affect the balance of hardship or justice between the parties … Therefore the criterion by which the degree of probability of future injury must be established is not fixed or invariable but rather depends on the various other relevant circumstances of the case. Hence the greater the prejudice or inconvenience that may be caused by the apprehended injury, if it occurs, the more readily will the court intervene despite uncertainties and deficiencies of proof … The court will take account of all relevant matters and will make such orders as appear most just in view of the various interests of the parties and of third persons.[8]

INJUNCTIONS AND CONTRACTS

24.59   Generally, the equitable enforcement of contractual rights is by means of an order for specific performance which requires the defendant to carry out his or her contractual obligation. This is the order that is usually sought in relation to positive contractual obligations. However, where there is a negative contractual obligation, the injunction is the usual equitable relief that is sought. A negative contractual obligation is one where inactivity on the part of the promisor is the essence of the obligation. It is irrelevant as to whether the obligation is expressed in positive language: *Wolverhampton & Walsall Railway Co v London & North West Railway Co* (1873) LR 16 Eq 433 at 440. Negative contractual obligations can be express or implied. As to implied negative contractual obligations, in *O'Keefe v Williams* (1910) 11 CLR 171 at 211, Isaacs J observed that '[e]very exclusive licence imports a negative, and the person who confers it impliedly enters into a

---

7.   On appeal, the decision in this case was overruled on grounds unrelated to the granting of the injunction. Indeed, the Court of Appeal indicated that, but for these grounds, the injunction had been properly granted: *Lennard v Jessica Estates Pty Ltd* (2008) 71 NSWLR 306.

8.   Spry, *The Principles of Equitable Remedies*, note 3 above, pp 379–80.

negative understanding to do nothing to contravene it'. Furthermore, every promise that is positive in substance, logically contains an implied negative promise. In *Whitwood Chemical Co v Hardman* [1891] 2 Ch 416 at 426, Lindley LJ said:

> Now every agreement to do a particular thing in one sense involves a negative. It involves the negative of doing that which is inconsistent with the thing you are to do.

The classical illustration of an enforceable negative contractual obligation is a reasonable restraint of trade.

24.60   In *Doherty v Allman* (1878) 3 App Cas 719 at 720, it was stated that the court had no discretion in these cases and had to grant the injunction. However, in *Dalgetty Wine Estates Pty Ltd v Rizzon* (1979) 141 CLR 552; 26 ALR 355, this view was rejected. Mason J, at CLR 573–4; ALR 373, said that matters going to the court's discretion included the nature of the stipulation, the nature of the contract in which it was located, the effect which enforcement would have on the relationship of the parties under the contract and the character of the order required to enforce the obligation. Furthermore, traditional equitable defences can be raised in opposition to the injunction. Thus, in *Harrigan v Brown* [1967] 1 NSWR 342, the application for the injunction was refused because of the plaintiff's unclean hands: see 31.8–31.12. As to whether damages at common law are adequate and, therefore, a bar to granting equitable relief, Brereton J suggested in *Tullett Prebon (Australia) Pty Ltd v Purcell* [2008] NSWSC 852 at [97], that, 'in the context of negative contractual stipulations, that will be so only in an exceptional case'. However, as was pointed out by Campbell JA in *Lucas Stuart Pty Ltd v Hemmes Hermitage Pty Ltd* [2010] NSWCA 283 at [10], this 'is an empirical generalisation, not a legal principle'. In relation to why damages will usually be an inadequate remedy when an employer seeks to enforce a restraint of trade against a former employee, in *Emeco Internatinal Pty Ltd v O'Shea* [2012] WASC 282 at [21], Edelman J said that the reasons include: '(i) the difficulty of detection of breaches of the obligations; (ii) the difficulty of establishing causation between any loss of business with customers and any actions of the ex-employee; and (iii) the difficulty of the calculation of the quantum of any damage arising from loss of business'.

24.61   An important illustration of injunctive relief being sought to enforce negative contractual obligations is with restraints in the context of employment contracts to prevent the employee from working for another employer during the currency of the employment contract. This is in contrast to a restraint of trade clause aimed at preventing an employee working for another employer after the employment contract has come to an end. It can be noted that such a restraint of trade clause is generally more difficult to enforce than is the case with a clause that prevents an employee working for another employer during the currency of the employment contract. In the latter case, such clauses are generally held to be reasonable and thus, prima facie, enforceable, although in appropriate cases the court will exercise its discretion to refuse enforcement by means of an injunction against the employee: see 24.70–24.73. The typical example of cases where an employee is prevented from working for another employee during the currency of the employment contract occurs when X, a person with particular skills and talents, promises to provide those skills and talents for the benefit of Y (the positive contractual obligation), but also promises not to provide those skills and talents for the benefit of anybody else (the negative contractual obligation). If X attempts to breach the express negative contractual obligation, Y will seek to enforce it by obtaining injunctive relief to prevent X performing those services for some other person.[9] The usual reason that X wants to breach the negative contractual obligation is that he or she no longer wants to perform the positive contractual obligation and wants to offer his or her skills and talents to Z. Y's motivation for seeking the injunction is that, if X is prevented from offering his or her skills and talents to Z, X will decide to perform his or her positive contractual obligation. Y will rarely seek to obtain an order against X for specific performance of the positive contractual obligation because it will, in most cases, be refused on the basis that contracts for personal services are rarely specifically enforced: see 23.41–23.43.

24.62 In deciding cases involving the enforcement of such negative contractual obligations the courts have been careful not to grant injunctive relief if the effect of the order would be tantamount to ordering specific performance of the positive contractual obligation. In *Tullett Prebon (Australia) v Purcell* at [74], Brereton J summarised the approach of the courts in such cases as follows:

> Equity will ordinarily enforce an express negative contractual stipulation. However, one of the exceptional circumstances in which equity will not do so is where to grant such relief would have the effect, directly or indirectly, of enforcing a contractual obligation to perform personal services. A court of equity will not permit an injunction to be used as an instrument of achieving indirectly what it would not enforce directly by a decree of specific performance. While equity will enforce by injunction negative contractual stipulations notwithstanding that they are terms of a contract for personal services, it will not do so in such a manner as has the practical effect of compelling performance of a contractual obligation to render personal services.

24.63 Historically, courts initially refused to grant injunctions forbidding an individual from working for a competitor: *Kimberley v Jennings* (1836) 58 ER 621 at 621. The first significant decision in this area was *Lumley v Wagner* (1852) 42 ER 687. The background to this seminal case was a cut-throat battle between the managers of two London opera houses for the services of Johanna Wagner, a famous opera singer. Lumley, the manager of the established Her Majesty's theatre, was first to contract Wagner for a three-month season in 1852. Significantly, Wagner was held to have also promised that during that period she was 'not to use her talents at any other theatre, nor in any concert or reunion, public or private, without the consent of Mr Lumley'. Before her contract with Lumley started, Gye, the manager of the recently established Covent Garden opera theatre, negotiated a contract with Wagner for the opera singer to perform at Covent Garden. Performance by Wagner of her contract with Gye would have meant breaching the negative contractual obligation in her contract with Lumley. Lumley sought, and obtained, an injunction to prevent her from doing so. Lord St Leonards, at 693, observed that the effect of the injunction was only to prevent Wagner from appearing at Covent Garden and that it did not require her to fulfil her obligation to Lumley at Her Majesty's theatre, something which his Lordship said he could not directly enforce, although he conceded that the injunction could well tempt Wagner to perform her contract at Her Majesty's theatre. However, there is little doubt that his Lordship was not uncomfortable with the outcome of defendants in cases such as this choosing to fulfil their obligations as a result of the injunction. In a passage reflective of promissory theories of contract Lord St Leonards, at 693, said:

---

9. In the United States of America, in contrast to other common law jurisdictions, the courts will enforce an *implied* negative contractual stipulation in cases of this kind: N B Oman 'Specific Performance and the Thirteenth Amendment' (2009) 92 *Minnesota Law Review* 2020, p 2027.

> Wherever this Court has not proper jurisdiction to enforce specific performance, it operates to bind men's consciences, as far as they can be bound, to a true and literal performance of their agreements; and it will not suffer them to depart from their contracts at their pleasure, leaving the party with whom they have contracted to the mere chance of any damages which a jury may give.

24.64   *Lumley v Wagner* was followed in *Warner Bros Pictures Inc v Nelson* [1937] 1 KB 209, where Warner Bros movie studio obtained an injunction against Bette Davis, precluding the legendary movie star from starring in movies produced by other movie studios for a period of three years. Branson J, at 219–20, conceded that Davis could well be tempted to continue to make movies with Warner Bros, but ruled that this was no grounds for refusing the injunction. A crucial factor in his Honour's decision was the fact that Davis was an intelligent and capable woman who could readily obtain alternative employment if she resolved not to work for Warner Bros. The fact that this alternative employment would be less financially rewarding than acting was not relevant. This approach was followed in *Hawthorn Football Club Ltd v Harding* [1988] VR 49, where Harding, a qualified dental technician, was contracted to play football for the Hawthorn football club for three years and precluded by his contract from playing for any other football club during that time. In granting an injunction to restrain Harding from playing for any other club, Tadgell J, at 59, said:

> I am not satisfied that the granting of the injunction on the terms sought would have of itself the substantial and practical effect of enforcing the positive covenant that [Harding] play football for [Hawthorn]. To enjoin [Harding] … could not, in my opinion, produce the effect, either actually or metaphorically, that [Harding] would be left 'idle' or that he would 'starve', in the relevant sense unless he played football for [Hawthorn].

24.65   In *Curro v Beyond Productions Pty Ltd* (1993) 30 NSWLR 337, television personality Tracey Curro was prevented from taking up a position with the *60 Minutes* program on the Nine Network, while she was still contracted to work for the *Beyond 2000* program on the Seven Network. The Court of Appeal, at 348, viewed Curro's conduct in signing a contract to work on the *60 Minutes* program as a 'flagrant and opportunistic' breach of her contract with Beyond Productions, and held that the injunction would not force her to choose between performing her contract with Beyond Productions or remaining idle.

24.66   Decisions in the *Lumley v Wagner* mould seem to ignore — or at best be rather naïve about — the fact that enforcement of the negative covenant may very well result in performance of the positive obligations as a matter of practical, if not legal, compulsion. If a person such as Johanna Wagner is forbidden to sing elsewhere than at the theatre with which she has contracted, her options are either to not sing at all, in which case her income is presumably reduced and she will very probably face a damages claim for breach of contract, or to perform as originally intended by the terms of that contract. It is not hard to appreciate that she is more likely to do the latter and sing, albeit grudgingly. Lord St Leonards' acknowledgment of this, while also insisting that he was not indirectly enforcing the positive contractual obligation, is disingenuous in the extreme.

24.67   In *Warren v Mendy* [1989] 3 All ER 103 at 112, Nourse LJ, in referring to *Warner Bros v Nelson*, said:

> [The] judge's view that Miss Bette Davis might employ herself both usefully and remuneratively in other spheres of activity for a period of up to three years appears to have been extraordinarily

unrealistic. It could hardly have been thought to be a real possibility that an actress of her youth and soaring talent would be able to forgo screen and stage for such a period.

24.68 It can be noted that, in most of the cases where an injunction is granted, defendants do succumb to the temptation referred to by Branson J in *Warner Bros v Nelson* and perform their positive contractual obligations. Johanna Wagner was one of the exceptions, for, as Waddams records, 'in the end Wagner did not sing at either theatre, and the 1852 season was a disaster for Lumley, and for Her Majesty's theatre, which closed from 1853 to 1855, Lumley attributing the closure largely to Johanna Wagner's defection'.[10]

24.69 All the cases discussed above were concerned with the employment of specified individuals. In cases in which the parties to the contract are independent companies in which there is no issue of employment of specific individuals and the performance of services is not personal in nature as it was in the above cases, courts will be more readily inclined to grant the injunction, even if the practical effect of the injunction is to grant specific performance of the contract. Thus, in *Lauritzencool AB v Lady Navigation Inc* [2005] 1 WLR 3686, the owners of two commercial vessels chartered them to the charterer as part of a pool of vessels which the charterer managed on a fleet basis. The owners sought to withdraw their vessels from the pool before the time charters expired. The charterer sought, and obtained, an injunction preventing the owners from using the vessels in a manner inconsistent with the time charters or allowing the vessels to be fixed with any third party for the duration of the time charters. Speaking for a unanimous Court of Appeal, Mance LJ, at 3705, said:

> The present relationships are between business concerns who, in the event of such relief, can be expected to continue to make them work in their own interests, and to sort out any complaints in arbitration if necessary hereafter … [N]either the fact that the contracts involved were for services in the form of a time charter nor the existence under such contracts of a fiduciary relationship of mutual trust and confidence represents in law any necessary or general objection in principle to the grant of injunctive relief precluding the [owners] from employing their vessels outside the pool … Nor does it afford any such objection to the grant of such relief that the only realistic commercial course which it left to the [owners] was, as I am prepared to assume, to do what they have done, namely to continue to provide the vessels to the pool and to perform the charters.

24.70 By way of contrast to these cases, others have refused to grant injunctions. Thus, in *Whitwood Chemical Co v Hardman* [1891] 2 Ch 416, Hardman had been appointed as manager of Whitwood Chemical Co for a period of 10 years. By his contract he promised to work exclusively for the company. When he breached that obligation an injunction was sought, but the Court of Appeal rejected the application on the basis that the injunction, if awarded, would be tantamount to specifically enforcing Hardman's obligation to work for Whitwood. Granting the injunction would have left Hardman with the choice of being idle or working for Whitwood. Lindley LJ, at 428, viewed *Lumley v Wagner* as an anomalous case to be followed only in cases similar on the facts. Kay LJ, at 431, suggested that *Lumley v Wagner* was a case in which the power to order injunctive relief was taken 'to the extreme limit to which it could go'.

---

10. S M Waddams, 'Johanna Wagner and the Rival Opera Houses' (2001) 117 *Law Quarterly Review* 431, p 440.

24.71   In *Page One Records Ltd v Britton* [1967] 3 All ER 822, members of the pop group 'The Troggs' entered into a management and agency agreement with Page One Records for a term of five years and promised not to engage anyone else to be their manager and agent. The Troggs sought to engage another manager and agent. Page One Records sought an injunction to prevent them from doing so. In refusing the application, Stamp J, at 827, after referring to *Warner Bros v Nelson*, said:

> [W]here a contract for personal service contains negative covenants, the enforcement of which will amount either to a decree of specific performance of the positive covenants of the contract or to the giving of a decree under which the defendant must either remain idle or perform those positive covenants, the court will not enforce those negative covenants.

24.72   Stamp J doubted that The Troggs could continue to function without the services of a manager and agent or seek other employment, and considered that they would need a manager and agent to function successfully as a pop group. According to Stamp J, at 827, this was so because:

> The Troggs are simple persons, of no business experience, and could not survive without the services of a manager … I entertain no doubt that they would be compelled, if the injunction were granted, … to continue to employ [Page One Records] as their manager and agent … [I]t would be a bad thing to put pressure on the Troggs to continue to employ as a manager and agent one, who, unlike the plaintiff in those cases [such as *Lumley v Wagner* and *Warner Bros v Nelson*] who had merely to pay the defendant money, has duties of a personal and fiduciary nature to perform and in whom the Troggs, for reasons good, bad or indifferent, have lost confidence and who may, for all I know, fail in its duty to them.

24.73   In *Warren v Mendy*, Benn, a talented boxer with a bright future in front of him, entered into a three-year management agreement with Warren that contained the usual positive and negative contractual obligations. Within a few months Benn had become disenchanted with Warren and had sought out Mendy to be his new manager. Mendy indicated that he was willing to be Benn's manager. Warren sought an injunction, not against Benn, but against Mendy to restrain an alleged tort of interference with contractual relations. For the Court of Appeal, the central issue in assessing Warren's claim was whether the effect of the injunction would be to force Benn to continue to retain Warren as his manager. The court refused to grant the injunction. Speaking for the court, Nourse LJ, at 114, set out the following principles to be applied in cases of enforcement of negative contractual obligations in the context of personal service contracts:

> This consideration of the authorities has led us to believe that the following general principles are applicable to the grant or refusal of an injunction to enforce performance of the servant's negative obligations in a contract for personal services inseparable from the exercise of some special skill or talent … In such a case the court ought not to enforce the performance of the negative obligations if their enforcement will effectively compel the servant to perform his positive obligations under the contract. Compulsion is a question to be decided on the facts of each case, with a realistic regard for the probable reaction of an injunction on the psychological and material, and sometimes the physical, need of the servant to maintain the skill or talent. The longer the term for which an injunction is sought, the more readily will compulsion be inferred. Compulsion may be inferred where the injunction is sought not against the servant but against a third party, if either the third party is the only other available master or if it is likely that the master will seek relief against anyone who attempts to replace him. An injunction will less readily

be granted where there are obligations of mutual trust and confidence, more especially where the servant's trust in the master may have been betrayed or his confidence in him has genuinely gone. In stating the principles as we have, we are not to be taken as intending to pay anything less than a full and proper regard to the sanctity of contract. No judge would wish to detract from his duty to enforce the performance of contracts to the very limit which established principles allow him to go … To that end the judge will scrutinise most carefully, even sceptically, any claim by the servant that he is under the human necessity of maintaining the skill or talent and thus will be compelled to perform the contract, or that his trust in the master has been betrayed or that his confidence in him has genuinely gone. But if, having done that, the judge is satisfied that the grant of an injunction will effectively compel performance of the contract, he ought to refuse it.

INJUNCTIONS IN AID OF STATUTORY RIGHTS

24.74   Where there has been a breach of statute, there are a number of possibilities in so far as obtaining an injunction is concerned. First, the legislation may expressly or impliedly exclude any remedy other than those which it expressly provides for, thereby excluding the remedy of an injunction: *Ramsay v Aberfoyle Manufacturing Company (Australia) Pty Ltd* (1935) 54 CLR 230 at 239–40, 255–6.

24.75   A second possibility is that the statute directly confers upon a person or category of persons the right of enforcement. This often occurs in the context of local government legislation. Thus, in *Cooney v Ku-ring-gai Municipal Council*, the local council was authorised by s 587 of the then *Local Government Act* in New South Wales to seek injunctive relief to restrain the defendant from using premises for the purposes of a trade or business contrary to the provisions of a residential proclamation.

24.76   The third possibility is that, if no private right is infringed by a breach of statute, a person will be able to seek injunctive relief if he or she can bring themselves within the principles of *Boyce v Paddington Borough Council* [1903] 1 Ch 109 at 114: see 22.27–22.29.

24.77   If a person cannot come within either the second or third of the above possibilities, and no private right has been infringed, that person cannot bring an action for an injunction in his or her own name. The only way the proceedings can be pursued is by obtaining the fiat of the Attorney-General, in what are termed 'relator actions'.

24.78   In a relator action a person, called the relator, seeks the intervention of the Attorney-General who sues at the relation of that person. Of course, the Attorney-General can act of his or her own accord without the prompting of another person. In relator proceedings the relator generally conducts the case and is liable for costs. However, amendments to the proceedings, and any compromise or discontinuation, needs to be approved by the Attorney-General. If the Attorney-General refuses to intervene, that decision is not amenable to review by the courts and the individual has no standing to bring an action in his or her own name: *Gouriet v Union of Post Office Workers* [1978] AC 435 at 483; [1977] 3 All ER 70 at 85.

24.79   In exercising its discretion to grant relief, a court will grant an injunction only if the breach of statute also amounts to an infringement of public rights: *Ramsay v Aberfoyle Manufacturing Company (Australia)* at 239. Repeated infringements of the statute may constitute an infringement of public rights. In *Gouriet v Union of Post Office Workers* at AC 481; All ER at 83, Lord Wilberforce stated that the granting of relief in such cases was 'an exceptional power confined ... to cases where an offence is frequently repeated in disregard of a, usually, inadequate penalty or to cases of emergency'. In *Newport Borough Council v Khan* [1990] 1 WLR 1185 at 1193, Beldam LJ observed that the discretion to grant the injunction is not based upon the defendant's deliberate and flagrant flouting of the law. Rather, the court needs to draw the inference that the defendant's unlawful acts will continue unless and until effectively restrained by the law and that nothing short of an injunction will suffice to so restrain the defendant.

24.80 In *Attorney-General ex rel Meat and Allied Trades Federation of Australia v Beck* [1980] 2 NSWLR 77, as few as five prosecuted infringements were held to constitute an infringement of public rights. In this case, Beck operated a butcher shop during hours prohibited by statute. His competitors in the vicinity objected. Powell J ruled that the alleged loss that the competitors suffered did not amount to 'special damage' within the principles set out in *Boyce v Paddington Borough Council*, and that they could only succeed if the Attorney-General intervened. However, in this case the injunction was initially obtained without the involvement of the Attorney-General, who intervened at a later stage. It was argued that, because no 'special damage' existed at the time the injunction was initially granted, the Attorney-General's subsequent intervention could not have retrospectively cured that defect and, thus, the proceedings should have been dismissed. In rejecting this argument, Powell J, at 93, said:

> While ... Beck would, until the Attorney-General was substituted as plaintiff, have been entitled to an order dismissing the proceedings, it does not follow that the proceedings, to that time, were a nullity. Indeed, if that had been the correct position, the proceedings could not have been amended by substituting the Attorney-General as plaintiff. The result thus is, in my view, that the proceedings remain proceedings validly commenced on 14th September, 1979; and that, in the absence of any condition, imposed at the time of the grant of leave to amend, limiting the Attorney-General to such relief as he could have claimed at the time of his substitution as plaintiff the Attorney-General is entitled to claim such relief as he could have claimed, if the proceedings had originally been commenced in his name. The question of what order for costs is appropriate, however, attracts different principles.

24.81 Where the injury to the public relates only to its moral wellbeing, the granting of an injunction is less likely on the basis that the public can usually protect itself from such injury. In *Attorney-General ex rel Daniels v Huber* (1971) 2 SASR 142, the majority of the Full Court in South Australia upheld the granting of an injunction to restrain performance of the theatrical revue *Oh! Calcutta* on the basis that the revue breached legislation that criminalised obscenity. On the other hand, in relation to the same play the injunction was refused in Queensland in *Attorney-General v Twelfth Night Theatre* [1969] Qd R 319.

ANTI-SUIT INJUNCTIONS

24.82 An anti-suit injunction is an order issued by the court that prevents one party from commencing proceedings against the other party in another jurisdiction. In *Star Reefers Pool Inc v JFC Group Co Ltd* [2012] EWCA Civ 14 at [24], Rix LJ, summarising the circumstances in which such injunctions can be granted in England, said:

What was needed was *either* an agreement for exclusive English jurisdiction or, its equivalent, an agreement for arbitration in England, in which case the court would ordinarily enforce the parties agreement by granting an anti-suit injunction in the absence of strong reason not to do so; *or* else two other conditions had to be satisfied, namely England had to be the natural forum for the resolution of the dispute and the conduct of the party to be injuncted had to be unconscionable.

24.83   Although the grant of such injunctions is discretionary, in cases where there is an exclusive jurisdiction clause, such a clause will, if necessary, usually be enforced by the means of the anti-suit injunction so as to prevent proceedings being commenced in a jurisdiction other than that stipulated in the exclusive jurisdiction clause: *Donohue v Armco* [2002] 1 Lloyd's LR 425 at 435.

24.84   Anti-suit injunctions usually relate to proceedings in a foreign jurisdiction. However, anti-suit injunctions can also prevent proceedings being commenced in other Australian jurisdictions. The counterpart of an anti-suit injunction is the power of the court to stay proceedings before it on the basis that it is appropriate that the dispute between the parties be resolved before another court.

24.85   The anti-suit injunction is a descendant of the pre-judicature system common injunction (see 1.30) which was also available to prevent proceedings being commenced in Scotland and Ireland and eventually in the British colonies.[11] In *Masri v Consolidated Contractors International (UK) Ltd (No 3)* [2009] QB 503 at 519–21, Lawrence Collins LJ said:

> Prior to the Judicature Acts, the anti-suit injunction generally required the applicant to establish either that there was 'vexatious harassment' or that the respondent was proceeding abroad in a manner which was contrary to equity and good conscience. After the Judicature Acts … the essential basis for the injunction was the vexatious or oppressive conduct of the respondent. That was the test even in cases in which the applicant relied on a contract not to sue in the foreign court … Since [the mid-1980s] the vexation/oppression test has often been subsumed within the category of unconscionability.

24.86   An anti-suit injunction, being an *in personam* remedy, binds only the party enjoined and is thus effective only to the extent that that party is amenable to the jurisdiction of the issuing court so that the order can be enforced against him or her: *Société Nationale Industrielle Aérospatiale v Lee Kui Jak* [1987] AC 871 at 892; [1987] 3 All ER 510 at 519.

24.87   The jurisdiction of the court to stay proceedings before it or to grant an anti-suit injunction was detailed in *CSR Ltd v Cigna Insurance Australia Ltd* (1997) 189 CLR 345 at 391; 146 ALR 402 at 432–3, where Dawson, Toohey, Gaudron, McHugh, Gummow and Kirby JJ said:

> [T]he power to stay proceedings … is an aspect of the inherent or implied power which, in the absence of some statutory provision to the same effect, every court must have to prevent its own processes being used to bring about injustice. The counterpart of a court's power to *prevent* its processes being abused is its power to *protect* the integrity of those processes once set in motion. And in some cases, it is that counterpart power of protection that authorises the grant of anti-suit injunctions.

---

11. T C Hartley, 'Antisuit Injunctions and the Brussels Jurisdiction and Judgments Convention' (2000) 49 *International & Comparative Law Quarterly* 166, p 168.

24.88 Their Honours, at CLR 392; ALR 433–4, continued:

> Quite apart from the inherent power of a court to protect its own processes, a court may, in the exercise of the power deriving from the Chancery Court, make orders in restraint of unconscionable conduct or the unconscientious exercise of legal rights. If the bringing of legal proceedings involves unconscionable conduct or the unconscientious exercise of a legal right, an injunction may be granted by a court in the exercise of its equitable jurisdiction in restraint of those proceedings no matter where they are brought. The inherent power to grant anti-suit injunctions … is to be exercised when the administration of justice so demands or, in the context of anti-suit injunctions, when necessary for the protection of the court's own proceedings or processes. In some cases, the equitable jurisdiction to restrain unconscionable conduct may be exercised in aid of legal rights. Thus, … if there is a contract not to sue, an injunction may be granted to restrain proceedings brought in breach of that contract, whether brought here or abroad. Similarly, an injunction may be granted in aid of a promise not to sue in a foreign jurisdiction constituted, for example, by an agreement to submit to the exclusive jurisdiction of the courts of the forum.

24.89 In *TS Production LLC v Drew Pictures Pty Ltd* (2008) 172 FCR 433 at 447; 252 ALR 1 at 14–15, Gordon J (Stone J agreeing) said:

> [I]t must be remembered that the principles governing whether to grant a stay of the domestic action and whether to enjoin prosecution of a foreign proceeding are not the same. Therefore, the … contention that if the court set aside the order staying the Australian action, it automatically followed that an order should be made restraining the further prosecution of the [foreign] proceeding, must be rejected. Instead, the Court must independently be satisfied of the answer to the [following] question … That is, can it be said that restraining prosecution of the [foreign] proceedings is necessary for the administration of justice, whether for protection of this Court's own proceedings and processes or otherwise? For example, would the litigation in the [foreign] proceedings of any controversy about the factual substratum amount to vexation or oppression? Or alternatively, is it demonstrated that the central or dominant purpose of … instituting the [foreign] proceedings was to prevent continuation of the proceedings in [the Australian] Court?

24.90 Gordon J, at FCR 448; ALR 15, continued and said:

> Indeed, the High Court explicitly stated in [*CSR v Cigna Insurance* at CLR 393; ALR 434] that 'the mere co-existence of proceedings in different countries does not constitute vexation or oppression'. The [High] Court [at CLR 393; ALR 434] … went on to say that 'foreign proceedings are to be viewed as vexatious or oppressive only if there is nothing which can be gained by them over and above what may be gained in local proceedings'. As the presiding judge has noted and as the appellant accepted, '[s]omething more [than mere co-existence of proceedings] is needed': reasons of Finkelstein J [in this case] at [33]. In my view, [an applicant], in claiming an anti-suit injunction, must demonstrate a sufficient case showing that the further prosecution of the [foreign] proceedings pending the hearing and determination of the proceedings in this Court would be 'productive of serious and unjustified trouble and harassment' or 'severely and unfairly burdensome, prejudicial or damaging': *Oceanic Sun Line Special Shipping Co Inc v Fay* (1988) 165 CLR 197 [at] 247.

24.91   In determining whether to grant an anti-suit injunction, the international law notion of comity plays an important part. In relation to comity, in *Deutsche Bank AG v Highland Crusader Offshore Partners LP* [2010] 1 WLR 1023 at 1036, Toulson LJ said:

> An anti-suit injunction always requires caution because by definition it involves interference with the process or potential process of a foreign court. An injunction to enforce an exclusive jurisdiction clause governed by English law is not regarded as a breach of comity, because it merely requires a party to honour his contract. In other cases, the principle of comity requires the court to recognise that, in deciding questions of weight to be attached to different factors, different judges operating under different legal systems with different legal policies may legitimately arrive at different answers, without occasioning a breach of customary international law or manifest injustice, and that in such circumstances it is not for an English Court to arrogate to itself the decision how a foreign court should determine the matter. The stronger the connection of the foreign court with the parties and the subject matter of the dispute, the stronger the argument against intervention.

24.92   In *CSR v Cigna Insurance* at CLR 395–6; ALR 436, it was held that, although an anti-suit injunction is directed to the parties, it involves an indirect interference with the processes of the foreign court, and caution is required before the injunction is granted. Indeed, as was observed in *Masri v Consolidated Contractors International* at 693, '[c]omity may be decisive where the [Australian] court is asked to grant an anti-suit injunction when the case has no relevant connection with [Australia], since to grant an injunction in such a case may be a breach of international law'. Furthermore, an application for an anti-suit injunction must be issued 'promptly and before the foreign proceedings are too far advanced': *The Angelic Grace* [1995] 1 Lloyd's Rep 87 at 96.

25

MAREVA AND ANTON PILLER ORDERS

INTRODUCTION

25.1   In *Bank Mellat v Nikpour* [1985] FSR 87 at 92, Donaldson LJ aptly described Mareva and Anton Piller orders as 'the law's two "nuclear" weapons'. They are orders granted in exceptional circumstances whose purpose is 'to protect the court's jurisdiction against defendants bent on dissipating or secreting their assets or evidence in order to render inconsequential the judicial process against them': *Grenzservice Speditions GesmbH v Jans* (1995) 129 DLR (4th) 733 at 755. The Mareva order does this by freezing a defendant's assets pending the hearing and determination of a plaintiff's cause of action against the defendant. The Anton Piller order does this by preventing the defendant destroying evidence relating to the plaintiff's case.

25.2   The Mareva order was initially known as a Mareva injunction. However, in *Cardile v LED Builders Pty Ltd* (1999) 198 CLR 380 at 395–6, 401; 162 ALR 294 at 304, 308, Gaudron, McHugh, Gummow and Callinan JJ pointed out that the word 'injunction' was inappropriate and should be replaced with the word 'order' on the basis that the doctrinal basis of an injunction differs from that of the Mareva order. The difference stems from the fact that an injunction protects a claimant's legal or equitable rights whereas the purpose of a Mareva order is to prevent the frustration of the court process: *RFD Ltd v Harris* [2008] WASCA 87 at [37]. In *Cardile v LED Builders* at CLR 412; ALR 318, Kirby J preferred the term 'asset preservation order'. In England a Mareva order is generally now referred to as a 'freezing order'.

25.3   In relation to the fundamental purpose of the Mareva order, in *Jackson v Sterling Industries Ltd* (1987) 162 CLR 612 at 623; 71 ALR 457 at 464, Deane J said:

> [The Mareva order is] accepted as an established part of the armory of a court of law and equity to prevent the abuse or frustration of its process in relation to matters coming within its jurisdiction.

25.4   In relation to the fundamental purpose of an Anton Piller order, in *Long v Specifier Publications Pty Ltd* (1998) 44 NSWLR 545 at 547, Powell JA said:

> [T]he jurisprudential basis for [Anton Piller orders] being made [is] said to be the inherent jurisdiction of the court to ensure that justice be done between the parties to the proposed litigation.

MAREVA ORDERS

25.5   The Mareva order derives its name from the second case in which such an order was made, namely, *Mareva Compania Naviera SA v International Bulkcarriers SA* [1980] 1 All ER 213. The first such case was *Nippon Yusen Kaisha v Karageorgis* [1975] 3 All ER 282.

25.6   In *Fourie v Le Roux* [2007] 1 All ER 1087 at 1090, Lord Bingham of Cornhill described the purpose of Mareva orders as follows:

> Mareva (or freezing) injunctions were from the beginning, and continue to be, granted for an important but limited purpose: to prevent a defendant dissipating his assets with the intention or effect of frustrating enforcement of a prospective judgment. They are not a proprietary remedy. They are not granted to give a claimant advance security for his claim, although they may have that effect. They are not an end in themselves. They are a supplementary remedy, granted to protect the efficacy of court proceedings, domestic or foreign.

25.7   The granting of a Mareva order does not give the plaintiff any proprietary or security interest in the defendant's assets. In *Customs and Excise Commissioners v Barclays Bank plc* [2007] 1 AC 181 at 193; [2006] 4 All ER 256 at 264, Lord Bingham of Cornhill said:

> The purpose [of a Mareva order] is not to give a claimant security for his claim or give him any proprietary interest in the assets restrained. The ownership of the assets does not change. All that changes is the right to deal with them.

25.8   Nor does the Mareva order improve the position of the plaintiff in any insolvency of the defendant: *Jackson v Sterling Industries Ltd* at CLR 618, 639; ALR 459, 475. However, in *Cardile v LED Builders Pty Ltd* at CLR 403; ALR 310–11, the High Court made the following pointed observation:

> Nevertheless, those statements should not obscure the reality that the granting of a *Mareva* order is bound to have a significant impact on the property of the person against whom it is made: in a practical sense it operates as a very tight 'negative pledge' species of security over property, to which the contempt sanction is attached. It requires a high degree of caution on the part of a court invited to make an order of that kind. An order lightly or wrongly granted may have a capacity to impair or restrict commerce just as much as one appropriately granted may facilitate and ensure its due conduct.

Jurisdiction

25.9   The most controversial issue surrounding the Mareva order when it first appeared was the question of the jurisdiction of the court to make such an order. The Mareva order's effect was to prevent an alleged debtor from freely dealing with his or her assets. However, established authority had long ago declared that a person 'cannot get an injunction to restrain a man who is alleged to be a debtor from parting with his property': *Lister & Co v Stubbs* (1890) 45 Ch D 1 at 14. Initially the English courts asserted that the then successor provision to s 25(8) of the *Judicature Act 1873* (UK) granted them jurisdiction to make Mareva orders. Section 25(8) and its equivalent provisions in

Australian jurisdictions[1] enable the court to grant interlocutory injunctions in any cases where it is just and convenient to do so.

25.10 Following its enactment, two lines of authority on s 25(8) emerged. In *Smith v Cowell* (1880) 6 QBD 75 at 78, Brett LJ said of the section: 'Those words are very wide, and give all the divisions a larger power than the Court of Chancery possessed before'. On the other hand, in *Morgan v Hart* [1914] 2 KB 183 at 186, Buckley LJ said:

> [T]he section does not give to the Courts either of Law or Equity any wider jurisdiction than existed before, but enables such orders as could be made to be made in any proceedings, without commencing special proceedings in the Court of Chancery such as were necessary before the Act.

25.11 The approach evident in *Morgan v Hart* suggests that s 25(8) did not provide the court with the jurisdiction to grant Mareva orders. In 1981, six years after the first Mareva order was granted, the approach of *Morgan v Hart* was affirmed by the House of Lords in *Bremer Vulkan Schiffbau und Maschinenfabrik v South India Shipping Corporation Ltd* [1981] AC 909 at 979–80, 992, 994–5; [1981] 1 All ER 289 at 296–7, 306–76, 308. The uncertainty in England on the jurisdictional question was resolved by the enactment of s 37 of the *Supreme Court Act 1981* (UK) which provided an explicit statutory basis for jurisdiction.

25.12 In Australia, in *Riley McKay Pty Ltd v McKay* [1982] 1 NSWLR 264 at 269, the Court of Appeal rejected an argument that s 66(4) of the *Supreme Court Act 1970* (NSW) — the New South Wales equivalent of s 25(8) of the *Judicature Act 1873* (UK) — gave the court jurisdiction to grant Mareva orders. Rather, the court, at 276, based jurisdiction on either the court's inherent jurisdiction or s 23 of the *Supreme Court Act 1970* (NSW), which stipulated as follows:

> The Court shall have all jurisdiction which may be necessary for the administration of justice in New South Wales.

The court, at 270, doubted if there was any distinction between s 23 and the court's inherent jurisdiction.

25.13 In *Jackson v Sterling Industries Ltd* at CLR 617, 623, 639–40; ALR 459, 463–4, 476, the High Court followed the reasoning in *Riley McKay v McKay* and confirmed that the jurisdiction to grant a Mareva order stemmed from either the court's inherent jurisdiction or the equivalents of s 23 of the *Supreme Court Act 1970* (NSW) in other Australian jurisdictions. In all Australian jurisdictions the court rules now explicitly confer power upon the court to grant Mareva orders.[2]

25.14 It can be noted that, although the jurisdiction to grant Mareva orders has been accepted in much of the common law world, the Supreme Court of the United States has held that such orders

---

1. *Federal Court of Australia Act 1976* (Cth) s 23; *Supreme Court Act 1970* (NSW) s 66; *Supreme Court Act 1979* (NT) s 69; *Supreme Court Act 1995* (Qld) s 246; *Supreme Court Act 1935* (SA) s 29; *Supreme Court Civil Procedure Act 1932* (Tas) s 11(12); *Supreme Court Act 1986* (Vic) s 37; *Supreme Court Act 1935* (WA) s 25(9). In the Australian Capital Territory, the equivalent of s 25(8), set out in s 34 of the *Supreme Court Act 1933* (ACT), was repealed in 2006.
2. *Federal Court Rules* (Cth) O 25A; *Court Procedure Rules 2006* (ACT) rr 740–45; *Uniform Civil Procedure Rules 2005* (NSW) Pt 25 Div 2; *Supreme Court Rules* (NT) Order 37A; *Uniform Civil Procedure Rules 1999* (Qld) Ch 8 Pt 2 Div 2; *Supreme Court Rules 2006* (SA) r 247; *Supreme Court Rules 2000* (Tas) Pt 36 Div 1A; *Supreme Court (General Civil Procedure) Rules 2005* (Vic) O 37A; *Rules of the Supreme Court 1971* (WA) O 52A.

cannot be made by American courts: *Grupo Mexicano de Desarrollo SA v Alliance Bond Fund Inc* 527 US 308, 327–33 (1999).

Requirements for obtaining a Mareva order

25.15 In *Glenwood Management Group Pty Ltd v Mayo* (1991) 2 VR 49 at 49–54, Young CJ indicated that there are three basic requirements to be satisfied before a court will grant a Mareva order. They are: (i) that the plaintiff has a good arguable case; (ii) that there is a risk of dissipation or secretion of assets so as to render any judgment which the plaintiff may obtain nugatory; and (iii) that the balance of convenience favours the granting of a Mareva order. His Honour, at 54–5, also observed that 'the three elements overlap and that the granting of a Mareva [order] is always a matter of discretion'. For example, 'as the strength of the arguable case diminishes so the balance of convenience moves in favour of the defendants and vice versa'.

25.16 Before looking more closely at these requirements, two preliminary points need to be explained. First, reference must be made to the fact that in most cases the initial grant of a Mareva order is on an ex parte basis — without the defendant's presence. In such circumstances the plaintiff must disclose all material facts known to him or her and is required to draw the court's attention to all important factual, legal and procedural aspects of the application: *Memory Corporation plc v Sidhu (No 2)* [2000] 1 WLR 1443 at 1459–60. The duty of disclosure here is higher than almost any other circumstances where disclosures of this kind are required by a court: *Payabi v Armstel Shipping Corporations* [1992] QB 907 at 918. The disclosure requirement extends to facts which the plaintiff would have known if he or she had made proper inquiries: *Brink's-Mat Ltd v Elcombe* [1988] 3 All ER 188 at 192. The duty of disclosure continues for as long as the proceedings remain on an ex parte basis. Thus, the plaintiff must disclose subsequent material changes to circumstances after obtaining an order if the proceedings are still on an ex parte basis: *Commercial Bank of the Near East plc v A, B, C & D* [1989] 2 Lloyd's Rep 319 at 323.

25.17 Failure to comply with the disclosure requirements will usually result in the discharge of a Mareva order that has been granted to the plaintiff: *Garrard v Email Furniture Ltd* (1993) 32 NSWLR 662 at 678. The court may, in its discretion, continue a Mareva order in the event of non-disclosure of a material fact if the non-disclosure was innocent and if the order would have been granted had the disclosure been made at the time of the ex parte application. Even if both of these matters can be established, the discretion to continue the Mareva order will only be sparingly exercised: *Ali & Fahd Shobokshi Group v Moneim* [1989] 2 All ER 404 at 412–3. On the other hand, if the Mareva order is discharged this does not prevent a subsequent application for relief being successful, as was the case in *Hayden v Teplitzky* (1997) 74 FCR 7; 154 ALR 497.

25.18 The second preliminary point to make is that a plaintiff seeking a Mareva order will usually be required to give an undertaking as to damages: *Cardile v LED Builders* at CLR 401; ALR 309. The undertaking will require the plaintiff to compensate the defendant or any third party that is adversely affected by the grant of the Mareva order in the event that the plaintiff does not succeed in his or her cause of action against the defendant. However, a unanimous New South Wales Court of Appeal in *Frigo v Culhaci* [1998] NSWSC 393, as well as Kirby J in *Cardile v LED Builders* at CLR 428; ALR 330, were all of the view that a Mareva order should never be granted without there being an undertaking as to damages. In the rare cases in which courts have dispensed with the necessity of an undertaking as to damages, such as *Allen v Jambo Holdings Ltd* [1980] 2 All ER 1259 and *United States Securities and Exchange Commission v Manterfield* [2009] 1 Lloyd's Law Rep 399, it has generally been in circumstances where the plaintiff had an unusually strong cause of action against the defendant. The difficulty associated with the assessment of damages pursuant to an undertaking is one of the reasons for the care with which the courts approach granting Mareva orders: *Cardile v LED Builders* at CLR 404; ALR 311.

25.19   The court rules relating to Mareva orders stipulate that the undertaking as to damages should be accompanied by an appropriate bank guarantee from the plaintiff to support the undertaking. Although the court may dispense with the need for a guarantee, there is a duty upon a plaintiff or his or her lawyer to raise the matter explicitly with the court at the time of making the application. This matter was at the heart of the court's decision in *Heartwood Architectural Timber & Joinery Pty Ltd v Ors & Redchip Lawyers* [2009] QSC 195. In that case a counsel for the plaintiff deleted the references to providing a guarantee from the standard form documents prescribed by the court rules in the application papers lodged with the court. The reason for doing so was that the plaintiff at the time was in some financial difficulties and giving a guarantee would have made things more difficult for them. At the time of the ex parte application for the Mareva order this was not noticed by the court, nor was it raised by the plaintiff's counsel. Some months later the Mareva order was discharged and the defendant sought to enforce the undertaking as to damages. However, the plaintiff had by then gone into liquidation, rendering the undertaking worthless because of the absence of any bank guarantee. The court found that counsel's conduct constituted a serious dereliction of his duty to the court in relation to the obligation to make full disclosure to the court at the time of seeking the order. In relation to this matter, Applegarth J, at [5], said:

> An obvious matter of importance to the Court is that there be orders in accordance with the usual draft orders, or there be some reason for a departure. It may be that there are good reasons why the usual undertakings are not to be given. But if a party seeking an ex parte freezing order wishes not to give the undertakings that appear in the Practice Direction, that should be brought to the attention of the Court.

A risk of dissipation of assets

25.20   The risk that the defendant will dissipate assets before judgment refers to the underlying basis of the Mareva order and has been described as its 'heart and core': *Barclay-Johnson v Yuill* [1980] 3 All ER 190 at 194. There must be a real danger that the defendant will default if judgment is obtained against him or her. In this respect, the fact that the defendant has been dishonest is, of itself, not enough: *Irish Response Ltd v Direct Beauty Products Ltd* [2011] EWHC 37 (QB) at [29]. In relation to establishing such a risk, in *Ninemia Maritime Corp v Trave Schiffahrtsgesellschaft mbH & Co KG* [1984] 1 All ER 398 at 406–7, Mustill J said:

> It is not enough for the plaintiff to assert a risk that the assets will be dissipated. He must demonstrate this by solid evidence. This evidence may take a number of different forms. It may consist of direct evidence that the defendant has previously acted in a way which shows that his probity is not to be relied on. Or the plaintiff may show what type of company the defendant is (where it is incorporated, what are its corporate structure and assets, and so on) so as to raise an inference that the company is not to be relied on. Or, again, the plaintiff may be able to found his case on the fact that inquiries about the characteristics of the defendant have led to a blank wall. Precisely what form the evidence may take will depend on the particular circumstances of the

case. But the evidence must always be there. Mere proof that the company is incorporated abroad, accompanied by the allegation that there are no reachable assets in the United Kingdom apart from those which it is sought to enjoin, will not be enough.

25.21 In *Barclay-Johnson v Yuill* at 195, it was held that, if the defendant is reputable and accustomed to paying its debts and meeting its obligations, no order will be made regardless of the location of the defendant or his or her assets. In *Australian Iron & Steel Pty Ltd v Buck* [1982] 2 NSWLR 889, the defendant had gifted away property and was cashing in various assets by auction sales. This conduct prompted the granting of the Mareva order.

25.22 Formulating the degree of risk with any degree of precision is difficult, given that each case is dependent on its circumstances. In *Patterson v BTR Engineering (Aust) Ltd* (1989) 18 NSWLR 319 at 323–4, Gleeson CJ, in addressing this issue, said:

> The earlier cases, some of which need to be understood in the light of the original idea that these injunctions were only available to prevent a non-respondent defendant from removing assets from the territorial jurisdiction of the court, speak of 'danger of money being taken out of jurisdiction' or 'a danger of default if assets are removed from the jurisdiction', or 'a danger of default'. Other expressions used include 'a real cause to apprehend' that the plaintiff may be deprived of a remedy, a 'risk', a 'real risk', a 'risk demonstrated by solid evidence' or 'reason to believe that the defendant has assets … but may well take steps designed to ensure that these are no longer available'
>
> … [However], it would be undesirable for courts to endeavour to be more precise in relation to [this] question … There is no shortage of forms of language, all having more or less the same meaning, available in decided cases for the guidance of judges. Important guidance is also to be found in a consideration of the nature and purpose of the remedy in question.

25.23 His Honour, at 325, went on to reject the formulation of 'whether the plaintiff has established the likelihood in question upon the balance of probabilities' because it was open to 'conceptual difficulties involved in applying the standard of balance of probabilities to future, as distinct from past, events'. Furthermore, such a formulation was too inflexible, as there could be cases where the Mareva order should be granted 'even though the risk of such dissipation may be assessed as being somewhat less probable than not'.

The plaintiff's cause of action

25.24 A Mareva order can only be obtained if the plaintiff has a cause of action that is justiciable within the jurisdiction. If the Mareva order is not ancillary to some such pre-existing cause of action it will not be granted. In *Siskina v Distos Compania Naviera SA* [1979] AC 210 at 256; [1977] 3 All ER 803 at 824, Lord Diplock said:

> A right to obtain [a Mareva order] is not a cause of action. It cannot stand on its own. It is dependent upon there being a pre-existing cause of action against the defendant arising out of an invasion, actual or threatened by him, of a legal or equitable right of the plaintiff for the enforcement of which the defendant is amenable to the jurisdiction of the court. The right to obtain [a Mareva order] is merely ancillary and incidental to the pre-existing cause of action. It is granted to preserve the status quo pending the ascertainment by the court of the rights of the parties.

25.25 A plaintiff with no private cause of action, but with a statutory right to recover and redistribute proceedings to others adversely affected by the defendant, can obtain a Mareva order. Thus, in *Securities & Investment Board v Pantell SA* [1990] Ch 426; [1989] 2 All ER 673, the Secretary of State delegated to a plaintiff a statutory right to sue the defendant in relation to breaches of certain financial services legislation by which the defendant had offered unauthorised investment advice and services to a number of people who subsequently suffered losses as a result.

25.26 Although a plaintiff must have a cause of action against the defendant, he or she does not necessarily have to have commenced proceedings before obtaining a Mareva order. However, if the plaintiff has 'neither brought proceedings nor worked out what proceedings he was going to bring to which the freezing order would be relevant', a Mareva order is not available to that plaintiff: *Fourie v Le Roux* at 1104.

25.27 The plaintiff must establish that he or she has a sufficiently strong cause of action against the defendant. The strength of the cause of action has been variously described as 'a good arguable case' (*Glenwood Management Group v Mayo* at 49; *Groeneveld Australia Pty Ltd v Nolten Vastgoed BV* [2011] VSC 18 at [49]–[60]); 'a prima facie cause of action against the defendant' (*Patterson v BTR Engineering* at 321); and 'a serious question or fairly arguable case': *Official Receiver of the State of Israel v Raveh* (2001) 24 WAR 53 at 57. In *Patrick Stevedores Operations No 2 Pty Ltd* (1998) 195 CLR 1 at 46; 153 ALR 643 at 669, the High Court used the 'serious question' formulation, but in *Cardile v LED Builders*, at CLR 408; ALR 314, referred to a 'reasonably arguable case'.

25.28 These different formulations are substantively different. In *Ninemia Maritime Corporation v Trave Schiffahrtsgesellschaft mbH & Co KG* at 404, it was stated that a good arguable case is one 'which is more than barely capable of serious argument, and yet not necessarily one which the Judge believes would have a better than 50% chance of success'. However, a prima facie case means 'that if the evidence remains as it is there is a probability that at the trial of the action the plaintiff will be held entitled to relief': *Beecham Group Ltd v Bristol Laboratories Pty Ltd* (1968) 118 CLR 618 at 622.

25.29 Whatever the true formulation of the test may be, the strength of the plaintiff's case is significant for the reasons set out in *Ninemia Maritime Corporation v Trave Schiffahrtsgesellschaft mbH & Co KG* at 402–3, where Mustill J said:

> [T]he strength of the plaintiff's case is relevant in two distinct respects: (1) the plaintiff must have a case of a certain strength, before the question of granting Mareva relief can arise at all. I will call this the 'threshold'; (2) even where the plaintiff shows that he has a case which reaches the threshold, the strength of his case is to be weighed in the balance with other factors relevant to the exercise of the discretion.

25.30 It should also be kept in mind that the strength of the plaintiff's cause of action may very well contribute to establishing the requisite degree of risk that the defendant will dissipate his or her assets: *Patterson v BTR Engineering* at 325.

25.31 The plaintiff must also establish with some precision the value of the prospective judgment because a Mareva order should not unnecessarily tie up the defendant's assets and property: *Cardile v LED Builders* at CLR 428–9; ALR 331.

Balance of convenience

25.32 In exercising its discretion whether or not to grant a Mareva order, the court weighs up the strength of the plaintiff's cause of action and the risk that the defendant will dissipate his or her assets against various discretionary factors such as delay and whether there has been a full and frank disclosure by the plaintiff. In *Cardile v LED Builders* at CLR 380; ALR 311, the High Court said:

> Discretionary considerations generally also should carefully be weighed before an order is made. Has the applicant proceeded diligently and expeditiously? Has a money judgment been recovered in the proceedings? Are proceedings (for example civil conspiracy proceedings) available against the third party? Why, if some proceedings are available, have they not been taken? Why, if proceedings are available against the third party and have not been taken and the court is still minded to make a *Mareva* order, should not the grant of the relief be conditioned upon an undertaking by the applicant to commence, and ensure so far as is possible the expedition of, such proceedings? It is difficult to conceive of cases where such an undertaking would not be required. Questions of this kind may be just as relevant to the decision to grant *Mareva* relief as they are to a decision to dissolve it. These are matters to which courts should be alive.

Other points

25.33 In addition to the three essential requirements to be met before a court can grant a Mareva order, the following matters can also be noted:

- The court has the power to make ancillary disclosure orders in order to disclose assets. The purpose of such orders is to ensure that the Mareva order is effective: *Deputy Commissioner of Taxation v AES Services (Aust) Pty Ltd (No 2)* [2009] VSC 527 at [16]–[23].
- The rights of third parties cannot be affected by the granting of a Mareva order. Thus, assets cannot be frozen if the effect will be to prevent the defendant from meeting normal debt obligations owed to third parties, as well as his or her own reasonable living expenses: *Jackson v Sterling Industries* at CLR 642; ALR 478. Third parties are entitled to intervene in Mareva proceedings to seek a variation of an order so that their interests are not prejudiced.
- The most common asset to which the Mareva order will apply will be the defendant's bank accounts. This is because of the relative ease with which bank accounts can be closed and funds moved out of the jurisdiction. However, in the appropriate case, Mareva orders can be made against assets that cannot be so quickly realised and/or moved out of the jurisdiction. Thus, in *Praznovsky v Sablyack* [1977] VR 114, a Mareva order was made in relation to the defendant's land that was under a contract of sale.
- A Mareva order can be granted against a third party if that person is in possession of or in control of the defendant's property. An application for such an order 'must be supported by clear evidence showing exceptional grounds, even on the initial application made without notice. The jurisdiction to grant such [an order] must be exercised with great caution': *ETI Euro Telecom International NV v Republic of Bolivia* [2008] EWCA Civ 880 at [126]. The most common third party in this context is a bank. In *Cardile v LED Builders* at CLR 405; ALR 312, the High Court said the following:

> What then is the principle to guide the courts in determining whether to grant *Mareva* relief in a case such as the present where the activities of third parties are the object sought to be restrained? In our opinion such an order may, and we emphasise the word 'may', be appropriate,

assuming the existence of other relevant criteria and discretionary factors, in circumstances in which: (i) the third party holds, is using, or has exercised or is exercising a power of disposition over, or is otherwise in possession of, assets, including 'claims and expectancies', of the judgment debtor or potential judgment debtor; or (ii) some process, ultimately enforceable by the courts, is or may be available to the judgment creditor as a consequence of a judgment against that actual or potential judgment debtor, pursuant to which, whether by appointment of a liquidator, trustee in bankruptcy, receiver or otherwise, the third party may be obliged to disgorge property or otherwise contribute to the funds or property of the judgment debtor to help satisfy the judgment against the judgment debtor.

- A Mareva order can extend to the defendant's assets outside the jurisdiction if there are not sufficient assets within the jurisdiction to cover the potential liability of the defendant: *Derby & Co Ltd v Weldon (No 2)* [1989] 1 All ER 1002 at 1009–10, 1015–8, 1022. In contrast to the position in England, in Australia exceptional circumstances are not required for an extra-territorial Mareva order: *Talacko v Talacko* [2009] VSC 349 at [35]. The jurisdiction of the court to grant extra-territorial Mareva orders is based upon the fact that the order is *in personam* (see 2.52–2.53) in nature and, therefore, a court can order a defendant over whom it has jurisdiction to do or refrain from doing something outside the territorial jurisdiction of the court: *National Australia Bank Ltd v Dessau* [1988] VR 521 at 522. Originally, the Mareva order was confined to assets within the jurisdiction. In *Hospital Products Ltd v Ballabil Holdings Pty Ltd* [1984] 2 NSWLR 662 at 664, Rogers J pointed to the illogicality of this approach and said:

> [T]he purpose nominated as the raison d'etre for the remedy could fail to be satisfied in given circumstances if relief is restricted to assets within the jurisdiction. To take the most simple situation, let it be assumed that a defendant, within the jurisdiction, has assets overseas against which execution could be levied in the event of judgment being obtained against the defendant within the jurisdiction. Is the court powerless to prevent such a defendant from transferring the foreign assets into the anonymity of a numbered Swiss bank account in the face of clear statements by the defendant of an intention to do so? Putting the question another way, why should the attempt of a defendant, within the jurisdiction, to make himself judgment proof in relation to foreign assets be any more permissible or any less inimical to the proper administration of justice than similar action with respect to locally owned assets? ... In a similar way, a question arises as to the justification for treating an asset located in a foreign jurisdiction differently from that within the jurisdiction in circumstances where a defendant has been wise enough to remove an asset shortly before the grant of a Mareva injunction.

- A Mareva order can continue after judgment against the defendant, or applied to such judgment, 'if there are reasons to fear that assets of a judgment debtor might be dissipated, and execution thereby frustrated': *Fatimi Pty Ltd v Bryant* [2002] NSWSC 750 at [322]. The fact that judgment has been obtained does not diminish the need for the undertaking as to damages that is usually required: see 25.18; *Banco Nacional de Comercio Exterior SNC v Empresa de Telecommunicaciones de Cuba SA* [2008] 1 WLR 1936 at 1947–8.
- If a plaintiff fails at first instance to obtain a judgment in his or her cause of action against the defendant, an appellate court has jurisdiction to grant a Mareva order pending the resolution of the plaintiff's appeal against the decision of the trial judge: *Tomasetti v Brailey* [2012] NSWCA 6 at [13].

- The terms of a Mareva order should usually be made 'for a limited period, delimited either by a date or event or subject to a condition': *Tagget v Sexton* [2009] NSWCA 91 at [67].

ANTON PILLER ORDERS

25.34 The Anton Piller order derives its name from the case of *Anton Piller KG v Manufacturing Processes Ltd* [1976] 1 Ch 55; [1976] 1 All ER 779, in which the essential requirements for the making of such an order were first authoritatively set out.

25.35 An Anton Piller order is similar to a Mareva order in that it seeks to preserve property and prevent the defendant frustrating the administration of justice. But, rather than ensuring that the judgment debt will ultimately be met by the defendant, it aims to gather and protect evidence that is crucial to the plaintiff's case, which may be yet to commence. The Anton Piller order enables this by ordering the defendant to allow the plaintiff access to the defendant's premises so that the plaintiff may inspect, copy and collect material which is necessary for it to successfully bring its case but which it fears will be destroyed: *Long v Specifier Publications Pty Ltd* at 547. In *British Columbia (Attorney General) v Malik* (2011) 330 DLR (4th) 577 at 582, the Canadian Supreme Court said:

> An *Anton Piller* order is an exceptional remedy and should only be granted on clear and convincing evidence. It is a highly intrusive measure that, unless sparingly granted and closely controlled, is capable of causing great prejudice and potentially irremediable loss.

25.36 The context in which Anton Piller orders were originally developed was in the seizure of pirated recordings or materials in order to protect intellectual property rights that had been infringed in the making of such recordings and materials. Now, the order can be made in any type of case. A further important development concerning the use of Anton Piller orders is that it is no longer necessary for an Anton Piller order to nominate the identity of the persons against whom it is to operate — their names being provided upon execution of the order. This feature — present in so-called 'John Doe' Anton Piller orders (*Joel v Various John Does* 499 F Supp 791 (1980)), and 'roving' Anton Piller orders (*Tony Blain Pty Ltd v Jamison* (1993) 26 IPR 8) — was developed in response to the problem of the sale of unauthorised merchandise at stadium concerts by vendors whose identities were unknown until such time as the order was executed.

Jurisdiction

25.37 In *Simsek v Macphee* (1982) 148 CLR 636 at 640–1; 40 ALR 61 at 65, Stephen J, in a single instance decision in the High Court, stated that the power of the court to grant an Anton Piller order stemmed from the court's inherent jurisdiction. In other cases it has been said that the jurisdiction rests either on the inherent jurisdiction of the court or the statutory conferral of powers to aid the operation of the courts, such as s 23 of the *Federal Court Act 1976* (Cth): *Microsoft Corp v Goodview Electronics Pty Ltd* (1999) 46 IPR 159. In all Australian jurisdictions the court rules now explicitly confer power upon the court to grant Anton Piller orders.[3]

---

3. *Federal Court Rules* (Cth) O 25B; *Court Procedure Rules 2006* (ACT) rr 750–55; *Uniform Civil Procedure Rules 2005* (NSW) Pt 25 Div 3; *Supreme Court Rules* (NT) O 37B; *Uniform Civil Procedure Rules 1999* (Qld) Ch 8 Pt 2 Div 3; *Supreme Court Rules 2006* (SA) r 148; *Supreme Court Rules 2000* (Tas) Pt 36 Div 1B; *Supreme Court (General Civil Procedure) Rules 2005* (Vic) O 37B; *Rules of the Supreme Court 1971* (WA) O 52B.

25.38   It is important to note that an Anton Piller order is not a search warrant. The latter is not issued to private litigants but to authorities charged with the bringing of criminal prosecutions and is, consequently, a much stronger order. While an Anton Piller order commands the defendant to allow entry to premises and access to materials therein, it does not in any way authorise the plaintiff to force an entry. The order applies pressure to the defendant, rather than an unqualified licence to the plaintiff. If the defendant denies access then he or she suffers consequences for disobedience of the court order, but the plaintiff is effectively blocked.

Requirements for an Anton Piller order

25.39   Given their nature and purpose, applications for Anton Piller orders 'are invariably made ex parte': *Long v Specifier Publications* at 547. In making an application for an Anton Piller order the duty of disclosure required of the plaintiff or his or her counsel is similar to that required in relation to Mareva orders (see 25.16–25.17). In *Anton Piller KG v Manufacturing Processes Ltd* at Ch 62; All ER 784, Ormrod LJ set out the essential elements of obtaining this ex parte relief as follows:

> First, there must be an extremely strong *prima facie* case. Secondly, the damage, potential or actual, must be very serious for the applicant. Thirdly, there must be clear evidence that the defendants have in their possession incriminating documents or things, and that there is a real possibility that they may destroy such material before any application *inter partes* can be made.

25.40   The 'clear evidence' of both possession and risk of destruction required under the third element is certainly the greatest challenge to the plaintiff. Despite an early generosity by the courts in granting Anton Piller orders, it is apparent that more is needed these days than a mere suspicion that the defendant will shred the evidence. An Anton Piller order is not an investigatory order: *Microsoft Corp v Goodview Electronics Pty Ltd* (1999) 46 IPR 159 at 164; *Hytrac Conveyors v Conveyors International Ltd* [1982] 3 All ER 415 at 418.

25.41   But, conversely, advances in technology now mean that in some cases evidence of a destructive intent is almost immaterial. In *Universal Music Australia Pty Ltd v Sharman License Holdings Ltd* [2004] FCA 183, the ordinary use of a dynamic operating system meant that the information required by the plaintiffs would be frequently overwritten and therefore lost. So although the defendants pointed to a cooperative attitude in related litigation in the United States, Wilcox J still felt his earlier granting of Anton Piller orders was justified because, regardless of the defendant's intentions, the data which the plaintiff needed was inherently subject to alteration and erasure.

25.42   To these elements must almost invariably be added the requirement that the plaintiff give an undertaking as to damages. However, the courts require much more of a plaintiff than his or her guarantee of financial compensation. There are many ways in which the plaintiff is expected to protect the defendant from abuse, trauma and loss. These include matters relating to the timing of the search, the right of the defendant to be present during the search and to seek legal advice, and the placement of seized documents in the hands of an independent solicitor or lawyer: *Celanese Canada Inc v Murray Demolition Corporation* (2006) 193 DLR (4th) 193 at 211–14.

25.43   Clearly, the execution of an Anton Piller order is a complex matter, holding much opportunity and potential to provoke conflict unless it is carefully prepared and strictly adhered to. Thus, the court will expect a plaintiff to give very precise information so as to enable a court to formulate a clear and precise order. In particular, the plaintiff must identify the premises to which it requires access, the documents or things it needs to inspect, copy and remove if necessary, and the persons who will execute the order and over what length of time: *Long v Specifier Publications Pty Ltd* (1998) 44 NSWLR 545 at 548–50. These matters will be among those specified in the order given by the court, and it is an abuse of process for the plaintiff not to follow the order to the letter — for example, by copying materials other than those for which it came: *Columbia Picture Industries v Robinson* [1987] Ch 38 at 76–7; [1986] 3 All ER 338 at 371–2.

The rights of the defendant

25.44 A defendant who is confronted on his or her doorstep by a party of persons wishing to execute an Anton Piller order faces a fairly onerous task in resisting them. Refusal to comply with the court's order is, of course, contempt; and this will be found even when the defendant has refused to comply in order to launch an ultimately ill-fated application to have the order dissolved. The order may be challenged on the ground that any of the requirements the plaintiff was supposed to meet — including the manner of the order's execution — have not been properly addressed. Given that the court has placed upon the plaintiff the obligation of meeting these requirements, and stressed their high importance, prior to an order being granted, it is generally unlikely that such an order will be set aside upon application by the defendant — although *Columbia Picture Industries v Robinson* illustrates a situation where this did occur for several reasons. In relation to setting aside an Anton Piller order, in *Brags Electrics Pty Ltd v Gregory* [2010] NSWSC 1205 at [17], Brereton J made the following points:

> *First*, where an Anton Pillar order is made ex parte (as it ordinarily will be), an applicant to set the order aside bears an onus of showing some reason why it should be set aside. However, it may be a sufficient reason to set aside the order that the grounds for such an order were not satisfied. *Secondly*, where such an application is made on the ground that there has been bad faith or material non-disclosure, then the court may set aside the order *ab initio*, but otherwise a discharge will operate *in futuro* only. Thus, where an application is made to set aside or discharge the order on the basis that the grounds for making such an order were not established, that will be of little utility if made after the order has been executed. At least in the absence of bad faith or non-disclosure, the remedy for a defendant where it is shown ultimately that an Anton Pillar order ought not have been made, is not to have the order set aside, but pursuant to the undertaking as to damages. *Thirdly*, on an application to set aside an Anton Pillar order, the court may take into account on the hearing of the application the 'fruits of the order' – that is to say, any evidence or admission procured as a result of the order – and any further evidence adduced in the meantime.

25.45 The final point of which to be wary is the chance that an Anton Piller order may lead a defendant to self-incrimination. Thus, it is possible for the defendant to raise the privilege against self-incrimination so as to resist compliance with the order, although the court will take into account how likely it is that actual prosecution of a crime will ensue: *Rank Film Distributors Ltd v Video Information Centre (a firm)* [1982] AC 380; [1981] 2 All ER 76.

26

EQUITABLE COMPENSATION AND DAMAGES

INTRODUCTION

26.1 In equity there are two possible bases for an order for the payment of money by way of compensation to an aggrieved party. The first arises from the inherent jurisdiction of equity to make orders for monetary compensation as an appropriate means to remedy purely equitable wrongs such as breaches of fiduciary obligations. This is known as 'equitable compensation'. The second is the ability conferred by statute for an order of damages to be substituted for, or added to, specific performance or injunction where those remedies have been sought in respect of contracts, torts or any wrongful act. Thus, in certain situations, equity has the power to provide for a remedy of damages in respect of a common law wrong. This is referred to as 'equitable damages'.

EQUITABLE COMPENSATION

26.2 Although equity courts never ordered damages as a remedy for the infringement of equitable obligations, they did provide for monetary forms of relief. In *Ex parte Adamson* (1878) 8 Ch D 807 at 819, James and Baggallay LJJ noted that relief in such cases was by way of 'a suit ... for equitable debt or liability in the nature of a debt. It was a suit for the restitution of the actual money or thing, or value of the thing, of which the cheated party had been cheated'. Equitable compensation orders were originally restricted to cases involving breaches of fiduciary obligations. Thus, in *Re Dawson (dec'd)* [1966] 2 NSWR 211, a trustee who had improperly dealt with trust funds was ordered to pay equitable compensation to the trust to restore the trust to the position it would have been in had there been no default on his part.

26.3 In *United States Surgical Corporation v Hospital Products International Pty Ltd* [1982] 2 NSWLR 766 at 816, McLelland J said that equitable compensation could be ordered in the case of the breach of any equitable obligation. Thus, equitable compensation orders have also been held to be available in cases involving undue influence: *Mahoney v Purnell* [1996] 3 All ER 61 at 88–91.

26.4 The modern authority for the availability of equitable compensation is *Nocton v Lord Ashburton* [1914] AC 932, in which Ashburton sought to recover compensation from his solicitor, Nocton, for advice that had resulted in a loss for him, but an advantage for the solicitor. Ashburton's claim for common law damages in the tort of deceit failed, but the House of Lords was prepared to award monetary compensation on the basis of Nocton's breach of fiduciary obligations. Viscount Haldane LC, at 952, affirmed the longstanding ability of the equity courts to order monetary compensation, and said:

Operating in personam as a Court of conscience it could order the defendant, not, indeed, in those days, to pay damages as such, but to make restitution, or to compensate the plaintiff by putting him in as good a position pecuniarily as that in which he was before the injury.

26.5 This quote raises the purpose of equitable compensation, which is to place the aggrieved party in the position he or she would have occupied had the equitable obligation not been breached: *Hill v Rose* [1990] VR 129 at 144; *O'Halloran v R T Thomas & Family Pty Ltd* (1998) 45 NSWLR 262 at 272. In this respect, in New South Wales in *McCrohon v Harith* [2010] 67 NSWCA 67 at [61], McColl JA pointed out that 'unlike the general rule in contract and tort, the rule in equity is that the determination of the quantum of any pecuniary remedy for breach of equitable duty falls for determination "at the time of trial, using the full benefit of hindsight": *Canson Enterprises Ltd v Boughton & Co* [1991] 3 SCR 534 at 555'. A consequence of this approach is that equitable compensation cannot put the plaintiff in a better position than he or she would have been had the breach not occurred: *Old v McInnes and Hodgkinson* [2011] NSWCA 410 at [97], [237].

26.6 In many cases, plaintiffs will have a choice of remedies available to them. It is often the case that the choice is between an account of profits (see 30.25–30.31) or equitable compensation: *Visnic v Sywak* (2009) 257 ALR 517 at 518. The distinction between these two remedies is to be found in the fact 'that the remedy of an account looks to the gain made by the party in breach while the remedy of equitable compensation looks rather to the loss suffered by the aggrieved party': *Edmonds v Donovan* [2005] VSCA 27 at [78]. In relation to this choice, in *GM & AM Pearce & Co Pty Ltd v Australian Tallow Producers* [2005] VSCA 113 at [56], Warren CJ said:

> [A]n account for profits and an award of damages are alternative and not cumulative remedies. Normally, where both remedies are available, a plaintiff must elect between them. Ordinarily, the election need not be made before the trial starts and may be delayed until determination of the cause of action. There is therefore no difficulty where the plaintiff claims both equitable compensation and an account of profits in the prayer for relief, however, election must be made when (but not before) judgment is given. Where the plaintiff does not know which remedy is more favourable at the time of judgment on liability, the court may order discovery or other orders designed to give the plaintiff the information it requires to make the election.

The nature of equitable compensation

26.7 In achieving its goal of restoring the plaintiff to the position that he or she was in before the breach of equitable obligation occurred, equity's approach to compensation, like all other equitable remedies, is conditioned by its 'flexible character': *Cole v Manning* [2002] NSWCA 150 at [63]. The appropriate date for the assessment of equitable compensation is the date on which the court makes the order for compensation, and the quantum of compensation should reflect the amount that is necessary to put the plaintiff back into the position in which he or she would have been had there been no breach of equitable obligation: *McCrohon v Harith* [2010] NSWCA 67 at [60]–[61].

26.8 Assessment of compensation is very much influenced by the type of equitable duty that has been breached: *Talacko v Talacko* [2009] VSC 533 at [124]–[132]. In some cases the measure of compensation will be determined by reference to the defendant's gain (*Ferrari Investment (Townsville) Pty Ltd (in liq) v Ferrari* [2000] Qd R 359 at 371–2), especially so in cases of defaulting fiduciaries.[1] In other cases the measure of compensation will reflect the plaintiff's loss, rather than the defendant's gain: *Hill v Rose* at 143.

26.9 Finally, the assessment of compensation can be denied by discretionary factors such as hardship (see 23.55–23.59), unclean hands (see 31.8–31.12) and laches (see 31.13–31.22).

The relationship to the common law conception of damages

26.10 An important question in relation to equitable compensation is the extent to which equity's purpose of restoring a plaintiff to his or her original position differs from that of common law damages. Common law damages are also focused upon returning the plaintiff to the position he or she would have been in had the wrong not occurred: *Johnson v Perez* (1988) 166 CLR 351 at 355; 82 ALR 587 at 588; *Tabcorp Holdings Ltd v Bowen Investments Pty Ltd* (2009) 236 CLR 272 at 286; 253 ALR 1 at 6. Although both common law and equity share the aim of providing monetary compensation to a plaintiff, there are significant differences between them in relation to the principles to be applied in assessing the quantum of monetary relief. The most important of these differences is that the liability under equity for breach of trust or fiduciary obligation is more absolute than the liability that arises under the common law of contract or tort.

26.11 Dal Pont observes that the relative attractiveness of equity's approach to compensation over common law damages leads to 'the technique of pleading fiduciary duties simply as a vehicle to broaden the availability of relief, or create an entitlement to it' and that this 'often involves an attempt to characterise as a breach of fiduciary duty that which is in effect no more than a breach of a common law or equitable duty of care'.[2] However, the courts generally will refuse to make a finding that an equitable obligation has been breached simply to broaden the scope of remedies available to a plaintiff. Thus, in *Cubillo v Commonwealth of Australia* (2001) 112 FCR 455 at 577–8; 183 ALR 249 at 370, the Full Court of the Federal Court said:

> [T]here is no room for the superimposition of fiduciary duties on common law duties simply to improve the nature and extent of the remedies available to an aggrieved party. If [on the facts of this case] it had been the case that the removal and detention of the appellants were not authorised … (or otherwise justified by law), those who caused the removal or detention would be guilty of tortious conduct and liable at common law. There would be no occasion to invoke fiduciary principles.

26.12 Furthermore, commentators and courts have traditionally been keen to emphasise the differences between common law damages and equitable compensation. This traditional approach stresses the inapplicability, in the context of equitable compensation, of the principles of causation, remoteness, foreseeability and mitigation, to potentially reduce the assessment of compensation payable by the erring party. In *Re Dawson (dec'd)*, in a case concerning a defaulting trustee, the court determined that the trustee had to bear the burden of an exchange rate significantly worsened since the date of breach. In relation to the trustee's liability, Street J, at 214–15, said:

---

1. For a thorough discussion of equitable compensation in the context of where trust property has been misapplied by a trustee, and where a fiduciary has committed a breach of the no conflict rule by failing to disclose material facts to his or her principal see J Glister, 'Equitable Compensation' in J Glister & P Ridge (eds), *Fault Lines in Equity*, Hart Publishing, Oxford, 2012, p 143.
2. G E Dal Pont, *Equity and Trusts in Australia*, 5th ed, Law Book Co, Sydney, 2011, pp 1021–2.

The obligation of a defaulting trustee ... is of a personal character and its extent is not to be limited by common law principles governing remoteness of damage ... [I]f a breach has been committed then the trustee is liable to place the trust estate in the same position as it would have been in if no breach had been committed. Considerations of causation, foreseeability and remoteness do not readily enter into the matter.

26.13 Consistent with *Re Dawson (dec'd)*, in *Youyang Pty Ltd v Minter Ellison Morris Fletcher* (2003) 212 CLR 484 at 500; 196 ALR 482 at 491, the High Court said:

[T]here must be a real question whether the unique foundation and goals of equity, which has the institution of the trust at its heart, warrant any assimilation even in this limited way with the measure of compensatory damages in tort and contract. It may be thought strange to decide that the precept that trustees are to be kept by courts of equity up to their duty has an application limited to the observance by trustees of some only of their duties to beneficiaries in dealing with trust funds.

26.14 This statement suggests that in a trust relationship — and arguably any relationship governed by principles of equity — claims for equitable compensation arising out of any breach of obligation would be unaffected by common law rules, such as causation, remoteness and mitigation. However, there are indications in some cases of a trend towards a greater willingness on the part of courts to acknowledge the similarities and growing closeness between the ways in which equity and the common law approach the awarding of their respective monetary compensation remedies. This trend is examined in the context of the principles of causation, the plaintiff's contribution to his or her loss, mitigation, remoteness, exemplary damages and aggravated damages.

Causation

26.15 In *Target Holdings Ltd v Redferns* [1996] 1 AC 421 at 432; [1995] 3 All ER 785 at 792, Lord Browne-Wilkinson said:

At common law there are two principles fundamental to the award of damages. First, that the defendant's wrongful act must cause the damage complained of. Second, that the plaintiff is to be put 'in the same position as he would have been in if he had not sustained the wrong for which he is now getting his compensation or reparation'. Although, as will appear, in many ways equity approaches liability for making good a breach of trust from a different starting point, in my judgment those two principles are applicable as much in equity as at common law. Under both systems liability is fault-based: the defendant is only liable for the consequences of the legal wrong he has done to the plaintiff and to make good the damage caused by such wrong. He is not responsible for damage not caused by his wrong or to pay by way of compensation more than the loss suffered from such wrong. The detailed rules of equity as to causation and the quantification of loss differ, at least ostensibly, from those applicable at common law. But the principles underlying both systems are the same.

26.16 Although his Lordship required there to be a causal connection between breach and loss, this requirement faces a less rigorous examination at equity than at common law. In *Maguire v Makaronis* (1997) 188 CLR 449 at 473; 144 ALR 729 at 744, Brennan CJ, Gaudron, McHugh and Gummow JJ observed that, in equitable compensation cases, a commonsense view of causation required that there be 'an adequate or sufficient connection between the equitable compensation claimed and the breach of [equitable obligation]'.

26.17   A consequence of this approach is that a defendant in equity cannot resist a finding of adequate causation by arguing that there was a break in the causal connection between breach of loss suffered by reason of some intervening act (*novus actus interveniens*). Equity is not readily susceptible to such speculation about other possible causes for loss when there is a clearly identifiable breach present: *Bennett v Minister of Community Welfare* (1991) 176 CLR 408 at 426–7; 107 ALR 617 at 630. In *Brickenden v London Loan & Savings Co* [1934] 3 DLR 465 at 469, the Privy Council observed:

> When a party holding a fiduciary relationship, commits a breach of his duty by non-disclosure of material facts, which his constituent is entitled to know in connection with the transaction, he cannot be heard to maintain that disclosure would not have altered the decision to proceed with the transaction, because the constituent's action would be solely determined by some other factor, such as the valuation by another party of the property proposed to be mortgaged. Once the Court has determined that the non-disclosed facts were material, speculation as to what course the constituent, on disclosure, would have taken is not relevant.

26.18   In *Beach Petroleum NL v Kennedy* (1999) 48 NSWLR 1 at 92, the Court of Appeal in New South Wales said:

> It is important to emphasise that the proposition on which reliance is placed refers only to an act of non-disclosure by a fiduciary of 'material facts which his constituent is entitled to know in connection with the transaction'. The central word in the formulation in *Brickenden* is the word 'material'. Before applying the principle, it is necessary to identify a fact which is 'material' in the requisite sense. Once a fact is so identified, the principle establishes that the defaulting fiduciary will not succeed in an argument that, even with disclosure of this material fact, the transaction would still have gone ahead.

26.19   Facts will not be 'material' if the relevant loss would have happened if there had been no breach: *Maguire v Makaronis* at CLR 493; ALR 760. Thus, in *Bank of New Zealand v New Zealand Guardian Trust Co Ltd* [1999] 1 NZLR 664 at 687, Tipping J said that '[o]nce the plaintiff has shown a loss arising out of a transaction to which the breach was material, the plaintiff is entitled to recover unless the defendant fiduciary, upon whom is the onus, shows that the loss or damage would have occurred in any event, ie without any breach on the fiduciary's part'.

26.20   In *O'Halloran v R T Thomas & Family Pty Ltd* (1998) 45 NSWLR 262, the New South Wales Court of Appeal stated their opinion that while the standard of liability was generally strict in respect of liability for equitable compensation, this was itself to be subject to the particular issues arising in each case. *O'Halloran* concerned a company director's responsibility to not deal improperly with company assets. With respect to the standard of causation required on these facts, Spigelman CJ, at 274–5, said:

> [A] claim for equitable compensation for breach of a fiduciary obligation requires a causal link between the breach and the loss. Causation in equity is not, however, susceptible to the formulation of a single test. It is necessary to identify the purpose of the particular rule to determine the appropriate approach to issues of causation.

His Honour, at 277, continued:

> The strict standard applicable to a trustee of a traditional trust with respect to improper application of trust property is based on the vulnerability of beneficiaries with respect to the disposition of property by a trustee who has control over such disposition ... Policy favours a stringent test in the circumstances of this case. It is the vulnerability of a company which places its property in the power of directors, that makes it appropriate to adopt the approach to causation applicable to the trustee of a traditional trust in deciding issues of causation for the contravention by a company director of his or her duty not to exercise the power to dispose of property for an improper purpose.

The Chief Justice, at 278, concluded that the standard 'adopted for the trustee of a traditional trust should be applied to the exercise of this fiduciary power by a company director'. In relation to breaches of fiduciary duties, in *Eiszele v Hurburgh* [2011] TASSC 65 at [51], after discussing various authorities, Blow J ruled that '[t]here is no reason in principle why fiduciaries, in breach of their duties of disclosure, should receive different treatment from courts of equity depending on whether their conflicts were between interest and duty or between one duty and another duty'.

26.21   However, it is clear from the decision in *O'Halloran* that the test for causation may well be different in the context of other breaches by a fiduciary. In *Permanent Building Society (in liq) v Wheeler* (1994) 11 WAR 187, the Court of Appeal dealt with a director's duty to exercise care and skill. Speaking for the court, Ipp J, at 239, described that duty as follows:

> The director's duty to exercise care and skill has nothing to do with any position of disadvantage or vulnerability on the part of the company. It is not a duty that stems from the requirements of trust and confidence imposed upon a fiduciary ... [The] duty is not a fiduciary duty, although it is a duty actionable in the equitable jurisdiction of this court.

His Honour, at 247–8, then went on to say:

> There is a fundamental distinction between breaches of fiduciary obligations which involve dishonesty and abuse of the trustee's advantages and the vulnerable position of beneficiaries, on the one hand, and, honest but careless dealings which breach mere equitable obligations, on the other. There is ample justification on policy grounds for more stringent rules in the case of breaches of fiduciary obligations, but not where there has been honest but careless dealings ... [T]he tortious duty not to be negligent, and the equitable obligation on the part of a trustee to exercise reasonable care and skill are, in content, the same. There is every reason, in my view, in such circumstances, to apply the maxim that 'equity follows the law' ... In my opinion, the principles referred to in *Brickenden* ... apply only to breaches of true fiduciary obligations and not to breaches of the equitable obligation on the part of a trustee or director to exercise reasonable skill and care.

26.22   The consequence of the decision in *Wheeler* is that a plaintiff's claim for compensation against a director who has breached his or her duty of care and skill, will face barriers relating to matters such as causation, remoteness and limitation period legislation that the same plaintiff would not face if his or her claim related to the director's obligation of trust and confidence to the company.[3]

---

3.   For an analysis of the *Wheeler* decision see J D Heydon, 'Are the Duties of Company Directors to Exercise Care and Skill Fiduciary?' in S Degeling & J Edelman, *Equity in Commercial Law*, Law Book Co, Sydney, 2005, p 185.

Plaintiff's contribution to loss

26.23   In New Zealand and Canada, courts have held that a plaintiff's claim for equitable compensation may be successfully defended on the basis that his or her contribution to the loss may be a complete or partial defence to liability on the part of the defendant: *Day v Mead* [1987] 2 NZLR 443 at 451; *Canson Enterprises Ltd v Boughton & Co* [1991] 3 SCR 534 at 585; (1991) 85 DLR (4th) 129 at 151.

26.24   In Australia, however, this approach has been rejected by the High Court in *Pilmer v Duke Group Limited (in liq)* (2001) 207 CLR 165; 180 ALR 249. In this case, the facts concerned the takeover by Kia Ora Gold Corp Ltd of Western United Ltd, a company in which many of Kia Ora's directors held an interest. Under such circumstances, the law required the preparation of a report by 'independent qualified persons' for the information of shareholders whose approval was ultimately required at a general meeting. The firm of chartered accountants engaged by Kia Ora had, in fact, a long history of dealing with both that company and Western United Ltd. The report asserted that the price to be paid for the shares in Western United was fair and reasonable. In reality, this was not the case, with Kia Ora paying out around $26m for $6m worth of shareholdings and thus enabling huge personal profits to be made by the Kia Ora directors who held shares in Western United. Kia Ora subsequently brought an action against the partners of the accountancy firm seeking to recover for its loss.

26.25   The Full Court of the Supreme Court of South Australia in *Duke Group Limited (in liq) v Pilmer* (1999) 73 SASR 64 found the accountants to be in breach of the contractual, tortious and fiduciary duties which they owed to the company. Ultimately, the court measured the damages payable by the defendants using the principles relevant to breach of contractual duty, since these resulted in the higher figure. In doing so, their Honours were careful not to transgress the High Court's finding in *Astley v Austrust Limited* (1999) 197 CLR 1; 161 ALR 155, that considerations akin to contributory negligence have no place in an assessment of damages for breach of contract. However, although thus not strictly necessary to decide, the Full Court considered the effect which a plaintiff's contribution to loss would have upon an assessment of equitable compensation for breaches of fiduciary obligations. In this respect, the Full Court, at 250, said that it would be:

> … inherently unjust, and we would say, inequitable, to require a defendant, whose fiduciary breach unlocked the door to the plaintiff acting in obvious disregard of its own interests, to bear sole responsibility for the total loss thereby suffered by the plaintiff where the plaintiff's own conduct has made a material contribution to that loss.

26.26   The appeal to the High Court by the former partners of the accounting firm succeeded on the basis that the calculation of damages to compensate for Kia Ora's loss had been incorrect and also that no fiduciary obligation had been breached. Although Kirby J disagreed on the latter score, the court was of one mind in rejecting any place for reduction on the basis of the plaintiff's conduct in the determination of equitable compensation. The reasons included an appreciation of the essence of the fiduciary relationship in which the beneficiary has no obligation to protect himself or herself against the fiduciary and the nature of contributory negligence in tort law. McHugh, Gummow, Hayne and Callinan JJ, at CLR 201–2; ALR 274, said:

Contributory negligence focuses on the conduct of the plaintiff, fiduciary law upon the obligation by the defendant to act in the interests of the plaintiff. Moreover, any question of apportionment with respect to contributory negligence arises from legislation, not the common law. *Astley* indicates that the particular apportionment legislation of South Australia which was there in question did not touch contractual liability. The reasoning in *Astley* would suggest, *a fortiori*, that such legislation did not touch the fiduciary relationship.

26.27   Kirby J, at CLR 231; ALR 298, stressed the court's commitment to the pre-judicature division of principles, and said:

> Whatever might have been my inclination to explore the notion adopted by the Full Court prior to *Astley v Austrust Ltd*, I regard the holding in that case as a splash of cold water, discouraging any creative instinct in this connection. There, after all, the court was considering the development of an apportionment principle within the four walls of the common law and the applicable statute … In the face of that decision and the repeated recognition by this court that, in Australia, the substantive rules of equity have retained their identity as part of a separate and coherent body of principles, the attempt to push common law notions of contributory negligence, as now modified by statute, into equitable remedies collapses in the face of insurmountable obstacles.

Mitigation

26.28   Just as a plaintiff's contribution to his or her own loss is not a basis for disallowing or reducing the amount of equitable compensation, any duty to mitigate is, as Glover observes, 'likewise suspect'. But, as Glover also notes, 'it may not be just to make fiduciary defendants pay for the consequences of their victims' profligacy or connivance … The answer to this is equity's remedial discretion'.[4] Consistent with this sentiment, in *Canson Enterprises Ltd v Boughton & Co* at SCR 554; DLR 162, McLachlin J said:

> In negligence and contract the law limits the actions of the parties who are expected to pursue their own best interest. Each is expected to continue to look after their own interests after a breach or tort, and so a duty of mitigation is imposed. In contrast, the hallmark of fiduciary relationship is that the fiduciary, at least within a certain scope, is expected to pursue the best interest of the client. It may not be fair to allow the fiduciary to complain when the client fails forthwith to shoulder the fiduciary's burden. This approach to mitigation accords with the basic rule of equitable compensation that the injured party will be reimbursed for all losses flowing directly from the breach. When the plaintiff, after due notice and opportunity, fails to take the most obvious steps to alleviate his or her losses, then we may rightly say that the plaintiff has been 'the author of his own misfortune'. At this point the plaintiff's failure to mitigate may become so egregious that it is no longer sensible to say that the losses which followed were caused by the fiduciary's breach. But until that point, mitigation will not be required.

Foreseeability and remoteness

26.29   While causation and mitigation may have to some extent been absorbed into the practical operation of equitable compensation, it seems that remoteness and foreseeability are yet to gain any admission to this territory. These concepts are far removed from the basis of equitable obligations

---

4.   J Glover, *Equity, Restitution & Fraud*, LexisNexis Butterworths, Sydney, 2004, p 444.

and liability for their breach. However, just as causation was once perceived as being outside equity's absolute liability approach, it may well be that remoteness and foreseeability become increasingly relevant as equity and the common law continue 'mingling or interacting'. Indeed, in Canada, such is the case: *Canson Enterprises Ltd v Boughton & Co* at SCR 579–80; DLR 147; *Hodgkinson v Simms* [1994] 3 SCR 377 at 443; 117 DLR (4th) 161 at 201.

Exemplary damages

26.30   A traditional approach to equitable compensation would limit its calculation to what was actually suffered by the plaintiff and that exemplary or punitive damages were not recoverable for breaches of equitable obligations. This approach represents an historical point of distinction between equity and the common law in that such damages can be awarded in tort law. However, there is growing support in some jurisdictions for the view that exemplary damages can be awarded as part of an award of equitable compensation. Thus, the Supreme Court of Canada in *Norberg v Wynrib* (1992) 92 DLR (4th) 440, has ruled that exemplary damages are available against a party in breach of a purely equitable obligation. Similarly, in New Zealand, in *Skids Programme Management Limited v McNeill* [2012] NZCA 314 at [123], the Court of Appeal ruled that, although 'the origin of the cause of action [for breach of confidence' lies in equity, we do not consider that this factor should dictate the remedies that are available', with the result that 'exemplary damages are available in New Zealand for breach of confidence'. Finally, exemplary damages can be awarded for breaches of fiduciary obligations in the United States of America.[5]

26.31   In Australia, a much more cautious approach is evident, the leading case on the issue being that of *Harris v Digital Pulse Pty Ltd* (2003) 56 NSWLR 298. This case concerned an action by Digital Pulse against two former employees who had diverted work to their own company. This was in clear breach of the clause in their contracts of employment not to compete with Digital Pulse for business. At first instance, Palmer J also found that the defendants had been in breach of the fiduciary duty which they owed their employer. So flagrant was the defendants' behaviour that, in addition to other forms of relief, his Honour awarded $10,000 exemplary damages against each. An appeal was brought to the New South Wales Court of Appeal arguing that jurisdiction did not exist to order exemplary damages for breach of a fiduciary duty.

26.32   The majority of the Court of Appeal upheld the appeal and found that Palmer J had erred in awarding exemplary damages on these facts. Heydon JA, at 360–91, who authored the leading judgment, expressed a fundamental objection to the concept of damages as punishment at equity after a thorough canvassing of authorities. He rejected the persuasiveness of New Zealand and Canadian authorities. Indeed, his Honour's ultimate dismissal of exemplary damages in equity laid the blame for the suggestion at the door, not so much of Palmer J, but the New Zealand Court of Appeal. His Honour, at 416, said:

> What [that court] contemplated in the *Aquaculture Corporation* case was a form — perhaps a mild form, but a form nonetheless — of fusion. It was fusion in the sense of selecting a remedy from the common law range of remedies which a court of equity administering the law relating to equitable wrongs before the introduction of a judicature system would not have administered. What is contemplated is that the unified court administering the two systems may select a remedy

---

5.   T Frankel, *Fiduciary Law*, Oxford University Press, Oxford, 2011, pp 258–60.

historically granted by the courts of common law in relation to a wrong recognised only in the courts of equity. But whatever one calls the process, it must be recognised as a process involving a deliberate judicially-engineered change in the law.

26.33   Mason P dissented. His Honour, at 326, said:

Both 'Equity' and 'Common Law' had adequate powers to adopt and adapt concepts from each other's system well before the passing of the Judicature Act, and nothing in that legislation limits such powers. They are of the very essence of judicial method which was and is part of the armoury of every judge in every 'common law' jurisdiction.

His Honour, at 335–6, saw merit in Palmer J's 'novel remedy' due to the need to achieve coherency in the law — it was undesirable that the rationale of punishing a wrongdoer was given expression when the wrong was classified as tortious but unavailable when the wrong was part of the equity canon.

26.34   In the other majority judgment, Spigelman CJ, at 305, rejected the holistic coherency advocated by Mason P as 'incompatible with the traditional common law judicial method'. His Honour, at 307–10, also clearly favoured analogical reasoning, if at all appropriate, between contract and equity in preference to tort and equity. However, it is important to note the limitations of the Chief Justice's opinion which necessarily confined the impact of the refusal of the majority in *Harris v Digital Pulse* to award exemplary damages to those cases where the basis of the fiduciary duty was found in a contract between the parties. As his Honour, at 304, noted:

It is, in my opinion, unnecessary and undesirable to decide this case on the basis that a punitive monetary award can never be awarded in equity. Remedial flexibility is a characteristic of equity jurisprudence.

26.35   The case of *Harris v Digital Pulse* is of enormous significance in many ways. Primarily, for present purposes, it rejects the possibility of exemplary damages being awarded for breach of an equitable duty which arises out of a contractual relationship. However, and second, it sends a reasonably clear signal (although, note, it does not stand for the broader proposition) that exemplary damages may never be awarded at equity as it is a jurisdiction which does not aim to punish. Third, it demonstrates the vital relevance of the jurisdictional distinctions between the common law and equity — whether one seeks to maintain or blur them. Fourth, it invites appraisal of judicial attitudes to the limits of discretion and flexibility which inhere in the character of equity. Fifth, it brings attention to the very nature of equity and the purpose of the relief it offers. Finally, and in light of all the above, *Harris v Digital Pulse* is a striking illustration of a court grappling with equity's relationship to the common law and the degree of consistency which is desirable between the two.

26.36   The decision in *Harris v Digital Pulse* has been criticised on a number of bases. Dal Pont has commented as follows:

[The decision] is odd ... particularly as equity often provides more extensive relief to a plaintiff than allowed by the common law, principally on the ground that equitable duties (in particular, fiduciary duties) are of a higher nature than common law duties. It seems strange that equity, via equitable relief, is willing to be more stringent against defendants who breach these higher duties, but will not countenance greater relief (in the form of exemplary damages) for especially flagrant breaches of these duties.[6]

26.37   It has also been observed that the employees in *Harris v Digital Pulse* were 'fortunate that what they did happened to constitute an equitable wrong and not a tort'.[7] The fact that distinctions of jurisdiction can result in like cases actually *not* being treated alike poses a real challenge to one of the bedrock values of Anglo-Australian law.[8] The move to a broad and principled understanding of equity as just further instances of civil wrongs, and thus sharing in tortious remedies through that analogy, underlay, to various degrees, the decisions of Palmer J at first instance and Mason P on appeal. But this faces two forms of opposition, most observable by Spigelman CJ's insistence, first, that the law 'develops from the bottom up, not from the top down' (*Harris v Digital Pulse* at 305), and then his Honour's opinion that, if anything, equity is most usefully analogous to contract law, which similarly focuses on 'satisfying expectation': *Harris v Digital Pulse* at 308–10.

Aggravated damages

26.38   Aggravated damages relate to 'injury to the plaintiff's dignatory interest (in this context, injury to the plaintiff's feelings) which is heightened by reference to the defendant's reprehensible conduct'.[9] In *Giller v Procopets* (2008) 24 VR 1 at 104, Neave JA held that, '[s]uch damages are compensatory, not punitive'. Her Honour, at 105, went on to rule that, in the appropriate case, it was proper for a court to include a component for aggravation in an award of equitable compensation. In determining whether or not an order for compensation for aggravation should be made, a court will assess the defendant's conduct on criteria that are very similar to the assessment of whether an award of exemplary damages would be made against the defendant.

EQUITABLE DAMAGES

26.39   When dealing with the enforcement of common law rights, the Court of Chancery in its auxiliary jurisdiction had an inherent jurisdiction to award damages, but 'as a matter of practice and principle [it] ordinarily did not do so': *Break Fast Investments Pty Ltd v PCH Melbourne Pty Ltd* (2007) 20 VR 311 at 319. Historically, the general approach of equity was to leave claims for damages to the common law courts. A plaintiff whose claim for equitable relief of a common law wrong failed, had to commence fresh proceedings in the common law courts in order to pursue a claim for damages. This was of considerable practical inconvenience for litigants and significantly increased the complexity, length and cost of legal proceedings.

26.40   The resolution of these problems was the purpose behind the *Chancery Amendment Act 1858* (UK), more popularly known as Lord Cairns' Act, after the Solicitor-General who oversaw its introduction. The Act sought to enable the Court of Chancery to make awards of damages to parties who were seeking equitable relief before it in the form of orders for specific performance

---

6.   Dal Pont, *Equity and Trusts in Australia*, note 2 above, p 11.
7.   D Morgan, '*Harris v Digital Pulse*: The Availability of Exemplary Damages in Equity' (2003) 29 *Monash Law Review* 377, p 400.
8.   A Burrows, 'We Do This At Common Law But That In Equity' (2002) 22 *Oxford Journal of Legal Studies* 1.
9.   M Tilbury & G Davis, 'Equitable Compensation' in P Parkinson (ed), *The Principles of Equity*, 2nd ed, Law Book Co, Sydney, 2003, pp 797–839 at 809.

or an injunction. In this way, a party who was denied such relief on discretionary grounds could recover damages without having to re-commence proceedings before the common law courts.

26.41   The provisions of Lord Cairns' Act may properly be seen as a precursor to the far-reaching reforms of the *Judicature Acts* in England in the 1870s which fused the administration of equity and common law generally: see Chapter 3. The fusion of the courts of common law and equity has reduced the practical significance of Lord Cairns' Act. However, as will be shown below, in situations where there are limitations upon the use of common law damages, the Act does retain its potency as a means by which a plaintiff can obtain damages as a remedy.

26.42   Lord Cairns' Act exists in modern statutory form in all Australian states, except Queensland.[10] In Queensland, a statutory provision to this effect, set out in s 62 of the *Equity Act 1867* (Qld), has since been repealed. However, it has been held that the repeal did not affect the court's power to award such damages where the power is recognised by case law: *Barbagallo v J & F Catelan Pty Ltd* [1986] 1 Qd R 245.

26.43   In relation to Australia's two territories, it was held in *Brooks v Wyatt* (1994) 99 NTR 12 at 27–30, that s 62 of the *Supreme Court Act 1979* (NT) in effect re-enacted by reference Lord Cairns' Act in the Northern Territory. Section 62 stipulates as follows:

> Where a plaintiff claims to be entitled to an equitable estate or right, or to relief on an equitable ground against a deed, instrument or contract, or against a right, title or claim asserted by any defendant in a proceeding, or to relief founded upon a legal right that could in England immediately before the commencement of the Judicature Act only have been given by a Court of Equity, the Court shall give to the plaintiff the same relief as ought then to have been given by the English Court of Chancery in a proceeding for the like purpose.

On the basis of this authority the same result would apply in the Australian Capital Territory where s 26 of the *Supreme Court Act 1933* (ACT) stipulates that:

> In proceedings in the court, the plaintiff is entitled to equitable relief if, in pre-Judicature Act proceedings of the same type, the plaintiff would have been entitled to such relief.

26.44   However, there is another foundation upon which jurisdiction to award damages in the territories is based. In the Northern Territory s 14(1)(b) of the *Supreme Court Act 1979* (NT) states that the territory's Supreme Court has the same jurisdiction as did the Supreme Court of South Australia as at 1 January 1911. At that time the Supreme Court of South Australia had jurisdiction to award equitable damages pursuant to s 141 of the *Equity Act 1866* (SA). Similarly, s 11 of the *Seat of Government Act 1909* (Cth) may have the effect of giving the Supreme Court of the Australian Capital Territory jurisdiction to award equitable damages. This is on the basis that, at the time the territory's Supreme Court was established in 1933, its jurisdiction in this area was dependent upon the fact that New South Wales had such jurisdiction pursuant to s 9 of the *Equity Act 1901* (NSW). However, in *Financial Integrity Group Limited v Scott Farmer & Bravium Pty Limited* [2009] ACTSC 143 at [98]–[109], Refshauge J doubted that this was the proper basis

---

10.   *Supreme Court Act 1970* (NSW) s 68; *Supreme Court Act 1935* (SA) s 30; *Supreme Court Civil Procedure Act 1932* (Tas) s 11(13); *Supreme Court Act 1986* (Vic) s 38; *Supreme Court Act 1935* (WA) s 25(10).

upon which the Supreme Court of the Australian Capital Territory could be said to have acquired jurisdiction to award equitable damages.

26.45   The *Federal Court of Australia Act 1976* (Cth) has no explicit provision giving the Federal Court jurisdiction to award equitable damages. However, in *Matthews v ACP Publishing Pty Ltd* (1998) 157 ALR 564 at 571, in a case where the principal relief sought was an injunction, Beaumont J held that ss 5(2), 22 and 23 of the Act 'when read together, mean that [the Federal] Court, as a statutory court, has at least the same powers as a modern court of equity to award damages in addition to, or in lieu of, an injunction (or its equivalent)'.

26.46   An example of an Australian statutory provision is s 68 of the *Supreme Court Act 1970* (NSW) which states:

> Where the Court has power:
>
> (a) to grant an injunction against the breach of any covenant, contract or agreement, or against the commission or continuance of any wrongful act, or
> (b) to order the specific performance of any covenant, contract or agreement,
>
> the Court may award damages to the party injured either in addition to or in substitution for the injunction or specific performance.

The only significant variation from the provisions of s 68 is in Victoria, where there is no equivalent to the phrase 'any wrongful act' found in s 68(a).

26.47   In *Wentworth v Woollahra Municipal Council* (1982) 149 CLR 672 at 676; 42 ALR 69 at 72, Gibbs CJ, Mason, Murphy and Brennan JJ referred to the purpose of Lord Cairns' Act in the following terms:

> The main object of the Act was to enable the Court of Chancery to do 'complete justice' between the parties by awarding damages in those cases in which it formerly refused equitable relief in respect of a legal right and left the plaintiff to sue for damages at common law.

26.48   It is important to note that the power to award damages under Lord Cairns' Act related to cases where the court has jurisdiction to order specific performance or an injunction. Thus, the Act does not enable a court to award damages in lieu of an account of profits: *English v Dedham Vale Properties Ltd* [1978] 1 All ER 382 at 399. Nor does it empower a court to award damages in lieu of an injunction that is sought in relation to the breach of a statutory prohibition, unless the statute manifests an intention to create a private right of enforcement: *Wentworth v Woollahra Municipal Council* at CLR 679–83; ALR 74–7; *Matthews v ACP Publishing Pty Ltd* at 573. However, a plaintiff does not need to have actually made an application for specific performance or an injunction for the court to exercise its power to award damages. It is enough that the court had jursidiction to grant such equitable relief: *Giller v Procopets* at 95–6.

26.49   Given the rationale behind the legislation, in accordance with the maxim that equity follows the law, the court applies, as far as possible, common law principles in assessing the measure of damages under Lord Cairns' Act: *Johnson v Agnew* [1980] AC 367 at 400; [1979] 1 All ER 883 at 895–6. Thus, in relation to the assessment of equitable damages, common law rules apply as to matters such as remoteness (*Griffin v Mercantile Bank* (1890) 11 LR (NSW) Eq 231); mitigation

(*Dillon v Nash Properties Pty Ltd* [1950] VLR 293, at 301–2); certainty (*Edward Street Properties Pty Ltd v Collins* [1977] Qd R 399); the date for the assessment of damages (*Johnson v Agnew* at AC 400–1; All ER 896); and the once and for all lump sum rule: *Neylon v Dickens* [1987] 1 NZLR 402 at 407, 410.

Jurisdiction to award equitable damages

26.50   Before equitable damages can be awarded, the court must have the jurisdiction to order a decree of specific performance or an injunction. Thus, if such equitable relief is refused on the basis that damages at common law are adequate, the court has no jurisdiction to award equitable damages. In *Waterways Authority of New South Wales v Coal & Allied (Operations) Pty Ltd* [2007] NSWCA 276 at [94], Beazley JA, speaking for a unanimous Court of Appeal, observed that 'the adequacy of damages is fundamental to the question whether specific performance is an available remedy so as to provide the jurisdictional route for an award of [equitable] damages'. Furthermore, if equitable relief is impossible to grant at the time proceedings are commenced, and remains so to the date of judgment, there is no jurisdiction to award equitable damages. Thus, in *McMahon v Ambrose* [1987] VR 817, specific performance of a contract to assign a lease was sought, but because the lease had already expired before proceedings were commenced it was impossible to make the order, and therefore there was no jurisdiction to award equitable damages. However, if at the time of hearing it has become possible to order equitable relief, then there is jurisdiction to award equitable damages: *Oakacre Ltd v Claire Cleaners (Holdings) Ltd* [1982] Ch 197.

26.51   Where the court has no jurisdiction to award equitable relief, the court will leave the plaintiff to his or her common law remedy of damages. The practicalities of assessing common law damages was explained in *International Advisor Systems Pty Limited v XYYX Pty Limited* [2008] NSWSC 2 at [54] and [70], where Brereton J said:

> As the primary basis for refusing specific performance is that damages at law are a sufficient remedy, the traditional course would have been, not to order an inquiry as to damages under *Lord Cairns' Act* — which assumes that the case was one in which specific performance could have been ordered — but to dismiss the suit without prejudice to the plaintiff's right to proceed at common law. Since the [adoption of the judicature system] that course is no longer necessary, and damages at law can be assessed and awarded in the Equity Division … [In this case] it has not been established that damages are an inadequate remedy … Accordingly, I will refuse to grant specific performance, but I will give judgment for the plaintiff against both defendants for the damages (at common law) … such damages to be assessed.

26.52   The fact that equitable relief is denied on discretionary grounds does not disentitle a plaintiff to equitable damages. In *Wentworth v Woollahra Municipal Council* at CLR 678–9; ALR 73–4, Gibbs CJ, Mason, Murphy and Brennan JJ said:

> It is obvious that a discretionary defence to a claim for equitable relief does not, if made out, operate as a defence to a claim for common law damages for infringement of the legal right on which the case for equitable relief is based. Although damages under [Lord Cairns' Act] are not common law damages and they are expressed by the statute to be given in lieu of, or in addition to, the basic claim for equitable relief, it conforms to the main object of the statute if damages in such a case are awarded under the [Act], even though the claim for equitable relief is defeated by a discretionary defence such as laches, acquiescence or hardship. We are content to assume, without finally deciding, that this is so.

26.53   Although the High Court only assumed that the proposition was correct, later cases have regarded it as authoritative. Thus, in *Waterways Authority of New South Wales v Coal & Allied (Operations)* at [166], Beazley JA referred to the 'well understood principle that damages under s 68(b) of the *Supreme Court Act* can be awarded even if the court would not have made an order for specific performance or final injunction by reason of some discretionary defence'.

Equitable damages in addition to specific relief

26.54   The provisions of Lord Cairns' Act clearly envisage the making of an order for damages in addition to specific performance or injunctive relief. This is especially useful in enabling the court to address the issue of any losses caused to the plaintiff by the defendant's breach that are not properly addressed by an order for equitable relief. Thus, in *Ford-Hunt v Raghbir Singh* [1973] 2 All ER 700, equitable damages were awarded in addition to a decree for specific performance to a purchaser of land to compensate him for the losses occasioned by the vendor's delay in completing the contract.

Equitable damages in lieu of specific relief

26.55   The ability to substitute equitable damages for an order of specific performance or injunction remains the more significant aspect of the Lord Cairns' Act provisions. This issue needs to be considered in three contexts. The first is where specific relief is denied to a plaintiff on discretionary grounds such as laches or acquiescence. The second is where specific relief has been ordered but, for one reason or another, cannot be carried out. The third is where there is no discretionary bar to specific relief, but the defendant claims that equitable damages should nevertheless be granted to the plaintiff.

26.56   In the first situation, as already noted (see 26.52–26.53), the fact that specific relief is denied on discretionary grounds does not preclude the court from ordering equitable damages. Thus, in *Norton v Angus* (1926) 38 CLR 523, a purchaser contracted to buy two parcels of land with a combined area of 1280 acres. However, relevant legislation prevented one person from owning more than 1280 acres of land in that particular region of Queensland. If specific performance was granted, that would have required the purchaser to find a buyer for one of the parcels who was willing to live on the land and pay rent to the Crown. The sale price would probably have been less than the true value of the land. On the other hand, if the purchaser chose to transfer the land to a trustee, it was liable to be forfeited. In the circumstances, the High Court ruled that it would be unfair to grant specific performance in favour of the vendor and ordered equitable damages instead. According to Knox CJ, at 530, 'the best justice of which the case is capable will be done by giving damages … in lieu of specific performance'. However, in some cases the reason for denying specific relief will also be the reason for denying equitable damages. Thus, in *Sayers v Collyer* (1884) 28 Ch D 103, in a case concerning an application for an injunction to enforce a restrictive covenant, the plaintiff's acquiescence to the defendant's breach meant that the plaintiff lost his right, not only to an injunction, but also to equitable damages.

26.57   In relation to the second situation, where specific relief once ordered becomes impossible to carry out due to intervening circumstances, a court will readily make an order for equitable damages in lieu of specific relief. Thus, in *Johnson v Agnew*, a vendor's successful application for specific performance of a contract for the sale of land was made impossible because of the purchaser's failure to comply with the order coupled with the exercise of a power of sale of the land by the vendor's mortgagee. In these circumstances, the House of Lords vacated the order for specific performance and awarded equitable damages in favour of the vendor pursuant to Lord Cairns' Act.

26.58 One of the most prominent areas in which the question of substituting equitable damages for specific relief arises, is in the third situation This relates to cases where a plaintiff seeks an injunction to restrain a trespass or nuisance by the defendant and the defendant claims that equitable damages is the appropriate remedy. Prior to the enactment of Lord Cairns' Act, the protection of the plaintiff's proprietary rights in such cases was principally by means of an injunction, simply because common law damages were relatively ineffectual as a remedy. At common law, damages were not available until there was a breach of the plaintiff's rights, so that repeated or continuing breaches required fresh proceedings: *Break Fast Investments v PCH Melbourne* at 319. An injunction was far more effective in that it put a stop to repeated or continuing breaches. Lord Cairns' Act 'introduced the possibility of damages for, inter alia, trespass to freehold land, which could represent compensation "once and for all", in circumstances where the trespass was permanent or continuing, thus obviating repeated applications for relief': *Break Fast Investments v PCH Melbourne* at 319.

26.59 However, this did not mean that equitable damages became 'the standard remedy for trespass, whereby wrongful acts could routinely be sanctioned by the effective "purchase" of the landowners' rights': *Break Fast Investments v PCH Melbourne* at 319. Rather, the courts have insisted that such damages will be ordered only in exceptional circumstances. In *Shelfer v City of London Electric Lighting Co* [1895] 1 Ch 287 at 322–3, A L Smith LJ said that it was a 'good working rule' to award equitable damages in lieu of the injunction: '(1) If the injury to the plaintiff's legal rights is small, (2) And is one which is capable of being estimated in money, (3) And is one which can be adequately compensated by a small money payment, (4) And the case is one in which it would be oppressive to the defendant to grant an injunction'. In *Jaggard v Sawyer* [1995] 2 All ER 189 at 208, Millet LJ said that, although the *Shelfer* principles had 'stood the test of time', it had to be kept in mind that they were 'not … an exhaustive statement of the circumstances in which damages may be awarded instead of an injunction [or order for specific performance]'.

26.60 In relation to the principles set out by Smith LJ, in *Break Fast Investments v PCH Melbourne* at 335–6, in the context of a case involving an injunction to restrain a trespass, Dodds-Streeton JA, speaking for a unanimous Court of Appeal, said:

> [T]he alternative remedy of damages will be ordered exceptionally, as indicated by the working rule in *Shelfer* or by such other relevant considerations as may apply in a particular case. The authorities do not dictate or authorise the balancing of potential detriment to the parties on the basis of equivalent entitlement, or indicate that trespass may be negatived by undertakings to minimise its potential effect on future use. The tests embodied in the working rule of *Shelfer* are cumulative, and assume a significant inequality of entitlement between the parties (as the injury to the plaintiff from the trespass must ordinarily be small and the harm occasioned by an injunction to the defendant must be so disproportionate as to constitute oppression). Oppression in that context imports consideration of, inter alia, specific detriment, including disproportionate harm to the defendant relative to injury to the plaintiff, the deliberate or unintended quality of the trespass and all other relevant circumstances.

26.61 In *Jaggard v Sawyer*, damages in lieu of an injunction were granted. In that case Mr and Mrs Sawyer built a house in circumstances involving a breach of covenant and trespass. Jaggard had indicated its opposition to the building work but proceedings for an injunction were only commenced after the building work was completed. No application for interlocutory relief had been sought at any stage of the building work. The Court of Appeal found that the injury to Jaggard was small and was able to be properly compensated by a small damages award. In relation to the issue of oppression, Bingham MR, at 203, said:

> It is important to bear in mind that the test is one of oppression, and the court should not slide into application of a general balance of convenience test. But oppression must be judged as at the date the court is asked to grant an injunction, and … the court cannot ignore the reality with which it is then confronted. It is relevant that [Jaggard] could at an early stage have sought interlocutory relief, which she would seem very likely to have obtained; but it is also relevant that [the Sawyers] could have sought a declaration of right. These considerations are not decisive. It would weigh against a finding of oppression if the [Sawyers] had acted in blatant and calculated disregard of the [Jaggard's] rights, of which they were aware, but the judge held that this was not so, and [Jaggard's] solicitors may be thought to have indicated that damages would be an acceptable remedy.

26.62 An example of a case in which the court refused to grant equitable damages in lieu of a mandatory injunction is *Wakeham v Wood* (1982) 42 P & CR 40. In that case Wood purchased land and built a house upon it in violation of a restrictive covenant that protected Wakeham's view of the ocean. Waller LJ, at 44–5, said:

> The present case does not in my view qualify in any particular with paragraphs (1) to (4) mentioned by A L Smith LJ. Here is a man who had been living in his house for 33 years with a view of the sea protected by a restrictive covenant. [Wood] purchased the land subject to the restriction with knowledge of it at the time of purchase. He did not make any inquiry of [Wakeham] either directly or indirectly, he did not inform his architect of the restriction, he took no notice of his builder telling him of [Wakeham's] objection and he put the roof trusses up in spite of letters from [Wakeham's] solicitor. A more flagrant disregard of [Wakeham's] rights it is difficult to imagine. As I have already indicated the [trial] judge concluded that there was a serious interference with [Wakeham's] legal right to a view of the sea. I find it difficult to say that where one has a view protected by covenant the denial of that view is capable of being estimated in money terms and therefore it seems to me it cannot be adequately compensated by a small money payment. Indeed in this case the [trial] judge awarded a substantial money payment. It no doubt will be oppressive to [Wood] if a mandatory injunction is granted against him, but that is entirely his own fault for proceeding with the construction in breach of the covenant after warning.

26.63 In *Watson v Croft Promosport Ltd* [2009] 3 All ER 250, the Court of Appeal declined to award damages in lieu of an injuction in circumsatnces relating to nuisance caused to an adjoining landowner by the owners of land that was used for motor car racing. An injunction was ordered limiting racing on the land to 20 days per year. A factor that was considered was the interests of the public in that the defendants in this case operated a car racing facility that provided employment and entertainment for members of the public in circumsatnces where there were limited locations where car racing could take place. In relation to this matter Sir Andrew Morritt, at 263, said:

> In a marginal case where the damage to the claimant is minimal I can accept that, consistent with the principles of *Shelfer v City of London Electric Lighting Co*, the effect on the public of the grant of an injunction is properly to be taken into account. But the fact that the public benefit might be relevant in those circumstances does not mean that its existence can, alone, negate the

requirement of exceptional circumstances or oppression of the defendant which both *Shelfer v City of London Electric Lighting Co* and *Jaggard v Sawyer* clearly require. There was no evidence … as to the effect on the public interest of a restriction on the defendants' use of their circuit to their core activities. But even if there were I am unable to see how this could be regarded as a marginal case so as to let in consideration of the public interest.

The discretionary nature of equitable damages

26.64   Even if a court has jurisdiction to order equitable damages, it can refuse to do so on discretionary grounds: *Weily v Williams* (1895) 16 LR (NSW) Eq 190 at 195–6. For example, in *McMahon v Ambrose* at 852–3, equitable damages were refused on the ground of laches. Furthermore, discretionary factors may affect the quantum of damages to be awarded. For example, in *Malhotra v Choudhury* [1980] Ch 52; [1979] 1 All ER 186, the plaintiff's delay in seeking damages in substitution for specific performance led the court to assessing damages by moving back the date for valuing a property by one year from the date of judgment, the latter being the date that would otherwise have been applicable for the assessment of damages.

The continuing significance of Lord Cairns' Act damages

26.65   The point was made above that much of the impact of Lord Cairns' Act was diminished by the reforms of the *Judicature Acts* a few decades later: see 26.40. But it would be erroneous to regard the usefulness of Lord Cairns' Act as spent. Its continued existence ensures the ability of a litigant to obtain financial relief in equity in cases where common law damages would be unavailable: see 26.66–26.70.

Damages before injury

26.66   In equity, an injunction can be granted to preclude a threatened breach of a plaintiff's rights, whereas common law damages are not available for an apprehended breach of the plaintiff's rights. However, in permitting equitable damages to be granted in lieu of specific relief, Lord Cairns' Act enables a plaintiff to recover a monetary remedy for a threatened breach of his or her rights. For example, equitable damages can be obtained in lieu of a quia timet injunction: see 24.54–24.58.

Contracts not evidenced in writing

26.67   Statutory provisions requiring contracts for the sale of land or an interest in land to be evidenced in writing cannot be enforced by an award of damages at common law: see 23.67–23.70. However, if the doctrine of part performance is satisfied (see 23.77–23.89), specific performance of the contract is available, with the consequence that equitable damages may also be ordered in such a case: *Lavery v Pursell* (1888) 39 Ch D 508 at 519.

'Wrongful acts' at equity

26.68   There is considerable authority to the effect that equitable damages are available in relation to infringements of equitable rights. The basis for such claims is the reference to 'wrongful acts' or 'wrongs' in the relevant legislation. There has been significant debate over whether these terms in the legislation include infringements of purely equitable rights, or are confined to torts only. A broader interpretation of 'wrongful acts' in the context of the wording of the legislation may be logical enough. However, the question must be asked whether there is any particular need for

Lord Cairns' Act damages to be awarded for breaches of purely equitable obligations, given equity's inherent jurisdiction to make orders of compensation in respect of such breaches, as discussed earlier in this chapter. Meagher, Heydon and Leeming[11] make strong arguments based upon history and principle in favour of the narrower interpretation of the legislation.

26.69 However, on the basis of a significant body of cases that had adopted the broader interpretation of the legislation, members of the High Court in *Wentworth v Woollahra Municipal Council*, at CLR 676; ALR 72, affirmed that Lord Cairns' Act damages are available for purely equitable claims. In Victoria, the absence of any reference to 'wrongful act' or 'wrong' in s 38 of the *Supreme Court Act 1986* (Vic) means that there is no doubt that equitable damages can be awarded in any case where the court has jurisdiction to order specific performance or an injunction, including cases involving the infringement of equitable rights: *Giller v Procopets* at 95.

26.70 In ordering equitable damages for infringements of purely equitable rights, the courts have indicated that they retain considerable flexibility in terms of the basis of assessing such damages. This can be illustrated in the context of equitable damages for breaches of the obligation relating to confidential information. In *Seager v Coydex Ltd (No 2)* [1969] 2 All ER 718 at 720, in a case between a willing buyer and willing seller in the context of misused information about a carpet grip invention, the Court of Appeal assessed damages on the basis of the market value of the relevant information. It should be noted that the Court of Appeal did not specifically state it was awarding equitable damages pursuant to Lord Cairns' Act. However, in the later case of *English v Dedham Vale Properties* at 399, Slade J took the view that the damages awarded by the Court of Appeal were awarded in lieu of an injunction. On the other hand, in *Talbot v General Television Corporation Pty Ltd* [1980] VR 224 at 244, the *Seager* approach was held to be inappropriate in the context of information relating to an idea for a series of television programs on successful businessmen. Rather, Marks J, at 245, proceeded to assess the 'depreciation in the value of [the plaintiff's] right'. Despite the many contingencies which were involved in assessing the worth of the right and the precise diminution of value, his Honour, at 249, held that the court had the duty to make an assessment. His Honour's assessment of damages in this case was upheld by the Victorian Court of Appeal, at 250–4.

LORD CAIRNS' ACT AND *WROTHAM PARK* DAMAGES

26.71 In *Wrotham Park Estate Company Limited v Parkside Homes Limited* [1974] 2 All ER 321, Parkside purchased land that was subject to a restrictive covenant preventing it from building on the land without the consent of Wrotham Park, the owner of the adjoining land. Parkside built on the land without gaining Wrotham Park's consent. Wrotham Park sought a mandatory injunction to have the houses demolished. Brightman J determined that it would be inappropriate to grant the injunction and proceeded to award damages in lieu of the injunction under the English Lord Cairns' Act provision. His Honour, at 339, said:

> The basic rule in contract is to measure damages by that sum of money which will put the plaintiff in the same position as he would have been in if the contract had not been broken. From that basis, [Parkside] argue that the damages are nil or purely nominal, because the value of the Wrotham Park estate … is not diminished by one farthing in consequence of the construction

---

11. R Meagher, D Heydon & M Leeming, *Meagher, Gummow and Lehane's Equity: Doctrines and Remedies*, 4th ed, LexisNexis Butterworths, Sydney, 2002, pp 854–5.

of a road and the erection of 14 houses on the allotment site. If, therefore ([Parkside submits]) I refuse an injunction I ought to award no damages in lieu. That would seem, on the face of it, a result of questionable fairness on the facts of this case ... If, for social and economic reasons, the court does not see fit in the exercise of its discretion, to order demolition of the 14 houses, is it just that [Wrotham Park] should receive no compensation and that [Parkside] should be left in undisturbed possession of the fruits of their wrongdoing? Common sense would seem to demand a negative answer to this question.

His Honour, at 441, then concluded:

[T]he general rule would be to measure damages by reference to that sum which would place [Wrotham Park] in the same position as if the covenant had not been broken ... Parkside and the individual purchasers could have avoided breaking the covenant in two ways. One course would have been not to develop the allotment site. The other course would have been for Parkside to have sought from [Wrotham Park] a relaxation of the covenant. On the facts of this particular case [Wrotham Park], rightly conscious of their obligations towards existing residents, would clearly not have granted any relaxation, but for present purposes I must assume that they would have been induced to do so. In my judgment a just substitute for a mandatory injunction would be such a sum of money as might reasonably have been demanded by [Wrotham Park] from Parkside as a quid pro quo for relaxing the covenant.

26.72 It was originally argued that so-called *Wrotham Park* damages were confined to claims for damages pursuant to Lord Cairns' Act: *Jaggard v Sawyer* at 201 and 212. However, subsequent cases in England have held that the availability of such damages is not so confined: *Experience Hendrix Llc v PPX Enterprises Inc* [2003] EWCA Civ 323 at [34]–[35], Thus, in *WWF — World Wide Fund for Nature v World Wrestling Federation Entertainment Inc* [2007] EWCA Civ 286 at [54], Chadwick LJ made it clear that '[t]he power to award damages on a *Wrotham Park* basis does not depend on Lord Cairns' Act: it exists at common law'. His Lordship, at [59], went on to say:

When the court makes an award of damages on the *Wrotham Park* basis it does so because it is satisfied that that is a just response to circumstances in which the compensation which is the claimant's due cannot be measured (or cannot be measured solely) by reference to identifiable financial loss.

26.73 On this basis *Wrotham Park* damages is not an equitable remedy. Rather it is a common law remedy that is available when more traditional assessments of damages, based upon assessing the financial loss of the plaintiff, would result in what a court regards as an inadequate measure of compensation for the plaintiff. In particular, it appears to be necessary that such traditional methods of assessment of damages would result in the defendant gaining an advantage for free, in which case Wrotham Park damages results in a defendant paying reasonable compensation for the advantage gained at the plaintiff's expense as a result of infringing the plaintiff's common law rights.

26.74 It has recently been held that *Wrotham Park* damages is also applicable in the case of breaches of a purely equitable obligation. In *Force India Formula One Team Ltd v 1 Malaysia Racing Team SDN BHD* [2   012] EWHC 616 (Ch) at [393], in a case concerning a breach of the equitable obligation with respect to confidential information, Arnold J, after concluding that monetary relief can be awarded for such a breach, said:

The key issue is whether damages or equitable compensation should be assessed on a different basis if the obligation which has been breached is equitable rather than contractual. In particular, should a different approach be taken … where the claimant has suffered no financial loss?

After a consideration of the relevant authorities, his Honour, at [424], concluded that '[t]he same approach is to be adopted to the assessment of damages or equitable compensation whether the obligation of confidentiality which has been breached is contractual or equitable'.

26.75 Thus, the decision in *Force India Formula One Team Ltd v 1 Malaysia Racing Team SDN BHD* extends the availability of *Wrotham Park* damages to cases of breaches of purely equitable obligations, or at least it does so in relation to the equitable obligation with respect to confidential information.

27

RESCISSION

INTRODUCTION

27.1   Rescission is the right to set aside a contract or other transaction. This right is recognised both at common law and in equity. The right to rescind may arise in favour of an innocent party to a contract who is a victim of a vitiating factor such as misrepresentation, mistake, duress, unconscionability or undue influence. The purpose of rescission is to put the parties back into the position they were in before the transaction was entered into. Thus, in *McDonald v Dennys Lascelles Limited* (1933) 48 CLR 457 at 477, Dixon J said that '[w]hen a contract is rescinded because of matters which affect its formation … the parties are to be rehabilitated and restored … to the position they occupied before the contract was made'. This purpose is usually referred to by the Latin phrase *restitutio in integrum*, but is also, at times, referred to as 'counter-restitution'. Thus, in *Independent Trustee Services Ltd v GP Noble Trustees Ltd* [2012] EWCA Civ 195 at [54], Patten LJ said:

> The necessary condition for obtaining the assistance of equity in the rescission process is that the representee should make counter-restitution. In a contractual case this will ordinarily involve him restoring to the representor any benefits which he has himself received under the contract or their equivalent value.

Once a transaction is rescinded 'it is treated both at law and in equity as non-existing': *Newbigging v Adam* (1886) 34 Ch D 582.

27.2   However, a transaction remains 'effective in law and equity unless and until' it is rescinded: *Alati v Kruger* (1955) 94 CLR 216 at 242. Thus, a contract until rescinded remains valid, creates rights and duties in the parties and can result in property being transferred from one party to another. It is *not* void *ab initio* (as from the beginning). It is *voidable*, that is, capable of being set aside by the innocent party if he or she so elects, and there is no limitation on the right to rescind. It must be noted that the innocent party is not required to rescind the contract.

27.3   In order to rescind, an innocent party must, as a general rule, clearly and unequivocally communicate his or her election to rescind to the other party: *Immer (No 145) Pty Ltd v Uniting Church in Australia Property Trust (NSW)* (1993) 182 CLR 26 at 38–9; 112 ALR 609 at 617–18. In exceptional circumstances, such as where the other party has absconded and cannot be found, the requirement of communicating an election to rescind is not necessary and it will be sufficient if the innocent party has taken reasonable steps to make known that he or she wants to rescind the contract. Thus, in *Car & Universal Finance Co Ltd v Caldwell* [1965] 1 QB 525; [1964] 1 All ER 290,

Norris, a fraudulent buyer of a car from Caldwell, absconded, making it impossible for Caldwell to give notice of rescission to Norris. Caldwell immediately informed the police and the Automobile Association, seeking their assistance in recovering the car. Subsequently, Norris sold the car to a third party. Caldwell sought recovery of the vehicle from the third party. The English Court of Appeal upheld Caldwell's claim on the basis that he had done all that could have reasonably been expected of him to rescind the contract and that the rescission was effective prior to Norris' sale to the third party. Therefore, the sale to the third party was ineffective and Caldwell was entitled to recover his car.

27.4   The following analysis of rescission will examine the remedy under three broad headings:

1.   the meaning of *restitutio in integrum*;
2.   the nature of the remedy of rescission; and
3.   limitations on the right to rescind.

THE MEANING OF *RESTITUTION IN INTEGRUM*

27.5   As noted, the purpose of rescission is to bring about *restitutio in integrum*. If this cannot be achieved, a transaction cannot be rescinded: *A H McDonald & Co Pty Ltd v Wells* (1931) 45 CLR 506 at 512. Therefore, the practical meaning of *restitutio in integrum* must be properly understood. This, in turn, requires an understanding of the differences between the common law and equitable understandings of rescission.

27.6   At common law rescission is available in relatively limited circumstances. The most important instances are contracts induced by fraudulent misrepresentations or duress and, in the case of insurance contracts, for non-disclosure of material facts. In equity, rescission is not so limited and extends to transactions resulting from non-fraudulent misrepresentations, certain unilateral mistakes, unconscionable transactions and undue influence. A further distinction is that the common law takes a stricter approach to the requirement of *restitutio in integrum*.

27.7   The difference between the common law and equitable rules as to *restitutio in integrum* was explained by Dixon J in *Alati v Kruger*, at 223–4 as follows:

> [E]quity has always regarded as valid the disaffirmance of a contract induced by fraud even though precise *restitutio in integrum* is not possible, if the situation is such that, by the exercise of its powers, including the power to take accounts of profits and to direct inquiries as to allowances proper to be made for deterioration, it can do what is practically just between the parties, and by so doing restore them substantially to the *status quo*. It is not that equity asserts a power by its decree to avoid a contract which the defrauded party himself has no right to disaffirm, and to revest property the title to which the party cannot affect. Rescission for misrepresentation is always the act of the party himself. The function of a court in which proceedings for rescission are taken is to adjudicate upon the validity of a purported disaffirmance as an act avoiding the transaction *ab initio*, and, if it is valid, to give effect to it and make appropriate consequential orders. The difference between the legal and the equitable rules on the subject simply was that equity, having means which the common law lacked to ascertain and provide for the adjustments necessary to be made between the parties in cases where a simple handing back of property or repayment of money would not put them in as good a position as before they entered into their transaction, was able to see the possibility of *restitutio in integrum*, and therefore to concede the right of a defrauded party to rescind, in a much wider variety of cases than those which

the common law could recognize as admitting of rescission. Of course, a rescission which the common law courts would not accept as valid cannot of its own force revest the legal title to property which had passed, but if a court of equity would treat it as effectual the equitable title to such property revests upon the rescission.

27.8   The strictness of the common law here is illustrated by the decision in *Blackburn v Smith* (1848) 154 ER 707. In that case, a purchaser had briefly enjoyed possession of land under a contract that he subsequently wanted to rescind. The right to rescind was denied by the court on the basis that the purchaser's surrender of possession of the land would not have restored to the vendor the benefit that the purchaser enjoyed during the period of possession.

27.9   On the other hand, equity only requires *restitutio in integrum* in substance and allows rescission if the parties can, in substance, be put back into the positions they were in before the contract was entered into. In *Erlanger v New Sombrero Phosphate Company* (1878) 3 App Cas 1218 at 1278, Lord Blackburn said rescission in equity was available 'whenever, by the exercise of its powers, [the court] can do what is practically just, though it cannot restore the parties precisely to the state they were in before the contract'. Thus, if property that has to be handed back to the other party has deteriorated or depreciated in value, compensation payments can be ordered in favour of the affected party. In other cases an account of profits can be ordered to achieve substantive *restitutio in integrum*. Thus, in *Balfour & Clark v Hollandia Ravensthorpe NL* (1978) 18 SASR 240, rescission of a contract for the purchase of a house was permitted, notwithstanding that the house had deteriorated since being occupied by the purchasers. The deterioration that was attributable to the acts of the purchasers was dealt with by the purchasers being ordered to pay compensation to the vendors.

27.10   In *Brown v Smitt* (1924) 34 CLR 160, a purchaser had entered into a contract to purchase a farm, entered into possession, made improvements to the property, and incurred losses carrying on a business on the land. In relation to rescission of the contract on the ground of the vendor's fraudulent misrepresentations, the purchaser sought compensation for improvements made to the farm and for losses incurred in carrying on the business. The High Court awarded compensation for the improvements to the farm but not in relation to the business losses. In relation to the improvements, Knox CJ, Gavan Duffy & Stake J, at 164, said:

> Where the property the subject matter of a contract remains unchanged, no difficulty arises. Where it has been wholly or substantially destroyed by the default of the party seeking rescission, there can be no rescission because there can be no restitution. But where the property has been improved or deteriorated by the act of the purchaser, and yet remains in substance what it was before the contract, equity adjusts the rights of the parties by awarding money compensation to one or the other, and so substantially putting each party in the position which he occupied before the contract was made.

In relation to business losses, Knox CJ, Gavan Duffy & Stake J, at 165–6, said:

> [P]utting the parties in the position they were in before the contract, replacing them *in statu quo*, does not involve replacing them in the same position in all respects, but only in respect of the rights and obligations created by the contract which is rescinded. A party, in case of rescission, cannot ask the Court to award him compensation for all collateral losses which he may have sustained

by reason of the fact that he entered into the contract, such as losses incurred in carrying on a business, but only such compensation as will restore the *status quo ante* in relation to the subject matter of the contract.[1]

27.11   A practical consequence of the different approaches to the meaning of *restitutio in integrum* is that if a contract cannot be rescinded at common law because the common law understanding of *restitutio in integrum* cannot be satisfied, equity, pursuant to its concurrent jurisdiction, may rescind it, provided *restitutio in integrum*, as understood in equity, can be achieved. Thus, in *Halpern v Halpern (Nos 1 & 2)* [2008] QB 195 at 222; [2007] 3 All ER 478 at 484, Carnwath LJ said that 'rescission for duress should be no different in principle from rescission for other "vitiating factors".'

27.12   Finally, a court will be more willing to uphold a rescission by using its powers to bring about *restitutio in integrum* in cases where the conduct of the defendant has been wilful or deliberate. Thus, in the case of fraudulent, rather than non-fraudulent, misrepresentations, Lord Wright in *Spence v Crawford* [1939] 3 All ER 271 at 288, said:

> The court will be less ready to pull a transaction to pieces where the defendant is innocent, whereas in the case of fraud the court will exercise its jurisdiction to the full in order, if possible, to prevent the defendant from enjoying the benefit of his fraud at the expense of the innocent plaintiff.

Controversial developments

27.13   The principle that substantial *restitutio in integrum* must be capable of being achieved before rescission in equity is possible has been challenged in recent times. In *JAD International Pty Ltd v International Trucks Australia Limited* (1994) 50 FCR 378 at 387, the Full Court of the Federal Court said that a court is justified in ordering rescission even if substantial *restitutio in integrum* is not achieved. A similar approach was hinted at in *Halpern v Halern* at QB 222; All ER 484, where Cranwath LJ said that 'perhaps ... for the purposes of "practical justice", the primary objective may not always need to be to restore *both* parties to their previous positions'. However, these suggestions fly in the face of accepted authority to the effect, in the words of the Court of Appeal in New South Wales in *Kirwan v Cresvale Far East Ltd (in liq)* [2002] NSWCA 395 at [140], that '[t]he notion of doing what is practically just is concerned with practicality. It does not deny that there must be restitution'. Furthermore, O'Sullivan, Elliott and Zakrzewski argue that 'the idea that practical justice should be done at the expense of restoring the parties to their original positions is difficult to understand' because '[i]t is not clear what alternative criterion of justice is being proposed'.[2] They suggest that this approach to rescission may have been influenced by the 'long shadow [of] the Trade Practices Act 1974',[3] in particular, the wide rescission power pursuant to s 87 of the said Act.

27.14   A more controversial issue is whether the court can order a partial rescission, thereby only partially bringing about *restitutio in integrum*. In *Vadasz v Pioneer Concrete (SA) Pty Ltd* (1995) 184 CLR 102; 130 ALR 570, Vadasz agreed to guarantee the payment to Pioneer Concrete for the supply of concrete to Vadipile Drilling Pty Ltd. Vadasz was told by Pioneer Concrete that the guarantee

---

1.   The High majority noted that the purchaser may have had an action in the tort of deceit (see Chapter 33) if the representation related to the business as opposed merely to the land.

2.   D O'Sullivan, S Elliott & R Zakrzewski, *The Law of Rescission*, Oxford University Press, Oxford, 2008, p 312.

3.   This legislation has subsequently been re-named as the *Competition and Consumer Act 2010* (Cth).

related only to future supplies of concrete. However, the guarantee that Pioneer Concrete got Vadasz to sign also covered earlier supplies of concrete that had not been paid for by Vadipile. When called upon to honour the guarantee, Vadasz claimed it was unenforceable on the basis that he had been told it related only to future supplies of concrete. There was no issue before the High Court as to whether Pioneer Concrete had acted fraudulently in this case. In relation to the guarantee, the High Court effectively partially rescinded it by ruling that it was valid only as to supplies of concrete made after the guarantee was entered into. In effect, the High Court ruled that Vadasz had given a valid consent to a limited obligation, namely, the guarantee for the payment of future supplies of concrete, and that this lesser obligation was not vitiated by Pioneer Concrete's misrepresentation. In ordering a partial rescission the High Court rejected traditional authority to the effect that rescission was an all-or-nothing remedy in the sense that a contract was either rescinded in its entirety or not at all.

27.15   The decision in *Vadasz* has met with a mixed reception. Thus, Seddon and Ellinghaus welcome the flexibility it has introduced into the law on rescission, and state:

> This case represents a significant development in the law of rescission under the general law because it has to a large extent removed the all-or-nothing character of rescission, which could in some cases produce an unfair result. It is relevant in deciding whether a court should set aside a contract in its entirety, or only in part, to ask whether the respresentee, had he or she known the truth, would not have entered into the contract at all (in which case full rescission is appropriate) or would have asked for a suitable modification to its terms (in which case partial rescission may be appropriate). This approach is not without its difficulties ... [T]here are problems in applying one test in determining whether a misrepresentation is actionable (it is so long as it was *an* inducement to enter the contract) and a different test at the stage of determining a remedy.[4]

27.16   On the other hand, Meagher, Heydon and Leeming express a less charitable opinion of *Vadasz*, opining that the case 'invents a doctrine of partial rescission, which might well have some interesting consequences in the hands of a more erratic judge'.[5]

27.17   Although *Vadasz* was a case concerning a fraudulent misrepresentation, there does not appear to be any reason why partial rescission could not be available in cases involving non-fraudulent misrepresentations, unilateral mistakes, duress, unconscionable bargains and undue influence. However, it has been held by the High Court that partial rescission is not appropriate in cases of rescission of contracts where there has been a breach of fiduciary obligations by one of the parties: *Maguire v Makaronis* (1996) 188 CLR 449 at 472; 144 ALR 727 at 744.

THE NATURE OF THE REMEDY OF RESCISSION

27.18   The nature of the remedy of rescission raises the issue of whether rescission is the act of the party that has a right to rescind or whether it is an order of the court in the same sense that damages at common law or specific performance are orders of the court. The significance of the issue lies in ascertaining the date on which a transaction is rescinded. If rescission is the act of the

---

4.   N C Seddon & M P Ellinghaus, *Cheshire and Fifoot's Law of Contract*, 9th Aust ed, LexisNexis Butterworths, Sydney, 2008, pp 533–4.

5.   R Meagher, D Heydon & M Leeming, *Meagher, Gummow and Lehane's Equity: Doctrines and Remedies*, 4th ed, LexisNexis Butterworths, Sydney, 2002, p 862.

party, rescission takes place when the party seeking to rescind gives notice of rescission to the other party. If rescission is an order of the court, rescission takes place when the court order is made. The resolution of the issue depends upon whether the rescission is one at common law or in equity.

27.19   At common law, rescission is viewed as the act of the party. The decision to rescind a contract is made by the innocent party to the contract, not the court, with the result that the contract is rescinded as at the date of the notice of rescission. The court's role is confined to ascertaining whether there exists a basis upon which the innocent party is entitled to rescind and, if such a basis exists, to dismiss any claims to enforce the contract.[6] It is for this reason that the common law insists upon exact *restitutio in integrum*. As a result, common law rescission is essentially confined to contracts where: (i) the defendant's obligations are purely executory; (ii) the defendant has only paid money; or (iii) the property transferred by the defendant consists of chattels that have not been used and remain in the same condition.

27.20   However, this is not the case in equity. A plaintiff in equity must seek a court order setting aside a transaction and obtaining any consequential relief that is necessary to bring about *restitutio in integrum*, with the consequence that the rescission is only effective when such orders are made.[7]

27.21   In *Alati v Kruger*, the facts concerned the sale of a fruit shop by Alati to Kruger, where the contract of sale was induced by a fraudulent misrepresentation. Although rescission at common law is available in such cases, it was not available in this case because exact *restitutio in integrum* was not possible. However, pursuant to equity's concurrent jurisdiction in relation to cases of fraudulent misrepresentation, rescission in equity was available in this case. In relation to the two forms of rescission, Dixon CJ, Webb, Kitto and Taylor JJ, at 223–4, said the following:

> If the case had to be decided according to the principles of the common law, it might have been argued that at the date when [Kruger] issued his writ he was not entitled to rescind the purchase, because he was not then in a position to return to [Alati] in specie that which he had received under the contract, in the same plight as that in which he had received it. But it is necessary here to apply the doctrines of equity, and equity has always regarded as valid the disaffirmance of a contract induced by fraud even though precise *restitutio in integrum* is not possible, if the situation is such that, by the exercise of its powers, including the power to take accounts of profits and to direct inquiries as to allowances proper to be made for deterioration, it can do what is practically just between the parties, and by so doing restore them substantially to the status quo. It is not that equity asserts a power by its decree to avoid a contract which the defrauded party himself has no right to disaffirm, and to revest property the title to which the party cannot effect. Rescission for misrepresentation is always the act of the party himself. The function of a court in which proceedings for rescission are taken is to adjudicate upon the validity of a purported disaffirmance as an act avoiding the transaction *ab initio*, and, if it is valid, to give effect to it and make appropriate consequential orders. The difference between the legal and the equitable rules on the subject simply was that equity, having means which the common law lacked to ascertain and provide for the adjustments necessary to be made between the parties in cases where a simple handing back of property or repayment of money would not put them in as good a position as before they entered into their transaction, was able to see the possibility of *restitutio in integrum*, and therefore to concede the right of a defrauded party to rescind, in a much wider variety of

---

6.   O'Sullivan et al, *The Law of Rescission*, note 2 above, p 61.
7.   O'Sullivan et al, *The Law of Rescission*, note 2 above, p 62.

cases than those which the common law could recognize as admitting of rescission. Of course, a rescission which the common law courts would not accept as valid cannot of its own force revest the legal title to property which had passed, but if a court of equity would treat it as effectual the equitable title to such property revests upon the rescission.

27.22   In *Alati v Kruger*, at 224, the High Court noted that, in cases where the right to rescind in equity is at stake, the role of a court is to adjudicate upon the *validity* of the rescission. Although *Alati v Kruger* was, as noted, a case of equity acting in its concurrent jurisdiction, the role of the court is the same in cases where rescission is available only on the basis of equitable principles, such as transactions concerned with undue influence, unconscionable transactions and innocent misrepresentations. Assuming that a basis for rescission exists, the validity of the rescission becomes an issue of whether *restitutio in integrum*, as understood in equity (see 27.9), has been, or can be, achieved. In relation to this issue, in *Kramer v McMahon* [1970] 1 NSWLR 195 at 206, Helsham J noted that the validity of rescission from the perspective of achieving *restitutio in integrum* can be viewed in three different sets of circumstances. First, in a purely executory contract where neither party has done anything towards the performance of their respective contractual obligations, a notice of rescission will bring about a valid rescission because the giving of the notice itself restores the parties to their pre-contractual position. Second, if the contract has to some extent been performed by the parties, and if the notice of rescission or the subsequent acts of the parties themselves restore the parties to their pre-contractual positions, then the rescission is also valid. Third, if the contract has to some extent been performed by the parties and the only way in which the pre-contractual position of the parties can be restored is for the innocent party to approach the court for orders to bring about *restitutio in integrum*, the rescission will only be valid if the court can, through the various orders that it can make, bring about *restitutio in integrum*. If it cannot do so, the rescission is invalid.

27.23   In making its orders a court can require that the rescission be on terms to be complied with by the innocent party. Thus, in *Maguire v Makaronis*, where a loan transaction was set aside, the High Court required the innocent party that had borrowed the money to repay all moneys advanced to them together with interest to the lender.

LIMITATIONS ON THE RIGHT TO RESCIND

27.24   The right to rescind is not an absolute right. In some circumstances the right is lost, leaving the innocent party to seek alternative remedies. For example, in cases of fraudulent misrepresentation, common law damages in the tort of deceit will be available. The relevant limitations or bars to rescission are analysed in the following paragraphs.

Affirmation

27.25   Given that an innocent party has a right to rescind, he or she can elect not to do so, thereby affirming the transaction. Election involves unequivocal 'words or conduct … that is consistent only with the exercise of one of the two sets of rights and inconsistent with the exercise of the other': *Sargent v ASL Developments Ltd* (1975) 131 CLR 634 at 646; 4 ALR 257 at 266. O'Sullivan, Elliott and Zakrzewski state that an election to affirm occurs when the party entitled to rescind 'unequivocally manifests an intention to affirm [the transaction] once free from the effects of the vitiating factor'.[8]

---

8.   O'Sullivan et al, *The Law of Rescission*, note 2 above, p 516.

Affirmation can be by words or conduct. Once the election to affirm has been made, the right to rescind is lost. The innocent party cannot later change his or her mind and choose to rescind: *Coastal Estates Pty Ltd v Melevende* [1965] VR 433 at 451. Examples of conduct that may amount to an election to affirm a transaction include:

• invoking or asserting contractual rights or in some way continuing to perform the contract: *Strive Shipping Corporation v Hellenic Mutual War Risks Association (The Grecia Express)* [2002] 2 Lloyd's Rep 88 at 163;

• remaining in possession of leased or purchased premises unless, in all the circumstances, the innocent party has no real choice but to retain possession: *Tenji v Henneberry & Associates Pty Ltd* (2000) 98 FCR 324 at 350–1; 172 ALR 679 at 705–6; and

• reselling or attempting to resell property that has been acquired: *Re Cape Breton Company* (1885) 29 Ch D 795 at 803, 811.

27.26 Before any words or conduct can amount to affirmation, the innocent party must be shown to have been aware of the circumstances that gave rise to the right to rescind. Whether he or she must also have been aware of the right to rescind because of these circumstances is a matter of some dispute. The Victorian Full Court decision in *Coastal Estates v Melevende* states that, in general, knowledge by the innocent party of both the circumstances giving rise to the right to rescind as well as of the right to rescind must be established before any question of affirmation can arise.

27.27 In *Coastal Estates v Melevende*, Melevende was induced by a fraudulent misrepresentation to enter into an instalment contract to purchase property. The contract was entered into in September 1960. Melevende became aware of the misrepresentation in early 1961. He continued to make instalment payments and even tried to sell the land. In September 1962, after seeking legal advice, he became aware of his right to rescind. The issue before the Victorian Full Court was whether Melevende's conduct in trying to sell the land amounted to affirmation of the contract, on the basis that such conduct was inconsistent with maintaining a right to rescind the contract for the misrepresentation.

27.28 The Full Court upheld the validity of the rescission. Adam J, at 452–3, observed that *generally* there cannot be any question of affirmation in the absence of knowledge by the innocent party of the fact that he or she has a right to rescind. His Honour pointed out that affirmation could, strictly speaking, only be said to occur when there was a choice between known alternative courses of conduct. In other words, actions undertaken in circumstances where the innocent party merely knows that there was a misrepresentation are not enough to establish affirmation. There must exist a knowledge that alternative courses of action are available; that is, a choice between rescission and affirmation. However, this general proposition is qualified by the principle that, if the innocent party exercises rights under the contract that would adversely affect the other party in circumstances where the innocent party only knows of the fact of misrepresentation, there is affirmation, even though the innocent party does not know of his or her right to rescind. The qualification to the general rule could not really be seen as a true species of affirmation, given that the innocent party can hardly be said to have affirmed a contract when he or she was unaware of the right to rescind it. Adam J offered a number of possible theoretical explanations of the qualification, including that it was an application of estoppel principles, or simply based upon general considerations of justice. Sholl J, at 443, opined that an example of the qualification could arise where, in a contract for the purchase of land, the innocent party as purchaser entered into possession of the land or accepted some benefit from the vendor who had been guilty of a misrepresentation. However, payments of instalments of the price and rates on the property, or trying to sell the land, were not prejudicial to the vendor on the facts of this case. Accordingly, none of Melevende's conduct amounted to affirmation in the proper sense, nor did it come within the qualification noted by Adam J, as the conduct was not prejudicial to the vendor.

27.29 The correctness of the *Coastal Estates v Melevende* decision is not beyond dispute. There is considerable opinion and authority to suggest that knowledge of the right to rescind is not necessary before it can be said that one has affirmed the contract. Thus, in *Re Hoffman; Ex parte Worrell v Schilling* (1989) 85 ALR 145, Pincus J rejected the distinction made in *Coastal Estates v Melevende* and ruled that conduct undertaken with mere knowledge of the misrepresentation is enough to lead to affirmation. A similar approach was taken by Chesterman J in *Southern Cross Mine Management Pty Ltd v Ensham Resources Pty Ltd* [2005] QSC 233 at [632] and by Stevenson J in *Land Enviro Corp Pty Limited v HTT Huntley Heritage Pty Limited* [2012] NSWSC 382 at [201]–[211]. In *Sargent v ASL Developments Ltd*, at CLR 645, 648; ALR 265, 276, the High Court left open the correctness of *Coastal Estates v Melevende*. In *Baburin v Baburin (No 2)* [1991] 2 Qd R 240 at 244, McPherson J was of the view that the correctness of *Coastal Estates v Melevende* had not yet been finally resolved. In *Moore v The National Mutual Life Association of Australasia Limited* [2011] NSWSC 416 at [79], Ball J also noted that the issue had not been resolved. On the other hand, the *Coastal Estates v Melevende* approach of requiring knowledge of the right to rescind before there can be any question of affirmation was supported by the English Court of Appeal in *Peyman v Lanjani* [1985] Ch 457; [1984] 3 All ER 703, which in turn was endorsed in *Garside v Black Horse Ltd* [2010] EWHC 190 at [28]. A slightly qualified approach to the issue of requiring knowledge of the right to rescind is found in *Crown Aluminium Ltd v Northern & Western Insurance Company Ltd* [2011] EWHC 1352 at [97], where Edwards-Stuart J concluded that, for election to occur, 'what is required is an unequivocal communication, whether by express statement or by the assertion of an inconsistent right, by a person who has knowledge of the relevant facts and, probably, of his legal rights — at least, in general terms'.

27.30 O'Sullivan, Elliott and Zakrzewski argue, as follows, that the *Coastal Estates v Melevende* approach is wrong:

> Ignorance of the law is usually irrelevant to the incidence of civil obligations, and there is no good reason for an exception here. More importantly, there are significant practical difficulties in applying the [*Coastal Estates v Melevende*] rule. It casts on the party alleging affirmation a burden of proof that is very difficult to discharge given the contraints of legal professional privilege.[9]

27.31 It should be noted that *Coastal Estates v Melevende* was a case concerned with rescission for fraudulent misrepresentation. In *Hunter BNZ Finance Ltd v C G Maloney Pty Ltd* (1988) 18 NSWLR 420 at 436, Giles J left open the question of whether the principle in *Coastal Estates v Melevende* applied in the case of rescission for an innocent misrepresentation. Furthermore, in cases of rescission on the basis that a transaction was entered into as the result of undue influence or unconscionability, it has been held that affirmation can occur even if the affected party did not know that he or she had a right to rescind the transaction: *Baburin v Baburin* at 257.

---

9.   O'Sullivan et al, *The Law of Rescission*, note 2 above, p 530.

Rights of third persons

27.32   If property has passed between the parties pursuant to a voidable contract, and a third person subsequently, in good faith and for consideration, obtains an interest in such property, then the contract cannot be rescinded: *Hunter BNZ Finance v C G Maloney* at 433–4. The rights of such a third person are paramount to the rights of the contracting parties. The rationale for this approach was explained in *Waters Motors Pty Ltd v Cratchley* (1963) 80 WN (NSW) 1165 at 1177, where Else-Mitchell J said that 'its true basis in equity is not simply that third parties have acquired an interest in the subject matter but that rescission would cause injustice to such third parties who would be punished for no fault of their own'.

27.33   The paramount nature of a third person's rights can be explained on the basis of the fact that if A passes property to B pursuant to that contract, there is a transfer of title to that property from A to B even though a contract between A and B may be voidable. If the contract is validly rescinded by A, title reverts back to A. However, if B passes the property to a third person (C), *after* the contract has been rescinded, C only obtains possession of the property. C does not get title to the property because, the contract having been rescinded, B had no title to pass to C. C must, therefore, return the property to A. This was the situation in *Car & Universal Finance v Caldwell*: see 27.3. On the other hand, if B had passed the property in question to C *before* the contract was rescinded, title would also have passed to C. This is because B, at the time of transferring the property to C, had acquired title to the property from A pursuant to the, as yet, unrescinded contract, which he or she then passed on to C. In this situation C's title prevails over A's contractual right — a mere equity — to rescind his or her contract with B. Effectively, A has no right to rescind the contract. However, A may have an action against B. For example, if the contract was induced by a fraudulent misrepresentation, A can sue B for damages in the tort of deceit.

Laches

27.34   Laches, or delay (see 31.13–31.22), by the plaintiff in rescinding a contract operates as a bar to rescission in equity. The mere lapse of time of itself will not deprive the innocent party of his or her right to rescind. It may, however, be a relevant factor in relation to whether he or she has affirmed the contract and has thereby lost the right to rescind. Thus, a failure to rescind within a reasonable time will amount to an election to affirm the contract: *Clough v London and North Western Railway Co* (1871) LR 7 Exch 26 at 35.

27.35   For laches to arise in the context of rescission it appears that the court needs to be satisfied that the period of time that has elapsed from the making of the contract is sufficient for the innocent party to have discovered the circumstances giving rise to a right to rescind. In *Leaf v International Galleries* [1950] 2 KB 86; [1950] 1 All ER 693, an attempt to rescind a contract formed five years earlier was rejected, even though the innocent party sought to act as soon as they became aware of the circumstances giving rise to the right to rescind. In cases of *fraudulent* misrepresentations, time begins to run from the time the fraud is discovered, not the date of contracting.

The rule in *Seddon's* case

27.36   Derived from the decision in *Seddon v North Eastern Salt Co* [1905] 1 Ch 326, this rule, in its modern variation, stipulates that if a contract for the sale of land has been executed, that is, if it has proceeded to settlement or completion, the right to rescind for an *innocent* misrepresentation is lost. Rescission is available prior to settlement or completion. The rule does not apply in the context of other vitiating factors that give rise to a right to rescind.

27.37 Whether the rule in *Seddon's* case applies beyond the scope of contracts for the sale of land is somewhat controversial. In *Seddon*, it was suggested that it applied to shares and in *Vimig Pty Ltd v Contract Tooling Pty Ltd* (1986) 9 NSWLR 731, it was applied to a contract for the sale of a business. However, other cases indicate that the rule does not extend to cover contracts involving personal property: *Grogan v 'The Astor' Ltd* (1925) 25 SR (NSW) 409; *Leason Pty Ltd v Princes Farm Pty Ltd* [1983] 2 NSWLR 381. In any event, the rule has now been abolished by statute in New South Wales[10] in relation to sale of goods contracts, and in Victoria[11] in relation to consumer contracts for the supply of goods. In the Australian Capital Territory and South Australia[12] the rule has been abolished with respect to all contracts.

Sale of goods

27.38 Whether rescission is available where a contract for the sale of goods has been induced by an innocent misrepresentation is the subject of some doubt. The doubt stems from a common provision in sale of goods legislation in all Australian jurisdictions which states that 'the rules of the common law … shall continue to apply to contracts for the sale of goods'.[13] On a narrow interpretation of the words 'common law', it has been argued that, because rescission for an innocent misrepresentation was not available at common law, the provision's reference to 'common law' meant that rescission of contracts for the sale of goods was only available for fraudulent misrepresentation: *Watt v Westhoven* [1933] VLR 458.

27.39 On the other hand, there is authority that has rejected such a narrow interpretation of the legislation, holding that rescission is available in relation to a contract for the sale of goods that is induced by an innocent misrepresentation: *Graham v Freer* (1980) 35 SASR 424. Furthermore, legislation to that effect has been adopted by the Australian Capital Territory and New South Wales,[14] and in Victoria legislation permits rescission for innocent misrepresentation in cases of consumer contracts for the supply of goods.[15]

Exclusion clauses

27.40 A contract may contain a term to the effect that pre-contractual statements cannot be relied upon by the parties to the contract. Such terms can have the effect of excluding a right of rescission for non-fraudulent misrepresentation: *Life Insurance Co of Australia Ltd v Phillips* (1925) 36 CLR 60 at 82, 87. The preclusion of the right to exclude the right to rescind for a fraudulent misrepresentation is probably based upon the view that such a right would be contrary to public policy and therefore void.[16] In the Australian Capital Territory and South Australia, legislation demands that clauses that

---

10. *Sale of Goods Act 1923* (NSW) s 4(2A)(b).
11. *Fair Trading Act 1999* (Vic) s 32OA(1).
12. *Civil Law (Wrongs) Act 2002* (ACT) s 173(b)(ii)–(iii); *Misrepresentation Act 1971* (SA) s 6(1)(b).
13. *Sale of Goods Act 1954* (ACT) s 62(1); *Sale of Goods Act 1923* (NSW) s 4(2); *Sale of Goods Act 1972* (NT) s 4(2); *Sale of Goods Act 1896* (Qld) s 61(2); *Sale of Goods Act 1895* (SA) s 59(2); *Goods Act 1958* (Vic) s 4(2); *Sale of Goods Act 1896* (Tas) s 5(2); *Sale of Goods Act 1895* (WA) s 59(2).
14. *Sale of Goods Act 1954* (ACT) s 62(2); *Sale of Goods Act 1923* (NSW) s 4(2A)(a).
15. *Fair Trading Act 1999* (Vic) s 32OA(1).
16. J W Carter, E Peden & G J Tolhurst, *Contract Law in Australia*, 5th ed, LexisNexis Butterworths, 2007, p 427.

exclude the right to rescind must, in the context of the contract, be reasonable.[17] However, in *Byers v Dorotea Pty Ltd* (1986) 69 ALR 715 at 725, it was held that such clauses do not exclude the statutory right of rescission that may otherwise be available where a contract has resulted from a violation of the statutory prohibition against misleading or deceptive conduct set out in s 18 of the *Australian Consumer Law*.

Statute in the Australian Capital Territory and South Australia

27.41   In the Australian Capital Territory and South Australia legislation[18] provides that a court may, after consideration of all the circumstances of a case before it in which a person is entitled to rescind or has rescinded, if it is just and equitable to do so, declare a contract to be subsisting and award to the innocent party damages that the court deems to be fair and reasonable. These provisions effectively preclude rescission where it has not yet occurred or reinstate a contract where it has occurred. Although the right to rescind is thus lost, the court has the discretionary power to award damages in favour of the innocent party.

27.42   The Australian Capital Territory provision is confined to non-fraudulent misrepresentations whereas the South Australian provision applies to all misrepresentations. However, as Seddon and Ellinghaus observe, 'it is difficult to conceive of a situation where a court would exercise its discretion to deny the remedy of rescission to a victim of fraud'.[19]

27.43   Seddon and Ellinghaus also observe that the purpose of these provisions is 'to provide a way of avoiding possibly precipitate consequences of rescission' as well as being 'clearly … useful in a case where the representee wished to rescind for a relatively trivial (but nevertheless actionable) misrepresentation'.[20]

---

17. *Civil Law (Wrongs) Act 2002* (ACT) s 176; *Misrepresentation Act 1971* (SA) s 8.
18. *Civil Law (Wrongs) Act 2002* (ACT) s 175; *Misrepresentation Act 1971* (SA) s 7.
19. Seddon & Ellinghaus, *Law of Contract*, note 4 above, p 546.
20. Seddon & Ellinghaus, *Law of Contract*, note 4 above, p 545.

28

CONSTRUCTIVE TRUSTS

INTRODUCTION

28.1   A constructive trust is a trust imposed by law. Because a constructive trust arises by operation of law, it is often said that the intention of the parties subject to a constructive trust is irrelevant to its application. Unlike an express trust (which needs actual or implied intention to be valid) and a resulting trust (which arises by way of a presumed intention on the part of a creator), the constructive trust can arise in circumstances where there was no actual, implied or presumed intention to create a trust.[1] However, as shall become clear below, it is wrong to state that the intention of the parties to a relationship is completely irrelevant to constructive trusts as there are forms of constructive trust that arise by way of common intention and agreement. In that sense it is preferable to say that intention is not a *necessary* element of the constructive trust, as it is for both express and resulting trusts: *Crafter v Crafter* [2011] FamCA 122 at [77]–[79].

Differences between constructive trusts, express trusts and resulting trusts

28.2   The first major difference between constructive trusts and express and resulting trusts is that constructive trusts are imposed by the court and do not necessarily rely on the intention of the creator for their validity (and in that sense are not subject to the requirement of certainty of intention).

28.3   The second major difference is that a constructive trustee is not necessarily subject to the full gamut of fiduciary responsibilities. Thus, in *Lonhro v Fayed (No 2)* [1991] 4 All ER 961 at 971–2, Millett J said:

> It is a mistake to suppose that every situation in which a constructive trust arises the legal owner is necessarily subject to all the fiduciary obligations and disabilities of an express trustee.

28.4   Under a constructive trust the trustee's main duty is to disgorge the trust property and, by doing so, the trust is extinguished. For this reason Dal Pont states that the constructive trust is similar to a bare trust where the only duty is to deliver up trust property to the beneficiaries.[2]

---

1.   G E Dal Pont, *Equity and Trusts in Australia*, 5th ed, Lawbook Co, Sydney, 2011, p 1115.
2.   Dal Pont, *Equity and Trusts in Australia*, note 1 above, p 1116.

28.5 The third major difference is that constructive trusts are not always subject to the requirement of certainty of subject matter.[3] While earlier authority suggested that identifiable property was a necessary element of a constructive trust (*Re Barney* [1892] 2 Ch 265), in *Westdeutsche Landesbank Girozentrale v Islington LBC* [1996] AC 669 at 705; [1996] 2 All ER 961 at 988, Lord Browne-Wilkinson said:

> In order to establish a trust there must be identifiable trust property. The only apparent exception to this rule is a constructive trust imposed on a person who dishonestly assists in a breach of trust who may come under fiduciary duties even if he does not receive identifiable trust property.

28.6 In *Giumelli v Giumelli* (1999) 196 CLR 101 at 112; (1999) 161 ALR 473 at 475, Gleeson CJ, McHugh, Gummow and Callinan JJ endorsed a similar view and found that some constructive trusts create or recognise no proprietary interest but rather impose a personal liability to account for losses sustained by constructive beneficiaries. In that situation there is no identifiable trust property. For example, in *Bofinger v Kingsway Group Ltd* (2009) 239 CLR 269; 260 ALR 71, the High Court adopted this approach and employed a constructive trust to force a mortgagee to properly account for payments made by guarantors to reduce a mortgage liability.

REMEDY OR INSTITUTION?

28.7 Because a constructive trust is not dependent on the intention of the parties for its validity it is markedly different in operation from express trusts and resulting trusts. Both the express and the resulting trust are forms of *property institution*. This means that the express and the resulting trust reflect defined relationships between parties that come into existence at a time determined by the conduct of those parties. Once in existence, the relationship is governed by the institution of trust, meaning that rights, powers and duties of trust should be exercised and honoured between the parties.

28.8 Over the last few decades there has been a continuing debate over whether the constructive trust is a property institution (like the express and resulting trust) or whether it is a remedy, to be employed to address certain types of wrongdoing.[4] A remedy differs from a property institution in the time of its availability and its discretionary nature.[5] If the constructive trust is an equitable remedy it will exist from the time that an order is made by the court: *Re Polly Peck International plc (in administration) v MacIntosh* [1998] 3 All ER 812 at 825. However, if the constructive trust is a property institution it arises upon the parties engaging in certain forms of conduct and will exist from that time onwards: *Westdeutsche Landesbank Girozentrale v Islington LBC* [1996] AC 669 at 714; [1996] 2 All ER 961 at 997. Similarly, if constructive trusts are treated as an equitable remedy, they will be discretionary in nature. A judge could refuse to order a constructive trust if it was a remedy, whereas if the trust is an institution it would exist independently of the judge's exercise of discretion.[6]

---

3. A J Oakley, *Constructive Trusts*, 3rd ed, Sweet & Maxwell, London, 1997, pp 2–3.
4. S O'Connor, 'Happy Partners or Strange Bedfellows: The Blending of Remedial and Institutional Features in the Evolving Constructive Trust' (1996) 20 *Melbourne University Law Review* 735.
5. D M Wright, *The Remedial Constructive Trust*, Butterworths, Sydney, 1998, p 57.
6. O'Connor, 'Happy Partners or Strange Bedfellows: The Blending of Remedial and Institutional Features in the Evolving Constructive Trust', note 4 above, p 738.

28.9   In *Muschinski v Dodds* (1985) 160 CLR 583 at 612–4; (1985) 62 ALR 429 at 450–1, Deane J attempted to provide a compromise model of the constructive trust, by referring to it as a 'remedial institution':

> The nature and function of the constructive trust have been the subject of considerable discussion throughout the common law world for several decades … At times, disputing factions have tended to polarise the discussion by reference to competing rallying points of 'remedy' and 'institution'. The perceived dichotomy between those two catchwords has, however, largely been the consequence of lack of definition. In a broad sense, the constructive trust is both an institution and a remedy of the law of equity. As a remedy, it can only properly be understood in the context of the history and the persisting distinctness of the principles of equity that enlighten and control the common law. The use or trust of equity, like equity itself, was essentially remedial in its origins … Like express and implied trusts, the constructive trust developed as a remedial relationship superimposed upon common law rights by order of the Chancery Court. It differs from those other forms of trust, however, in that it arises regardless of intention. For that reason, it was not as well suited to development as a conveyancing device or as an instrument of property law. Indeed, whereas the rationale of the institutions of express and implied trust is now usually identified by reference to intention, the rationale of the constructive trust must still be found essentially in its remedial function which it has predominantly retained … The constructive trust shares, however, some of the institutionalised features of express and implied trust. It demands the staple ingredients of those trusts: subject matter, trustee, beneficiary (or, conceivably, purpose), and personal obligation attaching to the property … When established or imposed, it is a relationship governed by a coherent body of traditional and statute law. Viewed in its modern context, the constructive trust can properly be described as a remedial institution which equity imposes regardless of actual or presumed agreement or intention (and subsequently protects) to preclude the retention or assertion of beneficial ownership of property to the extent that such retention or assertion would be contrary to equitable principle.

28.10   The intended effect of Deane J's reclassification was to allow courts to choose the time from which a constructive trust arises, and, in that sense, the remedial function of the trust is given effect through the imposition of the institution of trust. If a judge has decided to impose a constructive trust retrospectively, equity regards as done that which ought to have been done and the trust is considered to have existed as an institution from that time onwards, rather than from the time of the order: *Muschinski v Dodds* at CLR 614; ALR 451.

Impact on third parties

28.11   The problem with the exercise of such discretion is the uncertainty it generates for third parties who have an interest in the property in question. This is particularly the case in insolvencies where the parties are jostling for priority to access property to satisfy their debts. The institutional view of a constructive trust might be significantly unfair to unsecured creditors who were not aware of the existence of a constructive trust, but may nevertheless find their claims cannot be satisfied because the property is held on trust: *Sui Mei Huen v Official Receiver* (2008) 248 ALR 1 at 22; *Draper v Official Trustee in Bankruptcy* (2006) 236 ALR 499 at 522. In *Re Osborn* (1989) 25 FCR 547, Pincus J refused to impose a constructive trust on the basis that one of the parties had become bankrupt and it was in the public interest for bankruptcy law to operate with certainty. In *Disctronics Ltd v Edmonds* [2002] VSC 454, Warren J refused to impose a constructive trust because she was not satisfied that third party creditors would not be unfairly disadvantaged. In *Victoria University of*

Technology v Wilson [2004] VSC 33, Nettle J was similarly troubled by the possible detrimental effects on third parties caused by a constructive trust.

28.12   Nevertheless, there is a strong line of authority which states that institutional constructive trusts will arise even where the interests of third parties will be prejudiced: *Re Jonton Pty Ltd* [1992] 2 Qd R 105; *Re Sabri* (1996) 137 FLR 165. In *Parsons v McBain* (2001) 109 FCR 120, when discussing the imposition of common intention constructive trusts (see 28.55–28.90), the Full Federal Court held that the trust was created by the conduct of the parties and arose at that time, even if that had the effect of defeating unsecured creditors.

28.13   This has been followed in later cases: *Jabbour v Sherwood* [2003] FCA 529; *Parianos v Melluish (Trustee)* (2003) 30 Fam LR 524. In *Clout v Markwell* [2003] QSC 91 at [21], it was said that creditors should be expected to be aware of constructive trusts which may arise when the debtor is married or in a de facto relationship. In *Varma v Varma* [2010] NSWSC 786 at [507], Ward J said:

> As a matter of general principle, it seems to be the accepted position under Australian and English law that a constructive trust will be treated as coming into existence at the time of the conduct which gives rise to the trust … In such a case, the doctrine of priorities would apply and, where the equities are equal, the beneficiary of the constructive trust would be entitled to priority over the holder of a later equitable interest, a later legal interest (providing they are not a bona fide purchaser for value without notice) or an unsecured creditor of the constructive trustee.

28.14   The problem with a purely institutional view is that it has the potential to render the operation of the law too uncertain and place far too great a burden on creditors.[7] It therefore seems that the better approach is to require the court to consider the impact of the order on third parties and mould relief accordingly: *Varma v Varma* at [510]–[518]. If third parties to the action would be detrimentally affected by the imposition of a trust, it is preferable to order relief in the form of a monetary sum secured through a charge or lien, rather than a constructive trust: *Tim Barr Pty Ltd v Narui Gold Coast Pty Ltd* [2010] NSWSC 29 at [569]; *Varma v Varma* at [501]; *Victoria University of Technology v Wilson; West v Mead* [2003] NSWSC 161; *Distronics Ltd v Edmonds* [2002] VSC 454; *Bathurst City Council v PWC Properties Pty Ltd* (1998) 195 CLR 566; 157 ALR 414; *Giumelli v Giumelli*. In *Draper v Official Trustee in Bankruptcy* the court was able to order an equitable accounting between co-owners, as an alternative to imposing a constructive trust. In *Australian Building and Technical Solutions Pty Ltd v Boumelhem* [2009] NSWSC 460, parents had provided funds to their son to purchase land and build duplexes on it, one of which was to be transferred into the parents' names on completion. The parents had increased the mortgage on their own home to get the funds. The son had also used the property as security on debts owed by his business. When the business collapsed, the parents claimed an interest under both a resulting trust (to secure their initial contribution) and a constructive trust (for later contributions they made to the building effort). These claims were resisted by the son's creditors. Ward J declared that there was a resulting trust for the contributions to the purchase price but did not order a constructive trust over the further amounts paid by the parents. These amounts were instead secured by equitable liens which could then be ranked against the other security interests held by the creditors.

---

7.   G E Dal Pont, 'Timing, insolvency and the constructive trust' (2004) 24 *Australian Bar Review* 262.

When do constructive trusts arise?

28.15 The institution/remedy dichotomy also has implications for the question of when constructive trusts should be employed by the courts. The traditional institutional approach focuses on established categories of transaction or sets of circumstances that trigger the imposition of a constructive trust.[8] Contrastingly, the remedial approach to constructive trusts focuses on broad types of wrongdoing (such as unconscionability/unconscientiousness or unjust enrichment: see 28.185–28.186) and applies constructive trusts to whatever circumstances are affected by such wrongdoing.

28.16 One of the perceived benefits of the institutional approach is that it limits constructive trusts to defined sets of circumstances and, by doing so, limits the judge's discretion in deciding when and how to adjust a person's beneficial entitlements. The institutional approach, according to this argument, provides certainty and stability to the operation of constructive trusts, whereas the remedial approach can lead to arbitrariness.

THE NEW MODEL CONSTRUCTIVE TRUST

28.17 During the 1970s the United Kingdom's Court of Appeal, led by Lord Denning MR, adopted a free-ranging remedial basis for constructive trusts and came to the view that a constructive trust is 'imposed by law whenever justice and good conscience require it': *Hussey v Palmer* [1972] 3 All ER 744 at 747. Lord Denning referred to this as the 'new model' of constructive trust which could be imposed whenever the court believed it fair to do so: *Binion v Evans* [1972] 3 All ER 744; *Eves v Eves* [1975] 3 All ER 768 at 771–2. While the new model had obvious benefits of flexibility, its main effect was to replace (moderately) certain rules with arbitrary judicial fiat.

28.18 Later English decisions rejected the new model of constructive trust: *Lloyds Bank v Rosset* [1991] 1 AC 107; [1990] 1 All ER 1111. It never took a foothold in Australia where it was criticised as a form of 'palm tree justice': *Bryson v Bryant* (1992) 29 NSWLR 188 at 196.

28.19 When affirming the remedial element of constructive trusts in *Muschinski v Dodds* (1985) at CLR 615–6; ALR 452, Deane J was careful to distance himself from Lord Denning's new model:

> [T]here is no place in the law of this country for the notion of 'a constructive trust of a new model' which, 'by whatever name it is described, … is … imposed by law whenever justice and good conscience' (in the sense of 'fairness' or what 'was fair') 'require it'. Under the law of this country — as, I venture to think, under the present law of England - proprietary rights fall to be governed by principles of law and not by some mix of judicial discretion, subjective views about which party 'ought to win' and 'the formless void of individual moral opinion'. Long before Lord Seldon's anachronism identifying the Chancellor's foot as the measure of Chancery relief, undefined notions of 'justice' and what was 'fair' had given way in the law of equity to the rule of ordered principle which is of the essence of any coherent system of rational law. The mere fact that it would be unjust or unfair in a situation of discord for the owner of a legal estate to assert his ownership against another provides, of itself, no mandate for a judicial declaration that the ownership in whole or in part lies, in equity, in that other.

---

8. Wright, *The Remedial Constructive Trust*, note 5 above, p 19.

28.20 This chapter will now proceed by examining the situations that give rise to the imposition of a constructive trust, with regards to both the institutional and remedial aspects. This chapter examines constructive trusts that:

1. arise in incomplete sales of property;
2. arise in incomplete gifts;
3. remedy fraudulent transactions;
4. arise in secret trusts;
5. arise in mutual wills;
6. arise in estoppel;
7. are imposed on parties with a common intention concerning property;
8. remedy breach of fiduciary duty;
9. are imposed on third parties to a breach of trust;
10. are imposed on stolen property;
11. are imposed on moneys paid by mistake;
12. arise in cases of unlawful killing; and
13. arise in response to unconscientious conduct.

INCOMPLETE CONTRACTS FOR THE SALE OF PROPERTY: THE RULE IN LYSAGHT V EDWARDS

28.21 It has been said that the moment a valid contract for sale of property comes into existence the vendor becomes a constructive trustee for the purchaser, and the beneficial ownership passes to the purchaser, leaving the vendor with a right to the purchase money, a charge or lien with respect to that money, and a right to retain possession until paid: *Lysaght v Edwards* (1876) 2 Ch D 499 at 506. This is sometimes known as equitable conversion.[9] The basis of the rule is the maxim that equity looks on that as done which ought to be done; see 2.46–2.48.[10] The rule applies to both real property and personal property: *Acorn Computers Ltd v MCS Microcomputer Systems Pty Ltd* (1984) 6 FCR 277; *Shaw v Foster* (1872) LR 5 HL 321; *Re Wait* [1927] 1 Ch 606.

'Specific performance' or some alternative form of equitable protection must be available

28.22 Equitable conversion is subject to a number of qualifications. The first of these is that the interest of the purchaser must be one which equity will protect. Traditionally, it was said that the contract had to be specifically enforceable: *Re Wait* [1927] Ch 606; [1926] All ER Rep 433. The rules regarding the grant of specific performance are explained in Chapter 23. It has often been said that the strength of the interest of the purchaser is commensurate with the availability of specific performance: *Tanwar Enterprises Pty Ltd v Cauchi* (2003) 217 CLR 315 at 333; 201 ALR 359 at 371; *Atwell v Roberts (No 3)* [2009] WASC 96 at [106]–[107].

28.23 However, other judgments have not necessarily required strict compliance with the availability of specific performance: *GPT Re Ltd v Lend Lease Real Estate Investments Ltd* [2005]

---

9. Oakley, *Constructive Trusts*, note 3 above, p 275.
10. S Worthington, 'Proprietary Remedies: The Nexus between Specific Performance and Constructive Trusts' (1996) 11 *Journal of Contract Law* 1 at 3; C Boge, 'A buyer's "interest" in land under an uncompleted contract: A return to principle' (2008) 82 *Australian Law Journal* 266.

NSWSC 964 at [53]–[55]. In *Stern v McArthur* (1988) 165 CLR 489 at 522–23; 81 ALR 463 at 485, Deane and Dawson JJ said:

> Specific performance in this context does not mean specific performance in the strict or technical sense of requiring the contract to be performed in accordance with its terms. Rather it encompasses all of those remedies available to the purchaser in equity to protect the interest which he has acquired under the contract. In appropriate cases it will include other remedies, such as relief by way of injunction, as well as specific performance in the strict sense. As Sir Frederick Jordan put it: 'Specific performance in this sense means not merely specific performance in the primary sense of the enforcing of an executory contract by compelling the execution of an assurance to complete it, but also the protection by injunction or otherwise of rights acquired under a contract which defines the rights of the parties': Jordan, 'Chapters on Equity in New South Wales', *Select Legal Papers*, 6th ed (1947), p 52, n(e).

28.24   While this relaxation of the requirement for specific performance was doubted by Meagher JA in *Chief Commissioner of Stamp Duties v ISPT Pty Ltd* (1998) 45 NSWLR 639 at 654 5, it now appears that the interest of the purchaser will be recognised when equity will protect it via other remedies, such as an injunction: *Ehrenfeld v Crosscity Enterprises Pty Ltd* [2007] WASC 308 at [66]. Therefore, the fact that there may be an unfulfilled condition that prevents specific performance will not be fatal to equity's recognition of the purchaser's proprietary interest, as long as equity is prepared to offer some assistance to the purchaser. It will, however, be difficult for equity to protect the purchaser's interest without a right to specific performance, particularly if the purchaser is in breach of an essential condition of the sale: *Marchesi v Apostolou* [2007] FCA 986 at [110].

Unconditional transfer

28.25   The second qualification, which is related to the first, is that the obligation to transfer the property must be unconditional.[11] This requirement depends on the nature of the condition. If it is intended by the parties that no interest will pass to the purchaser until the satisfaction of a condition, then the condition is a condition precedent and there is no interest that can arise which will be protected by a constructive trust.[12] However, the parties may not have intended a condition to operate in that fashion and in such cases the condition will not be a bar to an equitable interest being granted to the purchaser. Similarly, if the contract does not propose to pass any interest in the property at all, but rather grant a license, it will not create an equitable interest: *Snowy Hydro Limited (ACN 090 574 431) v Commissioner of State Revenue (Vic)* [2010] VSC 221 at [61]. Finally, if the agreement is varied so that the legal obligation to pass property to a particular purchaser disappears then the constructive trust will fail: *Gangemi v Osborne* [2009] VSCA 297 at [73].

28.26   Controversy exists over whether the purchaser is required to have paid the purchase price. It is certainly clear that if the purchase price has been paid, the vendor holds the property on trust for the purchaser. In contracts for the sale of land there is authority to suggest that a constructive trust arises upon exchange of contracts and that payment of price is not necessary for the constructive trust to arise: *Kern Corporation Ltd v Walter Reid Trading Pty Ltd* (1987) 163 CLR 164 at 191; 71 ALR 417

---

11.   Worthington, 'Proprietary Remedies: The Nexus between Specific Performance and Constructive Trusts', note 10 above, p 10.
12.   Dal Pont, note 1 above, pp 1003–4.

at 435; *KLDE Pty Ltd v Commissioner of Stamp Duties (Qld)* (1984) 155 CLR 288 at 296–7. This result is inconsistent with the fact that, until settlement, the vendor is entitled to all rents and profits from the land. Additionally, in cases of sales of personalty, such as company shares and copyright, the vendor is entitled to all income from that property until the purchase price has been paid: *Hawks v McArthur* [1951] 1 All ER 22; *Performing Right Society v London Theatre of Varieties* [1922] 2 KB 433.

28.27   The better view is that in cases of unpaid vendors of realty and personalty the vendor is not a bare trustee of the property but rather holds an equitable interest on trust, the strength of which is dependent on the availability of specific performance or other equitable remedy. The more the purchaser has paid towards the purchase price, the stronger the equitable rights of the purchaser will be: *Trust Company of Australia Ltd v Commissioner of State Revenue* (2007) 19 VR 111 at 117; *Bunny Industries Ltd v FSW Enterprises Pty Ltd* [1982] Qd R 712 at 715.

28.28   Another problem relates to transfers that are conditional on the actions of third parties. In earlier cases it was said that if the contract was conditional on the actions of a third party (such as the creation or registration of titles), the purchaser had no interest and a constructive trust did not arise until the third party satisfied the condition: *Brown v Heffer* (1967) 116 CLR 344. But in later cases, following the relaxed approach to the requirement of specific performance, courts have found that an interest will arise in equity, as long as the purchaser's rights are ones which the court is prepared to protect: *Kuper & Kuper v Keywest Constructions Pty Ltd* (1990) 3 WAR 419; *Jessica Holdings Pty Ltd v Anglican Property Trust Diocese of Sydney* (1992) 27 NSWLR 140; *Forder v Cemcorp* (2001) NSWLR 486.

Identified property

28.29   The third qualification to the rule in *Lysaght v Edwards* is that the transfer must relate to identified property, meaning that the property must not be unascertained. In *Re Goldcorp Exchange Ltd (in rec)* [1995] 1 AC 74; [1994] 2 All ER 806, a large number of unsecured investors had bought gold off a company and stored it with the company. The gold that was the subject of each contract remained unascertained (gold had not been identified as belonging to individual investors). When the company went into receivership the investors were unable to claim equitable ownership on constructive trust.

Doubts over the trust status of the rule in Lysaght v Edwards

28.30   There are continuing difficulties in this area in relation to specific performance and unconditional sale which have led some judges to doubt whether the application of the rule truly gives rise to a constructive trust. In *Chang v Registrar of Titles* (1976) 137 CLR 177 at 190, Jacobs J said:

> Where there are rights outstanding on both sides, the description of the vendor as a trustee tends to conceal the essentially contractual relationship which, rather than the relationship of trustee and beneficiary, governs the rights and duties of the respective parties.

Similarly, in *Kern Corporation Ltd v Walter Reid Trading Pty Ltd* (1987) 163 CLR 164 at 192, Deane J said:

> It is both inaccurate and misleading to speak of the unpaid vendor under an uncompleted contract as trustee for the purchaser.

28.31   Both quotes from these cases were relied on by the majority in *Tanwar Enterprises Pty Ltd v Cauchi* at CLR 333; ALR 371. In this case the High Court found that a contract for the sale of land had been validly terminated by a termination notice and that the purchaser's equitable interest had been extinguished. Given this finding, Gleeson CJ, McHugh, Gummow, Hayne and Heydon JJ found that the constructive trust analogy was 'no longer accepted'. However, this comment was made after an endorsement of the notion that a right to specific performance would give rise to an equitable interest. To that extent, the rule in *Lysaght v Edwards* will still give rise to a constructive trust but only in those cases where equity will intervene to protect the interests of the purchaser, because the purchaser is entitled to specific performance, an injunction or some other equitable remedy. This understanding of *Lysaght v Edwards* is also supported by the observation of Williams J in *Fairweather v Fairweather* (1944) 69 CLR 121 at 154, where his Honour noted that a contract that was at one stage specifically enforceable may, at a later stage, cease to be so, so that 'the trusteeship of the vendor, which exists only while the contract is specifically enforceable, then comes to an end'. In making that observation his Honour referred to *Central Trust and Safe Deposit Company v Snider* [1916] AC 255 at 272, where Lord Parker of Waddington said that:

> If for some reason equity would not enforce specific performance, or if the right to specific performance has been lost by the subsequent conduct of the party in whose favour the specific performance might originally have been granted, the vendor or covenantor either never was, or has ceased to be, a trustee in any sense at all.

INCOMPLETE GIFTS

28.32 Some gifts of property will fail in law because legal title has not passed to the donee. In equity, if a donor does all the things that are necessary to pass the title that are exclusively the donor's responsibility, equity will perfect the gift: see 5.103–5.116. Any legal title will be held on constructive trust for the intended donee to give effect to the gift.

CONSTRUCTIVE TRUSTS AND FRAUDULENT TRANSACTIONS

28.33 Another species of constructive trust exists in fraudulent transactions where one party commits fraud in an agreement to transfer property, which, while not creating a contractual obligation, equity finds would be fraudulent to deny: *Chattock v Muller* (1878) 8 Ch D 177. In *Avondale Printers and Stationers Limited v Haggie* [1979] 2 NZLR 124 at 163, Mahon J stated:

> Where property is conveyed or proprietary rights released in consideration of an oral promise by the transferee that the transferor will retain or later acquire a beneficial interest in the property in question, and where retraction of the promise amounts to a fraud upon the transferor, then the transferee will be held a constructive trustee for the benefit of the transferor of either the whole property or of the relevant interest therein. The key to this type of enquiry in my opinion lies in the question whether the transferor would have parted with his property but for the oral undertaking of the transferee. If the question is answered in the negative, then renunciation of the promise or disavowal of the common intention will operate in equity as a fraud on the transferor and entitle him to the appropriate remedy.

28.34 In *Lonrho plc v Fayed (No 2)* at 969–970, Millett J said:

> Equity will intervene by way of constructive trust, not only to compel the defendant to restore the plaintiff's property to him, but also to require the defendant to disgorge property which

he should have acquired, if at all, for the plaintiff. In the latter category of case, the defendant's wrong lies not in the acquisition of the property, which may or may not have been lawful, but in his subsequent denial of the plaintiff's beneficial interest. For such to be the case, however, the defendant must either have acquired property which but for his wrongdoing would have belonged to the plaintiff, or he must have acquired property in circumstances in which he cannot conscientiously retain it as against the plaintiff.

28.35 One of the leading cases here is *Pallant v Morgan* [1953] Ch 43. It involved an auction sale where two neighbours had each engaged an agent to bid on a piece of undeveloped land near their properties. The agents agreed that one would bid and then they would split the land if successful at the auction. The agreement was unclear on how this would be done, and was not specifically performable. The defendant then reneged on the agreement. Harman J found that the land was owned equitably between the plaintiff and the defendant and that the property should be sold and the proceeds be, after subtracting the purchase price paid by the defendant (plus interest), split equally. This type of proprietary right is sometimes referred to as the *Pallant v Morgan* equity.

28.36 Another important case is *Avondale Printers and Stationers Limited v Haggie* where the plaintiff and defendants were both leaseholders in the same premises. The plaintiff had made plans to redevelop the premises and had entered into a contract to purchase the property. It later released its contractual rights to purchase the property to the defendants, but on the proviso that the defendant would contribute $30,000 to the redevelopment and offer the property for sale to the plaintiff in two years' time. After substantial improvements had been effected by the plaintiff, the defendants notified the plaintiff that they would no longer be offering the property for sale. Mahon J found that the defendant's assertion of ownership was fraudulent and ordered a constructive trust over the property, subject to the plaintiff reimbursing the costs of the purchase.

28.37 In *Last v Rosenfeld* [1972] 2 NSWLR 923, there was agreement by one party to sell their share in a property for $8500 which was subject to an oral agreement to transfer the share back after a year for the same amount. The purchaser reneged on the agreement and sold the property to a third party. Hope J held that a constructive trust arose over the property when the original transfer was created and that a share of the proceeds would be held on constructive trust. A similar trust arose in *Cockburn v Coburn* [2005] NSWSC 993 where a mother transferred her titles in land to her son but on the basis that the title would be re-transferred at a later time when debts on the land had been discharged.

28.38 In *Banner Homes Group plc v Luff Developments Ltd* [2000] Ch 372 at 397–9; [2000] 2 All ER 117 at 138–9, Chadwick LJ proposed the following requirements:

(1) A *Pallant v Morgan* equity may arise where the arrangement or understanding on which it is based precedes the acquisition of the relevant property by one of those parties to that arrangement. It is the pre-acquisition arrangement which colours the subsequent acquisition by the defendant and leads to his being treated as a trustee if he seeks to act inconsistently with it. Where the arrangement or understanding is reached in relation to property already owned by one of the parties, he may (if the arrangement is of sufficient certainty to be enforced specifically) thereby constitute himself trustee on the basis that 'equity looks on that as done which ought to be done'; or an equity may arise under the principles developed in the proprietary estoppel cases. As I have sought to point out, the concepts of constructive trust and proprietary estoppel have much in common in this area …

(2) It is unnecessary that the arrangement or understanding should be contractually enforceable. Indeed, if there is an agreement which is enforceable as a contract, there is unlikely to be any need to invoke the *Pallant v Morgan* equity; equity can act through the remedy of specific performance and will recognise the existence of a corresponding trust …

(3) It is necessary that the pre-acquisition arrangement or understanding should contemplate that one party (the acquiring party) will take steps to acquire the relevant property; and that, if he does so, the other party (the non-acquiring party) will obtain some interest in that property. Further it is necessary, that (whatever private reservations the acquiring party may have) he has not informed the non-acquiring party before the acquisition (or, more accurately, before it is too late for the parties to be restored to a position of no advantage/no detriment) that he no longer intends to honour the arrangement or understanding.

(4) It is necessary that, in reliance on the arrangement or understanding, the non-acquiring party should do (or omit to do) something which confers an advantage on the acquiring party in relation to the acquisition of the property; or is detrimental to the ability of the non-acquiring party to acquire the property on equal terms. It is the existence of the advantage to the one, or detriment to the other, gained or suffered as a consequence of the arrangement or understanding, which leads to the conclusion that it would be inequitable or unconscionable to allow the acquiring party to retain the property for himself, in a manner inconsistent with the arrangement or understanding which enabled him to acquire it.

(5) That leads, I think, to the further conclusions: (i) that, although, in many cases, the advantage/detriment will be found in the agreement of the non-acquiring party to keep out of the market, that is not a necessary feature; and (ii) that, although there will usually be advantage to the one and co-relative disadvantage to the other, the existence of both advantage and detriment is not essential—either will do. What is essential is that the circumstances make it inequitable for the acquiring party to retain the property for himself in a manner inconsistent with the arrangement or understanding on which the non-acquiring party has acted. Those circumstances may arise where the non-acquiring party was never 'in the market' for the whole of the property to be acquired; but (on the faith of an arrangement or understanding that he shall have a part of that property) provides support in relation to the acquisition of the whole which is of advantage to the acquiring party. They may arise where the assistance provided to the acquiring party (in pursuance of the arrangement or understanding) involves no detriment to the non-acquiring party; or where the non-acquiring party acts to his detriment (in pursuance of the arrangement or understanding) without the acquiring party obtaining any advantage therefrom.

28.39   The constructive trust will not be imposed if the agreement is too vague and uncertain to be enforced: *Yeoman's Row Management Ltd v Cobbe* [2008] 4 All ER 713; *London and Regional Investments Ltd v TBI plc* [2002] EWCA Civ 355.

28.40   In *Crossco No 4 Unlimited v Jolan Ltd* [2011] EWCA Civ 1619, the Court of Appeal attempted to characterise the nature of the *Pallant v Morgan* equity. Etherton LJ, at [85], refused to describe the equity as an example of a common intention constructive trust of the *Stack v Dowden* [2007] 2 AC 432; [2007] 2 All ER 929 variety (see 28.65–28.75), finding that such common intention constructive trust should not be applied in commercial contexts. Etherton LJ also stated that the underlying rationale for the equity was the presence of a fiduciary duty, such as the agency roles in *Pallant v Morgan*. Arden LJ disagreed and found that cases like *Banner Homes Group plc v Luff Developments*

Ltd clearly established that the equity is a form of common intention constructive trust: see 28.55. MacFarlane LJ found that, absent an express declaration from the Supreme Court, the decision in *Banner Homes* should be followed.

28.41   It is, with respect, hard to find any attractiveness in the attempted classifications in *Crossco No 4 Unlimited v Jolan Ltd*. None of them appear correct. The *Pallant v Morgan* equity does not require the existence of a fiduciary relationship and Etherton LJ's refusal to apply common intention constructive trusts outside of the domestic sphere is not supported by authority. These constructive trusts are similar to common intention constructive trusts in that they are often based in agreements but they differ in the requirement for detriment and the way that one of the parties seeks to defraud the other. If there is a common intention in these cases it is not a shared intention but a false one created by fraudulent behaviour and it is this falsity which attracts equitable intervention.

SECRET TRUSTS

28.42   Secret trusts are discussed at 16.145–16.165. Secret trusts have been characterised as constructive trusts. The argument for their recognition is very similar to the argument in favour of imposing trusts in cases of fraudulent transactions.[13]

MUTUAL WILLS

28.43   Mutual wills are wills made as part of an agreement, whereby the parties promise not to revoke their wills after one of the parties dies: *Dufour v Pereira* (1769) 21 ER 332; *Albrow v Cunningham* [2000] NSWSC 103.[14] Equity protects and enforces the rights created by such an agreement, and will impose a constructive trust on property to give effect to the agreement, should testators breach the agreement and revoke their wills: *Birmingham v Renfrew* (1937) 57 CLR 666 at 682–3. In *Barns v Barns* (2003) 214 CLR 169; (2003) 196 ALR 65 at 85, Gummow and Hayne JJ described the operation of mutual wills in the following steps:

> (i) it is the disposition of the property by the first party under a will in the agreed form and upon the faith of the survivor carrying out the obligation of the contract which attracts the intervention of equity in favour of the survivor; (ii) that intervention is by the imposition of a trust of a particular character; (iii) the subject-matter is 'the property passing [to the survivor] under the will of the party first dying' [*Birmingham v Renfrew* (1937) 57 CLR 666 at 689]; (iv) that which passes to the survivor is identified after due administration by the legal personal representative [*Easterbrook v Young* (1977) 136 CLR 308 at 319–320] whereupon 'the dispositions of the will become operative' [*Attenborough v Solomon* [1913] AC 76 at 83]; (v) there is 'a floating obligation' over that property which has passed to the survivor; it is suspended during the lifetime of the survivor and 'crystallises' into a trust upon the assets of the survivor at death [*Birmingham v Renfrew* (1937) 57 CLR 666 at 689–690]. (case references inserted)

To illustrate, in *Birmingham v Renfrew* a husband and wife had created mutual wills which left the entire estate to whoever survived on the condition that the estate would then pass on death of the survivor to the wife's relatives. The husband survived the wife but then changed his will. The new

13.   J D Heydon & M J Leeming, *Jacobs' Law of Trusts in Australia*, LexisNexis Butterworths, Sydney, 2006, p 294.
14.   R A Croucher, 'Mutual Wills: Contemporary Reflections on an Old Doctrine' (2005) *Melbourne University Law Review* 390.

will did not leave the estate to the wife's relatives. After the husband died the High Court held that the estate was held on constructive trust for the wife's relatives.

Agreement not to revoke will

28.44   The essential characteristic of mutual wills is that there be an agreement between the parties not to revoke their wills: *Baird v Smee* [2000] NSWCA 253. The mere fact that two persons make corresponding wills 'in the sense that the existence of each will is naturally explained by the existence of the other will is not sufficient to establish a binding agreement not to revoke wills so made': *Birmingham v Renfrew* (1937) 57 CLR 666 at 674–5; *Gray v Perpetual Trustee Co Ltd* (1928) 40 CLR 558 at 564–5. The agreement not to revoke may be implied from all the circumstances: *Hudson v Gray* (1927) 39 CLR 473 at 487; *Brigg v Queensland Trustees Ltd* [1990] 2 Qd R 11 at 14; *Low v Perpetual Trustees WA Ltd* (1995) 14 WAR 35 at 42–3.

28.45   Any new will written in breach of the agreement is not void, it merely is ineffective in equity with regards to its dispositive effect: *Charles v Fraser* [2010] EWHC 2154 (Ch) at [59].

Evidence of mutual wills

28.46   There is an obvious need for caution when examining a claim of mutual wills, given the effects that mutual wills have on subsequent testamentary dispositions: *Birmingham v Renfrew* at 674–5. As such, mutual wills 'can be established only by clear and satisfactory evidence': *Birmingham v Renfrew* at 681–2; *Re Cleaver* [1981] 1 WLR 939 at 947; *Osborne v Osborne* [2001] VSCA 95; *Hussey v Bauer* [2011] QCA 91 at [30]–[31]. Such evidence can consist of written or oral evidence of statements of intention, any substantial consideration offered for the promise not to revoke, the number of times the statement was made, the language used by the parties, the context (formal or informal) in which the promise was made, the nature of the relationship between the parties, and the certainty of the terms: *Albrow v Cunningham* [2000] NSWSC 103; *Radalj v Di Francesco* [2003] WASC 57; *Pridham v Pridham* [2010] SASC 204 at [29]. A court will *not* imply or infer the existence of an agreement not to revoke wills simply from the fact that similar wills have been made: *Fry v Densham-Smith* [2010] EWCA Civ 1410 at [3]. The agreement may be incorporated in the will or proved by extraneous evidence and it may be oral or in writing: *Charles v Fraser* at [58]. Mutual wills are commonly evidenced in codicils which expressly recognise an agreement not to revoke: *Olins v Walters* [2009] Ch 212.

Rights of the survivor to deal with the property

28.47   The survivor is free to write another will as the doctrine does not make wills irrevocable. Nor does it invalidate a will that has been changed in breach of an agreement. Rather, such a will stands but the property is held by the beneficiaries on constructive trust: *Fazari v Cosentino* [2010] WASC 40 at [18].

28.48   The survivor can also deal with property as they wish during their life, as long as transactions are not aimed at effectively destroying the agreement between the parties: *Fazari v Cosentino* at [45] [47]. In *Birmingham v Renfrew* at 689, Dixon J said:

> The purpose of an arrangement for corresponding wills must often be, as in this case, to enable the survivor during his life to deal as absolute owner with the property passing under the will of the party first dying. That is to say, the object of the transaction is to put the survivor in a position to enjoy for his own benefit the full ownership so that, for instance, he may convert it and expend the proceeds if he choose. But when he dies he is to bequeath what is left in the manner agreed upon. It is

only by the special doctrines of equity that such a floating obligation, suspended, so to speak, during the lifetime of the survivor can descend upon the assets at his death and crystallise into a trust. No doubt gifts and settlements, inter vivos, if calculated to defeat the intention of the compact, could not be made by the survivor and his right of disposition, inter vivos, is therefore, not unqualified. But, substantially, the purpose of the arrangement will often be to allow full enjoyment for the survivor's own benefit and advantage upon condition that at his death the residue shall pass as arranged.

28.49   In *Palmer v Bank of New South Wales* (1975) 133 CLR 150 at 162, Barwick CJ said that the survivor was not prevented from making testamentary gifts during their lifetime:

> It was conceded in *Birmingham v Renfrew* that the making of an agreement for mutual wills did not preclude the alienation of property during the lifetime of the promisors. When in that case Dixon J spoke of 'gifts and settlements, inter vivos ... calculated to defeat the intention of the compact' he no doubt had in mind gifts and settlements which were either testamentary in nature or which were in contravention of the terms of the particular contract, spelled out of the expressions actually used, bearing in mind the circumstances in which it was made.

28.50   In *Palmer v Bank of New South Wales* the opening of a joint bank account was found not to be testamentary in nature. Nor was it aimed at undermining the promise not to revoke the will. Contrastingly, in *Healey v Brown* [2002] EWHC Ch 1405, the survivor was found to have broken the compact for mutual wills by transferring her house into her name and the name of her son as joint tenants. David Donaldson QC, at [14], said:

> I would, in line with the observations of Dixon J, have had little difficulty in concluding that a sale at arm's length or market price by the survivor, Mr Brown, to permit personal enjoyment of the proceeds was not precluded by the agreement of the parties. But 'gifts and settlements, inter vivos, if calculated to defeat the intention of the compact' would plainly be in breach of it. Had Mr Brown sold the flat and used the proceeds to fund a place in a nursing home, there would have been no basis for complaint. But to give away the flat to his son — with immediate effect as to a 50% undivided share, and with effect on death as to the remainder by operation of the doctrine of survivorship — could scarcely run more directly and fully counter to the intention of the mutual will compact that the flat should pass to his deceased's wife niece on his own death.

Nature of the constructive beneficiary's interest

28.51   The interest of the constructive beneficiary, after the death of one of the contracting parties but prior to the death of the survivor, was described by Latham CJ in *Birmingham v Renfrew* at 675, as protected by a 'kind of floating trust'. This interest has been found to be strong enough to support a caveat (*Fazari v Cosentino* [2008] WASC 149) and has also been strong enough to give constructive beneficiaries standing to bring an action to remove an executor: *Russo v Russo* [2009] VSC 491. Once the survivor dies, the interest then 'crystallises', giving rise to a full equitable interest: *Birmingham v Renfrew* at 689–690; *Fazari v Cosentino* at [20].

ESTOPPEL

28.52   The law concerning equitable estoppel is discussed in Chapter 12, but for present purposes it should be recalled that the courts will allow an estoppel to be raised when one party makes a representation that is relied on by another to their detriment. If the first party then resiles from that representation in circumstances that are unconscientious, an equity arises in favour of the representee. Constructive trusts will often be employed as a way of enforcing the equity: *Harrison v Harrison (No 2)* [2012] VSC 74.

28.53   Before a constructive trust is imposed to enforce an estoppel, the court should firstly decide whether there is an appropriate equitable remedy which falls short of the imposition of a trust: *Flinn v Flinn* [1999] 3 VR 712. If third parties to the action would be detrimentally affected by the imposition of a trust, it is preferable to order relief in the form of a monetary sum rather than a constructive trust: *Giumelli v Giumelli*.

BREACH OF CONFIDENCE

28.54   The law of confidential information is discussed in Chapter 8. Constructive trusts are a major remedy for breach of confidence, not only for breaches of agreements to keep information confidential, but also for situations where information has been acquired by stealth: see 8.80–8.82.

COMMON INTENTION CONSTRUCTIVE TRUSTS

28.55   Where parties have entered into a relationship with a common intention that property is to be held between them in a particular way, equity may enforce that common intention by the imposition of a constructive trust: *Jin v Yang* [2008] NSWSC 754. While the parties may have had a shared intention or an agreement as to how property is to be held, such an agreement may not be enforceable as a contract because the agreement is not in writing, or because the parties may not have evidenced a sufficient intention to enter into legal relations.[15] Equity will enforce such an agreement if a party relies on the common intention to their detriment: *Bannister v Bannister* [1948] 2 All ER 133.

The development in England

28.56   The 'common intention constructive trust' has often been employed in the context of domestic property disputes. Prior to the introduction of statutory mechanisms for resolving property disputes following the breakdown of domestic relationships, it was necessary to frame any proprietary claim within equity. The role of the resulting trust as a mechanism for resolving such disputes is discussed in Chapter 18. During the 1970s, constructive trusts were also called on with increasing frequency as a way of determining beneficial entitlements to family-owned assets.

28.57   In England, prior to the introduction of the *Matrimonial Causes Act 1973* (UK), constructive trusts were initially employed as a way of resolving property disputes on marital breakdown. The trend began with *Pettitt v Pettitt* [1970] AC 777; [1969] 2 All ER 385, which involved a claim made by a husband for the proceeds of sale of a house legally owned by his wife. The husband made the claim on the basis of modest capital contributions that he made in the form of improvements to the house and garden. The House of Lords recognised that such a trust could arise if it could be shown that it was the common intention of the parties that such a beneficial interest was to be granted to the husband. The intention had to be actual intention or inferred from the circumstances. On that ground the claim failed as there was no evidence of a common intention to confer a beneficial interest upon him.

---

15.   H A J Ford & W A Lee, *Principles of the law of trusts* (Online), Thomson Reuters, Sydney, [22350].

28.58   These findings were confirmed in *Gissing v Gissing* [1971] AC 886; [1970] 2 All ER 780, where a wife failed to establish a beneficial interest in a house held in her husband's name. Her claim was based on the fact that she had helped to lay out a lawn and provided furniture. Lord Diplock, at AC 905; All ER 790, in what was to become a troubled passage, said:

> A resulting, implied or constructive trust — and it is unnecessary for present purposes to distinguish between these three classes of trust — is created by a transaction between the trustee and the *cestui que* trust in connection with the acquisition by the trustee of a legal estate in land, whenever the trustee has so conducted himself that it would be inequitable to deny to the *cestui que* trust a beneficial interest in the land acquired. And he will be held so to have conducted himself if by his words or conduct he has induced the *cestui que* trust to act to his own detriment in the reasonable belief that by so acting he was acquiring a beneficial interest in the land.

28.59   These comments of Lord Diplock gave encouragement to Lord Denning MR who thereafter launched the Court of Appeal on a journey down the dead end of the 'new model constructive trust': see 28.17–28.19. However, the House of Lords in both *Gissing* and *Pettitt* made it clear that constructive trusts should only be employed when the common intention was either expressed or could be inferred from the circumstances: *Gissing* at AC 906; All ER 790–1. The principles enunciated in *Gissing* and *Pettitt* are equally applicable to de facto relationships: *Burns v Burns* [1984] Ch 317; [1984] 1 All ER 244; *Grant v Edwards* [1986] Ch 638; [1986] 2 All ER 426. They can also be applied to other family relationships, such as loans between family members: *Re Sharpe (a bankrupt)* [1980] 1 All ER 198.

28.60   A finding of expressed common intention can be made on the basis of evidence of intention prior to or at the time of purpose: *Gissing v Gissing* at AC 908; All ER 791. Evidence may also be admissible of intention in the immediate aftermath of purchase: *Lloyd's Bank plc v Rossett* [1991] 1 AC 107 at 132; [1990] 1 All ER 1111 at 1118.

28.61   In the past, in the absence of evidence of express agreement, inferences of a common intention to grant a beneficial interest arose when the party made a direct financial contribution to the acquisition of the property. Indirect contributions, such as homemaking, were not considered unless there was an express agreement to recognise them: *Lloyd's Bank plc v Rossett* [1991] 1 AC 107 at 132–3; [1990] 1 All ER 1111 at 1119.

28.62   It has been argued by Wong that the focus on direct financial contribution for evidence of inferred common intention is sexist because it devalues domestic contributions that are, by and large, made by women via the sexual division of labour.[16] This discriminatory effect appears to have been lessened somewhat by the decision in *Midland Bank v Cooke* [1995] 4 All ER 562, where the Court of Appeal found that, once some direct financial contribution had been made (however minimal) it was then open to the court to calculate the beneficial interests on the basis of all contributions, whether direct or indirect. Moreover, the court could make inquiries as to the nature of all contributions, whether they were made at the time of purchase or beyond it.

---

16.   S Wong, 'Constructive trusts over the family home: lessons to be learned from other Commonwealth jurisdictions?' (1998) 18 *Legal Studies* 369.

Express, inferred and/or imputed intention

28.63 The cases above show that the court's inquiry goes towards the issue of whether the parties actually had an express intention that the beneficial interest in the property would be shared differently than the legal interest. That intention might also be inferred in light of the actions of the parties.

28.64 But what is the rule when parties have made financial contributions but have never discussed how they were to share the property? In *Oxley v Hiscock* [2005] Fam 211 at 246, Chadwick LJ said that in the absence of an agreement, the courts could impute an intention to the parties based on their course of dealing:

> It must now be accepted that (at least in this court and below) the answer is that each is entitled to that share which the court considers fair having regard to the whole course of dealing between them in relation to the property. And, in that context, 'the whole course of dealing between them in relation to the property' includes the arrangements which they make from time to time in order to meet the outgoings (for example, mortgage contributions, council tax and utilities, repairs, insurance and housekeeping) which have to be met if they are to live in the property as their home.

28.65 The House of Lords accepted this approach to common intention constructive trusts, with some modification, in *Stack v Dowden* [2007] 2 AC 432; [2007] 2 All ER 929: see 19.66. In that case the parties had lived in a de facto relationship since 1975 and had had four children. Over the years, the woman in the relationship had earned more money and had contributed nearly two- thirds to the costs of acquiring the home in which the family lived. The property was registered as jointly owned and on the breakdown of the relationship the man sought a half-share of the house. Baroness Hale, who gave the leading speech in the House, felt that the starting point in such disputes should be to follow the law. If the property was held jointly the beneficial interests will be treated as equivalent. Conversely, if the property is held in a single name, the starting point will be to presume that that was what was intended. The effect of this decision was to reject resulting trust analysis (as understood in Australia) altogether: see 19.66–19.68. The next question is to ask whether the parties had a common intention to hold the property differently from what was recorded in the legal title. That common intention could be actual, inferred or imputed: *Stack v Dowden* at AC 455; All ER 950. Should a party seek a different distribution to that provided by law, the onus of proving a different beneficial ownership rests on the person asserting it. Baroness Hale did warn the court that, in discerning the common intention of the parties, it should not impose its own view of what is fair but rather look for what the parties intended: *Stack v Dowden* at AC 456; All ER 951.

28.66 In *Stack v Dowden* at AC 459; All ER 953, Baroness Hale set out the following factors which are relevant to the determination of the parties' intention:

> Many more factors than financial contributions may be relevant to divining the parties' true intentions. These include: any advice or discussions at the time of the transfer which cast light upon their intentions then; the reasons why the home was acquired in their joint names; the reasons why (if it be the case) the survivor was authorised to give a receipt for the capital moneys; the purpose for which the home was acquired; the nature of the parties' relationship; whether they had children for whom they both had responsibility to provide a home; how the purchase was financed, both initially and subsequently; how the parties arranged their finances, whether

separately or together or a bit of both; how they discharged the outgoings on the property and their other household expenses. When a couple are joint owners of the home and jointly liable for the mortgage, the inferences to be drawn from who pays for what may be very different from the inferences to be drawn when only one is owner of the home. The arithmetical calculation of how much was paid by each is also likely to be less important. It will be easier to draw the inference that they intended that each should contribute as much to the household as they reasonably could and that they would share the eventual benefit or burden equally. The parties' individual characters and personalities may also be a factor in deciding where their true intentions lay. In the cohabitation context, mercenary considerations may be more to the fore than they would be in marriage, but it should not be assumed that they always take pride of place over natural love and affection. At the end of the day, having taken all this into account, cases in which the joint legal owners are to be taken to have intended that their beneficial interests should be different from their legal interests will be very unusual.

On the facts of the case it was decided that because the woman had contributed far more financially than the man, and the parties had never pooled their financial resources, the court could impute that it was not their intention to grant equal half-shares. On that basis the shares were adjusted 65 per cent to the woman and 45 per cent to the man.

28.67 There are a number of difficulties with the decision of the majority, not least the decision to jettison the presumption of resulting trust with little or no discussion: see 19.65. Lord Neuberger, in dissent, thought the idea that the court could impute an intention, rather than find an actual or inferred intention, was wrong in principle and was difficult, subjective and uncertain. His Lordship expressed unhappiness at the notion that the courts could apportion property based on what was fair. His Lordship, at AC 476; All ER 970, said:

> First, fairness is not the appropriate yardstick. Secondly, the formulation appears to contemplate an imputed intention. Thirdly, 'the whole course of dealing … in relation to the property' is too imprecise, as it gives insufficient guidance as to what is primarily relevant, namely dealings which cast light on the beneficial ownership of the property, and too limited, as all aspects of the relationship could be relevant in providing the context, by reference to which any alleged discussion, statement and actions must be assessed. As already explained I also disagree with Chadwick LJ's implicit suggestion in the same paragraph [of *Oxley v Hiscock*] that 'the arrangements which [the parties] make with regard to the outgoings' (other than mortgage repay ments) are likely to be of primary relevance to the issue of the ownership of the beneficial interest in the home.

28.68 Regardless of these criticisms, the decision was soon after affirmed by the Privy Council in *Abbott v Abbott (Antigua and Barbuda)* [2007] UKPC 53, where it was again said that the court could find an actual or inferred intention, or impute one to the parties, based on their conduct. However, it has been said that the courts should be slow, in the absence of an express agreement, to vary the legal ownership of property: *James v Thomas* [2007] EWCA Civ 1212 at [24]; *Matter of Edwards* [2011] EWHC 1688 (Admin) at [34]. In *James v Thomas* the Court of Appeal could not find a common intention constructive trust where the property in a relationship had been acquired by the man prior to the relationship commencing and no statement had been directly made which would have evidenced an intention to grant the woman an interest in the home.

28.69 This judicial reluctance to disturb legal title is also illustrated by the decision in *Fowler v Barron* [2008] EWCA Civ 377, where a de facto couple, who had been in a relationship for 23 years, had joint legal ownership of the domestic property. The man had provided the purchase moneys but an amount was secured by a mortgage that both parties had agreed to. The mortgage loan was repaid by the man alone. At trial (which was conducted prior to the decision in *Stack v Dowden*) the judge employed a resulting trust to find that the property was beneficially owned by the man. On appeal, the Court of Appeal found that, following *Stack v Dowden*, the starting point was of joint beneficial ownership as the parties had chosen to adopt this form when the property was acquired. The man failed to disprove the presumption of equal beneficial ownership flowing from the legal estates. The evidence suggested that while the woman's income did not go towards the mortgage it was used for the household. The parties had wills which gave each other the rights over the home. In light of these facts, there was not enough evidence to displace the presumption of a shared intention of equal ownership.

28.70   The Court of Appeal found similarly in *Morris v Morris* [2008] EWCA Civ 257, in a case which involved a married couple fighting over interests in a farm. The farm had belonged to the husband and his mother. The wife had worked on the farm, and eventually ran a horse riding business on it. She had provided a small sum which went towards the construction of a manège (a riding school) but this was used for her business and for her benefit. The wife succeeded at trial in claiming a half-share in the farm. This was overturned on appeal by the Court of Appeal, which could find no evidence of any intention to grant the wife a beneficial interest. Sir Peter Gibson J, at [17], said:

It is one thing to say that the claimant believed herself to be an integral part of a business conducted on particular land. It is another to find that the claimant has established an interest in the land itself.

28.71   The Supreme Court of the United Kingdom revisited *Stack v Dowden* in *Jones v Kernott* [2012] 1 AC 776; [2012] 1 All ER 1265. This case concerned an unmarried couple who purchased a property in their joint names with the woman paying the deposit and the rest of the purchase price being secured by a joint mortgage. The man provided a small weekly amount for household expenses and the woman made all the payments on the mortgage, a life insurance policy and other household bills. When the couple separated it was agreed that they each held an equal share in the house. They attempted to sell the property but were unsuccessful. Instead they cashed in their life insurance policy and the man was able to put his share towards purchasing his own home. Ten years later the man claimed a beneficial interest in the original house as he remained on the title. The woman claimed the total beneficial interest. At trial the judge found that the parties had altered their beneficial positions when they separated and that the appropriate way to discern that alteration was to consider what was just and fair in the circumstances. The judge awarded 90 per cent of the beneficial ownership to the woman and 10 per cent to the man. The decision was overturned by the Court of Appeal, which found that there was no evidence to overturn the presumption of joint ownership. The Supreme Court disagreed and restored the original trial decision.

28.72   In their joint judgment, Lord Walker and Baroness Hale, at AC 783–4; All ER 1270, drew a distinction, between cases where the property was held in joint names as opposed to the name of one of the parties, and said:

To the extent that we recognise that a 'common intention' trust is of central importance to 'joint names' as well as 'single names' cases, we are going some way to meet that hope. Nevertheless it is important to point out that the starting point for analysis is different in the two situations.

That is so even though it may be necessary to enquire into the varied circumstances and reasons why a house or flat has been acquired in a single name or in joint names … The starting point is different because the claimant whose name is not on the proprietorship register has the burden of establishing some sort of implied trust, normally what is now termed a 'common intention' constructive trust. The claimant whose name is on the register starts (in the absence of an express declaration of trust in different terms, and subject to what is said below about resulting trusts) with the presumption (or assumption) of a beneficial joint tenancy.

28.73　Lord Walker and Baroness Hale, at AC 786; All ER 1273, made it clear that the presumption of resulting trust no longer had any role in cases of family homes held in joint names for married or unmarried couples, and, at AC 788; All ER 1275, affirmed that the intention of the parties may be imputed in cases where it is not possible to discern an actual or implied intention. Applying this to the facts, they agree with the trial judge's assessment, although they stated that the trial judge did not need to impute an intention as there was enough evidence on the facts to infer an intention from the parties' behaviour.

28.74　Lord Walker and Baroness Hales, at AC 794; All ER 1280, concluded by summarising their position as follows:

(1) The starting point is that equity follows the law and they are joint tenants both in law and inequity. (2) That presumption can be displaced by showing (a) that the parties had a different common intention at the time when they acquired the home, or (b) that they later formed the common intention that their respective shares would change. (3) Their common intention is to be deduced objectively from their conduct: 'the relevant intention of each party is the intention which was reasonably understood by the other party to be manifested by that party's words and conduct notwithstanding that he did not consciously formulate that intention in his own mind or even acted with some different intention which he did not communicate to the other party': Lord Diplock in *Gissing v Gissing* [1971] AC 886, 906. Examples of the sort of evidence which might be relevant to drawing such inferences are given in *Stack v Dowden* [2007] 2 AC 432, [69]. (4) In those cases where it is clear either (a) that the parties did not intend joint tenancy at the outset, or (b) had changed their original intention, but it is not possible to ascertain by direct evidence or by inference what their actual intention was as to the shares in which they would own the property, 'the answer is that each is entitled to that share which the court considers fair having regard to the whole course of dealing between them in relation to the property': Chadwick LJ in *Oxley v Hiscock* [2004] 3 All ER 703 at [69]. In our judgment, 'the whole course of dealing … in relation to the property' should be given a broad meaning, enabling a similar range of factors to be taken into account as may be relevant to ascertaining the parties' actual intentions. (5) Each case will turn on its own facts. Financial contributions are relevant but there are many other factors which may enable the court to decide what shares were either intended (as in case (3)) or fair (as in case (4)).

28.75　Lord Collins agreed with Lord Walker and Baroness Hale. Lord Kerr SCJ, at AC 799; All ER 1285, expressed concern that the 'court should anxiously examine the circumstances in order, where possible, to ascertain the parties' intention but it should not be reluctant to recognise, when it is appropriate to do so, that inference of an intention is not possible and that imputation of an intention is the only course to follow'. Lord Kerr said that he would find it difficult to find an inferred intention on the facts but felt it was a simple task to impute an intention, which corresponded with the trial judge's decision. Lord Wilson followed a similar approach to Lord Kerr. His Lordship agreed with the result, but felt that it was not possible to infer a common intention on the facts. The only way forward was to impute an intention that equated to the proportions ordered by the trial judge.

Common intention constructive trusts in Australia

28.76 The common intention constructive trust has been recognised and accepted by Australian courts: *Stowe v Stowe* (1995) 15 WAR 363; *Engwirda v Engwirda* [2000] QCA 61; *Minassian v Minassian* [2010] NSWSC 708 at [69]. As in the English cases, it is necessary to show that the common intention actually existed, either by proving actual or inferred common intention: *Muschinski v Dodds* at CLR 595; ALR 436; *JACA Nominees Pty Ltd v Waldarra Pty Ltd* [2010] VSC 546; *Jeffrey-Potts v Garel* [2012] VSC 237 at [279]–[280]. In *Shepherd v Doolan* [2005] NSWSC 42 at [34], White J said:

> Where a constructive trust is imposed, based upon the parties' common intention as to the ownership of property upon which the claimant has acted to his or her detriment, the inquiry is as to the actual intention of the parties. The law does not impute a presumed intention to the parties based upon what the Court considers fair and reasonable persons in the position of the parties would have intended had they turned their minds to the issue.

Evidence of intention

28.77 Statements made by the parties such as 'it's for you and me' or 'this is your house', 'our house' have been taken as sufficient to prove a common intention to grant a beneficial interest: *Hohol v Hohol* [1981] VR 221; *Zaborskis v Zaborskis* (1982) 8 Fam LR 622; *Parianos v Melluish (Trustee)*. Evidence of statements after that time is only admissible against interest: *Charles Marshall Pty Ltd v Grimsley* (1956) 95 CLR 353 at 365; *Shepherd v Doolan* at [39]. The nature of payments to the acquisition of the property may also aid in construing intention: *Jin v Yang* at [50].

28.78 In *Shepherd v Doolan* at [37]–[38], White J summarised the law as follows:

> There may be an agreement between the parties as to how the property should be held. There may be express statements as to their intention. Their intention may be inferred from their conduct. The question of what acts demonstrate an agreement or common intention referable to the beneficial enjoyment of the property is one of evidence, not law. A common intention that a party have a beneficial interest in a property owned by another will not be inferred merely from their joint occupation of property, nor the carrying out of household duties, nor the bringing up of children on the property, nor the doing of repairs, renovations, maintenance, decoration or improvement, nor the provision of furniture …. The intention may be inferred from financial contributions, direct or indirect, to the acquisition of property, including the paying off of mortgages, or the payment of expenses which free up funds for that purpose … This is a wider enquiry than whether a contribution was made to the purchase money such as to give rise to a presumption of a resulting trust. Whilst both enquiries address the inferences to be drawn as to the parties' actual intentions, a contribution to the purchase price creates a presumption of beneficial ownership in the proportion which the amount contributed bears to the price. For a 'common intention' constructive trust, a contribution, direct or indirect, to the costs of acquisition of the property is a matter from which an intention that the claimant have a beneficial interest in the property might be inferred. There is a difference between a fact from which an inference can be drawn, and a fact from which a rebuttable presumption arises. The significance of the difference will depend upon the strength of the presumption. In the case of the 'common intention' constructive trust, there is

no presumption that the beneficial interest is in proportion with the contribution to the purchase price (references omitted).

Detriment

28.79   Once common intention has been proven, a constructive trust will arise if a party has acted with detrimental reliance on the basis of that intention: *Green v Green* (1989) 17 NSWLR 343 at 357; *Carruthers v Manning* [2001] NSWSC 1130 at [124]; *Brandling v Weir* [2003] NSWSC 723. In assessing detriment, the court will examine what interests are held by the claimant and compare them with the parties' common intention: *Thompson v Leigh* [2006] NSWSC 540. Absent detriment a claim for a constructive trust will fail: *Chippindale v Wyatt* [2010] NSWSC 927 at [97].

28.80   In *Allen v Snyder* (1977) 2 NSWLR 685, during the course of a de facto relationship, a couple purchased a house that was financed through a loan granted by the War Homes Services Department. A condition of granting the loan was that the woman, Allen, make a declaration that she was financially dependent on the man, Snyder. An additional condition of the loan was that the title of the house should only be held by the man. During the course of the relationship, Allen paid for furniture and Snyder made a will in which his interest in the house was to pass to Allen. After the breakdown of the relationship, Allen claimed that she was entitled to an equal beneficial share on the basis that it was the parties' common intention that she be granted such an interest.

28.81   Glass JA, at 689, began his judgment by noting that the rules of equity in these circumstances applied to heterosexual couples, homosexual couples or relationships between multiple parties. His Honour examined the judgments in *Pettitt* and *Gissing* and accepted that a trust could arise through the common intention of parties, as long as the party asserting the interest made some contribution in reliance on the agreement. Interestingly, his Honour, at 692, found that the trust was an express trust that lacked writing. The trust was enforceable because it would be fraudulent to deny the interest that was intended. Most importantly, Glass JA, at 694, stressed that the intention must be an actual or inferred intention. It could not be an imputed intention, that being an intention ascribed to the parties by operation of law. The factual evidence pointed out that there was a common intention that Allen be granted an interest in the house upon the occasion of the parties getting married, or on the death of Snyder. However, there was no intention to grant her an interest during the course of the de facto relationship.

28.82   Samuels JA agreed with Glass JA. His Honour, at 699, also found that the trust was an express trust based on an implied common intention. Mahoney JA, at 706, also agreed with the findings of fact by Glass JA, but pointed out that while the court should not impose constructive trusts on the grounds of fairness, the principles of constructive trust might develop to embrace property interests that need to be protected according to 'justice and good conscience'.

28.83   In Australia it appears that it is not necessary to show that the detriment suffered was in relation to the acquisition or maintenance of the property, as long as the detriment relates to the parties' common intention: *Australian Building and Technical Solutions Pty Ltd v Boumelhem* at [115]; *Cambouya Pty Ltd v Buchanan* [2005] NSWSC 743 at [39]–[41]. In *Ogilvie v Ryan* [1976] 2 NSWLR 504, an agreement between a testator and his house-keeper to grant her a life interest in a house in his will in return for her services, was upheld on the basis that it would be fraudulent to allow the legal title holder to receive the benefit of care without granting the agreed beneficial interest.

28.84 In contrast, in *Public Trustee v Smith* [2008] NSWSC 397, a claim on behalf of a deceased testatrix for a beneficial interest in a discretionary trust failed. The testatrix had created a discretionary trust but never formally made herself a beneficiary. The fact that she had acted during her lifetime as if she were entitled to a beneficial interest did not evidence a common intention to grant her one. She had not acted or refrained from acting because of any agreement with the corporate trustee (which she controlled). Nor did she suffer any detriment which was referable to a common intention.

Movement towards unconscionability/unconscientiousness

28.85 There seems to be a recent trend to look for unconscientious behaviour as opposed to detriment in common intention constructive trusts. In *Shepherd v Doolan* at [31], White J said:

> One class of case where equity will intervene to prevent the unconscientious denial by the legal owner of another party's rights, is where the parties agreed, or it was their common intention, that the claimant should have an interest in the property owned by the other, and the claimant acted to his or her detriment on the basis of that agreement or common intention.

28.86 It is not necessary for there to be actual unconscientiousness, as long as a possible denial of interest will have that effect. Nor is it necessary that the unconscientiousness originate from the behaviour of the other party to the relationship for the trust to arise. In *Clout v Markwell* [2003] QSC 91, it was argued that the wife could not claim an interest in property (even though there had been a common intention with her husband) because her husband had not denied her interest. Instead, the husband had gone bankrupt and the trustee was denying the existence of the wife's interest. Aktinson J dismissed this argument and said that a common intention constructive trust does not require there to have been an actual denial, but rather it arises because such a denial *would be* unconscientious.

28.87 A similar result occurred in *Parianos v Melluish (Trustee)* where the court found a common intention that the wife in a marriage would be given a share in the matrimonial home, even though it was placed solely in the husband's name. The marriage had broken down but before final resolution of the divorce the husband died. He died insolvent and the trustee of his estate sought to retain the house for creditors. The wife succeeded in claiming an interest under a common intention constructive trust but on the basis that it was unconscientious for the trustee in bankruptcy to deny the common intention created by the husband and acted upon by the wife to her detriment.

The quantum of beneficial interest

28.88 The courts will base the plaintiff's quantum of interest on what was agreed to by the parties: *Australian Building and Technical Solutions Pty Ltd v Boumelhem* at [116]. If the parties did not agree as to the exact nature of the interest the court can impose a constructive trust which best gives effect to the intentions of the parties: *Shepherd v Doolan*.

Problems with the application of the common intention constructive trust

28.89 The common intention constructive trust has unfortunately proven to be a clumsy tool for resolving disputes, particularly in the context of de facto relationships. The main problem is that there will always be numerous couples, married and unmarried, who have no discussion about ownership, make no agreement, and are therefore beyond the reach of the common intention constructive trust: *Midland Bank v Cooke* [1995] 4 All ER 562 at 575. In an effort to do justice between the parties the courts will often be tempted to stretch legal imagination and find evidence of common intention where there was none.

28.90 An equally regrettable feature of the decisions is that the terminology of all three types of trust has been used by courts to describe common intention constructive trusts: *Gissing v Gissing* at AC 905; All ER 790 (resulting, implied or constructive trust); *Allen v Snyder* (express trust); *Midland Bank v Cooke* (resulting trust); *Stowe v Stowe* (1995) 15 WAR 363 (constructive trust).

28.91 The common intention constructive trust is arguably better understood as a form of express trust. Dal Pont has argued that the trust must be a form of express trust given the focus on intention or, alternatively, it can be viewed as a constructive trust arising in response to an estoppel.[17] However, the bulk of Australian authority favours the description of these trusts as 'constructive': *Shepherd v Doolan* at [35].

28.92 As noted above, the cases also evidence a drift in authority from common intention constructive trusts towards unconscionability/unconscientiousness-based constructive trusts, discussed below at 28.184–28.231. Perhaps it may be more suitable to subsume common intention constructive trusts within the category of unconscionability/unconscientiousness-based constructive trusts, leaving common intention as a sub-category which triggers equitable intervention: *Shepherd v Doolan* at [31].

CONSTRUCTIVE TRUSTS TO REMEDY BREACH OF FIDUCIARY DUTY

28.93 In various cases the High Court has referred to the role of constructive trusts in providing a remedy for breaches of fiduciary obligations: *Muschinski v Dodds* at CLR 616; ALR 452; *Chan v Zacharia* (1984) 154 CLR 178 at 199; 53 ALR 417 at 433. However, constructive trusts should be seen as a final option for remedying breach, after careful analysis of the nature of the property; the relevant powers and obligations of the fiduciary; and the relationship between the profit made and the fiduciary's powers and obligations: *Bathurst City Council v PWC Properties Pty Ltd* (1998) 195 CLR 566 at 585; *Iacullo v Remly Pty Ltd* [2012] NSWSC 191 at [129]. In *John Alexander's Clubs Pty Limited v White City Tennis Club Limited* (2010) 241 CLR 1 at 45; 266 ALR 462 at 492, the High Court said:

> A constructive trust ought not to be imposed if there are other orders capable of doing full justice … [C]are must be taken to avoid granting equitable relief which goes beyond the necessities of the case. Another point … is that third party interests must be borne in mind in deciding whether a constructive trust should be granted. [Legal authority] does not permit a constructive trust to be declared in a manner injurious to third parties merely because the plaintiff has no other useful remedy against a defendant.

28.94 One of the difficult areas for the imposition of a constructive trust is where a breaching fiduciary has established a competing business. In such circumstances there are two main remedial alternatives: a constructive trust over the business (with a just allowance being given to the fiduciary

---

17. G E Dal Pont, 'Equity's Chameleon — Unmasking the Constructive Trust' (1997) 16 *Australian Bar Review* 46 at 67–9.

for his/her efforts) or some form of compensation or account where the profits relating to the breach of fiduciary duty are made payable to the plaintiff: *Hospital Products Ltd v United States Surgical Corporation* (1984) 156 CLR 41 at 110; 55 ALR 417 at 462–3.

28.95   In such circumstances the remedy of a constructive trust is obviously attractive to the plaintiff as it enables the plaintiff to take the new business as an ongoing concern. In *Timber Engineering Co Pty Ltd v Anderson* [1980] 2 NSWLR 488, the fiduciaries had, in breach of fiduciary duty, diverted business away from the plaintiff, to their own rival business. Kearney J held that the defendant's business could be held on constructive trust with allowances made to the defendants for their work and skill, as well as for any resources they had brought to the business that had not come from the breach of fiduciary duty.

28.96   That result can be contrasted with *Warman International Ltd v Dwyer* (1995) 182 CLR 544; 128 ALR 201. In this case a manager, Dwyer, worked for an Australian company, Warman, which had an agency agreement to distribute gearboxes made in Italy by Bonfiglioli. Bonfiglioli approached Warman about setting up a manufacturing joint venture in Australia, but Warman declined to be involved. In breach of fiduciary duty, Dwyer pursued the opportunity himself and set up his own businesses as a joint venture with Bonfiglioli. Later Bofiglioloi terminated the agency agreement with Warman, and the agency was taken over by Dwyer's companies. At trial the judge refused to order a constructive trust as this would have thrust the parties into a continuing relationship and instead ordered an account of profits. This decision was upheld by the High Court which ordered an account of the first two years of the businesses' operations.

28.97   The constructive trust that arises in response to a breach of fiduciary duty is institutional, in that it arises on the occurrence of the breach, not the court order: *Zobory v Federal Commissioner of Taxation* (1995) 129 ALR 484.

Loans in breach of fiduciary duty

28.98   A constructive trust is not automatically imposed upon money being lent in circumstances that give rise to a breach of fiduciary duty: *Hancock Family Memorial Foundation Ltd v Porteous* [2000] WASCA 29 (aff'd *Hancock Family Memorial Foundation Ltd v Porteous* (2000) 201 CLR 347). In *Daly v The Sydney Stock Exchange Ltd* (1986) 160 CLR 371; (1986) 65 ALR 193, Daly invested money with stockbrokers. The stockbrokers breached their fiduciary duty by advising Daly to invest in their firm rather than in the stock market. The stockbrokers knew the firm was in financial difficulties and, on the event of the firm becoming insolvent, Daly sought compensation from the fidelity fund established by the *Securities Industry Act 1975* (NSW). Gibbs CJ (with whom Wilson and Dawson JJ agreed) held that, while a fiduciary duty was breached by the stockbrokers, it was also necessary to show that the moneys were received by the stockbrokers as trustees before a constructive trust would be imposed. Gibbs CJ, at CLR 379; ALR 197–8, said:

> [I]n the present case it was not necessary to find that a constructive trust existed in order to ensure that the firm was not unjustly enriched. The benefit which the firm obtained in consequence of its breach of fiduciary duty was a loan of money, and the firm, as a debtor, was bound to repay the debt to the creditor, [Daly] … In deciding whether or not the money should be held to have been subject to a constructive trust it is not unimportant that the ordinary legal remedy of a creditor would have been adequate to prevent the firm from being benefited at the expense of [Daly]. Further, the consequences of holding the money to be subject to a constructive trust and

thereby transforming the creditor into a beneficiary suggest that it would be contrary to principle to recognize the existence of a constructive trust in a case such as the present.

Because legal remedies were available to pursue the amounts in debt, it was unnecessary to impose a constructive trust on the breach of the fiduciary duty. Additionally, another reason for not imposing a trust was that a constructive trust could have a detrimental effect on the claims of other creditors in the insolvency.

Voidable contracts

28.99 If a breach of fiduciary duty has the effect of rendering a contract voidable, until such time as the contract is made void the contract will dictate the relationships between the parties and no constructive trust will be imposed: *Guinness Plc v Saunders* [1992] AC 663; [1990] 1 All ER 652; *Lonrho Plc v Fayed (No 2)*. This was made clear in *Greater Pacific Investments Pty Ltd (in liq) v Australian National Industries Ltd* (1996) 39 NSWLR 143 at 153, by McLelland AJA when he said:

> In general, where there is a contract for the sale of property by A to B made in breach of fiduciary duty owed to A by B (or by C in whose breach B knowingly participated) pursuant to which the legal title to the property has been transferred from A to B, the transaction is in equity voidable at the instance of A, who may (if necessary) obtain an order for rescission setting it aside. Unless and until A effectively avoids the transaction and (if necessary) obtains an order for rescission, B's property rights as a result of the transaction remain unaffected. However if A does effectively avoid the transaction and (if necessary) obtain an order for rescission, the parties will be treated in equity as if the transaction had never been effected; in other words, equity will treat B as if he had held the property in trust for A, that is, as a constructive trustee *ab initio*. A constructive trust arises in such circumstances as a consequence of the effective avoidance or rescission of the transaction. Where, for whatever reason, the transaction has not been and cannot be effectively avoided and rescission is unavailable, it remains effective and no constructive trust can arise.

Bribes and secret commissions

28.100 Difficult questions arise in relation to the ownership of bribes received by fiduciaries in the course of their duties.[18] Older authority suggested that bribes taken by defaulting fiduciaries would be held as debts and not under constructive trusts: *Tyrrell v Bank of London* (1862) 10 HL Cas 26; *Re Caerphilly Colliery Company (Pearson's case)* (1877) 5 Ch D 336; *Metropolitan Bank v Heiron* (1880) 5 Ex D 31. In *Lister & Co v Stubbs* (1890) 45 Ch D 1, an agent, who was given authority to make purchases for his principal, received secret commissions from vendors as an incentive to order from them. The Court of Appeal declined to order the existence of a constructive trust over the commissions and instead ordered that the moneys were held in debt. In *Attorney-General for Hong Kong v Reid* [1994] 1 NZLR 1, the Privy Council, on appeal from the New Zealand Court of Appeal, overturned *Lister v Stubbs*, and found that the proprietary remedy of constructive trusts should be imposed on bribes received by fiduciaries.

---

18. D Hayton 'Proprietary Liability for Secret Profits' (2011) 127 *Law Quarterly Review* 487; R Goode, 'A Reply' (2011) 127 *Law Quarterly Review* 493; G Virgo, 'Profits Obtained in Breach of Fiduciary Duty: Personal or Proprietary Claim?' [2011] *Cambridge Law Journal* 502.

28.101   However, the English Court of Appeal revisited its position in *Sinclair Investments (UK) Ltd v Versailles Trade Finance Group* [2011] 4 All ER 335. This case concerned a director (Cushnie) of a company (TPL) who was argued to have inflated the share price of another company (VGP) by misusing money owned by TPL via a practice known as 'cross-firing' (which basically involved moving money through accounts to artificially increase the appearance of a company's turnover). Once the share price was inflated Cushnie sold his significant shareholding in VGP to make a profit (around twenty nine million dollars). It was argued that the proceeds of sale of the shares represented an unauthorised gain made by Cushnie in the course of his fiduciary relationship with TPL, which were held on constructive trust.

28.102   The Court of Appeal overturned this finding. While the case was not strictly concerned with bribes, Lord Neuberger MR (giving the judgment of the court) discussed the history of *Lister v Stubbs* and *Reid* and found that *Reid* (as a Privy Council decision on New Zealand law) was not binding on the Court of Appeal. Lord Neuberger MR, at 357, said:

> For the reasons I have given, previous decisions of this court establish that a claimant cannot claim proprietary ownership of an asset purchased by the defaulting fiduciary with funds which, although they could not have been obtained if he had not enjoyed his fiduciary status, were not beneficially owned by the claimant or derived from opportunities beneficially owned by the claimant. However, those cases also establish that, in such a case, a claimant does have a personal claim in equity to the funds. There is no case which appears to support the notion that such a personal claim entitles the claimant to claim the value of the asset (if it is greater than the amount of the funds together with interest), and there are judicial indications which tend to militate against that notion.

Lord Neuberger MR's views were followed in *Cadogan Petroleum plc v Tolley* [2011] EWHC 2286 (Ch) at [17]–[22].

28.103   What is the position of *Lister v Stubbs* in Australia? Prior to the decision in *Reid*, *Lister v Stubbs* was accepted as good authority (albeit in obiter discussion) by the High Court in *Ardlethan Options Ltd v Easdown* (1915) 20 CLR 285 at 292 and in *Daly v The Sydney Stock Exchange Ltd* at CLR 379; ALR 198. However there are Australian cases which view the decision in *Lister* as an anomaly: *DPC Estates Pty Ltd v Grey and Consul Development Pty Ltd* [1974] 1 NSWLR 443 at 470–1. After *Reid* was handed down a number of Australian cases received it favourably: *Jones v Southall & Bourke Pty Ltd* [2004] FCA 539; *Mainland Holdings Ltd v Szady* [2002] NSWSC 699 at [69]–[70]. Nevertheless doubts remained about which case, *Lister v Stubbs* or *Reid*, should be followed.

28.104   The Australian position was reviewed by the Full Court of the Federal Court in *Grimaldi v Chameleon Mining NL (ACN 098 773 785) (No 2)* (2012) 200 FCR 296; 287 ALR 22. This case concerned a mining exploration, Chameleon Mining NL (Chameleon). Grimaldi was engaged by the directors of Chameleon to raise capital and came to act as a de facto director of Chameleon. Grimaldi was also a director and the controlling mind of Murchison Metals Ltd (Murchison). Murchison had entered into an agreement with Winterfall, a company which was attempting to purchase the rights over a large iron ore deposit known as the 'Iron Jacks tenements'. For setting up this 'Murchison/Winterfall' agreement, Grimaldi (and another director of Chameleon) received a 'spotter's fee' of several million shares and options in Winterfall for helping it complete the purchase. Grimaldi improperly used Chameleon shares and money from Chameleon to fund the Winterfall purchase of the Iron Jacks tenements. Winterfall later commenced operations but Murchison eventually came to take over complete ownership of the project, which was valued at over one billion dollars. Chameleon sued Grimaldi for breach of directors' duties and fiduciary duties in relation to the above transactions. It was argued, amongst other things, that the spotter's fee was a secret commission that could be beneficially claimed by Chameleon.

28.105   The Full Court of the Federal Court, at FCR 427; ALR 149, found that, while the taking of the spotter's fee was a breach of fiduciary duty, it was incorrect to characterise it as a bribe or secret commission because the fee arose separately from Grimaldi's actions in improperly using Chameleon shares and monies to fund the Winterfall/Murchison agreement. Nevertheless, the Full Court saw fit to review the authorities on bribes and rejected *Lister v Stubbs* as being good authority in Australia.

28.106   The Full Court, at FCR 421; ALR 143, was critical of the practical effect of *Lister v Stubbs*, and said:

> To exclude the bribed fiduciary from the deterrent effect of the constructive trust is, in our view, to make it unavailable in the very situations where deterrence is likely to be the most needed. Bribery at its most naked breeds the crudest form of fiduciary infidelity. To privilege the dishonest fiduciary in this way is to create an incentive which should not be tolerated. This is particularly so in relation to public sector fiduciaries. In combating the corrupt public official, the full range of equity's remedies and techniques (including tracing and following illicit gains) are important instruments of deterrence. The courts of the common law countries have recognised this, as has the Privy Council in *Attorney-General (Hong Kong) v Reid*.

28.107   While the Full Court accepted that constructive trusts could arise over bribes and secret commissions, it did recognise that the constructive trust was not the only remedy available. The Full Court, at FCR 422–3; ALR 145 said:

> [T]o accept that money bribes can be captured by a constructive trust does not mean that they necessarily will be in all circumstances. As is well accepted, a constructive trust ought not to be imposed if there are other orders capable of doing full justice ... Such could be the case, for example, where a bribed fiduciary, having profitably invested the bribe, is then bankrupted and, apart from the investment, is hopelessly insolvent. In such a case a lien on that property may well be sufficient to achieve 'practical justice' in the circumstances. This said, a constructive trust is likely to be awarded as of course where the bribe still exists in its original, or in a traceable, form, and no third party issue arises.

The rule in *Keech v Sandford*

28.108   On the basis of the decision in *Keech v Sandford* (1726) 25 ER 223, a trustee of a tenancy who obtains a right to renew that tenancy holds that renewal on constructive trust for the beneficiaries. Upon renewal by the trustee, an irrebuttable presumption arises that the renewal is held on trust. The rule extends beyond trustees to other fiduciaries (such as agents, executors and partners) and those in similar positions (mortgagees and tenants for life). In *Chan v Zacharia* at CLR 200; ALR 434–5, Deane J recognised that there was a controversy concerning whether the rule was a manifestation of the principle that a fiduciary was unable to make secret gains or whether the rule was an independent doctrine of equity. Deane J, at CLR 201; ALR 435, preferred to consider the rule as one concerned with the operation of presumptions in the application of general fiduciary principles.

CONSTRUCTIVE TRUSTS THAT ARISE AGAINST THIRD PARTIES TO FIDUCIARY RELATIONSHIPS: THE RULE IN *BARNES V ADDY*

28.109   In *Barnes v Addy* (1874) 9 Ch App 244, Lord Selborne LC, at 251–2, said:

> Those who create a trust clothe the trustee with a legal power and control over the trust property, imposing on him a corresponding responsibility. That responsibility may no doubt be extended in equity to others who are not properly trustees, if they are found either making themselves trustees *de son tort*, or actually participating in any fraudulent conduct of the trustee to the injury of the *cestui que* trust. But, on the other hand, strangers are not to be made constructive trustees merely because they act as the agents of trustees in transactions within their legal powers, transactions, perhaps of which a court of equity may disapprove, unless those agents receive and become chargeable with some part of the trust property, or unless they assist with knowledge in a dishonest and fraudulent design on the part of the trustees.

28.110   Lord Selbourne's comments make it clear that third parties ('strangers' to trusts) can be made constructive trustees in three ways:

(i)   by acting as a trustee without authority (trustee *de son tort*);

(ii) through knowing receipt of trust property (sometimes referred to as the first limb of *Barnes v Addy*); and

(iii) through knowingly assisting in a breach of trust (sometimes referred to as the second limb of *Barnes v Addy*).

The impositiotn of a constructive trust in these cases is remedial in that it imposes a liability to compensate for losses occasioned to the trust. This remedial purpose can be contrasted to the remedy of tracing, which has the purpose of recovering the actual trust property.

Trustees de son tort

28.111   A trustee *de son tort* is a person who has intermeddled in the affairs of the trust without proper authority and has, in effect, become a trustee through his or her wrongdoing: *Dubai Aluminium Co Ltd v Salaam* [2003] 2 AC 366; *Mara v Browne* [1896] 1 Ch 199 at 209. To qualify as a trustee *de son tort* the person must have assumed some measure of control of the trust property: *Re Barney* [1892] 2 Ch 276.

28.112   A trustee *de son tort* will be liable even if they have acted honestly: *Life Association of Scotland v Siddai* (1861) 45 ER 800. This approach differs greatly from cases of knowing assistance and knowing receipt where dishonesty has become a touchstone of liability (at least in the United Kingdom).

28.113   Constructive trusts may also be imposed on intermeddlers in other relationships. Someone who acts as an executor without authority can also be considered a constructive trustee: *James v Williams* [2000] Ch 1; *Nolan v Nolan* [2004] VSCA 109.

Knowing receipt

28.114   In *The Bell Group Ltd (in liq) v Westpac Banking Corporation (No 9)* (2008) 225 FLR 1 at 537, Owen J, after a thorough review of authorities, set out the requirements for knowing receipt as follows:

    (a) there must be a 'trust';

    (b) the trustee must have misapplied 'trust property';

    (c) the third party must have received trust property;

    (d) at the time of receiving the trust property, the third party must have known of the trust and of the misapplication of the trust property; and

    (e) the third party will be taken to have 'known' in the relevant sense if the third party:

        (i) as actual knowledge of the trust and the misapplication of trust property; or

        (ii) has deliberately shut his or her eyes to those things; or

        (iii) has abstained in a calculated way from making such enquiries as an honest and reasonable person would make, about the trust and the application of the trust property; or

        (iv) knows of facts which to an honest and reasonable person would indicate the existence of the trusts and the fact of misapplication.

28.115 This formulation was not disturbed on appeal: *Westpac Banking Corporation v The Bell Group Ltd (In Liq) (No 3)* [2012] WASCA 157. The Bell Group of companies was a large corporate conglomeration which primarily represented the interests of the late Robert Holmes A'Court. The stock market crashed in 1987 and the Holmes A'Court's interests were sold to the Bell Group. After discovering the poor financial state of the Bell Group a number of Australian banks requested that their securities be refinanced. The effect of the refinancing was to vastly improve the banks' security position to the detriment of other investors. Later the Bell Group group failed. Liquidators were appointed who claimed (amongst many things) that the directors had breached their fiduciary duties when agreeing to the financial restructure and that the banks had knowingly received property which they knew was being provided in breach of fiduciary duty.

28.116 At trial, Owen J found that the banks were subject to the first limb of the rule in *Barnes v Addy* (knowing receipt) and had breached it. The claim that the banks had also knowingly assisted in the breach of trust failed as Owen J found that the directors had not engaged in a dishonest and fraudulent design, and that the banks had no actual knowledge of there being such a design: see 28.143. On appeal, a majority of the Court of Appeal of Western Australia (Lee and Drummond AJJA; Carr AJA dissenting) upheld Owen J's decision on knowing receipt but overturned his findings on knowing assistance, therefore finding that liability had been established in both limbs of *Barnes v Addy*.

The need for property

28.117 The first limb of *Barnes v Addy* requires property to have been received: *St Vincent de Paul Society Qld v Ozcare Ltd* [2009] QCA 335 at [75]. If property has not been received there cannot be any role for the first limb: *Delryk Pty Ltd v Mckay Atf the Kaylin Retirement Fund* [2009] WASC 305 at [21]. The property can be real or personal property or take the form of a security interest like a mortgage: *Super 1000 v Pacific General Securities* [2008] NSWSC 1222 at [211]. In *Westpac Banking Corporation v The Bell Group Ltd (In Liq) (No 3)* at [2156], Drummond AJA said:

> There is no justification for confining 'trust property' for the purposes of *Barnes v Addy* to tangible things. Importantly, that expression includes, as the respondents submit, choses in action comprising incorporeal property not reducible into physical possession, such as rights arising under a contract which are enforceable by action.

28.118 In *Farah Constructions Pty Ltd v Say-Dee Pty Ltd* (2007) 230 CLR 89; 236 ALR 209, a claim under the first limb failed for the absence of trust property. The case concerned a real estate joint venture between two companies, Farah Constructions Pty Ltd (Farah Constructions) and Say-Dee Pty Ltd (Say-Dee). Together they had purchased a block of units for redevelopment. The local council declined to approve the redevelopment because the area of land was too small, but indicated that the project might have a chance of approval if the land were joined with neighbouring properties. The owner of Farah Constructions (Mr Elias) exploited this opportunity but only after Say-Dee had been informed and invited to purchase the adjoining land. Mr Elias organised for his wife and daughters to acquire some of the adjoining blocks through their own companies. The joint venture later collapsed after Elias had attempted to purchase the joint venture land. Farah Constructions sought to have a trustee appointed for sale. Say-Dee cross-claimed, saying that the adjoining properties held by the Elias family were held on constructive trust.

28.119   A claim under the first limb of *Barnes v Addy* was made against Mrs Elias and the daughters but it failed because they had not received any property which was subject to a fiduciary duty. The adjoining land was not trust property. Nor was the information about the council's decision. While the information regarding the council's reasons for refusing the application may have been subject to a fiduciary duty, it was public knowledge and not confidential. The High Court also said that even if it was confidential it was not of a kind that would give rise to property rights (like a trade secret): see 8.6–8.14, 8.88.

'Trust' property or property protected by a fiduciary relationship?

28.120   It has been said that the first limb of *Barnes v Addy* could apply to strangers who receive property not just from a trustee but from any fiduciary in breach of duty, including directors: *DPC Estates Pty Ltd v Grey and Consul Development Pty Ltd* [1974] 1 NSWLR 443 at 459–460; *Belmont Finance Corporation Ltd v Williams Furniture Ltd (No 2)* [1980] 1 All ER 393 at 405; *El Ajou v Dollar Land Holdings plc* [1994] 2 All ER 685 at 700; *Hancock Family Memorial Foundation Ltd v Porteous* (1999) 32 ACSR 124 at 140. In other cases, it has been said that the first limb can only be applied to trust property in a 'strict sense': *Rogers v Kabriel* [1999] NSWSC 368 at [173].

28.121   In *Farah Constructions Pty Ltd v Say-Dee Pty Ltd* at CLR 141; ALR 244, the High Court, unfortunately, failed to resolve this issue, but merely noted that it had often been assumed, but not decided, that the first limb could be applied to breach of fiduciary duty.

28.122   Since *Farah Constructions Pty Ltd v Say-Dee Pty Ltd* the Court of Appeal of New South Wales in *Kalls Enterprises Pty Ltd (in liq) v Baloglow* [2007] NSWCA 191 at [153]–[157] found that the first limb could be applied to property subject to the fiduciary duties of directors. Muir J found differently in *Benzlaw and Associates Pty Ltd v Medi-Aid Centre Foundation Ltd* [2007] QSC 233 at [105]–[107], preferring that the property be trust property. In *The Bell Group Ltd (in liq) v Westpac Banking Corporation (No 9)* at 543, at trial, Owen J found that 'first limb *Barnes v Addy* jurisprudence can extend beyond trust property in the strict sense and may include property to which a fiduciary duty attaches' and on that basis decided to follow *Kalls Enterprises Pty Ltd (in liq) v Baloglow* rather than *Benzlaw and Associates Pty Ltd*. In *Super 1000 v Pacific General Securities* at [204], White J expressly acknowledged that the first limb could apply to transfers in breach of fiduciary duty. Bergin CJ in Eq found similarly in *Cassegrain v Gerard Cassegrain & Co Pty Ltd* [2012] NSWSC 403 at [241].

28.123   More recently, in *Grimaldi v Chameleon Mining NL (ACN 098773 785) (No 2)* at FCR 359; ALR 82, the Full Court of the Federal Court said the first limb extended 'to property held or controlled subject to a fiduciary duty'.

28.124 In *Westpac Banking Corporation v The Bell Group Ltd (In Liq) (No 3)* at [2136], Drummond AJA said:

> On the authority of *Kalls Enterprises* and *Grimaldi*, the first limb in *Barnes v Addy* should, in my opinion, be regarded as extending to dispositions of company property made by a director in breach of his fiduciary duties to the company. This is the view Owen J reached at [4776] in reliance, in part, on *Kalls Enterprises*.

It is suggested that, given the preponderance of authority, it should be accepted that the first limb applies to all transfers of property in breach of fiduciary duty.

Receipt

28.125 For a person to have 'receipt' requires him or her to have possession of the trust property for his or her 'own use and benefit': *Stephens Travel Service International Pty Ltd v Qantas Airways Ltd* (1988) 13 NSWLR 331; *Spangaro v Corporate Investment Australia Funds Management Ltd* (2003) 47 ACSR 285 at 303. Banks will not generally be treated as having receipt of funds placed in accounts, unless they apply the proceeds to the reduction of an overdraft, or for security: *Evans v European Bank Ltd* (2004) 61 NSWLR 75.

Knowledge

28.126 Difficulties arise in relation to the requirement of knowledge. The fundamental issue in determining whether a constructive trust should be imposed on a recipient of trust funds is whether the conscience of the recipient is bound in equity: *In re Montagu's Settlement Trusts* [1987] 1 Ch 264 at 277; [1992] 4 All ER 308 at 323. This requires knowledge that the property is subject to a fiduciary duty and knowledge that the property is being misapplied: *Australian Financial Services and Leasing Pty Ltd v Hills Industry Ltd* [2010] NSWSC 267 at [94].

28.127 In *Baden v Societe Generale pour Favoriser le Developpment du Commerce et de L'Industrie en Franc SA* [1992] 4 All ER 161 at 235, Peter Gibson J stated that there were five categories of knowledge in a recipient that were relevant to the decision to impose a constructive trust. They were:

(i) actual knowledge;
(ii) wilfully shutting one's eyes to the obvious;
(iii) wilfully and recklessly failing to make such inquiries as an honest and reasonable person would make;
(iv) knowledge of circumstances which would indicate the facts to an honest and reasonable person;
(v) knowledge of circumstances which would put an honest and reasonable person on inquiry.

The first three categories are often collectively described as 'actual knowledge' while the last two are jointly referred to as 'constructive knowledge': *Chameleon Mining NL v Murchison Metals Limited* [2010] FCA 1129 at [719].

28.128 Controversy has arisen in relation to whether all five categories of knowledge in *Baden* should satisfy the requirement of knowledge in cases of knowing receipt. The courts appear to be split between acceptance of all five categories or with limiting liability to those cases of actual knowledge.

Strict liability for unjust enrichment

28.129   It has been argued that, in cases of receipt, the recipient gets the full advantage of the breach of trust and, as a result, the liability should be strict and cover all receipt regardless of knowledge: *Koorootang Nominees Pty Ltd v ANZ Banking Group Ltd* [1998] 3 VR 16 at 101–5; *Lurgi (Australia) Pty Ltd v Gratz* [2000] VSC 278 at [75]. This is said to be proof that the underlying rationale for recipient liability is restitution for unjust enrichment: *El Ajou v Dollar Land Holdings* [1993] 3 All ER 717 at 738; *Koorootang* at 101–5.

28.130   This approach was rejected by the High Court of Australia in *Farah Constructions Pty Ltd v Say-Dee Pty Ltd* at CLR 158; ALR 258, as 'unhistorical' as '[t]here is no sign of it in clear terms in any but the most recent authorities'. Moreover, the restitutionary approach was said to reflect a 'mentality in which considerations of ideal taxonomy prevail over a pragmatic approach to legal development'.

The English approach: dishonesty

28.131   The more recent English approach is to treat the *Baden* categories of knowledge as flexible aids to categorisation, rather than as concrete tests. In *Polly Peck International plc v Nadir (No 2)* [1992] 4 All ER 769 at 777, Scott LJ said:

> Liability as constructive trustee in a 'knowing receipt' case does not require that the misapplication of the trust funds should be fraudulent. It does require that the defendant should have knowledge that the funds were trust funds and that they were being misapplied. Actual knowledge obviously will suffice. Mr Potts has submitted that it will suffice if the defendant can be shown to have had knowledge of facts which would have put an honest and reasonable man on inquiry, or, at least, if the defendant can be shown to have wilfully and recklessly failed to make such inquiries as an honest and reasonable man would have made (see categories (iii) and (v) of the categories [sic] of mental state identified by Peter Gibson J in *Baden's* case [1992] 4 All ER 161 at 235). I do not think there is any doubt that, if the latter of the two criteria can be established against the Central Bank, that will suffice. I have some doubts about the sufficiency of the former criterion but do not think that the present appeal is the right occasion for settling the issue. The various categories of mental state identified in *Baden's* case are not rigid categories with clear and precise boundaries. One category may merge imperceptibly into another.

The reference to category (v) in the passage appears to be a misquote because it is hard to understand how it reflects the rest of the paragraph: *Koorootang Nominees Pty Ltd v ANZ Banking Group Ltd* at 93.

28.132   This relaxation in the use of *Baden* categories reached its zenith in *Bank of Credit and Commerce International (Overseas) Ltd v Akindele* [2001] Ch 437. Lord Nourse, at 455, when speaking for the Court of Appeal, expressed doubts about the utility of categories:

> What then, in the context of knowing receipt, is the purpose to be served by a categorisation of knowledge? It can only be to enable the court to determine whether, in the words of Buckley LJ in *Belmont (No 2)* [1980] 1 All ER 393 at 405, the recipient can 'conscientiously retain [the] funds against the company' or, in the words of Megarry V-C in *Re Montagu's Settlement Trusts*, '[the recipient's] conscience is sufficiently affected for it to be right to bind him by the obligations of a constructive trustee'. But if that is the purpose, there is no need for categorisation. All that is necessary is that the recipient's state of knowledge should be such as to make it unconscionable

for him to retain the benefit of the receipt. For these reasons I have come to the view that, just as there is now a single test of dishonesty for knowing assistance, so ought there to be a single test of knowledge for knowing receipt. The recipient's state of knowledge must be such as to make it unconscionable for him to retain the benefit of the receipt.

The Australian position: actual and constructive knowledge

28.133   In Australia, it appears that knowing receipt will be established in cases (i) to (iv) of the *Baden* categories, but confusion exists as to whether category (v), negligent failure to inquire, should be included: *Spangaro v Corporate Investment Australia Funds Management Ltd*. In *Consul Development Pty Ltd v DPC Estates Pty Ltd* (1975) 132 CLR 373; (1975) 5 ALR 231, the court was concerned with a case of knowing assistance, but made general comments relating to both knowing receipt and knowing assistance. Gibbs J, at CLR 398; ALR 252, said:

> It may be that it is going too far to say that a stranger will be liable if the circumstances would have put an honest and reasonable man on inquiry, when the stranger's failure to inquire has been innocent and he has not wilfully shut his eyes to the obvious. On the other hand, it does not seem to me to be necessary to prove that a stranger who participated in a breach of trust or fiduciary duty with knowledge of all the circumstances did so actually knowing that what he was doing was improper. It would not be just that a person who had full knowledge of all the facts could escape liability because his own moral obtuseness prevented him from recognising an impropriety that would have been apparent to an ordinary man.

28.134   Similarly, Stephen J, at CLR 412; ALR 264 (with whom Barwick CJ agreed), found that knowledge should not extend to category (v), that being negligent failure to inquire. This was followed in later cases: *US Surgical Corp v Hospital Products* [1983] 2 NSWLR 157; *K and S Corporation Ltd v Sportingbet Australia Pty Ltd* (2003) 86 SASR 312. However, other decisions appear to have accepted that liability can be imposed for negligent failure to inquire: *Ninety-Five Pty Ltd (in liq) v Banque Nationale de Paris* [1988] WAR 132. In *Hancock Family Memorial Foundation Ltd v Porteous* at 142, Anderson J said:

> As to recipient liability, there is less certainty about what must be proved to sheet home liability to the non-trustee but I adopt, with respect, the reasoning and conclusions of Hansen J in *Koorootang Nominees Pty Ltd v Australia & New Zealand Banking Group Ltd* [1998] 3 VR 16 on the question. In the first place, it is not necessary to establish that a recipient of trust property acted dishonestly or with want of probity. Recipient liability may be established if the defendant had actual or constructive knowledge at the time he received the relevant property that: (a) it was trust property; and (b) it was being misapplied. The defendant will be taken to have constructive knowledge if it is proved that he wilfully shut his eyes to the obvious; that he wilfully and recklessly failed to make such inquiries as an honest and reasonable man would make in the circumstances; and that he knew of circumstances which would indicate the true facts to an honest and reasonable man. If all that is proved is that the defendant had knowledge of circumstances which would put an honest and reasonable man on inquiry, that is not enough: see *Koorootang* (at 85 and 105).

28.135   In *The Bell Group Ltd (in liq) v Westpac Banking Corporation (No 9)* at 536, Owen J relied on this statement. His Honour, at 533, also rejected the suggestion that the first limb required that the recipient have been dishonest — what was needed was a type of knowledge which fell within the first four categories of *Baden*. The finding was repeated by the Court of Appeal of Queensland in *Quince v Varga* [2008] QCA 376 at [41] and in later cases: *Armstrong Scalisi Holdings Pty Ltd* *v Abboud* [2012] NSWSC 268 at [22]; *Fodare Pty Ltd v Shearn* [2011] NSWSC 479 at 57; *Varma v Varma* [2010] NSWSC 786 at [478]. More recently, in *Westpac Banking Corporation v The Bell Group Ltd (In Liq) (No 3)* at [2127]–[2131], Drummond and Court of Appeal of Western Australia agreed with Owen J's decision at trial that the relevant types of knowledge are those which fell within the first four categories of *Baden*. The Full Court of the Federal Court found similarly in *Grimaldi v Chameleon Mining NL (ACN 098773 785) (No 2)* at FCR 363; ALR 86 saying that this view was supported by 20 years of authority.

Imposition of liability: personal or proprietorial?

28.136   Once liability has been established in knowing receipt, the third party recipient may be subjected to proprietary or personal liabilities for receipt: *Re Montagu's Settlement Trusts* [1987] Ch 264 at 272–3; [1992] 4 All ER 308 at 318–19. As stated above (see 28.99) in cases where an impugned transaction is void, a constructive trust can arise immediately over the property which is subject to the fiduciary duty. In cases where the transaction is voidable, personal liability can be imposed immediately but a constructive trust cannot arise unless the contract is made void. In *Grimaldi v Chameleon Mining NL (ACN 098773 785) (No 2)* at FCR 359–60; ALR 82, the Full Court of the Federal Court said:

> Distinctly while the proprietary liability referred to depends upon the existence of trust property in the strict sense, 'trust property' for *Barnes v Addy* purposes extends beyond it to property held or controlled subject to a fiduciary obligation. Most importantly for present purposes, it extends to corporate property, ie property subject to the control and the fiduciary responsibilities of a company's directors. If the directors dispose of corporate property in a dealing which is beyond their authority, whether actual, ostensible or usual, the dealing ordinarily is void and no interest passes to the third party donee, purchaser, etc. However, if the dealing occurs in a transaction which is within the directors' authority but which is not in the company's interests (ie is an abuse of power) or is otherwise in breach of fiduciary duty, the transaction will only be voidable: *Richard Brady Franks Ltd v Price* (1937) 58 CLR 112 at 142; [1937] ALR 470 at 476. As Australian law now stands, even if the third party recipient falls within the knowing receipt limb of *Barnes v Addy*, the company will not ordinarily be able to bring a proprietary claim against the recipient as distinct from a personal one, unless and until the transaction itself has been avoided. Though we later question the correctness of this particular requirement, what needs to be emphasised is that it still allows that a knowing recipient can be held accountable *in rem* for such of that property (or its traceable proceeds) as remains extant in that person's hands.

Knowing receipt and the Torrens system

28.137   Knowing receipt principles have caused difficulties for the courts when applied to interests in land under the Torrens system. In the Torrens system, registered interests can be set aside if they have been procured by fraud, where fraud refers to actual fraud, personal dishonesty or moral turpitude: *Asset Co v Mere Roihi* [1905] AC 176; see 7.78–7.87. However, mere notice of an unregistered interest prior to registration does not amount to personal dishonesty: *Mills v Stockman* (1967) 116 CLR 61 at 78. In *Macquarie Bank Ltd v Sixty-Fourth Throne Pty Ltd* [1998] 3 VR 133, a majority of the Victorian Court of Appeal decided that a registered mortgage under the Torrens system could not be set aside in a situation where the mortgagee acted honestly but with constructive knowledge that the mortgage document was a forgery, in breach of trust. As such, both Winneke P and Tadgell JA found that recipients who act honestly, but in circumstances where they should have discovered a breach of trust, could not be said to have acted fraudulently under the Torrens system.

28.138 But what if the registered proprietor has *actual* knowledge that their interest came pursuant to a breach of trust? On this issue the authorities are divided. In *Tara Shire Council v Garner* [2003] 1 Qd R 556, a majority of the Queensland Court of Appeal accepted that knowing receipt would apply in circumstances where a registered proprietor had actual knowledge that the property was trust property *and* that the registered transaction was a breach of trust. A similar approach was taken in *Koorootang Nominees Pty Ltd v ANZ Banking Group Ltd* at 105, although that case is distinguishable because it involved actual dishonesty on the part of the registered proprietor, in addition to knowing receipt.

28.139 In contrast, the Full Court of Western Australia rejected this use of knowing receipt principles in *LHK Nominees Pty Ltd v Kenworthy* (2002) 26 WAR 517. Anderson, Steyler and Pullin JJ all found that, absent 'Torrens-style' fraud, knowledge of a breach of trust would not defeat a registered interest, and knowing receipt principles could not be applied to set aside a registered interest. The High Court accepted this as the correct approach in *Farah Constructions Pty Ltd v Say-Dee Pty Ltd* at CLR 169; ALR 267.

28.140 The Privy Council considered these issues in *Arthur v Attorney General of the Turks and Caicos Islands* [2012] UKPC 30. Public land had been sold by a Minister of the Turks and Caicos Islands government through a corrupt process to the appellant. The appellant then onsold the property to a third party at a substantial profit. The government later sought to undo the transaction and claimed that the property was held on trust, by virtue of the sale being a breach of fiduciary duty. Later the government dropped its claims against the property but still maintained a claim for the purchase price received by the appellant. The appellant claimed that he had received indefeasible title and applied to have the claim for knowing receipt struck out. The trial judge and the Court of Appeal both refused the application. The Privy Council, in upholding the decision of the Court of Appeal, distinguished the Australian approach to knowing receipt for Torrens land, primarily because the Torrens legislation in the Turks and Caicos Islands made express provision for the protection of trust property and for the requirement of good faith and lack of notice in registration for indefeasibility.

28.141 Another issue that arises in the Torrens system is the *in personam* exception to indefeasibility which arises when the registered proprietor owes an enforceable common law or equitable duty: see 7.88–7.102. Equitable remedies including constructive trusts have been employed to enforce such obligations. In *Farah Constructions Pty Ltd v Say-Dee Pty Ltd* at CLR 171; ALR 268, the High Court again refused to find that the rule in *Barnes v Addy* fell within the *in personam* exception. The court found that there was no analogy between the constructive trusts employed in those cases and those which can arise from application of the first limb of *Barnes v Addy*. They accepted the reasoning of Tadgell JA in *Macquarie Bank Ltd v Sixty-Fourth Throne Pty Ltd* at 157, where he said that such an approach would 'introduce by the back door a means of undermining the doctrine of indefeasibility which the Torrens system establishes'. In *Raulfs v Fishy Bite Pty Ltd* [2011] NSWSC 105 at [88] Rein J found similarly and said:

> [T]here seems to be considerable force in the proposition that in the absence of a claim that meets the requirements of *Barnes v Addy*, as laid down in *Consul Development* and confirmed in

Farah, and in the absence of conduct falling within the fraud exception, there is no scope for an *in personam* claim.

28.142 In *Super 1000 v Pacific General Securities*, at [236], White J recognised that, short of statutory fraud, registration prevented proprietary remedies under *Barnes v Addy* but queried whether registration would prevent a personal remedy, such as equitable compensation, being pursued. White J repeated this finding in *Ciaglia v Ciaglia* (2010) 269 ALR 175 at 200. In *Break Fast Investments Pty Ltd v Giannopoulos* [2011] NSWSC 1508 at [126], Black J agreed with White J's analysis but added that a personal claim might also include and action for moneys had and received.

Knowingly assisting a breach of trust

28.143 There are three elements to the claim of knowingly assisting a breach of trust. First, the defendant must know that a dishonest and fraudulent design is being implemented. Second, the defendant must know that his or her acts have the effect of assisting the design. Third, the knowledge of the assistant (or accessory) must be of actual facts and not knowledge of mere claims or allegations.[19] In *Young Investments Group Pty Ltd v Mann* [2012] FCAFC 107 at [56], The Full Court of the Federal Court said:

> In order to succeed in a case based on the second limb, it must be established that the fiduciary embarked upon a dishonest and fraudulent design. It must also be established that the alleged assistor had knowledge ... of that dishonest and fraudulent design. While dishonest and fraudulent designs can include breaches of trust as well as breaches of fiduciary duty, any breach of trust or breach of fiduciary duty relied upon must be dishonest and fraudulent.

28.144 In *Westpac Banking Corporation v The Bell Group Ltd (In Liq) (No 3)* at [2104], Drummond AJA said:

> (1) a defendant will be liable if he has assisted a trustee or fiduciary such as a company director with knowledge of the dishonest and fraudulent breach of trust or breach of fiduciary duty on the part of the trustee or fiduciary;
> (2) the defendant will have sufficient knowledge of the trustee or fiduciary's breach if his state of mind falls within any of the first four categories of knowledge described in *Baden v Société Générale pour Favoriser le Developpement du Commerce et de l'Industrie en France SA*;
> (3) dishonest and fraudulent designs sufficient for the purposes of the second limb can include both breaches of trust and breaches of fiduciary duty, but any such breach must be dishonest and fraudulent.

28.145 Once established, a claim of knowing assistance will generally render the third party jointly and severally liable with defaulting trustees and fiduciaries to pay equitable compensation for losses suffered by the beneficiaries: *New Cap Reinsurance Corporation Ltd v General Cologne Re Australia Ltd* [2004] NSWSC 781 at [34]; *George v Webb* [2011] NSWSC 1608 at [263]. However, in *Michael Wilson & Partners Ltd v Nicholls* (2011) 244 CLR 427 at 457; 282 ALR 685 at 709, Gummow ACJ, Hayne, Crennan and Bell JJ said:

> [T]he relief that is awarded against a defaulting fiduciary and a knowing assistant will not necessarily coincide in either nature or quantum. So, for example, the claimant may seek

---

19. S Barkehall Thomas, 'Knowing Receipt and Knowing Assistance: Where Do We Stand?' (1997) 20 *University of New South Wales Law Journal* 1 at 14–15.

compensation from the defaulting fiduciary (who made no profit from the default) and an account of profits from the knowing assistant (who profited from his or her own misconduct).

The United Kingdom approach: dishonesty of the accessory

28.146   In the United Kingdom, the *Baden* categories of knowledge were employed in cases of knowing assistance, with the bulk of authority favouring the imposition of a constructive trust when the assistant had knowledge consistent with categories (i)–(iii): *Agip (Africa) Ltd v Jackson* [1991] Ch 547; [1992] 4 All ER 385.

28.147   However, the *Baden* categories have been discarded in the United Kingdom for cases of knowing assistance and replaced with a more general test of 'dishonesty'. In *Royal Brunei Airlines Snd Bhd v Tan* [1995] 2 AC 378 at 390–1; [1995] 3 All ER 97 at 107, Lord Nicholls stated that the test of dishonesty was an objective test of whether the person acted as 'an honest person would in the circumstances' in light of what the person actually knew at the time, rather than what a reasonable person would have known. His Lordship, at AC 390–1; All ER 107, expressly differentiated dishonesty from carelessness and said:

> The individual is expected to attain the standard which would be observed by an honest person placed in those circumstances ... When called upon to decide whether a person was acting honestly, a court will look at all the circumstances known to the third party at the time. The court will also have regard to personal attributes of the third party, such as his experience and intelligence, and the reason why he acted as he did.

28.148   Lord Nicholls, at AC 385; All ER 102, also stated that it was dishonesty of the third party accessory which was relevant and not the dishonesty of the trustee.

28.149   This test of dishonesty was restated in *Twinsectra Ltd v Yardley* [2002] 2 AC 164; [2002] 2 All ER 377, where a combined test was proposed, encompassing objective and subjective elements. The test (as proposed by Lord Hutton) required a finding that the defendant's conduct was dishonest by ordinary standards of reasonable and honest people, and that the defendant realised that, by those standards, he or she had acted dishonestly. Lord Millett, in his dissent, was critical of this test as he believed that the test should not have to take account of whether the defendant actually knew he or she was acting dishonestly.

28.150   The Privy Council returned to the dishonesty test in *Barlow Clowes International Ltd (in liq) v Eurotrust International Ltd* [2006] 1 All ER 333. At trial the judge had found that the conduct of the defendant had been dishonest by objective standards but that the defendant was not liable because subjectively his own standards meant that he had not acted dishonestly. The Privy Council, at 338, did not agree with that assessment and said:

> Their Lordships accept that there is an element of ambiguity in these remarks which may have encouraged a belief, expressed in some academic writing, that the *Twinsectra* case had departed from the law as previously understood and invited inquiry not merely into the defendant's mental state about the nature of the transaction in which he was participating but also into his views about generally acceptable standards of honesty. But they do not consider that this is what Lord Hutton meant. The reference to 'what he knows would offend normally accepted standards of honest conduct' meant only that his knowledge of the transaction had to be such as to render his

participation contrary to normally acceptable standards of honest conduct. It did not require that he should have had reflections about what those normally acceptable standards were. Similarly in the speech of Lord Hoffmann, the statement that a dishonest state of mind meant 'consciousness that one is transgressing ordinary standards of honest behaviour' was in their Lordships' view intended to require consciousness of those elements of the transaction which make participation transgress ordinary standards of honest behaviour. It did not also require him to have thought about what those standards were.

Later English cases have continued to apply this objective assessment: *Starglade Properties Limited v Roland Nash* [2010] EWCA Civ 1314 at [23]–[30].

The Australian approach: knowledge of the accessory

28.151   There are some Australian cases which support the test of dishonesty set out in *Royal Brunei Airlines* and *Twinsectra*: *Macquarie Bank Ltd v Sixty-Fourth Throne Pty Ltd*; *Voss v Davidson* [2002] QSC 316; *Maher v Millennium Markets Pty Ltd* [2004] VSC 174. In *Gertsch v Atsas* [1999] NSWSC 898 at [42], Foster AJ (when discussing recipient liability) attempted to bring the two lines of authority together and found that:

> … the acceptance of the first four *Baden* categories, even though they now have no prominence in England, amounts really to no more than accepting a standard of honesty appropriate in the circumstances. The reference in category (iv) to 'the facts' sufficiently indicates, in my view, that a person receiving, for his own use, trust property, whilst in the state of knowledge posited, would not, relevantly, be acting honestly.

28.152   Nevertheless, the orthodox approach has been to employ the *Baden* categories and to stick with the formulation of Gibbs and Stephens JJ in *Consul Development Pty Ltd v DPC Estates Pty Ltd*. In *Equiticorp Finance Ltd v Bank of New Zealand* (1993) 32 NSWLR 50, Kirby P, at 104, (in dissent, but the only judge to comment on the issue), said:

> In Australia, the only guidance of the High Court is to be found in [*Consul Development Pty Ltd v DPC Estates Pty Ltd*]. It appears to be suggested that, in the case of participation in a breach of trust, a stranger to the trust will be liable at least if the 'requisite degree of knowledge' in the categories 1 to 4, as stated in *Baden*, are made out. In such a case, the stranger will be liable to compensate the beneficiary.

28.153   In *NCR Australia v Credit Connection* [2004] NSWSC 1 at [168]–[169], Austin J summarised the position as follows:

> What seems to emerge from these observations is that liability arises where the defendant has assisted in the trustee's dishonest and fraudulent design and:
>
> • has actual knowledge of the dishonest and fraudulent design; or
> • has deliberately shut his or her eyes to such a design; or
> • has abstained in a calculated way from making such inquiries as an honest and reasonable person would make, where such inquiries would have led to discovery of the dishonest and fraudulent design; or
> • has actual knowledge of facts which to a reasonable person would suggest a dishonest and fraudulent design.

But there is no liability if the defendant merely knows facts that would have been investigated by a reasonable person acting diligently, thereby discovering the truth, where the defendant has innocently but carelessly failed to make the appropriate investigations.

28.154   A similar approach was advocated by Bryson JA in *Yeshiva Properties No 1 Pty Ltd v Marshall* (2005) 219 ALR 112, where his Honour found that the Australian courts should follow the *Consul Developments* approach to knowledge rather than the English dishonesty approach. Bryson JA, at 118, said:

In the application of Stephen J's test it is not necessary that the fraudulent scheme or purpose of the fiduciary or trustee should be fully known, or should be understood in any detail at all; the test is complied with if the known facts would communicate to a reasonable person a general understanding that there was a fraud, breach of trust or breach of fiduciary duty.

28.155   In *Farah Constructions Pty Ltd v Say-Dee Pty Ltd* at CLR 160; ALR 260, the High Court described any suggestion which discounted the differences between the traditional approach (as set out in *Consul Developments*) and that adopted in *Royal Brunei* as 'not soundly based'. In relation to the issue of whether it is the trustee or the stranger who have must have acted dishonestly, the High Court rejected Lord Nicholl's view that it was the stranger's dishonesty that was relevant. The traditional focus of the second limb was said to rest solely on whether the 'defendant assists a trustee or fiduciary with knowledge of a dishonest and fraudulent design on the part of the trustee or fiduciary': *Farah Constructions Pty Ltd v Say-Dee Pty Ltd* at CLR 159; ALR 259.

28.156   However, because Say-Dee's arguments had not been based on the approach in *Royal Brunei*, the court declined to decide whether it should be adopted in Australia. The High Court, at CLR 163–4; ALR 262–3, said:

Consul supports the proposition that circumstances falling within any of the first four categories of *Baden* are sufficient to answer the requirement of knowledge in the second limb of *Barnes v Addy*, but does not travel fully into the field of constructive notice by accepting the fifth category. In this way, there is accommodated, through acceptance of the fourth category, the proposition that the morally obtuse cannot escape by failure to recognise an impropriety that would have been apparent to an ordinary person applying the standards of such persons. These conclusions in *Consul* as to what is involved in 'knowledge' for the second limb represent the law in Australia. They should be followed by Australian courts, unless and until departed from by decision of this court (references omitted).

28.157   After the dire warnings against judicial innovation in *Farah*, Australian courts have unanimously toed the line of authority established by *Consul Development*: *Corporate Systems Publishing Pty Ltd v Lingard (No 4)* [2008] WASC 21 at [325]; *AED Oil Ltd v Back (No 2)* [2010] VSC 43 at [35]; *Sewell v Zelden* [2010] NSWSC 1180 at [81]; *Taverners J Pty Ltd v Saxo Bank A/S* [2011] VSC 27 at [12]–[13]; *Shepard v Mladenis* [2011] NSWSC 1431 at [61]; *Australian Receivables Ltd v Tekitu Pty Ltd* [2011] NSWSC 1306 at [166]; *Break Fast Investments Pty Ltd v Giannopoulos* at [129]; *Dometic Pty Ltd v Bach* [2011] VSC 651 at [9]; *Hraiki v Hraiki* [2011] NSWSC 656 at [61]; *Eden Energy Ltd v Drivetrain Usa Inc* [2012] WASC 192 at [102]–[103]; *Nicholson v Morgan (No 2)* [2012] WASC 296 at [21]; *In the matter of Wan Ze Property Development (Aust) Pty Ltd* [2012] NSWSC 722 at [42]. In *Grimaldi v Chameleon Mining NL (ACN 098773 785) (No 2)* at FCR 262; ALR 84, the Full Court of the Federal Court said:

For the purposes of the 'knowing assistance' liability, *Farah Constructions* has indicated beyond question in this Court that 'knowledge/notice' falling within the first four categories, but not the fifth, represents Australian law. The matter we would emphasise is that that limb of *Barnes v Addy* is based manifestly on the third party's own wrongdoing in the circumstances.

In *Westpac Banking Corporation v The Bell Group Ltd (In Liq) (No 3)* at [1122], Lee AJA said:

[The trial judge's] confinement of 'knowing assistance' to circumstances where the party actually knew that what was being done was improper did not reflect the law set out in *Farah Constructions*. *Farah Constructions* ... accepted that four of five divisions of knowledge suggested in *Baden Delvaux v Société Générale pour Favoriser le Developpement du Commerce et de l'Industrie en France SA* were of assistance in determining whether requisite knowledge had been established for the purposes of a *Barnes v Addy* claim.

Dishonest and fraudulent design

28.158 The breach of fiduciary duty must be dishonest and fraudulent for liability to arise: *Young Investments Group Pty Ltd v Mann* [2012] FCAFC 107 at [56]. Earlier decisions indicated that this required the fiduciary to have acted with some form of moral reprehensiveness (according to the rules of equity), but that the test did not require behavior to be criminal: *Selangor United Rubber Estates Ltd v Cradock (No 3)* [1968] 1 WLR 1555; *Consul Development Pty Ltd v DPC Estates Pty Ltd* at CLR 398; ALR 252. This formulation was adopted by Owen J in *The Bell Group Ltd (in liq) v Westpac Banking Corporation (No 9)*, who found that the fiduciary's behaviour needed to be more than a mere breach of duty and had to involve some conscious wrongdoing. On appeal, in *Westpac Banking Corporation v The Bell Group Ltd (In Liq) (No 3)*, the majority disagreed and found that this test set the bar too high. Drummond AJA, at [2123], said:

I understand the court in *Farah* to have said that a trivial breach or a breach of trust or fiduciary duty of the kind that would be excusable under provisions such as s 75 of the *Trustees Act* and s 1318 of the *Corporations Act* will not be sufficient to show 'dishonest and fraudulent' conduct on the part of the trustee or fiduciary for the purposes of the second limb but that conduct by a trustee or fiduciary that involves a breach of duty more serious than that will be sufficient to constitute 'dishonest and fraudulent' conduct. The court in *Farah* cannot I think be understood as requiring behaviour on the part of the trustee or fiduciary so egregious as to be described as 'morally reprehensible', even if not criminally dishonest.

Liability when the fiduciary and accessory are controlled by the same person

28.159 How should the knowledge requirement work in situations where the fiduciary and the accessory are effectively controlled by the same person? In *Kation Pty Ltd v Lamru Pty Ltd* (2009) 257 ALR 336, the Court of Appeal of New South Wales upheld a finding of accessorial liability in a situation where the breaching fiduciary and the accessory were both corporations controlled by the same individual. The fact that both companies were controlled by the same person did not mean that there was not a dishonest and fraudulent design on the part of the fiduciary company. The same picture emerges when the accessory is a corporation that is owned and controlled by a breaching fiduciary who is a natural legal person. In such a case the knowledge of the breaching fiduciary will automatically be held to be the knowledge of the third party corporation: *Barescape Pty Limited v Bacchus Holdings Pty Limited (No 9)* [2012] NSWSC 984 at [219]–[220]; *Holyoake Industries (Vic) Pty Ltd v V-Flow Pty Ltd* [2011] FCA 1154 at [123]; *Menkens v Wintour* [2011] QSC 7 at [146].

Accessorial liability and non-trustee fiduciaries

28.160 As with knowing receipt, it has been recognised that the second limb of *Barnes v Addy* also attaches to assistance given to non-trustee fiduciaries, such as company directors: *Westpac Banking Corporation v The Bell Group Ltd (In Liq) (No 3)*; *Grimaldi v Chameleon Mining NL (ACN 098773 785) (No 2)*. In *City of Sydney v Streetscape Projects (Australia) Pty Ltd* [2011] NSWSC 1214 at [491], Einstein J went even further and decided that the doctrine of knowing assistance could be applied to breaches of confidence (at least those arising with features of a fiduciary relationship). The facts concerned the City of Sydney which had contracted with Streetscape and its director, Obeid, to produce Smartpoles in preparation for the Sydney Olympics. Einstein J found that the City held confidential information in the Smartpoles and that the defendants use of the Smartpoles outside the terms of the agreement was a breach of confidence. Additionally, Einstein J found that the defendants' behavior was that of knowingly assisting Streetscape to breach its duty to the City.

THIRD PARTY LIABILITY FOR INDUCING AN INNOCENT BREACH OF TRUST

28.161 The High Court recognised in *Farah Constructions v Say-Dee* that there was a line of authority prior to and separate from *Barnes v Addy* which imposed liability on a third party who knowingly induced or immediately procured breaches of duty by a trustee in situations where the trustee had acted innocently or with no improper purpose: *Midgley v Midgley* [1893] 3 Ch 282; *Elders Trustee and Executor Co Ltd v EG Reeves Pty Ltd* [1987] 78 ALR 193 at 238–239; *Symri v Hinds* [1996] NTSC 57 at [34]–[35]; *Armstrong Strategic Management and Marketing Pty Limited v Expense Reduction Analysts Group Pty Ltd* [2011] NSWSC 704 at [15].

28.162 This rule is sometimes referred to as the principle in *Eaves v Hickson* (1861) 54 ER 840. In this case, the father of two beneficiaries to a will knowingly provided a forged certificate of his marriage to trustees to trick them into paying out funds to his children. The trustee innocently made the payment. The father was held liable for the loss caused by the payment because he knew that his actions would trick the trustees into breaching the trust.

28.163 In *Othman v Stanley* [2012] VSC 211, at [6], Mukhtar AsJ said:

> [I]t is safe to say … it would need to be pleaded that the wrongdoer (i) had knowledge of the trust and its terms; (ii) perpetrated acts of inducement with the intention of procuring a breach of trust; and (iii) the inducement caused the breach.

In *Australian Super Developments Pty Ltd v Marriner* [2010] VSC 41 at [162], the Victorian Court of Appeal found that the levels of knowledge required by the third party are the same levels of knowledge applied to cases of knowing assistance, namely, *Baden* categories 1–4.

28.164 In *Manildra Laboratories v Campbell* [2009] NSWSC 987, the facts concerned a claim of knowing assistance as well the alternative claim of knowingly procuring an innocent breach of fiduciary duty. Neither of the claims succeeded on the facts. A manager of a flour mill, owned by the plaintiff, created a company with a view to purchase another flour mill at Young that would be in competition with the plaintiff's mill. It was argued that the new company and the vendors of the Young mill had induced the manager to breach his fiduciary duties and that they had knowingly participated in a dishonest and fraudulent design. McDougall J dismissed the actions. The vendors of the Young mill had been approached by the manager and thought he was acting on behalf of his employer. The claims against the new company also failed because, while the manager had breached his implied contractual obligation of fidelity to his employer, this did not constitute a dishonest and fraudulent design.

CONSTRUCTIVE TRUSTS AND STOLEN PROPERTY

28.165   It has been said that a thief holds stolen property on constructive trust for the true owner, even in the absence of a prior fiduciary relationship. In *Black v S Freedman & Co* (1910) 12 CLR 105, an employee stole money from his employer and deposited some of it into his wife's bank account and purchased circular notes with the rest. The High Court found that the employer's money could be traced into both the account and the notes and that both were held on constructive trust: see Chapter 29 and *The Uniting Church in Australia Property Trust (NSW) v Vincent* [2009] NSWSC 375. Tracing normally requires a pre-existing fiduciary relationship, which was present in this case given there was a relationship of employer and employee. However, O'Connor J's decision in *Black v S Freedman & Co* was not predicated on the existence of a fiduciary relationship, but was purely based on the fact that when property is stolen the thief should be found to hold the property on trust for the true owner.

Theft or fraud

28.166   The constructive trust arises in cases of theft but also in cases of fraud. For example, in *Allianz Australia Insurance Ltd v Olver* [2003] VSC 101, a constructive trust arose over funds received by a boat owner who had scuttled his boat as part of an insurance scam. In *MBF Australia Ltd v Malouf* [2008] NSWCA 214, funds from a fraudulently misappropriated cheque were found to be held on constructive trust. In *Westpac Banking Corporation v Palasty* [2011] NSWSC 1478, Bryson AJ was prepared to apply the doctrine to a case of fraudulent misrepresentation. The trust that arises in these cases does so when the fraudster obtains the property: *Hraiki v Hraiki* at [39].

Third party recipients

28.167   If the thief makes a gift of the stolen property to a third party that third party will also be held liable to restore either the original property or its traceable proceeds, as equity does not assist a volunteer: *Heperu Pty Ltd v Belle* (2009) 76 NSWLR 230 at 154–5; 258 ALR 727 at 762–3; *Toksoz v Westpac Banking Corporation* [2012] NSWCA 199 at [4]. The volunteer's equitable obligation arises on the volunteer's discovery of the wrongful conduct.

28.168   If the third party provides consideration, he or she may be able to claim a defence as a bona fide purchaser for value without notice: *Black v S Freedman & Co* at 110. As with volunteers, the constructive trust will only become effective when the third party acquires knowledge of the theft: *Lurgi (Australia) Pty Ltd v Gratz* [2000] VSC 278 at [74]. The onus lies with the recipient to prove a lack of notice: *MBF Australia Ltd v Malouf* at [52].

28.169   Third parties may also be liable under both limbs of the rule in *Barnes v Addy*: see 28.114 28.164; *Break Fast Investments Pty Ltd v Giannopoulos* at [92]. In *Orix Australia Corporation Ltd v Moody Kiddell and Partners Pty Ltd* [2005] NSWSC 1209 at [160], White J held that *Barnes v Addy*:

... applies not only where the third party has provided knowing or dishonest assistance to a breach of fiduciary duty, but to a breach of trust or a fraud which arises independently of a pre-existing relationship of principal and fiduciary, or trustee and beneficiary.

Conflict with the *nemo dat* rule

28.170   This line of authority appears to conflict with the *nemo dat quod non habet* rule which states that the thief acquires no title to the property and cannot, therefore, pass title on to others, even a bona fide purchaser.[20] If the thief has no title, how can they be said to be a trustee? In *Shalson v Russo* [2005] Ch 281 at 318, Rimer J said:

> [A] thief ordinarily acquires no property in what he steals and cannot give a title to it even to a good faith purchaser: both the thief and the purchaser are vulnerable to claims by the true owner to recover his property. If the thief has no title in the property, I cannot see how he can become a trustee of it for the true owner: the owner retains the legal and beneficial title. If the thief mixes stolen money with other money in a bank account, the common law cannot trace into it. Equity has traditionally been regarded as similarly incompetent unless it could first identify a relevant fiduciary relationship, but in many cases of theft there will be none. The fact that, traditionally, equity can only trace into a mixed bank account if that precondition is first satisfied provides an unsatisfactory justification for any conclusion that the stolen money must necessarily be trust money so as to enable the precondition to be satisfied. It is either trust money or it is not. If it is not, it is not legitimate artificially to change its character so as to bring it within the supposed limits of equity's powers to trace: the answer is to develop those powers so as to meet the special problems raised by stolen money.

28.171   Tarrant has argued that this analysis confuses the difference between title to property, in the sense of ownership, and possessory title to property. The owner of property has the title or ownership of that property but they may give another person a right or title of possession, such as in a bailment. In fact, any person in possession receives a title to possession: *Islamic Republic of Iran v Barakat Galleries Ltd* [2009] QB 22; [2008] 1 All ER 1177. In the case of a thief that title is very weak and is easily destroyed by the true owner's assertion of rights. However, if the thief transfers possession to a third party prior to the true owner regaining possession, the third party receives the thief's weak possessory title. Tarrant argues:

> If the thief were to sell his title to a third party and deliver the stolen goods to the third party then the thief's property right to the goods will transfer to that third party purchaser. After the sale the victim still has their title to the goods which is a right to possession. The title formerly held by the thief was vulnerable to the victim's right to possession. The thief's property right has transferred to the purchaser and according to the nemo dat rule that property right is still vulnerable to the victim's property right. So the thief is able to transfer *a title* to the third party purchaser but, consistent with the nemo dat rule, that title is not *the title*. Accordingly, the nemo dat rule provides no difficulty in the operation of the theft principle (emphasis in original).[21]

---

20.   S Barkehall-Thomas, 'Thieves as Trustees: The Enduring Legacy of *Black v S Freedman & Co Ltd*' (2009) 3 *Journal of Equity* 52; S Barkehall-Thomas, 'Thieves, owners, and the problem of title: Part 1 — Chattels' (2011) 5 *Journal of Equity* 228; S Barkehall-Thomas, 'Thieves, owners, and the problem of title: Part 2 — Money' (2012) 6 *Journal of Equity* 1.

21.   J Tarrant, 'Thieves as Trustees: In Defence of the Theft Principle' (2009) 3 *Journal of Equity* 170.

28.172   Therefore, the better argument is that the constructive trust fastens over the possessory legal title enjoyed by the thief and third parties who receive the property from the thief.

Constructive trust or resulting trust?

28.173   In *Evans v European Bank Ltd* (2004) 61 NSWLR 75 at 99, Spigelman CJ thought that such a trust was better described as a resulting trust because of its automatic nature and institutional characteristics. A similar approach was adopted in *Port of Brisbane Corp v ANZ Securities Ltd* [2003] 2 Qd R 661, a case involving the theft by an employee of several million dollars from a company, which was then invested in a trust account with the defendant bank. By the time the theft had been discovered the trust moneys had been dispersed from the trust account. The plaintiff company argued (among other things) that the defendant bank had held the moneys on resulting trust for it and that the disbursement of those funds was a breach of that trust. In dismissing this claim, the Court of Appeal accepted the resulting trust analysis. It was said that these resulting trusts exist immediately on the transfer of trust property but that third parties are not subject to them until they become aware of their positions. It was also said that this resulting trust was not a fiduciary relationship. Finally, it was said that the resulting trust could not exist if the trust property had disappeared by the time of the judgment.

28.174   It is hard to see how the classification of these trusts as resulting trusts can be correct. It is true that there is no intention on the part of the victim to bestow a beneficial estate upon the thief, and this could arguably be a basis for the presumption of resulting trust. But, according to the presumptions of resulting trust, all the thief need do to destroy the trust is prove that there was no trust intended by the victim (which will always be the case). Given these trusts are imposed regardless of the intentions of the parties they are better classed as constructive trusts, albeit of an institutional kind. Later cases have confirmed that these trusts, whether they are resulting or constructive, are institutional: *Wambo Coal Pty Ltd v Ariff* [2007] NSWSC 589 at [40]–[41].

28.175   In *Westdeutsche Landesbank Girozentrale v London Borough Council* at AC 715–16; All ER 997, Lord Browne-Wilkinson said:

> I agree that the stolen moneys are traceable in equity. But the proprietary interest which equity is enforcing in such circumstances arises under a constructive, not a resulting, trust. Although it is difficult to find clear authority for the proposition, when property is obtained by fraud equity imposes a constructive trust on the fraudulent recipient: the property is recoverable and traceable in equity. Thus, an infant who has obtained property by fraud is bound in equity to restore it. Moneys stolen from a bank account can be traced in equity.

CONSTRUCTIVE TRUSTS AND MONEYS PAID BY MISTAKE

28.176   A constructive trust will arise when a person makes a mistaken payment for no consideration and the recipient denies the payer's right to have the money repaid: *Credit Union Australia Ltd v Lyons* [2009] NSWSC 1188. In *Chase Manhattan Bank v Israel-British Bank (London) Ltd* [1981] Ch 105, the plaintiff bank mistakenly paid the defendant bank twice for the same transaction. It was held that a person who paid money under a mistake could claim beneficial ownership of the funds because the recipient of the funds was bound in good conscience to repay the money from the moment the money was received. However, in *Westdeutsche Landesbank Girozentrale v Islington*

London Borough Council at AC 714; All ER 996, Lord Browne-Wilkinson qualified this finding by saying that the right to a constructive trust over money mistakenly paid only arose after the recipient had notice of the mistake. In *Wambo Coal Pty Ltd v Ariff* at [42], White J said:

> I do not see why, in principle, a constructive trust arising from the retention of moneys known to have been paid by mistake, and for which there was no consideration, would not arise from the time the payee acquired such knowledge, if the moneys paid could still be identified at the time such knowledge was acquired. Such a trust is as much an institutional trust as a trust imposed on property in the hands of the thief.

28.177 In *Young v Lalic* (2006) 197 FLR 27, Brereton J applied the principle to a payment which was made for a limited purpose with the intention that the payer retained beneficial ownership. Money had been provided by a woman to her future mother-in-law on the basis that it would be used to complete the construction of a home for the family to live in. The marriage ended after a few months and Brereton J ordered a constructive trust over the land for the value of the payment.

Third party recipients

28.178 As in cases of stolen property, third party volunteers who receive the money from the recipient will also be subject to the trust: *Strang v Owens* (1925) 42 WN (NSW) 183; *Addstead Pty Ltd (in liq) v Liddan Pty Ltd* (1997) 70 SASR 21. Bona fide purchasers for value without notice will have a complete defence, but the burden of proving that defence lies on the third party recipient: *Westpac Banking Corporation v Ollis* [2007] NSWSC 956 at [43]. Notice includes actual, constructive and imputed notice: *Espin v Pemberton* (1859) 44 ER 1380 at 1383.

CONSTRUCTIVE TRUSTS AND FORFEITURE FOR UNLAWFUL KILLING

28.179 The common law applies a forfeiture rule which operates to prevent a person who unlawfully kills another person from benefiting financially from the victim's estate: *Cleaver v Mutual Reserve Fund Life Association* [1892] 1 QB 147. In *Rasmanis v Jurewitsch* (1970) 70 SR (NSW) 407 at 412, Jacobs JA said:

> I think that the primary rule to be enforced is that the felon must not be allowed to retain any benefit flowing to him from the slaying and that he is required to hold any such benefit which flows at law upon trust for someone other than himself.

The rule does not always require equity's intervention but on occasion it will be necessary to impose a constructive trust to ensure that the killer does not obtain a benefit from the killing. The most obvious situation that calls for equitable intervention occurs when the killer and victim are joint tenants of property. In that situation equity will impose a constructive trust over the victim's half-share so that it will not pass to the killer on survivorship.

28.180 The rule applies in all cases of homicide. In earlier cases it was suggested that the rule would not be applied in cases where there was no intention to bring about a benefit from the estate of the deceased: *Permanent Trustee Co Ltd v Freedom from Hunger Campaign* (1991) 25 NSWLR 140. In other cases, it was suggested that the rule was flexible and may not be applied in cases where there was no unconscientiousness: *Public Trustee v Evans* (1985) 2 NSWLR 188; *Re Keitley* [1992]

1 VR 583; *Public Trustee v Fraser* (1987) 9 NSWLR 433. However, these decisions were overturned in *Troja v Troja* (1994) 33 NSWLR 269, a case involving a manslaughter by diminished responsibility. Speaking in the majority, Meagher JA, at 299, said:

> The law as laid down in *Cleaver's* case is that all felonious killings are contrary to public policy and hence, one would assume, unconscionable. Indeed, there is something a trifle comic in the spectacle of Equity judges sorting felonious killings into conscionable and unconscionable piles.

28.181 An acquittal in a criminal trial does not operate to conclude the issue of a person's innocence or guilt for the purposes of the rule: *Helton v Allen* (1940) 63 CLR 691. If a person has been charged but not convicted of the killing(s), they are not disentitled to property but cannot necessarily rely on their beneficial rights to call on the estate of their victims, prior to administration: *Gonzales v Claridades* (2003) 58 NSWLR 211.

28.182 The common law rule has been amended in New South Wales by the *Forfeiture Act 1995* (NSW). The Act allows the court to modify the effect of the rule 'if justice demands it'. However, the Act does not allow the court to intervene in cases of murder. If the killer has been found not guilty of murder by reason of mental illness, an interested person may apply to the Supreme Court for an order that the rule apply as if the offender had been found guilty of murder: s 11(1). The court may apply the forfeiture rule if it is satisfied that justice requires it: s 11(2). To determine this the court must consider the conduct of the offender, the conduct of the deceased person, the effect of the application of the rule on the offender or any other person, and other matters which appear material to the court.

28.183 In *Estate of Fitter and the Forfeiture Act 1995* [2005] NSWSC 1188, a woman, after also being attacked by her daughter, was stabbed to death by her husband and son. The husband, son and daughter were all found not guilty of murder by reason of mental illness but were detained under the *Mental Health Act 1990* (NSW). The victim's sister applied to the court to have the husband, son and daughter treated as murderers for the purpose of the forfeiture rule. The judge acceded to that request and ordered that the husband hold one half-share of the matrimonial home on constructive trust for the deceased's estate and that the husband and the children be prevented from taking any interest in the victim's superannuation.

CONSTRUCTIVE TRUSTS TO REMEDY UNCONSCIONABLE/ UNCONSCIENTIOUS CONDUCT

28.184 The courts have had pressure placed on them in recent times to expand the remedial basis of constructive trusts. One factor in this movement appears to be the failure of resulting trusts to deal with property disputes in the breakdown of emerging family structures, such as de facto relationships. Be that as it may, across the common law world there has been a search for some unifying principle that can be employed to justify the imposition of the remedial constructive trust.

Unjust enrichment

28.185 In Canada, the principle of unjust enrichment has been adopted as the fundamental principle justifying the remedial constructive trust: *Rathwell v Rathwell* (1978) 83 DLR (3d) 289. In *Pettkus v Becker* (1980) 117 DLR (3d) 257, the Supreme Court of Canada accepted that, in the absence of some common intention between the parties, a constructive trust should be imposed to remedy unjust enrichment in a domestic property dispute. Unfortunately, the decision in *Pettkus v Becker* gave rise to the belief that constructive trusts could only be imposed when there was unjust enrichment.[22] However, the Supreme Court has since modified its view and found in *Soulos v Korkontzilas* [1997] 2 SCR 217, that unjust enrichment is merely one ground upon which a constructive trust may be imposed.

Unconscionability/unconscientiousness as the touchstone

28.186   In Australia, unjust enrichment has not yet been accepted as a ground for the imposition of a constructive trust: *Stephenson Nominees Pty Ltd v Official Receiver* (1987) 16 FCR 536; *Rush v Keogh* [2000] NSWSC 624; *Crafter v Crafter* at [70]. The governing principle is that equity will impose a constructive trust to prevent the unconscionable or unconscientious retention of benefit. This is sometimes referred to as a 'windfall equity': *Henderson v Miles (No 2)* [2005] NSWSC 867 at [19]; *Crafter v Crafter* at [69].

28.187   The acceptance of unconscionability/unconscientiousness as the touchstone of the remedial constructive trust began with *Muschinski v Dodds*. In this case Muschinski claimed that she was the absolute beneficial owner of land at Picton. The land was held in the names of Muschinski and Dodds as tenants in common. Muschinski claimed that Dodds' half-interest was held on trust for her. Dodds sought an order for the sale of the land and the division of the net proceeds into equal shares.

28.188   Muschinski had provided the entirety of the purchase price of $20,000 from the sale of her previous home. The property was in a bad state of repair and the parties planned on restoring it, building a new prefabricated house on the land, and using the land to run an arts and crafts business. The parties agreed that they would use the proceeds of the sale of Muschinski's house to provide the purchase moneys and that Dodds would use his earnings and whatever moneys he obtained from his divorce settlement to pay for the prefabricated house.

28.189   The parties' plans never came to fruition. Some repair work was done by Dodds and the total respective financial contributions of the parties upon the breakdown of their relationship were $25,259.45 from Muschinski and $2549.77 from Dodds.

28.190   At trial, and on appeal to the Court of Appeal, the matter was treated as one of resulting trust, with a presumption arising in Muschinski's favour. Both the trial judge and the Court of Appeal found that the presumption of resulting trust had been rebutted by the evidence of Muschinski's intention to grant Dodds an interest in return for his promises to work on the property and in the proposed business. No constructive trust was found to have arisen.

28.191   A majority of the High Court (Gibbs CJ, Mason and Deane JJ; Brennan and Dawson JJ dissenting) found that a constructive trust should be ordered to protect Muschinski's beneficial interest. Interestingly, the majority judges differed in the way they approached Muschinski's arguments for recognition of her beneficial ownership and rights to compensation. Gibbs CJ believed that there should be an equitable accounting on the sale of the property, on the basis that the parties were joint and several debtors. Gibbs CJ recognised that Muschinski had a right to contribution against Dodds for the recovery of one-half of the amount paid under the contract,

---

22.   R Chambers, 'Constructive Trusts in Canada' (1999) 37 *Alberta Law Review* 173 at 174–5.

unless the parties had agreed (either expressly or impliedly) that no such right would arise between them. Gibbs CJ could find no evidence of such an agreement and therefore saw no impedient to an order for contribution (although it should be noted that his Honour agreed with the orders proposed by Deane J).

28.192   Deane J (with whom Mason J agreed) took a more radical approach. His Honour began by finding that the presumption of resulting trust had been rebutted, but that a constructive trust should be imposed. Deane J expressly disagreed with the approach of Gibbs CJ regarding Muschinski's right to claim an equitable contribution from Dodds. Instead, Deane J thought it more appropriate to consider Dodds' obligations as arising from the joint endeavour of the parties. To that extent the parties' relationship was akin to a joint venture and the principle could be applied. Denae J, at CLR 619; ALR 456 said:

> [J]oint venturers are entitled to the proportionate repayment of their capital contributions to [an] abortive joint venture. This is so notwithstanding that it was the common understanding or agreement that the funds advanced were to be applied for the purposes of the joint venture and that the return from them would take the form, not of a repayment of capital contributed but of a share in the proceeds of the joint venture when it was carried to fruition.

28.193   This principle was said by Deane J to reflect a wider equitable principle, that where a joint relationship or endeavour fails, equity will not permit one party to assert or retain the benefit of property if it would be unconscionable for that party to do so. Deane J, at CLR 619–20; ALR 456, said:

> [T]he principle operates in a case where the substratum of a joint relationship or endeavour is removed without attributable blame and where the benefit of money or other property contributed by one party on the basis and for the purposes of the relationship or endeavour would otherwise be enjoyed by the other party in circumstances in which it was not specifically intended or specially provided that other party should so enjoy it. The content of the principle is that, in such a case, equity will not permit that other party to assert or retain the benefit of the relevant property to the extent that it would be unconscionable for him so to do: cf *Atwood v Maude* [1858] LR 3 Ch App 369 at pp 374–375 and per Jessel MR, *Lyon v Tweddell* (1881) 17 Ch D 529 at 531.

28.194   The test of unconscionability was said to be a legal test. Deane J was careful to contrast the principle of unconscionability with general notions of fairness. His Honour, at CLR 621; ALR 456, said:

> Notions of what is fair and just are relevant but only in the confined context of determining whether conduct should, by reference to legitimate processes of legal reasoning, be characterised as unconscionable for the purposes of a specific principle of equity whose rationale and operation is to prevent wrongful and undue advantage being taken by one party of a benefit derived at the expense of the other party in the special circumstances of the unforeseen and premature collapse of a joint relationship or endeavour.

28.195   Deane J found that Dodds' behaviour was unconscionable, in particular, his assertion of legal title in the face of the contributions made by Muschinski. It followed that equity required a constructive trust to adjust the rights and obligations of the parties to compensate for the disproportion between the parties' contributions to the purchase price. However, Deane J did not believe that it was unconscionable for Dodds to retain his half-share in the residue of the proceeds of sale of the property, once each party had been reimbursed for their contributions to the purchase price and improvements.

28.196 Deane J, at CLR 617; ALR 453, expressly rejected unjust enrichment as a ground for the imposition of a constructive trust in Australia:

> It may well be that the development of the law of this country on a case by case basis will eventually lead to the identification of some overall concept of unjust enrichment as an established principle constituting the basis of decision of past and future cases. Whatever may be the position in relation to the law of other common law countries … however, no such general principle is as yet established, as a basis of decision as distinct from an informative generic label for purposes of classification, in Australian law. The most that can be said at the present time is that 'unjust enrichment' is a term commonly used to identify the notion underlying a variety of distinct categories of case in which the law has recognised an obligation on the part of a defendant to account for a benefit derived at the expense of a plaintiff …

28.197 Brennan J (with whom Dawson J agreed), also found the presumption of resulting trust to have been rebutted. Brennan J found that, as Dodds had received his legal interest as a result of his promise to improve the property, he was bound by a personal equitable obligation to compensate for his failure to make substantial improvements. However, as Muschinski had chosen to make a proprietary claim, and not a claim of personal equitable obligation, Brennan J believed her appeal should be dismissed.

28.198 Additionally, Brennan J, at CLR 609; ALR 447, found that no constructive trust could arise as it was not unconscionable for Dodds to retain his interest:

> [T]he parties agreed, after much discussion and some contest of wishes, on the foundation on which they hoped to build their future relationship, and that that foundation included making Mr Dodds an independent owner of property which he might devote to their common purposes as a manifestation of his commitment to their relationship. Their omission to provide for the winding up of their relationship reflects their inability to see what course that relationship might follow, but does not suggest that the foundation of the relationship on which they had ultimately agreed should be changed if the relationship ceased. Once it appears that the condition that the assurances be fulfilled was not intended to work a forfeiture of the interest given in the event of non-fulfilment, how can it be unconscionable to retain the interest? His separation from Mrs Muschinski was in breach of no equitable obligation and it can make no difference that that event occurred before the work was complete.

28.199 It was not until *Baumgartner v Baumgartner* (1987) 164 CLR 137; (1987) 76 ALR 75 that Deane J's approach was accepted by a majority of the High Court. This case concerned a claim made by a de facto wife that she owned a beneficial interest in half of a property purchased during the course of the relationship. The property had been purchased in the de facto husband's name. A number of statements were made by the de facto husband to the effect that the property was being purchased for both parties to enjoy. A child was born during the relationship, which required the wife to suspend her employment for three months. Apart from that period, the wife was employed and contributed to the running of the household. The parties pooled their incomes and this had the effect of reducing the mortgage debt on the home unit more quickly. At the end of the relationship the wife took furniture worth approximately $7000.

28.200   The trial judge found that there was no intention to create a trust, that there were no circumstances giving rise to a constructive trust and that there was nothing unconscionable or inequitable in the appellant retaining the full legal and equitable title. A majority of the Court of Appeal overturned this finding stating that there was ample evidence from which an inference could be drawn of actual common intention to create a trust.

28.201   On appeal to the High Court, Mason CJ, Wilson and Deane JJ first dealt with the question of whether a common intention could be inferred from the circumstances. Their Honours felt that as the existence of a common intention was a matter of fact, it was not a legitimate exercise for an appeal court to overturn the findings of the trial judge that there was no common intention. Their Honours then proceeded to examine whether a constructive trust might be imposed.

28.202   Mason CJ, Wilson and Deane JJ accepted the proposition raised by Deane J in *Muschinski v Dodds*, that the constructive trust could serve as a remedy, imposed by equity to prevent the unconscionable retention of benefit. The circumstances were examined for unconscionability and their Honours, at CLR 149; ALR 84, concluded:

> The case is accordingly one in which the parties have pooled their earnings for the purposes of their joint relationship, one of the purposes of that relation ship being to secure accommodation for themselves and their child. Their contributions, financial and otherwise, to the acquisition of the land, the building of the house, the purchase of furniture and the making of their home, were on the basis of, and for the purposes of, that joint relationship. In this situation the appellant's assertion, after the relationship had failed, that the Leumeah property, which was financed in part through the pooled funds, is his sole property, is his property beneficially to the exclusion of any interest at all on the part of the respondent, amounts to unconscionable conduct which attracts the intervention of equity and the imposition of a constructive trust at the suit of the respondent.

28.203   Their Honours, at CLR 149; ALR 85, then examined the question of how the parties should hold their respective shares under the trust and found that equity would normally favour equality especially 'in circumstances where the parties have lived together for years and have pooled their resources and their efforts to create a joint home, there is much to be said for the view that they should share the beneficial ownership equally as tenants in common'.

28.204   The court's role was to 'give effect to the notion of practical equality, rather than pursue complicated factual inquiries which will result in relatively insignificant differences in contributions and consequential beneficial interest': *Muschinski v Dodds* at CLR 150; ALR 85.

28.205   However, the general starting point was said to be subject to adjustment where it was necessary to avoid injustice: *Muschinski v Dodds* at CLR 150; ALR 85. The de facto wife was credited with the equivalent of three months' earnings, which she forwent to have the couple's child. This left the contributions of the parties at 55 per cent by the husband and 45 per cent by the wife. The de facto husband was also credited with the net proceeds of the sale of his former property, which were used to purchase the property, less the amount of payments of instalments under the mortgage over the unit that were made from the pooled earnings during the period of cohabitation. He was also entitled to be repaid the instalments under the mortgage over the property that he had paid after the termination of the relationship. A final adjustment was made in the husband's favour for an amount equivalent to the value of the furniture taken by the wife.

28.206   Gaudron J agreed with Mason CJ, Wilson and Deane JJ, stressing that in many cases it might be necessary to account for non-financial contributions.

28.207   Toohey J also agreed with Mason CJ, Wilson and Deane JJ, but was more willing to accept unjust enrichment as a basis for the imposition of a constructive trust. His Honour, at CLR 152–3; ALR 88, stated that there was little real difference between a constructive trust imposed on unconscionability grounds, and those imposed under Lord Denning's new model, or the Canadian unjust enrichment model. All of these types of constructive trust examine the pooling of assets in the acquisition of property for any unconscionable retention of benefit, or unjust enrichment. According to Toohey J, the approach of Mason CJ, Wilson and Deane JJ could be understood from any of the above standpoints.

The elements of the unconscionability/unconscientiousness constructive trust

28.208   The combined effect of *Muschinski* and *Baumgartner* was summarised by Pincus JA in *Turner v Dunne* [1996] QCA 272 at [4]–[5] as follows:

1. A constructive trust may be imposed even though the person held to be trustee had no intention to create a trust or hold property on trust.
2. An intention to create a trust may be imputed where it is necessary to do so 'in good faith and in conscience'.
3. A principle which may be applied is that which restores to a party contributions made to a joint endeavour which fails, when the contributions have been made in circumstances in which it was not intended that the other party should enjoy them.
4. Contributions, financial and otherwise, to the purposes of the joint relationship are relevant for this purpose.

28.209   In *West v Mead* [2003] NSWSC 161, Campbell J provided a more detailed breakdown of the requirements of the *Muschinski/Baumgartner* trust. Campbell J listed three requirements:

- There must be both a joint relationship or endeavour, where funds are spent towards a common benefit;
- The joint relationship or endeavour must have come to an end 'without attributable blame'; and
- There must be unconscionability/unconscientiousness — it must be unconscionable for the benefit of contributions provided by one party to be retained by the other.

Joint relationship or endeavour

28.210   Both the judgment of Deane J in *Muschinski v Dodds* and the judgment of Mason CJ, Wilson and Deane JJ in *Baumgartner* referred to the 'general equitable principle' that restores contributions to a party to a joint endeavour which later fails. The requirement for a joint endeavour was discussed in *West v Mead* at [59], where Campbell J said:

> In accordance with this approach, a plaintiff needs to establish that there is indeed a joint endeavour between the parties, in which expenditure is shared for the common benefit. It is also necessary to identify what the scope of that joint endeavour is. It is a question of fact, for any

couple, what the scope of the joint endeavour they are engaging in is. Further, for any couple, the scope of the joint endeavour they are engaged in might change from time to time. If, within the scope of a joint endeavour which lasts for years, an asset is acquired, as a result of contributions both parties have made, and for a purpose of the ongoing joint endeavour of the parties, this gives rise to the presumption that the beneficial interest ought be shared equally. That presumption can be displaced if one party is able to show that the contributions, both financial and non-financial, to that asset should be regarded as unequal. In practical terms, this way of proceeding will place the onus of attributing a value to non-financial contributions on the person who asserts that the title should be held unequally.

28.211   Agreements between the parties, expressed in writing or orally, may be relevant in assessing whether there was a relationship of joint endeavour: *Waterhouse v Power* [2003] QCA 155. Such agreements may assist the court in assessing the unconscionability of any denial of interest: *Meehan v Fuller* [1999] QCA 37 at [28]. Alternatively, if parties have entered into binding agreements, such agreements will ordinarily be enforceable: *West v Mead* at [63]. However, should the agreement prove unconscionable, the court will overturn the agreement and apply a constructive trust.

28.212   The absence of an express agreement is not fatal to a claim for a constructive trust. In *Brown v Manuel* [1996] QCA 65, a constructive trust was ordered in circumstances where the man had not, by anything which he had said or done, created an expectation in the woman that she would acquire a proprietary interest in any of their homes. The Court of Appeal of Queensland considered that it was not necessary that there be conduct inducing such an expectation in order that a constructive trust be applied, nor was it necessary that the parties should have pooled their resources. What was needed was a mutual expectation that the parties were contributing to the acquisition of the home.

28.213   However, the mere fact that parties are sharing living arrangements does not give rise to the existence of a joint endeavour. In *Barker v Linklater* [2008] 1 Qd R 405, the parties had co-resided but the plaintiff had not expended any money on improvements to the home and had not contributed a disproportionate amount to the household expenditure. Nor had she performed the majority of household chores. Muir JA, at [73], said:

> Their contributions did not differ to any significant degree from contributions of the kind commonly made by persons sharing rented accommodation or, for that matter, by a person renting accommodation in a house owned by the other occupant, save that the appellant maintained the yard. Those are not circumstances in which a monetary or other contribution is made without an intention that the other party should enjoy the benefit provided by the contribution. Nor do such circumstances render it unconscionable for a house owner such as the deceased to retain whatever benefits may have been provided by the other person during the cohabitation. Any denial by the deceased that the appellant had an interest in the house would not have been unconscionable. The circumstances under consideration, in themselves, would not give rise to a reasonable expectation on the part of either of the appellant or the deceased that the appellant had acquired an interest in the property.

28.214   Nor does the fact that one party is paying money which is going towards the beneficial acquisition of property give rise to a joint endeavour. In *Downham v McCallum* [2008] TASSC 81, the plaintiff failed to establish the existence of a joint venture in a situation where the defendants, who were leasing a property, agreed to purchase it by paying off the owner's loans and the rates and charges on the property. Porter J, at [102], found that:

> These were not joint ventures or relationships for the purposes of acquisition, development or use, such that the plaintiff's contributions were made for joint purposes. There was no relationship involving co-ownership or literal co-occupation, nor any element of mutual trust and confidence beyond that to which ordinary contractual principles might give rise.

28.215 Similarly, in *Draper v Official Trustee in Bankruptcy* a wife's payment of all the mortgage instalments on a property did not give rise to a constructive trust. The husband and wife had bought the property the day before the husband was declared bankrupt. The effect of the sequestration order was to sever the joint tenancy and place one-half of the title in the trustee's hands. When the property was sold the trustee claimed the half-share, even though all the instalments had been paid by the wife. The Full Court of the Federal Court found that, absent an agreement, the payment of mortgage debt did not automatically give rise to a constructive trust. In any event, the woman's contribution could be taken into account by alternative means, namely an equitable accounting between co-owners.

28.216 The existence of a joint endeavour is not limited to domestic property relationships. Assets acquired by business partners can also be held on constructive trust as long as there has been a pooling of assets as part of a joint endeavour and the retention of the legal title proves unconscionable: *Carson v Wood* (1994) 34 NSWLR 9. However, a valid commercial contract dealing with ownership of property will ordinarily prevent any claim for a constructive trust: *Clancy v Salienta Pty Ltd* [2000] NSWCA 248.

Termination without attributable blame

28.217 'Attributable blame' is a essential element of relief: *Raulfs v Fishy Bite Pty Ltd* [2012] NSWCA 135 at [73]; *Tasevska v Tasevski* [2011] NSWSC 174 at [71]–[79]; *Quinn v Bryant* [2011] NSWSC 1153 at [95]; *Palinkas v Palinkas* [2009] NSWSC 92; *Taylor v Streicher* [2007] NSWSC 1006 In *Kriezis v Kriezis* [2004] NSWSC 167 at [22]–[23], Burchett AJ said:

> Where an interest in property is put in the name of one party on the basis and for the purposes of a relationship with another party, who pays for that interest in property, and the substratum of the relationship is removed without attributable blame, so that unless equity intervenes, the former party would enjoy the benefit of the property in circumstances in which it was not specifically intended or specially provided he or she should enjoy it, the Court may hold that for him or her to do so would be unconscientious ... An interesting application of the same principle was made by Bryson J in *Bennett v Horgan* (unreported, 3 June 1994), where his Honour said:
>
>> The concept of attributable blame must be understood and applied with some tolerance; in my view it does not call for a judgment attributing blame among members of a family for the continuing relationship becoming intolerable, unless perhaps in particularly gross cases ... Leaving gross cases involving criminality or similarly reprehensible behaviour on one side, it should usually be understood, in my opinion, that where personal relationships deteriorate and the sharing of a dwelling becomes intolerable to some or all of those concerned, there is, within the meaning of Deane J's expressions, no attributable blame and the case is one for equitable adjustment.

28.218 The test of 'attributable blame' does not require the court to work out which one of the parties to the relationship was at the greater fault for its demise: *Henderson v Miles (No 2)* at [18].

In *Australian Building and Technical Solutions Pty Ltd v Boumelhem* at [99], White J made the following comment:

> [P]erhaps the answer is that if the joint endeavour comes to an end due to some wrongful conduct of the party seeking the imposition of a constructive trust this might impact on whether it is unconscionable for the other party in those circumstances to retain the benefits of the joint endeavour. In other words, a lack of focus on the 'without attributable blame' part of the *Muschinski* formulation of the test may be explicable if it is bound up in the question of unconscionability.

28.219   Examples of cases where the relationship ended without attributable blame include *Kriezis v Kriezis* (where the relationship between the mother and daughter had irretrievably broken down), *Cetojevic v Cetojevic* [2007] NSWCA 33 (where the joint endeavour was terminated due to the death of the plaintiff's son by drowning) and *Australian Building and Technical Solutions Pty Ltd v Boumelhem* (where the son declared bankruptcy).

Unconscionability/unconscientiousness

28.220   The final requirement for the imposition of a constructive trust is that one party must unconscientiously retain the benefit of contributions and deny the interests of the other party: *Drayson v Drayson* [2011] NSWSC 965 at [77]. In *Sivritas v Sivritas* (2008) 23 VR 349 at 374, Kyrou J said:

> In determining the scope of any *Muschinski v Dodds* constructive trust, a court can take into account direct financial contributions to the purchase price of the property and incidental costs such as stamp duty, registration fees, solicitors' fees and bank fees. However, a court is not limited to such expenditure. It can also take into account the pooling of financial resources, other financial contributions even in the absence of pooling, contributions of labour, and non-financial contributions or contributions in kind such as homemaking and parenting contributions. Further, the inquiry into whether the assertion by a party of his or her legal rights would be unconscionable can encompass events that occurred after the property was initially acquired. Expenditure on repairs and renovations of the property by a person asserting a constructive trust in respect of the property, where the expenditure is accepted by the legal owner of the property in the knowledge that it would improve the home and add to its value, can be considered as a contribution in quantifying the first person's equitable interest under the constructive trust.

28.221   Obviously, if claimants have made financial contributions as part of the joint endeavour, it is much easier for them to prove unconscientiousness when those interests are denied. Evidence of the pooling of financial resources will support such claims (*Hibberson v George* (1989) 12 Fam LR 725) but other valuable contributions, such as the provision of labour in renovations, will also support a claim: *Miller v Sutherland* (1989) 14 Fam LR 416. In *Saliba v Tarmo* [2009] NSWSC 581, the care and support provided by the claimants to the deceased was found to support a claim because the care and support was given on the basis that the deceased would grant them a half-interest in her home. On the other hand, in *Swettenham v Wild* [2005] QCA 264, the failure of a daughter to care for her father after he had purchased a property for them to live in and then transferred it into her name, was also found to be unconscionable. The parties had an agreement that the father would be cared for and when that no longer became possible due to the breakdown in their relationship, it was unconscionable for the daughter to retain the legal title.

28.222   If it is clear that the relationship is not a committed one and that one partner is free to leave at any time with any property acquired during the relationship, it will be hard to show unconscientiousness in the property interests lying where they fall when the relationship ends: *West v Mead* at [64]. It will also be difficult to prove unconscientiousness in cases where the joint endeavour took the form of a contract which spelt out how the assets were to be divided when the relationship broke down. In such cases it will not be unconscientious to act in accordance with the agreement. In *Raulfs v Fishy Bite Pty Ltd* at [83], it was not unconscientious for money that had been paid by one partner to the partnership to be retained and distributed according to the terms of the partnership dealing with termination.

Non-financial contributions and unconscionability/ unconscientiousness

28.223 While non-financial contributions must be considered in the assessment of unconscientiousness, difficulties have arisen in the value attributed to such contributions. For a constructive trust to arise, it must be shown that the claimant's financial or non-financial contribution actually helped to acquire or improve the property the subject of the alleged trust: *Brown v George* [1999] FCA 285. In that sense there must be more than the mere provision of love, care and support in a relationship: *Lloyd v Tedesco* (2002) 25 WALR 360 at [30]; *DPP v Mattiuzzo* [2011] NTSC 60 at [50]. This is especially difficult to prove with non-financial contributions where the benefits to the acquisition of assets are indirect.

28.224 This is illustrated by *Bryson v Bryant* (1992) 29 NSWLR 188, where a couple, who had been married for 60 years, died within a few months of each other. The wife predeceased the husband. The husband had legal title to the matrimonial home and had left the house to charity. The couple had no children and the sole beneficiary of the wife's estate brought a claim on the estate's behalf. It was claimed that an equitable half-share was held by the husband on constructive trust for the wife. It was also claimed that the retention of benefit by the husband's estate was unconscientious because the wife had laboured on the house and had been the sole breadwinner during the Depression. The trial judge dismissed the claim on the basis that the evidence indicated that the wife's labour was given for love and affection and not with the purpose of establishing an equitable interest in the house. A majority of the Court of Appeal (Sheller and Samuels JJA) found that it was not unconscientious for the husband's estate to retain the legal estate. Sheller JA, at 222, would have been willing to grant the wife a life interest on constructive trust had she survived her husband. As she had not done so there was nothing unconscientious in the husband taking the entirety of the house after her death. Samuels JA, at 231, agreed with the trial judge that the wife's duties were performed out of love and affection. More-over, the contributions she made as a homemaker could not be shown to have contributed to the acquisition or improvement of the property.

28.225 Kirby P dissented. His Honour, at 201, found that there was no reason for regarding the contribution of the homemaker as inferior and that equity should approach such contributions in a similar way to the legislative schemes that recognise domestic contributions. According to Kirby P, at 204, it was unconscientious that the husband's will should operate to the exclusion of the wife's wishes, given that she had made valuable contributions to the property.

28.226 It has been argued by Bailey-Harris that *Bryson v Bryant* proves equity's inability to fully recognise non-financial contributions made by homemakers.[23] However, later cases have gone

---

23. R Bailey-Harris, 'Property Disputes in De Facto Relationships: Can Equity Still Play a Role?' in M Cope (ed), *Equity: Issues and Trends*, Federation Press, Sydney, 1996, p 197.

further to fully recognise domestic contributions. In *Turner v Dunne* it was held that non-financial contributions of homemaking and parenting should be accounted for, otherwise parties who paid for homemaking services out of their own pockets would receive equitable aid, whereas parties who chose to do such tasks themselves would be left without a remedy.

Denial by third parties?

28.227   As in the case of common intention constructive trusts, it is not necessary for the party with legal title to have actually denied the interests of the other, for the constructive beneficiary to have an interest. As explained in *Australian Building and Technical Solutions Pty Ltd v Boumelhem* at [107], where Ward J said:

> The test of unconscionability must, at least in circumstances such as this, be framed by reference not simply to whether it is unconscionable for the other party to the relationship to deny the claimed benefits but by reference to whether, had that party been in a position to do so, it would have been unconscionable for it to deny the benefits.

This was doubted in *DPP v Ali (No 2)* [2010] VSC 503 at [86], but in that case the acquisition and ownership of the family home was not the result of any joint endeavour or undertaking in any case.

28.228   This effectively allows constructive beneficiaries to pursue their interests when the denial comes from a third party to the relationship, such as a creditor or trustee in bankruptcy. In *Young v Lalic*, a payment of $50,000 by the plaintiff to her future mother-in-law for contribution to the construction costs of a home that she, her husband and mother-in-law would reside in, was not returned by the mother-in-law after the marriage broke down. Brereton J found that the mother-in- law's denial gave rise to a 'windfall equity' that was unconscionable for her to retain.

Remuneration

28.229   The retention of benefits by one party of a relationship will not be unconscionable if the other party has been given remuneration for their non-financial contributions. In *Engwirda v Engwirda* [2000] QCA 61, a de facto wife claimed an equitable share in her husband's substantial business assets, which were largely acquired before the commencement of the relationship. The claim was dismissed on the grounds that there was no joint endeavour between the parties and that the de facto wife had been paid at commercial rates for any services she provided to the business.

28.230   Alternatively, it will not be unconscientious to deny an interest in circumstances where the claimant was given other forms of consideration in exchange for their contributions. In *Hill v Hill* [2005] NSWSC 863, Campbell J refused to find unconscientiousness in circumstances where a son had contributed improvements to his mother's property, but she had, in turn, allowed the son and his family to live there for 12 years, as well as guaranteed his business debts.

The effect of the Torrens system on unconscionability/ unconscientiousness-based constructive trusts

28.231   As *Muschinski v Dodds* makes clear, constructive trusts can arise over land, including Torrens land. The concept of indefeasibility is discussed at 7.75. The *Muschinski v Dodds* constructive trust ordinarily takes the form of an *in personam* exception to indefeasibility: see 7.88. In *Greffeld v Greffeld* [2012] FamCAFC 71, it was argued that the indefeasibility provisions prevented a claim for a constructive trust which was made by the sister of the husband, for moneys that the husband had wrongfully withdrawn from the sister's German bank account. The husband had taken the money and spent them in the purchase of land that was registered solely in the wife's name. The wife claimed that her registered and indefeasible interest was protected against the sister's claim. The Full Court of the Family Court rejected this argument and found that the sister's claim for a constructive trust was an *in personam* exception to the wife's indefeasibility. The husband had, by expending his sister's money, been acting as his wife's agent in the purchase. As such, the husband's knowledge of where the money had originated was imputed to the wife and she was caught by the personal equity that arose.

LEGISLATION AND CONSTRUCTIVE TRUSTS IN THE FAMILY CONTEXT

28.232   Most jurisdictions in Australia have legislated to grant courts powers to resolve disputes in the breakdown of marriage and de facto relationships, without the need for reliance on constructive trusts.

Breakdown of marriage and de facto relationships

28.233   Section 79 of the *Family Law Act 1975* (Cth) provides that the court may make orders for the settlement of property on the breakdown of marriage. Section 79(4) requires that the court take into account, among other things:

> (a) the financial contribution made directly or indirectly by or on behalf of a party to the marriage or a child of the marriage to the acquisition, conservation or improvement of any of the property of the parties to the marriage or either of them, or otherwise in relation to any of that last-mentioned property, whether or not that last-mentioned property has, since the making of the contribution, ceased to be the property of the parties to the marriage or either of them;

> (b) the contribution (other than a financial contribution) made directly or indirectly by or on behalf of a party to the marriage or a child of the marriage to the acquisition, conservation or improvement of any of the property of the parties to the marriage or either of them, or otherwise in relation to any of that last-mentioned property, whether or not that last-mentioned property has, since the making of the contribution, ceased to be the property of the parties to the marriage or either of them;

> (c) the contribution made by a party to the marriage to the welfare of the family constituted by the parties to the marriage and any children of the marriage, including any contribution made in the capacity of homemaker or parent;

> (d) the effect of any proposed order upon the earning capacity of either party to the marriage.

28.234   Traditionally all states and territories had their own legislation dealing with the resolution of property disputes between de facto partners.[24] The legislation generally gave the court power to make orders for the division of property between the partners. The court must consider a similar range of factors as those identified under the *Family Law Act 1975* (Cth). However, in 2008 the *Family Law Act 1975* (Cth) was amended to bring de facto relationships within its ambit.[25] The new

---

24. *Domestic Relationships Act 1994* (ACT); *Property (Relationships) Act 1984* (NSW); *De Facto Relation-ships Act 1991* (NT); *Property Law Act 1974* (Qld) Pt 19; *Domestic Partners Property Act 1996* (SA); *Relationships Act 2003* (Tas); *Relationships Act 2008* (Vic); *Family Court Act 1997* (WA) Pt 5A.
25. *Family Law Amendment (De Facto Financial Matters & Other Measures) Act 2008* (Cth).

scheme applies to de facto relationships that break down after 1 March 2009, although it is possible for parties to a relationship which broke down before that time to both opt into the scheme: s 86A. It is an exclusive jurisdiction that prevents proceedings from being initiated unless they are brought under the *Family Law Act*: s 39A(5). All state and territories have joined the scheme apart from Western Australia which has kept its own state-based court to administer family law.

28.235   The amendments mean that the laws with regards to relationship breakdown that previously applied to married couples now apply to de facto partners including provisions concerning property settlements, spousal maintenance, superannuation splitting, financial agreements and bankruptcy.[26] The definition of a 'de facto relationship' in s 4AA is as follows:

(1) a person is in a de facto relationship with another person if:

(a) the persons are not legally married to each other; and

(b) the persons are not related by family; and having regard to all the circumstances of their relationship, they have a relationship as a couple living together on a genuine domestic basis.

It encompasses both opposite sex and same sex de facto relationships: s 4AA(5). The section also provides a list of factors that may indicate that a person is in a de facto relationship, which are:

(a) the duration of the relationship;

(b) the nature and extent of their common residence;

(c) whether a sexual relationship exists;

(d) the degree of financial dependence or interdependence, and any arrangements for financial support, between them;

(e) the ownership, use and acquisition of their property;

(f) the degree of mutual commitment to a shared life;

(g) whether the relationship is or was registered under a prescribed law of a State or Territory as a prescribed kind of relationship;

(h) the care and support of children;

(i) the reputation and public aspects of the relationship.

28.236   In addition to being in a de facto relationship, it is necessary for the couple to satisfy 'gateway' provisions before they can commence proceedings set out as follows in s 90SB:

(a) that the period, or the total of the periods, of the de facto relationship is at least 2 years; or
(b) that there is a child of the de facto relationship; or
(c) that:
  (i) the party to the de facto relationship who applies for the order or declaration made substantial contributions of a kind mentioned in paragraph 90SM(4)(a), (b) or (c); and

---

26.   D Kovacs, 'A federal law of de facto property rights: The dream and the reality' (2009) 23 *Australian Journal of Family Law* 104.

(ii) a failure to make the order or declaration would result in serious injustice to the applicant; or

(d) that the relationship is or was registered under a prescribed law of a State or Territory.

Relationships which are not de facto relationships but which were regulated by the state and territory schemes will remain controlled by those schemes.[27]

28.237 The Australian Capital Territory, New South Wales, South Australia And Tasmania Have Also Expanded Their Legislative Regimes To Include Claims Made By Parties In 'Domestic Relationships' (In The Australian Capital Territory And New South Wales), 'Close Personal Relationships' (In South Australia) And 'Personal Relationships' (In Tasmania).[28] These Terms Cover Relationships Existing Between Adults, Whether Or Not Related By Family, Who Are Living Together, One Of Whom Provides The Other With Domestic Support And Personal Care Without Remuneration.[29] In Victoria, The One Definition Of 'Domestic Relationship' Covers Both The Traditional De Facto Relationships And These Relationships Of Care And Support.[30]

The remaining importance of equity

28.238 The legislative regimes at the federal, state and territory levels have largely done away with the necessity of framing claims for domestic assets within equity.

28.239 However, equity remains important. This is for four reasons. First, the legislative regimes do not cover all relationships. Most jurisdictions require cohabitation for a minimum period (normally two years) before a claim can be made under the legislation: see, for example, *Property (Relationships) Act 1984* (NSW) s 17(1). Second, most jurisdictions expressly preserve the rights of the parties to bring traditional equitable claims.[31] However, it should be noted that Western Australia has removed equitable jurisdiction over de facto disputes.[32] Third, equitable claims may be able to be brought after the expiry of the limitation period for claims under the statutory schemes: *Cooper v Lees* [2009] SASC 386. Fourth, equity has not been displaced in cases where a claim is made by a third party against the parties to a domestic relationship. For example, in bankruptcy, claims by domestic partners to the beneficial ownership of family assets must be proven in equity before they can take their place in the priority disputes between creditors. Admittedly, the *Bankruptcy and Family Law Legislation Amendment Act 2005* (Cth) has changed this to some extent by granting the Family Court power to sequestrate the property of parties to Family Court proceedings, even where that may affect the interests of creditors.

28.240 Nor has equity been discarded when claims are made against the assets of a deceased estate. If, however, a relationship has broken down before the death of a party and an application has been made to the Family Court prior to the death of one party, the court retains jurisdiction to finalise the proceedings: s 90SM(8).

---

27. G Watts, 'The de facto relationships legislation' (2009) 23 *Australian Journal of Family Law* 122.
28. *Domestic Relationships Act 1994* (ACT) s 3; *Property (Relationships) Act 1984* (NSW) s 5; *Domestic Partners Property Act 1996* (SA) s 3; *Relationships Act 2003* (Tas) s 6.
29. *Domestic Relationships Act 1994* (ACT) s 3; *Property (Relationships) Act 1984* (NSW) s 5; *Domestic Partners Property Act 1996* (SA) s 3; *Relationships Act 2003* (Tas) s 5.
30. *Relationships Act 2008* (Vic) s 35.
31. *Domestic Relationships Act 1994* (ACT) s 5; *Property (Relationships) Act 1984* (NSW) s 7; *De Facto Relationships Act 1991* (NT) s 52; *De Facto Relationships Act 1996* (SA) s 16; *Relationships Act 2003* (Tas) s 9; *Property Law Act 1958* (Vic) s 277.
32. *Family Law Act 1997* (WA) s 205V.

29

TRACING

INTRODUCTION

29.1   Beneficiaries have a right to pursue trust property that has been wrongfully taken by trustees or placed in the hands of third parties.[1] This proprietary right is given shape under the doctrine of tracing. Tracing allows beneficiaries to pursue their equitable rights to trust property through the hands that receive it, as well as into the new property that may have been created from or mixed with the trust property.

29.2   The advantage that tracing has over the personal remedies against the trustee lies in its proprietary form. Personal remedies will be of little value if the trustee is insolvent because any judgment must be satisfied out of the insolvent estate (which may or may not have enough money to satisfy the personal claim). A tracing claim will allow beneficiaries to reclaim trust property and, at the same time, keep it immune from the claims of other creditors in the insolvency.

COMMON LAW AND EQUITABLE TRACING

29.3   Tracing is available as a remedy in common law as well as in equity: *Commonwealth Bank of Australia v Saleh* [2007] NSWSC 903 at [22]. Common law tracing differs from equitable tracing in that equity recognises that a beneficiary retains his or her property rights over trust property in cases where the trust property is mixed with other property or converted into a new type of property: *Brady v Stapleton* (1952) 88 CLR 322. At common law, once a mixture or conversion takes place, the property rights of the plaintiff end and only a right to damages remains: *Puma Australia Pty Ltd v Sportsman's Australia Ltd* [1994] 2 Qd R 159.

29.4   While it is commonplace to refer to tracing as a remedy or claim, it is better described as an evidential 'process': *Re Magarey Farlam Lawyers Trust Accounts (No 3)* (2007) 96 SASR 337 at 371; *Re Global Finance Group Pty Ltd (in liq)* (2002) 26 WAR 385 at 406; *Boscawen v Bajwa* [1995] 4 All ER 769. In *Foskett v McKeown* [2001] 1 AC 102 at 128; [2000] 3 All ER 97 at 120–1, Lord Millett said:

> Tracing is thus neither a claim nor a remedy. It is merely the process by which a claimant demonstrates what has happened to his property, identifies its proceeds and the persons who have handled or received them, and justifies his claim that the proceeds can properly be regarded as representing his property. Tracing is also distinct from claiming. It identifies the traceable proceeds of the claimant's property. It enables the claimant to substitute the traceable proceeds

---

1.   M Christie, 'Tracing' in P Parkinson (ed), *The Principles of Equity*, 2nd ed, Lawbook Co, Sydney, 2003.

for the original asset as the subject matter of his claim. But it does not affect or establish his claim
… The successful completion of a tracing exercise may be preliminary to a personal claim (as in
El Ajou v Dollar Land Holdings [1993] 3 All ER 717) or a proprietary one, to the enforcement of
a legal right (as in *Trustees of the Property of FC Jones & Sons v Jones* [1996] 4 All ER 721; [1997]
Ch 159) or an equitable one.

29.5   The differences between common law and equitable tracing have been down-played: *Trustee
of the Property of FC Jones & Sons (a firm) v Jones* [1997] Ch 159 at 169–70; [1996] 4 All ER 721
at 729. In *Foskett v McKeown*, both Lord Millett and Lord Steyn believed that there was no real
difference between common law and equitable tracing as both were rules of evidence that helped
to identify assets but that said nothing about common law or equitable rights to those assets. These
comments have been favourably cited in Australia: *Heperu Pty Ltd v Belle* (2009) 76 NSWLR 230
at 252; 258 ALR 727 at 749; *Re Magarey Farlam Lawyers Trust Accounts (No 3)* at 371; *Evans v European
Bank Ltd* (2004) 61 NSWLR 75 (appealed on other grounds in *European Bank Ltd v Robb Evans of
Robb Evans & Associates* (2010) 240 CLR 432; (2010) 264 ALR 1).

29.6   Because tracing is an evidential process, judges are free to assess the evidence and make
reasonable inferences based on common sense. In *Toksoz v Westpac Banking Corporation* [2012]
NSWCA 199 at [9], Allsop ACJ, in relation to tracing stolen funds, said:

> Where the facts as proved are sufficient to permit the inference that moneys have been received
> or property bought without there being an honest source available to explain the wealth and the
> sums or value can be seen as referable to the following party's property wrongfully obtained, such
> that the inference is open that the wrongfully obtained funds were the source of the wealth, the
> funds can be so treated. One does not need to be able to show every link in the chain of accounts
> from and through which the money passed. Inferences will be more easily drawn, as here, in
> circumstances where the funds were stolen, the person who is said to have provided the funds was
> one of the thieves who stole money from the follower, when the recipient has an apparent close
> relationship with the thief, which recipient gave no value for it, has no personal source of income
> and gives no explanation as to the source or circumstances of the receipt of the money or any
> honest source of it.

SOURCE OF THE JURISDICTION TO TRACE — FIDUCIARY DUTY

29.7   The existence of a prior fiduciary relationship is an essential prerequisite to a claim of tracing
in equity: *Agip (Africa) Ltd v Jackson* [1991] Ch 547 at 566; [1992] 4 All ER 451 at 466; *Sinclair
v Brougham* [1914] AC 398. This is because the remedy of tracing comes from equity's exclusive
jurisdiction to deal with purely equitable claims, rather than from the auxiliary jurisdiction where
equity comes to the aid of common law rights: see 2.9–2.11.

29.8   The effect of grounding tracing in the exclusive jurisdiction is to substantially limit its
availability. Many commentators have been critical of this view of tracing's origins because, in the
absence of a prior fiduciary relationship, any person whose property is stolen by a thief will be
unable to trace that property in common law or equity, if the thief mixes the property.[2] Moreover,
courts are tempted to expand the definition of fiduciary relationships to avoid the injustice that
might arise in such a situation. This can cause significant damage to the doctrinal clarity of fiduciary

---

2.   G E Dal Pont, *Equity and Trusts in Australia*, 5th ed, Lawbook Co, Sydney, 2011, p 1024.

relationships.[3] The better approach would be to remove the prerequisite of fiduciary duty and allow tracing to stem from the auxiliary, as well as the exclusive, jurisdiction of equity.

29.9 In *Foskett v McKeown* both Lord Millett and Lord Steyn were critical of the necessity for a fiduciary relationship to exist as a precondition to tracing, but their comments fell short of removing the requirement. In *Shalson v Russo* [2005] Ch 281, Rimer J stated that even after *Foskett* the traditional differences between common law and equity remain and the requirement for a pre-existing fiduciary relationship still existed.

29.10 In Australia there appears to be more movement towards jettisoning the requirement. In *Commonwealth Bank of Australia v Saleh* at [29], Einstein J said that 'the better view' was that tracing protects property rights, rather than enforcing fiduciary relationships.

29.11 To that extent, it would appear that the trend of authority is away from requiring a fiduciary duty. It may also be that the developments of other equitable remedies, like constructive trusts based on unconscientiousness, may outflank the limited use of tracing, if it continues to be based on the requirement of a pre-existing fiduciary relationship.[4]

The need for property

29.12 In addition to the requirement that there be a pre-existing fiduciary duty between the parties, a claimant seeking to trace trust property must also establish that he or she had an equitable interest in the property prior to the breach of fiduciary duty and that the property now lies in the hands of the defendant. To that extent it is necessary to ascertain the trust property and identify it as being held by the defendant. In equity it does not matter, for the purpose of identification, that the property has become mixed with other property: *Re Hallett's Estate; Knatchbull v Hallett* (1880) 13 Ch D 696. Nor does it matter that trust funds have been used to purchase other property. Equity presumes that the trust property continues to exist in both situations: *Re Diplock* [1948] Ch 465 at 531–2; [1948] 2 All ER 318 at 352–3.

29.13 However, if the property has been dissipated or destroyed, the right to trace ceases. In *Raulfs v Fishy Bite Pty Ltd* [2012] NSWCA 135, Raulfs entered into a partnership agreement with Fishy Bite Pty Ltd (Fishy Bite). Fishy Bite was owned and controlled by Ajaka. Raulfs paid $400,000 as a contribution to the capital of the partnership. Ajaka withdrew the money and used it to pay out a mortgage over a house he owned with his de facto partner, Ablett. The commercial partnership broke down quickly and consent orders were entered for a winding up. Around the same time, Ajaka and Ablett's relationship broke down and they entered into a termination agreement in accordance with Part 4 of the *Property (Relationships) Act 1984* (NSW). Ablett became the sole registered owner of the house. Raulfs claimed that she could trace her partnership contribution into the house and sought to secure her rights by way of a charge over the house.

29.14 The New South Wales Court of Appeal found that Raulfs could not trace the proceeds. When the money was paid to the partnership it became a partnership asset and it was no longer

---

3. J D Heydon & M J Leeming, *Jacobs' Law of Trusts in Australia*, LexisNexis Butterworths, Sydney, 2006, pp 670–71.

4. D Murr, 'Recovering lost assets: Tracing at common law and in equity' (2006) 27 *Australian Bar Review* 174 at 186.

hers. Raulfs had no claim over the money once the money was paid and, as such, she had no property to trace.

29.15   The most common example of dissipation is when trust funds are placed in another account and that account is exhausted or overdrawn. In such a case, equity treats the trust property as being dissipated: *Bishopsgate Investment Management Ltd (in liq) v Homan* [1995] Ch 211; [1995] 1 All ER 347; *Viscariello v Bernsteen Pty Ltd (in liq)* [2004] SASC 266. In *Chong v Chanell* [2009] NSWSC 765, large sums of money held on trust had been gambled away leaving nothing to trace into (although fortunately for the plaintiff some of the moneys could be traced into a house).

29.16   Similarly, payment into an overdraft account will also destroy the possibility for tracing, as an overdraft account is a debit account: *Re Rowena Nominees Pty Ltd* [2006] WASC 69; *Grocers of Wyong v Retech Global* [2004] NSWSC 488; *Re Goldcorp Exchange Ltd* [1995] 1 AC 74; [1994] 2 All ER 806. For example, in *Williams v Peters* [2010] 1 Qd R 475, a purchaser of a luxury car was unable to trace the purchase moneys as they had been deposited in an overdraft account (in addition to there being no intention for the moneys to be held on trust).

29.17   Further deposits into the account will not automatically be treated as restorations of trust funds: *James Roscoe (Bolton) Ltd v Winder* [1915] 1 Ch 62 at 67–9; *Taylor v London & County Banking Co* [1901] 2 Ch 231; *Re Grey (No 2)* (1900) 26 VLR 529. In *Re Global Finance Group Pty Ltd (in liq)* at 408, McLure J found that subsequent deposits by a trustee into a mixed fund will be impressed with the trusts in favour of the beneficiaries if the trustee intended to make restitution to the trust by appropriating the funds to the replacement of the trust moneys. In *Australian Receivables Ltd v Tekitu Pty Ltd* [2011] NSWSC 1306 at [154], Ward J agreed and said:

> Insofar as the allocation of withdrawals and treatment of payments out of a mixed account of this kind is based on a presumption as to the trustee's intention, an actual intention by the trustee (or the third party) to treat moneys subsequently paid in as replenishing the trust fund would permit the conclusion that the trust connection was not lost.

Backward tracing

29.18   There is some authority to suggest that the rule against tracing into an overdraft is not absolute. One possible exception is 'backward tracing' where the moneys placed into an overdraft are used to reduce the overdraft so that further funds can be withdrawn to purchase an asset. In backward tracing the beneficiaries claim the ownership of the asset purchase with the reduction in overdraft. In *Hagan v Waterhouse* (1992) 34 NSWLR 308 at 358, Kearney J said:

> Just as it is no answer to a beneficiary's claim to an investment acquired with moneys drawn from a mixed current account in credit to say that the trustee's own moneys in the mixture could have sufficed to effect the purchase, so it is no answer in the case of such a purchase from an overdrawn account for the trustee to rely upon the extensive nature of his overdraft arrangements.

29.19   In *Bishopsgate Investment Management Ltd (in liq) v Homan* [1995] Ch 211 at 216–7; [1995] 1 All ER 347 at 351, Dillon LJ, when referring with approval to the trial judge's suggestion, said:

> The judge gave as an instance of such a case what he called 'backward tracing' — where an asset was acquired by [the defendant] with moneys borrowed from an overdrawn or loan account and

there was an inference that when the borrowing was incurred it was the intention that it should be repaid by misappropriations of [the plaintiff's] moneys. Another possibility was that moneys misappropriated from [the plaintiff] were paid into an overdrawn account of [the defendant] in order to reduce the overdraft and so make finance available within the overdraft limits for [the defendant] to purchase some particular asset.

29.20   In *Shalson v Russo* at 328, Rimer J expressed his agreement with Dillon LJ's observations in *Bishopsgate Investment Management Ltd v Homan* but could not find evidence to support the contention that the overdraft had been reduced to purchase and assets. In *Conlan v Connolly* [2011] WASC 160 at [80], Simmonds J found similarly, agreeing that the exception was available but finding that there was insufficient evidence to support the claim.

TRACING INTO PROPERTY IN THE HANDS OF TRUSTEES

29.21   The essence of trust law is that trustees are not entitled to enjoy trust property for their own purposes. If trustees misappropriate trust property and use it exclusively to purchase other property in their own name, equity allows the beneficiaries to trace the funds into the newly acquired property: *Fibre-Tek (Gold Coast) v Bennett* [2006] NSWSC 150; *Re Lovett* [1966] VR 65; *Frith v Cartland* (1865) 71 ER 525 at 526. For example, in *Lake v Bayliss* [1974] 1 All ER 1114, a trustee sold trust property and bought a ring with the proceeds. The ring was then given to a friend who sold it and banked the proceeds into a savings account. The beneficiary was entitled to trace the trust property into the proceeds, then the ring and then into the savings account. The beneficiaries can choose to enforce their beneficial interests in the new property by either asserting beneficial ownership of it, or by bringing a personal claim against the trustee for breach of trust. This claim can be enforced by an equitable lien or charge over the new property: *Foskett v McKeown* AC at 109; All ER at 122; *Chong v Chanell* at [39]; *Dennis Hanger Pty Ltd v Brown* [2007] VSC 495 at [36]. If beneficiaries choose the former option, and the newly acquired property has appreciated, they are entitled to keep the gain for themselves, as the trustee is not entitled to retain any profit from a breach of trust.

Mixed property — the rule in Re Hallett's Estate

29.22   Different approaches are taken where the newly acquired property has been purchased with a mixture of trust funds and the trustee's own funds. The first approach is known as the rule in *Re Hallett's Estate; Knatchbull v Hallett*. In this case, a solicitor-trustee sold trust property and mixed the funds from the sale with his own money in a bank account. The solicitor later died insolvent and a dispute arose between the beneficiaries and other creditors of the estate over who was entitled to the funds remaining in the account. Sir George Jessel MR found that the beneficiaries had a right to trace the proceeds of sale into the remaining account funds. Equity presumes in such circumstances that, once funds are mixed in an account, any following transactions come from the trustee's personal funds first. Any funds remaining in the account are treated as trust funds.

29.23   The rule in *Re Hallett's Estate* applies not only to money but to the mixing of other property as well. In *Brady v Stapleton* (1952) 88 CLR 322 at 337–8, the High Court said:

> [I]t would be a great mistake to suppose that the great case of *Re Hallett's Estate* … lays down a doctrine peculiar to money. On the contrary, it extends to money paid into a bank account, and so losing its identity as money, a doctrine which equity would never have had the slightest hesitation

in applying to money physically existing or to any other kind of personal property to which it could, as a matter of practical possibility, be applied. And there is no difficulty, and we do not think that equity would ever have had the least difficulty, in applying the same doctrine to shares or bonds ... Equities are not defeated if a trustee mixes trust moneys with his own moneys and with the mixture purchases a grey horse and a black horse, or a grey horse alone. In such a case equity imposes a charge on the two horses or the one horse. But, where it is possible to give effect to the rights of a *cestui que trust* by simply taking out so much money or so many bonds or so many shares, the *cestui que trust* may elect whether he will take property *in specie* out of the mass or have a charge on the mass.

The lowest intermediate balance rule

29.24   The lowest intermediate balance rule states that the beneficiaries' claim is limited to the lowest account balance in the period starting from the date of mixture to the date of the claim against the account. After *Re Hallett's Estate*, questions arose as to how to calculate beneficial proprietary interests in cases where deposits and withdrawals are made over time to accounts of mixed funds. In *James Roscoe (Bolton) Ltd v Winder*, a debt collector deposited over £400 of his clients' money into his own account. Over a period of time a number of withdrawals and deposits were made. The lowest balance recorded during the period was £25. At the time of the claim there was over £300 in the account. The beneficiaries sought to employ the rule in *Re Hallett's Estate* to claim the remaining funds. However, the court found it could not presume that the deposits made after the mixture were intended by the fiduciary to reimburse the trust. The only available balance was the lowest balance in the intermediate period between the breach of fiduciary duty and the claim, that being £25.

Tracing valuable purchases from a mixed fund

29.25   An exception to the rule in *Re Hallett's Estate* applies when the fiduciary makes a purchase of valuable property from the mixed fund and then proceeds to dissipate the rest of the account. In such circumstances the fiduciary is not entitled to use the rule in *Re Hallett's Estate* to prevent tracing into the valuable property. In *Re Oatway* [1903] 2 Ch 356, a trustee misappropriated trust funds by placing them in his account and then proceeded to use two-thirds of the money to buy shares. The rest of the account was then dissipated. The court found that the trust property should be traced into the shares, overturning the presumption in *Re Hallett's Estate* that transactions come from the trustee's personal funds first. In *Young v Lalic* [2006] NSWSC 18, a woman gave $50,000 to her fiancé and future mother-in-law to contribute towards the costs of construction of a new house on the mother-in-law's land. The money was expended but the marriage later broke down. The husband and mother-in-law refused to pay back the $50,000. Brereton J allowed the woman to trace the funds into the land and granted her a charge over the land worth $50,000. In *Shepard v Mladenis* [2011] NSWSC 1431, a Dr Wallman, a recently divorced obstetrician and gynaecologist was defrauded by an introduction agency, called Hearts United. Wallman paid $200,000 for personal relationships counseling. Hearts United arranged for Wallman to be introduced to 'Lily', who was described as being Australian/Chinese with blonde hair with a surname 'Bolivique'. She may or not have been a fictitious person. Hearts United convinced Wallman to pay large sums of money to enable him to marry Lily. Lily then requested larger sums ($200,000) that she could borrow from Wallman to help her organise the release of her father's estate in Croatia. Further amounts were requested which totaled two million dollars. All the moneys were paid to Hearts United. Mladenis, the director and owner of Hearts United used the funds to purchase a number of items including real estate, a Porsche, a Lexus, a BMW, and a Lamborghini. Pembroke J found that the money was held on a Quistclose trust and that the funds could be traced to the purchases.

29.26   It should be noted that, once funds have been traced into the newly acquired property, the beneficiaries cannot elect to take total beneficial ownership of the property (like they may when property is purchased solely with trust funds). Instead, the beneficiaries can only assert a lien or charge over the property, which is equal to the value of the trust moneys. The reasoning behind this limitation is that the property was not solely purchased using trust moneys. In *The Uniting Church in Australia Property Trust (NSW) v Vincent* [2009] NSWSC 375 at [9], Einstein J summarised the position as follows:

> Where a trustee acquires property using exclusively trust money, the beneficiary has a proprietary interest in the property acquired, however, where a trustee acquires property using trust money mixed with his own the beneficial owner does not have a proprietary interest in the property because it was not acquired only with trust property. Instead the beneficiary is entitled to a charge over the property to secure the amount of the fiduciary's liability … The charge gives rise to an entitlement to have the property restored to the beneficiary by restitution and arises as soon as the wrongful conversion or mixing occurs (references omitted).

29.27   Some commentators have read down this limitation on the beneficiaries' right of election. For example, Heydon and Leeming state that the decision does not exclude the beneficiaries from electing to take a *proportionate* beneficial share of the property.[5] The beneficiaries are merely prevented from claiming the entirety of the property. This reading of the rule in *Re Hallett's Estate* is supported by later cases in Australia and England: *Scott v Scott* (1963) 109 CLR 649; *In re Tilley's Wills Trust; Burgin v Croad* [1967] Ch 1179; [1967] 2 All ER 303; *Australian Receivables Ltd v Tekitu Pty Ltd* at [146]; *Shepard v Mladenis* at [65]. In *Foskett v McKeown* at AC at 131; All ER at 123–4, Lord Millett confirmed that beneficiaries could elect between claiming proportionate beneficial ownership and asserting a charge or lien:

> Where a trustee wrongfully uses trust money to provide part of the cost of acquiring an asset, the beneficiary is entitled *at his option* either to claim a proportionate share of the asset or to enforce a lien upon it to secure his personal claim against the trustee for the amount of the misapplied money. It does not matter whether the trustee mixed the trust money with his own in a single fund before using it to acquire the asset, or made separate payments (whether simultaneously or sequentially) out of the differently owned funds to acquire a single asset.

The key issue for the beneficiary will be whether the asset has appreciated or depreciated. If the property has increased in value then a proportionate share will be more attractive. If the asset has depreciated a charge is more attractive as its contents are fixed in value.

29.28   It is not clear whether this exception to *Re Hallett's Estate* can be applied where property has been purchased and the account of mixed funds still retains some funds. In *The Uniting Church in Australia Property Trust (NSW) v Vincent* at [9], Einstein J thought that it should and said:

> Where a fund mixed with trust money is used to acquire other property, the beneficiary is entitled to charge both the fund and any property acquired from that fund, *Re Oatway* [1903] 2 Ch 356

---

5.   Heydon & Leeming, *Jacobs' Law of Trusts in Australia*, note 3 above.

at 361; *Sutherland Re; French Caledonia Travel Service Pty Ltd (in liq)* (2003) 59 NSWLR 361 at 386. The charge may be asserted over both the fund and the property to its full value in the sense that the beneficiary must exhaust either first before recouping the full balance out of the other ... The rationale for this is that until the trustee has fulfilled his fiduciary duty to restore the trust property he will not be heard to claim his own interest in the acquired property, *Westpac Banking Corporation v Ollis* [2007] NSWSC 956 at [58].

29.29   Why should the beneficiaries only receive a proportionate amount of any increase? Beneficiaries should be entitled to the entirety of any gain, given that trustees are duty bound to not make unauthorised profits from a trust. This indeed has been the finding in some cases where fiduciaries have made profitable purchases with a mixture of trust funds and bank loans: *Paul A Davies (Australia) Pty Ltd v Davies* [1983] 1 NSWLR 440; *Australian Postal Corp v Lutak* (1991) 21 NSWLR 584. However, the general position outside of this type of case appears to be that only a proportionate share of profit will be made available to beneficiaries and specific evidence has to be led regarding the nature of the contributions made by the defaulting trustees before the proportionate approach is displaced: *Mavaddat v Lee* [2007] WASCA 141.

Mixed property in the hands of trustees from more than one trust

29.30   So far the discussion has concentrated on the mixture of trust property from a single trust with the trustee's property. However, it is not unusual for defaulting trustees to mix funds from more than one trust. In cases where the trust records are clear and exact it may be possible to discern which trust funds have been used in which expenditures. In such a case the losses will be attributed to the specific beneficiaries, and the remaining beneficial interests will be unaffected.

29.31   In *Re Stillman and Wilson* (1956) 15 ABC 68 at 72, Clyne J said:

> I think, though with some hesitation, that where a trustee has the control of a mixed trust fund belonging to a number of beneficiaries and he purports to withdraw from this fund money on behalf of one of the beneficiaries and then uses this money not on behalf of the beneficiary but for his own purposes, the money so withdrawn should be regarded as that of the beneficiary on whose behalf it purported to be withdrawn. The matter depends upon the intention of the trustee.

29.32   In *Re Global Finance Group Pty Ltd (in liq)* at 424, McLure J said that there were three reasons for following the trustee's intention in the case before her:

> First, and most importantly, the trust ledger records are reliable ... Prima facie, they provide a substantially accurate factual foundation for moulding an appropriate solution to the competing proprietary claims. All payments into and out of the trust account can be tracked. Secondly, the trust account records reflect the trustee's contemporaneous intentions. Thirdly, reliance on the record is consistent with the statutory framework in which the trustee is permitted to mix trust funds coupled with a requirement to account separately for the moneys the subject of different trusts.

29.33   Her Honour's approach was adopted in *Re Magarey Farlam Lawyers Trust Accounts (No 3)*. In this case a clerk working for a firm of solicitors stole over four million dollars from one of the firm's trust accounts over 13 years. The accounts were reliable and accurate and it was clear which beneficiaries had lost money. Given the degree of certainty, Debelle J ordered that the funds be distributed as according to their balances. Debelle J, at 373, said:

There are instances where a pro rata distribution is appropriate. I have already mentioned the case where money has been misappropriated from a trust account but not debited against the ledger of any particular client or clients. In that case, there is no other course available. It is also the only available course where records are not available so that it is impossible to identify the money belonging to each person who has contributed to a common or mixed fund. A typical example is an investment scheme where it is impossible to identify the funds of any particular investor with a particular investment ... The pro rata distribution was approved in *Keefe v Law Society of New South Wales* (1998) 44 NSWLR 451 at 461. I do not understand the reasoning in that case to stand in the path of a distribution according to the balances shown in the trust account ledgers in a case where misappropriations have occurred over as long a period as 13 years. In some cases, it is possible to trace the moneys invested to one or more particular investments but it is not possible to do so in the case of most investors. In that instance, the court will attribute an investment to those whose money can be identified with an investment but distribute the balance of the fund remaining pro rata among the remaining investors: see *Australian Securities Commission v Buckley* (19967) 7 BPR 15,024 and *Russell-Cooke Trust Co v Prentis* [2003] 2 All ER 478.... It is clear that the remedy must be tailored to the facts of each individual case. There is no principle of universal application. By contrast with the cases just mentioned, the record-keeping in this case was so complete that the only proper method is to distribute according to those records.

The general approach — pari passu

29.34 In other cases it may not be possible to discern which trust monies have been expended in which transactions. In this situation two rules can be applied to apportion whatever property remains between the different beneficial interests traced into the mixed fund.

29.35 The general rule is that beneficiaries have an interest in a mixed fund proportionate to their contributions to the fund: *Lord Provost of Edinburgh v Lord Advocate* (1879) 4 App Cas 823. For example, if $3000 from Trust A together with $2000 from Trust B were used to purchase 500 shares of equal value, 300 shares would be held in favour of Trust A and 200 shares in favour of Trust B.

29.36 In some cases of mixed funds, there will not be enough funds remaining to satisfy all the beneficial interests being claimed. For example, if $2000 from Trust A were mixed with $1000 from Trust B, but only $1000 was left in the account, the courts would apply $666.67 to Trust A and $333.33 to Trust B. In these situations, there are ordinarily poor accounting records and it is not clear which beneficial interests have been defrauded, so it is generally preferable for the remaining funds to be spread among the beneficiaries on a *pari passu* basis. Similarly, in investment schemes, where it is not possible to identify the funds of particular investors, a proportionate spread of remaining funds will be employed: *Australian Securities and Investments Commission v Nelson* [2003] NSWSC 129; *Australian Securities and Investments Commission v Enterprise Solutions 2000 Pty Ltd* [2001] QSC 82.

29.37 Alternatively, if funds have been taken out of a trust account in breach of trust but only part of those funds taken can be attributed to particular beneficiaries, then the court may attribute that loss to the beneficial interests which can be identified, but then distribute the balance of the remaining funds on a proportionate basis: *Australian Securities Commission v Buckley* (1996) 7 BPR 15,024; *Russell-Cooke Trust Co v Prentis* [2003] 2 All ER 478.

The rule in Clayton's case

29.38   The rule in *Deveynes v Noble: Clayton's case* (1816) 35 ER 781, applies to mixed funds held in bank accounts. It displaces the *pari passu* rule and states that all beneficial interests in a mixed bank account are subject to a 'first in, first out' rule.

29.39   To illustrate with an example, presume that a trustee mixes $1000 from Trust A with $2000 from Trust B and $3000 from Trust C, in successive days, totaling $6000. On the next day the trustee withdraws $2000 from the account, leaving a balance of $4000. Under the rule in *Clayton's case* the withdrawal is presumed to come from Trust A's funds and from Trust B's funds. The remaining funds in the account are therefore said to be traced to Trust B for an amount of $1000, and Trust C for an amount of $3000. The beneficiaries of Trust A will be unable to trace their funds into the account at all, and the beneficiaries of Trust B will only be able to trace half of what was taken from their trust into the mixed account. Of course, should the trustee have purchased assets with the funds, the beneficiaries of Trust A and B will be able to trace their funds into those assets. However, if the funds are merely dissipated, the beneficiaries of Trust A and B will be left only with personal claims for the withdrawn amounts.

29.40   It should be noted that the rule only applies to the bank balance at the end of the day and not to several transactions during one day: *The Mecca* [1897] AC 286; *Micro Minerals Pty Ltd v Grossberg* [1998] FCA 1795.

29.41   The rule in *Clayton's case* is difficult to apply where the facts concern large estates with complex bank accounts. It also works unfairly against the first victims of a breach of trust, by practically eliminating their attempts to trace. The rule has been discarded on occasion in New Zealand because of this reason: *Re Registered Securities* [1991] 1 NZLR 545. In England, judges have not overruled the case but have found ways to readily distinguish it: *Russell-Cooke Trust Co v Prentis* [2003] 2 All ER 478 at 494.

29.42   In Australia, it has been found that if there are large numbers of beneficiaries it is better to apply the *pari passu* rule to prevent injustice: *Re Australian Home Finance Pty Ltd* [1956] VLR 1; *Georges v Seaborn International* (2012) 288 ALR 240 at 262. In *Sutherland Re; French Caledonia Travel* (2003) 59 NSWLR 361 at 368–417, Campbell J reviewed the history of the rule in *Clayton's case* and decided that it should not be applied in Australia. The case concerned a travel agency which had become insolvent and placed under administration and then liquidation. The company had received funds held on trust, but adequate records had not been kept. Claims totaled $1.43 million but the trust account held only $97,000. The only other account was a cash deposit account totaling $75,000. The liquidator sought directions from the court as to how to distribute the funds. In the circumstances, Campbell J found against the application of *Clayton's case* as a matter of principle, regardless of whether there was enough information upon which to allocate withdrawals to particular deposits. Additionally, Campbell J found that the rule was not appropriate to the situation at hand where money was drawn from the account to pay the expenses of particular travellers, regardless of whether that traveller's moneys had been the first in, last in or somewhere in between.

29.43   Campbell J's reasoning was followed by Debelle J in *Re Magarey Farlam Lawyers Trust Accounts (No 3)*, where the breaches of trust had occurred over 13 years but records as to trust balances were very accurate. In that case the judge relied on the trust account ledger rather than

Clayton's case to determine what trust monies were still available. Debelle J, at 376–7, doubted the utility of the rule:

> The rule in *Clayton's Case* might have a limited utility in respect of appropriating payments into bank accounts as between trustee and beneficiary but it has been held in a number of jurisdictions in Australia to have no utility as between competing beneficiaries whose moneys have been deposited in a mixed fund.

TRACING PROPERTY INTO THE HANDS OF THIRD PARTIES

29.44   Bona fide purchasers for value without notice of the breach of trust are immune from tracing claims: *Boscawen v Bajwa* at 776. However, if a third party recipient has actual or constructive knowledge of the breach of fiduciary duty, or if the recipient is a volunteer, the property may be traced into his or her hands: *Strang v Owens* (1925) 42 WN (NSW) 183; *Chong v Chanell*; *Armstrong Scalisi Holdings Pty Ltd v Abboud* [2012] NSWSC 268 at [29].

29.45   In *Commonwealth Bank of Australia v Saleh* at [39], Einstein J summarised the principles of recovery against third parties as:

- where trust property is transferred to a volunteer who takes without notice, and there is no question of mixing, then the volunteer will hold the property on trust for the rightful beneficiaries;
- where the trust moneys were used to pay off a secured creditor, the trust was not entitled to be subrogated to the rights of the secured creditor who was repaid;
- if the volunteer purchased property with a mixed fund including trust moneys then the beneficiary would be allowed a charge over the property in order to secure repayment of the trust moneys used for the purchase;
- if an asset is purchased with mixed funds and it increases in value, the beneficiary will not be entitled to any proportionate share in *that increase* in value. In this respect, careful consideration needs to be given to renovations or improvements made upon real property.

29.46   Einstein J's summary is based on the earlier English case of *Re Diplock*. Diplock had created a will giving his executors discretion to distribute large sums to over 100 charities. The moneys had been mixed with the charities' own funds or used to improve assets (by making renovations or discharging debts). A settlement was reached with the executors but the beneficiaries decided to bring recovery actions against the charitable recipients. The beneficiaries were allowed to recover sums against charities who still held the funds separately, and they were entitled to recover a proportionate amount from mixed funds (which took into account what had been received from the executors). The other moneys, which had been expended on capital improvements or on debt reduction, were not recoverable, as this would have worked an inquity on the charities.

The rule against subrogation into securities

29.47   The rule (coming out of *Re Diplock*) that beneficiaries could not be subrogated to the rights of the secured creditor who was paid by the volunteer with trust moneys, has been questioned in more recent times. Subrogation is an equitable process whereby one person is taken to have received the rights of another without an assignment, because they have reduced that liability and it would be unconscientious not to allow the payer to take up the rights of the recipient. Unlike tracing, the beneficiary does not follow his/her own property into the security, but rather is substituted for the existing security holder. In cases of tracing, subrogation might allow beneficiaries to stand in the shoes of the mortgagee whose debt was paid with trust moneys. In *Boscawen v Bajwa*, moneys were advanced to fund the purchase of property on the condition that the funds were only to be released to fund the completion of the sale and were to be returned should the sale fall through. The funds were released prior to sale and were used to reduce a mortgage liability. The sale fell through and the moneylender sought to be subrogated to the rights of the mortgagee. Millett LJ, at 777, raised this as a possibility as follows:

> If the plaintiff succeeds in tracing his property, whether in its original or in some changed form, into the hands of the defendant and overcomes any defences which are put forward on the defendant's behalf, he is entitled to a remedy. The remedy will be fashioned to the circumstances. The plaintiff will generally be entitled to a personal remedy; if he seeks a proprietary remedy he must usually prove that the property to which he lays claim is still in the ownership of the defendant. If he succeeds in doing this, the court will treat the defendant as holding the property on a constructive trust for the plaintiff and will order the defendant to transfer it in specie to the plaintiff. But this is only one of the proprietary remedies which is available to a court of equity. If the plaintiff's money has been applied by the defendant, for example, not in the acquisition of a landed property but in its improvement, then the court may treat the land as charged with the payment to the plaintiff of a sum representing the amount by which the value of the defendant's land has been enhanced by the use of the plaintiff's money. And if the plaintiff's money has been used to discharge a mortgage on the defendant's land, then the court may achieve a similar result by treating the land as subject to a charge by way of subrogation in favour of the plaintiff.

29.48   There are a number of decisions which favour the use of subrogation in these cases: *Gertsch v Atsas* [1999] NSWSC 898 at [19]–[20]; *National Australia Bank Ltd v Rusu* [2001] NSWSC 32 at [51].

29.49   In *Cook v Italiano Family Fruit Company Pty Ltd (in liq)* (2010) 276 ALR 349 at 369–70, Finkelstein J reviewed both *Boscawen v Bajwa* and *Diplock* and said:

> In my view, the *Boscawen* approach is to be preferred to that in *Diplock*. I would only make a few additional comments in relation to *Diplock*. First, the reasoning in *Diplock* should be confined to land and, perhaps, other property of a special nature. Principles regarding specific performance might be relevant by analogy. Thus, if, for example, the subrogation claim related to paying off a debt incurred to fund an investment, the claim would have been allowed in *Diplock*. Second, as Millett LJ said in *Boscawen* (at 783), in *Diplock* an order might have been framed to avoid the perceived injustice of forcing a sale of land under a charge. For example, the charities might have been given reasonable opportunity to obtain finance to meet the beneficiaries' claims. This would have put the charities back as close as possible to their original position and prevented them retaining a windfall at the beneficiaries' expense. Third, there is much to be said for the view that *Diplock* was not intended to create an absolute rule, and should be confined to its peculiar facts: see eg *George v Biztole Corporation Pty Ltd* (unreported, Supreme Court of Victoria, Ashley J, 26 February 1996). Fourth, in applying *Diplock* it is important to distinguish between tracing and subrogation. It is undoubtedly the case that a claimant cannot trace into funds which have been paid by a volunteer to discharge a debt — the assets have ended up in the hands of a bona fide, for value and without notice, creditor. But it is altogether a different matter whether there remains a right of subrogation against the volunteer. Cases establishing the non-entitlement to tracing are sometimes cited, erroneously in my opinion, for similarly denying a right of subrogation: see for

example *Re J Leslie Engineers* [1976] 2 All ER 85 ... Fifth, there is considerable force in the argument that if a volunteer has applied misappropriated funds to discharge a debt, the volunteer should not be in a better position than if he had applied the funds to purchase an asset. In either case, the volunteer's assets have effectively been swollen. This is not to suggest that the circumstances in which subrogation and other equitable remedies are available should be identical.

29.50 While Finkelstein J's judgment seeks to suggest that *Diplock* may still be good law when applied to mortgages over land, in *Heperu Pty Ltd v Belle* (2009) 76 NSWLR 230; 258 ALR 727, the Court of Appeal of New South Wales accepted tracing into a reduction of a real property mortgage liability. The case involved a fraudster who had misappropriated cheques and deposited them into his wife's accounts. Funds were withdrawn from those accounts and used to make mortgage repayments for the wife (amongst other things). The victims of the fraud sought to recover the funds from the wife. The wife was innocent of any wrongdoing, but nevertheless the Court of Appeal felt that there were actions in both law and equity to trace the funds into the wife's property to recover whatever value remained in her hands, given her status as a volunteer. Allsop JA, at NSWLR 262; ALR 759, giving the judgment of the Court of Appeal, stated that the views of Millett LJ in *Boscawen v Bajwa* were to be preferred to the views expressed in *Re Diplock*. Allsop JA's preference was reaffirmed by Campbell JA for the New South Wales Court of Appeal in *Raulfs v Fishy Bite* at [95] (although in that case there was no proprietary right to give rise to a tracing claim): see 29.13–29.14.

29.51 In the *Heperu* litigation orders were made for further inquiries into tracing the funds: *Heperu Pty Ltd v Belle (No 2)* [2010] NSWCA 13. In *Heperu Pty Ltd v Belle* [2011] NSWSC 1151, Slattery J examined the claims for tracing. During the relevant period a total of $1,744,402.50 was misappropriated. During the same period the total mortgage payments made out of the account totaled $211,040.23. Heperu sought to recover the whole amount of these payments on the basis that it could be inferred that this amount was totally used to pay the mortgages. Slattery J refused to make such an inference and said that he was bound to use the ordinary rules of tracing to determine which payments were made from the stolen monies to pay the mortgages. On that analysis only $118,932.10 could be traced from the stolen funds to the mortgage payments. However, the mortgage payments included amounts for interest as well payments for the principal debt. Slattery J, at [51]–[54], found that Belle should only be liable for the reduced amount of principal debt, not the interest payments:

> In my view the appropriate measure of Ms Belle's obligation to restore funds derived from her husband's misappropriations to the extent as a volunteer she retains those funds, is to identify what benefits are in her hands when she receives notice of Heperu's claim. In my view that is the reduction on the principal indebtedness to the mortgagees ... brought about by the use of the application of the misappropriated funds. That is a figure already identified of $86,970.01. The Court of Appeal has already indicated in its preliminary view of the authorities on this question that 'it is not self evident that the interest payments increase the value of her equity. Of course payments of interest kept alive the opportunity of the equity redemption and capital appreciation thereof. The relevance of this to a restitutionary claim is not however self evident': *Heperu Pty Ltd v Belle* (2009) 76 NSWLR 230 at [156] ... In my view it is consistent with these authorities that the monies that Ms Belle paid in interest to maintain the equity of redemption in the Coffs Harbour and Potts Point properties are not properly part of the fund that she retains against which Heperu may have an order for restoration. That means that the actual mortgage payments made when there were misappropriated funds in the Westpac account totalling $118,932.10, which mortgage

payments included interest and principal, are not the correct measure of the misappropriated funds Ms Belle retained when she received notice of the Heperu's claim. Rather, it is the figure of $86,970.01, which is the reduction in principal indebtedness on the mortgages, excluding any reduction in indebtedness attributable to non misappropriated funds.

29.52   Slattery J's analysis of interest might be questioned if one emphasises the fact that interest is compounded and charged in real property mortgages for the life of the mortgage. The total amount of interest and capital is then charged out in the installments. If the interest is charged to the land, it eats away at the equity of the owner. Conversely, if interest is paid, the owner's equity has been improved because such interest is not compounded and charged onto the land. On this view of interest payment, it is arguable that they improve the equity and should therefore be recoverable against the volunteer as a received benefit.

Calculation of proportionate share

29.53   Another complicated issue arose in *Foskett v McKeown* concerning how one calculates the proportionate share in tracing cases involving a mixed fund which comes into the hands of volunteers. In this case a trustee misappropriated money from the trust fund and used it to pay the last two of five premiums on a life insurance policy. The policy was in favour of the trustee's children. After the trustee's suicide, the children received the policy money. How should tracing reflect the interests of the beneficiaries in the policy moneys?

29.54   The beneficiaries under the trust claimed that they were entitled to trace their money through the policy into the sum paid out by the insurers. They believed they were entitled to a proportionate share of the policy money. The majority of the Court of Appeal upheld the beneficiaries' claim but limited it to the amount of the two premiums together with interest. The beneficiaries were denied a proportionate share of the policy proceeds. The majority found no causal link between the misappropriation of the funds and the right to the policy proceeds, as the right to whole-of-life cover arose after the first two premiums, and was not causally related to the misappropriated funds.

29.55   A majority of the House of Lords in *Foskett v McKeown* upheld an appeal by the beneficiaries. In the leading speech, Lord Millett, at AC 137; All ER 129, dismissed the causal arguments raised by the Court of Appeal as follows:

> In my opinion there is no reason to differentiate between the first premium or premiums and later premiums. Such a distinction is not based on any principle. Why should the policy belong to the party who paid the first premium, without which there would have been no policy, rather than to the party who paid the last premium, without which it would normally have lapsed? Moreover, any such distinction would lead to the most capricious results.

29.56   Lord Browne-Wilkinson gave a separate judgment in agreement with Lord Millett. His Lordship stated that the crucial factor to appreciate was that the beneficiaries were claiming a proprietary interest in the policy moneys and that such proprietary interest is not dependent on any discretion vested in the court. As such, issues of fairness were irrelevant. Lord Browne-Wilkinson, at AC 108–109; All ER 102, said:

> Those equitable interests under the purchasers' trust deed are also enforceable against whoever for the time being holds those assets other than someone who is a bona fide purchaser for value of the legal interest without notice or a person who claims through such a purchaser. No question

of a bona fide purchaser arises in the present case: the children are mere volunteers under the policy Trust. Therefore the critical question is whether the assets now subject to the express trusts of the purchasers' trust deed comprise any part of the policy moneys, a question which depends on the rules of tracing. If, as a result of tracing, it can be said that certain of the policy moneys are what now represent part of the assets subject to the trusts of the purchasers' trust deed, then as a matter of English property law the purchasers have an absolute interest in such moneys. There is no discretion vested in the court. There is no room for any consideration whether, in the circumstances of this particular case, it is in a moral sense 'equitable' for the purchasers to be so entitled. The rules establishing equitable proprietary interests and their enforceability against certain parties have been developed over the centuries and are an integral part of the property law of England. It is a fundamental error to think that, because certain property rights are equitable rather than legal, such rights are in some way discretionary. This case does not depend on whether it is fair, just and reasonable to give the purchasers an interest as a result of which the court in its discretion provides a remedy. It is a case of hard-nosed property rights.

29.57 Lord Browne-Wilkinson continued by accepting that the situation before him was analogous to a mixed bank account. By paying two premiums out of trust moneys, the trustee had wrongly mixed the trust funds with the chose in action, represented by the value of the policy. It followed that the policy moneys belonged to the trustee's children and to the trust fund, in proportionate shares.

29.58 Lord Hoffmann also agreed with the speech of Lord Millett. Lord Steyn and Lord Hope dissented on the grounds that the children's right to policy moneys arose with the first premium and that there was no link between the misappropriated funds and the children's right to the policy money.

30

OTHER EQUITABLE REMEDIES

RECTIFICATION

30.1 The principal area in which rectification arises is with written contracts, although it can arise with other written documents. Thus, if there is fraud in the execution of a will, rectification can be ordered. The discussion of the remedy in this chapter will be confined to the context of contracts. In *Green v AMP Life* [2005] NSWSC 370 at [171], Campbell J defined rectification as follows:

> Rectification is an equitable remedy which enables a document which sets out legal rights in a way different to the way the parties intended, to be corrected so as to give effect to their intention. Insofar as rectification is granted of contracts, it is only of those contracts which were intended by the parties to be wholly expressed in writing, or of those parts of the partly written contract which were intended to be expressed in writing.

The remedy of rectification is a manifestation of the maxim that 'equity looks to the intent rather than the form'. Its purpose is the prevention of unconscientious conduct: *Ryledar Pty Ltd v Euphoric Pty Ltd* (2007) 69 NSWLR 603 at 667.

30.2 It is important to keep in mind that rectification refers to rectification of documents. It is not a means of reformulating the terms of an agreement set out in a document. In *Mackenzie v Coulson* (1869) LR 8 Eq 368 at 375, James V-C said:

> Courts of equity do not rectify contracts; they may and do rectify instruments purporting to have been made in pursuance of the terms of contracts.

30.3 In relation to the orders that a court makes when ordering rectification, in *Franklins Pty Ltd v Metcash Trading Ltd* (2009) 76 NSWLR 603 at 711; 264 ALR 15 at 118, Campbell JA said:

> The remedy that is granted is, as with all equity's remedies, one that will seek to undo, so far as is in practice possible, the departure, that the litigation has shown to exist, from equity's standards of conscientious behaviour. The way this is achieved, when a remedy of rectification is granted, is by rewriting the contract so that it no longer departs from the common intention of the parties. The rewriting is done in a quite literal sense — the proper form of order identifies the precise words of the contract that are to be struck out, the precise words that are to be inserted, and where those words are to be inserted. As well the order usually … involves calling in the original document and actually endorsing the order on the instrument that is to be rectified. In that way the executed contractual document is no longer able to be a potential source of error and confusion, by appearing to state legal relations that in truth are not as the document says.

30.4   A clear and convincing proof that the document does not accurately reflect the parties' intention is needed before a court will order rectification: *Commissioner of Stamp Duties (NSW) v Carlenka Pty Ltd* (1995) 41 NSWLR 329 at 345. This burden of proof is particularly onerous in circumstances where there have been prolonged negotiations between the parties that have resulted in a formal instrument in the preparation of which the parties were advised by skilled lawyers: *Franklins Pty Ltd v Metcash Trading Ltd* at NSWLR 713–4; ALR 120–1. Thus, in *Waldorf Australia Pty Ltd v Elias Construction Group Pty Ltd* [2010] NSWSC 164 at [14], Barrett J said:

> The insistence upon a high degree of proof in this area is a recognition of two realities: first, that persons who take the trouble to record their agreement in writing (particularly when they are, as here, assisted by lawyers) must generally be presumed to intend their written bargain to prevail over what they have not written; and, second, that it is easy for one such party, upon becoming dissatisfied after the event with some element of the written compact, to seek to brand it as inaccurate.

In addition to these reasons, in *Franklins Pty Ltd v Metcash Trading Ltd* at NSWLR 713; ALR 120, Campbell JA noted that, short of such clear and convincing evidence, there is a danger of imposing a contract on party that he or she did not make.

30.5   In satisfying this high standard of proof, a party seeking rectification will not be defeated by a clause in the agreement which states that the agreement is a complete agreement and supersedes and cancels all prior arrangements, understandings and negotiations. Such clauses do not preclude the grant of an order for rectification of the contract: *MacDonald v Shinko Australia Pty Ltd* [1999] 2 Qd R 152 at 155–6. Although the parol evidence rule applies in relation to entirely written contracts, it does not apply to exclude extrinsic evidence that goes towards establishing that the contract does not reflect the intention of the parties and should therefore be rectified: *Ryledar Pty Ltd v Euphoric Pty Ltd* at 657–8.

30.6   Being an equitable remedy, rectification can be denied on discretionary grounds such as unclean hands (see 31.8–31.12), laches (see 31.13–31.22) or acquiescence: see 31.23–31.24. In relation to the exercise of the court's discretion in cases of rectification, in *Metlife Insurance Ltd v Visy Board Pty Ltd* [2007] NSWSC 1481 at [39]–[40], Brereton J said:

> [T]he discretion … to decline rectification as an equitable remedy involves different considerations from those that arise in cases of specific performance (and for that matter injunctions), where ordinarily the plaintiffs are entitled to alternative relief in damages. That is because, if rectification is refused, the document remains in existence in an uncorrected form, and generally there is no available alternative relief. It is clear that mere delay is insufficient, although laches and acquiescence may justify declining relief. It is not enough to justify declining relief that rectification will cause hardship or prejudice to the defendant merely because performance on his part under the rectified document is more difficult than under its original form.

Furthermore, if a third party has acquired rights bona fide and for valuable consideration in property transferred under a contract that would otherwise be amenable to an order for rectification, the order will be refused: *Harris v Smith* [2008] NSWSC 545 at [49].

30.7   On the other hand, simply because there is an error in the written contract does not usually mean that rectification is the appropriate remedy. It may be that the true meaning of the document can be determined by applying rules of construction. Thus, in case of ambiguity, applying the rules of construction rather than ordering rectification is the appropriate way to resolve the ambiguity. Thus, in *Metlife Insurance v Visy Board*, at [22], Brereton J said:

> [W]hat must be shown with precision is the *form* which the instrument ought to have taken — that is to say, the words which ought to have been inserted in or omitted from it. Thus precision is required as to the words to be used, rather than the meaning of those words: rectification is concerned with the form of the instrument, as opposed to its meaning. Meaning is a matter of construction, not rectification, and ambiguity in the meaning of agreed words is not a bar to rectification, if they were, in fact, the words that the parties intended to use. Any such ambiguity can be resolved by the process of construction.

Similarly, obvious typographical or grammatical errors can usually be corrected pursuant to the rules of construction rather than by ordering rectification: *Fitzgerald v Masters* (1956) 95 CLR 420 at 426–7. However, in some cases such errors will be the subject of an order for rectification as occurred in *Sekisui Rib Loc Australia Pty Ltd (ACN 008 040 800) v Rocla Pty Ltd (ACN 000 032 191)* [2012] SASCFC 21 at [131]–[134], where a missing comma in a document was the subject of an order.

30.8   Rectification of a written contract generally requires there to be a common mistake by all the parties to it to the effect that the written contract fails to give expression to their true intention. However, in special circumstances, rectification is available in cases of unilateral mistake. Furthermore, voluntary agreements entered into by way of a deed can attract the remedy of rectification. In any of the cases, the mistake can be one of fact or law: *Allnutt v Wilding* [2007] EWCA Civ 412 at [6].

Rectification for common mistake

30.9   Rectification for common mistake relates to a situation where an earlier or prior agreement between the parties has been put into a written contractual document, but there has been a mistake in recording the earlier agreement in the written contractual document. In relation to the essential principles that apply to rectification for such a common mistake, in *International Advisor Systems Pty Limited v XYYX Pty Limited* [2008] NSWSC 2 at [21], Brereton J said:

> (1) … though there need not be a concluded antecedent contract, there must be an intention common to both parties at the time of the contract to include in their bargain a term which by mutual mistake is omitted from it; (2) … that a plaintiff must advance convincing proof that the written contract does not embody the final intention of the parties; and (3) … the omitted ingredient must be compatible of such proof in clear and precise terms, so that the Court must not assume for itself the task of making the contract for the parties.

30.10   The onus of proof in establishing the need for rectification rests with the party alleging that the written instrument needs to be rectified: *Australian Gypsum Limited v Hume Steel Limited* (1930) 45 CLR 54 at 64. It is not enough to establish that the written agreement does not represent the common intention of the parties. One has to also establish what the true intention of the parties was: *Ryledar Pty Ltd v Euphoric Pty Ltd* at 655. However, if one of the parties is mistaken, but the other's intention is in accordance with the written document, rectification will not be ordered: *Slee v Warke* (1952) 86 CLR 271.

30.11 In establishing common intention, the traditional view was that the written document had to contain some outward expression of common intention which the contract failed to express. This matter raises the issue of whether the common intention is to be determined objectively or subjectively. *Joscelyne v Nissen* [1979] 2 QB 86 at 98; [1970] 1 All ER 1213 at 1222, suggests that 'some outward expression of accord' is necessary. This requirement has been said to be an evidential factor rather than a strict legal requirement: *Beasley v Munt* [2006] EWCA Civ 370 at [36]. Other cases, however, suggest that an outward expression of common intention is not needed: *Bishopgate Insurance Australia Ltd v Commonwealth Engineering (NSW) Pty Ltd* [1981] 1 NSWLR 429 at 431; *Elders Trustee & Executor Co Ltd v E G Reeves Pty Ltd* (1987) 78 ALR 193 at 253–4.

30.12 In *Muriti v Prendergast* [2005] NSWSC 281 at [109], while White J conceded that an outward expression of intention was not always necessary, his Honour went on to say that:

> … in many cases … objective evidence of the parties' intentions will be necessary, as a practical matter, to provide the clear and convincing evidence of the parties' intentions sufficient to displace the presumption that they intended to be bound by the agreement expressed in the document which they signed.

To similar effect, in *Ensham Coal Sales P/L v Electric Power Development Co Ltd* [2005] QSC 236 at [17], McMurdo J said that 'the parties' intentions cannot remain undisclosed, so that whilst the parties need not have disclosed their intentions to each other, the intentions must have been manifested in their words or conduct'.

30.13 In *Commissioner of Stamp Duties (NSW) v Carlenka Pty Ltd* (1995) 41 NSWLR 329 at 332, Mahoney A-P said that, in the context of rectification, intention 'refers to what was subjectively seen as to be brought about and the consequence of it. It refers to that which is subjectively foreseen and intended to be effected by the document'. Therefore, evidence of what a party intended to agree to when he or she entered a particular contract is admissible: *NSW Medical Defence Union Ltd v Transport Industries Insurance Co Ltd* (1986) 6 NSWLR 740 at 751–2. The common intention must be such 'that the Court can conclude, with the appropriate clarity, both the substance and the detail of the precise variation which needs to be made to the wording of the instrument': *Bush v National Bank Ltd* (1992) 35 NSWLR 390 at 407. The requirement of clarity and precision is necessary so that an order for rectification reflects the intention of the parties rather than the court 'making a contract for [them]': *Muriti v Prendergast* at [134]. This does not, however, require that the parties have a common intention 'as to the precise words in which the term should be expressed': *Muriti v Prendergast* at [137]. The exact form of words in which the common intention is to be expressed is immaterial, if in substance and in detail the common intention can be ascertained: *Hicklane Properties Ltd v Bradbury Investments Ltd* [2008] EWCA Civ 691 at [10].

30.14 In *Ryledar Pty Ltd v Euphoric Pty Ltd*, at 642, Tobias JA (Mason P and Campbell JA agreeing) summarised the law on ascertaining the common intention of the parties as follows:

> [F]irst, the common intention which must be established by clear and convincing proof to justify rectification must be the actual or true common intention of the parties. Second, evidence of that intention may be ascertained not only from the external or outward expressions of the parties manifested by their objective words or conduct but also from evidence of their subjective states of mind. Third, where, for instance, the correspondence between and/or conduct of the parties establishes a positive lack of an 'objective' common

intention, then that evidence must be taken in conjunction with the evidence (if any) of their subjective states of mind to determine whether the necessary common intention has been established … Fourth, … a party subsequently acting as if the instrument stood in the form into which it is sought to be rectified was strong evidence of that party's intention at the time to execute the instrument in its rectified form. Such conduct is obviously of significance but, depending on other evidence, if any, is not necessarily conclusive although in the absence of any such evidence it may be. Fifth, it follows that where the correspondence and/or conduct positively establishes the necessary common intention, then assertions by the party opposing rectification of his or her subjective state of mind which is inconsistent with that party's outward manifestation of his or her intention, being unexpressed and uncommunicated, is unlikely to trump his or her expressed intention. But this is because that party is unlikely to be believed. Sixth, where … the outward expression of the parties' common intention is at best inconclusive, then establishing that the subjective states of mind of the parties evinces the relevant common intention becomes critical if the necessary standard of proof to support an order for rectification is to be achieved.

30.15   Whether rectification can apply to a situation where both parties intend to use certain language but are mistaken as to the meaning and effect of the language is somewhat in doubt. In *Frederick E Rose (London) Ltd v William H Pim Junior & Co Ltd* [1953] 2 QB 450; 2 All ER 739, the parties intended to use the word 'horsebeans', but mistakenly believed that 'horsebeans' were the same as feveroles. The English Court of Appeal declined to order rectification.

30.16   However, more recent authority suggests that rectification can be ordered where the mistake was as to the legal effect of the words used. In *Allnutt v Wilding* at [11], Mummery LJ said that rectification can be ordered:

> … when, owing to a mistake in the drafting of the document, it fails to record the [parties'] true intentions. The mistake may, for example, consist of leaving out words that were intended to be put into the document, or putting in words that were not intended to be in the document or, through a misunderstanding by those involved about the meaning of the words or expressions that were used in the document. Mistakes of this kind have the effect that the document, as executed, is not a true record of the [parties'] intentions.

This approach was endorsed by the New South Wales Court of Appeal in *Ryledar Pty Ltd v Euphoric Pty Ltd* at 631–3, and by the Court of Appeal in Western Australia in *Tipperary Developments Pty Ltd v Western Australia* (2009) 38 WAR 488 at 548; 258 ALR 124 at 184.

30.17   However, rectification is not available where the parties' mistake is as to the legal consequences of the document. In *Allnutt v Wilding*, the parties had created a discretionary trust. They believed that the creation of a discretionary trust would be a potentially exempt transfer for the purposes of inheritance tax. It was not. If they had appreciated that legal consequence, their claim was that they would have created an interest in possession trust. The court ruled that a change in the document from one which created a discretionary trust into one which created an interest in possession trust was outside the ambit of rectification.

30.18   For rectification for common mistake there is no need that the prior agreement be a contract. In *Maralinga Pty Ltd v Major Enterprises Pty Ltd* (1973) 128 CLR 226 at 350; 1 ALR 169 at 178, Mason J said:

It is now settled that the existence of an antecedent agreement is not essential to the grant of relief by way of rectification. It may be granted in cases in which the instrument sought to be rectified constitutes the only agreement between the parties, but does not reflect their common intention.

30.19 However, the common intention must continue unaltered until the document is executed. In *Maralinga v Major Enterprises*, land owned by Major Enterprises was put up for auction. The auctioneer announced that Major Enterprises would allow a mortgage back to the vendor for a portion of the price. Maralinga was the successful bidder. The draft contract did not contain the mortgage back provision. When signing the contract both parties were aware of the omission, although Maralinga believed that it could still have the benefit of the auctioneer's promise as to the mortgage back. Maralinga later sought rectification of the contract on the basis that, at the end of the auction, there was an agreement which included the mortgage back provision which was not included in the written contract. The High Court refused to order rectification on the ground that there was no mistake as to what the written contract contained and that the written contract differed from any agreement that arose with the completion of the auction. Maralinga was unable to establish that the common intention of the parties was that the written contract would record the agreement that arose at the completion of the auction.

Rectification for unilateral mistake

30.20 Rectification of a contract when unilateral mistake is involved will only be ordered in exceptional circumstances because it 'has the result of imposing on the defendant a contract which he did not, and did not intend to, make and relieving the claimant from a contract which he did, albeit did not intend to, make': *George Wimpey UK Ltd v V I Construction Ltd* [2005] EWCA Civ 77 at [75]. What is usually required is 'an element of sharp practice on the part of the non-mistaken party, in circumstances where it would be unconscionable for that party to take the benefit of the other party's mistake': *Igloo Homes Pty Ltd v Sammut Constructions Pty Ltd* [2005] NSWCA 280 at [199]. In *Chartbrook Ltd v Persimmon Homes Ltd* [2008] EWCA Civ 183 at [137], Lawrence Collins LJ described rectification for unilateral mistake as 'a species of equitable estoppel that precludes the party who knows of the other party's mistake from resisting rectification'.

30.21 In *Thomas Bates & Son Ltd v Wyndhams (Lingerie) Ltd* [1981] 1 All ER 1077 at 1086, it was held that, for a written contract between A and B to be rectified for unilateral mistake, the following elements had to be established:

(i) A is mistaken as to whether a particular term of the contract is or is not included;
(ii) B knows of A's mistake;
(iii) B fails to draw A's attention to the mistake in circumstances where equity would require B to take some step or steps, depending on the circumstances, to bring the mistake to A's attention; and
(iv) the mistake must be one calculated to benefit B.

30.22 The critical element here is that of knowledge. English cases adopt the position that knowledge extends to: (i) actual knowledge; (ii) wilfully shutting one's eyes to the obvious; and (iii) wilfully and recklessly failing to make such inquiries as an honest and reasonable person would make: *George Wimpey v V I Construction* at [42]–[45]; *Daventry District Council v Daventry & District Housing Ltd* [2012] 1 WLR 1333 at 1357–8. In Australia, in *Misiaris v Saydels Pty Ltd*

(1989) NSW Conv R 55–474, Young J took the view that it is sufficient if B 'must have known' or 'strongly suspects' that A made a mistake.

30.23   The principles in *Thomas Bates & Son v Wyndhams (Lingerie)* do not need to be established if B's conduct amounts to fraud or other unconscientious conduct, or where there is a fiduciary relationship between A and B: *George Wimpey v V I Construction* at [74]. Thus, in *Commission for the New Towns v Cooper (Great Britain) Ltd* [1995] Ch 259 at 280; 2 All ER 929 at 946, Stuart-Smith LJ offered the following illustration:

> I would hold that where [B] intends [A] to be mistaken as to the construction of the agreement, so conducts himself that he diverts [A]'s attention from discovering the mistake by making false and misleading statements, and [A] in fact makes the very mistake that [B] intends, then notwithstanding that [B] does not actually know, but merely suspects, that [A] is mistaken, and it cannot be shown that the mistake was induced by any misrepresentation, rectification may be granted. [B]'s conduct is unconscionable and he cannot insist on performance in accordance to the strict letter of the contract; that is sufficient for rescission. But it may also not be unjust or inequitable to insist that the contract be performed according to [A]'s understanding, where that was the meaning that [B] intended that [A] should put upon it.

Rectification of voluntary deeds

30.24   The principles governing the power to order rectification in the special context of a voluntary settlement set out in deed form were stated by Brightman J in *Re Butlin's Settlement Trusts* [1976] Ch 251 at 262; 2 All ER 483 at 489, as follows:

(i)   a settlor may seek rectification by proving that the settlement does not express his or her true intention, or the true intention of himself or herself and any party with whom he or she has bargained, such as a spouse in the case of an ante-nuptial settlement;

(ii)   it is not essential for him or her to prove that the settlement fails to express the true intention of the trustees if they have not bargained; but

(iii)   the court may in its discretion decline to rectify a settlement against a protesting trustee who objects to rectification.

Brightman J, at Ch 63; All ER 489, qualified the last point by noting that rectification would not be ordered in the face of a reasonable objection by a trustee who had accepted that position on the basis of the settlement document as written and in ignorance of the mistake.

ACCOUNT OF PROFITS

30.25   The essence of the remedy of an account of profits is the recovery of net gains that a defendant has made pursuant to a breach of duty owed to the plaintiff. The remedy stems from 'the principle that no one should be permitted to gain from his own wrongdoing': *Attorney-General v Guardian Newspapers Limited (No 2)* [1990] 1 AC 109 at 262; [1988] 3 All ER 545 at 644. The purpose of the remedy is not to punish the defendant, but rather to prevent the unjust enrichment of the defendant: *Dart Industries Inc v Decor Corporation Pty Ltd* (1993) 179 CLR 101 at 114–15; 116 ALR 385 at 390. Thus, the remedy is not compensatory in nature. In this respect, in *Nicholls v Michael Wilson & Partners Limited* (2010) 243 FLR 177 at 211–2, Young JA said:

There is a vital difference between an order for account of profits and an order for the payment of equitable compensation. In the former case, the plaintiff adopts what the defendant did, virtually as its agent and asks the agent to pay over the profits the agent made. In the latter case, the defendant is treated as a wrongdoer and is liable to pay what the plaintiff lost by its wrongdoing.

30.26 The power to order an account of profits is confirmed in the rules of court of Australia's High Court and Federal Court as well as the Supreme Courts of the states and territories. In *Warman International Ltd v Dwyer* (1995) 182 CLR 544 at 558; 128 ALR 201 at 209, the High Court observed as follows:

> The assessment of the profit will often be extremely difficult in practice; accordingly it has been said that '[w]hat will be required on the inquiry … will not be mathematical exactness but only a reasonable approximation'. [*My Kinda Town Ltd v Soll* [1982] FSR 147 at 159]. What is necessary however is to determine as accurately as possible the true measure of the profit or benefit obtained by the fiduciary in breach of his duty.

30.27 In the context of equitable rights, an account of profits is always available if such a remedy is necessary to give effect to the equitable right, provided that there is 'a sufficient connection' between the breach of equitable duty and the profit derived: *Visnic v Sywak* (2009) 257 ALR 517 at 523. One of the most common instances where the remedy arises is in the context of breaches of fiduciary obligations. In ordering an account of profits the court can, in appropriate circumstances, make some measure of allowance or recompense for the defendant's effort and skill in generating the profit. In *Chirnside v Fay* [2007] 1 NZLR 433 at 471, Blanchard and Tipping JJ, in the context of a defaulting fiduciary, summarised the relevant principles here as follows:

> [A] fiduciary who has acted in breach of fiduciary duty, and against whom an account of profits is ordered, may nevertheless be given an allowance for the skill and effort employed in obtaining the profit which he has to disgorge. This will be done when … it would be inequitable for the beneficiaries to step in and take the profit without paying for the skill and labour which produced it … [T]his power is used sparingly out of concern not to encourage fiduciaries to act in breach of duty. But if making an allowance in a particular case cannot sensibly be regarded as giving that encouragement, the rationale for a sparing approach is reduced.

30.28 In *Warman International Ltd v Dwyer* (1995) 182 CLR 544; 128 ALR 201, where the fiduciary's breach consisted of a misappropriation of the goodwill of a business, the breach was remedied by ordering an account of profits of the new business for a period of two years only. This was on the basis that profits after that period could safely be considered to be attributable to the defaulting fiduciary's own efforts in running the new business. In coming to this conclusion the High Court, at CLR 561–2; ALR 211–2, said:

> In the case of a business it may well be inappropriate and inequitable to compel the errant fiduciary to account for the whole of the profit of his conduct of the business or his exploitation of the principal's goodwill over an indefinite period of time. In such a case, it may be appropriate to allow the fiduciary a proportion of the profits, depending on the particular circumstances. That may well be the case when it appears that a significant proportion of an increase in profits has been generated by the skill, efforts, property and resources of the fiduciary, the capital he has introduced and the risks he has taken, so long as they are not risks to which the principal's property has been

exposed. Then it may be said that the relevant proportion of the increased profits is not the product or consequence of the plaintiff's property but the product of the fiduciary's skill, efforts, property and resources. This is not to say that the liability of a fiduciary to account should be governed by the doctrine of unjust enrichment, though that doctrine may well have a useful part to play; it is simply to say that the stringent rule requiring a fiduciary to account for profits can be carried to extremes and that in cases outside the realm of specific assets, the liability of a fiduciary should not be transformed into a vehicle for the unjust enrichment of the plaintiff. It is for the defendant to establish that it is inequitable to order an account of the entire profits … Whether it is appropriate to allow an errant fiduciary a proportion of profits or to make an allowance in respect of skill, expertise and other expenses is a matter of judgment which will depend on the facts of the given case. However, as a general rule, in conformity with the principle that a fiduciary must not profit from a breach of fiduciary duty, a court will not apportion profits in the absence of an antecedent arrangement for profit-sharing but will make an allowance for skill, expertise and other expenses.

30.29   In relation to common law rights there are relatively few circumstances in which an account of profits is available. These include the dissolution of a partnership or agency relationship, and intellectual property and industrial property cases. In this context, in *Southern Equity Pty Limited v Timevale Pty Limited* [2012] NSWSC 15 at [110], Brereton J said:

> [E]quity will not decree an account where there is a sufficient legal remedy; but where the legal remedy is an imperfect one, equity has a large discretion to intervene … [W]hile there are no hard and fast rules [for granting such an account in equity's auxiliary jurisdiction], relevant factors that will incline the court to order an account include that it would otherwise be difficult for the plaintiff to establish the true state of affairs, as the defendant is in possession and control of the relevant information and documents; and that the accounts are too complex to be fairly resolved in a common law trial, that is to say to be left to a jury.

30.30   In the context of breaches of contract involving no equitable wrong, the House of Lords has held that in exceptional circumstances an account of profits can be ordered: *Attorney-General v Blake (Jonathan Cape Ltd Third Party)* [2001] 1 AC 268 at 285. However, this approach was rejected by the Full Court of the Federal Court in *Hospitality Group Pty Ltd v Australian Rugby Union* (2001) 110 FCR 157 at 195–6. On the other hand, in *Town and Country Property Management Services Pty Ltd* [2002] NSWSC 166 at [83], Campbell J said that 'if an account of profits is sometimes available in circumstances where there has been a breach of contract, something more than a mere breach of contract is needed to demonstrate the appropriateness of awarding the equitable remedy'.

30.31   Where a plaintiff has the choice of pursuing common law damages or an account of profits, generally he or she must elect which of the two remedies to pursue: *Colbeam Palmer Ltd v Stock Affiliates Pty Ltd* (1968) 122 CLR 25 at 32; see 26.6. However, if there is a breach of an equitable obligation and a breach of an independent common law obligation such as a breach of contract, the former may give rise to a remedy of an account of profits, whereas the latter gives rise to damages at common law, which can be pursued in addition to the remedy of an account of profits. Thus, in *Timber Engineering Co Pty Ltd v Anderson* [1980] 2 NSWLR 488, an employer obtained an account of profits and common law damages in relation to an employee's actions, which constituted a breach of fiduciary obligations owed to the employer as well as a breach of a contractual duty of good faith. However, where the two remedies arise out of the same facts, the plaintiff would not be permitted to recover both the full profits and damages on the basis of the rule that precludes double recovery.

Similarly, if an account of profits and equitable compensation are alternative remedies, a plaintiff is required to elect between the alternatives: *Attorney-General (UK) v Guardian Newspapers Ltd (No2)* [1990] 1 AC 109 at 286.

RECEIVERS

30.32 One of the oldest equitable remedies is the appointment of a receiver. The appointment of a receiver and manager is of more modern origin. The distinction between a receiver, on the one hand, and a receiver and a manager, on the other, in the context of a partnership, was explained by Jessell MR in *Re Manchester & Milford Rly Co; Ex parte Cambrian Rly Co* (1880) 14 Ch 645 at 653, as follows:

> A 'receiver' is a term ... meaning a person who receives rents or other income paying ascertained outgoings, but who does not ... manage the property in the sense of buying or selling or anything of that kind ... If a receiver was appointed of partnership assets, the trade stopped immediately. He collected the debts, sold the stock-in-trade and the assets, and then ... the debts of the concern were liquidated and the balance divided. If it was desired to continue the trade at all, it was necessary to appoint a manager, or a receiver and manager as it was generally called. He could buy and sell and carry on the trade.

30.33 Receivers can be appointed out of court or by order of the court. In practice, a receiver appointed out of court will usually seek to restore the financial prosperity of the business he or she has been appointed to administer. A court-appointed receiver will usually be simply concerned with preserving the assets of the business for those who will ultimately take them: *Duffy v Super Centre Development Corp Ltd* [1967] 1 NSWR 382 at 383–4.

Out of court appointment

30.34 A common example of an out of court appointment of a receiver is pursuant to a mortgage. Often, the loan instrument will expressly empower the lender to appoint a receiver with powers of sale and of management of the land pending its sale. The most common ground justifying the appointment is the borrower's failure to meet interest or principal repayments. The powers of the receiver stem from, and are governed by, the terms of the mortgage document. In the absence of express powers contained in a mortgage, a lender may have recourse to a statutory power of appointment.[1]

30.35 A receiver appointed pursuant to a mortgage, unless otherwise provided for by the mortgage document, will be deemed to be the agent of the borrower.[2] The consequence of this is that the lender is not liable for any liabilities incurred by the receiver. The receiver's duties include 'the duty to exercise his powers in good faith (including a duty not to sacrifice the mortgagor's interests recklessly); to act strictly within, and in accordance with, the conditions of his appointment; to

---

1. *Conveyancing and Law of Property Act 1898* (ACT) s 91(c); *Conveyancing Act 1919* (NSW) ss 109(1)(c), 115A; *Law of Property Act 2000* (NT) s 96; *Property Law Act 1974* (Qld) s 83(1)(c); *Law of Property Act 1936* (SA) ss 47(1)(c), 55A; *Conveyancing and Law of Property Act 1884* (Tas) s 21(1)(c); *Property Law Act 1958* (Vic) ss 101(1)(c), 109; *Property Law Act 1969* (WA) s 57(1)(c).
2. *Conveyancing and Law of Property Act 1898* (ACT) s 98; *Conveyancing Act 1919* (NSW) s 115(2); *Law of Property Act 2000* (NT) s 96(2); *Property Law Act 1974* (Qld) s 92(2); *Law of Property Act 1936* (SA) s 53(2); *Conveyancing and Law of Property Act 1884* (Tas) s 26(2); *Property Law Act 1958* (Vic) s 109(2); *Property Law Act 1969* (WA) s 65(2).

account to the mortgagor after the mortgagee's security has been discharged, not only for the surplus assets, but also for his conduct of the receivership': *Expo International Pty Ltd (Receivers and Managers Appointed) (in liq) v Chant* [1979] 2 NSWLR 820 at 834.

30.36 If a receiver acts *ultra vires*, fraudulently or not in good faith, he or she is personally liable to the lender. In *State Bank of New South Wales Ltd v Chia* (2000) 50 NSWLR 587 at 625–6, Einstein J described the position of a receiver appointed out of court as follows:

> The purpose of the appointment of a receiver out of court is somewhat different; they are not appointed for the benefit of the company but for the purpose of realising the security held by the appointer. The appointment of such a receiver is performed by the mortgagee, however, it is invariably the case … that the instrument under which the receiver is appointed provides that the receiver is the agent of the mortgagor. It has been said that the agency is 'a very special' and 'limited' one. The purpose and effect of rendering the receiver the agent of the mortgagor is to relieve the mortgagee from the liabilities which the law casts upon a mortgagee going into possession and to place upon the mortgagor the liability for the acts and defaults of the receiver. To make the receiver the agent of the mortgagor is, of course, something of a contrivance. As Starke J said in *Visbord v Federal Commissioner of Taxation* (1943) 68 CLR 354 at 376, '[w]e must not lose sight of the substance of the appointment. It was made for the benefit of the mortgagee and to protect the mortgagee from liability as mortgagee in possession or as principal'. Yet it is a contrivance which has the effect of removing a receiver appointed out of court from those classes of persons who may be said to be fiduciaries … [T]here are no reasons for the imposition of fiduciary obligations where, although one party agrees to act for or on behalf of another, the other party is able to control what powers are exercised for or on his or her behalf or able to control the manner of its exercise … [T]he receiver appointed out of court is the only genuinely non-fiduciary agency. To say that a receiver appointed out of court is not, generally, a fiduciary, is not to say that they are in no circumstances a fiduciary nor to say they owe no duties in the conduct of their receivership. Outside of those imposed by Statute, the general law imposes at least three duties upon a receiver. In the first place, the receiver has a duty to the mortgagee to collect and realise the assets of the company for the purpose of discharging the security. In the second place, the receiver holds in trust for the mortgagor, any proceeds from the sale of the company's assets after the satisfaction of the claims of the mortgagee and subsequent creditors. In the third place … the receiver, as the donee of a power, must exercise the powers and duties granted to him or her in good faith and for a proper purpose.

30.37 In relation to the special kind of agency relationship referred to in the above passage, in *Sheahan v Carrier Air Conditioning Pty Ltd* (1997) 189 CLR 407 at 419; 147 ALR 1 at 6, Brennan CJ said:

> Although a receiver appointed with powers such as those contained in [the mortgage debenture] is the agent of the debtor company so that, in his dealings with third parties, his acts are binding on that company, the receiver is not treated as an ordinary agent of the company in exercising powers (including the power of sale of the company's assets) which are conferred for the purpose of realisation of the security by the mortgagee. The receiver is appointed not for the benefit of the company but for the benefit of the mortgagee. The special nature and limited extent of a receiver's duty to the company in exercising his powers do not deny to the receiver's acts done in exercise of those powers the character of acts done by the company's agent.

Court appointment

30.38   All Australian jurisdictions have statutory provisions enabling a court to appoint a receiver in all cases in which it appears to be just or convenient to do so.[3] In order to persuade a court to make an appointment under this statutory power, 'generally an applicant must show a right which will be protected and enforced by the appointment and that no other available remedy is adequate for that purpose': *Liquor National Wholesale Pty Ltd v The Redrock Co Pty Ltd* [2009] NSWSC 1418 at [98]. In *Fonu v Merrill Lynch Bank and Trust Company (Cayman) Ltd* [2011] 4 All ER 704 at 718, the Privy Council stated that the following principles applied in relation to the statutory power to appoint receivers:

(1) the demands of justice are the overriding consideration in considering the scope of the jurisdiction ...; (2) the court has power to ... appoint receivers in circumstances where ... no ... receiver [would have been] appointed before [the *Judicature Act*] 1873; (3) a receiver by way of equitable execution may be appointed over an asset whether or not the asset is presently amenable to execution at law; and (4) the jurisdiction to appoint receivers by way of equitable execution can be developed incrementally to apply old principles to new situations.

30.39   Because a receiver is appointed by the court, he or she is an officer of the court and not an agent for any parties to the litigation. A court-appointed receiver 'owes fiduciary obligations to all persons interested in the subject property': *State Bank of New South Wales Ltd v Chia* at 625. The function of the receiver is to preserve assets and their potential to earn future profits: *Duffy v Super Centre Development Corporation Ltd* [1967] 1 NSWR 382 at 383–4.

30.40   The powers of the receiver in such circumstances are determined by the court making the appointment. In *Mariconte v Batiste* (2000) 48 NSWLR 724 at 737, Austin J held that the court can also 'give directions with respect to the discharge of the functions for which the appointment is made — at any rate, where ... such directions are necessary in a practical sense to enable the receiver to carry out those functions without exposing himself to a real risk of litigation'.

30.41   Any unauthorised interference with a court-appointed receiver in the carrying out of his or her duties and functions is a contempt of court. Because such a receiver is not an agent of any of the parties, if he or she contracts, he or she does so as principal and is thus personally liable on any such contract: *Moss Steamship Co Ltd v Whinney* [1916] AC 254 at 259. However, if the receiver merely causes an existing contract to continue to be performed, there is no personal liability attached to the receiver in relation to events arising out of that contract: *Parsons v Sovereign Bank of Canada* [1913] AC 160.

30.42   The appointment of a receiver by a court does not vest any property in the receiver: *Bolton v Darling Downs Building Society* [1935] St R Qd 237. Thus, the receiver has no right of action in his or her name for recovering property that is subject to the receivership. In such cases, the receiver must apply for leave to sue in the name of the person or entity entitled to sue: *Wilton v Commonwealth Trading Bank* [1974] 2 NSWLR 96. However, with contracts made by the receiver after appointment, because they are made by the receiver as principal, the receiver sues in his or her name to enforce them.

---

3.   *Supreme Court Act 1933* (ACT) s 34A; *Supreme Court Act 1970* (NSW) s 67; *Supreme Court Act 1979* (NT) s 69; *Supreme Court Act 1995* (Qld) s 246; *Supreme Court Act 1935* (SA) s 29(1); *Supreme Court Civil Procedure Act 1932* (Tas) s 11(12); *Supreme Court Act 1986* (Vic) s 37; *Supreme Court Act 1935* (WA) s 25(9).

30.43 A receiver appointed by a court is subject to duties of a fiduciary nature to the relevant parties. In particular, this precludes the receiver purchasing property that is the subject of his or her appointment: *Nugent v Nugent* [1908] 1 Ch 546.

30.44 Typical situations involving court appointments of receivers include:

* Cases of partnerships being wound up or dissolved.
* Cases of mortgages where an out of court appointment cannot be made for some reason and the security is in jeopardy. Thus, in *McMahon v North Kent Ironworks Co* [1891] 2 Ch 148, a mortgagor was insolvent but not yet in default under the mortgage. The court was persuaded that, in the circumstances, the security was in jeopardy and appointed a receiver.
* Cases involving vendors and purchasers where a receiver can be appointed if the property produces income but there is a dispute between the parties. A receiver may be appointed pending resolution of the dispute: *Gibbs v David* (1875) LR 20 Eq 373.
* Cases where creditors have a right to be paid out of a particular fund where a receiver may be appointed to prevent dissipation of that fund.

DELIVERY-UP AND CANCELLATION OF DOCUMENTS

30.45 A court exercising equitable jurisdiction can make orders for the delivery-up and cancellation of documents in circumstances where such documents are either void at common law or voidable in equity. The main purpose of such orders is to prevent persons who have possession of such documents perpetrating any injustices: *Langman v Handover* (1929) 43 CLR 334 at 352. However, the orders will not be made if the invalidity is obvious on the face of the documents: *Langman v Handover* at 358. Nor will they be made if the documents are only partially void: *Ideal Bedding Co Ltd v Holland* [1907] 2 Ch 157 at 173–4. Such a case would include where a document is void only as against creditors.

30.46 In cases where the document is void on grounds of illegality, delivery-up and cancellation will not be refused simply because the parties to the transaction are involved in the illegality. To refuse to make the order in such cases would be tantamount to perpetuating the illegality and would serve to undermine the rationale of the remedy, namely, the protection of the public by the prevention of injustices based upon the tainted document. In *Money v Money (No 2)* [1966] 1 NSWR 348 at 352, Jacobs J noted that in such cases equity will intervene 'to prevent further performance of the illegal transaction since public policy itself requires that it should interfere'.

30.47 In appropriate circumstances the order for delivery-up and cancellation will be on terms imposed upon the plaintiff by the court. Thus, in *Lodge v National Union Investment Co Ltd* [1907] 1 Ch 300, certain securities were provided pursuant to a money-lending transaction. The securities were illegal under relevant legislation. The court ordered delivery-up and cancellation of the securities on terms that the borrower repaid the outstanding amount of the loan. However, such terms will not be imposed where such an imposition is precluded by the legislation that renders the transaction illegal: *Kasumu v Baba-Egbe* [1956] AC 539; [1956] 3 All ER 266.

31

EQUITABLE DEFENCES

INTRODUCTION

31.1 This chapter will briefly outline a number of general equitable defences, namely, those of illegality, unclean hands, laches, acquiescence, limitations legislation, equitable set-off and waiver. Other equitable defences arise, but have been discussed in other parts of this book, such as in Chapter 23, because it is more appropriate to deal with them there. Furthermore, the principles of equitable estoppel can also operate as a defence to a plaintiff's proceedings (see Chapter 12), and the defence of the bona fide purchaser taking for value and without notice is critical in the context of priorities: see 7.48.

31.2 Generally, one may not contract out of the defences discussed in this chapter. As was pointed out in a case involving a defence of unclean hands to an application for specific performance, '[o]nce the court is asked for the equitable remedy of specific performance, its discretion cannot be fettered': *Quadrant Visual Communication Ltd v Hutchinson Telephone (UK) Ltd* [1993] BCLC 442. However, in the case of equitable set-offs, they can be contracted out of, either expressly or impliedly (*Gilbert-Ash (Northern) Ltd v Modern Engineering (Bristol) Ltd* [1974] AC 689 at 712; [1973] 3 All ER 195 at 210), or by the terms of a relevant statute: *Webster v Bread Carters' Union of New South Wales* (1930) 30 SR (NSW) 267 at 276.

ILLEGALITY

31.3 Equity will refuse to grant its remedies if the relevant transaction is illegal on the basis of the maxim that 'one who comes to equity must come with clean hands'. Straightforward instances of illegality include the formation of contracts prohibited by statute and the commission of a prohibited act. An example of the latter is that equity will not enforce an agreement to recover an illegal gambling debt: *Quarrier v Colston* (1842) 41 ER 587.

31.4 The more difficult area of illegality relates to transactions that may be illegal because they are associated with some illegal purpose, even though the transactions or acts per se are not prohibited. The approach of the courts in such cases is that laid out by the High Court in *Nelson v Nelson* (1995) 184 CLR 538; 132 ALR 133.

31.5 In *Nelson v Nelson*, Mrs Nelson, as an 'eligible person' under the *Defence Service Homes Act 1918* (Cth), was eligible for a subsidised loan from the Defence Service Home Corporation. She had two children, Peter and Elizabeth. In 1987 Peter and Elizabeth purchased a property at Petersham in Sydney. The deposit and the balance of the purchase price were provided by Mrs Nelson. The purpose of the transaction was to enable Mrs Nelson to later purchase another house with the benefit of a subsidised loan from the Corporation. Mrs Nelson would not have been eligible for the subsidised loan if she already owned another house. In 1989 Mrs Nelson, with the assistance of a subsidised loan, purchased a house in Paddington in Sydney. At the time, Mrs Nelson declared that she did not own or have any interest in any other property. In 1990 Peter and Elizabeth sold the Petersham property, with the proceeds of sale being placed into a solicitors' trust account. In 1991 Mrs Nelson and Peter commenced proceedings in which they sought a declaration that the solicitors held the balance of the proceeds of sale of the Petersham property on trust for Mrs Nelson. By way of cross-claim, Elizabeth sought a declaration that she had a one-half interest in the proceeds of sale. The issues before the court were: (i) whether Elizabeth was entitled to one-half of the sale proceeds of the Petersham property; and (ii) whether Mrs Nelson was entitled to any benefit in the proceeds of sale in light of the unlawful conduct that led to her purchase of the Paddington property.

31.6 The High Court unanimously held that Elizabeth was not entitled to any interest in the proceeds of sale of the Petersham property on the basis that she and Peter held it on trust for Mrs Nelson, on the basis of principles relating to resulting trusts: see Chapter 19.

31.7 In relation to whether Mrs Nelson was entitled to the proceeds of sale, the High Court majority (Deane, McHugh and Gummow JJ) started from the proposition that equitable relief should not be refused on account of the illegal purpose if granting such relief would not frustrate the purpose of the relevant legislation. This was particularly so if the legislation itself provided some mechanism for dealing with the illegal purpose. However, where the granting of equitable relief could frustrate the purpose of the legislation, but the threat could be met by moulding appropriate relief, then the court should grant such relief. It was on this latter point that the majority held that Mrs Nelson was entitled to the proceeds of sale subject to being denied the benefit that she obtained by her unlawful conduct. The minority (Dawson and Toohey JJ) held that Mrs Nelson was entitled to the proceeds of the trust unconditionally, on the basis that the question of any illegal conduct by her was a separate issue to be taken up by the Defence Service Homes Corporation if it chose to do so.

UNCLEAN HANDS

31.8 The maxim that 'one who comes to equity must come with clean hands' requires a plaintiff in equity not to be guilty of some improper conduct, or else relief will be denied. This is so because '[n]o Court of Equity will aid a man to derive advantage from his own wrong': *Meyers v Casey* (1913) 17 CLR 90 at 124. For example, specific performance of a contract will be refused if the plaintiff procured the contract as the result of equitable fraud even if the defendant has not rescinded the contract. The application of the unclean hands defence is difficult, if only because one judge can legitimately take one view and another judge the opposite view on whether the facts of a particular case give rise to the defence. This 'uncertainty is the necessary result of a notion as imprecise as that of "clean hands"': *ANZ Executors & Trustees Ltd v Humes Ltd* [1990] VR 615 at 635.

31.9 For the conduct of the plaintiff to fall within the maxim, it must have: (i) an 'immediate and necessary relation to the equity sued for' and (ii) 'a depravity in a legal as well as in a moral sense': *Dering v Earl of Winchelsea* (1787) 29 ER 1184 at 1184–5. In relation to the first test, in *Carantinos v Magafas* [2008] NSWCA 304 at [58] and *Kation Pty Ltd v Lamru Pty Ltd* (2009) 257 ALR 336 at 339 and 375, the New South Wales Court of Appeal suggested a more flexible test of 'whether the disentitling conduct had a sufficiently close relationship to the equity sued for'. In relation to the second test, general depravity by the plaintiff will not bar equitable relief. The depravity must be related to the plaintiff's cause of action in equity: *Moody v Cox and Hatt* [1917] 2 Ch 71 at 87–8. However, as was pointed out by Campbell J in *Black Uhlans Incorporated v New South Wales Crime Commission* [2002] NSWSC 1060 at [181], although these two tests are a necessary condition for the application of the maxim they are not sufficient because, '[e]quitable relief is always discretionary, and other factors can influence the exercise of the discretion'. Thus, in *Mrs Pomeroy Ltd v Scalé* (1907) 24 RPC 177, it was held that if a plaintiff who seeks an injunction has previously engaged in conduct of a type which, if continuing, might have provided a ground for refusing the injunction on the basis of the maxim, but prior to trial the plaintiff has ceased that activity and undertaken not to continue it, an injunction might be granted. In *Carantinos v Magafas*, the plaintiff was not denied equitable relief on the basis of the unclean hands defence in circumstances where the plaintiff and the defendant had been involved in a scheme designed to defraud tax authorities and financiers. Even though the plaintiff had not fully and frankly disclosed his fraudulent and illegal conduct, relief by way of an account of profits was granted subject to conditions that there was to be no distribution of any funds to the plaintiff until such disclosure had been made.

31.10 The operation of the two 'necessary' tests of the maxim can be illustrated by the following two cases. In *Black Uhlans v New South Wales Crime Commission*, Wilson, a member of the Black Uhlans motorcycle club, stood to have his property forfeited as a result of his conviction for drug trafficking. The club's clubhouse was in Wilson's name and the issue was whether it was to be forfeited along with Wilson's other property. The club established that it provided part of the funds used to acquire the clubhouse, which meant that Wilson held a proportionate share of the property on trust for the club pursuant to principles relating to resulting trusts: see Chapter 19. The Commission argued that the club could not invoke the principle of resulting trusts because it did not come before the court with clean hands. This was because it had been implicated in Wilson's false application for a loan that provided the balance of the money used to purchase the clubhouse. However, Campbell J held that the club's fraudulent activity did not deprive it of its entitlement pursuant to the principle of resulting trusts, as that conduct related only to how Wilson obtained the loan and did not relate to the club's contribution to the funds for the purchase of the clubhouse.

31.11 In *Bolianatz v Simon* (2005) 264 DLR (4th) 58, Bolianatz died leaving a will in which Simon was a beneficiary. Unknown to Bolianatz, Simon had stolen money from him, a crime for which he was subsequently convicted and ordered to make restitution. The issue before the Saskatchewan Court of Appeal was whether the unclean hands maxim meant that Simon was disentitled from receiving his inheritance pursuant to Bolianatz's will. The court held that the maxim was not applicable for two reasons. First, the maxim only applies against a plaintiff to proceedings before the court. In this case Simon was the executor of Bolianatz's will. Second, the court held that there was not a sufficient connection between Simon's crime and the inheritance pursuant to Bolianatz's will. Richards JA, at 75, noted that '[b]equests are not denied because a beneficiary is of bad character, has behaved immorally or has been involved in criminal activity'. His Honour noted that, had Simon obtained his bequest as the result of fraud on his part, or coerced Bolianatz to make the provision in his will, his conduct would have invalidated his inheritance.

31.12 The unclean hands principle is somewhat related to the defence of illegality. In *Nelson v Nelson*, at CLR 550–1; ALR 142–3, Deane and Gummow JJ were of the view that if the defence raised by the defendant was in essence a matter of illegality, there was no scope for the operation of the unclean hands defence.

LACHES

31.13   In seeking equitable relief, a plaintiff must act promptly and diligently: *Smith v Clay* (1767) 27 ER 419 at 420. Equity will not allow defendants to remain for too long in a position of not knowing whether equitable relief will be ordered against them. It would be unconscientious to do so. Laches, or undue delay, by the plaintiff in commencing or prosecuting an application for an equitable remedy will lead a court to deny the application: *Eads v Williams* (1854) 43 ER 671 at 678. The defence of laches does not apply in relation to common law remedies. In *Lindsay Petroleum v Hurd* (1874) LR 5 PC 221 at 239–40, Sir Barnes Peacock described the nature of laches as follows:

> [T]he doctrine of laches in Courts of Equity is not an arbitrary or a technical doctrine. Where it would be practically unjust to give a remedy, either because a party has, by his conduct, done that which might fairly be regarded as equivalent to a waiver of it, or where by his conduct and neglect he has, though perhaps not waiving that remedy, yet put the other party in a situation in which it would not be reasonable to place him if the remedy were afterwards to be asserted, in either of these cases lapse of time and delay are most material. But in every case, if an argument against relief, which otherwise would be just, is founded upon mere delay, that delay of course not amounting to a bar by any statute of limitations, the validity of that defence must be tried upon principles substantially equitable. Two circumstances, always important in such cases, are the length of the delay and the nature of the acts done during the interval, which might affect either party and cause a balance of justice or injustice in taking the one course or the other, so far as relates to the remedy.

31.14   In *Crawley v Short* (2009) 262 ALR 654 at 678, Young JA, speaking for the Court of Appeal on this matter, said:

> The elements of the defence of laches are: (i) knowledge of the wrong; (ii) delay; and (iii) unconscionable prejudice caused to the opponent by the delay … The result of a successful plea of laches is that the plaintiff's equitable claim is dismissed.

31.15   In relation to the element of knowledge the cases give very little guidance. In most cases there is no real doubt that knowledge of the wrong exists. In *Crawley v Short* at 678, Young JA stated that 'the degree of knowledge required … [is] a question of fact and degree in each case to be taken together with all the other facts of the particular case'.

31.16   In relation to the second and third elements of laches set out in *Crawley v Short*, it is clear that, for the laches principle to apply, the delay must be unreasonable and, in all the circumstances, it must render the grant of equitable relief against the defendant unconscientious: *Re Loftus (dec'd)* [2006] 4 All ER 1110 at 1124. It is often said that mere delay — that is, delay that has had no adverse consequences for the defendant or any third party — is not enough to establish laches: *Lamshed v Lamshed* (1963) 109 CLR 440 at 453. This is so, even in cases of long periods of delay. Thus: (i) in *Burroughes v Abott* [1922] 1 Ch 86, the court granted rectification of an instrument after a delay of twelve years; (ii) in *Weld v Petre* [1929] 1 Ch 33, a mortgagor's redemption suit was held not time-barred despite a delay of twenty-six years; and (iii) *Fitzgerald v Masters* (1956) 95 CLR 420, the High Court granted specific performance twenty-six years after the cause of action arose.

31.17   However, in *P & O Nedlloyd BV v Arab Metals Co (No 2)* [2007] 1 WLR 2288 at 2312, the English Court of Appeal stated that it 'would not wish to rule out the possibility that the court would regard it as inequitable to allow a claim to be pursued after a very long period of delay, even in the absence of evidence that the defendant or any third party had altered his position in the meantime'. The court went on to say that in all cases '[t]he question for the court … is simply whether, having regard to the delay, its extent, the reasons for it and its consequences, it would be inequitable to grant the claimant the [equitable] relief he seeks'.

31.18   The time from which delay is measured is the time at which the plaintiff has knowledge of the facts upon which his or her equitable remedy is based: *Lindsay Petroleum Co v Hurd* at 241. Where a plaintiff has knowledge of the relevant facts, he or she is presumed to have knowledge of his or her rights to a cause of action. Furthermore, the availability of the means of getting the knowledge is as good as having the knowledge: *The Bell Group Ltd (in liq) v Westpac Banking Corporation (No 9)* (2008) 225 FLR 1 at 763. In cases involving undue influence time begins to run with the cessation of the influence: *Goldie v Getley [No 3]* [2011] WASC 132 at [234].

31.19   In determining whether laches arises in any given case the court will not rely on earlier cases to any great extent. The question of whether the plaintiff has acted with sufficient promptness is almost exclusively dependent upon the individual facts and circumstances of any given case: *Lamshed v Lamshed* at 453. In *Eastern Services Ltd v No 68 Ltd* [2006] 3 NZLR 335 at 347, Anderson J, delivering the judgment of the court, said:

> [T]he doctrine of laches requires a balancing of equities in relation to the broad spectrum of human conduct. In the abstract, facts and the weight to be given to them are infinitely variable. But in a particular case they have to be identified and weighted for what they are, as a singular exercise.

However, it must also be noted that the court takes the view that there are cases which require special promptitude, including claims to establish a constructive trust, setting aside a contract for undue influence and claims generally for the rescission of contracts: *Streeter v Western Areas Exploration Pty Ltd [No 2]* (2011) 278 ALR 291 at 407.

31.20   In *Lamshed v Lamshed* there was a delay of several years in prosecuting a claim for specific performance of a contract for the sale of land, and laches was established. The prejudice to the defendant vendor was in the fact that the vendor should not have been left indefinitely in a position of not knowing whether or not the contract would be enforced and thus not knowing whether he could safely deal with the property on the basis that the contract would not be enforced against him. On the other hand, in *Eastern Services v No 68*, a purchaser's application for specific performance of a contract for the purchase of a right-of-way was granted notwithstanding a delay in completion of the contract of 26 years. The vendor was unable to establish any prejudice to itself arising from the delay. In reaffirming the necessity of establishing prejudice to the defendant, the New Zealand Supreme Court recognised that the length of delay and the nature of acts done during the period of delay could lead to an inference being drawn that the delay had prejudiced a defendant. Other examples of where significant delays were held not to constitute laches include *Burroughes v Abott* [1922] 1 Ch 86, where the court granted rectification of an instrument after a delay of 12 years and *Weld v Petre* [1929] 1 Ch 33 where, despite a delay of 26 years, a mortgagor's redemption suit was held not to be time-barred.

31.21   When laches is successfully raised in relation to the enforcement of common law rights, such as in a claim for specific performance of a contract, the plaintiff is left to his or her common law remedies. However, when purely equitable rights are involved, denial of relief on the grounds of laches means that the plaintiff, in effect, has no rights at all. It is for this reason that courts are somewhat reluctant to find laches in such cases. Thus, in the case of enforcement of express trusts, relief will only be denied to a plaintiff if there is 'gross laches' on his or her part: *Hourigan v Trustees Executors and Agency Co Ltd* (1934) 51 CLR 619 at 650. In *Orr v Ford* (1989) 167 CLR 316 at 341; 84 ALR 146 at 160, Deane J said that gross laches referred to 'circumstances where inaction or standing by (with knowledge) by a plaintiff over a substantial period of time assumes an aggravated character in that it will, if the plaintiff is granted the relief which he seeks, give rise to serious and unfair prejudice to the defendant or a third party'.

31.22   In *Orr v Ford* at CLR 341–2; ALR 160–1, Deane J outlined the limited circumstances in which laches could arise in relation to express trusts as follows:

> Ordinarily, it is difficult to envisage circumstances, falling short of waiver, release, election or estoppel, in which the laches of a beneficiary would produce a situation in which it was inequitable and unreasonable to grant relief in proceedings for the enforcement of an express trust in relation to trust property which remained in the possession of the trustee (or his personal representative). There are, however, at least two categories of case where that is not so. The first is where there is or has been dispute or mistake about the existence of the trust or the identity or extent of the trust property. The second category is where prejudice to third parties, such as other beneficiaries, is involved. In the first category of case, unreasonable delay in instituting proceedings to enforce the claim may of itself give rise to the serious and unfair prejudice necessary to constitute 'gross laches' in that it may bring about a situation in which the means of resisting the claim, if it be unfounded, have perished. In determining what constitutes 'unreasonable delay' regard must be had to all the circumstances, including the nature of the claim and the conduct of the parties. It may well be that the modern availability of proceedings for declaratory relief to negate a claim by a beneficiary makes it unlikely that such serious and unfair prejudice would be found to exist in a case where the defendant had been aware of the existence of such a claim at relevant times … In the second category of case, regard is paid to the prejudice which would be caused to third parties in assessing whether the plaintiff's laches has brought about a situation in which it would be inequitable and unreasonable to grant the relief which he seeks. The two categories of case are not mutually exclusive.

ACQUIESCENCE

31.23   Related to, and to some extent overlapping with, the defence of laches is the defence of acquiescence. Although the notion of acquiescence has various shades of meaning, for present purposes it refers to a situation where the plaintiff has expressly or impliedly assented to the defendant's conduct and the defendant has altered his or her position as a result: *Archbold v Scully* (1861) 11 ER 769 at 778. In *Byrnes v Kendle* (2011) 243 CLR 253 at 279; 279 ALR 212 at 233, Gummow & Hayne JJ stated that 'acquiescence … is best understood as requiring calculated (that is, deliberate and informed) inaction … or standing by'. In such a situation the plaintiff will be denied equitable relief. Although delay by the plaintiff may contribute to establishing acquiescence, it is not an essential element of the defence of acquiescence: *Sayers v Collyer* (1884) Ch D 103.

31.24 The decision in *Shaw v Applegate* [1978] 1 All ER 123 illustrates the closeness of acquiescence to the defence of laches. In that case Shaw had the benefit of a covenant attached to land, the terms of which prevented Applegate from using the land for the purposes of an amusement arcade. Over a period of time Applegate brought onto the property gaming tables, slot machines and various amusement machines whereupon eventually he, in fact, began to operate an amusement arcade on the property. Finally, Shaw sought an injunction to restrain the breach of covenant. Applegate argued that equitable relief should be refused on the grounds of acquiescence. The Court of Appeal rejected this argument on the basis that, although Shaw had full knowledge of what Applegate had been doing, Shaw was unsure as to when Applegate's conduct amounted to a breach of the covenant. His doubts in this respect precluded a finding of acquiescence on his part. However, the delay of three years in commencing proceedings would have, in all the circumstances, severely prejudiced Applegate if the injunction had been granted. Accordingly, the injunction was refused on the ground of laches, with the court ordering that equitable damages be assessed pursuant to the provisions of Lord Cairns' Act: see Chapter 26.

STATUTE OF LIMITATIONS

31.25 In Australian jurisdictions there are two broad categories of limitations legislation. The first relates to the Australian Capital Territory and Western Australia where, unless otherwise stipulated in the legislation, a plaintiff has six years to commence an action for equitable relief.[1] The second relates to the other jurisdictions where the limitations legislation has little direct application to equitable remedies. An important exception in these jurisdictions relates to equitable interests in land which, because the relevant definitions of land in the legislation include equitable interests in land, means that the same limitations apply to them as for legal interests in land. Another exception relates to the various time limitations within which actions against trustees for breaches of trust must be commenced.[2]

31.26 However, in the absence of express statutory provisions, equity applies statutory limitation periods if an analogous common law right exists which would have been successfully defended by a plea of the statute. In some states this power to apply the statute by analogy is recognised by legislation.[3] The use of limitations legislation by analogy is a manifestation of the maxim that 'equity follows the law'. In relation to equity's jurisdiction to apply statutory limitation periods by analogy, in *Knox v Gye* (1872) LR 5 HL 656 at 674–5, Lord Westbury said:

> [W]here the remedy in Equity is correspondent to the remedy at Law, and the latter is subject to a limit in point of time by the *Statute of Limitations*, a Court of Equity acts by analogy to the statute, and imposes on the remedy it affords the same limitation … Where a Court of Equity frames its remedy upon the basis of the Common Law, and supplements the Common Law by extending the remedy to parties who cannot have an action at Common Law, there the Court of Equity acts in analogy to the statute; that is, it adopts the statute as the rule of procedure regulating the remedy it affords.

1. *Limitation Act 1985* (ACT) s 11; *Limitation Act 2005* (WA) s 13.
2. *Limitation Act 1969* (NSW) ss 47(1) (e), 48(a); *Limitation Act 1981* (NT) ss 32(1)(e), 33(a); *Limitations of Actions Act 1974* (Qld) s 27(2); *Limitations of Actions Act 1936* (SA) s 32(1)(a); *Trustee Act 1893* (SA) ss 45, 46; *Limitation Act 1974* (Tas) s 24(2); *Limitations of Actions Act 1958* (Vic) s 21(2).
3. *Limitation Act 1969* (NSW) s 23; *Limitation Act 1981* (NT) s 21; *Limitation Act 1974* (Tas) s 9.

31.27   Although the notion of delay is inherent in applying limitations legislation by analogy, the principle that equitable claims can be barred in this way is quite separate and distinct from the defence of laches. In *Williams v Minister, Aboriginal Land Rights Act 1983* (1994) 35 NSWLR 497 at 509, Kirby P suggested that '[t]he considerations that may be relevant to a defence of laches will be different from (or not exactly the same as) the considerations relevant to the application of the [legislation]'.

31.28   In assessing whether the statute applies by analogy, in *Johns v Johns* [2004] 3 NZLR 202 at 224, Tipping J said as follows:

> There will be a bar by analogy only when the fiduciary claim parallels the statute-barred claim so closely that it would be inequitable to allow the statutory bar to be outflanked by the fiduciary claim. In order to determine how close the parallel is the Court must examine not only the underlying facts but also the nature of the relationship between the parties and the policy and purpose of the different causes of action. If there is a sufficient difference in any material respect, the suggested parallel is unlikely to be close enough to make it appropriate in equity to apply an analogous bar … [However, the issue cannot] be concluded solely by reference to the degree of concurrence of the factual allegations. That of course must be the first focus because, if there is no sufficient degree of concurrence in that respect, the suggested analogy is likely to fail at that point. If, however, there is factual concurrence in the sense that the different causes of action are simply different ways of putting the same factual complaint, and there are no policy or other reasons militating against it, the case for an analogous bar is likely to have been made out.

31.29   In *Metropolitan Bank v Heiron* (1880) 5 Ex D 319, it was held that the liability of a fiduciary to account for bribes received by him or her was the equitable equivalent of the liability of a defendant that is sued at common law on an action for money had and received, with the result that the limitation period applicable to the common law action also applied to the equitable remedy of account. Similarly, the limitation period applicable to claims against a defendant at common law for breaches of professional duty can be applied by analogy to relief against that defendant based upon 'dishonest' breaches of fiduciary obligations: *Aussie Ideas Pty Ltd v Tunwind Pty Ltd* [2006] NSWCA 286 at [22]–[24]; *Gerard Cassegrain & Co Pty Limited v Cassegrain* [2011] NSWSC 1156 at [231]–[235]. However, it is much more difficult to do so in cases involving 'innocent' breaches of fiduciary obligations. In *The Bell Group Ltd (in liq) v Westpac Banking Corporation (No 9)* at 760, Owen J made the following observations:

> [A]n 'innocent' breach of fiduciary duty … has less overlap with common law actions. It is one of equity's unique creatures whose ambit extends into circumstances in which the common law is reluctant to go. For example, a fiduciary can be held to account for profiting from an opportunity presented by his or her position, even though that opportunity could not have been utilised by the other party. Accordingly, in cases of non-dishonest breaches of fiduciary duty, the analogy is problematic … [Furthermore, where] plaintiffs seek proprietary remedies rather than mere compensation, … the analogy is more difficult to draw.

31.30   However, a court will only apply a statutory limitation period by analogy if the equitable remedy corresponds to the action affected by any statutory limitation period. By way of illustration, it can be noted that in all Australian jurisdictions except the Northern Territory, limitations legislation stipulates that claims based upon a simple contract must be commenced within six years of the date on which the cause of action arises.[4] In the Northern Territory the period is three years.[5] In New South Wales, the Northern Territory, Queensland, Tasmania and Victoria, the legislation also stipulates that these provisions do not apply to claims for an order for specific performance or an injunction, except in so far as any such statutory limitation period may be applied by the court by analogy.[6]

31.31 In *P & O Nedlloyd BV v Arab Metals Co (No 2)* at 2302–10, the English Court of Appeal held that there was no scope for an order for specific performance of a contract to be refused by the application by analogy of those or any other existing limitations legislation provisions. This approach was followed in *Italiano Oliveri v Invocare Australia Pty Ltd* [2008] NSWSC 1138 at [48], where it was held that the statutory limitation period in relation to a claim for damages for breach of contract could not be applied by analogy to a claim for specific performance of the contract. It is suggested that the principles in these two cases would apply equally to cases where an injunction is sought to enforce a contract.

EQUITABLE SET-OFF

31.32 A set-off exists when a defendant, in answer to a plaintiff's claim, is able to successfully plead that he or she has a countervailing claim against the plaintiff that absolves him or her, wholly or partially, from liability to the plaintiff. A set-off must be distinguished from a counter-claim. A set-off is a defence which precludes the plaintiff from enforcing his or her claim, either in whole or in part. It is 'not a denial of the [plaintiff's claim] but rather a plea against its enforcement': *IBM Pacific Pty Ltd v Nudgegrove Pty Ltd* [2008] QSC 195 at [11]. A counter-claim is a separate action in its own right by the defendant against the plaintiff. If a plaintiff discontinues his or her claim, the set-off also comes to an end. However, if the defendant has filed a counter-claim, the counter-claim continues, notwithstanding the discontinuance of the plaintiff's claim. Unlike a set-off, a counter-claim is not a defence.

31.33 Historically, set-offs were unknown at common law until introduced by statute in the *Insolvent Debtors Relief Act 1728* (UK) and the *Set-Off Act 1735* (UK). The essence of these Acts was to give a right to set off mutual debts between the parties, thereby enabling competing claims to be heard together, rather than in separate cases. By mutual debts, it was meant that the claims had to be between the same parties in respect of the same right. In *Stooke v Taylor* (1880) 5 QBD 569 at 575, Cockburn CJ said that the statutory plea of set-off 'is available only where the claims on both sides are in respect of liquidated debts, or money demands which can be readily and without difficulty ascertained'. This legislation applies in the Northern Territory, South Australia, Tasmania, Victoria and Western Australia as part of the English law that applies in Australia pursuant to the doctrine of reception. In New South Wales there is modern legislation that re-enacts the old English legislation.[7] In the Australian Capital Territory and Queensland the legal right to set-off appears to have been

---

4. See *Limitation Act 1985* (ACT) s 11(1); *Limitation Act 1969* (NSW) s 14(1); *Limitations of Actions Act 1974* (Qld) s 10(1)(a); *Limitations of Actions Act 1936* (SA) s 35(a); *Limitation Act 1974* (Tas) s 4(1)(a); *Limitations of Actions Act 1958* (Vic) s 5(1)(a); *Limitation Act 2005* (WA) s 13.
5. *Limitation Act 1981* (NT) s 12(1)(a).
6. *Limitation Act 1969* (NSW) s 23; *Limitation Act 1981* (NT) s 21; *Limitations of Actions Act 1958* (Vic) s 5(8); *Limitations of Actions Act 1974* (Qld) s 10(6)(a); *Limitation Act 1974* (Tas) s 9.
7. *Court Procedures Act 2004* (ACT) s 122–123; *Civil Procedure Act 2005* (NSW) s 21.

repealed.[8] The statutory right to set-off for mutual debts also exists in bankruptcy and company liquidation legislation.[9]

31.34   Set-off in equity pre-dated the statutory set-off provisions noted above. In equity, the classical set-off jurisdiction 'exists in cases where the party seeking the benefit of it can show some equitable ground for being protected against the adversary's demand. The mere existence of cross-demands is not sufficient': *Rawson v Samuel* (1841) 41 ER 451 at 458. An equitable set-off does not extinguish the plaintiff's claim. The claim still exists, but, to the extent of the set-off, equity regards it as unconscientious for the plaintiff to enforce it: *IBM Pacific Pty Ltd v Nudgegrove Pty Ltd* at [11]. However, an equitable set-off may be denied if, in all the circumstances, it would be unjust that a set-off should occur. Thus, the conduct of the parties may be relevant to the question of the availability of equitable relief by way of set-off: *Re Interesting Developments Pty Ltd* [2009] VSC 12 at [36]. Furthermore, the right to equitable set-off can be excluded by a clearly worded contractual term to that effect: *Norman; Re Forest Enterprises Ltd v FEA Plantation Ltd* (2011) (195) FCR 97 at 117–8; 280 ALR 470 at 492.

Contrasts between set-offs at common law and equity

31.35   In relation to equitable set-off, the following points can be noted. First, equity does not require the existence of mutuality in the same way as does the common law: *Ex parte Stephens* (1805) 32 ER 996. However, this difference explains equity's concerns with there being a sufficient connection between the respective demands of the parties: see 31.38–31.40.

31.36   Second, equitable set-offs can be pleaded against unliquidated claims, whereas at common law, set-offs are only available against liquidated claims: *Re K L Tractors Ltd* [1954] VLR 505 at 508. Thus, at common law there can be no set-offs in relation to tortious actions.

31.37   Third, at common law, set-offs can only be raised in relation to common law claims. However, equitable set-offs can be raised in relation to both common law and equitable claims. Indeed, the most common context for equitable set-offs is in response to claims for liquidated damages at common law.

The test for the availability of equitable set-off

31.38   The availability of set-off in equity has been described in various formulations. On the one hand, there is the view that the set-off must go to the root of, or impeach, the title of the plaintiff's claim. This so-called 'impeachment' formulation has been expressed in a variety of ways. In *British Anzani (Felixstowe) Ltd v International Marine Management (UK) Ltd* [1980] QB 137 at 145; [1979] 2 All ER 1063 at 1068, it was said that the cross-demand must go to 'the very root of the plaintiff's claim'. In *Tooth v Brisbane City Council* (1928) 41 CLR 212 at 224, it was said that the cross-claim must flow out of, and be inseparably connected with, the dealings and transactions which also give rise to the claim. In *Hamilton Ice Arena Ltd v Perry Developments Ltd* [2002] 1 NZLR 309 at 312, it was said that the link between the respective demands of the plaintiff and defendant had to be, in effect, interdependent.

---

8.   G E Dal Pont, *Equity and Trusts in Australia*, 5th ed, Law Book Co, Sydney, 2011, p 913.

9.   *Bankruptcy Act 1966* (Cth) s 86; *Corporations Act 2001* (Cth) s 553C.

31.39   More recently, in *Forsyth v Gibbs* [2009] 1 Qd R 403 at 406, Keane JA accepted the impeachment test when he said:

> Consistently with the technique of equity, which does not seek to define what an elephant is but knows one when it sees one, the principles governing the availability of equitable set-off of cross-claims are couched in open textured terms, such as 'sufficient connection' and 'unfairness'. In some cases, it will be necessary to engage in an evaluation of a range of facts which might establish 'sufficient connection' or 'unfairness' of the relevant kind. But the principles to be applied are not so vague or subjective that it is never possible to determine, for the purposes of an application for summary judgment, that the facts alleged by a defendant simply fall short of what is required. It is important to emphasise that the availability of an equitable set-off between cross-claims does not depend upon an unfettered discretionary assessment of whether it would be 'unfair' in a general sense for a plaintiff to insist on payment of the debt owed to it while the cross-claim remains unpaid. It is essential that there be such a connection between the claim and cross-claim that the cross-claim can be said to impeach the claim so as to make it unfair for the claim to be allowed without taking account of the cross-claim.

This statement of principle, together with other cases applying the impeachment test, was endorsed by the Full Court of the Federal Court in *Norman; Re Forest Enterprises Ltd v FEA Plantation Ltd* at FCR 112–4; ALR 487–8.

31.40   In *Geldof Metaalconstructie NV v Simon Carves Ltd* [2010] 4 All ER 847 at 848, Kay LJ, speaking for the Court of Appeal in England, said that the impeachment 'should no longer be used' and went on to describe the approach that the English courts now favour in terms of there needing to be a 'close connection' between the dealings and further that 'it needs to be unjust to enforce the [plaintiff's] claim without taking into account the cross-claim'. Kay LJ, at 849, concluded as follows:

> Although the test for equitable set-off plainly therefore involves considerations of both the closeness of the connection between claim and cross-claim, and of the justice of the case, I do not think that one should speak in terms of a two-stage test. I would prefer to say that there is both a formal element in the test and a functional element. The importance of the formal element is to ensure that the doctrine of equitable set-off is based on principle and not discretion. The importance of the functional element is to remind litigants and courts that the ultimate rationality of the regime is equity. The two elements cannot ultimately be divorced from each other. It may be that at times some judges have emphasised the test of equity at the expense of the requirement of close connection, while other judges have put the emphasis the other way round.

However, as Aitken observes, '[i]t remains a question whether or not the English approach will be adopted in Australia'.[10]

31.41   Equitable set-offs have been successfully raised in a variety of contexts. In *Young v Kitchin* (1878) 3 Ex D 127, a set-off of damages was allowed for delay or defective work against moneys due under a building contract. In *Government of Newfoundland v Newfoundland Railway Company*

---

10.   L Aitken, ' "Recognising and Elephant": Equitable Set-Off, "Impeaching Title" and the Modern Position on "Sufficient Connection"'(2011) 85 *Australian Law Journal* 51, p 58.

(1888) 13 App Cas 199, the Privy Council allowed a set-off of damages for failure to complete construction of a railway line against a claim for payment of a subsidy in respect of that part of the construction that was completed under the contract to build the railway line. In *Morgan & Son Ltd v Martin Johnson & Co Ltd* [1949] 1 KB 107, a claim for damages for the loss of a stored vehicle was allowed to be set off against the charges for storing a number of vehicles. In *Hanak v Green* [1958] 2 QB 9, a builder's claim for extras and for damages for refusal of access to the site was allowed as a set-off against the client's claim for damages for defective work. In *Knockholt Pty Ltd v Graff* [1975] Qd R 88, a tenant's claim for the landlord's breach of a covenant to repair the leased premises was set off against the landlord's claim for unpaid rent. In *Hill Corcoran Constructions Pty Ltd v Navarro & Anor* [1992] QCA 017, the plaintiff sued for a debt owing under a deed of loan. The purpose of the loan was to facilitate the construction by the plaintiff of a home unit building for the defendant under an existing building contract. A claim for damages for defective building work in respect of that construction was allowed to be set off against the plaintiff's claim.

WAIVER

31.42   In *The Bell Group Ltd (in liq) v Westpac Banking Corporation (No 9)* at 771, Owen J noted that '[t]he equitable defence of waiver … applies where a party has made a conscious decision to relinquish a right to seek an available remedy'. Thus, if a person has waived a right or remedy, he or she will be denied the right to subsequently pursue that right or remedy against another person. In *Agricultural and Rural Finance Pty Limited v Gardiner* (2008) 238 CLR 570 at 588; 251 ALR 322 at 335, Gummow, Hayne and Kiefel JJ defined waiver as 'an intentional act, done with knowledge, whereby a person abandons a right by acting in a manner inconsistent with that right'. Thus, 'a waiver must be in clear and unequivocal terms and must be communicated to the other party': *Bowen v Alsanto Nominees Pty Ltd* [2011] WASCA 39 at [16], [98].

31.43   The precise definition of waiver is difficult to pin down as the term is used in different ways in different contexts. However, in that regard, a useful statement is found in *Pacific Brands Sport & Leisure Pty Ltd v Underworks Pty Ltd* (2006) 149 FCR 395 at 421; 230 ALR 56 at 81, where Finn and Sundberg JJ said:

> The term 'waiver' is commonly used loosely to encompass doctrines as diverse as election, estoppel and contract variation … To the extent that waiver has an independent province — and this is a matter of some contest in Australian law — the best that probably can be said is that it applies to those circumstances in which the law recognises a voluntary or intentional relinquishment or renunciation of a known right, claim or privilege.

In *Commonwealth of Australia v Verwayen* (1990) 170 CLR 394 at 427; 95 ALR 321 at 343, Brennan J said:

> As a right is waived only when the time comes for its exercise and the party for whose sole benefit it has been introduced knowingly abstains from exercising it, a mere intention not to exercise a right is not immediately effective to divest or sterilize it.

31.44   In *Commonwealth v Verwayen*, the Commonwealth made statements to the effect that it would not plead limitations legislation as a defence to a claim for damages by Verwayen. The High Court, by a bare majority, held that the Commonwealth could not resile from its statements. Two of the majority judges found for Verwayen by applying the principles of equitable estoppel. However, the other two judges (Toohey and Gaudron JJ) based their judgments on the doctrine of waiver.

31.45 There has been considerable debate as to whether there exists a doctrine of waiver that is independent of the law of contract and the doctrines of estoppel and election. However, the prevailing view is that an independent waiver doctrine does exist: *Badat v DTZ Australia (WA) Pty Ltd* [2008] WASCA 83 at [51]–[52], [141]–[148]. In any event there is considerable overlap between the doctrine of waiver and other forms of discharge or release. Thus, in *Agricultural and Rural Finance v Gardiner*, at CLR 587, ALR 334, Gummow, Hayne and Kiefel JJ said:[11]

> Waiver has often been used in senses synonymous with election or estoppel. It has been suggested that waiver is indistinguishable from one or other of those doctrines. Sometimes, although expressed in terms of waiver, the reasoning adopted in cases reveals the elements for applying a more specific principle, typically election or estoppel. And it may be that in cases of the several kinds last mentioned, the term is used as no more than a conclusionary word stating the consequences of the operation of that more specific principle, rather than as indicating the application of any distinct and independent principle. Nonetheless, it is clear that there are cases in which the word has been used in senses other than those embraced by principles of election, estoppel or variation of contract. So, for example, waiver has been used in the sense of rescission where what has occurred is 'an entire abandonment and dissolution of the contract'. It has been used in connection with a party not insisting upon a term of a contract which is identified as a term for that party's sole benefit. And from time to time 'waiver' has been used to describe some modification of the terms of a contract without the formalities, or consideration, necessary for an effective contractual variation.

31.46 At common law, rights under a deed can be waived by another deed or by an agreement for valuable consideration. Rights arising outside the scope of a deed can be waived at common law by a deed or by accord and satisfaction: *McDermott v Black* (1940) 63 CLR 161 at 187–8. Accord and satisfaction refers to the purchase of the release from a debt obligation. Often the payment is less than what is owed. The accord is the agreement to discharge the obligation and the satisfaction is the consideration for the agreement.

31.47 In equity, an agreement for valuable consideration to waive a right is in all cases effective, and this rule applies to both legal and equitable rights.

31.48 Whether *legal* rights can be waived in equity in the absence of valuable consideration is not clear. The weight of authorities suggests that, in these circumstances, equity will not recognise a waiver unless it has been waived in law. (In law an obligation entered into in a deed can be released by a deed, even if the latter deed is not one for valuable consideration.) Meagher, Heydon and Leeming suggest that there are some exceptional circumstances in which departures from this view are possible.[12]

---

11. For analyses of this case see C Bevan, 'Waiver of Contractual Rights: A Non Sequitur' (2009) 83 *Australian Law Journal* 817; R Purslowe, 'Waiver of Contractual Rights — An Analysis of *Agricultural and Rural Finance Pty Limited v Gardiner*' (2009) 11 *University of Notre Dame Law Review* 112.

12. R Meagher, D Heydon & M Leeming, *Meagher, Gummow and Lehane's Equity: Doctrines and Remedies*, 4th ed, LexisNexis Butterworths, Sydney, 2002, p 1028.

31.49 With respect to the waiver of *equitable* rights in the absence of an agreement for valuable consideration, such rights can be waived under hand or even orally. Furthermore, a waiver can be inferred by conduct: *Re Hall* [1941] 2 All ER 358 at 370. However, a mere promise to waive or a mere expression of intent to waive is insufficient: *Avtex Airservices Pty Ltd v Bartsch* (1992) 107 ALR 539. But, for the equitable waiver to be effective in these circumstances, it must be shown that the plaintiff fully appreciated the nature and circumstances of the transaction from which his or her right arose, and that he or she had at least constructive knowledge of the equitable right against the defendant: *Grant v John Grant & Sons Pty Ltd* (1954) 91 CLR 112 at 129–30.

Index

References are to paragraphs